Twentieth-Century Literary Criticism

Topics Volume

Guide to Gale Literary Criticism Series

For criticism on	Consult these Gale series
Authors now living or who died after December 31, 1959	*CONTEMPORARY LITERARY CRITICISM (CLC)*
Authors who died between 1900 and 1959	*TWENTIETH-CENTURY LITERARY CRITICISM (TCLC)*
Authors who died between 1800 and 1899	*NINETEENTH-CENTURY LITERATURE CRITICISM (NCLC)*
Authors who died between 1400 and 1799	*LITERATURE CRITICISM FROM 1400 TO 1800 (LC)* *SHAKESPEAREAN CRITICISM (SC)*
Authors who died before 1400	*CLASSICAL AND MEDIEVAL LITERATURE CRITICISM (CMLC)*
Authors of books for children and young adults	*CHILDREN'S LITERATURE REVIEW (CLR)*
Dramatists	*DRAMA CRITICISM (DC)*
Poets	*POETRY CRITICISM (PC)*
Short story writers	*SHORT STORY CRITICISM (SSC)*
Black writers of the past two hundred years	*BLACK LITERATURE CRITICISM (BLC)*
Hispanic writers of the late nineteenth and twentieth centuries	*HISPANIC LITERATURE CRITICISM (HLC)*
Native North American writers and orators of the eighteenth, nineteenth, and twentieth centuries	*NATIVE NORTH AMERICAN LITERATURE (NNAL)*
Major authors from the Renaissance to the present	*WORLD LITERATURE CRITICISM, 1500 TO THE PRESENT (WLC)*

ISSN 0276-8178

Volume 74

Twentieth-Century Literary Criticism

Topics Volume

**Excerpts from Criticism of Various Topics
in Twentieth-Century Literature, including Literary
and Critical Movements, Prominent Themes and
Genres, Anniversary Celebrations, and Surveys
of National Literatures**

Jennifer Gariepy
Editor

Thomas Ligotti
Associate Editor

GALE

DETROIT · NEW YORK · TORONTO · LONDON

STAFF

Jennifer Gariepy, *Editor*

Thomas Ligotti, *Associate Editor*

Susan Trosky, *Permissions Manager*
Kimberly F. Smilay, *Permissions Specialist*
Steve Cusack, Kelly A. Quin, *Permissions Associates*

Victoria B. Cariappa, *Research Manager*
Michele P. LaMeau, Andrew Guy Malonis, Barbara McNeil, Gary J. Oudersluys, Maureen Richards, *Research Specialists*
Julia C. Daniel, Tamara C. Nott, Tracie A. Richardson, Norma Sawaya, Cheryl L. Warnock, *Research Associates*

Mary Beth Trimper, *Production Director*
Deborah L. Milliken, *Production Assistant*

Ninette Saad, *Desktop Publisher Assistant*
Randy Bassett, *Image Database Supervisor*
Robert Duncan, Michael Logusz, *Imaging Specialists*
Pamela Reed, *Photography Coordinator*

Library of Congress Catalog Card Number 76-46132
ISBN 0-7876-2018-1
ISSN 0276-8178

Printed in the United States of America
10   9   8   7   6   5   4   3   2   1

Contents

Preface vii

Acknowledgments xi

Preface

Since its inception more than fifteen years ago, *Twentieth-Century Literary Criticism* has been purchased and used by nearly 10,000 school, public, and college or university libraries. *TCLC* has covered more than 500 authors, representing 58 nationalities, and over 25,000 titles. No other reference source has surveyed the critical response to twentieth-century authors and literature as thoroughly as *TCLC*. In the words of one reviewer, "there is nothing comparable available." *TCLC* "is a gold mine of information—dates, pseudonyms, biographical information, and criticism from books and periodicals—which many libraries would have difficulty assembling on their own."

Scope of the Series

TCLC is designed to serve as an introduction to authors who died between 1900 and 1960 and to the most significant interpretations of these author's works. The great poets, novelists, short story writers, playwrights, and philosophers of this period are frequently studied in high school and college literature courses. In organizing and excerpting the vast amount of critical material written on these authors, *TCLC* helps students develop valuable insight into literary history, promotes a better understanding of the texts, and sparks ideas for papers and assignments. Each entry in *TCLC* presents a comprehensive survey of an author's career or an individual work of literature and provides the user with a multiplicity of interpretations and assessments. Such variety allows students to pursue their own interests; furthermore, it fosters an awareness that literature is dynamic and responsive to many different opinions.

Every fourth volume of *TCLC* is devoted to literary topics. These topic entries widen the focus of the series from individual authors to such broader subjects as literary movements, prominent themes in twentieth-century literature, literary reaction to political and historical events, significant eras in literary history, prominent literary anniversaries, and the literatures of cultures that are often overlooked by English-speaking readers.

TCLC is designed as a companion series to Gale's *Contemporary Literary Criticism,* which reprints commentary on authors now living or who have died since 1960. Because of the different periods under consideration, there is no duplication of material between *CLC* and *TCLC*. For additional information about *CLC* and Gale's other criticism titles, users should consult the Guide to Gale Literary Criticism Series preceding the title page in this volume.

Coverage

Each volume of *TCLC* is carefully compiled to present:

- criticism of authors, or literary topics, representing a variety of genres and nationalities

- both major and lesser-known writers and literary works of the period

- 6-12 authors or 3-6 topics per volume

- individual entries that survey critical response to each author's work or each topic in literary history, including early criticism to reflect initial reactions; later criticism to represent any rise or decline in reputation; and current retrospective analyses.

Organization of This Book

An author entry consists of the following elements: author heading, biographical and critical introduction, list of principal works, excerpts of criticism (each preceded by an annotation and a bibliographic citation), and a bibliography of further reading.

- The **Author Heading** consists of the name under which the author most commonly wrote, followed by birth and death dates. If an author wrote consistently under a pseudonym, the pseudonym will be listed in the author heading and the real name given in parentheses on the first line of the biographical and critical introduction. Also located at the beginning of the introduction to the author entry are any name variations under which an author wrote, including transliterated forms for authors whose languages use nonroman alphabets.

● The **Biographical and Critical Introduction** outlines the author's life and career, as well as the critical issues surrounding his or her work. References to past volumes of *TCLC* are provided at the beginning of the introduction. Additional sources of information in other biographical and critical reference series published by Gale, including *Short Story Criticism, Children's Literature Review, Contemporary Authors, Dictionary of Literary Biography,* and *Something about the Author,* are listed in a box at the end of the entry.

● Some *TCLC* entries include **Portraits** of the author. Entries also may contain reproductions of materials pertinent to an author's career, including manuscript pages, title pages, dust jackets, letters, and drawings, as well as photographs of important people, places, and events in an author's life.

● The **List of Principal Works** is chronological by date of first book publication and identifies the genre of each work. In the case of foreign authors with both foreign-language publications and English translations, the title and date of the first English-language edition are given in brackets. Unless otherwise indicated, dramas are dated by first performance, not first publication.

● Critical excerpts are prefaced by **Annotations** providing the reader with information about both the critic and the criticism that follows. Included are the critic's reputation, individual approach to literary criticism, and particular expertise in an author's works. Also noted are the relative importance of a work of criticism, the scope of the excerpt, and the growth of critical controversy or changes in critical trends regarding an author. In some cases, these annotations cross-reference excerpts by critics who discuss each other's commentary.

● A complete **Bibliographic Citation** designed to facilitate location of the original essay or book precedes each piece of criticism.

● Criticism is arranged chronologically in each author entry to provide a perspective on changes in critical evaluation over the years. All titles of works by the author featured in the entry are printed in boldface type to enable the user to easily locate discussion of particular works. Also for purposes of easier identification, the critic's name and the publication date of the essay are given at the beginning of each piece of criticism. Unsigned criticism is preceded by the title of the journal in which it appeared. Some of the excerpts in *TCLC* also contain translated material. Unless otherwise noted, translations in brackets are by the editors; translations in parentheses or continuous with the text are by the critic. Publication information (such as footnotes or page and line references to specific editions of works) have been deleted at the editor's discretion to provide smoother reading of the text.

● An annotated list of **Further Reading** appearing at the end of each author entry suggests secondary sources on the author. In some cases it includes essays for which the editors could not obtain reprint rights.

Cumulative Indexes

● Each volume of *TCLC* contains a cumulative **Author Index** listing all authors who have appeared in Gale's Literary Criticism Series, along with cross references to such biographical series as *Contemporary Authors* and *Dictionary of Literary Biography.* For readers' convenience, a complete list of Gale titles included appears on the first page of the author index. Useful for locating authors within the various series, this index is particularly valuable for those authors who are identified by a certain period but who, because of their death dates, are placed in another, or for those authors whose careers span two periods. For example, F. Scott Fitzgerald is found in *TCLC,* yet a writer often associated with him, Ernest Hemingway, is found in *CLC.*

- Each *TCLC* volume includes a cumulative **Nationality Index** which lists all authors who have appeared in *TCLC* volumes, arranged alphabetically under their respective nationalities, as well as Topics volume entries devoted to particular national literatures.

- Each new volume in Gale's Literary Criticism Series includes a cumulative **Topic Index,** which lists all literary topics treated in *NCLC, TCLC, LC 1400-1800,* and the *CLC* yearbook.

- Each new volume of *TCLC,* with the exception of the Topics volumes, includes a **Title Index** listing the titles of all literary works discussed in the volume. In response to numerous suggestions from librarians, Gale has also produced a **Special Paperbound Edition** of the *TCLC* title index. This annual cumulation lists all titles discussed in the series since its inception and is issued with the first volume of *TCLC* published each year. Additional copies of the index are available on request. Librarians and patrons will welcome this separate index; it saves shelf space, is easy to use, and is recyclable upon receipt of the following year's cumulation. Titles discussed in the Topics volume entries are not included *TCLC* cumulative index.

Citing Twentieth-Century Literary Criticism

When writing papers, students who quote directly from any volume in Gale's literary Criticism Series may use the following general forms to footnote reprinted criticism. The first example pertains to materials drawn from periodicals, the second to material reprinted from books.

[1]William H. Slavick, "Going to School to DuBose Heyward," *The Harlem Renaissance Re-examined,* (AMS Press, 1987); excerpted and reprinted in *Twentieth-Century Literary Criticism,* Vol. 59, ed. Jennifer Gariepy (Detroit: Gale Research, 1995), pp. 94-105.

[2]George Orwell, "Reflections on Gandhi," *Partisan Review,* 6 (Winter 1949), pp. 85-92; excerpted and reprinted in *Twentieth-Century Literary Criticism,* Vol. 59, ed. Jennifer Gariepy (Detroit: Gale Research, 1995), pp. 40-3.

Suggestions Are Welcome

In response to suggestions, several features have been added to *TCLC* since the series began, including annotations to excerpted criticism, a cumulative index to authors in all Gale literary criticism series, entries devoted to criticism on a single work by a major author, more extensive illustrations, and a title index listing all literary works discussed in the series since its inception.

Readers who wish to suggest authors or topics to appear in future volumes, or who have other suggestions, are cordially invited to write the editors.

Acknowledgments

The editors wish to thank the copyright holders of the excerpted criticism included in this volume and the permissions managers of many book and magazine publishing companies for assisting us in securing reproduction rights. We are also grateful to the staffs of the Detroit Public Library, the Library of Congress, the University of Detroit Mercy Library, Wayne State University Purdy/Kresge Library Complex, and the University of Michigan Libraries for making their resources available to us. Following is a list of the copyright holders who have granted us permission to reproduce material in this volume of *TCLC*. Every effort has been made to trace copyright, but if omissions have been made, please let us know.

COPYRIGHTED EXCERPTS IN *TCLC*, VOLUME 74, WERE REPRODUCED FROM THE FOLLOWING PERIODICALS:

American Literature, v.XLIII, January, 1972. Copyright © 1972 by Duke University Press, Durham, NC. Reproduced by permission.—*American Philosophical Quarterly*, v. 12, 1975 for "Existentialism and the Fear of Dying" by Michael A. Slote. Reproduced by permission.—*American Quarterly*, v. XVIII, Summer, 1966. Copyright 1966, American Studies Association. Reproduced by permission of The Johns Hopkins University Press.—*Arizona Quarterly*, v. 20, Summer, 1964. Copyright © 1964 by Arizona Quarterly. Reproduced by permission of the publisher.—*College Literature*, v. XV, 1988. Copyright © 1988 by West Chester University. Reproduced by permission of the publisher.—*Comparative Literature Studies*, v. IV, 1967 for "Uses of the Visible: American Imagism, French Symbolism" by Warren Ramsey; XVIII, September, 1981 for "Ezra Pound's Imagism and the Tradition" by P. E. Firchow. Copyright © 1967, 1981 by The Pennsylvania State University. Both reproduced by permission of The Pennsylvania State University Press.—*Comparative Literature*, v. 11, Summer, 1970. Reproduced by permission./ v. 36, Spring, 1984 for "Learning the Hard Way: Gothic Pedagogy in the Modern Romance Quest" by Patricia Merivale. Copyright © 1984 by University of Oregon. Reproduced by permission of the author.—*Critical Quarterly*, v. 23, Summer, 1981. Reproduced by permission of Blackwell Publishers.—*Criticism*, v. VII, Winter, 1965. Copyright © 1965 Wayne State University Press. Reproduced by permission of the publisher .—*Critique*, v. XVII, April, 1976. Copyright © 1976 Helen Dwight Reid Educational Foundation. Reproduced with permission of the Helen Dwight Reid Educational Foundation, published by Heldref Publications, 1319 18th Street, NW, Washington, DC 20036-1802.—*Cumberland Poetry Review*, v. VII, Fall, 1987. Copyright © 1987 by Poetics, Inc. Reproduced by permission.—*ELH*, v. 40, Fall, 1973. Copyright © 1973 by The Johns Hopkins University Press. All rights reserved. Reproduced by permission.—*Essays in Criticism*, v. XXII, April, 1973 for "Fear in `Macbeth'" by P. Rama Moorthy. Reproduced by permission of the Editors of *Essays in Criticism*.—*Extrapolation*, v. 28, Spring, 1987. Copyright © 1987 by Kent State University Press. Reproduced by permission.—*Harper's Magazine*, v. 201, August, 1950 for "Mencken and the 'Mercury,'" by William Manchester. Copyright © 1950 by Harper & Row, renewed 1978 by William Manchester. All rights reserved. Reproduced by permission of Don Congdon Associates, Inc.—*Journal of Modern Literature*, v. 12, July, 1985. Reproduced by permission.—*The Journal of Narrative Technique*, v. 2, May, 1972 for "The Sun Also Rises: One Debt To Imagism" by Linda W. Wagner. Reproduced by permission of the publisher and the author.—*Journal of Popular Culture*, v. 7, Winter, 1973. Reproduced by permission of the Bowling Green State University Popular Press.—*Journal of the Otto Rank Association*, v. 9, Winter, 1974-75 for "Fear and Growth: Reflections on The Beast of the Jungle" by Vern Haddick. Copyright © 1975 by The Otto Rank Association. Reproduced by permission of the author.—*Journalism Quarterly*, Summer, 1974. Reproduced by permission.—*Lost Generation Journal*, v. 3, Spring-Summer, 1975. Reproduced by permission.—*Menckeniana*, v. 47, Fall, 1973; No. 78, Summer, 1981; No. 89, Spring, 1984. All reproduced by permission.—*Modern Fiction Studies*, v. 15, Winter, 1969-70. Copyright © 1970 by Purdue Research Foundation, West Lafayette, IN 47907. All rights reserved. Reproduced by permission of The Johns Hopkins University Press.—*Modern Language Quarterly*, v. 44, March, 1983. © 1993 University of Washington. Reproduced by permission of Duke University Press.—*Modern Philology*, v. 90, August, 1992 for "Ezra Pound, Yone Noguchi and Imagism" by Yoshinobu Hakutani. Copyright © 1992 by The University of Chicago. All rights reserved. Reproduced by permission of the publisher and the author.—*Mosaic*, v. 24, Winter, 1988. Copyright © 1998 by Mosaic. Reproduced by permission.—*The New Republic*, v. 131, September 13, 1954. Copyright 1954 The New Republic, Inc. Reproduced by permission of *The New Republic*.—*New York Literary Forum*, 1980. Copyright © New York Literary Forum 1980. All rights reserved. Reproduced by permission.—*PMLA*, v. 84, March, 1970. Copyright © 1970 The Modern Language Association of America. Reproduced by permission.—*Sagetrieb: A Journal Devoted to Poets*, v. 4, Spring, 1985 for "H. D. and the Origins of Imagism" by Cyrena N. Pondrom. Copyright © 1985 by Cyrena N. Pondrom. Reprinted in *Signets: Reading H.D.*, edited by Susan Stanford Friedman and Rachel Blau DuPlessis. University of Wisconsin Press, 1990. Reproduced by permission of the author.—*South Atlantic Quarterly*, v. 46, April, 1947. Copyright 1947, renewed 1974 by Duke University Press, Durham, NC. Reproduced by permission./ v. 60, Summer, 1961; v. 83, Winter, 1984. Copyright © 1961, 1984 by Duke University Press, Durham, NC. Both reproduced by permission.—*South Dakota Review*, v. 30, Winter, 1992. Reproduced by permission.—*Studies in Black Literature*, v. 6, Summer, 1975. Copyright ©1975 by the editor. Reproduced by permission.—**Studies in Short Fiction**, v. 17, Fall, 1980; v. 29, Fall, 1992. Copyright © 1980, 1992 by Newberry College. Both reproduced by permission.—**Studies in the Novel**, v. 6, Summer, 1974. Copyright © 1974 by North Texas State University. Reproduced by permission of the publisher.—**Symposium**, v. 31, Fall, 1977. Copyright © 1977 Helen Dwight Reid Educational Foundation. Reproduced with permission of the Helen Dwight Reid Educational Foundation, published by Heldref Publications, 1319 18th Street, NW, Washington, DC 20036-1802.—**Triquarterly**, v. 11, Winter, 1968 for "The Rhetoric of Fear and of Hope" by Jean H. Hagstrum. Copyright © 1968 by *TriQuarterly*, Northwestern University. Reproduced by permission of the author.—**Ulbandus Review**, v. 1, Spring, 1978 for "Russian Acmeism and Anglo-American Imagism" by Elaine Rusinko. Reproduced by permission of the publisher and the author.—**The University Review**, v. 37, Autumn, 1970 for "Hamlet's Fear of Death" by Virgil Hutton. Copyright © 1970 The Curators of the University of Missouri. All rights reserved. Reproduced by permission of the publisher and the author.—**Wordsworth Circle**, v. 15, Winter, 1984. © 1984 Marilyn Gaull. Reproduced by permission of the editor.—**World Literature Today**, v. 69, Autumn, 1995. Copyright © 1995 by the University of Oklahoma Press. Reproduced by permission.

COPYRIGHTED EXCERPTS IN *TCLC,* VOLUME 74, WERE REPRODUCED FROM THE FOLLOWING BOOKS:

Cederstrom, Lorelei. From "Walt Whitman and the Imagists" in **Walt Whitman of Mickle Street: A Centennial Collection**. Edited by Geoffrey M. Sill. The University of Tennessee Press/Knoxville, 1994. Copyright © 1994 by The University of Tennessee Press/Knoxville. All rights reserved. Reproduced by permission of The University of Tennessee Press.—Coffman, Jr., Stanley K. From **Imagism: A Chapter For The History Of Modern Poetry**. University of Oklahoma Press, 1951. Copyright 1951 by the University of Oklahoma Press. Renewed 1979 by Stanley K. Coffman, Jr. Reproduced by permission.—Duffey, Bernard. From "Ezra Pound and the Attainment of Imagism,"in **Toward a New American Literary History: Essays in Honor of Arlin Turner**. Edited by Louis J. Budd, Edwin H. Cady and Carl L. Anderson. Duke University Press, 1980. Copyright © 1980 by Duke University Press, Durham, NC. Reproduced by permission.—Edmund S. de Chasca. From **John Gould Fletcher and Imagism**. University of Missouri Press, 1978. Copyright © 1978 by The Curators of The University of Missouri. All rights reserved. Reproduced by permission.—Fletcher, Ian. From **A Catalogue of The Imagist Poets**. J. Howard Woolmer, 1966. Copyright © 1966 by J. Howard Woolmer. Reproduced by permission of the author.—Gale, Steven H. From "John Osborne: Look Forward in Fear" in **Essays on Contemporary British Drama**. Edited by Hedwig Bock and Albert Wertheim. Max Hueber Verlag, 1981. © 1981 Max Hueber Verlag. Reproduced by permission of the editors.—Indick, Ben P. From "What Makes Him So Scary" in **Discovering Stephen King**. Edited by Darrell Schweitzer. Starmont House, Inc., 1985. Copyright © 1985 by Darrell Schweitzer. Reproduced by permission.—Mott, Frank Luther. From **A History of American Magazines: Volume 5: Sketches of 21 Magazines, 1905-1930**. Harvard University Press, 1968. Copyright © 1968 by the President and Fellows of Harvard College. All rights reserved. Reproduced by permission of the publisher.—Perkins, David . From **A History of Modern Poetry: From the 1890s to the High Modernist Mode**. The Belknap Press of the Harvard University Press, 1976. Copyright © 1976 by the President and the Fellows of Harvard College. All rights reserved. Reproduced by permission.—Pinto, Vivian de Sola. From **Crisis In English Poetry: 1880-1940**. Hutchinson's University Library, 1951. Reproduced by permission.—Rajan, B. From **Modern American Poetry**. Dennis Dobson, Ltd., 1950. All rights reserved. Reproduced by permission of the author.—Roberts, Neil. From "Lawrence, Imagism and Beyond" in **British Poetry, 1900-50: Aspects of Tradition**. Edited by Gary Day and Brian Docherty. St. Martin's Press, 1995 and Macmillan Press, Ltd., 1995. Copyright © 1995 by the Editorial Board, Lumiere (Co-operative) Press Ltd. Copyright © Gary Day and Brian Docherty. All rights reserved. Reproduced by permission of Macmillan, London and Basingstoke. In North America by St. Martin's Press, Inc.— Shapiro, Michael J. From **Reading the Postmodern Polity: Political Theory as Textual Practice**. University of Minnesota Press, 1992. Copyright © 1992 by the Regents of the University of Minnesota. All rights reserved. Reproduced by permission.—Stempel, Daniel. From "Lafcadio Hearn's Translations and the Origins of Imagist Aesthetics" in **Comparative Literature East and West: Traditions and Trends**. Edited by Cornelia N. Moore and Raymond A. Moody. The College of Languages, Linguistics and Literature, University of Hawaii and the East-West Center, 1989. Copyright © 1989 by The College of Languages, Linguistics and Literature, University of Hawaii and the East-West Center. All rights reserved. Reproduced by permission.—Wagniere, Harriet Helms. From **The Old Century and the New: Essays in Honor of Charles Angoff**. Edited by Alfred Rosa. Associated University Presses, 1978. Copyright © 1978 by Associated University Presses. Reproduced by permission.

The *American Mercury*

INTRODUCTION

The *American Mercury* was an influential journal of opinion and literature that debuted in January 1924 and gained a wide audience under the editorial control of its cofounders, George Jean Nathan and H. L. Mencken. Known for the caustic satire of its editorial essays, the monthly review created a sensation among intellectual circles during the 1920s, with its debunking of such cultural icons as Abraham Lincoln and Walt Whitman and its mixture of fiction, literary criticism, political analysis, and cultural comment. Counting such authors as Sherwood Anderson, Ernest Boyd, William Faulkner, Sinclair Lewis, and Eugene O'Neill among its contributors, the *American Mercury* reached the height of its popularity in the mid to late 1920s, when its circulation numbered more than 75,000 per month.

Among the most sensational episodes connected with the *American Mercury* was the 1926 "Hatrack affair," in which Mencken and the *American Mercury* became the targets of an obscenity charge by the Massachusetts Watch and Ward Society. Taking offense to "Hatrack," a profile of a small-town prostitute which appeared in the April 1926 issue, Watch and Ward secretary Jason Frank Chase led the campaign to ban sales of the magazine in Boston. On the advice of attorney Arthur Garfield Hays of the American Civil Liberties Union, Mencken traveled to Boston and before a throng on onlookers personally sold a single copy of the issue to Chase. Mencken was promptly arrested and appeared in court the following morning, where the charge of distributing immoral literature was summarily dismissed. All related legal proceedings were subsequently decided in favor of the *American Mercury,* and the chief result of the affair was to heighten the scandalous reputation of the magazine and to augment its circulation.

Following ongoing editorial disputes with Mencken, Nathan resigned his coeditorship in July 1925 but remained a contributing editor and oversaw the "Theater" section and the "Clinical Notes" department until 1930. Circulation of the *American Mercury* began to decline in the early 1930s as Mencken's iconoclastic style lost its appeal under the altered national mood of the Great Depression. He resigned his editorship of the magazine in 1933. Publisher Alfred A. Knopf sold the *American Mercury* in 1935 to Paul Palmer and Lawrence E. Spivak, who instituted a number of format and editorial changes throughout the 1930s and 1940s in an effort to achieve profitability. A succession of owners and editors continued to publish the *American Mercury* as a journal of conservative opinion for several decades, although the magazine never regained the prominence and influence it had known during the Mencken era.

Frank Luther Mott

SOURCE: "The American Mercury," in *A History of American Magazines: Volume 5: Sketches of 21 Magazines, 1905-1930,* Harvard University Press, 1968, pp. 3-26.

[*In the following essay, Mott discusses the content and contributors of the* American Mercury *from the 1920s through the 1960s.*]

By 1923 H. L. Mencken and George Jean Nathan were tired of their connection with the *Smart Set* and hopeful of something better. For some fifteen years they had written critical articles for that magazine, and during the last half of that term they had been in editorial charge. They had won a wide reputation and an enthusiastic following, especially among the young and skeptical; and Mencken, through his forthright and biting essays collected in a series entitled *Prejudices,* had become a prophet of modern apostasy. They were ready for a more impressive and dignified forum than that afforded by a magazine with the cheap name and rather sleazy tradition of the *Smart Set.*

Thus, when Alfred A. Knopf offered to set up a monthly review, giving them a one-third working interest in it as editors, they were quick to accept. Such titles as "The Blue Review," "The Twentieth Century," and "The Portfolio" were suggested; that of *The American Mercury*[1] was adopted when Knopf and Nathan outvoted Mencken.[2]

The first number was dated January 1924 and came out early in the preceding month. It made an impressive appearance as a whacking big octavo with 128 double-column Garamond-set pages bound in green covers. Elmer Adler was the designer. It was clearly planned for the more thoughtful reader of a free-thinking sort who had fifty cents to spend on a magazine in these inflationary years. For such a reader the contents of the new review were both intellectually exciting and to the last page entertaining.

And so it caught on. The original print order was for ten thousand copies; and two reprints were called for, bringing the total to 15,500. By the time the second number was in press, Vol. I, No. 1 was selling to collectors for ten dollars.[3] By the end of its first year, the *Mercury* was printing 55,000 copies, which was pretty good for a magazine whose projectors had counted on a circulation of 20,000.[4] Of this total, more than two-thirds were newsstand sales. Average net paid circulation went on climbing until it reached, in the magazine's second year, about 75,000.[5]

That first ten-dollar number is worth examining, since it set the pace that the magazine followed rather consistently for more than five years. It opens with a "debunking" article by Isaac R. Pennypacker on "The Lincoln Legend," which emphasizes the prominence of the family from which he sprang on the one hand, and his shortcomings as a military leader on the other. A later article in the number, by Harry Elmer Barnes, "The Drool Method in History," attacks the historians for their capitulation to school boards and legislatures that forbid any disrespect to established idols and mores. A good little chapter on Stephen Crane by Carl Van Doren, a collection of personal letters to various friends from the late James Huneker, and a literary colloquium between George Moore and Samuel C. Chew (more notable for its novel form and its badinage than for any new ideas) constitute the literary criticism of this initial number. "Santayana at Cambridge," by the daughter of Hugo Münsterberg, is more a character sketch than a philosophical dissertation; and Woodbridge Riley's "The New Thought" is a rather muddled, satirical account of that school and its connection with Christian Science, which is called "Eddyism." "Aesthete: Model 1924," by Ernest Boyd, is a satire on editors of the "little magazines." The two political articles are a satirical sketch of Hiram Johnson by John W. Owens and a factual analysis of "The Communist Hoax" in the United States by James Oneal. Two pieces dealing with military matters are anonymous—one a sober and statistical review of actual disarmament since the adoption of the Anglo-Japanese-American Treaty of 1922; and the other a short essay, "On a Second-Rate War," in which "the struggle of 1914-1918" is discussed in a summary studded with words like "jumble," "childish," "unpreparedness," and "strategic error."

The only poems in the number are an undistinguished group by Theodore Dreiser. There are three short stories—Ruth Suckow's fine genre piece from Iowa entitled "Four Generations," Leonard Cline's funny and fanciful satire on "cops" called "Sweeny's Grail," and John McClure's sketch of Cairo street-life, "The Weaver's Tale."

Of departments there are six scattered through the book. The first is a four-page "Editorial." "The Editors," writes Mencken, "are committed to nothing save this: to keep to common sense as fast as they can, to belabor sham as agreeably as possible, to give a civilized entertainment." He provides a little advance list of his bêtes noires in this passage:

> The ideal realm imagined by an A. Mitchell Palmer, a King-Kleagle of the Ku Klux Klan or a Grand Inquisitor of the Anti-Saloon League, with all human curiosity and enterprise brought down to a simple passion for the goose-step, is as idiotically utopian as the ideal of an Alcott, a Marx, or a Bryan. . . . It will be an agreeable duty to track down some of the worst nonsense prevailing and to do execution upon it—not indignantly, of course, but nevertheless with a sufficient play of malice to give the business a Christian and philanthropic air.[6]

Ah, that is the authentic Mencken! Turn on twenty pages and you come to the second department—one which be-

came, as the months passed, perhaps the most popular feature of the magazine—"Americana." Herein are gathered bits of this "worst nonsense," geographically classified. This first batch begins as so many later ones did, with Alabama, wherein it is noted that Birmingham's Commissioner of Safety W. C. Bloe had ordered the city's "exclusive clubs" to cease and desist allowing the playing of Sunday golf, billiards, and dominoes; and it ends with the state of Washington, in which Bellingham's Garden Street Methodist Church had come up with a report, printed in a national publishers' journal, that "$100 worth of advertising had brought in more than $1,700 in silver plate collections."

The department called "Clinical Notes" is edited in this number by Mencken and Nathan jointly; later Nathan carried it on alone. Here are short expressions of "prejudices," opinions, comment on social and artistic matters, mostly heterodox, sometimes calculated to shock, occasionally sophomoric, often commonsense without conventional camouflage. "The more the theologian seeks to prove the acumen and omnipotence of God by His works, the more he is dashed by evidences of divine incompetence and irresolution." Mencken is displeased by "such dreadful botches as the tonsils, the gall-bladder, the uterus, and the prostate gland."[7]

"The Arts and Sciences" is one of the best of the magazine's departments. In this first number, it dips into "Architecture" with a short piece by C. Grant La Farge about the new city skylines, into "Medicine" with a sensible little article about glands and rejuvenation by L. M. Hussey, and into "Philology" with an admirable essay by George Philip Krapp about acceptability of language usages. Later nearly all categories of human knowledge were tapped in the short pieces in this department—the various sciences, law, theology, economics, pedagogy, the fine arts, poetry, radio, and so on. The other two departments are Nathan's "The Theater," with his always incisive and informed commentary on current plays and the affairs and personalities of the playhouse; and "The Library," with reviews of new books by Mencken and others. In this initial issue, the "others" were James Branch Cabell, Ernest Boyd, and Isaac Goldberg; later Mencken did them all himself, and there was also a "Check List of New Books" including brief notices. Most of these departments were carried over from the old *Smart Set,* where they had made much of the success of that magazine—"Americana," Mencken's reviews and Nathan's theatrical criticism, and the "Clinical Notes." These last fortunately lost, in the transition, their former heading "Répétition Générale."

Readers of this first number of the *American Mercury* found that all of its articles were short, most of them running from four to seven pages. They also noted that the review was preoccupied with American topics; if they did not, they were reminded in the "Editorial": "In general *The American Mercury* will live up to the adjective in its name. It will lay chief stress at all times upon American ideas, American problems, and American personalities because it assumes that nine-tenths of its readers will be Americans and that they will be more interested in their own country than in any other."[8]

Further, readers must have been impressed with the prominence of satire in the magazine—a satire that often ran into iconoclasm and "debunking," as the term went in those days. Said the *New Republic,* a severe critic from the first: "'Iconoclastic' is a word which one fears will be frequently applied to our *Mercury.* A better word will have to be invented to describe someone who loves to hear the crash of empty bottles quite as much as that of ikons, who often can't tell the difference between them, and who always uses the same crowbar on both. The resulting noise is so loud as almost to sound like a philosophical system, and many people have been fooled accordingly."[9]

This leaves unanswered the question as to whether the *New Republic* considered Hiram Johnson, for example, an ikon or an empty bottle; but indisputable ikons in the *Mercury*'s range were Lincoln and Whitman. The Lincoln article, noted above, presented views which have since had wide acceptance; the one on Whitman, by Ernest Boyd, expressed opinions even then out of date and destined with passing years to seem more and more unperceptive. Boyd saw Whitman as "the first of the literary exhibitionists whose cacophonous incongruities and general echolalia are the distinguishing marks of what is regarded as poetry in aesthetic circles today. . . . With the lapse of time, his false position has reached the last degree of unreality."[10] According to Assistant Editor Angoff, this article was "the subject of heated controversy in the office," and "Mencken himself eventually admitted that the author was overstating his case."[11] A number of other pieces in early numbers of the *Mercury,* it must be added, treated Whitman and his work more tenderly.

But, ikons or empty bottles, there is no doubt that Mencken had great fun smashing what he considered to be "frauds," and most of his readers enjoyed the game no less. In the magazine's fifth anniversary number, he wrote a paragraph that is worth quoting for its catalogue of the objects of Mercurial attack:

> In this benign work [of exposing frauds] it has covered a considerable range, and tried to proceed with a reasonable impartiality. The chiropractors and the Socialists, the Holy Rollers and the homeopaths, the pacifists and the spiritualists have all taken their turns upon its operating table. It has exhibited, mainly in their own words, the dreams and imbecilities of the prophets of high-powered salesmanship, vocational guidance, osteopathy, comstockery, and pedagogy. It has brought to notice, in the chaste, dispassionate manner of the clinic, the hallucinations of Rotary, the Gideons, the D. A. R., the American Legion, the League of American Penwomen, the Methodist Board of Temperance, Prohibition, and Public Morals, and a multitude of other such klans and sodalities, many of them highly influential and all of them amusing.[12]

But in the same editorial, Mencken points out that his review has done much more than expose "frauds": "It has given a great deal more space to something quite different, namely, to introducing one kind of American to another." And he mentions such articles as those of the lumberjack James Stevens, later famous for his "Paul Bunyan" stories; the convict Ernest Booth, whose series about bank-robbing and such were cut short by prison authorities; and the musician Daniel Gregory Mason, who, in his stories of the Chautauqua, poked fun at the yokels whose favor he had once courted on the platform. There were also Jim Tully, who wrote of "hobo" life; George Milburn, with his Oklahoma sketches; Mary Austin, who told Indian tales, and so on.

Other favorite topics in Mencken's *Mercury* were the American newspaper, often treated with understanding, sometimes with severity; advertising and press-agentry, usually assailed; folk literature, superstitions, and anthropology; the American Negro, his progress and his problems; philology, with emphasis on American usages; American history, particularly unswept corners and picturesque personalities and events; and literary figures such as Poe, Whitman, and Melville.

George S. Schuyler was a leading writer on the racial problem, and his article "A Negro Looks Ahead" created a sensation not only in the South but throughout the country. It concluded: "The Aframerican, shrewd, calculating, diplomatic, patient and a master of Nordic psychology, steadily saps the foundation of white supremacy. Time, he knows, is with him. . . . By 2000 A.D. a full-blooded American Negro may be rare enough to get a job in a museum, and a century from now our American social leaders may be as tanned naturally as they are now striving to become artificially."[13]

All regions came in for occasional lashings in the pages of the *Mercury*—the Midwest's "Bible Belt," puritanical New England, the culturally arid West—but the South perhaps caught it hardest. Wrote W. J. Cash in "The Mind of the South": "There *is* a new South, to be sure. It is a chicken-pox of factories on the Watch-Us-Grow maps; it is a kaleidoscopic chromo of stacks and chimneys on the club-car window as the train rolls southward from Washington to New Orleans. But I question that it is much more. For the mind of that heroic region, I opine, is still basically and essentially the mind of the Old South."[14]

Political articles of a serious nature were rare in the *Mercury*. Most of those about contemporary political figures and most of Mencken's editorials in this field were designed to puncture the balloons of popular reputations. The most famous of such pieces was the mercilessly contumelious editorial about Bryan, published in the October 1925 number, shortly after that statesman's death. It is still amusing reading, the real, distilled Mencken. There was really not much politics in it; it was a postscript to what Mencken had written (chiefly for the Baltimore *Sun*) about the Scopes trial. One astute critic of Mencken's total work has written: " . . . It was significant that one of the cruelest things he ever wrote, his essay on Bryan, was probably the most brilliant."[15]

Though contemporary literature was often treated in the *Mercury*'s articles, it was in Mencken's own book reviews that the heart of the magazine's comment on the writing of the day appeared. These reviews were, indeed, one of the most interesting features of the *Mercury*. In them Mencken expressed, in striking and exuberant style, his devotion to basic actualities and his contempt of gentility and sentimentality, his stout support of writers who defied conventionality and popular inhibitions, and his scorn for the idols of mass culture. Carefully discriminated and qualified book reviews are often dull; Mencken's never were, partly at least because he usually condemned or praised, and no nonsense about it. Let us take two examples more or less at random. In the second number of the *Mercury*, a review of *The Great Game of Politics*, by Frank R. Kent, a colleague of the reviewer on the Baltimore *Sun*, began:

> Astonishingly enough, this is the first book ever written in America which describes realistically and in detail the way in which the mountebanks and scoundrels who govern 110,000,000 free and brave people obtain and hold their power.[16]

And a year or more later appeared the following succinct review of Ernest Hemingway's second book, *In Our Time:*

> The sort of brave, bold stuff that all atheistic young newspaper reporters write. Jesus Christ in lower case. A hanging, a carnal love, and disembowellings. Here it is, set forth solemnly on Rives handmade paper, in an edition limited to 170 copies, and with the imprimatur of Ezra Pound.[17]

Like a good journalist, Mencken did give his readers much information about the new books; but many read his reviews more for the Mencken in them than for anything else. They were always readable, sometimes amusing. Mencken was "at least half Puck," observed a later critic, and added. "He loved to hear the rumble of his own hyperboles."[18]

"Menckenism" became a common word to describe a compound of prejudices, hyberbole, and a kind of free-wheeling diction just this side of rant. Certain words were overused: imbecile, mountebank, oaf, nincompoop, rascal, wowser, swine, pusillanimous, perfidious, fraudulent. To this "Menckenese" must be added two invented terms which have gained a considerable acceptance in the language: *booboisie* and *Homo Boobus,* the latter corrected by the more learned Boyd, we are told, to *Homo Boobiens.*[19] Contributors had to submit their copy to editing which, if it did not include "a proper salting of Menckenese," at least brought it into harmony with the tone of the magazine.[20]

"Mencken was always eager to print authors for the first time," according to his assistant editor, "and to that end he carried on a huge correspondence with young men and women in all parts of the country."[21] This was a practice he had brought from the *Smart Set;* in the two magazines, he introduced to a larger public many writers virtually unknown before. Such a list would include Ruth Suckow, James Stevens, Jim Tully, and many others.

But the *Mercury*'s table of contents was loaded with plenty of names well known to the reading public. In addition to those mentioned in other places in this chapter, we may list here a few representative frequent contributors: Gerald W. Johnson. Chester T. Crowell, Robert L. Duffus, Fred Lewis Pattee. Henry F. Pringle, C. Hartley Grattan, Louis Adamic, Duncan Aikman, Marquis W. Childs, Margaret Mead, Nelson Antrim Crawford ("A Man of Learning," August 1925), Benjamin deCasseres, Lewis Mumford, Louis Untermeyer, and William E. Dodd.

The *Mercury* printed many short stories of considerable distinction. Some of them had regional settings, like those of Ruth Suckow, Winifred Sanford, James Stevens, George Sterling, Idwal Jones, and William Faulkner. It is said that Mencken did not like Faulkner, and accepted "That Evening Sun Go Down" (March 1931) under protest.[22] Sinclair Lewis provided both non-fiction and fiction ("The Man Who Knew Coolidge," January 1928) from his busy typewriter.

Mencken looked upon his own early book of verse as a youthful indiscretion, and had little respect for contemporary poetry.[23] In his *Mercury* salutatory, he promised "some verse (but not much)."[24] This meant, apparently, a poem or two in each number. Some of them were very good, indeed. Favorites were the Midwesterners Vachel Lindsay, Edgar Lee Masters, and Carl Sandburg; the Negroes Countee Cullen and James Weldon Johnson ("Go Down, Death!" April 1927); and the Westerner George Sterling; as well as Joseph Auslander, Grace Stone Coates, and Gwendolen Haste.

The *Mercury* also published some works in dramatic form, notably Eugene O'Neill's "All God's Chillun Got Wings" (February 1924), and several short pieces in dialogue by James M. Cain. Incidentally, Mencken was "violently" opposed to publishing the O'Neill play, but Nathan is said to have "threatened to resign" if it was rejected.[25]

The most dramatic episode of the magazine's early history was the result of the publication in the issue for April 1926 of a sketch by Herbert Asbury entitled "Hatrack." This was one of a series presenting the author's recollections of the religious life of a small town, later published as *Up From Methodism;* and since evangelists sometimes preached realistically against sexual misdemeanors, Asbury found an opportunity here to bring in a little character sketch of a village prostitute. It was all in the best tone of stag-party hilarity. That it exaggerated and gibed a phase of the religious and social life of the small town, and that it offended tastes more refined than those of Asbury and Mencken there can be no doubt; but surely there were few readers of the *Mercury* who considered it obscene or corrupting to morals. Harlotry doubtless has its humorous phases, and "Hatrack" followed a not unfamiliar literary tradition.

That was not the attitude of Boston's Watch and Ward Society. It seems clear that Mencken courted some overt action by this unofficial organization; his biographer says that he had anticipated it.[26] He had baited the society in September of the preceding year by publishing an article entitled "Keeping the Puritans Pure," by A. L. S. Wood of the *Springfield Union,* in which Jason Frank Chase, then secretary of the society, was ridiculed. So when the "Hatrack" number appeared, Chase notified the dealers' trade agency in Boston that it was "objectionable"; and the dealers, accustomed to unquestioned yielding to the threat of prosecution implied in a Chase edict, stopped the sale of the April *Mercury*. Thereupon Mencken and Knopf enlisted Arthur Garfield Hays, famous attorney of the American Civil Liberties Union, in behalf of the *Mercury;* and Hays suggested that Mencken make a clean-cut case of it by himself selling a copy of the banned periodical to Chief Watcher and Warder Chase within the pure precincts of Boston. Mencken agreed, Chase agreed. Wrote Hays in his recollections: "On April 5, 1926, a milling, enthusiastic, and hilarious mob of thousands gathered at the corner of Park and Tremont streets in Boston, the crowd running over onto the Boston Common. Word had leaked out that at two o'clock in the afternoon the April number of The American Mercury was to be sold. There was a huge demand for the magazine at almost any price. People were wildly waving one, five, and ten dollar bills."[27]

But only one copy was sold, and that to Chase by Mencken at fifty cents. The clowning Mencken tested the coin with his teeth. Immediately after the transaction Mencken was arrested and taken to the police station, where he furnished bail. The next morning there was a judicial hearing on the charge of selling "obscene, indecent, and impure literature . . . manifestly tending to corrupt the morals of youth." Somewhat to the surprise of the defendant,[28] the charge was dismissed. "I cannot imagine," said the judge, "anyone reading the article and finding himself or herself attracted toward vice."[29]

There were sequels to this hearing. The April *Mercury* was suppressed in many cities and towns throughout the country. A Cambridge dealer who had sold it to Harvard "youths" was actually fined a hundred dollars, which the *Mercury* paid. A week later an injunction was obtained to prevent further interference with the sale of the moot number of the magazine. But most embarrassing was the action of the United States Post Office Department in refusing to accept the April *Mercury* for mailing. Eventually Hays had to get a federal injunction to force acceptance; and then the case was carried to the Circuit Court of Appeals, which decided that the question was "academic," the April number being by that time far out of date.[30]

The case cost the *Mercury* some ten thousand dollars, which nearly exhausted its reverse.[31] Newspapers generally disapproved the ribaldry of "Hatrack" and were inclined to sympathize with the censors. A leading editorial in the *New York Herald Tribune* began: "The incurable vulgarity of Mr. H. L. Mencken is mixed with a considerable amount of business acumen. In his latest escapade he has been alert to capitalize to the utmost the egregious bad taste of an article to which the Boston authorities took exception. The case is flagrant enough to urge a stocktaking of current standards of decency in print." The writer goes on to admit that "Hatrack" was "neither obscene nor suggestive," though vulgar and indecent; and after this exercise in semantics, he adds that Mencken "is scarcely worth his space in a good jail."[32]

According to Angoff, Mencken later regretted having printed "Hatrack."[33] Commercially, as the *Herald Tribune* suggested, it was probably good business. The *Mercury*'s average net circulation for 1926 rose to about seventy thousand, and the next year it added some five thousand more. The years 1926-1928 brought the magazine's greatest prosperity.[34] Issues occasionally ran to 140 pages, of which 11 might be advertising. Book "ads" led; but clothing, foods, cosmetics, cigarettes, travel aids, and investment opportunities took much space. An amusing feature of the advertising section in these years was the series of full pages taken by manufacturers (such as the Lambert Pharmacal Company, distributors of Listerine) to criticize the *Mercury* itself and satirize its famous editor.

In July 1925, Nathan retired from his co-editorship to the position of contributing editor in charge of the departments "Clinical Notes" and "The Theater." He felt that the magazine was losing the esthetic and cultural tone that he valued most, and in 1930 he severed his connection with it entirely and sold his stock to Knopf.[35] Charles Angoff, a young Harvard graduate with a brief experience on Boston newspapers, joined the *Mercury* in 1925 as assistant editor, and eventually outstayed his chief on the staff.

The early thirties marked the end of an era of American life, and they also marked the end of the Mencken *Mercury*. The magazine's circulation dropped from 62,000 in 1930 to a little more than half of that in 1933. Relations between editor and assistant editor were often strained.[36] Samuel Knopf, the publisher's father and a heavy stockholder, died in 1932. In the probation of his will, the value of the magazine was placed at zero;[37] and this was supported by a comptroller's affidavit which declared that the *Mercury* was "a one-man magazine catering to a very selective class of readers who are followers of its editor," and that it must be reorganized to survive.[38]

The fact was that the beginning of the depression had coincided with a marked recession in the popularity of H. L. Mencken. In 1926 Walter Lippmann had called Mencken "the most powerful personal influence on this whole generation of educated people," though he had added the observation that "the man is bigger than his ideas," which are "sub-rational"—that is, he appeals to "those vital preferences which lie deeper than coherent thinking.''[39] But the "vital preferences" of the twenties were not those of the thirties. Wrote Angoff many years later: "The world was leaving him behind. Even the college boys had begun to sneer at him. . . . The clippings from the [college] newspapers were becoming more and more unfavorable, and one literary editor on the West Coast referred to him as 'The Late Mr. Mencken.' "[40]

The sober counsel of the more "coherent" thinkers was beginning to prevail under the stresses of the thirties. The *Mercury* formula was no longer so acceptable, even to the young intellectuals. Norman Cousins, trying to account for the failure of the review under Mencken, once wrote:

> There was something wrong with its basic diagnosis. America was not the home of the fools and the land of the boobs they [the editors of the *Mercury*] thought it was. There was plenty of surface stuff that made us look silly, but there was also solid stuff far more significant that had to be recognized. The items that appeared in the *Mercury*'s Americana were part of the froth and not of the essence. . . . The pulsebeat of historical America failed to come through in the *Mercury*. . . . To be totally without respect for the mechanism of hope in man as were the editors of the *Mercury* was to live in the wrong century.[41]

Doubtless the decline of Mencken's popularity had something to do with his growing wish to retire from the editorship of the *Mercury*, but there were other reasons. Because of the magazine's financial straits, he was drawing no salary.[42] He was tired and unwell. When he visited Upton Sinclair in California in the late twenties, that worthy, always a severe critic of the review "with the arsenical green covers," remarked upon his tiredness. Sinclair argued with Mencken over the *Mercury*'s emphasis on "the absurdities of democracy," and later said: "If you ask Mencken what is the remedy for these horrors, he will tell you they are the natural and inevitable manifestations of the boobus Americanus. If you ask him why then labor so monstrously, he will say that it is for his own enjoyment, he is so constituted that he finds his recreation in laughing at his fellow boobs. But watch him a while, and you will see the light of hilarity die out of his eyes, and you will note lines of tiredness in his face, and lines of not quite perfect health, and you will realize that he is lying to himself and to you; he is a new-style crusader, a Christian Anti-Christ, a propagandist of no-propaganda."[43]

Mencken retired as editor of the *American Mercury* at the end of 1933. He was succeeded by Henry Hazlitt, who had been literary editor of the *Nation*, but who had spent most of his professional life as a financial writer for newspapers. The retiring editor wrote of his successor: "He is the only competent critic that I have ever heard of who was at the same time a competent economist . . . one of the few economists in human history who could really write." He would continue the review's established policy, playing "a bright light over the national scene, revealing whatever is amusing and instructive."[44] But Hazlitt's ideas, it soon developed, did not fit with the *Mercury* pattern, and after a few months he resigned the editorship to Angoff.[45]

Changes in editorship, however, did not restore prosperity. The magazine continued to decline both in the zestful and uninhibited spirit that had once been its fundamental elixir and, more alarmingly, in circulation. And so, in 1935, Knopf sold the *Mercury*[46] to Paul Palmer and Lawrence E. Spivak, the former coming from the newspaper field, and the latter from magazine work. Palmer took over the editorship and Spivak the publisher's chair. A new policy was proclaimed: the review would renounce its left-wing tendencies and become a kind of combination *Forum-New Yorker-Collier's*. Lombard C. Jones was managing editor briefly; he was succeeded by Gordon Carroll. Angoff, offered an associate editorship, declared that he "would rather go out and shovel manure . . . than associate myself with the publication they have in mind."[47]

Whatever Angoff preferred to shovel, the *Mercury* handled much excellent and well-written material under the new management. Laurence Stallings wrote the book reviews in "The Library." "The Clinic" had some resemblance to the old "Arts and Sciences" department; it contained short articles on social, scientific, and economic matters. Among contributors were Katharine Fullerton Gerould, William Henry Chamberlin (on Russia), Ralph Adams Cram, Ford Madox Ford, and Anthony M. Turano. Mencken contributed two articles attacking Roosevelt in 1936.

But circulation continued on the downward curve. A strike of the office staff called by the Office Workers' Union in June 1935, which triggered picketing for fourteen weeks, did not help matters.[48] Advertising had fallen off dangerously and circulation had dropped below thirty thousand when, in the fall of 1936, radical changes in format, price, and editorial policy saved the magazine. The pocket, or "digest," size was adopted, with 128 double-column pages. The old fifty-cent price was cut in half. The magazine took a strong conservative stand— anti-New Deal, pro-capitalism. "President Roosevelt," declared an editorial in 1938, "no longer desires recovery under the present Capitalist system."[49] A strong drive against Stalinism and against Soviet infiltration in America was initiated; Eugene Lyons was the chief contributor in this field. Topics related to sex were common in the magazine for a few years. Havelock Ellis wrote on "Studies in Sex: A History" (January 1936) and Mencken on "Utopia by Sterilization" (August 1937); but the articles that provoked the most scathing replies in the "Open Forum" were two by anonymous women—"I Believe in the Double Standard," by "A Wife" (April 1937) and "Chastity on the Campus," by "A Co-Ed" (June 1938). A rather plaintive reply to the latter by a Brooklyn girl declares her intention to remain chaste in spite of everything.[50]

Departments were reshuffled. "Americana" was retained, of course, though shrunken to two or three of the smaller pages. John W. Thomason, Jr., reviewed books in "The Library"; and "The Check List," repository of brief reviews, was eventually taken out of the advertising section to appear in the body of the book. "Open Forum," a revival of "The Soap Box," which had appeared toward the end of the Mencken regime, invited short letters from irate or pleased readers; it occasionally ran to nearly twenty pages. "Book Preview," giving extracts from forthcoming books, and "The Other Side," in which prominent liberals were given their say, were short-lived departments. A little nature essay by Alan Devoe appeared each month under the heading "Down to Earth." "Poetry" was a departmental heading for a few years; later the poems were again distributed through the magazine. Perhaps the best of the new departments was one in which Albert J. Nock for a few years discussed public affairs, speaking for the editorial board. And, finally, Nathan came back in 1938 to do a theater department for the ensuing twelve years.

Among leading contributors during the Palmer editorship were Harold Lord Varney, Benjamin Stolberg, and Stewart H. Holbrook. An article by Varney in the number for December 1936 accusing the American Civil Liberties Union of undue sympathies for Russia brought on a libel suit. When Mencken entered the picture by protesting that the suit was a threat to the freedom of the press, for which the A. C. L. U. had always stood, Director Arthur Garfield Hays of the Union suggested that Mencken act as arbitrator. The idea of Mencken the extremist judicially weighing the matters in dispute was ludicrous, but he did just that. The printing of his report in the *Mercury* was supposed to settle the whole matter; but inasmuch as he found against both contestants, there was an aftermath of replies. "I am substantially right," Mencken concluded, "and decline to change a word."[51]

The new *Mercury,* in the smaller size and at the smaller price, more than doubled its circulation in a short time, but it lost advertising. American Mercury Books—reprints of popular books in soft covers at twenty-five cents—proved to be a money-maker, however. It began in 1937, with James M. Cain's "The Postman Always Rings Twice," advertised as "a classic of the tough school of American fiction"; and the series developed into the extensive business of Mercury Publications, Inc., publishers of mystery and science fiction magazines and books.[52] This was the first successful modern paperbound series in America. It was a Spivak idea, and it furnished the profits to keep the *Mercury* going during the Spivak administration.

Lawrence E. Spivak, son of a New York dress manufacturer, was a Harvard graduate and had been assistant publisher of *Hunting and Fishing* before he came to the *Mercury* as business manager in 1933. When he purchased complete control of the magazine in 1939, he installed Eugene Lyons as editor. Russian-born Lyons had been brought to New York as a child and there, after

some work at City College, he had become very interested in Communism. He edited *Soviet Russia Pictorial 1922-1923,* and became an assistant director of Tass, the Russian news and propaganda agency; but he never joined the Communist Party. A term of six years as United Press correspondent in Russia brought him into close touch with events and situations and broke the spell that the Soviet ideology had held over him; and after his recall in 1934 at the demand of the U.S.S.R. authorities, he became one of the most prominent anti-Soviet writers in America. Under Lyons' editorship and Spivak's management, the *Mercury* became a leader in the attack on Stalin and in exposing Communist "penetration" in the United States. In this crusade he was assisted by John Roy Carlson, whose *Under Cover* was a sensational and controversial best-seller in 1943; Jan Valtin, whose *Out of the Night* scored a similar success in 1941; and others.

Another cause strongly and repeatedly presented in the *Mercury* in these years was that of the importance of the air force in our military system. Major Alexander P. de Seversky wrote many articles about the superiority of air attack and defense in the early forties. These were supported by several contributions of Colonel Hugh J. Knerr in 1942.

Articles were usually short, as they had been since the change to the smaller size, and content was varied. An outstanding article of Lyons' editorship was Thomas Wolfe's "The Anatomy of Loneliness" (October 1941). Mary M. Colum had charge of "The Library" for a year or two; thereafter the reviewing was shared by several hands. Associate editors for short terms were Allen Churchill, William Doerflinger and John Tebbel; in 1943 Angoff dropped his shovel and came back to the *Mercury* to serve first as literary editor and then as managing editor as long as Spivak remained as publisher.

With the number for July 1944, Lyons retired from the editorship to take charge of the new magazine *Pageant;* and Spivak became both editor and publisher. He and Angoff filled the *Mercury* with stimulating articles on lively questions. Kingsbury Smith's series about the workings of the State Department was outstanding. The magazine, on the whole, took a more liberal position than it had once occupied. Norman Angell and Russell Davenport were contributors, along with many writers comparatively unknown. Nathan and Devoe continued their departments, and in 1948 Bergen Evans started a new one on popular superstitions headed "Skeptic's Corner." More attractive covers than the magazine had ever known were supplied by Al Hirschfield; they carried colored caricature-portraits of public figures.

In the years 1943-1945, the *Mercury* gradually increased its circulation, reaching an average of eighty thousand per issue, the highest of its history; then it began to slide down again. In a day of mass circulations, the *Mercury* was a midget. Spivak was losing about $100,000 a year on the magazine, making up its deficits out of the profits of Mercury Publications, Inc.[53] In 1949 the price per copy was raised to thirty-five cents, and circulation declined to forty thousand. The absorption of *Common Sense,* an anti-Communist monthly, did not help much. In the fall of 1950 Spivak sold the magazine to Clendenin J. Ryan for about $50,000,[54] and thereafter devoted himself to "Meet the Press," which had started on radio in October 1945 and moved to television in November 1947. Four years later Spivak sold Mercury Publications, Inc., to Joseph W. Ferman, who had been associated with him for several years on the magazine and in the publishing concern.

Ryan, the new owner, was the son of Thomas Fortune Ryan, and a man of wealth who could afford to experiment with a magazine of famous name and lively spirit. He had once been an assistant to Mayor La Guardia of New York City, and was interested in political reform. He now associated himself with William Bradford Huie, lecturer, author, and air-power devotee, who was given "complete autonomy of policy and action" in the conduct of the magazine. Huie at once declared his intention to "re-create the magazine in the Mencken tradition," but with a difference: "The boobs," he said, "have become bureaucrats; the censors have become commissars; the yahoos have been marshaled into pressure groups." But he added, "We are more interested in manners, morals, and the arts than in politics."[55] Angoff was succeeded as managing editor by Susie Berg. The price was again placed at twenty-five cents.

Manners and morals did indeed occupy much space in what was for a short time called *The New American Mercury.* The editor found time, between lecture engagements and television broadcasts, to write much for the magazine himself, including a fiction serial of 1951 entitled "The Revolt of Mamie Stover," which was announced as "a serious book about a whore."[56] Alfred Towne's "Homosexuality in American Culture" ran in the fall of 1951. And so on. Lee Mortimer, author of *Washington Confidential* and such classics, was a steady contributor.

But the magazine was not all sex. Huie hated Truman, and in an open letter to General Eisenhower advised him to break with the President and announce himself openly as a candidate for the Republican nomination for the presidency.[57] The magazine was now throughly conservative in politics. Too much of its literary criticism was on the level of one writer's dismissal of Irving Howe's analysis of Sherwood Anderson: "The silliest damn statement I've heard in years."[58] But the *Mercury* retained as contributors such writers from the Spivak regime as Nathan, Holbrook, Devoe, Tebbel, Stolberg, and Evans.

Two years of paying deficits were enough for Ryan, and in 1952 he sold the magazine to J. Russell Maguire, multimillionaire oil man and munitions-maker. The new owner was not as complaisant toward his editor's policy as Ryan had been; and beginning February 1953 Huie was supplanted by John A. Clements, who had been promotion director of the Hearst magazines, with Joseph B. Breed as managing editor. The price went to thirty-five cents.

The emphasis on sex now disappeared, and the anti-Red theme was resumed with vigor. The *Mercury* defended Senator Joseph McCarthy in his drive against Soviet "infiltration"; and, in general, it took a strong right-wing Republican position. J. B. Matthews was chief editorial writer, assisted, especially in the crusade against Communism, by the indefatigable Lyons and Varney, as well as by Ralph de Toledano and Alan Set. George Fielding Eliot, John T. Flynn, and Harry T. Brundidge were frequent contributors. There were many short departments. Variety and brevity were watchwords; forty or more articles might appear in a single number, each from one to four pages in length. There were a few full-page cartoons.

A clean sweep changed the editorial management of the magazine in the fall of 1955. Editor Clements and his chief associates and contributors went out, and owner Maguire carried on until the appointment of William La Varre to the editorship in 1957. La Varre, explorer and feature writer, had the assistance of Natasha Boissevain, who had become managing editor on Clements' retirement; and Maguire continued to write editorials. Maurine Halliburton succeeded to the editorship in the summer of 1958.

The editorial policy was now very clear: the *Mercury* was an organ of rather extreme right-wing Republicanism. It published short contributions by United States senators, members of Congress, and governors belonging to that faction; and its editorials supported that school of thought. Many of its articles dealt with international affairs, but there was still a wide variety in its offering outside of politics. The "Forum" departments for readers' letters were lively and interesting. Articles on the popular religious movement had some prominence; Billy Graham, J. Howard Pew, and James Hargis wrote in that field. Circulation advanced gradually in the fifties to some seventy thousand.

It is impossible to measure such an intangible as the "influence" of a magazine. One cannot doubt, however, that the *American Mercury* under most of Mencken's editorship had a considerable effect on the thinking of many people—chiefly, perhaps, in the younger and more literate groups. Also, it seems evident that the magazine under the Spivak management in the forties had a notable impact on public opinion. Its later advenures in sex problems and "McCarthyism" were less impressive. In the fifties it was in some ways a spokesman for conservatives in politics. But in 1960, when one sees the magazine on a news-stand, one is likely to exclaim, "Oh, is the *American Mercury* still published?"*

[1] TITLES: *The American Mercury.* (*The New American Mercury,* Dec. 1950 Feb. 1951 only.)

FIRST ISSUE: Jan. 1924. Current.

PERIODICITY: Monthly, 1924-62. 3 vols. yearly, 1924-40 (1-51); 2 vols. yearly, 1941-61 (52-93); 1 vol. yearly,

1962-current. Monthly, 1962 except for Summer (May, June, July) and Sept.-Oct.; quarterly, 1963-current (Fall, 1965, omitted).

PUBLISHERS: Alfred A. Knopf, Inc., 1924-35 (Samuel Knopf, business manager, 1924-32, Lawrence Edmund Spivak, 1933-35); L. E. Spivak, 1935-36; Paul Palmer, 1936-39; L. E. Spivak, 1939-50 (Joseph W. Ferman, bus. man., 1940-50); Clendenin J. Ryan, 1950-51; J. Russell Maguire, 1952-60 (Robert C. Hodgson, bus. man., 1953-56; Leslie J. Yarbrough, 1956-60); all New York. Defenders of the Christian Faith, Inc. (Gwynne W. Davidson, chairman; M. L. Flowers, bus. man.), 1960-62; Oklahoma City. The Legion for the Survival of Freedom, Inc. (E. Wiltsie Platzer, chairman, 1963-66; Bruce Holman, chairman, 1966-current), 1963-66. The Legion name is missing from Fall and Winter, 1966, but Holman is still listed as "Chairman of the Board." (Edwin A. Walker states in the Sept. 1965 issue that he was publisher Dec. 1964—Sept. 1965.) McAllen, Texas, 1963-65; Houston, Texas, 1966; Torrance, Calif., 1966-current.

EDITORS: Henry Louis Mencken and George Jean Nathan, 1924-25; H. L. Mencken, 1925-33; Henry Hazlitt, 1934; Charles Angoff, 1934-35; Paul Palmer, 1935-39; Eugene Lyons, 1939-44; L. E. Spivak, 1944-50; William Bradford Huie, 1950-53; John A. Clements, 1953-55; J. R. Maguire, 1955-57; William La Varre, 1957-58; Maurine Halliburton, 1958-60; Gerald S. Pope, 1960-62; Marcia C. J. Matthews, 1963; Jason Matthews, 1963-64; Edwin A. Walker (man. ed.), Dec. 1964-65; La Vonne Doden Furr, 1966-current.

INDEX: *Readers' Guide* to 1961.

REFERENCES: Anon., "The Importance of Charles Angoff," *Little Review,* v. 4, August 1917, pp. 37-48; M. K. Singleton, *H. L. Mencken and the American Mercury Adventure* (Durham, N.C., 1962); Johnny L. Kloefkorn, "A Critical Study of the Work of H. L. Mencken As Literary Editor and Critic of *The American Mercury,*" Emporia State Research Studies, v. 7, no. 4 (Kansas State Teachers College, 1959); Stephen E. Fitzgerald, "The Mencken Myth," *Saturday Review,* Dec. 17, 1960, pp. 13-15, 71; Lawrence E. Spivak and Charles Angoff, eds., *The American Mercury Reader* (Philadelphia, 1944).

2 William Manchester, *Disturber of the Peace: The Life of H. L. Mencken* (New York, 1951), pp. 148-49. The author is indebted to this work for many facts pertaining to the Mencken editorship of the *Mercury,* which Mr. Manchester derived from personal communication with his subject.

3 *New Republic,* v. 37, Feb. 6, 1924, p. 274.

4 Mencken, in *American Mercury,* v. 30, Dec. 1933, p. 387.

5 See circulation figures month by month, *Mercury,* v. 6, Dec. 1925, pp. xlii-xliv; also *N. W. Ayer & Son's Directory of Newspapers and Periodicals* (Philadelphia, 1925-

current). Circulation figures given later in this chapter are based chiefly on *Ayer.*

6 *American Mercury,* v. 1, Jan. 1924, pp. 27-28.

7 *Ibid.,* v. 1, Jan. 1924, pp. 75-76.

8 *Ibid.,* v. 1, Jan. 1924, p. 30.

9 *New Republic,* v. 37, Feb. 6, 1924, p. 274.

10 *American Mercury,* v. 6, Dec. 1925, pp. 451, 458.

11 *New Republic,* v. 131, Sept. 13, 1954, p. 19.

12 *American Mercury,* v. 15, Dec. 1928, pp. 407-8.

13 *Ibid.,* v. 19, Feb. 1930, p. 220.

14 *Ibid.,* v. 18, Oct. 1929, p. 185.

15 Alfred Kazin, *On Native Grounds* (New York, 1942), pp. 203-4.

16 *American Mercury,* v. 1, Feb. 1924, p. 248.

17 *Ibid.,* v. 5, Aug. 1925, p. xxxviii. This appeared in the "Check List," a department of brief notices, but I have the word of Mr. Angoff, then assistant editor, that Mencken wrote it (Angoff to Mott, June 13, 1959).

18 Eric F. Goldman, *Rendezvous With Destiny* (New York, 1952), p. 316.

19 H. L. Mencken, *The American Language,* 4th ed. (New York, 1936), p. 560, n. 1.

20 Manchester, *Disturber of the Peace,* pp. 153-54. For comment on this assimilative process in contributions to the *Mercury,* see Oscar Cargill, *Intellectual America* (New York, 1941), p. 494.

21 Charles Angoff in the *New Republic,* v. 131, Sept. 13, 1954, p. 21.

22 Charles Angoff, *H. L. Mencken: A Portrait From Memory* (New York, 1956), pp. 107-8.

23 Angoff, *Mencken,* p. 83 and chap. vii. Angoff says Mencken in later life bought up any stray copies of his *Ventures Into Verse* when he found them, and destroyed them. No wonder: see quotations from the volume in Cargill, *Intellectual America,* p. 484.

24 *American Mercury,* v. 1, Jan. 1924, p. 30.

25 Statement made to Lawrence E. Spivak by Angoff, and reported in a letter (Feb 10, 1959) to Mott.

26 Manchester, *Disturber of the Peace,* p. 187. The fullest accounts of the "Hatrack" episode are in chap vii of this

book and in Arthur Garfield Hays, *Let Freedom Ring,* revised ed. (New York, 1937), pp. 157-85.

[27] Hays, *Let Freedom Ring,* p. 160.

[28] Manchester, *Disturber of the Peace,* p. 196.

[29] Hays, *Let Freedom Ring,* p. 169.

[30] *The American Mercury v. Kiely, Postmaster, et al.,* 19 Fed. (2d) 295 (1927).

[31] Manchester, *Disturber of the Peace,* p. 207.

[32] *New York Herald Tribune,* April 7, 1926, p. 22, col. 1.

[33] Angoff, *Mencken,* p. 52.

[34] Lawrence E. Spivak, later business manager of the magazine, writes (Jan. 30, 1959): "According to my figures, the *Mercury* reached its highest volume of business—close to $415,000—in 1927, but it reached its highest profit of $16,000 on a volume of $373,000 in 1926. The profit in 1927 was only $6,000; in 1928 it was $8,500; and in 1929 the magazine lost about $15,000. It continued to lose money through 1939, with the exception of 1933, when it made $900 largely because of vigorous cuts in expenditures." Letter quoted with permission of the author.

[35] Manchester, *Disturber of the Peace,* pp. 219-20.

[36] Angoff, *Mencken,* pp. 217-18.

[37] *Newsweek,* v. 8, Sept. 26, 1936, p. 48.

[38] Manchester, *Disturber of the Peace,* p. 266.

[39] *Saturday Review of Literature,* v. 3, Dec. 11, 1926, p. 413. This article was reprinted in pamphlet form by Knopf.

[40] Angoff, *Mencken,* p. 225. Manchester, a much more sympathetic biographer, agrees about the decay of Mencken's popularity; *Disturber of the Peace,* pp. 266-67.

[41] *Saturday Review of Literature,* v. 37, June 12, 1954, p. 22.

[42] Letter from Spivak, Jan. 30, 1959. Spivak adds: "According to my recollection Mencken never drew more than $9,000 a year." Letter quoted with permission of the author.

[43] Upton Sinclair, *Money Writes!* (New York, 1927), pp. 131-32. Chaps. viii and xxvi in this volume are devoted to criticisms of Mencken.

[44] *American Mercury,* v. 30, Dec. 1933, pp. 385, 386.

[45] Hazlitt joined the editorial staff in the fall of 1933, and announcement of the change was made in the papers on October 5; but his name did not appear as editor until January 1934. Angoff took over with the May 1934 issue, though he was not given the title of editor until August.

[46] This statement oversimplifies a complicated deal by which Business Manager Spivak bought the magazine in January 1935 for its debt ($38,000) to be paid out of problematical profits; but, as Spivak remembers it, Palmer a little later advanced some cash and he and Spivak divided the stock equally. In April, under this ownership, Spivak became publisher and Palmer editor. A year later the company needed money and Spivak gave up his half of the stock when Palmer put up more cash. Spivak then resigned as "publisher," but continued as business manager (Spivak letter, Jan. 30, 1959).

[47] *Newsweek,* v. 5, Feb. 2, 1935, p. 26.

[48] Much attention was given to the issues of this labor contest by the *New Republic,* v. 83, July 10, 1935, p. 254, and the *Nation,* v. 140, June 26, 1935, p. 741, and v. 141, July 31, 1935, pp. 128-29. [The strike was called by the Office Workers' Union after the dismissal of two employees from the *Mercury* staff, which had joined the union only a few days before. The union chose to interpret the dismissal as reprisal for union affiliation, which would have been against the law according to NRA regulations; Spivak and Palmer disavowed previous knowledge that the staff had been unionized, and insisted the cause of firing was "inefficiency." The dispute was taken to the Regional Labor Board which, in May, handed down a decision favorable to the strikers. However, the Supreme Court decision of that same month voided the NRA, resulting in the National Labor Relations Board dropping the *Mercury* case. Palmer had ignored the decision anyway, and tried to ignore the continued picketing and to carry on as usual. Mass picketing which developed in mid-June continued into July, with rough behavior causing many police problems. After fourteen weeks, the strike was called off in August, although a boycott continued. Spivak in the June 26 *Nation* attributed the trouble to a "radical group" which disapproved of the recent editorial change in the *Mercury* from an extreme left position of the previous editor to that of "liberalism" which was "always its tradition." It is of interest to note that in 1949 the C.I.O. took action to expel the Office Workers' Union from its membership because of Communist domination.]

[49] *American Mercury,* v. 45, Nov. 1938, p. 257.

[50] *Ibid.,* v. 45, Sept. 1938, p. 117.

[51] *Ibid.,* v. 45, Oct. 1938, p. 240.

[52] See Frank L. Schick, *The Paperbound Book in America* (New York, 1958), pp. 62-65.

[53] Correspondence with Spivak, Jan. 30, 1959.

[54] About half in cash and half in subscription liabilities (Spivak correspondence).

[55] All quotations in this paragraph are from the editor's statement, *American Mercury,* v. 71, Dec. 1950, pp. 665-68.

[56] *Ibid.,* v. 72, March 1951, p. 280.

[57] *Ibid.,* v. 73, Dec. 1951, pp. 3-8.

[58] *Ibid.,* v. 72, May 1951, p. 616.

* This historical sketch was written in 1960. In 1966 the *American Mercury* was not likely to be seen on a newsstand, but it was still published, presumably by the Legion for the Survival of Freedom, Inc. (see n. 1). In the issue for June 1966, it was stated that *Western Destiny, Folk,* and *Northern World* had merged with the *Mercury.*

The magazine proclaims it has been "published continuously since it was founded by H. L. Mencken and George Jean Nathan," but certainly the only continuity is in name and volume numbering. It is now a vehicle for severe criticism by the ultra-conservatives.

In 1959 Lawrence Spivak wrote that if he had known what was going to happen to the *Mercury* when he sold it in 1950 to Clendenin J. Ryan, he "would have buried it. . . . It is a shame that the magazine that contributed so much and earned a great name in its day, should come to its present low state" (Spivak to Mott, Jan. 30, 1959, quoted with permission of author). Since 1960 the magazine has shifted ever further to the right in its editorial policy.

Harriet Helms Wagniere

SOURCE: "Behind the Scenes: Charles Angoff and the American Mercury," in *The Old Century and the New: Essays in Honor of Charles Angoff,* edited by Alfred Rosa, Associated University Presses, 1978, pp. 79-93.

[*In the following essay, Wagniere emphasizes Charles Angoff's role in editing the* American Mercury *from 1925 to 1935.*]

The *American Mercury* magazine entered the world of quality journalism with its first issue in January 1924, co-founded and co-edited by George Jean Nathan and H. L. Mencken. They were fresh from their triumphs as co-editors of the *Smart Set,* where they had already established a following. Mencken, however, had begun to shift his emphasis away from literature toward the political and social scene in America. Nathan, on the other hand, had hoped to focus on belles-lettres in the new journal. Early in the days of the *Mercury,* Mencken and Nathan would "split" ostensibly over Nathan's insistence that Eugene O'Neill's play, *All God's Chillun Got Wings,* appear in the magazine. The play had been written by O'Neill especially at Nathan's request for material for the magazine's first issue. Mencken objected to its publication on grounds that it shed no light on the workings of American democracy. Despite this disagreement, *All*

God's Chillun Got Wings was printed in the February 1924 issue; Nathan had won the battle, but was to lose the war. In addition to their diverging interests, Mencken claimed that Nathan was not doing his share of the editorial work. It was a matter of time before Mencken approached Alfred Knopf, the *Mercury*'s publisher, with an ultimatum, and Nathan was soon out as co-editor, although he continued to write two columns, "The Theatre" and "Clinical Notes."

The Nathan-Mencken "split" was the reason for Charles Angoff's catapult into the offices of the *American Mercury.* Mencken became anxious to find someone capable of assisting him with the editorial work. Later Mencken confided to Angoff that of the thousands of applicants for the job, he was the only one with "the good sense" to include samples of his writing.[1] Once chosen, Angoff was given only three days of orientation before Mencken left him in charge of the entire operation of that notable magazine to return to his home in Baltimore. A young man, just graduated from Harvard in 1923, Angoff was an intellectual who, like Nathan, had a literary bent, and whose presence on the *Mercury,* after Nathan's relegation to "The Theatre" and "Clinical Notes" contributions, would serve to offset the heaviness of Mencken's preponderance with politics. Many of the important pieces of literature that saw print on the pages of the *Mercury* in the early days were, of course, due to Nathan's influence. But there was also an important area in which Angoff had a hand.

Because of the heavy responsibilities that were placed on him (and as time passed he would take an ever-growing share of the editorial burden), Angoff would also be "developing into one of the best managing editors in the country."[2] The highly efficient office of the *American Mercury* was the result of two things: Angoff's diligence and ability, and Mencken's Prussian influence. His first instructions from Mencken on his duties were simple but authoritative. He had twenty-four hours to answer mail and no time to lose in handling manuscripts. As M. K. Singleton notes, Angoff's jobs, the many "hats" he has had to wear, included the following:

> Angoff soon learned the facts about the monthly: the buying policy did not permit accumulation of manuscripts, nor was he to buy serial features or essays dealing with . . . non-American matters; a knowledge of legal restrictions on the republication of the *Mercury* material was acquired and he soon became familiar with Mencken's habits of arranging the format early every month (the regular mailing date was the fifteenth of every month); most important, he became sensitive to his boss's personal preferences, and he tried assiduously to follow them.[3]

Angoff had been hired as what Mencken "called 'a slave.' With one, he predicted to Knopf, he could get the business of the magazine done and dispense with Nathan."[4] It had been Nathan's refusal to do routine editorial work that had created this opportunity for Angoff, an enormous challenge that he proved capable of meeting.

Mencken was delighted to have Angoff. He now had relief from the oppression of dealing with the six or seven hundred manuscripts that arrived at the *Mercury* office each month.[5] On the third day after Angoff's arrival, Mencken announced that he was leaving New York for his home in Baltimore. If that was not a sufficient enough shock, Mencken also said that he would be gone three or four weeks.[6] "'Anyway,' said Mencken, 'the office is yours. I don't want to hear from you unless it's something very urgent. If any masterpieces come in, hold them till you hear from me, but they won't come in. . . . So you're the general from now on. Bye.' And he was off."[7] Angoff's natural response was, as he recalled it, that "I was terrified. I worked as I had never worked before."[8] Mencken was to be well-satisfied, and in a letter to his friend Phil Goodman on February 4, 1925, he wrote, Angoff "turns out to be very good. He has already relieved me of much of my routine drudgery, and I hope to put even more on him."[9] When Mencken returned to New York three weeks later, he praised Angoff for the work he had done and told him he would not only be kept on the *Mercury*, but that he was asking Knopf to raise his salary.[10]

In retrospect Angoff remarked, "The reason Mencken took so much from me, was that he needed me. It would have taken four people, at least, to replace me."[11]

Angoff did almost everything on the magazine. Besides looking through the manuscripts as they came in and rejecting them or passing them on to Mencken when it was warranted, he also wrote to authors with suggestions for manuscript revisions.

> I was the first reader of all manuscripts. There were no second or third or fourth readers as on so many magazines, for Mencken said: "A number of readers on a magazine only means that the magazine is overstaffed . . . that no one of its editors is really competent. . . . An editor is an editor in all things."[12]

Angoff was also to write brief reviews for the *Mercury*'s "Check List" of new books. This job, in addition to everything else, was assigned to Angoff within the first three days. Small wonder that he would say, "My head was in a whirl, and I wondered how on earth I could handle what seemed like so complicated an administrative task. . . ."[13] Mencken also gave Angoff the important job of proofreader. Mencken's instructions were: "The proofs—you read them and keep the master proof, for the make-up. I may read some proofs, and I may not. We send proofs to all authors. Add their corrections to your own."[14] The responsibility for making certain that there were no typographical or other errors in the final pages of the *Mercury* was an awesome one, one that was usually handled by several proofreaders on other magazines. Angoff was to become superior in this area of the technical aspects of editing. He would later routinely allow "plenty of time to polish it [the final make-up]—the writing, the layout, the typography, the order of the articles."[15] Angoff commented that "one of the things both Mencken and I were especially proud of was the reputa-

tion the *Mercury* had won for its excellent technical editing." An amusing story about how well Angoff would perform this job took place in the *Mercury* office between Angoff and Mencken. There were only two days before the issue was to go to the printer, and Angoff was anxious to get started. When he pressed him to begin, he was told by Mencken, who was in one of his frequently humorous moods:

> I know what you have on your mind, Meester Angoff. You want time to read the proofs again, and give it a final touch. Well, I think we ought to have a couple of typos in the next issue. Pearl [Raymond Pearl, the noted biologist of Johns Hopkins University] was telling me the other day that he spent two whole nights on the last issue looking for a grammatical or typographical mistake. He gave up in disgust and filled himself with English beer, the worst in the world.[16]

Despite his joking, Mencken felt strongly about the importance of having an editor perform this function instead of a full-time proofreader. He told Angoff that

> having a full-time proofreader on a magazine . . . was worse than a waste of money. It was an assurance of bad proofreading, for [to him] there was more involved in proofreading than checking spelling and typographical errors. A good proofreader, he believed, was ready to violate grammar and "good usage" in order to preserve the author's special flavor and style, and the only one who could be such a proofreader, therefore, was the editor who knew all the reasons why the manuscript was bought and who was eager to preserve those reasons in the printed page.[17]

In the matter of accepting manuscripts, Mencken and Angoff had a similar arrangement to the one that Nathan and Mencken had adopted, with the exception that Mencken had the final word with regard to Angoff's decisions. However, it is an indication of the respect that Mencken had for Angoff's ability, that he was often able to persuade Mencken to accept an article or story after he had initially refused it. On one point, though, Mencken was relentless. His Prussian insistence on the speedy flow of manuscripts was part of this demand for efficiency. He told Angoff, "Get rid of all manuscripts, one way or another, within a day, never longer than two days. It's impolite to keep anything longer."[18]

The fact that the important job of reading and selecting manuscripts was relegated to a half a dozen readers on each of such magazines as the *Forum*, the *Century*, the *Atlantic*, and *Harper's*, was considered "preposterous" by Mencken, notes Angoff. Therefore, full burden for first readership on the *American Mercury* was thrown on Angoff's shoulders as well. Mencken informed him of this responsibility as follows:

> Run through the manuscripts. If you see anything you like real well and think we ought to buy, let me see it, otherwise reject it. Except, of course,

stuff that is all right but needs repairing. In that case tell them how you want it repaired. If they come through with an acceptable manuscript, send it on to me. Otherwise, send it back for further repairs. . . . Most of the manuscripts stink on sight. . . . If a first reader doesn't know the difference between a good and a lousy manuscript, he should be fired. Every editor should be a potential chief editor, ready to take over on an instant's notice.[19]

Mencken was right in this respect, and one day Angoff would take over the editorship of the *Mercury*. This insistence on editorial competence by Mencken is also analogous to Nathan's demand that the dramatic acuity of critics and their knowledge of their craft be such that they should be able to tell the quality of a play "within twenty minutes."

Angoff, who like Nathan had intense literary interests, was responsible for getting "Ballad of the Gallows Bird" by Edwin Markham for the *American Mercury*. The poem had been "rejected by Mencken before Angoff's arrival,"[20] but when he heard of it he contacted Markham by phone and in less than a week he had the poem on his desk. The original piece, if uncut, would have taken "eleven pages in the *Mercury*."[21] Angoff saw approximately twelve stanzas that could be deleted without harming the poem. He says he had to muster his courage to call Markham and suggest the cuts because of his great respect for his work, especially "The Man with the Hoe."[22] Angoff was surprised and pleased when Markham agreed to the changes. There still remained the problem of Mencken's approval about printing it, since even after the cuts it would take up ten pages. Angoff informed Markham of the situation, and assured him that he would do everything possible to get that approval. Markham "chuckled and merely said: 'God bless you, young man.'"[23]

Angoff immediately called Baltimore to tell Mencken. When Mencken "exclaimed" over the length, Angoff said he did a little fibbing to get him to come around. "That's the best I could do," he told Mencken. "I argued and argued with Markham and I had a hell of a time getting him to agree to the cuts. Either we take it now with the cuts, or we send it back."[24] Mencken asked Angoff to read several stanzas to him. Then Mencken said, "You'll never be an actor or an elocutionist, my boy, but the stuff has swing to it. All right, buy it. But if he gives you any more trouble, send the damn stuff back to him." Angoff knowingly replied, "He won't."[25] In August 1926 "Ballad of the Gallows Bird" was printed in the *Mercury*, all ten pages of it after editing.[26]

Because of this little episode, Markham and Angoff became friends—"as much as a man in his early twenties and a man in his sixties could be friends."[27] The thought occurred to Angoff that Markham "might have, at the bottom of one of his trunks," some other poetry, or an article that the *Mercury* would print.[28] Mencken gave Angoff the day off, as he had asked, to go to Staten Island to Markham's home. But Mencken warned him not to expect to get any material.

Angoff said that Mencken turned out to be right. Markham, it seems, "preferred to talk about a new religion, Unity, in which he was greatly interested." Then he said, "Young man, . . . would you like to be saved?"[29] Angoff answered "yes" and Markham replied, "Fine. Give me a dollar, and I'll see you get some fine, inspiring, uplifting literature for a whole year."[30] Angoff handed over a dollar and Markham "continued to talk about the glories of Unity."[31] Despite Angoff's attempts to return to the subject of Markham's contributing something else to the *Mercury*, he could not be dissuaded from talking about Unity.

> "It is the New Light come to enlighten the world," he said in a quavering voice, "and it is young men like you, with the light of old wisdom in their eyes and the strength of the New Order of Evolution, who must help spread it upon the earth and among the people."[32]

Angoff began his [writing] career with a boom; his first article, "Boston Twilight," appeared in December 1925. A long-time resident of Boston, he denounced "the cultural poverty of Irish elements in the Hub city and made passing remarks about censorship."[33] This article was followed by two others: "The Baptists," in February 1926, and "The Methodists," in April 1926.[34] Both were written under the pseudonym James D. Bernard. In "The Methodists" Angoff once again took a crack at the Watch and Ward Society, a group of Boston censors led by the Reverend T. Frank Chase.

Kemler says that Mencken felt that the articles did not do "justice to the subject,"[35] but it soon became obvious that they had hit their target. They would produce sufficient ill feeling in Boston to cause the Watch and Ward Society to ban the April issue of the *American Mercury* and bring legal action because of a story in that number, "Hatrack," which would lend its name to the famous censorship fight known as the "Hatrack" case. Kemler records the incident as follows:

> After the December attack, Chase advised his friends that the *Mercury* was such a filthy magazine that sooner or later he would have to suppress it. After looking at the April attack he soon found the pretext he was looking for. It was "Hatrack," a study of a prostitute. At once he issued the order outlawing the issue. . . . On March 30 he issued press releases explaining that "Hatrack" was immoral, "unfit to read," "full of filthy and degrading descriptions" . . . the injustice of the thing fell full upon him [Mencken]. Months before, Mencken had selected "Hatrack" from Herbert Asbury's forthcoming book about his boyhood in Farmington, Missouri. . . . It ["Hatrack"] ridiculed the evangelists who went through town, railing against imaginary bawdy houses, while it spoke very compassionately about the town's one and only prostitute, called Hatrack because of her figure, who accommodated her customers in the cemetery.[36]

What happened is now history. Mencken went to Boston, himself, deliberately to be arrested selling an issue on

Brimstone Corner to Frank Chase, to dramatize the situation. "By the daring of his defiance, he would attract widespread public attention, rallying a nationwide opposition to the Boston censorship."[37] In the trial that then took place, the judge dismissed the case after stating his opinion of the *Mercury*'s April issue: "I have read every article in the magazine . . . and find them all intellectual and of a serious nature. . . . I do not find anything in any other article that touches upon sex except 'Hatrack,' but there the subject is not made attractive—in fact the contrary is the case."[38] Kemler notes that Mencken was told by a "Knopf Boston book agent that the city's Irish politicians had really been outraged and had become 'anti-Mencken' because of the 'Boston Twilight' article, and the 'Hatrack' story had only been a pretext to confiscate the *Mercury*."[39]

The *American Mercury* and Mencken had won an important and well-publicized victory. But as Angoff later wrote: "The whole case did not sit so well on the literary conscience of the *Mercury* nor was it very comfortable in his [Mencken's] own mind. There was something shabby and flamboyant about it."[40] Mencken had felt that the whole thing had been a mistake; "If you're going to fight the moralists, fight them with something that has high literary value in itself, that you're not ashamed of."[41]

In the course of Angoff's career on the *Mercury*, several of his articles would draw intense reactions, both negatively, as the "Boston Twilight" article had, and positively. One article that caused favorable comment and even resulted in his being offered a fabulous job, was "Railroads at Bay," which appeared in January 1928. Angoff considered the piece a "hack job from beginning to end. I wrote it because Mencken asked me to," he said. Soon after its appearance, he was offered a job as a traffic manager by the vice-president of a Southern railroad who had called him long distance.[42] He had been so impressed by the knowledge displayed in the article that he wanted Angoff to handle his company's traffic problems. When Angoff explained that the article contained everything that he knew about railroads, the executive still persisted. Angoff refused. Both he and Mencken would laugh over the incident, and Mencken said that "It would have served them right if he [Angoff] had accepted the job."[43]

In 1930 Angoff had been corresponding with William Faulkner. Early in 1931 Faulkner sent him his short story, "That Evening Sun Go Down." Angoff was "thrilled," but Mencken, who said he saw no sense in Faulkner, refused to publish the story. "It is gibberish," he contended. "My God, the man hasn't the slightest idea of sentence structure or paragraphing."[44] Angoff defended the story on the grounds of "its impact, of its weird yet powerful characterization, of its truly magnificent writing."[45] In an attempt to over-ride Mencken's objections, Angoff suggested they submit the story to a third party for an opinion. They agreed to have Sara Haardt (a contributor who became Mencken's wife in 1930) read the story, and if she liked it, it would be printed.[46] "To Mencken's dismay" and Angoff's delight, Sara liked the story and it was printed in the March 1931 number. This incident has a resemblance to Mencken's and Nathan's dispute back in 1925, about publishing Eugene O'Neill's play *All God's Chillun Got Wings*. That issue had been mediated, too, but by Alfred Knopf. However, the similarity ends there. The ill will between Mencken and Nathan over the event was to cause Nathan to leave his co-editorship of the *Mercury*. The situation with Angoff and Mencken was one of friendly dispute, which took on a sense of humor with the mediation by Sara. Although Mencken was surprised at the outcome, no eruption in his and Angoff's relationship occurred as a result.

Mencken would take a last crack at Angoff by suggesting that the first two pages of the story should be cut out.[47] Angoff, who left that they should be retained, "left them in and said nothing to Mencken."[48] He was "pretty sure that Mencken would not read the proof . . . [he] took another chance when make-up time came around . . . [and] suggested that . . . [they] lead off with the Faulkner story."[49] Mencken took the whole thing with good spirits: "Have it your own way," he said. "You have me buffaloed, but you'll pay for this stupidity some day, and your stay in purgatory will be eternal."[50]

Because of the falling circulation during the depression years, Mencken and Angoff printed a three-part series called "The Worst American State," which appeared in September, October, and November 1931. Angoff says, "The idea for the series was Mencken's."[51] However, it was Angoff who did all of the research work, which involved looking up hundreds of statistics on life, death, health, education, incidence of various diseases, and book buying among other things. The first draft was also written by Angoff.[52] It was an effort to "enliven the magazine"[53] and to lighten its tone during the somber days of the depression. The article concluded that Mississippi was the "worst state." It did not help circulation from falling, but much to Angoff's and Mencken's astonishment, "the series became source material for many important academic studies on sociology."[54] In addition, the series was heavily used as source material for the last major book, *Mainsprings in Civilization* (published in 1945), by Ellsworth Huntington, Yale's late distinguished geographer.[55] In fact, five years after it was printed in the *Mercury*, a New York publisher had wanted to issue the series in book form, but by that time both Mencken and Angoff had lost interest in the project.

There is a statement about the *Mercury* regarding its source of articles that needs correction. When DeWitt Wallace, who began the *Reader's Digest*, came to Angoff back in the twenties, he asked if, for a yearly amount, he could have the exclusive right, for a period of three months after an article appeared in the *Mercury*, to digest whatever he wanted. The author was to get a fee, and so was the *Mercury*, for each article used.[56] Angoff, because he felt sorry for Wallace, said that he would not tie him up legally, but if within a month after an article appeared in the *Mercury*, he wanted to digest it, he could so do.[57]

However, in Peterson's *Magazines of the Twentieth Century,* the following statement appears:

> In the mid-thirties, having money enough to commission the sort of nonfiction he wanted, Wallace began offering original articles to other publications in exchange for the right to "condense" and reprint them. Editors of some magazines with small budgets, welcomed articles they could not otherwise afford. A dozen magazines like . . . the *American Mercury* . . . took advantage of this offer.[58]

This statement is very misleading. Angoff, who was editor of the *American Mercury* from August 1934 until March 1935, and who had been with the magazine since 1925, denies this statement.[59] He said that during the entire time that he was there no such articles were purchased. But Peterson's remark implies that the practice was quite prevalent, and that many articles of this nature went into the *Mercury.* Perhaps, Angoff noted, when Paul Palmer became editor these articles were received from Wallace, but this was not the case at any time during his stay as managing editor or as editor.

In 1933 Mencken would finally leave the *Mercury.* He was succeeded as editor by Henry Hazlitt. Hazlitt did not remain on the *Mercury* long. Within little over a year, in August 1934, Angoff assumed the editorship. Although he was politically liberal during his editorship, Mencken would write, "Angoff took the *Mercury* far to the Left, and became the hero of all the New York Reds, who regarded the conquest of the *American Mercury,* with plenty of reason, as a notable feat."[60] This, however, was not the case from Angoff's point of view. He said, "I printed articles in defense of the New Deal. And I never printed Mike Gold as Mencken did. In fact, the Communists didn't like me, even though they tried to court me, because I said favorable things about Trotsky."[61] In any event, circulation of the *Mercury,* which had begun a downward swing in 1929, continued to decline. Knopf, who had long wanted to unload the magazine, was given an offer by Paul Palmer, and he sold the *Mercury.* Angoff left in March 1935.

NOTES

[1] Charles Angoff lecturing at the Theodor Herzl Institute, November 4, 1975.

[2] Edgar Kemler, *The Irreverent Mr. Mencken* (Boston: Little, Brown and Co., 1950), p. 191.

[3] M. K. Singleton, *H. L. Mencken and the American Mercury Adventure* (Durham, N.C.: Duke University Press, 1962), p. 60.

[4] Carl Bode, *Mencken* (Carbondale and Edwardsville, Ill.: Southern Illinois University Press, 1969), p. 234.

[5] Singleton, *Mercury Adventure,* p. 59.

[6] Charles Angoff, *H. L. Mencken: A Portrait from Memory* (New York: Thomas Yoseloff, Inc., 1956), p. 29.

[7] Ibid.

[8] Ibid.

[9] Singleton, *Mercury Adventure,* p. 59.

[10] Angoff, *Portrait,* p. 29.

[11] Interview with Charles Angoff, May 12, 1973.

[12] Angoff, *Portrait,* p. 186.

[13] Ibid., p. 28.

[14] Ibid., p. 27.

[15] Ibid., p. 38.

[16] Ibid.

[17] Ibid., p. 190.

[18] Ibid., p. 26.

[19] Ibid.

[20] Singleton, *Mercury Adventure,* p. 80.

[21] Angoff, *Portrait,* p. 91.

[22] Ibid.

[23] Ibid.

[24] Ibid.

[25] Ibid.

[26] Singleton, *Mercury Adventure,* p. 80.

[27] Angoff, *Portrait,* p. 92.

[28] Ibid.

[29] Ibid.

[30] Ibid.

[31] Ibid.

[32] Ibid.

[33] Kemler, *Irreverent Mencken,* p. 192.

[34] Ibid.

[35] Ibid., p. 193.

[36] Ibid., pp. 193-94.

[37] Ibid., p. 194.

[38] Ibid., pp. 203-4.

[39] Ibid., p. 199.

[40] Angoff, *Portrait,* p. 52.

[41] Ibid., p. 53.

[42] Ibid., p. 155.

[43] Ibid.

[44] Ibid., p. 107.

[45] Ibid.

[46] Ibid., p. 108.

[47] Ibid.

[48] Ibid.

[49] Ibid.

[50] Ibid.

[51] Ibid., p. 203.

[52] Ibid.

[53] Singleton, *Mercury Adventure,* p. 220.

[54] Angoff, *Portrait,* p. 204.

[55] Ibid.

[56] Charles Angoff, *The Tone of the Twenties* (New York: A. S. Barnes and Co., 1966), p. 44.

[57] Ibid.

[58] Theodore Peterson, *Magazines in the Twentieth Century* (Urbana, Ill.: University of Illinois Press, 1956), p. 215.

[59] Interview with Charles Angoff, May 12, 1973.

[60] Singleton, *Mercury Adventure,* pp. 238-39.

[61] Interview with Charles Angoff, August 27, 1973.

William Manchester

SOURCE: "Mencken and the Mercury," in *Harper's Magazine,* v. 201, No. 1203, August, 1950, pp. 65-73.

[*In the following essay, Manchester discusses H. L. Mencken's collaboration with George Jean Nathan on the* Smart Set, *their founding of the* American Mercury, *and Mencken's contributions to the editorial content and early success of the magazine.*]

The end of the first world war found H. L. Mencken climbing over a personal parapet, throwing up a batch of signal flares, and advancing with fixed bayonet into the wacky no man's land which was public life in the nineteen-twenties. The image may not be altogether apt—Mencken detested physical exercise, and a month before the Armistice he had written a friend, with some bitterness, that the draft would probably snare him "despite my asthma, piles, tongue trouble, hay fever, alcoholic liver, weak heels, dandruff, etc."—but it is certainly true that the coming of the new era brought him extraordinary recognition and that he met that recognition more than half-way. The first edition of his *American Language* (which he called "a heavy indigestible piece of cottage cheese") was a smashing success; everywhere his name was identified with liberating influences, and from the indiscriminate came a chorus of praise and abuse—a chorus which delighted him, though he took it with small seriousness. The center of American cultural gravity had shifted. It had swung toward Mencken. And it sent him, as his most hostile critic put it, off "at a hard gallop, spattered with mud . . . high in oath."

It was during this period of unrest and change that Mencken's individual and specific impact upon the national letters reached its height. He was still regarded, and still regarded himself, as primarily a literary critic, and the swarms of young and promising authors drew him, more and more frequently, to New York. He remained, on these visits, the hick from Baltimore, but the city was now teeming with hicks who had something to say, and the cosmopolitan tone of the literati, together with the tremendous esteem in which he was now held, served to temper his painful self-consciousness. Alfred Knopf, his publisher, drew his friends together when he was in town, and Mencken's suite at the Algonquin was thrown open to late parties, with illegal hooch and subversive statements carrying the insurgents through until dawn.

George Jean Nathan, back on his feet after a bout with influenza, was as delightful as ever. Together he and Mencken redecorated the walls of their *Smart Set* office, tacking up a Hoover-for-President poster, a one-sheet of Louis Robie's "Crackerjacks," and a batch of temperance posters Edna Ferber had sent them from Paris. They sent out requests for a gilt chair which would collapse if a fat lady poet sat in it, photographs of the late Czar Nicholas, Bishop Manning, and Lillian Russell (in tights), and a concrete bust of a leading reformer.

When delighted friends responded, the two editors promptly announced for the Republican Presidential and Vice-Presidential candidacies, and they published in their magazine a platform including promises to take the Statue of Liberty out beyond the three-mile limit and dump it, to wear no cutaway coats or plugged hats, to abolish the Y.M.C.A., to establish enormous arenas in which to turn clergymen loose upon one another, and to turn the Philippines over to Japan. Word of the announcement spread, to the indignation of Harding bigwigs, and even in London there was a brief, solemn flurry of interest over the "surprise candidates." In the New York *Sun,* Berton Braley pretty well summed up the attitude of their contemporaries to all this in the opening lines of his satirical "Mencken, Nathan, and God":

> There were three who sailed away one night
> Far from the maddening throng
> And two of the three were always right
> And everyone else was wrong
> But they took another along, these two,
> To bear them company,
> For He was the only One ever knew
> Why the other two should be.
> And so they sailed away, these three—
>
> Mencken,
> Nathan,
> And God.

No issue was serious to them, no figure exempt from the harlequinade. Every topic of importance, it seemed, wound up on the vaudeville stage as a sort of burlesque of itself. Nathan, who loved the theater, and Mencken, who hated it, spent much time defending their respective positions, but when the difference reached the dignity of debate, it was slapped down mightily by Nathan. He had, that season, discovered a play by Dario Niccodemi which, in sheer awfulness, surpassed anything ever seen on the New York stage. Indeed, so terrible was the performance that, fascinated, he sat through the last curtain. Back at his apartment in the Royalton Hotel he wrote Mencken, with great seriousness, that however much a man might dislike the theater, he should not miss the greatest drama since Ibsen's debut. Mencken was doubtful, but if Nathan said so. . . .

Up he came to New York, dressed to kill for the great occasion. Nathan tipped off John Williams, then Charles Frohman's right-hand man, and the three took a box at the Morosco. Mencken was placed in the center. There he sat, bolt upright, looking, as Nathan told him later, like Harding, while his hosts, during the performance, murmured ecstatically to one another, "Oh, this scene!" . . ."Isn't it tremendous?" . . ."What a speech!" etc. Mencken at first said nothing—Nathan was a drama critic, he ought to know—but as the farce wore on, he protested over and over again, more and more loudly, "Pishposh!" At the very end, he caught on, eyed Nathan and Williams with great severity, and lustily croaked. "PISHPOSH!" And the dignified debate was over.

Mencken's reputation, like himself, was most stimulated among other aliens in New York or among writers in other parts of the country. His New York friends, like Mencken, were strangers to Broadway; in New York they might cavort, free from the taboos of the home town. His most enthusiastic followers lived in the provinces, and their number seemed to increase in direct proportion to the ridicule directed at rural regions. All over America the reaction against patriotism had set in, and if the local boomers fumed when a specific locale was singled out for *Smart Set* abuse, the local literati flourished. No more violent attack was printed in these years than the "Sahara of the Bozart," and none stirred up greater enthusiasm among Southern poets. The South, Mencken wrote, was "that stupendous region of fat farms, shoddy cities, and paralyzed cerebrums . . . that gargantuan paradise of the fourth-rate" which stretched, "a vast plain of mediocrity, stupidity, lethargy, almost of dead silence," between "senile" Virginia and "crass gross, vulgar, and obnoxious" Georgia. Contemplating its letters, Mencken thought of "Asia Minor, resigned to the Armenians, Greeks, and wild swine, of Poland abandoned to the Poles."

As Mencken's popularity zoomed, he devoted his social energies to cultivating and whooping up the young talent which had sought out the *Smart Set.* Characteristically, he met the new excitement with great industry and incessant grumbling. He acknowledged that "a hundred thousand second-hand Coronas rattle and jingle in ten thousand remote and lonely towns, and the mail of every magazine editor is as heavy as the mail of a get-rich-quick stockbroker," but the manuscripts pouring in from every direction, he wrote to a friend, were "mainly crap." It may be that he actually thought so, but if so, his interests had suddenly and completely turned to the soliciting, reading, and purchasing of crap. Every young man who approached either Mencken or Nathan was cordially received and his talents thoroughly investigated. When a bacteriologist named Paul de Kruif sat down one afternoon in the old Hotel Pontchartrain in Detroit and wrote Mencken, asking if he could combine science and writing, he was invited to the *Smart Set* for succor. When a playwright named Eugene O'Neill timidly ventured to cross recognized dramatic horizons, his plays were printed and he was urged to go still further. And when three young Princeton graduates—John Peale Bishop, Edmund Wilson, and F. Scott Fitzgerald—stormed the Royalton one morning after the war, they were wined, victualed, and warned by Nathan that failure to submit stories to the magazine would be taken as a personal affront. It was this same critical tutelage, given the first faltering steps of nearly every major writer of the twenties, which accounts for Mencken's elevation to critical sainthood by the first war generation. For almost a decade there was scarcely a major writer in the country who did not trace his career from a first acceptance by the *Smart Set.*

Mencken and Nathan still avoided literary parties, partly because of the people they drew, but also because they had no time for such frivolity. In the first year after the war, they were lured to but one such affair. It turned out to be the most ghastly experience of their careers to date—and by all odds the most profitable. Tom Smith of the *Century* insisted they drop by "just for one drink." Mencken complained vigorously in the cab, and as soon as the door opened he knew he had made a dreadful mistake.

They were greeted by a tall, skinny redhead, obviously quite drunk, who wrapped one arm around Mencken's neck and another around Nathan's. Resistance was quite useless; he had them by the esophagi, and as Nathan groaned and Mencken grunted pitifully, this apparition from another planet yelled into their flinching eardrums, "So you guys are critics, are you? Well, let me tell you something. I'm the best goddam writer in this here goddam country and if you, Georgie, and you, Hank, don't know it, you'll know it goddam soon. Say . . ."

There was no escape, at least not for the present. While Smith shrugged and the other guests, amused, looked on, the summit of their fears held forth on his own abilities and the necessity for favorable notice in the *Smart Set*. At the end of a half hour the door of the flat opened and Mencken and Nathan, wild-eyed, fled down the stairs and into the first cab that passed, sympathizing with one another and vowing never again to come within shouting distance of Smith's place.

But their troubles with "the louse," as Mencken called their persecutor for want of a name, were not over. Next morning, dropping by the office on his way back to Baltimore, Mencken was amazed to find the proofs of a novel, together with a note from the publisher, thanking him for the praise he had allegedly bestowed on the author at Smith's party. Disgusted, he was about to toss the sheets in the wastebasket when he suddenly remembered he had nothing to read on the train. In Jersey City he became interested. In Philadelphia he was fascinated, and back at Hollins Street that afternoon he excitedly wrote Nathan: "Grab hold of the bar-rail, steady yourself, and prepare for a terrible shock! I've just read the advance sheets of the book by that *lump* we met at Schmidt's and, by God, he has done the job! It's a genuinely excellent piece of work. I begin to believe that perhaps there isn't a God after all. There is no justice in the world."

The novel, as many will have guessed, was *Main Street;* the redhead, Sinclair Lewis. His performance that first night had not been out of character, but Mencken had learned to be tolerant with men of talent, and once he and Nathan had extracted a promise to "keep your goddam hands off our goddam necks," they got along famously. Between them, on Mencken's visits to New York, they gave bar patrons as bizarre a show in the perversion of American mores as even that jaded audience had ever seen, with Mencken quoting from Prohibition pamphlets and Lewis delivering a lecture on the merits of Rotary or a sermon on the beauty of the Church of God. By January of 1922, Lewis was looking to Mencken for critical tutelage. "You ask about the new novel—which won't be out till next September," he wrote from London:

> It's curiously associated with yourself. A year ago in a criticism of *Main Street* you said that what ought to be taken up now is the American city— not NY or Chi but the cities of 200,000 to 500,000—the Baltimores and Omahas and Buffalos and Birminghams, etc. I was startled to read it

because that was precisely what I was then planning, and am now doing. But your piece helped me to decide on this particular one as against one or two others which, at the time, I also wanted to do.

> I think you'll like it—I hope . . . you do. All our friends are in it—the Rotary Club, the popular preacher, the Chamber of Commerce, the new bungalows, the bunch of business men jolliers lunching at the Athletic Club. It ought to be at least 2000% American, as well as forward-looking, right-thinking, optimistic, selling the idea of success, and go-getterish.

> The central character is a Solid Citizen, one George F. Babbitt, real estate man, who has a Dutch Colonial house out on Floral Heights. . . .

II

For some time Mencken had been anxious to get rid of the *Smart Set*. For one thing, the title was distasteful. To him and, he felt, to many of his readers, it meant a fashion magazine. Since the days when he and Nathan had dreamed of a periodical to be called the *Blue Review,* he had nursed plans for a new magazine with an American motif, and when Knopf brought up the idea on his own hook, Mencken fairly seethed with enthusiasm. There was but one obstacle. He found Nathan, who was little interested in Mencken's talk of a periodical dealing with the political ramifications of the national scene such ramifications, lukewarm. Literary and artistic interests were quite enough for him, and he viewed as alarming Mencken's increasing absorption with things political. Knopf was acceptable—eminently acceptable—as a publisher, but if Knopf wanted a magazine, why couldn't it be the *Smart Set?* Mencken, doubtful, approached Knopf, and Knopf, after huddling with his father, business manager of the firm, returned their verdict. It was No. A new magazine or none was Knopf's position, and Nathan, somewhat dubious, was drawn into the scheme.

Nor were Nathan's doubts his alone. Knopf had seen, as Mencken had not, the growing breach between the editorial enthusiasms of of the two editors, and a new politically minded magazine, he believed, would be best edited by Mencken alone. But Mencken's sense of loyalty balked at this. Nathan had always been with him, and, he vowed, Nathan always would be. There had to be two editors for the new project, and they had to be Mencken and Nathan. Thus it was that two of the three sponsors for the *Smart Set*'s heir—Nathan and Knopf—went into the inaugural conference with grave misgivings.

The first squabble developed over a name. Mencken and Nathan liked the *Blue Review,* probably for sentimental reasons, but Knopf vetoed it. Then a long series of prospective titles was proposed: the *Twentieth Century,* the *Capitol,* the *Defender,* the *Sovereign,* the *Regent,* the *Chancellor,* the *Portfolio,* the *Pendulum,* the *Other Man's Monthly,* the *Gray Monthly,* the *Colonnade,* the

Inter-Continental Review, the *Athenaeum,* the *Colonial Review,* and the *New Review.* Finally, Nathan suggested the *American Mercury.* Mencken protested at once; it would, he argued, be interpreted as an imitation of the London *Mercury,* the *Mercure de France,* or the *Mercurio Peruano.* Knopf, however, voted for the *American Mercury,* and the *American Mercury* it became.

Next came the problem of the *Smart Set.* Before any sort of contract could be written between the publisher and his editors, Mencken and Nathan must first get rid of their *Smart Set* stock. Hearst was approached, but refused to buy. Mencken suspected that he was really interested, however, and an ingenious scheme was devised. The stock was sold to a friend, with the understanding that if Hearst would buy within a year, the editors should share in the proceeds. Sure enough: in a few months, Hearst was nibbling. He bought the *Smart Set* and turned it over to a sub-editor, who for six years turned out a sleazy product. This done, Mencken and Nathan signed with Knopf, assuming complete editorial responsibility and the ownership of one third of the magazine. Offices were to be at Knopf's at 730 Fifth Avenue.

Throughout 1923 Mencken and Nathan shaped the details, conferring with Knopf over problems of typography and format and writing prospective contributors, asking for manuscripts which might fit the tone of the *Mercury.* The magazine, designed by Elmer Adler, was to be green-backed; the type, Garamond—again, over objections from Mencken, who was afraid it would look "too damned Frenchy." Letters went out each week to such men as Upton Sinclair, Dreiser, Hergesheimer, Gerald W. Johnson, Gamaliel Bradford, Jim Tully, a newcomer to the *Smart Set,* and Dr. Raymond Pearl of Baltimore, whom Mencken then knew only as one of the scientific writers he was patronizing. Later, as Pearl contributed more and more frequently to the *Mercury* he became one of Mencken's closest friends, but in August he was simply "Dear Dr. Pearl":

> I am preparing to set up a new monthly review in New York, and turn to you in the hope that you may be interested in it. . . . I am trying to get together a group of collaborators who at least know their subjects and may be depended upon to tell the truth as they see it. For example, Lowie in anthropology, Chafee and Pound in law, Grant La Farge in architecture, Watson in psychology, and so on. . . .

To Sinclair [Lewis] he wrote more frankly:

> I shall try to cut a rather wide swathe with it, covering politics, economics, the exact sciences, etc., as well as belles-lettres and the other fine arts. . . . You know me well enough to know that there will be no quarter for the degraded cads who now run the country. I am against you and the Liberals because I believe you chase butterflies, but I am even more against your enemies.

Certain features were carried over from the *Smart Set:* the collection of "Americana," Mencken's literary article, Nathan's drama criticism, and the column of observations on the human comedy, written by Mencken and Nathan in the *Smart Set* under the heading "Répétition Générale," henceforth to be known as "Clinical Notes" and written by Nathan alone. It was a time which augured well for infant publications—the *Reader's Digest* was founded in 1922, *Time* in 1923, and the *New Yorker* in 1925—and Mencken and Nathan were full of high hope as they put the finishing touches on the first issue.

It was hope well justified. The opening number, for January 1924, came out just before Christmas, and was swept off the news-stands. By December 28 they were on the presses with the second edition of the number, and Knopf excitedly sent Mencken word from New York that the circulation department was already 670 subscriptions behind. "Knopf has bought thirty new yellow neckties," Mencken wrote a friend, "and has taken a place in Westchester County to breed Assyrian wolf-hounds."

Within a month the issue had been reprinted a second time and the February number was headed for a twenty-five-thousand circulation—this in a fifty-cent magazine which its editors had never expected to go over twenty thousand. So rapidly did the subscription lists mount that the printers, who had taken credit for the first new numbers, were paid off at once and the *Mercury,* in effect, had financed itself. Nor was the end in sight. An average monthly circulation of 38,697 in 1924 soared to 77,921 in 1926, and never dropped below sixty-five thousand until the Depression. Knopf's business department, stunned at first, immediately plunged into advertising in the big cities, whence most of the subscribers came, and in the college towns, where circulation seemed to approximate population. Mencken was delighted. "Prayer still has its old power," he wrote Carl Van Doren.

III

In The *Mercury* office he was regarded with a mixture of awe, respect, and affection. Knopf had set aside a tiny room for the magazine, and this was divided by a partition, with Mencken, Nathan, and Edith Lustgarten, their editorial secretary, on one side, and ten advertising and circulation workers on the other. These ten worked at extremely close quarters, huddled among great piles of figures, bills, and copy layouts, and to reach the editors visitors had to step warily between them. Once through to the other side of the partition, they found a bare and only slightly less crowded closet furnished by three desks and the great brass spittoon Mencken had rescued from his gaudy *Smart Set* quarters.

To this office he now came on his periodic visits to New York, which began Monday morning and extended through Wednesday afternoon. All outstanding business in the editorial offices was settled Monday. Letters were dictated, and the few authors who had to be seen were interviewed. As a general rule, he and Nathan avoided the company of writers outside the office, and lunch hours and evenings were spent with old friends. Often, just as Mencken had settled down to some particularly absorbing editorial chore at the *Mercury,* the phone would ring: Knopf, anxious to show off his prize dog, had a distinguished visitor in his office. Mencken would swear a bloody oath—part of Miss Lustgarten's necessary equipment, she had been told, was a pair of asbestos ears—and after methodically washing his hands he would trot off to the front office.

To his desk each day came between fifty and sixty letters, from authors, aspiring authors, admirers, and, more often, assailants of the *Mercury.* "I have just read your magazine, and it certainly is nothing I would want my fourteen-year-old daughter to read" a matron would write; or, "If you don't like the good old U. S. A., the boats are still sailing for Russia, buddy." At first, their terrific labor brought the editors small financial return; despite the *Mercury*'s soaring circulation, the initial expenses soaked up most of the income, and Mencken found himself working at a frantic pace with little difference to his bank book save the money drawn out for New York trips. "The increasing business of the *American Mercury* is working me to death," he wrote Gamaliel Bradford. "I find that I am now a business man in active practice, with many of the duties that also belong to the pants business." The 1924 Democratic convention, which he spent sweating naked in a New York hotel room, furiously editing *Mercury* articles between Baltimore *Evening Sun* editions, nearly broke his health, and he began to cast around for help.

He found it in a wide-eyed young product of the Boston slums, fresh out of Harvard and full of desire to crash the magazine business. Charles Angoff had submitted examples of his work to a number of magazines, the *Mercury* among them. A correspondence with Mencken prospered, they met in New York, and ultimately he was offered the job of assistant editor. It was a bid half of young intellectual America might have snapped at, and Angoff took it without a question. Twenty-four hours later, he found himself, terrified and confused, in complete charge of the magazine: Mencken, sick of routine, had introduced him to the office staff and then blithely left for Baltimore on the next train. Angoff's only instructions were to answer all letters the day they arrived and to return all manuscripts within twenty-four hours. There was, he had been told, no excuse for not doing either.

Angoff proved capable, however, and henceforth he handled most of the correspondence and made up each month's issue. In matters of detail, he found, Mencken was completely irresponsible; indeed, his irresponsibility was at times alarming. When, during his first weeks on the *Mercury,* Angoff received a formal request for the magazine's circulation, and asked Mencken what it was, he was told it hovered at two hundred twenty-five thousand. The information was sent out; then he looked it up and came back to Mencken on the run.

"It's under fifty thousand," he gasped. "Why did you say that?"

"Well," said Mencken, with a nonchalant flip of his Uncle Willie cigar, "It's a good round figure."

His *Mercury* work, as with the *Smart Set,* was done at Mencken's Hollins Street home in Baltimore. There he solicited and received manuscripts and there his critical articles and editorials were written. He remained, as always, the delight of authors exasperated with the cavalier manner of editors. Rarely was a manuscript held over three days, and before it went into the magazine, the author was given the opportunity to inspect the proofs for error. His consideration for contributors was remarkable. If, reading a manuscript, he thought it might be sold to a magazine paying more money, the author was so advised, and Mencken offered to withdraw. Stories of promise which, for various reasons, did not suit the *Mercury* were returned with notes suggesting magazines they *did* suit.

In return for this, Mencken asked his contributors to bear with him through several revisions of each manuscript before it saw print.

"When it goes into the *American Mercury,*" he wrote Jim Tully after the *n*th rewriting of an article, "I want it to be perfect"—by which he meant an integral part of the expression of his personality which the magazine had come to be. Twenty years before, as city editor of the Baltimore *Morning Herald,* he had written new leads until the managing editor had ordered him to stop; now, with no managing editor over him, he rewrote incessantly, inserting the word or phrase which gave the piece the proper salting of Menckenese. Titles were changed constantly ("The Decline of the Negro Churches" became "Black America Begins to Doubt") for this same reason, and no suggestion for a projected article went out without detailed instructions for its writing.

Back the manuscripts would go, again and again, with notes describing Mencken's bouts with his editorial conscience, usually beginning, "My eyes are streaming with tears as I write, but the bald fact remains . . . ," and winding up with an embellished request for another try. In the end, authors generally got the idea: everything which came under Mencken's pencil had to have something of him in it before it could get his stamp of approval. If it did not, the author wound up with the original story and the short note:

> Mr. Mencken has just entered a Trappist monastery at Gethsemane, Ky., and left strict orders that no mail was to be forwarded. I am returning the enclosed for your archives.
>
> Sincerely yours,
> Edith Lustgarten

Such editorial conduct would have been irritating had it not succeeded so enormously. What his readers were buying, after all, was Mencken, and if the contents had strayed far from his interests, they would have doubtless been as disappointed as would he. The scraps of "Americana" printed each month—sweet tributes to Edgar A. Guest; news items of ministers wearing black ties presented by silk manufacturers, singing "Blest Be the Tie That Binds," and offering to eat their straw hats if the word of God were proven untrue—were surely not representative of America. They were representative only of the editor's absorption and of the vital, iconoclastic personality he was vending. Open a copy of the *Mercury* for these years—say that for December 1924—and you find his stamp on virtually every page: in the essay on Bryan by Edgar Lee Masters; in the study of the jury system; in the article on patent medicine and fake food tonics; in the report on letters to congressmen by their constituents; in the James M. Cain attack on the blowziness of statesmen; in the notes on the Ku Klux Klan, on Dr. Frank Crane, on journalism, on the ancient Greeks.

Was it a one-man magazine? Not quite—not yet. Nathan still wrote his monthly theater article and the "Clinical Notes" department; to it he still brought authors who were his special proteges. But more and more, as Mencken threw himself into the enterprise with all of his unbelievable energy, it became a product of the peculiar maelstrom which he had created, and in which he now lived. Through its pages each month he brawled and bellowed with the gusto of a Norfolk whore, the finesse of a Spanish fencer, and the independence of a Maine farmer. "The news that the *American Mercury* is 'lacking in constructive points of view' is surely not news to me," he wrote Upton Sinclair in answer to criticism. "If any such points of view ever get into it, it will only be over my mutilated and pathetic corpse. The uplift has damn nigh ruined the country. What we need is more sin."

Significantly, perhaps, Sinclair, who was one of the *Mercury*'s sharpest critics, was also one of its greatest benefactors. Like many an established writer who disagreed with Mencken's basic tenets, he was moved to admiration for the tremendous energy and positiveness of his editorship, and so sent him the names of deserving young writers who crossed his horizons.

It was this channeling of raw talent toward Baltimore, combined with Mencken's sharp eye for merit in unsolicited manuscripts, which brought to the magazine so high a level of writing. As a quality magazine unafraid to make the common man respectable, the *Mercury* was working in a virgin field, and hence was untroubled by competition. Stories by jailbirds on penitentiaries, by prostitutes on whoredom, by vagrants on how to bum a meal—all found an eager reader in Mencken. From Ernest Booth, behind bars, came "A Texas Road Gang," "We Rob a Bank," "I Face a Jury of My Peers," and "Ladies of the Mob"; from Robert Tasker, another convict, came "The First Day." Rightists, Leftists, geniuses, boobs—if they could write, it was enough. There was room for them between the Paris-green covers of the *American Mercury*.

IV

Yet the most distinguishing characteristic of the *Mercury,* which gave it its very special flavor and for which it is best remembered, was not the quality of its contributions, not even the saucily edited articles on the Klan and the Babbitts, but the pieces from Mencken's own pen. While he tenderly cultivated budding talent and spread himself with courteous gestures before all authors, this other side of Mencken—this curious combination of Voltaire, Frederick the Great, Thomas Jefferson, and Main Street—thundered closer and closer, as the twenties grew older, to an absolute in philosophical nihilism never before approached in America.

His stupendous gift for invective had now reached heights so incredible, so breath-taking, so awe-inspiring, so terrible in its indictment of the national culture that it wrung monthly gasps from sixty thousand readers and porcupined the hair of intellectuals, army officers, bond salesmen, and garage mechanics in St. Paul, St. Louis, St. Joseph, and St. Cloud. How could so violent a hymn of hate be sung so jubilantly?

Hear it:

> The normal American of the "pure-blooded" majority goes to rest every night with the uneasy feeling that there is a burglar under the bed, and he gets up every morning with a sickening fear that his underwear has been stolen.

Of the farmer:

> No more grasping, selfish, and dishonest mammal, indeed, is known to students of the anthropoidea; he deserves all that he suffers under our economic system and more.

Of the war:

> That combat was carried on, at least from this side of the fence, in a grossly hysterical, disingenuous, cowardly, and sordid manner.

Of religion:

> The church itself, as it has grown more sordid and swinish, has only grown more prosperous.

Of the yearning of yokels to put down culture:

> They dream of it behind the egg-stove on winter nights, their boots off, their socks scorching, Holy Writ in their hands. They dream of it as they commune with Bos taurus, Sus scrofa, Mephitis mephitis, the Methodist pastor, the Ford agent. It floats before their eyes as they scan the Sears Roebuck catalogue for horse liniment, porous plasters, and Bordeaux mixture . . . This Utopia haunts and tortures them, they long to make it real. They have tried prayer, and it has failed; now they turn to the secular arm. The dung-fork glitters in the sun as the host prepares to march. . . .

And as he howled across the union, month after month, back came the answering refrain, from delighted college students, from posturing preachers, from disillusioned intellectuals, from infuriated matrons of the D. A. R.:

H. L. Mencken!

"He is one of the smart type who, having no constructive ability and lacking in depth—to judge from his writings—directs his energies to undermining and pulling down. His magazine misrepresents in the interest of the anarchists, supports subversive movements, and is widely circulated among the Reds." Thus Representative Blanton in Congress.

At George Washington University, students debated whether the *Mercury* or *Captain Billy's Whiz Bang* was the more stimulating. In the vote, Mencken won by a yokel.

H. L. Mencken!

In Los Angeles, Dr. Remsen D. Bird, president of Occidental College, stormed, "Mencken's opinions are unsound, immoral, and un-American."

The Reverend John Roach Stratton, addressing four hundred students at Harvard, compared Bryan to Gladstone and opened an attack on Mencken. He was heckled to a halt by boys waving green-backed magazines. "Why are there lightning rods on church steeples?" shouted a sophomore. "God expects people to use their heads," stammered Stratton.

H. L. Mencken!

"These literary poseurs, Harold [*sic*] L. Mencken and Sinclair Lewis, mean little in the busy lives of 100,000 Rotarians," declared Alexander MacFarlane, international director of Rotary. "These highbrow writers attack Rotary because of its popularity, and it is their motto to attack everything that is popular."

In the *Saturday Review of Literature,* Walter Lippmann called him "the most powerful personal influence on this whole generation of educated people."

H. L. Mencken!

"The buzzard of American literature says that 'one bold and intelligent editor could save Mississippi from the blight of Fundamentalism,'" wrote Frederick Sullens in the Jackson, Mississippi, *News.* "It is only wild-eyed, loud-mouthed jackasses like Mencken who seek to destroy mankind's faith in the fundamentals of Christianity."

Co-ed debating teams from Stanford and the University of California argued the question of whether Mencken was fit to associate with nice people. They decided he was.

H. L. Mencken!

"If a buzzard had laid an egg in a dunghill and the sun had hatched a thing like Mencken," cried the Reverend Dr. Charles E. Jones in the *Gospel Call,* "the buzzard would have been justly ashamed of its offspring."

In the *Peninsula Daily Herald* of Monterey, California, appeared the advertisement: "Wanted—Young woman would like position as housekeeper for single gentleman of simple tastes. Subscriber to the *American Mercury* preferred."

And throughout the Republic, in shabby Kansas city-rooms, one-building colleges, and brokers' offices; along San Francisco docks, Main Street drug counters, and Broadway bars; behind Vermont barns, stockyard fences, and Westchester hedges; in twenty-room mansions and one-room shacks; under chandeliers and freight cars—wherever thoughtful men rebelled against the brassy, shoddy atmosphere of a Model-T culture—the name became a challenge and a talisman:

H. L. MENCKEN!

Johnny L. Kloefkorn

SOURCE: "An Introduction to the Mercury," in *Emporia State Research Studies,* v. 7, No. 4, June, 1959, pp. 5-47.

[*In the following essay, Kloefkorn offers a detailed description of the history and contents of the* American Mercury, *examining H. L. Mencken's role as literary editor and analyzing his achievement as a literary critic through book reviews published in the* American Mercury.]

AN INTRODUCTION TO THE MERCURY

> Daffy-Down-Dilly has come up to town,
> In a yellow petticoat, and a green gown.
> > —Anonymous

The yellow-hued mood of melancholy and disillusionment which settled over the nation's literature following World War I had just begun to assert itself when, in late December of 1923, the first issue of the green-backed *American Mercury,* dated January, 1924, appeared. The editors of this new periodical, as the large black print on the cover made clear, were H. L. Mencken and his associate of long-standing, George Jean Nathan. The publisher was New York City's Alfred A. Knopf, a man with whom Mencken had been connected since 1917, when Knopf published Mencken's *A Book of Prefaces.* Planned as a quality magazine that would appeal to only a small group of intellectuals, the *Mercury* surprised its editors by being immediately received with enthusiasm and acclaim throughout the country. William R. Manchester, Mencken's biographer, vividly described the event:

> The opening number . . . was swept off the newsstands. By December 28 they were on the presses with the second edition of the issue, and Knopf excitedly sent Mencken word from New York that

the circulation department was already 670 sub-scriptions behind. Within a month the number had been reprinted a second time and the February issue was headed for a twenty-five-thousand circulation—this in a fifty-cent magazine which its editors never expected to go over twenty thousand. So rapidly did the subscription lists mount that the printers, who had taken credit for the first few numbers, were paid off at once and the *Mercury,* in effect, had financed itself.[1]

With this encouraging beginning, the *Mercury* was soon firmly established in the top ranks of the quality periodicals of the day, and the coeditors were jubilant.[2] Actually, however, Mencken had been planning the *Mercury* for some time. While he and Nathan served as joint editors of *The Smart Set* (1914-23), Mencken had nurtured the thought of founding a new magazine "to give American intellectuals of the Twenties the magazine for which they were yearning."[3] In the main, *The Smart Set* was concerned with art and literature, and Mencken, by that time, wanted a vehicle through which he could voice his opinions about things political, as well as literary. Returning from a trip to Europe early in 1923, Mencken found Knopf willing to take the step.[4] Since Mencken and Nathan had been partners for so long, there was little question but that they should continue as such in the new enterprise. However, Nathan, unconcerned with politics and quite content to deal exclusively with the literary aspects of the American scene, was skeptical.[5] Nevertheless, he accompanied Mencken into the new project, despite his lack of enthusiasm. But the partnership was doomed to be short-lived, for Nathan's distaste for the political carnival that Mencken loved so well soon pulled him away from the editorial responsibilities, and, a year after the magazine appeared, Nathan withdrew and Mencken became its sole pilot. After that time, Nathan merely contributed theatre reviews and wrote a department called "Clinical Notes"; Mencken was then free to direct the magazine as he chose.

Once Knopf had agreed to speculate on the *Mercury,* Mencken and Nathan were kept busy making preparations and decisions about the content of the magazine. Throughout 1923, they discussed the formation of the periodical with Knopf, and wrote numerous letters to their friends in an attempt to solicit manuscripts for the new publication.[6] Several of the departments that they placed in the *Mercury* were carried over from *The Smart Set.*[7] Thus the final version of the *Mercury* was a blending of the old and the new.

The aims of the *Mercury* were outlined in an editorial in the first issue, which stated that the editors were "committed to . . . keep the common sense as fast as they can, to belabor sham as agreeably as possible, to give a civilized entertainment."[8] The intent was to direct the magazine to the "Forgotten Man—that is, the normal, educated, well-disposed, unfrenzied, enlightened citizen of the middle minority."[9] As for *belles lettres,* the editors would

welcome sound and honest work, whatever its form

or lack of form, and carry on steady artillery practise against every variety of artistic pedant and mountebank. They [the editors] belong to no coterie and have no aesthetic theory to propagate. They do not believe that a work of art has any purpose beyond that of being charming and stimulating, and they do not believe that there is much difficulty, taking one day with another, about distinguishing clearly between the good and the not good.[10]

The plan, in reference to fiction, was to include "one or two short stories in each issue, such occasional short plays as will merit print, some verse (but not much), and maybe a few other things, lying outside the categories."[11] Book reviews were to cover only those works which the editors chose to comment upon.[12] All in all, the primary aim was "to attempt a realistic presentation of the whole gaudy, gorgeous American scene,"[13] and to "ascertain and tell the truth,"[14] hoping, meanwhile, "to introduce some element of novelty into the execution of an enterprise so old."[15]

These were the aims of the *Mercury* when it entered the arena in late 1923, dressed in a Paris-green cover, and filled with the things that the young intellectuals had, judging from its immediate popularity, been thirsting for.

The original format of the *Mercury,* conceived by Mencken, Nathan, and Knopf in 1923, was changed very little during Mencken's ten years with the magazine. It was designed by Elmer Adler and printed in Garamound type.[16] The first issue of the magazine carried, in addition to the main body which encompassed essays, articles, short stories, plays, poetry, an editorial, and various other unclassifiable pieces from contributors, eight special sections, or departments. These were labeled "Americana," "The Arts and Sciences," "Clinical Notes," "The Theatre," "The Library," "*The American Mercury* Authors," "Check List of New Books," and "Editorial Notes." Some comment about the purpose and general content of each of these departments follows:

"Americana"—In this section of the magazine, several pages (usually three, four, or five) were devoted to a recording of brief excerpts which Mencken culled from newspapers, periodicals, pamphlets, and various other sources. Primarily humorous in content, the excerpts were chosen to illustrate a multitude of shenanigans, absurdities, and imbecilities which showed up in the nation's provincial press. Mencken listed the quotations alphabetically, by states, and wrote a short introductory paragraph for each. Typical of the entries in this department were the following two concerning the state of Kansas:

KANSAS

From resolutions adopted by the Lyon county W.C.T.U.:

Passages in Mother Goose which mention tobacco or alcoholic beverages should not be read by children, and songs which mention tobacco should not be tolerated at state music contests.[17]

Marvel reported by the alert Fredonia *Herald:*

A hog bit part of John Eisenbrandt's left thumb off Monday while Eisenbrandt was engaged in putting a ring in the hog's nose on his farm near Fort Scott. Whether it was the quickness of the bite or the sharpness of the animal's teeth is not known, but it is a fact, acording to Eisenbrandt, that he did not know that the hog had bit him until he chanced to look down and saw the end of his thumb was missing. It was the sound of the hog's teeth clinking together that caused him to look down.[18]

Mencken made no comments about the material he inserted in "Americana"; the items were allowed to speak for themselves.

"The Arts and Sciences"—Included in this department were articles of varying lengths by authorities in the scientific fields. Discussions of almost every recognized scientific subject—chemistry, astronomy, medicine, and the like—were placed under this heading. For instance, the first issue carried articles dealing with architecture, medicine, and philology, and covered a total of nine pages. The number of pages given over to the section varied slightly with each issue.

"Clinical Notes"—This section began as a joint enterprise by Mencken and Nathan, and it remained in the periodical until February, 1930. However, the department was written exclusively by Nathan after 1925. The articles in the section ranged in size from lengthy essays to brief, three- or four-line witticisms, and the discussions dealt with everything from advice to bachelors ("Toward men, ever an aristocrat; toward women, ever a commoner—that way lies success."[19]) to tracts on hedonism. An entry which captures the mood of the section:

Text for a Wall-Card—It is lucky for a young woman to be just a bit homely. The fact helps her to get a good husband, and, what is harder, to keep him after she has got him. The flawless beauty has no durable joy in this life save looking in the glass, and even this departs as she oxidizes. Men, knowing her intolerable vanity, are afraid of her, and, if snared into marriage with her, always look for the worst.[20]

"The Theatre"—Covering the whole panorama of the New York stage, Nathan wrote this section each month until February, 1930. Here he commented on every conceivable facet of the drama as it was then conducted in New York.

"The Library"—In this section, Mencken reviewed one or more books each month, sometimes singly and sometimes in groups according to subject. Other reviewers had a hand in the section for the first few issues of the magazine, but this practice was soon discontinued, and thereafter, Mencken wrote all of the reviews. . . .

"The American Mercury Authors"—Appearing on the final page of the magazine, this department contained brief, one-paragraph notes about the authors whose works were printed in that particular issue of the magazine. Various bits of information concerning the author's life and writings were included in these informal discussions.

"Check List of New Books"—This department was placed with the advertisements at the end of the magazine, and included short comments about many new books and reprints.

"Editorial Notes"—Also placed with the advertisements in the latter pages of the *Mercury,* this section was utilized by Mencken to air topics which consisted, in the main, of comment about the publication of the magazine—circulation, editorial policy, contributors, and so forth.

Advertisements were confined to the outside pages of the *Mercury,* and were printed on slicker, better quality paper than was the integral portion of the magazine. As mentioned previously, few alterations were made by Mencken in the format of the magazine during the decade. Beginning in January, 1931, he introduced a section called "Music," and this department, consisting of discussions of that phase of the fine arts by outside contributors, continued to appear throughout the remainder of that year. The name of the department was changed to "The Music Room" in January, 1932, and its purpose was much the same as that of its predecessor. However, "The Music Room" survived for only a few months, and was dropped from the magazine in September, 1932. Another section, called "The Soap Box," became a part of the *Mercury* in October, 1932. Here Mencken printed letters from readers, along with subscribers' queries and their answers. The plan allowed the readers a portion of the magazine wherein they could contact other readers to make requests for all types of relatively obscure information. Outside of the addition of these innovations and the loss of Nathan's contributions, only insignificant changes were wrought on the *Mercury.* Toward the end of his editorship, Mencken discontinued writing his usual editorial, and substituted for it a monthly article called "What's Going on the World." This article served as the lead story in several of the last issues, but its tone and general contents differed little from that of the editorials.

By far, the majority of the *Mercury*'s space was allotted to articles dealing with some segment of American life. A glance at the *Mercury* for those years attests to the heterogeneous nature of the articles which Mencken selected to bring before his readers. Manchester discussed the matter as follows:

As a quality magazine unafraid to make the common man respectable, the *Mercury* was working in a virgin field, and hence was untroubled by competition. Stories by jailbirds on penitentiaries, by prostitutes on whoredom, by vagrants on how to bum a meal—stories which could never have got beyond the slush heaps in the *Atlantic Monthly* or *Harper's*—found an eager reader in Mencken.[21]

Since so many pages were given over to the articles and departments, only a relatively small amount of space was granted to the publication of imaginative prose and verse—less than ten percent of the *Mercury* was allowed to *belles lettres*.

The overall size of the *Mercury* was ten by seven and one-half inches, and was priced at fifty cents a copy or five dollars a year. Even when the magazine began to suffer drastic losses in circulation, Mencken did not reduce the price. Charles Angoff, Mencken's assistant editor, reported that Mencken was "delighted that the *Mercury* sold at fifty cents a copy and five dollars a year, and that it was so expensively put up,"[22] and he quotes Mencken as saying, "'If we printed the same sort of stuff in a magazine selling for twenty-five cents or even thirty-five cents, . . . we'd we ruined. They'd think we were a bunch of tramps, not worth listening to.'"[23] The pages in the magazine were numbered consecutively, by volume, and each volume included four issues of one hundred and twenty-eight pages each. This was the general make-up of the magazine that occupied the national spotlight when Mencken was at its helm.

When Nathan and Mencken deserted their posts on *The Smart Set* to found *The American Mercury,* Mencken's reputation was soaring higher than it ever had before. Moreover, he was not only a popular writer; he was also an astute literary critic who had made some worthwhile contributions to the field of letters in America. For, as Manchester concluded in a study of Mencken's work as critic on *The Smart Set,* Mencken was "fighting a battle. . . . His reviews . . . were annihilating the writers of romance and helping pave the way for the disciples of realism."[24] The same study ended with this evaluation of Mencken's literary efforts on *The Smart Set:*

> Mencken stands, despite his obloquy, his iconoclastic style, and his seeming nihilism, as an achiever who, as critic and thinker, reaffirmed certain basic beliefs, such as liberty of expression and intellectual honesty, who called for artistry in creativity and an end to cant in American life, and who prepared the way for the cultural renaissance which was to produce a coherent American literature for a nation which had known only a handful of talented writers.[25]

During World War I, Mencken's political viewpoints forced him to remain silent, and, during those turbulent years, when the people's patriotic zeal precluded their championing the "original, and hence subversive, ideas"[26] which were the core of Mencken's existence, he retreated into what amounted to an almost self-imposed retirement. But, at war's end, the national climate shifted to the opposite pole, and the services of his bombastic pen were highly in demand. As Manchester described the phenomenon,

> Something had happened. A war had ended, but more: a new era had begun. The day of the American protective league, of the war saboteurs, of the *Evening Mail*'s pussyfooting and Theodor Hemberger's terror, the day when to be German was to be suspect,

when . . . Dreiser and Mencken [could be] gagged—that day had passed . . . It was 1919. The Twenties were on the threshold. And so was H. L. Mencken.[27]

Another factor in elevating Mencken's reputation had also occurred at this time—the publication of his massive philological work, *The American Language.*

> The impact of the book was terrific. With one powerful stroke he had hewed in half the umbilical cord which philologically bound this nation to England. Later strokes were to come—and he [Mencken] was to deliver them—but the immediate effect of that first edition, coming as it did with the dying echoes of rifle fire in France, was tremendous.[28]

In the end, the upshot of these propitious happenings was that Mencken's fame received a tremendous boost, and, what was even more significant, he once again had a chance to express his opinions in whatever manner he chose. Within the next five years, he had published four books (the series of his *Prejudices*) and co-authored, with Nathan, two others (*Heliogabalus: A Buffoonery in Three Acts,* and *The American Credo*). Naturally, these works aided in keeping Mencken's name in the limelight. He was immediately adopted by the war generation as a saint, and his renown gathered steam accordingly.[29]

> Thus did the Twenties come to Mencken. The champion of intellectual unrest, of disillusion, he tapped this new vein with a flourish and zeal that staggered the Philistines and brought the jaded literati flocking. In the gaudy covered *Smart Set* and in his stream of books and magazine articles, they found their unspoken thoughts brilliantly couched.
>
> . . . . .
>
> He was compared to Juvenal, Dryden, Swift, Voltaire, and in the Glasgow *Herald,* to Sam Johnson. Overnight, it seemed, his face became international.[30]

The accolades which Mencken attracted during this period were not all, of course, prompted by his writings about aesthetic matters; but, in terms of reputation, the results were the same—he was being listened to, and the ranks of admirers swelled daily. There were detractors, too, but, as is always true, his popularity with the opposite wing was merely increased by their invective.

In the area of *belles lettres,* Mencken's "social energies were devoted to cultivating and whooping up the young talent which had sought out *The Smart Set.*"[31] Mencken tooted his horn for such writers as Theodore Dreiser, Sinclair Lewis, Eugene O'Neill, and F. Scott Fitzgerald, and Manchester wrote that

> it was this critical tutelage, given the first faltering steps of nearly every major writer of the Twenties, which accounts for Mencken's elevation to critical sainthood by the first war generation. For almost

a decade there was scarcely a major writer in the country who did not trace his career from a first acceptance by *The Smart Set*.[32]

Needless to say, Mencken's activities did not go unnoticed by other critics of the day. Writing in 1923, Carl Van Doren said of Mencken that "no one holds out a quicker hand of encouragement to any promising beginner in literature or scholarship."[33] Perhaps the best testimony to Mencken's reputation and influence during those years came from Angoff, who grew up with the war generation and was one of the young intellectuals who cherished Mencken's leadership:

> Like so many other young men of my generation, I had been a faithful reader of *The Smart Set*. . . . The stories in *The Smart Set* seemed like no stories in any other magazine. The same was true of the articles and poems, but it was H. L. Mencken's book reviews and George Jean Nathan's drama reviews that attracted most of the young people I knew. They were dazzlingly written, and they expressed the rebellion that we all felt. Groups of us would discuss these reviews—always enthusiastically. Some of us could recite by heart paragraph upon paragraph of certain reviews by Mencken and Nathan.[34]

So it was that when Mencken and Nathan produced a new magazine, a large following awaited them. Mencken's writings in *The Smart Set,* his books, his magazine articles—all had served to place him in the spotlight, and he was in a position to attract an even larger audience and to continue his role of intellectual leadership in *The American Mercury.* "The war played into his hands . . . as into those of hardly any other literary American,"[35] and, from his tower atop the *Mercury,* he was free to manipulate the gushing flow of literature in the United States.

MENCKEN AS LITERARY EDITOR OF THE MERCURY

> Hark, Hark,
> The dogs do bark,
> The beggars are coming to town!
> Some in rags,
> And some in tags,
> And one in a velvet gown.
>
> —Anonymous

Like the unknown beggars in the nursery rhyme, the nation's writers responded to H. L. Mencken's clarion-like call for manuscripts that would conform to the tone and standards of his new magazine. The manuscripts, too, were like the beggars—some were dressed in rags, some in tags, and a few in velvet gowns. It was Mencken's task to choose the velvet ones, and he knew what he wanted, as the following letter from Mencken to Sinclair Lewis, written when Mencken was soliciting manuscripts a few months before the *Mercury* appeared, clearly illustrates:

> I shall try to cut a rather wide swath with it, covering politics, economies, the exact sciences, etc., as well as *belles lettres* and the other fine arts. I have some promises of stuff from men who

have something to say and know how to write, and I hope to stir up the animals. In politics it will be, in the main, Tory, but *civilized* Tory. You know me well enough to know that there will be no quarter for the degraded cads who now run the country. I am against you and the Liberals because I believe you chase butterflies, but I am even more against your enemies.[1]

Motivated by letters such as this one and advance advertising, the writers scurried to ship their "stuff" to Mencken and thus make a bid for space in the *Mercury.* For Mencken, then, the problem that remained was one of selection, and it is this process which is interesting here. In fact, perhaps the most rewarding evidence pertaining to Mencken's critical acumen while editor of the *Mercury* is to be found, not in his editorials and book reviews, but in the articles, stories, plays, and poems which he selected for publication within the magazine's covers. The writings he bought reflect directly upon his tastes and abilities as editor and critic.

Works by approximately seven hundred writers appeared in the *Mercury* while Mencken was its editor, but a large percentage of the articles which found their way into the periodical were concerned with politics, economics, science, prohibition, and a host of other subjects outside the realm of pure literature. As mentioned previously, short stories, poetry, plays and other articles which could be classified as fiction constitute less than ten percent of the total volume of the *Mercury.*

Of the one hundred and seventy-five authors of fiction whose writings Mencken published, more than a third sold only one story to the *Mercury.* Other authors, some having a story, poem, or play in the magazine almost on the average of once each year, were more prolific, and it appears that Mencken, having made a decision about a certain writer, gave the author his unwavering support by publishing that writer's offerings again and again. All of the articles of a reportorial nature are of no concern here, except to note that they consistently dominated the contents of the magazine; the others, the works of imaginative fiction, along with the men and women who wrote them, deserve consideration. However, it would be unfair, it not impossible, to evaluate each contribution in terms of its literary importance and significance. It was felt that the best test of Mencken's critical insight as editor of the *Mercury* was to discover how the magazine's contributors have fared in the world of letters; to explore their contribution to *belles lettres;* to ascertain, as closely as possible, their positions among American writers and their reputations as craftsmen in the art of fiction. To accomplish this investigation, the author has, of course, utilized his own knowledge of the field. However, as must naturally happen, many of the people who wrote for the *Mercury* and who attained some distinction as writers, are practically unheard of today and would be only names to the student of literature. Therefore, three well-known reference works which list authors of importance were consulted in this investigation: William Rose Benét's *The Reader's Encyclopedia;* James D. Hart's

The Oxford Companion to American Literature; and *Twentieth Century Authors,* by Stanley J. Kunitz and Howard Haycraft.[2] It can only be assumed that a writer who is not listed in one or more of these three works has failed to make any notable contribution to the field of American letters.

No attempt has been made to classify the writers according to their reputations or to place them in the order that their works appeared in the *Mercury.* Therefore, the authors are listed in alphabetical order according to last names. The first section covers prose writers and the second deals with writers of poetry. The *Mercury's* prose writers:[3]

Abdullah, Achmed—This British author published one story in the *Mercury,* and is mentioned in *Encyclopedia* and *Authors.* Mencken's antipathy towards the English is well-known, and Abdullah is one of the few men from that country to make the grade in the magazine.

Adamic, Louis—All three references list Adamic. He published twice in the *Mercury.*

Anderson, David Merrill—No mention of this author is to be found in any of the three references. One piece by Anderson was in the magazine.

Anderson, Nels—This author, who appeared once in the *Mercury,* receives no attention in the references.

Anderson, Sherwood—It almost goes without saying that Anderson is listed in all three references, for his place in American letters is a high one. It is to Mencken's credit that three stories by Anderson appeared in the magazine.

Armstrong, John—Although this man published twice in the *Mercury,* he has earned no particular distinction among writers, and is not listed in the references.

Barrett, Richmond—This author, who published one story in the magazine, is also not mentioned in the reference works.

Beach, Joseph Warren—The *Oxford Companion* recognizes this writer, who has done some notable literary criticism. He is not mentioned in the other two references. He published twice in the Mercury.

Beer, Thomas—Listed in all three references, Beer is a fairly well-known novelist. One work by him appeared in the magazine.

Bercovici, H. LeB.—One story by Bercovici found its way into the magazine. He is not mentioned in the reference works.

Blake, Robert—Blake had one play in the *Mercury.* He is not cited by the references.

Booth, Ernest—One work of fiction by this author was in the magazine. He is not listed in the references.

Boyd, Albert Truman—Apparently a writer of no distinction, Boyd printed one article in the *Mercury.* No mention of him is found in the references.

Boyd, Thomas—This writer, who published once in the magazine, has written two or three novels of merit. He is listed in all three of the references.

Brody, Catherine—One work of fiction by this writer appeared in the *Mercury.* The three references contain no mention of her.

Brown, Bob—Having made one prose contribution to the magazine, Brown is not listed in the references.

Burnett, W. R.—This writer's novels, of which *Little Caesar* is perhaps the best, have earned him some distinction. He published once in the *Mercury,* and is noted in all three references.

Cabell, James Branch—Probably no student of literature has not heard of Cabell, who was one of America's most prolific writers. He was one of Mencken's favorites. . . . He wrote three times for the magazine, and is listed in all the references.

Cahill, Holger—This writer published once in the *Mercury.* He is not listed in the reference works.

Cain, James M.—Six short plays and three stories by Cain were printed in the *Mercury.* He gained some fame through his novel, *The Postman Always Rings Twice,* and is hence cited by the references.

Caldwell, Erskine—A writer who published once in the periodical and whose popularity as a novelist makes comment unnecessary, Caldwell is mentioned by all the references.

Cautela, Giuseppe—The references do not list this man, who printed one story in the periodical.

Chew, Samuel C.—The *Encyclopedia* refers to Chew, although the other two reference works do not. He wrote one play for the *Mercury.*

Clarage, Eleanor—Not mentioned by the references, this writer printed one work in the magazine.

Clark, Emily—Three stories by this writer appeared in the magazine. She is not listed in the reference works.

Conroy, Jack—Although neglected by the other two references, Conroy is cited by the *Oxford Companion.* His novel, *The Disinherited,* is worth mention. He published five times in the *Mercury.*

Crowell, Chester T.—Two works of fiction by Crowell were printed in the magazine. He is not listed in the references.

Davidson, H. Carter—No recognition is given to Davidson by any of the references. He published once in the *Mercury*.

Davis, H. L.—This writer's novel, *Honey in the Horn*, won for him a Pulitzer prize. His works appeared seven times in the magazine, and he is listed in all three references.

DeCasseres, Benjamin—Listed in all three references, DeCasseres published two times in the *Mercury*.

Dickinson, May Freud—This writer published once in the magazine. She is not mentioned by the references.

Dobie, J. Frank—This writer's fame as folklorist-novelist is relatively well established. Mencken printed one of Dobie's stories in the magazine, and he is mentioned by both the *Encyclopedia* and the *Oxford Companion*.

Douglas, W. A. S.—One of the magazine's most frequent contributors, Douglas appeared nine times during the ten years. However, he receives no space in the references.

Dreiser, Theodore—Since he has been recognized as one of America's best novelists in the naturalistic vein, Dreiser's name naturally appears in all three references. It is somewhat surprising that only one story by Dreiser appeared in the *Mercury*, because he was another of Mencken's favorites.

Eaton, Walter Prichard—Listed in the *Encyclopedia* and *Authors*, Eaton published one story in the *Mercury*.

Fante, John—Five stories by Fante appeared in the magazine, and he is cited by the *Oxford Companion* and *Authors*.

Farrell, James T.—This writer's stories about the character, Studs Lonigan, as well as several others, have earned him a high place in American letters. He is mentioned by all the references. He published three times in the *Mercury*.

Faulkner, William—A giant among American novelists, Faulkner is recognized as one of the best novelists in the United States. His many novels dealing with the deep South are all well known. Four of his works appeared in the *Mercury*, and he is listed in all three references.

Fergusson, Harvey—An author of several novels of secondary importance, Fergusson printed once in the magazine. He is mentioned by all three references.

Fitzgerald, F. Scott—This writer's novels, and particularly *This Side of Paradise* and *The Great Gatsby*, went far towards capturing the mood of the Twenties, and he is today regarded as a sort of symbol of the cynicism and disillusionment of that era. He published two stories in the *Mercury*, and is listed in all three reference works.

Forsling, Elizabeth Paxton—Not mentioned by the references, this writer had one story in the magazine.

Francis, Owen—One work by Francis appeared in the *Mercury*. The references do not list him.

Gale, Zona—A short story writer of some distinction, this writer published twice in the magazine. She is listed by all the references.

Garey, Robert B.—Not listed in the references, Garey had one article in the periodical.

George, W. L.—Listed in the *Encyclopedia* and *Authors*, George had one story in the *Mercury*.

Gilman, Mildred Evans—This author is represented in the magazine by one story. She is not listed in the references.

Gold, Louis—This writer, who is not mentioned by the reference works, printed one story in the magazine.

Gold, Michael—A writer of minor importance who published twice in the *Mercury*, Gold is listed in all three reference works.

Grafton, Samuel—Not listed in the references, Grafton wrote two stories for the periodical.

Greene, Ward—Listed only in *Authors*, Greene appeared three times in the magazine.

Haardt, Sarah—Not mentioned in the references, this writer printed four pieces in the *Mercury*. She was Mencken's wife.

Hackett, Francis—One-time editor of *The New Republic*, Hackett is referred to in all three works. He printed one story in the magazine.

Hale, Nancy—This writer published two stories in the *Mercury*. She is listed in the *Encyclopedia*.

Hall, Leonard—Never mentioned by the references, Hall wrote two pieces for the magazine.

Halper, Albert—This writer has a few novels to his credit, all of which are of minor importance. Five of his stories were bought by Mencken, and his name appears in all three references.

Hanko, Arthur—Represented by one story in the magazine, Hanko is not listed in the reference works.

Hanley, Hugh—This writer also had one story in the *Mercury*. He is not mentioned by the references.

Hartswick, F. Gregory—Another writer with a single entry in the magazine, Hartswick is not listed in the references.

Hecht, Ben—An author of many novels and plays, Hecht appeared in the magazine once. He is listed in all of the three reference works.

Herbst, Josephine—A minor novelist, this author is mentioned by all the references. Four stories by her appeared in the *Mercury*.

Herrmann, John—Not cited by the references, Herrmann had two stories in the magazine.

Hess, Leonard—This writer printed one piece in the magazine. He receives no mention by the references.

Heth, Edward Harris—The references do not list this author, whose writings appeared once in the *Mercury*.

Holbrook, Stewart H.—Not mentioned by the references, Holbrook had two stories in the *Mercury*.

Hughes, Langston—A Negro writer, Hughes is mentioned by all the references. Two of his stories found their way into the *Mercury*.

Hussey, L. M.—This author published three pieces in the magazine. He does not appear in the reference works.

Huston, John—Represented in the *Mercury* by two stories, Huston is not listed by the references.

Jeans, Robert—Also not included in the references, Jeans published three stories in the magazine.

Joffe, Eugene—A single work by this author went into the periodical. He is not listed in the references.

Jones, Carter Brooke—Although four stories by Jones appeared in the magazine, he is not mentioned by the references.

Jones, Idwal—Another writer who published often in the *Mercury*—six times in all—Jones is not listed in the references.

Kelm, Karlton—The references neglect Kelm. He printed two stories in the magazine.

Lanke, J. J.—Mentioned only by the *Encyclopedia*, Lanke is represented in the magazine by one story.

Lea, M. S.—This writer published one story in the *Mercury,* and is not listed in the reference works.

Lee, B. Virginia—One story by this author went into the magazine, and she is neglected by the references.

Leenhouts, Grant—This writer, with one story in the *Mercury,* is not cited by the references.

LeSuer, Meridel—This writer's name is absent from the references. She had one story in the periodical.

Levitt, Saul—Another writer of no particular merit, Levitt published one piece in the *Mercury*. The references do not list him.

Lewis, Sinclair— . . . Mencken championed Lewis's works. This writer's *Main Street* and *Babbitt,* both first-rate novels, secured for him a high place in the nation's letters. He is listed by all three references, and he printed one story in the *Mercury*.

Lindsay, Malvina—One story by this writer appeared in the magazine. None of the references lists her.

McClure, John—Listed only in the *Encyclopedia,* McClure published seven stories in the *Mercury*.

McIntosh, K. C.—Represented in the magazine by one story, McIntosh's name is not included in the reference works.

Manlapaz, Ignacio—Ignored by the references, Manlapaz printed one piece in the magazine.

Mason, Gregory—Published once in the magazine, Mason is mentioned only by the *Encyclopedia*.

Maynard, Lawrence M.—Not listed in the reference works, Maynard had one story in the *Mercury*.

Meyer, Ernest L.—A writer who published once in the magazine, Meyer receives no mention in the reference works.

Milburn, George—With thirteen stories to his credit, Milburn was the most frequent contributor to the *Mercury*. His reputation today is of no consequence, and none of the references includes him.

Miller, Harlan—Also not cited in the references, Miller wrote one story for the magazine.

Moore, Muriel—This writer contributed one story to the *Mercury*. She is not listed in the references.

Mulhern, Alice—One article by this writer appeared in the magazine, and she is not mentioned by the reference works.

Mullen, Kate—A single story by this author appeared in the magazine. None of the references lists her.

Newman, Frances—A novelist with little reputation today, this author sold one story to the *Mercury*. She is listed in the *Encyclopedia* and *Authors*.

Nuhn, Ferner—Not mentioned by the references, Nuhn had three stories in the magazine.

Odum, Howard W.—Two stories by Odum were printed in the *Mercury*. He receives no mention in the references.

O'Mara, Patrick—This author sold two stories to the *Mercury*. He is not cited in the reference works.

O'Neale, Albert Lindsay Jr.—Mencken purchased one story by O'Neale. He is not listed in the references.

O'Neill, Eugene—One of America's most famous playwrights, O'Neill is represented in the *Mercury* by one play. As a writer considered by many critics as the nation's greatest dramatist, O'Neill naturally receives attention in all the references.

Parker, Dorothy—This writer's reputation as a satirist is fairly well established, particularly through her verse. She published one story in the magazine, and is listed in all three references.

Peterkin, Julia—This writer, who has won some fame as a novelist and was once awarded a Pulitzer prize, sold one story to the magazine, and is included in all three references.

Peters, Paul—Author of one story that appeared in the *Mercury,* Peters is not listed in the references.

Purdy, Nina—This writer also sold one story to the magazine. None of the reference works lists her.

Purroy, David—Mencken bought one of Purroy's stories. He is not listed in the references.

Roberts, Elizabeth Maddox—This novelist has a minor reputation in the United States. She is represented in the magazine by one story, and she is mentioned by all three references.

Rosenfeld, Louis Zara—Another writer who published one story in the *Mercury,* Rosenfeld receives no mention in the references.

Sampson, Charles—Three stories by Sampson appeared in the magazine. He is not listed in the reference works.

Sanford, Winifred—This writer's works appeared frequently in the periodical—eight times in all, but is seldom mentioned today, and is not cited in the references.

Sawyer, Ruth—Listed in the *Encyclopedia* and *Authors,* this writer has only a slight reputation. She published one story in the periodical.

Sayre, Joel—Although five stories by Sayre were purchased by Mencken, none of the references mentions him.

Schuyler, George S.—Two stories by Schuyler found their way into the *Mercury*. He is not included in any of the references.

Sherwin, Louis— Ignored by the references, Sherwin published one play in the magazine.

Snider, Charles Lee—Also neglected by the references, Snider had one play in the periodical.

Sonnichsen, Erich—Two stories by this writer were in the magazine. He is not cited in the references.

Stevens, James—A writer of folk tales, Stevens is noticed by all three references. He published five stories in the *Mercury*.

Strong-Wolfe, Elela—This writer, who sold one story to the magazine, is not listed in the references.

Stuart, James—Not mentioned in the references, Stuart had one story in the *Mercury*.

Suckow, Ruth—This writer's fiction has earned for her a fair distinction among American authors. Mencken printed nine of her stories, and she is recognized by all three reference works.

Sullivan, Maurice S.—Two of Sullivan's stories appeared in the magazine. None of the references lists him.

Tanaquil, Paul—This writer sold one article to the *Mercury*. He is not listed in the references.

Tanner, Myron T.—Another writer not mentioned in the reference works, Tanner had one story in the *Mercury*.

Tasker, Robert Joyce—None of the references lists this writer, who contributed one story to the magazine.

Thomas, Dorothy—One of the most frequent contributors to the *Mercury,* this writer had eight stories in the magazine. She is not noticed in the references.

Toogood, Granville—One story by this writer went into the magazine. He receives no mention in the references.

Tully, Jim—At one time a popular novelist, Tully, whose reputation is based on such books as *Circus Parade* and *Shanty Irish,* holds only a minor position among the nation's writers. He was one of Mencken's favorites, as is shown by the fact that seven of his stories were printed in the *Mercury*. He is listed in all three references.

Walker, Stanley—This writer had two stories in the magazine. None of the references lists him.

Weisberg, Goldie—Represented in the periodical by one story, this writer receives no mention in the reference works.

Wembridge, Eleanor Rowland—One story by this writer appeared in the magazine. She is not listed in the references.

Whitman, Stephen French—Another writer who had one story in the magazine, Whitman is not cited in the references.

Whitney, Parkhurst—One story by Whitney was printed in the *Mercury*. None of the references lists him.

Wilson, Charles Morrow—This writer is mentioned in the *Encyclopedia*. One of Wilson's stories was printed in the *Mercury*.

Wimberly, Lowry Charles—Five stories by Wimberly were printed in the magazine, but he is neglected by the reference works.

Wimberly, Merritt—Also disregarded by the references, this writer had three stories in the periodical.

Winslow, Thyra Samter—Mentioned in both the *Encyclopedia* and the *Oxford Companion*, this writer has gained some recognition for her short stories. Three of her stories appeared in the *Mercury*.

Zugsmith, Leane—One story by this writer, whose novels have earned her a minor position in the world of letters, was printed in the *Mercury*. She is cited by all three references.

The writers of verse:

Aiken, Conrad—One poem by Aiken appeared in the magazine. He is a well-known poet, and is listed in all three reference works.

Anderson, Sherwood—Although Anderson is more widely recognized as a prose writer than as a poet, one of his works in verse appeared in the *Mercury*. The three references list him.

Auslander, Joseph—A top-notch poet, Auslander published one piece in the magazine. He is recognized by all of the references.

Bodenheim, Maxwell—One poem by this author, whose reputation among American poets is fairly well established, was printed in the magazine, and he is listed in all three references.

Brown, Bob—One of Brown's poems went into the *Mercury*. None of the references lists him.

Cooksley, S. Bert—Three poems by this writer, who receives no attention in the references, were sold to the magazine.

Cullen, Countee P.—This Negro poet, who is included in both the *Encyclopedia* and the *Oxford Companion*, had one work in the *Mercury*.

Davidson, Eugene—Another writer who had one poem in the magazine, Davidson is not listed in the references.

Davis, H. L.—Primarily a prose artist, Davis, who is cited by all three references, published one poem in the periodical.

Dreiser, Theodore—One poem by Dreiser found its way into the *Mercury*. His position among American writers has been noted. All three references lists him.

Dunne, Edith Hart—Not mentioned in the references, this writer contributed one verse item to the magazine.

Elmendorf, Mary J.—Two poems by this author were printed in the magazine. None of the references mentions her.

Ferril, Thomas Hornsby—Mencken obviously liked Ferril's work, since five of his poems appeared in the magazine. None of the references lists him.

Frost, Frances M.—Only the *Encyclopedia* includes information about this writer, who published four poems in the magazine.

Hackett, Francis—This writer's position on *The New Republic* has been referred to. He contributed one poem to the *Mercury*, and is listed by all three reference works.

Heyward, DuBose—One poem by Heyward appeared in the periodical. The author of the novel, *Porgy*, which was the basis of the famous drama, *Porgy and Bess*, Heyward is listed in all three references.

Hoffenstein, Samuel—A writer of only slight reputation, Hoffenstein sold two poems to the *Mercury*. The *Encyclopedia* and *Authors* list him.

Hubbell, Lindley Williams—Not included in the reference works, Hubbell had one poem in the magazine.

Jeffers, Robinson—One of America's foremost craftsmen in verse, Jeffers printed one poem in the *Mercury*. It goes without saying that all the references devote considerable space to this poet.

Jenkin, Oliver—No mention of this writer is given in any of the reference works. One of his poems was published in the magazine.

Johns, Orrick—Listed in the *Encyclopedia* and *Authors*, Johns's place among the nation's poets is a minor one at best. A single poem by him appeared in the *Mercury*.

Johnson, James Weldon—A writer who has attained some recognition through his poetry and who is cited in all three reference works, Johnson also had one poem in the periodical.

Kenyon, Bernice—Unnoticed by the references, this writer published three poems in the *Mercury*.

Kimball, Alice Mary—The magazine contains two poems by this writer, who is neglected by the references.

Lechlitner, Ruth—One poem by this writer appeared in the magazine. She receives no mention in the references.

Lee, Lawrence—Also represented in the *Mercury* by one work, Lee is not discussed in the references.

Lee, Muna—The *Mercury* contains four poems by this writer. None of the reference works lists her.

Lindsay, Elizabeth—This writer had one poem in the periodical. She is not noticed by the references.

Lindsay, Vachel—In view of Lindsay's eminence as a poet, it is to Mencken's credit that he bought two of his poems. Lindsay is, of course, discussed in all the references.

Lundbergh, Holger—One poem by this writer, who is ignored by the reference works, appeared in the magazine.

McClure, John—Referred to in the *Encyclopedia*, McClure had one poem in the magazine.

Masters, Edgar Lee—No student of literature is not familiar with this writer's *Spoon River Anthology*, and he is generally considered as one of America's best poets. He is listed in all three reference works, and three of his works were printed in the *Mercury*.

Moore, Virginia—Not listed in the references, this writer sold one poem to the magazine.

Morton, David—The author of several books of poems, Morton's reputation is a minor one. Only the *Encyclopedia* lists him. One of his poems was published in the *Mercury*.

Prosper, Joan Dareth—Also the author of one poem printed in the magazine, this writer receives no mention in the references.

Rorty, James—Three poems by Rorty appeared in the magazine. He is neglected by the references.

Sandburg, Carl—Another titan of American letters, Sandburg published three works in the magazine. He once won a Pulitzer prize for his verse, and is naturally listed in the reference works.

Speyer, Leonora—A famous American poet and winner of a Pulitzer prize for her poetry, this writer appeared twice in the *Mercury*. She is discussed in all three references.

Sterling, George—A relatively well-known poet, Sterling had three poems in the magazine. He is recognized by all three references.

Stuart, Jesse—A writer of some merit, Stuart published two poems in the magazine. He is noticed by all three reference works.

Untermeyer, Louis—Three poems by this widely known artist were included in the *Mercury*. He is mentioned by all three references.

Walton, Eda Lou—Listed in the *Encyclopedia,* this writer published two poems in the magazine. Her work as a poet is of minor significance.

Widdemer, Margaret—Winner of a Pulitzer prize, this writer's poetry deserves attention. One poem by her was printed in the *Mercury,* and she is listed in all three references.

Wood, Clement—A minor poet, Wood published one piece in the magazine. He is discussed in ᵗʰe *Encyclopedia* and *Authors*.

Wylie, Lou—Not mentioned in the reference works, this writer is represented in the *Mercury* by four poems.

Although no concrete conclusions pertaining to Mencken's editorial skills and prejudices can be drawn from the foregoing, the investigation provides a basis for several general observations. The first is that Mencken gave relatively little space to *belles lettres* in the *Mercury;* the second, that many of the most frequent contributors to the magazine have, since that time, either stopped producing or have been totally neglected by the nation's readers and critics. Of the writers who published in the *Mercury,* only forty-five percent are recognized by the *Encyclopedia,* and even less—thirty-one percent—by the *Oxford Companion* and *Authors.* The large number of contributors who have failed to make the ranks in the world of letters is an indication that Mencken often printed works by authors with little or no reputation.

Angoff's statement that "Mencken's abiding heroes as fiction writers were Joseph Hergesheimer, James Branch Cabell, Ambrose Bierce, Ring Lardner, and George Ade"[4] seems out of place in relation to this study: of these writers, only Cabell's fiction appeared in the *Mercury.*

THE BOOK REVIEWS IN THE MERCURY

> Peter White will ne'er go right:
> Would you know the reason why?
> He follows his nose wherever he goes,
> And that stands all awry.
>
> —Anonymous

Angoff, who was possibly Mencken's closest professional associate during his days on the *Mercury,* has since brought forth the charge that

> Mencken's ambitions and envy eventually landed him into the writing of literary criticism and scholarly works. Heaven knows he tried hard enough, but it became apparent to the discerning at once, as it has become clear to nearly everyone now, that he didn't have the necessary gifts.[1]

The charge went even further when Angoff declared that Mencken "was in the main, for or against an author depending upon the agreement of the author's general outlook on life with his own."[2] These are, of course, devastating assaults on Mencken's critical acumen, and they suggest that, as critic, he merely followed his nose. But whether they are totally accurate, only partially correct, or completely false and prejudiced appraisals of Mencken's abilities is still a matter for dispute. Writing as late as 1956, Henry Hazlitt recalled that Mencken "was the outstanding American literary critic of his generation, its most influential stylist, its most prominent iconoclast."[3] Evidently, then, the feud over Mencken's critical talents continues unabated.

To form a basis for evaluating Mencken's work as literary critic on *The American Mercury,* pertinent comments from his book reviews have been taken from the magazine. The works he reviewed which could be classified as pure fiction have, of course, been ignored, for they shed no light on his critical alertness.

Only two groups of books of verse were reviewed during the decade, and the reflections Mencken recorded about them indicate that he was not interested in the form. In October, 1925, he examined twenty-nine volumes of poetry,[4] and concluded the following:

> What I get from them is mainly the impression that we are passing into an era of flabby stuff— that the fine frenzy which seized the poets fifteen years ago has spent itself, and they are laid up for repairs. It was something of an adventure in those days—or even so lately as five years ago—to review the current verse. There was an immense earnestness in it, and a great deal of originality, some of it almost hair-raising.
>
> . . . . .
>
> And in the rubbish there were some pearls. But I can find none in the volumes now under review. There is a great deal of respectable writing in them, but the old glow is gone.[5]

Included in those twenty-nine volumes were one each of the works of Edgar Lee Masters, Edwin Arlington Robinson, and William Butler Yeats, to name a few. Thus it is evident that Mencken's interest in poetry had expired by that time, and he was ready to turn his back on it. However, in June, 1926, he presented the last poetry review to appear in "The Library" while he was with the magazine.[6] He devoted less than three pages to a review of sixty-one volumes, and summarized his opinion of them by remarking:

> I offer this appalling list as proof beyond cavil that the art and mystery of the poet still flourishes among us, despite Coolidgism and Rotary, despite even the collapse of the New Poetry Movement. The general average of the current poetry is very high.[7]

The contradictory nature of his two reviews is immediately apparent, and this, considering the fact that he wrote the second only eight months after the first, is an indication that he was, perhaps, either confused in his decisions or eager to disregard verse altogether. The meager quantity of poetry examined in the *Mercury* certainly tends to support Angoff's recollection that Mencken's

> attitude toward poetry was a strange combination of shame over his own youthful verses . . . and of a peculiar theory he had developed, namely, that poetry was almost entirely an occupation of the young and was not worth the serious attention of mature people.[8]

The fact also upholds Manchester's comments about Mencken's feelings toward the medium:

> Mencken was at his funniest and least discriminating in the field of poetry. Distrust of the emotions without which poetry cannot live killed his own poetical urge . . . and his concept of verse—that it should sing a song pleasantly and never attempt an idea—was downright medieval. . . . He found little worth supporting in contemporary poetry. Poets were treated as children and their poems subjected to the sharpest gibes. Free verse was scorned.[9]

At any rate, the inconsistency of Mencken's judgments does anything but lend credit to his criticism. The main point, though, is that he obviously was not interested in the writers of poetry, and consequently, failed to give them a hearing in the *Mercury.*

The field of prose got a better hearing, however, and a total of eighty-nine works by fifty-eight different authors was reviewed by Mencken during the ten years. A look at these reviews should provide ample evidence for an appraisal of Mencken's work as literary critic. The following list was arranged alphabetically, by the author's last names, rather than by any system of chronology. Included under each name are the author's works, or work, and Mencken's appraisal of each.

Anderson, Sherwood—Reviewing *Horses and Men,* a volume of short stories, the critic thought Anderson owed a big debt to Theodore Dreiser, and that the tales were "of the very first rank. They are simple, moving, and brilliantly vivid." About the lead story, Mencken declared, "There is a vast shrewdness in it; there is sound design; there is understanding; above all, there is feeling."[10] When *Dark Laughter* was published, Mencken shouted that Anderson "has at last found his method, and achieved his first wholly satisfying book." He thought the book had defects, but that Anderson made his characters "breathe and move."[11]

Atherton, Gertrude—Mencken ventured the opinion that parts of *The Crystal Cup* were very sensational, and probably "sugar for the movie lads." A quote on the cover of the book which praised the author in glowing terms brought this comment from Mencken: "God save the Republic!"[12]

Benefield, Barry—A review of Benefield's volume of short stories, *Short Turns,* concluded that the "stories are essentially well-made and situation is more important in them than character . . . but after all, Maupassant said most of it long ago."[13]

Bodenheim, Maxwell—*Replenishing Jessica* smacked too much of Greenwich Village to please Mencken, and the author was "completely devoid of humor." Employing a dash of invective, Mencken called the work "a show of marionettes, and the philosophizing that goes with that show is simply the doctrinaire tosh that passes for profound in the Village."[14]

Burke, Kenneth—This author's *The White Oxen and Other Stories* also incited a flow of harsh criticism. He said the "early pieces are . . . simply bad. His later ones are such muddy, indignant stuff as thrills the bold minds of the Cafe Rotonde."[15]

Cabell, James Branch—Five books by Cabell were reviewed during the period, and, except for the last one, Mencken gave all of them his highest praise. *The High Place* had minor defects, but, overall, was done "in the manner of the celebrated *Jurgen*," and was, "in brief, the melancholy story of a dream come true."[16] *The Silver Stallion: A Comedy of Redemption* had, he believed, "its lacks, but as a piece of writing it is Cabell at his best." All in all, the book was packed with "sly and devastating jocosities, lovely rows of musical words, turns of phrase and thought that bring one up with a gasp."[17] As for *Something About Eve*, Mencken surveyed it and posed the question, "Who can match him at his diabolical best?" and gave Cabell a stirring ovation: "As year chases year the position of Cabell gradually solidifies, and it becomes manifest that his place among the American writers of his time, seen in retrospect, will be at the first table."[18] *The White Robe*, too, drew resounding acclaim, and Mencken mused that Cabell "has never done a better piece of work." This judgment was followed by a statement about Cabell's position as a writer: "No man writing in America today has a more strongly individualized, or, on the whole, a more charming style."[19] The final book by Cabell that was examined, *The Way of Ecben*, left Mencken "discontented" because "things that get into it have no place in it." But even this work, he thought, had its merits. "It might have been much better, but the worst of Cabell is surely not bad."[20]

Cather, Willa—In his reviews of three of this author's novels, Mencken consistently applauded her skillful writing, but regretted her lack of form. The first, *A Lost Lady*, was "excellent stuff, but it remains a bit light." Nevertheless, he believed that the story had "an arch and lyrical air; there is more genuine romance in it than in half a dozen romances in the grand manner."[21] "A somewhat uncertain grasp of form" was discovered in *The Professor's House*, but the surface was "so fine and velvety in texture that one half forgets the ungraceful structure beneath." All in all, it was "an ingratiating piece of work."[22] The narrative of *Death Comes for the Archbishop* occasionally fell "to the level of a pious tale. But . . . not often. If there is a devotée in her, there is also an immensely skillful story-teller." Miss Cather had done

stories "far richer in content, but . . . never exceeded *Death Comes for the Archbishop* as a piece of writing."[23]

Clark, Emily—Mencken declared, in a discussion about *Stuffed Peacocks*, that the author displayed "plain signs of a fine talent." The sketches of characters had "brilliant color, fine insight, and a sort of hard, scientific mercilessness."[24]

Cohen, Lester—*Sweepings*, wrote Mencken, seemed "dull. . . . It bears the air of an enterprise a bit beyond the author's skill." Mencken felt that the reason for this was that Cohen had not collected enough observations for a full-length book. "Before he has gone fifty pages his characters begin to stiffen, and after that the thing is less a chronicle of human beings than an elaborate and somewhat improbable fable."[25]

Conrad, Joseph—Two of Conrad's books were held up to the critical light. *The Rover* was a tale with "a beginning, a middle and an end; it moves smoothly and logically; it is nowhere discursive or obscure; in truth, it is almost well-made." And, overall, a "capital tale, done by a great master."[26] Mencken did not judge *Suspense* to be an equivalent of Conrad's top work. "It begins clumsily, but after the first chapter it is a truly superb piece of writing." But, despite the awkward opening, the book was "well-nigh perfect. Sheer virtuosity could go no further."[27]

Crawford, Nelson Antrim—The only book by Crawford reviewed during the decade, *A Man of Learning*, aroused loud guffaws from the critic, but he gave it only brief notice. He thought Crawford's well-drawn picture of an American college president was a "superb piece of cruel buffoonery."[28]

Croy, Home—This writer's *R.F.D. No. 3* was a "dreadful drop" from Croy's earlier one, *West of the Water Tower*. "The novel proceeds, not from cause and effect, but by leaps. No step, true enough, is overlooked, but no step is made quite plausible." The writer's best qualities were in his character sketches, which were "by no means without a grim, compelling realism." A characteristic Menckenism slipped out when he described one character as a "sort of third-rate Promeseus chained to a manure pile."[29]

Dennis, Geoffrey—A "story-teller of unusual talent, with a great deal of originality" was Mencken's summation of Dennis, and his *Harvest in Poland* was an "impossible story told in terms of the most meticulous realism." And the author invested this combination with "new life by widening the spread between its two parts." Lavish praise for Dennis's style followed: "His prose has a Carlylean thunder in it; he knows how to roll up gorgeous sentences. And he has humor."[30]

Dixon, Thomas—Discussing Dixon's *The Love Complex*, Mencken was astounded to discover in the author a "Baptist who can dream." After this remark, Mencken neither blasted nor praised the book; but he recommended "this lush and thoughtful work to all students of American *Kultur*."[31]

Dos Passos, John—The two books by Dos Passos examined during the period were both viciously attacked. The plot of *Streets of Night* was "simply a series of puerile and often improbable episodes in the lives of two silly boys and an even sillier girl." The author had not explained his characters enough to "make their conduct intelligible and plausible," and the book was thus "depressingly disappointing." The work caused Mencken to offer the thought that the United States needed someone to understand and depict the Young Intellectual. He believed Dos Passos was obviously not equipped for the task, and concluded that "if Sinclair Lewis could only lay eggs and hatch young of his own kind there would be hope."[32] As for *Manhattan Transfer*, Mencken judged it "incoherent, and not infrequently very dull," and doubted that any human being would "ever be able to read it—that is, honestly, thoroughly, from end to end." Mencken surmised that the extremely favorable reception of Dos Passos's first book, *Three Soldiers*, had ruined him: "His first book was far too successful: a very unfortunate thing for a young novelist. His later volumes have shown him hard at it, but making extremely heavy weather."[33]

Dreiser, Theodore—This writer, whom Mencken had long supported, was the subject of two reviews, wherein Mencken flogged him for his wordiness, but, in general, lauded his books. The two-volume *An American Tragedy* was seen as a "vasty double-header, . . . a shapeless and forbidding monster—a heaping cartload of raw materials for a novel, with rubbish of all sorts intermixed—a vast, sloppy, chaotic thing." Parts of the novel were overwritten, filled with "dreadful bilge." However, Mencken thought the overall effect of the book was extremely satisfying, and that the latter portions were very well done. His advice: "Hire your pastor to read the first volume for you. But don't miss the second."[34] Dreiser's book of twelve character sketches, *A Gallery of Women*, also received mixed comment. He thought the author was "full of pretty phrases and arch turns of thought . . . [that] seldom come off." But, despite Dreiser's shortcomings, Mencken mused that his books were the best in modern American fiction.[35]

Eaton, G. D.—Mencken decided that the protagonist in Eaton's first book, *Backfurrow*, was well drawn. As a whole, the work elicited mild praise. "There is not much finesse in the story, but it is moving. Few first novels show so much seriousness or so much skill."[36]

Elser, Frank B.—*The Keen Desire* was "immensely better than any of its predecessors," although Mencken found that Elser over-worked the "device of projecting his hero's acts against a background of his hero's thoughts." But the author had a "sensitive feeling for character" and his main character was "depicted with great insight and unfailing skill."[37]

Ferber, Edna—The critic ventured a guess that Miss Ferber's virtues had been marred by her popularity, and that, in portions of *Show Boat*, she seemed to be writing only for her huge audience. Mencken lauded her for having a "sharp eye for character," and was impressed that she could "evoke genuine feeling."[38]

Fergusson, Harvey—The first of Fergusson's two books discussed during the period, *Women and Wives*, was moderately acclaimed. Mencken thought his competence lifted the "familiar story of the novel out of the commonplace," and that the method was "unhackneyed and effective." The author, he thought, had "very solid talent."[39] The other book, *Wolf Song*, was an "extraordinarily brilliant and charming story," and better than anything Fergusson had ever done. "Full of acidulous humors," the novel's descriptions were very life-like: "The Old Southwest is made to palpitate with such light and heat that they are felt almost physically, and the people that gallop across the scene are full of the juices of life."[40]

Fitzgerald, F. Scott—Although Mencken was not impressed by the story in *The Great Gatsby*, he declared that it was "full of evidences of hard, sober toil," and that it was an indication that Fitzgerald was making "quick and excellent progress" in his writing. With the novel, the critic believed Fitzgerald had changed from a "brilliant improvisateur to . . . a painstaking and conscious author." His final decision: "As a piece of writing it is sound and laudable work."[41]

Glasgow, Ellen—This author's works were met with a blend of applause and abuse. *Barren Ground* left Mencken "rather in doubt" because the author exhibited "no sign of an intimate knowledge of the poor, flea-bitten yokels she sets before us." Altogether, it was "a novel somehow weak in its legs. There is, in detail, excellent work in it. It is boldly imagined and competently planned. But it is not moving."[42] Her next book, *They Stooped to Folly*, drew plaudits for its satirical approach in a story about the South, for Mencken thought satire was the "immemorial refuge of the skeptic who has abandoned hope." The story was meritable because it had a "local vestiture and a local significance." The author, he decided, wrote "very skillfully. She knows how to manage situations and she has an eye for the trivialities which differentiate one man or woman from another."[43]

Gold, Michael—This writer's *Jews Without Money* was highly praised, and Gold's writing reminded Mencken of Jim Tully's, although there were "important differences." Gold's tale was "one of the most eloquent stories that the American press has disgorged in many a moon."[44]

Greene, Ward—Greene's first novel, *Cora Potts*, went a "good deal beyond mere promise." It was a "gorgeous panorama of the New South," and "full of a hearty gusto . . . despite the fact that now and then it edges over the borders of the probable."[45]

Hackett, Francis—"A novel that misses its goal by an inch" was Mencken's summation of *That Nice Young Couple*. He thought Hackett was a better essayist than story-teller, but that the essays were "unfailingly exhilarating. They are full of novel phrases . . . and . . . shrewd observation and penetrating wit." Mencken decided Hackett was a "beginning novelist who has seen something of life in this world, . . . and acquired a genuinely resilient and charming English style."[46]

Harrison, Henry Sydnor—Acid comments followed the publication of *Andrew, Bride of Paris.* It contained "only a pathetic hollowness" and was "childishly transparent— a moral tale that even schoolboys—nay, schoolmasters, must laugh at."[47]

Hecht, Ben—*Count Bruga* impressed Mencken as somewhat of a paradox because, although the story was "deliberately artificial," Hecht "gets so much gusto into the writing of it, and adorns it with so many flashes of insight into motive and character, that the impossible . . . takes on a sort of possibility." His writing was often "careless, but . . . never banal."[48]

Hemingway, Ernest—A book of short stories, *Men Without Women,* led Mencken to write that the author was "somewhat uncertain about . . . characters." He thought the praise Hemingway had been receiving stemmed from his "technical virtuosity," and that "hard and fundamental thinking . . . must get [him] on if [he is] to make good [his] high promise." The book's lead story, "The Killers," was a "thing to be sincerely thankful for."[49] The merit of *A Farewell to Arms* was in its "brilliant evocation of the horrible squalor and confusion of war." Mencken decided that toward the end of the book the main characters "fade into mere wraiths, and in the last scenes they scarcely seem human at all." Hemingway's dialogue was lauded for being "fresh and vivid," but, "otherwise, his tricks begin to wear thin. The mounting incoherence of a drunken scene is effective once, but not three or four times."[50] *Death in the Afternoon* was seen as an "extraordinarily fine piece of expository writing, but . . . it often descends to a gross and irritating cheapness." He thought Hemingway's observations and style were excellent: "The narrative is full of the vividness of something really seen, felt, experienced, . . . done in English that is often bald and graceless, but . . . with great skill." The primary objection to the book had to do with Hemingway's obscene language. Mencken shouted that the "four-letter words are as idiotically incongruous as so many boosters' slogans or college yells" and that they would probably "give the Oak Park W.C.T.U. another conniption fit." Hemingway digressed too often in the book to "prove fatuously that he is a naughty fellow." Mencken's departing words: "The Hemingway boy is really a case."[51]

Hergesheimer, Joseph—The critic found little lacking in *Tampico,* and the book's appearance occasioned Mencken to remark that it was Hergesheimer's "business to evoke . . . the hideous, and he does it with easy skill and vast effect." The novel was "full of the glow that he knows how to get into a narrative. It is carefully designed. There is color in every line."[52]

Hoyt, Nancy—*Roundabout* was deemed charming despite its "load of somewhat naive melodrama," and Mencken

liked it. "It is a tale of calf love—not done with superior snickers, but seriously and even a bit tragically."[53]

Huxley, Aldous—The critic had little to say about *Antic Hay* other than that it was "full of a fine gusto." But he rendered an opinion that Huxley "suffers from the fact that the burlesque modern novel is very hard to write— that the slightest letting down reduces it to mere whimsicality and tediousness."[54] He was considerably more elated over *Two or Three Graces:* "All his sure and delicate skill gets into the telling of it. It is rich with searching and frolicsome humors. It is a capital piece of writing."[55]

Kennedy, Margaret—A pat on the back was awarded for *The Constant Nymph*'s "excellent workmanship," but Mencken said the author had "by no means penetrated to the secrets of the harmonic soul; she has simply done us a set of amusing Bohemians."[56]

Komroff, Manuel—A book of short stories, *The Grace of Lambs* was testily dismissed. Mencken found "nothing in the pieces save a vague desire to be poetical and profound. They have no direction, and only too often they have no sense."[57]

Lardner, Ring W.—Lardner's *How to Write Short Stories,* mainly a volume of his own works, evoked lofty acclaim. The stories were "superbly adroit and amusing; no other contemporary American, sober or gay, writes better." But Mencken feared that they would not endure, because "our grandchildren will wonder what they are about." Mencken also made another prediction: "The professors will shy at him until he is dead at least fifty years. He is doomed to stay outside where the gang is."[58] *The Love Nest, and Other Stories* was "satire of the most acid and appalling sort—satire wholly removed, like Swift's, . . . from the least weakness of amiability, or even pity," and the characters were "unmistakably real." Mencken reckoned that "few American novelists, great or small, have character more firmly in hand," and championed Lardner for "trying to get the low-down Americano between covers."[59] Reviewing *Lose With a Smile,* Mencken recalled his earlier prediction, and maintained that the "professors continue to look straight through him, just as they looked through Mark Twain in 1900 and Walt Whitman in 1875." He decided the professors did not like Lardner because he denied the "doctrine that the purpose of literature is to spread sweetness and light." The book, itself, was "vastly amusing, but there is a great deal more in it than a series of laughs."[60]

Lewis, Sinclair—Six books by Lewis were reviewed during the decade, and Mencken's evaluations of them fluctuated between lofty accolades and spicy denunciations. *Arrowsmith* was "five hundred pages of riotous and often barbarous humor, yet always with a sharp undertone of irony in it, always with a bitter flavor," and it was "well thought out and executed with great skill." In the book, Mencken found no "uncertainty of design. There is never any wavering in theme or purpose."[61] The characters in *Mantrap* were "only a herd of stuffed dummies. They are never real for an instant." After guessing that "perhaps the book is a mere pot-boiler, done with the left hand," Mencken wrote, "I have presented *Mantrap* to my pastor, and return joyfully to a re-reading of *Babbitt*."[62] *Elmer Gantry* evoked a different tune: "For the third time Lewis knocks one clear over the fence." Mencken suggested that it would go higher than *Babbitt* or *Main Street*. The book was "American from the first low cackle of the prologue to the last gigantic obscenity," and Mencken opined that it would "consolidate and improve his position in his craft." Lewis was, he thought, "within his bounds, an artist of the first calibre."[63] *The Man Who Knew Coolidge* spurred the comment that Lewis had "created characters of genuine flesh and blood, and not merely two or three of them, or half a dozen, but whole companies." The protagonist in this book was excellent, but not as good as Babbitt: "The wistful earnestness of Babbitt is not in him; he is the First Gravedigger rather than Hamlet." Babbitt, he decided, would "haunt historians of the Ford Age long after Ford himself sinks into a footnote."[64] Dodsworth was a "somewhat sombre work," mainly because the characters' actions were not accounted for rationally, and some of the dialogue between the two principal characters was "simply impossible." Here Mencken noted that Lewis's work was "uneven. From the best scenes of *Babbitt* to the worst of *Mantrap* there is a drop as dizzy as that from a string quartette to a movie."[65] *Ann Vickers* was, primarily, "flubdub." Mencken thought the main character "simply gets away from him." It was a "kind of patchwork, partly very good, but mainly bad."[66]

Lewisohn, Ludwig—"Soberly composed, devoid of the usual novelists' tricks, and full of excellent writing" was Mencken's judgment of *The Case of Mr. Crump*. He decided the author's future would be a bright one: "Lewisohn is a man of fine talents, and I believe that his best books are ahead of him. He has learning . . . and a sense of beauty, a rather rare combination."[67]

Loos, Anita—*Gentlemen Prefer Blondes* filled Mencken with "uproarious and salubrious mirth." The laughter came from a "farce full of shrewd observation and devastating irony," and from her dashes of "fresh humor, not too formal and refined."[68]

Masters, Edgar Lee—This author presented a paradox to Mencken, because his verse ranged from the eloquent and profound *Spoon River Anthology* to a "great mass of feeble and preposterous doggerel." The same was true for Master's novel, *Mirage*. It was "one of the most idiotic and yet one of the most interesting American novels that I have ever read." He admitted that the book's "fascination lies in its very deficiencies as . . . a work of art—in its naive lack of humor, its elaborate laboring of the obvious, its incredible stiltedness and triteness."[69]

McFee, William—Mencken was not impressed by *Race*, which he thought was "a challenge to all the dull English practitioners of stewed tea realism." McFee was "unable to come to grips with his characters; they never got beyond a feeble whimsicality."[70]

Millin, Sarah Gertrude—Three works by Miss Millin were reviewed in the *Mercury*. Discussing *God's Stepchildren*, Mencken asserted that the author had a "truly astonishing capacity for narrative," and that the book was a "searching and mordant treatise, often brilliant, upon the effects of racial mixtures." All in all, it was an "extremely artful, knowing and moving piece of work."[71] The story in *Mary Glenn* was "achieved with great plausibility and effect," and was "a splendid thing, indeed—vivid, highly dramatic, and full of a poignant eloquence."[72] As for *An Artist in the Family,* Mencken thought she had "done better work," but, though not the best of her books, it offered "something very delicate and fine."[73]

Montague, C. E.—A reprint of this English writer's book, *A Hind Let Loose,* was met with high approval. Mencken declared it "satire in the grand manner," satire managed "superbly." The work was a "charming and uproarious piece of buffoonery, carried on with the utmost dexterity from start to finish."[74]

Muilenburg, Walter J.—The critic was not "moved" by the author's "peasants" in *Prairie,* and the characters bore the brunt of his criticism:

> . . . they never seem real to me for an instant. I can't get rid of a feeling that they are set up in front of me, not by one who has lived among them and sweated with them, but by a spectator from . . . some agricultural experiment station.[75]

Norris, Charles G.—*Pig Iron* was read "with immense interest, and enjoyed . . . unflaggingly," and Mencken insisted that Norris's novels "have received a great deal less critical attention than they deserve." His books, Mencken thought, had "solid substance in them, and a fine dignity."[76]

Odum, Howard W—The author's *Rainbow Round My Shoulder* was a "work of art that lives and glows," a "story of extraordinary fascination," and one "managed with the utmost skill." Mencken did not spare his praise. "Walt Whitman would have wallowed in it, and I suspect that Mark Twain would have been deeply stirred by it too."[77]

Parrish, Anne—"Written with quite unusual skill," *The Perennial Bachelor* was a "work of sound virtues." Mencken thought this new novelist's talent was "unmistakable," and that the "narrative moves without a hitch; there is not a false note; the final effect is achieved surely, and even brilliantly."[78]

Remarque, Erich Maria—*All Quiet on the Western Front* received thunderous applause as a "brilliantly vivid and poignant story of man in war—unquestionably the best story of the World War so far published." Somewhat tartly, Mencken hoped the book would teach the leaders of the American Legion the "difference between falling safely upon a starved and exhausted foe and fighting against great odds for four long years."[79]

Scott, C. Kay—*Siren* displayed a "great deal of genuine novelty," and the critic thought the author's "effort to enter into the very minds of his characters" was ingenious. Mencken judged this technique as a "novelty that lifts itself above the general run of such things. Mr. Scott is intelligent, and has something to say."[80]

Sergel, Roger L.—This author was dismissed as a second-rate Dreiser and *Arlie Gelston* was acidly abused. The main character was "stupid and dull without being pathetic; her story has the impersonal emptiness of a series of fractions," and the book was called a "respectable, but entirely undistinguished work."[81]

Smits, Lee J.—*The Spring Flight* summoned forth the highest approbation. Mencken wrote that he could not "recall a first novel of more workmanlike dignity. There is absolutely no touch of amateurishness in it . . . It would be absurd to say that it shows merely promise." The writer had handled his "machinery . . . in an extremely dexterous manner" in producing "an extraordinarily sound and competent piece of work."[82]

Stevens, James—The book on folklore, *Paul Bunyan*, received exceedingly high acclaim, and the author was lauded both for his style and for recording the material. "He is a skillful writer of English, with a simple, ingratiating style. He is full of a rich, wholly masculine humor, and hence thoroughly in rapport with the extravagant Rabelaisian humor of Bunyan himself."[83]

Stribling, T. S.—*Teeftallow*, Mencken declared, approached "perilously near to the border of moral indignation. But . . . in no other volume known to me is there a more truthful picture of life among the Tennessee hillbillies." The work accomplished the mammoth task of rendering the Scopes trial "comprehensive to the bewildered unbeliever."[84]

Suckow, Ruth—Mencken reviewed Miss Suckow's first book, *Country People*, and found it "quite bare of the usual obviousness and irresolution of the novice." He evaluated the work as "curiously impressive" and thought she had a "profound understanding of simple and stupid people." Miss Suckow's future was seen as "unquestionably secure."[85] His praise flowed again when *The Odyssey of a Nice Girl* appeared, and he wrote that she "can discern and evoke the eternal tragedy in the life of man." The work was "genuinely moving, . . . never banal."[86] The book of short stories, *Iowa Interiors*, too, elicited lofty approval. "Who . . . has ever published a better first book of short stories than this one? Of its sixteen . . . , not one is bad—and among the best there are at least five masterpieces." The characters were "overwhelmingly real, and not a word can be spared."[87] However, Mencken's zeal diminished somewhat when *The Bonney Family* was published, and, in a scanty review, he wrote that she had "done better work."[88] His customary praise returned when *Cora* appeared, but he still harbored a "feeling that this is not her best." The main character was "a sort of case history in a thesis: one has an uneasy sense that she is

being used to prove something." Nevertheless, the story was "very deftly put together; with each successive book, indeed, Miss Suckow writes with greater skill."[89]

Tully, Jim—*Jarnegan* was given a relatively unfavorable reception because Tully had managed the story badly "by succumbing to the charms of a moving-picture ending." But Mencken was convinced that the work showed improvement over Tully's earlier efforts. The story was "immensely interesting—a bravura piece done at high pressure. There is a great deal more than a picturesque part in Tully; he has begun to learn his trade."[90]

Van Vechten, Carl—Three works by this author were examined during the period. Only brief comments were made about *The Blind Bow-Boy*. Mencken was not impressed by it, but he conceded that it never "grows dull, even when it grows thin."[91] Much the same was true for *Fire-Crackers*, and Mencken concluded that it "does not lift me." Perhaps, the critic thought, his own "mounting troubles" had put him "out of the mood" for Van Vechten's type of story.[92] *Nigger Heaven* evoked mild praise. "The scenes of revelry in the book, to borrow a Confederatism, are genuinely niggerish. And the people, in the main, are very real."[93]

Wells, H. G.—Two books by Wells were criticized during the decade, and the appraisals of them struck opposite poles. *Christina Alberta's Father* was "dreadful stuff," a "thoroughly bad piece of work—muddled in plan, carelessly written, and full of characters that creak in every joint." He declared that Wells had resorted to "all sorts of fly-blown devices—the omniscient scientist, the long-lost father, and so on." Mencken refrained from describing the book, and gave this advice: "Go read it yourself—if you have the endurance."[94] But Wells regained Mencken's favor with *The World of William Clissold*, and the critic gushed with praise. He thought it was "extraordinarily meritorious. It is not only a good book; it is an amazing book." Mencken decided he could recollect "no more penetrating discussion of sex in general, or of its social implications, including marriage," and concluded that there were "weak spots in it, as there are in Holy Writ, but taken as a whole it is unquestionably a sound and brilliant performance."[95]

Wilder, Thornton—A short notice followed publication of *The Bridge of San Luis Rey*. Mencken decided that after reading the "most surprising bravura passages" he still had some "doubt as to what it is all about." The book often seemed "fragmentary: it charms without leaving any very deep impression. But that is a defect that the years ought to cure."[96]

Winslow, Thyra Samter—Mencken bestowed moderate praise upon *Show Business*, and found the author to be "an ironist both subtle and merciless." He was pleased that the "stage is neither a region of romance to her nor a hell of sin. It simply amuses her, and she gets her own sardonic delight in it into her book."[97]

Young, Francis Brett—The critic's perusal of *Sea Horses* led him to believe that Young was a "disciple of Joseph Conrad, and . . . he surely does no discredit to his master." The tale was "very deftly managed. It is the work of a man whose talent is obvious."[98]

The inferences to be drawn from the preceding mass of reviews are, in number, several; in significance, highly important; and, in respect to Mencken's interest in literature while pilot of the *Mercury*, devastating. One fact about the reviews presents itself with resounding force. It is the fact that an overwhelming percentage of them are, overall, extremely favorable, which makes it appear that Mencken was trying to appease rather than criticize. Evidently, he judiciously selected the books he reviewed, and, in the main, chose only works by writers he liked. Some support for this judgment is gained from disclosing the number of books of fiction that were criticised each year; in 1924, fourteen works were reviewed; in 1925, twenty-four; in 1926, twenty-five; in 1927, five; in 1928, eight; in 1929, five; in 1930, five; in 1931, none; in 1932, one; and in 1933, two. Surely, this information indicates that Mencken's interest in literature declined steadily throughout the ten years. In fact, since he discussed only thirteen books during the last half of his stay on the magazine, it seems foolish to regard him as an active literary critic during those years. Furthermore, only three works were reviewed during the last three years: *Death in the Afternoon, Lose With a Smile,* and *Ann Vickers*—all three by writers who had been prominent and popular for several years. Therefore, it seems likely that, while on the *Mercury,* Mencken lost touch with America's swirling flow of fiction, and merely coasted on his reputation from *The Smart Set.* Angoff has pointed out that, "In spite of Mencken's reputation as a discoverer of new writers, during the *Mercury* days he read very few of the new novels, generally only those by established authors."[99] All the evidence certainly bolsters this statement.

What Mencken *did* primarily choose to review in "The Library" was far removed from pure literature. Most of his examinations were of books about such subjects as religion, politics, and sociology. A general idea as to the types of books he discussed may be derived from a list of titles which were lifted, at random, from the pages of the *Mercury.* All of the following books were reviewed in the magazine between February, 1929, and August, 1933: *Protestantism in the United States*[100]; *The Nature of the Physical World*[101]; *Washington Merry-Go-Round*[102]; *The Beliefs of 700 Ministers*[103]; *What Is Life*[104]; *Liberalism in the South*[105]; *Genetic Studies of Genius*[106]; *The Prohibition Experiment in Finland*[107]; *England's Crisis*[108]; *Arctic Village*[109]; and *Life in Lesu.*[110]

The very titles of these books—typical examples of the majority of works reviewed by Mencken—almost preclude the necessity for pointing out the obvious fact that Mencken's main interests during the period were not in things literary.

CONCLUSION

Humpty Dumpty sat on a wall,
Humpty Dumpty had a great fall;
All the king's horses
And all the king's men
Couldn't put Humpty Dumpty
Together again.

—Anonymous

H. L. Mencken's years on *The American Mercury* were exciting ones, for his sparkling treatment of the American scene was thoroughly in tune with the times. His audience, throughout most of the Twenties, was both large and appreciative; his writings were read widely; he was quoted and revered by the nation's young intellectuals; he was regarded as somewhat of a literary dictator; and, in brief, he was the darling of the Jazz Age. The green-backed *Mercury* was his mouthpiece, and through it he trumpeted and hooted—and was heard. But he was, like Humpty Dumpty, doomed for a fall, and, when he fell, the *Mercury* began to collapse, too. The postwar spirit had ushered him into power, but when the tenor of the times changed, he was swept back out again. As Angoff has pointed out, Mencken's descent was caused by the depression: "In the years 1918-1928 Mencken's name seemed to be on the tongue of every literate man and woman. His decline was almost coincidental with the beginning of the depression in the United States."[1] Somehow, Mencken's antics were no longer appreciated after bread became precious, and, by December, 1933, his audience had dwindled away, and he left the *Mercury* with that month's issue. The announcement that he was quitting his post stimulated the following editorial, which appeared in the October, 1933, edition of *The Christian Century.* It aptly sums up the reasons why Mencken's brand of leadership suddenly went out of fashion.

> The retirement of Mr. Mencken from the editorship of the *American Mercury* may not mark an epoch in American literature but it has significance as one of the signs of the passing of a type of criticism which during the past decade has had a vogue disproportionate to its value. Mr. Mencken's scorn of the 'booboisie' and his Rabelaisian laughter at the queer antics of the 'Bible Belt' have been his conspicuous contributions to the interpretation of American culture. . . . One had already begun to sense a disquieting untimeliness in these keen cynicisms which professed to be so absolutely timely. Their subject matter was of today, but their spirit was of yesterday. We are fed up with cynicism. 'Oh yeah' has lost its charm. Criticism must pass into a somewhat more sober and disciplined mood to get a favorable hearing. We no longer relish being told that we are fools. We have heard it often enough, and have admitted it. . . . Mencken's abandonment of his post as the mentor of American mores is symptomatic of a change in the American mood.[2]

Upton Sinclair, a long-time adversary of Mencken's, had predicted the fall as early as 1927:

Mencken has 'made his school,' as the French say; he has raised up a host of young persons as clever as their master, and able to write with the same shillelah swing. For the present that is all that is required; that is the mood of the time. But some day the time spirit will change; America will realize that its problems really have to be solved.[3]

The prediction was fulfilled, and Mencken retreated because, just as he had been unable to change his views and was hence forced to become silent during World War I, "the entire world had shifted key, and C Major, the only tone he knew, was suddenly discordant and out of tune."[4] The *Mercury* rapidly lost circulation as the depression became more and more severe, and, as Manchester remarked, it could not be saved.

> An affidavit filed by Joseph C. Lesser, comptroller at Knopf's . . . summed up the predicament of the magazine when it contended that the depression had struck it especially hard because it was dependent entirely on 'the activity, ingenuity, and popularity' of Mencken. Class magazines, Lesser pointed out, must be revamped and reorganized if they were to survive, but that could not be expected of the *Mercury* since it was a 'one-man magazine catering to a very selective class of readers who are followers of its editor.'[5]

At any rate, Mencken was jilted. His reign as literary dictator had ended before his last edition appeared in late 1933, and he never regained the power and influence that was his for so many years.

However, Mencken's work on the *Mercury,* both as editor and literary critic, has never been forgotten, although the various critics differ broadly in their evaluations of the man and his writings. No one denies his onetime influence, though, not even the critic Louis Kronenberger, who had no praise for Mencken's literary abilities. He once stated that "the editorials and book reviews in *The Smart Set* and the earlier issues of *The American Mercury* proved formidable instruments—probably the most formidable of their day—in creating literary trends and reputations,"[6] and this judgment is supported by practically everyone who has ever written about Mencken. But, as mentioned previously, opinion concerning Mencken's abilities and contributions is more divided. One observer, L. B. Hessler, writing in 1935, accused Mencken of founding a school of "bad boy" criticism[7]; namely, meaningless, ill-founded criticism:

> No attempt is made by practitioners of this spiteful school of criticism to give an unbiased and honest appraisal of the work under observation or to concern themselves with the reader at all. Since it is much easier and vastly more interesting to throw brickbats, mud, and rotten eggs . . . at others, the bad boy does so.[8]

To be sure, Mencken threw many "brickbats" and "rotten eggs" in his reviews, but they were not always aimed in the wrong direction. For this reason, Hessler's attack on

Mencken's critical acumen seems a bit too general. More truth is to be found in Kronenberger's assertion that Mencken lacked

> . . . an esthetic judgment to match his common sense. A very good pamphleteer, he turned out to be a very bad critic. Once he got into the temple of art, he seemed no better than an adventurer. He drummed up bad novelists and talked good ones down.[9]

Nevertheless, when Mencken reviewed a book by someone who has since been awarded a high place among the nation's writers, he was usually correct in his decisions. He was completely wrong about Dos Passos, of course, and his judgment of Dreiser's *An American Tragedy* now seems a bit cruel, but these are exceptions to the rule. The statement that Mencken "drummed up bad novelists" is a true one. Surely, he wasted many superlatives on such writers as Cabell and Hergesheimer, writers who have now faded into literary oblivion.

However, not all of the criticism about Mencken has been adverse. Burton Rascoe, for one, thought that Mencken, along with Nathan and Cabell, had

> taken part in all of the important socio-literary affairs of their day— . . . each of them having done in his time mightier and more successful battles against Philistinism and Pharisaism, against the stultifying and repressive forces of ignorance, censorship, prejudice and other enemies of liberty and freedom of conscience than all the Hickses, Forsythes, Cowleys and fellow-travellers put together.
>
> . . . . .
>
> Mencken has not only honored Twain's memory; he has carried on the Mark Twain tradition in the American language and literature.[10]

The truth is that Mencken was not altogether a bad critic and editor while on the *Mercury,* and he made some worthwhile contributions. He was always eager to give a hearing to young and inexperienced writers, and he published much of their work in the magazine. Angoff recorded that

> Mencken was always eager to print authors for the first time, and to that end he carried on a huge correspondence with young men and women in all parts of the country in the hope that they would come through with a printable piece. . . . No wonder he was called the managing editor of all the young hopeful writers all over the nation. There has been no one like him in this respect ever since he gave up *The Mercury* . . . , and the life of all beginning writers has been so much the harder and so much the lonelier.[11]

However, it is not to Mencken's credit that the vast majority of the beginning writers he championed so lustily failed to gratify the promise he evidently saw in them. In brief, his attitude toward new writers is estimable, although his critical judgment was seldom sound.

The most stirring indictment to be made about Mencken's treatment of *belles lettres,* and one that the evidence renders irrefutable, is that he tended to give increasingly less attention to literature in the *Mercury* as time went by. Little by little, whatever literary erudition he possessed, whatever interest he had in the ebb and flow of the nation's fiction, and whatever grasp and understanding of *belles lettres* he owned were supplanted by an attachment for the more superficial movements of the day. The energy he had devoted to fiction while critic for *The Smart Set* and during the early years of the *Mercury* was eventually burned up in his writings about the political carnival, and he apparently had little left for the arts. Mencken made only a feeble effort in his book-review department to cover the literature that was published during the Twenties, and, if the small number of works he examined in "The Library" is any indication of the amount he read, it is likely that by the time the *Mercury* lost its popularity he was merely floundering somewhere in the murky backwaters of American literature; the main stream had passed him by. And not only did Mencken fail to listen to the writers who were, at that time, literary nonentities, but he also ignored the authors who were receiving thunderous applause from every corner of the country—people who were molding and transforming the nation's literature. His failure to review books by such writers as William Faulkner, Thomas Wolfe, and John Steinbeck, to list but a few, presents conclusive testimony to the fact that he had relinquished his grasp on American literature. Granted, Mencken tooted his horn for several writers who have since been awarded a select niche in the ranks of America's top-flight novelists, but his support of, and contribution to, *belles lettres* while editor of the *Mercury* was in no way commensurate to that which has often been accorded him by many of the country's leading critics.

Manchester's assertion that Mencken had, by the time the depression struck,

> . . . not only lost touch with the older writers he had championed, i.e., Dreiser, Boyd, Anderson, Cabel, *et al.;* he had lost that very contact with borning fiction upon which his reputation as a literary critic was predicated. He had become completely the magazine editor and social philosopher and had, in so doing, defaulted a role for which, intrinsically, he was far better suited.[12]

is, perhaps, slightly exaggerated, although it misses the mark only by an inch; Mencken had kept a finger in the nation's literary pie, but it was the little one.

Another thing that is inferred by an examination of Mencken's *Mercury* is his distrust of innovators. His highly unfavorable reviews of Dos Passos's works definitely attests to the assumption. And, according to Angoff, Mencken was never impressed by Faulkner and his experiments with the stream-of-consciousness technique, a literary device that he manipulated such that it figured prominently in securing for him the fame he now has.

> Mencken could not see him at all. He claimed that 'there is no more sense in him [Faulkner] than in

the wop boob, Dante,' and 'he has no more to say than do Hawthorne and all those other New England female writers. My God, the man hasn't the slightest idea of sentence structure or paragraphing.'[13]

Angoff also recorded that Mencken was opposed to printing Faulkner's short story, "That Evening Sun Go Down," which appeared as the lead story in one issue.[14] And, wrote Angoff, during the argument between him and Mencken, the latter said, "It is gibberish, Angoff, I tell you it is gibberish."[15] This reluctance to embrace the new trends which were then being developed in the short story and the novel is another facet of Mencken's relations with *belles lettres* which makes him appear out of tune with the flow of literature that was passing across his desk.

A note of confusion about literature and a strong indication of a declining zeal for it was sounded by Mencken, himself, in his writings in the *Mercury*. Apparently, when he assumed the editorship in January, 1924, his old fire was still burning, for, in June of that year he urged a novelist to write a book about a marriage that succeeds,[16] and the reasons he presented indicate that his campaign for realism was still in motion. "The more novels get away from what is typical," he maintained, "the less substance and vitality they have. The odd, the strange, the fantastic—these things belong to the romance, not to the novel."[17] As the years passed, however, such comments became less and less frequent, and, in September, 1927, he ventured the following:

> The new novels show a vast facility, but one must be romantic, indeed, to argue that they show anything else. The thing vaguely called creative passion is simply not in them; they are plausible and workmanlike, but they are never moving. The best fiction of today is being written by authors who were already beginning to oxidize ten years ago; the youngsters, debauched by the experiments of such men as James Joyce, wander into glittering futilities. One hears every day that a new genius has been unearthed, but it always turns out, on investigation, that he is no more than a clever sophomore. No first book as solid and memorable as *McTeague* or *Sister Carrie* has come out since the annunciation of Coolidge.[18]

Today it seems somewhat unbelievable that Mencken wrote this at a time when Hemingway, Wolfe, Faulkner, Fitzgerald, and Dos Passos were publishing fairly regularly. And, according to a piece he wrote less than a year later, he did not believe it himself. In "The Library" for May, 1928, he reviewed a group of six new books—three novels and three volumes of short stories. The novels were by Sarah Gertrude Millin, Ruth Suckow, and Nelson Antrim Crawford, and the short stories by Emily Clark, Ernest Hemingway, and Thornton Wilder. The review began with an overwhelming ovation:

> The amazing thing about the current fiction is how good it is. Is the novel, as certain croakers allege, an outworn form, with no more juice of life in it? Then let them read such things as these . . .

. . . . .

And is the short story, squeezed between the O. Henry curse and the *True Confessions* curse—I assume that a curse can squeeze, as it can undoubtedly hiss—is the short story, as one hears, empty, artificial and passe? Then let whoever believes it give attention to these pieces . . . [19]

The appalling inconsistency of these diatribes requires no elaboration; they shout for themselves.

A few months later, in December, 1928, the pendulum had swung back the other way, and Mencken penned yet another contradiction when he explained his attitude toward letters in an editorial which summed up the first five years of the magazine's existence:

The American Mercury has not neglected *belles lettres,* but it makes no apology for devoting relatively little space to mere writing. Its fundamental purpose is to depict and interpret the America that is in being; not to speculate moonily about Americas that might be, or ought to be. It would print more short stories if more good ones could be found. But not many are being written in the United States today.[20]

At the same time, Mencken speculated that few short stories were then being produced because the form, itself, was in decay and the market for inferior stories was too good; money, he thought, was contaminating the writers' artistic standards.[21] And this at a time when such notables as Lardner, Katherine Anne Porter, Willa Cather, Faulkner, John O'Hara, Steinbeck, and Hemingway were turning out some of the most admirable stories that the country has ever produced!

The state of poetry was also a sad one: "In the field of poetry there are similar doldrums. An immense mass of verse is being written, but not one percent of it has any merit whatsoever."[22] Here, again, Mencken's views seem extremely shallow, for these top-flight poets were producing at the time: E. E. Cummings, Robert Frost, William Carlos Williams, John Crowe Ransom, Roy Campbell, Stephen Spender, Edna St. Vincent Millay, Ezra Pound, T. S. Eliot, Allen Tate, Robert Penn Warren—the list is long and mighty, and it goes on and on. Mencken's inconsistency in evaluating verse has already been mentioned, and it would be pure repetition to belabor the point further.

The reason why Mencken's opinions were so jumbled and confounding seems obvious: he simply was not giving *belles lettres* its just due. Instead of keeping only a little finger in the literary pie, he should have either removed it entirely or shoved his whole fist in, for a glance at his *Mercury* reveals two things: Mencken was not always walking with the *avant garde* of American letters during his ten-year stay on the magazine, and, when he was, he was often out of step.

The final conclusion can only be that, despite whatever weight Mencken's literary efforts may have carried dur-

ing the Twenties, he was neither a profound literary critic nor an astute judge of America's beginning writers during his years on the *Mercury*. Anyone who thinks that he was either of these things while editor of the magazine is mistaken, because, in the light of this study, it appears certain that he virtually neglected *belles lettres* throughout the decade. It is likely that Mencken's reputation will dwindle in the future, and, if he is revered at all fifty years from now, it will be for his humorous iconoclasm and for his inimitable writing style, which was, perhaps, the best of its type that America has ever seen.

NOTES

AN INTRODUCTION TO THE *MERCURY*

[1] William R. Manchester, *Disturber of the Peace, The Life of H. L. Mencken* (New York: Harper and Brothers, 1951), pp. 150-51.

[2] *Ibid.,* p. 151.

[3] *Ibid.,* p. 148

[4] *Ibid.*

[5] *Ibid.*

[6] *Ibid.,* p. 149.

[7] *Ibid.,* p. 150.

[8] H. L. Mencken, "Editorial," *The American Mercury,* 1:23, January, 1924.

[9] *Ibid.*

[10] *Ibid.,* p. 29.

[11] *Ibid.,* p. 30.

[12] *Ibid.*

[13] *Ibid.*

[14] *Ibid.,* p. 27.

[15] *Ibid.*

[16] Manchester, *Disturber of the Peace, The Life of H. L. Mencken, op. cit.,* p. 149.

[17] H. L. Mencken, "Americana," *The American Mercury,* 4:45, January, 1926.

[18] H. L. Mencken, "Americana," *The American Mercury,* 5:37, May, 1925.

[19] H. L. Mencken, "Clinical Notes," *The American Mercury,* 1:77, January, 1924.

20 *Ibid.*, p. 75.

21 Manchester, *Disturber of the Peace, The Life of H. L. Mencken, op cit.*, p. 155.

22 Charles Angoff, *H. L. Mencken, A Portrait from Memory* (New York: Thomas Yoseloff, Inc., 1956), p. 192.

23 *Ibid.*

24 William R. Manchester, *A Critical Study of the Work of H. L. Mencken as Literary Critic for the Smart Set Magazine, 1908-1914* (A thesis presented to the graduate school of the University of Missouri, August, 1947), p. 213.

25 *Ibid.*, p. 215.

26 Manchester, *Disturber of the Peace, The Life of H. L. Mencken, op. cit.*, p. 105.

27 *Ibid.*, p. 116.

28 *Ibid.*, p. 115.

29 *Ibid.*, p. 134.

30 *Ibid.*, p. 125.

31 *Ibid.*, p. 133.

32 *Ibid.*, p. 134.

33 Carl Van Doren, "H. L. Mencken: A Gadfly for Democracy," *The Century Magazine*, 105:796, March, 1923.

34 Angoff, *H. L. Mencken, A Portrait from Memory, op. cit.*, p. 19.

35 Van Doren, *op. cit.*, p. 791.

MENCKEN AS LITERARY EDITOR OF THE *MERCURY*

1 Manchester, *Disturber of the Peace, The Life of H. L. Mencken, op. cit.*, p. 150.

2 When referring to one of these works in this chapter, the author has used, for the sake of brevity, the following abbreviations: *Encyclopedia* for *The Reader's Encyclopedia; Oxford Companion* for *The Oxford Companion to American Literature;* and *Authors* for *Twentieth Century Authors.*

3 The names of authors listed in this section were taken from *The American Mercury* for the ten years, January, 1924, to December, 1933. Anyone interested in knowing what fiction was contributed by the writers in this compilation should consult the magazine for those years.

4 Angoff, *H. L. Mencken, A Portrait from Memory, op. cit.*, p. 104.

THE BOOK REVIEWS IN THE *MERCURY*

1 Charles Angoff, "Mencken Twilight," *North American Review*, 246:218, Winter, 1938-39.

2 *Ibid.*, p. 221.

3 Henry Hazlitt, "Mencken: A Retrospect," *Newsweek*, 47:90, February 20, 1956.

4 H. L. Mencken, "Poetry," *The American Mercury*, 6:251, October, 1925.

5 *Ibid.*, p. 252.

6 H. L. Mencken, "Books of Verse," *The American Mercury*, 8:252, June, 1926.

7 *Ibid.*

8 Angoff, *H. L. Mencken, A Portrait from Memory, op. cit.*, p. 83.

9 Manchester, *Disturber of the Peace, The Life of H. L. Mencken, op. cit.*, p. 46.

10 H. L. Mencken, "Three Volumes of Fiction," *The American Mercury*, 1:252, February, 1924.

11 H. L. Mencken, "Fiction Good and Bad," *The American Mercury*, 6:249, October, 1925.

12 H. L. Mencken, "The Gland School," *The American Mercury*, 6:249, October, 1925.

13 H. L. Mencken, "Certain Works of Fiction," *The American Mercury*, 9:381, November, 1926.

14 H. L. Mencken, "Novels Good and Bad," *The American Mercury*, 5:507, August, 1925.

15 H. L. Mencken, "Fiction Good and Bad," *The American Mercury*, 6:379, November, 1925.

16 H. L. Mencken, "Three Gay Stories," *The American Mercury*, 1:380, March, 1924.

17 H. L. Mencken, "Fiction," *The American Mercury*, 8:509, August, 1926.

18 H. L. Mencken, "A Comedy of Fig-Leaves," *The American Mercury*, 12:510, December, 1927.

19 H. L. Mencken, "The Story of a Saint," *The American Mercury*, 16:508, April, 1929.

20 H. L. Mencken, "Fiction by Adept Hands," *The American Mercury*, 19:126, January, 1930.

21 H. L. Mencken, "Three Volumes of Fiction," *op. cit.*, p. 252.

[22] H. L. Mencken, "Fiction Good and Bad," *The American Mercury,* 6:379, November, 1925.

[23] H. L. Mencken, "The Desert Epic," *The American Mercury,* 12:508, December, 1927.

[24] H. L. Mencken, "Fiction," *The American Mercury,* 14:127, May, 1928.

[25] H. L. Mencken, "Certain Works of Fiction," *op. cit.,* p. 381.

[26] H. L. Mencken, "Three Volumes of Fiction," *op. cit.,* p. 252.

[27] H. L. Mencken, "Fiction Good and Bad," *The American Mercury,* 6:379, November, 1925.

[28] H. L. Mencken, "Fiction," *The American Mercury,* 14:127, May, 1928.

[29] H. L. Mencken, "Fiction," *The American Mercury,* 5:124, May, 1925.

[30] H. L. Mencken, "Novels Good and Bad," *op. cit.,* p. 507.

[31] H. L. Mencken, "A Reverend Novelist," *The American Mercury,* 6:122, September, 1925.

[32] H. L. Mencken, "Rambles in Fiction," *The American Mercury,* 2:380, July, 1924.

[33] H. L. Mencken, "Fiction Good and Bad," *The American Mercury,* 7:506, April, 1926.

[34] H. L. Mencken, "Dreiser in 840 Pages," *The American Mercury,* 7:379, March, 1926.

[35] H. L. Mencken, "Ladies, Mainly Sad," *"The American Mercury,* 19:254, February, 1930.

[36] H. L. Mencken, "Fiction," *The American Mercury,* 5:124, May, 1925.

[37] H. L. Mencken, "Certain Works of Fiction," *op. cit.,* p. 381.

[38] H. L. Mencken, "Three Novels," *The American Mercury,* 9:127, September, 1926.

[39] H. L. Mencken, "Rambles in Fiction," *op. cit.,* p. 380.

[40] H. L. Mencken, "The Desert Epic," *op. cit.,* p. 508.

[41] H. L. Mencken, "New Fiction," *The American Mercury,* 5:382, July, 1925.

[42] H. L. Mencken, "New Fiction," *op. cit.,* p. 382.

[43] H. L. Mencken, "Two Southern Novels," *The American Mercury,* 18:251, October, 1929.

[44] H. L. Mencken, "The Life of the Poor," *The American Mercury,* 19:381, March, 1930.

[45] H. L. Mencken, "Two Southern Novels," *op. cit.,* p. 251.

[46] H. L. Mencken, "Novels Good and Bad," *op. cit.,* p. 507.

[47] H. L. Mencken, "Fiction Good and Bad," *The American Mercury,* 7:506, April, 1926.

[48] H. L. Mencken, "Fiction," *The American Mercury,* 8:509, August, 1926.

[49] H. L. Mencken, "Fiction," *The American Mercury,* 14:127, May, 1928.

[50] H. L. Mencken, "Fiction by Adept Hands," *op. cit.,* p. 126.

[51] H. L. Mencken, "The Spanish Idea of a Good Time," *The American Mercury,* 27:506, December, 1932.

[52] H. L. Mencken, "Certain Works of Fiction," *op. cit.,* p. 381.

[53] H. L. Mencken, "Fiction," *The American Mercury,* 8:509, August, 1926.

[54] H. L. Mencken, "Three Gay Stories," *op. cit.,* p. 380.

[55] H. L. Mencken, "Three Novels," *op. cit.,* p. 127.

[56] H. L. Mencken, "New Fiction," *op. cit.,* p. 382.

[57] H. L. Mencken, "Fiction Good and Bad," *The American Mercury,* 6:379, November, 1925.

[58] H. L. Mencken, "Ring W. Lardner," *The American Mercury,* 2:376, July, 1924.

[59] H. L. Mencken, "A Humorist Shows His Teeth," *The American Mercury,* 8:254, June, 1926.

[60] H. L. Mencken, "Pongo Americanus," *The American Mercury,* 29:254, June, 1933.

[61] H. L. Mencken, "Arrowsmith," *The American Mercury,* 4:507, April, 1925.

[62] H. L. Mencken, "Fiction," *The American Mercury,* 8:509, August, 1926.

[63] H. L. Mencken, "Man of God: American Style," *The American Mercury,* 10:506, April, 1927.

[64] H. L. Mencken, "Babbitt Redivivus," *The American Mercury,* 14:251, June, 1928.

[65] H. L. Mencken, "Escape and Return," *The American Mercury,* 16:506, April, 1929.

[66] H. L. Mencken, "A Lady of Vision," *The American Mercury,* 28:382, March, 1933.

[67] H. L. Mencken, "Portrait of a Lady," *The American Mercury,* 10:379, March, 1927.

[68] H. L. Mencken, "Brief Notices," *The American Mercury,* 7:127, January, 1926.

[69] H. L. Mencken, "Edgar Lee Masters," *The American Mercury,* 2:250, June, 1924.

[70] H. L. Mencken, "Rambles in Fiction," *op. cit.,* p. 380.

[71] H. L. Mencken, "Novels Good and Bad," *op. cit.,* p. 507.

[72] H. L. Mencken, "Fiction Good and Bad," *The American Mercury,* 7:506, April, 1926.

[73] H. L. Mencken, "Fiction," *The American Mercury,* 14:127, May, 1928.

[74] H. L. Mencken, "Rambles in Fiction," *op. cit.,* p. 380.

[75] H. L. Mencken, "Fiction Good and Bad," *The American Mercury,* 6:379, November, 1925.

[76] H. L. Mencken, "Fiction Good and Bad," *The American Mercury,* 7:506, April, 1926.

[77] H. L. Mencken, "Black Boy," *The American Mercury,* 15:126, September, 1928.

[78] H. L. Mencken, "Fiction Good and Bad," *The American Mercury,* 6:379, November, 1925.

[79] H. L. Mencken, "Im Westen Nichts Neues," *The American Mercury,* 17:510, August, 1929.

[80] H. L. Mencken, "Fiction Good and Bad," *The American Mercury,* 7:506, April, 1926.

[81] H. L. Mencken, "The Husk of Dreiser," *The American Mercury,* 1:509, April, 1924.

[82] H. L. Mencken, "Fiction," *The American Mercury,* 5:124, May, 1925.

[83] H. L. Mencken, "An American Saga," *The American Mercury,* 5:254, June, 1925.

[84] H. L. Mencken, "Fiction," *The American Mercury,* 8:509, August, 1926.

[85] H. L. Mencken, "Rambles in Fiction," *op. cit.,* p. 380.

[86] H. L. Mencken, "Fiction Good and Bad," *The American Mercury,* 7:506, April, 1926.

[87] H. L. Mencken, "Certain Works of Fiction," *op. cit.,* p. 381.

[88] H. L. Mencken, "Fiction," *The American Mercury,* 14:127, May, 1928.

[89] H. L. Mencken, "Fiction by Adept Hands," *op. cit.,* p. 126.

[90] H. L. Mencken, "Certain Works of Fiction," *op. cit.,* p. 381.

[91] H. L. Mencken, "Three Gay Stories," *op. cit.,* p. 380.

[92] H. L. Mencken, "Fiction Good and Bad," *The American Mercury,* 6:379, November, 1925.

[93] H. L. Mencken, "Three Novels," *op. cit.,* p. 127.

[94] H. L. Mencken, "The English Novel," *The American Mercury,* 6:509, December, 1925.

[95] H. L. Mencken, "Wells Redivivus," *The American Mercury,* 9:506, December, 1926.

[96] H. L. Mencken, "Fiction," *The American Mercury,* 14:127, May, 1928.

[97] H. L. Mencken, "Fiction," *The American Mercury,* 8:509, August, 1926.

[98] H. L. Mencken, "New Fiction," *op. cit.,* p. 382.

[99] Angoff, *H. L. Mencken. A Portrait from Memory, op. cit.,* p. 103.

[100] H. L. Mencken, "The Gods and Their Agents," *The American Mercury,* 17:123, May, 1929.

[101] H. L. Mencken, "The Riddle of the Universe," *The American Mercury,* 16:509, April, 1929.

[102] H. L. Mencken, "The Men Who Govern Us," *The American Mercury,* 24:251, October, 1931.

[103] H. L. Mencken, "The Pastors and Their Dogmas," *The American Mercury,* 17:509, July, 1929.

[104] H. L. Mencken, "The Origin of Life," *The American Mercury,* 16:253, February, 1929.

[105] H. L. Mencken, "The Agonies of Dixie," *The American Mercury,* 28:251, February, 1933.

[106] H. L. Mencken, "Superiority in the Young," *The American Mercury,* 23:126, May, 1931.

[107] H. L. Mencken, "Coroner's Inquest," *The American Mercury,* 24:381, November, 1931.

[108] H. L. Mencken, "The Panting Motherland," *The American Mercury,* 23:380, July, 1931.

[109] H. L. Mencken, "Utopia in Little," *The American Mercury*, 24:124, May, 1933.

[110] H. L. Mencken, "How People Live," *The American Mercury*, 29:506, August, 1933.

CONCLUSION

[1] Angoff, "Mencken Twilight," *op. cit.*, p. 230.

[2] "Mr. Mencken Leaves the *Mercury*," *The Christian Century*, 50:1292, October 18, 1933.

[3] Upton Sinclair, "Mr. Mencken Calls on Me," *The Bookman*, 66:255, November, 1927.

[4] Manchester, *Disturber of the Peace, The Life of H. L. Mencken, op. cit.*, p. 262.

[5] *Ibid.*, p. 266.

[6] Louis Kronenberger, "H. L. Mencken," *The New Republic*, 88:245, October 7, 1936.

[7] L. B. Hessler, *op. cit.*, p. 215.

[8] *Ibid.*, p. 223.

[9] Kronenberger, *op. cit.*, p. 245.

[10] Burton Rascoe, "Mencken, Nathan and Cabell," *The American Mercury*, 49:365, March, 1940.

[11] Charles Angoff, "The Inside View of Mencken's *Mercury*," *The New Republic*, 131:21, September 13, 1954.

[12] Manchester, *Disturber of the Peace, The Life of H. L. Mencken, op. cit.*, p. 220.

[13] Angoff, *H. L. Mencken, A Portrait from Memory, op. cit.*, p. 107.

[14] *Ibid.*

[15] *Ibid.*

[16] H. L. Mencken, "Clinical Notes," *The American Mercury*, 2:186, June, 1924.

[17] *Ibid.*, p. 187.

[18] H. L. Mencken, "Editorial," *The American Mercury*, 12:35, September, 1927.

[19] H. L. Mencken, "Fiction," *The American Mercury*, 14:127, May, 1928.

[20] H. L. Mencken, "Editorial," *The American Mercury*, 15:409, December, 1928.

[21] *Ibid.*

[22] *Ibid.*, p. 410.

Menckeniana

SOURCE: "H. L. Mencken, George Jean Nathan and the American Mercury Venture," in *Menckeniana*, No. 78, Summer, 1981, pp. 1-10.

[*The following essay presents Alfred A. Knopf's account of the professional and personal breakup between H. L. Mencken and George Jean Nathan.*]

H. L. Mencken first met his future collaborator, George Jean Nathan, in 1908 in the offices in New York of *The Smart Set* magazine, where both were being interviewed for editorial positions. Mencken was offered the job of literary critic and Nathan that of drama critic. According to Mencken's biographer. Dr. Carl Bode, Nathan's work in *The Smart Set* didn't actually begin to appear until 1909, almost a year after their first meeting.

Such was the chemistry between the two men that an extraordinary friendship developed, both literary and personal. It would last until 1923 when, with the assistance of an innovative young publisher, Alfred A. Knopf, the two founded the *American Mercury*, perhaps the most influential literary magazine of the time. Mr. Knopf was publisher.

Shortly after the first issue appeared in January of 1924, it became apparent that there were differences between Mencken and Nathan. The following story was written by the surviving member of the team that created one of the most sensational literary magazines in the history of publishing.

Only one man could write this story and it is a view from the inside. Much of the other writing concerning the Mencken-Nathan break-up has been scholarly speculation over the intervening half-century.

This chapter concerning H. L. Mencken, George Jean Nathan, and the *American Mercury* is drawn from Mr. Knopf's memoirs, an undertaking he now describes as "a task long since abandoned." It was written during the 1960's.

Mr. Knopf has graciously granted *Menckeniana* the privilege of publishing this account. He has also included an entry from his diary, dated October 7, 1925, which further sets the stage for this exciting story.

The text is uncut and appears as Mr. Knopf wrote it almost twenty years ago.

A somewhat edited version of this story appeared on the "Other Voices" page of the Baltimore *Evening Sun* and was published between June 22-25, 1981.

In writing to Op-Ed page editor, Gwinn Owens, Mr. Knopf said: "I gave my chapter no further thought until in the special edition of *Menckeniana,* issued as part of the centenary celebration of Henry's birth last September 12, I read 'HLM and

GJN: The Editorial Partnership Re-examined' by Carl Dolmetsch (author of an admirable work on *The Smart Set* magazine), which is a paper he had given at a seminar on Mencken at the Newberry Library in Chicago the previous May. I found this piece so inadequate, ignoring so much of what I knew was missing, that I determined to publish my own record."

I find in a diary dated October 7, 1925, the following: "Pow-wow with HLM this morning. His soreness for George Nathan seems deep-seated and growing. The more he gets from George in the way of getting rid of the old-fashioned old partnership, the more he wants. Nothing in the end will satisfy him but complete divorce. It looks like Henry's one weakness. He insists that George isn't our friend any more than the friend of the *Mercury*—that he talks much of what books he gets for us (exactly none) and what financial sacrifices he made leaving his own books with us. Meanwhile, George is more friendly personally than ever before. Henry can force a row if he will, but I hope he won't, because after all George is within his rights and only his taste in not long ago clearing out from where he so clearly isn't wanted could be questioned. It's just another example of how the best of friends, when they once fall out, become the bitterest of enemies. Outwardly all is calm and amiable; actually Henry will never rest till he ruins George. Poor game it seems to me for Henry—not worthy of his ammunition. What a story the true history of the rise and fall of the Mencken/Nathan partnership will make some day." . . .

Long before this, differences between Henry and George had become acute, and Henry determined either to leave the magazine himself or to get rid of his associate. He somehow never seemed to realize that George couldn't just be wished or ordered off the premises. After all, he owned one-sixth of the property and would sooner or later have to be bought out.

October 15th (probably 1924) Mencken wrote Nathan, "After a year's hard experience and due prayer, I come to the conclusion that the scheme of the *American Mercury* as it stands is full of defects, and that to me at least it must eventually grow impossible. We can go into my reasons at length if necessary next week. I am proposing to Alfred that a meeting be called for Wednesday. For the present I state only my conclusions.[1] They are:

(1) That the magazine is fast slipping into the formalism which ruined *The Smart Set*—in other words, that we are beginning to depend upon rubber stamps rather than upon ideas.

(2) That this decay is due mainly to the need to stay within the narrow (and progressively narrowing) circle of our common interests—in brief, to the duality of editorial control.

(3) That no remedy is worth anything that doesn't strike at the root of the difficulty.

"I therefore propose the following alternatives:

(1) I will as of January 1st next take over complete control of the editorial department, put in a managing editor, run the office and operate the magazine as Sedgwick operates the *Atlantic*, or (2) I will retire from all editorial duties and responsibilities and go upon the same footing that other contributors are on. My inclination at the moment is to choose Number Two. I can see nothing ahead under the present scheme save excessive and uninteresting drudgery and a magazine growing progressively feebler.

"You may not agree with my conclusions even after you hear my reasons, but the point is that it is not necessary that they be correct. It is only necessary that I believe them. I don't want to begin to think of the editorship as a job and a nuisance. Either it must be something to interest me greatly or it is something to be got rid of.

"If case No. 2 is adopted I am willing to cancel my stock in the company or to turn it into the treasury. I offer to write one article a month for the magazine at the same rate paid to other contributors."

A few days later he wrote another and much longer letter to Nathan.

"What I am thinking of is the future—two, five, or ten years hence. In particular, I am thinking of my own future. As things stand, I see nothing ahead save a round of dull drudgery, with no chance to life the magazine out of casualness and triviality and to make it of solid dignity and influence. Its present apparent success (i.e., that of the *Mercury*) I believe is largely illusory. It is appealing mainly to a superficial and unstable class of readers. Their support is not to be depended on. They buy it at the newsstands and gabble about it intermittently, but they are not permanently interested in ideas. What the magazine needs is a sounder underpinning. It must develop a more coherent body of doctrine, and maintain it with more vigor. It must seek to lead not a miscellaneous and frivolous rabble, but the class that is serious at bottom, however much it may mock conventional seriousness. There is great significance, I believe, in the fact that the most successful thing we have ever printed, and by long odds, was the Kent[2] article on Coolidge.

"You mention *The Smart Set* and say that I was wrong about it. I believe on the contrary that I was right every time. *The Smart Set* went to pot because it was too trivial, because it interested intelligent readers only intermittently, and then only when they were in trifling moods, when they were, so to speak, a bit stewed intellectually. Eventually many of them tired of it because it got nowhere. Their reading of the magazine became irregular, and so its circulation declined. As you will recall, I proposed at least a dozen times that we put more solid stuff into it. We could never agree as to the character of the solid stuff, and I thus lost interest in it. During its last three or four years I certainly put no hard work and thought into it, I simply slopped along. I don't want to do this with the *American Mercury*. On *The Smart Set* we could hide behind the obvious handicaps, the absurd name, the wretched printing, the imbecility of Warner (Elting F. Warner, its owner) and so on. But now we are out in the open with the harsh sunlight on us.

"I believe that either of us convinced of all this, and with a simple and vigorous policy, could make the *Mercury* something very much better than it is, and give it eventually the sort of position of the *Atlantic,* or even a better position. Its chances are not unlike those which confronted the *Atlantic* in the years directly after the Civil War. It has an opportunity to seize leadership of the genuinely civilized minority of Americans. But I doubt that the job just presented is one for two men. Divided counsels make for too much irresolution and compromise. In particular I doubt that you and I could carry it off together. Our interests are too far apart. We see the world in wholly different colors. When we agree, it is mainly on trivialities. This fundamental difference was of relatively small consequence on *The Smart Set,* where neither of us took the magazine very seriously. The presence of Warner made it impossible. But it is different with the *American Mercury*. I see no chance of coming closer together. On the contrary, I believe that we are drifting further and further apart. I note an obvious proof of it: we no longer play together. Another: when we sit down to discuss the magazine itself, we are off it in ten minutes.

"What is to be done I don't know. But I believe the matter ought to be talked out. I can see clearly only what is ahead for myself. My current job tends to irritate me. I am tied to routine, and much of it is routine that shouldn't be thrown on me—for example, watching the printer, and especially the make-up man. Page 374 in the November issue is in point. If I get out of contact with the office for three days my desk is in chaos. All this makes it a practical impossibility for me to do what I ought to do, and what Sedgwick does—that is, track down ideas, manuscripts and authors. I have duties that are antagonistic, and that kill each other. If I go on I'll slide inevitably, in self protection, into the easier of them. In other words, I'll do precisely what I did on *The Smart Set*. I could work with a competent slave, but I can't work when I must be that slave myself."

"But I don't want to make this a roster of grievances. You have your own troubles, and some of them are worse than mine. All I suggest is that we sit down and look at the situation realistically, and try to remedy it if it can be remedied. It goes without saying that I am willing to go on as now until a remedy can be found. But nothing is to be gained by evasions. It ought to be clearly understood by all hands that I am dissatisfied with the present scheme, and that its continuance is bound to make me less and less useful to the magazine. Look at my December book article: it is dreadful stuff. I therefore propose a palaver. Why should we quarrel? Either I am right or I am wrong. If I am right, I assume that everyone will agree. If I am wrong, I engage to shut up."

January 17th, 1927, Henry wrote me:

"Keep off the subject of the *Mercury* as much as possible. I have laid a good foundation, I think, for an absolute divorce. The details need not be hurried. There is plenty of time. I have told George that under the agreement which I propose to observe very strictly and even pedantically, I shall:

(a) Refuse to take any salary for five years.

(b) Hand over no manuscripts to him that come into the office.

(c) Refuse absolutely to put his name on letter paper or to do anything else not required by the agreement clearly and specifically."

But whatever this agreement may have been, it was never signed. So the two continued to quarrel. From time to time they would report to me that they had reached an agreement and were ready to tell us about it. Blanche, Father, and I would then sit down with them around a table in my father's office prepared for good news but within a matter of minutes they would be quarrelling again and the meeting would break up. This happened over and over again.

Meanwhile, we had managed to convince Henry that, if George were to be got rid of as Henry insisted, we would have to buy him out. This led to discussions between the two of them at which we of course were not present. Their nature is shown by this letter from Henry to me:

"The status of affairs on the editorial side is as follows:

"George asked me to make an agreement with him, in advance of any agreement he might make for his stock with your father, for his continuance as a contributor to *The American Mercury*. He said the completion of such an agreement with me would materially condition the demands he would make for his stock. I told him that it was impossible to discuss the matter, save most informally. I told him I had agreed with you and your father to make no arrangement with him until the stock business was settled.

"In the course of the informal discussion, which he insisted upon I told him:

"1. That, no matter what arrangement he made about the stock, I would discontinue Clinical Notes at the end of the year, my reason being that I did not think they fitted into the scheme of the magazine.

"2. As for his theatre reviews, I told him that my mind was open. I said I could not decide until the stock matter was settled and I had had a chance to discuss the future of the magazine with you and your father. In case we decided that we should head in the direction of the *Atlantic Monthly,* I would be against printing theatre reviews.

On the contrary, if we decided to make a lighter magazine I'd be inclined to continue them.

"He asked for an immediate decision on the ground that, if the reviews were dropped, he would have to make other arrangements as soon as possible. I told him that it was out of the question to decide until the stock matter and the question of the magazine's future plans were out of the way, but that if the decision were against the reviews I would naturally protect him until he could make other arrangements. He then asked if I'd be willing to make a long-term contract with him, in case we decided to go on with the reviews. I told him no. I said that I'd protect him against being thrown out without notice, but couldn't go any further.

"All these discussions were at his request, and I couldn't avoid them. I offer this exact account of their conclusions in order to prevent misunderstanding. The essence of the matter is that George tried to make his editorial status a condition of the negotiations about the stock, but that I refused absolutely to agree. As things stand, I have made no promise whatever, save to treat him decently in case we decide against continuing him as a contributor. So much, of course, goes without saying. To sum up:

"1. In case he and your father come to terms and you continue to publish his books, I'll follow your advice about printing his theatre reviews. I am not eager for them, but am willing to carry them on (without any contract) so long as you print his books.

"2. In case you part with him as his publisher, I shall notify him at once that his reviews will be terminated not later than January 1st next (and at once if he says so). In other words, I won't print him at all if you cease publishing his books.

"3. In either case the Check List will cease not later than January 1st.

"If you want me to come to New York during the week a wire will bring me at once. I believe the time has come to clear up the whole situation. We have all been harassed enough."

Stock in the American Mercury, Incorporated consisted of one hundred and fifty shares divided as follows: Samuel Knopf, fifty, Blanche, twenty-five, Henry, twenty-five, George, twenty-five, and twenty-five for me. At a meeting held January 9th, 1928, the board of directors of Alfred A. Knopf, Incorporated resolved that the corporation should acquire all the *Mercury* stock in exchange for seven hundred and fifty shares of preferred stock in Alfred A. Knopf, Incorporated and five hundred shares of its Class B capital stock—all, that is, except twenty-five shares held by Nathan. An agreement had finally been reached by which his connection with the *Mercury* ceased with the February, 1925, issue, although his name would remain on the cover of the magazine up to and including the July issue of that year. It was more

than four years, however, before we were finally able to purchase George's twenty-five shares, and the price finally arrived at was twenty-five thousand dollars, which we paid him in four equal installments, the first November 20th, 1929, the last May 20th, 1931. This was a good sale for George, for as things turned out our publishing house had acquired stock that in the end had no value whatever.

While from then to the time of his death George did what he could to create a public impression that there had been no breach between the two old friends, he would have been more than human did he not continue to hold a grudge against Henry, though he had only himself to blame for suffering the indignities to which he was subjected when the partnership broke up.

Thus Henry ordered Nathan's name to be removed from the directory in the lobby at 730 Fifth Avenue and his desk—he insisted on having one in the office somewhere—moved to an inner office where most of the stenographers worked.

But matters didn't end here, and those of us who knew both men were not unaware of how things really stood. Nathan shortly became the prime mover in the establishment of the *American Spectator,* which he edited with the collaboration of Ernest Boyd, Theodore Dreiser, James Branch Cabell, and Eugene O'Neill.

It began as a monthly and the first issue appeared in November, 1932. There were no issues in April and May of '35 and after November, 1936, it became a bimonthly. Richard R. Smith was the President of the company and claimed that the magazine was "circulated simultaneously in England, France, Germany, Austria, and Italy." The last issue bore the date April-May, 1937, and the masthead named Charles H. Fingerhood President and Publisher and M. Lehman Editor.

A more serious matter arose when Reynal and Hitchcock announced the forthcoming publication of *The Smart Set Anthology,* to be edited by Burton Rascoe and Groff Conklin.

Rascoe first approached Henry with regard to this book in his letter of June 28th, 1934, and two days later Mencken replied, declining to participate in the venture. He wrote with regard to Nathan, "We ceased to publish jointly at least ten years ago, and I am against resuming. Why in hell didn't you write to me when the project was first proposed? Your letter is my first news of it." And to this Rascoe replied, "Unless I hear from you to the contrary, I shall consider your decision final."

Mencken wrote again, "I hate like hell to sit on my rights, but the whole *Smart Set* enterprise belongs to the far past and I don't want to revive it. If you want to say that I decline to enter upon it go ahead, but don't quote this letter or my last. *I think you understand my objection.*" (My italics.)

Then Rascoe July 11th, "O.K. on all counts—with, of course, regrets."

And Mencken on the 14th, "Very good. I trust to your discretion."

In the light of what developed, it seems clear that Rascoe did not understand Henry's objection, and Henry was mistaken in trusting to Rascoe's discretion. Indeed it would have been more sensible all round had Henry spelled out to Rascoe quite frankly what his relations with Nathan had become.

July 12th, 1934, Henry wrote me:

"Rascoe wrote to me about that book a week or so ago. I refused absolutely to let him use anything of mine. He reports that Nathan is eager to see the thing go through, but I am teetotally opposed to appearing with him in any manner or form, now or hereafter. I can't, of course, prohibit the publication of the book, but I can at least prohibit the publication of any of my own stuff. Rascoe asked Sara[3] for permission to reprint one of her early stories, and I advised her to refuse it, which she did."

The explanation of Rascoe's animus is, of course, extremely simple: to publish a *Smart Set Anthology* with nothing in it by Mencken would be like a performance of *Hamlet* without the Prince. Rascoe tells in his preface how in 1919 Mencken asked and received his permission to reprint in a pamphlet which we called "Fanfare"[4] a piece he had written in November, 1917, for the Chicago Sunday *Tribune*. Seventeen years later, in his preface to the *Smart Set Anthology,* he stated for the first time that "permission was not asked of the Chicago *Tribune* . . . and the Chicago *Tribune*'s copyright on the article," and that this meant that his article could now "be reprinted by anybody legally, without my consent and without payment to me."

He went on, "I should not consider it proper to mention, also, that I was paid nothing by Alfred A. Knopf or by Mencken for my contribution to this pamphlet, if an ironical situation had not arisen when Mr. Conklin and I sought permission from authors and publishers for work to be included in this anthology. All of the authors, but one, whose permissions we particularly sought, granted it with enthusiasm, Mencken being the one exception. All, but one, of the publishers controlling copyrights, whose permissions were necessary, granted them with grace and alacrity, Alfred A. Knopf being the one exception.

"I had written to Carl Van Vechten, asking his permission to include an essay which had appeared in the *Smart Set* and later included in a book issued by Knopf. Mr. Van Vechten readily granted the permission, expressed enthusiasm about the project. . . . He told me it was necessary to get Knopf's permission, since the latter controlled the copyright.

"Knopf granted the permission and sent me the necessary papers to sign. . . . The next day a letter arrived from Knopf, saying that since granting the permission he had learned that H. L. Mencken was not to be represented in the anthology and that, on talking it over with Mr. Van Vechten, Mr. Van Vechten had decided that he did not want to appear in a *Smart Set* anthology in which Mencken was not represented."

Rascoe went on to say that he did not know the cause of the break between Mencken and Nathan, "but I do know that on Mencken's part it has been complete, uncompromising and, as the above singular action on Knopf's part of once granting and then withdrawing copyright permission, appears almost vindictive." But note what follows:

"In all the conversations I have had with Nathan from the time the break was supposed to have occurred until the other day, he had given me no indication that a rupture of their long friendship had ever occurred, his references to Mencken have always been as affable and affectionate as they ever were."

Through all of this Rascoe, usually knowledgeable, seems to me to have acted with great naïveté. Certainly the breach between Mencken and Nathan was no secret, and he could have learned the facts easily enough had he consulted me. But Nathan must have bemused him, for he solemnly writes, "I asked Nathan recently (about the break) and he replied that there was no break as far as he was concerned; and that the only thing he could figure out that had made Mencken sore at him was something he said, in a jest, about Mencken's collar. 'He thought I was making fun of him and got very angry,' said Nathan." Rascoe adds, "But this sounds so preposterous that it must be dismissed as improbable"—a magnificent understatement which makes one wonder why, if he felt that way about it, Rascoe saw any need to print it.

It seems clear from this record that Mencken wanted a complete divorce from Nathan, and it was just as obvious to me—though there was naturally no written record to support this—that the one thing Nathan *didn't* want was that kind of a divorce. After all, the theater and HLM were, I think, the two great experiences of his life.

As advance-of-publication promotion, Reynal and Hitchcock printed in pamphlet form the introduction which Rascoe had written. This contained matter that Henry and I regarded as clearly libelous. For example:

"Mencken broke with Dreiser,[5] because Dreiser would not contribute to a fund to defend the *American Mercury,* a Knopf publication which was profiting handsomely in circulation by reason of the fact that the issue of the magazine containing the story, "Hatrack," by Herbert Asbury had been banned in Boston. Mencken went up to Boston, sold the magazine on the Boston Common, and got himself arrested as a test case. Mencken later said he bore the expense of the trial himself, and that all who were interested in the freedom of American literature should have contributed to the cause. He thought Dreiser should do so particularly because, when *The Genius* was suppressed, Mencken got up a petition to procure release of the book. But Dreiser himself bore the cost to him of the impounding of *The Genius*. He pointed out that Knopf had not contributed any support to Dreiser's cause, even moral support in that case. He saw no reason why he should contribute money to defend a case which was proving the very best advertisement a Knopf property could get. If Mencken bore the entire legal fees, court costs, and other expenses without calling upon Knopf that, according to Dreiser, was Mencken's lookout. That's Dreiser's side of the break with Mencken as Dreiser related it to me."

The facts: the *American Mercury* paid all expenses of the "Hatrack" affair, Mencken never approached Dreiser or anyone else nor, of course, did I, for any financial help. Indeed, no such conversation or correspondence between Dreiser and Mencken as Rascoe describes ever took place. Finally, we took no advantage whatever of the publicity given the *American Mercury,* by the "Hatrack" case because, as I have stated earlier, we never reprinted the issue of the magazine and, at the time of the acquittal of Mencken by Judge Parmenter in Boston, we did not have a single copy of it for sale. And in any case it would have been mighty hard for anyone who knew Mencken— and Rascoe surely claims he did—to imagine him ever passing the hat.

November 20th Henry wrote me:

"The pamphlet has just come in, and I have had time only to read the paragraph on page 33. I incline to agree with you that Rascoe has gone mashuggah. It is not infrequently the fate of peasants who try to make the grade as intellectuals. The whole paragraph is a mass of humorless imbecilities. I'll read the rest of the pamphlet before the end of the day.

"The truth is that I have had no communication with Dreiser, either direct or indirect, since December 12, 1925. I remember the day precisely because it was the day before my mother died. Drieser came to Baltimore with his girl and disgusted me so greatly that I resolved to have no more to do with him in this life. The Hatrack case did not break until April 2, 1926. The American Mercury company, of course, paid all the expenses of the action. It even refunded to me my expenses on the trip to Boston. Before I left Baltimore Paul Patterson, of the Baltimore *Sun,* came to me with an offer of any financial support that I might need. He remembers this clearly, and is willing to make oath that I refused. Obviously, if I refused the help of a plainly solvent man, I was not soliciting money from Dreiser.

"At the time of the raid on *The Genius* there was no trial of any one, and hence no war chest was needed. But a protest of American authors was got up, and I financed the tedious business of getting signatures. My stenographer worked on it for weeks, and all of this correspon-

dence is in my vaults, so there can be no question about my participation. After the protest was finished, Dreiser insisted on adding the names of a number of Greenwich Village women—the primeval female larvae of what are now known as proletarian authors. I thereupon washed my hands of the matter.

"I enclose copies of my correspondence with Rascoe. As you will observe, I was polite to him. Moreover, you will note that he showed no signs of indignation himself. Yet more, you will note that Nathan agreed to further the enterprise after learning that I would refuse to have anything to do with it."

When Dreiser learned how he had been misrepresented by Rascoe, he responded nobly and wrote his old friend: "What the devil do you mean by imagining things and putting them in my mouth? Mencken, outside of an occasional request for a story or article, never asked me for anything, or to support him in any way, and in this particular case, at that time, if he had asked me I most certainly would have contributed, provided my means, which were slight enough, would have permitted.

"I know that you never willingly misstate anything. So there must be some yarn of some kind, either in connection with someone else or some statement that I have made which has stuck in your mind but which can have nothing to do with this. In consequence you must arrange, as I know you will, with Reynal and Hitchcock to retract this in a satisfactory form.

"I can't be angry with you because I care for you too much. But I must be just to all concerned and so must you."

On the same date, November 20th, Dreiser wrote Mencken, sending Henry a copy of a letter I had written him and saying, "My first reaction to it is that Rascoe has lost his mind. . . . I am writing Rascoe, mailing him a copy of this letter to you and also sending one to Knopf. Regardless of Burton's feelings, and I care for him very much, I am in common decency bound to address Reynal and Hitchcock, his publishers, in regard to it."

And to them he wrote, "In justice to myself, Mencken, and for that matter, Rascoe, since I never questioned his desire for accuracy, something must be done about it. Neither the public nor the critics can be left with the conviction that something occurred which never did occur."

Next day Mencken replied to Dreiser:

"It goes without saying that I never suspected you for an instant of saying anything of the sort. Putting aside the wanton libel on Alfred Knopf and the distress I knew it must have given you to be involved in it, the pamphlet gave me a loud laugh, rare enough in these last days before the Second Coming. The source of some of Rascoe's more grotesque statements is only too obvious. The poor fellow is himself a ridiculous object. He got a stout kick in the pants, and now he is running around rubbing his backside and complaining that it hurts. He has been silly before, and he will be silly again.

"I am seriously thinking of doing my literary and pathological reminiscences, probably in ten volumes folio. This is my solemn promise to depict you as a swell dresser, a tender father, and one of the heroes of the Argonne.

"My best thanks for your letter. It was decent of you to go to the bat so promptly. The libel on Knopf—perhaps the squarest man in money matters ever heard of—was really filthy and disgusting."

November 19th Reynal and Hitchcock sent a circular letter to those who had received Rascoe's pamphlet, which read in part, "The paragraph on page 33 referring to Mencken's break with Dreiser, which was intended for obvious reasons to have been omitted, was included in the copy that was sent you. This paragraph contains certain implications we find are not in accordance with the facts, and it was not our intention to give distribution to any statement containing such implications." They asked for the return of the original copy, "which we will replace with a corrected copy of the pamphlet."

As I had always been friendly with Eugene Reynal—I hardly knew Curtice Hitchcock—I said I was satisfied with this notice, but Mencken felt differently and I think now he was right. He wrote me:

"I have a letter from Hitchcock, enclosing a copy of his circular withdrawing the Rascoe pamphlet, and a copy of his letter to Dreiser. I suppose you have seen the last named. It is a cool piece of effrontery, and expresses surprise that you should have written to Dreiser, inasmuch as you had approved the circular. Obviously, this Hitchcock is a bounder comparable to Rascoe himself. He nowhere expresses any regret for his palpable libel on you, and he lies deliberately when he says that it was included in the pamphlet by error. I think you should make him come across with a more frank and categorical disclaimer. I shall not reply to him."

But in the end, because Rascoe's animus was so great, Henry and I agreed with our attorney, Benjamin H. Stern, that we couldn't possibly do ourselves any good by taking any sort of recognition of it and that it was best to drop the matter. Which we did.

Later Henry wrote me: "I gather from a note in Walter Winchell's column that Rascoe's introduction to his so-called *Smart Set Anthology* is largely devoted to Nathan's side of our late unpleasantness. So far as I am concerned, I don't care what either Nathan or Rascoe writes or says. It may be well, however, for you to examine the story with some care. We made a great error in being merciful to Nathan. We should have thrown him out on his backside and let him yell. It is foolish to be decent in dealing with a rat."

[1] This account is based on a manuscript history of the Hatrack case, which Mencken later wrote for his private records.

[2] Frank R. Kent, *Baltimore Sun* columnist.

[3] Mrs. Henry Mencken.

[4]"H. L. Mencken: Fanfare" by Burton Rascoe; "The American Critic," by Vincent O'Sullivan; "Bibliography" by F. C. Henderson (pseudonym), pamphlet published by us in 1920. Rascoe's article, a review of "A Book of Prefaces," was first published in his column in the Chicago Sunday *Tribune* November 11th, 1917.

[5]Kemler, *The Irreverent Mr. Mencken,* page 301, writes, "George Jean Nathan insists that Dreiser's break with Mencken had absolutely no connection with his. As I see it, the two incidents had their origin in the same remote cause—namely, Mencken's transformation into a political pundit."

Gerald Schwartz

SOURCE: "The West as Gauged by H. L. Mencken's American Mercury," in *Menckeniana,* No. 89, Spring, 1984, pp. 1-14.

[*In the following essay, Schwartz examines editorial attitudes toward the American West in the* American Mercury *through a bibliographic survey of works about the West and by Western regional writers that appeared in the magazine during the Mencken era.*]

So given was H. L. Mencken to criticism of the South, that in 1974 there appeared a lengthy monograph by Fred C. Hobson, entitled *The Serpent In Eden,* dealing with the Sage's treatment of that region. There seems to be less awareness among Menckenophiles of H.L.M.'s attitudes toward another vast and distinctive region, the trans-Mississippi West. With this in mind the present author tackled the pages of Mencken's *American Mercury,* in an attempt at discerning such attitudes on the part of Mr. Mencken, his peers and disciples.

The prospects for a bibliographic essay focusing on the West appeared none too good, since the *Mercury*'s editorial staff was comprised exclusively of professional Easterners, both urban and urbane. In addition to the Baltimore iconoclast and his co-editor, the cosmopolitan drama critic George Jean Nathan, the crew which got out the monthly publication included Charles Angoff, a young Bostonian, fresh out of Harvard.

But Mencken's maiden editorial informed his readers that *"The American Mercury* will live up to the adjective in its name. It will lay chief stress at all times upon American ideas, American problems and American personalities because it assumes that nine-tenths of its readers will be Americans."[1]

. . . . .

While the *Mercury* was in the planning stage, Mencken proclaimed that the publication would become "the gaudiest and damnedest ever seen in the republic."[2] This prediction proved not mere hyperbole, but rather close to the mark. For half a dozen years or more, the attractive green cover was ubiquitous in college dormitories and fraternity houses, in libraries, in the reading rooms of the best clubs and resorts, and in the homes of the intelligentsia.

The Depression marked the end of the honeymoon between Mencken and his *Mercury* on the one hand, and the "civilized minority" on the other. Unable and unwilling to revise his nineteenth-century liberalism, and to shed his anachronistic world-view grounded in the philosophies of Nietzsche, Spencer, William Graham Sumner, and their like, Mencken declined swiftly in popularity, and the *Mercury* declined along with him.

The Baltimore Sage remained as editor through 1934, but the publication was pretty much moribund from 1931 onward. It was in the Fall of that year that the *Mercury*'s editors received a manuscript entitled "The Tragedy of the Sioux," by Chief Sitting Bull. The chief was "hoping to bring about a more just appraisal of the Sioux people and to relieve them from wardship."[3] Mencken waxed enthusiastic over the article. Angoff dismissed it as "dull and pointless," a piece that "might have found a place in the *Atlantic Monthly* around the turn of the century."[4] The younger man warned the editor that the *Mercury* would become a laughing stock if Sitting Bull's article occupied the lead position in the November, 1931 issue.[5] The altercation, though eventually resolved, seemed an appropriate cut-off point for the scope of this article. Fittingly, it related to a Western theme. More, it had turned out that the present author's initial fears about a paucity of Western material had been unwarranted. Happily, *The American Mercury* devoted an abundance of space to Western authors, Western history, Western social criticism, and, in keeping with its generally iconoclastic tone, to Western buffoonery, as well.[6]

. . . . .

No region, save the Deep South, which H. L. Mencken labeled "The Sahara of the Bozart," in one of his most provocative satirical essays, came in for harsher treatment in the *Mercury*'s "Americana" section each month, than the Far West. This regular feature, compiled jointly by Mencken and Nathan, was enormously popular among the journal's readers, according to both editors. It had as its purpose the mocking of the values of "the booboisie," and Babbitts, both secular and ecclesiastical. Items of a nature guaranteed to amuse, or outrage *Mercury* readers, were extracted from selected publications and reprinted in "Americana."

At times the items chosen were downright macabre, such as the advertisement in the Yakima (Wash.) *Morning Herald* which announced the Annual Benefit Dance, re-

plete with "Snappy Music," sponsored by the Wenas Cemetery Association, or the news from Medford, Oregon, that a young resident of that community, upon reading in a physical culture magazine that fasting would improve his health, proceeded to forsake food, and died some days later, of starvation.[7]

The editors delighted in reporting ludicrous and undignified acts committed by eminent Westerners. Did Dr. C. H. Marvin, President of the University of Arizona, "camouflaged as a bewhiskered white wing—help State American Legion Commander Dougherty sweep a Phoenix thoroughfare because Phoenix defeated Tucson in a Legion membership campaign"?[8] Then the *Mercury* was quick to lend national publicity to the item. Did Washington's governor, Roland H. Hartley, boast that he emphatically would not approve the purchase of expensive spittoons for the new State Capitol building, and then proceed to sign a voucher authorizing the buying of fifty-six cuspidors, valued at up to $100 apiece, and did this same Hartley dance a jig for high school students near Spokane, and then invite them to Olympia in the best Babbitt-like fashion, to "sit in a chair that cost $1,000, and I'll show you through the Governor's office, which is filled with furniture valued at $40,000."?[9] Then it was not long before the *Mercury*'s sophisticated readers were chuckling over the incident in the "Americana" column.

Perversions of individual liberty induced intense disgust in the *Mercury*'s editors, assuaged only by the gales of pejorative laughter, at the antics of such types as Oregon's Governor Walter M. Pierce, who was quoted as saying that "Time has modified the old adage that every man's home is his castle and sanctuary, and in the future Oregon homes must be kept in such condition that a visit from an inspector of the State Prohibition forces will be welcomed at any time."[10]

Ridiculed too, under the caption "Free Speech in Salt Lake City," was the pronouncement by the Utah Associated Industries, to the effect that "The antecedents of speakers, should first be known, and the nature of their attitude be ascertained before hospitality is extended to them."[11]

A Westerner won his town's volunteer fire department spitting championship.[12] Another was divorced by his wife because he was in the habit of drinking milk directly from his goat's udder at the breakfast table.[13] Yet another, this time the pastor of a Bellingham, Washington, church, proudly boasted that newspaper advertising was helping to bring on the Kingdom of God, since "$100 worth of advertising had brought in more than $1,700 in silver plate collections."[14] A Santa Paula, California, editorial writer mocked hand-kissing as a prime example of European decadence.[15] All found their way into the pages of "Americana."

Criticism of Western manners and morals, both past and present, was not restricted to "Americana." California, or more specifically the Southern portion of the state, was referred to by the *Mercury* as "Moron-Land."[16] The state was "controlled by moronic Babbitts."[17] It was a fitting home for the obscene mob-master William Randolph Hearst whose gaucheness led him to "hold court in Cecil de Mille magnificence," and for success oriented Stanford University, where academic credit was given to sophomores who registered for a course in cheer leading.[18]

Mencken summed up the Golden Gate State as "an Alsatia of retired Ford agents and crazy fat women—a paradise of Rotary."[19] He bewailed the failure of California to live up to its original promise of producing "a charming and enlightened civilization." At one time there had been "a touch of tropical balm in its air, and a touch of Latin and even oriental color in its ideas. Like Louisiana it seemed likely to resist Americanization for many years."[20] But, alas, under the influence of hordes of invading garden-variety American dullards, the state had slid downhill and the "civilized minority" was in despair. Small wonder that despite the potential along the gorgeous California coast for "an almost Latin elegance and voluptuousness," the inhabitants "insisted upon conducting themselves precisely as if they lived in Iowa or Mississippi."[21]

A thousand or more miles to the East, Kansas stood as a "resplendent jewel which sends out rays of Holy Thinking," a state so revolting, so dominated by cranks and uplifters, and so oriented toward evangelical crusading and fundamentalism, that it was only a shade above California on the scale of civilization.[22]

Between the two loomed Bernard de Voto's Utah, which the young historian whose early literary reputation was largely made between the *Mercury*'s covers, characterized as "a commonwealth of greengrocers who have lifted themselves from the peasantry."[23] To Edgar Lee Masters, who had declared that were he a young artist he would flee not to Paris, but to Salt Lake City, the home of "a whole people who loved, respected, encouraged and produced beauty," de Voto replied

> I defy—anyone—to find one artist or even a quasi-artist in all the wide expanse of Utah, from Soda Springs to Hurricane, from Roosevelt to St. George. No artist ever lived there ten minutes after he had the railroad fare out. If the presence of one should become known, the Mormons would damn him as a loafer and the Gentiles would lynch him as a profligate.[24]

Nor did other Western states fare better at the hands of the *Mercury*'s editors and authors. From the Dakotas to Arizona, from Washington to Texas, all suffered at one time or another similar stings of biting social criticism.

It is not to be supposed, however, that the *Mercury*'s editorial policy directed toward the West that variety of Eastern chauvinism which such Western authors as Vardis Fisher would later persistently decry. Quite to the contrary, the West, according to Mencken, Nathan, Angoff, and their underlings and contributors, had once been a gloriously romantic place, peopled by lusty giants. That it had been reduced, by the prohibition era, to a mere replica of the disgustingly tame and "cultured" East, was a tragedy for America. It was an especially poignant tragedy for the type of men and women who in an earlier day had been lifted out of the doldrums of mundane living to the ennobling adventure implicit in the migration to a new, mysterious and challenging land. Here is de Voto telling *Mercury* readers about the Great Migration of the eighteen-forties:

> for all the anguish of the trail, the expedition had, reminiscently, a glamor beyond anything else in our national experience. Oregon never quite came up to the advertisement it had had, and few emigrants attained the bliss they expected there, but the wandering itself was a glorious success. It had brought daily adventure into ordinary lives. It had keyed limited souls to the vastness of the plateaux and the sonoras. It had made of the commonplace folk veteran wanderers of the wilderness, who had dared the impossible and survived it. For thousands, the months along the trail were the climax of experience, a crescendo of vigor and intensity and wild color, which they could never attain again. It was for a season life at the highest pitch, something splendid and heroic beyond expression.[25]

The Old West had been free-wheeling, wide-open, a perpetual carnival. "Seattle," H. L. Davis informed readers, "got its start from having the only first-rate sporting house on Puget Sound: Portland forged ahead of the other cities of Oregon largely through the social popularity of its North End."[26]

The Western spirit at its freest had been exemplified by those towns which sprang up and flourished as a result of the discovery of mineral wealth. Virginia City, in the days of the Comstock lode, was "the sublimated essence of the mining town, it was the superlative extreme of the mineral West."[27] The town's saloons were supplemented as places of entertainment by lecture halls and opera houses as well as by brothels and gambling dens. "The itinerant performers of America, from trained fleas to transcendentalists, from Schuyler Colfax and Samuel Bowles to Artemus Ward and Orpheus C. Kerr, followed the serious money to the Comstock."[28]

Duncan Aikman maintained that Deadwood afforded the ultimate in Western *joie de vivre*. The town was prepared to revel in "Whatever was violent, whatever was grotesque, or carried a stench above the gulch's high evening shadow line," he wrote in an article entitled "Deadwood The Dreadful."[29] By the time of Deadwood's birth the technique of "staging a new mining town," had been perfected and Westerners flocked in

> to show off before one another all the tricks they had learned from Abilene to Walla Walla, and from Poker Flat to the furthest geographic reaches of Mr. Beadle's collection. In 10 years time the old-timers would be in Hell with their boots on or forgetting their lore through age and apathy, the promising youngsters would be reformed by the process of civilization or the penitentiaries—But

in Deadwood, "300 miles from nowhere," with the Sioux riding about them on the warpath, with no state, or even territorial government to claim jurisdiction, the veterans of a hundred minor duchies of the Kingdom of Hell on Wheels gathered for their last appearance in their prime. Here they indulged their vanity for grotesque splendors, and strutted the last refinements of their arts and sciences of living before it was too late.[30]

This nostalgia for a paradise lost, that is to say, for a Nietzschean paradise lost, runs like a motif throughout those pages of the *Mercury* devoted to the West. Of Phoenix, Arizona, her adopted home, the Polish born Goldie Weisberg lamented, "the champion bull-dogger of other days has been replaced by the champion golfer."[31]

The Southwest had fared perhaps worst of all at the hands of progress. An El Paso writer compared "the paved, pious and stolid city," of his advanced years with the "rough, uncouth and very gay town," in which he had been born, and could not repress a deep sigh of regret. "Where life was once cheerful, filled with alarms and worth living," he complained,

> it is now flat, decorous and commonplace; where men were once publicly and delightfully naughty and openly bellicose they are now only surreptitiously so; where the leading citizens once wore six-shooters and Winchesters they now wear wrist watches and golf sticks, and where—God save the race! the communal sports, in days past, were wont to drink hard liquor out of the original carboys and to play poker with the North Star as the limit they now absorb coca-cola with a dash of tequila in it, and bet on mah jong at a twentieth of a cent a point.[32]

San Antonio, too, had once been a splendid place in which to live, wrote another *Mercury* contributor. The town, before the reign of George F. Babbitt, and his ilk, had boasted gaudy gambling houses. "Chili queens dispensed smiles and indigestion on the plazas."[33] Tourists delighted in the many saloons and in the bustling redlight district, which was widely regarded as a major business asset. Good music, good theatre, good food, all abounded. "Holidays and fiestas were greeted with acclaim. Life was very gay."[34]

Butte, Montana, was one of the few Western communities which remained, well into the post World War I era, relatively uncorrupted. It was in fact lauded by a native author, whose tribute to its glories was entitled "Hymn to an Oasis."[35] The city was admittedly controlled by Anaconda Copper as a fief of sorts, but so what? Though the blatant capitalist exploitation produced scores of radicals, it produced too a lack of delusions about The American Way of Life. "It is," the writer proclaimed, "a wise, weary, sardonic burg, this copper camp pigeon-holed away in the remoter Rockies; a wild one, a Rabelaisian, bad and bold."[36] The typical jealous Montanan from the less fortunate reaches of the state, "loathes Butte with the acrimony that only the inferiority complex engenders."[37]

But Butte, and the hardy breed that peopled it, was an exception. James Stevens bemoaned the demise of the rough living "savages" who once filled railroad construction gangs, in an article appropriately entitled "The Uplift on the Frontier."[38] These men, among whom the wildly talented Stevens had long lived and worked, were "savages" no more. They had been reduced to the comfortable, respectable, but sorry status of "mere laborers," by such civilizing forces as the Loyal Legion of Loggers and Lumbermen, which had sprung up during the war. These tamed milk-shake drinkers and movie-goers "belonged to the tribe whose calked boots once crashed on the floors, and whose bellows once rattled the glasses of the bars on Burnside Street and Yesler Way," Stevens lamented.[39]

Even San Francisco, which had at one time given promise of developing into the most charming city on the continent, was fast sliding downhill. By 1925, "The merry and turbulent days were dying out."[40] Americanization was proceeding at an alarming rate. Local color was fading from that very Chinatown, which in happier days had been the home of paper dragons and porcelain-faced prostitutes.[41]

Mencken and his editorial associates, with their characteristic delight in tweaking the noses of the bourgeoisie, extolled the virtues of Western "bad men," and inhabitants of the *demi monde*. The professional gambler of an earlier day, reported D. I. Potter, basing his conclusions we may conjecture on Bret Harte's Oakhurst and Jack Hamlin, was a gentleman in the classic meaning of the term. He

> dressed, shot, swore, played, drank, ate, looked— no doubt slept—harder than any other men. He had his adventures more openly. He took his code of debts and honor more seriously. He flung way his cash more recklessly upon charity, debauchery and display. He was more ostentatiously sentimental in his reverence for "decent ladies." In New Mexico, and Arizona, in territorial days, he took a solemn and decently exposed pride in the fact that the taxes on his concessions were the most lucrative source of the public school funds. He flourished in the hairy 70's and 80's, so his beard and moustachios were of the fiercest. He came and went trailing his gusto in life as he found it. He did not cheat.[42]

Conventional Western heroes like Boone, Crockett, and Kit Carson fared less well on the pages of the *Mercury*. Sam Houston, was depicted as a mundane frontiersman, whose career paled when contrasted with that of his colorful adversary, Santa Anna, "The Napoleon of the West."[43] Brigham Young, the Mormon's "first pope," was "a serpentine politician," and "a mob-master of the first order."[44] John C. Fremont was tormented by delusions of grandeur, and was "tragically symbolic of the youthful visions, the fatal optimism, the inability to reconcile crude fact and beautiful ideals, the sordidness and pretense—that form the true history of the United States."[45]

The cowboy, personification of frontier heroism, was, contrary to the myth makers, not at all a dashing and romantic figure given to prodigious drinking, dramatic gambling bouts, gunfighting, and an intense appreciation of nature's beauties. He was rather a prosaic fellow, who drank and gambled merely as an escape from boredom, rarely fought, and was devoid of esthetic perception. That he hated his environment and longed to be shut of it, was evidenced by the sentiment of such ballad lyrics as "Oh bury me *not* on the lone prairie."[46]

The *Mercury*'s Western heroes were of a different stamp. "Jesse James is deep in the hearts of his 100% countrymen," wrote Benjamin DeCasseres, a frequent contributor to the journal.[47] "He is the manifestation of romantic lawlessness. Jesse James has achieved immortality. He is a great American. When I was a boy he was looked upon as *the* great American by all the boys I knew."[48]

The hero of H. L. Mencken's youth, according to the editor, knew "no such posthumous eminence as Jesse James—although he was a far more gallant and engaging figure." He was Billy The Kid, who Harvey Ferguson, echoing Mencken's sentiments in a *Mercury* feature, called a "quixotic romantic, who cared nothing for money—who lived and died an idealist."[49] Billy, according to Ferguson, was "the key figure of an epoch—the primitive pastoral epoch in the history of the West."[50]

"All of us who were boys in the 80's remember Billy the Kid," wrote Mencken, in a review of Walter Noble Burns' biography of the noted killer:

> and with a veneration that is still bold and unaffected. He was one of the glories of that purple decade along with Sitting Bull, Geronimo and General Nelson A. Miles. He ranked far above Buffalo Bill, for Bill's butcheries were confined to Indians and horned cattle, whereas Billy was covered with Christian blood.[51]

The Indian generally emerged from the columns of the *Mercury* a heroic figure, at least when contrasted with his white oppressor. Anthropologist Robert H. Lowie, whose features on Western tribes frequently appeared, fairly gloated over the "—vast contrast between the standardized Anglo-American civilization of today with its ubiquitous radios, automobiles, and cinemas, and the widely varied patterns of its predecessors on the same soil."[52]

George A. Custer was portrayed as a treacherous egomaniac, his adversary Rain In The Face, as a noble and fierce warrior, by Eli L. Huggins.[53] The Indians of Oklahoma were being "swamped in the flood of Babbittry," *Mercury* readers learned.[54] "The old, tolerant, helpful, help-yourself West is gone or going," but the red-man remains relatively unimpaired.[55] The "well-to-do Oklahoma Indians approach more closely the type of the English country gentleman than any other group in the United States," wrote Stanley Vestal, paying them the supreme compliment.

> They have been taught to exalt personal qualities, to believe that character is more important than

achievement. They had a rigid code of honor, and they have been, until lately, quite indifferent to property. Like an English country gentleman, the Indian prefers a small, sure income from the lease of his inalienable lands—to a finer home and no certain income. His chief interests have always been war, politics, and charity—to his friends or to the needy—and, of course, sport. These are precisely the interests of the English governing classes.[56]

The Indian, be he Cheyenne from the Plains, Hopi from the Pueblos, or Yurok from the Pacific Coast, "thumbed his nose at the economic interpretation of history."[57] He was very much a noble savage, or, in brief, a natural gentleman.

Alone among the effete whites to be in a position, moral or otherwise, to look down upon the first-Americans, was the scout and Indian fighter. Captain James Cook, who had "devoted more than thirty years of his life to herding, hunting, scouting and trailing from Mexico to Montana," was such a man."[58] Captain Cook had known Geronimo, Lone Wolf, Chief Joseph, and others of their ilk, and while they remained for him mere "savages," he was loud in the praise of their bravery. "The most pleasant thought," he concluded, "in connection with the battle scenes during the wars with the Western savages is that such scenes will never be reenacted."[59]

H. L. Mencken delighted in the adverse criticism heaped on the *Mercury* by more conventional humanists, who extolled the values of progress and civilization, and were proud of the taming of the West. "The news that *The American Mercury* is 'lacking in constructive points of view' is surely not news to me," he wrote to Upton Sinclair. "If any such points of view ever get into it, it will only be over my mutilated and pathetic corpse. The uplift has damn nigh ruined the country. What we need is more sin."[60]

Historians who have subscribed to Dr. Turner's thesis, and either lamented the passing of the free-land frontier, noted by the master in his 1893 address, or substituted other kinds of frontiers in the manner of Lucy Hazard, or David Potter, likely have overlooked the type of "New Frontier," proclaimed by Mencken in 1925. "No one seems to have noticed, so far" he wrote,

> that the science of bootlegging has restored the frontier to the Republic.—Today the Indian-trails are jammed with Fords, and the soughings of Rotary resound in the Sierras and up the flanks of Pike's Peak. The young idealists of the Union no longer run away from home to follow Buffalo Bill and General Nelson A. Miles; if they stir from the village at all it is to become movie actors or bond salesmen.

But in the rum runners, a new frontier hero has sprung up. "In them is all the romance of the old-time trailblazers and Indian fighters. They have restored the frontier to American history."[61]

Though Mencken had, on the eve of launching *The American Mercury,* written a friend that he and George

Jean Nathan were "abandoning belles-lettres for more serious literature," quality fiction remained a foremost concern of the journal throughout his reign.[62] If California were indeed "The Champion," i.e., the very worst of the forty-eight states, in the Sage's hierarchy of values, it nevertheless was discussed at great length in the *Mercury,* as a well-spring of literature.

Ludicrous, according to George P. West, was the proclamation of the Los Angeles Chamber of Commerce pledging its "ceaseless efforts for Bigger and Better Art."[63] Outrageous was the notion of California dilettantes that since the state was "physically another Greece," and since "its Spanish background and romantic past constitute a rich and stimulating tradition," art would flow from it in abundance.[64] West pointed out that "Bret Harte vented a positive dislike of the California climate and scenery in waspish verses now buried deep in the old files."[65] Twain, despite all the benefits to his literary career which emanated from California, "disliked the State and never revisited it. His friends of the 'Jumping Frog' days knew him no more after that first sensational success."[66] But a group of excellent California writers could not be overlooked. Among them were Ambrose Bierce, Jack London, George Sterling, and Frank Norris, who captured "the essence of San Francisco" in his books.[67]

The relative merits of California writers were debated at length by *Mercury* critics. Norris had, according to Charles C. Dobie, "helped to rescue the California scene from the languishing sentimentalities of Bret Harte."[68] He was, Dobie continued, "both a story teller and a novelist, something that in these days of bastard sophistication is continually under critical surveillance and suspicion."[69] The literary tradition of Carmel, California was examined at length. The town had housed and inspired not alone George Sterling and Jack London, but Charles Warren Stoddard, Ray Stannard Baker, Lincoln Steffens and a host of other literati.[70] Appropriate homage was paid to *The Golden Era,* a mining boom publication, which had "influenced the pre-Civil War humorists, definitely colored Mark Twain's prose style, made the fame of Petroleum V. Nasby, and terminated in the writings of the Danbury *News* Man and Bill Nye."[71]

Carey McWilliams proclaimed that current West-coast writing, "reveals a self-conscious enthusiasm for a genuinely Western spirit. It seems that this spirit must be defined, if at all, in a negative way; that is, it consists in freedom from the prevailing Eastern vices of sex interest, morbid psychology and realism."[72]

But Mencken and his associates threw open the pages of the *Mercury* to all writers of talent, and Western writers, not merely Californians of course, but Oregonians, Oklahomans, and countless representatives of points-in-between, if they did not quite dominate the magazine's columns were nonetheless very much in evidence.

Such a writer was H. L. Davis, a native and longtime resident of the Pacific Northwest, who had worked as printer's devil, sheepherder, harvest hand, deputy sheriff and county editor, before he began his professional writing career. Though a group of Davis' poems had been awarded the Levinson Prize in 1919, he was, in essence, discovered by Mencken, and first encouraged by the Baltimorean to launch a serious literary career.

Davis was of the opinion that "the past century of settlement and conquest in the Oregon country was a greater historical epoch than the migrations of the Israelites from Egypt, and that it has for the most part been written up with the same sentimentality."[73] In a series of lustily written narratives, centering about the wheat and cattle country of Eastern Oregon, he attempted to rectify this condition, and to write in a *genre* which transcended mere realism, and approached what Hamlin Garland termed "verityism."

If H. L. Davis loved the land about which he wrote, then it was with the love of the battle-scarred career soldier for his tattered company. In such stories as "Cow Town Widows," "A Town in Eastern Oregon," and "Old Man Isbell's Wife," he poignantly portrayed a tired and much-abused species, living out their mediocre lives in a desolate and lonely land, struggling in the manner of Sherwood Anderson's grotesques, for communication and love, but usually without success. Davis was skeptical about the human condition, at least as it was manifested in his native region. His observations about wheat farmers echo Mencken's earlier sentiments about tillers of the soil, which the latter had expressed in his famous essay "The Husbandman." That is to say, they were characterized as uncivilized louts, to whom "sportsmanship was wholly foreign."[74] In his amusing piece entitled "Water On The Wheat," Davis describes the effects of a sudden measure of affluence on a community of Northwestern "Scissorbills."

> They built a community hall, and held meetings and made speeches once a week, with resolutions condemning gambling, bootlegging and the holding of dances in public schoolhouses in the rest of the country. The sheriff's office began to get letters from them, tattling on each other for making kitchen-beer. They demanded remission of county taxes, a Federal law pricing wheat at $3 a bushel, laws compelling the railroads to haul wheat for nothing, a law compelling farmhands to work for a maximum of $2.50 a day, a law forbidding people to use substitutes for butter, a law compelling all prisoners in the county jail to work during harvest for nothing.[75]

Davis' Menckenesque loathing of boosterism, particularly of the variety which the Babbitts of preposterous Oregon cow towns attempted to foster, is vented in his hilarious story entitled "Hand-Press Journalist." In this tale a small town editor, driven by intolerable social pressures to escape the hamlet, runs off a final edition of his journal prior to fleeing. Beneath the masthead which proclaims "The City With A Future . . . Pure Air, Clear Water, Clean Surroundings . . . And Other Public Enterprises Too Numerous To Mention," he prints the banner headline "A Stink In Nature's Nostrils," and proceeds to lambast the town and all of its residents.[76]

Mencken was proud of his "discovery," and a couple of years after he had left the *Mercury* expressed the opinion, in private correspondence with Davis, that "*Honey In The Horn* seems to me to be the best first novel ever printed in this country, and I incline to believe that it is the best novel of any sort since *Babbitt*."[77]

James Stevens was another of the *Mercury*'s literary "finds." Stevens' first contribution to the *Mercury*, the magazine boasted editorially, midway through Mencken's decade of tenure,

> dealt with his adventures and observations as a lumberman in the Northwest. He was working at the time in a lumber mill, and there was a sharp reality in his story that no professional writer save the most adept could have hoped to match. The response of readers was immediate and he was encouraged to try his hand further.[78]

Stevens took to retelling the Paul Bunyan legends in the *Mercury*. Soon readers of the green-covered journal were familiar with the great Western lumberman's hero, and with Babe the Blue Ox, "who ate 300 bales of hay at a meal, wire and all"; Hels Helsen, "the Big Swede and bull of the woods, who muddied the Missouri river forever with one Spring bath"; Johnny Inkslinger, "the time-keeper who figured with a fountain pen fed by hose lines from two barrels of ink"; Hot Biscuit Slim; Cream Puff Fatty; and a host of other woodsey characters.[79] The contributions of James Stevens were not restricted to the Paul Bunyan legends, which he later expanded into a book, but they constituted the high-point of Steven's work.

Louis Adamic, a Yugoslavian-born dock-worker from San Pedro, California, made his literary debut in the *Mercury*. George Milburn, an Oklahoma college student, whose sensitive and perceptive personality and local color sketches had hitherto reached only the subscribers of an obscure and insignificant anthology, was introduced to a considerably wider reading public. Milburn, according to Charles Angoff, "was one of Mencken's finest discoveries."[80] His stories, Angoff continued, were "among our most magnificent fictional pieces," and who, after having been introduced to the intensely human, if often pathetic Oklahomans who people Milburn's work, would dispute this?[81]

The number of "single-shot," Western authors, writing about Western themes, who were published by the *American Mercury* is far too great to warrant their inclusion in an article of this length. The same is true of the many obscure poets from Montana, Idaho, Oregon, and elsewhere, whose works appeared in the journal. Ballads of Belle Starr, of Kit Carson, of star-lit nights on the plains, and in the Rockies, all found their way into the *Mercury*, along with Thomas Hornsby Ferril's "Fort Laramie," and Carl Sandburg's "Santa Fe Sketches."

It was quite a publication, Mr. Mencken's *Mercury*, in the days before the harsh realities of the depression shifted the national spotlight from that ring wherein the gaudily colored brass-bands played, to the one in which the somber-hued economic determinists held forth. Many and significant were its contributions. Among the greatest of these was that its Western authors transmitted to the "civilized minority" in the brownstones and row-houses of Boston, New York, Philadelphia, and points East, what it felt like to amble down Main Street, as a lad, and see "—a Pueblo buck string a bow and shoot at a bird on a telegraph wire."[82]

[1] (H. L. Mencken), "Editorial," *The American Mercury* (January, 1924), p. 30.

[2] Carl R. Dolmetsch, "Mencken As a Magazine Editor," *Menckeniana* (Spring, 1967), p. 1.

[3] "Editorial Notes," *The American Mercury* (November, 1931), p. XXVIII.

[4] Charles Angoff, *H. L. Mencken: A Portrait From Memory* (New York, A. S. Barnes and Co., Inc., 1956), p. 213.

[5] *Ibid.*

[6] *The American Mercury* continued publication for many years after Mencken's departure, though it underwent several changes in editorship, format and policies.

[7] The first item is derived from "Americana," *The American Mercury* (October, 1930), p. 173. The latter is from the same monthly feature and journal (February, 1924), p. 179.

[8] "Americana," *The American Mercury* (July, 1926), p. 296.

[9] The first item is derived from "Americana," *The American Mercury* (December, 1927), p. 420. The latter is from the same monthly feature and journal (May, 1928), p. 175.

[10] "Americana," *The American Mercury* (April, 1924), p. 431.

[11] "Americana," *The American Mercury* (March, 1927), p. 305.

[12] "Americana," *The American Mercury* (February, 1927), p. 181.

[13] "Americana," *The American Mercury* (July, 1925), p. 302.

[14] "Americana," *The American Mercury* (January, 1924), p. 50.

[15] "Americana," *The American Mercury* (May, 1931), p. 48.

[16] Louis Sherwin, "The Walrus of Moron-Land," *The American Mercury* (February, 1928), p. 190.

[17] Jim Tully, "Two-Time Losers," *The American Mercury* (March, 1928), p. 311.

[18] The first item is derived from George P. West, "Hearst: A Psychological Note, *The American Mercury* (November, 1930), p. 297. The latter is from "Americana," the same journal (April, 1924), p. 429.

[19] (H. L. Mencken) "The Champion," *The American Mercury* (October, 1924), p. 197.

[20] *Ibid.*

[21] Duncan Aikman, "Santa Barbara Has A Fiesta," *The American Mercury* (January, 1925), p. 50.

[22] Charles B. Driscoll, "Why Men Leave Kansas," *The American Mercury* (October, 1924), p. 178.

[23] Bernard de Voto, "Utah," *The American Mercury* (March, 1926), p. 322.

[24] *Ibid.*, p. 321.

[25] Bernard de Voto, "The Great Medicine Road," *The American Mercury* (May, 1927), p. 112.

[26] H. L. Davis, "Three Hells: A Comparative Study," *The American Mercury* (July, 1930), p. 257.

[27] Bernard de Voto, "Brave Days In Washoe," *The American Mercury* (June, 1929), p. 231.

[28] *Ibid.*

[29] Duncan Aikman, "Deadwood The Dreadful," *The American Mercury* (November, 1927), p. 341.

[30] *Ibid.*, p. 337.

[31] Goldie Weisberg, "Panorama: Phoenix, Arizona," *The American Mercury* (May, 1929), p. 100.

[32] Owen P. White, "El Paso," *The American Mercury* (August, 1924), p. 437.

[33] Chester T. Crowell, "Strange News From Texas," *The American Mercury* (March, 1925), p. 324.

[34] *Ibid.*

[35] Arthur O'Dane, "Hymn To An Oasis," *The American Mercury* (October, 1925), p. 190.

[36] *Ibid.*, p. 193.

[37] *Ibid.*, p. 194.

[38] James Stevens, "The Uplift On The Frontier," *The American Mercury* (April, 1924), p. 418.

[39] *Ibid.*

[40] Idwal Jones, "San Francisco: An Elegy," *The American Mercury* (August, 1925), p. 478.

[41] Idwal Jones, "Cathay On The Coast," *The American Mercury* (August, 1926), p. 460.

[42] D. I. Potter, "Gentlemen All," *The American Mercury* (September, 1924), p. 112.

[43] Sam Acheson, "Sam Houston," *The American Mercury* (August, 1927), pp. 487-495.

[44] H. L. Mencken, Review of *Brigham Young,* by M. R. Werner (New York: Harcourt Brace & Co.), *The American Mercury* (July, 1925), p. 510.

[45] Robert L. Duffus, "Fremont And Jessie," *The American Mercury* (November, 1925), p. 289.

[46] Chester T. Crowell, "Cowboys," *The American Mercury* (October, 1926), pp. 162-169.

[47] Benjamin DeCasseres, "The Complete American," *The American Mercury* (February, 1927), p. 144.

[48] *Ibid.*

[49] Harvey Ferguson, "Billy The Kid," *The American Mercury* (June, 1925), p. 224.

[50] *Ibid.*

[51] H. L. Mencken, Review of *The Saga of Billy The Kid,* by Walter Noble Burns (Garden City, N.Y.: Doubleday Page & Co.), *The American Mercury* (May 1926), pp. 125-126.

[52] Robert H. Lowie, "American Indian Cultures," *The American Mercury* (July, 1930), p. 366.

[53] Eli L. Huggins, "Custer and Rain In The Face," *The American Mercury* (November, 1926), p. 339.

[54] Stanley Vestal, "The First Families of Oklahoma," *The American Mercury* (August, 1925), p. 493.

[55] *Ibid.*

[56] *Ibid.*, p. 494

[57] Robert H. Lowie, "Prestige Among Indians," *The American Mercury* (December, 1927), p. 448.

[58] "Editorial Notes," *The American Mercury* (June, 1931), p. XXVIII.

[59] James H. Cook, "The Art of Fighting Indians," *The American Mercury* (June, 1931). p. 179.

[60] Letter from H. L. Mencken, Guy J. Forgue (ed.), *Letters of H. L. Mencken* (New York: Alfred A. Knopf, 1961), p. 273.

[61] H. L. Mencken, "The New Frontier," *The American Mercury* (January, 1925), pp. 59-60.

[62] Adele G. Nathan, "Mencken and The Little Theatre Movement," *Menckeniana* (Winter, 1962), p. 6

[63] George P. West, "The California Literati," *The American Mercury* (July, 1926), p. 281.

[64] *Ibid.*

[65] *Ibid.*

[66] *Ibid.*

[67] *Ibid.* p. 284.

[68] Charles C. Dobie, "Frank Norris, or Up From Culture," *The American Mercury* (April, 1928), p. 422.

[69] *Ibid.,* p. 423

[70] Mary Austin, "George Sterling At Carmel," *The American Mercury* (May, 1927), pp. 70-71.

[71] Idwal Jones, "Plumes and Buskins," *The American Mercury* (March, 1928), p. 297.

[72] Carey McWilliams, "Swell Letters in California," *The American Mercury* (September, 1930), p. 47.

[73] "Editorial Notes," *The American Mercury* (April, 1930), p. XXVIII.

[74] H. L. Davis, "Water On The Wheat," *The American Mercury* (February, 1930), p. 140.

[75] *Ibid.,* p. 144

[76] H. L. Davis, "Hand-Press Journalist," *The American Mercury* (April, 1930), p. 485.

[77] Letter from H. L. Mencken, Guy J. Forgue (ed.), *Letters of H. L. Mencken* (New York: Alfred A. Knopf, 1961), p. 394.

[78] H. L. Mencken, "Editorial," *The American Mercury* (December, 1928), p. 408.

[79] Most of the characters listed appear in James Stevens, "Why Poker Was Invented," *The American Mercury* (October, 1928), pp. 129-138.

[80] Charles Angoff, *H. L. Mencken: A Portrait From Memory* (New York: A.S. Barnes and Co., Inc., 1956), p. 111.

[81] *Ibid.*

[82] Harvey Ferguson, discussing his New Mexico boyhood, quoted in *The American Mercury.*

Jack Salzman

SOURCE: "Conroy, Mencken, and *The American Mercury*," in *Journal of Popular Culture*, v. 7, No. 3, Winter, 1973, pp. 524-28.

[*In the following essay, Salzman traces H. L. Mencken's support of writer and radical Jack Conroy through their personal correspondence and the publication of Conroy's work in the* American Mercury *during the early 1930s.*]

By 1930, so we frequently have been told, both *The American Mercury* and its brilliantly iconoclastic editor, Henry Louis Mencken, had lost most of their once-formidable influence. The Depression may have been the pivotal event; or perhaps, as one historian of the *Mercury* contends, "the glorious heyday of the green monthly was over by the time of the great upheaval."[1] Whatever the exact moment, there seems to be little disagreement that by 1930 there was a drastic deterioration in the quality of *The American Mercury*. Everyone apparently was angry with its editor: Mencken was too conservative, too bourgeois, too pro-German, and too anti-Semitic. He failed to grasp the import of the stock market crash. His friendships with George Jean Nathan and Theodore Dreiser had ended several years earlier, and Mencken no longer had anyone of Dreiser's stature—no Sinclair Lewis or Sherwood Anderson—to champion. He was scorned by Left and Right alike. And the journal which he had edited since its inception in 1924 was now attracting "fewer first-rate, and even second-rate, minds."[2]

In the mid-twenties, before hard times fell upon Mencken, the *Mercury,* and the nation in general, Jack Conroy, who already "had begun to write some verse and have some of it published,"[3] went to Hannibal, Missouri, to work in a rubber heel plant. Not long after, he moved to Toledo, where he worked in the Willys-Overland automobile factory during the day and wrote poems and stories in the evening. In the winter of 1930, when the workers were being laid off weeks at a time, he found a job picking carrots. Years later, Conroy was to recall: "That's one of the hardest jobs I had: picking carrots out of the frozen ground, I swore then I'd never look a carrot in the eye as long as I lived because part of the arrangement was to take carrots home as part-pay. We'd have creamed carrots, fried carrots, every kind of carrots you could think of. Finally, things got to such a state that we had to make it back to Missouri where we had relatives."[4] At the same time, he was publishing his writings in such places as *The Northern Light, The Morada,* and *New Masses;* and, with

Ralph Cheyney, he was editing *Unrest: The Rebel Poets Anthology*. With all this happening, Conroy may have been too busy to hear about Mencken's "decline." At any rate, it was at this time that he began to correspond with the *Mercury*'s editor, who became, in Conroy's words, "one of the best friends I ever had."[5]

It was typical of Conroy, who has devoted much of his energy to getting the works of other writers published, that he initiated his correspondence with Mencken by telling him about a promising young writer, Joseph Kalar, and asking him at the same time to look at some material by a writer whom Conroy would unsuccessfully try to dub the Bard of the Ozarks, H. H. Lewis.[6] Mencken, in a letter dated October 24, 1930,[7] thanked Conroy for his tip about Kalar, and told him that he was indeed interested in several of the pieces by Lewis which Conroy had sent him. Mencken was strongly tempted by Lewis' "School Days," but felt that it would have to be cut before it could be published in *The American Mercury*. He also was intrigued by Lewis' "Marathon diary" and an article about a mail-order swindle, although he thought that "Lewis ruins [the latter] by his socialistic fulminations. They seem to be dragged in without point. After all, suckers would still be suckers under Bolshevism." Lewis would not alter the mail-order piece and Mencken would not publish it as it was. Nor did he get to publish the "Marathon diary." But Mencken did publish "School Days." He made a few minor changes, retitled the piece, "School Days in the Gumbo"—that seemed "less flat"— and included it in the January, 1931, issue of the *Mercury*.

In the meantime, Mencken, who clearly was not as oblivious to the Depression as some people have made him out to have been, had asked Conroy to do a piece about his winter in Toledo, to be called "A Hard Winter." When Conroy wrote that he would do the article, Mencken replied on November 13, 1930, "It is good news that you will tackle 'A Hard Winter.' It should make a capital piece. But get it in before the winter is over. We make up January tomorrow, and February on December 15." Conroy made the December 15 deadline, and "Hard Winter" was the feature piece in the February, 1931, *American Mercury*.

In the same issue, Mencken published a notice of the 1930 number of *Unrest*. He earlier had written Conroy that the notice was not to be altogether favorable: "It seems to me that there is some dreadful bilge in the book," Mencken wrote on November 13, 1930. "But also some very good stuff." The notice was not altogether favorable, but it was a good notice nonetheless. Mencken refrained from calling any of the poems "dreadful bilge"—"banal doggerels" was his term for the poorest poems—and he spoke glowingly of the "eloquent pieces" by Michael Gold, James Rorty, and Jack Conroy. Gold's "A Strange Funeral in Braddock" was somewhat puzzling, for Mencken could not understand how the episode of a worker trapped in a steel ingot was a reflection upon the capitalistic system: "Precisely the same accident might have happened in a Soviet steel-mill," Mencken

wrote, "and there is no reason to believe that the Bolsheviki would have been more successful in separating the corpse from the steel than Charlie Schwab's hirelings were at Braddock." Still, despite his reservations, Mencken found that *Unrest* "makes good reading. Not a few of the radicals write well, and all of them are in deadly earnest."[8] It was very much like Mencken not to allow his political disagreements with the Left to determine his aesthetic judgments. For several years, Mencken had been vilified by the Left in general and Mike Gold in particular (who called Mencken "one of the salon singers" who was popular because he "has expressed the philosophy of the *nouveaux riches*").[9] Yet he published some of Gold's *Jews Without Money* sketches in the *Mercury,* he had kind words for *Unrest*—including Gold's contributions—and, as he wrote Conroy on November 30, 1930, he published more articles in *The American Mercury* in favor of the Soviet Union than against it, "though my own feeling is that they [the Soviets] have failed."

Mencken's iconoclasm made him a perfect editor for Jack Conroy. If the material was interesting, Mencken would publish it. In a three year period, he accepted and published six of Conroy's sketches (the checks for which, Conroy has said "kept me alive for months").[10] Five of the sketches became part of *The Disinherited*. In May, 1931, three months after the publication of "Hard Winter," the *Mercury* published Conroy's "Boyhood in a Coal Town." This sketch, together with one published in August, 1932, "Life and Death of a Coal Miner" (a title which Mencken changed from "Shot Firer") became the essence of "Monkey Nest Camp," the first section of *The Disinherited*. In February, 1932, Mencken read Conroy's sketch based on his experiences in the rubber heel factory in Hannibal. "It is capital stuff," he wrote Conroy on February 6, 1932, "and I'll be delighted to take it." A few cuts were made, "for the article is rather long as it stands," the title was changed to "Rubber Heels," and Mencken included the piece in the April, 1932 issue of *American Mercury*. Later, it was printed in *The Disinherited* as part of Section VII of "Bull Market." And, in September, 1932, Mencken published "Pipe Line," which Conroy incorporated into the last section of *The Disinherited,* entitled "The Hard Winter" (which begins with the sketch Conroy had written in 1930, at Mencken's request, about his winter in Toledo).

The last work of Conroy's to be published in *The American Mercury* was "The Siren." It appeared in the May, 1933, issue, and was the only one of the *Mercury* sketches not to be incorporated into *The Disinherited*. Although the setting for "The Siren" once again is Monkey Nest, the story did not go into *The Disinherited,* as Erling Larsen explained in his article on "Jack Conroy's *The Disinherited* or, The Way It Was," "perhaps because the 'I,' no doubt Larry Donovan, is here only an observer and narrator and not a heavily involved participant." And perhaps, as Larsen also notes, "the substance of the story would not here fit into the book Professor [Daniel] Aaron calls 'a good example of the American picaresque novel.'"[11] Larsen's essay considers most of the important aspects of Conroy's story. Little need be added to it, except to note that some of the ambiguities which Larsen finds in the opening pages of "The Siren" may be due to Mencken's request—or insistence—that Conroy cut the story to fifteen or sixteen pages of typescript: "You have some capital material here," Mencken told Conroy on January 25, 1933, "and it seems to me that you handle it very well. Unluckily, the story, as it stands, is a bit long. Worse, it gives the *effect* of being a bit long. . . . I believe that you could make some easy cuts in the earlier parts. If you agree, let me have the manuscript back." Conroy agreed. He also accepted Mencken's suggestion that it would be less theatrical to have Hassem "escape actual execution" (as he apparently did not in the original manuscript), and concluded the story, as Mencken advised, "at the time of [Hassem's] departure for home."

On October 6, 1933, the New York *Times* carried a statement of Mencken's resignation as editor of *The American Mercury.* The new editor was to be Henry Hazlitt, and on November 25, 1933, Mencken wrote Conroy, "I think you'll find Hazlitt very hospitable, even though he did fail to take one of your manuscripts. Don't forget that you and I used to differ also, at least now and then." But Conroy did not try *The American Mercury* again. *The Disinherited* was published by Covici-Friede in 1933, the first issue of *The Anvil* appeared in May of that year, and there was a lot of work to do. Mostly, though, it was Mencken whom Conroy respected, and with his departure the *Mercury* no longer seemed as receptive as it once had been.

The American Mercury never did get to publish anything by Joseph Kalar, nor did it publish anything by Moe Bragin, the author of "Cow," whom Conroy also urged upon Mencken. But it did include Lewis' "School Days in the Gumbo," and the September, 1931, issue contained a piece entitled "Ohio Town," by Hugh Hanley, the man who had been an assistant editor of *The Spider,* the American college radical magazine, of which Jack Conroy had been the managing editor. As for Conroy, Mencken not only published his sketches; he also was a constant source of encouragement. When Conroy wrote the Baltimore sage that he wanted to find a wider market for his sketches, Mencken, in a letter dated March 6, 1931, immediately suggested the liberal weeklies: *"The New Freeman* would probably be delighted to print parts of it, and maybe you could also sell some to the *New Republic."* When Conroy had difficulty finding a publisher for *The Disinherited,* Mencken wrote on December 23, 1932, "Please don't be discouraged about your book. Keep it moving among publishers, and soon or late it will find a place. I suggest that the younger firms are more likely to take it than the older ones." And when Conroy told him that the book was to be published by Covici-Friede, Mencken wrote on April 1, 1933, "I am delighted to hear that Covici is to do your book. At the moment the publishing business is completely paralyzed, but there are already signs of a picking up and by September business should be fairly good again. It goes without saying that

I'll want to print a notice of the book in The American Mercury [sic]. . . . "

Perhaps by 1930 the heyday of *The American Mercury* was indeed over. Yet from 1930 to Mencken's resignation in 1933, the *Mercury* published works by Maxwell Bodenheim, Erskine Caldwell, James T. Farrell, John Fante, William Faulkner, Albert Halper, Josephine Herbst, James Rorty, and Leane Zugsmith. Not a bad record. Most impressive of all, however, was the series of six sketches by Jack Conroy. He succeeded brilliantly in doing just what he wanted to do: "to be a witness to the times, to show how it feels to be without work, and with the imminent fear of starving, to move people to think about it, and what's more important, to do something about it."[12] In large part, Mencken made Conroy's success possible, and his importance during this period of our cultural history must be recognized. For it was, after all, *The American Mercury,* not *New Masses,* which first published the sketches which were to form the base for Jack Conroy's *The Disinherited,* one of the few essential testaments of the 1930s.

NOTES

[1] M. K. Singleton, *H. L. Mencken and The American Mercury* (Durham, N. C.: Duke University Press, 1962), p. 214.

[2] Carl Bode, *Mencken* (Carbondale: Southern Illinois University Press, 1969), p. 256.

[3] Jack Conroy, "'Home to Moberly,'" *Missouri Library Association Quarterly,* XXVIX (March, 1968), pp. 41-50.

[4] Interview with Robert Lefley, Radio Station WFMT, Chicago. Reprinted in Chicago *Daily News,* May 18, 1963, p. 9.

[5] Interview with Lefley.

[6] See Jack Conroy, "H. H. Lewis: Plowboy Poet of the Gumbo," *December,* XI (1969), 203-206.

[7] Copies of H. L. Mencken's letters were lent me by Jack Conroy, whose cooperation I gratefully acknowledge.

[8] "Check List of New Books," *American Mercury,* XXII (February, 1931), xiv.

[9] Michael Gold, "America Needs a Critic," *New Masses,* October, 1926.

[10] Interview with Lefley.

[11] Erling Larsen, "Jack Conroy's *The Disinherited* or, The Way It Was," *Proletarian Writers of the Thirties,* ed. David Madden (Carbondale: Southern Illinois University Press, 1968), p. 90. Daniel Aaron's quote is to be found

in his Introduction to the Hill & Wang reprint of *The Disinherited.*

[12] Interview with Lefley.

Leo M. J. Manglaviti

SOURCE: "Faulkner's 'That Evening Sun' and Mencken's 'Best Editorial Judgement'," in *American Literature*, v. LIII, January, 1972, pp. 649-54.

[*In the following essay, Manglaviti compares extant versions of William Faulkner's "That Evening Sun," which was first published in the* American Mercury *in March 1931, focusing on Mencken's role in the revision process.*]

H. L. Mencken's *American Mercury* published William Faulkner's "Honor" in July, 1930, and "Hair" in May, 1931. In October, 1930, Faulkner sent to Mencken still another contribution, the typescript of "That Evening Sun Go Down," which in the permanent Faulkner canon became "That Evening Sun." The final version of the story is one of Faulkner's most critically discussed short prose pieces. Following by two years *The Sound and the Fury*, it is a sequel to the world of the Compson children in which Quentin narrates a few hours in the life of Nancy, Dilsey's relief servant, who fears becoming the victim of a husband seeking retribution. Mencken printed the story in March, 1931, with alterations and omissions made in the original typescript,[1] itself a revision of a manuscript entitled "Never Done No Weeping When You Wanted to Laugh."[2] The present version, "That Evening Sun," restored excisions and changes in the *Mercury* version and was included in *These 13* in the fall of 1931, and later in Faulkner's *Collected Stories* (1950).[3] The story has thus had four versions, only three of which have been studied.

After 40 years the missing text in the chronology, the typescript which Mencken received, is available as part of the H. L. Mencken Papers in the Manuscript Division of the New York Public Library. When Mencken died in 1956, he restricted from public use for 15 years the estimated 30,000 items in the correspondence deeded to the library. This restriction was lifted on January 29, 1971, on the fifteenth anniversary of Mencken's death. Mencken the arbiter of American letters is again apparent, his protégé no less than the Faulkner newly becoming established as the directing force of the Southern literary renaissance.

Bearing Faulkner's interim title of "That Evening Sun Go Down," the typescript consists of 26 letter-sized pages, with autograph corrections by both Faulkner and Mencken. In addition, pages four and five have been completely retyped by Faulkner, in accord with suggestions by Mencken. Mencken's criticism and Faulkner's notes in reply are also contained in the slim Faulkner folder of the Mencken Papers.[4] This correspondence clarifies Mencken's role in the revisions, as Norman Holmes Pearson speculated in an essay written when Yale acquired the manuscript in 1954. In noting the change of Nancy's husband's

name from Jesus to Jubah in the *Mercury* printing, Mr. Pearson concludes:

> Whether the substitution was Faulkner's own idea of improvement or expressed his fear of an unintentional blasphemy, or whether it was the editor of *The American Mercury* who was more conservative than he liked to appear, I do not know.

Leaving aside the question of Mencken's elusive attitude, it is not difficult to agree with Mr. Pearson that the restoration of the name Jesus gave back to the story a "certain paradoxical tension which was otherwise lost." Faulkner's decision to restore the name Jesus also is essential for resolving at least one conflict in the story (*MT*, p. 10; *AM*, p. 261; *CS*, pp. 296-297), where the dialogue holds in painful suspension Nancy's fear of the Lord and a dread of her husband's revenge sworn on her prostitution with white men. And Mencken was more concerned with this aspect, and with Faulkner's portrayal in his explicit fashion of Nancy's sinful pregnancy.

The substitution of the name Jubah was indeed precipitated by Mencken, as was a major alteration in dialogue and imagery. After receiving the typescript, Mencken wrote to Faulkner a letter of impeccable composition, dated simply "November 7th." The editor writes:[6]

> This is a capital story and I certainly hope to use it, but it leaves me with doubts about two points. One has to do with the name of Nancy's husband. I see no reason why he should be called Jesus—it is, in fact, a very rare name among Negroes, and I fear using it would make most readers believe we were trying to be naughty in a somewhat strained manner.
>
> Don't you think the story would be just as effective if it were changed to some more plausible name?
>
> Secondly, it seems to me that the dialogue about Nancy's pregnancy, on pages four and five, is somewhat loud for a general magazine? [*sic*] I believe it could be modified without doing the slightest damage to the story.
>
> I hesitate extremely to make such suggestions to an author of your skill, but such is my best editorial judgment. If you care to carry them out, let me have the MS. back at once. It is a fine piece of work, and I'd like very much to print it.

Faulkner returned the typescript with an undated typed note, on which Mencken later penciled "1931":[7]

> Here is the story, corrected according to your letter. Will you please have them hold the check until you hear further from me? I expect to be in New York in November. I'll be obliged to you.

His trip to New York probably included a visit to Cape and Smith to settle affairs in the publication of *These 13*. In this collection of stories, Faulkner restored the deletions agreed upon for the March, 1931, issue of the

American Mercury, where "That Evening Sun Go Down" was printed on the very first page, having been given a prominent position on the cover.

In addition to his typed letter, Faulkner at some point curiously returned Mencken's "November 7th." letter.[8] On the reverse Faulkner penned unsigned notes for what may have been the first draft of an abandoned longer letter. In a characteristically near illegible hand (with two cancellations, as shown below) are recorded his thoughts on the changes he made in the typescript:

> I did not delete the section, the dialogue about the pregnancy, altogether, because it seems to me that it establishes Judah [*sic*] as a potential factor of the tragedy as soon as possible. [and so *crossed out here*] Otherwise, to me, the story would be a little obscure [until *crossed out here*] for too long a time. However, if you think best, it might be taken out completely. I am glad you like the story; I think it's pretty good myself.
>
> I did remove the "vine" business. I reckon that's what would outrage Boston.

Thus the retyped section (*MT,* pp. 4-5) represented William Faulkner's temporary compromise with the popular taste which H. L. Mencken helped legislate for many busy years.

The sensibilities of Boston or Mencken notwithstanding, Faulkner later restored the "vine business" and the final version now reads (*CS,* p. 292):

> "It never came off of your vine, though," Nancy said.
>
> "Off of what vine?" Caddy said.
>
> "I can cut down the vine it did come off of," Jesus said.

The fruit in question is Nancy's unborn bastard child. This exchange follows Jesus's telling the Compson children that Nancy's pregnant stomach was really a watermelon under her dress. In the typescript, where Jesus becomes Jubah, Faulkner inserted "And it was winter, too" immediately before the revision of the vine metaphor, thus softening the original sexually violent effect (*MT,* p. 4; *AM,* p. 258):

> "Where did you get a watermelon in the winter?" Caddy said.
>
> "I didn't," Jubah said. "It wasn't me that give it to her. But I can cut it down, same as if it was."

Also removed here as unnecessary (though the ambiguous "cut it down" remains) was Caddy's bewilderment at the original double entendre: "Off of what vine? . . . What vine?" These lines were also restored in *Collected Stories* (p. 292).

In its final form "That Evening Sun" also includes a line, omitted from the *Mercury* version, immediately after the

description of Nancy found hanging "stark naked" in her attempted jail suicide: "her belly already swelling out a little, like a little balloon" (*CS,* p. 292). In the revised typescript Faulkner had written (*MT,* p. 4):

> " . . . her belly swelling a little, paling a little as it swelled, like a colored balloon pales with distension."

This entire phrase has been penciled out, and subsequently did not appear in the *Mercury.* Did Mencken's "judgment" again exercise the final say? Faulkner had recently implied the granting of such a prerogative, in his unsigned notes, and apparently it was Mencken himself who acted as censor.

Mencken was the proofreader, or at least one of the readers of the revised typescript. The first page has a byline for Faulkner in Mencken's hand, as well as a note to himself about payment for the story. In one long paragraph (*MT,* pp. 16-17; *AM,* p. 263) Mencken's pencil substituted "she" and "her" for "Nancy" and "Nancy's," changes which Faulkner eventually incorporated into his rewriting (*CS,* p. 301). And Mencken no doubt made the scattered paragraph divisions, later kept by Faulkner, a few more pronominal changes, capitalizations ("Negroes," "Winter," "Summer"), and the Roman numeral insertions for an arrangement into five sections. Faulkner later modified the last of these changes to six sections, and he restored the lower case to "winter" and "summer." Faulkner's own changes in the typescript, in addition to retyping the "vine" dialogue, consist of neat blue-inked substitutions of "Jubah" for "Jesus," the removal of the superfluous line about "the other Jesus" in Nancy's frightful wailing (*MT,* p. 10; *CS,* p. 297), and a few typing corrections. A third hand has inserted lines and Arabic numerals, probably indicating galley sheet pagination. Mencken would thus emerge as the reader who probably removed the description of Nancy's swollen belly.

Faulkner prevailed in the end, reworking the final draft of "That Evening Sun" from both the Yale manuscript and the *Mercury* version.[9] It is not likely that he saw the typescript again during the revision process. For a line in his typed story was apparently accidentally omitted from the *Mercury* printing (*AM,* p. 260) and likewise does not appear in *Collected Stories* (p. 295). While Nancy is cursing the possibility of Jesus' having slept with another woman, she threatens to cut off his arm (*MT,* p. 9). She reiterates: "Ara hand that touched her, I'd cut it off." This is intact in the typescript but has mysteriously disappeared from the printed versions. The reason may never be known, but possibly revelatory reminiscences may be forthcoming in 1981, when Mencken's five-volume diary is opened for public view in the Enoch Pratt Free Library in Baltimore. Mencken noted in his Faulkner file, on his customary small scrap of orange paper, a diary entry for what appears to be December 16, 1931. Joseph Blotner's forthcoming biography of Faulkner will no doubt illuminate the editorial relationship with Mencken from perspectives far south of Baltimore. As for Mencken, perhaps he felt the world unworthy of access all at once to his privacy, where he helped negotiate for all ages the position of Faulkner and others in the annals of literature.

[1] Hereafter referred to as the Mencken Typescript and cited in the text as *MT*. Originally published as: "That Evening Sun Go Down," *American Mercury*, XXII (March, 1931), 257-267, hereafter cited in the text as *AM*.

[2] This manuscript is now at Yale. See Norman Holmes Pearson's essay (cited below), "Faulkner's Three 'Evening Suns,'" in *Yale University Library Gazette*, XXIX (Oct., 1954), 61-70.

[3] "That Evening Sun," in *Collected Stories of William Faulkner* (New York, 1950), pp. 289-309. This version will hereafter be cited as *CS*.

[4] The typescript is apparently the only one of Faulkner's five contributions kept by Mencken. Besides the letters printed below, Mencken in this collection retained only three exchanges of 1948 in which Faulkner promised to ask Random House to send copies of his works to a friend of Mencken's in the University of Berlin.

[5] Pearson, p. 65. The essay documents Faulkner's extensive revisions of his original manuscript, and analyzes as well the dramatic movements in the story.

[6] For permission to quote this letter in full I am indebted to Mr. William G. Frederick, Vice President of the Mercantile-Safe Deposit and Trust Company of Baltimore, which administers the Mencken Trust.

[7] I am grateful to Faulkner's daughter, Mrs. Paul D. Summers of Charlottesville, Virginia, for permission to quote this letter to Mencken, and for my citations (below) of both the complete text of Faulkner's explanatory notes and occasional sections of the unpublished Mencken Typescript.

[8] This autographed Mencken letter is a rarity in his papers. Mencken did not keep carbons, and his own letters generally appear as transcripts later typed by his secretary from her notes.

[9] Mr. Pearson discusses this development, citing particularly Faulkner's thorough revision of the ending of the story. See his essay, especially pp. 67-70.

Theodore Maynard

SOURCE: "Mencken Leaves The American Mercury," in *Catholic World*, v. 139, April, 1934, pp. 10-20.

[In the following essay, which was written on the occasion of H. L. Mencken's resignation from the American Mercury, *Maynard offers a consideration of his influence and career.]*

Let me make two preliminary remarks. The first is that I know Henry Mencken and have a great respect and liking for him. Therefore perhaps I write with a bias in his favor, though it should be said that I respected him long before I knew him. The second remark is that I do not propose offering here a general discussion of the life and miracles of the Sage of Baltimore, or even of his literary work as a whole. My concern is primarily with his editorship of *The American Mercury*.

Of his early work on Baltimore newspapers, or on *The Smart Set* from 1908-23, I do not know enough to speak with any competence, though I am aware that this should be considered in any final estimate of Mencken. But as nothing so ambitious as such an estimate is to be attempted, there is hardly any need for an apology. And, after all, *The Smart Set* was conducted in a mood of sardonic cynicism, the trashy stories being offered to what Mencken loves to call the "booboisie," and the mordant criticism (which was the real purpose of the magazine) to what some people, but never Mencken himself, love to call the "intelligentsia." It was in *The American Mercury* that Mencken really set up a pulpit from which he could address the country. So distinctive a thing did he make of it that it is difficult to conceive of it without him. We may get a very good magazine from Mr. Hazlitt, but it is bound to be a different magazine under the old name. I wish it all success, but the terms "Mencken" and "Mercury" will remain always inseparable in my mind. I shed a few tears of regret before continuing.

In January, 1924, the first number of *The American Mercury* appeared under the editorship of H. L. Mencken and George Jean Nathan. All the characteristic features of the magazine had been carefully thought out, so that during ten years it has received practically no modification. From the beginning it was a smashing success, the first issue having to be printed twice. In fact, its success was greater at the start than later on. The depression caused sales to drop off; but even had the Coolidge boom kept up, *The Mercury* would probably have declined somewhat. Mencken had done his work so thoroughly that everybody who had read the early issues had a pretty good inkling as to what would be in the later ones. He had thumped his point home so well that there was no longer much need of doing any thumping at all. Yet I am reliably informed that *The Mercury* was almost alone among magazines of its class in the fact that it ended 1933 with a profit.

From the start it was Mencken's magazine. He had, indeed, stipulated that Nathan should be associated with him; but it was plain that the association was merely nominal. There were for some time joint "Clinical Notes" (mainly written by Nathan), and some pages of dramatic criticism, wholly written by him. But it is clear that his function was that of an advisory contributor. After the first year it was announced as such, and eventually he retired altogether. It is no reflection upon him to say that he never really fitted into *The Mercury*. His keen intelligence takes little interest in the turbulent life of the world, though nobody could make more bitingly satirical comments upon some of its more superficial aspects. In politics he has no interest whatsoever. As Mencken once said of him, he probably could not name the Vice-President of the United States. Without precisely living in an ivory tower, his life is mainly spent in the theater.

But Mencken's preoccupation was with the whole of American life, though his riotous taste in humor led him to prefer its gaudier manifestations. His gusto at first sight leaves one with the impression that he was willing to gobble everything down without discrimination. But with that gusto goes a delicate epicureanism: none of his cannibal banquets is quite complete without a Methodist bishop or a dry senator to grace the board. These were his larks' wings and nightingales' tongues. On the other hand, those Anti-Saloon League ecclesiastics and politicians who thought of Mencken as a dreadful ogre who could be satisfied with nothing except their raw flesh, were in error. He enjoyed morticians and beauticians and horticians almost as much. On lean days he would even tear a Lion limb from limb, and track a Shriner to the inmost recesses of his shrine. He has even been known to make do upon such coarse fare as insurance company executives, realtors, publicity experts, shoe-salesmen, radio-announcers, chiropractors and taxi-drivers, with a little juice squeezed out of the bones of bootleggers and baseball-players as a sauce. Not always could he roll upon his voluptuous tongue the blood of Y. M. C. A. secretaries or prohibition enforcement officers. No doubt Mencken is a monster, but only on holydays of obligation did he fasten his vampire teeth on a justice of the Supreme Court or a founder of a new religion.

Yet in spite of somewhat rowdy fun at times, *The Mercury*'s articles were almost always well-informed. Mencken saw to that. If he had a way of jazzing up the contributions to his magazine, he was also careful to check statements of fact. One may think his point of view warped, or dislike his style, but I cannot recall where any of his critics convicted him of serious error. Never once has he been sued for libel, despite his years of outspoken controversy. *The Mercury* told us many things which we could not easily learn about elsewhere; and it was generally safe to rely upon what we were told. Despite his fondness for wild humor, Mencken has an extremely orderly mind, chock-full of practicality and common sense, and detests inaccuracy as much as any other form of slovenly inefficiency.

The Mercury was above all else *The American Mercury,* and confined itself to life in this country. It never contained articles about happenings in Europe, unless they were concerned with the way Americans disported themselves in, say, Paris or Majorca. Even European books received scant attention, when they were noticed at all.

Many Americans were very naturally indignant at some of the aspects of the American scene that were exposed, and at the irreverence with which many of their most cherished traditions were handled. As Mencken himself

put it, he for years spilled ink "denouncing that hypocrisy that runs, like a hair in a hot dog, through the otherwise beautiful fabric of American life." With loud scoffs he derided all the politicians and wowsers and members of Rotary who unctuously proclaimed that their lives were dedicated to the social uplift. Take this, for instance, upon Rotary:

> One hears of its spokesmen announcing that Moses, or Homer, or St. Francis, or Martin Luther, or George Washington was the first Rotarian, and arguing gravely that, when the next war threatens, only Rotary will be able to stop it. The members of this party wear the club emblem as if it were the Garter, and spend a great deal of their time worrying over such things as the crime wave, necking in the high schools, the prevalence of adenoids, the doings of the League of Nations, and the conspiracy of the Bolsheviki to seize the United States and put every Cadillac owner to the sword. They have a taste for rhetoric, and like to listen to speeches by men with Messages. The boys of the other party are less concerned about such high matters. When there is nothing better afoot they go to the weekly luncheons, gnaw their way through the chicken patties and green peas, blow a few spitballs across the table, sing a few songs, and then, when the speech-making begins, retire to the washroom, talk a little business, and then prevail upon Fred or Charlie to tell the new one about Judd Gray and the chambermaid at Hornellsville, N. Y.

No doubt Mencken would be the first to admit that Rotarians are a very harmless bunch of fellows. If he derided them, it was because they laid themselves wide open to the shafts of satire. He understood very well that by making them look absurd he would help to discredit all those other well-meaning but fatuous groups of people whose complacent good-nature tends to smother the spread of ideas. It was no good trying to argue with them; indeed there was nothing very much that one could argue about. The only thing that could be done was to try and laugh them out of existence.

As these were the very people that the mass of Americans had been taught to admire and imitate, there was a good deal of bewilderment and indignation when they were attacked. Mencken was therefore denounced by them as being un-American, a dangerous radical, a Jew, the Teuton Blond Beast, an Anglophile, and what not. He laughed at the anger he aroused, kept (and later published) a scrapbook of the terms of abuse used against himself, and let fly another quiver of arrows—with devastating effect. There was no need for him even to take the trouble to defend himself against the charge of being un-American. Though a German in blood he has none of the marks of a German about him, unless it be a liking for beer and music and methodical industry. But so far from being ponderous or stodgy, his mind clicks to a hairtrigger, and his flow of ideas is fantastic and prolific rather than deep. It would be hard to find a more representative American. However much he might make fun of American life and American institutions, one could not imagine him living anywhere except in America, or having been produced by any country but America. He had nothing in common with those aesthetic fellow-countrymen of his who, after a brief acquaintance with England or France, are never able to be happy again anywhere except abroad. When Mencken is asked why he does not clear out of the United States, since he holds the opinions he does, he answers very simply that it is because he would not for worlds miss the spectacle of rich absurdity provided for his entertainment here. That is his way of saying that he likes America too much to leave. He might add (but as he never will, I must do it for him) that he loves America too much to leave. He would warmly repudiate any suggestion that he stays for his country's good. He loathes all reformers and up-lifters. But he is doing what he can to increase the dignity and honesty and charm of American life. No doubt he does relish to the full the antics of the people he derides; but were he merely the detached spectator he would at most sneer at them. His furious and boisterous propaganda at their expense would have no meaning, did he not hope to do his part in exterminating them as pests. It would be a sad day for him when the last of them perished; but upon his conscience there rests the inexorable duty of working towards that day.

If Mencken has, as his chief assets, humor and honesty and good sense, his chief deficiency would seem to be philosophical. Not that he is without a philosophy, but it does not strike one as being very important. Thousands will laugh and cheer when he goes on the warpath against the Babbitts, where hardly one will listen when he begins to expound his system. He may be said to have a huge following, but no disciples. As Ernest Boyd says in his book on Mencken, he has had "a Nietzschean education, and he is loyal to his old teacher, but his philosophy of life and art has little of Nietzsche in it, and their points of contact are probably fewer than their points of divergence. Their one fundamental point of agreement is their rejection of Christianity and democracy." Even if we are to take the somewhat sportive *In Defense of Women* (thoroughly repudiated by Mencken in practice since his marriage) as owing something to Nietzsche, it would still be true that Mencken is a Nietzschean in a Pickwickian sense. Even where the views of the two philosophers coincide—that is concerning Christianity and democracy—the coincidence is far from perfect. With little of Nietzsche's bitter rancor, Mencken attacks a corrupt congressman rather than the philosophical idea of democracy; Elmer Gantry rather than Christianity. A believer in Christianity and democracy must not only approve of all this, but the more sincere his conviction, the stronger must be his approval. In the specific case Mencken is nearly always right; his general principle may be unsound, but is of little consequence one way or the other.

I must confess having always been mildly amused at Mencken's announcing himself as an aristocrat. For he is the most sociable and accessible of mortals, without a particle of "side," a good mixer, positively exuding bonhomie. Now I am aware that a real aristocrat has no need

to cultivate an icy aloofness. In fact that is generally the mark of the parvenu. But the easy and affable manners of the aristocrat will have also at all times a touch of distinction. Mencken, on the other hand, is thoroughly *bourgeois,* though in the best sense: cheerful, sturdy, independent, comfortable. I do not question the sincerity of his aristocratic principle. But I recall another, and a far more fierce, upholder of that principle: Coventry Patmore. He was all that Mencken is not: arrogant, intolerant, but quite content to let the world go to the devil in its own way. If I am obliged to applaud his greater consistency, I confess that I much prefer Mencken's "aristocracy" on all other grounds.

Mencken's political theory boils down to this: that there should be honesty and competence in politics, and that under the parliamentary system we rarely get either. Both points may be admitted by the firmest believer in democracy. But it must be immediately added that the aristocratic system offers no better guarantee of our obtaining them, if as good a one. All that a man of intelligence and public spirit can be expected to do is to expose chicanery and stupidity wherever they appear. This Mencken always does. His practice being what it is, his political theory may be whatever he chooses to call it.

Moreover, Mencken, being the man he is, does not stop to argue with anyone of whom he disapproves. He takes a battle-ax, and tries to split his enemy's skull—which, after all, is the most effective method of controversy. He is deterred by no feelings for exalted personages, or by any concessions to respectability. Presidents Harding, Coolidge and Hoover were each in turn served in much the same way; and, though at the time many people thought Mencken was using almost blasphemous language, it would seem that the country has come very generally to share his opinions of its former heroes. Take this from an editorial written in 1930:

> It is very hard to understand such a man. By what standard of values does he judge himself? What is his honest verdict when he looks into his shaving-glass of a morning? The Presidency is in his hands, and there is nothing higher for him to look for in this world. One would naturally expect a man in that situation to give some thought to the essential decencies—to devote himself to making sure, not of his immediate benefit, but of his ultimate reputation. But Dr. Hoover seems either unwilling or unable to take that view. He prefers to go on as he came in—playing shabby politics, consorting with creatures from the abyss, contributing his miserable mite to the destruction of free government among us.

It should be remembered that when he wrote this (and indeed on the very eve of the 1932 election), Mencken believed that Mr. Hoover's reëlection was certain. But he was determined that it should not occur without his protest. It should be remembered also that this comes, not from a wild radical—for Mencken is one of the few "rugged individualists" left among us—not from a Socialist, but from the reverse of one. Though in Mr. Roosevelt he has found a President whom he can respect, he has indicated clearly his disapproval of the policies of the present administration.

What it all comes to is this: Mencken makes no pretense to being a "constructive critic." He is purely destructive, but is, as such, decidedly beneficial to society. Contrary to what is generally held concerning a destructive critic, I cannot see that he is obliged to have something better to put in the place of the evil thing he would destroy. By sitting down to write a perfect constitution for future generations, he would give the scoundrels he was out to attack every chance to escape, or, perhaps, even to go, still secure in place and profit, to their graves.

The criticism I have offered of Mencken's political philosophy—that it is valuable only when it tackles specific cases—I should be equally prepared to make regarding his animadversions upon religion.

In 1930 his *Treatise on the Gods* appeared. The book is written in a sober style—as though to ward off the possibility of any charge of brutal iconoclasm—and perhaps for that reason is very dull, quite the dullest thing Mencken has ever produced. His object, he says, "may be roughly described as one of amiable skepticism. I am quite devoid of the religious impulse, and have no belief in any of the current theologies. But neither have I any active antipathy to them, save, of course, in so far as they ordain the harassing of persons who do not believe in them." That is a reasonable position to take up, and it must be admitted that Mencken writes his *Treatise* with moderation and fairness, even holding himself in leash against his old enemies the Baptists and Methodists. But the service he has done to religion (which, in my estimation is considerable) was in the smiting of religious humbug and intolerance. He is at his weakest when he attempts to systematize his unbelief.

Just as I believe that criticism, however severe, of those in high political position, can do nothing but good when it is well founded, so I hold the same thing of religious criticism. It is upon the basis of powerfully argued objections to the various articles of the Faith that St. Thomas Aquinas builds up the edifice of the *Summa Theologica*. There can be no firm faith until those objections have been met. And while naturally I should not force immature minds to consider a powerfully argued case against religion, I should not think a mind mature that had not weighed that case. It is in this way that a theologian is formed.

Furthermore, putting theology out of the discussion, it is good for every religious body (including Catholics) to be criticized, on the ground of the methods they employ, their ecclesiastical or personal manners, their educational standing, or their I. Q. Upon the whole Mencken has let Catholics down very lightly, and what criticism he has made of us has, as a rule, been deserved. But were I a Methodist (and intelligent) I think that, however much the lash laid by him upon Methodist backs might smart,

I should be grateful, and try to correct my behavior, if for no other reason than that of avoiding the lash in future. I am speaking, of course, only of fair criticism; unfair criticism I should resent.

To what extent Mencken's criticism of certain Protestant sects has been fair, and to what extent unfair, I must leave those sects themselves to determine. But there can be no doubt whatever that, however noble the motive may have been, this country has lain under the harrow of the Anti-Saloon League, and that this was a machine of outrageous religious tyranny. There can be no doubt that American Catholics have suffered from intolerance and bigotry, deliberately directed against them by the same ecclesiastical groups who ran the Anti-Saloon League. On this score Catholics are deeply indebted to Mencken. He has done valiantly in helping to discredit our bitterest enemies.

But it is not merely because Mencken has been the enemy of those groups from which we have suffered most, that Catholics owe him a debt of gratitude. His friendly feelings towards us are shown in more positive ways. His references to the Church are kindly and respectful, because, as he says, "It is manifestly more honest, intelligent and urbane than any of the dominant Protestant sects." Now and then, it is true, he has pilloried Catholics in "Americana"; but only rarely has this happened. I recall one such case. A Catholic family in New Jersey while eating a dessert of Jello, found that the fragments left upon one of the plates resembled a statue of the Little Flower. The miraculously formed statue was exhibited to their pious (and moronic) neighbors. Well, I believe such assininity ought to be ridiculed. There are fools among Catholics, as among other people. Whether it is because Catholics more rarely make fools of themselves than, say, Baptists, which I hope is the reason, or whether it is because Mencken has a more friendly feeling for Catholics, it is certainly true that they have no reason to complain of their treatment at his hands. There is no human likelihood of his ever becoming a Catholic. Nevertheless Catholics have received a good deal of aid and comfort from him.

But if Mencken had never said a word in our favor, his strenuous fight against cant and sentimentality and humbug, by clearing the air, tends to our advantage. With the battle over literary censorship the Church officially has no concern. We have our own *Index,* which is designed primarily as a barrier against the dissemination of heresy. The individual conscience has to be the guide with regard to works stained with pornography.

When the law steps in at this point the question becomes hopelessly confused. All Catholics of course hold that works likely to have an immoral effect should be neither written nor read; and some Catholics have supported their suppression by the State. The result is merely that works which may not be sent through the mails, may be sent by express. Furthermore it would seem to be impossible for the law to decide intelligently as to what works are immoral. I take a case in point. James Joyce's *Ulysses* has until recently been banned. Now that enormous work has sections in which the limit of obscenity is reached, in the sense of Joyce's using all the nine unprintable Anglo-Saxon monosyllables. Nevertheless *Ulysses* is about as far as anything could be from an incitement to sin. On the other hand books of all kinds which assume the right to adultery and the rectitude of abortion are freely circulated.

I am aware that I am not making an adequate discussion of the censorship. All I am trying to maintain is that there are practical as well as theoretical difficulties in its way, so that a protest against Comstockery is both valid and valuable. While Mencken has fought against the censorship, he is not obsessed on the subject, and *The Mercury* has been very harmless in the nature of its contributions. Even the attempt, some years ago, to suppress an issue of *The Mercury* in Boston because of a story it contained, resulted, after Mencken went there to force his arrest, in his acquittal, and in the death of the local Comstock shortly after from chagrin. The story was a mild affair.

Mencken's literary criticism has really been directed against exploding every form of hokum. The man, being perfectly honest and forthright, has a keen sense of the possession or lack of these qualities in other people. He has been all in favor of vigorous writing by people who have something to say, and against, as he says in *The American Language,* "the typical literary product of the country . . . a refined essay in *The Atlantic Monthly* manner, perhaps gently jocose but never rough."

Against the whole tribe of professors he has waged unceasing war. Of one of these gentlemen he says that he "devotes a chapter to proving that 'of the 10,565 lines of *Paradise Lost* 670, or 6.3 per cent, contain each two or more accentuated alliterating vowels,' another to proving that in such word-groups as *rough and ready,* 68 per cent put the monosyllable first and the dissyllable second, and 42 per cent put the dissyllable first and the monosyllable second."

Experimental psychology is treated just as savagely. Here is a sample:

> Lately I was reading the elaborate report of a professor who exhibited 'a set of French photographs of a pornographic nature' to twenty or thirty subjects, including two young women and a boy, and then solemnly photographed and measured their grimaces. That done, he read to them 'several of the most pornographic case histories from Ellis' *Psychology of Sex*.' Then he shoved their hands into buckets containing live frogs. Then he ordered them to cut off the heads of rats with butcher knives. To what end are such puerile obscenities? Who was in any doubt that the gals would jump when their hands touched the frogs, that they would shrink from butchering the rats, that the French photographs would make them blush and giggle? Yet American psychological literature is made up very largely of just such tosh and bosh.

A great day for him was when, in 1925, Boni and Liveright published a novel by a Baptist minister. Mencken's long review of it was screamingly funny, but is too long to quote. Here, however, is the knock-out blow:

> Dr. Dixon is a Baptist clergyman. The Baptists are not commonly regarded as artists. One hears of them chiefly as engaged in non-aesthetic or anti-aesthetic enterprises—ducking one another in horse-ponds, scaring the darkeys at revivals, acting as stool-pigeons for Prohibition agents, denouncing the theater and the dance, marching with the Klan. But here is one who has felt the sweet kiss of beauty; here is a Baptist who can dream.

Since Dr. Dixon's preposterous novel was rather easy game, it should be said that Mencken does not hesitate to take the button off the foils with writers like H. G. Wells, Arnold Bennett, Stuart Sherman and Paul Elmer More. Nor do his friends escape when they write nonsense, as may be seen by his reviews of Edgar Lee Masters' *Mirage* and Sinclair Lewis' *Ann Vickers*. Here is criticism that is always astringent and bracing. The only serious defects I can find in it are a comparative failure to appreciate delicate shades of meaning in prose, and a suspicion of poetry. Yet he reads verse, though he regards it as nothing but charming lying; and his first book was in verse. Much of it is not at all bad (though Mencken has since completely repudiated it) being ingenious and well-constructed. One might describe it (by slightly altering a line of Belloc's) as

> Much in the style of Kipling,
>   only worse.

This attempt, never since then renewed, at the writing of verse proves that Mencken, whatever else he is, is not a poet.

But we cannot expect everything. If Mencken's mind lacks sensitiveness, he makes up for it by his grip upon actuality, his coarse refreshing common sense. And he writes in a style which, if heavily loaded with slang, is for that reason all the more pungent. There is never any doubt about what it is that he is trying to say, or his complete ability to say it. Masculine, sinewy and lucid— we must put him, despite important differences, with Swift and Cobbett. All three are earth-bound, but all three make a virtue of their limitations.

It is a question whether any of Mencken's work is likely to survive. So essentially journalistic is it, that I must confess that (despite the pleasure I always take in his writing when I first read it) I find it hard to go back to it. The effect is immediate, not lasting. Probably of all men who have ever written, Mencken is least concerned with the judgment of posterity. It is sufficient for his purpose that he can arrest the attention of his contempories, if only for a fleeting instant. This is writing thrown out because of the urgent spur of the occasion, and may be considered as merely printed conversation. His talk is in exactly the same vein, rapid-fire, explosive, humorous. We should take what he writes in the same way, as the expression of what he means at the moment, but about which he may change his mind, and which in any case is not to be taken too literally. He should be allowed a little leeway for the play of fancy. At the same time his sincerity should be acknowledged: we must not confound seriousness and solemnity.

The man, upon a first personal acquaintance, may surprise, and yet he and his work constitute a single entity. However cruel some of his criticism seems, it all springs from his honesty. Here is a man kindly and courteous, who, though he talks exuberantly, is quite willing to listen to what other people may have to say, however dull it may be. This pitiless foe of Babbittry is unmasked as a man full of all the common and commonplace virtues. There is about him nothing of the aesthete. Literary men do not often look the part, yet few of them look less like it than Mencken. A man of his somewhat squat stocky figure, and large round face suggests the proprietor of a thriving delicatessen store. His ties look as though they had been picked in a hurry from the fifty cent bargain counter. He is the very embodiment of normality.

His cordiality puts one instantly at ease. Nobody can meet him and not like him, and his amiability is so great that when, after having fought a man upon paper for years, Mencken encounters him in the flesh, his sociability has a way of overcoming his aversion.

The first time I met him was shortly after his marriage. It was entertaining to see how tremendously he was enjoying being married, and to notice the attitude of his young wife towards her celebrated husband. She looked at him with the eye a mother would cast upon a precociously clever urchin, admiration and indulgence mingled together.

At lunch he ate voraciously of a Southern dish, the recipe for which he had got, so he told me, from Carl Van Vechten. And it pleased him that I enjoyed my food, and took a second and third helping. He apologized that he was at the moment out of beer—for he is vain of his prowess as a brewer—but, as a bottle of wine was produced, I was content to forego even the best Volstead-era home-brew. Then he said, "Maynard, look behind you! That was a wedding-present from my brother." It was a picture six feet by four that must once have hung in a saloon, and it showed a brewery going full blast.

Some time afterwards, G. K. Chesterton told me how his host in New York had written to Mencken, in the hope of bringing the two men together. Mencken had replied, "I am very sorry I cannot go to meet Chesterton. For I have long cherished an ambition to take him out and make him drunk, and then hand him over to the police while he was in that condition, to the shame of Holy Mother Church."

I told Mencken afterwards of Chesterton's comment: "Why, I could put Mencken under the table any day!" "Yes," said Mencken, "I suppose he could."

What he will do now that he has left *The Mercury,* I do not know. A treatise on morals is in preparation, and this, I think, is likely to be better than his excursion into theology. But it is not likely to contain anything new. His work is completed. His plea that no magazine should keep an editor for more than ten years, can be only a way of his admitting that he has said what he had to say, that there is no more to say. *The American Mercury* has fulfilled its destiny.

For several years past it had grown steadily less interesting. Not that the actual value of its contents declined; but subjects suitable for treatment in its pages were growing fewer. Even "Americana" was less funny than in the days of yore. Was it that Revivalists and Rotarians had, because of the *Mercury* lash, become more circumspect in their behavior? Whatever the reason, the crop of absurdity was thinning. And as Burton Rascoe has said of Mencken, he is now in the unhappy position of a born disputant who finds no one to disagree with him.

But if he has been a little too successful, the country should still be grateful to him. It is a better place to live in now (despite the depression) than it was in the old boom days. And while it would be fantastic to suggest that the higher level of intelligence is due to Mencken, it is no more than plain justice to acknowledge his efforts in behalf of decency and honesty. There is much that escaped his ken. His range is limited. There is no prophetic fire in the man. He has never itched to steer humanity in any particular course. He set himself one task—exposing fools and hypocrites. And that task has been accomplished.

George T. Warren

SOURCE: "The Mercury Idea," in *Menckeniana*, v. 47, Fall, 1973, pp. 25-6.

[*In the following essay, Warren offers personal reminiscences of H. L. Mencken as a journalist in Baltimore during the 1910s and suggests a possible early stimulus for the conception of the* American Mercury.]

When and where did HLM conceive of the *American Mercury?* I may have the answer.

In 1911, when I was twenty-one, I encountered HLM's books on Shaw and Nietzsche in the Houston, Texas, Public Library. A year later our family moved to Baltimore, where I was delighted to discover that this penetrating author, who had the American language so firmly by the tail, was doing a daily column for the Baltimore *Evening Sun.* What great sport he had lampooning the politicians and "the rev. clergy."

One hot June day I got up enough courage to climb the back stairs to the *Sun's* editorial room, expecting to find a cantankerous, blustery individual of fifty or sixty. What a surprise awaited me. Then only thirty-two, HLM proved to be the most amiable of men. He sat at his desk in shirt sleeves, proofreading his column. I had just returned from Philadelphia and while there had made a little pilgrimage to the Mickle Street cottage where Walt Whitman spent his last years. I naturally mentioned this to HLM (as a kind of excuse for calling) whereupon he countered with a story about his Philadelphia friend and literary idol, James Huneker, noted dramatic and literary critic. It was an enjoyable fifteen minutes. I think the "Free Lance" was pleased to receive this token of homage from a youngster lately come east from the Lone Star State.

Mencken was certainly not the typical hollow-chested, bespectacled author. He could pass as a husky meatcutter with a stall in Lexington Market, or a jovial drummer from New York or Chicago. Just why he gravitated into journalism when he could have so easily followed in his father's and uncle's footsteps and become a wealthy cigar manufacturer mystifies me. Maybe it would have been too easy. Like the transformation of Jack London from a swashbuckler on the San Francisco water front into a king of storytellers, answering not a "call of the wild" but a call to greater things.

Our little visits were invariably on Saturday afternoons about 2 o'clock when Henry was winding up things for the week. One time I recall wrapping up a dozen books he was taking home to wade through on Sunday for review in the *Smart Set*. What a glutton for punishment, although he loved to pose as a beer-drinking loafer!

One of those afternoons I found HLM pleasantly excited over a new periodical entitled the *Unpopular Review*. [The critic adds in a footnote that this journal "Appeared from January, 1914, to June, 1919, then continued to March, 1921, as *Unpartizan Review*."] Bound in somber brown, few if any advertisements, edited by Henry Holt the publisher. HLM asked me to take it home, browse through it, and jot down comments. I willingly complied, returning it the following week. As I look back it seems to me that we have here the initial pattern or stimulus that eventually resulted in the *American Mercury*. Since the appearance of *The Letters of H. L. Mencken* I find, on pages 255 to 260, that the London *Mercury* and the *Mercure de France* at much later dates were probably deciding factors. Nonetheless, Henry Holt's *Unpopular Review* could have started sowing the seed that later brought forth the *American Mercury* with its iconoclastic articles and stories calculated to jolt the members of the Establishment out of their easy chairs.

I pasted a few of Henry's letters in one of my Memory Books. This excerpt is typical of his wit and brevity: "My sincere congratulations on your marriage. This is the only noble state of man and I myself would marry tomorrow if I could find a widow whose former husband's clothes fitted me. Unluckily I am so fat and irregular of contour that such widows are rare." A year later, upon learning of the birth of my son, he wrote, "Dear Warren, Here's looking at the newcomer. May he avoid literature and devote himself, in the years to come, to supporting his father."

Charles Angoff

SOURCE: "The Inside View of Mencken's Memory," in *The New Republic,* v. 131, September 13, 1954, pp. 18-22.

[*In the following essay, Angoff recalls editorial and administrative policies during the Mencken years of the* American Mercury, *and assesses the influence of Mencken's literary criticism and political ideas.*]

I have before me, as I write this article, a letter from one of the most distinguished historians in the United States today, in which he says, "It is good to hear from you again. I didn't know that you are still connected with *The American Mercury,* which has certainly changed—and not for the better in my opinion." And only yesterday I spent an hour with the editor of one of the most intellectual, most respected and most successful periodicals in America—it has a circulation that runs well over a million a week—and the first thing he did was to hold up the very latest issue of *The Mercury* and say, "Shame on you." This editor prides himself upon the factual soundness of every article in his magazine. One of his celebrated boasts is, "We don't want writers on our magazine, we want reporters, men and women who respect facts, facts, and nothing but facts, men and women who make no statement without checking it first at least three times." And yet he, like the aforementioned historian, didn't know that I haven't been associated with *The Mercury* in any way since 1950.

But these, of course, are not the most disturbing things I hear and read about *The Mercury.* I am far more disturbed by the growing legends about the magazine and its editors, especially H. L. Mencken, most of them more colorful than true, and also by the strange and often unfair interpretations of the place of *The Mercury* and of its editors in American cultural and journalistic history. One such interpretation appeared in the *Saturday Review* a few weeks ago, written by the editor, Norman Cousins, under the title, "Our Times and *The Mercury.*" The piece was vigorously and plausibly written. There was, indeed, much truth in it, but it wasn't the whole truth or even a major part of it, not at least from the point of view of one who was associated with the old *Mercury* and with Mencken for about ten years, during a part of which both largely set the tone of the thinking of many college students and recent college graduates, when Mencken's every sneer and smile were tantamount to royal commands among those whom he called "the civilized minority."

It is true, unfortunately, that many of the articles in the old *Mercury* were, as Mr. Cousins points out, of a debunking character, and hence, inevitably, of inferior quality. Mr. Cousins refers to a shabby article on Abraham Lincoln, questioning the legends about his social origins and casting doubts upon his status as one of America's great historic figures. Also, there were many other such articles—even worse ones.

Re-reading old copies of Mencken's *Mercury* can be a very depressing experience. There was an article arguing that the public utilities were almost unanimously true public servants and that all those who dared to criticize them were "quacks, ignoramuses, and hired lackeys of the kept liberal press." There was another article in which the author proved to his own satisfaction that Walt Whitman was not a poet of even the second class but a word monger and a general phony. There was a third article presenting in quick fashion "The Case Against Large-Scale Farming," that has failed to make much sense to hundreds of thousands of farmers since it was first published in 1932. There was a fourth article insisting that all religion began "as a conditioned reflex." There was a fifth article making such merciless fun of "the stupid pedagogues" that an overly impressionable reader might have despaired of the whole future of our country. Indeed, there were a dozen articles loaded with carefully selected "facts" and proving even to "professors and other such inferior beings" that all public schools were "a fraud and delusion, a drain upon the public treasury, and a stench to the nostrils of all decent, well-informed and well-disposed men and women."

There were many dozens of articles sneering at democracy in general and at virtually all Senators and Congressmen and Governors and mayors except those that passed Mencken's acid test to be considered civilized, namely, whether they were for or against Prohibition. And Mencken's editorials and book reviews, to a large extent, were one long harangue against all the people and things that most Americans respect and hold dear: education, the home, marriage, love, religion, the United States Supreme Court, the Presidency, the radio, children as a class, all women who haven't the "decency to keep quiet when their menfolk talk, particularly when they talk about matters beyond the ken of the female mind," the whole science of psychology, the whole science of astronomy ("You can't tell me that there is any sense to this rubbish about stars being away—hundreds of thousands of miles away—that's pish posh"), all clergymen ("a man of the cloth is *ipso facto* a fraud and to be watched, especially when there are young girls or young boys about"), and so on *ad infinauseam*. And in his very last book review for the old *Mercury* (December, 1933), he saw nothing really to worry about in the rise of Hitler, and at the same time expressed some views that made many of his friends wonder where he stood on Nazism.

Mencken himself—and so powerfully did he impress his personality upon *The Mercury* that he and it were virtually one as long as he edited it—was a man of few basic ideas, and perhaps half of them were absurd, cheap, and simply not true. He believed that there were congenitally inferior and congenitally superior people, that the people of wealth "and substance" were largely the congenitally superior, that public school education was mostly a waste of money because the congenitally inferior children naturally could not be improved and the congenitally superior needed little education or such education as they needed could be supplied by their wealthy parents, that democ-

racy was the worst form of government and the tool of "all the poltroons and mob masters in this life," that benevolent despotism of the Frederick the Great variety was the only government that made sense, and so on.

His gift for literary criticism in the grand sense was very limited. He tended to like only those novelists who "showed up" Americans or other human beings, but chiefly Americans, as "boobs, dupes, and lackeys." Poetry was almost an unknown world to him. He claimed time and again that only "women, damaged men, perennial adolescents, and others who are ill at ease in the world of sound ideas write poetry." Painting, dancing and sculpture were, to him, "obviously third-rate arts."

He was against all political and economic reforms because reforming the "congenitally inferior" was foolish; genuine statecraft attempted to keep these "congenitally inferior" in their "proper place," which, of course, consisted in serving the "congenitally superior." America was the most benighted land in creation, or, to use one of his phrases, "America is the backside of the universe."

Finally, despite all his praise of "genuine scholarship," he himself was not much of a scholar. *The American Language* makes entertaining reading, but philologists, in the privacy of their libraries, have smiled at it. One of them, an eminent lexicographer, has called *The American Language* "an elephantine newspaper feature story." This is probably too cruel a characterization, but there is truth in it. There can be little doubt, however, that Mencken's *Notes on Democracy, Treatise on the Gods* and *Treatise on Right and Wrong,* are not much better than journalistic quickies.

And yet, despite these criticisms—and I have deliberately refrained from qualifying them, as I easily could have done, in order to forestall any charge that I am being too kind to my old teacher and friend—it is a mistake to undervalue Mencken and *The Mercury.* As a thinker Mencken probably had only a temporary vogue, for his fund of knowledge was limited and his ideas, as I have said, were few and largely dubious. But as a journalist, his influence was immense. Indeed, he was one of the greatest editors in all our history.

Of course, there was considerable froth in the pages of *The Mercury.* The Americana department was all froth, and nobody realized it better than Mencken himself. There was also excitement for sheer excitement's sake. For example, the aforementioned article on Whitman, which was the subject of heated controversy in the office, finally went in, though Mencken himself eventually admitted that the author was overstating his case, simply because, as Mencken said, "Oh, hell, Angoff, you may be right, and I guess I can't answer all that goddamn Harvard learning of yours, but I think we ought to print the piece if only to get the professors sore. For years they said Whitman was a bum, now they say he's an angel. Let's keep them hopping and squirming." And he wrote some of those dreadfully unfair things about Woodrow Wilson and William Jennings Bryan and Stuart P. Sherman and Henry Van Dyke, not because he believed every word he put down but also to "stir up the animals."

Sometimes his conscience would bother him, as when, in reviewing Sherman's posthumous book, he said some very nice things about him, taking back a large part of the abuse he had heaped upon him while he was alive. When I asked him why he did this he turned his face away and said, "It's the Christian in me, I guess. That baptismal water they poured over me when I was a boy, and against my wish, is powerful stuff. But really, there were some good things in Sherman, there really were."

Sometimes, when I would get his manuscript for the Editorial or the Library departments, I would cut out the passages that seemed in especially bad taste to me, without telling him. I imagined he knew what I had done, but he never reprimanded me, except once, when he had called somebody an "Episcopalian *litvak*," and I had cut it because I thought in that particular instance he was hitting below the belt. "Well, Angoff," he said, "so you cut out 'Episcopalian *litvak*.' I wish you hadn't. I'm fond of that phrase. Actually, in all honesty, it's not my own. I went to a *briss* [festival of circumcision] the other day, and the rabbi used that phrase in describing some mutual friend, a married man, who was carrying on with a *shikse* [Gentile girl]. If they had taught you how to drink like a man at Harvard, you would have had enough sense to let that phrase stand."

This sort of high-jinx was probably a bit adolescent, but that very fact to a considerable extent contradicts Mr. Cousin's remark that "the pulse-beat of historical America failed to come through in *The Mercury*." What is the pulsebeat of America? Of course, it is many varied things, but I believe that one of its dominant characteristics is high-jinx, sheer excitement, wild exaggeration, grand apostrophizing, the organ roll in prose, the "yawping from the housetops" in poetry. It is to be found in Melville and in Mark Twain and in Walt Whitman and in Thomas Hart Benton and in Charles Ives and in Thomas Wolfe and even in the fantastic debates and deliberations of Congress and the various state legislatures and the city councils. Mencken and his *Mercury* were anything but cold. They were always in a state of frenzy—and this frenzy was generally the frenzy of love, love of America and of its history and traditions, people and customs, heroes and rogues, saints and sinners and clowns . . . the American plains and mountains and rivers and cities and villages, and glories and aberrations, and dreams and hopes and regrets and miseries and . . . all that is America.

In fact, *The Mercury* printed more Americana than all the other so-called quality magazines put together. It was *The Mercury* that brought the whole Paul Bunyan folk-lore before literate America; before that it was known chiefly to folk-lore specialists. It was *The Mercury* that for years printed at least two articles in every issue on American history—and among the men who wrote those articles,

incidentally, were William E. Dodd, Charles A. Beard, and Howard Odum. There were articles on life on the plains of Iowa and Montana and Nebraska, American horses and coyotes, old-time preachers and modern radio "spiritual counsellors"; there were articles on virtually every hero and rogue of more than local interest . . . on Daniel Boone and James Audubon and Bishop Asbury and Bishop Seabury and Samuel Adams and John Adams and Jim Corbett and Jim Jeffries and P. T. Barnum and, coming down to more recent times, Oswald Garrison Villard of *The Nation* and Roger Baldwin of the American Civil Liberties Union, and scores of others. *The Mercury* loved everything that was American, the good, the bad, and the in-between.

Despite all his diatribes against America, Mencken was an ardent patriot, and he infused *The Mercury* with his patriotism. That was the chief reason why he had so much contempt for the expatriates of the twenties and early thirties. He looked upon them as virtual traitors. "Only third raters go off to Paris and Nice and those other frog dumps," he said to me. "A real writer stays home and writes about his own people. Look at Red [Sinclair] Lewis. You'll never see him guzzling that French wine in Paris and diddling the French girls, who, by the way, are not the cuties they are cracked up to be. They're mostly ugly as sin. But, as I say, Red Lewis stays home and writes about Sauk Center and Zenith. I tell you, not a goddam line worth reading will come out of that whole gang on the Left Bank."

What Mencken actually accomplished was nothing less than a revolution in American journalism. Though he denounced America month in and month out, and especially "the democratic bilge that is called a political philosophy," he democratized quality journalism. He brought the kitchen and the hayloft and the living room and the circus tent and the skid row and the loggers' camp and the camp meeting tent and the barber shop and the railroad yard right into the august pages of a fifty-cent magazine. The intellectuals of the big cities were thrilled to read all about this America that only the newspapers had hitherto dealt with, and skimpily at that. It is true that *The Mercury* sometimes overpraised the writers of the aforementioned articles—Mencken was indulging in hyperbole when he called the Jim Tully of "Circus Parade" and "Shanty Irish" "the American Gorki"—but it is also true that the readers of Tully and Holbrook and James Stevens and Frank Dobie learned about an aspect of America that they could not have learned in *Harper's* or *The Atlantic* or *Scribner's* or *The Century* or *The Forum*. Those who knew this best of all were the editors of these magazines. And the fact is that *Harper's* and *Atlantic* and the other "quality magazines" were never the same again after *The Mercury* got going.

The Mercury also vitalized the political articles. In the other magazines in its class political articles generally were written by professors who wrote about Washington and state politics from above, and who took great pains to be objective and calm, both admirable virtues but of little value when not based upon intimate knowledge of the subjects they were writing about. When *The Mercury* wanted an article on President Coolidge—what type of person he was, what he dreamed about when alone, what he talked about to his wife, what he actually read, who his heroes were—it did not go to a professor of history at the University of Wyoming, one who had never been within a thousand miles of Washington. *The Mercury* went to Frank Kent, a Washington reporter of long experience (and the original TRB of the *New Republic*) who saw Coolidge week in and week out, watched him smile, heard him speak, heard him stammer, talked to Senators and Congressmen who expressed their frank opinions about Coolidge. The result was something new in the field of the political article: a truly well-informed, vigorously written analysis by a man who knew him and who had a point of view. The article, which appeared in August, 1924, holds up remarkably well, and is still probably the best brief appraisal of Coolidge that has so far appeared in print.

The profile, which has become so integral a part of *The New Yorker,* and by which it has been deservedly praised, was actually born in the offices of *The Mercury.* Mencken realized that so-called second-class men—men who seldom make the front pages of newspapers but do occasionally appear at the bottom of page 17—often make better material for articles than do so-called first-class men. And he also had the same kind of abiding interest in revealing trivia that Harold Ross had: he wanted to know the kind of flower Grover Whalen prefers to have in his lapel and why, what type of suspenders Gene Talmadge of Georgia likes and why, the kind of poetry Senator Borah used to write in high-school, what type of popular songs Charles Evans Hughes generally hums when by himself. . . . Thus *The Mercury* printed excellent profiles by Henry Pringle and Herbert Asbury and Stanley Walker and others.

Since Mencken was interested in medicine and chemistry, he insisted that *The Mercury* print at least one and preferably two scientific pieces in every issue. This was something quite new in quality journalism. What was even more new was the treatment that Mencken called for. He demanded accuracy and completeness, but he also demanded humanity and clarity. So that in time *The Mercury* department of The Arts and Sciences became a model for other magazines. Lee Foster Hartman, late editor of *Harper's Magazine,* was especially taken with this department. He once asked where Mencken got so many good ideas. I told Mencken, and he instructed me to tell Hartman that "prayer and whiskey and the Holy Ghost are my only guides in this vale of tears."

Mencken had no respect whatever for "names." His principle was, "when a man wins the right to say what he pleases, he generally has very little to say, and he certainly has nothing worth printing." He found special delight in printing whole issues of *The Mercury* without a single "name." He especially liked to print issues where the names on the Table of Contents were "foreign"—

Goldberg, Weissberg, Cautella, Krout, Halper. We once had an issue almost of this sort; near the bottom there was the name of Ralph Adams Cram, the celebrated Boston architect. Mencken looked and looked and then said to me, "How in hell did that Angoff-Saxon name get into decent society?"

Mencken was always eager to print authors for the first time, and to that end he carried on a huge correspondence with young men and women in all parts of the country in the hope that they would come through with a printable piece. He would send them long letters of advice on how to rewrite their articles, and he would suggest where they seek subjects. I was instructed to do the same. The young people were thrilled, and many of them did come through. What pleased them especially was that here was an editor who was not above corresponding with them, as was the case with the editors of some of the other "toney" magazines; here was a man who bubbled over with the same enthusiasms that possessed them, an editor who was truly desirous of printing good pieces about sheriffs and policemen and Governors and mayors and district leaders—and by good pieces Mencken did not mean stuffy pieces about "the socio-political implications of government on the lower levels." He meant honest, well-written, human pieces. No wonder he was called the managing editor of all the young hopeful writers all over the nation! There has been no one like him in this respect ever since he gave up *The Mercury* twenty years ago, and the life of all beginning writers has been so much the harder and so much the lonelier.

Mencken's respect for good writing and lively thinking amounted to a religious fervor. Frequently he would accept articles whose burden of ideas offended him, but he was so impressed by the writing or by the logic that he printed them nevertheless. The politics or "the religious aberration" of a writer didn't interest him; if his story or article or poem was good, he printed it—and then took the author out and argued with him about politics or religion. He printed chapters from Michael Gold's *Jews Without Money* though he detested Communism. "In politics Mike has the mind of a cat's behind," said Mencken, "but the man can write, at least he can write about the East Side of his mother." Mencken also printed sections from Emma Goldman's autobiography, though her anarchism seemed like "garbage" to him. And he once printed an article on Charles S. Peirce, perhaps the most original philosopher America has produced so far, though he looked upon most philosophers as "idiots and worse" and sneered at metaphysics and epistemology. "I'll be damned if I know why I am accepting this article," he said, "but there's something about Peirce that appeals to me, and the writing is very powerful. Don't tell any of my friends that I agreed to the publication of the piece."

Why, then, did Mencken's *Mercury* collapse? I haven't any sure answers. It could be, as Mr. Cousins says, that *The Mercury*'s politico-economic philosophy, such as it was, made no sense after the crash of 1929 and after the New Deal went into office. *The Mercury* scoffed at all "constructive ideas," and the times called for such ideas.

It may also be that *The Mercury* was becoming less *Mercuryish,* so to speak—Mencken was getting fed up with editing and wanted to devote more time to his books. As Mencken was getting less interested in magazine editing, he began to listen more and more to advice from others, and the magazine began to lose personality, began to be less and less Mencken's *Mercury* but a sort of raffle barrel, a variety store.

Perhaps the 50-cent price was too steep for a time when there were apple-vendors on every corner of Fifth Avenue. Perhaps . . . perhaps. . . . Nobody really knows why one magazine dies, and another keeps on hobbling along. Why did *The Bookman* die—and why does *The Atlantic Monthly* live on? Why did *The Dial* pass out—and why does *Harper's* continue? *The Atlantic* and *Harper's* deserve to live on, but weren't *The Dial* and *The Bookman* also worthy periodicals? Of course they were, and for a while they were superb, but they died, and I don't believe anybody really knows why.

But some magazines die and are forgotten. Others die and are never forgotten. I don't think *The Mercury,* will ever be forgotten. It was the mouth-piece of a whole era in American cultural history.

Despite all its faults, *The Mercury* was very much a part of its times, even of its century. It sold for fifty cents but anybody with twenty-five cents to spare could understand it and enjoy it, for *The Mercury* gloried in printing articles, stories and poems about all the people, so long as these articles were interesting. Through one side of his mouth Mencken prattled about the beauties of political aristocracy and of benevolent despotism, but through the other he would instruct me, "watch out especially for the manuscripts that come in, written in pencil, on butcher paper. The pearls of great price are to be found there, not in the fancy manuscripts, with pink and blue ribbons all about them. Read extra carefully all things, in prose or fiction, about the unknowns, the people who rub against you in the subway and on the street, the people you see as the train rushes along on the way to your lousy town, Boston. These people are worth all the politicians and all the preachers and all the moralists in Christendom. All art is about them and the still, small voice within them. They're all that matters."

Thus spoke the man who railed against the "booboisie." He was a man of contradictions and absurdities, and puerilities and even cheapness, but he was a great editor, and his *Mercury* was, all in all, a great magazine.

Fenwick Anderson

SOURCE: "Inadequate to Prevent the Present: The American Mercury at 50," in *Journalism Quarterly,* Summer, 1974, pp. 297-302.

[*In the following essay, Anderson assesses the influence of the* American Mercury *on the occasion of its fiftieth anniversary.*]

This year marks the 50th birthday of *The American Mercury,* one of the chief intellectual stimulants of the Roaring Twenties. From its founding in 1924 by H.L. Mencken and George Jean Nathan, the little green-backed monthly "debunked the idols and ridiculed the mores of middle-class America."[1] For admirers of Mencken and the magazine, however, it is a very unmerry birthday indeed, because *The Mercury* has been sinking into the quicksand of right-wing extremism for two decades.

By 1933, when Mencken departed, the magazine's iconoclasm was no longer palatable in the despair of the Great Depression. Publisher Alfred Knopf sold it in 1935 to Paul Palmer and Lawrence Spivak, later moderator of the radio-TV show "Meet the Press." They tried to make it a responsibly conservative journal, but financial problems soon forced them to imitate *Reader's Digest* in size and format. After Spivak purchased full control in 1939, it lost as much as $100,000 a year but was supported by his pioneering efforts in paperback book publishing.[2]

Millionaire banker Clendenin J. Ryan bought *The Mercury* in 1950, with William Bradford Huie as editor mixing sex, sensationalism and sophisticated conservatism. When Ryan pulled out in 1952 to escape mounting deficits, Huie—who said he was desperate enough to take money from Hitler or Stalin—found an angel of sorts in J. Russell Maguire. Maguire had amassed a fortune in wartime munitions production and Texas oil speculation, but the Securities and Exchange Commission had ended his career as a Wall Street broker for "flagrant violations" of the law, and he had unsavory connections with anti-Semitic groups.[3] Huie stayed on for several months, gambling that he could retain control of editorial policy, but failed and left at year's end.[4]

Shrillness soon increased with a series of articles on Communist penetration of American life by J.B. Matthews, a former fellow-traveler turned professional anti-Communist. Matthews' *modus operandi* was to claim that the reds had dangerously infiltrated a profession, to carefully document the leftist records of a few of its members, and then to let readers assume he had proven his premise. The first article asserted that Kremlin agents had so successfully infiltrated higher education that the nation would be better off if all colleges had been closed for the preceding 35 years. Educators accounted for about 30% of the fellow-travelers in the Communist-front apparatus, he wrote.[5]

Matthews could attack professors with impunity, but his article, "Reds and Our Churches," caused a national furor. It claimed that "The largest single group supporting the Communist apparatus in the United States today is composed of Protestant clergymen." In numbers of fellow-travelers, the clergy bested even educators by a 2-1 margin and, aside from the official Communist Party leadership, "the five top pro-Soviet propagandists in this country are all Protestant clergymen."[6]

The article was condemned by conservatives such as Virginia Sen. Harry Byrd, religious leaders and ultimately President Eisenhower. Senate Democrats on Joseph McCarthy's subcommittee investigating alleged subversion successfully pressured the senator to fire Matthews from his new job as executive staff director.[7]

The Mercury was relatively tame in 1954-55, though one issue lionized the "Powerhouse in Pecos," an enterprising young businessman named Billie Sol Estes, whose amazing career was traced from his first flock of sheep to his first million. His later implication in massive frauds involving grain storage and non-existent ammonia tanks demonstrated that the sheep were only the first ones fleeced. "If you want to succeed in this world, you just keep God's Commandments and fear no man," Estes explained, although "I got lots of friends, and friends are money in the bank." Accused of being too open-handed for loaning money to blacks and Mexican-Americans, he replied: "If we don't help these folks, the Communists will win them over with promises."[8]

If the magazine's content was quiet, its office was not. Late in 1955 there was a blowup at *The Mercury,* with editor John Clements and other editors or contributors, including Matthews, quitting in October. Most of them would say only that they disagreed with editorial policy, but a reporter who knew them said it was because they felt "that attempts were being made to introduce anti-Semitic material . . ."[9]

Perhaps they were right. Within little more than a year, the magazine was featuring G. (for George) Lincoln Rockwell, soon to lead the American Nazi Party until his assassination in 1967. Rockwell's first article said Marxist ideas had turned the descendants of Iceland's Vikings into "spoiled, alcohol-bemused, welfare-worshipping, security-loving, responsibility-shirking people . . ." Iceland had the ability to defend itself but lacked the will, and was headed for the junk heap of history. Despite the deteriorating situation, "the same healthy blood which is still coursing in young Icelandic veins *can* perform the spiritual and economic miracle which the country needs."[10]

Later Rockwell warned that the Marine Corps' fighting spirit and iron discipline were endangered by public opinion against brutalities in training. As long as the horrors of war threaten, he advised, "we must be prepared to participate *successfully* in these horrors." Criticism of brutality was part of a red plot to soften up Americans, because military training meant learning

> the art of killing to enforce the will of the nation . . . And when you practice the art of killing, somebody's likely to get hurt. If we're not willing to accept that risk like men, we don't deserve to survive any longer as a nation.[11]

In a similar vein, Harold Lord Varney predicted doom because consistent cowardice left no more room for maneuver: "America has reached the end of its tether . . . The next crisis threatens to be the last." Echoing Rockwell, he moaned that Americans lacked some inner steel in their character, which was doubly sad because they could have ruled the world:

> 1947 saw us standing upon a pinnacle from which we could have dictated terms to the world . . . and could have pulverized the cities and industries of any country, including Russia, which defied our will.[12]

When his prediction of doom was not vindicated quickly, Varney warned again that "the United States stands upon the very precipice edge of national disaster." Things were brighter from 1921-33, good years for the nation despite "some carping egghead voices"—such as H.L. Mencken.[13] (After a prolonged absence, Varney returned for a 1964 encore which sadly intoned: "The unhappy truth is that we are losing the Cold War . . . Unless we speedily change our course, we are certain to be surpassed in a few more years." Evidently the country was no longer on the precipice edge, but he argued that it ought to face the showdown as soon as possible.[14]

Anti-Semitism, which grew slowly and sporadically at first, increased in the late 1950s. One writer suggested that Communism was popular among Israelis because 20% of them backed leftist parties, and because the *kibbutz* was based on Marxist principles. This demonstrated that red influences were not flukes but "direct manifestations of the deeper and more lasting influence Communism exercises over the minds, hearts and aspirations of large groups of the Israeli people."[15]

Despite the magazine's pretense that it opposed only Zionists, Hilary Grey put the cards on the table with his statement that the U.N. Declaration of Human Rights "guarantees rights to the religious and racial minority responsible for communism . . ."[16] An anonymous series called "Termites of the Cross" denied that Jews were persecuted in Russia because "If this were true, Jews . . . would constitute the most hostile group of anti-Communists in the country—whereas almost the exact opposite is true."[17]

The general counsel for B'nai B'rith's Anti-Defamation League, Arnold Forster, charged that the magazine had betrayed its proud heritage. "It has become the single most important anti-Semitic publication in the United States," he said. Because of such accusations, three printers refused to produce it, and *Mercury* wholesalers dropped in 1960 from more than 600 to fewer than 200.[18]

The magazine denied everything, then carried on with more of the same. Maguire editorially decried the tyranny planned by "Zionist egocentric maniacs possessed of an insatiable and ruthless lust to rule or ruin all mankind." Miscegenation was also involved in the plot, so Maguire thundered that "Mongrelized, bestialized human dogs beget only miserable, slinking human curs."[19] One of many anonymous fillers revealed that "Chronic flouride poisoning not only blunts the intellect, *but also helps to limit population by causing chemical castration—and finally* cancer!"[20] Another announced, with no further explanation, that "Black magic is being used on the people of this country without their knowledge."[21]

The conspiracy was so pervasive that it took in even Ernest Hemingway's *The Old Man and the Sea* and the Salk polio vaccine. A review of the film version of Hemingway's book explained that "the huge fish which the old man cannot control is the capitalist system" and that "The sharks are obviously a symbol of the invincibility of the Communist underground procedures."[22] Another article referred to the Salk serum as "monkey juice" and asserted that the shots "are being used to weaken and enslave the people" by causing epidemics.[23]

Maguire said farewell in January 1961, telling readers that the magazine was now owned by a patriotic organization, The Defenders of the Christian Faith, Inc., which would print *The Mercury* in its own plant.[24] Gwynne W. Davidson, Defenders president and new board chairman, promised that the same policies and "vigorous editorial thrust" would remain in force.[25] Editorial offices, which had been in New York for more than 35 years, were moved to Oklahoma City. Nobody bothered to mention that the magazine had dropped from 164 to 132 pages since the last issue of 1960.

The promise of editorial vigor was fulfilled by Maj. George R. Jordan who asserted that the Soviets had established a hospital in Ethiopia to train Russian-speaking witch doctors. Trainees were already "carrying the Kremlin's orders to the firesides of all the tribes."[26] Longtime rightist Kenneth Goff, meanwhile, exulted that the death of United Nations Secretary-General Dag Hammarskjold in a Congo airplane crash had saved America from world government. Goff said it seemed "that the very hand of God smashed the plane into the hillsides, proving once again that He is still ruler of the universe and holds the fate of man in His hands."[27] Despite such extremism, the general level of vituperation decreased under Davidson's editorship in 1961-62, and anti-Semitism ceased to be a staple feature.

After the April number, financial problems hampered production in 1962, and only three more issues were printed. In a frank editorial, Davidson admitted the difficulties made obvious by the combined summer issue, which was only half the usual thickness. Nevertheless, many publications were in trouble and *The Mercury* considered its difficulties serious but not fatal.[28] *The Mercury* and the Defenders parted at year's end, however.

The magazine made one more attempt at monthly publication in 1963 under the ownership of The Legion for the Survival of Freedom, Inc., and the editorship of broadcaster Marcia Matthews, who contributed such novel terms as "commuliberal" and "commUNism." But she died after the April issue, and only two more were printed the rest of the year, though all were back up to 96 pages. The magazine's address was listed as a post office box in McAllen, Texas.

Her husband, Jason Matthews, became managing editor and in the October issue announced the impending death of the Republican Party. He was sure that the movement to draft Senator Barry Goldwater would fail because patriots had been unable to nominate a candidate in 30 years. His own credentials as an expert were that he once assisted President Hoover, advising him to renounce Prohibition in 1932:

> Our indices had shown that if both parties had in their National platforms a promise of Repeal, the Republicans would win by an overwhelming majority in spite of the depression . . . [29]

The following September he predicted Republican victory in spite of his earlier prediction that Goldwater could not be nominated. Matthews foresaw a Goldwater landslide of 433 electoral votes and opinion polls to the contrary meant nothing because it was the first time since 1932 that "the people have had an opportunity to vote for their own survival." *The Mercury* touted the analysis as that of a man who was right in 1936 when *The Literary Digest* forecast victory for Alf Landon.[30] Matthews died shortly after the electoral debacle.

During 1964 *The Mercury* settled into its present quarterly publication schedule. Although the first issue was 96 pages, the second and third were only eight oversized pages (8 1/2" x 11") each, and the final issue 16. Military Editor Gen. Edwin A. Walker, who had accused the Kennedy administration of muzzling the military, assumed editorship with the December issue, which returned to the familiar digest size.

In an election post-mortem, Walker charged that "Not Johnson but the Communist Party acquired a 42-million vote mandate . . ." which raised the question whether the administration and voters would accept red leadership. His answer was in the affirmative, probably because of the infiltration of "cryptos" and "ism-mystics."[31]

The first three issues of 1965 were written almost solely by Walker, sometimes using transparent aliases. Possibly because he was a target of Lee Harvey Oswald, Walker returned often to the subject of President Kennedy's assassination, declaring that "If one-half the homes in the United States had been flying the U.S. Flag . . . on Nov. 22, 1963, your president would not have been killed. No one would have dared."[32] Later, he wrote that Lyndon Johnson's supporters in 1964 had voted "with the communists and the criminals involved in the assassination . . ."[33]

With the final issue of the year, Walker relinquished the editorship, and the headquarters shifted to Houston. As *The Mercury* acquired a board of contributors to replace personal control, it slowly grew back to 68 pages and forged an alliance with an intelligence newsletter, *The Washington Observer*. (The newsletter dispenses four pages of inside political gossip on a biweekly basis.) *Mercury* offices soon were moved again to Torrance, Calif., so it could "help to strengthen the forces of sanity" there.[34]

Yet in 1967 it seemed more eager to strengthen the forces of racism. One article purporting to ask "What Do We

Owe the Negroes?" answered that they "enjoyed a slavery unparalleled in history for mildness and humanity"
and later were freed by the magnanimous white man at
little cost to themselves. Blacks had failed miserably to
take advantage of their opportunities, which suggested
that "perhaps the White man is at fault for making the
road too easy for the emancipated Negro."[35] Another
writer demonstrated his white superiority by asserting
that "every intelligence test [*sic*] . . . have proven conclusively that Negroes are intellectually inferior."[36] *The
Mercury* concurred. "It is a simple fact that Negroes have
never, at any time or place in the entire history of the
world, created or maintained a culture above that of the
stone age," it declared.[37]

As for the Vietnamese, one writer advocated bombing
them back to the Stone Age. He advised America "to
overwhelm the enemy with irresistible force, to smash
and crush and destroy until the last quiver of resistance is
wiped out."[38] An editorial said the American peace movement was financed by Zionists and "must be suppressed—by force if necessary . . ." Or as *The Mercury*
summed up, "PUT THE TRAITORS IN JAIL!"[39]

While supporting the presidential campaign of George
Wallace in 1968, the magazine perceived rampant anarchy. Congressman James B. Utt believed anarchy had
already gone so far that "the only salvation may be a
military dictatorship." Of course, he defined anarchy
rather broadly, describing the Poor People's March on
Washington that summer as "an invasion intended to
overthrow the government by force and violence."[40]

Frank Capell, chiefly known for libeling former Sen.
Thomas Kuchel as a homosexual, discovered anarchy at
the Democratic National Convention in Chicago. He informed readers that Vaseline for protection against tear
gas "does not grow by the wayside" and reviled the dem-
onstrators' "bizarre (and dangerous and/or disgusting)
weapons." He concluded that "We seem to have conspiracy all over the place here."[41]

As a panacea for growing anarchy, *The Mercury* offered
the fascist rhetoric of the National Youth Alliance. Dennis C. McMahon, Alliance vice-president, issued a battle
cry for the "annihilation of the campus red front" because, at last, there was "an organization with determination to liquidate the enemies of the American people . .
." One of the Alliance's major goals was driving mari-
juana dealers off the campus with tar and feathers, but
that would be only the beginning. Soon "the Left will be
forced to cower in the sewers underground as they hear
the marching steps of the NYA above them."[42]

Oddly enough, *The Mercury* soon reprinted an article which
incidentally referred to McMahon as a "psychopathic-liar"
and to NYA President John Acord, who had contributed an
adulatory piece on Wallace, as an "arch conman."[43]

Whatever *The Mercury* thought of McMahon, it concurred with his principles. Explaining that all civilization

depends on violence, it argued that "Violence that is used
to maintain law and order . . . is a positive good." Furthermore, if government failed to use enough violence,
"the people have the right and obligation to enforce the
law themselves!"[44] After all, as Revilo Oliver put it, since
the Constitution was dead the niceties no longer counted.
Evidently it was a poor Constitution anyway since it was
"inadequate to prevent the present."[45]

Similarly, Austin App applauded ignoring the niceties
abroad, terming the My Lai massacre "this execution of
109 probable Vietcong accomplices." When civilians
cooperated with an uncivilized enemy which wore no
uniforms, "harsh countermeasures are not only necessary
but justified." Thus until liberals demanded trials for
atrocities by the other side, "the call for trials against the
U.S. boys who destroyed My Lai is essentially nothing
but pro-Communist progaganda."[46]

Meanwhile, *The Mercury* upheld the high standards of
Western culture with a poem by an "Unrepentant
Westerner":

> This doctrine of 'Equality'
> Is just a tool of treason,
> Let's heed the voice of History:
> Adhere to Race and Reason! . . .
>
> . . . . .
>
> The Spirit of the Age decrees
> Oppose these evil forces!
> Our Heritage demands that we
> Use all of our resources![47]

Somewhat belatedly, *The Mercury* decided that Maguire
had failed to use all his resources. It revealed that his
daughter Marina had died in a Tulare, Calif., jail cell
following an overdose of methadone. She arrived at this
fate even though she had inherited $20 million. Despite
the good Maguire did through *The Mercury,* it said, he
had supported it with tax-deductible advertising charged
off to his other businesses. The magazine's judgment of
its former owner was:

> What a shame that Russell Maguire did not spend
> his twenty million dollars in more direct action—
> action that he couldn't charge off against profits.
> If he had, his daughter might be alive today.[48]

Former owner Spivak's judgment of the magazine was
equally harsh: "It's become a disgraceful sheet. Instead
of selling out in 1950, I'm sorry I didn't bury it. I would
rather have done that than see it dragged in the mud."[49]
Instead of being buried, *The Mercury* has simply sunk
deeper in the mire and been forgotten by all but roughly
10,000 subscribers. For a magazine which once had influence on public opinion far exceeding its circulation,
early senility may be a fate less merciful than death.

[1] Theodore Peterson, *Magazines in the 20th Century*
(Urbana: University of Illinois Press, 1964), p. 431.

2 Frank Luther Mott, *A History of American Magazines,* Vol. V (Cambridge: Harvard University Press, 1968), pp. 18-20, 22-4.

3 "Trouble for the *Mercury,*" *Time,* Dec. 8, 1952, p. 42.

4 "Number Three for *Mercury,*" *Time,* Dec. 15, 1952, p. 59.

5 J.B. Matthews, "Communism and the Colleges," *The American Mercury* (hereafter abbreviated *AM*), May 1953, pp. 111-12, 120.

6 Matthews, "Reds and Our Churches," *AM,* July 1953 pp. 3, 7.

7 "Joe Stubs Toe," *Newsweek,* July 20, 1953, pp. 29-30 and "Joe's Bloody Nose," *Time,* July 20, 1953, p. 15.

8 Karl Detzer, "Powerhouse in Pecos," *AM,* October 1955, p. 50.

9 "Blowup at *The Mercury,*" *Time,* Oct. 3, 1955, p. 69.

10 G. Lincoln Rockwell, "No Wonder Iceland Hates Us!," *AM,* January 1957, pp. 7-9, 13.

11 Rockwell, "Who Wants Panty-Waist Marines?," *AM,* April 1957, pp. 119, 122.

12 Harold Lord Varney, "Our March to Catastrophe," *AM,* February 1957, pp. 29-30, 33.

13 Varney, "Our Feeble Foreign Policy," *AM,* December 1958, pp. 5-6.

14 Varney, "Why We Retreat in the Cold War," *AM,* January 1964, p. 77.

15 Fayez A. Sayegh, "Communism in Israel," *AM,* March 1958, pp. 50-1.

16 Hilary Grey, "U.N.—The New Cominform," *AM,* July 1959, p. 19.

17 "Termites of the Cross," *AM,* October 1959, p. 5.

18 "Mencken's *Mercury* Now," *Newsweek,* March 14, 1960, p. 92.

19 Russell Maguire, "You Too May Soon Be a Slave!," *AM,* February 1960, pp. 26-7.

20 "Do You Know?," *AM,* December 1959, p. 118.

21 "Do You Know?," *AM,* February 1960, p. 60.

22 "How We Swallowed 'The Old Man and the Sea'," *AM,* August 1959, pp. 75-6.

23 Barbara Hansen, "Salk-Serum Saddled Americans Still Get Polio—in Epidemics," *AM,* January 1960, pp. 91-2.

24 Maguire, "*Mercury* Moves Forward," *AM,* January 1961, p. 64.

25 Gwynne W. Davidson, "To Bear Witness to the Truth," *AM,* January 1961, p. 65.

26 George R. Jordan, "African Witches' Brew Concocted in Moscow," *AM,* February 1961, p. 19.

27 Kenneth Goff, "Setback in the U.N.," *AM,* December 1961, pp. 105-6.

28 Davidson, "Optimism Prevails at *Mercury* Headquarters," *AM,* Summer 1962, p. 7.

29 Jason Matthews, "Will Any Republican Ever Again Be President?," *AM,* October 1963, pp. 40, 44.

30 Matthews, "The Rigged Polls and the Coming Election of Barry Goldwater," *AM,* Summer-September 1964, p. 6.

31 Edwin A. Walker, "The November Mandate—1964," *AM,* Fall-December 1964, p. 7.

32 Walker, "The U.S. Flag," *AM,* Winter 1965, p. 14.

33 Walker, "A Letter to a Republican and a Democrat," *AM,* Summer 1965, p. 16.

34 "Great Leap Westward," *AM,* Winter 1966, p. 5.

35 Robert E. Kuttner, "What Do We Owe the Negroes?," *AM,* Spring 1967, pp. 8-9.

36 Raymond F. Treadwell, "Suppressed Document Rises to Haunt Politicians," *AM,* Spring 1967, p. 14.

37 "Fashion of the Future," *AM,* Fall 1967, p. 3.

38 Richard W. Edmonds, "Soldiers' Lives for Votes," *AM,* Summer 1967, p. 14.

39 "Is Dissent Treason?," *AM,* Winter 1967, p. 4.

40 James B. Utt, "Anarchy—U.S.A." *AM,* Fall 1968, pp. 11-12.

41 Frank Capell, "Conspiracy in Chicago," *AM,* Winter 1968, pp. 57-60.

42 Dennis C. McMahon, "The National Youth Alliance," *AM,* Spring 1969, pp. 61-3.

43 C.B. Baker, "James J. Kilpatrick—Conservative Quisling," *AM,* Fall 1969, pp. 55-6.

44 "Freedom and Violence," *AM,* Summer 1969, p. 3.

[45] Revilo Oliver, "After Fifty Years," *AM,* Fall 1969, p. 19. Oliver won notoriety in 1964 by suggesting that President Kennedy was killed because he failed to advance the Communist cause fast enough.

[46] Austin J. App, "My Lai, Dresden and War-Crimes Trials," *AM,* Spring 1970, pp. 12-13.

[47] "Oppose These Evil Forces!," *AM,* Spring 1970, p. 56.

[48] Ian Bruce MacLeod, "Maguire's Folly," *AM,* Fall 1971. p. 13.

[49] Mencken's *Mercury* Now," *Newsweek,* March 14, 1960. p. 92. Anti-Semitic mud remains an integral part of the magazine. In the Summer 1973 issue, for example, one article declared that "the world would be a far better place to live if Germany had won—*even if it had meant the defeat of American arms!*" because Hitler would have saved the white race from liberalism, juvenile delinquency and integration. Yet the magazine smugly editorialized in its 50th anniversary issue (Spring 1974) that if

Mencken returned, he would approve of its editorial policies. An accompanying article by Joseph P. Kamp, though marred by factual errors and fulsome obeisance to the current editor, provided inside explanations for events discussed here. He claimed the 1952 staff shakeup was the work of an ADI *agent provocateur.*

Further Reading

Secondary Sources

Chielens, Edward E. "The *American Mercury*" in his *The Literary Journal in America, 1900-1950: A Guide to Information Sources,* pp. 39-43. Detroit: Gale Research, 1977.

    Annotated bibliography of writings about the *American Mercury.*

Fear in Literature

INTRODUCTION

The subject of fear, whether in the form of neurotic anxiety or supernatural terror, is among the most prevalent in literature. A common element in the motivation of character and a dominant motif in contemporary fiction, the psychological and aesthetic qualities of fear have demanded the attention of literary critics since classical antiquity. Generally, critics see the specifics of literary fear both as a function of historical time and as a constant feature aroused by the human dread of the unknown or unknowable. The latter sort of fear has since been largely identified with the term *Gothic,* which was culled from the eighteenth-century vogue of the romantic novel of terror in a medieval setting. Popularized by such writers as Ann Radcliffe and Matthew "Monk" Lewis, the Gothic novel gave way to the modern genre of horror fiction with its ubiquitous treatment of supernatural forces that conspire to victimize and destroy human beings. Writers in this vein exploit what have become stock effects—the physical isolation of the protagonist, suspense and misdirection, and the introduction of a shadowy "other" or mysterious evil—to excite readers. A parallel line of development in the literature of fear is illustrated by the work of Edgar Allan Poe, in which psychological aberration coupled with an evocation of the uncanny and the macabre play the primary roles in creating an atmosphere of terror.

The sensationalism of Gothic horror fiction does not account for the totality of that which is fear-inducing in literature. Critics observe in the modern period a literature of anxiety that draws its impetus from the cultural moment, such as the concrete fears of wartime dramatized in Stephen Crane's *The Red Badge of Courage* or in Jean-Paul Sartre's "Le mur" ("The Wall"). Additionally, neurotic fears that may exist as part of the ordinary psychological make-up of everyone in many ways characterize the literature of the modern era. This tendency is perhaps no more clearly expressed than in the novels and short stories of Franz Kakfa, works that dramatize an all-consuming anxiety created by the emotional isolation of a bureaucratic age.

OVERVIEWS

André de Lorde

SOURCE: "Fear in Literature," in *New York Literary Forum,* 1980, pp. 247-51.

[*In the following essay which was originally published in* La Revue Mondiale *in 1927, de Lorde broadly surveys fear in literature from the Gothic novels of the eighteenth century to dystopian visions in science fiction of the early twentieth century.*]

An entire literature of Fear exists.

Why should this be astonishing? Each one of us has in his innermost being a secret longing for violent emotions. At all times, in all parts of the globe, horror shows have drawn large audiences. The huge amphitheaters in Rome were too small to hold the citizens eager to see the gladiators slaughter one another and the Christians thrown to the lions. If the Inquisition had made public its interrogations conducted on the rack, they would have had to turn people away. To witness the hideous torture of Damiens, the crowd surged towards the square as though to holiday festivities.

"Bah!" you will say, "Times have changed; in our days, the progress of civilization has made such barbarous pastimes unthinkable." True enough. Still, set men, bulls, and horses at one another in an arena, and excited spectators will shriek with joy; at break of day guillotine some human wreck half-dead with fright, and there won't be enough soldiers, their bayonets fixed, to hold back the pushing throng of those who want to *see.* And don't those tender hearts, who are revolted by such spectacles, seek out at fairs the most violent and horrific "attractions"? Don't they derive acute pleasure at the circus or music hall from watching the most dangerous feats? If I perspire with anxiety as I follow the movements of the dancer along the tightrope, if my breathing stops with the music when this young person in pink tights is about to attempt what she herself calls *the death leap,* it is because I actually imagine an atrocious death for her, her battered corpse bloodying the sand in the ring. No doubt, if I were sure that the accident was going to happen, I would be the first to rush forward to prevent it; but if, on the other hand, I was certain that it would not happen, I would lose interest in the show. A most curious compromise on the part of our conscience is at work here. If my sensibility steps forth to reproach me for the odious satisfaction that I find in thus anticipating a calamity, I immediately assuage these scruples by involving the law of probabilities. There is only one chance in a thousand that the accident will happen precisely today; but as soon as this reassuring thought runs the risk of dulling my pleasure, I revive it again by calling up in my mind's eye the image of the fall, despite what seems possible. I would not be as ferocious as that Englishman who went to every show of a wild animal act in order to be present when the lion tamer would get eaten; but, by going once quite by chance, I

81

have a slight hope, without admitting it to myself, that today will be the day, more or less in the same way that I dream—without daring to believe it—that my lottery ticket will be the winning one. . . .

Fear has always existed, and each century has stamped upon its literature the mark of the fears that tormented it, but the primitive caveman and the contemporary businessman have not shuddered for the same reasons. The sources of fear have varied, but not fear itself, which is eternal and immutable. . . .

Feeble as they are, the Gothic novels had a real vogue; not only were Anne Radcliffe and Monk Lewis imitated by a host of minor writers, they also had the honor of inspiring two of England's greatest authors, Walter Scott and Lord Byron, to write many a picturesque descriptive passage. In France, *The Monk* and *The Mysteries of Udolpho,* translated in 1797, were read, appreciated, and plagiarized; the novelists, from Ducray-Duminil to Eugène Sue, went to them for stirring subjects for many, many years, and the playwrights along the Boulevard of Crime brought to the stage the principal episodes of these works.

As early as 1799, Guilbert de Pixérécourt, the father of melodrama, stages at the Ambigu his *Château des Apennins,* borrowed from Anne Radcliffe's novel, but where the horror is considerably attenuated. This astute dramatist knew how to turn a famous novel to good profit in the theater; he neglected no "effect" capable of moving or astounding the spectators: *Victor, ou l'enfant de la forêt, l'Homme à trois visages, Le Monastère abandonné,* quite like *Le Château des Apennins,* are full of ingenious situations. In one of his plays, *Christophe Colomb, ou la découverte du Nouveau Monde* (1814), whose action in part unfolds in the Antilles, Pixérécourt, on the look-out for novelties, was even convinced that he should, "for the sake of greater verisimilitude," have his savages speak the language of the Antilles taken from Father Breton's Caribbean dictionary. The results are not without savor, as witness this piece of dialogue between King Oranko and his subject Kavaka:

> ORANKO. Cati louma.
>
> KAVAKA. Amouliaca azackia Kereber *(Oranko hestitates).*
>
> ORANKO. Inolaki . . . Chicalama . . .
>
> KAVAKA. Hava a moutou Koulé Ouékelli.
>
> ORANKO. Areskoui, azakia, kavaïti avou.
>
> ALL. Anakilika!
>
> ORANKO. Ouallou hougousou!

And so it goes on and on . . . for whole scenes the actors carry on the dialogue in Caribbean. . . .

The true genius of fear is, in actual fact, incarnated in Edgar Poe, and his work brings together all the seeds of terror that can blossom in the human soul: physical horrors, moral anxieties, painful apprehensions of the other world and even this sensation previously unrecorded in literature, *the fear of being afraid,* that tortures the unfortunate Roderick Usher. The dominant trait of this exceptional talent is the conjunction of unbridled imagination and imperturbable logic, the fusion of nightmare and truth. In the midst of his most hallucinatory dreams, Poe always keeps one foot firmly planted in reality. In his work, macabre fantasy and meticulous precision conducive to verisimilitude become intertwined, overlap, and grow inseparable. There results from this union an impression of dread that no one else, not even Dante, has ever produced. As the reader enters into contact with Poe, a secret terror softly steals and glides into his soul, then takes possession of him, clasps him tightly, makes him shudder. The strongest nerves can offer no resistance; willy-nilly, we follow Poe into a hell, to which his art has been able to lend a semblance of life. First he rocks us on the waves of a raging sea, and then he suspends us on the edge of a bottomless abyss; vertigo seizes us, anguish makes our throat contract. . . . "Panic-stricken" genius is the phrase that Barbey d'Aurevilly has used in speaking of Poe: no epithet could be more fitting. . . .

Poe's literary influence has been immense. Strangely enough, it was felt in France before showing any signs in his own native country. In the second half of the nineteenth century, while Charles Nodier, Gérard de Nerval, Théophile Gautier, and Erckmann-Chatrian continue the Hoffmann tradition and write fantastic rather than terrifying works, we see the example of the American master inspire numerous disciples. . . .

His influence can be seen on many writers, including some of the greatest: above all on Baudelaire, who translated almost all of Poe and who is indelibly marked by his work; there are many poems in *Les Fleurs du mal* where we catch reminiscences of Edgar Poe, and it can be asserted that without him, Baudelaire would not have realized all his capabilities.

Poe's mark is no less visible on Barbey d'Aurevilly and Villiers de l'Isle-Adam. Both read Poe (Barbey has even devoted some magnificent pages to him), both have been subject to his authority; but *Les Diaboliques* and the *Contes cruels* are very far removed from Poe's *Tales of the Grotesque and Arabesque.* That is because Barbey and especially Villiers are unrepentant romantics. They can only conceive fear with a stately train of situations and antitheses in the style of Victor Hugo; the veiled figures, the funeral processions, the cloistered leper in Villiers's *Duke of Portland* are scarcely more believable than the coffins in Hugo's *Lucrèce Borgia* or the drowned bodies in Dumas père's *Tour de Nesle.* All of this literary satanism is hardly frightening; it has a musty smell of old bric-a-brac and the property room.

Much more realistic in their sober precision, Mérimée's novellas achieve effects of terror that strike you with unexpected rapidity like a gypsy girl's dagger. *Colomba, Lokis,* and *La Vénus d'Ille* surpass by far in emotional intensity the best of the *Contes cruels.* The true spiritual heir of Edgar Poe is uncontestably Marcel Schwob—with the difference that separates talent from genius. Strange affinities exist between these two spirits: the same sarcastic and terrifying imagination is characteristic of each of them; they both possess the same "meditative faculty" which Poe bestows upon his Egaeus in the tale "Berenice." The painful anxiety of the one, and the Jewish sensibility of the other, reach by different routes the same goal. There is in Schwob's *Sur les dents* a ferocious irony that closely connects this tale to Poe's "Loss of Breath" or "The Man Who Was Used Up," and *L'Homme voilé* equals in phlegmatic horror *"The Cask of Amontillado"*. . . .

Writers could not simply go on imitating Poe indefinitely, still less could they outdo him. They were obliged to renew the genre. This is what has been attempted by the creators of the *scientific-marvelous,* a rich source of terror and delight. The progress of the sciences, the quasi-fabulous discoveries of the past thirty years, and the publicity given to research accomplished by inventors have contributed to arousing our minds to new objects of curiosity. Science has gone from the laboratory to the novel.

Jules Verne confined himself to considering as accomplished certain discoveries that already exist to all intents and purposes. Wells, Rosny the elder, and Maurice Renard go much further still: they are not concerned with what *will be,* but with what *could be,* and, boldly wielding the hypothesis, they venture out into the vast expanses of the unknown. Here, it should be observed, there is no question of the supernatural, which for science does not exist. At most, they propose for our scrutiny facts susceptible of a dual interpretation, the one miraculous, the other rational (Wells's *Pollock and the Porroh Man* and Maurice Renard's *Le Singe);* the true domain of these storytellers remains the uncertain and the not yet known. That is how Wells imagines perilous journeys through time, that is how Rosny supposes the intrusion onto our planet of one of those invisible worlds that fill the emptiness of infinite space, that is how Maurice Renard makes us perceive the diabolical experiments conducted by the magician Lerne who understands human cross-breeding as well as Dr. Alexis Carrel. Pure imagination? No, certainly, not, since such tales offer us, as applied to the study of imaginary phenomena or of monsters, the most rigorous methods of investigation. We find in Wells the study pursued with a perfect logic—except in one point—of what would happen *if* a man succeeded in making himself invisible by the discoloration of his blood. Thus these authors create new subjects of terror, which are addressed less to the nerves than to the understanding and which answer to our desire for the truth while at the same time giving sustenance to the need for shudders which is a part of our nature.

Douglas Fowler

SOURCE: "The Pleasures of Terror," in *Extrapolation,* Vol. 28, No. 1, Spring, 1987, pp. 75-86.

[*In the following essay, Fowler traces aesthetic conditions for the enjoyment of horror in literature and film, including an undisclosed source of terror, the physical confinement of the protagonist, and reader/viewer identification with a protagonist who is aware of the source of terror but cannot convince others within the story.*]

The importance of humanity's own cruelty and destructive impulses in the experience of literature and film has never been given anything like the attention it deserves, and the very vocabulary needed to begin discussing the subject—*sadism, masochism, suicide*—is still contaminated with hospital odors and those connotations of criminal deviation few are likely to assign themselves casually. And yet terror, violence, irrevocable loss, and catastrophic suffering are some of the most obvious properties of literature, and it seems long past the time when a smack of dainty parlor radicalism should still cling to a claim that art is sometimes a dream state wherein readers can act out fantasies of destruction and self-immolation they cannot allow themselves to act out in the real world. The business of artists is not really to salvage souls or mend the world, but to create, in any way they can, a world of intensity in which for privileged moments boredom can be forgotten. The great omission of all fantastic narrative is almost, by definition, the reality that it leaves behind, the one readers escape. And it is also too easily forgotten that this moment must be *virtually* inconsequential—without consequence. *Inside* the artistic experience, readers participate but should not have to pay. Literary theorists have too quickly turned away from the large and obvious dissimilarities between the fantastic world and the real one. Fantastic art offers a moment of incandescent intensity that makes use of commonplace realities solely as a disguise; nothing could be less suitable as a design for living or as a vehicle for comment on life.

Kingsley Amis is correct when he points out that a readerly taste for pretended horror is "no more connected with an appetite for real horror, real blood, than [it is with] an interest in the Theatre of Cruelty or the bullfight" (209). Why keep on denying that those destructive thrills are attractive *as long as they are only make-believe?*

For this discussion all modes of terror-creating narrative (horror-fantasy, science fiction, fantasy) are included in the term *gothic,* with apologies for my thriftiness by identifying them only by a useful oversimplification (better to be thought willful than naive). *Gothicism* is really a spiritual-cultural term, of course, nothing less than immense cathedral-shadow of Western history, but no other abbreviation even begins to offer itself as an accurate and finite substitute for all the modes of horror-fantasy.

M. H. Abrams gives a shorthand definition of the mode of gothicism centering on its creator's attempt to "evoke chilling terror, by exploiting mystery, cruelty, and a variety of horrors" (69), and he points out that the term is now usefully applied not simply to the ugly mysteries of an Ann Radcliffe monastery or the bizarre decay of a great and ancient family in a story of Poe's, but also to a type of terror-intending fiction that may do without medieval trappings as long as its events are "uncanny, or macabre, or melodramatically violent." Abrams also notes that the source of gothic terror is now frequently an "aberrant psychological state," not just a supernatural evil. One element that also must be interwoven into any complete definition is the presence within the form, shaping its structures and energies, of the world as a nightmare; as Joe David Bellamy points out, "nightmares antedate and are the true prototype of all gothic forms" (11). So although the definition can only be approximate, the term "gothicism" indicates the importation of nightmare into art. Leslie Fiedler remarks this crucial importation and points out that the essential burden of the gothic tale is to take readers "out of the known world into a dark region of make-believe . . . which is to say, [into] a world of ancestral and infantile fears projected in dreams" (114). Dream forms are the key to the imaginative resonance of the form.

Where, then, does the contemporary artist find the materials for his gothic terror, for the dream-become-art? Given that problem, we might consider and then immediately turn away from our century's most prodigious catastrophes—Verdun, Auschwitz, Hiroshima—and this in itself tells a good deal about the aesthetics of terror: the pleasurable beauty of terror lies at the heart of gothicism. The fact that trench warfare, extermination camps, and the experimental destruction of large civilian populations by means of atomic weapons were *real* perhaps has something to do with the revulsion with their uses as merely aesthetic properties and materials, but then Truman Capote creates a gothic masterpiece out of real murders no less hideous for his "non-fiction novel" *In Cold Blood* (1966). Other non-fiction accounts of grisly crimes—such as Joe McGinnis's *Fatal Vision* (1983), Shana Alexander's *Nutcracker* (1985), and the Michaud-Aynesworth study of Ted Bundy, *The Only Living Witness* (1983)—draw us irresistibly into their spiderwork.

What is the difference? Perhaps this: at Verdun, Auschwitz, and Hiroshima, human life counted for nothing at all, and the pleasurable terrors of gothicism depend upon the assumption that human life counts for everything. The gothic is not an absurd or existential mode; it is a romantic one. The difference between these perspectives is nothing less than the difference between no-meaning and meaning. Speaking about the extermination camps in his excellent study *Violence in the Arts*, John Fraser remarks that the essential horror of the camps was that "the actual intensity of suffering . . . [the] heightened sense of the consciousness of other people" (98) was utterly benumbed, for the horrors of the Final Solution all center on the perfect *indifference* of administrator, guard, and functionary to the human life it was their duty to destroy. It is this indifference that disqualifies Auschwitz from gothic possibilities. Thomas Pynchon can parody *The White Devil* (1608) in *The Crying of Lot 49* (1966) by having his wicked usurper Niccoló grind and dye the

bones of his enemies into writing ink—the grisly joke is still then a matter of *passion,* the intense emotion of hatred, the intense satisfaction of having that hatred revenged. But the technological fact that the human body can actually be rendered down into soap loses its *artistic* usefulness when it becomes clear that at the destruction complexes of the Third Reich this rendering was not a matter of passionate feeling at all. It was a matter of bureaucratic momentum, a scrupulous attention to duty, orders, and the task at hand. The real terrors of the Final Solution are not in its fantastic excesses of cruelty and sadism, and Fraser points out the utter falsity of what he calls the "most common cliché image" from the camps, that of "the shaven-headed prisoner being whipped to work by the glossy-booted S.S. man" (100). The history of humanity is fraught with savage murder, burnings, ritual sacrifices, exterminations, to say nothing of slave labor. What these modern camps made appallingly obvious was the complicity its victims could be induced to take *in their own destruction,* the degree to which sheer attention to the routines and processes of destruction, even to the routines and processes that conduct to one's own destruction, can be the supreme motive force in human affairs. The moral conscience of the twentieth century has been writhing from impalement on the terrible fact that such things as Auschwitz were even possible, but the aesthetic unsuitability of the camps gives the real insight into the core of their unique horror. It is a horror that seems only initially to derive from the sheer magnitude of the numbers killed, but the final horror of Auschwitz lies in the terrifying recognition that the energies of a great many people were engaged in operating, as efficiently as possible, the most astonishing social machinery in all history: a vast and intricate killing device the function of which was genocide and the operation of which was left to indifferent bureaucrats and complicit victims. A sure litmus test for gothic material is simply to ask if it can be parodied, for parody is the comic exaggeration of excess and demands overinflation of its subject. Auschwitz cannot be parodied because there is no emotion to be exaggerated or it is beyond hyperbole.

The importance of this is central to the understanding of modern efforts to create pleasurable terror. The more successful examples from the last two decades avoid the enormities of recent history and reveal a pronounced tendency to return to primitive, pan-cultural dream forms (*Jaws, Deliverance, Harvest Home, Carrie, Alien, Close Encounters, Cocoon, E.T., Halloween, Poltergeist*) or to rummage in the attic for religious paraphernalia so far gone into neglect that its reappearance seems purposefully anachronistic and playful as children dressing up in their grandparents' Sunday clothes (*Rosemary's Baby,* all four *Omen* films, *The Exorcist,* etc.). It is revealing to notice that by the mid-1980s the religious subgenre had already been exploited and abandoned, for like every other sort of fossil fuel the Christian imaginative heritage in the West proved to be finite. Sensing this exhaustion, contemporary writers and filmmakers went on to strip-mine *the imaginative forms themselves,* now drawing their energies from pure nostalgia and semi-ironic reanimations of the beloved kitsch of their own youths: Indiana Jones is simply a glossier, sexier reincarnation of Johnny Weismuller as Jungle Jim, Lex Barker as Tarzan, Stewart Granger in *King Solomon's Mines,* and Cornel Wilde as the white hunter in a half-dozen B-grade jungle flicks. High tech and low camp would also be called on to bring back to life the undead in resurrection jobs like *An American Werewolf in London, King Kong, Dracula, The Thing, Invasion of the Body Snatchers, The Bride* (a remake of *The Bride of Frankenstein* as a vanity vehicle for English rock star Sting), and others.

Leslie Fiedler points out that science fiction is "the gothicism of the future" (508) and that just beneath its moral pretensions and pseudo-scientific hocus-pocus, it is essentially terror fiction dressed in the trappings of imagined technology. "The gothic," says Fiedler, is always "half serious enterprise, half fashionable vice" (122). The horror-fantasy *mise en scène* must not be frankly serious or demand a strenuously moral response. One symptom of this playfulness is our tacit recognition and approval of preposterous gothic locales: Bram Stoker's Transylvania; those archaeological digs William Peter Blatty swipes out of Hollywood's Mummy series for *The Exorcist* (since recycled into *Omen* movies and their like, by no coincidence); H. G. Wells's lost tropical isle peopled only by mad scientists and his South American valleys peopled only by blind men; any and all photogenic castle / mansion / monastery or inhabitable planet out there beyond Alpha Centauri. The significant feature linking all these places together is their patent anti-reality—their ingenuous, childlike, vaguely ridiculous invitation just to pretend. It should not really be a surprise that one of the most successful motion pictures ever made (a fine example of the subgenre Sentimental Gothic, incidentally) takes place a long time ago in a galaxy far, far away, amidst a biology and physics that makes *Peter Pan* look as realistic as Zola in comparison. That's just the point: we go to the gothic for play, not instruction, and it is anything but art for the soul's sake, with edifying fright as its central mechanism.

Yet, like all play, the gothic is created out of the tension between freedom and restraint, the collision between anarchic energy and inviolable boundary. At heart, imaginative participation in the game involves three paradoxes, and the (half-serious) creators of gothic experience must satisfy these three conditions to succeed. First, the artists must keep the *source* of terror out of direct line of sight. Second, they must create a sense of menacing physical confinement. Third, they must involve us (by means of our empathetic identifications with surrogates) in what I will call the "Cassandra Situation."

Each of these premises needs to be amplified and illustrated, but it is first appropriate to note that these conditions all serve to expedite the return on the part of the readers or viewers in to the imaginative kingdom of childhood, for the genre of gothic horror-fantasy is par excellence a voyage *back* and *down*. As Roger Schlobin puts it, to "horror writer and reader, creation is a dark

force, and its twisted spawn are a seminal part of the character of the universe" (5:2263). The wellspring of this spawn is, of course, the human dream, where creation never ceases with a Seventh Day and the oldest fears reclaim us every night. Back and down, then, the imagination is led to re-explore the frightening wilderness of childhood terrors beneath human pretenses of reasonability and the tacit covenant that adults have entered into, which professes that the universe is all IBM cards and fluorescent light, decimal places, second hands, and yardsticks one-yard long. Julia O'Faolain has described the psychic residue of childhood with the wonderful phrase "rage-charred" because of its astonishing and inexplicable capacity for terror, and she claims that gifted artists reawaken these first memories and eldest nightmares, surviving undiminished by later experience, reminding us "that we were once pre-sane" (14). The laws governing the pleasures of terror are thus the conditions of the *descensus ad inferos,* the descent to the underworld, the journey down into the primal pre-sane dream-stuff. "The geography of the *descensus* is always the geography of dream," as Bernard F. Dick explains (45). We are Dante; the artist is Virgil; the Inferno lies within. In *The Romantic Fantastic,* Tobin Siebers points out that this "descent into the mind" is transformed by horror-intending artists into "a descent into hell, thereby recuperating and enthroning superstition" (185). The attraction of this hell-bent imaginative experience is anathema to liberal, "progressive" assumptions—the substrate of the Humanities Establishment and its universities, publications, and foundations. Donald Thomas brilliantly summarizes the eternal appeal of that archetypal hero of superstition and the "twisted spawn" of madness, the Marquis de Sade: "the one undeniable quality of his writing is that he stands the easy optimism of the *philosophes* and progressives on its head. The self-destructive power of the human race is the supreme power, in Sade's view, and the extinction of the species is inevitable and not to be regretted." Thomas holds that the astonishing endurance of Sade's legacy stems from his reaffirmation that "mankind is caught in the toils of a terrible aboriginal calamity" (207) and that the Enlightenment itself was a fatuous illusion. Did not the guillotine blades of the French Revolution prove him right? From a contemporary perspective, we might ruefully confirm Sade's exalted ferocity and annihilating cynicism as one more stage in the distillation of that mystical-intellectual nitroglycerine with which sorcerer's apprentices like Hitler, Lenin, and Mao have blown history off the rational iron rails laid down so smugly for it by the Rousseaus, Darwins, and Adam Smiths in the preceding centuries. The world pretends to want evolution and light, but in its marrow it really desires a bang, not a whimper. The enormous success and staying-power of the horror-fantasy narrative is simply this same human impulse, writ small. Sweeping generalizations, perhaps, but the first questions and not the fine print always seem to be slighted in an organized discussion of intellectual phenomena.

Far from enlightening readers and viewers, then, the creators of horror-fantasy are, in fact, involved in ushering them away from the sunshine and down into interior fantasies older even than firelight flickering on the wall of a cave. Charles Lamb said these restless shadows "predominate in the period of our sinless infancy," and behind the marvelous quaintness of his nineteenth-century phrasing, is real insight. Freud himself, always aware that the interior energies of literature are simply the reactuated fantasies of childhood naiveté, said it no better for *this* century when he concluded that the great creators of magic tales succeed by "betraying us to the superstitiousness which we have ostensibly surmounted . . ." (17:250). The manner in which this "betraying" must be accomplished is the focus of the description which follows.

> . . . But that I am forbid
> To tell the secrets of my prison-house
> I could a tale unfold whose lightest word
> Would harrow up thy soul, freeze thy young
>   blood. . . .
>   (*Hamlet*, I.v.13-16)

The words are Hamlet's, but the strategy they illustrate is Shakespeare's, and any artist who ever wanted to achieve the effect of pleasurable terror will recognize the necessity of this evasion. Words are only words; none exist that can "harrow up thy soul." There is no way to present any alternative reality without using *this* reality as a point of departure, or as a metaphor. And in the paradoxical realm of fiction, where a gifted artist can use madness, disease, or death to give the most intense kind of pleasure, terror seems to be bred most potently in the *interval* between inference and fact, between the suspected and the known. To confront the source of suspense directly, to consummate the process of discovery, would destroy the effect. Conrad's *Heart of Darkness* (1902), perhaps the purest example of gothicism in our century, is a perfect illustration of this first condition needed to produce pleasurable terror.

To say that *Heart of Darkness* is a study of what one critic calls "the mortifying diseases of nineteenth-century imperialism" (Chace 199) is to be at once correct and ridiculous—like describing Thomas Pynchon's *Gravity's Rainbow* (1973) as a book about V-2 rockets. Making extravagant use of purple inks on loan from Poe, Conrad created a sort of prose Rorschach blot, and the impossibility of reducing its convolution, shading, and haunting symmetries to any sort of adequate paraphrase is one proof of the tale's success. Notice how little *happens* in the story—a man named Marlow tells at length (at incredible length!) of a European ivory-agent named Kurtz whose methods of getting treasure from the native cannibals were both utterly unsavory and wonderfully successful. Evidently this Kurtz chap went native in some fashion or other, and then he died—and died of no simple medical affliction, we are given to understand. He left a fiancée this side of death, and his personal magnetism and singular genius were such that we expect she will never get over him. Period.

Little enough action for a tale of over thirty-thousand words, one would assume, but then an extraordinary pro-

portion of those words are really not words at all, but fragments of magic incantation, the verbal cinders of otherworldly energies, a language that can only point in the direction of an experience no language can describe. *Uncontrollable, unspeakable, ineffable, inscrutable, impenetrable, intolerable* [to thought], at once *exalted and incredible* [degradation], *inconceivable, indefinable, unearthly, inappreciable, impossible, invincible, inexplicable, implacable, unfathomable, insoluble, unapproachable, irresistible:* perhaps no story in literary heritage surrenders itself to a vocabulary more difficult to paraphrase or more fraught with menacing abstractions that words can neither define nor picture. Conrad's tale takes the evils of the white man's burden for its starting point, but these human, racial evils are only "mere incidents of the surface" (13), and Marlow assures that the "inner truth is hidden—luckily" (65). He himself has *almost* seen it, but he tells us (more than a dozen times) that he cannot convey in words the smallest fraction of those unholy terrors. And nothing can be said about the story that will pull its central mystery into the light, for here the artist has recognized the first principle of aesthetic terror—that an ogre's approaching footsteps are immeasurably more frightening than any portrait of the ogre himself, fangs and all. One of the most brilliant and useful insights from Tom Stoppard's *Rosencrantz and Guildenstern Are Dead* (1967) is on the diminishment of the wonderful by the ordinary—for the ordinary is simply the wonderful seen too often. One man sees a unicorn, and the vision may be either real or a hallucination; then a second man sees the unicorn, too:

> "My God," says [the] second man, "I must be dreaming, I thought I saw a unicorn." At which point, a dimension is added that makes the experience as alarming as it will ever be. A third witness, you understand, adds no further dimension but only spreads it thinner, and a fourth thinner still, and the more witnesses there are the thinner it gets and the more reasonable it becomes until it is as thin as reality, the name we give to common experience. . . . (Stoppard 21)

Like Conrad, Stoppard knows that to give a local habitation and a name to the wonderful is inevitably to trivialize it, to dissolve the magic terrors of the glimpsed and the guessed in the universal solvent of everyday reality. As Fiedler puts it, "for the abominable, to be truly effective, must remain literally unspeakable" (121).

The second artistic condition of the gothic tale, that of physical confinement, is a premise so simple and obvious as to have been frequently ignored. Eino Railo took *The Haunted Castle* as the title of his 1927 study of gothic fiction, and literary people have perhaps been too quick to involve themselves in psychological speculation as to the religious and cultural implications of the word "haunted" at the expense of even noticing the sheer fact that isolation and confinement are in themselves important aesthetic conditions. The castle, monastery, or decaying great house may have their guilty ancestral secrets to whisper, but isn't the simple fact that both characters and readers are alone to face them really at the core of fear? Railo, Fiedler, and others have all theorized brilliantly about the characteristic gothic premise of the past revenging itself on the present (as with the racial guilt of the South that underlies the fiction of Faulkner, O'Connor, and McCullers, for example), but those who have seen *Night of the Living Dead* should agree that the sheer terror of finding themselves in an anonymous farmhouse while the night outside yields up destroying ghouls is more than sufficient proof that most audiences know first-hand what it means to be threatened by isolation and immobility, with the shadows of the enormous night breeding God-knows-what. All of which is to say that the artists' uses of the past for gothic effect may imply a significant cultural situation, but that they cannot make us afraid unless they return us to our *own* childhood.

Jaws (the original, *not* its sequels and imitations) was an effective terror film largely because Stephen Spielberg understood how to use his medium to achieve both a sense of mystery and a sense of confinement. The shark playing the title role is very little *seen* for almost the entire length of the film, remember, and frequently it is kept from sight by the clever expedient of substituting its sight for ours. In the final confrontation, the characters played by Robert Shaw, Richard Dreyfuss, and Roy Scheider are physically isolated and mortally vulnerable because they have no choice but to take on their antagonist in its own kingdom, and the fishing boat *Orca* is, at that point in the movie, as fearful a gothic locale as the House of Usher. Interestingly enough, a guilty, revenging past was also introduced into the film *Jaws* (it was not in the novel): Quint, the Ahabesque sea captain of the *Orca* (as played by Robert Shaw) had in the past helped commit the supreme Frankensteinian impudence of this century: during World War II he had been aboard the Navy vessel that delivered the Hiroshima bomb to its flight crew on the island of Tinian. Returning from this mission, the ship had been torpedoed by the Japanese, and so many of its [life-jacketed] survivors had been destroyed by sharks that Quint has resolved never to [wear a life-jacket] again. And of course he won't and is destroyed, for again the guilty past revenges itself on a present desperately attempting to cut itself free. In gothic art, anything that might rationally be captioned "Just Some Silly Native Superstition" must always come true. The gothic is a fairy tale told for adults, and its creators do not hold a mirror up to nature so much as step through a looking glass into a realm governed by magic, wish, and dream.

Whatever the device, it is essential that artists' use of a sense of physical confinement or inadequacy resurrect with alarming clarity childhood vulnerabilities. To be effective, terror narrative must return us to those moments in early life when we found ourselves at the mercy of a world built to a scale far larger and for purposes more threatening and mysterious than any we could recognize in ourselves. Regardless of the official sentimentality about the supposed happiness of childhood—childhood as Eden before the apple—isn't childhood always at least partially an experience when we were dauntingly

aware of the larger and more brutal energies which surrounded us? It is no accident that *Alice in Wonderland* has continued to haunt the imagination of our culture for more than a century, for Carroll's great fairy tale is the purest account—one might almost say the most faithful *transcription*—of the universal dream-stuff of the childish mind: from Red Queen to Jabberwocky, from Mad Hatter to magic potion, *Alice* is the distilled essence of the exquisitely vulnerable Self set upon by the irrational and tyrannically powerful Other. Carroll's vision is the very paradigm of childhood finding itself at the mercy of the monstrous adversary world that always waited just beneath the daylight English garden. The art of terror is the art of returning to the child who lives on within.

The third condition of pleasurable terror, the "Cassandra Situation," seems at first glance to be the most curious paradox of all. However, it is the essence of childhood to *know* and not to be believed, and in successful terror-art, the protagonist comes to know the terrible danger but cannot convince others of its reality. In *Dracula* or *Rosemary's Baby,* for example, the partisans of Our Kingdom are in possession of facts that are only preposterous to the others. The participative tension the audience feels derives its power not only from watching the supernatural forces from the Other Kingdom intrude into this world, but also from the indifference, opacity, and even hostility of those who need to be convinced of the desperate necessity of defending against that incursion. All of us were children, and all children are Cassandras; their gift and curse of living inside their own fantasies is one reason they are quarantined off from adult "reality." They know that the Under-the-Bed is deadly but that no one can be convinced to defend them from it; that magic, fairy tale, and the supernatural are real possibilities; and that those ancient shadows at the bottom edge of consciousness will not "resolve only into toy horses and Biedermeyer furniture," as Oedipa Maas's psychiatrist explains in *The Crying of Lot 49.* The condition is universal; its resurrection deeply resonant.

One of the most impressive examples of the Cassandra Situation is that in Ira Levin's *Rosemary's Baby* and the Roman Polanski film made from it. Levin has inverted a fairy tale to form the core of his tale—Immaculate Conception becomes Satanic Conception—and he has illustrated in the process F. Scott Fitzgerald's wonderful dictum that the cleverly expressed opposite of any generally accepted idea is worth a fortune to somebody. Society must insure that pregnancy is a desirable state, but for the expectant mother herself there are atavistic fears of that alien presence commandeering her body: she is *literally* possessed, and something may go unspeakably wrong. Levin masterfully enlarges this fear. Rosemary is both isolated and confined *within* her pregnancy—how could the terror be brought any closer?—and both isolation and confinement are essential in creating fear. As the first step in making Rosemary a Cassandra, Levin arranges for her to lose her friend Hutch, who urged Rosemary and her husband not to move into the Manhattan-Gothic Bramford because it has a history of what he primly refers to as "ugly and unsavory happenings" (17)—a pair of Victorian spinsters who practiced cannibalism, a high incidence of suicides, a dead infant wrapped in newspapers, even a practicing witch named Adrian Marcato who claimed in the best "Just Some Silly Native Superstition" manner to have "succeeded in conjuring up the living Satan" (16). Hutch, an active threat to the man Rosemary will discover is Adrian Marcato's son, is conjured into a coma and eventually destroyed by the devil worshippers. The unsuitable young woman whom Rosemary is to replace as Mother of the Antichrist "suicides" from the seventh floor of the "Black Bramford" only days after Rosemary and Guy move in. Guy's sudden success as an actor is achieved at the expense of the mysterious blindness that afflicts his chief rival for a part. Her husband, her physician, and her neighbors all conspire against her: Rosemary is absolutely and utterly alone with her terrible revelation.

Because any tale of the supernatural is potentially absurd—science fiction and horror are genres that always verge on the ridiculous—Levin has expertly controlled reader disbelief at every point. For example, instead of long, gloomy descriptions of the Bramford's brooding evil (traditionally done in those purple inks on loan from Poe), Levin allows the bright chirp of a near-acquaintance of Rosemary's to encapsulate the apartment building's photogenic eccentricity: "I'm *mad* about it! If you ever want to sub-let, I'm first, and don't you forget it! All those weird gargoyles and creatures climbing up and down between the windows!" (13). But even if the voice describing those chic monstrosities is inane, Levin still gets to have his monstrosities—Poe smuggled in under a plain brown wrapper. Viewed simply as a technical accomplishment, Levin's book (and Polanski's film) are masterfully satisfying, and the use of a Cassandra Situation is crucial to their effects.

But the largest question of all continues to perplex, down behind any merely technical discussion of the processes of creating terror: why is fear, in art, a *pleasurable* emotion in the first place? Do we really purge ourselves of it in the artistic experience, as Aristotle claimed? Searching my own responses to terror art leads me to suspect a simpler explanation, and one that squares better with the paradoxical fact that the *sufferings* of soap opera heroines exert a spellbinding fascination on millions and millions of viewers and listeners: narrative art is a machine we use to create emotions for ourselves under conditions where we don't have to pay for them. I suggest that the fundamental conception of human nature from Aristotle through Freud has assumed that humanity wants to be returned to some sort of primal equipoise, a steady state of tranquility, balance, and adjustment. But aren't the silliest, lamest words in all the world *happily ever after?* We all live out here in ever after, and I'm afraid we find it obvious and tiresome: better *any* sort of intensity than *this*. Of course, the implications of this claim are so unflattering that it will be reflexively dismissed by the humanities establishment as a coarse, vulgar heresy. Nevertheless, the pleasure in terror is real, and the task must be to account for that fact, not to dismiss its reality with some unconvincing pieties.

WORKS CITED

Abrams, M. H. *A Glossary of Literary Terms.* New York: Holt, Rinehart & Winston, 1971.

Amis, Kingsley. *What Became of Jane Austen? and Other Questions.* London: Russell and Russell, 1966.

Bellamy, Joe David, ed. *Superfiction.* New York: Random House, 1975.

Chace, William M. *The Political Identities of Ezra Pound and T.S. Eliot.* Stanford: Stanford Univ. Press, 1973.

Conrad, Joseph. *Heart of Darkness.* Ed. Robert Kimbrough. New York: Norton, 1963.

Dick, Bernard. "*The Waste Land* as *Descensus ad Inferos.*" *Canadian Review of Comparative Literature* Winter 1975: 35-46.

Fiedler, Leslie. *Love and Death in the American Novel.* New York: Dell, 1966.

Fraser, John. *Violence in the Arts.* Cambridge: Cambridge Univ. Press, 1974.

Freud, Sigmund. *The Standard Edition of the Complete Psychological Works of Sigmund Freud.* Ed. and trans. James Strachey. Vol. 17. London: Hogarth Press, 1953-74. 24 vols.

Levin, Ira. *Rosemary's Baby.* New York: Random House, 1967.

O'Faolain, Julia. "Erotic Fantasy." *London Magazine* June/July 1977: 5-34.

Pynchon, Thomas. *The Crying of Lot 49.* New York: Bantam, 1967.

Schlobin, Roger. "Fantasy Versus Horror." *Survey of Modern Fantasy Literature.* Ed. Frank N. Magill. Vol. 5. Englewood Cliffs, N.J.: Salem, 1983. 5 vols.

Siebers, Tobin. *The Romantic Fantastic.* Ithaca, N.Y.: Cornell Univ. Press, 1984.

Thomas, Donald. *The Marquis de Sade.* Boston: Little, Brown, 1976.

William Eickhorst

SOURCE: "The Motive of Fear in German Literature," in *Arizona Quarterly,* Vol. 20, No. 2, Summer, 1964, pp. 147-63.

[*In the following essay, Eickhorst surveys fear in German literature from the thirteenth century to the mid-1960s, highlighting works by Johann von Schiller, Johann Wolfgang von Goethe, Rainer Maria Rilke, Franz Kafka, Ernst Barlach, Thomas Mann, Gottfried Benn, Hermann Hesse, and Friedrich Dürrenmatt, among others.*]

No other word denoting a state of mind has been allotted more synonyms by standard dictionaries than fear. The most frequently employed terms among these synonyms are anxiety, terror, and fright—all designating that painful emotion experienced when one is confronted by impending danger, imaginary or real. In modern German writings *Angst* (anxiety) is usually the expression for this sensation rather than *Furcht* (fear), unless the reference is to *Gottesfurcht* (fear of God). In the intellectual and religious realms anxiety is thought of as a consequence of guilt; in philosophy, according to Heidegger, it originates from merely being in this world. Freud believed that anxiety developed from anticipation of sexual denial.

There is a consensus among medical authorities that anxiety can derive from emotional disturbances. Sensitive people react to disagreeable impressions and painful experiences with anxiety. Melancholy, schizophrenia, delirium, and compulsion are regarded as resulting from anxiety. The vastly increased feeling of insecurity after war or any other cultural crisis leads to a corresponding increase of neurotic susceptibility. A state of anxiety can be produced also by a faulty education or by violent occurrences with which an immature mind cannot cope. Kierkegaard, who has exerted a far reaching influence on modern thought, was obsessed by anxiety all his life. He thought that anxiety was a teaching emotion necessary for self-evaluation and for solving the predicaments of ordinary life.

The word fear has appeared in literature since its beginnings. It occupies a dominant place in the Old Testament. Since the Hebrew word *Moró* (fear) resembles very much *moréh* (teaching), the often quoted passage "The fear of the Lord is the beginning of wisdom," might read "The guidance of the Lord is the beginning of wisdom." Accordingly, the belief of the theologian Kierkegaard that God guides through anxiety goes back to the Scriptures. The Greeks regarded fear as a necessary element of tragedy. Aristotle stated that tragedy by arousing fear and pity effects a purge of the emotions.

Walther von der Vogelweide wrote of a general anxiety among youth during the decline of knighthood at the beginning of the thirteenth century: "Woe, how miserably the young act now, who formerly were jovial in a courtly manner. Now they know how to worry only: Woe, why are they acting this way?" Anxiety as a literary theme, however, played no decisive role in German letters until the seventeenth century, after war, pestilence, and the swift progress of science had shattered the long persisting belief that man was the center of the universe. Although rife with terror and sorrow, the literary compositions of the Middle Ages, the epics, chapbooks, fairy tales, and folksongs, lack characters with chronic fear complexes. People on all levels of society, including those who were at odds with the Church and those who had come in contact with mysticism, were uniform in their hope for forgiveness of sins and in their belief in life hereafter. Even Doctor Faustus of the sixteenth-century chapbook prayed for salvation of his soul. Dürer wrote that his old mother had shown great fear of dying (*Todesfurcht*) but had not been afraid of coming before the Lord.

During the period of the Baroque, at the time of the Thirty Years' War, German literature was permeated by the anxiety-ridden poetry of hymn writers such as Gerhardt, Neander, and Rinckart, as well as by that of the predominantly secular lyricists, Gryphius, Hofmannswaldau, and von Zesen. For the members of these two groups, *Angst* or *Furcht* became the words most frequently used to express emotion. A deep religious conviction safe-guarded the writers of church songs from fear of life, but their more worldly fellow-poets revealed in their verses an anxiety similar to that with which many people today are afflicted. They were plagued not only by insecurity and the burdensomeness of life but also by anxiousness about the transitory and futile nature of existence. For instance, Gryphius, the most productive poet of the Baroque period, possessed a split personality. His thoughts vacillated from the worldly to the divine, from lust to prayer, from almost blasphemous rebellion against God to an almost remorseful humility. Fear and belief were the two poles of his poetic inspirations. In "At the End" the lyricist mourned, "I have spent my time in burning anxiety," and in "Evenings" he prayed, "Let not woe, splendor, lust, nor anxiety lead me astray. Thine eternally bright glory be around and over me."

In spite of the pious note on which this work ended, Gryphius' excessive feeling of anxiety betrayed a pathological state. Even when he celebrated a joyous occasion in verse, as in his poem "On the Birth of Jesus," Gryphius used *Furcht, Höllenangst* (fear of Hell) and *Schrecken* (horror) to signify dread blessedly dispelled: "And fear, the terror of Hell, and horror all were lost." In the Christian era it was not until the eighteenth century that death was conceived of as a possible friend of man (Claudius' "Death and the Girl").

Even Gerhardt, whose mighty hymns are as stirring now as they were during his lifetime, gave intense expression to his fear of dying in "The Suffering Countenance of Jesus Christ."

> When the time comes for me to depart
> Do not depart from me;
> When the time comes for me to suffer death,
> Then come forth;
> When fear most powerfully
> Sizes upon my heart,
> Snatch me away from anxiety
> Through Thy anguish and suffering!

In writings of the eighteenth century there was comparatively little evidence of anxiety in literature. Exponents of the German classical period (Lessing, Goethe, and Schiller) had their protagonists adhere to a theory of accepted order in the world. These characters seldom express fear of existence (Werther is the outstanding exception) and suffer only an anxiety induced by actual threats of pain or death.

The historian and playwright Schiller, who used "anxiety" and "fear" more than did any of the other representatives of the German classical school, viewed history as man's judgment on earth (Kierkegaard could see no significance in the occurrences of events). Schiller's Don Carlos speaks of *Todesangst* (mortal terror) when referring to his love for his stepmother, but fright does not inhibit his capacity for making decisions.

> . . . This way
> Can only lead to madness or the scaffold.
> I love with no hope—sacrilegiously
> At peril of my life, in mortal terror—
> I see this, yet I go on loving.

Schiller's Philip II hopes to extract useful information from persons he suspects of being possessed by innate fear and therefore may be more easily persuaded to reveal secrets simply through threat of torture. In *The Maid of Orleans* Schiller wrote of the terror the British manifest of Joan of Arc and of her fearlessness because she is fighting with God's sword. Diego in *The Bride of Messina* states: "One must have something to fear for, to hope for, and to worry about on the next morning in order to be able to bear the difficulty of existence." He assumes that concern and apprehension will give the thoughts controlling man's activities a balance which will aid him in bearing a humdrum existence. (This idea resembles Kierkegaard's assertion that fear fulfills a salutary purpose.) Schiller used the term *Schrecken* in "The Lay of the Bell" to signify the terror of the masses during a revolution:

> But the most fearful horror of all horrors
> Is man in his purblind delusion.

Goethe, who believed in immortality and the final goodness of the world, was aware of the conflict in all existence and honored it in "The Harper's Song":

> You lead us into life,
> You let the poor wretch incur guilt,
> Then you leave him to his torment,
> For all guilt brings vengeance upon itself on earth.

Goethe ended the poem *Proemion* with this conception of man's relation to God:

> We should surrender all to God, fear him,
> and, if it is possible to put our fear and
> awe of him aside, love him.

Hölderlin, who achieved perfection in his poetry, broke on the imperfection of life. Even though the poet possessed strong faith in the unity of man and divine nature, as well as firm hope in mankind's future, he suffered immeasurably from the dualism of existence. This unfortunate genius gave stronger expression of the dread of man in his loneliness and uncertainty than did any of his contemporaries; but, strangely enough, he never used the words "fear" or "anxiety" in his rich collection of poems. His "Hyperion's Song of Destiny" conveys the hopelessness of mankind's lot, a condition which the twentieth century disciples of "Overt Anxiety" have declaimed (Auden, Camus).

> But we are destined
> Nowhere to repose;
> They fall, they vanish,
> The suffering mortals,
> Blindly driven
> From hour to hour,
> Like water tossed
> From cliff to cliff
> Years long down to uncertainty.

The developments during the nineteenth century that led to the modern crisis of anxiety went hand in hand with disbelief in the teachings of traditional religion. Although such gifted German playwrights as Büchner and Grabbe doubted the divine order of things, they created protagonists who showed no particular fear of either life or death. While the dramatist Hebbel predominantly dealt with the doom of individuals and cultures in his plays, he believed, nevertheless, that God in His grace would not allow mankind to destroy itself: "And the Lord will abate his ominous threatening as much as he can, and tie together again all these threads which have been rendered asunder."

With the exception of Heine, who at times was convinced of the futility of all human efforts, of Lenau, who was full of "sadness at the doubtful doom of humankind," and of E. T. A. Hoffmann, who maintained that "the devil dips his tail into everything," the German Romanticists held to the belief that a Heavenly Father guides us all. Even though their verse is permeated with melancholy and longing, they rarely betrayed fear in their works.

Lenau bewailed the hopeless isolation of one dispossessed of both love and faith in his poem "Loneliness":

> That he, scared by his loneliness, frightened,
> Jumps up from the solid cliff
> Full of fear, stretching out his arms for the wind.
> Without love and without God: the road is
>   horrible.
> The draft blows cold in the streets; and you?—
> The whole world is sad to desperation.

E. T. A. Hoffmann, whose realistic horror stories have excited readers since their first publication, occupied himself in his life, as well as in his tales, with automatons. Olympia, the puppet from *The Doll* (1817), has become best known through Offenbach's opera *The Tales of Hoffmann*. The versatile creator Hoffmann was haunted by the possibility that an almost perfect and human-like machine might soon be constructed, a monster that would turn the entire world into an abyss of fear.

After Darwin's theories of biology, Schopenhauer's of tragedy (man's worst guilt is to be born at all), and Nietzsche's of decadence had become general knowledge, belief in the ultimate goodness of nature and a better future diminished in the same proportion as general anxiety among people increased. At the turn of the century there appeared many books describing the general state of instability which allegedly prevailed among the upper classes of society. Not only were a dozen artistic family novels on disillusionment and decadence (Ricarda Huch's *Memoires of Ludolf Ursleu, the Younger*, 1892; Fontane's *Effi Briest*, 1894; Rudolf Huch's *Family Hellmann*, 1908) released, but also a vast number of narratives about subtilized youths and children being consumed by various kinds of anxieties (Hermann Hesse's *Under the Wheel*, 1905; Friedrich Huch's *Mao*, 1907; and Ernst Wiechert's *The Story of a Boy*, 1907). The protagonists of the genealogical novels all come to the conclusion that life on earth has very little meaning. Huch's Ludolf Ursleu compares life to a turbulent sea which human beings never leave while alive. The harshest indictment of man's existence comes from Tom Buddenbrooks after he becomes acquainted with Schopenhauer's philosophy:

> Was not every human being a mistake and a blunder? Was he not in painful arrest from the hour of his birth? Prison, Prison bonds and limitations everywhere! The human being stares hopelessly through the barred windows of his personality at the high walls of outward circumstances till Death comes and calls him home!

Rilke's *The Notebooks of Malte Laurids Brigge* (1909), the embodiment of anxiety in modern literature, contains all the elements of the two genres mentioned above. It initiated the works of fiction which represent practical applications of Kierkegaard's conception of anxiety such as Wassermann's *World's Illusion* (1919) and Gertrud Le Fort's *The Last at the Scaffold* (1910). The chief characters in these narratives combat their crushing aversions and anxieties in order to come nearer to God. The following excerpts from Rilke's account of the last scion of an old, aristocratic family presents some of the monstrous forms that the fears of a modern decadent might assume. These hallucinations resemble some of the weird phenomena in Kafka's tales. (*The Metamorphosis*, 1916.)

> So here and there on my coverlet lie lost things out of my childhood and are as new. All forgotten fears are there again. The fear that a small, woolen thread that sticks out of the hem of my blanket may be hard, hard and sharp like a steel needle; the fear that this little button on my nightshirt may be bigger than my head, big and heavy; the fear that the torn border of an opened letter may be something forbidden that no one ought to see, something indescribably precious for which no place in the room is secure enough; the fear that if I fell asleep I might swallow the piece of coal lying in front on the stove; the fear that some number may begin to grow in my brain until there is no more room for it inside me; the fear that it

may be granite I am lying on, grey granite; the fear that I may shout, and that people may come running to my door and finally break it open; the fear that I may betray myself and tell all I dread; and the fear that I might not be able to say anything, because everything is beyond utterance,—and the other fears . . . the fears.

The counterpart of this bulk of fiction peopled with bewildered human beings is the group of excellent poems which tell of big city dwellers who live anxiously and sinfully. Thus in Hugo von Hofmannsthal's poem "Ballad of the Outer Life," Rilke's "For Lord, The Big Cities Are Lost and Disintegrated," and Trakl's "Occident" ("You mighty cities, built of stone . . . , you dying peoples! Pallid wave breaking on the shore of night, falling stars.") are echoed the anxieties hovering over urban civilizations.

The despair and loneliness of our *Age of Anxiety* culminated in the dream visions of Franz Kafka. While most protagonists of the family novels still harbored a faith in reaching "a sheltered haven" after spending their days on a "boundless and bottomless" sea of life, the chief characters of Kafka's narrations cannot look forward to any kind of solace after death since in their crises they have no access to God. Kafka's heroes, who symbolize twentieth-century man, are condemned to the utmost loneliness. Often their nearest kin reject them. But what makes their dilemma hopeless is the fact that they cannot be unburdened from guilt; for God, as judge, is out of their reach and, therefore, can never set them free. The hero of *The Trial* (1925), Joseph K., resembles the man in the "Legend of the Law," a parable related to Joseph K. by a priest. The man lets himself be frightened by the manner of the gatekeeper until the end of his days and so is kept from entering the door of the law, which would be opened only for him, until he, dying, learns: "This entrance was destined for you only." Joseph K. never understood the meaning of this legend. Blaming others for his misfortune, he receives, unprepared, his death sentence. Kafka, whose fiction is almost devoid of the words fear and anxiety, discusses these phenomena at length in his diaries in which he advocates that people should follow the example of animals that subject their fear and take a stand in danger. Von Hofmannsthal also emphasizes this idea in his later plays, for example, in the motto of *The Woman Without a Shadow* (1926): "Have reverence! Courage! Fulfill your destiny!" A number of critics claim, without giving real evidence, that Kafka was profoundly religious, having been influenced by Kierkegaard. Perhaps they had in mind a view similar to that of August Closs who states in his *Medusa's Mirror* (1959), that the theme of Kafka's terrifying trilogy of utter human melancholy, *The Trial; The Castle*, 1926; *America*, 1927, is related to Kierkegaard's assertion which Closs states as being

> . . . that only through fear and despair can people find their salvation, as they compel us to the decision of our inmost freedom, a freedom which we thus owe to ourselves. In this struggle to decide

our own fate we stand alone, but God's eyes watch over us. [August Closs, *Medusa's Mirror* (London: The Camelot Press, Ltd., 1959), p. 104.]

A short note among Kafka's literary remains summarizes his grim verdict on life: "There is no possessing, only an existence, an existence yearning for the last breath, for suffocation." Kafka's most specific reference to anxiety is contained in the following statement:

I constantly try to communicate something which cannot be communicated, explain something that cannot be explained, relate something which I have in my bones and which can be experienced in these bones. It is perhaps basically nothing except that anxiety which has been so often discussed, just that anxiety which has been extended to everything, anxiety of the most powerful force and the most insignificant, and the anxiety of expressing a word. However, this fear is perhaps not merely fear, but also a yearning for something, which goes beyond anxiety.

The twentieth-century playwrights Ernst Barlach and Bertolt Brecht and the novelist Thomas Mann have all shown special interest in the subject of the annihilation of civilization.

Ernst Barlach attempted in his sculpture and plays to convey his mystic conception of God. The philosophy of his play *The Deluge* (1924) is contained in a discourse between Noah, the obedient servant who has complete faith in his vengeful god's righteousness, and Calan, the rebel who asserts that his baseness comes from Noah's god but his strength from a greater, unavenging god that changes with the world in its evolution.

There is a god of the floods in whose image it is said, "The world is tinier than nothing and God is everything." However, I see the other God of whom it will be said, "The world is great, and God is tinier than nothing—a period, a glimmering, and everything begins in him and everything ceases in him." He is without shape and voice.... Everything originates from Him and everything returns to the base of His strength. He creates and is newly created by the one He created. . . . God grows because of me and continues to change with me to something new—how beautiful it is, Noah, that I too no longer have shape and am absorbed in the strength and depth of God—already I am sinking towards Him—He has become I and I He—He with my lowliness, I with His glory—a single entity.

Bertolt Brecht in his third version of *The Life of Galileo* (1955) blamed Galileo not only for the moral dilemma in which present civilization finds itself, but also for the doubt and fear that mark it. In the play Galileo says of himself:

As a scientist I had a unique possibility. During my time astronomy reached the public. Under these special circumstances, the steadfastness of a man could have produced great revolutionary changes.

Had I resisted, natural science could have developed a code similar to the Hippocratic Oath, a vow to use their power only for the benefit of mankind. The way science is now, the highest one might hope for is a race of inventive dwarfs who can be hired to do anything.

In spite of the desolate outlook which Brecht presented, he could not avoid being impressed by the dynamic force of life in people. In his poem "Of the Friendliness of the World" he paid homage to man's devotion to his planet.

From the earth filled with cold wind
You all depart covered with scabs and manage.
Before he is covered with dust
Almost everyone has learned to love the world.

Thomas Mann in his *Doctor Faustus* (1947) portrayed the hero and his German people on their way to certain destruction, because the Germans have been denied integration as individuals and as a people. Their deficiency causes them not only to war among themselves but also with other peoples. They have become criminal worshipers of an idealism that is out of tune with the world. The abstract, mystic musician Doctor Faustus reflects the mind of the German people and their unhappy relationship to the world. They cannot find harmony but they yearn to hear satanic music expressive of highest order and chaotic irrationality.

The expressionist poet of nihilism and detachment Gottfried Benn asserts that absolute existence and permanence can be ascribed only to a work of art and that form alone is capable of producing faith and action, while life must be regarded as a vulgar illusion. This feeling of bankruptcy which intellectuals often confess in respect of their own philosophy of life is phrased in Benn's poem *Lost Ego*.

Lost ego, disrupted by stratospheres, victim of
    the ion, lamb of the gamma-rays, particle and
    field, chimaeras of infinity on your grey stone
    of Notre-Dame.
The days pass for you without night and
    morning, the years without snow and fruit bear
    infinity threateningly hidden—the world as
    flight.
Where do you end, where do you camp, where
    do your spheres extend—loss, gain—a game of
    beasts, eternities, you flee past their bars.
The glance of the beast: the stars as tripes, death
    in the jungle as reason of being and creation,
    man, Battles of the Nations, Catalaunian
    Fields, down the beast's gullet.
The world thought to pieces. And space and time
    and what wove and weighed mankind, only a
    function of eternities. The myth lied.
Where to? Where from? Not night, not morning,
    no Evoe, no requiem, what you want is a
    borrowed slogan—but borrowed from whom?
Oh, when they all bowed towards one centre and
    even the thinkers only thought the god, when
    they branched out to the shepherds and the
    lamb, each time the blood from the chalice had
    made them clean

and all flowed from the one wound, all broke the
bread that each man ate—oh, distant compelling fulfilled hour, which once enfolded
even the lost ego.

Notwithstanding this sad status quo in which Benn saw
modern mankind, he admired people's courage. Man is
neither the strongest nor perhaps the most gifted of animals, yet he has survived every cataclysm and developed
lasting arts and ideas. People struggle day after day, enduring pain and misfortune, and still they cling to life.

Benn, who introduced the concept of science into his
terse and unadorned rhythms, created with his challenging intellectual metaphors a form for literature as characteristic of our age as the New Coventry Cathedral is for
architecture.

At a time when "Overt Anxiety" had not been adopted as
a byword of writing about the "Modern Condition" and
the term "Outsider" for socially isolated persons was not
in general use, Hermann Hesse in *The Steppenwolf*
(1927) had already presented in Harry Haller a recluse
living in a time that was out of joint. In Haller's mind
there is constantly raging a savage battle between a
primitive, rebellious spirit and an intellectual, saintly
one. In addition to his inner conflict, Haller suffers from
living in an impersonal, mechanized, and superficial society. In spite of apparently insurmountable odds, the
protagonist at the end learns to rearrange, whenever necessary, the various elements of his personality in order to
adjust to the multiple adversities of life and to achieve
integration—a solution which is unconvincing.

Harry Haller blames his difficulties in life on the fact that
he belongs to a generation caught between two ages:

He said to me once when we were talking of the
so-called horrors of the Middle Ages: "These
horrors were really non-existent. A man of the
Middle Ages would detest the whole mode of our
present-day life as something far more than horrible,
far more than barbarous. Every age, every culture,
every custom and tradition has its own character,
its own weakness and its own strength, its beauties
and ugliness; accepts certain sufferings as matters
of course, puts up patiently with certain evils.
Human life is reduced to real suffering, to hell,
only when two ages, two cultures and religions
overlap. A man of the Classical Age who had to
live in medieval times would suffocate miserably
just as a savage does in the midst of our civilization.
Now there are times when a whole generation is
caught in this way between two ages, two modes
of life, with the consequence that it loses all power
to understand itself and has no standard, no security,
no simple acquiescence. Naturally, everyone does
not feel this equally strongly. A nature such as
Nietzsche's had to suffer our present ills more than
a generation in advance. What he had to go through
alone and misunderstood, thousands suffer today.

Two prominent contemporary authors, Friedrich Dürrenmatt
and Gertrud von Le Fort, have focused in their writings

considerable efforts on different phenomena of fear.
While the mystic Gertrud von Le Fort believes that in
our cosmos nothing happens outside its divine order,
Dürrenmatt allows an element of chance in his world.

Dürrenmatt regards terror as a means for awakening sympathy in people. He gives shock treatments of fear to his
readers rather than to his characters because he wishes to
frighten his callous contemporaries into a realization of
their criminal indifference toward suffering. In his play
The Visit (1958) the solid citizens of a Swiss village
consent to the murder of one of their closest friends because they are afraid that otherwise they might lose
their possessions. Fear is likewise the keynote of the
playwright's radio play *The Mission of the Vega* (1959).
The Vega, a spaceship, lands on Venus, the inhabitants of
which came from the earth. They have become accustomed to a primitive life of hardship which, brought out
in the following conversations, lacks the injustice existing on earth. The general atmosphere of danger and the
precarious living conditions have forced upon the people
freedom from want and freedom from fear, a state which
has compelled them to live together in peace.

Wood: You say that as if it is something easy, to
die!

Bonstetten: Every necessity is easy. One must only
accept it. And the most necessary, the most natural
presence on this planet is death. It is everywhere,
at all times. The heat is too great, the radiation too
intense. Even the sea is radio-active. Everywhere
there are worms which burrow under our skin and
into our intestines, bacteria which poison our blood,
viruses which destroy our cells. The continents are
full of impassable swamps, boiling seas of oil and
volcanoes everywhere, and stinking giant animals.
We do not fear your bombs, for we live in the
midst of death and have had to learn to fear it no
more.

As a final example in these discussions of fear in literature Gertrud von Le Fort's epistolary narrative *The Last
at the Scaffold* (1931) will be mentioned. This existential
masterpiece was transformed by Bernanos into a successful play which in turn served as a libretto for an opera by
Poulenc. Gertrud von Le Fort presents in this *Novelle* a
background fused out of reality and illusion, a combination reminding one of the mysterious world of E. T. A.
Hoffmann. Most of the action is laid in the cloister of the
Carmelites near Paris in the horror-haunted days of the
French Revolution. The heroine Blanche de la Force can
neither live in the castle of her skeptic father nor find
solace in the monastery or among the revolutionaries
since she is unconsciously longing for a divine world.
Blanche de la Force suffers from an inborn fear, the result of a frightful mistreatment of her mother by the mob.
The fear of the pregnant mother endured during the assault produces in the child a permanent condition of horror. The author suggests that this anxiety reflects the
mortal terror of an epoch coming to an end. There is a
constant fear in the child's eyes because she is obsessed
with visions of destruction of her secure existence. Such

fear leads her to seek refuge with a Carmelite order, although she does not share the deep convictions of its members. Blanche has a subconscious feeling that her mortal fear is religious in nature. When she and the nuns pray the famous hymn of their patron saint, Saint Theresa of Ávila:

> Yours am I, born for you,
> What will you do with me?
> Give me riches or poverty,
> Give me consolation or grief,
> Give me rejoicing or sadness,
> Sweet life, sunlight without a veil,
> Since I gave myself to you completely:
> What will you do with me?

she substitutes the line "Give me asylum or mortal terror" for "Give me rejoicing or sadness." During the death struggle of the prioress, Blanche becomes so terrified that the headmistress of the novices considers her unqualified to take the vows. Later, when religious communities are being dissolved by the revolutionaries, the new prioress hastily orders Blanche to be admitted to the order. She is given the name "Jesus in Gethsemane," for she is to experience within herself the death of Christ's fear and the awakening of a will to survive, a will that corresponds to the reality of things, the terror of the world. As a revolutionary commission appears to arrest the nuns, Blanche is overwhelmed by her fear and flees to her home. There she has to witness the killing of her father, whom she herself was unable to save because she could not obey the mob's alternative to the slaughter; she could not drink a cup of human blood. Protected by pitying market women, she is taken to witness many killings and is presented to the mob as an aristocrat converted to the cause of the revolution. One day while watching executions she sees the sisters ascending a scaffold singing "Veni creator." She loses her fear and exalted by a spiritual awakening joins the Carmelites in their hymns. Before it is her turn to be beheaded, the market women snatch her away and beat her to death. Defenseless man in his moment of greatest fear thus joins God in a state of infinite security. Rilke's famous saying, "Who is talking about being victorious?—to have come through is everything," is applicable not only to the protagonist of this *Novelle* but also to those in his own and Kafka's novels.

Although the number of literary works and motives producing fear considered in the discussion above are comparatively few, there seems to be enough material evidence from the beginning of German literature to the present of variations in intensity in the general state of fear. A minimum of overt anxiety was expressed during periods when there appeared to be a sense of unity in man's life, that is, when his struggle for existence did not conflict with his intellectual needs. The two periods showing the greatest harmony and the least anxiety were the time of the portrait sculptors and court romances, and the age of Goethe. The states of anxiety described in German works always reached their heights after a sharp decline in civilization.

During the decay of courtly culture, Walther von der Vogelweide lamented the general anxiety among youth.

Three centuries later, coinciding with the Baroque movement, the second period of general depressions made its appearance. The aftermath of war, disease, and scientific progress with its heliocentric theory had robbed man of his security and faith. The third wave of fear and pessimism invaded German letters after the Napoleonic Wars and the Industrial Revolution. From the writings of the later romanticists, Heine, Lenau, and Hoffmann, as well as those of the apostle of pessimism Schopenhauer, emanated a philosophy of skepticism, anxiety, and despair. After Darwin's theory of biology and Nietzsche's of the decay of faith had become generally known, fear among people increased considerably. At the turn of the century many narratives appeared disclosing alleged skepticism and anxiety prevailing in the upper classes of society. Big-city civilizations were depicted as breeding places of unrest, fear, and hopelessness. The great genealogical novels dealing with upper- and middle-class families and fiction about subtilized children and youths incapable of making adjustments to life were filled with accounts of anxiety and instability.

Since the First World War, writers have uninterruptedly turned out literary works wrestling with "the modern dilemma." They have attempted analyses of our times and have proposed philosophies compatible with our precarious existence. Gertrud von Le Fort, Rilke, von Hofmannsthal, Kafka, Brecht urge men, even though their sacrifices are in vain and never will be recognized, to combat their fears and fulfill those destinies they believe to be theirs. These authors share with Kierkegaard the belief that we can achieve innermost freedom only if our decisions are forged by fear and despair.

The narrator in Hermann Hesse's *Steppenwolf* argues that many gifted people suffer from a state of anxiety because they are caught between two ages. If this were true and if Nietzsche's assertions were valid that architecture and painting grow first out of a particular culture, literature second, and music last, one might conjecture that in the expressionist movement and its outgrowths western civilization is passing through a last phase of romanticism and has arrived at the threshold of a predominantly classical period evidenced by unadorned architecture.

Many recent German literary works contain romantic and mystic overtones. Gertrud von Le Fort and Barlach give a Christian answer to modern perplexities as did the mystics of the fourteenth century and the pietists of the eighteenth. Gottfried Benn labels the sum of contemporary experience as a nothing, the enigmatical conclusion of being able to explain everything, and he suggests that man strive for aesthetic perfection in some art form.

There are indications that people have made progress in the last few years in learning to live with overt anxiety and in time might come to look at fear as did the exiles to Venus in *The Mission of the Vega*. The international crises of the last two years have been accepted more calmly by news media than have any other world threats since the invention of nuclear weapons. The following occurrences might be taken as good omens that the recent wave of anxiety has crested: When such clichés as "the frustration in our atomic age" have been humorously treated in the comic strips ("Beetle Bailey"), when Auden's *The Age of Anxiety* has begun to sound like yesteryear's jazz, when T. S. Eliot's hymns on decaying and dying are parodied by Henry Reid ("Chard Witlow") and Eliot's recording voice is mocked by Dylan Thomas, when assembly-line fiction of world destruction brought about by unscrupulous scientists and power maniacs is dismissed summarily by its continental reviewers and readers, when students are vociferously rejecting Dürrenmatt's *The Mission of the Vega* as "another *1984*," and when the newspapers hail or bewail the end of the beatnik generation, the symbol of instability, there are signs in the air that the dawn of a new epoch is breaking, a period in which a greater sense of unity might prevail.

Charles Child Walcutt

SOURCE: "Fear Motifs in the Literature Between Wars," in *South Atlantic Quarterly,* Vol. 46, April, 1947, pp. 225-38.

[*In the following essay, Walcutt describes interwar literature as characterized by guilt following World War I, fear during the 1930s, and confrontation during the early years of World War II.*]

"If we had only heeded our writers! The poets saw the second war coming and realized its horror, early in the thirties. . . ." A hundred versions of these sentiments have been uttered in recent years. It is a commonplace of criticism to say that the poet is more aware of historical trends than the historian, of social currents than the sociologist, of spiritual values than the theologian. E. B. White has declared that he envies the poets their wisdom. This superior insight of the poets undoubtedly is a fact. It is also a universal truth of history that mankind has not heeded its wise men. But the relation of literature to society, particularly with respect to the problem of war in this century, cannot perhaps be adequately described as merely a clear warning unheeded by unheeding men. It is more complicated and more significant than that.

From World War I to World War II there has been a cycle or pattern of attitudes toward war; this pattern appears both in literature generally and in the changing moods of particular writers. It begins with guilt, turns into fear, and purges itself in confrontation. Immediately after the first war came guilt and remorse. These were imperceptibly transformed into fear of the coming war. This fear almost entirely disappeared in the literature of confrontation after the war began.

After World War I there was let-down, despair, and—inevitably—guilt. People found that they had not won a brave new world. All the old problems remained as daily reminders, fears, and threats—many of them indeed intensified by the war which had proposed to eliminate them. The simple people who had fought were soon selling apples on street corners. This is mentioned not to use a trite figure, but to recall a powerful symbol of guilt: the apple-seller was the concrete embodiment of a tremendous failure. The war had generated bigness—centralized power—which combined with public exhaustion to make people believe that they were less than ever in control of their fate. Guilt spread with the grim realization that life and time had been squandered without producing any fundamental change in the nature of man or the constitution of society. The causes of war were unaltered, and men recoiled in guilt and remorse.

Guilt, remorse, and despair were the binding elements—the mortar—of the literature of the 1920's. Treatises exposed the munitions industry; pamphlets attacked profiteers; we lacerated our flesh by decreeing that no man should ever again make a cent of profit from wartime production—but this of course came later: at first our guilt was such that we could not even imagine the possibility of another war. In fiction we immediately think of Hemingway. In *The Sun Also Rises* there is a kind of pastoral cynicism which constitutes a protest against all the hypocrisies, the sentimentalities, and the superficialities which led us into war. This protest is an expression of guilt. Hemingway's war novel, *A Farewell to Arms,* is also heavy with a sense of waste and futility: it says that the war is meaningless, that society is drenched with evil, and that only the simple emotions of separate people are good. The same generalizations apply to the early writings of John Dos Passos and to dozens of other novelists. They likewise apply to much of the poetry of the twenties. Robinson Jeffers, for example, cries out against civilization and warns us to

> . . . be in nothing so moderate as in love of man, a
>   clever servant, insufferable master.
> There is the trap that catches noblest spirits, that
>   caught—they say—God, when he walked on
>   earth.

Guilt informs the early novels of Aldous Huxley, and it is the backbone of the tremendous figure of social protest in the fiction of the twenties. Guilt is thus diffused in such other emotions as bravado, recklessness, cynicism, indignation, and social protest. Such emotions are partly compensatory, partly mere elaborations on the underlying guilt.

The time comes when the dark night of guilt is penetrated by the first red gleams of a new and bloodier day. Men watched the Nazis grow stronger, but their guilt prevented them from acting. They were caught in a death-impulse of expiation. Terror mounted as they watched the menace grow. It was the terror that accompanies inaction, the painful stretching tension that grows while the thunder in the cloud does not strike. An example of sheer terror is H. G. Wells's *The Croquet Player* (1937), in which the brooding evil that haunts a certain spot in England is traced to the bones there of prehistoric men, which have been disturbed by diggers: the spirits of these wild brutes return, and the inhabitants are infected with terror and cruelty. But this, we find, is only a myth by which a sensitive doctor conveys his terror of the frightful violence that man is about to release. "He has made up that story . . . because the realities that are overwhelming him are so monstrous and frightful that he has to transform them into this fairy tale about old skulls." What he fears is "endemic panic . . . a contagion in our atmosphere. A sickness in the very grounds of our lives"—the return of the Beast. "And now we see him here face to face and his grin derides us. Man is still what he was. Invincibly bestial, envious, malicious, greedy. Man, Sir, unmasked and disillusioned, is the same fearing, snarling, fighting beast he was a hundred thousand years ago. These are no metaphors, Sir. What I tell you is the monstrous reality. The brute has been marking time and dreaming of a progress it has failed to make. . . ." A single passing reference to children killed by bombs connects this terror to the immediate future.

It is often said that our poets anticipated all the horrors of the war during the 1930's and were therefore well ahead of their time. We should consider not only the fact of this anticipation but also its emotional and intellectual qualities and perhaps question the kind of social "usefulness" that can be expected of it. Guilt and fear, but particularly guilt, depend upon a concept of personal responsibility for social evil. The poet looks at the fearful misapplication of life and knowledge and resources against the dark background of political manipulation, individual greed, and moral apathy which precede, underlie, and succeed the sacrifice of the war effort. The contrast appalls him. Disgust with mankind and indignation are ethical responses to these blacks and whites. The poet, moreover, is in a special situation: being the sensitive conscience of society, he feels his guilt more painfully than ordinary men; not being a man of action, he feels in double measure the guilt of society's inaction. He suffers because he knows and because he does not act.

To keep this guilt from becoming intolerable, the poet may—instead of protesting or of retreating into cynicism—make an aesthetic object of it and of his fear, which he will subject to fascinated contemplation and from which he may wring a poetry that will exercise a hypnotic effect of forgetfulness that is just as real an escape as the cynicism of the early Hemingway. Such a poet is Frederic Prokosch, who has wrought so brilliantly with the problem of fear that it has been almost wholly transformed in some of his poems into a gilded arabesque. His poems in *Death at Sea,* published early in 1940, are almost exclusively concerned with the approaching catastrophe. The sea in the title, which appears again and again in the poems, is his symbol for the death instinct in modern man. It is the yearning for annihilation, and Prokosch renders it so perfectly that he appears to be identified with it. For example, "The Heroes" deals with an embarkation of young Nazi soldiers. A contrast is made between their fanatical devotion to their cause and the consequent drying up in them of love, represented by the grief-stricken women who watch the departure and

are, it appears, despised for the weakness which their grief reveals. That is how the poem appeared to me. But to a group of very intelligent students with whom I discussed it in 1940 it appeared that Prokosch had a certain admiration for these "transported" soldiers—if not admiration, they certainly would not concede that he saw them as objects of horror and despair. He was, they said, merely interested and even fascinated. The horror I found in the situation came from my own idealism, not from the poet's intention. Reading this poem now, we may wonder whether "fear" of war induced by it should have heightened people's awareness of social realities, or whether its effect might not rather have been hypnotic or distracting:

THE HEROES

And then they moved. Sunlight covered them like
    a song.
They turned their clipped, indifferent heads once
    more,
They smiled, and seemed to wait: their long
Brown arms shone like water and the shore

Muttered, like a gigantic animal in pain.
The women and children were no more than birds
Or leaves, or drops of rain.
They were incapable of thoughts or words.

And these tall smiling figures, legendary,
Though a week before they had been only men,
Stood on the brink of the past; all the fury
And hallucination of the past rose up again,

Rose up and covered them like fever, or a song.
They were statues. They scarcely seemed to move,
As they moved away. They had grown tall and
    strong,
Their eyes glowed with a new and hidden love.

The women did not understand at all. They stood
And waited till the ship was gone. Their grief
Was like the warm rain falling or a leaf
Falling into the hollow of a wood.

No amount of exposition could convince my students that the poet presented these "heroes" with distaste or even disgust. They saw no ethical attitude at all in it—only fascinated contemplation of a situation, flavored, some said, with admiration.

Another poem in the same volume, "Molière," presents the apparently shallow formality and rationalism of the rococo as a conscious defense against the bestiality and violence of man. It is the artifice by which the brute is held at bay, even as the glow of approaching revolution deepens. Here are the first twelve lines:

Molière, with his deliberate eye and urbane
Pen, pierced the skull: in the tart elegance of his
    verse
As in a collector's palm, lay man's split,
    membranous brain.

What he said about avarice, affectation, death,
Was clad in such lucidity—it almost seemed

That there was little he intuitively discerned or
　even dreamed

Of that horrible disorderly whirlpool, man's
　desire:
The hooked, retaliating nightmare, the dirty tears,
　the hissing breath—
To tell of these would demand a pen dipped not in
　ink but in fire!

And yet, he knew, he knew; and all those others
　knew as well.
Through the clipped and ordered park, the salon,
　the avenue,
They walked, rosy with the approaching glow and
　spectacle of hell.

The poem concludes with the statement that this civilization "Lies lost as wholly as Othello's howl, or Dido's echoing cave." The implication is that a similar catastrophe is about to break on the modern world and that modern man goes on with the trivia of daily life, aware but heedless, rosy with the approaching glow and spectacle of hell. This is fearful, indeed, but being approached through a sort of historical parallel it appears as inevitable, and the effect is fascination and wonder rather than incitement to action or even a very keen sense of society's predicament. These poems do not render a richer ethical apprehension of the modern problem, but rather they offer an escape from it in the contemplation of their glittering patterns of inevitableness and decay. Guilt has given way to fear, after which the scarcity and impotence of ethical consciousness in a world of blind masses and death-struck intellectuals is then acknowledged and this knowledge is itself made an object of detached aesthetic contemplation.

II

If the fear motif has thus been used as an escape from the dilemma of individual responsibility in a world where the responsible individual feels himself to be not only impotent before the hugeness of the problem but also corrupted by his own participation in the comforts of materialism, it has doubtless been so because modern society lacks values which can compete successfully with our despised but luscious chrome-plated fleshpots. The weakening of values is an aspect or cause of the aimlessness, the lack of purpose, which begets fear. But we have gone further than this. What happens when certain values have wavered or diminished to the point where we are no longer sure whether fear is a permissible emotion? Such a tendency is revealed in current treatments of two most "fearful" matters. Insanity and the supernatural are today subjects of astonishing literary equivocation.

A century ago the supernatural was a constant reality, not to say obsession; and it was not to be trifled with. From the horrors of Poe to the humor of Artemus Ward is a long step with much land between. Today we are not supposed to believe in ghosts and goblins. We are timid and somewhat shamefaced about ESP, revivalism, and the new mysticism. And we now have, in movies about zombies, in the *New Yorker Magazine,* and elsewhere, a blend of humor and the supernatural which is unique. We shiver with fear at the same time that we laugh at ourselves for these primitive fears. Insanity is receiving the same ambivalent treatment. Whereas science seeks to explore and define it, popular literature now considers it something of a virtue, not to say an accomplishment. Plays like *Harvey* and a host of other documents one could mention are saying that the world is so mad that a reasonable man had better abandon his reason or he will go mad with thinking on the unthinkable. Here daffiness becomes a virtue, and we scream with shrill laughter at a world that is out of control. This desperate burlesquing of insanity and the supernatural is an attempt to destroy the values underlying our deepest fears. Fears do not make us face problems. We evade them by a safety valve of maniacal laughter.

III

First guilt and remorse. Then we shuddered with apprehension or embroidered our terror into fantastic patterns as the inevitable war moved toward us. Then, when the fury broke, there was relief from tension. There was the outlet of participation. Guilt was quite gone, because now it was too late to prevent what had come. There was curiosity, even absorption in the details of war. Never have we had such accurate and objective reportage as, for example, in the articles in the *New Yorker, Collier's,* the *Post,* and in volumes of the various correspondents. It appears that such reportage was intended at the beginning of the war to let the full horror of the facts speak for itself. Fear of war had been so great during the thirties that one thought no imaginative treatment of it would be necessary or indeed possible when it came. During the years of fearful waiting we assumed that the real thing would be even more fearful. But it was not. Perhaps our reporters failed to reckon on the cathartic effect of action. Perhaps they failed to see how interesting war could be. Surely they must have failed to anticipate that it would have its humorous aspects and that restraint and dryness of style would be appropriate. And they probably had not counted on the intense interest of Americans in machinery and speed and power, the eagerness of a depression-starved generation for new gadgets. In any event, this reporting did not convey any horror comparable to the prewar expectation, nothing remotely approaching the terror of H. G. Wells, the morbid absorption of Prokosch, or the anguish of Auden. Wartime reportage is jolly by comparison with these. *A Walk in the Sun,* for example, or *A Bell for Adano,* contains none of the terror expected in 1937. Marquand in *Repent in Haste* complains of the monotony of battle stories: a few crashes, a few deaths, a few operations by sea or air—and after that they are all alike, he says. This attitude would have been truly inconceivable to the fear-ridden thirties. The complete change of mental climate involved in the turn from fear to confrontation accounts for the way people in America were troubled by Hemingway's *For Whom the Bell Tolls.* This book straddled the line between fear and confrontation. It dealt with the real confrontation in Spain, but to America in 1940 this was still imaginary and hence in the domain of fear. People did not know how to take the book.

Cecil Day Lewis has recently published a volume of poems, *Short Is the Time,* written between 1936 and 1943, that illustrate the generalizations offered here. Most of them deal with some aspect of the contemporary world, with war as the binding element. In "February, 1936" Lewis writes of fear and guilt using metaphors of childhood and sacrifice. The poem is heavy with guilt:

> Whether to die,
> Or live beneath fear's eye—
> Heavily hangs the sentence of this sky.
>
> Now to the fire
> From killing fells we bear
> This new-born lamb, our premature desire.
>
> We cannot meet
> Our children's mirth, at night
> Who dream their blood upon a darkening street.
>
> Stay away, Spring!
> Since death is on the wing
> To blast our seed and poison every thing.

In "Bombers" (1938) themes of guilt and fear are united with metaphors of childbirth, suffering, and blood. Here, even as late as 1938, guilt is almost as strong as fear. Yet the latter is clearly seen to have taken possession of the poem. Here are the last three stanzas:

> Black as vermin, crawling in echelon
> Beneath the cloud-floor, the bombers come:
> The heavy angels, carrying harm in
> Their wombs that ache to be rid of death.
>
> This is the seed that grows for ruin,
> The iron embryo conceived in fear.
> Soon or late its need must be answered
> In fear delivered and screeching fire.
>
> Choose between your child and this fatal embryo.
> Shall your guilt bear arms, and the children you
>   want
> Be condemned to die by the powers you paid for
> And haunt the houses you never built?

In these lines a chill of dread unites with pathetic images of children's suffering, and the poignancy carries to the point where reader and poet are identified with the helplessness of the children. The poem states guilt but conveys first dread and then helplessness, the latter again a sort of escape from impossible responsibilities. Guilt, particularly war-guilt, follows the inflicting of pain and death. Expiation comes through identification with the injured: to suffer is to repay. Rebecca West has described the hypnotized immobility with which guilt-stricken England, embracing the idea of sacrifice, waited like a black lamb for the Nazi knife at its throat. Something of that

spirit informs this poem: the guilty wait fearfully the self-inflicted doom of war.

Nor is Lewis unaware of the motives behind the death impulse. Addressing Death, he refers to those who have sought Him out:

> I grant you the last word. But what of these—
> The criminal agents of a dying will
> Who, frantic with defeat, conspire to force your
> Earlier intervention?
> It is they, your damned auxiliaries, must answer
> For the self-slain in the foodless, fireless room,
> For stunted hearts that droop by our olive-green
> Canals, the blossom of children untimely shattered
> By their crazed, random fire, and the fear like a
>   black frost
> Foreshortening our prospect, metallic on our
>   tongues.
> If I am too familiar with you, sir,
> It is that these have brought you into contempt.
> You are in nature. These are most unnatural.

The poet's war is with death's "free-lance and officious gunmen," who betray mankind. Their betrayal has consisted of commerce and appeasement—of all the activities that characterized the years during which war grew steadily more inevitable while everyone watched and no one acted. But who "sought" death? The appeasers who enjoyed their profits and would enjoy war when it came—or the poet who raptly gazes at an evil which he cannot control and which he takes unto his bosom for an object of aesthetic investigation? Does the poet err in supposing that his guilty fear is a true image of society's conscience? Does not the poet lacerate his own tender conscience with a thorn whip woven of all society's guilt? Were he a man of action he would not think so painfully, whereas to think demands traits of mind and character which set him apart from society and cause to flower in him the guilt of which society bears the unconscious seeds. The poet condemns society for failing to act by a conscience that it does not have.

With the confrontation of war the tone of Lewis's poems shifts unmistakably to vigor and affirmation through action:

> Here in a parched and stranger place
> We fight for England free,
> The good our fathers won for her,
> The land they hoped to see.

Everything is simplified. These spirited rhythms carry us back to an earlier century of British confidence. And we ask, Is this what the fear-ridden, the guilt-striken poet of the thirties was looking forward to? Had his anguished absorption with evil, with irresponsibility, with the coming deaths of little children prepared him only for simple exultation in action like that experienced by any vigorous boy of eighteen?

Yet Lewis cannot be satisfied with the simple escape of action, not completely or not always. That he carries his guilt into and through the war appears in "Will It Be So Again?," written between 1941 and 1943. The question asked is bold to the point of being prophetic; its tone is weariness, grief, resignation:

> Will it be so again
> That the brave, the gifted are lost from view,
> And empty, scheming men
> Are left in peace their lunatic age to renew?
>
> . . . . .
>
> Will it be so again—
> The jungle code and the hypocrite gesture?
> A poppy wreath for the slain
> And a cut-throat world for the living? that stale imposture
> Played on us once again?

The poet knows, alas, that it will be so again—and where in another mood he enjoyed the catharsis of confrontation, here he shows that this catharsis has failed to cleanse, and the sick spirit carries the fever of guilt and fear into the frenetic tumult by which he vainly tries to rid himself of his ailment. The poet perhaps sees that his activity is desperate and is therefore evidence of his malady. But nevertheless the malady is unbearable and drives him on. What the poet does not see is that the moral indignation contained in such phrases as "hypocrite gesture," "stale imposture," and "scheming men" presents us with a *cul de sac* walled with the hard granite of fact—a granite not of moral guilt but of a society both too massive and too complicated to be stormed with such a weapon. It is as if the poet sought to melt this granite wall with his tears, and the futility of this enterprise reminds us of Prokosch's arabesques: both draw away from the social problem.

Properly exploited, guilt and fear are drugs. Already we see signs that the atomic bomb is being worked up into a dreadful symbol with which we shall divert ourselves from the problems and responsibilities that confront us in these years following the war. On a lower level, horror movies abound, filling the same need. It is to be doubted, however, that the literature of the next decade will follow the same pattern of guilt-fear-confrontation. Guilt is the rebound of betrayed idealism. But this time most of the intellectuals have not expected the war to make the world safe for democracy. They have considered it anything from a blind folly at one extreme to a desperate necessity at the other, but between these extreme attitudes has been no confidence that victory would affect the conditions of human nature or of modern society which produce wars. Writers will therefore not experience new guilt, although, as we have seen in the case of C. Day Lewis, they may carry some of the old unpurged guilt along with them. Some of them will doubtless investigate the question of ethical responsibility in a world whose complexity increases while the amount of disinterested ethical force exercised in it becomes proportionately smaller. This problem will evoke cold analysis from some and pure terror of a new sort from others.

Patricia Merivale

SOURCE: "Learning the Hard Way: Gothic Pedagogy in the Modern Romance Quest," in *Comparative Literature,* Vol. 36, No. 2, Spring, 1984, pp. 146-61.

[*In the following essay, Merivale focuses on "Gothic pedagogy," or learning by fear.*]

A series of works—from Mozart's *The Magic Flute* (1791) through Goethe's *Faust* (1806, 1832), Flaubert's *La Tentation de St. Antoine* (1856), James Branch Cabell's *Jurgen* (1919), David Lindsay's *A Voyage to Arcturus* (1920), and Hermann Hesse's *Steppenwolf* (1927) to John Fowles's *The Magus* (1966)—employ the devices of what I call "Gothic pedagogy" in their dramatic or narrative structures. Inner artifacts—pageant, vision, performance—provide the hero of each of these "internalized romantic quests"[1] with an astonishing, terrifying, yet phantasmagorical sequence of lessons, made up of separate episodes chiefly connected with each other by the fact that the hero experiences them. These "Gothicized" hero-quests, or *Bildungen,* are also Gothicized godgames, for a Magus, devil-god and stage-director, has devised and produced them to reinforce his didactic manipulations of the hero. Gothic pedagogy is the linkage between such a godgame and such a hero-quest: its inner artifacts are, so to speak, the strings by which the puppets are controlled.

The *Walpurgisnacht* pattern of *Faust* II, as found in *St. Antoine, Jurgen, Steppenwolf,* and *The Magus* (as also in *Peer Gynt*) is perhaps the clearest, as well as the most definitively "Gothic" narrative structure for Gothic pedagogy, but the episodic, linear journey of *Arcturus* and the explicit initiation ritual of *The Magic Flute* are made up of similarly discrete, eclectic, terrifying, and ultimately educational "performances."

The chief goal of education by fear has commonly been disillusionment, usually qualified by an ambiguous moral improvement and an increased knowledge of the world or self, but approaching, in *St. Antoine* and *Arcturus,* an unrelieved pessimism. The heroes of three modern existential quests, those by Cabell, Hesse, and Fowles, are able, by the end, to start building up their identity again on relatively illusionfree foundations, yet without reaching the communal affirmations of the Mozartian or Goethean initiations, as seen in *The Magic Flute* and in *Wilhelm Meister.*

"Teaching through fear," by means of allegorical pageants, rituals, or other inner actions of the sort found in *The Magic Flute* and *Faust,* constitutes the whole of the action in Flaubert's *La Tentation de St. Antoine* and almost the whole in *A Voyage to Arcturus* and *The Magus.* These works are part of the long tradition of the godgame. (An early example is Shakespeare's *Tempest,* where a benevolent Prospero manipulates the action in order to educate and initiate.) "Mozart," again, is the patron of the educational phantasmagoria in the Magic

Theater of Hesse's *Steppenwolf*. The most recent godgame, as familiar, memorable, and specious as it is Gothic, is Fowles's *The Magus,* in which a far more ambiguously benevolent magician manipulates actions and feelings through allegedly educational, highly melodramatic, phantasmagorical pageants. In such works, stages or stations of a hero's journey of education may be marked both by manipulated actions, in which the hero unwittingly enacts the plan of the higher powers, and by explicitly "theatrical" performances, like those Mephisto puts on for Faust, which not only enlighten the hero but require him, as intermediary audience, to respond on our behalf with the Gothic emotions of terror and astonishment.

Such initiatory sequences tend to be distinctly eclectic. The rise of Comparative Religion and Mythology toward the end of the eighteenth century seems to be one cause of the "bricolage"—the piecing together from any and all available sources—of such episodes in texts from *Faust* and *The Magic Flute* (if not earlier) to the present day. Mozart's hero is led episodically toward enlightenment, a visionary as well as a social initiation, whose symbolic patterns and stages are put together from the repertoire of gimmicks available in folklore, traditional religions, subversive heresies, new cults, leftovers from old cults, Christianity, Rosicrucianism, alchemy, numerous other subdivisions of the occult, and of course especially the—in themselves eclectic—rituals of Freemasonry. Our judgment of the literary merits of the *Magic Flute* libretto is less relevant here than its evident importance, for more than musical reasons, to every author I am discussing. The recipes are similar for works much influenced by *The Magic Flute:* Goethe's sequel *Die Zauberflöte zweiter Teil,* his novelle *Das Märchen* (both 1795), various German romantic tales, *Faust,* and eventually Strauss's *Die Frau ohne Schatten,* however much subtler and more complex they may be in their allegorical intentions. Allegory in *The Divine Comedy,* though multi-layered, is controlled by a single "true" perspective; allegory in *The Magic Flute* and its successors is eclectic, for truth is seen as multiple and therefore relative, or inaccessible, or non-existent.

"Eclectic allegories" borrow mythologies from all over the place and juxtapose them abruptly, in bricolage, rather than blending them. Their heroes go through one discrete experience after another; each experience is separately significant and representative, but they signify in different ways, according to different patterns of belief, or even take place in different mythological realms. "We three have met like characters out of three separate romances which the Author has composed in different styles," says a character in Cabell's *Jurgen.*[2] Such episodes are connected more, as I have suggested, by the hero's experiencing of them than by any logic of cause and effect; they add up, in the end, to a sort of summary world view in terms of the slow accretion of the hero's identity. Eclectic allegories are marked by the synecdochal inclusiveness characteristic of the "internalized romantic quest," of which they are, in my view, a major subdivision, distinguished by their strongly episodic, almost encyclopedic structures.

The quickest and most entertaining way to see how eclectic allegory works is to read *Jurgen,* an elegant, frivolous spoof of a heroic quest for identity. Cabell lays under contribution every literary mythology available (including especially *Faust*), to accumulate a potpourri of fantasy experiences and dramatic roles all the more appropriate for such a hero if he is, as so many of them are, an artist-hero as well. Jurgen circles, like a good hero of internalized romantic quest, back to the doubtfully Goethean Ewig Weibliche who was his starting point (cf. Abrams)—back home, after journeys, like Peer Gynt's or Faust's, made up of teeming fantasies from his own brain, to the woman he abandoned. All these works are shaped biographically, but all these heroes—even Jurgen—are in some degree representative of Man. The biographical is a synecdoche for the historical: the Life of Man is foreshortened into the life of a man.

John Fowles seems to be pointing in the direction of eclectic allegory, when in his most explicit definition of the godgame he offers an alternative title for *The Magus:* "*The Godgame.* I did intend Conchis to exhibit *a series of masks representing human notions of God,* from the supernatural to the jargon-ridden scientific; that is, a series of human illusions about something that does not exist in fact, absolute knowledge and absolute power. The destruction of such illusions seems to me still an eminently humanist aim" (my italics).[3] The stripping away of a series of illusions: as I have suggested, this formula will recur continually in our discussion of eclectic allegories from Flaubert to the present. As a definition of godgame, however, this does not entirely square either with general critical usage or with Fowles's own usage in the text. His palinode at the end of *The Magus,* "The godgame is over . . . Because there is no God, and it is not a game" (p. 637), evidently refers in the more familiar sense to the complex structure of deity manipulating protagonist by the overlapping devices of rigged actions and educational inner artifacts. Seemingly Fowles intends us to distinguish the microcosmic game which has made up most of his book from the macrocosmic game in which we and Nicholas perhaps still half believe, even at the end, insofar as we still (mistakenly) suppose that there is some analogy between Conchis's complex "game" and the way the world works. A similar palinode occurs at the end of *Jurgen:* we and Jurgen have supposed from the beginning that the course of his quest is determined by some alliance between Koshchei, the god "who made things as they are" (p. 6) and the goddess Sereda, who "[takes] the color out of all things" (p. 25). "Do you think . . . that I am frowzing in this underground place by my own choice? and knew your name by accident?" asks the Centaur (p. 6). When Jurgen checks on this at the end, however, he is exposed to the "humiliating fact" (p. 248) that Koshchei has had much more important things to do than worry about Jurgen—that Jurgen, indeed, like his own Quixotic horse, has been free to choose his own way all along (p. 24). Both authors get the benefit of the firm narrative structure of the godgame while renouncing the philosophical commitments that it implies. Whatever ambiguities have maintained tension throughout the microgame as to the malevolence or benevolence of the "deity" are resolved in the macrogame into the awful though sometimes bracing fact of his indifference (Fowles, Cabell, Flaubert). On the other hand such godgames as *The Magic Flute,* G. K. Chesterton's *The Man Who Was Thursday,* and *A Voyage to Arcturus* depend for much of their significance on the supposition that the microgame that the protagonist goes through *is* in some sense a representation of the macrogame, or the way things are. The episodes in each are "a series of confidence tricks" played by Sarastro or Sunday or Krag, in their demonic disguises, whose seeming malevolence will ultimately be revealed as somehow benevolent (as indeed it also is *within* Fowles's microgame).

Mozart's librettist has provided a pre-Romantic link between the initiations undergone by Spenser's Red-Crosse Knight, or the baroque godgames of Calderón, Cervantes, and Shakespeare, and the more secular and apparently randomly inclusive quests of the Romantics. In Mozart, as in *Wilhelm Meister,* initiation into manhood and humane community is under the control of Higher Powers; it is, as the term "godgame" implies, something of a rigged performance. There is more emphasis on initiation into, or at least toward, transcendence and less on community in the Romantic story tellers (Novalis, Hoffmann, and others), despite the strong influence of Mozart on their eclectic and allegorical internalizations of quest. The staged initiation rituals of *Das Märchen,* more lighthearted than Goethe's own sequel but almost equally operatic, the rituals of Novalis's *Heinrich von Ofterdingen* (1798), and those of Hoffmann's *Der goldene Topf* (1814) are all more explicitly visionary in culmination than *The Magic Flute* and more nearly synonymous (as *Faust* is also) with the entire life quest of their respective heroes. They adapt to more visionary purposes patterns of arcane gimmickry like those found in Mozart: the emblems of rose, lily, and crystal, the alchemical deployments of precious metals and the four elements, and much else. Although they deal far more in the uncanny and the downright supernatural, and it is thus easier to call them Gothic, if anything they educate more by beauty and less by fear than Mozart does. Hoffmann and Novalis, in turn, helped to shape the Christian allegories of George Macdonald (and, through him, C. S. Lewis), as well as Lindsay's allegorical romance, thinly disguised as science fiction, *A Voyage to Arcturus,* which, like Flaubert's *St. Antoine,* is a secular godgame and an ironically Faustian visionary quest; both provide useful analogies to such contemporary godgames as *The Magus* and Thomas Pynchon's *The Crying of Lot 49.*

In the *Magic Flute-Faust*-Flaubert sequence, shifting emphases in the dialectic of Gothic and rational nullify, by the time of Flaubert, the benevolent results of Gothic pedagogy as employed in the godgames of *Faust* or *The Magic Flute.* In *St. Antoine* the operations of Hilarion's Gothic pedagogy undermine the Saint's always fragile identity. As in Ibsen's *Peer Gynt,* for instance, and later in *Arcturus,* the Faustian "existential" accretion of identity changes direction: it becomes a reductive process, of stages coming ever closer to nonidentity.

Faust II is made up largely of Mephistopheles's stage-managed sequence of episodes, representing from every angle the variety of choice both of action (or mode of life) and outlook available to the questing spirit. These episodes "exhaust symbolically a circle of human possibilities"; they are all "little independent worlds, which, each being complete in itself . . . yet come but little in contact . . . to express a manifold world [in which] the hero [acts] merely as a sort of thread," as Eckermann said of the episodes of *Faust.*[4] In *Faust* such a structure is of course dramatic; in other works it may be lyric, narrative, or even operatic. Goethe himself, in conversation, stressed the connections between Mozart and *Faust:* "the higher import [of the Helena scene in *Faust* II] will not escape the initiated—as with *The Magic Flute*" (Hamlin, p. 415); he and others frequently alluded to the "operatic" nature of *Faust* II, which he felt should have been set to music by Mozart (or Meyerbeer).

Mozart's quest-hero, Tamino, is controlled by the patterns of ritual, which provide a degree of psychological safety, for the audience at least. *Faust* is, in formal or fictional terms, a game between God and Satan, which God, like Sarastro, is bound to win. Much of Faust's education takes place in smaller inner duplications of the main action within that larger frame of benevolent, rational, divine control. The phantasmagorical theatricals—*Walpurgisnacht,* Witches's Kitchen, Helena episode, Classical *Walpurgisnacht,* and others, are set up by stage-director Mephistopheles. However dark and chaotic the Gothic metadramas spun from the mind of Faust which give Mephisto his raw material, the outer structure remains rational, if not always reasonable, and the goal is still, as in Mozart or the romantic tales, an "enlightened" or quasi-visionary equivalent of salvation. Faust, curiously passive, as the heroes of eclectic allegory usually are (St. Antoine is an extreme case), is at best in these scenes one of Mephisto's performers (Mephisto is, in turn, one of God's), but more often almost as much the spectator as we are.

Mephistopheles, the quintessence of Faustian Gothic, appears suddenly and looms darkly; in visual terms, he takes up an excess of space and cuts off light, like the Queen of the Night, Sarastro, or the Moor Monostatos in any even moderately Gothic production of *The Magic Flute,* or the ever-enlarging Hilarion-devil in *St. Antoine,* or the black nurse-bodyguard in *The Magus.* To loom darkly is only part of Sarastro's role; it is the whole function of that papier-maché Gothic villain, Mozart's Moor. Both perform in the service of education, as the comic cowardice of that reluctant student and failed hero-quester, Papageno, reveals: their loomings are, like all the terrifying stage effects and threats of damnation in the script, a Gothic pedagogy. In another sense, however, Faust is his own teacher, for stage-manager Mephisto *is* his dark double. W. H. Auden has commented that "in an ideal production, Faust and Mephisto should be played by identical twins."[5]

"Fostered alike by beauty and by fear" is Wordsworth's summary phrase for his own late eighteenth-century, pre-

Romantic education, evidently a more balanced one—like Faust's—than those of, say, Heinrich von Ofterdingen, who was largely educated by beauty, or of Mary Shelley's Victor Frankenstein, who was largely educated by fear. Frankenstein's most plangent terror is that induced by the sight of his Monster, dark against the night sky, looming at casements, shutting him into spaces too small, or, shadowy on the ice, pursuing him over spaces too large, dead, and empty. The Gothic pedagogues, like Racinean kings Gothicized by Roland Barthes, or like Wordsworth's vengeful mountain pursuing the small guilty boy across the lake in his stolen boat, educate through fear.

Sarastro employs the figures of apparent evil to teach his would-be initiates; the God of Faust can in the end turn all Mephisto's evil inclinations to good effects. Frankenstein, on the other hand, although the "god" of Mary Shelley's story, can by no means control the monster he creates. His intellectual pretensions—to know everything and to grant life—are a Faustian mockery of the rational control exercised, Prospero-like, by these other rulers; he only achieves, by more advanced and "scientific" systems, what Faustian magic does: he conjures up his own dark double. Perhaps Frankenstein and the Monster, or Flaubert's St. Antoine and Hilarion, should also, like Auden's Faust and Mephisto, be played by identical twins. A text like *Frankenstein,* whose Chinese-box narrative structure makes it inappropriate as an example of eclectic allegory, may nevertheless, because of its role as a pure Gothic novel, help to underline some of the Gothic elements in these other works. It could be considered a flawed godgame, in which god and creature change roles and two strong identities cancel each other out. It is also a repertoire of relevant Gothic conventions—dark doubling, looming, phobic spatiality (agoraphobic and claustrophobic), and an internal quest ending in annihilation. Most interesting are the elements of Gothic pedagogy: the Monster's education through beauty is undermined by his subsequent education through fear. In an inversion of Tamino's education, enlightened benevolence gives way to Gothic vengefulness. Witnessed performances serve as mediated educational experiences, though texts and manuscripts serve an even more important role as inner artifacts. As god and creator change places, so do teacher and pupil: the Monster teaches by terror the master who has become his slave.

In *St. Antoine* and *Arcturus,* as also in *Peer Gynt,* Faustian accretion is turned, ironically, into reduction.[6] All three texts are built upon a peeling off of layers of illusion: self-illusion in *Peer,* ideological illusion in *St. Antoine,* the illusions which make up the whole of our (this) world of illusions in *Arcturus.* The sequence of episodic experiences cast in the Gothic shapes of terror, pain, and the grotesque, especially in Flaubert and Lindsay but also in *Peer Gynt,* instead of building up identity reverse the process and reduce it to "nothing": the raw material of Peer's casting-ladle, the undifferentiated matter of the Saint's final temptation, the food of further illusion in Lindsay.

Flaubert's St. Antoine, a doleful nobody in a null world, is sole audience of a series of terrifying pageants, de-structive of every possible faith, each of which is enacted with encyclopedically minute erudition.[7] Here the encyclopedic tendency inherent in eclectic allegory, always on a collision course with the romantic self-consciousness of the internalized romantic quest, brings questing to a standstill before finally demolishing it, in Flaubert's *Bouvard et Pécuchet,* a few years later. St. Antoine's is the Solipsist's Progress from nowhere to nowhere by way of the Gothic pageants projected onto the stage of his own imagination. These artifacts, as in Petrarch's *I Trionfi,* say, move processionally past the stationary hero, who undertakes no spatial journey at all. His quest is not even negative in its results (like Frankenstein's): it is ultimately pointless. St. Antoine is his own playwright, as well as his own god; the world of the play is demonstrably the creation of "un Dieu en délire" (p. 77) and Antoine's pageant-drama is that of a poet hallucinated, a pseudo-drama generated from the Book, his only tangible artifact. The parade of monstrosities that comes by—"des idoles de toutes les nations et de tous les âges, en bois, en métal, en granit, en plumes, en peaux cousues" (p. 163)—accompanied by the corrosive cynicism of Hilarion's Mephistophelean commentary, constitutes a Gothic pedagogy covering eclectically all myths, religions, and histories, and climaxing in hybrid grotesques, Lovecraftian monstrosities, and beast-gods from the slime. Hilarion, growing larger in every scene, looms ever more claustrophobically; eventually, like Frankenstein's monster, he blocks out the sky.

The parallels with *Faust* are complex and deliberate: like *Peer Gynt, St. Antoine* adapts, even parodies, Faust's education through visions of horror.[8] Terror and temptation meet and overlap in a perpetual *Walpurgisnacht,* as Hilarion exploits Antoine's inclination to morbidity. These are Gothic visions well on the way to decadence: the godgame of the Romantic Agony in which the erotic, the fearful, and the grotesque perpetually intermingle, tainting the very questions of faith and intellect which trigger them off. Like Frankenstein, St. Antoine creates his own god-monsters (they are "un écho de sa pensée,—une réponse de sa mémoire," p. 232), but unlike him, he can de-create them by fainting from terror and then waking up. His last temptation is to become unconscious, undifferentiated matter; waking after that vision, he drifts back to the blank pretenses of his hermithood.

From the perverse temptations of sainthood in the desert for St. Antoine it is a surprisingly short step to the perverted temptings of the Desert Saints in *Jurgen* (p. 127). The "stations" of Jurgen's heroquest are not only the most consistently and archetypally erotic of any I discuss; they are also by far the most cheerfully so. Jurgen "deals fairly" in turn with all the avatars of the Goddess and with all the archetypal abridgements of allegorical possibilities which they represent. Though Jurgen's tastes are fundamentally more wholesome than most of what he is offered, his *Leitmotif,* "I will taste any drink once," suggests the irrepressible curiosity particularly suitable for the hero of eclectic allegory, and all the more necessary in an essentially benevolent godgame, in which the teeth of Gothic terror have been filed down, if not extracted. Even Antoine's fear warred with his curiosity; Jurgen's curiosity is sharply flavored with "doubt" (i.e., skepticism); for Fowles's hero, curiosity, as we shall see, is almost the whole of his reason for staying in the "game." Helen, Anaïtis, and Guinevere—a very Faustian amalgam of mythic possibilities—are the major avatars, but a hamadryad and a vampire are also among those who jostle for Jurgen's favors. Jurgen's journey, which takes either a year or a day, depending on one's sense of time, begins and ends on *Walpurgisnacht* on a wild, Faustian heath; his Faustian rejuvenation, to the accompaniment of the babble of witches, takes place in a garden of illusions. The gods Jurgen encounters *chez* Anaïtis are as "zoölogically muddled" (p. 121) as his adventures are mythologically muddled; the theological disputation (p. 102) and the animal hybrids and grotesques might almost have been copied from *St. Antoine* (the latter are copied again later, in deliberate pasteboard, in the trial scene of *The Magus*).

The eclectic mythographies Cabell summons up for reinforcement are an elegant blend of erudition and faking. The decadence of Anaïtis's court becomes especially Gothic in the scene of a Crowleyesque erotico-religious ritual involving, among other distressing stage properties, a live, crucified toad, and punctuated by the motto "Do that which seems good to you," adapted from Aleister Crowley's "Do what thou wilt shall be the whole of the Law."[9]

Among Cabell's numerous appropriations of Gothic motifs, perhaps the most powerful is the haunting shadow of the goddess who bleaches everything: it looms over all Jurgen's frivolities and pleasures. Such Gothic pedagogies educate Jurgen out of his profligacy and some of his idealism, but he is more like Candide than like Faust when he returns to settle down to growing old with his own aged, disagreeable Cunégonde: "For hereabouts [in Heaven] are none of my illusions . . . and I must now return to such illusions as are congenial" (p. 228). There is some easy sentimentality in the ending; Jurgen, in the final analysis, is a Biedermeier Tamino or bourgeois St. Antoine. Although in this book, too, there is a steady peeling off of illusions, Jurgen gets nowhere as near to the "nothing" at the center of the Gyntian onion as do Maskull, the Steppenwolf,[10] St. Antoine, and Peer himself. He is left with a slender but still minimally adequate supply of "congenial illusions."

Jurgen, we are often reminded, is also a poet. In one episode he is offered the ecstatic terror of the vision of Pan—or Everything—often vouchsafed to poets of Swinburnian impulses.

"What are you about to show me?"

". . . All."

. . . "Merlin would have died without regret if [he] had seen what you have seen."

". . . have you not just seen that which you may not ever quite forget?" (pp. 98-100)

He finds the vision too strong (and perhaps too life-denying); but having seen it, the "state of [his] nervous system was deplorable" (p. 101).

Possibly David Lindsay borrowed a line or two from this scene for an episode in *A Voyage to Arcturus,* which appeared in 1920. The artist Earthrid (who stretched out between earth and water, and whose instrument is a lake) plays music which is a mystical experience bringing pain and death: "Real life resembles my music . . . Neither you, nor any other person, can endure the thoughts which I put into my music."[11] In a later scene Lindsay's hero Maskull asks, "What do you propose to show me?" and is told that "if you are true-hearted, you will see things you will not easily forget" (p. 216). A curious, perhaps coincidental link (the American edition of *Jurgen* came out in 1919) between the cheeriest and the most consistently somber of our texts.

Maskull is more nearly heroic than any protagonist since Faust, and in some ways, though he is no thinker, the most nearly Faustian. His adventures begin at a séance in a strange country house to the accompaniment of the Temple music from *The Magic Flute* (Shaping's music of delusory harmony, to go by the argument of the Earthrid chapter). But Maskull, unlike Tamino, is the victim of a godgame where the "gods" are not on his side; more than any other protagonist I am discussing, he "learns the hard way," and the lesson is that the world, insofar as it is not pain, is illusion. The pain is at least true; and the god of pain is perhaps on his side.

A sinister, demonic master of ceremonies, Krag, sends Maskull to Tormance, the aptly-named planet of Arcturus, and seems, Sarastro-like, or Magus-wise, to be pulling the strings of the performers Maskull encounters there. Like our other heroes, though in an even more strictly linear journey, Maskull moves over the planet Tormance encountering, episodically, in a true eclectic allegory pattern, ontologies made concrete: those beings who stand bizarrely and vividly for certain types of experience, attitudes toward experience, and especially ways of perceiving experience. The séance scene is in the Gothic mode of the 1890s (of Conan Doyle, Algernon Blackwood, and others), but most of the book subtly transposes Gothic myths (and other myths, like Charon, Daphne, the Sirens, all Gothicized) into the new images appropriate to Lindsay's distant planet. Forms of vampirism and "belles dames" dominate several episodes; Maskull once describes his experiences as "a series of heavy enchantments" (p. 150). Maskull, as susceptible as Jurgen but as fiercely misogynist as St. Antoine, almost always succumbs to these strange temptresses but kills them afterwards; he is no passive hero, but his mode of action is commonly destruction. Lindsay's Dantean topography of chasms and ledges is the backdrop for superhuman (and doubtless allegorical) feats of mountain-climbing; likewise Dantean (or Faustian) are not only his interstellar journey but also his short-haul flight on the back of the grotesque shrowk. At the end Maskull almost yields to the perverse temptations of sainthood itself. In short, Lindsay is at least as eclectic in source and point of view and at least as Gothic in his ways of applying his discrete ontologies to the fear and pain centers of his "overtested" hero (p. 266) as any author since Mary Shelley. As one of the few critics of this book says (unwittingly stressing the eclecticism of Lindsay's allegory), "one comes to admire every episode equally *each for a different reason*" (my italics).[12]

Each possibility tempts and traps the hero. Each is seen in turn to be delusory. These encounters are partly impositions upon Maskull by the Master of the Quest: Krag? Surtur? Crystalman? These deities are name- and shape-shifters, too. More than once Maskull must ask the would-be initiate's key question, implied in St. Antoine's "Qui donc es-tu?" (p. 229), or in Tamino's uncertain approach to the Temple, "Am I serving the right god?" In the end Krag tells us, as we too "must have known," that his "name on Earth . . . is pain" (p. 287). These episodes are also partly, as in the other quests, extrapolations of the protagonist's own psychic needs, partly startling accounts of strange beings, perceptually adapted to nonterrestrial circumstances, partly Everyman's brave and desperate encounters with all those categories of experience that add up to an education in the intolerableness of life. Like Childe Roland's quest as seen by Harold Bloom, this journey, through the psychic landscape of torments, is a "gnostic nightmare." Tamino can't help but win; Maskull can't help but lose. They are both quest-heroes of great strength of character, but in very different philosophical worlds; Enlightenment optimism and sense of community have given way to a Schopenhauerian pessimism and sense of solitude. Like St. Antoine, Maskull loses a lot of faiths.

Two authors more popular among our contemporaries than any I have so far discussed, Hermann Hesse and John Fowles, have returned, largely with the aid of Jung, to a more affirmative, less wholly ironic, much more communal version of the "Mozartian" and Faustian quest. The puzzling, grotesque, and terrifying phantasms of Pablo/Mozart's and of the Magus's magic theaters educate the Steppenwolf and Nicholas Urfe, respectively, out of despair and into taking on life again, into choosing, with existential free will, to go on learning:

> Somewhere behind me I heard [Mozart's] ghastly laughter . . . A glimpse of [life's] meaning had stirred my reason and I was determined to begin the game afresh . . . I would traverse, not once more, but often, the hell of my inner being.

> One day I would be a better hand at the game. One day I would learn how to laugh. Pablo was waiting for me, and Mozart too. (p. 248; cf. *The Magus*, p. 540)

Hesse seems a detailed source for much more in *The Magus* than the Mozartian laugh of Fowles's Immortals;

he is an intermediary between Fowles and those other lovers of both Mozart and visionary quests, the German romantics (especially Novalis and Hoffmann), in all of whom "Bildung" is an affirmative if partially ironic concept. No one would have asked St. Antoine or Maskull to learn to laugh, or would have supposed that their rough education would make them even marginally nicer to other people. In both *Steppenwolf* and *The Magus,* a more or less benevolent (as it turns out) governing committee operates on Enlightenment premises (as in *Wilhelm Meister* or *The Magic Flute*) qualified into a sort of Jungian existentialism by two centuries of closer acquaintance with the irrational. This group backs up the manipulations of the Magus figures to guide the Steppenwolf and Nicholas to new self-awareness. Yet Fowles's Immortals still echo the cruelty of Hardy's, even when Nicholas reassures us—"some deeper, wiser, [more] esoteric society" (p. 527)—that they are as kindly and reasonable as Hesse's or Goethe's: indeed, these echoes clash. This committee of the Elect sits uneasily in its archetypal disguises out of Freemasonry, Tarot, and the Mysteries; perhaps it has not advanced as far beyond the "Club of Reason" mocked early in the book as Conchis (or even Fowles) thinks it has.

Nicholas's explicitly theatrical experiences—the bulk of the book—seem to derive much of their structuring artifice from Hesse's Magic Theater, and thus more remotely from Goethe's *Walpurgisnacht*. The captions for the "Polymus Films" which "project" one of Nicholas's climactic tests resemble the signboards advertising the Magic Theater as well as the names on those rooms in the theater designating (spatially) its separate (temporal) scenes. The judgment or "Execution" of the Steppenwolf at the end of the book closely parallels Nicholas's trial by the psychologists. Scenes in both books shift phantasmagorically in the manner of German Romantic tales; music accompanies the mimes and pageants, as well as serving as a prime part of the conceptual frame of each story. Scenes of temptations to suicide, or of phantasmagoric, nonmotivated murders, are set up for the heroes (as in all the Faustian eclectic allegories, including *Arcturus*) as tests of their power to choose rightly. All these theatricals resemble a *Walpurgisnacht* in combining ritual with revel, in being unnerving and often fearful, in shifting levels of reality and probability faster than the hero's (or reader's) responses can stabilize them, in combining the grotesque and the erotic in equal proportions (as in Flaubert), and in extrapolating and projecting these horrors of one's inward being into the imagery of beast-gods from muddled mythologies, who provide a fragmented vision of oneself in a hallucinatory, distorting set of mirrors.

Fowles's wonderfully eclectic intertextuality will keep commentators busy for some time to come. They have already noted, for instance, patterns from the Tarot cards, with special reference to the Fool's Journey toward the hope of learning something next time, episodes from Shakespeare's *The Tempest,* so frequently alluded to in the text (though it seems more seriously applied in Fowles's other, more concentratedly Gothic, novel *The*

Collector), motifs from Orphic and Eleusinian mysteries, and from the Orpheus and Eurydice story itself, none of which are guaranteed not to be red herrings, plus several forms of popular and pulp literature, cunningly transposed by Fowles into mythic patterns—war stories, Sadic pornography, soppy romance. Another set of pulp fictions could be added: those based more or less loosely on the career of Aleister Crowley, first as the Magus of a suburban villa-temple (Maugham, 1908; Cabell's spoof of 1919, see note 9; and Crowley's own fictionalization of 1922), and then as Magus of a Mediterranean island (John Buchan, 1926; Simon Raven, 1961). Although none of these authors deviates from the purity of schlock Gothic adventure stories into anything more philosophical than the eroticized black masses of Crowley himself, in life and in art, it is perhaps no wonder that Conchis has a bit of Crowley in him ("doctor Crowley, I presume," p. 510), as well as a bit of Prospero.

Conchis also seems at times as if he might be a voyeur-stage director in the Henry James or Witold Gombrowicz mode, a purveyor of the "aesthetics of perversion," villainously turning other people's lives into his own work of art.[13] Nicholas has several such metaphors for Conchis: "a novelist . . . creating with people, not words . . . a Svengali" (p. 247; cf. p. 277); Bourani as a "gallery of automata" with "real human beings [as] his puppets" (p. 327; see Arthur Machen for another version of that prize automaton, the Iron Maiden); Nicholas concludes that Conchis's "gratuitous cruelty [was] closer to tormenting dumb animals than any true teaching" (p. 393). In the context of the book, however, these suggestions of a more psycho-aesthetic definition of the Gothic are rather lightly sketched in: these are the angry accusations Nicholas makes, rather like Tamino accusing Sarastro of all possible villainies, when neither of them yet understands the situation. This context does not prevent Nicholas's view from being *part* of the truth about Conchis, if not a serious and consistent pattern, and certainly *part* of Conchis's fascination, in "art" as in "life."

Fowles's Gothic repertoire is evidently very extensive: a phobic spatiality comparable to *Frankenstein*'s, cat-and-mouse mental cruelties of Ambrosian quality, dark loomings and sudden, silent, unaccountable appearances serving as transitions between episodes (as also in *Arcturus*): again and again Nicholas suddenly sees, for instance, "a man standing . . . ashily silhouetted against the night sky" (p. 378). "That great [melo] dramatic skill, the art of timing one's surprises" (p. 215) is a large part of Fowles's success at Gothic theatricals, whether in the inner performances or in the outer text. Conchis's creeping up behind Nicholas brandishing a four-foot axe prepares the latter to hear the story of Conchis's encounter with the axe-wielding Norwegian messianic madman: two different Gothic teaching devices. The book is a mosaic of Gothic elements, none of which is as fearful for an instant as the Monster looming at Frankenstein's window, or his shadow on the ice. Of the two great motivating forces of the heroes of internalized romantic quests, fear and curiosity, Nicholas's motive, like Jurgen's, is over-whelmingly curiosity; more than any of the others he *volunteers* "to play [his] part" in the masque (p. 173). And what he witnesses is, as he realizes, self-conscious Gothic "camp," for the looming black mute, who, like Monostatos, so often bars his way, displays the "over-done macabreness of a horror-magazine illustration" (p. 203).

If *The Magus* is not wholly successful in the company of the tales of Mozart, Goethe, Flaubert, Hesse, Cabell, and Lindsay, it is perhaps because Fowles wants to have the advantages of realism as well as those of melodramatic, mythic fable. Nicholas is too "much" of a character to be Tamino or Maskull, not "enough" of one to be Faust. I agree with the first critic (it was Nicholas Urfe himself) to note the disproportion (to speak in novelistic terms) of setting the whole panoply of the Immortals into expensive and often cumbersome motion merely to cure Nicholas (like Jurgen) of profligacy. What I call the "speciousness" of *The Magus* is found there, where a split between novel and fable has not been adequately mended. All the same, it is a textbook example of Gothic pedagogy in operation, both for clarity and inclusiveness. As in all the eclectic allegories, Fowles's narrative and dramatic structures are staged, episodic, theatrical, disjunct, held together by the hero's character in its dynamic relationship with its Magus and dark double, who forces upon him visions which are lessons as well as tests. One could do worse, in studying the role of Gothic pedagogy in the internalized quest romance, than to work back from *The Magus*, like a quest-hero returning to his origins, in order to arrive (again) at *The Magic Flute* and *Faust*.

NOTES

[1] See M. H. Abrams, *Natural Supernaturalism* (New York, 1973), esp. pp. 190-92; hereafter cited in the text.

[2] *Jurgen* (New York, 1946), p. 161; hereafter cited in the text.

[3] "Introduction," *The Magus: A Revised Version* (New York, 1978), p. 10. See Robert Rawdon Wilson, "Spooking Oedipa: On Godgames," *CRCL*, 4 (1977), 186-204. Wilson, using the original edition, discusses only the more familiar definition.

[4] References to *Faust* are to the Walter Arndt translation, ed. Cyrus Hamlin (New York, 1973); "Hamlin" indicates quotations from the editorial material of this edition. Wolfgang Binder, "Goethe's Classical Conception of *Faust*" (Hamlin, p. 580); "Conversations with Eckermann" (Hamlin, p. 425).

[5] See Auden's introduction to his translation of *The Magic Flute*. Again freely adapting Hegel, Abrams comments on the "bewildering metamorphoses . . . 'a slow procession and sequences of *Geister,* a gallery of pictures' . . . This protagonist . . . is also his own antagonist . . . in altering disguises, so that one actor plays all the roles in the drama" (pp. 230-31); a life-and-death struggle

for domination results, "in which master and servant change places" (p. 232).

[6] For a fuller discussion of this point, see my article, *"Peer Gynt:* Ibsen's *Faustiad," CL,* 35 (1983), 126-39.

[7] *La Tentation de Saint Antoine,* ed. Edouard Maynial (Paris, 1968); hereafter cited in the text. See the translation by Kitty Mrosovsky, *The Temptation of Saint Antony* (London, 1980), for an exceptionally clear and useful extended introduction.

[8] "An imitation of imitations of Faust," said Flaubert's friend Maxime du Camp, as quoted in Flaubert, *Selected Letters,* ed. Francis Steegmuller (Freeport, N.Y., 1953), p. 6. The anonymous *Nachtwachen des Bonaventura* (1804) and Melville's *The Confidence Man* (1857) resemble *St. Antoine* as sequential unmaskings, ultimately meaningless and leading nowhere. Each suggests the structure of a godgame, but *Bonaventura* lacks a Magus-figure, or instructor, while Melville's Protean proliferation of manipulative Magi ("to say that there are more than one to a book, is good presumption there is none at all," Ch. xliv) finds no one competent to be *in statu pupillari.* Something further may follow of these Masquerades.

[9] Pp. 110-13. Crowley himself, incidentally, was not unmoved by Cabell's tribute to his "Gnostic Mass" in this scene; he praised *Jurgen* effusively, with particular stress on the book's making concrete "infinitely diverse orders of being," i.e., its eclecticism (*Confessions,* New York, 1969, p. 738). No doubt Crowley and Cabell were both familiar with Rabelais's Thélème, of which Cabell's Cocaigne seems a Gothicized branch office.

[10] *Steppenwolf,* trans. Basil Creighton (New York, 1969), p. 69: "Man is an onion made up of a hundred integuments . . . unmasking the illusion of the personality."

[11] *A Voyage to Arcturus* (New York; 1963), p. 181; hereafter cited in the text. See Kathryn Hume, "Visionary Allegory in David Lindsay's *A Voyage to Arcturus," JEGP,* 77 (1978), 72-91, for a full and satisfying account of Lindsay's allegoric significances; the concept of concretized ontologies is hers. Eric Rabkin, "The Conflation of Genres and Myths in *A Voyage to Arcturus," JNT,* 7 (1977), 149-55, while promising more than it, in brief compass, delivers, makes the interesting comment that *Arcturus* is episodic in the same way *Alice through the Looking-Glass* is, and less helpfully, that Maskull's northward journey resembles Frankenstein's. See also Jack Schofield, "Cosmic Imagery in *A Voyage to Arcturus," Extrapolation,* 13 (1971), 146-51. His unpublished M.A. thesis, "David Lindsay's *A Voyage to Arcturus:* Allegorical Dream Fantasy as a Literary Mode" (University of British Columbia, 1972), is the best critical account of *Arcturus* to date. In my book *Pan the Goat-God: His Myth in Modern Times* (Cambridge, Mass., 1969), I give a fuller discussion of the terrifying vision of Pan in Machen, Swinburne, and Meredith as it relates to the

scene in *Jurgen,* as well as of the Crowleyesque visions of Somerset Maugham and others.

[12] Colin Wilson et al., *The Strange Genius of David Lindsay* (London, 1970), p. 52. Shrowk-like journeys or cosmic flights also occur in Fowles, Flaubert, and Ibsen. The closest analogue to Lindsay's is in a book very like *Arcturus* but much inferior, H. P. Lovecraft's *The Dream-Quest of Unknown Kadath* (1927).

[13] See my articles, "The Aesthetics of Perversion: Gothic Artifice in James and Gombrowicz," *PMLA,* 93 (1978), 992-1001, and "The Raven and the Bust of Pallas: Classical Artifacts in the Gothic Tale," *PMLA,* 89 (1974), 960-66. The implacably smiling Cycladic head (p. 150), "famous Poseidon" (p. 215), and the "pompous," ultimately empty, white statues in Regent's Park are some rather good examples from Fowles of the Gothicized classical artifact.

James M. Keech

SOURCE: "The Survival of the Gothic Response," in *Studies in the Novel,* Vol. 6, No. 2, Summer, 1974, pp. 130-44.

[*In the following essay, Keech defines the Gothic novel in terms of its effect—the ability to evoke "fear characterized by foreboding and intensity"—and extends the Gothic genre to include George Orwell's* Nineteen Eighty-Four *and other works which reflect the modern sense of individual "impotence in a fearfully incomprehensible world."*]

Traditionally, the Gothic novel has been regarded as a work defined by its common elements, a sort of formula novel employing standard atmospheric trappings and stereotyped characters. Conceptually, it has meant a set of stock devices used to evoke terror and horror: ruined castles and abbeys, dank dungeons, gloomy tyrants, mad monks, imperiled maidens, secret chambers, haunted galleries, creaking doors, mysterious portraits, ghosts, "skulls and coffins, epitaphs and worms." Scholars, such as Tompkins, Summers, and Varma, have divided it into types: the historical Gothic, the terror Gothic, and the horror Gothic, or "Schauer-Romantik"; but it has rarely been seen beyond these types as any more significant than those "horrid" novels that captivated Catherine Morland in Jane Austen's *Northanger Abbey.* Reeking of excessive romanticism, employing farfetched terrors, such as Walpole's statue with the nosebleed, and beset with imitation rather than creative originality, the Gothic novel has been viewed as little more than a literary curiosity.

It is not my purpose to revaluate the worth of the Gothic novels of the past, though this in many ways needs to be done, for they have received short shrift for too long in the literary marketplace. Rather, in this essay, I intend to focus on some of the limitations of the traditional perspective of the Gothic novel which blinds us to its consideration as an element of the literary vision after 1820. The Gothic novel needs redefinition in order for this to be done.

Recently there have been attempts to expand the range of the Gothic novel's definition and to broaden its application. Lowry Nelson, Jr., and Robert D. Hume,[1] for example, have seen such novels as *Wuthering Heights, Moby-Dick,* and *Sanctuary,* as falling within the Gothic mold. Both critics have, essentially, chosen to see the Gothic novel not so much as a set of rigid trappings and devices as an effect produced by certain elements common to all Gothic novels. Though Nelson or Hume have not gone far enough in freeing the definition of the Gothic novel from its reliance upon traditional devices or in clarifying the distinction between the trappings and the effects these trappings produce, they have made significant steps toward a needed rethinking of what is called Gothic in fiction.

Basically, the Gothic novel should be seen as attempting to evoke a particularized response, and its stock devices as merely one means to that end. All literary artists attempt to involve the reader in a series of manipulated responses leading, hopefully, to an overall effect. The devices they use, call them setting, plot, character, imagery, shape the work to provoke that desired cumulative response. The response of the Gothic novel is fear, universally inherent in every man's nature, primitive and basic, and existing regardless of time, place, or culture. Imitation has rendered the traditional castle and Byronic villain, along with clanking ghosts, dungeons, and skeletons, as a hackneyed method of approaching that fear; and time, too, has changed the nature of what we regard as fearful. Certainly, at one time however, the stock devices worked. The early Gothic novels of the romantic period were not necessarily regarded as belonging to an inferior type of fiction. Until the flood of inferior Gothic imitations of the 1780-90s made the type recognizable and their inferior quality made them laughable enough to be ridiculed, as in *Northanger Abbey,* the first Gothic novels affected their readers with genuine power. Thomas Gray was made afraid of sleep at night by reading *The Castle of Otranto;* Byron called *Vathek* his Bible; Ann Radcliffe's novels established her to the age as a major novelist; Coleridge gave *The Monk* serious critical consideration in *The Critical Review* and thought it the "offspring of no common genius"; and genuine originality and serious literary skills were noted in Mary Shelley's *Frankenstein* and Maturin's *Melmoth the Wanderer.* That their power and emotional force can still be felt, in part, today gives added weight to the need for legitimate recognition of the Gothic as a meaningful literary experience.

The best of the Gothic novels were, and still are in part, successful works of art because they produced a universal and enduring response that is also inherent in later literature of Gothic nature: in "The Rime of the Ancient Mariner," *Wuthering Heights, Great Expectations,*

Moby-Dick, Heart of Darkness, Absalom, Absalom!, and *Nineteen Eighty-Four.* The element common to all these is not a set of stock devices but the production of an effect of fear and foreboding that carries the reader to the realm of the nightmare by means of a variety of techniques of which the traditional Gothic trappings is but one. A definition of the Gothic novel should outline not the dated means but the simplest elements common to its effect.

One of these common elements is the particular quality of the Gothic response of fear, a fear characterized by a necessary presentiment of a somewhat vague but nevertheless real evil. It is a fear of shadows and unseen dangers in the night. Explicitness runs counter to its effectiveness, for Gothic fear is not so much what is seen but what is sensed beyond sight. The fearful inventions of J. R. R. Tolkien's imagination in *The Lord of the Rings,* the Night Riders and Gollum for example, are perfect illustrations of the power of the impressionistic over the concrete. Always seen as vague shapes or veiled in nebulous shadows, Tolkien's evil creations are genuinely fearful, and they impart a decidedly Gothic aura to his trilogy. In similar fashion, the fear in a traditional Gothic novel is created not only by that which frightens, the darkness of the underground passageways in Otranto's castle when the maiden's lamp is accidentally extinguished, but by the foreboding that magnifies its dangers: Isabella's apprehensions of her fate if captured by Manfred in this darkness. It is not only Victor Frankenstein's horror at the monster's brutal murder of his brother, but the premonition of those future atrocities which the monster's anguished hatred is both capable and desirous of inflicting. In *The Monk,* this fear is created not by Ambrosio's acts of murder and rape alone, but also by the presentiment that his process of moral corruption will intensify with further dreadful consequences. Thus, fear in a Gothic novel moves beyond the concrete in allowing the imagination to build upon and shape foreboding outlines into a sustained fear which is verified periodically by peaks of intense concrete terror or horror.

This association of fear and foreboding is not merely that suspense and dread to be found in those Gothic novels typed under the novel of terror, namely the works of Walpole and Radcliffe. It is present there in various plenty, of course, but it forms a vital part of the response in those novels classified by Varma as the "Schauer-Romantik," or romance of horror: the novels of Lewis, Shelley, Maturin. Horror does not negate fear, though Mrs. Radcliffe felt it did: "Terror and horror are so far opposite, that the first expands the soul, and awakens the faculties to a high degree of life; the other contracts, freezes, and nearly annihilates them. . . . "[2] Rather, the repulsive horrors of Lewis, Shelley, and Maturin magnify the apprehensions that characterize Gothic fear. Agnes's awakening in the tomb and touching the maggots bred in the putrified flesh of adjacent corpses brings shudders of disgust and repulsion to *The Monk,* but it does not eliminate the dreaded fears of the future horrors that she might experience. Agnes can still suffer and the Prioress of St.

Clare is still frighteningly capable of further atrocities. The mind is not closed by horror to the vicarious experience of the sublimity of fearful apprehensions (except to the reader who at this point closes the novel and reads no more), but rather enlarged by a greater intensity. The real distinction between novels of terror and of horror is not a difference in kind but in degree. D. P. Varma implies that the nature of the difference lies in their degree of intensity: "The difference between Terror and Horror is in the difference between awful apprehensions and sickening realization: between the smell of death and stumbling upon a corpse."[3] Horror is not the finality of terror, but the magnification of it. Though we may be thoroughly shocked by man's, or a monster's, hitherto undreamt of acts, we also stand in greater fearful awe of the limits further acts may approach. The horrible sufferings of Moncada in *Melmoth the Wanderer* do not end the reader's fears, but build them toward some awful crescendo that promises to reveal what man's final capacity for inflicting horror will be.

Indeed, the fearful response in the better Gothic novels is marked by the common element of intensity. They depict violations of moral and religious norms that are fearful by their excess. The acts that create fear and presage even more in the Gothic novel are supreme. They are grievous sins, not mere wrongs—the worst of what man or devil is capable. They stem not from accident or simple human frailty or corruption, but from an agency evaluated by the reader's moral perspective as approaching the ultimate in evil. The Gothic novel, therefore, deals not with gambling, thievery, or simple murder, but with matricide, rape, incest (*The Monk*); murders of innocent children and virginal brides (*Frankenstein*); blasphemy, infectious spiritual pollution, and damnation (*Vathek, Melmoth the Wanderer, Dracula*).

It is not surprising, therefore, that the best and most intense of Gothic novels employ hero-villains of Promethean proportions, giants among mortal men in their strength, in the intensity of their emotions, in their faculty for evil. They evoke terror not only by what they do but also by the presentiment of their dreadful capacities. Manfred, in *The Castle of Otranto,* fails materially to intensify the novel's effect, for he is merely a bad man, incapable of reaching beyond petty intrigue and impulsive murder. But Ann Radcliffe's Montoni in *The Mysteries of Udolpho* is truly fearful, for we sense that he is capable of extraordinary acts of human depravity. Shelley's monster, Maturin's Melmoth, and Stocker's Dracula are even more frightening, for, possessed of supernatural abilities, they possess a propensity for malevolence that exceeds human comprehension.

Though the better Gothic novels possess such Promethean hero-villains, they should not be seen as a basic defining characteristic of the Gothic, but merely a device for creating a high level of intensity of effect. Not all Gothic novels use them. They do not appear in *The Castle of Otranto, The Monk,* and *Vathek,* but the response of fear is still evoked, though at a somewhat lower level of intensity than, say, *Melmoth.* Any agency of absolute power would suffice to produce a similar intensity of fear, and the Inquisition was frequently so used in the Gothic novel, for example in *The Monk* and *Melmoth the Wanderer.*

Attendant to those novels that employ the hero-villain protagonist is the problem of what Robert Hume calls "moral ambiguity," a confusion in the reader's moral evaluation of the protagonist because of the coexistence of malevolent values and admirable heroic qualities. Though the reader may reject the evil the villain embodies, he is fascinated by his heroic greatness: by Montoni's strength of will and defiance of conventional moral and legal restraints, by Frankenstein's monster's alienation and superhuman physical powers, by Melmoth's tragic capacity for cynical suffering. This moral ambiguity imparts to the Gothic novel a greater complexity and dimension, and removes those novels which possess it from the morass of shallow sensationalism which is the major raison d'être of the inferior novel. It is not necessary for moral ambiguity to be present for a novel to be Gothic: there is no moral doubt of Dracula's status as monster, pure and simple. Ambrosio is also obviously corrupt and contemptible. But it seems vital for a great Gothic novel, accounting in great measure for the serious literary consideration given *Frankenstein* and *Melmoth the Wanderer.*

The term "Gothic," as I see it, consequently means a response, or effect, of fear characterized by foreboding and intensity rather than a set of traditional stock devices. The devices are merely a time-honored method of producing the effect with a minimum of artistic originality. Unfortunately, the word will never, perhaps, divorce itself from this association with ruined castles, graveyards, skeletons, ghosts, and imperiled maidens. It will always mean to some the stock elements. Perhaps, the modifier "traditional" should be used in conjunction with "Gothic" to imply, with some pejorative associations of imitative and hackneyed, the stock devices, and the term "Gothic" alone used to imply the response. Certainly, such a practice would emphasize that the traditional trappings are not necessary for a novel to be Gothic, but the response is, and it would distinguish between works which are Gothic by device, such as *The Old English Baron,* and works which are Gothic by effect, such as Conrad's *Heart of Darkness.*

Nevertheless, though the stock devices are neither primary nor exclusive to the Gothic novel, they cannot be dismissed, for their use does reflect another common element vital to the Gothic response. In order for the abbey, tower, tomb, skeleton, or ghost to activate the imagination and evoke the sense of fear, an appropriate atmosphere must be created. This atmosphere is primary to the necessary effect. With the proper atmosphere a child's playhouse can be chillingly terrifying and a castle safe, warm, beautiful, and romantic. Robert Hume has perceptively noted that "The key characteristic of the Gothic novel is not its devices, but its atmosphere. . . . The setting exists to convey the atmosphere."[4]

The essential nature of the atmosphere which produces the Gothic response is ominousness. Redolent of isolation, evil, death, the images which convey this ominousness are those of darkness, danger, grotesqueness, and gloom. To the romantic sensibilities of the early Gothic novelists, medieval castles and wild scenery suggested this atmosphere, but it is by no means inherent solely in them. A scientist's laboratory, through emphasis of the proper atmosphere, can be just as Gothic as the Castle of Montoni:

> It was on a dreary night of November that I beheld the accomplishment of my toils. With an anxiety that almost amounted to agony, I collected the instruments of life around me, that I might infuse a spark of being into the lifeless thing that lay at my feet. It was already one in the morning; the rain pattered dismally against the panes, and my candle was nearly burnt out, when, by the glimmer of the half-extinguished light I saw the dull yellow eye of the creature open. . . . [5]

In similar fashion, though the ostensible framework for *Vathek* is oriental, its basic character, as established by its atmosphere, is essentially Gothic:

> A death-like stillness reigned over the mountain and through the air; the moon dilated on a vast platform the shades of the lofty columns, which reached from the terrace almost to the clouds; the gloomy watch-towers, whose number could not be counted, were covered by no roof; and their capitals, of an architecture unknown in the records of the earth, served as an asylum for the birds of night, which, alarmed at the approach of such visitants, fled away croaking.

The more pervasive this ominous atmosphere and the greater its consistency of mood, the greater the sense of the Gothic response to the work. Manfred's dungeons in *The Castle of Otranto* are only mildly ominous: the passageways are intricate, silent, windy, dark, and ultimately "dismal," but so scant is the atmospheric detail that the novel's force is weakened. In comparison, the catacombs in Poe's "The Cask of Amontillado" are the essence of Gothic fear: dark, damp with dripping nitre, filled with skeletons and air so foul that torches glow instead of burn. The images that produce the atmosphere are so plentiful and so orchestrated in their connotative harmony that the story produces that supreme single effect that Poe demanded from a short story. Thus the extent of the development of atmosphere will, more than any other element, determine the placement of a work in the Gothic category, for it is the key distinguishing mark of the Gothic response.

Other key elements of the Gothic are certain basic characters or agents. These characters are not so much stereotypes as embodiments of traits whose conflict produces the feelings of apprehension and fear. First, there must be at least one character or agency, such as the hero-villain or the Inquisition, whose essence is unrestrained power or force or passion; and, secondly, at least one character who embodies meekness or helplessness and serves as the artistic surrogate for the reader's feelings of inadequacy. The agent of power is the focal point of the Gothic novel's production of apprehensive fear. His powers may stem from the human resources of strength, will, or intelligence, such as the powers of Manfred, Vathek, and Montoni, or they may be supernatural in origin, as are the powers of Ambrosio, Frankenstein's monster, Melmoth, and Dracula. In either case these powers are extraordinary and awesome. They are also powers either partially or totally perverted, even if innocent of conscious evil intent, as is Victor Frankenstein's pursuit of the secret of life. Only evil or misfortune comes from the exercise of these extraordinary powers, for some sort of moral corruption is at their core.

The character, or agent, or power appears magnified by his opposite, the character who represents helplessness, usually the persecuted maiden in the traditional Gothic novel but who can be any sort of victimized humanity. His helplessness stems either from the contrast of his ordinary mortality in conflict with superhuman powers or his meekness or vulnerability in conflict with greater human resources. This character reflects a moral norm which the reader finds acceptable, and consequently his persecution and his injuries seem terrifying or horrible when there is a shocking discrepancy between his moral position and undeserved calamities. This character's humanity and acceptable moral position enable the reader to identify with him and thus be drawn vicariously into the victim's world of fear and undeserved evil. There he finds himself in the frightening uncertainty of what appears to be a moral no-man's-land where ethical values and moral laws have no apparent weight, where the powerful ignore such standards with an ease and absence of conscience that bring the very validity or existence of the moral laws into question. If this process of victimization by the powerful is extended far enough, as it is in *The Monk, Frankenstein, Melmoth,* and in *Dracula,* the ultimate Gothic fear is momentarily reached, that surrealistically horrible recognition of a world of moral chaos where only power has meaning.

These, then, as I view them, are the basic defining characteristics of the Gothic novel: it evokes fear characterized by foreboding and intensity; this fear is created by an atmosphere of ominous detail and by the frightening supremacy of power and evil over weakness and good. If the concept of the Gothic can be divorced from the traditional reliance upon definition by stock devices, the word "Gothic" becomes liberated and timeless. It can be applied to identify minor effects or the essence of whole works, from the eighteenth century to the present. It also enables us to perceive something thematically meaningful in the writer's perception of terror and horror that goes beyond mere sensationalism, the traditionally regarded graveyard for the early Gothic novelists's attempts to approach sublimity through fear.

I suggest that the Gothic as a literary response neither ended with Maturin, nor did it degenerate further into the drugstore bookracks as cheap popular literature. Rather, I believe, serious novelists, after the traditional Gothic novel had ended its vogue, recognized something aesthetically meaningful in the Gothic novel: that it conveyed a universal and timeless response that could be used as a metaphor with thematic weight. Indeed, traditional Gothic novels such as *Frankenstein* and *Melmoth the Wanderer* employ the Gothic scene as metaphor. Mary Shelley used it to characterize the moral horror of Victor Frankenstein's experiments, and Maturin used the Gothic as a thematic reflection of the dark horror of spiritual despair. Later novelists, though not known as writers of Gothic novels, for example the Brontes, Dickens, Conrad, Wells, Faulkner, have utilized the Gothic response for thematic emphasis.

The Victorian novelists first saw the literary potential of the Gothic effect separated from its traditional heritage. Charlotte Bronte, perhaps more unconsciously than voluntarily, sensed within the Gothic novel certain symbolic elements that would convey thematic meanings of power, fear, and awe within a more realistic background. Mr. Rochester, ugly, powerful, willfully defying convention and law in his passionate love for Jane, is in direct descendency from Manfred, Montoni, and Melmoth. This Gothic hero-villain symbolized for Charlotte Bronte the power of the masculine essence and its sexual force: dominating, ugly yet fascinating, instilling a fearful helplessness in the female. In her novel Gothic fear metaphorically imparts a thematic moral perspective of complete free will divorced from social duty. Emily Bronte's Heathcliff is also a symbolic embodiment of power, will, sexual force, and passion—as perfect a Byronic hero-villain as any in a traditional Gothic novel. It is Heathcliff as Gothic villain, who stands as her central metaphor for fearful sexual passion, perhaps even a reflection of the subconscious sexual yearnings of Emily Bronte's own dark Id.[6]

Charles Dickens also utilized the Gothic effect for its metaphorical meanings of fear and horror. Dickens was drawn not by the symbolic power or sexual energy inherent in the hero-villain, but by the metaphorical connotations of Gothic atmosphere. There is, however, a difficulty in determining Dickens's conscious use of the Gothic in his novels, for his symbolic atmosphere is complex, blending social misery with Gothic effect in such a way that it becomes impossible to separate his vision of bleak misery, imprisoned humanity, and spiritual poverty from that of horror and terror. The images of misery and Gothic fear are similar: decay, death, darkness, disease; they belong as much to slums such as Tom-all-Alone's as they do to castles and dungeons. There are occasions in Dickens's novels, however, when he seemed to be consciously thinking in terms of the traditional Gothic effect. This Gothic strain in Dickens's work runs from the inset stories of *Pickwick Papers* to the ominous cathedral crypt and tower of *Edwin Drood:* in the undertaker's shop and city slums of *Oliver Twist;* in the miserly decay of Scrooge's office of *A Christmas Carol;* in Krook and his shop, in the Ghost's Walk of *Bleak House;* in the gro-

tesque specimens of Mr. Venus of *Our Mutual Friend;* in the gloomy prison of the Clennam house of *Little Dorrit;* and especially in Satis House of *Great Expectations.* In evoking the Gothic response to these settings, Dickens used thematic atmosphere to imply that fear and foreboding are integral elements of a society which esteems self or money more than people. The reader's expected shudder when encountering these settings of Dickens was to be one of moral horror, in the reflection that the Gothic was not necessarily an imaginary fancy in a cheap novel but a part of the very nature of normal society.

This influence of the Gothic novel upon the Brontes and Dickens has long been recognized; but, once this recognition has been noted and suitably filed in the correct pigeonhole of literary history, analysis of the author's purposeful uses of the Gothic fails to follow. The Gothic has, quite simply, too frequently been regarded as an end in itself. Thus the thematic intentions of the novelist's Gothic effects, that metaphorical equation through device and atmosphere of the fearful in the Gothic world and the fearful in his own world, becomes ignored. It is this thematic function of the Gothic that needs to be recognized in the fiction not generally associated with the Gothic tradition.

This metaphorical function of the Gothic becomes even more unnoticed in modern novels which produce the Gothic response without employing the traditional devices. It is with these works that a definition of the Gothic based on effect becomes critically meaningful. Joseph Conrad's *Heart of Darkness,* for example, is a novel colored throughout by a sense of the Gothic; and Kurtz's whispered cry, "'The horror! The horror!'" at the thematic climax of the novel, precisely focuses the novel's essence. *Heart of Darkness* is a novel of Gothic horror.

Though it has no tormented victim and no Promethean villain of power (unless Kurtz can be seen as filling both roles simultaneously), the novel's atmosphere is profoundly Gothic. This atmosphere serves as an extended metaphor to characterize the dark submerged bestiality at the core of man's biological nature as fearful and horrible. Marlowe's search for Kurtz is like that of Browning's Childe Roland for the dark tower: a mythic quest through a frightening symbolic wasteland dominated by Gothic scenery which impressionistically imparts the work's theme. Atmosphere in *Heart of Darkness* is symbolically meaningful, and that atmosphere is decidedly and consistently Gothic.

The novel opens with the contrast of the morally neutral sea, luminous in the evening haze, with the land, long tainted by the darkness of man's potential for brutality: "The air was dark above Gravesend, and farther back still seemed condensed into a mournful gloom, brooding motionless over the biggest, and the greatest, town on earth." The symbolic landscape is further developed into a Gothic metaphor with Marlowe's summation of the historical heritage of England hidden behind its present civilized facade:

"And this also . . . has been one of the dark places of the earth. . . . I was thinking of very old times, when the Romans first came here, nineteen hundred years ago. . . . The very end of the world, a sea the color of lead, a sky the color of smoke. . . . Sandbanks, marshes, forests, savages—precious little to eat fit for a civilized man, nothing but Thames water to drink. No Falernian wine here, no going ashore. Here and there a military camp lost in the wilderness, like a needle in a bundle of hay—cold, fog, tempests, disease, exile, and death—death sulking in the air, in the water, in the bush."

This Gothic atmosphere metaphorically imparts its foreboding to all segments of Marlowe's quest: to the vision of the African river on the map as "an immense snake uncoiled . . . its tail lost in the depth of the land"; to the Belgian trading company on "a narrow and deserted street in deep shadow, high houses . . . a dead silence, grass sprouting between the stones," with its fatal women "guarding the door of darkness, knitting black wool as for a warm pall"; to the dark continent itself with its sense of decayed civilization imparted by ruined machinery, enslaved natives, solitude, and silence.

The forest itself is the principal Gothic metaphor in the novel, for its darkness, fearful and fascinating, conceals the mystery of Kurtz and of man that Marlowe seeks. The forest is the equivalent of the Gothic agent of power, suggesting the very strength of those primal urges to which Kurtz succumbs: "The great wall of vegetation, an exuberant and entangled mass of trunks, branches, leaves, boughs, festoons, motionless in the moonlight was like a rioting invasion of soundless life, a rolling wave of plants, piled up, crested ready to topple over the creek, to sweep every little man of us out of his little existence." Above all, the forest, symbol of concealment and strength, is fearful; for its black shadows hide mysteries far more ominous than those behind *The Mystery of Udolpho*'s black veiled recess: "the forest, the creek, the mud, the river—seemed to beckon with a dishonoring flourish before the sunlit face of the land a treacherous appeal to the lurking death, to the hidden evil, to the profound darkness of its heart."

Heart of Darkness is a Gothic novel. It is not traditional; it has no castles and dungeons, no skeletons and ghosts; but it fully embodies what is basically Gothic: apprehensive fear, ominous atmosphere, the sense of frightening power inherent in evil. Conrad saw this evil as an inherent part of man, not in a collection of literary trappings, and metaphorically used the Gothic effect in a meaningful way as the major symbolic force in his novel.

The fiction of William Faulkner has similar Gothic elements. Indeed, Faulkner was primarily regarded in the 1930s as a follower of Poe and Ambrose Bierce.[7] Though this was a narrow perspective, the early critics of Faulkner perceived, even if they did not value, the Gothic strain that underlies much of Faulkner's chronicle of Yoknapatawpha County. An examination of the Gothic in his novels would show that Faulkner, rather than creating mere gory sensation, was artistically utilizing the Gothic to capitalize upon a stock response that metaphorically emphasizes the innate horror underlying certain aspects of Southern tradition.

Malcolm Cowley, in his famous introduction to *The Portable Faulkner,* first recognized this purposeful use of Gothic materials. In discussing *Absalom, Absalom!* he said: "It seems to belong in the realm of the Gothic romances, with Sutpen's Hundred taking the place of the haunted castle on the Rhine, with Colonel Sutpen as Faust and Charles Bon as Manfred. Then slowly it dawns on you that most of the characters and incidents have a double meaning; that besides their place in the story, they also serve as symbols or metaphors with a general application."[8] These applications are varied, but they do form discernible thematic patterns in Faulkner's work.

One pattern can be noted in Faulkner's use, as metaphor, of an equivalent of the Gothic castle or haunted abbey: the ruined Southern antebellum mansion, such as the houses of Emily Grierson, Thomas Sutpen, Joanna Burden, the Compsons, the McCaslins, and the old Frenchman place. Each suggests a conventional Gothic device, yet the complex metaphorical implications go much further toward the suggestion of themes. The atmosphere of romantic decay accompanying the traditional device thematically conveys the sense of decline of the South's vanished glory, implying the need for the region to recognize the advent of a new age and to accept a new culture based on new values. Tragically, perhaps, neither the Compsons nor Emily Grierson can, and their Gothic houses symbolize the unyielding heritage of the past that plagues the South. But also, like the grandeur of a medieval castle, these mansions also convey other meanings: the worthy essence of a chivalric tradition, that gentleman's code of honor of the Compsons and Sartorises, which is crumbling under the less noble values of industrialization and the morally corrupt entrepreneurship symbolized by the rising Snopeses. There is also associated with these mansions a latent horror, a kind of Gothic curse, arising from their associations with slavery. The symbolic ghosts that haunt Sutpen's Hundred and the ledgers of the McCaslins are as fearful in their moral implications as the literal specters of Gothic galleries. The attitude toward the black man that evolved from slavery was the curse that doomed Thomas Sutpen, Joanna Burden, and Joe Christmas and which torments their descendents. The atmosphere surrounding the Gothic architectural setting was the perfect metaphor for Faulkner to use to convey the shadowy sense of doom and terror underlying Southern values.

The Gothic villain is another Gothic device that Faulkner employs for symbolic implications. As Robert Hume has argued, *Sanctuary*'s Popeye is the impotent, vicious monster symbolic of the inescapable evil in life.[9] Thomas Sutpen, a more classic hero-villain of the Byronic stamp, represents the heroic will needed to create a civilization from raw wilderness, but he also serves as a metaphor symbolizing the fearful elements of Southern values: the self-destructive moral rigidity, the inhumanity of the South's caste system, the failure to acknowledge the brotherhood of all men because of race. Like Melmoth and Heathcliff, Thomas Sutpen belongs to the hazy regions of moral ambiguity. He is a gloriously dynamic mixture of admiration and Gothic horror who symbolized the ambiguity of the South, for Quentin Compson and also for William Faulkner.

The Gothic in nontraditional literature has, therefore, become a means of evoking a response, both emotional and moral, to those aspects of life which we fear, or ethically should fear, most. To the Brontes and Dickens Gothic fear was equated with sexual energy and inhuman materialism. To Conrad it was an integral element in the nature of man, and to Faulkner it was slavery and the distorted values of caste and honor. It may be interesting to now ask: what major fears of today find symbolic reflection as Gothic metaphors in our current fiction, and what does their use tell us about the way current novelists view contemporary society? Since the Gothic has become a metaphor for the ominous, destructive forces in life, the Gothic in today's art forms will point a finger of moral condemnation at those fearful elements of life that make man seem the impotent victim of the currently terrifying.

Novelists of today, I feel, find the Gothic responses of horror in an increasingly complex and amoral technology, in giant industry, giant government, and giant bureaucracy. When millions can die with the push of a single button on a machine, or fall victim to the perversity of a computer, or sense the very air they breathe is toxic, the Gothic becomes an apt evaluation for the nature of existence. The ordinary man is seen as a powerless victim of life's incomprehensible forces. The Byronic hero-villain recedes as an object of fear to be replaced by abstract agencies, evoking a correspondent Gothic horror, which, though more vague, are just as powerful, frightening, and inhuman. Instead of Manfreds, Montonis, and Melmoths, the new evil forces in life given Gothic substance by modern novelists are Big Brother government, scientifically controlled humanity, the suppression of individual freedom in a world grown too complex for ordinary comprehension.

Science, with its nuclear bombs and nerve gases, is one of today's monsters. The relationship between science and the Gothic response is an old one, existing as early as Mary Shelley's *Frankenstein* and continuing through nineteenth-century fiction with Wilkie Collins's depiction of the horrors of vivisection in *Heart and Science* and H. G. Wells's *Island of Doctor Moreau*. A Gothic atmosphere was thus seen very early as a means of symbolically expressing the cold objectivity of science and the sense of fearful power resident in the control of natural forces. In the twentieth century, this attitude toward science has been coupled with an awareness of the basic inhumanity of man's institutions; and novelists's projections of the future, in such novels as *Nineteen Eighty-Four*, *Fahrenheit 451*, and occasionally in *Brave New*

World, significantly impart a sense of Gothic gloom and apprehension to their political-technological antiutopias. Each novel opens with the creation of a Gothic atmosphere which shapes initial attitudes to the narrative that follows: *Fahrenheit 451* with a glimpse of lurid, fiery destruction; *Brave New World* with the Central London Hatchery, a cold, grey skyscraper equivalent of the Gothic castle; and *Nineteen Eighty-Four* with scenes of ruin and decay. In addition, each novel contains scenes of a clearly Gothic horror: the mechanical hound in *Fahrenheit 451;* the Pavlovian conditioning room in *Brave New World;* Winston Smith's tortures in the Ministry of Love in *Nineteen Eighty-Four*. Thus each novel utilizes the metaphorical implications of the Gothic response thematically to project the sense of fear surrounding a future built upon our present tendencies and values.

Of the three novels, only *Nineteen Eighty-Four* can be called primarily Gothic, for only it contains all the elements necessary to place it within the Gothic type. The other novels use the Gothic as an occasional metaphor to suggest possible reactions to future life; *Nineteen Eighty-Four* sees a future under Big Brother government as synonymous with Gothic horror. Its passive victim is Winston Smith. Big Brother is the symbolic representative of ominous power. The prevailing atmosphere is one of gloom, decay, and fear. Its horrors are equal to any in *The Monk*. For example, the apprehensive terror of Room 101 in the Ministry of Love builds to a crescendo of genuine Gothic horror:

> "The rat," said O'Brien, still addressing his invisible audience, "although a rodent is carnivorous. You are aware of that. You have heard of the things that happen in the poor quarters of this town: In some streets a woman dare not leave her baby alone in the house, even for five minutes. The rats are certain to attack it. Within quite a small time they will strip it to the bones. They also attack sick or dying people. They show astonishing intelligence in knowing when a human being is helpless." There was an outburst of squeals from the cage. . . .
>
> . . . . .
>
> "I have pressed the first lever," said O'Brien. "You understand the construction of this cage. The mask will fit over your head, leaving no exit. When I press this other lever, the door of the cage will slide up. These starving brutes will shoot out of it like bullets. Have you ever seen a rat leap through the air? They will leap onto your face and bore straight into it. Sometimes they attack the eyes first. Sometimes they burrow through the cheeks and devour the tongue."

With this response of absolute horror evoked, the Gothic is seen as the prevailing metaphor characterizing the nature of existence under the political system of *Nineteen Eighty-Four*.

Undoubtedly, the Gothic will be used in other works as a metaphor for the scientific-bureaucratic future or for the present. Perhaps, like the absurd, it will become a dominant motif used to characterize perspectives of modern life by novelists who find our present existence not only meaningless but fearful or horrible. Kurt Vonnegut, in *Slaughterhouse Five* for example, demonstrates how the two metaphors can operate concurrently. In a description of an Iron Maiden, Vonnegut imparts a brief but powerful moment of traditional horror, thematically establishing an historical precedent for man's brutal nature, which is further augmented by a flippant repeated phrase which emphasizes the absurdity of his concomitant callousness:

> Weary's father once gave Weary's mother a Spanish thumbscrew in working condition—for a kitchen paperweight. Another time he gave her a table lamp whose base was a model one foot high of the famous "Iron Maiden of Nuremburg." The real Iron Maiden was a medieval torture instrument, a sort of boiler which was shaped like a woman on the outside—and lined with spikes. The front of the woman was composed of two hinged doors. The idea was to put a criminal inside and then close the door slowly. There were two special spikes where the eyes would be. There was a drain in the bottom to let out all the blood.

So it goes.

Certainly the Gothic response offers significant potential to the modern writer, not only in conjunction with the absurd, but on its own as a metaphor of fear and horror. We have seen it advance from a perspective of the romantically fearful medieval past to a metaphor for contemporary evils and fears: sexual passion, materialism, the hereditary savagery of man. Today it reflects the individual's sense of impotence in a fearfully incomprehensible world. As a metaphor, the Gothic response is still alive and functioning with properly disturbing effectiveness.

NOTES

[1] Lowry Nelson, Jr., "Night Thoughts on the Gothic Novel," *Yale Review*, 52 (Dec. 1962), 236-57; Robert D. Hume, "Gothic Versus Romantic: A Revaluation of the Gothic Novel," *PMLA*, 84 (March 1969), 282-90.

[2] *New Monthly Magazine*, 8 (1826).

[3] *The Gothic Flame* (New York: Russell and Russell, 1966), p. 130.

[4] Hume, p. 286.

[5] Mary Shelley, *Frankenstein*.

[6] See Thomas Moser, "What Is the Matter with Emily Jane? Conflicting Impulses in *Wuthering Heights*," *PMLA*, 27 (June 1962), 1-19.

[7] See Granville Hicks, "The Past and Future of William Faulkner," *Bookman*, 74 (Sept. 1931), 17-24.

[8] (New York: Viking Press, 1961), p. 13.

[9] Hume, p. 288.

Michael A. Slote

SOURCE: "Existentialism and the Fear of Dying," in *Language, Metaphysics, and Death,* Second Edition, Fordham University Press, 1994, pp. 80-100.

[*In the following essay, Slote uses concepts developed in the writings of Blaise Pascal, Søren Kierkegaard, Martin Heidegger, and Jean Paul Sartre to explain how the fear of death accounts for many aspects of human behavior.*]

In this paper I shall present a fairly systematic "existentialist" view of human anxiety about death and human responses to that anxiety, based on the work of Pascal, Kierkegaard, Heidegger, and Sartre. My main purpose is constructive, rather than exegetical. What seems to me most distinctive and important about the work of these existentialist authors is their approach to the fear of dying—or at least the relevance of what they say to that subject, for sometimes, when they deal with other topics, what they say can (I shall attempt to show) be used to illuminate the nature of human responses to the fear of death. But I think that much of what these authors say about the fear of dying is inchoate, confusing, or incomplete, and requires supplementation, clarification, and systematization of the kind I shall be attempting to provide here.[1]

I

Perhaps the central locus of discussion, by an Existentialist, of human attitudes toward and responses to death is the section of Kierkegaard's *Concluding Unscientific Postscript* called "The Task of Becoming Subjective." According to Kierkegaard, becoming subjective is "the most difficult of all tasks in fact, precisely because every human being has a strong natural bent and passion to become something more and different."[2] But what is it to be subjective or to be objective, and why is the former so difficult and the latter so tempting? Part of Kierkegaard's explanation involves him in a contrast between the subjective and objective acceptance of Christianity. But Kierkegaard also applies the subjective/objective distinction to attitudes toward life and death generally. And what unites Kierkegaard in the "Becoming Subjective" section of the *Postscript* with such non-religious Existentialists as Heidegger and Sartre is the fact that he has something to say about human attitudes toward life and death that presupposes no particular form of religiosity and that has not, I think, been said by anyone outside the existentialist tradition. And it is this aspect of Kierkegaard's work that I shall be examining.

According to Kierkegaard, to have an objective attitude toward one's life is to have the kind of attitude toward one's life encouraged by an Hegelian view of the world.

On such a view, one is part of a larger "world-historical" process of the self-realization of Reason or Spirit, and one's life takes on significance if one plays a role, however minor, in that world-historical process. One does not have to be an Hegelian to think in this kind of way. One can be thinking in a similar way if, as a scientist or philosopher, e.g., one devotes oneself to one's field in the belief or hope that one's life gains significance through one's contribution to something "bigger."

Kierkegaard says that people with such an attitude have an objective attitude toward their lives; and he wants each of us to dare to become subjective and renounce this "loftily pretentious and yet delusive intercourse" with the world-historical.[3] Those who live objectively are, according to Kierkegaard, under a delusion or illusion, and if so, then surely he has a real argument in favor of being subjective. For Kierkegaard, at least part of the illusion is, I think, the belief that by living objectively, one's dividend, what (good) one gets from life, is greater.[4] In the first place, even if a certain world-historical process of development is a great good, it is a good that is divided up among those participating in that development into many parts, none of which, presumably, is large in relation to the whole, and so perhaps the good to be derived from participating in that development will be less than the good to be gained by living subjectively. But Kierkegaard then seems to question whether indeed there is *any* good to be gained from living for some world-historical process, since one who does so may not be around when it comes to fruition. But it is not clear that the good of such a process of development must all come at the end of that development, so I think Kierkegaard has still not given us any very strong reason for believing that one who lives objectively is under some kind of illusion that his life is better.

However, in the *Postscript* Kierkegaard attempts to tie up his discussion of living objectively, i.e., of living for the world-historical, with certain illusory "objective" attitudes toward death. One who lives world-historically will sometimes say: "What does it matter whether I die or not; the work is what is important, and others will be able to carry it forward." But this is to think of one's death as nothing special, as just one death among others, as a "something in general." And Kierkegaard seems to believe that one who thinks this way is under an illusion, the illusion that his own death has no more significance *for him* than the death of (random) others, or, to put it slightly differently, that he *should be* no more concerned about his own death than about that of others. However, various Stoic philosophers would, I think, tend to argue that it is Kierkegaard's belief that one should be especially concerned about one's own death that is an illusion, an illusion born of irrational self-centeredness. So it is not obvious that Kierkegaard is correct about the illusory nature of objective living, or about the advisability of living subjectively. In any case, the attitude of people who live for the world-historical toward their own death is of some interest: they are, at least at some level, not as afraid of dying as they might be or as some people are.

And I think there are interesting implications to be drawn from this fact that have some of the spirit of what Kierkegaard says in the *Postscript*.

II

Those who live world-historically for some enterprise like science or philosophy seem not to be very anxious about dying. And I would like to suggest, what Kierkegaard never actually says, that we may be able to *explain* the tendency to live for the world-historical as resulting from our characteristically human fear of dying. For no one wants to live in fear, and since one who lives objectively, for the world-historical, does not feel the fear of dying that some of us do, there is reason and motive for people who have experienced anxiety or fear at the prospect of dying to (try to) adopt an objective existence, including an objective attitude toward their own deaths. But what are the psychological mechanisms by which living world-historically assuages someone's fear of death? Here I can only suggest, not establish, an answer, and what I shall say is intended as exploratory and somewhat speculative.

Consider the claim that people who live for the world-historical sometimes make that they will *be or become immortal through their works,* or that they will *live on through their works.* Why do people ever say such things; if what they are saying is just metaphorical, why do they use *that* metaphor and why do they seem to take the metaphor seriously?[5] It seems to me that such claims of immortality or living on are not (if there is no afterlife along traditional religious lines) literally true. It is not even literally true to say that part of one lives on in one's works, for books, e.g., are not literally parts of those who write them. Moreover, even if there is a traditional religious type of afterlife, one presumably does not live on *through one's works.*[6]

When we say that we shall live on or be immortal through our writings, e.g., I think we sometimes make that claim in a serious spirit. We are not just joking or deliberately speaking loosely. But when someone points out that what we are saying is not literally true, I think that most of us are willing to admit that what we have said is not literally true. How is this possible? It is my conjecture that someone who says he will live on, at least unconsciously believes that what he has said is (literally) true. Part of the evidence for the *unconsciousness* of the belief, if it exists, is the fact that when someone brings it to our attention that it cannot literally be true, we are ready, at least on a conscious level, to admit that this is so. What (further) supports the idea that the belief exists on some unconscious level is the fact that we at first express it in a serious vein and are not fully conscious that what we are saying is not literally true. We have to be reminded that what we have said is not literally true, and in this respect are not like someone who says that a certain person has a heart of gold. In the latter case, one is quite clear in one's mind *ab initio* that what one is saying is not the literal truth. One is, I think, often less clear, and in some sense more confused, about the literal falsehood of what one says when one says that one will live on in one's works. And this unclarity or confusion, as compared with the "heart of gold" case, is some evidence that one who speaks of living on in his works unconsciously believes that he will do so, inasmuch as the existence of such an unconscious belief is one very obvious possible explanation of that unclarity or confusion.[7] But what lends the greatest support to the view that such an unconscious belief exists in those who live world-historically and say they will live on in their works is the generally accepted fact that human beings naturally tend to fear dying. It is to be expected that men will try to avoid that fear and repress it, if possible. One way of doing this would be to convince oneself that one was immortal through one's works, so that death was not really or fully the end of one's existence. It would be hard to convince oneself of such a claim on a conscious level, just because of its literal falseness. But such belief in one's immortality could perhaps survive on an unconscious level where it would be less subject to rational scrutiny, and perhaps be capable of counteracting one's fear of death. The unconscious delusion of one's immortality (or living on) through one's works can, if we adopt Freudian terminology, be thought of as an unconscious defense mechanism of the ego that protects us from conscious fear about death by repressing that fear and counterbalancing it in such a way that it for the most part remains unconscious.[8] And this would explain why people who live for the world-historical are not consciously afraid of dying much of the time, and, in effect, why people so often live for the world-historical.[9]

Let me carry my speculation further. At one point in the *Postscript* (p. 274), Kierkegaard says that to live for the world-historical is to forget that one exists. This curious claim is, I think, more plausible or forceful than it may seem at first. Consider a person who lives objectively and unconsciously believes that he will live on through his books. Such a belief is not just false, but necessarily false, since it involves both the idea that one is alive and the idea that the existence of certain works like books is sufficient for one's continued existence; and nothing whose continued existence is entailed by the existence of such works can be *alive*. Moreover, the belief that one's books's existence is sufficient for one's continued existence seems to involve the idea that one has roughly the same kind of being as a book or series of books. So I think there is something to the idea that one who lives objectively somehow thinks of himself as not existing as a person, and as not being alive. But he presumably does not think this on a conscious level, for much the same reason that one does not on a conscious level think that one is going to live on through one's works. On the other hand, the *unconscious* delusion that one is not alive (or is of the same kind as a series of books) would seem capable of counteracting and allaying anxiety about dying just as easily as the unconscious belief that one is immortal through one's works does so. If one is going to live on in books, one is not going to lose one's life and there is nothing to fear from death, so that fears about dying may be prevented from becoming conscious by

being allayed on an unconscious level. Similarly, if one is not really alive, or is of the same "stuff" as books, then one also has nothing to fear from dying; and one's ceasing to be, if it occurs, will be no more tragic than the ceasing to be of a book.[10] So if one believes this kind of thing on an unconscious level, it is again not hard to see how one's fear of death may be allayed and kept unconscious.[11] Thus it would seem that people so often live for the world-historical because such living involves unconscious beliefs (delusions) that help them, more or less successfully, to avoid conscious fears about dying.[12]

According to Kierkegaard, however, not only does one who lives for the world-historical forget that he exists, but such a person at least to some extent ceases to exist as a person, ceases to live.[13] For if we use our lives as a means to the existence of certain works and/or to be mentioned in some paragraph or footnote of some authoritative history of our field of endeavor, then we are valuing our lives no more than we value the existence of certain works or our being mentioned in paragraphs or footnotes. And when we unconsciously think of ourselves as immortal through our works, we are in effect thinking that what we lose when we die cannot be that important or valuable. And to do and think in this way is to put a low value on one's living. But if one places a low value on actual living, one will not take full advantage of one's life (living) and that is a bit like already being dead, or not alive. So I think there really is something to Kierkegaard's claim that to live world-historically is to some extent to cease to exist as a person, to cease to be alive. The claim constitutes, not literal truth, but a forceful and penetrating metaphor.

It is well known that the fear of dying is a prime source of much of human religiosity. Belief in an afterlife of the traditional religious sort is one way that men can assuage their anxiety about dying. What is perhaps not so well known is how the fear of dying can give rise to (and explain) certain attitudes and activities of people who are not in any ordinary way religious, and perhaps also certain attitudes and activities of religious people that are not generally associated with religion. What I have tried to show here is that there are in Kierkegaard's *Concluding Unscientific Postscript* insights about our attitudes toward life and death that can be used to help us understand how certain nonreligious aspects of human life result from the fear of dying.

In doing so, I have assumed that people who live objectively and say that they are not terribly anxious about dying are nonetheless afraid of dying at some level. And this may seem high-handed. However, I am inclined to think that in general people living world-historically (who do not believe in some traditional religious type of life after death) continue to be subject to a certain welling-up of death anxiety that can overtake them in the midst of their daily lives.[14] Despite my own tendencies toward the world-historical, I have often experienced this sudden welling-up of death anxiety, and I think that the fact that this phenomenon is widespread among non-religious world-historical people (and indeed among people in general) is evidence that fear of dying never entirely ceases to exist in (such) people, but always continues to exist at least on an unconscious plane. For it is easier to imagine such a sudden welling-up of fear as the "return of the repressed" and as indicating a certain inefficiency of one's repressive mechanisms than to think of it as resulting from the sudden regeneration of death fears within one. What could plausibly explain such a sudden rebirth of death anxiety *in medias res?* Moreover, the earlier-mentioned fact that world-historical people (people who live for the world-historical) sometimes seriously say that they will be immortal through their works, without being clear in their own minds that this is just a metaphor, is, as I have already argued, evidence that such people unconsciously believe that they are immortal through their works (or that they are not alive). But why should they have such unconscious beliefs, except as part of a mechanism to relieve and keep repressed their fear of dying? So even such seemingly innocuous locutions as that we shall be immortal through our works indicate the existence of death fears even on the part of people who live for the world-historical and claim not to be afraid of dying. Let us now turn to Pascal's *Pensées* to see how the fear of dying affects other aspects of human life.

III

There is a famous long passage in the *Pensées* where Pascal talks about diversion, its role in human life, and its sources. Men "cannot stay quietly in their own chamber" alone and meditating, for any length of time.[15] We need or think we need diversion and activity and cannot be happy without diverting ourselves from ourselves because of the "natural poverty" of our feeble and mortal condition, so miserable that nothing can comfort us when we think of it closely."[16] Now, Pascal does not go on to decry the vanity of human diversion and claim that life would be less vain if we thought more about ourselves and our mortality. He is not arguing for the vanity of worldly human concerns in the timeworn manner of Ecclesiastes. He has an entirely new perspective on where the vanity of human life really lies. The vanity of our lives consists, for Pascal, in the fact that when we divert ourselves (from ourselves), we typically deceive ourselves about our motives for behaving as we do.[17] For example, a man who gambles often convinces himself that obtaining the money he is gambling for would make him happy (at least for a while). He focuses on the getting of the money and forgets that his real or main purpose is to divert himself. Thus if he were offered the money on condition that he not gamble, he would be (at least temporarily) unhappy, because he seeks diversion. On the other hand, if he were offered the diversion, say, of playing cards without being able to gamble for money, he would also be unhappy. For it is not just diversion he seeks; he must also have some imagined goal which he focuses on in such a way that he does not see that diversion is his real or main goal. Pascal does not, however, explain why men cannot simply seek diversion without

fooling themselves about their goal. But an explanation can be given along lines that Pascal might have approved. Imagine that we divert ourselves in order not to have to think of ourselves, and also realize that this is so. Shall we not *ipso facto* be thrust back into that very awareness of self which we sought to avoid through diversion? To realize that one wants not to think of oneself because it is unpleasant to dwell on one's feeble and mortal condition is *ipso facto* to be thinking of oneself and opening oneself up to the very unpleasantness one wishes to avoid. And if those who want to avoid thinking of themselves must remain ignorant of that fact if they are to succeed in not thinking of themselves, how better to accomplish this than by focusing on something outside themselves and thinking of it as their goal?

This explanation of human striving and activity applies not just to gambling, but, as Pascal says, to the waging of campaigns in love or in war and to many other human activities. Many of us fool ourselves about our motives much of the time when engaged in such activities. One objection to this analysis, however, would be that to explain so much human activity in terms of the fear of, or desire not to be, thinking of oneself is to offer a gratuitous explanation of our behavior. Why not just say that as animals we have an instinctive desire for certain activities which typically involve a lack of self-consciousness and which are called "diversions?" But the instinct theory of the origin of our diversions has, as it stands, no obvious way of explaining the self-deception Pascal points out. If we simply have an instinct for certain activities, activities that in fact tend to divert us from ourselves, why do some of us much of the time and many of us some of the time deceive ourselves into thinking that it is winning a certain victory or honor or woman that is our main goal, when it is the diverting activity leading up to that winning that is our main goal? On the theory that we do not like thinking about ourselves, however, the fact of self-deception can be explained along the above lines; so the assumption of a desire not to think of oneself is not gratuitous.

Furthermore, there is good independent evidence that people do not like to think about themselves. There is, for example, an experience that I have sometimes had, and that I think the reader will probably also have had; in the middle of thinking about something else I have all of a sudden thought to myself: "All this is being done by *me* and all these people are talking about *me*." I hope this description will suffice to convey the kind of experience I have in mind. What is interesting, but also perplexing and distressing to me, are the following facts. When I have this experience of myself, there seems to me to be something precious about it; and I think: "This is the moment when I am most alive; it is very good to have this experience." (There is, after all, a long tradition in which self-consciousness is a great, or the greatest, good.) I usually also think that though I am at that moment too busy to prolong the self-consciousness, I shall definitely set aside a good deal of time in the future to take full advantage of this kind of experience of self-awareness. But somehow that never happens. And when I am again momentarily self-conscious in the way I have been describing, I again put off a long bout of such self-consciousness to the future, despite my typical accompanying conviction that the experience of being self-conscious is a wonderful one that I really should and shall take greater advantage of. All this needs explaining, and the obvious explanation, I think, is that I really do not like the experience of self-consciousness, as Pascal suggests.

But why, in the end, should we not want to think about ourselves? Pascal suggests that the reason is that thinking about ourselves makes us think of our feeble and mortal condition. He also says about man: "to be happy, he would have to make himself immortal; but, not being able to do so, it has occurred to him to prevent himself from thinking of death."[18] Presumably, then, Pascal thinks that there is a connection between thinking about oneself and thinking unpleasant thoughts about one's death; and this seems to me to be quite plausible. For at least while we are absorbed in things outside us, we do not think of ourselves, or thus, it would seem, of our death; whereas if and when one does think about oneself, one might very easily think about one's death. It would seem, then, that the explanation of our diverting ourselves from (thinking about) ourselves is that this at least to some degree enables us to avoid thinking anxiously about our mortality. And so we have now clarified two general areas or aspects of human life in terms of the fear of dying. Let us turn next to Heidegger.

IV

Men's attitudes toward death are a major theme in Heidegger's *Being and Time*.[19] For Heidegger, in everyday life we exist in a mode that Heidegger calls the "they" (*das Man*). Heidegger characterizes this mode of existence as inauthentic, at least in part because in it, one is forgetful of the fact that death is one's ownmost possibility and cannot be outstripped. By this he means something close to the Kierkegaardian idea that one's own death has greater significance for one than does the death of others. Heidegger says that such a mode of existence is tempting because it tranquilizes one's anxiety in the face of death.[20] So it would seem that Heidegger can be thought of as providing a psychological explanation of certain aspects of human life, which he calls collectively "(being lost in) the 'they,'" and thus that Heidegger is doing something similar to what we have seen Kierkegaard doing in the *Postscript* and Pascal doing in the *Pensées*.[21]

According to Heidegger, one important aspect of our average everyday lostness in the "they" is its typical modes of discourse, chatter, and idle talk, and the busybody curiosity that characterizes such discourse. Heidegger points out that when people are idly and curiously talking about whether John and Mary will get divorced, the actual event, the divorce, if it occurs, actually disappoints the idle talkers; for then they are no longer able to con-

jecture about and be in on the thing in advance. The curiosity of everyday idle talk is concerned with the very latest thing(s), with novelty; and what interests in anticipation may be "old hat" or out of date when it occurs. Horse races and even pennant races in baseball seem to me to be good examples of this tendency. We have the keenest interest in who will win, but it is hard to maintain much interest in such races once we know their outcome; there is even a certain disappointment or let-down sometimes when the results of such things finally become known.[22] Heidegger's discussion here seems to have a good deal in common with what Pascal says about diversion, for one way of diverting ourselves from ourselves would be to be constantly curious about the latest things. But why not be interested in things that are not new and be diverted by them? The answer here—though it is not one that Heidegger actually gives—seems to me to lie precisely in the desire not to think of oneself that Pascal lays such emphasis on. What is newer is less well known, and the more there is to learn about something, the less likely one is to get bored with it or to cease being absorbed in it, and so be thrust back into thoughts about oneself. Furthermore, our earlier discussion of Pascal can help us to explain why we are sometimes let down when a certain event we have (only) conjectured about occurs, even though in advance we thought that "nothing would make us happier" than to know exactly when and how the event would occur. For if our goal is distraction from ourselves through conjecturing, we cannot very well admit this to ourselves without (running a grave risk of) defeating that goal; so we somehow fool ourselves into thinking that what we want is to know for sure about the character of the event we are conjecturing about, as a means to our real goal of diverting ourselves through conjecturing about something or someone outside ourselves; and when we cannot conjecture any more, then of course we are let down.

There may be a further reason why the desire for novelty is so pervasive in human life—though what I shall now be saying is perhaps more speculative than anything else I have to say here. As Heidegger says (p. 217), when one has the desire for novelty, it is as if one's motive were to have known (seen) rather than to know (see); for as soon as one has known (seen) something, one no longer wants to know (see) it. And there seems to be a certain vanity in such a way of dealing with things. Now consider what is implicitly involved in wanting, say, to have seen Rome, but not to see (keep seeing) Rome. There are tours whose advertising has the feeling of: "Come to Europe with us and you will see 8—count 'em, 8—countries in 8 days;" and such advertising and such tours appeal to many people who want to (say that they) have been, e.g., in Rome, but who do not much want to *be* in Rome. When one makes such a tour, one often even wishes the tour were already over so that one (could say that one) had already been to Rome in Italy (and to the other seven countries). The actual touring, with its "inconveniences," is often not desired or enjoyed. But to want the eight days and the trip to be already over with is in a certain sense to want a part of one's life over with in exchange for a being able to say one has been. This desire is in many cases unconscious. Sometimes some of us say, with an air of seriousness, that we wish that a certain trip or period of time were already over. But when confronted with the implications of what we have said, we almost inevitably recoil from what we have said and say that of course we do not *really* want a certain part of our life to be already over, perhaps adding that we were only speaking loosely or jokingly in making our original remark. In that case our desire to have a certain part of our life over with exists, if at all, only on an unconscious level. Evidence that there *is* such an unconscious desire comes from the fact of our original seriousness in saying that we wished a certain trip over with and from the fact that we are by no means clear in our own minds that we do not mean our statement literally, the way a hungry man is, for example, when he says that he could eat a mountain of flapjacks. I think this initial unclarity is best explained by (and thus evidence for) the existence of an unconscious desire to have a certain part of our life over with.[23] And perhaps for the very purpose of keeping this desire out of consciousness, we convince ourselves at least temporarily that we really want to *be* in Rome, or *feel* its living antiquity, etc. But then, after we have spent the tour rushing about, impatient with tarrying in one place too long, we *may*, upon reflection, recognize that we wanted the having seen more than the seeing of the places, like Rome, that we visited.

The logical extension of the wish to have a certain portion of one's life already over with is the wish to have one's whole life over with, and I would like now very tentatively to argue that at some deep level many of us have this latter wish, and so want not to be alive. Part of the reason for thinking so consists in the way we deceive ourselves about the extent of our desires to have portions of our lives over with. We sometimes think: if only it were a week from now so that I knew whether *p*, everything would be all right. But then when the time comes at which everything is supposed to be going to be all right, we soon find another reason for thinking things are not all right and for wishing other parts of our lives over with. I think that the initially implausible assumption that some people unconsciously wish their whole lives over with, wish not to be alive, provides the best explanation of this whole perplexing phenomenon. For if one has the unconscious desire to have one's whole life over with, there will be mechanisms in force to prevent it from becoming conscious. If one were conscious that one wanted *many different parts* of one's life over with *seriatim,* one would be dangerously close to being conscious that one wanted one's *whole life* over with. So it might reasonably be expected that someone with the unconscious wish or desire that his whole life be over with would be (made to be) unaware of the extent to which he wanted particular portions of his life over with before they were lived. Thus I think there is reason to believe that people who deceive themselves in this way unconsciously wish not to be alive.[24]

It will perhaps seem more plausible to hold that such a wish exists if I can show how it is explained by our fear of dying. One way of allaying fear of the loss of something is a kind of denial that one might call the technique of "sour grapes in advance." We can convince ourselves that the thing we may lose is not worth having or that we do not really want it. (This recalls the studies psychologists have done on the resolution of "cognitive dissonance.") An unconscious desire not to be alive might, then, help us to counterbalance or to keep repressed our fear of dying. The existence of such a desire can thus be supported in various ways and fits well into the kind of theory about our attitudes toward death so far proposed. But there is no time to speculate further in its favor.[25]

We argued earlier that if someone thinks of himself as not alive, he will not take full advantage of his life and it will be as if he is not (fully) alive. The same can be said for someone who wants not to be alive. We saw earlier the force of the metaphor that some of us are dead. Since it is as if some of us are dead because of what we have, unconsciously, done to ourselves, there is also force to the metaphor that some of us have killed ourselves. To live for the having seen and known of things is, metaphorically speaking, not to be alive, and to have killed oneself.[26] And one can also say this about those who live for the world-historical. I have a tendency to put myself entirely into my work and to live for something "bigger," philosophy. But sometimes I recoil from such an existence and from myself, and I feel that I have really just thrown my life away, have been personally emptied, through world-historical living. At such a time the metaphor of killing oneself seems particularly compelling.

We have thus far characterized those who live world-historically as assuaging the fear of dying via the *beliefs* that they are immortal and/or that they are not alive. But I think that such people also sometimes unconsciously wish not to be alive in the manner of those who divert themselves with novelties.[27] (Of course, those who live world-historically can be diverting themselves as well, e.g., with busy research or advocacy of causes.) For one thing, as we have already seen, people who live world-historically unconsciously think that they are not alive. And they want to think this, at least unconsciously, as a means to less fear or anxiety. But presumably if one wants to think one is not alive, that is because one wants not to be alive. This kind of inference from what one wants to think to what one wants is surely *usually* in order. Secondly, there is evidence that world-historical people tend to want parts of their lives over with in much the same way that seekers after novelty do. Someone writing a book that is intended to advance some field in the long run will often wish that the next six months of his life were already over so that he could see the book in finished form and have the writing of it over with. If only this were possible, everything would start being all right, he thinks, and he would be ready really to live his life again. Such a person, however, will, in many cases, be fooling himself about the extent to which he wants to "put off living" by missing parts of his life. As soon as there is another book to write, or academic appointment in the offing, he may very well once again want some part of his life already over with. Saying that such a man really wants to live, but only wants to avoid certain tense or burdensome parts of his life, does not really allow us to understand why he so often on such slight pretexts (is writing a book really so unpleasant and tense, considering the rest of the things that can be going on in one's life at the same time?) thinks up reasons for wanting to postpone living by omitting some parts of his life. Just as a man who is always *just about* to take a vacation and really live (it up) for a change, but who never does, can be plausibly suspected of preferring his work to a vacation or to "life" despite his protestations to the contrary, the perplexing behavior of one who lives world-historically and keeps wanting parts of his life over with while remaining unconscious or unaware of the extent to which this is so can, I think, only be made sense of in terms of an unconscious desire not to be alive.[28] Such a desire is strange and perplexing, perhaps, but no more so than the behavior it is supposed to explain.

Heidegger says many more interesting things about the "they." Idle talk and curiosity seem to be interested in anything and everything, though in fact, unbeknown to us, limits have been set on what we are to be interested in. For example, one is not, in the midst of curious talk, supposed to bring up the tragedy of life or the inevitability of death. Anyone who brings up such things is told not to be "morbid." Heidegger suggests that idle talk and curiosity function as a way of keeping us from thinking of our own death. For one thing—if I may borrow again from our discussion of Pascal to supplement what Heidegger is saying here—the illusion of interest in everything is an excellent means for blocking off thought about dying and its consequent anxiety, since if we believed, while we were engaged in idle talk, that we were not supposed to be deeply talking about death, we might very easily be thrust back into the very anxiety that idle talk was supposed to avoid. Moreover, the very self-assurance and harshness with which someone who brings up death in the midst of idle talk is branded as morbid tends to encourage and rationalize our avoidance of the topic of death.

Another device by which everyday living in the "they" keeps us from fears of death is by branding such fears as cowardly. Heidegger, however, thinks that it is more cowardly *not* to face death anxiously. Now there certainly seems to be room for disagreement on this issue. Some of the Stoics seem to have thought that it was irrational, rather than courageous, to be anxious about one's own death because death was a matter of indifference. And this latter philosophy of death may be correct; but it might be interesting at this point to make some educated guesses about the psychology of those who have advocated the "Stoic" view of death. For to my mind there is something strange and suspicious about (holding) the view that one's own death is not an evil. I have already discussed the fact that despite our best repressive mechanisms, the fear of dying sometimes comes upon (some of) us suddenly in the midst of life. When others tell us that

it is morbid or cowardly to worry about death, we are given an excuse or motive not to worry about death, and such advice may well help us to get rid of the conscious fear of death at least temporarily. The philosophical view that it is irrational to worry about death because death is a matter of indifference may have a similar function to play in the psychic lives of those who propound it. Philosophers pride themselves on being rational, and by branding the fear of dying as "irrational" they may give themselves a motive for ceasing consciously to worry about death and actually help themselves to get rid of the conscious fear of dying. I am inclined to think, then, that the view that it is irrational, and not courageous, to fear death, because death is no evil, may well be motivated, in many of those who propound it, by the fear of death itself, a fear that they are consequently able to repress, but not to get rid of. If so, then those who are helped to repress their fear of dying by holding a "Stoic" view of death are under an illusion when they claim as rational philosophers to be totally indifferent to death. But it might be better to live under such an illusion without consciously worrying about death than to know that one was not indifferent to death because one *was* consciously afraid of death. In the light of these complexities, it would seem hard to decide between Heidegger, on the one hand, and the Stoics and the "they," on the other, as to whether it is courageous to be (consciously) anxious in the face of dying.

Heidegger suggests yet further ways in which existence in the "they" tranquilizes our anxiety about dying. In the "they" there is an emphasis on keeping busy doing things, as the means to, or sign of, a full and good life. When someone suggests that one might do better to be more reflective and less busy, the response of the "they" is that by keeping busy, one is living "concretely" and avoiding self-defeating and morbid self-consciousness; this encourages the person who hears this to keep busy and not reflect on himself, and thus functions as a means to keeping us from the conscious fear of dying. (Consider, in particular, how the old, who are especially subject to fears of death, are told to keep busy and active.)

Heidegger points out that someone lost in the "they" will *admit* that death is certain and that one (everyone) dies in the end. According to Heidegger, in speaking of what happens to "everyone" or to "one" eventually, we "depersonalize" and "intellectualize" death. In thus depersonalizing death, it is as if the person were saying that death has nothing to do with *him right now,* and this enables him to talk about death without focusing on himself or having that particularly intimate experience of self-awareness described earlier or, thus, having fearful thoughts about death. Also, talk about the inevitability or certainty of death, etc., may be part of a process of "isolation of affect" in which one intellectualizes (about) a certain phenomenon to keep away from (consciousness of) certain related feelings.[29] Heidegger also points out that social scientists often seek to create "typologies" and systematic theories about humanity in the belief that they are thereby penetrating to the deepest level on which one can understand humanity and oneself, but that such intellectual "hustle and bustle" may entirely ignore the question of the significance for men of their own death and death anxiety; such intellectualization, he suggests, may serve to keep one from anxious thoughts about death by convincing one that one has reflected as deeply as it is possible to do. And the very stuffiness and detachment with which some sociologists, psychologists, etc., sometimes declare their desire to plumb the depths of the human spirit is, I would think, some evidence that they have a deeper need to avoid the *feeling* of their own mortality.

An important further point that is due to Kierkegaard rather than to Heidegger is that one can even overintellectualize one's response to a work, like that of Kierkegaard or Heidegger, which attempts to reveal in an "existential" manner the importance of our attitudes toward dying.[30] Spinoza has said that "passive" feelings like fear tend to dissipate when we scrutinize them, and this may well mean that it is difficult at one and the same time both intellectually to focus on and learn the significance of death anxiety and to *feel* that significance. And so there seems to be a real danger that someone who reads the writings of Existentialists will only intellectually understand and agree with what they say, and thus fail to derive all the benefit one could or should get from reading them. Of course, Spinoza's dictum also implies that it is difficult to think intellectually about death anxiety while feeling such anxiety. And one reason why I and others may be so interested in thinking and writing about death anxiety is that such thinking and writing may, in effect, involve an isolation of affect about death.[31]

In discussing Heidegger, we have brought in Kierkegaard and Pascal to help "deepen" his analysis of how death anxiety affects large portions of human life. I would like now to make use of certain ideas of Sartre's (in ways that Sartre undoubtedly would not approve) to point out yet another aspect of human life that can be explained in terms of the fear of dying. (However, I shall not discuss Sartre's own views on death, which in fact run counter to much of what we have to say on that subject.)

V

Being and Nothingness is perhaps most famous for its discussion of what Sartre calls "bad faith," which consists in being or putting oneself under the illusion that one is not free and cannot do other than what one in fact does.[32] For Sartre, one is in bad faith when one says: I have to get up and get to work; I can't stay in bed, I have a family to feed. Bad faith is involved because one does not *have* to get up and go to work.

Some people will immediately object to what Sartre is saying on the grounds that if determinism about human behavior is true and a certain person in fact will not stay in bed, then he is under no illusion when he says that he cannot stay in bed. Since, despite anything Sartre says, it is by no means obvious to me that such determinism is

not (approximately) true or that human beings possess free will, I would like now to (re)interpret Sartre's "bad faith" in such a way as to avoid assuming either human indeterminism or human free will.

Someone who says he has to go to work in the morning will sometimes say: "I have no choice in the matter." But I think that he does have a choice, even if a determined and unfree one, and that if he cannot stay at home, that is in part *because* of his (perhaps determined and unfree) choice. Moreover, I think that someone who is reminded of these facts will typically be willing to take back his original claim to have no choice in some matter, will grant that he had been speaking loosely or metaphorically. But it seems to me that such a person will typically not have been clear in his own mind about all this at the time when he originally claimed to have "no choice." And for reasons we have already gone into at length, I think this indicates that the person making such a claim unconsciously believes that he has no choice in a certain matter, even though he really does have a (possibly determined and unfree) choice in that matter and can be brought to conscious awareness of that fact. Such a person is under an illusion about the part he (and his choosing or deciding) plays in certain events or situations, and it is *this kind* of illusion that *I* shall call "bad faith."

Bad faith in this new sense is clearly related to bad faith in Sartre's sense. And, assuming that the new kind of bad faith does exist, it would be good if we could give some sort of explanation of it. Sartre's explanation of bad faith in the old sense will not be of much help to us here, since it assumes not only that human behavior is undetermined but also (implausibly enough) that human beings basically realize (believe) that this is so. My suggestion is that we explain bad faith in my new sense in much the same way that we have been explaining various other phenomena—namely, in terms of the fear of dying. (Indeed, Heidegger hints at this idea in *Being and Time*, p. 239.) I think that we can explain bad faith in terms of the fear of dying, if we suppose that the illusion of bad faith helps to repress such fear and if we borrow one further idea of Sartre's. According to Sartre, someone in bad faith (in his sense) who denies his own freedom is, in effect, thinking of himself as a thing or object, since things and objects are unfree, etc. I would like tentatively to claim that people who unconsciously believe that they have no choice, say, about getting up in the morning are, in effect, thinking of themselves as things or objects,[33] since things and objects really do lack choice. If we make this assumption, we can explain how bad faith in my sense enables one to relieve or repress death fears. For objects cannot die, and so unconsciously thinking of oneself as an object is unconsciously to think that one has nothing to fear from death.[34] (And if one passes away but is a mere object, then that is no more tragic than the passing away of a rock.)

Bad faith in the new sense seems to have much in common with living for the world-historical. In the latter case, one thinks of oneself as not alive; in the former, one thinks of oneself as a mere thing; and one might wonder whether there is much difference here either in the content of these unconscious beliefs or in the way they act on the fear of dying. Furthermore, just as one who lives for the world-historical can aptly be described metaphorically as not alive[35] and as having killed himself, one who lives in bad faith is, metaphorically speaking, a mere thing and not alive, and since he has (unconsciously) done this to himself, he has, metaphorically speaking, turned himself into a thing. And given the fact that the only way a person really can turn himself into a thing is by turning himself into a corpse, it is perhaps metaphorically appropriate to describe someone who is (constantly) in bad faith as having killed himself. Sartre holds that someone who thinks of himself as a mere thing wants (among other things) to *be* a mere thing. And I think we could argue that people in bad faith in my sense sometimes unconsciously want to be things in something like the way we earlier argued that people living for the world-historical want not to be alive. Furthermore, the unconscious desire to be an object would seem capable of countering the fear of dying in much the same way that the unconscious desire not to be alive does so, and so there is this further similarity between living in bad faith and living for the world-historical.

VI

If what has been said here is on the right track, then it would seem that Pascal, Kierkegaard, Heidegger, and Sartre all describe phenomena that pervade our lives and that are best explained in terms of their efficacy in relieving or repressing the fear of dying. Our explanation has made use of a Freudian type of view of repression and of the unconscious. This will certainly make our arguments here suspect in the eyes of some people. I have in effect been "practicing" a kind of "existential psychoanalysis," and though this term is one that was originally used by Sartre in *Being and Nothingness* to describe some of his own procedures, it may well apply more accurately to the kinds of things I have been doing here. For Sartre does not posit an unconscious, but I have followed Freud in doing just that.[36] In any case, I hope that this paper may bring to light an area, or areas, where Existentialism and Psychoanalysis can be mutually enlightening.

Of course, in addition to using psychoanalytic ideas, I have also frequently appealed to my own experience and intuitions, to how things strike me and to the "feel" of certain ideas. Though some things, I trust, will strike readers the way they have struck me, this will no doubt not always be the case; and when it is not, my appeals to how things feel to me, etc., are bound to seem like special pleading. Perhaps I *am* guilty of this, but I do not know how to avoid it in a paper like this where personal experience may be more relevant to seeing certain points than abstract arguments. And perhaps some of the ideas or intuitions I have relied on will seem more palatable to the reader if he "lives with them" and takes the time to see whether they do not, perhaps, make sense in and of his experience of himself and the world. For it is in

something like this way that many of the ideas and intuitions of this paper have become acceptable to me.

In this paper, I have pieced together various ideas from Pascal, Heidegger, Sartre, and Kierkegaard, as well as extrapolated beyond what any of them has said, to provide a fairly general picture of how the fear of dying accounts for many aspects of human life. The explanatory "theory" we have presented links together phenomena that the various Existentialists discussed separately, and as such should, given any standard account of scientific method, be more plausible than the accounts of the various Existentialists taken separately. So I hope I have helped to support and fill out the basically existentialist notion that the quality of a (non-religious) man's life greatly depends on his attitude toward his own death. And even if this idea is not particularly prevalent in Sartre, we can use things Sartre says to substantiate it.

Some people will complain that I have only been doing psychology, not philosophy. But it may not be important whether this accusation is true. And I also think that when psychology is general enough and speaks directly to the human condition, it can also count as philosophy. If, as we have argued, the main motive for world-historical (or busily self-distractive) participation in certain enterprises comes from (desire to avoid) the fear of dying, then a good many intellectuals, scientists, and others may be less pure in motive, less selfless, than they are often thought to be.[37] And this fact, if it is one, is surely very relevant to our understanding of the human condition, and so counts in favor of calling what we have been doing philosophy.[38]

NOTES

[1] I shall by no means, however, be discussing all the things these authors say on the topic of death.

[2] *Concluding Unscientific Postscript* (Princeton, 1960), p. 116.

[3] *Ibid.,* p. 133.

[4] *Ibid.,* pp. 130ff.

[5] Horace in the *Odes* (3, xxx) seems to be an example of someone who takes the metaphor seriously.

[6] I think that people who talk of gaining immortality through their children also say what is literally false, and their psychology is, I think, significantly similar to the psychology of those who talk of living on through their books.

[7] Kierkegaard hints at the idea that world-historical people believe they live on through their works when he implies (*Postscript,* p. 140) that such people need to be reminded that "in the world-historical process the dead are not recalled to life."

[8] For examples of reasoning similar to that just used that appear in the psycho-analytic literature, see, e.g., S. Freud's "Splitting of the Ego in the Defensive Process" (in his *Collected Papers* [London, 1956], 372-75) and Otto Fenichel's *The Psycho-analytic Theory of Neurosis* (New York, 1945), pp. 479-84. For another *philosophical* use of an argument like mine above, see M. Lazerowitz' *The Structure of Metaphysics* (London, 1955), pp. 69ff. and *Studies in Metaphilosophy* (London, 1964), pp. 225ff., 251. I am indebted to Lazerowitz' account for some of the structure of my own analysis.

[9] J. P. Sartre (in *Being and Nothingness* [New York, 1956], p. 543) says that "to be dead is to be a prey for the living." And Thomas Nagel (in "Death," Ch. 1) has tentatively claimed that a man can be harmed or unfortunate as a result of things that happen after his death, e.g., if his reputation suffers posthumously. I wonder whether these views are not, perhaps, indicative of some sort of unconscious belief that people live on in their works.

[10] The unconscious belief that one is going to live on and the unconscious belief that one is not alive seem to counteract the unconscious belief or fear that one is going to die in contradictory ways, the former with the "message" that we are not really going to lose what we have, the latter with the "message" that we really have nothing to lose. But we have already seen that the unconscious belief that one lives on in books is itself contradictory or necessarily false, so it should not, perhaps, be so surprising that the unconscious uses mutually contradictory means to repress death-fears. On this see Freud's *The Interpretation of Dreams,* ch. 2. For similar use of the (metaphorical?) notion of unconscious "messages," see Otto Fenichel's *Outline of Clinical Psychoanalysis* (New York, 1934), esp. pp. 13, 30, 33, 52, 250, 260, 275f.

[11] In "A Lecture on Ethics," *The Philosophical Review,* 74 (1965), 8ff. Ludwig Wittgenstein speaks of the feeling people sometimes have of being safe whatever happens. He claims that such a feeling or belief is nonsensical; but perhaps this occasional feeling is better thought of as the expression of a meaningful, but necessarily or clearly false, unconscious belief that we are safe whatever happens, a belief that counteracts the fear of dying and that is roughly equivalent to the unconscious belief that one is not alive. For one is absolutely safe (from death) if and only if one is not alive.

[12] I do not want to claim that everyone dedicated to some "cause," to something "bigger" than himself, is living world-historically. Such dedication may result from altruism or "conviction" and may not involve the world-historical psychology if it is not accompanied by delusions of immortality through one's works or actions, or the view that one's own death is unimportant.

[13] *Ibid.,* pp. 118, 175, 271, 273.

[14] See Heidegger's *Being and Time* (New York, 1962), pp. 233f.

[15] (New York, 1958), p. 39.

[16] *Ibid.*

[17] *Ibid.,* p. 40.

[18] *Ibid.,* p. 49.

[19] Our discussion here will be based on sections 27, 35-42 and 47-53 of *Being and Time.*

[20] Heidegger uses "fear" only with respect to things in the world. For death "anxiety" is reserved; but this is not necessarily dictated by ordinary usage.

[21] Of course, some philosophers will say that by treating Heidegger as an explanatory psychologist, I am treating him as if he were operating on the "ontic" level, whereas Heidegger thinks of himself as operating on an "ontological" level deeper than the "ontic" level on which science, psychology, and most pre-Heideggerian philosophy typically function. However, despite many efforts, I myself have never been able to make satisfactory sense of the ontic/ontological distinction. If the distinction is viable, Heidegger may have a good deal more to say than I shall be giving him credit for; but we can at least credit him with insights on a level with those of a Pascal or a Kierkegaard.

[22] Of course, some people constantly dwell on past (sporting) events (and their part in them), but I do not think this is incompatible with the general tendency I am describing.

[23] Compare here our earlier argument for the existence, in world-historical people, of an unconscious belief in their immortality through their works.

[24] Our earlier argument that we do not like thinking about ourselves can be strengthened along the lines of our present argument for the existence of an unconscious wish not to be alive. Similar self-deception occurs in the two cases.

[25] I have posited the wish not to be alive as an unconscious defense mechanism of the ego that responds to (prior) fear of dying. Freud, on the other hand, late in his career posited a basic (id-based) death instinct to account for various phenomena. See *Beyond the Pleasure Principle* (New York, 1950). The two sorts of views are incompatible, and so the explanation given just now in the text may be mistaken. However, there is some reason to prefer it. Our ego-theory of the death wish fits in better with our earlier-discussed theories about the ego's unconscious handling of the fear of dying. Moreover, other things being equal, it is better to treat a phenomenon as a derived phenomenon, within a theory, than to treat it as basic, within that theory. In addition, there is the sheer unintuitiveness of supposing that we have death wishes *ab initio,* rather than acquiring such (irrational) wishes in the *neurotic* process of repression. Finally, it is by no

means clear that a basic death instinct is needed to account for clinical phenomena. On this see Otto Fenichel's "A Critique of the Dead Instinct" in *The Collected Papers of Otto Fenichel,* first series (New York, 1953), pp. 363-72.

[26] I think we have some inkling of this metaphorical killing when we speak of "killing time" at moments when we want to have something over with, want a certain (perhaps boring) part of our lives over with. Use of that phrase may be a disguised conscious expression of the unconscious desire not to be alive.

[27] Kierkegaard's claim in the *Postscript* (p. 137) that one whose eye is on world-historical things has perhaps found "a highly significant way of . . . killing time" seems to indicate some awareness on his part that world-historical people want not to be alive and have, metaphorically speaking, killed themselves. Whose time, after all, does one kill except one's own? And one's time is one's life. Incidentally, it is natural to say that world-historical people "bury themselves in their work," and this metaphor seems to suggest the very same things that our use of the metaphor of killing time does.

[28] Cf. Emerson's remark in his *Journals* (April 13, 1834) that "we are always getting ready to live, but never living."

[29] Cf. O. Fenichel's "Outline of Clinical Psychoanalysis," *op. cit.,* pp. 190f., for ideas about "isolation of affect" that are related to some of the things we have said here and earlier in the paper.

[30] *Postscript,* pp. 166f.

[31] Heidegger also points out that the force of living in the "they" is such as to make people lost in the "they" scoff at his analysis of such lostness. Once one is aware of one's tendencies to cover up certain anxieties, it may be harder to use the mechanisms one has previously used in doing so; so one who wishes at some level to keep covering up his anxiety has a motive to reject Heidegger's analysis and, indeed, our analysis here.

[32] See *Being and Nothingness,* Pt. 1.

[33] I hope I shall be forgiven for ignoring plants.

[34] This recalls the Simon and Garfunkel song that goes: "I am a rock, I am an island; and a rock feels no pain, and an island never cries." The idea that we sometimes want to think of ourselves as things to avoid the pain of life or of facing death is not new or silly. Moreover, even if people in bad faith only think of themselves, unconsciously, as *similar to* mere things, that thought may itself be capable of relieving the fear of death.

[35] Kierkegaard says that such a person is also a "walking stick," which suggests the similarity of such a person to someone in bad faith who exists as a mere object.

[36] Sartre rejects the unconscious for reasons that seem to me to be interesting, but ultimately unacceptable.

[37] This is not to say that such people should stop doing science, etc., with their present motives. They may be happier than they are otherwise likely to be, and may be contributing to the intellectual or practical good of other people. Also see note 12, above.

[38] I am indebted to G. Boolos, E. Erwin, B. Jacobs, D. Levin, S. Ogilvy, and M. Wilson for helpful comments on earlier drafts of this paper.

PRE-TWENTIETH-CENTURY

LITERATURE

Elizabeth R. Hatcher

SOURCE: "Chaucer and the Psychology of Fear: Troilus in Book V," in *ELH,* Vol. 40, No. 3, Fall, 1973, pp. 307-24.

[*In the following essay, Hatcher discusses Chaucer's realistic presentation of Troilus's anxiety over Criseyde's infidelity in Book V of* Troilus and Criseyde *through comparison with a parallel passage in Boccaccio's* Il Filostrato.]

> If . . . fear increases so much as to disturb the reason, it hinders action even on the part of the soul. But of such a fear the Apostle did not speak.
>
> —St. Thomas Aquinas, *Summa Theologica*[1]

Despite St. Paul's omission and St. Thomas's *caveat,* medieval literature frequently gave allegorical or stylized accounts of the way fear paralyses the human mind. Prudentius, when he allows Avaritia and her unsavory followers, including Anxietas, Cura, and Metus, to strip the valuables from the corpses of the fallen Luxuria and her allies, suggests that avarice burdens the miser with a host of anxieties—fears lest he lose his possessions—which even turn him against his own fleshly cravings. The poets of courtly love discussed those species of anxiety[2] accompanying the desire for and possession of the lady's love. Stylized versions of what we might call the *anxiety of anticipation* crowd the pages of courtly literature: Dante the youth of the *Vita Nuova,* Petrarch the lover of the *Sonnets,* Tristan, Troilo, Troilus, and other heroes without number lose sleep and appetite, grow pale, tremble, and dream. The *anxiety of loss,* real or imagined, occurs less often; when it does appear, it too is stylized in expression. When young Prince Floris is separated for a fortnight from the servant-child Blanchefleur, he is obsessed with the thought of her; his companions' joy fails to cheer him; he sighs and cannot study; a single day seems to drag on like three; and when the time is up and she still does not come, he can neither eat nor drink. Adult heroes thwarted in love often go mad and become sylvan "wild men" like Sir Orfeo and Yvain. In *Il Filostrato,* Boccaccio similarly treats Troilo's outward signs of inward pain upon losing Criseida as stylized, operatic gestures, without exploring them as symptoms of mental agony.[3]

Not so Chaucer. In the part of the *Troilus* which goes from Criseyde's departure to Troilus's discovery of the brooch,[4] Chaucer's alterations of his Italian source's speech, characterization, and plot—particularly in Troilus's boar dream and its aftermath—result largely from the intention to explore the psychological realities behind the symptoms of Troilus's anxiety: to show how, despite his courtly idealization of Criseyde, Troilus's knowledge that she might desert him preys upon his mind.[5] This knowledge adds an inarticulate fear to his loneliness, poisons his dreams, and haunts him with the need to verify his ideal image of her;[6] ironically, it sends him to his death believing she is a far worse traitor than she really is.

Did Chaucer, like other poets of his day, learn about love—and about fear—from scholastic psychology? Only in part. For Aquinas, love causes fear, "since it is through his loving a certain good, that whatever deprives a man of that good is an evil to him, and that consequently he fears as an evil."[7] Aquinas also finds the siege of a town an apt metaphor for the physiological "contraction of heat and vital spirits towards the inner parts" of the body which he believed to accompany fear: "the inhabitants of a city, when seized with fear, leave the outskirts, and, as far as possible, make for the inner quarters."[8] Thus Chaucer is making an association natural to his times in using a story of siege as the setting for an analysis of a lover's anguish. Aquinas further observes that this "contraction" resulting from fear also causes trembling in the body's outer members, because the lack of heat, "whereby the soul moves those members," induces loss of control.[9] This was the physiological basis for elaborate descriptions of the trembling lover for Dante, Petrarch and other poets known to Chaucer.

But Chaucer goes further than Aquinas in analysing fear's psychological effects. Aquinas says that moderate fear, "without much disturbance of the reason. . . . conduces to working well, in so far as it causes a certain solicitude, and makes a man take counsel and work with greater attention."[10] He balks, however, at discussing the effects upon the mind of *im*moderate fear (I have quoted the passage as an epigraph) and skips to a new topic. Chaucer rushes in where the Angelic Doctor feared to tread, and with his characteristic sensitivity shows how Troilus's immoderate fear fatefully distorts perception.

In both the Italian and the English poems, this part of the story falls into three sections. Section 1 (*Filostrato* V, 15-71; *Troilus* V, 197-686) describes Troilus's misery after the exchange and ends with a scene-shift to the Greek camp. Section 2 (*Filostrato* VI; *Troilus* V, 687-1099) shows Diomede's seduction of Criseyde. Section 3 (*Filostrato* VII, 1-VIII, 10; *Troilus* V, 1100-1666) describes Troilus's protracted uncertainty as Criseyde fails to return and ends with the discovery of the brooch. In the *Troilus,* but not in *Il Filostrato,* each section acts differently to expand our understanding of Troilus's anxiety. In Boccaccio's version of Section 1, Troilo and Pandaro candidly doubted Criseida's infidelity; Chaucer rewords or suppresses their skepticism. This change shows that Troilus reacts to stress differently from Troilo. Speaking indirectly of his dread, he tries to ignore it, but this effort only makes the dread infect his actions more pervasively than it does Troilo's. In Boccaccio's version of Section 2, Criseida did precisely what Troilo expected she might do—deserted him for another lover. No ironic discrepancy separated her real nature from his image of her. He suspected she would play the whore, and she did. Chaucer makes Criseyde not a libidinous opportunist but an angry, frightened woman plagued by superb hindsight. This change enables him in turn to modify the boar dream so that it reveals the ironic effect of anxiety on Troilus's image of Criseyde. In Boccaccio's version of Section 3, the boar dream's meaning (VII, 23-24) was as obvious to Troilo as to the reader, and triggered such spectacular gestures as Troilo's suicide attempt, Pandaro's eloquent speech against suicide, Deifebo's intervention, and Cassandra's cattiness. Chaucer instead draws us to compare the troubled Criseyde of the betrayal scene with the vile Criseyde of the dream, and to see that Troilus's attempt to ignore his fear has given him a much uglier image of her than her real nature warrants. Chaucer makes Troilus obsessed by this dream. It so degrades his lady that he loyally struggles to reject its message. Tormented by it, he seeks everywhere for a substitute interpretation until the brooch confirms the fact of her betrayal and seems to confirm his mistakenly degraded view of her.

I

After Criseyde's departure, the heroes of both poems regret not having acted to keep her and feel frustration at her loss. Both anxiously while away the ten days killing time at Sarpedon's, rereading their old love letters, sorrowfully revisiting Criseyde's empty house, and reliving the high points of the affair at the sites where they occurred (*Filostrato* V, 40-48, 51-55; *Troilus* V, 435-501, 528-81). Both constantly fear she may never return. But whereas Troilo frequently articulated his fear, Troilus cannot speak ill of his lady. He only expresses doubt in veiled terms and in moments of great stress.[11] Complaining to Pandaro, Troilo stated outright that he expected never to see Criseida again and asked whether she had forgotten him.[12] Troilus merely utters a vague question in the solitude of his chamber: "Whan shal she come ayeyn? / I not, allas!" (V, 225-26). Desperate that she might long for him, Troilus (but not Troilo) wishfully imagines how ghastly she will look after the ten days: "O pitous, pale, and grene / Shal ben youre fresshe wommanliche face / For longynge, or ye torne into this place" (V, 242-45).

Unlike Troilo, Troilus strives to dismiss his anxiety about her return.

> Another tyme he sholde myghtyly
> Conforte hym self, and seyn it was folie,
> So causeles swich drede for to drye,
> And eft bygynne his aspre sorwes newe.
> (V, 262-65)

As he returned from Serpedone's, Troilo asked outright, "O Dio! / Trovero io tornato l'amor mio?" and Pandaro answered just as frankly that he doubted she would ever return.[13] In contrast, Troilus is so hopeful of finding Criseyde returned before her day that he sings as he rides (V, 502-04). Pandarus is as skeptical as his Italian counterpart, but he keeps his doubt to himself. He assuages Troilus's anxiety with lies, encouraging him to trust that she will come soon.

> "Ye, haselwode!" thoughte this Pandare, . . .
> But natheles he japed thus, and pleyde,
> And swor, ywys, his herte hym wel bihighte,
> She wolde come as soone as evere she myghte.
> (V. 505, 509-11)

In both poems the hero prays to Love for the lady's return. But Troilo's prayer mainly showed his sensual desire for Criseida, while Troilus's springs from his fear of Criseyde's betrayal—fear intellectualized to a matter of theological importance. Troilo wanted Criseida because she was a pleasurable object which he merited by his devotion:

> Ritornala [l'alma mia] nel suo primo piacere,
> Stringi Criseida sì come mi fai,
> Sì ch'ella torni a dar fine a' miei guai.[14]
> (V, 57)

Troilus asks Cupid to avert his Old-Testament countenance of wrath and to turn toward him his New-Testament aspect of mercy and grace:[15]

> "Wel hastow, lord, ywroke on me thyn ire,
> Thow myghty god, and dredful for to greve.
> Now mercy, lord; thow woost wel I desire
> Thi grace moost of alle lustes leeve."
> (V, 589-92)

He wants Criseyde to *care enough about him* to attempt the return:

> "Distreyne hire herte as faste to retorne
> As thow doost myn to longen hire to see;
> Than woot I wel that she nyl nat sojorne."
> (V, 596-98)

The God's failure to constrain Criseyde in this way would be cruelty as prominent as Juno's wrath which ruined Thebes (V, 599-602). Thus Troilus's fear of betrayal has reached epic proportion in his mind. Half-articulated, it exceeds Troilo's overt doubt and sensual want.

At the city gates, Troilo again wondered aloud if Criseida would come back;[16] Troilus again alludes only obliquely

to his doubt: "Here I dwelle out cast from alle joie, / And shal, til I may sen hire eft in Troie" (V, 614-16). After describing (as does Boccaccio) his hero's conviction that people are noticing his misery and wondering about its cause, Chaucer emphasizes (as Boccaccio does not) Troilus's anxiety: "Swich lif right gan he lede, / As he that stood bitwixen hope and drede" (V, 629-30). Troilo's song in *Filostrato* V, 62-66 is a long, elaborate prayer for death; Troilus's is a single stanza metaphorically expressing his fear of desertion.

> "O sterre, of which I lost have al the light,
> With herte soore wel oughte I to biwaille,
> That evere derk in torment, nyght by nyght,
> Toward my deth with wynd in steere I saille;
> For which the tenthe nyght, if that I faille
> The gydyng of thi bemes bright an houre,
> Mi ship and me Caribdis wol devoure."
> (V, 638-44)

Finally, Troilo's fantasy that the breezes from the Greek camp were Criseida's sighs (*Fil.* V, 70) becomes Troilus's laboriously reasoned delusion, symptomatic of anxiety in its desperate concern for "proof":

> "And hardily this wynd, that more and moore
> Thus stoundemele encresseth in my face,
> Is of my ladis depe sikes soore.
> I preve it thus: for in noon othere space
> Of al this town, save onliche in this place,
> Fele I no wynd that sowneth so lik peyne;
> It seyth: 'allas, whi twynned be we tweynne?'"
> (V, 673-79)

These differences show that wherever Troilo or Pandaro coolly doubted Criseida's return, Chaucer suppresses or mutes the reference. He makes Troilus state his fear obliquely, metaphorically, or hysterically. He makes Pandarus conceal his skepticism and talk assuredly of her return, encouraging Troilus to believe what Pandarus himself does not. In this way Chaucer generates greater tension than does Boccaccio because he depicts an anxiety so great that Troilus cannot articulate it clearly. As one fears to name a dread disease, Troilus dares not state outright that Criseyde might stay away willingly. Instead, he sometimes assures himself nothing is amiss and sometimes succumbs to a nameless fear which becomes an obsession. His prayers and songs take shape from his worry. And his hidden doubt exaggeratedly expresses itself in his boar dream, more damning of Criseyde than her actual behavior.

II

Before the dream, both poems shift scene to Criseyde's betrayal. This scene is crucial to Chaucer's depiction of Troilus's anxiety because, unlike the betrayal in *Il Filostrato,* it illustrates the ironic disparity between Criseyde's real nature and the anxious Troilus's image of her. Hence it is no digression to show how Chaucer modifies the betrayal to further his audience's understanding of Troilus's anxiety. He does so mainly by making Criseyde less sensual and more bewildered than

Criseida. Since we see the betrayal while Troilus does not, we can understand if not excuse Criseyde's failure to return. When Troilus's anxiety surfaces in the boar dream, we—but not he—can see how deeply he misunderstands her.

Boccaccio's Troilo feared Criseida would desert him for another lover, and the betrayal in Part VI of *Il Filostrato* fulfilled his expectation. In the Greek camp, Criseida was sexually frustrated (VI, 2), lonely (3), worried that her unhappiness was wrecking her beauty (4), and angry that her separation from Troilo prevented her from seizing the day for love (5). The lovestruck Diomede urged her to give up her Trojan lover because he would certainly not survive the city's fall (15-18). He appealed to her snobbery by praising Greek refinement over Trojan boorishness (21); he asserted his own royal lineage (22). Much to his delight, Criseida said she would indeed consider loving him if Troy fell (31). She did not seem greatly to fear for the city; but since she believed strongly in the *carpe diem* philosophy, it was only logical that she not remain loyal to a lover whose days were numbered. After Diomede had gone, Boccaccio told us that the Greek's good looks and smooth tongue had won her heart.

Chaucer changes all this. He mitigates Criseyde's sensuality (V, 720-21) by burying it among a host of largely non-sexual apprehensions. To loneliness (727-28) he adds dismay that, despite her complex scheming, she has underestimated the difficulty of getting back to Troy (692-93); anger at her father's refusal to let her return (694-95); worry about what Troilus will think if she is late (696-700); and fear of being caught as a spy or raped by a sentinel if she should try to escape (701-07). Instead of pouting about the loss of her beauty or about the waste of time for love, Chaucer's heroine bemoans her lack of prudence (744-49).

To a woman with such complicated uncertainties, Chaucer's politic Diomede is a more formidable enemy than Boccaccio's amorous warrior would be. As a tour de force of amatory prowess, he has decided to defy the old saw warning that "men shal nat wowe a wight in hevynesse" (V, 791) and to win Criseyde's heart while she still mourns her Trojan love (792-98). What a grand topic for barracks-room boasts! Although his conversation with her (855-945) closely follows Boccaccio, his prediction of doom for Troy has greater impact on a woman who so fears for her safety. Her flustered, disconnected reply reveals this impact. She rambles over all the facts which make staying put her only safe alternative, offering weak objection after weak objection (960-76). Thus preoccupied, only mid-speech (982) does the usually honor-obsessed Criseyde realize that Diomede has insulted her by suggesting she has a Trojan lover (877). She rebukes him accordingly (981-83). But if she must stay in the camp, she will need a champion, so she qualifies her rebuke: she dare not be too rough with Diomede. She would rather die than love; she may, of course, change her mind later—but not yet; he may come back tomorrow, if he doesn't mention love; though if ever she

did love a Greek, it should be he; but that does not mean that she *will* love him; "ny sey nat nay; but in conclusioun, / I mene wel, by god that sit above" (984-1004).

Under other circumstances, Diomede's "wordes" and "grete estat" (1024-25) would not threaten Criseyde's loyalty to Troilus. But Troy is in peril (1025); Criseyde is alone (1026). Had she *not* mourned—had she *not* grieved at losing Troilus and feared the danger of trying to get back to him—Diomede *could not* have seduced her. He has little reason to crow, for circumstances only happen to be on his side.[17] To Boccaccio's Criseida, the fate of Troy mattered less than Diomede's handsome looks and friendly persuasion (VI, 33-34). To Chaucer's Criseyde, the fate of Troy makes the crucial difference.

Part VI of *Il Filostrato* ended here. Having admirably illustrated his theme "Giovane donna è mobile, e vogliosa / È negli amanti molti" (*Fil.* VIII, 30), Boccaccio shifted back without further comment to Troilo's vain wait. At the corresponding part of *Troilus,* Chaucer interpolated twelve stanzas (V, 1016-99), explicitly defending Criseyde but implicitly underscoring her insensitivity, which hone the irony of her infidelity to a keen edge.[18] Mixing sympathy and disappointment, the narrator describes the slow ripening of Criseyde's ambivalence into betrayal; because she is sorry for what she has done, she can hardly be called fickle. Her hesitation at attempting escape gives Diomede further time for courtship; his courtship ends her sighs for her former lover (1034-36). She gives Diomede Troilus's horse, which he has won in battle (1038-39); she lets him wear "a pencel of her sleve" (1043); worst of all, she gives him a brooch Troilus gave her—the brooch which will prove her betrayal (1040; cf. 1661). All this seems damning evidence. But perhaps she is only trying to do the expected courtly thing; perhaps she simply is unaware that two of these gifts are more than courteous gestures. Like a tragic version of Pope's Belinda, she does not see the difference between a Bible and a billet-doux. Excess of pity, not whim, causes her final failure (1045-50). Recognizing the irony that she, not Troilus, is destroying her honor, she determines to be loyal to Diomede (1071) and exculpates her former lover (1075-84). The narrator urges forbearance: "Iwis, I wolde excuse hire yit for routhe" (1099). Criseyde's guilt is real, not only because she truly does wrong, but because she begins—and ends—as we all do, in weakness. Boccaccio's betrayal scene demonstrated that his heroine was fickle; Chaucer's demonstrates that she is only human.[19]

The reader (or listener) now knows Criseyde more intimately than Troilus does, because he has watched her thoughts as she betrays her lover. Now he is ready to see that Troilus's secret fear of betrayal, confronted with her failure to return, ironically yields in the boar dream a harsher judgment against her than she deserves.

III

In the *Troilus,* the section extending from the tenth day to the discovery of the brooch closely follows Boccaccio only as far as the boar dream.[20] Chaucer drastically alters the dream itself (*Fil.* VII, 23-24) and Troilo's reaction to it (25-31).[21] In *Il Filostrato,* Troilo had been worrying aloud, from the moment of separation until the night of the dream, that Criseida might desert him. The dream directly and without irony reflected this worry: it showed Criseida doing exactly what he had said she might do, and what we had already seen her do.

> In sogno vide il periglioso
> Fallo di quella che 'l facea languire:
> ... gli sembrava
> Un gran cinghiar veder che valicava.
>
> E poi appresso gli parve vedere
> Sotto a' suoi pie Criseida, alla quale
> Col grifo il cor traeva, ed al parere
> Di lui, Criseida di così gran male
> Non si curava, ma quasi piacere
> Prendea di ciò che facea l' animale.[22]
> (VII, 23-24)

To what Troilo already knew, the dream added only the symbolic animal identifying the lover, and Troilo immediately understood it all. He awoke enraged, called Pandaro, interpreted the dream correctly, and tried to stab himself.

Chaucer changes the dream so that it distorts reality. In it, after uttering not one clear word of complaint against the tarrying Criseyde,[23] Troilus in his sleep abruptly experiences a brazen, hideous image of her.

> He mette he say a boor with tuskes grete,
> That slep ayein the bryghte sonnes heete;
>
> And by this boor, faste in hire armes folde,
> Lay, kissynge ay, his lady bright, Criseyde.
> (V, 1238-41)

We know that while Criseyde has indeed betrayed him, she hasn't behaved like this. Troilus's is a "sick" dream whose characters behave unnaturally and unpleasantly. Boccaccio's boar charged; Chaucer's, for all his "tuskes grete," sleeps "ayein the brighte sonnes heete." Boccaccio's Criseida took conscious pleasure in the aggression; Chaucer's Criseyde lavishes her kisses upon an indolent and unresponsive swine. Why does Troilus suddenly dream that she falls for this pig much as the bewitched Titania falls for Bottom the Ass?

I believe Chaucer means to imply that Troilus has the brutal dream *because* he has not uttered his doubt. The dream startlingly blends two types which, according to medieval lore, are incompatible. Because it tells Troilus that Criseyde has betrayed him, the dream reflects the truth and hence qualifies as a *somnium,* according to Macrobius: "one that conceals with strange shapes and veils with ambiguity the true meaning of the information being offered, and requires an interpretation for its understanding."[24] But at the same time, it savagely blackens Criseyde's real behavior and hence is an *insomnium,* a "nightmare" or lying dream, which Macrobius said "may

be caused by mental . . . distress, or anxiety about the future. . . . As examples of the mental variety, we might mention the lover who dreams of possessing his sweetheart or of losing her. . . . Such dreams . . . are noteworthy only during their course and afterwards have no importance or meaning."[25] This paradoxical fusion of true and false dreams conveys to the reader a psychological irony to which Troilus (because he does not know the circumstances of Criseyde's betrayal) is necessarily blind: the harder one tries to whitewash one's legitimate distrust, the more deceptive that distrust becomes. For a thousand lines Chaucer has been developing this theme by muting Troilo's every overt reference to his anxiety over Criseida's return, and by showing that Criseyde fails to return through terror and indecision rather than through lust. Now the theme becomes an image in a dream that fuses two categories of mental experience which the poet's age believed disjunct. Because Troilus has tried so hard to ignore his anxiety, the dream tells him that her seducer need not even try to win her heart— she would throw herself upon his indifferent sensuality. We the audience can see, as Troilus cannot, precisely how true—and how false—his dream is.

Chaucer plays his theme out to its end by describing Troilus's efforts to dispel his anxiety. Each effort is ironic because, whether Troilus accepts or rejects the dream, he is doomed to be wrong. Perhaps the greatest brilliance of Chaucer's description is his use of the trope "the unbelievable Cassandra." He animates the trope as do few classical or medieval authors by basing Troilus's incredulity on a plausible and ironic psychological situation.

Like Troilo, Troilus first accepts the dream's message without question: "O Pandarus, now knowe I crop and roote /. . . . My lady bright, Criseyde, hath me bytrayed" (1245, 1247). Pollyanna Pandarus questions the boar's identity in order to reassure his friend.

> "Paraunter, ther thow dremest of this boor,
> It may so be that it may signifie,
> Hire fader, which that old is and ek hoor,
> Ayeyn the sonne lith in poynt to dye,
> And she for sorwe gynneth wepe and crie,
> And kisseth hym, ther he lith on the grounde;
> Thus sholdestow thi dremes right expounde."
> (V, 1282-88)

In Troilus's dream, the boar has great tusks, hardly symbolic of decrepitude, and Criseyde's behavior displays sexual rather than filial devotion.[26] However, eager to disprove his intuition, Troilus immediately agrees to test Criseyde by writing her a letter. Her reply[27] rules out Pandarus's interpretation but settles nothing else (V, 1424-31). Troilus thus continues in an agony of uncertainty.

At this point, where Boccaccio introduced a new thread of plot,[28] Chaucer shows Troilus driven to seek further advice on the dream's meaning. He both wants the truth and dreads that the dream *is* the truth.

> This drem, of which I told have ek byforn,
> May nevere come out of his remembraunce;
> He thoughte ay wel he hadde his lady lorn,
> And that Joves, of his purveyaunce,
> Hym shewed hadde in slep the signifiaunce
> Of hire untrouthe and his disaventure.
>   (V, 1443-48)

He consults the seeress Cassandra. "She gan first smyle"; then, drawing on the boar's heraldic derivation as the device of Diomede's house, she gives name and reality to the vague animal upon whom Criseyde lavishes her kisses.

> "This Diomede hire herte hath, and she his.
> Wepe if thow wolt, or lef; for, out of doute,
> This Diomede is inne, and thow art oute."
>   (V, 1517-19)

In resolving the dream's one ambiguity, Cassandra puts her skill in support of Troilus's intuition and forces him to accept or reject the dream's version of Criseyde's betrayal. Without knowing it, she thus reinforces the irony of Troilus's position. She is no more able than he to separate the true part of the dream from the false part, the *somnium* from the *insomnium*. She cannot free Troilus from the need to choose between two beliefs, both wrong: either Criseyde is true and the dream false, or she is horribly false and the dream true. The idealistic Troilus takes the *nobler* option: honoring his vow as a courtly lover, he rejects both the dream and its interpreter.

> "Thow seyst nat soth," quod he, "thow sorceresse,
> With al thy false goost of prophecye!
>
>   . . . . .
>
> Awey," quod he, "ther Joves yeve the sorwe!
> Thow shalt be fals, paraunter, yit to-morwe!"
>   (V, 1520-21, 25-26)

His refusal to believe Cassandra, ironic in its double use of "fals," leaves Troilus where he was before he consulted her—desperately needing some solution besides what is now, to him, the obvious one. Furious that Cassandra substantiates his secret doubt, he springs from bed "as though al hool hym hadde made a leche" (1537); from then on "he gan enquere and seche / A sooth of this, with al his fulle cure" (1538-39). This suggests that he busily consults other soothsayers and interrogates envoys or couriers who might know of Criseyde's actions in the Greek camp.[29] As he reacted to Cassandra, so we may well imagine he reacts to the findings of these fevered inquiries, rejecting whatever suggests Criseyde's betrayal, believing whatever gives him hope. He cannot learn the truth because his anxiety, now at panic level, prevents him from appraising the evidence objectively. Even after Criseyde writes him a forked-tongued letter—accusing him of insubmission to the gods, lechery, indiscretion, and deceit (1604-17)—"he ful ne trowen myghte, / That she ne wolde hym holden that she hyghte" (1635-36). His longstanding inability to accept the doubt symbolized by the boar dream has blinded him to reality until the brooch unquestionably confirms his worst fears, the true *and* the false. Even then his recognition is understated: "now ful wel he wiste, / His lady nas no lenger on to triste" (1665-66).

The irony Chaucer introduces by contrasting Criseyde's actual behavior with Troilus's dream of it is the bitterest of his hero's tragic career. Troilus dies believing his idealized lady has revealed her utter unworthiness. Only later in literary history would the "fals" Criseyde of his dream—the unreal traitress—become the *real* Criseyde: the sensual, callous, sluttish Cressid, the cynical, self-indulgent Cressida, of the Elizabethan lyrics and of Shakespeare's play.[30] The grief Troilus carries to his pyre is the more pathetic for being, in part at least, unwarranted.

This interest in an ironic psychological theme, sustained throughout most of Book V, is present in *Troilus* but not in the corresponding part of *Il Filostrato*. As he rewrote this part of Boccaccio's poem, Chaucer supplemented, deleted, and changed his source in order to depict one of his hero's psychological mechanisms. What is true of this part is probably true of the whole poem. We cannot in any case understand Chaucer's purpose as he wrote unless we understand how the *Troilus* differs from *Il Filostrato*. The two poems have been endlessly compared and the comparison may be a tedious aspect of Chaucer criticism, but it does what "readings" and background studies do not do: it reveals Chaucer's touch, the intimate details of his reworking, like fingerprints left by his manipulations. It reveals what we are rarely privileged to know about poems: the artist's intention. We find intention in what is unique in Chaucer's poem. Despite recent critical preoccupations, the unique is not the display of rhetorical virtuosity, not the illustration of moral dogma, but the realistic development of character giving rise to psychological irony. The best "novelistic" criticism from earlier in this century (such as that of Kittredge and Lewis) recognized the importance of rhetoric, doctrine, and allegory, though it knew less about them than we do now; but even the worst of it (such as that of Cook and Van Doren) was right to admire the realism added—even invented—by Chaucer.

Where did he learn this psychological realism? Certainly he had behind him the tradition of faculty psychology, which from Aristotle to Aquinas and beyond had gauged the moral value of human acts by anatomizing the soul into a hierarchy of separate but interdependent functions and describing the effects upon them of every desire, hatred, and aspiration that had entered into the heart of man. Certainly he had behind him the whole range of romancers, sonnetteers, and satirists, from Dante to Jean de Meun, who had exalted or degraded human sexuality according to their taste. What he had that they did not was the instinct to perceive how people's minds work—in the case of Criseyde to perceive that weakness meets treachery at a hairline juncture, in the case of Troilus to perceive that anxiety is most destructive when it is least articulated.

[1] I-II, 44, 4, resp.; tr. the Fathers of the English Dominican Province (New York: Benziger Bros., 1947), I, 775.

[2] St. Thomas defined "anxiety" (*agonia*) as fear of unforseeable future misfortunes and ranked it with the four other "species" of fear: laziness (fear of work), shame-facedness (fear of disgrace), amazement (fear of unpredictably great evil), and stupor (fear of the unwonted) (*ibid.*, I-II, 41, 4, resp. [p. 766]). Despite its ancient occurrence in Latin (cf. reference to Prudentius), the word "anxiety" did not enter English until 1525, when St. Thomas More used it in *Of the Four Last Things* (OED). The MED lists "anxiety" as the first definition for ME "angwisshe," whose other meanings are (1b) "loving-longing," (2) physical torment, (3) "the pangs of childbirth," (4) "distressing circumstances, hardship," and (5) "ill will, hostility." Thus, ME associated love with the painful contemplation of the uncertain future, but it did not allot this mental pain a word to itself. I describe Troilus's condition as "anxiety" ("uneasiness or trouble of mind about some uncertain event"—OED) because the notion if not the word itself is what the love poets, and Chaucer in particular, had in mind as they portrayed the lover's "angwisshe."

[3] Boccaccio was interested in these deeds—Troilo's re-reading of his old letters, his visit to Criseida's empty house, his wanderings about the city (he did not specifically mention the temple as does Chaucer in V, 566)—primarily as symbols of desolation. He did not probe the mental state behind them because he wanted to portray Troilo as a martyr-like victim of the fickleness to which Criseida, like all women, was by nature subject. Troilo might be compared to Chaucer's Constance as the subject of a "tragedy of victimization": cf. Morton W. Bloomfield, "The Man of Law's Tale: a Tragedy of Victimization and a Christian Comedy," *PMLA*, 87 (1972), 384-90; previously published in Italian as "*Il Racconto dell' uomo di legge:* la tragedia di una vittima e la commedia cristiana," *Strumenti Critici*, 9 (1969), 195-207.

[4] *Troilus and Criseyde* V, 197-1666; *Il Filostrato* V, 15—VIII, 10. Editions quoted throughout are Robert K. Root, ed., *The Book of Troilus and Criseyde by Geoffrey Chaucer* (1926; rpt. Princeton, N. J.: Princeton Univ. Press, 1954); and Nathaniel E. Griffin and Arthur B. Myrick, eds., *The Filostrato of Giovanni Boccaccio* (1929; rpt. New York: Biblo and Tannen, 1967). Numerical references are to lines in *Troilus*, stanzas in *Il Filostrato*. In the notes I give the Griffin-Myrick translation of *Il Filostrato*.

[5] Donald R. Howard analyses the love affair's psychological development through Books I-III in *The Three Temptations: Medieval Man in Search of the World* (Princeton, N. J.: Princeton Univ. Press, 1966), pp. 109-35: "There *is* psychological realism in the poem, added by Chaucer to the material of the *Filostrato*" (p. 134; the whole page is relevant). But Howard does not treat of this realism in the area I am concerned with here.

[6] "The intensity of his grief can only be explained by the fact that in his heart he is desperately afraid that Criseyde will not return, but he cannot admit this to himself and so rejects the inferences of her delay and Cassandra's interpretation of his dream. . . . Chaucer . . . has arranged, modified, and sharpened [detail invented by Baccacio] to create a convincing and deeply moving psychological study of the painful and relentless disintegration of hope" (Alfred David, "The Hero of the *Troilus*," *Speculum*, 37 [1962], 579).

[7] St. Thomas, I-II, 43, 1, resp; p. 771.

[8] I-II, 44, 1, resp.; p. 773.

[9] I-II, 44, 3, resp.; p. 774.

[10] I-II, 44, 4, resp.; p. 775.

[11] Ida L. Gordon suggests Chaucer's concern in this part of the poem: "in the description of Troilus' reactions to Criseyde's departure from Troy, which leads up to [his apostrophe to her empty house], the reader's sympathy for Troilus has been steadily built up by implicit appeals to the fellow-feeling that anyone must have who has ever waited, alternating between hope and doubt, for something or someone desperately longed for" (*The Double Sorrow of Troilus: A Study of Ambiguities in "Troilus and Criseyde"* [Oxford: Clarendon Press, 1970], p. 132). She takes her cue from C. S. Lewis: "All men have waited with ever-decreasing hope, day after day, for some one or for something that does not come, and all would willingly forget the experience. Chaucer spares us no detail of the prolonged and sickening process to despair. . . . The thing is so painful that perhaps no one without reluctance reads it twice. In our cowardice we are tempted to call it sentimental" (*The Allegory of Love: A Study in Medieval Tradition* [1936; rpt. New York: Oxford Univ. Press (Galaxy Books), 1958], p. 195).

[12] *Fil.* V, 24, 25:

Io non la credo riveder giammai.

. . . . .

Di' che fa' tu? or étti punto nella
Mente di me, o messo m' hai in oblio
Per lo tuo padre vecchio ch' ora t' have?

"I do not believe that I shall ever again cast mine eyes upon her. . . . Say, what doest thou? Hast thou now any thought of me in thy mind or hast thou forgotten me for thine aged father, who hath thee now?"

[13] *Fil.* V, 48, 49: "O God, shall I find my love returned?"

Ma Pandar seco diceva altrimente,
Come colui che conosceva intera
L'intenzion di Calcas pienamente:
Questa tua voglia sì focosa e fiera
Si potrà raffreddar, s' el non me mente

Ciò ch'io udii infin quand' ella c'era;
Ed il decimo giorna, e'l mese e l'anno
Pria la rivegghi, credo passeranno.

But Pandarus, as one who fully knew the whole intent of Calchas, spake otherwise with him. "This wish of thine, so fierce and fiery, may be cooled, if I be not deceived by what I heard even when she was here. I believe that the tenth day and the month and the year will pass before thou dost see her again."

[14] "Restore it [my soul] to its first pleasure; constrain Cressida as thou dost me, so that she may return to put an end to my woes."

[15] Robertson would no doubt interpret this prayer, like the religious imagery in Book III, as unwitting blasphemy: "the religious imagery serves to show the corruption of the higher reason in Troilus as it submits completely to the wiles of the lower reason in pursuit of sensual satisfaction" (*A Preface to Chaucer: Studies in Medieval Perspectives* [Princeton, N. J.: Princeton Univ. Press, 1962], p. 487). Howard's comment on Chaucer's use of the suggestion-delectation-consent pattern can apply as well to the other "psycho-religious" language in the poem, including this prayer: "The psychological language of Christian morality is used . . . not *primarily* to depict Troilus and Criseyde as sinners (though the implication may be found); it is used because it was the only psychological explanation which the Middle Ages had for demonstrating a moral act" (p. 122). Here, the anxious Troilus uses his knowledge of theology as a bargaining point with God: he will live and die a believer if Cupid (described as though he were the Judaeo-Christian God) will manifest his wrath-turned-to-mercy by returning Criseyde (V, 593-95).

[16] *Fil.* V, 59:

> Deh vedrott' io
> Giammai tornar colli tu' atti adorni,
> A rallegrarmi sì com' hai promesso?
> Deh fia omai, deh or foss' egli adesso!

"Ah, shall I ever see thee return to delight me with thy comely ways, even as thou hast promised? Ah, will it ever be? Ah, would it were even now!"

[17] Cf. Howard's comment on her falling in love with Troilus: "Circumstance plays a greater role [than in Criseida's case] in her final acquiescence" (p. 127). And Lewis: "The situation, in itself, is half the battle for Diomede; but Diomede, in any situation, would have been a dangerous wooer to Criseyde" (p. 188). Dangerous, perhaps; successful, no—for the reason Lewis himself gives: since Troilus fulfills her craving for protection, "it is not to be believed that she would ever have been faithless to Troilus, ever less than a perfect lover to him, as long as he was present" (p. 187).

[18] The very movement of the stars is ironic: cf. Gordon, pp. 111-12, on ll. 1016-29. She misses one small facet of the irony. Troilus has already (I, 1074) been described as a lion. But now "Cynthea hire charhors overraughte / To whiele out of the Leoun, if she myghte" (V, 1018-19). The fickle moon goddess driving her horse (conventionally a symbol of sexual passion) out of the constellation Leo is the astral prototype of Criseyde deserting her lover. The reference to Cynthia's eagerness casts suspicion on her earthly counterpart's feelings; at the same time, the mere fact that Cynthia is doing what she is doing suggests that she may be influencing Criseyde's decisions and thus mitigating the latter's responsibility for them.

[19] Critics clash on this point. Mrs. Gordon denies the contrast I suggest: she thinks that "amorousness . . . determines her response to both [Troilus and Diomede]" and that "there is no radical alteration of her character [from Boccaccio's Criseida]" (p. 110). Howard recognizes the contrast in the first part of the two poems: "Boccaccio's Criseida is much closer to the medieval anti-feminist picture of womanhood: she is passion's slave, where Chaucer's heroine is a rational creature" (p. 122). But he too believes that in the betrayal scene Criseyde "becomes the fickle and treacherous woman of the antifeminist tracts" (p. 150). Lewis hits what I think is the right note: Criseyde is "a tragic figure in the strictest Aristotelian sense, for she is neither very good nor execrably wicked. . . . But there is a flaw in her"—the fear that Lewis describes as her "ruling passion" (pp. 184, 187, 189). The best discussion of V, 1016-99 is E. T. Donaldson, "Criseide and Her Narrator," in *Speaking of Chaucer* (New York: Norton, 1970), pp. 79-82.

[20] In neither poem is this dream a clinical nightmare, though, as will be seen, it has features of Macrobius's *insomnium* ("nightmare") or lying dream. Ernest Jones lists the "three cardinal features" of nightmares as "(1) agonizing dread; (2) sense of oppression or weight at the chest which alarmingly interferes with respiration; (3) conviction of helpless paralysis" (*On the Nightmare* [1931; rpt. New York: Grove Press (Evergreen Ed.), 1959], p. 20). The second and third features never appear in either dream, and the first appears only after Troilo and Troilus wake up. See Helen Storm Corsa, "Dreams in *Troilus and Criseyde*," *American Imago*, 27 (1970), 52-65, for the argument that Chaucer's treatment of the dreams adds "unmistakable oedipal vibrations" to the poem in order that the love story might "dramatize metaphorically one of man's most inevitable experiences, that of primal loss" (63). On the same page Corsa quotes Jones to support her contention that the boar dream *is* a nightmare; but this contention depends primarily on the correctness of her "oedipal" thesis.

[21] In *Il Filostrato*, the section from dream to brooch takes up 728 lines (VII, 25-VIII, 10); in *Troilus*, it takes up 424 (V, 1242-1666). Here Chaucer for once simplifies and condenses Boccaccio instead of complicating and expanding him. Interested not in spectacular gesture but in psychological irony, he leaves out Troilo's suicide attempt following the dream (*Fil.* VII, 32-36) and conse-

quently those parts of Pandaro's speech denouncing suicide as cowardly. He shortens Troilo's letter to Criseida by half (*Fil.* VII, 51-75; *Troilus* V, 1310-1421). He eliminates Deifebo from this part of the poem and changes Cassandra's role, depriving Troilo of his discourse on that well-worn courtly-love topic, the superiority of virtue to pedigree in measuring *gentilesse* (*Fil.* VII, 89-104).

[22] In a dream he saw the perilous sin of her who made him languish. . . . He seemed to behold a great charging boar.

And then afterward it seemed to him that he saw beneath its feet Cressida, whose heart it tore forth with its snout. And as it seemed, little cared Cressida for so great a hurt, but almost did she take pleasure in what the beast was doing.

[23] Describing the wait directly before the dream, Chaucer has continued to tone down Troilo's and the narrator's verbally expressed suspicions of her. When Troilo and Pandaro returned to the city walls on the eleventh day, Boccaccio's narrator bluntly said, "ad altro già ell' avea dritto il pensiero" ("to another had she directed her thought," *Fil.* VII, 14). Chaucer is more vague: "al for naught; his hope alwey him blente" (V, 1194-95). When the eleventh day passed without her return, Troilo "forte comincio a rammaricarsi / E di [Criseida] e d'amor" ("began to complain more bitterly 'gainst her and Love," *Fil.* VII, 15). In contrast, Troilus simply does not know what to think—or if he does, he cannot say so: "He nyste what he juggen of it myghte, / Syn she hath broken that she hym bihighte" (V, 1202-04).

[24] William H. Stahl, tr., *Macrobius' Commentary on the Dream of Scipio* (New York: Columbia Univ. Press, 1952), p. 90.

[25] *Ibid.,* pp. 88-89.

[26] Cf. Corsa, p. 61.

[27] Chaucer has heightened the test's suspense and hence its irony. In Boccaccio, when she did *not* reply (VII, 76) to Troilo's accusation of "novello amore" (58), her meaning was clear. Not until much later when she did write (106) had Troilo any reason for new hope. In the interim he may have been miserable, but at least he *knew* he was spurned.

[28] In *Il Filostrato*, Deifebo visited Troilo, overheard him mourning for Criseida, and got his brothers to send their ladies to comfort him. Among them, Cassandra had in turn overheard Deifebo say that Troilo loved Criseida. She reproached Troilo for wasting his affection on "la figlia d'un prete scellerato, / E mal vissuto e di piccolo affare" (VII, 87: "the daughter of a wicked priest, a man of evil life and of small importance"). Troilo denied her charge, rebuked her, and defended Criseida in his long courtly discourse (89-104).

[29] In *Fil.* VIII, 3, Troilo sent Pandaro to reproach her.

[30] After writing this sentence, I discovered Gretchen Mieszkowski's superb monograph, "The Reputation of Criseyde: 1155-1500," *Transactions of the Connecticut Academy of Arts and Sciences,* 43 (Hamden, Conn.: Archon, 1971), 71-153. Analysing Criseyde's character as developed by her portraitists before Chaucer, Mieszkowski argues convincingly that "even in Chaucer's time, Criseyde was [already] a figure to laugh at or moralize over, a traditional example of a woman who changes lovers too easily, a type of the fickle woman" (pp. 73-74). Mieszkowski shows that Chaucer's picture of Criseyde in *Troilus* did not subsequently deflect the tradition (pp. 105-40). I believe she definitively banishes the notion that Criseyde was not thought of as a slut until the fifteenth or sixteenth century. Therefore, my sentence—founded on Rollins's and Tatlock's errors—is wrong. However, I also believe that the prior existence of a tradition need not of itself force a poet to accept its limits; that, humanist and prober of the female psyche that he was, Chaucer felt impelled to humanize the stereotype. The *Troilus* is in part a book *about* Criseyde's reputation, exploring both its justifications and its inhumaneness. Mieszkowski (like her mentor Donaldson) skillfully discusses the narrator's constantly-collapsing efforts to defend his heroine. For all that, the depth of understanding in Chaucer's portrait of Criseyde forbids us to snicker or moralize over her. If Chaucer's immediate audience and poetic successors thought he wanted them to do so, then they misread his text. It would not be the first time a work was misread in its own day—and certainly not the last.

P. Rama Moorthy

SOURCE: "Fear in Macbeth," in *Essays in Criticism,* Vol. XXII, No. 2, April, 1973, pp. 154-66.

[*In the following essay, Moorthy identifies fear as the thematic core of* Macbeth, *pervading the atmosphere and guiding the actions of Macbeth and Lady Macbeth.*]

The ambiguity of Macbeth's character is likely to be perpetuated as long as we identify the imaginative truth of the play with its moral faith. The play is, in an important way, more than its preoccupation with good and evil; its imaginative complex extends beyond its moral intention. There has been a certain romanticising of evil in *Macbeth* criticism. In calling the play 'a statement of evil'[1]—'*Macbeth* defines a particular kind of evil—the evil that results from a lust for power'[2]—L. C. Knights has made it morally central and, in doing so, abridged the work's imaginative scope and freedom. This approach has led to the diminution of both the play and its protagonist apparent in statements like—'We may indeed call *Macbeth* the greatest of morality plays';[3] '(Macbeth) though a tragic hero, (is) yet a criminal';[4] and 'to all intents (Macbeth is) a contracting character'.[5] Such a magnification of its moral structure results in a dwarfing of the spiritual, non-moral content of the tragedy, and diminishes the imaginative complexity of Macbeth's character. What has been lost is a certain vital mystery that relates Macbeth, amorally, to the bear (to which Macbeth compares himself) that 'must fight the course'.

The play, before it is about evil, is about something anterior to evil, something of which evil is a reductive part—an elemental ground that creates the kind of world that Macbeth inhabits and also is a product of. It is a world *in extremis* and of elemental turmoil, of thunders and lightning, and of the utterness of blood, blackness and death. It is a world that has jumped its nature and norms—a world of aberrations (like the witches), of unnatural happenings (like the horses eating each other), and of inversions (like unsexing, unmanning). It is a world of doubleness of character, incident and action; of the doubleness of language—of equivocation, ambiguity and antithesis. In it there is a confusion of values, a mixing of opposites—fair and foul. It generates dreams and nightmares, vision and voices and in it 'nothing is but what is not'. It is on the verge of life and death, and crisis is its norm.

The tension that holds Macbeth and his world is the tension of fear. Fear is the medium and also the material of the play. Lady Macduff, in her anguished utterance, states the theme: 'All is the fear, nothing is the love'. Fear, like the elemental happenings, strikes both the innocent mother and the child. Fear has its own diabolic operations and it creates what it apprehends. The gruesome murder of Lady Macduff and her child come as the apalling fulfilment of her own fears: 'When our actions do not, our fears do make us traitors.' Fear wills its own sinister creation, supplanting the natural one.

What Macbeth is combatting beneath the haze of ambition and moral scruple, is fear—or death that fear symbolises. The thought of murdering Duncan throws up an image of fear that threatens Macbeth's vital being. He is himself a bewildered witness of fear

> Whose horrid image doth unfix my hair,
> And make my seated heart knock at my ribs,
> Against the use of nature.
> (I. ii. 135-7)

The horror is so dire that Macbeth fears a division in his 'single state of man'. Nevertheless he dares it, and in spite of his vision and voices, holds himself together, while his wife, deeply affected by the horror of the deed, breaks down, suffers a division, and dies. It is the peculiar fate of Macbeth that he is condemned to begin, to dwell, and to endure where Mr. Kurtz (*Heart of Darkness*) ended crying—'The horror, the horror!'. It is Macbeth, therefore, that speaks, most obsessively, the word fear and its synonyms (there are about fifty of them in the text)—two out of every three invocations of fear being Macbeth's, and the third one, almost always, Lady Macbeth's. Haunted by fear, they both go through the travail of life like the condemned. Lady Macbeth suc-

cumbs to fear before long; but Macbeth rides it until the death of a soldier puts an end to his tragic career.

Macbeth's first reflex at the suggestion of the crown by the witches is, significantly, a startle—a fright: 'Good Sir,' asks Banquo in surprise, 'why do you start and seem to fear Things that do sound so fair?'. It is important to examine whether in his first soliloquy the suggestion of the crime comes to him as sin, a disgusting act of moral depravity, a fall, or as sheer horror which the image of retribution, a daring of the forbidden, engenders. Is it horror as revulsion, as in Oedipus, or horror as fear, as in Mr. Kurtz, or both? Here is a confession of Macbeth's nature by himself when he hears the cry of women:

> I have almost forgot the taste of fears.
> The time has been, my senses would have cool'd
> To hear a night-shriek; and my fell of hair
> Would at a dismal treatise rouse, and stir,
> As life were in't
> (V. v. 9-13)

No moral question is involved in this. Yet 'a night-shriek' or 'a dismal treatise' disturbs Macbeth as deeply as does the thought of murdering Duncan. The reaction in both the cases is identical.

Examining Macbeth's susceptibility to fear in the passage above, A. C. Bradley observes that Macbeth's fear is 'a native disposition',[6] and 'that it belongs to a time before his conscience was 'burdened'.[7] The word 'native' in the phrase appropriately identifies the origin and depth of Macbeth's fear, but we have to consider whether the 'horrid image' of murdering Duncan carries in it an element of 'conscience burdened'.

'Most readers have felt', affirms L. C. Knights, 'that after the initial crime there is something compulsive in Macbeth's crimes'. But the germ of the compulsiveness is already there in him and his 'initial crime' is itself the result of the compulsiveness we discern in Macbeth's killings in the battlefield. Macbeth who

> Unseam'd him from the nave to the chops,
> And fix'd his head upon our battlements
> (I. ii. 23-4)

and who 'didst make Strange images of death' betrays, in the relished violence, excess and picturesqueness of his killings, a compulsiveness of which the 'initial crime' is a further dramatisation. 'Strange' is a keyword here, suggesting elements of both the unnatural ('I have seen Hours dreadful and things strange'—II. iv. 3) and the obsessional ('strangely-visited people, All swoln and ulcerous'—IV. iii. 150). This is a streak peculiar to Macbeth's mind and Macbeth's confessions of his mental state further reinforces it: 'My strange and self-abuse Is the initiate fear, that wants hard use' (III. iv. 141-2)—mark the word 'initiate'. Are not both Macbeth and his wife speaking the truth when Lady Macbeth says in the Banquet scene—'My Lord is often thus, And hath been from his youth'? Macbeth confirms it by saying 'I have a strange infirmity which is nothing To those who know me'.

Fear has been the most trying, deeply unsettling ordeal that Macbeth is fated to go through. Rather than dare it, he would avoid it, seek excuses to be exempted from it. Perplexed and helpless he hopes, almost childishly, that somehow 'Chance', 'Time and the hour' will resolve the problem for him: 'If Chance will have me King, why, Chance may crown me without my stir'. He seeks, in desperation, the support and help of Banquo by frequently reminding him of his share in the prophecy: 'Do you not hope your children shall be kings . . . ?', 'Think upon what hath chanc'd', 'It shall make honour for you'. In writing the letter to his wife about the prophecy he betrays his need for strength and encouragement from his 'dearest partner of greatness'.

The 'horrid image' of murdering Duncan symbolises for Macbeth a terrible daring fraught with fatal consequences. He is himself taken aback by the image that suddenly springs into his consciousness. He asks incredulously, 'why do I yield to that suggestion', as if it is an involuntary happening of which he has no control. Macbeth's responses here are clearly the reflexes of a terrified man. The issue is, crucially, of life and death, whatever else it may be later to his rational thinking.

It is in the soliloquy 'If it were done . . .' that the state of Macbeth's mind and the truth of his motivations are clearly revealed. The beginning of the passage is conditional, the mood subjunctive, and the tone is defensive and argumentative, and even veiledly apologetic—there are two 'if's and five 'but's in the passage. The whole passage of 28 lines, except for the last two and half lines, is lopsidedly devoted to the issue of why the deed should *not* be done, which suggests that Macbeth is already emotionally decided on the issue and that he is seeking intellectual and moral support for his disinclination. First, it is the practical aspect of the issue that occupies his mind and then, to reinforce it, comes the moral question which, turning to religion, rouses the horror image of outraged pity. The moral question, in its order of occurrence, and position in the passage, suggests its auxiliary nature, its importance as a reinforcement of the claims of practicality and prudence—for there is no feeling on Macbeth's part, either before or after the deed, of a kinsman, host, or subject towards Duncan, and there is no revulsion towards himself either of having violated those bonds. It is, for Macbeth, only the 'deed'—'I have done the deed', a doing or a daring for the 'soldier', for the 'man'. But what acts as an *effective* deterrent or support for his unwillingness is the image of horror in the guise of pity:

> And Pity, like a naked new-born babe,
> Striding the blast, or heaven's Cherubins, hors'd
> Upon the sightless couriers of the air,
> Shall blow the horrid deed in every eye
> That tears shall drown the wind
> (l. vii. 21-5)

But how subsidiary the question of morality or even consequence is to Macbeth is brought home to us in the image of the 'intent' as horse ('I have no spur To prick the sides of my intent'). This 'horse' has to oppose the 'horse' of the new-born babe ('Striding') and the heaven's Cherubins ('hors'd') who 'shall blow the horrid deed in every eye, That tears shall drown the wind'—the power suggested in those words symbolising the power of the 'horse' to be opposed. And in relation to the 'horse', Macbeth's ambition is a 'rider' ('Vaulting ambition'), and is on par with 'spur'. There is regret in the words—'I have no spur', 'but only'—and Macbeth is, deep down, deploring his helpless condition. But the 'horse' of the intent is there in its vitality (mark, also, the tension the word *intent* suggests), and it is Lady Macbeth that provides the 'spur'.

It is the 'male' and the 'man' in Macbeth, that his wife prods and rouses to action. But to rouse the 'elemental' male in Macbeth, she has to be herself the elemental female, a possessed Agave tearing her child to pieces, in the frenzied passage:

> I would, while it was smiling in my face,
> Have pluck'd my nipple from his boneless gums,
> And dash'd the brains out
> (I. vii. 56-8)

Lady Macbeth's words have the desired effect on Macbeth. Macbeth's words witness the response of the 'male', the 'man' in Macbeth:

> Bring forth men-children only!
> For thy undaunted mettle should compose
> Nothing but males
> (I. vii. 73-5)

Macbeth has to be his elemental biological self, the male, to deal with the elemental fear. And, what is more, Lady Macbeth also seeks to be 'Unsex'-ed, to be the 'male' or 'man'. They both repeat the word 'man' so frequently and obsessively that the word itself becomes a kind of chant to charge them into that state.

For Macbeth, being a soldier is not a mere profession. It is bound up with the fact of his fear—'native disposition'—and his consequent obsession with being 'man'. His soldiership is his self-expression and his style of dealing with fear. How else would Macbeth, except as a soldier, dramatise his fears in making 'Strange images of death' and thus reassure himself of his bravery? Lady Macbeth knows that her words go home and draw the proper response from Macbeth when she says in the sleep-walking scene: 'Fie, my Lord, fie, a soldier, and afeard?'. So intimate is the role of a soldier for Macbeth that it is almost indistinguishable from his character. Macbeth is more soldier than Lear is king. Towards the end, when Macbeth feels that there is no possibility of hope for him and the thought of suicide occurs to him, he asks:

> Why should I play the Roman fool, and die
> On mine sword? Whiles I see lives, the gashes

        Do better upon them
        (V. viii. 1-3)

Macbeth cannot abdicate his role, in life or in death, for to do so is to falsify what is obviously his life-time involvement with fear. It is in the role of a soldier he lives most vividly, and though he knows, on confronting Macduff, that Macduff 'hath cow'd my better part of man', yet he cannot but be a soldier—'before my body I throw my warlike shield'—and there is the final challenging of death by Macbeth in his cry:

        lay on, Macduff;
        And damn'd be him that first cries,
        'Hold, enough!',
        (V. ix, 33-4)

Fear, therefore, is both the destiny and the fate of Macbeth. It whets him where it hurts him. It is through fear—fear which is the tension between life and death—that Macbeth apprehends life as vividly as he does death. Referring to Macbeth's daring of death in the Banquet scene ('approach thou like the rugged Russian bear . . .'), Bradley observed: 'These, when they arise, hold him spell-bound and possess him wholly, like a hypnotic trance which is at the same time the ecstasy of the poet.'[8] Macbeth's horror does have the vividness and vitality of a poet's vision. When he speaks of the 'taste of fears', there is a poet's relish of the emotion. In the passage:

        I have almost forgot the taste of fears
        The time has been, my senses would have cool'd
        To hear a night-shriek . . .
        (V. v. 9-11)

there is regret that he has 'almost forgot the taste of fears', and a nostalgia in the tone.

Macbeth's fear is also his measure of sensitivity, his test of being alive. Macbeth needs fear for his conviction of the reality of life and death. It is the peculiar medium of his acute perceptions. To take away fear from him is to take away his *taste* of both life and death. Twice Macbeth is 'rapt' in the dream of kingship—once when the witches prophesy it ('He seems rapt withal'), and again when Ross announces the new honour ('Look, how our partner's rapt'). Macbeth himself confesses his ecstasy to his wife—'I stood rapt in the wonder of it'. 'Rapt' and 'wonder' are the apt terms that identify the poetic sensibility of Macbeth for whom life in its joy strikes as a vision just as death in its horror affects him as a nightmare. The ecstasy is a lived dream, a dream that holds him in a trance as he experiences it in the exquisite phrase—'the swelling act of the imperial theme', the expansion ('swelling') into the grandeur of supreme power that Rome ('imperial') symbolises. Macbeth who has been pursued by death and is desperately seeking freedom from it, and the power to secure that freedom, realises in that phrase both freedom ('swelling', 'cabin'd, cribb'd, confin'd') and supreme power ('imperial theme')—his beatific vision of life, which the words 'rapt' and 'wonder' precisely identify.

It is in vivid sensuous concretes that the experiences of life—and death—come to Macbeth. The 'wine of life is drawn' from a life without significance; age is 'days fallen into the sere, yellow leaf'; sleep is 'the balm of hurt minds, sore labour's bath', death is sleep 'after life's fitful fever'; murdered Banquo shakes his 'gory locks'; murdered Duncan has his 'silver skin lac'd with the golden blood'. There is also a certain largeness and richness to Macbeth's conception of life. A rich life is 'honour, love, obedience and troops of friends', to drink happily is to 'Be large in mirth' and to ask to 'Give me some wine, fill full', and freedom is to be' broad and general as the casing air'.

And because life is so rich and sensuous, death which is an annihilation of this, strikes Macbeth as horror—horror which is apprehensible to the senses, vivid and dire, to his poetic sensibility. The horror is 'the naked new-born babe, Striding the blast'; fear is 'gory locks'. But the horror or the fear, while it deters him, also draws out the soldier in him. He responds to the challenge with the verve and dash of a soldier—the 'bravura of bravery',[9] to use Robert B. Heilman's phrase. It is the warrior that leaps to the defence of the poet—and Macbeth is, in a profound sense, a 'warrior poet'.

Macbeth is 'king'—in taste ('swelling act of the imperial theme'), valour ('valour's minion') and royal blood ('I am his kinsman'). It is only the law, the law of morality, that stands in his way. It does not seem 'unreasonable' that he should desire to be king. His vital impulsions are such that it seems almost inevitable that he should do what he is doing in order to realise them. There is behind his doings a subtle force of a claim, a compulsion which a claim induces, a sense of obligation ('an appalling sense of duty'[10] as Bradley put it), a vital impulsion beneath what is apparently a criminal compulsion. Therefore, the moral issue in the problem does not strike Macbeth as 'true', and when he talks of the moral implications of the deed before murdering, he is not 'really' there: he is 'rationalising' his fear.

To dare the 'terrible feat' Macbeth has to be part of what he is daring; he has to work himself into the state of horror. In the soliloquy before the murder of Duncan ('Is this a dagger . . .') the imagery points to the charged state of Macbeth before he proceeds to murder Duncan. Macbeth sees a vivid vision of a dagger—'thy blade, and dudgeon, gouts of blood' (mark the apostrophising 'thy' which further dramatises the 'reality' of the dagger)— invokes the diabolism of 'Pale Hecate's Off'rings' and the lust of 'Tarquin's ravishing strides', and hopes that no distraction takes 'the present horror from the time which suits it'. And he proceeds, as the bell strikes, in the 'present horror', to do the murder.

A certain incredibility or a kind of possessedness goes with Macbeth's murdering of Duncan. Macbeth had to do what was to him the ultimate in his daring. Both in that *he* did it because he must, and in that, perhaps, *something else* did it through him, Macbeth has to feel 'innocent' about the deed. Naturally, immediately after the murder, he asks, perplexed and anguished: 'But wherefore could not I pronounce "Amen"? I had most need of blessing'. The word 'wherefore' has a greater force than 'why' and acquires further emphasis when followed by 'but', for Macbeth knows that there is no culpable *'there'* to his 'crime' to account for a 'therefore' in it for the denial of 'blessing' to him. (And, further, when Macbeth says 'Glamis hath murther'd Sleep, and therefore Cawdor Shall sleep no more, Macbeth shall sleep no more!', he is pointing to the apparent illogicality of 'Cawdor' and 'Macbeth' being punished for the crime of 'Glamis'—implying thereby that what he did as Glamis has no more culpable bearing on him than if he had done it in a state of possession or trance.) In saying that he had 'most need' of blessing, he not only implies his innocence as to the guards, but emphasises a greater deserving or need of protection against the external evil than them, for he has been haunted by it more than they. There is deep anguish in his persistent dwelling on it in spite of his wife's attempts to dissuade him from it.

It is significant that Macbeth, unlike Othello who, in a similar situation of murder, invites damnation—'whip me ye devils, From the possession of this heavenly sight. Blow me about in winds. Roast me in sulphur'[11]—regards himself as an innocent victim of it and agonises over the fact that the blessings of God are denied to him. Othello sees and recognises his guilt, but Macbeth cannot; his involvement in the deed is of a different dimension. So much so, that after the knocking, seeing his own hands of blood, he asks incredulously, 'What hands are here?' and agonises: 'Ha! They pluck out mine eyes'. Macbeth cannot pluck out his eyes like a sinner who has seen his sin, for unlike Oedipus he is not there in the sin. It is not because he is too close to the crime, and too dazed to recognise his guilt. It is just that the nature of his involvement and responsibility is of a different kind, for long after the crime he could still say, with innocence:

> They have tied me to a stake: I cannot fly,
> But, bear-like, I must fight the course
> (V, vii. 1-2)

Nor is there any statement of remorse on his part, anywhere in the play, as from a sinner or a criminal: there is anguish and agony, but Macbeth does not see them as something that he deserves. He is a victim in a hostile universe and he is fighting, 'bear-like . . . the course'. When he learns, towards the end, that 'Macduff was from his mother's womb Untimely ripp'd' he finds that 'it hath cowed my better part of man' and says 'I'll not fight with thee', but, nevertheless, with the better part of him cowed in him, he still dares to fight him with a challenging cry—'lay on . . . '. Where there is a suggestion of regret, remorse or a sense of guilt, there is a curious process of rationalisation. The Macbeth who says

> Of all men else I have avoided thee:
> But get thee back, my soul is too much charg'd
> With blood of thine already.
> (V. viii. 5-7)

is either 'rationalising' or 'placating' Macduff, as Kenneth Muir and Robert B. Heilman suggest. Quoting Chambers who thinks that it is 'the only touch of remorse in Macbeth'—mark the word *only*—Muir asks: 'Or is he rationalising?'[12] Heilman adds: 'Possibly too, he is unconsciously placating the man.'[13] To authenticate remorse or a sense of guilt on the part of Macbeth it would be necessary to establish Macbeth's recognition of the crime and his moral responsibility in regard to it. The problem is bound up with Macbeth's integrity as 'man' of which his being a soldier is the self-expression. It is his nature—'yet do I fear thy nature'—that determines the kind of involvement he has in his conflict with the world. Macbeth has to fight, he is condemned to fight, and in his fighting he has his peculiar being.

But Macbeth cannot kill himself. To destroy something, the preservation of which has been his life-time obsession, would be to falsify the fight, his relation to the world and, above all, the truth of his being. It has been given to Macbeth to look into the face of Horror and begin his career where Mr. Kurtz's ended: Mr. Kurtz comes to Horror corrupted, and the Horror he looks into spells his death. Macbeth's peculiar privilege is to face it, combat it and thus achieve the vital dignity that fighting confers on the fighter—the bear, that must 'bear-like . . . fight the course'. In comparing himself to the bear Macbeth identifies the vital streak in his character. Macbeth in being 'man', is being vividly himself when he is fighting soldier-like or dying soldier-like on the battlefield. And in this battle, Macbeth's sorrow is still in vital terms. His sorrow in this struggle is not his realisation of the outrage of human morals, but the tragic awareness of his dwindling energy, age and battle fatigue—'I have liv'd long enough: My way of life Is fall'n into the sere, the yellow leaf . . .'; time stretches endlessly for him and there is no end, no respite of death: 'Tomorrow, and to-morrow, and to-morrow, Creeps in this petty pace from day to day . . .' and 'I 'gin to be aweary of the sun / And wish th'estate o'th' world were now undone. . . .'

Macbeth has to be judged in terms of the ethics that govern his own involvement in life. To induct the play's moral prejudice into Macbeth's vital consciousness, and consequently into the imaginative consciousness of the play, is to destroy the autonomy of Macbeth's vital—and the play's imaginative—integrity. The play is bifocal: the moral truth in the play is subjacent to its imaginative one. Illustratively Macbeth is evil; but experientially Macbeth is life-in-death. The 'evil Macbeth' points to himself: the 'vital Macbeth' points to something that issues beyond himself, something that sustains him and what he fights, both the perplexed Ahab and his intangible whale. His anguished cry 'But wherefore could not I pronounce "Amen"' is taken beyond society, to the realm of religion, and his very protest is the establishment of his 'innocence' before God.

NOTES

[1]L. C. Knights, *Explorations,* London, 1958: p. 18.

[2]L. C. Knights, *Some Shakespearean Themes,* London, 1959: p. 120.

[3]Kenneth Muir, *Macbeth,* London, 1964: p. lxxii.

[4]Ibid., p. lix.

[5]Robert B. Heilman in *Shakespeare Survey 19.* (Ed.) Kenneth Muir, Cambridge, 1996: p. 13.

[6]A. C. Bradley, *Shakespearean Tragedy,* London, 1961: p. 296.

[7]Ibid., p. 296.

[8]Ibid., pp. 296-7.

[9]*Shakespeare Survey 19,* p. 19.

[10]A. C. Bradley, op. cit., p. 300.

[11]*Othello:* V. vii. 278-9.

[12]Kenneth Muir (Ed.), *Macbeth,* p. 165.

[13]Robert B. Heilman: *Shakespeare Survey 19,* p. 16.

Virgil Hutton

SOURCE: "Hamlet's Fear of Death," in *The University Review,* Vol. 37, No. 1, Autumn, 1970, pp. 11-19.

[*In the following essay, Hutton calls attention to Hamlet's last soliloquy in a discussion of Hamlet's changing attitude toward death.*]

The soliloquy that Hamlet pours forth in response to seeing Fortinbras and his army has suffered the twilight fate of a poor, unmarried, female relation: kept on because it is "there," but neglected as one of Shakespeare's expendable superfluities. Stage productions not only generally omit the soliloquy, as does the Folio text, but often go beyond the Folio in excising Fortinbras from the play altogether. And the cut, at least of the soliloquy, has seemed justified by the desperately needed saving of time at the expense of little that is new. For the soliloquy appears to be simply a delayed replay of the second soliloquy, where Hamlet berates his inaction, raises the issues of cowardice and honor, and finally whips himself into a resolution of action just as he does after seeing Fortinbras.

One of Granville-Barker's footnotes, however, provides hints for believing that Hamlet's last soliloquy may contain far more significance than it has been granted.[1] Although believing Dover Wilson "goes too far" in concluding that "The Fortinbras scene was patently written in order to give occasion to the soliloquy," Granville-Barker earlier in the footnote raises a query that supports Wilson's contention. After pointing out how Shakespeare

"undisguisedly" clears the stage for the soliloquy by simply having Hamlet tell Rosencrantz to get out of sight, Granville-Barker ponders the implications of this indifferent stagecraft:

> Shakespeare was not interested, it would seem, in nice stagecraft for its own sake. Still, he seldom, in his maturity, takes refuge in such simplicities as this. Its verisimilitude will pass, *just* pass. Is his mind so occupied with the *matter* of the scene, that his sense of the theater is in momentary abeyance?

If Granville-Barker's unanswered question possesses substance, we must certainly be encouraged to reexamine the soliloquy in hopes of discovering the something new in its "matter" that would so engage Shakespeare's mind.

I wish to suggest that the new matter is the soliloquy's presentation of Hamlet's fear of death, which seemingly has escaped or been rejected by the minds of probing critics for perhaps the same reason Hamlet is unable to give it direct expression: unconsciously Hamlet would be loath to admit a fear that smacks of cowardice; and critics may have been similarly reluctant to uncover yet another apparent blemish in their hero. C. S. Lewis, sensing that "death is the subject of *Hamlet,*" toys with the prospect of tracing Hamlet's delay to his fear of death, but then backs off for lack of sufficient evidence:

> If I wanted to make one more addition to the gallery of Hamlet's portraits I should trace his hesitation to the fear of death; not to a physical fear of dying, but a fear of being dead. And I think I should get on quite comfortably. . . . But this is not what I am going to do. Shakespeare has not left in the text clear lines of causation which would enable us to connect Hamlet's hesitations with this source.[2]

But I believe sufficient evidence exists both in the soliloquy itself and in the surrounding context of the play to demonstrate that Shakespeare utilizes the fear of death in order to establish not a lesser but a greater heroism in Hamlet by the end of the play than would otherwise be possible.

Since critics, like hounds following a clever fox, have been thrown off the scent by bits of evidence from early in the play that indicate Hamlet's lack of fear of death, we must consider whether or not this evidence is sufficient to prevent further consideration of the issue. The evidence consists of statements in which Hamlet vents his willingness to die or to commit suicide:[3]

> Or that the Everlasting had not fixed
> His canon 'gainst self-slaughter.
> (I, ii, 131-32)

> Why, what should be the fear?
> I do not set my life at a pin's fee,
> And for my soul, what can it do to that,
> Being a thing immortal as itself?
> (I, iv, 64-67)

You cannot take from me anything that I
  will more
willingly part withal—except my life, except
my life, except my life.
  (II, ii, 211-13)

Against the first quotation, we may note that Hamlet never does commit suicide and that the invocation of suicide stresses his extreme disgust with the ways of the flesh and of the world rather than his intention of actually killing himself. Furthermore, it is safe for him to invoke something that, because of his beliefs, is beyond his reach. The third quotation, which is partially attributable to Hamlet's antic disposition, again emphasizes a disgust with the world that might make him willing to accept death, but his following exclamation, "These tedious old fools!" reveals that his impatient thoughts lie elsewhere.

The second quotation is the most important because it explains Hamlet's fearless attitude toward death early in the play. He is the pure, idealistic young Christian mouthing conventional pieties: since the world and the flesh are evil I would gladly be rid of them in order that my soul, freed from its bondage, could enjoy the delights of immortality. Feeling no spots on his soul, he need fear no harm from death. And if this attitude had persisted, it would indeed be fruitless to pursue his fear of death later in the play, but Hamlet's second and third soliloquies betray decisive changes in his thinking. His early carelessness but mirrors thoughtless youth, which laughs at death because it seems so far away.

In the Hecuba soliloquy, perhaps the main unconscious block to Hamlet's action is that the weight of his revengeful bitterness is still directed toward his mother, against whom, according to the Ghost's command, he must do nothing. But in addition, a further obstacle unexpectedly appears. For the first time we hear Hamlet recognizing and fearing the possibility of his own damnation, a fear that would undoubtedly be sharpened by the Ghost's vivid intimations of purgatorial horrors. No longer bolstered by the secure feeling of automatic purity, he admits the tormenting supposition that the very act he is required to perform may make his soul as sullied and worthy of destruction as his flesh. As yet, however, his fear remains within the Christian framework of future damnation or salvation.

Following after a brief interval of only fifty-five lines, Hamlet's famous third soliloquy reveals that his concern with death, which arose almost as a minor afterthought at the end of the preceding soliloquy, has become a matter of great urgency to a mind so quick to grasp and run down the various complexities and difficulties of a problem once it has arisen to his attention. And already we can notice a further shift in Hamlet's thoughts on death. Although his oft-quoted lines on the inhibiting power of conscience show that his will to action, unlike Claudius's, is at least partially paralyzed by the Christian fear of being damned, his generalized statements on death transform his specific fear of damnation into a vague fear of the unknown. Even those who still persist in interpreting the soliloquy as a meditation on suicide must admit that Hamlet is restrained from action not only by doctrine but also by a fear of death's hidden terrors. He can only speculate on "what dreams may come," and he speaks of death as "The undiscovered country" that may contain ills "we know not of."

How ironically remote now seems Hamlet's earlier defiance of death, "Why, what should be the fear?" But surely we need not view his progression as merely a downward descent toward cowardly inactivity brought on by "thinking too precisely on th' event." Though losing some of his former Christian assurance, Hamlet gains in humanity and universality. The pure young prig has been forced, through a recognition of his own vulnerability, to grapple not only with the specific Christian fear of damnation but also with the universal fear of death itself.

At last we are ready to approach Hamlet's Fortinbras soliliquy, wherein resides much of the "mystery" in Hamlet because for the first time he berates his inactivity without being able to produce any reason for it. In the second soliloquy he specifically cites his fear of being damned by a deceptive devil; in the third soliloquy he specifically names "conscience"; but here, although his hesitation remains, he can offer nothing to explain it. Nor is the answer readily evident to us, since all of the previous obstacles have seemingly been cleared away: Hamlet has had it out with his mother, and, through his mousetrap, he has justified the Ghost's call for vengeance. In Hamlet's final soliloquy, then, resides a mocking sphinx whose riddle must be solved.

Since the specific explanations for Hamlet's inaction appear toward the end of his second and third soliloquies, it is likely that the same pattern will recur in his final soliloquy; only this time, because Hamlet has run out of respectable excuses, the explanation must be expressed indirectly. As we examine the last half of the soliloquy, we begin to perceive that what most impresses Hamlet is the easy carelessness toward death displayed by Fortinbras and his soldiers as they march to battle. Fortinbras is admired because his spirit

> Makes mouths at the invisible event,
> Exposing what is mortal and unsure
> To all that fortune, death, and danger dare,
> Even for an egg-shell.

Hamlet realizes that on grounds of honor he has enormously greater cause for acting than Fortinbras has (just as before, Hamlet had realized that his motives for passion were much stronger than the player's) and feels shamed by the contrast between the other person's action and his own inaction. But now the lines disclose a second, implied comparison that explains the source of Hamlet's present inaction and shame:

> And let all sleep, while to my shame I see
> The imminent death of twenty thousand
>   men

> That for a fantasy and trick of fame
> Go to their graves like beds. . . .

Since Hamlet "sees" these things only through the eyes of his imagination, his words unconsciously expose the thought that these men, unlike himself, can act because they are not inhibited by a fear of death—they can "Go to their graves like beds." And Hamlet feels doubly shamed because this braving of death seems demonstrated not only in the heroic Fortinbras but even in the common soldiers. Thus, through the insistent pattern of death imagery, Shakespeare expresses, as plainly as psychological verisimilitude admits, Hamlet's basic fear of death stripped of its former clothes of conscience and fear of damnation.

That Hamlet assumes his own death will accompany the fulfillment of his task may be deduced from his second and third soliloquies; but, significantly, this assumption reappears in the lines immediately preceding the passages we have been examining:

>   —I do not know
> Why yet I live to say "This thing's to do,"
> Sith I have cause, and will, and strength,
>   and means,
> To do't.

Incidentally, we may note how these lines eliminate a whole series of conventional explanations for Hamlet's delay in order to clear the way for the revelation to follow. But the curious wording of the second line is our main concern here. Though at first the line merely seems to stress the fact of Hamlet's delay, a further implication arises from the phrase "Why yet I live." Suddenly we realize that Hamlet is linking his continued existence to his unfulfillment of the revenge—if this thing were done, Hamlet would not still be alive. The soliloquy's closing bloody resolution announces Hamlet's determination to imitate Fortinbras and his men—to make "mouths at the invisible event."

Having grasped the significance of Hamlet's final soliloquy, we can discover fresh meanings in the graveyard scene, for which commentators have been hard pressed to supply an adequate *raison d'être*. Certainly it provides comic relief, further delineates Hamlet's meditative bent, and may symbolize the corrupt state of Denmark. But none of these functions accounts for the length of the scene: such extended symbolism simply becomes belabored, Macbeth's porter provides brilliant comic relief in less than 50 lines, and we surely do not require 200 lines to inform us anew that Hamlet is prone to meditation.

G. Wilson Knight, in his perverse way, insists on the overriding importance of the death motif in *Hamlet;* but by positing Hamlet himself as death's symbol, Knight misjudges Hamlet's relation to death. Granville-Barker finds in Hamlet's graveside meditations evidence of a detached, despairing, intellectual nihilism that turns "away to wistful sentiment and idle fancy" in a momentary effort to forget the duty he still has to perform.[4]

Contrary to these and other representative views of Hamlet's progression as a downward one into the coils of evil and toward intellectual and spiritual defeat, I propose that the graveyard scene dramatizes his philosophical and emotional reconciliation with death, though not until later do we learn the result of his extended meditations over the skulls casually cast up by the gravedigger. Here Hamlet confronts death fully and squarely in all of its ugly, smelly details. Far from indulging in idle speculations as a form of escape from his burdensome task, Hamlet is battling to overcome the last major block to the performance of his revenge. Like the traditional Christian or Stoic moralist, he is coming to terms with death through an imaginative reexperiencing of the vanity of life's ephemeral glories and triumphs: death annihilates both class distinctions and all the great achievements one might have boasted of while alive—Alexander's bones would give off the same stench as the Jester's bones; the lawyer no longer has his "quiddities," the lady her beauty, nor the conqueror his gains.

At this point we should mark Hamlet's crucial shift from a concern with what death might bring—fear of damnation, fear of the unknown, fear of the physical reality of death—to a concern with what death must take away. Having mastered his previous fears, Hamlet faces the final temptation, the final obstacle that may underlie all our fears of death: our over fondness for our worldly existence. Two questions arise: first, where does Shakespeare represent Hamlet mastering his fears of what death might bring; and second, how can the contention that in the graveyard Hamlet is quelling his love of the world be reconciled with his previous expressions of disgust with the world:

> How weary, stale, flat, and unprofitable
> Seem to me all the uses of this world!
> (I, ii, 133-34)

Taking up the first question, we must remember that although Hamlet does not appear on stage between his last soliloquy and the graveyard scene, we are informed of his offstage activities through two letters, one to Horatio and one to Claudius. Both letters reveal Hamlet deliberately acting, for the first time since his encounter with the Ghost, without overmuch regard for the consequences. In the letter to Horatio, we see Hamlet so far in the forefront during the battle with the pirates that he was the only one to board the enemy ship. But of equal significance is an image which flows so naturally from Hamlet's pen that we hardly notice it: "Let the King have the letters I have sent, and repair thou to me with as much haste as thou wouldest fly death." (IV, vi, 20-21)

Through his own trials, Hamlet has been brought to feel the fear of death, and, characteristically generalizing on the basis of his particular experience, automatically attributes this fear to all, including the even-tempered Horatio, who is not "passion's slave." But if this fear is universal, true bravery consists not in a lack of fear but in being able to act in spite of it, which Hamlet is attempting to do. And his cryptic, mockingly obsequious note to Claudius is an audaciously provoking challenge to the shocked King, who receives it just as he is about to tell Laertes of Hamlet's death. Further evidence of Hamlet's efforts to fulfill the bloody resolution at the end of his last soliloquy appears in his proud recital of how efficiently he thwarted Claudius's treachery and dispatched Rosencrantz and Guildenstern to their deaths. It is, then, through his offstage adventures that Hamlet proves to himself that he too can be a Fortinbras.

As for the second question concerning Hamlet's stated disgust with the world, it is apparent that the stronger his avowals of disgust the stronger was his love for the "uses of this world," just as his violent reaction against his mother only proves his love for her. Ophelia's memory portrays Hamlet as embodying the Renaissance ideal of being well practiced in all the worldly arts:

> The courtier's, soldier's scholar's eye, tongue,
>   sword,
> Th' expectancy and rose of the fair state,
> The glass of fashion and the mould of form. . . .
>   (III, i, 147-49)

And Hamlet's use of tongue and rapier in Act V proves that Ophelia's description is not simply love's flattery. Hamlet's initial quarrel with the world is a temporary one induced by the unexpected frailty of his mother; and as his rage against his mother cools, so must his rage against the world. Furthermore, the graveyard scene comes precisely when Hamlet, fresh from his foiling of Claudius's plot and his brave encounter with the pirates, is enjoying a new sense of power and self-confidence.

We reach the end of our particular thread of Hamlet with his speeches to Horatio immediately before the King and his retinue enter to witness the proposed duel. Hamlet feels a foreboding fear but will not yield to it: "It is but foolery, but it is such a kind of gain-giving as would perhaps trouble a woman." (V, ii, 195-96)

The importance of Hamlet's speeches at this point lies in their mood of calm but firm determination. Hamlet has conquered himself. He can acknowledge his fear because he is now able to master it, and he can provide the philosophical basis for this mastery: "We defy augury. There is special providence in the fall of a sparrow. If it be now, 'tis not to come; if it be not to come, it will be now; if it be not now, yet it will come. The readiness is all."

Through the image of the sparrow's fall, Hamlet not only combines stoic fatalism with Christian providence but also conveys a profound sense of humility in relation to the overwhelming force that guides all things to their conclusion. Since a sparrow can scarcely be imagined as preparing itself for a fall, the "readiness" must chiefly consist in providence's ordering of things until all is ready for the fall. But Hamlet's own feeling of readiness is what enables him to propound this philosophy, and his own readiness derives from his reconciliation with the prospect of death that he exposes in his next sentence.

The Folio reads, "since no man ha's ought of what he leaves. What is't to leave betimes?"; whereas the Second Quarto reads, "since no man of ought he leaves, knowes what ist to leave betimes, let be." To make sense out of the Second Quarto's reading, editors who follow the Quarto here perhaps most commonly shift the comma to make the line read, as it does in the Norton text, "Since no man of aught he leaves knows, what is't to leave betimes? Let be." Naturally, the textual discrepancies have provoked much critical speculation over Hamlet's meaning; but since the Folio is relatively plain, most of the theorizing has focused on the Quarto's less concrete wording.

Warburton provides a model interpretation of the Quarto's version: "It is true that, by death, we lose all the goods of life; yet seeing this loss is no otherwise an evil than as we are sensible of it; and since death removes all sense of it, what matters it how soon we lose them? Therefore, come what will, I am prepared."[5]

Not wholly content with this, Dr. Johnson suggested an interpretation that would ally Hamlet more closely with the Greek's tragic understanding of life's uncertainty: "Why should he dread an early death, of which he cannot tell whether it is an exclusion of happiness or an interception of calamity?"

Furness agrees with Clarke's preference of the Quarto on the basis of Johnson's interpretation: "Clarke prefers the Qq on what, I think, is the true ground, so finely paraphrased by Johnson: That it is more characteristic of Ham. to think little of leaving life, because he cannot solve its many mysteries, than because he cannot carry with him life's goods."

Dover Wilson offers an even subtler reading: "Hamlet's argument is: 'early' or 'late' is no matter, so long as one is prepared; and since we can gather from nothing in this life whether we are leaving it early or late, why bother about it?"[6]

But Granville-Barker rejects this etherealizing trend and prefers the Folio because, as he candidly admits, he understands it whereas he does not understand the Quarto. Further, he attempts to blunt the rationale behind Johnson's argument by denying that Hamlet "is merely thinking—with St. Paul and the Burial Service—of the worldly goods a man must leave behind":

> Surely it is his loss of other things that he has in mind, of things he loved and valued; his father's care, his faith in his mother, the ideal love for Ophelia, hers for him. He could keep nothing of all this. And so, with things such as this, it still would be. What is it, then, to leave betimes, before he has lost more? But let us own that, whatever the meaning may be, it is more than vaguely conveyed.[7]

Granting a degree of vagueness and admitting that in these matters certainty cannot be expected, I nevertheless believe that much of the interpretative mystery here remains because Hamlet's line has not been viewed as the end of a carefully plotted progression in Hamlet's attitudes toward death, and more specifically because the line has not been interpreted as the conclusion Hamlet has drawn from his graveyard meditations. Once we recognize Shakespeare's preparation for the line, its basic meaning should no longer prove so puzzling.

None of the interpretations we have presented lays sufficient stress on Hamlet's "betimes," for what Hamlet is forced to accept is the giving up not of what he already has but of what he might gain or achieve in the future. Hamlet's personal tragedy is to be cut down before having a chance to prove his greatness. In turning back to the graveyard scene, we can now more fully appreciate why Hamlet dwells on people who had achieved their worldly aims of power, wealth, wit, and beauty—the politician, courtier, lawyer, landowner, jester, lady, conqueror, emperor—and why his meditations climax with Alexander and Caesar, who are reduced to the basest of uses.[8] Just as Hamlet instinctively admires Fortinbras, so he cannot help but hear, through the names of ancient heroes, the siren call of fame and glory. But since, as Hamlet perceives, death strips even the mightiest of their gains, how can it be of such great importance whether he dies before having had a chance to become a hero? Both the Folio and Quarto rendering of Hamlet's reconciliation to an early death convey essentially the same meaning: since once dead we neither possess literally nor are aware of what we gained or achieved while alive, what does it matter if we die before we have had the opportunity to become rich, learned, or famous?

Thus, Hamlet has come full circle. At the beginning of the play he is braving death and rejecting the world; at the end he is braving death and rejecting the world. But to miss the difference between the two is to miss not only perhaps the most important aspect of Hamlet's internal strife but also his triumph.

Hamlet's inconspicuous achievement may be likened to the progress of a Zen master as described by Seigen Ishin: "Before a man studies Zen, to him mountains are mountains and waters are waters; after he gets an insight into the truth of Zen . . . mountains to him are not mountains and waters are not waters; but after this when he really attains to the abode of rest, mountains are once more mountains and waters are waters."[9]

Shakespeare has created not, of course, a Zen master but a man who, in conquering himself through a fusion of Stoic and Christian philosophy, can assume his rightful title as a tragic hero.

A major stumbling block to Hamlet critics has been their tendency to portray him as either consistently heroic or, more usually, consistently anti-heroic (too weak, meditative, or melancholic to perform his duty). Tracing the course of Hamlet's changing attitudes toward death has produced the important side effect of exposing the inadequacy of such static interpretations. In *Hamlet*, Shakespeare depicts a figure with heroic potential who, though no hero at first, is compelled through a sudden and devastating confrontation with evil acts outside his control to scramble through trial and error toward heroism as rapidly as possible. In this respect, Hamlet's progress may be likened to that of Lear, who, though old and already long a king, must endure a harsh apprenticeship of suffering and madness before he can rightfully bear the mantle of a hero.

Static interpretations have also, I believe, obscured Shakespeare's handling of the age of Hamlet, who from the beginning of the play is described by everybody in terms of his youthfulness, and yet in the graveyard scene is assigned the precise age of thirty. If we argue that Hamlet is consistently young, we must dismiss the figure stated by the gravedigger as a mistake of some sort by Shakespeare or his transcribers and printers. On the other hand, if we accept the gravedigger's statement of Hamlet's age, we are hard put to explain the play's earlier stress on his youthfulness. Finally, if in frustration we say with Bradley, "It matters little here whether Hamlet's age was twenty or thirty . . . ,"[10] we still have failed to explain why it apparently mattered to Shakespeare. Once we concede, however, that Shakespeare uses age, as he uses time, dramatically rather than realistically, we can readily resolve the seeming discrepancies. Through the gravedigger's figure of thirty, Shakespeare is telling his audience that young Hamlet has now grown up, has matured because of his trials and suffering. In actual time Hamlet has aged only a few months, but in dramatic and psychological time Hamlet has leaped years into full maturity or, to be more precise, into herohood.

The irony of Hamlet's tragic destiny lies not so much in his own death's occuring at the moment of his triumph over his enemy as in his death's following so closely his triumph over himself—a triumph that insures his worthiness to assume the burdens of life, kingship, and greatness. For only by the end of the play are we ready to hear and to believe Fortinbras's most fitting epitaph for Hamlet:

> For he was likely, had he been put on,
> To have proved most royal. . . .

NOTES

[1]Harley Granville-Barker, *Prefaces to Shakespeare* (Princeton, 1946), footnote 43, I, 115-116.

[2]C. S. Lewis, "Hamlet: The Prince or the Poem," in *Proceedings of the British Academy* (London, 1942), XXVIII, 147-152. Reprinted with abridgments in Cyrus Hoy, ed. *Hamlet* (A Norton Critical Edition, 1963), pp. 214-218.

[3]For my quotations from *Hamlet* I have followed the text and line numberings of the Norton Critical Edition of *Hamlet* edited by Cyrus Hoy.

[4]Granville-Barker, I, 136, 254-256.

[5]This and the following two interpretations are quoted from Horace Howard Furness, *A New Variorum Edition of Shakespeare: Hamlet* (Dover reprint of the 10th edition, 1963), I, 440.

[6]J. Dover Wilson, *The Manuscript of Shakespeare's 'Hamlet' and the Problems of its Transmission* (New York, 1934), II, 214.

[7]Granville-Barker, footnote 23, I, 146.

[8]In IV, iii, 19-30, Hamlet had wittily demonstrated how "a king may go a progress through the guts of a beggar" simply in order to deflate Claudius.

[9]Quoted by D. T. Suzuki in William Barrett, ed., *Zen Buddhism: Selected Writings of D. T. Suzuki* (Doubleday Anchor Books, 1956), p. 14.

[10]A. C. Bradley, *Shakespearen Tragedy* (Meridian Books reprint, 1955), p. 101.

Jean H. Hagstrum

SOURCE: "The Rhetoric of Fear and of Hope," in *Triquarterly,* Vol. 11, Winter, 1968, pp. 109-23.

[*In the following essay, Hagstrum analyzes the philosophical positions on the nature of fear and hope advanced by Samuel Johnson and William Blake.*]

In 1749 Samuel Johnson, often considered the last classical rationalist, asked, "Where then shall Hope and Fear their objects find?" In 1793 William Blake, sometimes called the first Romantic, declared, "Fear & Hope are—Vision."

These famous sentences seem to unite the two qualities. But by nature fear and hope, like volatile gases, tend to fly apart or consume one another. Indeed, to keep them together or even to keep them safely interacting requires strenuous doing. One of our authors, in order to cast out destructive fear, had to create a rhetoric of hope, and the other, in order to tame delusive hope, had to create a rhetoric of fear. That kind of separation having been forced by the nature of the two emotions, Blake and Johnson now seem to confront each other across a deep gulf in the landscape of cultural history. For one thinker sought to steady the mind by committing it to the *objects* of outside reality while the other sought to relieve the mind by projecting its *visions* upon outside reality.

But the sentences that unite the two qualities are by no means untypical, and in the days of Johnson and Blake fear and hope were often associated to form more than one kind of pattern. The two had, for example, been immemorially united in a kind of holy wedlock whenever anyone contemplated man's fate or future. They were also linked with the fortunes of trade, and the commercial English—traders, investors, and colonists—were thought to have been peculiarly agitated by hope and fear. And the artistic culture that followed Johnson and was contemporary with Blake made the movement from fear to hope—or something very close to it—a basic aesthetic configuration. Beethoven progressed from storm to calm in the Sixth Symphony, from fear of fate to a joyous triumph over it in the Fifth and Ninth Symphonies, and from illness to health in the A minor Quartet.

But none of these happy unions or sequences of fear and hope help us much in understanding Johnson and Blake. For these writers allowed the two emotions to be wrenched asunder. They then brought them together again—only after hard and harrowing experience—into rhetorical structures that were forced, unstable, unnatural, and combustible—but also highly illuminating and intensely human.

1. PERSONAL TERROR

"It takes a worried man to sing a worried song." If Woody Guthrie's aesthetic philosophy seems a bit simple, we should remember that it was held by Samuel Johnson himself—and also by Horace, Fielding, Dennis, Hume, Tolstoy, and I. A. Richards—all of whom used the test of sincerity in their literary criticism. Following these somewhat plain paths, we shall consider the personal fears that shattered the quiet, first of Johnson and later of Blake. We then turn to fear and hope as they appear in the moral and intellectual positions of each writer.

Modern study has made it impossible to say simply that Johnson was a conservative who loved the old and feared the new. His conservatism, if that indeed is the word for it, was a life-long discipline imposed by the man himself on a strong disposition to revolutionary violence. "Sir," he said of his earliest days with Garrick in Walpole's London, "I was mad and violent." Nor can it be said today, without qualification and careful definition, that Johnson was a neoclassical rationalist of limited sensibility. His diaries reveal a man of "tumultuous imaginations" (the phrase is his) which he expended enormous psychological energies to reclaim. The rational, classical discipline of mind and art that Johnson recommended to others seems to have first had the more personal task of calming the raging sea of the man's own obsessive fantasies. Behind the phrase, "Dangerous Prevalence of Imagination" (so often taken as a sign of the traditional and unambitious classicism attributed to Johnson), lay the acutest personal suffering and mental anguish.

Fear is a word used frequently by Johnson in his religious and political writings, and it is often taken as a sign of the man's timid withdrawal from intellectual and spiritual adventure. But if one looks at the life behind the language, one soon learns that *fear* (powerful though that word is) is much too tame to describe the emotions we discover. In 1761 Johnson refers in his diary to "my terrors and perplexities"; in 1766 he is "harrassed with vain terrors"; in 1768 he buys a padlock which he later entrusted to Mrs. Thrale along with his dark secret, about which we can only guess; and in 1771 he records in Latin "an insane thought about foot-fetters and manacles."

What terrorized this man, whose stout sanity as a writer has become legendary? Death, annihilation, Judgment—but above all what he described as "the uncertain continuance of reason," the most alarming of all the uncertainties that beset man. Of the poet Collins who had suffered mental alienation, Johnson said, "Poor dear Collins! . . . I have often been near his state," and of his own "vile melancholy" Johnson said that it had made him mad all his life, "at least not sober." When he was 68 years old, he cast a retrospective eye on his past life: "I discover nothing but a barren waste of time with some disorders of body, and disturbances of mind very near to madness."

Of William Blake's mental state in the late nineties the word *terror* is also appropriate. In the year 1800, when he signed himself as an "enthusiastic, hope-fostered visionary," he also wrote, "I begin to Emerge from a Deep pit of Melancholy, Melancholy without any real reason for it, a Disease which God keep you from & all good men." This terror he related to his visions of the revolutions in America and France:

> terrors appear'd in the Heavens
> above
> And in Hell beneath, & a mighty and awful
> change threatened the Earth.
> The American War began. And all its dark horrors
> passed before my face
> Across the Atlantic to France. Then the French
> Revolution commenc'd in thick clouds
> And my Angels told me that seeing such visions I
> could not subsist on the Earth
> But by my conjunction with Flaxman, who knows
> how to forgive Nervous Fear.

There are profound differences between Blake's terrors and Johnson's. Johnson's were those of a man of an extremely scrupulous conscience and an enormous sense of responsibility, who may also have suffered from feelings of sexual guilt. Blake, a man of the tenderest sensibilities and a lover of *all* life, suffered pangs over having to encourage destructive energy and revolutionary violence. Johnson feared the imaginative delusion that would break his contact with reality. Blake encouraged imaginative visions, and he desperately wanted them authenticated as even more valid than outside nature. In spite of these differences, the two are alike in this—that each was almost overwhelmed by psychic energies, which, undirected, might have darkened the light of his mind.

No one in the eighteenth century could have suffered as Blake and Johnson suffered without being haunted by images of the institutions their society had created for the insane. Both the French and the English Enlightenment imprisoned mental sufferers. In France, from 1657, when the Hôpital Générale was opened, the mad were confined—at first with debtors, beggars, drunkards, voluptuaries, and other varieties of outcast. In England the Bethlehem Hospital had received lunatics as early as 1405; but in 1675 the quarters were enlarged and a new handsome and spacious building was erected at Moorfields. Some of the inmates of "that magnificent palace," as Steele called it, we can today contemplate in the coldly brilliant satire of Swift, who made them the mirror of society; or in the last engraving of Hogarth's *Rake's Progress,* where Tom has reached his nadir and is chained to the bare floor of Bedlam. Or we can see their Spanish counterparts in the art of Goya, where they are seen in their vast, monotonous, obsessive freedoms, silhouetted against the darkness, without the landscape that Brueghel and Bosch had given their grotesques—no star in their dark night, solitary and communing only with themselves. Such creatures as these provoked the curiosity of men, women and children in the eighteenth century, who paid their two-pence to tease and taunt the sufferers. Johnson's curiosity was also aroused, for he went to Bedlam at least twice; but his own tortured mind must have been seared by what he witnessed—the straw, the chains, the bare stones, the wooden bowls for food, the pacings, the grimaces. On his many nocturnal rambles through London he may even have heard the midnight screams and the rattling chains. When Johnson presented his padlock to Mrs. Thrale and perhaps asked for confinement in her quarters, he knew what he wanted to escape.

Swift saw contemporary society in Bedlam. Blake saw Bedlam in society. His fear-driven contemporaries he beheld as living in pits of melancholy, in caves of despair, in houses with barred windows, or still in wombs from which they could not emerge. . . . In the society William Blake castigated, the once proud human form is bent in fear and humility, bowing before authority, kneeling before altars, crouching, cringing, and sometimes rolled up into a foetal ball. Many of these images must have come directly from Bethlehem Hospital, where, Blake said, were built the "Dens of Despair," where there were stones and rocks only, "for human form was none."

The minds of Johnson and Blake were haunted by more than their own, subjectively induced spectres. Society itself helped to provide a grim and palpable setting for the fears of their lonely hours.

2. JOHNSON AND A RHETORIC OF FEAR

In her *Anecdotes* Mrs. Thrale, the friend to whom Johnson committed his padlock and his dark secret, refers to his "over-anxious care to retain without blemish the perfect sanity of his mind." Such a standard would have been austere for almost anyone; for a man of Johnson's tumultuous imagination it was impossible. But there were compensations—for us and, we hope, for him also. His personal triumph was great—the achievement in all his writings and most of his conversations of a clear-eyed, steady, humane rationality, free of hysteria and even strain—and this by a man whose mind, as Boswell said, resembled a place of caged lions and tigers ready to spring out.

Quite apart from the force of his personal example, Johnson's comments on the mind itself constitute an impressive layman's analysis. His discussions, which anticipate Freud and many modern practices, surely ought to be useful in a discipline where descriptive and terminological accuracy has not yet been reached. We should always welcome a mind of large general powers which has been exposed to relevant experience operating on difficult and elusive problems. Such credentials are especially welcome in diagnosing and prescribing for the "diseases of the imagination."

Consider, for their contemporary ring and relevance, some of Johnson's comments on the obsessed mind. On madness and fear, for example: "A madman loves to be with people whom he fears; not as a dog fears the lash; but of whom he stands in awe." Consider his comment on the sensuality of the deranged: "Madmen are all sensual in the lower stages of the distemper. They are eager for gratifications to soothe their minds and divert their attention from the misery which they suffer: but when they grow very ill, pleasure is too weak for them, and they seek for pain." Or consider the differences between a Boswell, who thinks that Johnson in deep error, confused madness, and melancholy, and Johnson himself, who sees all of us as prone to what can end in mania and who seems to have understood the alternations of the manic-depressive cycle and of the transformations of gloom into hysteria and vice-versa. Or again, and in greater detail, consider the analysis of the astronomer's paranoia in *Rasselas*—for the humanity as well as for the shrewdness of the discussion. The scientist's mania—that he can control the seasons—is grotesque but not inhuman: all men, in whom any power of fancy predominates over reason, are, to the extent of that predominance, obsessed. Such plays of fancy, mild in their onset but totally obsessive in their culmination, attack the learned who isolate themselves from life, who preoccupy themselves with the mind, and who give themselves over to "silent speculation." Obsessive fancies are related to a man's displeasure with himself, and the reality from which airy gratifications woo him is his own psyche—its shortcomings, its frustrations. Unsatisfied personal pride drives man to "unattainable dominion" and "impossible enjoyments," which if progressively indulged will make all other intellectual gratifications tasteless compared with the feast on "luscious falsehood." After such a repast, what other satisfactions can possibly gratify? Man, recalled by nature or custom, "enters peevish into society, because he cannot model it to his will." A cold and stubborn community with its own necessary rules cannot compete with the delights that dance around a man in the semi-slumbers of fancy, and so he deserts life once more. The cycle continues until in the end fictions operate as realities, and one gives oneself over to dreams of rapture or anguish.

Johnson on the mind is wholesome, abrasive, and complex—so complex that the following reduction of his thought to its three essential points does it some injustice. (1) *Man is responsible for his mental condition.* Johnson saw madness as the culmination of a progressive series of ego-flattering choices that could, at several earlier points, have been interrupted. He was of Hogarth's view, who said that the inmates of Bedlam had themselves effaced the "stamp of Heaven." Johnson saw moral value in the proximity to Bedlam of new and fashionable residences: "I would have those who have heated their imaginations live there, and take warning." Johnson was wrong in fastening responsibility on the disturbed, a burden that he himself could scarcely bear. But there was no position that he defended more passionately than man's freedom to choose and his obligation to choose wisely. To those ends Johnson thought that a man should be willing, if necessary, to sacrifice even the calm of his mind. (2) *Mental suffering is caused by an empty mind.* There is a hunger of imagination that preys incessantly on life, and rushes into the vacuum that nature always abhors. The intellect "will embrace anything, however absurd or criminal, rather than be wholly without an object." (3) *It is therefore prudent to fill the mind with proper objects from outside reality.* Johnson asked no more essential question than the one with which we began the lecture: "Where then shall Hope and Fear their objects find?"

This question brings us back from the mind in general to the emotions of hope and fear. I wish now to analyze Johnson's carefully constructed intellectual position involving fear—what the title calls his rhetoric of fear. The paradox is that the man whose mind was harrowed by fear soberly recommends fear to others and expects that fear will cast out fear.

"Fear is one of the passions of human nature, of which it is impossible to divest it." This being true, fear must have an object, for without an object it remains *Angst,* or anxiety, an emotion that preys upon the mind and threatens purposelessly and permanently to upset its balance. With an object, that emotion becomes salutary. "Holy fear" is of demonstrable "efficacy to the great purposes of our being"; in the fear of God is embraced "the whole system of moral and religious duty." That general fear can be divided into fear of punishment for offence and fear of the offence itself. Such a view, which dismayed many of Johnson's contemporaries (both the giddy and the gloomy, in Boswell's phrase) is essentially the view that man is a responsible creature in a universe of moral law. Even Johnson's shocking outburst at Oxford is—if one deducts the passion, of course—a perfectly logical conclusion from his premises. When asked by the amiable Dr. Adams of Merton College what he meant by being damned, Johnson replied "passionately and loudly": "Sent to Hell, Sir, and punished everlastingly." This was in 1784. In 1741 William Dodwell said in a sermon at the same university that men have now "learnt to wear off the Apprehension of Eternal Punishment." That apprehension Johnson did not want worn off himself or other men. Although he must surely have been a modern enough man to hope for the moral equivalent of literal hell-fire, he could not possibly have denied either the presence of or the need for a potentially punitive moral law, however one defined it or wherever one placed it. "Faith," he once wrote, or copied from someone else, is "in some proportion to Fear."

Johnson was no better than an indifferent commentator on *Macbeth*. But *Macbeth,* that play of fear, provides an excellent gloss on Johnson's conception. Macbeth starts and shakes in raptures of alternating hope and fear, tosses "in restless ecstasy," and ends with a mind "full of scorpions." His condition is subject to a precise Johnsonian analysis, although Johnson himself, unaccountably, never made it. Macbeth suffers from a "dangerous prevalence of imagination," because his hopes *before* his crime were attached to the wrong object and became vaulting ambition, and also because his fear *after* his crime had no object at all. That fear had at first been monitory and could have been salutary; but, overborne by criminal hope, and now unattached, devouring, illusory, it drives the man to break down all the defences of personal, moral, and social safety. And his object-less fear ravages the whole state, where men now know not what they fear. Hecate describes to the witches the ethical and psychological situation of the play, again in the precise terms of Johnson's rhetoric of fear: security is a "mortal's chiefest enemy"; illusion will draw Macbeth on to his destruction.

> He shall spurn fate, scorn death, and *bear*
> *His hopes 'bove* wisdom, grace, and *fear.*

Ethical confusion leads inevitably to psychological confusion, which in turn leads to mischief and crime. Ambitious hope, unchecked by humble and ethical fear, is one formula of tragedy.

Macbeth says to his Lady before he has screwed his courage up to the sticking point of murder: "I dare do all that may become a man, / Who dares do more is none." Johnson said of this line and a half that it "ought to bestow immortality on the author, though all his other productions had been lost." Such praise seems excessive until we realize that Shakespeare has epitomized in memorable, aphoristic language what Johnson regarded as man's central task: transforming vague and destructive *Angst* into useful and ethical fear and making it serve the purposes of life. Salutary fear is essentially the fear of transcending the limits placed by reality on our nature and on our powers. Let no man dare to be more than man!

Johnson's rhetoric of fear, which in this manner enforced respect for the facts, the laws, and the limitations that nature imposes on us, had enormous consequences in his practical criticism of life, literature, and manners. Johnsonian fear deflated the hero, discouraged hero-worship, and scorned the heroic in history. Remembering that Alexander the Great knew himself a mere man only because of his need for sleep, Johnson adds dryly, "the body which required such frequency of renovation gave but faint promises of immortality." Johnsonian fear led to a distrust of every social, political, and personal nostrum his age provided, and Johnson damned with wit or in-

dignation the inevitable law of progress, the inevitable law of regress, the noble savage, the healing power of outdoor nature. His fear of the vaguely awesome made him discourage religious poetry—religion was a subject too awful for the wings of wit—and it made him scorn most religious philosophy as impiously and foolishly ambitious. His fear made him distrust the whole system-building penchant of cosmological and metaphysical man: "To such meditations humanity is unequal!" It led him to satirize every metaphor imposed upon physical reality—the great chain of being, for example—and every proposed organization of psychic life—the law of association, the rule of a dominant passion. In refuting Berkeley he kicked a stone and rebounded from it, as if to show the power as well as the presence of hard, irrefutable, inescapable material reality.

Thus Johnson's deflationary laughter, born of a basic fear of the pretentious, the ambitious, and the illusory, rests on his unwavering respect for nature. Outside reality—always including both the natural and the human—was for him not only a healing and healthful restraint but an intellectual challenge; and it is on this property, so narrow in one sense, so spacious in another, that Johnson erected his house of hope. Here—and only here—can man "invigorate himself by reason and reflection." This is so because reason and nature were almost synonymous, because reason and virtue were also almost synonymous, and because therefore virtue and nature, being equal to the same thing (reason), are also equal to each other. Confronting nature, man becomes truly free to create and free to hope. Acting to increase the "hereditary aggregate of knowledge and happiness," he witnesses his irrational fears depart, and he achieves the dignity of a truly reasonable being, owing his achievements to the "call of choice" instead of to brute necessity. Here he can choose as objects of his mind those topics in science and art never yet undertaken. Here lie innumerable combinations of fact and observation, uncounted opportunities for the hypotheses of reason and the metaphors of the imagination, and of course unimpeachable ways of correcting error and sobering the fancy.

On man's transactions with nature Johnson placed few limitations. In fact, since it is precisely that contact with reality that can conquer false fears, the law of limitation does not apply. In other areas, as we have seen, Johnson's scorn withers the ambitious and the rash. But here he encourages bold enterprise, and his scorn is reserved for "intellectual cowardice"—for those men of the academy who specialize in chimerical terrors and in frightening the young from intellectual adventure by revealing the bugbears of their own minds. Granted, boldness even here can, without good sense, become rashness, but "heady confidence" is always better than "heartless pusillanimity." The vehement and the active are "always hastening to their own reformation," but the timid man of letters or of science is suffering from a disease of the mind obstinate and fatal.

The realm of endeavor to which Johnson summons the scholar and the scientist he placed under the generic title of either *literature* or *science*—words virtually synonymous. This was a much broader domain than *belles lettres* alone, although it of course included them. *Literature* (or *science*) embraced all the great enterprises of a modern University, from laboratory to stage; and the inner fences were low. All these enterprises, in which man's mind was applied to nature, Johnson respected, because they were concerned with the real, the experimentally and verifiably real, and were thus the effectual enemy of illusion. They provided the foundation of Johnson's hope. That foundation no fear could shake, because the enterprises of the mind operating upon nature were themselves the antidote of unhealthy fear and were themselves sanctioned by salutary fear.

3. BLAKE AND A RHETORIC OF HOPE

Johnson builds hope on fear, but Blake builds hope in fear's despite. In establishing his rhetoric of hope, Blake found it necessary directly to attack all the limits that Johnson found good. The chief villain of Blake's myth, the hoary, frosty god of the Establishment, the anti-Man, Urizen, is named after *horizon* (that is, limit or boundary). . . . That bearded and venerable oppressor is in fact always creating frontiers, as he wields the plummet line, applies the geometer's compass, weaves nets, or makes bars and grids. Blake's rhetoric of hope is *not* based on the outside world and nature (which Blake hated as intellectually stifling) but on internal desire. One of his designs shows a man on earth leaning a ladder on the moon and crying out, "I want! I want!" An early aphorism says that "More! More! is the cry of a mistaken soul, less than All cannot satisfy Man." Blake conceded that opaqueness had limits—black apparently can be no blacker than black—and one cannot contract beyond a certain point. "But there is no Limit of Expansion!" he said.

Johnson encouraged salutary fear. But Blake hated all fear and saw it as the result of deliberate repression and oppression. His Milton says to Satan:

Thy purpose & the purpose of thy Priests & of thy
　　Churches
Is to impress on men the fear of death; to teach
Trembling & fear, terror, constriction.

Consider the verbal images with which Blake describes the present state of man. He is "Weak! wither'd! darken'd!" living as he does in wintry repression. Huddled into himself and shivering, he lives in a den: "Over the doors Thou shalt not: & over the chimneys Fear is written." Infancy, "fearless, lustful, happy," is now a fading memory, and the loving, laughing little girl has become "the pale Virgin shrouded in snow."

For Johnson limitation is discipline. For Blake it is inhibition. And inhibition guides old Urizen's "obdurate" pen as he writes the scroll of the future, tracing "the wonders of Futurity in horrible fear of the future."

Salvation is effectuated by erect, proud, nude, defiant, young men and women, rising to newness of life in the full sunlight, impelled by fires within as they combat the winter of man's discontent. . . . The act that redeems is an act of bold rebellion, and it has cosmic effects:

When I had my Defiance given
The Sun stood trembling in heaven.

In those lines Blake refers to his own salvation from fear. Let us look more closely at that event as Blake recounts it in his myth. Los, the painter-prophet-poet, in the oppressive society that rules by fear, has become what he beholds. He is now a frustrated, divided, fearful being, struggling with and wasting the energies of his body, lacking confidence in his work, and lamenting the past or raging at the present in unproductive alternations. In such a state he can no longer enjoy the beauty of Enitharmon, his wife, who has shriveled into herself—the bursting grape now "Shut up in a little purple covering." Love is transformed into the jealous and possessive fears that accompany the frozen marriage bed.

Then comes the change. Enitharmon beholds the Lamb of God in his second coming. Her first response is fear, fear that she and Los will suffer eternal death—a natural response since she had been taught by the churches that the returning God comes to judge and punish. But seeing her husband's fires rekindle at the vision, she warms to her "lovely terrible" mate and urges him to work on—now, however, in "sweet moderated fury." Certain of her faith in him and understanding now that the Lamb returns to love man and not accuse him, the poet-painter plants his right foot firm on an iron crag of Urizen's prison (society, that is) and leaps aloft in a mighty arc to the heavens above (the realm of artistic-prophetic vision). . . . There on the sky he draws his giant forms, and Enitharmon colors them in blushing love. (We remember that Catherine Blake often applied the color to her husband's pages.) Their collaboration produces the shapes even of Blake's spiritual foes, who are now in his power as an artist. These former enemies of the poet's spirit are not destroyed or even tamed. They are released into a new life of meaning and beauty in the very art of the poet himself.

Los wonders at the mystery of it, and Blake remained convinced to his dying day that the Last Judgment was the casting out of bad art by good art, that the gifts of the Holy Spirit were artistic endowments, and that the forgiveness of sins was the practice of art. Or, put in another way, loving your enemy is absorbing him into your imaginative life and giving him a place in your myth— that is, in your understanding of the world, in your vision of the life of things. Thus does Blake re-interpret—and perhaps subvert—the fundamentals of Christianity.

There is little, then, that the human mind cannot do. And surely, if it can destroy one world and make another, imaginative self-expression can get us through the day. Blake's vision, for all its grotesque and grandiose assertiveness, does not in fact neglect the nasty, stubborn psychological realities of routine life.

I was angry with my friend;
I told my wrath, my wrath did end.
I was angry with my foe:
I told it not, my wrath did grow.

You either express yourself in love and hope or repress yourself in anger and fear. If the latter, you create a "Poison Tree"—that is, you make a poisoned society of poisoning fear.

Blake's method of relieving the breast of the perilous stuff that infects it is at once classical and modern. It is a therapy capable of infinite refinement and is likely to figure centrally in everything we do about the mind.

Blake's system of redemption through imaginative expression is rivaled only by another, Johnson's method of excavating the rock of outside reality and so healing the mind. I say "rock," but actually Johnsonian nature is far from being a soil ungrateful to the tiller's care. Its productiveness should not be estimated by Johnson's crops alone, but even these are not inconsiderable. His quick adaptation to his own literary criticism of the new doctrine of the sublime; his practice of the empirically oriented psychological criticism whose domain he extended; his destruction of the paralyzing and perennial analysis of literary works by genres; his own observations of the mind at work; his naturalization into the English language of the new vocabulary of physical science; his countless social, political, aesthetic, moral definitions inside and outside his dictionary; his distillation into proverb and epigram of so much human experience—all these achievements arose from encounters with nature and reality, of almost literal struggles between man's reason and external nature.

It would be easy—much too easy—to say that we must have both the Johnsonian nature that slowly creates a usable heritage and Blakean mind that burns up one universe and breathes another into being. But I cannot let the contrasts stand in balance, see-saw, teeter-totter. For truth is sometimes best served by the reconcilement, not merely the retention, of opposites. I wish you would therefore consider in conclusion what will have to remain a paradox only, since I am not wise enough to transform it into an insight.

If we do not let the sapphire-studded glories of Blake's New Jerusalem blind us, we can discern the outlines of Johnsonian law. Remember the psychological chaos of present life, as Blake saw it: "grief and fear and love and desire: And now I hate & now I love." What replaces those emotions and their destructive alternations and cycles? Blake calls it "Intellect," or "*mental* pleasures and energies," or "fitness and order." Within the new man an unmistakable hierarchy of faculties and appetites keeps the sexual desires in their proper place, the loins, from whence they no longer invade the mind and heart. Looking back from order upon chaos and its cause, Blake says, recalling Shakespeare and Johnson, "Attempting to be more than Man / We become less." Is it possible that Blakean imagination and Johnsonian nature turn on the same pivot?

W. H. Auden has written that Blake

even as a child could pet
The tigers Voltaire never met.

Voltaire may never have met them, but Johnson had. Both he and Blake knew tigers of wrath and serpents of fear. It was no easy path that led each to the repose of intellectual order. To that realm of stable form each of our writers applied the word *science,* not in its modern restricted sense but in the older meaning that included all the activities of the mind, discursive and creative. In a very real sense, therefore, both men end in the University—an ideal University where "sweet Science reigns" and where all the activities of the mind are first tamed and then honored.

Patricia Meyer Spacks

SOURCE: "Horror Personification in Late Eighteenth Century Poetry," in Studies in *Philology,* Vol. 59, No. 3, July, 1962, pp. 560-78.

[*In the following essay, Spacks traces the personification of the supernatural in English poetry of the late eighteenth century and its influence on the presentation of supernatural entities in poetry of the early nineteenth century.*]

Although eighteenth-century attitudes toward the reality of the supernatural were various and frequently ambiguous, even highly rational critics commonly felt that supernatural personages had a legitimate place in poetry and drama, where they could function as imaginative creations. The precise nature of that place, however, remained through most of the century a vexed question, and efforts to answer the question produced an appalling, if historically interesting, bulk of bad poetry. One solution, attempted frequently, was based on that favorite eighteenth-century variety of metaphor, the personification. Addison early noted the connection between personifications and other forms of imaginary being; later critics followed him in considering ghosts, furies, and personifications as creatures much like one another, and poets exploited the similarity by creating fresh personifications, or re-creating classic ones, in which supernatural figures were labeled Revenge, Despair, Envy, and the like.

Personifications, however, were essentially different from other imaginary beings because of their special function: to reinforce an abstract idea by a concrete image and thereby to achieve one sort of rhetorical sublimity. By uniting personification with the imaginative power of the unearthly, a more intense sublimity might be attained. Poets usually relied on the frightening supernatural in attempting such unions: terror was, as Burke and many before him had pointed out, an essential component of sublimity.[1] The exemplification of an abstraction by a ghost or demon, then, would produce not merely the rhetorical sublimity of *all* personification, but the additional, more profound (because achieved by subject rather than style) sublimity derived from the very notion of the supernatural. And not only would the image of a ghost reinforce the abstraction it symbolized; the abstraction—representing undeniable reality—would also justify the ghostly image, removing it from the realm of controversy.

Although personifications of this sort flourished throughout the eighteenth century, between 1750 and 1800 certain significant changes took place in their use, changes which appear to lead directly toward the unqualified and serious introduction of more originally conceived supernatural personages in the early nineteenth century. The nature of these changes is hinted by the period's criticism of personification in general.[2] Early in the century, critics who considered personification tended to emphasize its didactic value. Addison was exceptional when, in his famous *Spectator* essay on "The Fairy Way of Writing," he stressed its significance for enlarging imaginative scope. More typical was John Hughes, who insisted upon the double function of allegory, which "amuses the Fancy, whilst it informs the Understanding."[3] His emphasis is upon the second function; he says, indeed, that allegory, because of its imaginative license, "wou'd be shocking and monstrous, *if the Mind did not attend to the mystick Sense contain'd under it*" (I, xxiv; italics mine).

Some years later, on the other hand, we find Thomas Warton relatively unconcerned with "the mystick Sense." "Instead of boldly cloathing these qualities with corporeal attributes, aptly and poetically imagined," Warton writes of Gower's personifications, "he coldly yet sensibly describes their operations, and enumerates their properties."[4] The objection is to Gower's considering personifications primarily as abstractions (with possible didactic functions) instead of making them into convincing beings. Joseph Warton, writing of Pope, wishes that the epithets for the allegorical personages in "Windsor Forest" "had been particular and picturesque, instead of general and indiscriminating."[5] He too cares about personifications as functioning individuals in the poem more than as conveyors of moral truth.

The vigor with which Dr. Johnson and Lord Kames insist upon the necessary limitations of personification surely is partly accounted for by the abundance of critical opinion which seems to ignore such limitations, as well as by the increasing looseness of poetic practice. The Warton brothers are representative of a large group; Dr. Johnson seems to speak for a minority when he insists that "to exalt causes into agents, to invest abstract ideas with form, and animate them with activity, has always been the right of poetry. But such airy beings are, for the most part, suffered only to do their natural office, and retire. Thus Fame tells a tale, and Victory hovers over a general, or perches on a standard; but Fame and Victory can do [no] more. To give them any real employment, or ascribe to them any material agency, is to make them allegorical no longer, but to shock the mind by ascribing effects to

non-entity."[6] The view of personifications as imaginatively conceived beings should not, in other words, interfere with consciousness of their strictly allegorical purposes.

Lord Kames, also concerned with the necessity of preserving propriety in the actions attributed to personifications, has categorical objections to the device on the grounds of its essential unnaturalness. "It gives an air of fiction to the whole; and prevents that impression of reality, which is requisite to interest our affections, and to move our passions." No moral effect can be hoped for, he continues, from contemplating the actions of "beings who act not upon the same principles with us."[7] Personification, in this view, is essentially self-defeating. Its very imaginative potency, its power to create an entirely new sort of being, prevents it ultimately from having a moral or didactic effect—from fulfilling its primary purpose.

The critical opposition, then, is between those who, like Johnson and Kames, are conscious of instruction as the ultimate function of poetry, and those who consider entertainment to be equally important: John Langhorne, for example, who says that poetical description "borrows its chief powers and graces" from personification, and that without it "moral and intellectual painting would be flat and unanimate" and even scenery would be "dull."[8] These opposed attitudes have in common, however, the assumption that personifications are imaginary beings in their own right, to be judged as potential actors in a poem, not merely as emblems of moral and intellectual truth. If the more analytical and serious critics felt obliged repeatedly to warn poets that personifications were *not* simply characters, that special laws must govern their use, their warning was certainly necessary, at least in the area of horror-personification. Yet the poets who ignored it, paradoxically, produced the most significant and interesting results.

I

It is difficult to recapture the attitude of contemporaries toward eighteenth-century horror-personification, and the characteristics of the device which seem most striking to a twentieth-century observer are likely to prove misleading. One conspicuous aspect of many horror-personifications was their lack of descriptive development. In 1751 John Brown published "An Essay on Satire, Occasioned by the Death of Mr. Pope." It contained a reference to "the demon shame" and a line stating that "snake-hung envy hisses o'er his [Pope's] urn."[9] Such simple identification seemed sufficient to him, and throughout the century to many other poets. The laureates Thomas Warton, H. J. Pye, and Southey would label abstractions spectres, demons or fiends, and do no more with them; their contemporaries were equally perfunctory. They could afford to be perfunctory—they could, indeed, hardly afford *not* to be—because they were working, by and large, within elaborately defined traditions. Behind "snake-hung envy" stood the figure of Envy in Ovid, the Virgilian and Ovidian Furies, and perhaps, by association, the image of Medusa. Such images had long existed not only in poetry, but in painting: Joseph Spence's *Polymetis* is one of many eighteenth-century treatises which insist upon the relation between the two arts with specific reference to personification.[10] Personification provided a possible mode for exploiting the rich resources of the classics, and as such it was abundantly used. Classical machinery was almost unanimously disallowed for modern poets; since it had no sanction even of popular belief in the eighteenth century, it could not be accepted. But the same objections did not apply to personification, and Alecto, for example, was after all very close to being a personification in the first place. It is not surprising, consequently, that a favorite device of eighteenth-century personification was to label Terror, Ruin and Suspicion "furies" and to provide for them descriptive details taken directly from classic tradition.

The effort to utilize classic tradition was not self-justifying; poets employed it as part of their attempt to provide emotional richness in poetry. In relation to this goal descriptive fullness was not merely unnecessary; it might actually be undesirable. "A circumstantiate description [of a personification]," wrote Lord Kames, "dissolves the charm, and makes the attempt to personify appear ridiculous."[11] He was, to be sure, no proponent of personifications at their best. But Erasmus Darwin, an enthusiastic if misguided user of the device, felt that it was better suited to poetry than to painting precisely because in poetry allegorical figures are generally described indistinctly and consequently do not seem improbable.[12] Emotional effect, then, was thought to depend partly on obscurity. And there was a yet more specific justification for descriptive vagueness; it is suggested by a monody printed anonymously in the *Annual Register* for 1774.

> Behind, stood Death, *too horrible for sight,*
> In darkness clad, expectant, prun'd for flight;
> Pleas'd at the word, the shapeless monster sped . .
> .
> Terrific horrors all the void invest,
> Whilst the Archspectre issues forth confest.[13]

The truly horrible is by its nature undescribable; moreover, Burke had insisted emphatically on the poetic value of obscurity: "To make any thing very terrible, obscurity seems in general to be necessary."[14] The anonymous monodist is no Milton, but he is clearly attempting to use Miltonic technique, to suggest the dreadful rather than delineate it, to achieve a sense of terror by such words as "shapeless," to make "terrific horrors" evoke in a reader a strong emotional response to the unknown. Many late eighteenth-century writers used the same technique in their presentation of horror-personifications.[15] But the problem was not, after all, so easily solved. All these poets evidently wished to impart "sublimity to objects [or qualities] which naturally have it not, by giving them a relation to others":[16] a goal announced by Alexander Gerard, who uses as a prime example of sublimity-by-association Homer's Discord, given grandeur, like so many eighteenth-century personifications, by being assigned supernatural qualities (p. 25). But classical references, as a good many twentieth-century critics have noted, were wearing out; reliance on tradition could not supply all the answers. And the poetry of obscurity, admirable as it might be in Milton, proved surprisingly difficult to imitate.

One new recourse of many poets writing late in the century was to avoid the problem of description by emphasizing function rather than appearance. Rachel Trickett has pointed out the characteristically static quality of Augustan personifications;[17] by 1762, on the other hand, Daniel Webb was insisting that "such images as are in motion, and which, by a gradual enlargement, keep our senses in suspense, are more interesting than those, which owe their power to a single impression, and are perfect at their appearance."[18] Yet the attempt to put images into motion frequently produced singularly static activity:

> Come, *Melancholy,* spread thy raven wing, . . .
> To the dark charnel vault thy vot'ry bring,
> The murky mansions of the mould'ring dead. . . .
> Soon as to life our animated clay
> Awakes, and conscious being opes our eyes,
> Care's fretful family at once dismay,
> With ghastly air a thousand phantoms rise,
> Sad *Horror* hangs o'er all the deep'ning gloom,
> *Grief* prompts the labour'd sigh, *Death* opes the
>   marble tomb.[19]

The atmosphere is familiar from graveyard verse; the personified figures themselves are not described, except in the reference to Melancholy's raven wing. We are told what they do rather than how they look. If they are phantoms they seem phantoms in the sense of figments of the imagination rather than ghosts. Indeed, the personifications of the final couplet seem more essentially abstractions than physical beings; we may even feel, with Coleridge, that their status as personifications depends entirely upon the printer's use of capitals, since the function of personified grief is precisely the same as that of grief the emotion. Dr. Johnson's restrictions are being carefully observed; the result here is that the abstraction is given no real physical existence. What has been added is merely atmosphere; the abstractions have been placed in a slightly new emotional context.

Yet new emotional contexts themselves could be significant, in ways which point directly toward some of the triumphs of the Romantic Movement. For poets now began to use personifications for the direct and emphatic communication of psychic stress: horror-personifications became emblems of psychological states, and were used thus with some specific theoretical justification. John Ogilvie suggested that our idea of imaginary personages, such as personifications, may be "more distinct and particular" than our ideas of real people[20] not, as Erasmus Darwin was to theorize, because of tradition, but because of psychology. We may have trouble forming a concept of the physical being of *people* in literature because we do not fully know their characters, but there can be no such problem with personifications, for which the originals exist in our own minds (I, cv). We have a notion of what terror is; the physical being of personified Terror must follow directly from that. The true power of personification, then, derives from the fact that it merely objectifies images already implicit in all human minds.

Consider this excerpt from John Brown's long poem, "The Cure of Saul":

> The unchain'd furies come!
> Pale melancholy stalks from hell:
> Th'abortive offspring of her womb,
> Despair and anguish round her yell.
> By sleepless terror Saul possess'd,
> Deep feels the fiend within his tortur'd breast.
> Midnight spectres round him howl:
> Before his eyes
> In troops they rise;
> The seas of horror overwhelm his soul.[21]

This is sufficiently over-wrought, but the stress on the activities of the abstractions as persons (melancholy stalks, despair and anguish yell) makes possible a special sort of economy: the poet suggests simultaneously the physical effects of melancholy, through the physical roles of the personifications, and, through the insistent association of emotions and fiends, the full dreadfulness of the psychological effects which precede them.

There was, of course, nothing new about personifying Remorse or Despair; these were obvious and familiar subjects for such treatment. What *was* new in a considerable mass of late eighteenth-century poetry was the degree to which emphasis now rested more on the effects of the emotion than on its physical embodiment. Poetic interest now centered on the way it *feels* to be suspicious or remorseful; the more theoretical problem of how the qualities of terror, say, could be given concrete reality was characteristically subordinated to communication of the personal suffering involved in being terrified. And personification, of course, offered a simple method of stressing the universal relevance and power of an emotion rather than its merely individual manifestations. Early in the century the connection between disturbed psyches and the seeing of ghosts had been a cause for deprecating both the supernatural and believers in it. Addison, taking a stroll in a walk reported to be haunted, enjoys the atmosphere and does not wonder that "weak minds" should fill such a scene with apparitions.[22] His tone of aristocratic superiority was echoed by innumerable poets, who likewise dismissed belief in the supernatural as a property solely of weak minds. The transition to an interest in the precise nature and causes of various forms of "weak-mindedness," the new attempts to emphasize rather than discount the significance of mental disturbance through associating it with the supernatural, obviously mark an important intellectual shift. If it did not immediately bear fruit in good poetry, it foreshadowed a major mode of poetic accomplishment.

Another important development in late eighteenth-century horror-personification, also derived from interest in emotional effect, continues rather than reverses an earlier technique. The early personifications of the century had been frequently pictorial, decorative. Now new modes were discovered for producing decorative effects; they characteristically involved treating personifications as beings like any other, and placing them in non-allegorical contexts. The contexts, and the descriptive detail devoted to the personification itself, might be Christian ("See how war, with dreadful stride, / Marches at the Lord's command"[28]) or classic, or, with increasing frequency, it might derive from folk tradition. The developing interest in German and Scandinavian mythology produced new possibilities for personification. Thus, in a poem called "Odin":

> Ah! see where on the savage heath,
> Half hid amidst the gloomy storm,
> And dancing hand in hand with Death,
> Moves many a rude and ghastly form!
> There Terror, cheated Fancy's child,
> Files o'er the mountains shrieking wild . . . [24]

Several other abstractions inhabit this scene, but none seem much like personifications: the labels attached to them are titles, not descriptions. Yet these beings are as vivid as any other inhabitants of the poem because the context lends them reality, "character," without any necessity for description. This tendency to treat personifications as beings of precisely the same order as other supernatural personages was also to lead ultimately to important developments in English poetry.

II

Major poets and good poetry have been conspicuously absent from this discussion thus far, and with good reason. Johnson, Cowper, Burns: none of these used horror-personification to any significant extent; even Gray employed it only very deviously. All may have been conscious of weaknesses that seemed inherent in the device, weaknesses manifested in the examples that have been quoted: the extent to which personification relied on fast-dying traditions; the remotely decorative and unreal effect it tended to have; the triteness of most of the figures that seemed conceivable. And at the other extreme were the dangers that we know Johnson to have been conscious of: any attempt to make personifications truly fresh might result in total destruction of rhetorical bounds, removing altogether the formal significance of the figure.

The tendencies in late horror-personification that have been mentioned so far have been essentially conservative in their manifestations: the withholding of descriptive detail, the reliance on association rather than elaboration of the figure itself are far from radical solutions to the problem of giving personifications vigor. Late in the century, however, a group of minor poets began to experiment with more radical methods. Theoretically as well as practically concerned with the nature of personification, they tried to expand its possibilities, and prepared the way for Blake and Coleridge by their efforts to create truly "original" horror-personifications, with a new sort of elaboration added to the material of tradition. Ogilvie, for example, in a non-allegorical poem, presents Envy thus:

> Envy! thou Fiend, whose venomed sting
> Still points to Fame's aspiring wing;
> Whose breath, blue sulphur's blasting stream,
> Whose eye the basilisk's lightning-gleam:
> Say, through the dun ile's solemn round,
> Where Death's dread foot-step prints the ground,
> Lovest thou to haunt the yawning tomb,
> And crush fallen Grandeur's dusty plume?
> Or, where the wild Hyaena's yell
> Reigns thro' the hermit's cavern'd cell,
> Moves thy black wing its devious flight?
> (Thy wing that bloats the cheek of Night)
> There oft beneath some hoary wall
> Thy stings are dipt in scorpion's gall;
> Thence whizzing springs the forky dart,
> And spreads its poison to the heart.[25]

We are offered here the familiar atmosphere of graveyard poetry, but in a new way: emphasis now is on the nature of the personage itself, and the multiplication of details suggests the poet's concern to turn his personification into a vivid character in its own right. He does not succeed, because he is not a good poet. ("Is there not imagination in them [Ogilvie's poems], Sir?" asked Boswell. Johnson: "Why, Sir, there is in them what *was* imagination, but it is no more imagination in *him,* than sound is sound in the echo."[26]) The sting which originally points toward Fame's aspiring wing eventually flies to the heart; the wing of Envy "bloats the cheek of Night" in no clearly discernible fashion. The conception of Envy as fiend, in short, is not consistently developed; the personification is convincing neither as personage nor as figure of speech. Personifications of this sort have, as Donald Davie observes, "little or nothing to do with language,"[27] and, as Dr. Johnson hinted, almost as little to do with imagination. Yet the effort they represent is significant; they foretell a development of personification away from its function as a rhetorical device, toward a new place—a duplication, indeed, of a very old place—as a provider of imaginative expansion.

In *The Triumphs of Temper* (1781), the popular poet William Hayley made a serious attempt to widen the imaginative resources of poetry. His poem alternated realistic cantos, dealing with the heroine's daytime activities, with fantastic ones, recounting her inspired dreams. Every night, Serena visits the Cave of Spleen. Hayley explains in his preface that his conception derives from Pope's in "The Rape of the Lock," and that he feels such material should be treated more seriously: he insists on the relation of his method to Dante's.[28] The Cave of Spleen, naturally, is rich in allegorical figures—extended personifications.

> Th'infernal Portress of this doleful dome,
> With fiery lips, that swell'd with poisonous foam,
> Pale Discord, rag'd; with whose tormenting tongue,
> Thro' all its caves th'extensive region rung:
> A living Vulture was the Fury's crest;
> And in her hand a Rattlesnake she prest,
> Whose angry joints incessantly were heard
> To sound defiance to the screaming Bird.[29]

The poem is composed largely of groups of such set pieces. Hayley, like so many of his contemporaries, tries systematically to associate spleen and ennui with hell in order to make a didactic point; and he works harder than most to accomplish this association. He gives heavy weight sometimes to physical appearance, sometimes to activity, sometimes to a combination of the two. Throughout the poem, in the "realistic" as well as the avowedly fantastic sections, he presents fiend-personifications from various points of view, with various sorts of emphasis, concentrating always on sheer vividness of evocation. And the more convincing his personifications are as monsters, the more detail is devoted to them, the less relation they seem to have with the abstractions they nominally represent. Hayley demonstrates dramatically the accuracy of Dr. Johnson's fears about the results of lack of restraint in dealing with personification: the figure of speech becomes a figure no longer. Erasmus Darwin, more bizarre in his attempts than Hayley or Ogilvie, illustrates the same point: turning plants into sorceresses and imps with lavish use of completely automatic references to tradition, he produces personifications which function effectively neither as abstractions nor as supernatural beings.

The attempt to re-vivify personification by concentrating more intensely on the nature of the created personages, then, would seem to be a failure. As the century approached its close, horror-personifications moved in all their elaboration toward meaninglessness. The figures might be superficially vivid, but their details often seemed mechanically selected and used, drawn still from lifeless traditions. Yet the vividness, however superficial, frequently obscured the *conceptual* reality of the personifications. It is possible to criticize the earlier personifications of the century, the simpler ones, on many grounds, but they do not have the peculiar emptiness so often found in Ogilvie and Hayley and Darwin. When John Brown wrote of despair and anguish as "Th'abortive offspring of [melancholy's] womb," he used the word *abortive* in a rich sense, suggesting on one level a concept of despair and anguish as monstrous, foetus-like creatures; on another level, the fact that melancholly tends to keep the emotional life from coming to full fruition. When he described Saul as possessed by sleepless terror, he suggested another personification, a monster surpassing human limitations in never needing to sleep; he conveyed also the horrible, never-ending quality of terror as an emotion. He, too, depended on convention: these personifications are furies, they come from hell, and Brown certainly believed in furies as inhabitants of hell no more than Darwin believed in witches re-animating the dead. Yet his furies are more convincing because they serve a genuine purpose of clarification and emphasis. By many of its later users, personification was intended to decorate rather than illuminate—and its decoration is frequently shoddy.

III

Wordsworth's *caveat* about personification in the 1802 preface to *Lyrical Ballads* is well-known; so is the fact that Wordsworth employed personifications fairly often.

Horror-personification was particularly appealing to the early Romantics; a comparison between Blake and an anonymous predecessor suggests the transformation they effected in it. The *Annual Register* for 1758 contains the following passage from "The Pleasures of the Mind."

> Last, Winter comes to rule the year,
> In sweet vicissitude severe;
> See him on *Zembla*'s mountains stand,
> He stretches out his palsied hand,
> And all his magazines unfold
> Their copious hoards of ice and cold: . . .
> Deep-bellowing bursts of thunder roll,
> And pleasing horror swells the soul.[30]

Here is Blake:

> He [Winter] hears me not, but o'er the yawning
>   deep
> Rides heavy; his storms are unchain'd, sheathed
> In ribbed steel; I dare not lift mine eyes,
> For he hath rear'd his sceptre o'er the world.
>
> Lo! now the direful monster, whose skin clings
> To his strong bones, strides o'er the groaning
>   rocks:
> He withers all in silence, and in his hand
> Unclothes the earth, and freezes up frail life.
>
> He takes his seat upon the cliffs; the mariner
> Cries in vain. Poor little wretch! that deal'st
> With storms, till heaven smiles, and the monster
> Is driv'n yelling to his caves beneath mount
>   Hecla.[31]

The comparison between a very good and a very bad poet is, of course, automatically unfair, but some of the reasons for success and failure here may be significant. The earlier personification is at least *honest* in the sense that John Brown's personification is honest; it is a genuine attempt to express in figurative terms certain essential qualities of winter, and to evoke a vaguely paradoxical attitude toward these qualities ("sweet vicissitude severe," "pleasing horror"). But the image intended to sum up qualities and attitudes is itself hazy: Winter never really emerges as a figure, and the personification appears to accomplish nothing that could not be achieved equally well without it. Blake, too, is honest in intention: the basic purpose of his personification seems identical to that of the earlier one. His greater success in achieving this purpose depends on the genuine creation of an image of power and horror in his Winter, whose relations with men are complex and complexly perceived. This Winter is a being, not merely a season; he seems, indeed, to acquire symbolic overtones that go far beyond any ordinary conception of the season. His defeat by the smiles of heaven suggests an essentially diabolic quality; he is both a time of year (his functions are all appropriate to the nature of winter) and far more than that, a truly direful monster, physically as well as theoretically conceived. But his vivid realization as a monster is an implicit threat to the allegorical limitation required by the nature of personification: the same problem existed for Blake as for Hayley.

Coleridge, too, made lavish use of personification in his early poems. In "Ode on the Departing Year" (1796) these lines occur; they are addressed to England.

> The Nations curse thee! They with eager
>   wondering
> Shall hear Destruction, like a vulture, scream!
> Strange-eyed Destruction! who with many a dream
> Of central fires through nether seas up-thundering
> Soothes her fierce solitude; yet as she lies
> By livid fount, or red volcanic stream,
> If ever to her lidless dragon-eyes,
> O Albion! thy predestined ruins rise,
> The fiend-hag on her perilous couch doth leap,
> Muttering distempered triumph in her charmed
>   sleep.[32]

The "fiend-hag" Destruction, implicitly compared with a vulture, is the product of individual imagination, not tradition. She is not, of course, automatically more effective for this reason, but Coleridge's treatment produces a very striking image. Emphasis on the physical being of the creature is restricted to her eyes: first "strange-eyed," she is later given "lidless dragon-eyes," which define her strangeness and suggest an association with the dragon as traditional enemy of God. (In the Book of Revelation, Satan appears as a dragon; the dragon was in the Middle Ages the characteristic antagonist of the Christian knight; the early Hebrews conceived it as cosmic enemy.) Her surroundings and her triumphant muttering, the more horrible for being part of a charmed sleep, increase the enveloping sense of terror. One may remember the image long after forgetting what it represents.

Coleridge writes often in similar vein; his war eclogue, "Fire, Famine, and Slaughter," is an extended instance. Even his Greek ode on astronomy, translated by Southey in 1793, is rich in this sort of material. "The Ancient Mariner" offers perhaps the most dramatic example of a description in which personification has moved far from the typical eighteenth-century modes. In the 1798 version included in *Lyrical Ballads*, the description of the spectre-woman and her mate concludes,

> Her skin is as white as leprosy,
> And she is far liker Death than he;
> Her flesh makes the still air cold.[33]

It was not until the revision for the 1817 *Sybilline Leaves* that the lines became,

> Her skin was as white as leprosy,
> The Night-mare Life-in-Death was she,
> Who thicks man's blood with cold.[34]

In the same revision, the marginal gloss identified the spectres as Death and Life-in-Death.

The minor alterations, of course, among other things, change a spectre into a personification. And it makes little difference to the effect of horror whether the beings are explicitly identified; for emotional, if not thematic, purposes, the line between the allegorical and the non-allegorical seems not particularly significant. We have here another indication of how close the relationship between personifications and supernatural beings might be.[35]

One is not likely to react to Blake and Coleridge, however, with the irritation he may well feel at the attempts of such poets as Ogilvie and Darwin to use personifications which are in no real sense limited by the conventions of rhetoric. The reason is clear enough: Blake and Coleridge in one sense revivified the very convention they were also destroying. Their personifications do not lack propriety in achieving vividness: to think of Winter as striding over groaning rocks, freezing frail life in his hand, does not take us far from a normal conception of winter—it merely dramatized normal conceptions; to image Destruction as associated with volcanic streams amplifies rather than violates our ordinary notions of destruction. These are, in short, from one point of view far better personifications than the others we have examined: their authors have elaborated them without losing sight of the original reason for their existence.

Yet the elaboration remains none the less a threat to the whole notion of personification. As a matter of fact, it is far *more* a threat in such truly imaginative forms as we have been examining than in the mechanical developments of lesser poets. Darwin's sorceress is more a sorceress than a plant; Hayley's Spleen, more a spectre than an emotion. Yet they are not very convincing as sorceress or spectre, either, because they seem to be composed of building blocks. But Coleridge's spectre-woman is truly a ghostly figure, whether she is called Life-in-Death or simply a spectre: the realized imaginative effect, the consciousness of terror, remain the same in either case. If the first version is more powerful than the second, it is because of the differences in the last line—not because of the presence or absence of a label. The image itself is intense: the vision of the fiend-hag is stronger than the idea of destruction; the monster striding over the world engages our attention more than the idea of winter which justifies the conception. The images provoke an emotional response so strong that we forget the intellectual connections which need to be made. The abstract idea, in other words, adds little to the vividness of the image, and the image is so intense in its own right that it can no longer be said to reinforce the abstraction. Instead, it overpowers the abstraction. And when the imagined personage becomes so clearly stronger than the idea it embodies, it is a small step to direct presentation of a being itself with no reference to the limiting idea.

The process, indeed, parallels the conjectured ancient development of mythology. First of all the primitive mind personifies, creating a pseudo-animal or human image for, say, thunder. But as such images become firmly established they gradually acquire more and more attributes, until there is no longer a deity equivalent to thunder but instead a god, a Jupiter, one of whose powers is the control of thunder. So it was with horror-personifications: their most successful elaborations helped to make it possible for the supernatural to make its frequent undisguised appearances in nineteenth-century poetry. And they also helped to make possible, as the process came full circle, precisely the sort of unemphatic personification that was so frequently attempted, so seldom with full success, in the eighteenth century. When Blake personifies Earthquake, he does so with considerable elaboration:

> Earth, thus I stamp thy bosom! rouse the
>   earthquake from his den,
> To raise his dark & burning visage thro' the
>   cleaving ground,
> To thrust these towers with his shoulders! let his
>   fiery dogs
> Rise from the center, belching flames & roarings,
>   dark smoke![36]

Only a few years later, when Shelley has occasion to use a similar personification, the effect is vastly different:

>   Is this the scene
> Where the old Earthquake-daemon taught her
>   young
> Ruin? Were these their toys? or did a sea
> Of fire envelop once this silent snow?[37]

The contexts, of course, are very different, but the difference in tone between the two passages derives partly from their different approaches to personification. For Blake, the personification is a highly-charged device which must be created in emphatic detail. For Shelley, only the most allusive details are necessary—partly because of the sort of elaboration his predecessors have used, which created a fresh and vigorous tradition, made the demon-side of a personification seem as "real" as the abstraction-side, so that Shelley could expect from his readers not only associations with past earthquake-personifications, but also with a long line of "real" demons from Grendel's dam on.

The eighteenth-century experimenters with horror-personification were seldom good poets; yet the history of their efforts suggests to a considerable extent the origins of much other-worldly subject matter in the nineteenth century and the evolution of some characteristic practices in its evocation.

NOTES

[1] Edmund Burke, *A Philosophical Enquiry into the Origin of our Ideas of the Sublime and Beautiful,* ed. with introduction and notes by J. T. Boulton (London, 1958), p. 73. Mere horror, however, seemed to offer a satisfactory substitute for terror: Burke himself blurs the distinction by speaking of a "sort of delightful horror, which is the most genuine effect, and truest test of the sublime" (p. 73). Indeed, the distinction between terror and horror does not seem to have been important through most of the eighteenth century.

[2] For a fuller account of personification criticism in the eighteenth century, see Earl R. Wasserman, "The Inher-

ent Values of Eighteenth-Century Personification," *PMLA*, LXV (1950), 435-63, and Chester F. Chapin, *Personification in Eighteenth-Century English Poetry* (New York, 1955). A brilliant account of the values of personification is offered by Bertrand H. Bronson, "Personification Reconsidered," *New Light on Dr. Johnson,* ed. F. W. Hilles (New Haven, 1959), pp. 189-232.

[3] John Hughes, "An Essay on Allegorical Poetry," prefaced to *The Works of Mr. Edmund Spenser,* 6 vols. (London, 1715), I, xxix.

[4] *The History of English Poetry,* 3 vols., II (London, 1778), 4.

[5] *An Essay on the Genius and Writings of Pope,* 2nd ed., 2 vols., I (London, 1762), 28.

[6] "Life of Milton," *The Works of Samuel Johnson,* 11 vols. (London, 1787), II, 169.

[7] Henry Home, Lord Kames, *Elements of Criticism,* ed. Abraham Mills (New York, 1838), p. 421.

[8] *The Poetical Works of William Collins,* with Observations on His Genius and Writings by J. Langhorne (London, 1765), p. 145.

[9] [Robert Anderson, ed.], *A Complete Edition of the Poets of Great Britain,* 14 vols. (London, 1790-94), X, 878, 877. The use of lower case initial letters for the personifications is interesting, even though it is presumably the product of late editing or printing. In this connection a recent observation by Professor Bronson might be noted. He remarks on the early eighteenth-century habit of capitalizing all nouns. "Personifications, naturally, were no exceptions to the rule—but neither did they give rise to it. That they became exceptions because of the general proscription of capitals in printing of the latter half of the century is doubtless a natural consequence of their affinity to proper names. Once a typographical shift had occurred, a certain class of images was thrown into high relief, that before had claimed no more notice than what intrinsically was the due of each. . . . To restore the balance, we ought never to capitalize personification in a modernized text." Bertrand H. Bronson, *Printing as an Index of Taste in Eighteenth Century England* (New York, 1958), pp. 17-18.

[10] See specifically Joseph Spence, *Polymetis: Or, an Enquiry Concerning the Agreement Between the Works of the Roman Poets, and the Remains of the Antient Artists* (London, 1747), pp. 292-301. Jean H. Hagstrum, *The Sister Arts* (Chicago, 1958) treats the relation between personification and pictorial tradition.

[11] *Elements of Criticism,* p. 358.

[12] Erasmus Darwin, *The Botanic Garden,* Part II, containing *The Loves of the Plants,* 2nd ed. (London, 1790), p. 53.

[13] "From a Monody, on the Death of Dr. Oliver Goldsmith," *The Annual Register,* XVII (for 1774; 2nd ed. 1778), 204. Italics mine.

[14] *Philosophical Enquiry,* p. 58.

[15] Chapin believes that "eighteenth-century poets do not ordinarily attempt the fabrication of 'obscure' personifications in their own verse. They may admire instances of this in Milton, but if their own personifications are 'obscure,' this is rarely, if ever, from design" (*Personification,* note 33, p. 144). Questions of design or intention must necessarily remain ultimately unresolved in most cases, but it seems to me that there are clear indications, at least in this special realm of horror-personification, that the attempt at obscurity was a fairly common and significant device.

[16] Alexander Gerard, *An Essay on Taste* (London, 1759), p. 28.

[17] Rachel Trickett, "The Augustan Pantheon: Mythology and Personification in Eighteenth-Century Poetry," *Essays and Studies* N.S. VI (1953), 76.

[18] Daniel Webb, *Remarks on the Beauties of Poetry* (1762), from Hans Hecht, *Daniel Webb, Ein Beitrag zur Englischen Ästhetik des achtzehnten Jahrhunderts mit einem Abdruck der Remarks on the Beauties of Poetry* (Hamburg, 1920), p. 94.

[19] Thomas Denton, "Immortality: or, the Consolation of Human Life," *A Collection of Poems in Six Volumes, By Several Hands* (London: R and J. Dodsley, 1763), V, 229.

[20] John Ogilvie, *Poems on Several Subjects,* 2 vols. (London, 1769), I, cii.

[21] John Brown, "The Cure of Saul" (1763), Anderson X, 881-2.

[22] *The Spectator* #110, July 6, 1711; 11th ed., 8 vols. (London, 1733), II, 108.

[23] John Newton, "Death and War" (1778), *Works,* 4 vols. (New-Haven, 1824), II, 545. Of the Seatonian Prize poems from Cambridge, all on religious subjects, twenty of the thirty-seven between 1762 and 1799 contain horror-personifications. See *Cambridge Prize Poems,* 2 vols. (Cambridge, 1817).

[24] George Richards, *Poems,* 2 vols. (Oxford, 1804), I, 29-30.

[25] "Jupiter and the Clown," *Poems,* I, 124.

[26] James Boswell, *The Life of Samuel Johnson, LL.D.,* 2 vols. (London, 1952), I, 261.

[27] *Purity of Diction in English Verse* (London, 1952), p. 40.

[28] His own account of his influences: "I wished, indeed . . . for powers to unite some touches of the sportive wildness of Ariosto, and the more serious sublime painting of Dante, with some portion of the enchanting elegance, the refined imagination, and the moral graces of Pope." Preface, *The Triumphs of Temper* (London, 1781), p. x.

[29] *Triumphs of Temper,* pp. 6-7.

[30] *The Annual Register,* I (for 1758; 6th ed. 1777), 414.

[31] "To Winter," *The Complete Writings of William Blake,* ed. Geoffrey Keynes (London, 1947), p. 3. The poem was first printed in *Poetical Sketches* (1783).

[32] *The Poetical Works of Samuel Taylor Coleridge,* ed. James Dykes Campbell (London, 1938), p. 81.

[33] *Lyrical Ballads, with a Few Other Poems* (London, 1798), p. 18.

[34] *Works of Coleridge,* p. 100.

[35] This close relationship seems to be implicitly denied by Chapin in his generalizations about eighteenth-century personification. "Collins may believe in the reality of his abstractions as creatures of a spirit-world, but Collins is an exception. Personifications became 'real' to the eighteenth-century mind when they are felt as dramatizations of the values, affections, or qualities which relate to the activities of man in the empirical world—not when they are projected as figures from a world of vision" (*Personification,* p. 132). Horror-personifications, to be true, represent a special case which would naturally tend to include abstractions "projected as figures from a world of vision." Collins, who wrote before the mid-point of the century, set the tone for much of the development of the late eighteenth century toward personifications treated more as imaginative than as rhetorical devices.

[36] "Tiriel," *Complete Blake,* p. 106.

[37] "Mont Blanc: Lines Written in the Vale of Chamouni," *The Poetical Works of Percy Bysshe Shelley,* ed. Harry Buxton Forman, 4 vols. (London, 1877), I, 75.

Patricia Meyer Spacks

SOURCE: "The Eighteenth-Century Collins," in *Modern Language Quarterly,* Vol. 44, No. 1, March, 1983, pp. 3-22.

[*In the following essay, Spacks argues for a less-Romantic, rational view of the poetry of William Collins (1721-1759), whose central emotions and preoccupations—namely anxiety and the demonic—have led to his increased reputation among late twentieth-century critics.*]

William Collins sounds different now from the Collins we used to know. For example, Paul S. Sherwin claims,

"Collins feels, all right; but what he feels most urgently is his estrangement from the passionate integrity of unself-conscious or 'unmixed' feeling. Impatient and aching, he is a fever of himself, his intensity springing directly from baffled desire."[1] This feverish figure, "one of the doomed poets of an Age of Sensibility," to use Harold Bloom's words,[2] reveals, like Smart and "the great Romantics," a "struggle with his vocation," the fate of the post-Miltonic writer.[3] He explores problems of sexuality as well as of literary creativity;[4] he resembles Satan more than Milton (Sherwin, p. 32); his imagery partakes of the demonic.[5] Tormented, colorful writer of tormented, colorful verse, he does not much resemble an "eighteenth-century" poet.

Critical allegations of this sort imply a version of literary history (often a Freudified and personalized version) which blurs the century between Milton and Pope, a period that has long caused trouble for critics of poetry. Collins in his most conspicuous recent avatars gains stature mainly by his intimations of the future: a false teleology. The currently fashionable view privileges poetic sensibility, posits discernible relations between psyches and the texts they originate, appropriates Collins to the values of Romanticism. I shall argue that he belongs, rather, to the century of Pope and Johnson, the century in which he lived. (He died in 1759, only fifteen years after Pope.) If, as I believe, Collins inhabits the second rank of eighteenth-century, not nineteenth-century, poets, one must wonder why, unlike such indubitably second-rate contemporaries as Joseph Warton and far more even than Thomas Gray, he has captured the attention of thoughtful and perceptive late-twentieth-century critics who hint that he has the stature of an important Romantic poet or condescend to him because he fails to be sufficiently Romantic.

The new defenders of sublimity, anxiety, and the demonic have acquired their authority partly by sheer intelligence, partly by astute public relations, partly by their ability to perceive enduring human concerns implicit in even the most convention-dominated texts of the past. Their version of Collins sounds worthy of attention because the poet, as they present him, cares about what we care about. Close examination of the critical texts, however, may raise questions about whether the "caring" belongs to Collins or to his recent interpreters.

The most compelling Collins-critics share a Freudian orientation at times startling in its single-minded intensity. Thus Thomas Weiskel, writing about the poet's use of Oedipus in the "Ode to Fear," comments, "It is exactly this ambivalent excitement and dread which the Freudians insist lie behind the mystery of the primal scene and its perceptional derivatives. Had Freud never lived, we would be driven to the hypothesis of the oedipal complex to make sense of these lines" (p. 116). Without Freud, in other words, Collins makes no sense. With Freud's help, critics discover in the poet a consistent substratum of torment. Consider Bloom, also on the "Ode to Fear": "at how high a price Collins purchases this indefinite rapture, this cloudy Sublime! For his poem is one with his deepest repression of his own humanity, and accurately prophesies the terrible pathos of his fate, to make us remember him always, with all his gifts, as Dr. Johnson's 'Poor Collins.'"[6] Or Sherwin: "Occasionally, as in the 'Ode to Evening,' [numinous or visionary possibilities] threaten to erupt, abandoning Collins to his anxieties, and while the temptation to range beyond even toward daemonic ground is scrupulously resisted, it is never completely subdued. For all its delicacy, Collins' Evening realm, like all of his art, is founded upon an unappeasable terror" (pp. 102-3).

Anxiety, the dominant emotion of the twentieth century, governs, in many of these perceptions, the eighteenth-century poet. We domesticate our forebears by discovering in them our own sufferings. Even Collins's most serene lyric, the "Ode to Evening," testifies to his "terror"; his interest in fear as poetic subject proclaims his uncertainties. Instead of inquiring why the poet concerns himself with the literary dynamics of fear, these critics ask what Collins is afraid of. "Here is Collins, invoking Fear," Bloom writes, "yet what has he to fear except himself and John Milton?" (*Anxiety of Influence*, p. 110). According to Paul Fry, "Collins's Fear, fear of nothing but his own hobgoblinry, is really anxiety" (p. 132). Sherwin tells us, "Collins' fear is that he doesn't feel, or fear, enough" (p. 77). The line between poetic speaker and living person blurs when Bloom can link an ode's evocation of fear to its author's subsequent insanity or Sherwin make confident assertions about Collins's own fears. The interest of the poetry depends on the possibility of making provocative claims about its author.

These critics concentrate almost entirely on four poems by Collins, and mainly on three of them. Because of its announced subject, "Ode to Fear" lends itself particularly well to exegesis of anxiety; it also exemplifies the "daemonic" side of Collins, which links him most obviously with the Romantics.[7] "Ode on the Poetical Character" deals explicitly with questions of origins and makes the writing of poetry its poetic subject; critics who associate anxiety with problems of poetic genealogy therefore delight in it. "Ode to Evening" attracts attention by its innovative form and by its clear relations to the poetic past and the poetic future alike. And, for at least some critics, "Ode on the Popular Superstitions of the Highlands of Scotland," which also demonstrates its author's awareness of the demonic and his concern with the sources of poetic power, merits close attention. The political odes, addressed to Peace or Liberty or mourning the death of a soldier in battle, are relatively neglected, as are the early eclogues and the odes on "The Manners" and "The Passions." On the whole these works perhaps lack the poetic merit of most of the widely discussed texts, but it is more relevant to point out that they seem less "interesting" than the others—which is to say, less immediately involved with issues that preoccupy twentieth-century readers. At any rate, the version of Collins that emerges from the most conspicuous current discussions depends on severe selectivity. A personification like "Observance" ("To me in Converse sweet impart, /

To read in Man the native Heart")[8] does not lend itself readily to speculation about terror or the demonic.

The critics concern themselves, of course, with accomplishment as well as psychology. "What is at stake [for "Collins, Smart, and the great Romantics"]," Geoffrey Hartman writes, "is, in fact, the erection of a voice" (*Fate of Reading*, p. 167). The problem of "voice" in Collins has provoked considerable discussion. Fry, concerned with the development of the ode in English, links Collins and Gray as practitioners. "The occasion of the ode is vocative, presentational, yet what it repeats over and over is the dispersion of voice and presence from the text that stands in their place. This is true of all odes, but nowhere more clearly true than in Gray and Collins, who show unexampled daring, if I may, in their willing submission to the conventions of 'vocal' writing" (p. 126). Repetition rather than argument, Fry notes, provides the important "semaphores" of the ode (p. 125); Collins's style depends heavily on generic tradition. Weiskel speaks of the "radical uncertainty of tone which the sublime poem exhibits"; he continues, "The poor 'I,' or voice of these poems, is often thrown into affectation or attitudinizing of one kind or another in its effort to stay afloat on the turbulence of ideological change." The problem of tone that he locates is "how to be at once impassioned, high sounding, and sincere" (p. 109). Noting the "histrionic, sometimes hysterical, character" of Collins's odes, Hartman attributes this character to their evocation of "a power of vision they fear to use"—the problem of voice and tone thus leading back once more to that of fear and anxiety (*Beyond Formalism*, p. 326). And Sherwin sees Collins as involved in an "ordeal of soul making" which "consists largely of his efforts—under Milton's aegis—to discover a voice that expresses his own individual genius" (pp. 11-12).

Although only Weiskel mentions "uncertainty of tone" as an aspect of Collins's writing, all these critics imply the same thing. In effect they both reiterate and defend against the kind of charge Gray long ago leveled at Collins: "a fine Fancy, model'd upon the Antique, a bad Ear, great Variety of Words, & Images with no Choice at all."[9] Fine fancy and richness of diction with little control, bad ear, lack of choice in images: such poetic attributes, with their implied indiscriminacy, might generate tonal uncertainty with no need to allege "turbulence of ideological change" as a cause. Collins struggles to find a voice, he falls into hysterical modes, he submits to necessities which he appears not fully to understand. His critics interpret these facts as aspects of his interest for twentieth-century readers.

One possible explanation for the generosity of such interpretations emerges in Sherwin's book-length treatment. "Contra Johnson," Sherwin writes, "it can be argued that dread of the imagination's more-than-rational energy bespeaks too narrow a conception of reason and suggests that it is the rational in us which needs cleansing" (p. 80). The critic offers this as his own insight, not Collins's; indeed, he adds that "Collins . . . remains a stranger to this saving wisdom" (p. 80). The observation, and its characterization as "saving wisdom," betray the bias that once produced the description of Pope and Dryden as classics of our prose. The forces of "reason" and "imagination" square off once more; Hartman and Bloom and Fry and Weiskel, allying themselves with imagination, claim Collins for the irrational, the suprarational. His uncertainties, like his anxieties, associate him with those who go beyond reason.

The notion of the eighteenth century as an "Age of Prose and Reason" vanished long ago, one might suppose. But when Sherwin writes of "the contagion of the age" (p. 43), he means the century's alleged overvaluing of the rational. "How can the enlightened mind rid itself of itself?" he inquires (p. 43), posing this question as central to Collins's undertaking. Later, he characterizes the poet's techniques in the "Ode to Fear" as "a Dionysiac gesture aimed at abolishing the various Enlightenment constraints prohibiting intercourse between his actual self and the self of his desire" (p. 68). Up-to-date vocabulary, an old-fashioned view. Even Hartman and Bloom, with more apparently complicated understandings of the eighteenth century, sometimes hint at less blatant versions of a similar interpretation. When Hartman writes, of a poetic line extending from Collins to Coleridge by way of Smart, Chatterton, and Blake, "The genius of Poetry becomes a genie once more, a compelling psychic force that works its own salvation in a man, and often as an adversary to accepted values" (*Beyond Formalism*, p. 325), he implies the superiority of this salvationary poetic force to the "accepted values" it combats, the values of the age. Or when Bloom comments, with an air of large concession, "The inherent values of eighteenth-century personification were undoubtedly very real," one can hardly doubt that he finds "Collins' mythical confrontations" far superior to the "traditional personification" they supplant, because larger, more "imaginative," than such personification could ever be (*Visionary Company*, p. 8).

If Collins can be made to stand for good imagination as opposed to bad reason, his current critical resurgence becomes more comprehensible. In *The Visionary Company* Bloom summarizes the "myth" of literary history which Collins accepted; there is reason to believe that Bloom accepts it too:

> Collins saw himself as a poet separated by the school of Waller from a main tradition of the English Renaissance, the creation of a British mythology: the Faery Land of Spenser, the green world of Shakespeare's romances, the Biblical and prophetic self-identification of Milton. This reading of English poetic history, with Waller and Pope in the Satanic role, is itself of course a poetic myth, and a very productive one, in Blake and the Romantics as much as in Collins and the Wartons. (p. 11)

Collins's revival by neo-Romantic critics who share this vision of the fruitful poetic line depends on the perception that at least this one eighteenth-century poet partici-

pates in the ennobling tradition of Shakespeare and Spenser rather than the enervating one of Pope and Waller.

One recent study of Collins, Richard Wendorf's *William Collins and Eighteenth-Century English Poetry,* tries to put the poet back where he belongs, among his contemporaries.[10] Wendorf understands Collins as developing from a fairly orthodox eighteenth-century position to take gradual possession of an original idiom, technique, and subject. Finally, however, he sees Collins as a poet of limitation.

> Collins's is, for better and worse, a poetry of limitation. It would be difficult to think of another poet who has been so successful in emphasizing his own limitations, in suggesting poems that might be written and welcoming powers that might be felt. Collins's most impressive poems are often paradoxical or ambivalent, devoted either to the difficulties involved in achieving poetical success or to certain effects and materials that are considered to lie just beyond this poet's reach. But a poetry that celebrates its own limitations is ultimately constrained by them. I think we sense, especially in Collins's final poem, his own realization that there were certain boundaries beyond which his innovative approach could not be pushed. (p. 188)

This balanced assessment comes as a relief after so much overheated language about terror and the demonic, yet it too may confirm old stereotypes about the eighteenth century. Dr. Johnson made thrilling poetry of man's confrontation with his mortal limits, but Collins's version, in this summary, sounds less than thrilling. A poetry that backs away from its own sense of possibility, a poet aware of Romantic powers and of the unlikelihood of using them, a pervasive realization of boundaries: although Wendorf does not suggest that these aspects of Collins depend on his inhabiting a period in which reason and moderation were highly valued, such a conclusion might tempt any reader. Wendorf's summary reverses the interpretation that finds Collins interesting because he defies the standards of his age; now the poet no longer sounds interesting.

The problem of interpretation which Collins raises, in other words, involves his literary period as well as his literary accomplishment. Understood as a poet struggling to escape the constraints of inhibiting conventions and values, he earns attention by his promise of a glorious future: Wordsworth and Keats achieve the fruition which their predecessor intermittently foretells. This view depends on the critical myth that the Romantic movement defines the great moment of Anglo-Saxon literary history. Collins and Smart prophesy the coming of nineteenth-century poetic saviors; lyric poetry (including the lyric epic of Wordsworth) epitomizes what all poetry aspires to.

Without discounting the importance of recent critical illuminations of the great Romantics, one yet may observe that other myths can uncover other aspects of past poetry.

For those writing in the eighteenth century, obviously, the early nineteenth century does not glimmer in the distance as the approaching era of poetic greatness. Despite their discomfort with aspects of available convention, poets like Collins and Smart write in and from their own time, not only against it. If Collins values Milton and Spenser and Shakespeare, so does Dr. Johnson (although, admittedly, for rather different reasons). Collins's themes in fact often duplicate those explored by contemporaries working in the tradition now understood as "classic" or "Augustan." Lack of clear commitment muffles his voice, but to read his confusions as daring and powerful inflates his reputation at the cost of obscuring the shape of his work. If we understand those confusions as marks of poetic insufficiency—thus returning to an old view of Collins—and see his utterance as analogous to that of quite un-Romantic contemporaries, we may discover different strengths.

First, however, it is worth thinking about why Collins has assumed his current aspect. His poetry provides an ideal text for "creative" criticism, the kind of criticism that inflates its own claims to literary power as well as the stature of its objects. Elements of the verse that fifty years ago provided grounds for critical reproach—dubious syntax, the poet's "mis-remembering" of earlier works, narrative confusion, abrupt shifts of tone, rhetorical vagueness—now increase the opportunities for interpretation; the poetry itself hardly restrains its readers. One can say almost anything about Collins while remaining within the limits of plausibility: a fact that may either unnerve or encourage the would-be critic. Verse that conspicuously fails to declare its own intent allows lavish exercise of critical power.

The poetic vagueness that generates critical freedom especially encourages antirational interpretations. Whatever Collins exemplifies, one could hardly claim him, in his poetic practice, as a proponent of reason. Imagination and originality have since Blake come to seem incontestable poetic virtues—indeed, virtues in life as well as literature. Collins's appeal for the critics and the attraction of their neo-Romantic elucidations depend partly on the seductiveness of such Romantic values. Readers encountering cloudy representations of personalized abstractions can forget the abstractions and discover a mythology by emphasizing the special ("imaginative") rather than the general ("conventional") aspects of such poetic figures. Critical empire-building has enlarged Romantic territory until Milton himself appears to inhabit it; such enlargement becomes possible only because imagination and originality have replaced reason and decorum and even moral energy as standards of accomplishment. To value the eighteenth century in its own terms risks the unexciting. Donne and Herbert speak to the twentieth-century reader of familiar spiritual and emotional dilemmas; Wordsworth's suffering and exaltations prefigure other odysseys of the individual soul; but the idea of a struggle for reason and control no longer thrills many readers.

The "Romantic" Collins has obvious appeal for a twentieth-century audience. He resembles us not only in his emotions ("terror," "anxiety," "uncertainty") but in his preoccupations (the nature of the inner life, the nature and possibility of poetry). Neo-Romantic criticism manages often brilliantly to assimilate the past to the present. Nothing any longer seems distant, different; strangeness itself becomes an aspect of familiarity. Critics emphasize how Collins humanizes or demonizes fear or fancy; they thus suppress the problematic and alien aspect of the personified abstractions that may seem to twentieth-century readers even more peculiar than demons. If commentators acknowledge in passing this conventional aspect of Collins's personages, they hasten to emphasize his innovations, his using abstractions in new ways, for new purposes.

Much of Collins's manipulation of characters with names like *Fear* and *Vengeance* actually conforms to Johnson's conservative strictures:

> To exalt causes into agents, to invest abstract ideas with form, and animate them with activity has always been the right of poetry. But such airy beings are for the most part suffered only to do their natural office, and retire. Thus Fame tells a tale and Victory hovers over a general or perches on a standard; but Fame and Victory can do no more. To give them any real employment or ascribe to them any material agency is to make them allegorical no longer, but to shock the mind by ascribing effects to nonentity.[11]

Johnson goes on to complain about Milton's Sin and Death: they should not build a bridge, since immaterial agencies cannot cause material effects. Unlike Sin and Death, Collins's character Fear in "The Passions," startled by the sound he himself has made, and the more complexly realized equivalent figure of the "Ode to Fear," both causing and suffering terror, meet Johnson's standards: the actions of the character interpret the abstraction he represents. Collins's strongest personifications convey power beyond their functions of explanation and emphasis, but they do not pass the boundaries of those "traditional values" which Hartman opposes to Collins's.

The best personifications create their effects by evocative physical or emotional detail. Collins's odes, however, also contain beings whose nature receives virtually no specification: "Young *Fancy*," for example, from "Ode on the Poetical Character," the subject of a good deal of recent discussion. She gives to chosen poets the magic girdle of poetic sanctity; she offers "Visions wild" and a vaguely inspirational "Flame" (22); she retires with the presiding deity of the poem to his sapphire throne; and, along with "Heav'n" (18), she finally overturns the inspiring bowers of the poet's Eden. She has no physical reality, and her functions remain at least partially obscure. In 1797 Laetitia Barbauld said of this mysterious retirement with God that the allegory was "neither luminous nor decent."[12] Subsequent commentators have by and large pursued the question of decency but ignored that of luminosity, which, with its implication of revelatory force as well as of clarity, is in fact an important issue. Mrs. Barbauld presumably means that it is difficult to figure out what happens in the epode of Collins's ode. That difficulty—which in various forms pervades the entire poem—only encourages twentieth-century critical inventiveness. The critics declare their certainty ever more emphatically as they confront Collins's uncertainty. Thus Weiskel, on a single page about the epode (p. 128), uses the locutions "clearly," "of course," "surely," and "pretty clearly," and he concludes, in an impatient outburst, "If this doesn't suggest sexual union I don't know what does." He protests too much: almost nothing in Collins's text is clear or sure or a matter of course, and little seems even "pretty clear." Luminosity, however, no longer implies an accepted critical standard; its opposite, obscurity, attracts far more attention. Obscurity suggests "depth," "complexity"; on the grounds largely of his obscurity, it seems, Collins claims the epithet of "visionary."

Compared with the personifications of his eighteenth-century predecessors and contemporaries, Collins's imagined figures, despite their elaborative detail, rarely manifest the kind of energy one would expect to find associated with terms like "visionary" and "demonic." In the "Ode to Fear," for instance, "Danger" inhabits an unusual setting and is "hideous":

> *Danger,* whose Limbs of Giant Mold
> What mortal Eye can fix'd behold?
> Who stalks his Round, an hideous Form,
> Howling amidst the Midnight Storm,
> Or throws him on the ridgy Steep
> Of some loose hanging Rock to sleep.
> (10-15)

I find him less scary than a more economically rendered group of personifications created by the young Pope in *Windsor-Forest:*

> Gigantick *Pride,* pale *Terror,* gloomy *Care,*
> And mad *Ambition,* shall attend her there:
> There purple *Vengeance* bath'd in Gore retires,
> Her Weapons blunted, and extinct her Fires:
> There hateful *Envy* her own Snakes shall feel,
> And *Persecution* mourn her broken Wheel:
> There *Faction* roar, *Rebellion* bite her Chain,
> And gasping Furies thirst for Blood in vain.
> (415-22)[13]

Drawing on an established iconographic tradition, Pope adapts it to his immediate poetic needs with brilliant selectivity: Envy stung by her own snakes, Rebellion biting her chain, Faction's roaring converted to an emblem of futility. In contrast, Collins's multiplication of actions sounds shrill, overinsistent. Unlike Pope, he sounds as though he does not quite know what he is doing.

Obscurity and confusion are not poetic virtues. A poet's insistence that his personifications are frightening does not make them so. Collins's determination to populate his odes with abstractions—some of them quite unrealized as poetic beings—does not constitute a triumph of poetic imagination, an escape from the constrictions of his age;

on occasion these abstractions (Fancy, for instance) testify to imaginative failure or confusion. On the other hand, Collins has his own more modest virtues. The project he pursues links him with his non-Romantic contemporaries—not only Gray and Smart, concerned like him with the conundrum of what modern poetry can do, but Johnson and Reynolds and Young, concerned like him with the nature and implications of human limits.

The shape of Collins's preoccupations begins to emerge through a closer look at a personification mentioned earlier, Observance, from "The Manners." Collins's poem appeared in his collection of *Odes* in 1747. Two years later, Samuel Johnson published *The Vanity of Human Wishes,* which opens,

> Let observation with extensive view,
> Survey mankind, from China to Peru;
> Remark each anxious toil, each eager strife,
> And watch the busy scenes of crouded life;
> Then say. . . .
> (1-5)[14]

Collins invokes "Observance" in these terms:

> O Thou, who lov'st that ampler Range,
> Where Life's wide Prospects round thee change,
>
>   . . . . .
>
> To me in Converse sweet impart,
> To read in Man the native Heart,
> To learn, where Science sure is found,
> From Nature as she lives around. . . .
> (21-28)

Although Observance's view proves intensive as well as extensive, his first attributed quality emphasizes his "Range." He looks about as well as within; like Observation, he both *sees* and *says* ("Converse sweet"), and he too teaches his invoker, supplying skills rather than knowledge of human experience. Collins's shorter couplets lack the weight and tension of Johnson's, but his reliance on a personification devoid of pictorial reality to distance the speaker from his own concerns and to authorize a project of psychological and social investigation foretells the technique of Johnson's poem. A phrase like "Converse sweet"—utterly un-Johnsonian—reveals that Collins interests himself also in immediate feelings; but he embeds references to emotion in an insistently generalized context.

Unlike *The Vanity of Human Wishes,* "The Manners" imagines earthly possibilities beyond futility. It *imagines* rather than *discovers* them. Despite his invocation of Observance, the speaker (unlike Johnson's persona) observes nothing. He conjures up further personifications: the Manners, uncharacterized; Humour and Wit, evoked mainly through their apparel; finally Nature, the object of another elaborate invocation drawing on many literary references. Nature, whose personified form possesses not even specified gender, provides the alleged source of "Each forceful Thought, each prompted Deed" (72) and, apparently, the origins of feeling as well. The ode concludes with the speaker's expressed desire "To rove thy Scene-full World with Thee!" (78).

Before the end of the poem, in short, Collins moves far from Johnson in his articulated concerns. But only the preoccupation he shares with Johnson, the belief in the value of observation, emerges with clarity. The confusion of the rest, when compared with Johnson's certainty and authority, becomes vivid. The speaker in "The Manners" does not know what he wants most, or even whether he values primarily the human or the literary. His desire to rove a "Scene-full World" seems a pallid substitute for experience. The problem of "scene," which does not exist for Johnson, often preoccupies Collins. "Scene" is a problem, and "self," and the relation of the one to the other. Johnson, still convinced of poetry's didactic function, subordinates self and scene alike to moral purpose. Collins, unable to commit himself to either a didactic or an expressive theory of poetry, remains uncertain also about poetry's appropriate subject matter.

The word *Scene* occurs crucially in another Collins poem, the "Ode on the Poetical Character," which concludes, after an evocation of Milton's Eden,

> And Heav'n, and *Fancy,* kindred Pow'rs,
> Have now o'erturn'd th' inspiring Bow'rs,
> Or curtain'd close such Scene from ev'ry future
>   View.
> (74-76)

Critics have pondered the role of Heaven and Fancy in this resolution. Sherwin, for instance: "The kindred powers of Heaven and Fancy—yet surely not Collins' kindred—have overturned the inspiring bower of Milton's mountain paradise, and he finds himself in a heaven-deserted age in which he must descend to the middle ground of the toiling moderns" (p. 88). Or Fry: "Why should Fancy wish to assist in her own disabling? . . . [Perhaps because] she is secretly a guardian and not a pioneer of psychological borderlands, a timid sorceress of vocal presence who fears her own calling and finally refuses to invoke beings whose response she dreads. Even the creative imagination itself, Collins must finally admit, screens its own workings from consciousness" (p. 109).

The "heaven-deserted age," "the middle ground of the toiling moderns," even the idea of fancy's "disabling"—these comprise extrapolations from the text. The poem actually says, not that Heaven and Fancy have abandoned the poet, but that they have destroyed or concealed one particular "Scene," exemplified by Eden. Milton lolls beneath a tree in this particular Eden, but the final lines do not affirm that no one can live there now. No one can any longer be *inspired* by this setting, or no one can *view* it: the lines state only these equivalent possibilities.

One must ask why Heaven and Fancy have acted thus, and the answer, since the poem itself supplies none, will depend on individual predilection. The possibility of a relatively benign interpretation exists among others. Perhaps Heaven and Fancy have not unaccountably reversed their usual functions; perhaps they have only altered the available sources of poetic inspiration. If the poet can no longer see this particular scene, he must look elsewhere: not to religion (the metaphorical Eden) or to the external world (the literal garden, the "Scene-full World"); possibly to the life within?

The question mark belongs tonally to Collins himself. The "Ode on the Poetical Character" does not resolve its implicit question about the source of contemporary inspiration, nor did Collins ever find a satisfactory answer. Inspiration and subject matter are virtually identical, in the final lines of "Ode on the Poetical Character," and Collins's problems about subject plague him to the end of his career. His apparent inability to commit himself to his intimations of possibility helps to account for the flabbiness of his weakest work. He backs away from what he has to say.

Perhaps poetic unsuccess only seems from outside like lack of courage. Collins may have suffered not failure of daring but failure of perception or of intellect as he explored the problem peculiar to his era, that of the extent and limits of the self's prerogatives. The boundaries of justifiable entitlement presented both a personal and a poetic dilemma. What am "I" allowed to do (roam the scene-full world, attend to my own feelings, concern myself with my country or my friends)? What can I write about? How do my public obligations as poet relate to my private impulses? Do my feelings impede or energize my verse? Wordsworth would write the poetry of the "egotistical sublime"; Collins, true to his moment in history, understood egotism as a difficulty: not something to be suppressed, necessarily, but something to be investigated. Just over half a century after his *Odes,* the literary world would fully discover the self as subject. We still live with that discovery and its consequences; Collins did not. His poetry asks questions which it provisionally and repetitiously answers; the answers amount to a late-Augustan compromise. The questioning itself generates much of the interest of Collins's poetry.

In the year of Collins's death, Edward Young, an old man, published *Conjectures on Original Composition.* A decade later, in a series of lectures delivered at the Royal Academy, Sir Joshua Reynolds insisted on the value of imitation and deprecated the notion of originality. Both men, unlike each other and unlike Collins in all obvious respects, dwell on versions of the question that preoccupies the poet: the rights of the creative self, the value of indulging it. The debate over originality only slightly disguises these issues. To go even farther afield, Fanny Burney's famous "shyness," her concern over what the role of author means to a female, transposes the same questions into a more modest mode; her character Evelina, silent in public, voluble on paper, struggles with similar issues. In another key, Dr. Johnson's musings in *The Rambler* and his agonized self-appraisals in his prayers and meditations also ponder the proper limits of the self's claims. "Dive deep into thy bosom," Young exhorts,

> learn the depth, extent, bias, and full fort of thy mind; contract full intimacy with the stranger within thee; excite and cherish every spark of intellectual light and heat, however smothered under former negligence, or scattered through the dull, dark mass of common thoughts; and collecting them into a body, let thy genius rise (if a genius thou hast) as the sun from chaos.[15]

Reynolds, Burney, and Johnson, conscious of dangers in such self-concentration, draw on external systems of authority to bound individual presumption. Artistic tradition, social decorum, and Christian faith provide standards and strategies for judging and controlling the self.

Collins, unwilling to trust the stranger within him, finds that faith, reason, and decorum offer slender support. Lacking the structure of established religious or secular mythologies, he generates his own pantheon, but his relation to actualities beyond himself remains uncomfortable. Much of his poetry consists of fantasy constructions which soothingly obscure literal facts of experience and perception. The "Scene-full World" contains possibilities more distressing than the gallery of florid figures like *"Vengeance"* ("Ode to Fear," 20), the *"Fiend of Nature"* ("Ode to Mercy," 15), or *Britannia*'s Genius" ("stain'd with Blood he strives to tear / Unseemly from his Seagreen Hair / The Wreaths of chearful *May*" ["Ode, to a Lady on the Death of Colonel Ross," 2, 4-6]). From time to time, the poetry affords a glimpse of what it largely suppresses. Thus, Collins's fourth eclogue, after describing Circassian maids with "Their Eyes' blue languish, and their golden Hair" (56), announces with alarming specificity, "Those Hairs the *Tartar*'s cruel Hand shall rend" (58)—a detail inadequately contained by the eclogue's careful Popean couplets. Such a line suggests why Collins relies so heavily on vagueness.

In the background is the horror of death. Johnson suffered over the idea of being sent to hell and damned everlastingly; Collins returns insistently to death's physical realities. He indeed has something to fear besides Milton and himself. In "Ode, to a Lady on the Death of Colonel Ross," where "ev'ry Sod . . . wraps the Dead" (41), the poet invokes a typical supporting cast: ghostly dead warriors, personified Freedom lying on the grass ("Her matted Tresses madly spread" [40]), "Imperial *Honor*'s awful Hand" (23), "Aërial Forms" (20). Then he acknowledges the possibility that "These pictur'd Glories" (50) may prove inadequate to soothe the survivor's grief for the dead man: "in Sorrow's distant Eye, / Expos'd and pale thou see'st him lie" (52-53). "Sorrow" sees an exposed corpse, not a set of fantasy figures. In "Ode Occasion'd by the Death of Mr. Thomson," a dead poet inhabits an "Earthy Bed" (21); neither dirges nor the tears of Love and Pity will do him any good, hidden as he is beneath the "cold Turf" (32). In "Ode on the Popular Superstitions of the Highlands of Scotland," a "luckless Swain" (104), drowned, becomes "a Pale and breathless Corse" (12), appearing to his sleeping wife with "blue swoln face" (131). (She shudders at the sight [130].) Collins confronts his own difficulty with such physical facts most directly in "Ode, Written in the beginning of the Year 1746," one of his best poems, which juxtaposes the "Mold," "Sod," and "Clay" of the dead soldiers with another troop of fanciful personages (Spring, Honour, Freedom, "Fairy Hands," "Forms unseen") to declare the superiority of truth, even the truth of death, over fancy. When Spring returns to deck the graves, the poem alleges, "She there shall dress a sweeter Sod, / Than *Fancy*'s Feet have ever trod" (5-6). Yet the second stanza, a series of personifications, dramatizes the need for fancy as the only defense against death. Like many of Collins's poems, this one struggles with its own indeterminate subject, to declare both the value of truth and the poet's compulsion to decorate intolerable fact with created figures.

The implications of this short poem summarize important aspects of Collins's theme. The *feeling* self, facing the fact of death, can do nothing. The *poetic* self can invent, decorate, imagine, create; as result, it distances painful reality. Dirges, like tears, do not help the dead, but they support survivors. Poems make pictures providing alternatives for fact. Poetry, in other words, does not imitate life, but neither does it openly express the feelings of the poet. It finds appropriate modes of disguise; its remoteness from external reality gives it value.

Read in the context of such a poetic program, the "Ode to Fear" assumes a rather different aspect. Full of "hobgoblinry," to appropriate Fry's term, it makes a point of its own factitiousness. As the opening lines insist, Fancy generates fear, which responds to "th' unreal Scene" (Collins's favorite kind of scene after all) only when Fancy lifts the veil obscuring it (3-4). The speaker's identification with his own personification ("Like Thee I start, like Thee disorder'd fly" [8]) consists mainly in his shared ability to create by fancy the unreal scene and then to respond to it. But Fancy also generates real emotional dangers: the threat of captivation by one's own fantasies ("Who, *Fear*, this ghastly Train can see, / And look not madly wild, like Thee?" [24-25]). The Greek tragic dramatists suggest a safe way of enjoying such emotion: through the role of reader, in which one can experience without penalty the "throbbing Heart" (42) of terror. The antistrophe, however, acknowledges that the world contains real causes for fear: rape, murder, the cries of drowning seamen—a sinister and disturbing set of evocations. With renewed ardency, therefore, an ardency of submission, the speaker returns to the position of reader, which alone protects him from an emotional reality he dreads. He will suspend disbelief in "each strange Tale" (57) he encounters, and he will avoid testing the authenticity of fearful legend. He begs Fear to teach him to "feel" like Shakespeare (69), able to imagine himself embracing at least this safely mediated form of terror, again the product of Fancy.

The "plot" of this poem resembles that of "Ode, Written in the beginning of the Year 1746" in its opposition between intolerable actuality—rape, murder, and the like— and necessary fancy. But fancy's necessity for Collins bears little relation to its urgency for Coleridge or Keats. Fancy implies a retreat from the "Scene-full World" which Collins desires but can neither inhabit nor interpret; "th' unreal Scene," more controllable, is thus safer.

"Ode on the Popular Superstitions of the Highlands of Scotland," Collins's last poem, which he did not complete, adumbrates a solution to the problem of self and scene: an Augustan reconciliation. Exploring what the speaker calls "Scenes that oer my soul prevail" (204), it uses imagination as a substitute for possibly threatening experience. The poet conjures up the landscape and legendry that engender excitement; he in effect "gives" the scene to his Scottish friend John Home, to whom it belongs by a right Collins cannot himself assert. He thus disclaims the imaginative possession that he demonstrates, adapting a strategy of disguise and defense comparable to that in the "Ode to Fear." The rhetorical framework of the later poem, however, conveys new assurance. "Popular Superstitions" begins and ends with discussions not of legend but of friendship. Home, returning to Scotland, is urged not to forget "that cordial Youth" (5) whom he and Collins have known, and not to forget the "social Name" of the poet himself (10): "But think far-off how on the Southern coast / I met thy Friendship with an equal Flame!" (11-12). (The competitive note just hinted at here—"I'm as friendly as you are"—perhaps foretells the speaker's appropriation of his friend's subject.) The emotional bond between the two men justifies the Englishman in prescribing Home's itinerary and interests. More important, by the ode's end it has generated the speaker's authority. Some day he too may roam the glens and heaths of Scotland. "Mean time," he invokes the "Pow'rs" (215) of that realm to protect his friend: "To Him I lose, your kind protection lend / And *touch'd with Love, like Mine,* preserve my Absent Friend" (218-19; my italics). His own love has become the talisman, source and symbol of magic preservation; instead of yearning to participate in the energy of mysterious "Pow'rs," he invites them to partake of his own emotional vitality.

Like the group of conventional personifications (*"Fancy, Friendship, Science,* rose-lip'd *Health"*) that appear unexpectedly at the end of "Ode to Evening" (50), this allusion to the social context returns the poem to safe eighteenth-century ground. But it also returns the speaker to feelings he can boldly claim. Agreeable emotions of friendship, which sanctioned the poetic enterprise in the first place, promise stability of relationship. (Even in Home's absence, the friendship endures; indeed, it seems to strengthen in the course of the poet's musings on his friend's travels.) Providing a point of return from the more troubling feelings evoked by the thought of drowned countrymen or buried kings, the speaker's love for his friend, something within him that he can trust, authorizes his imaginative excursions through the scene-full world and guarantees his safe return. Pope ended his *Essay on Man* with the vision that "true SELF-LOVE and

SOCIAL are the same" (396). Collins resolves his perplexity about what kind of freedom he can allow himself as poet by dissolving his solitary self into a social self—a social *name,* verbal equivalent for a self. His alliance with Home provides an organizing center, a point of view to clarify the purpose of imaginative wandering; it reduces the problem of subject and the problem of self by generating a focus that justifies the poet's fanciful exploring of the Highlands and alleviates the danger of self-absorption. He can at least imagine dealing with the *real*—the actual Highlands landscape—without dwelling only on death. Deprived of Eden, the poet can also look within, reveal his feelings about that landscape—as long as he assures himself of his continuing connection with another, his anchor in the world without. The presence of *Friendship* among the "Ode to Evening" personifications gives it equivalent importance to *Fancy;* the "Popular Superstitions" ode clarifies that importance. Friendship too is a generative force.

In comparison with the flamboyant distress of a soul grappling with the demonic, the resolution of poems and of problems through reliance on calm friendship sounds unexciting. But some of Collins's best poems, in my view, indeed achieve this sort of stasis: "Ode, Written in the beginning of the Year 1746," "Ode to Evening," "Ode on the Popular Superstitions of the Highlands of Scotland." This is the "eighteenth-century Collins": a quieter figure than the Romantic poet to whom we have become accustomed—and, on occasion, a better poet.

I read Collins's poems as a series of questions about the possibility of self-authorization. Aware that the poetic resources of both Milton and Shakespeare have vanished, and finding religious faith inaccessible (his dead inhabit the cold earth, not heaven), Collins discovers little outside himself to value securely. His contemporaries speculate about comparable problems, but locate solutions in various kinds of communal authority: religion (Johnson combating the horror of death and the dangers of the ego, Smart identifying himself with the heroes of his mythology) or social tradition (Churchill, Goldsmith). "Poor Collins" rarely succeeds in his search. Eden lost, the scene-full world posited but rarely discovered, he tries to convert his inner life to the kind of generalization that might substitute for external sanctions without making excessive claims for the self; he reveals the problematics of self as subject. His personifications of emotion (Pity, Fear, the Passions, Mercy, etc.) distance him from his own feeling by claiming its universality (not *my* pity, mankind's), although the poems in which he embeds these figures insistently, often confusedly, examine his own relation to such generalizations. His resort to social feeling at the end of the "Superstitions" ode involves another kind of externalization, possibly more successful because less desperate. The poetic self, Collins repeatedly concludes, dares do nothing alone. It must submit— to Shakespeare, to the subject matter belonging to a Scot, to the generalizations of the culture. Thus mediated, thus protected, it may generate poetry.

Like Johnson, Collins intermittently suspects that all predominance of imagination over reason is a degree of insanity. Many of his poems are more interesting to talk about than to read because of their uncontrolled imaginative explosions: in summary the poems sound visionary and exciting, but they do not compose any coherent poetic fabric. (The "Ode on the Poetical Character" is a conspicuous case in point.) The criticism that glorifies such writing for its intimations of a new sensibility—minimizing its incoherence and constantly deflected purpose, or attributing them to the bad influence of eighteenth-century rationality—ignores Collins's occasional true, modest achievement: a verse of quiet, faintly melancholy compromise.

NOTES

[1] *Precious Bane: Collins and the Miltonic Legacy* (Austin: University of Texas Press, 1977), p. 51.

[2] *The Visionary Company: A Reading of English Romantic Poetry,* rev. ed. (Ithaca: Cornell University Press, 1971), p. 14.

[3] Geoffrey H. Hartman, *The Fate of Reading and Other Essays* (Chicago: University of Chicago Press, 1975), p. 167.

[4] Thomas Weiskel, *The Romantic Sublime: Studies in the Structure and Psychology of Transcendence* (Baltimore: Johns Hopkins University Press, 1976), e.g., pp. 116, 118, 132; Paul H. Fry, *The Poet's Calling in the English Ode* (New Haven: Yale University Press, 1980), p. 103.

[5] Geoffrey H. Hartman, *Beyond Formalism: Literary Essays, 1958-1970* (New Haven: Yale University Press, 1970), pp. 325, 331; Weiskel, p. 132; Sherwin, e.g., pp. 57, 67, 103; Fry, pp. 124-25.

[6] *The Anxiety of Influence: A Theory of Poetry* (New York: Oxford University Press, 1973), p. 111.

[7] Cf. Hartman: "For Wordsworth personification may be trivial, but it is not innocent. Collins had restored the psychological and ritual link between it and the demonic persona" (*Beyond Formalism.* p. 331).

[8] "The Manners. An Ode," lines 25-26, in *The Works of William Collins,* ed. Richard Wendorf and Charles Ryskamp (Oxford: Clarendon Press, 1979). Subsequent quotations from Collins are taken from this edition.

[9] Gray to Thomas Wharton, 27 December 1746, *Correspondence of Thomas Gray,* ed. Paget Toynbee and Leonard Whibley, 3 vols. (Oxford: Clarendon Press, 1935), I, 261.

[10] Minneapolis: University of Minnesota Press, 1981.

[11] *Lives of the English Poets,* ed. George Birkbeck Hill, 3 vols. (Oxford: Clarendon Press, 1905), I, 185.

[12] *The Poetical Works of William Collins,* with a prefatory essay by Mrs. Laetitia Barbauld (London, 1797), p. xxiii.

[13] *Pastoral Poetry and An Essay on Criticism,* ed. E. Audra and Aubrey Williams, Twickenham Edition of the Poems of Alexander Pope, I (New Haven: Yale University Press, 1961).

[14] *The Poems of Samuel Johnson,* ed. David Nichol Smith and Edward L. McAdam (Oxford: Clarendon Press, 1941).

[15] *Edward Young's Conjectures on Original Composition,* ed. Edith J. Morley (London: Longmans, Green, 1918), p. 24.

W. P. Albrecht

SOURCE: "Hazlitt's 'On the Fear of Death': Reason Versus Imagination," in *Wordsworth Circle,* Vol. 15, No. 1, Winter, 1984, pp. 3-7.

[*In the following essay, Albrecht examines the dialectic of reason versus imagination that characterizes William Hazlitt's "On the Fear of Death," in which he concludes that fear of death can best be allayed by setting "a just value on life."*]

In February, 1822, Hazlitt had come to Scotland for a divorce in hope of marrying Sarah Walker. While staying at the Renton Inn, Berwickshire, he wrote eleven essays intended for the second volume of *Table-Talk.* Early in March, in a letter to P.G. Patmore, he listed the essays, nine already written and two more soon to be completed. He also told Patmore that this work had been done "magnificently."[1] We can agree, I think, that Hazlitt had reason to be well satisfied. P.P. Howe calls "the month at Renton . . . a month of hope."[2] But this was hope susceptible to bitter moods.

The seventh and least hopeful of the eleven essays is the one that closes Volume II of *Table-Talk,* "On the Fear of Death." An immediate and principal cause of Hazlitt's unhappiness was an unresponsive Sarah Walker. In fact, a passage deleted from the essay calls on "some creature"—clearly Sarah—for assurance of love lest "I . . . stagger into my grave . . . old before my time, unloved and unlovely. . . . "[3] But Hazlitt had other reasons for his gloom. His income was, as usual, precarious; and, as he reported to his son in "On the Conduct of Life" (another Renton essay), he feared that he might not live much longer (17.86). He underestimated the time he still had ahead of him, but he was already suffering from the "habitual indigestion" (probably cancer) that harassed him until he died of it in 1830 (12.354).[4] Furthermore, his emotions had never recovered from Napoleon's defeat at Waterloo. "My final hopes of happiness, and of human liberty," he wrote in "On Patronage and Puffing" (also of the Renton period), "were blighted . . . ; and since then

I have had no pleasure in any thing . . ." (8.292). This is an obvious exaggeration, but throughout his life Napoleon's downfall and its aftermath, in England as well as France, made recurrent contributions to Hazlitt's moods.

Hazlitt considered events in post-war England to have been as damaging to human rights as the restoration of the Bourbons. Hard times had provoked the landowners to enact sterner Poor Laws, and rioting for bread had incited brutal suppression. Hazlitt blamed not only the arbitrary power of the ruling class but also liberal reformers concerned too much with "dry formalities" and too little with "liberty and humanity" (11.129). In fact, he came to identify "the science of Political Economy" with "the *divine right* of landlords" (19.291). From his earliest to his last essays, Hazlitt attacked liberal political philosophy as "abstraction" that equates morality with self-serving calculation.

It is a measure of his despair that, for his argument in "On the Fear of Death," Hazlitt accepts the premises of what he called "the material, or *modern,* philosophy" (2.113). The assumption that man necessarily seeks pleasure and avoids pain underlies early nineteenth-century liberalism. On this assumption liberal writers such as Malthus, the Mills, John Austin, and, most elaborately, Bentham erected closely argued moral, legal, and political structures. Self-interest and reason emerged as the primary realities binding human beings together and self-preservation as the motive articulating civil society. Yet, as Eldon J. Eisenach has shown, such liberal writers as Hobbes, Locke, and J.S. Mill also recognized a higher authority than reason which, although acknowledging the freedom to act in one's self-interest, frees one from the necessity of doing so. This higher authority was variously defined as religion, public opinion, habit, imagination, sympathy, or history, or as some combination thereof. These writers believed that only through the force of such authority, represented by at least a few citizens, can a liberal political order be achieved and preserved.[5]

It is the first of these "two worlds of liberalism"—to use Eisenach's terms—that Hazlitt quarreled with. Like Hobbes, Locke, and Mill, Hazlitt thought selfish calculation useful in "limiting individual rights in society"; but also like Hobbes, Locke, and Mill he recognized a higher authority needed to put a true value on life and to sustain our moral and political obligations (19.303-304; 7.270). Morality requires "disinterestedness," or "benevolence." We become "disinterested" when imagination, stirred by sympathetic emotion, "creates" an idea of another's good that overrules the impulses of self-love. Habitual sympathy enhances this responsiveness; habitual selfishness checks it (1.1, 9-16, 26-38; 2.231; 20.162-80). For Hazlitt, then, the principal authority higher than reason is the *imagination,* strengthened by *habit.* But *history,* too, in testifying to "some degree of benevolence amongst men" independent of self-love, becomes for Hazlitt an authority transcending reason (2.224).[6]

Yet in "On the Fear of Death" Hazlitt places his argument within the first world of liberalism. The two worlds offer differing views of death. In the first, since reason leaves no room for supernatural religion or faith in an afterlife, the self, however cherished, must at last dissolve into eternal nothingness. In a world of some higher authority than reason, however, self-preservation is less urgent and death less fearsome. On the one hand, religion may hold out the prospect of life after death. On the other, life itself may offer rewards that allay the fear of death. The loss of self in serving others may make its ultimate extinction appear less dreadful. Those "more capable of deriving happiness from unselfish sources," wrote J.S. Mill, "will care less and less for . . . [the] flattering expectation" of eternal life.[7] Or, other incentives—such as those prompting the soldier, the mountain climber, or the criminal—may outweigh the risk of life and safety. Arguing in *The Edinburgh Review* for July, 1821, that capital punishment does not deter crime, Hazlitt had pointed out "the nature of passion to be blind to mere consequences" or, through habit, to "harden itself" against them. (19.244-45). Nevertheless, in "On the Fear of Death" it is "a *rational* cure . . . for the inordinate fear of death" that Hazlitt proposes (8.330; my italics). Having accepted the primacy of self-preservation as a human motive, he attacks it rationally, suppressing the imagination and abstracting almost as egregiously as he accuses Bentham of doing (11.8-9, 14-15). Countering the abstractions of logical argument, however, are the excursions of Hazlitt's imagination. Hence, a dialectic of reason versus imagination develops and runs through the four parts of the essay. The rational cure for the fear of death, although Hazlitt insists on it to the end, is qualified by implicit recognition of a higher authority than reason.

To abstract the concerns of life from the idea of death, Hazlitt begins "On the Fear of Death" with an analogy to prenatal non-existence: "Perhaps the best cure for the fear of death is to reflect that life has a beginning as well as an end. There was a time when we were not: this gives us no concern—why then should it trouble us that a time will come when we shall cease to be?" (8.321-22). Hazlitt continues cheerfully: "When Bickerstaff wrote his Essays . . . when Garrick was in his glory, and Reynolds was over head and ears with his portraits, . . . it was without consulting me: the debates . . . on the American war, or the firing at Bunker's Hill, disturbed not me: yet I thought this no evil . . . : I had not then looked out into this breathing world, yet I was well . . . To die is only to be as we were before we were born, . . . [when] we had lain . . . snug, out of harm's way; . . . at peace and free from care. . . . " (8.322). Hazlitt has sliced out a portion of nonexistence and labeled it good. "I neither ate, drank, nor was I merry, yet I did not complain . . ." (8.322). He becomes less light-hearted, however, as his imagination probes the life that death puts an end to. "The worst that we dread is, after a short, fretful, feverish being, after vain hopes, and idle fears, to sink to final repose again, and forget the troubled dream of life!" (8.322). Declarative sentences with short independent clauses give way to questioning in more complicated structures rich in alliteration; brisk colloquialism yields to formality; the pronouns "I" and "we" are replaced by the poetic "ye" and "thou":

> Ye armed men, knights templars, that sleep in the stone aisles of that old Temple Church . . . are ye not contented where ye lie? Or would you come out of your long homes to go to the Holy War? Or do ye complain that pain no longer visits you, . . . that you hear no more of the thickening phalanx of the foe, or your lady's waning love; . . . that . . . no sound shall ever pierce through to disturb your lasting repose, fixed as marble over your tombs, breathless as the grave that holds you! And thou, oh! thou, to whom my heart turns, . . . who didst love in vain . . . wilt not thou too rest in peace (or wilt thou cry to me complaining from thy clay-cold bed) when that sad heart is no longer sad, and that sorrow is dead which thou wert only called into the world to feel! (8.322-23)

(The reference to the dead mistress, according to Howe's note, "is elusive" [8.373n]. It was Hazlitt who "loved in vain.") Clearly death is not just like prenatal non-existence, for death is preceded by life and takes its coloring from life's hopes and fears. The knight's grave is "breathless" only because the body deposited there once breathed—was once part of that "breathing world" for which it exchanged non-existence. Ostensibly illustrating the painlessness of death, the knight and the lovelorn lady now suggest life choked off by death, asserting even from the grave the claims of the living.

" . . . There is nothing in the idea of a pre-existent state," Hazlitt must grant, that "excites our longing like the prospect of a posthumous existence." Or nothing that excites fear like the prospect of losing our beloved self. As the principal reason for fearing death, Hazlitt selects "an habitual attachment" to self—"an inveterate prejudice in favour of our immediate existence" (8.323-24). To make the ultimate extinction of self less fearsome, Hazlitt cannot turn to a higher authority than reason, for the rational context of his argument has suppressed such authority. He has only one course left, and that is to put reason on the side of death, not life. That is, he must represent the self as not worth preserving. To minimize the pain of loss that we project into the idea of death, he must minimize what we have to lose. It is impossible, of course, to form an idea of our own death untouched by imagination; we always find ourselves, as Freud wrote, "present as spectators."[8] But by reducing the imagination's contribution to life, Hazlitt can reduce its projections on death.

"No young man," to be sure, "ever thinks that he shall die," but what once seemed far away is soon at hand. Soon our "pleasures . . . have worn themselves out," and our "pains . . . have worn us out." We have no wish to live our lives over. "Once is enough. As the tree falls, so let it lie. We shut up the book and close the account once for all!" (8.324-25) Yet crisp certainty gives way to doubt. Once more we find the image of life choked off by death: life has been compared to "exploring of a passage that grows narrower and darker . . . and where we are stifled for want of breath at last" (8.325)[9]. Sentence

structure has become more elaborate, and now the pronouns change from first person plural to first person singular. At one time "I felt" more strongly "the greater thickness of the atmosphere"; it "seemed to suppress a thousand rising hopes. . . ." Now "I feel a thinness and want of support, I stretch out my hand to some object and find none, I am too much in a world of abstraction; the naked map of life is spread out before me, and in the emptiness and desolation I see Death coming to meet me. In my youth I could not behold him for the crowd of objects and feelings, and Hope stood always between us . . ." (8.325). In Hazlitt's world of abstraction, objects have lost the reality that only imagination, stimulated by emotion, can give them. Of course, to describe this world Hazlitt uses images and metaphors, such as "the shadows of age," "a dank, cold mist encircling all objects," and "dim, twilight existence" (8.325-26); but these images have been deadened by what Coleridge calls "the logic of grammar" rather than charged with "passion, the universal logic."[10] As in Coleridge's "Work without Hope," it is "thought," not passion, that in the abstracting mind "becomes image."[11] And thought offers "no inducement to look forward" or "interest in looking back to what has become so trite and common" (8.325). Without imagination both the world in Coleridge's poem and Hazlitt's world of abstraction are curtained off from hope.

Premising that self is paramount, the first world of liberalism limits passion to self-concern and ultimately, therefore, must offer only images of loss. A loss, which suddenly, Hazlitt finds intolerable: "If I had lived *indeed,* I should not care to die. But I do not like a contract of pleasure broken off unfulfilled. . . . My public and private hopes have been left a ruin, or remain only to mock me. I should wish them to be re-edified. I should like to see some prospect of good to mankind, such as my life began with. I should like to leave some sterling work behind me. . . . I have thought and suffered too much to be willing to have thought and suffered in vain" (8.325-26). Once more, as in the earlier passage on the dead knights and sorrowful lady, Hazlitt has allowed the train of association to challenge his argument for painless death. Once more, on the idea of death imagination has projected the claims of life; and death, not so abstract now, is more fearsome. Nevertheless, Hazlitt's wish to have his hopes "re-edified" is short-lived. His momentary waking from his "dim, twilight existence" has come too late. " . . . I had better return to my bookish chimeras and indolence once more!" (8.326) At this point the dialectic between imagination and reason—assertive identity and acceptance of death—subsides in resignation. "As our strength and beauty die, as our hopes and passions, our friends and our affections leave us, we begin by degrees to feel ourselves mortal!" (8.326)

There are still other imaginative projections that Hazlitt must suppress. The very sight of death is fearsome: "I have never seen death but once, and that was in an infant" (8.326). The infant was probably Hazlitt's son John, who died in 1816 while still less than a year old.[12] "It was not like death, but more like an image of life!"

(8.326) Viewing the dead child, Hazlitt becomes a spectator at his own death. Again the fear of breathlessness overtakes him. The child "seemed to smile at the short pang of life which was over; but I could not bear the coffin-lid to be closed—it almost stifled me; and still as the nettles wave in a corner of the churchyard over his little grave, the welcome breeze helps to refresh me and ease the tightness at my breast!" (8.326) But it is the *nettles* that Hazlitt remembers waving over the grave, their sting aired out perhaps, but still redolent of pain.

Thus the third part of the essay reverses the order in each of the first two parts. Here Hazlitt has begun (in the first person singular) with imaginative projections on death which (in the more general first person plural) he proceeds to strip away. The trouble, Hazlitt continues, is that we make death fearsome by "mixing up the idea of life with it" (8.327). Hazlitt would unmix these elements. We view an ivory or marble image—like Chantry's *Sleeping Children* in Lichfield Cathedral—"with pure delight," never fretting that it is not alive or fancying "that it has a shortness of breath," because "it never was alive" (8.326). Despite any comfort that religion, with its promise of life after death, may offer, we generally make death a "ghastly monster" by imagining "how we should feel, not how the dead feel" (8.327). Nor need we worry that others will greatly mourn our own passing. "The pathetic exhortation on country tombstones, 'Grieve not for me, my wife and children dear,' &c. is for the most part speedily followed to the letter." (8.327). Like Hazlitt's identification with the dead child, our concern that others will suffer from our death is only a projection of self-importance. "While we were living, the world seemed in a manner to exist only for us. . . . But our hearts cease to beat, and it goes on as usual, and thinks no more about us than it did in our lifetime" (8.327). Once more Hazlitt has resolved the imagination-reason dialectic in favor of reason. To be sure, he has not rid death entirely of self-projection. He still "mixes up the idea of life" with death, but what remains is the pessimistic, abstracted view of life with which age readies itself to die.

This view of life without hope does, indeed, cure the fear of death; but it is not a view that Hazlitt—in 1822, or at any later time—could sustain. Although gloom and illness continued to beset him, he did not succumb to a "world of abstraction" void of hope. When he wrote "On the Fear of Death," he was still in his forty-fourth year, with eight years of life remaining and almost half his collected works yet to be written. He did not give up his wish "to leave some sterling work behind [him]." His later books include what is probably his masterpiece, *The Spirit of the Age* (1825), and his intended masterpiece, the *Life of Napoleon* (1828-30). His political hopes might fade, but they could brighten. In his sickroom, the month before his death, he wrote: "The Revolution of the Three Days [July 27-29, 1830] was like a resurrection from the dead, and showed plainly that liberty too has a spirit of life in it . . ." (19.334n). Politically he remained an emphatic radical, attacking, on the one hand, the "monster, Legitimacy" and, on the other, political economy (12.136;

19.291). He continued to find the abstractions of the modern philosophy morally and politically irresponsible.

Even in "On the Fear of Death," particularly in the fourth and final part, Hazlitt questions the values of the modern philosophy. In each of the first three parts, the play of imagination stays largely within the first world of liberalism; that is, it remains in the service of self, confined by the logic of self-preservation. By questioning Hazlitt's rational cure, it only increases the fear of death; it does not offer any alternative cure. In the closing part of the essay, however, Hazlitt turns from his own society, with its predilection for abstract reasoning, to an earlier age and a different, less rational cure for the fear of death. Reverting to a favorite theme, Hazlitt draws on history to support imagination as an authority over reason: the imagination thrived on the passions of that "comparatively barbarous" age when the greatest poets, painters, and sculptors flourished, but in modern times it has been checked by scientific inquiry and speculative thought (4.160-62. See also 5.46,82; 6.37-38). The resulting abstractions Hazlitt now identifies with those of the modern philosophy: "The effeminate clinging to life as such, as a general or abstract idea, is the effect of a highly civilised and artificial state of society. Men formerly plunged into all the vicissitudes and dangers of war, or staked their all upon a single die, or some one passion, which if they could not have gratified, life became a burthen to them—now our strongest passion is to think . . ." (8.328-29). This part of the essay, like the third part, has begun with imagination dominating the dialectic. In "old histories and romances . . . the heroes and heroines . . . go to death as to a bridal bed. . . . " Romeo and Juliet would pay any price to consummate their love; but "the instant . . . [Romeo] finds himself deprived of his Juliet," he wishes only to die, and Juliet eagerly follows him in death. "There is at least more of imagination in such a state of things, more vigour of feeling and promptitude to act than in our lingering, languid, protracted attachment to life for its own poor sake" (8.329). The old readiness to die must have owed something to "a spirit of martyrdom as well as . . . the reckless energy of barbarism." Undoubtedly it was bolstered by religious belief that "embodied something beyond . . . [this life] to the imagination." Thus "the rough soldier, the infatuated lover, the valorous knight, &c." were all readier "to take a leap into . . . futurity, which the modern sceptic shrinks back from, with all his boasted reason and vain philosophy, weaker than a woman!" (8.329)

For reassurance that death can be less fearsome, however, Hazlitt still does not turn to the imagination, for time has drained away its vigor. Hazlitt had some grounds, of course, for identifying his own hopelessness—and enfeebled imagination—with that of a society enmeshed in its own desires. At any rate, he offers consolation within the values of that society: to allay the fear of death, we need only realize that life becomes no longer worth living. Shifting from the third person of the imaginative past to the more reasonable "we" of modern society, Hazlitt concludes the essay: "The most rational cure after all for the inordinate fear of death is to set a just value on life. If we merely wish to continue on the scene to indulge our headstrong humours and tormenting passions, we had better begone at once: and if we only cherish a fondness for existence according to the benefits we reap from it, the pang we feel at parting with it will not be very severe!" (8.330) Self-indulgent passion—like Hazlitt's for Sarah Walker, presumably—comes to nothing, and we are left with only the faded prospect of life diminishing into death.

Hazlitt wrote an additional paragraph to conclude "On the Fear of Death." This cancelled paragraph was first printed by Hazlitt's son in his edition of *Table Talk* (1845-46). It supports Hazlitt's rational cure as it further describes the sort of death that age visits upon life: time "anticipates the work of Death" and leaves "him but half his spoils; for we die every moment of our lives. . . . We . . . have drunk up the cup of life, and have left only the lees. . . . We drag about a mockery of existence long after all the life of life is flown. It is the sense of self alone that makes death formidable, and that hinders us from perceiving that our fleeting existence is long ago lost in itself" (8.374).

Having noted that in "On the Fear of Death" reason and imagination produce "contrasting (and contradictory) attitudes to death," Stanley Jones adds that Hazlitt, "trapped in a suicidal infatuation with a girl half his age," was never more conscious than during his stay in Renton of "the gulf between . . . the illusory simplifications of logic, and the reality . . . encompassed by the imagination."[13] A considerable ingredient in the reality encompassed by Hazlitt's imagination must have been his hopeless love for Sarah. In "On the Fear of Death" he would console himself by suppressing the imagination and looking at hopelessness rationally: hopelessness is inevitable with age. Our hopes die sooner than our bodies, and before we know it we are left with only a mockery of life. The last flickerings of imagination are delusive; reason tells us that we have nothing more to expect from life or to fear in death. Yet no more than a few days after completing "On the Fear of Death," Hazlitt restored imagination to the high place he characteristically gives it. In the eleventh and last of the Renton essays (listed as "On Individuality" in the letter to Patmore but published, as Jones has shown, as "On Reason and Imagination" in *The Plain Speaker* [1826]),[14] Hazlitt asserts that "logical reason and practical truth are *disparates*" (12.46) and argues for the moral authority of imagination over reason.

The last days at Renton had leavened the mood of "On the Fear of Death" with hope. Hazlitt felt the elation shown both in the letter to Patmore—written two days before completion of the last Renton essay—and in a letter to Sarah no later than the next day (Jones, pp. 424-25): "Do you know I *have done my work*, or shall by Saturday?" (*Letters*, p. 242). The version of this letter in *Liber Amoris* adds: "a volume in less than a month. This is one reason why I am better than when I came, and another is, I have had two letters from Sarah" (9.113).

The cup of life, it seems, now had more left in it than the lees. And, embracing a particularity that the abstractions of despair had excluded, imagination could challenge the urgency of self. What at the beginning of "On Reason and Imagination" Hazlitt calls "geographical reasoning" (12.45) was very likely prompted, as Jones points out (p. 247), by Hazlitt's "naked map of life" metaphor in "On the Fear of Death." But now Hazlitt would disown "geographical reasoning." Without "the crowd of objects and feelings (8.325) that once supported his hopes—hopes not only for himself but for mankind—Hazlitt's "world of abstraction" in "On the Fear of Death" is ruled by reason, not imagination. Its emotional thinness borders on what, in "On Reason and Imagination," Hazlitt calls the "cold indifference" that inhibits moral thought and action (12.47). Morality requires the identification of oneself with others; and only particular "objects" can arouse "the warmth of passion" that kindles the sympathetic imagination (12.46): "If we are imbued with a deep sense of individual weal or woe, we shall be awe-struck at the idea of humanity in general. If we know little of it but its abstract and common properties, . . . we shall care just as little as we know either about the whole or the individuals" (12.55). Now, shortly after writing "On the Fear of Death," Hazlitt has reasserted the authority of imagination over reason and is firmly back in the second world of liberalism.

Of course, in "On the Fear of Death" Hazlitt had not completely forgotten that second world or the shortcomings of the modern philosophy. The dialectic of reason versus imagination is not fully resolved in favor of the former. If Hazlitt finally defers to the authority of reason, he also questions it. In the last part of the essay history supports imagination as the higher authority. We recognize a common denominator in that "highly civilised" state of society described by Hazlitt and his rational cure for the fear of death: both assume the primacy of self-interest among human motives, and neither calls on imagination to overrule self-serving reason. The contrast between the old "heroes and heroines" and the "modern sceptic," weak despite his "boasted reason," not only defines but also trivializes the values of modern society; and at the same time the "reckless energy" of all those barbarous lovers, soldiers, knights, and martyrs questions whether reason offers the best cure for the fear of death. Imagination persists in qualifying the abstractions of reason.

NOTES

[1] W.C. Hazlitt, *Memoirs of William Hazlitt*, 2 vols. (1867), II, 68; or *Letters of William Hazlitt*, ed. H. Sikes, W.H. Bonner, and G. Lahey (1978), p. 237. Stanley Jones dates the letter to Patmore March 5, and shows that Hazlitt wrote the eleven essays between February 11, and March 7, ("Hazlitt's Missing Essay 'On Individuality'," *RES*, n.s., 28 [1977], 423-26).

[2] *Life of William Hazlitt* (1949), pp. 340-41.

[3] An almost identical passage in *Liber Amoris* names the creature "S.L.," as Hazlitt frequently calls Sarah in this

book (*Complete Works of William Hazlitt,* ed. P.P. Howe [1930-34], 9.114). Other references to Hazlitt's writings will be to this edition. For the deleted passage, see Stewart Wilcox, "A Manuscript Addition to Hazlitt's Essay 'On the Fear of Death'," *MLN,* 55 (1940), 45-47. For bitter thoughts of Sarah in other Renton essays, see "On the Disadvantages of Intellectual Superiority" (8.288), "On the Knowledge of Character" (8.305, 309), "On Dreams" (12.23), and "On the Conduct of Life" (17.98, 395-96n).

[4]Howe, *Life,* pp. 319, 342, 392, 416; Herschel Baker, *William Hazlitt* (1962), pp. 467-68.

[5]*Two Worlds of Liberalism* (1981).

[6]Hazlitt is quoting Bishop Butler. See *Works of Joseph Butler,* ed. W.E. Gladstone (1896), II, 36-37n, 96n.

[7]"Utility of Religion," *Collected Works of John Stuart Mill,* eds. F.E.L. Priestley and J.M. Robson (1963-77), X, 426. See also Eisenach, pp. 5, 214, 217.

[8]"Thoughts for the Times on War and Death," *Standard Edition of the Complete Psychological Works of Sigmund Freud,* trans. J. Strachey et al., (1955), XIV, 289-90.

[9]Whereas for Keats the dark passages promised to disclose the "ballance of good and evil" (*Letters of John Keats 1814-1821,* ed. H.E. Rollins [1958], I, 281).

[10]*Miscellaneous Criticism,* ed. T.M. Raysor (1936), pp. 163-64.

[11]*Collected Letters of S. T. Coleridge,* ed. E.L. Griggs (1956-71), V, 415-16. See also Edward Kessler, *Coleridge's Metaphysics of Being* (1979), pp. 139-41.

[12]Hazlitt had lost another infant son, William, in 1809. See Howe, *Life,* pp. 135, 212; Baker, p. 170n.; Howe's note in *Complete Works,* 8.373.

[13]Jones, *op. cit.,* pp. 427-28.

[14]*Ibid.,* pp. 421-26.

Joseph M. Garrison, Jr.

SOURCE: "The Function of Terror in the Work of Edgar Allan Poe," in *American Quarterly,* Vol. XVIII, No. 2, Summer, 1966, pp. 136-50.

[*In the following essay, Garrison seeks to reconcile Poe's preoccupation with horror with his quest for "Supernal Beauty."*]

Critics who want to challenge Henry James' snobbish judgment that "an enthusiasm for Poe is the mark of a decidedly primitive stage of reflection"[1] should not assume that Poe's reputation as an American master is se-

cure. It is not; in fact the lack of interest in Poe's work among undergraduate and graduate students grimly predicts that Poe, like his General in "The Man That Was Used Up," may turn out to be nothing more than an "exceedingly odd looking bundle of something."[2] With rare exceptions, extant arguments for Poe's front-rank status are inadequate and unconvincing, in some cases frivolous.[3] No student of American literature with any sense of proportion would elevate Washington Irving to the first echelon (although according to official opinions he fathered American literature), but there are students of literary history who put Poe there because he devised the formula for the detective story, because he was a versatile craftsman, because he anticipated some of Einstein's theories or because he influenced a bevy of Frenchmen.[4]

Such clumsy attempts at canonization simply do not rescue Poe from the strictures of hostile criticism—Yvor Winters', for instance—and until such criticisms are successfully refuted, or at least substantially qualified, they will continue to enjoy the influential currency which Winters' accusation has had:

> Poe's aesthetic is an aesthetic of obscurantism. We have that willful dislocation of feeling from understanding, which, growing out of the uncertainty regarding the nature of moral truth in general and its identity in particular situations which produced such writers as Hawthorne and James, was later to result through the exploitation of special techniques in the violent aberrations of the Experimental School of the twentieth century, culminating in the catastrophe of Hart Crane.[5]

This "heretical" judgment consigns Poe to obscurity on the grounds that his work lacks fundamental consistency and clarity of aim. If Winters is right, then Poe should surely meet with the fate which purposelessness deserves. But if he is wrong, it is the function of criticism at the present time—to use Arnold's apt phrase—to discover artistic integrity in Poe's work and thereby provide at least one substantial basis for an evaluation of his standing as a major American writer. The aim of this essay is to consider the existence of such an integrity in the work of Edgar Allan Poe and to suggest how it can resolve the ostensible tension between Poe's acknowledged commitment to "Supernal Beauty" as the poetic ideal and his preoccupation—especially in his prose fiction—with horror, madness and those demonic influences which paralyze personality, destroy social bonds and alienate men from spiritual environments.

Any study of Poe's literary principles which takes into consideration his practice of poetry and prose should perhaps begin where Poe himself began, with a theory of poetry. It is clear that Poe frequently employed the word *poetry* to describe any exercise of the creative imagination which has the creation of Beauty as its object. As George Kelly has observed, Poe's poetic principle embraced "all varieties of human artistry";[6] it was not confined to the disciplines of meter and rhyme. In his critical notices of literary forms other than the verse-poem, Poe uses the word *poetry* to identify any imaginative artifact which is informed with "the sentiment of Poesy . . . , the sense of the beautiful, of the sublime, and of the mystical" (VIII, 282). As early as 1835, the year in which he began contributing to the *Southern Literary Messenger,* he described John Pendleton Kennedy's prose style in *Horse-Shoe Robinson* as "richly figurative and poetical" (VIII, 9). If he was patronizing a mentor with this comment, he was certainly not motivated by indebtedness when he called De la Motte Fouqué's *Undine* a "superb *poem,*" one which was "altogether more in consonance with the true poetic sentiment" than Lowell's *Legend of Brittany* (XI, 247). Poe's comments on Thomas Moore's *Alciphron* are also relevant:

> The poem is distinguished throughout by a very happy facility which has never been mentioned in connection with its author, but which has much to do with the reputation he has obtained. We allude to the facility with which he recounts a poetical story in a *prosaic* way. By this is meant that he preserves the tone and method of arrangement of a prose relation, and thus obtains great advantages over his more stilted compeers. His is no poetical *style* . . . , but an easy and ordinary prose manner, *ornamented into poetry* (X, 68-69).

In these examples Poe implies a distinction between poetry in its most confined sense as versification and poetry as the "Creation of Beauty." This distinction is tacitly acknowledged in "The Poetic Principle": for example, poetry is defined in that essay as one of the "modes of inculcation" (XIV, 272), and as an attribute of Beauty which is evident in all the arts—"in Painting, in Sculpture, in Architecture, in the Dance—very especially in Music—and very peculiarly, and with a wide field, in the composition of the Landscape Garden" (XIV, 274). As if the point were not already sufficiently clear, Poe adds: "Our present theme, however, has regard only to its manifestation in words. . . . I would define, in brief, the Poetry of words as *The Rythmical Creation of Beauty*" (XIV, 274-75).[7] A passage from the preface to *Eureka* suggests that in the last years of his life Poe continued to use the word *poetry* in some contexts to describe any work of art which has as its object the creation of Beauty:

> To the few who love me and whom I love—to those who feel rather than to those who think—to the dreamers and those who put faith in dreams as in the only realities—I offer this Book of Truths, not in its character of Truth-Teller, but for the Beauty that abounds in its Truth; constituting it true. To those I present the composition as an Art-Product alone:—let us say as a Romance; or, if I be not urging too lofty a claim, as a Poem (XVI, 183).

Re-emphasizing the claim he had made in 1845, that poetry for him was "not a purpose, but a passion" (VII, xlvii), he concluded the preface to *Eureka* with a request: " . . . it is as a Poem only that I wish this work to be judged after I am dead" (XVI, 183).

The fact that Poe described one of his own prose compositions as a poem is highly significant for the possibility of artistic integrity in his serious work. His plea at the end of the preface to *Eureka* is suggestively applicable to many of his tales and sketches, and it supports some very educated guesses. Vincent Buranelli has pointed out similarities in tone, mood and theme between the poems and the tales; and he has reminded the forgetful reader that Poe freely introduced poems into his prose creations, and apparently introduced them without feeling that their inclusion would damage the effects.[8] The habit suggests that Poe considered the two genres compatible. "The Conqueror Worm," "To One in Paradise" and "The Haunted Palace" are incorporated in "Ligeia," "The Assignation" and "The Fall of the House of Usher" to sustain and intensify effects which have already been impressively accomplished by the prose narratives. Edward H. Davidson supports these observations when he says that Poe was encouraged, specifically in the Grotesques, "to leave behind the accepted naturalistic world around him and to explore the indeterminate regions which poetry had suggested." "These tales," Davidson adds, "are indeed 'poems,' and Poe always remained a poet even when he was contributing some of his most uninspired narratives to the periodicals. . . . "[9]

Poe's own comments on the craft of short fiction in the reviews and notices of Hawthorne's tales would suggest, moreover, that genre classification, as far as his own writing was concerned, was very artificial and arbitrary; in fact the only determinants he supports uniformly and systematically are the principles of originality, brevity, totality and single effect. Many of the observations in his discussions of Hawthorne's fiction are even appropriated from the early essays on poetry, such as the "Letter to B———" and "Drake-Halleck." His definition of the kind of tale which can provide "the fairest field which can be afforded by the wide domains of mere prose, *for the exercise of the highest genius*" (XIII, 151; italics mine) differs from his conception of the poem only in the intensity with which it can excite the soul. The objective of the stimulus is in both cases the same, the transmission of pleasure; and this is "the end of all fictitious composition" (XIII, 145).

The popular term *short story* is evidently much too inclusive to substitute for the word *tale* as Poe uses it. He clearly distinguishes Irving's "graceful and impressive narratives" (XIII, 153-54), or John Neal's "magazine stories" (XIII, 154), from "that class of composition [the tale] which, next to such a poem as I have suggested, should *best fulfil the demands and serve the purposes of ambitious genius,* should offer it the most advantageous field of exertion, and afford it the fairest opportunity of display . . ." (XIII, 152; italics mine). Such a tale should demonstrate "true or commendable originality, . . . a peculiarity springing from ever-active vigor of fancy—better still if from ever-present force of imagination, giving its own hue, its own character to everything it touches, and, especially, *self impelled to touch everything*" (XIII, 143).

The emphasis on originality in his discussions of the tale provides additional evidence for similarity between Poe's theories of the poem and the tale. He awarded William Cullen Bryant the highest poetical honors because he had executed original conceptions which were "of the very loftiest order of true Poesy" (IX, 302). Moreover, originality is one of the poetic prerequisites enumerated in *"Ballads and Other Poems"* (XI, 73). And Poe's own practical commitment to this poetic virtue is unequivocally recorded in "The Philosophy of Composition," where he says that in writing "The Raven" his "first object (as usual) was originality" (XIV, 203). The arguments for brevity, totality and single effect in the 1842 review of *Twice-Told Tales* also suggest that his poetic theory provided the basic assumptions that conditioned his definition of the tale. His discussion of these criteria draws explicit parallels between the characteristics of the two genres. The argument for brevity is a case in point: "The ordinary novel is objectionable, from its length, for reasons [analogous to those which render length objectionable in the poem] already stated in substance. As it cannot be read at one sitting, it deprives itself, of course, of the immense force derivable from *totality*" (XI, 107). The fact that Poe used an extensive discussion of his poetic principles as the introduction to his reviews of Hawthorne's tales offers of course the most substantial evidence that he considered the "brief prose tale" in its highest order an appropriate vehicle for the poetic sentiment, perhaps second only to the synthesis of poetry and music in verse.

This interpretation does not disregard the distinction between the poem and the tale which Poe tried to make in the 1842 review of *Twice-Told Tales*. However, it does necessitate a clarification in his critical terminology. Poe says:

> the tale has a point of superiority even over the poem. In fact, while the *rhythm* of this latter is an essential aid in the development of the poet's highest idea—the idea of the Beautiful—the artificialities of this rhythm are an inseparable bar to the development of all points of thought or expression which have their basis in *Truth*. But Truth is often, and in very great degree, the aim of the tale (XI, 108-9).

If we apply the conventional concepts of Beauty and Truth to Poe's own work, a glaring inconsistency between theory and practice torpedoes any serious attempt to consider his critical attitudes, his lyrics and his narratives of horror and terror as the result of a unified and coherent artistic purpose. Poems such as "The Conqueror Worm," "The City in the Sea," "The Haunted Palace" or even "The Raven," cannot be described as contemplations of the Beautiful, if Beauty is defined as "that evergreen and radiant Paradise which the true poet knows, and knows alone, as the limited realm of his authority— as the circumscribed Eden of his dreams" (VIII, 281).[10] In "The Conqueror Worm," to use an extreme example, there is nothing self-evidently or affirmatively Beautiful, as Patrick F. Quinn has observed,[11] about Poe's description of the worm as "A blood-red thing that writhes from out / The scenic solitude" (VII, 88). On the other hand, tales such as "The Fall of the House of Usher," "The

Masque of the Red Death," "The Black Cat" or "Mesmeric Revelation" do not seem to "have their basis in *Truth,*" if *"Truth"* designates an objective, expedient knowledge which can only make actuality—the world of extended stuff—intelligible to a rational knower. Poe's attitude toward this kind of truth is well known: he thought it was hostile to the work of the creative imagination. In "The Poetic Principle" he defines it as "that Truth which is the satisfaction of the Reason" (XIV, 290), that truth which a moral inculcates—Longfellow's didacticism, for example. Like the vulture in "Sonnet— To Science," this kind of truth preys on the poet's heart and isolates him from "the summer dream beneath the tamarind tree" (VII, 22). Poe registered his objections formally:

> The demands of Truth are severe. She has no sympathy with the myrtles. All *that* which is so indispensable in Song, is precisely all *that* with which *she* has nothing whatever to do. It is but making her a flaunting paradox, to wreathe her in gems and flowers. In enforcing a truth, we need severity rather than efflorescence of language. We must be simple, precise, terse. We must be cool, calm, unimpassioned. In a word, we must be in that mood which, as nearly as possible, is the exact converse of the poetical. *He* must be blind, indeed, who does not perceive the radical and chasmal differences between the truthful and the poetical modes of inculcation. He must be theory-mad beyond redemption who, in spite of these differences, shall still persist in attempting to reconcile the obstinate oils and waters of Poetry and Truth (XIV, 272).

The tales in which Poe dramatizes his characteristic themes certainly do not yield to "the demands of Truth." "The Fall of the House of Usher" or "The Masque of the Red Death" is no more didactic than "The Haunted Palace" or "The Raven"; in none of these examples does Poe absolutize "that Truth which is the satisfaction of the Reason." But if he really considered the tale "a class of composition" which next to the poem "should best fulfill the demands and serve the purposes of ambitious genius, should offer it the fairest opportunity of display," what did he mean when he said that "Truth is often, and in very great degree, the aim of the tale"?

Patrick F. Quinn's answer to the question is convincing and instructive and should provide exemplary stimulus for further serious critical considerations. The significance of Poe's work can be best understood, he says, "if we see it in relation to one of the great traditions in western thought, the tradition of the two realms of Existence and Essence":

> In a simple formulation, the first realm, Existence, is actual life as we all know it, "the real world," as we say, here and now. This is the realm of fact and diversity, made up of all the problems, joys, relationships, and decisions that daily life involves. The second realm, of Essence, is the realm of abstraction, of imagination, where there are no problems but only solutions, where there is permanence rather than change.[12]

Following up the implications of this distinction, Professor Quinn clarifies Poe's knotty remark that prose fiction aims at Truth by proposing a dualism in his understanding of the word *Truth*. Poe uses the word *Truth*, he says, to designate both Existence and Essence. *Truth* can refer to the Truth of didacticism, which "teaches the expediency" (XI, 71)—the Truth of science, which thrives on "dull realities" (VII, 22). This is the "severe" Truth "which is the satisfaction of the reason," the Truth which Poe keelhauls in his review of Richard H. Horne's *Orion:*

> grant this *truth* to be all which its seekers and worshippers pretend—they forget that it is not truth, *per se*, which is made their thesis, but an *argumentation*, often maudlin and pedantic, always shallow and unsatisfactory (as from the mere inadaptation of the vehicle it *must* be) by which this *truth*, in casual and indeterminate glimpses, is—*or is not*—rendered manifest (XI, 257).

But Poe also uses the word *Truth* to designate Essence, as in this passage from his review of Longfellow's *Voices of the Night:*

> And thus his productions are scintillations from the brightest poetical truth, rather than this brightest truth in itself. By truth, here, we mean that perfection which is the result only of the strictest proportion and adaptation in all the poetical requisites—these requisites being considered as each existing in the highest degree of beauty and strength (X, 72-73).

The evidence corroborates Professor Quinn's generalizations, but it also suggests that they are incomplete since they do not establish a "dialogical" relationship between Existence and Essence and do not identify the Truth that emerges from the interdependent relationship between these two philosophical categories. It would seem that Poe is referring to a synthetic Truth when he says that "Truth is often, and in very great degree, the aim of the tale." Truth, in this context, can be interpreted as the given human condition of man as a finite, dependent being—a creature—living a finite, dependent existence in the world of actuality, but a creature who is also seeking in various and sometimes wholly catastrophic ways to satiate "a longing unsatisfied, which he has been impotent to fulfill . . . , a wild effort to reach the beauty above" (XI, 71-72). For Poe, in other words, the Truth of Existence may be said to posit the Truth of Essence: "To look upwards from any existence, material or immaterial, to its *design*, is, perhaps, the most direct, and the most unerring method of attaining a just notion of the nature of the existence itself" (VIII, 281). In Poe's writings, the protagonists who fail to discover Existence as a stairway to Essence document the tragedy of the human struggle, as Poe understands it; but they also affirm Truth, in an indirect way, in that they demonstrate the inadequacy of finitude and actuality as foundations for total experiences, and in so doing suggest the possibility of another kind of resolution.

A Truth of Existence which posits Essence is thoroughly consistent with Poe's belief, sustained throughout his literary career—from "Tamerlane" through *Eureka*—that

the poetic instinct, in spite of man's demonic ability to pervert it, makes at least some degree of "Intellectual Happiness" accessible *in this world*. The concluding paragraph of *Eureka* envisions the eventual identity of Existence and Essence, but it does not reduce life in the world of actualities to meaninglessness:

> "Think that the sense of individual identity will be gradually merged in the general consciousness— that Man, for example, ceasing imperceptibly to feel himself Man, will at length attain that awfully triumphant epoch when he shall recognize his existence as that of Jehovah. In the meantime bear in mind that all is Life—Life—Life within Life— the less within the greater, and all within the *Spirit Divine*" (XVI, 314-15).

If life becomes meaningless and chaotic for some men, it is because they have denied their "proper identities" and have failed to experience the "faint indeterminate glimpses" of their eventual union with God; they have not been motivated by "the Human Aspiration for Supernal Beauty," an activity which Poe describes in "Drake-Halleck" as "the Hope of a higher Intellectual Happiness hereafter" and which he frequently identifies with the poetic sentiment; they have failed to discover the power which Tamerlane sought, a power which will "shrive me of the sin / Unearthly pride hath revell'd in . . ." (VII, 1).

Existential nonentities appear with uncomfortable regularity in Poe's work—in his tales and poems—but these pathetic figures work out their pathetic fates in contexts which are not incompatible with Poe's concept of Existence as an activity which *should* take place "within the *Spirit Divine*." Insofar as it confirms the note of assurance in the conclusion of *Eureka*, the Truth of Existence for Poe may be described as poetic, not oppressingly disillusioning. Truth and Poetry, then, as Poe uses the terms in the notices of Hawthorne's *Twice-Told Tales* would seem to be surrogates in a kind of Keatsian equation of Beauty and Truth, as formulated, for example, in this passage from *Eureka:*

> the sense of the symmetrical is an instinct which may be depended upon with an almost blindfold reliance. It is the poetical essence of the Universe— *of the Universe* which, in the supremeness of its symmetry, is but the most sublime of poems. Now symmetry and consistency are convertible terms:— thus Poetry and Truth are one. A thing is consistent in the ratio of its truth—true in the ratio of its consistency. *A perfect consistency, I repeat, can be nothing but an absolute truth.* We may take it for granted, then, that Man cannot long or widely err, if he suffer himself to be guided by his poetical, which I have maintained to be his truthful, in being his symmetrical instinct (XVI, 302).

When Poe says, therefore, that prose tales "have their basis in *Truth*," he is not excluding them from consideration as products of the Poetic Sentiment but is suggesting that they, like verse-poems, can and probably should record and encourage "the Human Aspiration for Supernal Beauty." The point is convincingly made toward the end of "The Poetic Principle":

> And in regard to Truth—if, to be sure, through the attainment of a truth, we are led to perceive a harmony where none was apparent before, *we experience, at once, the true poetical effect*—but this effect is referable to the harmony alone, and not in the least degree to the truth which merely served to render the harmony manifest (XIV, 290; italics mine).

It is not surprising that Poe, in his final essay on Hawthorne, deleted the paragraph which had attempted, but without success, to differentiate between the province of poetry and the province of prose.[13] For the serious artist, both modes can serve the same function—"to render the harmony manifest."

Considered from one point of view, Poe's tales of horror, therefore, seem to be subject to many of the principles which govern his verse-poems and may be considered investigations in prose of the same themes and ideas which he was projecting imaginatively in "Al Aaraaf," "Israfel" or "To Helen." These themes and ideas are presented differently in his prose work, it is true; but the differences do not provide a sound basis for a distinction between the function of verse and the function of prose. Some of Poe's poems do affirm the existence of a Supernal Beauty by attempting to envision it imaginatively as an ideal which exists and to which men should aspire. But this is not the method of all his poems. As Professor Quinn has previously noted, "The Conqueror Worm," or "The City in the Sea," do not rhythmically create Beauty, at least in any obvious or direct way.[14] How, then, can these poems, and the tales which support their conclusions, be classified as products of the Poetic Sentiment, according to Poe's terminology? In what way may they be said to arouse *"an elevating excitement of the Soul"* (XIV, 290)? Is there any angle from which they can be read as more than incriminating evidence for "the jarring and tumultuous chaos of human intelligence" (VIII, 281)?

An observation which Poe makes in his review of *Barnaby Rudge* offers a suggestive clue. Speaking of the principle of excellence as a standard for evaluative criticism, he says: "In teaching what perfection *is,* how, in fact, shall we more rationally proceed than in specifying what it *is not?*" (XI, 42) This statement may be read as a description of a method which Poe seems to use occasionally in his poems and frequently in his serious tales. It seeks to teach perfection—one of the equivalents for the Beauty which all poetry should struggle to create—by "specifying what it *is not.*" As a method it produces artifacts which are necessarily inferior to those which record the "true poetical effect," but ultimately its objective can be poetic, regardless of the literary genre in which it is contained. The only fundamental distinction between poetry and prose which Poe consistently supports in his critical essays is a qualitative one. There are different methods of presentation; but for the serious art-

ist there is only one "immortal instinct," and that is "the sense of the Beautiful" (XIV, 273). The serious artist, regardless of the medium in which he works, must keep his eye steadily on this object.

Excluding the facile burlesques and penny-a-line nonsense of such things as "The Angel of the Odd," "Three Sundays in a Week" or "Why the Little Frenchman Wears His Hand in a Sling," much of Poe's other prose work may be described as a versatile set of variations on the theme of Beauty, on "the sentiment of the beautiful . . . , that sense which speaks of God through his purest, if not his *sole* attribute—which proves, and which alone proves his existence" (XI, 255-56). In addition to his observation on perfection in the review of *Barnaby Rudge,* many other comments in his critical essays and in some of his tales and sketches support the argument for a thematic unity and consistency in his artistic vision. The major thrust of his vision is affirmed imaginatively in "Al Aaraaf" or *Eureka;* it is negatively sustained, by implication, in the works that seem to despair of man's quest for "Love—the true, the divine Eros—the Uranian" (XIV, 290). One cannot be horrified by Prospero's demise or the fall of the house of Usher, for example, without implicitly affirming principles which are antithetic to the world views to which these protagonists submit. The negative line of Poe's argument, in other words, may be compared with the method of the satirist, who condemns what he depicts with the hope of provoking restoration. In providing therapeutic contrast, the horrible can shape Poe's ideal—Beauty.

An investigation of Poe's occasional references to the functions of terror and horror in imaginative literature seems to indicate that he deliberately dramatized these effects in order to teach his reader to navigate the tempests of the human condition without losing the "spiritualizing" principle that enables him to repudiate "Vice solely on the ground of her deformity—her disproportion—her animosity to the fitting, to the appropriate, to the harmonious—in a word, to Beauty" (XIV, 273). Apprehension of Beauty is aesthetic pleasure, and it should be remembered that pleasure in Poe's opinion is "the end of every separate aim of our existence" (XI, 12). The possibility that terror and horror, if rightly understood, can and should yield pleasure by implication (when the reader is exposed vicariously to a human predicament with which he is encouraged to come to terms) provides a theoretical basis for Poe's argument, drawn in his critical essays, between the legitimate and illegitimate uses of these effects. Moreover, it seems reasonable to suggest that this distinction is applicable to his own creative work, especially in view of the evidence provided by the preface to the first edition of his collected tales, where he tries to answer the charge of gloomy "Germanism" which some of his contemporaries had leveled at him:

> the truth is that, with a single exception, there is no one of these stories in which the scholar should recognize the distinctive features of that species of pseudo-horror which we are taught to call Germanic,

for no better reason than that some of the secondary names of German literature have become identified with its folly. If in many of my productions terror has been the thesis, I maintain that terror is not of Germany, but of the soul,—that I have deduced this terror only from its legitimate sources, and urged it only to its legitimate results.[15]

The last part of Poe's rejoinder requires extended answers to the questions which it poses. What are the "legitimate" sources and results of terror?

Within the range of terrible spectacle, Poe pronounces the merely terrible—terror for terror's sake—illegitimate. This opinion is repeatedly maintained in his critical reviews. One of his early contributions to the *Southern Literary Messenger,* a review of William Gilmore Simms' *The Partisan,* censures the novelist for insensitiveness because he depicted acts of violence "in a manner too shockingly horrible to mention" (VIII, 157). Poe objects not to the fact that the murder committed by Frampton, and other violent scenes, were included in the book but that Simms delineated them with "a species of delight" and "with a smile"; because they only demonstrate "a love for that mere *physique* of the horrible which has obtained for some Parisian novelists the title of the 'French convulsives,'" they are instances of "bad taste—villainously bad taste" (VIII, 156). The same attitude toward indiscriminate use of horrible detail seems to buttress Poe's comment in the *Marginalia* that "Pure Diabolism is but Absolute Insanity" (XVI, 160). This attitude is also evident in his review of *Barnaby Rudge,* when he suggests that the hero's horror of blood is *"inconsequential."* In his recommendation for revision of the plot, moreover, he says that terrifying or revolting incidents should inculcate the standards by which they can be recognized and condemned as destructive:

> And here how fine an opportunity has Mr. Dickens missed! The conviction of the assassin, after the lapse of twenty-two years, might easily have been brought about through his son's mysterious awe of blood—*an awe created in the unborn by the assassination itself*—and this would have been one of the finest possible embodiments of the idea which we are accustomed to attach to "poetical justice" (XI, 62-63).

A clearer statement of belief in the redemptive possibilities of terror and horror appears in "The Premature Burial." The sketch records the story of a man who suffers from a serious cataleptic disorder and who consequently takes elaborate precautions to protect himself from being entombed in the suspended condition. Awaking from a dream in which he imagines that he actually has been buried alive, he says:

> The tortures endured, however, were indubitably quite equal, for the time, to those of actual sepulture. They were fearfully—they were inconceivably hideous; but out of Evil proceeded Good; for their very excess wrought in my spirit an inevitable revulsion. My soul acquired tone—acquired temper.

I went abroad. I took vigorous exercise. I breathed the free air of Heaven. I thought upon other subjects than Death. . . . In short, I became a new man, and lived a man's life (V, 273).

Out of horror, then, good certainly did proceed.

The narrator in "The Premature Burial" describes and demonstrates a method that places Poe's investigations of the process of self-dissolution in a new perspective. It suggests that many of his tales and some of his poems are designed to repudiate by indirection the terrifying conclusions which they contain. A statement previously cited from Poe's review of *Barnaby Rudge* corroborates this generalization: "In teaching what perfection *is,* how, in fact, shall we more rationally proceed than in specifying what it *is not.*" In other words, those moments of experience in which men alienate themselves from their ineffable source confirm the undeniable fact that this *is not* that, thereby implying a positive attribute. Horror and terror are legitimate effects when they are calculated to compel the reader to turn his attention and affections from a debilitating and terrifying analysis of the human condition to an alternative—an ideal—in Poe's case, "the sentiment of Intellectual Happiness here, and the Hope of a higher Intellectual Happiness hereafter."

The argument that Poe deliberately employed terror and horror, and the situations which evoke these responses, to advance negatively the ethereal "discoveries" announced in "Al Aaraaf" or *Eureka* seems to be substantiated by "The Imp of the Perverse," an essay-tale investigating one of "the *prima mobilia* of the human soul," perverseness, in order to determine "in what manner it might be made to *further the objects of humanity, either temporal or eternal*" (VI, 145; italics mine). Poe defines perverseness as "a *mobile* without motive, a motive not *motivirt,*" and he develops the idea in this way:

> Through its promptings we act without comprehensible object; or, if this shall be understood as a contradiction in terms, we may so far modify the proposition as to say, that through its promptings we act, for the reason that we should *not.* In theory, no reason can be more unreasonable; but, in fact, there is none more strong. With certain minds, under certain conditions, it becomes absolutely irresistible. I am not more certain that I breathe, than that the assurance of the wrong or error of any action is often the one unconquerable *force* which impels us, and alone impels us to its prosecution. Nor will this overwhelming tendency to do wrong for the wrong's sake, admit of analysis, or resolution into ulterior elements. It is a radical, a primitive impulse—elementary (VI, 146-47).

Two verses from Paul's letter to the Romans explicate one aspect of Poe's conception of perverseness. Speaking of man's natural inclination toward evil and the new life which he can find in Christ, Paul says: "For I know that nothing good dwells within me, that is, in my flesh. I can will what is right, but I cannot do it. For I do not do the good I want, but the evil I do not want is what I do."[16]

The narrator's acknowledged purpose in "The Imp of the Perverse," however, is to defend the position that perverseness can occasionally "operate in furtherance of good" (VI, 150). Under the influence of perverseness, he commits an act of murder without being detected, inherits his victim's estate and for a time enjoys "absolute security." Then perverseness begins to exert its influence again. At first the man is annoyed by "a haunting and harassing thought"; then he becomes plagued with the fear that in spite of his safety he may make some public acknowledgment; finally, at the very moment when he imagines that an "invisible fiend" strikes him on the back, "the long-imprisoned secret" bursts forth in passionate confession. Like the Ancient Mariner, the narrator seems to be telling his story in the hope that a reaffirmation of guilt will purge his soul; it seems to be clear, at least, that he relives the "horrible" experience not merely for the sake of reviving its terror but for the sake of rediscovering and perhaps sharing with the reader the enlightenment which the experience has produced. The Truth of the discovery is not a moral prescription, universally administered; in fact, "The Imp of the Perverse" repudiates one of the cardinal principles which undergirds didacticism—the "sentiment of satisfaction" that results from reflecting upon "absolute security." What the narrator and reader learn through the analysis of perverseness cannot be reduced to a formula, but we can say that they mature by discovering, among other things, that they are creatures who have perverted "the relations of human society—the relations of father and child, of master and slave, of the ruler and the ruled" but who can still turn their eyes "from Nature even to Nature's God" (VIII, 281-82) in search of Perfection, Beauty and Happiness. If this is the kind of Truth which Poe is trying to verify in this work, one paragraph in "The Imp of the Perverse" has especial interpretive consequence as a veiled statement of intention:

> I have said thus much, that in some measure I may answer your question—that I may explain to you why I am here—that I may assign to you something that shall have at least the faint aspect of a cause for my wearing these fetters, and for my tenanting this cell of the condemned. Had I not been thus prolix, you might either have misunderstood me altogether, or, with the rabble, have fancied me mad (VI, 150).

It seems feasible to conclude that Poe, like the narrator in "The Imp of the Perverse," deliberately wore his "fetters" and tenanted his "cell of the condemned" in order to shatter his readers' complacency, in order to convince them, in keeping with his poetic passion, that their most noble activity was and always would be the quest for "Supernal Beauty." This conclusion encourages a reinterpretation of Poe's tales of horror as vehicles for the sentiment of Poesy, subject to the same philosophy of art, the same philosophy of Beauty and the same philosophy of criticism that sustain him in his most idealistic imaginative flights "Out of Space—Out of Time."

NOTES

[1] *French Poets and Novelists* (London, 1878), p. 76.

[2] *The Complete Works of Edgar Allan Poe,* ed. James A. Harrison (New York, 1902), III, 269. Unless otherwise noted, all subsequent references in this essay to the Poe canon are to this edition—the Virginia edition—and will be parenthesized within the text.

[3] One of the exceptions is Patrick F. Quinn's "Four Views of Edgar Poe," *Jahrbuch Für Amerikastudien,* V (1960), 138-46.

[4] Even Arthur Hobson Quinn, whose biography of Poe is still authoritative, seems to lose his perspective in the eulogy which concludes *Edgar Allan Poe* (New York and London, 1941): "His fame is now secure. The America in which he could find no adequate reward treasures every word he wrote, and in every city in which he lived, except the city of his birth, stands a lasting memorial to him. He has become a world artist and through the translations of his writings he speaks today to every civilized country. He has won this wide recognition by no persistent clamor of a cult, but by the royal right of preeminence. For today, nearly a hundred years since his death, he remains not only the one American, but also the one writer in the English language, who was at once foremost in criticism, supreme in fiction, and in poetry destined to be immortal" (p. 695).

[5] "Edgar Allan Poe: A Crisis in the History of American Obscurantism," *American Literature,* VIII (Jan. 1937), 389.

[6] "Poe's Theory of Beauty," *American Literature,* XXVII (Jan. 1956), 526.

[7] Poe considered formally other manifestations of the poetic sentiment in "The Landscape Garden" (IV, 259-71), "The Domain of Arnheim" (VI, 176-96), and in "Landor's Cottage" (VI, 255-71). The architects and gardeners in these sketches are dedicated to "the *creation of novel forms of Beauty*" (V, 263).

[8] *Edgar Allan Poe* (New York, 1961), p. 87.

[9] *Poe: A Critical Study* (Cambridge, 1957), p. 154.

[10] A comment from Poe's review of *Ballads and Other Poems,* published in the same issue of *Graham's* that contained his first notice of *Twice-Told Tales* (Apr. 1842), would suggest that his notion of the Beautiful had not changed appreciably during the interim between "Drake-Halleck" and 1842: "Inspired with a prescient ecstasy of the beauty beyond the grave, it [poesy] struggles by multiform novelty of combination among the things and thoughts of Time, to anticipate some portion of that loveliness whose very elements, perhaps, appertain solely to Eternity" (XI, 72).

[11] *Jahrbuch Für Amerikastudien,* V, 140.

[12] *Jahrbuch Für Amerikastudien,* V, 144-45.

[13] Poe's final essay on Hawthorne was a review of *Twice-Told Tales,* including comments on *Mosses from an Old Manse,* which appeared in *Godey's Lady's Book* in 1847 under the title "Tale-Writing" (XIII, 141-55).

[14] *Jahrbuch Für Amerikastudien,* V, 140.

[15] *Tales of the Grotesque and Arabesque* (Philadelphia, 1840), p. 6.

[16] Romans 7:18-19; RSV.

Richard Badenhausen

SOURCE: "Fear and Trembling in Literature of the Fantastic: Edgar Allan Poe's 'The Black Cat,'" in *Studies in Short Fiction,* Vol. 29, No. 4, Fall, 1992, pp. 487-

[*In the following essay, Badenhausen focuses on "The Black Cat" to illustrate Poe's skill in eliciting a fearful, emotional response from the reader.*]

In an important article published in *PMLA* two decades ago, William Spanos discussed T. S. Eliot's incomplete verse drama *Sweeney Agonistes* in terms of existentialist theories about apprehending truth through a final encounter with death. Spanos pointed out that the events of *Sweeney* suggest "an action remarkably analogous to the movement from self-deception to authenticity that most existentialist philosophers describe as the archetypal life-journey of modern man" (8).[1] According to Heidegger's version of that experience, most individuals live "unauthentic" lives in which evasions of anxiety about death become the controlling action; only when confronted by extreme situations separating them from the rest of the world and bringing them face-to-face with death do individuals have the opportunity to achieve the humanized "I." Through this acknowledgement, death "comes to assume . . . a benign character in spite of its horror" (Spanos 9). Students of modern poetry will immediately sense how this argument has relevance not just for *Sweeney Agonistes* but for much of Eliot's work.

But the topic of this essay is instead a writer Eliot admired, Edgar Allan Poe, and his tale of horror, "The Black Cat" (1843).[2] In that story, a male narrator scheduled to be executed in 24 hours as punishment for the murder of his wife attempts to describe the events that lead to his downfall. After an uneventful childhood marked only by his "tenderness of heart" and a few blissful years of marriage, the narrator's behavior turns ugly (Poe, "Black Cat" 597).[3] His actions include carving out the eye of a household cat with a penknife; hanging that cat by the neck from the limb of a tree; attempting to murder a second cat that mysteriously resembles the first save for a haunting white blemish on its breast; burying an axe into the brain of his wife and hiding her body behind a wall in the basement; and, in a final moment of bravado in front of policemen investigating the disappearance, tapping his cane against the concealing wall

only to be answered by the wailing cat—the decomposing corpse is discovered along with the trapped cat that had been feeding on the human scraps.

The details are not unlike those of many of Poe's classic works of horror that depend on conventions like the haunting animal-figures, the isolated, self-conscious narrator on the brink of madness, the grisly murder and subsequent mutilation of the corpse, the dread of an evil eye, life-in-death existence, and the struggle with the fear of fear itself. "The Black Cat" also enacts perfectly Poe's famous conception of the short story in which the author

> has not fashioned his thoughts to accommodate his incidents; but having conceived, with deliberate care, a certain unique or single *effect* to be wrought out, he then invents such incidents—he then combines such events as may best aid him in establishing this preconceived effect. (*Essays* 572)[4]

In this instance, however, that definition applies in two ways, for the condemned narrator of "The Black Cat" mimics the role of the author by relating his story in a way that will produce a calculated response from the audience. Despite pledging to tell his tale "without comment," the narrator is constantly qualifying, correcting, and explaining, in the hope that the audience will see events from his perspective. Although announcing in the opening sentence that he "neither expect[s] nor solicit[s] belief" (597), the narrator is obsessively concerned with both activities: he hopes for understanding from his listeners and energetically pursues approval by employing the various manipulative tools of the storyteller. Like the Anglo-Saxon scop, he possesses the power to shape the events of history in this oral format. Because he is a man condemned to die, the "preconceived effect" is sympathy; yet coming from an unreformed criminal, the method is nervous accusation and compulsive denial. He is a very different fellow from, for example, the narrator of "The Cask of Amontillado," whose quick-paced bombastic rhetoric presents a series of events whose details have been finely crafted over the course of 50 years of reciting the account. If the narrator of "The Black Cat" had similarly managed to escape punishment for his crime, he surely would have shaded the particulars of his tale differently, possibly reining in one or two of the more extreme moments ("oh, mournful and terrible engine of Horror and of Crime" [603] comes to mind) or building up the suspense more dexterously, as in the later tale. In that respect, the outcome of the plot in Poe's tales is of paramount importance because it frequently determines how the narrator will sell his story to the reader.

At this point, I return to Eliot's lower-class simian, Sweeney, who "knew a man once did a girl in. . . . kept her there in a bath / With a gallon of lysol in a bath" (122). Spanos describes the effect of such an event in existential terms when he explains:

> The man who is capable of a decisive action (i.e., an irreversible movement activated by consciousness of his identity), even if it is a murder, is closer to

redemption than the dehumanized *das Man,* who, neutralized by the boredom of eternal recurrence, is capable of neither positive nor negative action. For the irreversible act of murder disengages the individual from the crowd, from the protective shelter of the "they," and thus condemns him to become a fully conscious individual without recourse to the explanation to others that domesticates anguish and anesthetizes the sting of guilt. . . . The decisive act of murder has disengaged the murderer from the safe familiarity of the crowd and thrust him into the realm of the uncanny (the "not-at-home"), where explanations cannot domesticate solitary dread. (12, 18-19)

When we come upon the narrator at the start of "The Black Cat," he has enacted the first part of this formula: through the murder of his wife he has disengaged himself from the everyday world. The degree of that complete separation is further signified by the narrator's very calm and inhuman response to the murderous act: he sets about "with entire deliberation, to the task" (603) of cleaning up his bloody mess, as if he were washing dishes after a quiet dinner at home.

When the structuralist critic Tzvetan Todorov speaks of "an experience of limits" (48) as the element that characterizes most of Poe's work, he comes close to describing a condition, through language echoing the existentialists—what Karl Jaspers calls *Grenzsituation* or "ultimate-situation"—where we face the "inescapable realities in relation to which alone human life can be made genuinely meaningful" (20).[5] But the narrator's response to that detachment from society differs significantly. Instead of embracing, before his execution, the opportunity for redemption of the self by authenticating the "I," the narrator chooses to address his final captive audience (the reader) with a hearty denial of his situation. In fact, he refuses even to acknowledge a disengagement from the human race by suggesting that his murderous actions differed in no way from the normal, everyday occurrences of the domestic realm; indeed, he preposterously calls the events of his tale "a series of mere household events" (597). The narrator actively campaigns for a position in the everyday crowd by confessing that he plans to "place before the world. . . . nothing more than an ordinary succession of very natural causes and effects" (597). With the reader playing the role of attentive jury, the narrator adopts the language of defense attorney and promises not the gruesome, graphic descriptions favored by prosecutors, but simple, sensible explanations. After describing how he raised an axe to kill the offending cat, the narrator notes that the blow was intercepted by the hand of his wife. Naturally, he continues, " . . . I withdrew my arm from her grasp and buried the axe in her brain. She fell dead upon the spot, without a groan" (603). Although a hopeless task, he tries to employ explanations to "domesticate [the] solitary dread," in Spanos's words.

Poe accentuates the effect by allowing his narrator to concentrate not on the murder itself (described in two short sentences) but on the grotesque methods considered for eliminating the body (seven sentences, including discussions of decapitation, burning, and burying) and achieving a final solution (11 sentences). The horror in Poe's tale originates not from the descriptions of murder or decomposing corpses (they are delivered with scientific precision, appropriate to the narrator's detachment from those acts), but from the reader's realization that the narrator is aggressively arguing his case and that given a last opportunity to humanize the self through a confrontation with death, he still flees in its face. The horror takes on more gruesome overtones if we read the story as John Harmon McElroy suggests, that is to view the narrator's remorse as feigned. The narrator's purpose in telling the tale is to mock the events, see humor in his own sadism, and finally "to get the reader to identify with him" (109). But then horror and humor have always stood close to one another in literature; indeed, many find "The Black Cat" difficult to read without laughing.

My reading of "The Black Cat" accords nicely with those critics who posit a fear-based conception of fantastic literature. In what he terms "fear-literature" or "weird" literature, H. P. Lovecraft sees

> A certain atmosphere of breathless and unexplainable dread of outer, unknown forces . . . a malign and particular suspension or defeat of those fixed laws of Nature which are our only safeguard against the assaults of chaos and the daemons of unplumbed space. . . . The one test of the really weird is simply this—whether or not there be excited in the reader a profound sense of dread . . . a subtle attitude of awed listening. (15-16)

Peter Penzoldt agrees in suggesting that "all stories of the supernatural are tales of fear that play on our doubt whether what we maintain to be pure imagination is not, after all, reality. . . . Fear is the basic emotion in all weird fiction" (9-10). In many respects, "The Black Cat" succeeds according to Lovecraft's definition because it puts its reader into that state of "awed listening" (with the murderer at the narrative controls) and then presents a sequence of events that will provoke different levels of fearful responses. Because the varying degree of those responses provides a commentary on the reader himself, the story challenges him to look inside himself and confront the view (in a like way, the murderer's actions have placed him in the same position).

Todorov criticizes such formulations of the fantastic partly because he is uncomfortable placing so much emphasis on the reader's response to the text and partly because he disagrees with the elevation of fear, above all other conditions, as a test for the form.[6] On the other hand, he acknowledges that literature of the fantastic does contain elements that serve specific functions, the first being to produce "a particular effect on the reader—fear, or horror, or simply curiosity—which the other genres or literary forms cannot provoke" (92). "The Black Cat" performs that function in allowing the narrator to address his comments directly to the reader: why else would a condemned man feel compelled to tell his tale remorselessly if not to evoke a final response that gives him pleasure before death?

Part of the artistry of Poe's tale is that the narrator's motivation is not so apparent when the story begins. Initially the narrator goes to great lengths to disguise that purpose by focusing the reader's attention away from his participation in the act of reading and toward the "homely narrative" itself and the speaker who delivers it. In the first eight sentences of "The Black Cat," the narrator refers to himself 13 times; and as the tale unfolds the first person pronoun virtually litters the page. Instead of referring to the current reader's response to his tale, the narrator imagines a *future* "intellect more calm, more logical, and far less excitable" (597) than his own to put the recent events in proper perspective, a wish assuring that the validity of his presentation of those events will never be challenged. We should start to question the intentions of the narrator upon realizing, despite all the references to himself, that he never divulges his name. Nor does he refer to his wife by name. Instead, the only named character is the first black cat, Pluto, thus reinforcing the message of the story's title: the initial object of the narrator's attention is the cat; only after he has carried out his murderous deeds does the speaker turn his attention to us. The dominance of the cat is all-important (it alone of all the domestic animals in the household, including "birds, gold-fish, a fine dog, rabbits, a small monkey[!], and *a cat*" [597], is referred to with emphasis), for it incorporates and signifies for the speaker all of his wicked and criminal ways.

Before explaining how the speaker wrestles with that symbol, I must return to Kierkegaard and his text, *The Concept of Dread* (1844), published coincidentally one year after "The Black Cat." There Kierkegaard lays out a distinction central to existentialist thought: the relationship between fear and dread. To oversimplify somewhat, fear is comprised of tangible worries, like the fear of death, which rational creatures can distance through various strategies and thus remain sane. Dread (*aengste*), on the other hand, is much more formidable because one cannot objectify the source; hence there is no way to conquer the feeling—the individual is left only to dwell on the feeling itself. Reidar Thomte's explanation (in the introduction to his edition of the slightly retitled *The Concept of Anxiety*) of Paul Tillich's view of anxiety is helpful here, because it draws from Kierkegaard's original model. Thomte explains that Tillich

> defines anxiety as "finitude in awareness": "Anxiety is the self-awareness of the finite self as finite." Like finitude, anxiety is ontological; it cannot be derived from anything. Anxiety differs from fear in that the object of anxiety is "nothingness," and nothingness is not an "object." Fear relates itself to objects—for example, a danger, a pain, an enemy—for it is psychological and can be conquered. Anxiety cannot be conquered, for no finite being can conquer its finitude. (xvi)

One way an individual plagued by anxiety might react is to become obsessively preoccupied with the physical manifestations of the problem instead of seeking to understand the behavioral patterns causing it. He turns increasingly inward (possibly toward eventual madness), instead of looking outward to where the source of the problem exists. This very thing happens in Hoffmann's "The Sandman" (1816)—a story essential to Freud's essay on the uncanny—when Nathanael falls in love with the automaton Olympia; upon sensing his mistake, he is "seized by a nameless dread" (163), and finally, "in a raging frenzy . . . [is] taken away to the madhouse" (164).

From what a reader can piece together from his tale, Poe's narrator begins to have problems in his life when he can no longer find an appropriate corresponding object for his terror. After confessing briefly to scolding his wife with "intemperate language" and even "offer[ing] her personal violence" (598), the narrator turns to the cat as a source of his problems even though he blames the demons haunting him on an alcoholic condition. That, however, seems only a convenient way to explain away or deny fairly typical behavior of a patient struck by an anxiety disorder: he suppresses the symptoms of anxiety by self-medicating with alcohol instead of trying to discover the real source of his psychic stress (most likely his new marriage, in this instance).

After committing his first crime—cutting out Pluto's eye—the narrator experiences a "sentiment half of horror, half of remorse" (599). Following the hanging of that same cat and seeing a relief of its figure appear on the wall of the recently destroyed house, he feels "wonder and . . . terror" (600). Having disposed of the first pet, the narrator replaces Pluto with a similar cat who only elevates his level of fear to what he calls "dread . . . not exactly a dread of physical evil—and yet I should be at a loss how otherwise to define it" (602). The progression of emotion from horror to terror to dread, each more indescribable than the previous (indeed, he can't "define" the final stage), nicely captures the speaker's descent into the valley of existentialist despair. In the opening paragraph of the tale, the narrator even foreshadows this sequence when he describes how "these events have terrified—have tortured—have destroyed" him (597).

Although he believes he can simply replace the previous cat that had served as an objectification of his fears, the narrator begins to encounter the unexplainable and more harrowing condition of Kierkegaard's dread. He confesses this fear is worse than the earlier emotion because the "terror and horror with which the animal inspired me, had been heightened by . . . the mark of white hair" (602) on its breast. As the response becomes more magnified—fear evolving into dread—the narrator focuses on more minute elements to objectify the feeling: first the cat and then a mark on the cat. Then that mark begins to assume

> a rigorous distinctness of outline. It was now the representation of an object that I shudder to name—and for this, above all, I loathed, and dreaded, and

would have rid myself to the monster *had I dared*—
it was now, I say, the image of a hideous—of a
ghastly thing—of the GALLOWS!—oh, mournful
and terrible engine of Horror and Crime—of Agony
and of Death! (602-03)

The narrative structure breaks down when the speaker
attempts to retell his experience at that moment, an appropriate response when one tries to relate his confrontation with the horror of human existence. Indeed, one
should not be able to articulate an experience that lacks
a corresponding object. As he tries to characterize the
mark, the narrator seems to experience one of those
moments in which there exists a "collapse of the limit
between subject and object; and . . . the transformation of
time and space" (Todorov 120). Only at this key moment—the one time during the actual telling of his tale—
are we reminded of the narrator's standing outside the
boundaries of his tale, awaiting those "GALLOWS."

From the speaker's description of the events leading up
to his imprisonment, it is clear that he has encountered
one of Jaspers's so-called "ultimate situations," that is,

> situations which we cannot evade or change. . . .
> In our day-to-day lives we often evade them, by
> closing our eyes and living as if they did not exist.
> We forget that we must die, forget our guilt, and
> forget that we are at the mercy of chance. . . . But
> to ultimate situations we react either by obfuscation
> or, if we really apprehend them, by despair and
> rebirth: we become ourselves by a change in our
> consciousness of being. (20)

Jaspers's reference to our "day-to-day lives" eerily echoes the narrator's insistence that the events of his story
are "mere household events." After killing his wife, the
narrator chooses the path of obfuscation, convincing himself that he has solved life's mysteries and his own difficulties through violent action. After that moment, the
speaker tells us, he slept "soundly and tranquilly," for he
believed the cat or

> the monster, in terror, had fled the premises forever!
> I should behold it no more! My happiness was
> supreme! The guilt of my dark deed disturbed me
> but little. . . . The glee at my heart was too strong
> to be restrained. (605)

The progression of feelings here—from tranquility to
happiness to glee—directly reverses the earlier descent
and suggests our speaker has not really left behind his
encounters with dread, despite his optimistic assertions
to the contrary. It seems, in fact, that he is merely
mimicking his earlier response with a hollow self-reas-
surance that all is well. Indeed, within minutes he will
be tapping a cane against the artificial crypt that conceals his wife. Because the individual plagued by anxiety mistakenly associates the anxious feelings with a
specific object (as we do with fear), he believes he can
rid the affliction by extinguishing the object. The horror heightens when the object is eliminated and the
anxiety returns.

Those familiar with Freud's theories about fear will have
recognized by now a number of echoes throughout my
discussion from his essay on "The 'Uncanny'" (1919),
which attempts to uncover "what arouses dread and horror . . . [and] what excites fear in general" (219). Freud
speculates that the "uncanny" brings about fear precisely
because the object that initiates the response "is *not*
known and familiar" (220). But what is more interesting
is Freud's use of an earlier work on the uncanny, attributed to E. Jentsch,[7] to observe the effect in literature,
suggesting that it not only occurs as a condition of a
particular figure's encounter with fear, but that it emerges
in readers as well. Freud cites Jentsch's contention that

> In telling a story, one of the most successful devices
> for easily creating uncanny effects is to leave the
> reader in uncertainty whether a particular figure in
> the story is a human being or an automaton, and
> to do it in such a way that his attention is not
> focused directly upon his uncertainty, so that he
> may not be led to go into the matter and clear it
> up immediately. That, as we have said, would
> quickly dissipate the peculiar emotional effect of
> the thing. (227).

Aside from being a suggestive precursor to Todorov's
definition of the fantastic as a kind of "hesitation" on the
part of a reader when confronted by supernatural phenomena, Jentsch's commentary invites comparison with
"The Black Cat" because the narrator has created a situation in which the reader is very much on the defensive.[8]
As mentioned earlier, Poe's narrator deflects attention
away from the reader early on so as to have him not
dwell on that "uncertainty." The dehumanization of the
"particular figure" (the narrator) occurs only later, when
we attempt to process his dispassionate description of the
gruesome events. Far from "dissipating the emotional
effect," the structure of Poe's tale heightens the uncanny
effect on the reader.

In retelling his tale for a captive audience, the narrator
possesses the opportunity and capability to receive pen-
ance for his deed. But when he relates his story (as a man
condemned to die, facing yet another final, boundary
situation), he tragically falls back on rhetorical tricks
instead of confronting his despair and reaching out for
possible rebirth. His response serves as the counterexample
to Ernest Becker's explanation for how one transcends
oneself: "By realizing the truth of his situation, by dispelling the lie of his character, by breaking his spirit out of
its conditioned prison" (86). Like Garcin, and even more
so Estelle, in Sartre's *No Exit,* Poe's narrator turns away
from the truth and as a result condemns himself to the
rhetorical prison of his tale, the actual prison in which he
awaits execution, and the imminent prison (following his
death) of an eternity in a universe apparently absent of
God. Instead of turning inward toward a discovery of the
authentic self, he chooses to manipulate the reader throughout his narrative with multiple evasions and explanations.
While this tactic proves the narrator's worth as a skillful
storyteller and allows him to succeed as a rhetorician, it
also induces him to fail as a human being.

But in actuality, the narrator is not the primary point of "The Black Cat," even if he has led us to believe that from the start. Instead, this is a tale that uses its tools to force a response from the reader and then asks him to consider the emotion it engenders. In many ways, Poe's story fulfills Todorov's definition for the first function of fantasy: provocation of fear, horror, or curiosity (92), the three responses intermingled in much the same way they are when a nation watches the gruesome details of televised accounts of mass murders—there is an uneasiness about how to watch, but we do still watch. If we find ourselves, as McElroy suggests, consciously identifying with Poe's narrator in any way, our response might be to shudder upon that recognition, to deny the identification, or to fear what that says about ourselves. If we sympathize with the narrator and recognize the existential underpinning of his situation, we replace the fear with alarm over his missed chance for redemption. If we find the entire sequence of events simply difficult to comprehend (and much modern fantasy by authors as wide-ranging as Robert Coover, Donald Barthelme and Moacyr Scliar puts the reader on the defensive in this manner), the only recourse is nervous laughter and the hope that we did not miss a joke understood by the rest of the audience. Our response to the narrator's language is finally what the tale is about; and as a result, it succeeds in breaking the fictional barrier by generating real fear in the reader. Unlike the strategy in "The Fall of the House of Usher," where the narrator functions, in Darrel Abel's words, as "a mere point of view for the reader to occupy" (177), the speaker in "The Black Cat" controls and distorts the point of view, leaving little room for the reader to pursue alternate directions. The trapped reader finally must face himself in the same way as the imprisoned and condemned narrator. That controlling feature must have been part of the attraction for Poe in choosing to employ the form.

In many ways, the final paragraph of "The Black Cat" illustrates how well the tale forces the burden of responsibility upon the reader. In the culmination of his story, the narrator explains how the police tore away at the basement wall and how the corpse of his murdered wife "stood erect" behind it with the ghastly cat sitting on her head: the animal had survived by feeding from the body. Indeed, that metaphor of an unknown and unseen terror symbolizes perfectly the problematic nature of anxiety. Poe's narrator then ends with a simple explanation: "I had walled the monster up within the tomb!" (606). How are we to react to this admission? The form of delivery almost mimics that of the punch line of a joke, with the narrator hitting his forehead wondering, "How could I have been so stupid?" Indeed, that line follows one of the tale's more tortured puns, when the narrator describes the wall's falling "bodily" (606) as the corpse itself appears. Why doesn't he then go on to explain the reaction of the police and their subsequent arrest of him? What happens to the narrator upon completion of his tale? Why doesn't Poe complete the framing device with the narrator returning us to his jail cell and mulling over his thoughts? These questions emphasize how the tale insistently turns over responsibility for making sense of the events to the reader. The story is finally a conduit through which the reader must discover and confront his own emotions and fears. In many ways the tale brings us to the same position in which our narrator found himself right before his own life began to fall apart: facing an unknown fear (that may develop into anxiety?) and trying to overcome it. The challenge for all readers is to make the right choice when encountering that fear.

WORKS CITED

Abel, Darrel. "A Key to the House of Usher." *University of Toronto Quarterly* 18 (1949): 176-85.

Becker, Ernest. *The Denial of Death.* New York: Free P, 1973.

Eliot, T. S. "American Literature." Rev. of *A History of American Literature,* vol. 2, ed. William P. Trent et al. *The Athenaeum* 25 (Apr. 1919): 236-37.

——.*Collected Poems 1909-1962.* San Diego: Harcourt, 1970.

——."'A Dream within a Dream.'" *The Listener* 25 (Feb. 1943): 243-44.

Freud, Sigmund. *The Standard Edition of the Complete Psychological Works of Sigmund Freud.* Ed. and trans. James Strachey. Vol. 17. London: Hogarth P, 1955. 24 vols.

Hoffmann, E. T. A. *Selected Writings of E. T. A. Hoffmann.* Ed. and trans. Leonard J. Kent and Elizabeth C. Knight. Vol. 1. Chicago: U of Chicago P, 1969. 2 vols.

Jaspers, Karl. *Way to Wisdom: An Introduction to Philosophy.* Trans. Ralph Manheim. 1954. New Haven: Yale UP, 1966.

Kierkegaard, Søren. *The Concept of Anxiety.* Ed. and trans. Reidar Thomte. 1844. Princeton: Princeton UP, 1980.

McElory, John Harmon. "The Kindred Artist; or the Case of the Black Cat." *Studies in American Humor* 3 (1976): 103-17.

Lovecraft, Howard Phillips. *Supernatural Horror in Literature.* New York: Ben Abramson, 1945.

Penzoldt, Peter. *The Supernatural in Fiction.* 1952. New York: Humanities P, 1965.

Poe, Edgar Allan. "The Black Cat." *Poetry and Tales.* Cambridge, England: Library of America, 1984. 597-606.

——. *Essays and Reviews.* Cambridge, England: Library of America, 1984.

——. "Instinct VS Reason—A Black Cat." *Poetry and Tales* 370-72.

——. *Poetry and Tales.* Cambridge, England: Library of America, 1984.

Spanos, William V. "'Wanna Go Home, Baby?': *Sweeney Agonistes* as Drama of the Absurd." *PMLA* 85 (1970): 8-20.

Todorov, Tzvetan. *The Fantastic: A Structural Approach to a Literary Genre.* Trans. Richard Howard. 1970. Ithaca: Cornell UP, 1980.

NOTES

[1] Although we are working with completely different material, I am indebted to Spanos's approach and its suggestiveness for my study of Poe.

[2] Like his attitude toward Whitman, Eliot's feelings about Poe evolved with time. Although critical of his American precursor early on—"Hawthorne, Poe and Whitman are all pathetic creatures," he remarked in 1919 ("American Literature" 237)—Eliot came to terms with American literary tradition by the 1940s and was comfortable enough to proclaim that "no American author has counted for more in European literature than Edgar Poe" ("A Dream" 243) and that although "there is no easy way of proving that Poe was a great poet: the best evidence is that once his poems have become part of your experience, they are never dislodged" (244).

[3] Poe himself owned "one of the most remarkable black cats in the world . . . [with] not a white hair about her . . ." ("Instinct . . ." 371). See Poe, "Instinct vs Reason—A Black Cat."

[4] The essay appeared originally as a review of Hawthorne's *Twice-Told Tales* in *Graham's Magazine,* May 1842, one year before "The Black Cat."

[5] The explanation of Jaspers's *Grenzsituation* is Manheim's.

[6] Todorov dismisses this view by declaring, "fear is often linked to the fantastic, but it is not a necessary condition of the genre" (35).

[7] I have been unable to locate the article by Jentsch entitled "Zur Psychologie des Unheimlichen" (1906).

[8] See Todorov on the "hesitation experienced by a person who knows only the laws of nature" 25.

D. Hampton Morris

SOURCE: "Variations on a Theme: Five Tales of Horror by Maupassant," in *Studies in Short Fiction,* Vol. 17, No. 4, Fall, 1980, pp. 475-81.

[*In the following essay, Morris discusses the structural similarity of Guy de Maupassant's "Lui," "La Chevelure," "Le Horla," "La Nuit," and "Qui sait?"*]

Considering Guy de Maupassant's voluminous production of short stories, Michael G. Lerner points out in his biography of this prolific author that an intriguing aspect of these tales is "the way Maupassant manages to use the same situation time and time again merely by altering the circumstances in some small way—a change in the location, a difference of age, a switching of relationships, or a fresh perspective from a new angle."[1] This persistent repetition of structure is particularly prominent in five apparently disparate tales of horror published within the last ten years of Maupassant's life, when the author began to suffer from increasing physical and mental torment: *Lui* (1883), *La Chevelure* (1884), *Le Horla* (1886), *La Nuit* (1887), and *Qui sait?* (1890).

Upon first reading these stories one might be tempted to say that they are entirely distinct, involving quite different subjects and themes. *Le Horla,* for example, is the story of a man frightened by a horrible invisible monster, whereas *La Chevelure* concerns a woman's hairpiece which becomes the fetish of a madman. A careful, attentive rereading of these texts reveals, however, the striking similarities among them. The frequent occurrence of structural parallels and the definite pattern they tend to present indicate that they are probably the result of an *idée fixe,* firmly implanted within the mind of the author, which surfaced each time during the creative process.[2]

Each story begins with a description of the happy solitary life of the protagonist. In *Le Horla* the narrator writes: "Quelle journée admirable! J'ai passé toute la matinée étendu sur l'herbe, devant ma maison, sous l'énorme platane qui la couvre, l'abrite et l'ombrage tout entière."[3] The narrator of *La Nuit* loves Night as if it were his mistress. When the sun disappears, he likes to wander alone in the shadows where he feels "tout autre, plus jeune, plus fort, plus alerte, plus heureux" (p. 1138). In the three other tales, this description follows a short introduction concerning the present situation of the narrator, but one still finds the picture of a peaceful life, with few complications or anxieties. The narrator of *Lui* tells his friend: "Autrefois je n'éprouvais rien de cela. Je rentrais tranquillement. J'allais et je venais en mon logis sans que rien troublât la sérénité de mon âme" (p. 854). In the notebook of the madman in *La Chevelure,* we find the following notation: "Jusqu'à l'âge de trente-deux ans, je vécus tranquille, sans amour. La vie m'apparaissait très simple, très bonne et très facile" (p. 936). Finally, the narrator of *Qui sait?* states that he has always been "un solitaire, un rêveur, une sorte de philosophe isolé, bienveillant, content de peu, sans aigreur contre les hommes et sans rancune contre le ciel" (p. 1186).

Suddenly, however, this tranquil existence of the narrators suffers a brutal interruption. A strange, incomprehensible event occurs which inspires in the narrators not only uneasiness and uncertainty, but also stark terror. Curiously, even if, through Maupassant's remarkable ability to create a mood or atmosphere with only a few strokes of the pen, the narrators' surroundings (the landscape, the time of day, the weather, etc.) contribute to an incipient feeling of malaise, it is always a physiological phenomenon which announces the manifestations of this bizarre interruption: a shudder, or uncontrollable trembling, which the narrators experience without understanding it. In *La Nuit* the solitary stroller is in the Bois de Boulogne when suddenly: "Un frisson singulier m'avait saisi, une émotion imprévue et puissante. . . . Pour la première fois je sentis qu'il allait arriver quelque chose d'étrange, de nouveau" (p. 1140). The madman obsessed with the hairpiece has an irresistible desire to see it again. Having previously caressed it, he relates that this time: " . . . je la repris, et je sentis, en la touchant, un long frisson qui me courut dans les membres" (p. 940). The narrator of *Lui?,* after having felt completely alone, experiences this same presentiment of an unusual happening: "Puis, soudain, un frisson de froid me courut dans le dos" (p. 855). In *Le Horla* the narrator experiences an inexplicable change of mood: "Je descends le long de l'eau; et soudain, après une courte promenade, je rentre désolé, comme si quelque malheur m'attendait chez moi.—Pourquoi?—Est-ceun frisson de froid qui, frôlant ma peau, a ébranlé mes nerfs et assombri mon âme?" (p. 1098). Several days later, walking alone in the forest, he experiences this feeling again, this time with the notion that someone is pursuing him: "Un frisson me saisit soudain, non pas un frisson de froid, mais un étrange frisson d'angoisse. . . . Tout à coup, il me sembla que j'étais suivi, qu'on marchait sur mes talons, tout près, à me toucher" (pp. 1100-1101). It is perhaps in *Qui sait?,* however, that one finds the best example of this sudden termination of a "normal" existence announced by a shudder. The narrator himself suggests this phenomenon as a presentiment of something incomprehensible: "En approchant de la maison, un trouble bizarre me saisit. . . . 'Qu'est-ce que j'ai donc?' pensai-je. Depuis dix ans je rentrais ainsi sans que la moindre inquiétude m'eût effleuré. . . . Qu'était-ce? Un pressentiment? Le pressentiment mystérieux qui s'empare des sens des hommes quand ils vont voir de l'inexplicable? . . . A mesure que j'avançais, j'avais dans la peau des tressaillements . . ." (p. 1189).

But what are the manifestations of these presages? In every case these unusual feelings are quickly followed by a series of bizarre and horrifying events. In *La Nuit* there is the experience of terrifying solitude. Night, which had been a benevolent "companion" for the narrator, suddenly becomes a malicious entity, an invisible monster intent upon crushing him in his solitude. "Il me sembla qu'il faisait froid, que l'air s'épaississait, que la nuit, que ma nuit bien-aimée, devenait lourde sur mon coeur. . . . Une voûte de nuages, épaisse comme l'immensité, avait noyé les étoiles, et semblait s'abaisser sur la terre pour l'anéantir" (pp. 1140-1141). Now he is totally afraid of the night. Its silence is overwhelming and the "non-response" of his former companion further horrifies him: "Personne ne me répondit. . . . Ma voix s'envola, sans

écho, faible, étouffée, écrasée par la nuit, par cette nuit impénétrable. . . . Mon appel désespéré resta sans réponse" (pp. 1141-1142). In a moment of despair, his watch becomes a consolatory object, its continuous ticking like the presence of a friend. Unfortunately, even this comfort is soon denied him. His watch suddenly stops, leaving him completely alone. He is convinced that there is "rien, plus rien," that Night is going to destroy everything, and that he is going to die with the Seine.

The madman in *La Chevelure,* who becomes completely obsessed by a woman's hairpiece that he found in some antique furniture, caresses the wig as if it were his mistress, and when he closes it up in the drawer, he feels its presence continually, "comme si elle eût été un être vivant, caché prisonnier" (p. 940). His obsession becomes more and more extreme. For one or two months he remains completely shut up in his room with the hairpiece: "Elle m'obsédait, me hantait. J'étais heureux et torturé, comme dans une attente d'amour, comme après les aveux qui précèdent l'étreinte" (p. 940). He finally realizes that he is actually awaiting the woman who possessed the hair. This woman does indeed finally come. He sees her, he takes her as his mistress, and he is immeasurably happy. But his happiness is of brief duration. According to the madman's account, someone comes and takes his mistress away and locks her up like a criminal. Without her, he is left in misery.

Returning home one evening, after having experienced an inexplicable shudder and a general feeling of discomfort, the narrator of *Lui?* sees someone seated in his armchair in front of the fire. Believing that it is one of his friends, he draws nearer, extends his hand, and suddenly there is no one there. The chair is empty. Try as he will, the narrator cannot free himself from the fear of seeing his counterpart again. He is convinced that "he" is always there: "Il demeure invisible, cela n'empêche qu'il y soit. Il est derrière les portes, dans l'armoire fermée, sous le lit . . ." (pp. 858-859).

The narrator of *Qui sait?* sees his furniture leave his house unaided by human hands. At Rouen he discovers it in the shop of a curious-looking antique dealer "gros comme un phénomène." After having made some inquiries, he finds that the strange man has disappeared and the furniture with him. Two weeks later the narrator receives a letter from his gardener who relates the mysterious return of all his furniture. But the narrator does not go back to his home. Instead, he seeks refuge in a rest home, continually fearing that the antique dealer might one day go mad and seek him out: "Les prisons elles-mêmes ne sont pas sûres" (p. 1199).

In *Le Horla,* perhaps the best of these stories, the narrator tells of his fear of an invisible being that he has felt in his presence. Once the being drinks water and milk during the night. Another time it picks a rose. It even reads a book, turning the pages. The narrator becomes obsessed with the idea of this invisible creature which he believes to be superior to man. By some sort of telepathic communication the narrator learns the name of the being: the "Horla"! Finally, the narrator glimpses the Horla in a mirror: "Ce qui me cachait ne paraissait point posséder de contours nettement arrêtés, mais une sorte de transparence opaque, s'éclaircissant peu à peu" (p. 1121). Pushed to the point of insanity by his obsession, the narrator decides to kill the Horla if he can. Completely forgetting his servants, he sets fire to his house after having locked the Horla in his bedroom. But this superior being is impervious to the accidents of chance; he will die only at the end of his natural lifespan. There is no alternative for the narrator: he must kill himself.

After each strange event, the narrators make various attempts at rationalization, but every effort fails. They ask themselves questions which they are actually incapable of answering, and, finally, the manifestations remain unexplained. For example, at the end of *La Nuit* the narrator asks only: "Que se passait-il? Oh! mon Dieu! que se passait-il? (p. 1142). It is in *Lui?* and *Le Horla* where the narrators try the hardest to "explain away" their unsettling experiences. The narrator of *Le Horla* believes that our senses are too imperfect to perceive everything around us: "Comme il est profond, ce mystère de l'Invisible! Nous ne le pouvons sonder avec nos sens misérables . . . [p. 1908] . . . . mon oeil est si faible, si imparfait, qu'il ne distingue même point les corps durs, s'ils sont transparents comme le verre!" (p. 1119). These protagonists also blame their condition on illness. The narrator of *Le Horla* reports: "J'ai un peu de fièvre depuis quelques jours. . . . Je suis malade, décidément! Je me portais si bien le mois dernier!" (pp. 1098-1099). And the narrator of *Lui?* states: "C'était fini, bien fini. J'avais eu la fièvre, le cauchemar, que sais-je? J'avais été malade, enfin" (p. 857).

In addition, the narrators try to interpret the apparitions as hallucinations. In *Lui?* the narrator explains the appearance of the man in the chair as the result of "un accident nerveux de l'appareil optique" (p. 856). Likewise, the narrator of *Le Horla* considers the invisible creature's actions as merely hallucinatory: "Certes, je me croirais fou, absolument fou, si je n'étais conscient, si je ne connaissais parfaitement mon état, si je ne le sondais en l'analysant avec une complète lucidité. Je ne serais donc, en somme, qu'un halluciné raisonnant" (pp. 1112-1113). In spite of all this "reasoning," however, the apparitions remain unexplained. Try as they might, the narrators cannot rid themselves of their obsession. Indeed, we might mention in this context that it is precisely this agonizing hesitation between extreme lucidity and irrational perception of nightmarish sensations which points to Maupassant as not merely a skillful "teller of tales," as he has often traditionally been viewed, but as a precursor of surrealism, of which the major principles are founded upon a seemingly "floating frontier" between illusion and reality.

Although these strange events are inexplicable, there is a key theme in these texts which can lead one to understand better the common "framework" of Maupassant's tales: solitude. For example, the narrator of *Qui sait?*

writes: "Nous sommes deux races sur la terre. Ceux, qui ont besoin des autres . . . et ceux que les autres, au contraire, lassent, ennuient, gênent, courbaturent, tandis que l'isolement les calme, les baigne de repos dans l'indépendance et la fantaisie de leur pensée" (p. 1187). The narrator of *Lui?* is convinced that "he" is there "parce que je suis seul, uniquement parce que je suis seul!" (p. 859). In *Le Horla* the narrator clearly emphasizes the importance of aloneness as a requisite condition for such bizarre experiences: "Quand nous sommes seuls longtemps, nous peuplons le vide de fantômes" (p. 1105). In fact the word "alone" *(seul)* is found quite frequently in these texts, and in this manner Maupassant accentuates the overwhelming effect of absolute solitude. In *Qui sait?*, for example, the narrator says before the appearance of the antique dealer: "J'étais seul. J'appelais, on ne répondit point. J'étais seul" (p. 1194). And in *Lui?* the narrator confesses to his friend that he is going to be married "pour n'être pas seul! . . . Je ne veux plus être seul, la nuit . . . parce que j'ai peur, tout seul" (p. 853).

In all of these stories it is indeed solitude which invokes the strange manifestations. It seems to create the ideal atmosphere for their appearance. However, this "aloneness" is incapable of explaining away completely all the supernatural events, for, as we shall see, Maupassant has cleverly integrated within his works several details which exclude a strictly psychological explanation.

All of these bizarre manifestations are confirmed by "external evidence," i.e., that which could not be reasonably discounted as hallucinations or the imaginings of the narrator's troubled mind. This evidence is offered either by other characters in the story who attest to the reality of the event or by objective facts which support a supernatural interpretation. We have already seen that there is an entire spectrum of attempts at rationalization in these tales. There is also a corresponding range of confirmation. For example, in *La Nuit,* there is only the watch which stops; however, in *Le Horla* one finds frequent examples of external evidence: the Brazilian ship which passes in front of the narrator's house, the article concerning an epidemic of madness in Brazil, and the illness of the coachman. In *Qui sait?* the valet witnesses to the mysterious disappearance of the furniture and the gardener, to its sudden return.

The presence of external evidence prevents the reader from applying a purely psychological interpretation to these stories. On the other hand, dismissal of these events as merely coincidental is equally unreasonable, for so many coincidences would be as unbelievable as the pure supernatural. By integrating both internal and external evidence, Maupassant very cleverly maintains the tension between the explicable and the inexplicable, a technique which is the hallmark of masterpieces of this genre.

After having carefully analyzed these texts, one discovers that their similarities are not accidental. They are actually identities slightly altered from tale to tale. Each narrator follows the same "itinerary," as represented in the following diagram:

happy solitude→shudder→bizarre event(s)→unhappy solitude

The presence of this common progression, the repetition of principal themes, and the regularity of their appearance at similar points in the narration indicate strongly that Maupassant did indeed follow a basic narrative structure of which he was probably sometimes conscious, sometimes unconscious, and that these five stories are actually only variations of a single tale.

Even in Maupassant's first novel, *Une Vie,* one discovers the same basic structure—a happy and peaceful life which becomes a miserable one filled with unhappiness. Maupassant, whose quite pleasant childhood was followed by continual personal deceptions and disappointments, may have been expressing in these stories the notion that life itself is only a process of perpetual disillusionment for each individual. It is quite significant that the author never gives names to his characters in the five texts discussed above. The narrators, then, although they represent strikingly singular pathological cases, may also betoken, in a generic sense, all men who must suffer in one way or another, sometimes through mental crises or terrifying confrontations with the unknown and the unknowable, deceptions which serve as only preparation for that supreme disillusionment—Death itself.

NOTES

[1] Michael G. Lerner, *Maupassant* (New York: George Braziller, 1975), p. 172.

[2] Lerner suggests that Maupassant's repetition of the same situation in his stories was "partly due to the fact that he often kept the basic ideas of his long stories or novels in his mind for a long while before he wrote on them in a definitive form and used them meanwhile in shorter tales to perfect his presentation of them as well as to continue to make a living" (p. 172). Other Maupassant scholars have indicated that the author's obsessive use of certain thematic choices, plot developments, and characterizations, particularly noticeable toward the end of his life, is directly related to his unbalanced state of mind during this period of his literary production. Cf. Paul Cogny, *Maupassant: l'homme sans Dieu* (Brussels: Renaissance du Livre, 1968); Paul Ignotus, *The Paradox of Maupassant* (New York: Funk and Wagnalls, 1968); Edouard Maynial, *La Vie et l'oeuvre de Guy de Maupassant* (Paris: Mercure de France, 1906); André Vial, *Guy de Maupassant et l'art du roman* (Paris: Nizet, 1954); and Albert H. Wallace, *Maupassant* (New York: Twayne, 1974).

[3] Guy de Maupassant, *Contes et nouvelles,* ed. Albert-Marie Schmidt and Gérard Delaisement (Paris: Editions Albin Michel, 1960), II, 1097. Subsequent citations are from this volume.

TWENTIETH-CENTURY LITERATURE

Vern Haddick

SOURCE: "Fear and Growth: Reflections on The Beast of the Jungle," in *Journal of the Otto Rank Association,* Vol. 9, No. 2, Winter, 1974-75, pp. 38-42.

[*In the following essay, Haddick discusses Henry James's "The Beast in the Jungle" in terms of Otto Rank's concept that human life is characterized by an inner struggle between forces of fear and growth.*]

Rereading Henry James' short story "The Beast in the Jungle" after several years' involvement with Rank's writings has been an exhilarating experience. With regard to Otto Rank, his insights into problems of contemporary life seem even more relevant when fleshed out with such a concrete example. And with reference to James, his tale of a man who shapes his surroundings after the pattern of a monstrous anxiety and then discovers that the world so created has denied his self its chance to unfold, vibrates all the richer against such a conceptual background as Rank's dyad of fear and growth.

On the surface James' story is that of John Marcher, who from early years feels marked off from others by the conviction that he will experience a unique fate. In time he pictures that lurking future "something" as both magnificent and monstrous, a sleek invisible beast. He engages his acquaintance May Bartram to watch for its spring with him. So he spends decades waiting for an imaginary encounter, while May, remaining beside him, perceives and tries to help him see also that his real affliction is an inability to love and grow. Thus on a deeper level the story can be taken as that of whole groups of us whose exaggerated fears conjure up chronic speculations and thereby keep us from relating to life in another way, ever at hand, that might support an equally natural self-development. On yet a third level, suggested by submerged hints especially toward the close of the tale, Marcher's case is that of Everyman—an inner dialogue between forces of fear and growth which Rank discussed as perhaps the central bipolarity of everybody's life.

James composed the story between July and October 1902. Somewhat atypically for him he entered in his notebook only a reticent clue to his inspiration for it, speaking impersonally of the instance of a man who indulges fears that haunt him and so fails to marry a woman who had always waited at his side. Yet according to Leon Edel, the James biographer, the seeds of the situation probably derived from a striking incident in James' life which proves that he too was an Everyman caught between the pulls of fear and growth (or love). Edel remarks that from adolescence James showed in both his behavior and writings a pronounced distrust of close involvement with women. However during his "middle years" in Europe he befriended the deaf lonely American novelist Constance Fenimore Woolson, who became warmly attached to him. When James eventually noticed the drift of their relationship he retreated to a safe distance, limiting their exchanges to occasional letters and one meeting a year. Then in Venice a winter night in 1894 she threw herself from her bedroom window and died of the injuries. James was appalled at the outcome, saw belatedly the wide gap in their regard for each other, and met Miss Woolson's heirs in Italy to help settle her estate and dispose of her personal effects. Yet even here, Edel speculates, two forces may have continued to influence James' behavior: his affectionate courtesy may have been yoked to the worry that Miss Woolson's private papers revealed too much about him. However, unlike John Marcher who so justified his fear that he achieved a negative fate, the author in real life arranged matters in Venice, if there were matters to arrange, and then cultivated the possibilities for late growth from the friendship until he produced a great piece of psychological fiction.

The outcome in the case is quite consistent with Rank's discussions of the Janus-type dyad. Rank proposed that the fear response is likely the first content of human consciousness; yet he did not see it as always winning the battle because of its early appearance upon the field. It has to contend with a strong urge and capacity for growth ("the will") which also seems to be present in men just as a consequence of their birth into the human species. Rank pointed to the long record of man's religions, art, institutions and products as demanding that the positive coping response be given its due. Even though separation and loss, having occurred once, may recur at any moment; even though if man focuses his attention on his feelings of negative difference he may make his life, like John Marcher's, a vast barren expanse; it is always open to a person to turn his energies in the opposite direction, cultivate the positive aspects of his individuality and respond with love to the same characteristic in others. Instead of dwelling on a possible future threat and drawing fearfully back from each new chance, so cutting himself off from opportunities which the new is always offering (like a May Bartram beside every man) he can choose to relate warmly to the other, the outer, and so involve both of them in richer present experience. Rank said in *Will Therapy* that overconcern for the future can serve as a means of denying the possible threat in the here and now; yet the model of psychotherapy which he described in the same work also took the immediate relationship between client and helper as the context from which more-productive selves may grow. Marcher's fixation upon his future meeting with the imaginary beast displaced successfully the threat he may have sensed in closest union with Miss Bartram; still that other companion was always present to remind him tactfully in endless ways that his forebodings might be read as perhaps due only to the "expectation— or at any rate the sense of danger, familiar to so many people—of falling in love." James presents the possibilities of growth through the relationship to May with a vividness and poignancy that reaches its climax when she confides just before her death, "I would live for you still—if I could—but I can't." Marcher in the grip of his obsession rejects even that appeal; and later he thinks of her demise as just another aggravation, the end of her usefulness in keeping the watch with him.

Then in the last two or three pages of the story (as in the last chapter of the James-Woolson friendship recorded by Edel, and in the final stage of successful therapy as described by Rank) the darker force is shown up as not necessarily invincible. Marcher shakes off the "neurotic" role he had embraced and takes an impressive step toward growth so long denied. In the cemetery while visiting May's tomb he sees at a nearby grave a man so completely the image of "scarred passion" as to cause Marcher to ask, "What had the man *had,* to make him by the loss of it so bleed and yet love? Something that *he,* John Marcher, hadn't. . . . No passion had ever touched him, for this was what passion meant." He realizes, even so late, that passive before the beast he had projected into the world he has turned his whole life into a long negative adventure when the many years might have been full of love shared with May. The pain of his lost opportunity cannot be undone. Yet, we feel, something of worth has come out of it in the end.

It is apparent that only two characters figure in the story, which is told so consistently from Marcher's point of view that it might be taken as his account of an hallucination in which May and the beast represent projections of a deep bipolarity in his nature. John Marcher chooses to identify with the beast until during his visit to the graveyard he suddenly rises to a new outlook. There among the tombstones he feels first that, on his travels away from London since May's death "he had been separated so long from the part of himself that alone he now valued." Then he realizes that, unacknowledged by him at the time, May Bartram (even whose name suggests a mirror-image of his own) had been something more than a useful fellow spectator. She had been, rather, "the truth of his life" in which he could have loved himself; she had been "his other younger self." Finally, he admits, to have loved her would have been precisely to have turned the tables on the beast and led a rich full existence. With that realization by his protagonist James ends "The Beast in the Jungle." It is a note in close harmony with the one Edel sounds in his final pages on the James-Woolson friendship. And the dual chord fixes vividly for us those poles of fear and love (or growth) to which Rank referred over and over in his writings.

So much for the novelist and John Marcher. Now I wonder if we Marchers and Jameses of a later decade can face down our own beasts more successfully than the poor solitary bachelor in the tale? The path through our years seems beset with even more threats than his: with specters of changed life styles, widely divergent outlooks, startling demands and proposals. To meet them with anxiety and skepticism is of course one natural response, as Rank would be the first to tell us—but at the same time he might add, "a futile sterile response, that." Another way, of course, is to grasp and use the chance for growth in relationship with "the other." John Marcher could not until too late see the opportunity presented by his other, younger half. He chose instead to justify his fear. I wonder if we shall too?

Alvin Starr

SOURCE: "The Concept of Fear in the Works of Stephen Crane and Richard Wright," in *Studies in Black Literature,* Vol. 6, No. 2, Summer, 1975, pp. 6-10.

[*In the following essay, Starr draws parallels between the responses to fear by protagonists in Stephen Crane's "The Blue Hotel" and* The Red Badge of Courage *and Richard Wright's "Big Black Good Man" and* Native Son.]

Richard Wright uses the concept of fear in at least three ways within his fiction which reflect similar utilizations of this concept within the fiction of Stephen Crane. Mainly, he follows Crane in the depiction of paranoiac fear. Secondly he uses fear in *Native Son* in much the same way that Crane does in *The Red Badge of Courage.* Finally Wright makes use of a more metaphysical concept of fear in two of his works ("The Man Who Lived Underground" and *The Outsider*), and this type of fear strangely resembles that which Crane used in "The Open Boat."

In Wright's story "Big Black Good Man" and in Crane's story "The Blue Hotel," the protagonists both share the same type of fear—namely paranoia. The Swede's lack of knowledge of the true nature of the West or of the brutishness of the American frontier causes him to have certain expectations about the people he meets in the Palace Hotel in Fort Romper, Nebraska. His "dime store novel" preconceptions cause him to see everyone in the hotel except the Easterner as willing to murder him with little or no provocation. Because of his prejudgments ("I suppose there have been a good many men killed in this room"),[1] the Swede eventually brings on his own death— not in the Blue Hotel, but at the hands of a polished gambler who happens to be carrying a knife to protect himself from bullies like the Swede. Various of the Swede's comments illustrate his paranoia:

> "Oh, I see you are all against me. I see." ("B. H.," p. 321).

> "I am going to be killed before I can leave this house!" ("B. H.," p. 321).

> "I won't stand much show against this gang. I know you'll all pitch on me." ("B. H.," p. 336).

The Swede sees everyone in the hotel as his enemy, yet there is little in the narrative to justify his fear of anyone but the hotelkeeper's son. In addition, the Swede does not know that the violent days of the Old West have almost totally disappeared from this area and that Nebraska is basically filled with agricultural communities whose notorious gamblers are now family men. He is living in a world of make-believe, where hotelkeepers are supposed to poison their guests and where everyone is out to mock or destroy the "tenderfoot." Only in the Swede's mind is everyone out to get him, but this fantasy brings on his death just as it almost does that of the hotelkeeper in Wright's "Big Black Good Man."

As in Crane's story, Wright's protagonist creates a fantasy world of fears based on unwarranted expectations. Having been a night porter in Copenhagen, the white Olaf Jenson had had somewhat limited opportunities to come into contact with blacks, except for sailors now and then; and none of those sailors were like the big black man that this story portrays.[2] When this "black giant" enters the Copenhagen hotel, Olaf, who is working behind the desk, is filled with unreasoned fears about what will happen to himself. Olaf, like the Swede, begins to recall the myths he has heard; but in this case Olaf is falling prey to a "pulp fiction" conception of blacks. At first, like Crane's Swede, he puts up a "front" to show this huge black man that he is unafraid of him: "Olaf moved about quickly, pulling down the window shades, taking the pink coverlet off the bed, nudging the giant with his elbow, to make him move as he did so. . . . That's the way to treat 'im. . . . Show 'im I ain't scared of 'im. . . ."[3] The reader will recall that the Swede is always aware of how he looks to the people he fears most. His statements about his not being a tenderfoot, his pride at winning the fight, and his attempt to force the gambler to drink, all show this reaction. In both the case of the hotelkeeper and of Olaf, this is the kind of arrogance which is a compensation for fear. Later, even though the night porter finds *this* customer's request for a woman and something to drink disgusting, he cooperates and meets both of these demands. But as Lena, a white prostitute, leaves the "black giant's" room, Olaf's hates and fears begin to fill his thoughts as they had in the case of Crane's Swede:

> . . . he could not shake off a primitive hate for that black mountain of energy, of muscle, of bone; he envied the easy manner in which it moved with such a creeping and powerful motion; he winced at the booming and commanding voice that came to him when the tiny little eyes were not even looking at him; he shivered at the sight of those vast clawlike hands that seemed always to hint of death. . . . ("B. G. M.," p. 81)

Also in the same manner as Crane's Swede, Olaf considers covering up his fears by voicing them belligerently to his antagonists. (The Swede actually does voice his fear and hatred; whereas, Olaf only *considers* saying what he feels.) After the fifth request by the black guest for Lena and whiskey, "Olaf was about to make a sarcastic remark to the effect that maybe he ought to marry Lena, but he checked it in time. . . . After all, he could kill me with one hand he told himself" ("B. G. M.," p. 82).

On the day that this gargantuan black man checks out, he demands that Olaf stand up. As Olaf arises he thinks, "This evil blackness was about to attack him, maybe kill him" ("B. G. M.," p. 83). His fears seem confirmed as the black man reaches up and puts his hands around his neck. Olaf is so afraid that he is about to die that he wets his pants and pleads, "Please don't hurt me" ("B. G. M.," p. 84). But after shunting aside Olaf's remark, the black man exits without harming him, or so much as threatening to do so. For a year Olaf dreams of vengeance on this black man by means of a "*white* shark," but finally he appears to have forgotten his adventure when his black customer returns and once again encircles Olaf's neck with his fingers. In reaction to this renewed assault, Olaf is about to shoot what he thinks is a black assilant when the black man suddenly pulls out the shirts he has been measuring Olaf for. Although the result of the paranoia of Wright's and Crane's main characters are different, it is still obvious that their "fears" are similar.[4]

In *Native Son,* even though most of Bigger's fears are justified, some of them stem from a deep-seated—seemingly unrealistic—paranoia. This again shows Wright using fear in the same manner that Crane had. As a black youth brought up in an extremely racist environment, Bigger's fear-filled reactions are often appropriate for assuring his survival. However, when Bigger's fears lose all but the faintest relationship to the situations that he is involved in, they become paranoiac and a part of the forces that destroy him. At the beginning of Book I, Bigger considers robbing a store whose owner is white. Bigger's exaggerated fear of pursuit by the white world gives the reader some feeling of the extent of his paranoia:

> They [Bigger, G. H., and Gus] had the feeling that the robbing of Blum's would be a violation of ultimate taboo: "It would be a trespassing into territory where the full wrath of the alien white world would be turned loose upon them; in short, it would be a symbolic challenge of the white world's rule over them; a challenge which they yearned to make, but were afraid to." (*N. S.,* p. 18)[5]

The assumption that the police will try harder to catch any Black who robbed a white-owned store in the ghetto is logical, but the feeling that "the full wrath of an alien white world would be turned loose upon the three of them" is an exaggerated and hence a paranoiac reaction that a racist society has implanted in Bigger's mind, and the mind of many other Blacks. Later when Bigger takes a gun and a knife to the Dalton home, he shows exactly the sort of fear which no longer distinguishes among enemies (paranoia). It is this inability to sort out individuals or even types among white people in Book I of *Native Son* that causes Bigger to hate Jim and Mary for their treatment of him instead of merely scoffing at the "liberal" gestures that they make toward him. If white racism had not caused Bigger to see all whites through a fog of fear, he might not have been so afraid of being caught with the Daltons's daughter in her room. Certainly he would have been fired by the self-righteous Daltons, but there is no reason why he should have been charged with rape, simply because of the Dalton's concern for their daughter's reputation.

This pattern of paranoia continues on into Books II and III of *Native Son*.[6] Wright's repeated usage of this type of fear in *Native Son* has also caused Edwin Berry Burgum to see part of Bigger's fears in terms of paranoia. Since his remarks give a kind of independent substantiation to my own interpretation of Bigger's conduct, I shall include them at this juncture. He suggests the following: "His [Bigger's] uncertain groping for some valid avenue of self-fulfillment before the murder now [after Bigger's arrest] gives way to the authority of his excitement. He enters a world of paranoiac fantasy in which his acts of frenzy seem to him not so much the clever concealment of his initial mistake as the unfolding of a grandoise plan of conquest."[7]

Pursuing the comparison I have made to "Blue Hotel" one step further, one may note that Bigger tries to act tough just as the Swede did in order to hide his fears. As I pointed out earlier, this is the typical compensation mechanism of the paranoiac. In addition, as with Crane's protagonist, paranoia is the main cause of Bigger's death. The main characters of four other of Wright's works ("The Man Who Lived Underground," *The Outsider, Savage Holiday,* and *Lawd Today*) often illustrate paranoiac fears; but the examples I have given so far are sufficient to show the similar use that Wright and Crane make of this syndrome.

Yet the paranoiac fear of "Blue Hotel" is not the only Crane-like use of fear that occurs in *Native Son*. Wright also portrays fear in a way that is very similar to the fear one finds in *The Red Badge of Courage*. As a basis for my study of the analogous type of fear one finds in *Native Son* and *The Red Badge of Courage,* I should like to cite Daniel Weiss' article, "'The Blue Hotel': A Psychoanalytic Study," which contains an excellent analysis of fear and the reactions fear causes as these phenomena occur in *The Red Badge of Courage*. Early in his analysis Weiss suggests three ways in which Henry Fleming reacts to his fears. I have found that each of these three reactions to fear also occurs with Bigger Thomas in *Native Son*. Because Henry Fleming is horrified by the prospect of going into battle, he sublimates these fears by viewing war in terms of the past or as a game, it is compared to a "Greeklike struggle" and the army is seen as a "blue demonstration." This flight from reality to avoid the terrors of what one is actually afraid of is also found in Bigger who sees the whites he fears in terms of a game called "White" in Book I of *Native Son*. Secondly, Weiss finds that Fleming avoids confronting the terror within himself by projecting his fears on others like Wilson. What else is Bigger doing than this when he tries to make Gus look like the one who is afraid to rob Blum's store? Moreover, Weiss suggests that Henry looks for refuge in various "parent figures."[8] Again it is easy to see that Max, and, to a lesser extent, Jan serve this same role for Bigger in *Native Son*.

Continuing his analysis of Crane's novel, Weiss suggests that Henry chooses both what Weiss calls the "flight to activity" and the "flight to passivity" in order to cover up his fears. "The flight to activity involves the primitive logic of becoming the thing or person one fears and then proceeding to intimidate others. Reassurance is bound up with the obsessive display of fierceness, seeming is being, pretensions are genuine. At such moments tensions clamoring for discharge convert fear into anger, hatred, and aggression."[9] These ideas so aptly describe what Wright was doing that they seem as if they had just come out of a critical study of Wright's novel. Note how the following statements by Edwin Berry Burgum parallel Weiss' idea of the "flight to activity" as applied to *Native Son:*

> Bigger kills the rat that has been frightening the women folks, and then frightens them the more by flaunting its dead body in their faces. His courage is that overcompensation for fear called bravado.
>
> Knowing that he cannot learn to fly an airplane, his helplessness creates an inner state of fear which (as it has been transformed by the healthy impulse of courage into bravado) sets up the direct motivation of hatred, and transforms what might have been a healthy social activity into petty thievery. But, to the uneducated boy, hatred for the whites is too remote and turns inward. It vents itself upon his family with their misguided notion that decency is rewarded, upon his black neighbors from whom his gang steals, upon the gang for the pettiness of its objectives, and upon himself for his inability to attain more grandoise ends.[10]

Here in an analysis of *Native Son* are precisely the same notions of the intimidation of others, the "display of fierceness," and fear being converted to "anger, hatred, and agression," that Weiss uses to discuss *The Red Badge of Courage.*

Not only does Weiss' idea of "flight to activity" fit Bigger's actions in Book I, it also sheds light on his actions in Book II as Bigger is forced to face up to the consequences of his accidental murder of Mary. Rather than collapsing because he is now what he has always wanted to avoid becoming, a murderer and a rapist in the eyes of white society, Bigger decides that the murder of Mary is the foundation for a new life that he can create for himself. Because his fears are greater than they have ever been before, he *willingly* accepts the fact that he is a murderer (at least he does so in his thoughts), and he even suggests that he looks forward with great anticipation to being able to tell white society of his deed after his inevitable capture. This is an enormous change from the Bigger who, at the beginning of Book I, "knew that the moment he allowed what his life meant to enter fully into his consciousness, he would either kill himself or someone else. So he denied himself and acted tough" (*N. S.,* p. 14). Even though this first "flight to activity" through acting tough failed because fate put Bigger in a room with a drunken girl and her blind white mother, Bigger has not learned enough not to try another "flight" from his fears. In his new role as a murderer, Bigger is able to *intimidate* the whites who have always struck terror into his heart. He does this both to the Daltons in

the ransom scheme and to the Communists (all of whom are white in Bigger's mind) in his attempt to blame them for Mary's murder. But this "flight" does not work any better than the wall of toughness he uses in Book I; so that when the pressures get too great his fear resurfaces as hate, and he kills Bessie. Thus it is clear that the pattern of analysis Weiss works in both Book I and II of *Native Son.*

The remainder of Weiss' treatment of *Red Badge of Courage* gives us an excellent tool for understanding Book III of *Native Son.* Weiss suggests that the second way that Henry reacts to fear is through a "flight to passivity." "The flight to passivity is describable in terms of Henry Fleming's readiness to accept protection, to yield rather than advance, to depend on the 'cheery man' who leads him back to his bivouac, . . ."[11] During Book III of *Native Son,* Bigger too is looking for protection—for something or someone to help him understand his life and to aid him to face his certain death. He even lets Reverend Hammond talk to him in the hope that this man will be able to help him; but Bigger finds out that religion can help him only to face death while it will not help him to really understand his own life. Then as Jan talks to him, Bigger starts to sense that this man holds the answer to both his queries, but Jan's talk with him is interrupted by other visitors. Later when Max talks to him and, even more importantly, lets Bigger talk, he decides that this man may be able to serve his needs for "protection" just as well as Jan could have. Afterwards when Max speaks so eloquently in his defense in court, Bigger is almost sure that he can help him with both of his problems. Although I do not feel that Max holds an answer for Bigger, it is still revealing that Bigger is willing to depend on him. Still it is clear that Book III may be seen in terms of what Weiss calls a "flight to passivity."

Richard Wright uses "fear" in one other way that Crane does. In "The Open Boat" the correspondent's unexpressed fear at the end of the story is not of death so much as it is of something that he comes to feel is just as essential. The experience of the correspondent on the open and uncaring sea had given him a chance to be an "interpreter" and brought him an insight into life that he had never had before. This insight is exemplified by his new understanding of the verse "a soldier of the Legion lay dying in Algiers, . . ." as being "stern, mournful, and fine."[12] Once the correspondent has this new knowledge, he has to confront the possibility of his inability to communicate what he knows, and the inability of society to understand what he has found out. Perhaps even the other two survivors will not understand. This fear is as true to him as the fear of death is to Henry or the Swede. This more metaphysical type of fear is shared by at least two of Wright's characters. When Fred Daniels (of "The Man Who Lived Underground") comes out of the sewer, he goes almost immediately to the police. He wants to communicate the nature and the content of his experiences below the city. No longer is he afraid of being falsely accused of murder. The reality he has seen *must* be communicated even if it costs him his life—it is more important than his life. As Fred tries to explain what he saw, his depiction seems almost surreal—human language is not a sufficient vehicle for conveying this reality. In addition, society, as represented by the police, is unwilling to heed his message ("You've got to shoot his kind. They'd wreck things.").[13] Discussing this story, Ronald Ridenour comes to just this evaluation of Fred Daniels' fear. It is, he writes, "not a fear of death but a fear that his knowledge will not be heard, will not be heeded because of its totally alien nature."[14] Likewise, Cross Damon (of *The Outsider*) is filled with a fear that mankind will not be able to see either the mistakes he has made or to understand the truth that he and others like him bring to the world. As he dies, he tells Houston about his anguish in the following terms:

> "I wish I had some way to give the meaning of my life to others. . . . To make a bridge from man to man. . . . Starting from scratch every time is . . . not good. Tell them not to come down this road. . . . The real men, the last men are coming. . . . Somebody must prepare the way for them. . . . Tell the world what they are like. . . . We are here already, if others but had the courage to see us. . . . "(*Outsider,* pp. 439-440).

Clearly Crane's correspondent, and Wright's Fred Daniels and Cross Damon have a common desire to be "interpreters," but they *fear* that their answers will fall upon deaf ears.

Wright then uses fear in at least three ways that are reminiscent of Crane. This similar use of fear by both authors certainly suggests some influence, whether conscious or unconscious, of Crane upon Wright.

NOTES

[1] Stephen Crane "Blue Hotel," *The Red Badge of Courage and Four Great Stories by Stephen Crane* (New York: Dell Publishing Co., 1964), p. 320. Hereafter all citations will be given in parenthetical entries.

[2] It is interesting to note that both Crane's protagonist and Wright's hotelkeeper are Scandinavians.

[3] Richard Wright, "Big Black Good Man," *Eight Men* (New York: Pyramid Books, 1961), p. 80. Hereafter all citations will be given in parenthetical entries.

[4] Indeed, it is also worth noting that the paranoia in Crane's work is tied to the experience of an alien environment, while it is connected with experiencing an alien race in Wright's work.

[5] Richard Wright, *Native Son* (New York: Harper and Row, 1966), p. 18. Hereafter all entries will be given in parenthetical entries.

[6] Typical examples of paranoiac reaction in Book II of *Native Son* include: Bigger's fear that his voice has changed since the murder, p. 97; Bigger's excessive fear of whites, p. 109; Bigger's concern over Bessie's questioning, p. 129; Bigger's fear that Britten is part of a plot to trap him, Bigger's guilt-filled dream in which he sees his own head severed from his body, p. 156; Bigger's pulling a gun on Jan, p. 162; Bigger's fear of the furnace (he will not clean out the ashes because of this fear), p. 183; Bigger's fear of the white cat, p. 190; and Bigger's murder of Bessie in order to save himself, p. 221.

Typical examples of paranoiac reactions in Book III include: Bigger's fear that Max and Jan are using him, p. 288; Bigger's fear that Reverend Hammond's gift of a wooden cross was an attempt to trap him, p. 313; Bigger's fear that Max is trapping him, p. 321; Bigger's driving Reverend Hammond away and his throwing coffee at a white priest, p. 386; Bigger's fear that Max has betrayed him because he is about to die.

[7] Edwin Berry Burgum, "The Promise of Democracy in Richard Wright's *Native Son*" in *The Novel and the World's Dilemma* (New York: Russell and Russell, 1963; rpt. in Richard Abcarian, ed., *"Native Son": A Critical Handbook* (Belmont, California: Wadsworth Company, 1970), p. 118.

[8] Daniel Weiss, "The Blue Hotel: A Psychoanalytic Study in *Stephen Crane—A Collection of Critical Essays,* ed. Maurice Bassan (Englewood Cliffs, New Jersey: Prentice Hall, 1967), p. 155.

[9] Weiss, pp. 155-156.

[10] Burgum, p. 117.

[11] Weiss, p. 156.

[12] Stephen Crane, "Open Boat," *The Red Badge of Courage, and Four Great Stories by Stephen Crane,* p. 209.

[13] Richard Wright "The Man Who Lived Underground," *Eight Men,* p. 74.

[14] Ronald Ridenour, "The Man Who Lived Underground: A Critique," *Phylon,* 31, No. 1 (1970), p. 57.

William Rossky

SOURCE: "The Pattern of Nightmare in *Sanctuary*; or, Miss Reba's Dogs," in *Modern Fiction Studies,* Vol. 15, No. 4, Winter, 1969-70, pp. 503-515.

[*In the following essay, Rossky sketches a pattern of stasis and paralysis which produces a nightmare effect in William Faulkner's* Sanctuary, *contributing to its criticism of modern society and its commentary on the human condition.*]

Having demolished the once popular judgment of *Sanctuary* as simply a potboiler, a notion which stemmed usually from an incomplete reading of Faulkner's own comments, critics and scholars have for some years regularly accorded the book the serious consideration warranted by the author's honesty of intention.[1] Chiefly the tendency of the commentary has been to see the novel in some way as an attack on the modern world—an outpouring of indignation at the mechanization and dehumanization, the immorality and loss of spiritual values in the twentieth-century wasteland.[2] This rather overwhelming consensus of critical opinion is, surely, at least partly correct. The difficulty, however, is that such light-of-day analyses in terms of modern life do not adequately convey the vast sense of nightmare which exists in the novel, nor the consequent largeness of meaning and effect. For nightmare pervades *Sanctuary,* and its terror is ultimately like the terror before the question posed by Job, *Oedipus,* and *Lear*—but without the satisfactions of acceptance or heroism and without the compensation of spiritual growth through suffering the incomprehensible.[3]

That some such effect is to be expected is suggested by Faulkner's own comment on *Sanctuary* as "an exposition of the terror and the injustice which man must face."[4] To be sure, the large and moving sense of terror may reflect, as Lawrence Kubie argues, the modern male's fear of sexual impotence.[5] For that matter, it may even be rooted in modern, or ageless, feelings of guilt and a consequent expectation of punishment that sometimes results in the projection into the universe of an ubiquitously threatening and imminent doom. But the possible existence of such psychological roots does not invalidate the fact that the terror emanates also—and perhaps principally—from the dark vision of an irrational, nightmarish universe. Indeed, the two sources would be likely to merge and to reinforce each other.

Much of the feeling of *Sanctuary* is the result of what we may well call a technique of nightmare. Although the word "nightmare" is hardly an original one for the novel, how thoroughly it applies requires emphasis. Repeatedly the narrative evokes moments of dreamlike horror typical especially of a certain kind of nightmare: The dreamer is caught in impotent terror; paralyzed, deeply frightened, trying, yet unable, to act or to scream.[6] And while they provide an appropriate atmosphere for the patterns of degenerate modernity, these many instances of paralysis-with-horror also contribute even more to a sense of cosmic nightmare; they accumulate to an experience of profound terror and powerlessness within and before the chaos and illogicality of the whole of existence.

This view is clarified and supported by the recurrent examples of nightmare imagery. And I do not refer here merely to what might be called modern variations on the conventions of the older Gothic novel—such matters as the moldering old ruin, the Frenchman's place, which duplicates the decaying medieval castle; the threat of a dark villain in Popeye's lean, lethal shadow extending over the house; or the figure of the half frightening and half protective retainer. Although such things contribute to the total tone, the chills inspired by these and similar conventional Gothic devices[7] arise clearly out of make-believe. Almost like the shudders of children listening to tales of haunted houses, they are the fears of "let's pretend." The effects are not deeply disturbing, not genuinely nightmarish, and Faulkner leaves them behind rather early in the book. More deeply woven into its texture, however, are the dreamlike images and scenes in which the principals—and the readers—are caught in a clotting motion, in a paralysis, or near-paralysis, of helpless terror. In its sense of slow, strange motion, the world of *Sanctuary* resembles, in a way, Poe's world of drifting fog; slow, falling water; and dripping moonlight. But even Poe sometimes inspires only the Gothic "make-believe" shudder as compared to the sense of cold paralysis, entrapment and terror which permeates *Sanctuary* and becomes a feeling about existence itself.

Certainly the persistence of images and incidents of slow motion or of total pause in Faulkner—"frozen moments"[8]—has often been noted. But what needs emphasis is that they occur not only with varying degrees of frequency from novel to novel but in a wide variety of uses. For example, the stillness with motion experienced as Lena Grove waits for the Armstid wagon early in *Light in August* conveys chiefly ripeness and placidity—it is an essentially Edenic moment—whereas in *Go Down, Moses* Ike McCaslin's "frozen moments" often mark experiences of mystical exaltation, awe or insight, while the tableau of Jewel mastering his horse in *As I Lay Dying* is a concentration of sublimated love and fury. *Sanctuary* is particularly full of such episodes of dreamlike retarded motion or stasis; but, even more important, despite subtle differences of effect among them, they are almost all nightmarishly terrifying.

These moments of fear-infused stasis that convey the sense of impotence of nightmare begin on the first pages with that still and threatening two-hour pause, broken only by an occasional bird call or the sound from the highway, during which Horace squats before the danger of Popeye at the spring. They appear repeatedly in the experience of Temple Drake and, incidentally, help to create a degree of identification with her that is sometimes overlooked. Especially at the Frenchman's place, Temple seems almost constantly in motion that yet remains terrifyingly fixed; she seems constantly wheeling to flee from one room to another and back again, yet remains in one place, in the circle of the house, cowering in the circle of her fear: "Still running her bones turned to water and she fell flat on her face, still running."[9] "Without ceasing to run she appeared to pause" (p. 56, and see p. 49), her face "fixed in that cringing grimace" of placating terror (p. 57). At one point she seems to stand still, helplessly watching "herself run out of her body, out of one slipper" (p. 109, and see p. 77). Other examples occur in the rigid tension of Temple as she cringes against the porch door (p. 76) or at the corner of the kitchen stove (p. 60), lies stiff on the bed as others muse in the darkness beyond (pp. 91, 94-5, and cf. pp. 81, 84), or thrashes impotently on the corn shuck mattress at Ruby's touch (p. 96). Especially as Temple retells it to Horace, that whole evening becomes a nightmare of strange pause in action and of active fantasizing without action. During the frenetic succession of transformations which Temple fantasizes as escapes from Popeye, she lies, seemingly without breathing, paralyzed—at one point she imagines herself dead in a coffin—even when her somehow impersonally frightened skin jerks before Popeye's cold moving touch. Popeye's whole visit in the darkness is an action shrouded, dreamlike, and, of course, incomplete. So too a sense of horrible, helpless lassitude pervades the atmosphere at Miss Reba's when Temple arrives. In the shuttered brothel into which light leaks with "a protracted weariness like a vitiated backwater beyond sunlight" (p. 172), Temple lies frightened, her blood seeping, and listens to the ticking of the clock or the watch, and the sounds outside her room are remote and strangely threatening as in nightmare. Even more pointedly applicable is the rape scene itself. The whole sequence is strange, dazed and still; action seems extremely remote, thus unreal; and sound appears suspended: " . . . it was as though sound and silence had become inverted" (pp. 121-122). Temple sits first in helpless paralysis, "her hands limp and palm-up on her lap" and, as the chapter closes, again lies "thrashing" in one place in the terrified impotence of motion which is non-motion.

The intense, choked horror of nightmare is also conveyed in the "silent" screams of the novel, in the stasis of Temple's long, unuttered "hopeless" cry as she rides with Popeye, "her mouth open and the half chewed mass of bread and meat lying upon her tongue" (p. 169) and in the scream which she finally utters in the rape scene, "like hot silent bubbles into the bright silence" (p. 122). The sense of stifled scream underlies almost all her experiences, until she begins to glory in her Memphis life— at which point she herself becomes part of the nightmare of others, particularly of Horace. And the soundless scream continues into the fiery tableau of Goodwin's lynching in which everything seems "soundless" and dreamlike, including the screams of a man burned by the oil from his exploding can (p. 355). In Faulkner only the castration of Joe Christmas in *Light in August,* with its background sound of the screaming siren like a searing iron upon raw nerves, may be said to evoke equally the feeling of intense paralyzed horror. Indeed it might not be very far wrong to describe the whole experience of agonized, stifled and unresolved terror in the novel as a kind of long soundless scream.

Even the courtroom scene subscribes to the dominant pattern. Once more Temple sits "hands . . . motionless, palm-up on her lap," "lax-ankled" in "motionless slippers" above a crowd in which the faces become "white and pallid as the floating bellies of dead fish" (p. 341). In a great gap of silence, Judge Drake's slow progress up the aisle is followed by the "slow gaping of the small white faces" to where Temple sits blank-eyed and immobile (p. 346). The whole scene is like the slow motion of bad dreams; and through it runs the fearful enormity of Temple's lies and the triumph of injustice. Before that enormity Horace himself seems paralyzed into impotence.

The complex of stasis or slow-motion and helpless horror which creates the effect of nightmare is also repeatedly conveyed in many smaller scenes and images. For example, it appears in little in the images of cigarette smoke drifting slowly past the viciousness of Popeye's face; in the picture of Ruby's sick child with "its curled hands above its head in the attitude of one crucified" (p. 160); in Temple's remembering the tableau of a group of co-eds poised threateningly about one frightened girl, "their eyes like knives" (p. 182); in Temple's encounter with the rat staring "eye to eye" (p. 111); in the one-handed, empty-faced clock at Miss Reba's which Temple watches to the "faint rasping sounds" of window shades (p. 177); even in the image of the wheel of Gowan's car spinning in the suddenly ominous silence after the accident (p. 45) or in the gruesome slow motion of Red's corpse rolling out of its casket (p. 299).

For that matter, the ostensibly ordinary, like the half-masticated gob of sandwich in the middle of Temple's unuttered scream, functions to accent the nightmare. Outside the central dark dream of *Sanctuary,* men pitch coins in front of the courthouse yard and crowds move about the square, "people buying comfortable things to take home and eat at quiet tables" (p. 197). The "normalcy" of the lives of Belle and Narcissa, which has a kind of horror of its own, helps to sharpen the larger nightmare of which they are unconscious. The somewhat overextended episode of the barber apprentices wandering blindly on the edge of adult evil serves by contrast to point up the dream horror and yet provides a change of pace that helps ultimately to sustain the horror which might otherwise pall. Even the comedy of Red's macabre funeral is a sort of porter-at-the-gate interlude; for the humor, which appears at first sight a departure from the pattern, contains chilling overtones which actually return us to it.

Indeed, the very prevalence of this atmosphere helps partially to clarify what are sometimes regarded as perplexing illogicalities in *Sanctuary:* Why doesn't Temple just escape into the woods at Goodwin's? Why on the trip to Memphis doesn't she slip away from Popeye at the gas station? And why doesn't Horace question Temple at the trial? Although there are others, one answer lies in the nightmare pattern of the book. As in nightmare, helplessly caught in stasis, they cannot do otherwise. The very fact that they do not do these perhaps expected things actually contributes to the atmosphere of horrible dream. The pattern also helps to answer questions about the title. The sense of helpless exposure, without sanctuary, deepens its irony.

Although more evidence will shortly be offered, enough has perhaps already been said to support the view, first, that images and actions of a special kind of nightmare— of terror-stricken impotence, of dreamlike fearful paralysis or near paralysis—do pervade the novel and, secondly, that, for the most part, they do not carry much by way of special implication about the modern world. What is particularly modern about Temple rigid upon the chattering shucks of the mattress, about the visits in darkness, about the lynching scene, or, for that matter, about any of the sequences presented? Even in the extended dreamlike hiatus of Popeye and Horace at the spring, the emphasis on the ugliness of modern mechanization in the description of Popeye is a fringe effect in respect to the central impression of a chilling mesmerizing pause. The matter of the novel is recognizably modern, but it contributes chiefly as a sort of imagistic base—what Faulkner might well have called a "tool"[10]—to the major effect of nightmare.

It is not that the comment on modernity is not there, then, but that Faulkner does more. To make Horace, Popeye, and Temple simply the arid twentieth-century figures suggested by the word "wasteland" is to reduce the nightmare. If modern aridity is a part of the point, the special kind of horror in the book also goes beyond this effect and beyond any simple application to social evils of the modern world. Indeed, it is difficult in a way to apply this nightmare—this sense of terrorized impotence—to the view of the novel as a condemnation simply of modern social ills. In the recent past at least, the very modernity of these evils would have suggested not fearful paralysis, but potential for change. Emotionally, the book's kind of nightmare does not blend very directly with such ills as may after all be listed, analyzed, and presumably resolved with daylight clarity. It is rather to a universal, cosmic terror that the nightmare of *Sanctuary* is most essentially related.

This view is supported not only by the very recurrence of the images and actions already cited but also by further analysis of some of them and by a series of other examples of the nightmare pattern which are clearly cosmic in implication. And these are moments in the novel which always cry out for attention—moments which, because of the reverberations they set in motion, insist on their large symbolic significance.

Pregnant with such meaning is the heaven-tree outside the jail. Perhaps, as William Van O'Connor thoughtfully suggests, the tree reflects "the evil inherent in human nature,"[11] but it is much more likely that this is true of the jail than of the tree which is, after all, not made by man. (One thinks here also of Faulkner's jail in *The Hamlet,* the walls sweating with years of accumulated human injustice.) But whether the tree speaks of something in man or not, surely it evokes even more a feeling about the universe beyond man. In another novel its trumpet-shaped blooms might well connote not merely the final Judgment Day, as O'Connor says, but even the angelic trumpets of the heavenly hosts and thus a possibility of heavenly good. But here these portents of heavenly fulfillment make only a severely ironic cosmic comment. For the pulsating heaven-tree throws an ominous "splotched shadow" upon the bar-slotted wall behind which lie not only the guilty but the innocent. As in nightmare, the shadow of this heaven symbol "shuddered and pulsed monstrously in scarce any wind" (p. 148). The effect is all stasis and menace. Only an existential fear is inspired by the "heaven" blooms that fall and become dead, slippery smears on the sidewalk. Not cosmic justice and order, but chilling and dark cosmic threat are communicated by Faulkner's handling of the nightmarish heaven-tree.

In the image of the one-armed and therefore slowly moving clock in Temple's room at Miss Reba's, it is as though Faulkner were again pausing to emphasize. This blank-faced symbol, initially an image of quiet dying, of "moribund time" (p. 180), becomes increasingly a chilling reminder of the universal menace. In the night, it becomes the world paralyzed within the cosmic whirl, a "disc suspended in nothingness, the original chaos," and then a "crystal ball holding in its still and cryptic depths the ordered chaos of the intricate and shadowy world upon whose scarred flanks the old wounds whirl onward at dizzy speed into darkness lurking with new disasters" (p. 181). The central suggestion is that of impotent exposure to a huge and enveloping threat. Even the surrounding "nothingness" is not absence of threat but rather a frightening "original chaos." The imagery and diction are full of menace, not only in "chaos," but in "scarred flanks," "wounds," "darkness," "lurking," "disasters." The whirling, "dizzy speed" actually emphasizes the sense of impotence, for it suggests our helplessness, the impossibility of controlling the motion. In this passage, the "ordered chaos" found in the "cryptic depths" of a "shadowy world" offers no comfort. For any notion of real order is dissolved not only by the words "shadowy" and "cryptic" but by the image of the globe whirling without progress in a black universe of constantly "new disasters." Within the larger chaos, any global order is illusory, "shadowy"; and "ordered chaos" is, hopelessly, still chaos. The phrase is frightening in its ironic implications.

The globe reappears as a principal image in Horace Benbow's thought on his return from visiting Temple in the Memphis brothel, and, again, with other images, it helps to convey the terrifying stasis of nightmare in a cosmic dimension. To review the references briefly: In language which echoes significantly that quoted earlier, Horace wishes all the participants, including himself, dead, "cauterized out of the old and tragic flank of the world" (p. 265), and he thinks then "of the expression he had once seen in the eyes of a dead child, and of other dead: the cooling indignation, the shocked despair fading, leaving two empty globes in which the motionless world lurked profoundly in miniature" (p. 266). Like the clock in Temple's room at Miss Reba's, which is also described as "mirrorlike" (p. 180), the vast globe is reflected in the little. Horace also sees the past few days as "a dream filled with all the nightmare shapes it had taken him forty-three years to invent." And, consequently, as he walks toward the house, the insect sounds of the night seem "the chemical agony of a world left stark and dying above the tide-edge of the fluid in which it lived and breathed" (p. 267). In a landscape of nightmare, "The moon stood overhead, but without light; the earth lay beneath, without darkness." After he enters, he thinks of the night sounds as "the friction of the earth on its axis" which may decide "to turn on or to remain forever still: a motionless ball in cooling space, across which a thick smell of honeysuckle writhed like cold smoke" (p. 267).

The images in this interior monologue merge effects of frustrating stasis or near paralysis and of chill and horror on a cosmic scale. The circles of moon and earth stand or lie eerily static, and both microcosmic eye and macrocosmic earth turn into cold, "motionless" globes; a world dying but fixed cannot reach the vanishing source of its life and turns into a "motionless ball." Where there is motion, it is impeded and slow. Rather like paralyzed action, it occurs only with nightmarish difficulty, with "friction" and by "writhing." A sense of strange cold in the spring night helps to create the growing shiver of fear: "Cooling indignation" suggests a series of images at the end of which the empty eyes and their reflected worlds turn completely cold; a chill surrounds the planet over which "cold smoke" moves and around which is only "cooling space." It is the cosmic bad dream. The nightmare which Horace has by his sheltered existence tried to deny for "forty-three years" has come alive. Just before he calls up the memory of the eyes of the dead, he thinks, at first sight somewhat cryptically, "Perhaps it is upon the instant that we realise, admit, that there is a logical pattern to evil, that we die . . ." (pp. 265-266). But in the context, the "logical pattern to evil" is simply the fact of the universal nightmare; when we recognize that everything is "evil," that this is the "logical pattern"—that is, the only pattern which logic permits us to discover and accept—then we must give up. And thus the position of Horace's fantasy at the end of this chapter also becomes explicable, for it is consistent that the sequence should end with his nightmare vision of a female, "bound" and impotent on the flat car, hurtled through a terrifying blackness and a stasis of roaring sound to strange peace as she swings "lazily" and distantly, indifferently, in the sky (p. 268). It is a symbolic moment, pinpointing much that has preceded, for she has passed through the dark nightmare of existence and, to use Horace's earlier phrasing, has been "cauterized out of the old and tragic flank of the world."

Even the old man, Goodwin's father, contributes to the sense of universal nightmare. Blind and deaf, slobbering over his food very much like Flaubert's old duc de Laverdière in *Madame Bovary,* the older Goodwin epitomizes, from one point of view, the horror of human decay, the effects of Time. In this way of looking, he becomes man as impotent victim of the cosmic condition. But, with his yellow-clotted eyes and tapping stick that seem to pursue the cringing Temple (e.g., pp. 60, 104), he also performs a function rather like that of the old blind beggar with the running eye sockets and the clattering stick who haunts Emma Bovary.[12] In both novels, the individual character's sense of being pursued enlarges until the reader understands that the blind men symbolize a universal threat. Thus in the heavy silence immediately before the rape, Temple imagines first that she shrieks at the absent "old man with the yellow clots for eyes." But, as she lies helplessly "tossing and thrashing" in one place, she ends by screaming only to two blind and revolting orbs, "the two phlegm-clots above her" (p. 122). Suddenly the disembodied, unseeing and indifferent "clots" expand in dimension and implication; suddenly

they also are like globes. They make cosmic this moment of agonizing dread and furious powerlessness. Sightless and disgusting, they offer a dreadful comment on the relationship of the cosmic to man.

In the climactic depiction of the inferno in which Goodwin burns, the paralyzed horror of dreams occurs again; and again the resonances are ultimately vast. At the center of the "circle" of humanity which Horace has entered, the huge flame blazes; "but from the central mass of fire there came no sound at all. It was now indistinguishable, the flames whirling in long and thunderous plumes from a white-hot mass . . ." (p. 355). Horace cannot hear Goodwin. He cannot hear the men. He cannot "hear the fire, though it still swirled upward unabated, as though it were living upon itself, and soundless: a voice of fury like in a dream, roaring silently out of a peaceful void" (p. 355).

"Like in a dream." The sequence is surely as clearly nightmarish as any. The sense of sound cut off, the strange and dreadful deafness of it all, evokes the suppressive effect of nightmare, as if a dreamer's scream can be neither uttered nor heard. The very silence of the auditory images—"thunderous," "voice of fury," and "roaring"—recreates the impossibilities of bad dreams and makes these ordinarily ominous sounds even more threatening. And, as in nightmare, the scene builds an effect of stasis in which powerlessness and enormous dread fuse. Indeed, the moment is one of tremendous and unusually portentous pause, again as though to mark it for significance. It is as if the world had stopped and the tableau of circle around burning center contained all existence. The bonfire becomes the mesmerizing conflagration at the heart of everything. Before it Horace stands immobilized and powerless. Images of the disembodied "voice of fury" (echo of a fearful but now impersonal Voice out of the whirlwind?) and of an ironically "peaceful void" also add huge dimensions to this nightmare. No vast Power intervenes in the barbarous immolation of Goodwin: there is only the frightening "voice" and vast emptiness. The peacefulness of the "void" is, in the context, ironically the equivalent of indifference; it is an extension of the fearful silence of the whole scene.

One generally ignored sequence epitomizes this major experience of paralyzed horror before the nightmare universe: In their fear Miss Reba's vicious poodles express in little the very heart of this feeling in the novel. In a dreamlike tension of "terrific silence," they crouch beneath Temple's bed, static in fright before the possibility of a senseless and murderous chaos—"the flatulent monotony of their sheltered lives snatched up without warning by an incomprehensible moment of terror and fear of bodily annihilation at the very hands [Miss Reba's] which symbolised by ordinary the licensed tranquility of their lives" (p. 186). Snarling and afraid, "crouching there in the dark against the wall" (p. 184) or "crouching against the wall under the bed in that rigid fury of terror and despair" (p. 190), they express, in their impotent fear before threatened annihilation by their ostensibly secure but now erratic universe, the essence of the human nightmare. Although this picture of the cringing animals appears at first sight a casual and unintegrated episode, it is perhaps no coincidence that it occurs at the very center of the book.

It is also striking that the experiences of both Temple and Horace reflect to a degree the symbolic pattern established by Miss Reba's poodles. Horace moves similarly from the secure, if blind, regularity of ordinary living to his exposure, in moments already described, to the nightmare of dark irrationality. Not only his expectation of order and justice in man and man's law, but also his comfortable belief in a just cosmic order is destroyed. Like the uninitiated and ineffectual Mrs. Compson in *The Sound and the Fury,* who exclaims that God would not permit her to be hurt because she is a lady, Horace somewhat fatuously tries to comfort Ruby with the notion of a polite cosmic order. He tells her that, although God may be "foolish" occasionally, "at least He's a gentleman" (p. 337). It is not, however, very long after that Horace, seeing the signs of spring, thinks, "You'd almost think there was some purpose to it" (p. 350). Significantly, in our last view of Horace, he has retreated into the shell of his conventional home—beneath his bed, so to speak—and, upon Belle's repeated insistence, is about to "lock the back door" (pp. 358, 360), locking behind him the fearful universe. The paralysis inspired by nightmare becomes his permanent condition.

Temple too undergoes a passage from security to nightmare. And between the helpless animals and Temple crouching in a corner of the kitchen or against the porch door of the old mansion, cringing in the bedroom or in the loft, rigid and trembling on chattering shucks or tossing and thrashing beneath the yellow eyes, the parallel is particularly strong. The lines which describe the dogs frozen in fear are immediately and perhaps pointedly followed by a description of Temple "cringing" and "thrashing furiously" but helplessly before Popeye's advance (pp. 190-191). Her journey through the horror impresses the reader, however, a good deal more than it does Temple, whose ultimate response is rather clearly superficial.

The role of the third principal, Popeye, does not, of course, follow the some pattern. Edmond Volpe aptly describes that function when he calls him "a link between human and cosmic evil."[13] Almost all the way through, Popeye is another aspect of the freezing menace of the nightmare. He is the gangsterism of the twenties raised to symbolic power. He thus resembles remarkably the gangster agents of a frighteningly accidental universe in Hemingway's "The Killers"—Faulkner may well have been influenced by the earlier story—and foreshadows, moreover, the cosmic chill evoked by Ionesco's killer in *Tueur Sans Gages.* But, as Volpe adds, in the last chapter Popeye is also seen as "victim of blind cruel fate."[14] As the agent of nightmare becomes the human victim, he contributes significantly to the sense of cosmic irrationality. This is not to say that the author has made it easy for the reader to accept the switch of Popeye from one role to the other. He hasn't. Although thematically appropri-

ate, the planting of Popeye in the world of men is too sudden, proportionately too brief, and (despite some earlier signs) too incompletely foreshadowed for the reader to accept. Technically, it fails.

Miss Reba's dogs also snap "viciously at one another" (p. 175), and in this they also seem almost to be commenting on the behavior of men within the nightmare world of the novel. Such a picture of men as vicious, snarling and even mad in their relationship emerges from the respectable cruelty of Narcissa, the calculating ruthlessness of Eustace Graham, the aggressive irrationality in the perverted lust of the mob even before the lynching, and the administration of justice in the trial and condemnation of Goodwin; it is reflected in Ruby's belief that Horace, like other men, must be helping her for what he can get out of it (pp. 330-331) and in the old mad woman's judgment that "the good folks live" in jail (p. 326). This complex of human viciousness, irrationality, and injustice becomes part of the total nightmare of the novel; it is itself terrifying and blends easily with the larger horror. And especially in the context of the greater fear, it becomes a most bitter comment on man. But it does not by itself produce that sense of deep horror and paralysis that suffuses the book. The purely human appears the lesser nightmare, a little culpable world within the devastatingly larger immensity.

To see *Sanctuary,* then, only as a criticism of modern society or even as an indignant satire on man's morality is, true as these views are, to miss much of Faulkner's vision. From the shudders of Gothic make-believe, the book moves into the pervasive horrors of authentic nightmare, that sense of clotting stasis, of cringing impotence and fear before threat, which finally dominates the novel. The paralyzed horror of ordinary nightmare, perhaps psycho-sexual in origin, expands and deepens here into the impotent terror before the nightmare of existence. As in great tragedy, the terror is not simply at the human but also at the cosmic condition; and if in *Sanctuary* Faulkner fails to offer the resolutions of great tragedy so that we never wake to real daylight, he also offers no pat solutions or forced redemptions. In later novels, he moves increasingly toward resolutions; and, significantly, images of the constellations begin then to wheel in seasonal order above men's little world. But the truth at this moment in the constant flux of Faulkner's development is the universal dream-horror of existence.

NOTES

[1] That Faulkner did extensively revise the book to meet the demands of his artistic conscience is clear not only from his introduction to the 1932 Modern Library edition and repeated statements before audiences in Japan and Virginia, but from the researches of Linton Massey, "Notes on the Unrevised Galleys of Faulkner's *Sanctuary,*" *Studies in Bibliography,* VII (1956), 195-208; James Meriwether, "Some Notes on the Text of Faulkner's *Sanctuary,*" *Papers of the Bibliographical Society of America,* LV (Third Quarter, 1961), 192-206; Michael

Millgate, "'A Fair Job': A Study of Faulkner's *Sanctuary*," *A Review of English Literature*, IV (October, 1963), 47-56, and *The Achievement of William Faulkner* (New York, 1966), pp. 113-117, 123.

[2] For discussions of *Sanctuary* as an attack on a mechanistic society or on modern immorality or explicitly as a *Waste Land* comment on modern life, see, for example, Wyndham Lewis, "William Faulkner: Moralist with a Corn Cob," *Men Without Art* (London, 1934), p. 63; George Marion O'Donnell, "Faulkner's Mythology," in *William Faulkner: Three Decades of Criticism*, ed. Frederick J. Hoffman and Olga W. Vickery (East Lansing, 1960), pp. 88-89; Malcolm Cowley, *The Portable Faulkner* (New York, 1946), p. 15; William Van O'Connor, *The Tangled Fire of William Faulkner* (Minneapolis, 1954), pp. 58-62; Irving Howe, *William Faulkner: A Critical Study*, rev. ed. (New York, 1962), pp. 193, 199; David L. Frazier, "Gothicism in *Sanctuary*: The Black Pall and the Crap Table," *Modern Fiction Studies*, II (Autumn, 1956), 114-124; Hyatt H. Waggoner, *William Faulkner: From Jefferson to the World* (Lexington, 1959), pp. 91-100; Douglas Cole, "Faulkner's *Sanctuary*: Retreat from Responsibility," *Western Humanities Review*, XIV (Summer, 1960), 291-298; Peter Swiggart, *The Art of Faulkner's Novels* (Austin, 1962), pp. 29-31; Millgate, "'A Fair Job,'" pp. 54-62, and *Achievement*, p. 119; Lawrance Thompson, *William Faulkner: An Introduction and Interpretation* (New York, 1963), pp. 99-116; Olga Vickery, *The Novels of William Faulkner*, rev. ed. (Baton Rouge, 1964), pp. 103-114; Frederick J. Hoffman, *William Faulkner*, 2nd ed. (New York, 1966), p. 66; Melvin Backman, *Faulkner: The Major Years* (Bloomington, 1966), p. 177. Waggoner, by considering that the *Waste Land* mood may be related to the view that there is "no meaning in nature, outside of man" (p. 97), and Thompson, by seeing the society of *Sanctuary* as a perversion of divinely planned order, offer in their analyses a metaphysical dimension.

[3] Critics who have noted, though for the most part briefly, the larger, cosmic implications of Faulkner's novel are André Malraux, "A Preface for Faulkner's *Sanctuary*," *Yale French Studies*, No. 10 (Autumn, 1952), 92-94; Rabi, "Faulkner and the Exiled Generation," in *William Faulkner: Two Decades of Criticism*, ed. Frederick J. Hoffman and Olga W. Vickery (East Lansing, 1954), pp. 132-133; Maurice E. Coindreau, "William Faulkner in France," *Yale French Studies*, No. 10 (Autumn, 1952), 88-89; Karl E. Zink, "Flux and the Frozen Moment: The Imagery of Stasis in Faulkner's Prose," *PMLA*, LXXI (June, 1956), 289; John Longley, Jr., *The Tragic Mask: A Study of Faulkner's Heroes* (Chapel Hill, 1963), pp. 102-103; Jean Pouillon, "Time and Destiny in Faulkner," in *Faulkner*, ed. R. P. Warren (Englewood Cliffs, N.J., 1966), p. 79; Cleanth Brooks, *William Faulkner: The Yoknapatawpha Country* (New Haven, 1963), pp. 127-138; and Edmond L. Volpe, *A Reader's Guide to William Faulkner* (New York, 1964), pp. 140-151, are primarily concerned with the novel as a discovery of the universal evil in man; Volpe, however, goes farther to see a "connection between human and cosmic evil" (p. 150).

[4] *Faulkner at Nagano*, ed. R. A. Jelliffe (Tokyo, 1956), p. 66. See also p. 64. In *Faulkner in the University*, ed. F. L. Gwynn and J. L. Blotner (Charlottesville, Va., 1959), pp. 111, 267, Faulkner speaks of man's living in an irrational universe.

[5] "William Faulkner's *Sanctuary*: An Analysis," *Saturday Review*, XI (October 20, 1934), 218, 224-226. See also Backman, pp. 47-49.

[6] Ernest Jones (*On the Nightmare*, London, 1949, p. 20) concludes that two of the three chief characteristics of nightmare are "agonizing dread" and "conviction of helpless paralysis." (His third is a physical sensation of "weight at the chest," which would seem almost an aspect of the second.)

[7] For other parallels to the Gothic novel, see David L. Frazier, "Gothicism in *Sanctuary*," cited above.

[8] See, e.g., R.P. Warren, "William Faulkner" in *William Faulkner: Three Decades of Criticism*, p. 124. See also "Robert Penn Warren," *Writers at Work: The Paris Review Interviews*, ed. Malcolm Cowley (New York, 1959), p. 201, and Zink, pp. 285-301. In "Shaping the World of *Sanctuary*," *University of Kansas City Review*, XXV (Winter, 1958), 137-142, James Brown calls attention to the tableaux in *Sanctuary*.

[9] *Sanctuary*, Modern Library edition (New York, 1932), p. 44. All references to *Sanctuary* in the text of this article are to this edition.

[10] See, e.g., "William Faulkner" in *Writers at Work*, p. 132, and *Faulkner in the University*, pp. 17, 68.

[11] *Tangled Fire*, p. 59.

[12] In *Sanctuary* the echoes of Flaubert's *Madame Bovary* are very strong and suggest that Faulkner was writing to a degree under its influence. Faulkner even refers directly to the black fluid that runs from Emma's mouth (p. 6), and the irony of the "four china nymphs" supporting the clock in the brothel (p. 177) parallels the irony of the simpering little bronze cupid on the clock in Emma and Leon's love nest.

[13] *A Reader's Guide*, p. 149.

[14] *A Reader's Guide*, p. 150.

Philip Bordinat

SOURCE: "Anatomy of Fear in Tolstoy and Hemingway," in *Lost Generation Journal*, Vol. 3, No. 2, Spring-Summer, 1975, pp.

[*In the following essay, Bordinat focuses on passages from Leo Tolstoy's* War and Peace *and Ernest Hemingway's* In Our Time *to define two types of battle narrative: "ac-*

tual," in which a soldier's real terror is disclosed, and "acceptable," in which the facts of war are recorded without reference to individual response.]

In 1934, Ernest Hemingway wrote in *Esquire*, "Read *War and Peace* . . . and see how true and lasting and important the people and the action are. . . . That is the hardest thing to do."[1] In 1925, Hemingway's first wife, Hadley, indicated that he carried *War and Peace* all over Spain the previous summer.[2] No attempt is made here to trace a Tolstoian influence, if indeed one exists. Rather, consideration will be given to Tolstoy's war writings to explain the effectiveness of two passages from *In Our Time;* the two vignettes may be the best things Hemingway ever wrote about man at war. Use will also be made of the non-fiction writings of Lord Moran and S. L. A. Marshall, who have each written penetrating analyses of men under fire.

S. L. A. Marshall, the United States Army military historian, describes the battlefield as, "the lonesomest place which men may share together. . . . [A man] can feel the danger, but there is nothing out there, nothing to contend against. It is from the mixture of mystification and fear that there comes the feeling of helplessness which in turn produces greater fear."[3] The feelings of loneliness and helplessness with the resultant feelings of fear are seldom described by those who have experienced them. It is difficult to admit debilitating fear even to oneself and nearly impossible to do so to others. Sometimes, however, through the anonymity of fiction, we get the unvarnished truth, though more often we get an account which is true in outline but with the facts shaped to provide an acceptable view of the writer-hero. Thus, there are two kinds of battle accounts, the *actual* truth and the *acceptable* truth. Ernest Hemingway provides excellent examples of both in *In Our Time*.

The first account undoubtedly arises from Hemingway's direct personal experience at Fossalta, in Northern Italy, where he suffered a serious leg wound. Reflected here is the fear with the resultant loneliness and helplessness that Marshall describes:

> While the bombardment was knocking the trench to pieces at Fossalta, he lay very flat and sweated and prayed, "Oh Jesus Christ get me out of here. Dear Jesus, please get me out. Christ, please, please, please, Christ. If you'll only keep me from getting killed I'll do anything you say. I believe in you and I'll tell everybody in the world that you are the only thing that matters. Please, please, dear Jesus." The shelling moved further up the line. We went to work on the trench and in the morning the sun came up and the day was hot and muggy and cheerful and quiet. The next night back at Mestre he did not tell the girl he went upstairs with at the Villa Rossa about Jesus. And he never told anybody.[4]

Here we have, expressed in a tone akin to the confessional, a raw fear that few men will admit, even to themselves. Self-respect has given way completely to self-

preservation, revealing the aptness of Norman Mailer's title, *The Naked and the Dead*. The young soldier, cowering in the bottom of his trench, has learned a truth about himself, about his susceptibility to abject terror, that must be clothed immediately for his own protection. The beginning of this suppression is seen in the final ironic line. "And he never told anybody."

Leo Tolstoy, whose *Sevastopol* established him as a great writer on war, presents a description of the wounding of a staff-captain that reveals the same kind of fear found in the Hemingway passage. As the captain awaits the explosion of a bomb which has landed a few feet from him,

> He mentally prayed to God, and kept repeating, "Thy will be done! What made me go into the military service?" . . . And he began to count: "One, two, three, four," making up his mind that if it exploded on an even number, he would live, but if on an uneven number, he would be killed. "Everything is ended; I am killed," he thought, when the bomb exploded (he forgot whether it was on an even or an uneven number), and he felt a blow and a severe pain in his head. "O Lord, forgive me my sins!" he said, swaying on his hands, and he rose, and fell down senseless on his back.[5]

There is in this passage the same appeal to the diety and the same use of repetition. Yet, Hemingway achieves a greater dramatic impact than Tolstoy does by giving us the words coursing through the terror-ridden mind, rather than the brief description, "and kept repeating." Both writers also resort to irony, as the hero moves to repress the experience. Hemingway's soldier "never told anybody." Tolstoy's captain, who has sustained a superficial head wound, chooses to remain in the line rather than go back for treatment.

> Mikhaylov hestitated for a moment, and would have followed Ignátev's advice, if he not suddenly thought of the many severely wounded at the ambulance. "It may be the doctors will only laugh at my scratch," thought the staff-captain, and resolutely, in spite of the drummer's persuasion, he went back to his company.[6]

With Hemingway's soldier and with Tolstoy's, now that the terror has subsided, there is an immediate consciousness of what the world will think. Self-respect once again asserts itself.

Self-respect, which so often can be re-established through what others think, is at the core of the successful soldier's response to his own excruciating "failure." Hemingway, of course, merely hints at the re-establishment of masculinity through the characteristic reaffirmation at the Villa Rossa, which is, in a sense, a symbolic act for his young man. Tolstoy's staff-captain avoids the possible humiliation that would come to him at the medical aid station. The key to the future is that the hideousness of ones own fear should remain secret. In *War and Peace*, Nikolai Rostov, on coming under fire for the first time, goes through the fear, the petition to God, and the relief that his fear was not noticed:

And the terror of death and of the stretchers, and the loss of the sunshine and life, all blended into one sensation of sickening fear.

> "Good God, Thou who art in that sky, save and forgive, and protect me," Rostov whispered to himself.

With the danger past, Rostov thinks back,

> "It's all over, but I am a coward, yes, I am a coward. . . ."

Then, with a sense of relief,

> "It seems as if no one noticed it, though," Rostov thought to himself. And indeed no one had noticed it at all. . . . [7]

Tolstoy, of course, explains it to us while, with Hemingway, the fear of discovery is implicit in the brief description itself.

Even soldiers of long battle experience can be shocked into humiliating recognition of their own capacity for fear. Commandos in World War II, who had prior to D-Day crossed the channel in successful operations behind German lines, in a number of cases suffered this kind of battle shock when they encountered shell-fire for the first time during the invasion of Normandy. Perhaps more impressive are the accounts of Lord Moran, who later become Churchill's personal physician, about his experiences as a medical officer with the Royal Fusiliers in the First Great War. In his book, *The Anatomy of Courage,* which, like S. L. A. Marshall's work, is an attempt to analyze the soldier's behavior under fire, he describes the fear that many men had of shelling:

> There were men in France who were ready to go out but who could not meet death in that shape. They were prepared for it if it came swiftly and cleanly. But the shattering, crude bloody end by a big shell was too much for them. It was something more than death, all their plans for meeting it with decency and credit were suddenly battered down; it was not so much that their lives were in danger as that their self-respect had gone out of their hands. [8]

The importance of self-respect is seen in Lord Moran's own experience:

> One day, nearly a year after joining the battalion, while we were being shelled I found myself shivering. It did not immediately occur to me that it was connected with the shells, and as it was a cold day I put on my British warm. But the trembling did not cease. I grew perturbed and was relieved to discover that my plight had passed unnoticed. For days I went about with fear in my heart lest I should do something foolish when times were bad. [9]

Again, there is the concern for what others will think, a fact that may account for the relative rarity of descrip-

tions of the *actual* experience of being under fire. More often what we get are descriptions which fall into the second category, the *acceptable*.

The *acceptable* description may square with the facts, but the facts are shaped to reflect well on the narrator. S. L. A. Marshall, in a lecture presented to the U.S. Army Staff College, Class of 1954,[10] described having interviews with American soldiers coming out of action in Korea. They spoke of rough times and of fear, but with a bravado that excited admiration in the listener. Marshall, detecting that he might be getting only a portion of the truth, moved much further forward and commenced interviewing men who were still shaking with fear. The stories now told of men cowering in the bottoms of their slit trenches, too frightened to fire their weapons. "The isolated man," says Marshall, "will develop a sense of having been deserted by his fellows, and he will reason to himself that if he does not shoot and expose his position the enemy will not fire back."[11] He was at last getting close to the answer to the shattering figures that evolved from World War II actions; only twelve to twenty-five percent of all combat soldiers who were in a position to fire at the enemy, in fact, did so. Our concern, on the other hand, is not how fire-power may be increased, but how quickly man fabricates a story to cover the fact of his own humiliating fear. Nikolai Rostov puts the acceptable account in perspective when he reflects, while listening to others talking of war experiences,

> After Austerlitz and the campaign of 1807, Rostov knew from his own experience that men always lie when they describe deeds of battle, as he did himself indeed.[12]

The lie is often one of omission, as it is in the *acceptable* description from Hemingway's *In Our Time*, where the narrator, a young British officer, covers his feelings by assuming a tone reserved for rugby or cricket matches back at the Old School;

> It was a frightfully hot day. We'd jammed an absolutely perfect barricade across the bridge. It was simply priceless. A big old wrought-iron grating from the front of a house. Too heavy to lift and you could shoot through it and they would have to climb over it. It was absolutely topping. They tried to get over it, and we potted them from forty yards. They rushed it, and officers came out alone and worked on it. It was an absolutely perfect obstacle. Their officers were very fine. We were frightfully put out when we heard the flank had gone, and we had to fall back.[13]

In this passage, Hemingway's young officer has revealed nothing of the fear nor of the horror of death. Rather he has presented the external facts in a tone out of keeping with the tragedy he is describing. Certainly, part of the explanation for the omissions and the alien tone may be found in the *acceptable* image presented of the narrator as a brave man with a will to fight—that is, the ideal soldier. Lord Moran sheds additional light on descriptions of this kind when he writes,

We simply could not afford to allow death to hover in the offing as the final mystery; it must be brought to earth and robbed of its disturbing influence, by rough gibes and the touch of ridicule. If it was firmly grasped like a nettle soon there was no sting left in it.[14]

One is reminded of John Donne's "Death Be Not Proud." The personification of death removes the sting. Each man, faced with the fear of death in battle, must learn to handle the reality of his own fear. Few can live with this unvarnished reality; they must fabricate an illusion that satisfies their self-image if they are to retain their self-respect.

Gertrude Stein and Sherwood Anderson, perhaps with a touch of vengeance, decided that Hemingway was "yellow." "But what a book, they both agreed, would be the real story of Hemingway, not those he writes, but the confessions of the real Ernest Hemingway."[15] The two passages from *In Our Time,* which are complete stories in themselves, could have been the clues that led Stein and Anderson to speculate on the "real Ernest Hemingway."

NOTES

[1]Philip Young, *Ernest Hemingway: A Reconsideration* (University Park: Pennsylvania State University Press, 1966), p. 141n.

[2]Carlos Baker, *Ernest Hemingway: A Life Story* (New York: Scribners, 1969), p. 161.

[3]*Man Against Fire* (New York: Morrow, 1947), pp. 44-45.

[4]*In Our Time* (New York: Scribners, 1958), p. 87.

[5]*A Landed Proprietor, The Cossacks, Sevastopol,* tr. Leo Wiener (Boston: Dana Estes, 1904), p. 374.

[6] . . . *Sevastopol,* pp. 375-76.

[7]*War and Peace,* tr. Constance Garnett (New York: Modern Library, n.d.), p. 132.

[8]*The Anatomy of Courage* (Boston: Houghton Mifflin, 1967), p. 63.

[9]*The Anatomy of Courage,* p. 30.

[10]Interview with Col. H. J. Sweeney, British Army, U.S. Army Staff College, Class of 1954.

[11]Bill Davidson, "Why Half Our Combat Soldiers Fail to Shoot," *Colliers,* 8 November, 1952, p. 18.

[12]*War and Peace,* p. 603.

[13]*In Our Time,* p. 43.

[14]*Anatomy of Courage,* p. 149.

[15][Gertrude Stein], *The Autobiography of Alice B. Toklas* (New York: Harcourt, Brace, 1933), pp. 265-66.

H. F. Peters

SOURCE: "Ernst Jünger's Concern With E. A. Poe," in *Comparative Literature,* Vol. X, No. 2, Spring, 1958, pp. 144-49.

[*In the following essay, Peters considers thematic affinities in the works of Edgar Allan Poe and Ernst Jünger, while noting their different attitudes toward salvation.*]

Frequent references to E. A. Poe in the works of Ernst Jünger, particularly in those written during and after World War II, raise two questions: First, what is it that attracts Jünger and Poe? And second, has Jünger's interest in Poe influenced his own writings? This paper addresses itself to the first question. Concerning the second, let me simply say that I do not think it is possible to trace any direct influences of Poe on Jünger. Undoubtedly Jünger sees in Poe more than the expert craftsman of grotesque tales and romantic fantasies, although the role of the romantic element in Jünger's work should not be underestimated. The relationship of the two authors is one of affinity rather than dependency, an affinity rooted in their common concern with one major literary theme—the theme of terror.

Terror, as a literary theme, is as old as literature itself. The Greeks considered it an essential element of tragedy. In German literature the romantic poets, notably E. T. A. Hoffmann, were past masters at it—so much so that, when the theme began to appear in Poe's writings, he was accused of plagiarizing the Germans. He defended himself against this charge by protesting that, "if in many of my productions terror has been the thesis, I maintain that terror is not of Germany but of the soul."[1]

It is surely no accident that Poe's terrors of the soul find an echo among contemporary writers. The ever-increasing complexities of our technological civilization, the threat of total destruction which hangs over us in the shape of mushroom clouds, give rise to deep-seated fears. We may dismiss such fears and refuse to talk about them; they are present nevertheless. For, as Jünger says:

> . . . was uns im Innersten beschäftigt, entzieht sich der Mitteilung, ja fast der eigenen Wahrnehmung. Da gibt es Themen, die sich geheimnisvoll durch die Jahre hindurch fortspinnen, wie etwa das der Auswegslosigkeit, die unsere Zeit erfüllt. Sie erinnert an das grossartige Bild der Lebenswoge der asiatischen Malerei, auch an den Malstrom von E. A. Poe.[2]

This entry in Jünger's war diary, *Strahlungen,* is dated Paris, November 18, 1941. The reference to Poe's "A Descent into the Maelström" is instructive. To understand its significance the reader must recall the events of the war winter of 1941. These were the months when

Hitler's armies suffered their first serious reverses in Russia. Under the impact of an unusually severe winter, they reeled back before Moscow. To Jünger, the author of the subtly anti-Nazi novel, *Auf den Marmorklippen,* it meant that the end was in sight, the revolution of nihilism drawing to a close. "Wir haben in diesen Wochen den Nullpunkt passiert," he noted in his diary. "Dennoch ist es merkmürdig, dass mich im tiefsten Grunde Zuversicht belebt."[3]

The narrator in Poe's story also passes through the "zero point" and is saved. Salvation from the jaws of death is one aspect of the terror theme. Jünger's image of the wave of life which carries man beyond destruction is exemplified by the manner in which Poe's hero is carried through the maelström and cast back into life. His brother is drowned because he lacks faith in the uplifting power of the waves. Paralyzed by terror, he clings to the ring bolt and is sucked down into the abyss.

The moral of Poe's story is that it is fatal to panic in the face of death. Terror is a test of character. If you succumb to it you are lost. It is a lesson that Jünger learned in two world wars. He feels it has a special meaning in our age. Are we not all standing at the brink of a maelström that may destroy us if we lose heart? That is why he says in a letter to me, dated January 9, 1957: "Der Malstrom erschien und erscheint mir noch als eine besonders gelungene Diagnose und Prognose unserer Zeit. Ihre Tendenz ist auf die knappste Formel gebracht."

An entry in an earlier diary, *Gärten und Strassen,* August 19, 1939, gives a clue to the nature of Poe's diagnosis as Jünger interprets it: "Die beste Schilderung des voll automatisierten Zustandes enthält die Erzählung 'Hinab in den Maelstrom' von E. A. Poe."[4] Man's fate in a world of vast and terrifying mechanical forces that seem to be beyond human control is one of Jünger's major concerns. He thinks that Poe anticipated such a state and therefore deserves the epithet, "der erste Autor des zwanzigsten Jahrhunderts,"[5] which the Goncourts bestowed upon him. Poe's image of the maelström is to Jünger a symbol of our age.

He gives a similar symbolic interpretation of Poe's story, "The Pit and the Pendulum."

> Die Wassergrube gibt uns das Bild des Kessels, der immer dichteren Umkreisung, der Raum wird enger und drängt auf die Ratten zu. Das Pendel ist das Sinnbild der toten, messbaren Zeit. Es ist die scharfe Sichel des Chronos, die an ihm schwingt und den Gefesselten bedroht, doch ihn zugleich befreit, wenn er sich ihrer zu bedienen weiss.[6]

"Kessel" refers here to the great battles of encirclement, the *Kesselschlachten* of the war in Russia, the classic example of which is Stalingrad. Jünger, the author of *In Stahlgewittern,* continues to think in military images. But there is this difference—while Jünger in his earlier books glorified war, his concern in his later books is with the isolated individual threatened with destruction by impersonal technical forces.

> Die immer künstlicheren Städte, die automatischen Bezüge, die Kriege und Bürgerkriege, die Maschinenhöllen, die grauen Despotien, Gefängnisse und raffinierten Nachstellungen—das alles sind Dinge, die Namen bekommen haben und die den Menschen Tag und Nacht beschäftigen.[7]

These themes also occupied Poe. He anticipated many of the mechanical horrors that have become reality in our time. But the real significance of Poe's nightmarish visions is that he analyzed them and uncovered the strange ambivalence of the soul, which can be fascinated by what terrifies it. In "The Imp of the Perverse" he lays bare that streak in man which makes him seek out the very dangers that threaten to destroy him. "There is no passion so demonically impatient, as that of him, who shuddering upon the edge of a precipice, thus meditates a plunge."[8] Modern psychologists call this fascination with terror the death wish of the soul. It is a theme that often occurs in Jünger. "Der Schwindel vor dem kosmischen Abgrund ist ein nihilistischer Aspekt,"[9] he writes with reference to Poe's essay "Eureka," and asks: "soll man, und sei es auch nur geistig, die äussersten Gewässer aufsuchen, die Katarakte, den Malstromwirbel, die grossen Abgründe?"[10] He answers yes. "In unserer Lage sind wir verpflichtet, mit der Katastrophe zu rechnen und mit ihr schlafen zu gehen, damit sie uns nicht zur Nacht überrascht."[11] Like Hölderlin ("wo aber die Gefahr ist, wächst das Rettende auch")[12] Jünger believes that the greater the dangers the better the chances of salvation. "Bei grossen Gefahren wird das Rettende tiefer gesucht werden, und zwar bei den Müttern, und in dieser Berührung wird Urkraft befreit. Ihr Können die reinen Zeitmächte nicht standhalten."[13]

The difference between Jünger and Poe lies in their attitude towards "das Rettende," which may perhaps be interpreted as Providence. In Poe's stories salvation is usually the result of a rational act on the part of the threatened. Lashing himself to the water cask was such a rational act which saved the narrator of "A Descent into the Maelström." Jünger too believes in the saving power of courageous action, but courage alone is not enough. Something else is necessary, the support of a transcendental force, a wholly irrational power of salvation. While Poe is fundamentally a rationalist who knows the irrational yearnings of the soul, Jünger has been tending more and more towards mysticism. Rationalism, he thinks, leads to mechanism and mechanism to torture.

> Zahllose leben heute, welche die Zentren des nihilistischen Vorganges, die Tiefpunkte des Malstromes passiert haben. Sie wissen, dass dort die Mechanik sich immer drohender enthüllt; der Mensch befindet sich im Inneren einer grossen Maschine, die zu seiner Vernichtung ersonnen ist. Sie mussten auch erfahren, dass jeder Rationalismus zum Mechanismus, und jeder Mechanismus zur Folter führt, als seiner logischen Konsequenz. Das hat man im 19. Jahrhundert noch nicht gesehen.[14]

Nor, we might add, did Jünger see it in his earlier writings. This difference in attitude towards salvation in Poe and Jünger accounts for the different emphasis in their treatment of terror. For Poe it is the fascination with terror that leads him back to the same theme time and again. Jünger emphasis is on salvation from terror. While in Poe's stories unrelieved terror often prevails, producing a melodramatic effect, Jünger imparts to his readers a sense of man's ultimate conquest of the powers of darkness. In a rather mystifying entry in *Strahlungen,* dated Paris, January 15, 1942, Jünger draws this distinction between himself and Poe. He quotes a letter he received from a friend concerning his "schwarze Fürstin": "Ich meine, dass Ihre Fürstin etwas vom 'Untergang des Hauses Usher' beeinflusst ist. Doch wird hier der Weg zur Heilung gezeigt. Das ist gut. Poe zeigte nur den Untergang."[15]

In a letter to me, January 9, 1957, Jünger explains that this entry refers to his story "Der Hippopotamus," published in *Das abenteuerliche Herz* (2nd ed., 1938). The heroine of his capriccio, as he calls it, is that unhappy Brunswick princess who was queen of England at the time of Napoleon. She was a victim of severe mental depressions, and the story deals with a method of treatment. As in Poe's "The Fall of the House of Usher," the narrator in Jünger's story faces a strange and threatening situation. He finds himself in the presence and at the mercy of a person who is obviously going mad. But, while in Poe's story madness finally overwhelms everything, with the narrator fleeing aghast from a scene of horror he has been unable to alleviate, Jünger presents a cure. It combines scientific and magical elements. Scientific are the prescriptions of sleeping drugs, magical the incantations the princess is to use when she feels the approach of her illness. This combination of scientific and magical elements is a distinguishing feature of Jünger's prose. It has given rise to the expression "magischer Realismus."

Scientific and magical elements also intermingle in Poe's work. But Poe saw in magic mainly a destructive force, a dark demonic power that both terrifies and fascinates the soul. To Jünger the magical forces in life are those that uplift man, carrying him beyond destruction. The mediaeval distinction between black and white magic might perhaps be applied to Poe and Jünger. The latter's concern is with man's ascent from the dark realm of demons. To his wife, who was living amidst the terrors of aerial bombardment, he wrote in June 1943: "Was Dich betrifft, so fühle ich mit Gewissheit, dass Du unbeschadet dem grossen Malstrom entrinnen wirst; verliere das Vertrauen zu Deiner eigentlichen Bestimmung nicht."[16] Poe did not have such faith to counterbalance the terrors of his soul.

Jünger is interested in Poe's world because it gives him insights into the "dark mathematics" of fate.

> Im Malstrom Edgar Allan Poes besitzen wir eine der grossen Visionen, die unsere Katastrophe vorausschauten, und von allen die bildhafteste. Wir sind nun in jenen Teil des Wirbels abgesunken, in dem die Verhältnisse in ihrer dunklen Mathematik,

zugleich einfacher und faszinierender, sichtbar werden.[17]

Both Poe and Jünger know that there are powerful and irrational forces that urge man to seek his own destruction. This knowledge terrified Poe and he communicates to his reader a sense of doom: "And my soul from out that shadow that lies floating on the floor / Shall be lifted—nevermore!" Jünger sees a challenge to rise above it, not merely through resolute action but through faith in God's saving grace. At the end of *Auf den Marmorklippen,* when after a night of terror the powers of darkness seem firmly established, the sound of an organ is heard and the words:

> Weil denn kein Mensch uns helfen kann
> Rufen wir Gott um Hilfe an.

It should be noted in conclusion that Jünger's religious position, as reflected by writings cited in this paper, has puzzled many readers of his earlier works. They are not convinced that the former champion of "total mobilization," the herald of the front soldier, the author of *Der Arbeiter,* has undergone a genuine conversion. They feel that his metaphysical speculations are forced and his dreams, visions, and belief in magic are at best a substitute for religion. Jünger himself has noted that an age of terror inevitably gives rise to "Ersatzreligionen von unabsehbarer Zahl."[18]

I would suggest that these critics ponder the significance of the maleström image which occupies such an important place in Jünger's later books. In its dual aspect of death and rebirth it symbolizes the human condition as all the great teachers of religion have taught us to see it. Like many writers of his generation in Germany and elsewhere—T. S. Eliot is a case in point—Jünger descended into the maeström, embraced nihilism or, as he put it, was for a time a fellow traveler of the "Mauretanians." But he did not stay there.

> Tatsächlich war, als ich diese Fabel ["Der Hippopotamus"] vor einem Besuch bie Kubin konzipierte, die Sehnsucht nach dem Aufstieg aus den dunklen Dämonenreichen des Malstroms in mir besonders stark. Man muss derartiges auch als Prognostikon betrachten, denn die erfundenen Figuren eröffnen den Schicksalsreigen, sie tanzen ihm bald lächelnd, bald schauerlich voran, und Dichtung ist unsichtbare, noch ungelebte Historie.[19]

Amidst the terrors of a world in chaos Jünger found "Das Rettende." That, it seems to me, is the heart of the matter.

NOTES

[1] *The Complete Works of Edgar Allan Poe,* ed. J. Harrison (New York, 1902), I, 150-151.

[2] Ernst Jünger, *Strahlungen* (Tübingen, 1949), pp. 65 f.

[3] *Ibid.,* p. 66.

[4] Ernst Jünger, *Gärten und Strassen* (Berlin, 1942), p. 48.

[5] *Ibid.,* p. 48.

[6] Ernst Jünger, *Der Waldgang* (Frankfurt, 1950), p. 43.

[7] *Ibid.,* p. 43.

[8] *The Best Tales of E. A. Poe,* Mod. Libr. ed., p. 111.

[9] Ernst Jünger, *Über die Linie* (Frankfurt, 1950), p. 23.

[10] *Der Waldgang,* p. 67.

[11] *Ibid.,* p. 68.

[12] Hölderlin, *Sämtliche Werke* (Stuttgart, 1951), II[1], 165.

[13] *Der Waldgang,* p. 55.

[14] *Ibid.,* pp. 121 f.

[15] *Strahlungen,* p. 82.

[16] *Ibid.,* p. 349.

[17] *Ibid.*

[18] *Über die Linie,* p. 24.

[19] *Strahlungen,* p. 82.

John C. Blankenagel

SOURCE: "Human Fears in Jakob Wassermann's Writing," in *Journal of English and Germanic Philology,* Vol. 50, No. 3, 1951, pp. 309-19.

[*In the following essay, Blankenagel catalogs such various fears as fear of death, fear of the loss of affection, fear of change, fear of the future, and fear of others in the works of Jakob Wassermann.*]

Among numerous recurring motifs in Jakob Wasserman's narratives, human fears have a conspicuous place. Doubtless the prominence of this motif is symptomatic of an age marked by turbulent conflicts, by unrest, doubt, suspicion, covetousness, intolerance, social injustice, persecution, racial prejudice, violence, political upheavals, economic stress, and waning spirituality. But in addition it should be borne in mind that, as a representative of a race that has long lived under the shadow of persecution, Wassermann was particularly sensitive to fears induced by evil, injustice, and man's inhumanity to man. In his *Selbstbetrachtungen* he stated his belief that no other feeling is transmitted so ineradicably from generation to generation as fear, particularly so when it has become the trauma of a race.[1] On recalling that during the first crusade one monk was responsible for the massacre and suicide of sixteen thousand Jews, he wondered why one man can bring forth so much evil, whereas a single individual can produce so little good. He inclined to the belief that by nature evil is much more active than the good, and that human activity is on the borderline between good and evil.[2] This conception of the power of evil underlies Wassermann's view that mankind inspires fear and is beset by fear.

The specter of fear is in evidence not only in those narratives by Wassermann which deal with the first World War and the ensuing years of political, economic, and spiritual uncertainty. Rather, it figures in his writings from *Melusine* and *Finsternis,* printed in 1896, to his last novel, *Joseph Kerkhovens dritte Existenz,* which was published posthumously in 1934. Human fears are presented as haunting life in various periods of history, in many countries, and among civilized as well as savage peoples. As the author's knowledge of human nature deepened, his treatment of fear became subtler.

Wassermann portrays the elemental fear of misers who tremble at the thought of losing their possessions, the fear of the superstitious savage surrounded by mysterious, unintelligible forces, and the terror aroused by seemingly hostile uncanny nature. And there is fear of life, death, the nebulous future, fate, change, loss of affection, security, prestige, position, and self-respect. But direst of all, and transcending all others, is man's fear of his fellows, of inhumanity prompted by cold indifference, jealousy, selfishness, hatred, vengefulness, greed, lust, sordid ambitions, and fanaticism. Fears are seen to be no less terrifying because they are merely rooted in the imagination. Indeed, morbid obsessions and the lurking dread inspired by intangibles prove to be particularly harrowing and devastating.

Melusine, the frail heroine of Wassermann's first novel, is filled with a nameless dread of human beings; she is afraid of life, whose darkness, violence, and hopelessness terrify her. But though she fears life and would like to end it, she is even more afraid of death. She longs for freedom, and yet in her timidity and helplessness she fears the very freedom she desires. Overwhelmed by her sense of economic dependence, she is haunted by evil dreams in which she is paralyzed by some hideous phantom that pursues her. Fearful that her dreams of happiness may not be realized, she dares not abandon herself to the passions of love. Fear fills her with a desolate feeling of frustration; it dulls her hopes, her thoughts, and her sensibilities.

A graphic portrayal of physical fear is to be found in *Finsternis,* one of Wassermann's early stories, which calls to mind tales of terror by E. T. A. Hoffimann and Edgar Allan Poe. Here the gruesomeness of a single night spent alone in the solitary Black Forest shatters a man's health and impairs his mind for years. The terrifying darkness holds him in its clammy embrace, chills him, congeals his blood, and paralyzes his judgment, his reason, and his whole body. Bloody red visions hover before him, colored lights dance before his eyes, uncanny sounds pursue him, and shudders creep over his back while his heart alternately races and stops beating. The night stares at him cruelly and relentlessly until he finally becomes delirious and insane.

In *Alexander in Babylon,* the great Macedonian conqueror is immune to fear until near the end of his life, when suddenly he is obsessed with terror at the idea of death. Then he shudders at the thought of the void into which he is about to step, before the path into darkness that opens threateningly before him. This fear is all the greater because, until the death of his friend Hephästion, it had never occurred to him that he, too, was mortal; hitherto death had seemed merely to be the lot of others. With this realization the former happy, naïve warrior becomes a brooding ponderer whose spontaneity of decision and action vanishes. To avoid death he rises in semi-delirium from the bed which seems to menace him, runs in amazement at the realization that his legs still carry him, and continues to run for fear that this strange resurgence of vigor will forsake him if he stops. And ironically enough, he literally runs to his death.

Mad fear of accusation in a baffling trial for murder is strikingly portrayed in *Clarissa Mirabel.* Terror impels innocent suspects to incriminate others in order to clear themselves, while a veritable vortex of fear engulfs a whole community. Imaginations are morbidly stimulated by insane dread, until overwrought minds can no longer distinguish between reality and the fictions of their own invention. Much of this terror arises from deep distrust, of so-called courts of justice which become ruthless under political pressure, resort to intimidation and chicanery, and yield to the clamor of an aroused public for a scapegoat. Clarissa herself is horrified by the awesome abyss of her own thoughts and emotions.

To a large extent the fears of the foundling Caspar Hauser are quite unusual, since many of them arise from his life in solitary confinement until the age of seventeen. Hence it is not surprising that he is frightened by the unaccustomed world of sights, sounds, and human beings. Wassermann has presented Caspar's timorousness in great detail. Natural phenomena, such as thunder, lightning, wind and rain, startle the youth so that he longs for the stillness of his former prison. When new sounds excite and torment his inordinately sensitive nerves, he trembles with alarm, his eyes roll nervously, he utters strange animal cries of fright, falls to the ground, and writhes in terror. For days after such agitation he remains feverish.

Caspar senses danger in everything new and strange. Even the thought of growth and change fills him with unaccountable dread. His first dreams, after years of dreamless slumber, are terrifying to him, for on awakening he feels as if something sinister and mysterious had happened to him somewhere and somehow. Has someone been in his room? Has somebody called or threatened him? When heartless clergymen endeavor to redeem Caspar's soul from pagan ignorance not by kind words

and an appeal for reverence, but by prattling about the wrath of God and punishment for sin, by threats and fulminations, the lad becomes more and more terrified.

But Caspar's greatest fear is that of idle curiosity-mongers who besiege him as they might a freak at a circus. Why, he wonders, are there so many of them, whence do they come, and why are their eyes and mouths so cruel? Scarcely has his consciousness been aroused when he begins to realize that his soul was untroubled only before he came into the world of men. And so he wishes that he might go into hiding or that he might have the face of a flower, so as not to be compelled to answer the staring looks of unfeeling men. "Trägheit des Herzens," designated by Wassermann as mankind's besetting sin of omission, prevents others from speaking words of kindness which might have dispelled Caspar's fears.

In the novel *Ulrike Woytich,* fears of various kinds play an important role. An opening scene vividly presents frantic fear of death in a burning theater where a wild panic ensues as frenzied men and women trample each other under foot. Like unreasoning beasts they forget all chivalry, all decency, and all consideration for others. Another kind of fear is that of Mylius, the wealthy miser, whose whole life centers about his possessions, and who lives in constant terror at the thought of losing them. His property alone lends meaning to his cramped, sordid existence. Likewise Ulrike is pursued by the fear of losing her ill-gotten gains; despite her great riches, she is plagued by the fear of poverty and the dependence it engenders. Josephe's anxieties are far more subtly portrayed. She is tormented by the thought that she may lose the affection of her newly-found granddaughter, that devotion may bring rude disappointment in her lonely life, and that warm attachment may yield nothing but sad disillusionment. After a long life of sorrow she is veritably afraid to love anew.

Eugen Faber, the central character of *Faber oder die verlorenen Jahre,* is harassed by the fears which are so characteristic of the returned soldier who has lost all initiative, feels uprooted, and is unable to resume life as a civilian. His very gait is that of a man who knows no goal. He returns from imprisonment in Russia and Siberia during World War I filled with dread at the thought of estrangement from his wife Martina, now that she has become economically independent of him, interested in a career, and absorbed in philanthropic work among abandoned children. He has long been afraid that an unknown Princess, the head of a charitable institution, may have come permanently between him and his wife. During Faber's long imprisonment Martina, too, has brooded with anxious forebodings over friends who had once lived together in very happy marriage but who became singularly incompatible after separation brought on by the war. The fear of finding each other unalterably changed became an obsession which neither Martina nor Faber could dispel. But whereas she found refuge in her new, absorbing duties, he, in solitary idleness, became introspective, gloomy, listless, morose, irresolute, and fearful of the future.

When they meet after years of separation, it is as if a specter were stalking between them, preventing resumption of their old, natural companionship and of free discussion. Fear is manifest in Faber's nervously rapid pulse on his return to his native city, in his dread of a reunion with Martina which impels him to mount the stairs to his dwelling and to descend again without entering, in Martina's trepidation at the possibility of changes in Faber, their uneasiness at the thought of resuming intimate marital relations, in Faber's troubled efforts to ascertain the nature of the Princess' influence on Martina and the constant anxiety that things can never again be what they once were. There are numerous shades of uneasiness, dread, alarm, consternation and agony.

Wassermann gives a vivid description of Faber's fears as he broods in the solitude of his Siberian prison:

> Er kennt sie, diese Angst; seine Augen sagen es, er muss es nicht aussprechen. Sie ist ihm auf der Brust gelegen wie ein Zentner Sand. Sie hat seine Gedanken finster und das Brot bitter gemacht. Woraus entstanden? Aus einem Nichts, einem Fetzen Einbildung, einem Traumgespinst, das sich darin geübt hatte, Argwohn und Entbehrung zu Gift zusammenzumischen. Keine harmlose Stunde und Beschäftigung mehr; daneben kriecht die Angst; aus jedem Gesicht grinst sie, aus jedem Schall wispert sie. Etwas hat sich verändert dort drüben, tausende von Meilen weit; aber was? Von all dem bohrenden Denken bleibt nur die Drohung übrig wie eine Kugel mit glühenden Stacheln. Auch er hat Martinas Briefe unzählige Male gelesen; auch er hat sie beinah alle auswendig hersagen können. Er hat die geschehene Wandlung gerochen an ihnen; die Schriftzüge haben ihm mehr verraten als die Worte; er hat es nicht zu denken und nicht zu fassen vermocht, und mit keiner Geisteskraft war dem abzuhelfen; es frass wie Wunde im Fleisch.[3]

Another kind of dread cramps the life of Faber's sister Klara. It arises from her unhappy marriage to a conceited, hypocritical moralizer with political ambitions. She describes her agonized fears as follows:

> Wer kann aber aussprechen, was das ärgste ist? Zusammensein ohne Herz, ermesst ihrs? Und die Furcht davor, Tag und Nacht die Furcht vor dem Schritt und vor der Stimme, und vor dem Wort, das man weiss, Wie grässlich die Furcht vor dem Wort, das man weiss, eh es noch gesprochen ist; mags gut oder böse sein, man verabscheuts.[4]

In *Der Aufruhr um den Junker Ernst,* Wassermann drew a sinister picture of the Inquisition in Germany in the seventeenth century. There is suspicion everywhere, a traitor hides in every company, and men shun each other for fear of denunciation before fanatical tribunals. Würzburg, the scene of the story, lives in dread of fiendish torture and cruel executions. There is uncanny fear in the eyes of the people, livid exhalations hide the sky, and the phantom of horrible death lurks in the very air. No family is spared, brides are dragged away from the wedding feast, suckling babes are snatched from their mothers, and tender women are hauled into the witches' court.

The bishop of Würzburg is obsessed with the superstition that man is beset on every hand by demons. He suspects all things and all people of being bewitched; even the air he breathes may be poisoned by insidious forces that have sworn to annihilate the kingdom of God. After Junker Ernst has been imprisoned, the bishop is beside himself with terror. He distrusts every man, every look, and every sound. The air seems full of distorted, threatening faces, and on all hands he hears mysterious uncanny noises. Hence it is not at all surprising that he is overcome with horror when Theodata accuses him of being possessed. He who has wrought the destruction of others now trembles at the thought that the devil may actually have approached him; he finally flees to escape the very tortures he cruelly prescribed for others.

Like other youths Ernst has had his boyhood fears, but his were all the greater because of his vivid imagination. But he never knows fear in its most terrifying form until he encounters sinister, silent Pater Gropp, the very personification of the Inquisition. In his presence Ernst realizes for the first time in his life what it means to be afraid of men. Man's fear of man, says Wassermann, is the worst of all fears. It is utterly unconquerable and incurable; its claws reach down into the very depths of the human soul.[5]

In *Der Fall Maurizius,* another form of fear is manifest in Robert Thielemann, Etzel Andergast's schoolmate, who suffers agony because of the constant dissension between his parents. He is ashamed to bring Etzel to his home for fear that the latter may witness his parents' hatred and their efforts to enlist the support of their children in their quarrels. In this novel, prisoners are seen to fear death and yet to long for death; they are harrowed by tormenting dreams, by the thought of going mad, and of becoming impotent. While he is in prison, Leonhart Maurizius' fears center about the passing of time. When, after having spent fifteen months of incarceration in a state of stupor, Maurizius becomes aware that so much time has passed of which he perceived almost nothing, he begins to fear that time, living time, may elude his grasp. This gruesome thought robs him of sleep; he is as if consumed by the fear that he may lose time by unawareness of its passing during imprisonment for life.

After he has been pardoned and liberated, Maurizius is troubled by the feeling that the period of time during which he was removed from the continuity of things outside of prison is like a gulf that can never be bridged. Broken in body and spirit, sexually impotent, listless, and devoid of purpose, he is unable to adjust himself to life outside of prison walls. And so, as his train crosses a viaduct, he steps from it to his death.

Major Irlen, in *Etzel Andergast,* is filled with apprehension for his country. Germany, says he, is like an uncanny man in black armor; the Germans are no longer a nation, but are like besieged people in a fortress, threatened with being shot if they rebel against the established order.[6] In those days before 1914 his fears grow as he sees his contemporaries lose all humility while they worship military power and drift irresistibly into war.

The postwar era with its collapse of hopes fulfills the fears expressed in the first part of *Etzel Andergast*. The general catastrophe is marked by moral disintegration, by a sense of the vanity of all effort, of sacrifice and devotion, by questioning of all values, by skepticism, capitulation and defeatism. In view of the threatened vitality, the alarming loss of resiliency, and the paralysis of the human will, Kerkhoven feels as if there were a cosmic disturbance which man is quite unable to combat.

In this German inferno, where mind, soul, and body are ravaged as by a pestilence, all those who are not firmly grounded are lost in a bottomless abyss. There are young people who despair because they can have no confidence in existing institutions. Without a goal, they become the victims of chance circumstance. War, political turmoil, and revolution have begotten neurotics lacking in will, energy, purpose, tenacity, and stability. Timorous, as many of them are, they band together in groups, but they find no constructive leadership. For, by slaying a generation, the war made a gap in the chain of life, and left an orphaned age-group devoid of the guidance and leadership it sorely needed.

But various other kinds of fear and uneasiness darken the lives of characters in *Etzel Andergast*. As a psychiatrist, Kerkhoven is seemingly ever engaged in dispelling the fears that burden human souls. He is familiar with the eloquently pleading look of those who want to be freed from the terrors of death. Nina, his first wife, is filled with paralyzing dread at the very thought of being supplanted in her husband's affections. Her anguished suffering renders her almost inarticulate; she resembles a frightened, wounded little bird, and fear helps to undermine her reason. Irlen tells the story of an African chief who tried to assure obedience to his commands even after his death by implanting the demon of superstitious fear in his followers. While wounded, Etzel waits in terror for Kerkhoven to dispel the insistent spooky voices that haunt him in darkness.

Few fears, however, can rival those of Marie during her unhappy liaison with another man during her first marriage. Terror grips her so that she can neither eat, drink, sleep, nor think. Her heart races, her vitals are in a tumult, her head is dizzy, she is unable to lie still, her brain is horribly convulsed, and she is overcome with nausea. Later on, the incomprehensibility of Etzel's moods terrifies her; there are times when she lives in fear of being unable to withstand the temptations of his impetuous affection. Yet her anxiety is even greater when his love seems to be waning. In his absence she is consumed with longing; in his presence she is seized with a vague, nameless dread which strikes her dumb.

Even Kerkhoven, the scrupulously conscientious physician, has days when everything he does seems condemned to futility, when the ship of life seems to be buffeted about beyond control, and when time and the world are like uncanny elements to which man can make no enduring adjustment. His sick, confused patients are like so many guilty, timorous victims, sentenced by fate to pursue a course from which they are powerless to deviate, but in which cause and effect are inexorably linked.

In his last novel, *Joseph Kerkhovens dritte Existenz,* Wassermann again portrays humanity as troubled by a wide range of fears, some of which are real, but many of which are rooted in morbid imagination. Marie Kerkhoven suffers inner torment as she becomes more and more conscious of this world's limitations, its barren worship of petty ends, its falseness, brutality, and bloodthirstiness. Her anguished fear is all the more poignant because the aim and meaning of life seem like a hopeless riddle. Mordann, who suffers from persecution mania, suspects even his faithful daughter of conspiring against him. This suspicion tortures him all the more because she knows all his secrets, and because he fears her admiration for him may be feigned in order to catch him off his guard. His anxiety is heightened by the very vagueness of any grounds for suspecting her.

Marie is afraid of losing her husband's affection. Jealousy of Kerkhoven fills Herzog with the fear of losing his wife Bettina. As a result of the intrigues of Ganna, his divorced wife, Herzog is obsessed with fear. Even the thought of her is a nightmare that pursues him in his sleeping as well as in his waking hours; it is an ever-growing burden which he is unable to throw off. In his sleep he is constantly on the defensive, trying to justify himself before her, and ever conscious of the futility of his efforts. Unfathomable fear of Ganna, of molestation, persecution, and lawsuits are a constant menace in his life. Her covetousness fills him with such dread of losing all his property to her that he becomes enslaved to his belongings.

Though fond of chess, Imst, a minor character, declines to play with Kerkhoven for fear that defeat may rob him, the ex-convict, of the slight spark of self-respect that still glows faintly within him. His wife Jeanne labors under the morbid delusion that she is still carrying on her struggle with Imst's deceased first wife; she is a prey to fear, to a sense of guilt and fancied persecution. She is troubled also by the haunting notion that her desire for the death of an enemy may actually have caused it to come about.

As an intelligent physician who experiments with new methods, Kerkhoven has fears of having sinned through neglect, through yielding to the spell of a fixed idea while diagnosing a case, and through failure to explore every symptom. Much of his practice as a psychiatrist and neurologist naturally reveals anxiety neuroses which he tries to remove from troubled, warped lives. He sees not only the physical but also the mental and spiritual suffering of the times. His patients are haunted by want, and overwhelmed by the struggle for bare sustenance; there are political fugitives, men whose vocations have crumbled away, people from all walks of life and of every age, a sorry pitiful, moving spectacle. Of forty cases, says he, ten are afflicted with mental obsessions, five or six have criminal instincts, and the others are notorious litigants and incurable neurotics, consumed with mysterious hatreds of their fellows. They look like any other passer-by, but they are hideous nihilists who think only of murder; they are sadists in disguise, people who torture themselves and whose shadowy lives are spent in tormenting others.

Marie's daughter Aleid is representative of a younger generation of cynics who scoff at all faith in a higher order of things. They are exposed to a mental and spiritual torment of which older generations have no inkling. Their uncertainties go deeper and are more devastating than the religious doubts of other centuries. They have no guides, teachers, masters, or rules of conduct; they know nothing but confusion and violence. They love death rather than life, with which they are surfeited; they worship power and scorn man, for their heritage is want, terror, and despair. Aleid's joy in living has been sapped by a spirit of negation, she lacks all capacity for devotion and sacrifice, and she regards science, art, and religion as lying expedients evolved by idiots and criminals for the purpose of holding mankind in subservience.

In various ways Wassermann's characters endeavor to free themselves from the fears that warp their lives. In *Das Gänsemännchen* Gertrud, Daniel Nothafft's first wife, commits suicide to end her despair. Baron von Auffenberg, in the same novel, seeks solace by withdrawing to a Dominican monastery. Likewise Eugen Faber's sister Klara embraces Catholicism as a refuge from a life of fear. Four major characters in *Joseph Kerkhovens dritte Existenz* seek and find comfort by turning their thoughts to religious faith and prayer. With Kerkhoven, Marie, Bettina, and Herzog the search for God and for a faith that transcends the fragmentary nature of human knowledge ultimately becomes the dominant interest. Caught in the mechanically rigid round of routine duties, beset with fears, and unsatisfied by the limited range of human experience and knowledge, they turn to the realm of the unseen and the eternal. Faith, Kerkhoven concludes, is one of man's highest achievements; genuine faith is comparable to writing *Faust* or composing the *Passion of Saint Matthew*. It must be preceded by readiness to believe; it is the final consummation of a long and difficult process; it represents a distinctly personal religious experience.

It is Wassermann's conviction that those who endeavor to liberate others from their fears are themselves redeemed from fear. This theme prevails in such novels of his early, middle, and late years as *Die Juden von Zirndorf, Christian Wahnschaffe,* and *Joseph Kerkhovens dritte Existenz.* Agathon Geyer, who figures in *Die Juden von Zirndorf* and in *Die Geschichte der jungen Renate Fuchs,* states this creed of service and liberation as follows:

> Denn das ist mein Glaube geworden: wer sich selbst erlost durch Leiden und durch Wissen, der erlöst alle Leidenden, die neimals wissen werden. Nichts geht verloren in der Welt, am wenigsten das stumme Opfer. . . . Wem ich die Hand drucke der

> gibt mir seine Angst und seine Sorgen, und ich nichte schweigend auf. Gütig sein ist alles, und gütig sein heisst: sehen und ertragen. Ein jeder ahnt in mir den Mitträger seiner Schuld und seines Elends, nur tausendiach vermehrt. Deshalb wächst seine Stärke und sein Leichtigkeitsgefühl, und er erscheint sich als der allein Verantwortliche über seinem Schicksal.[7]

Christian Wahnschaffe's final code of unselfish service is somewhat similar to Agathon's:

> Ich will nichts von mir wissen, ich bin mir gleichgültig, aber ich will alles von den Menschen wissen, denn die Menschen, siehst du, die Menschen, das ist das Geheimnisvolte das Furchtbare, das, was immer quält und schreckt und leiden macht. . . . Immer einen, immer zu einem, dann zum nächsten, dann zum dritten, und wissen, aufsperren jeden, das Leiden herausnehmen wie die Eingeweide aus einem Huhn.[8]

As a physician and psychiatrist, Kerkhoven, the hero of Wassermann's last novel, is engaged far more practically and effectively than Agathon and Christian in dispelling anxiety, alleviating suffering and bringing encouragement and balance into troubled lives that are a prey to haunting fears.

Wassermann believed that helpful kindness, the antipode of "Trägheit des Herzens," has the power not only to overcome evil and fear but also to establish some measure of justice. In his *Selbstbetrachtungen* he stated that the standard of justice which prevails in any group or community determines the sum total of joy, inspiration, contentment, and happiness which that group is capable of producing.[9] The striving for justice, a practical manifestation of kindness, is thus closely linked by Wassermann with the alleviation of human fears, so many of which are rooted primarily in the injustice that arises from man's inhumanity to man. Wassermann was well aware that men practice justice in proportion as they respect human dignity; he was convinced that in relations based on equity and consideration for others the devastating power of fear loses its sway over the lives of men.

NOTES

[1] *Selbstbetrachtungen.* (Berlin: S. Fischer, 1933), p. 60.

[2] *Ibid.,* p. 106.

[3] *Faber oder die verlorenen Jahre.* (Berlin: S. Fischer, 1924), pp. 160 f.

[4] *Ibid.,* p. 193.

[5] *Der Aufrahr um den Junker Ernst* (Berlin: S. Fischer, 1926), p. 74.

[6] *Etzel Andergast.* (Berlin: S. Fischer, 1931), p. 133.

[7] *Die Geschichte der jungen Renate Fuchs.* (Berlin: S. Fischer, 1930), p. 348.

[8] *Christian Wahnschaffe.* (Berlin: S. Fischer, 1932), p. 745.

[9] *Selbstbetrachtungen.* (Berlin: S. Fischer, 1933), p. 98.

Eben Bass

SOURCE: "Frost's Poetry of Fear," in *American Literature,* Vol. XLIII, No. 4, January, 1972, pp.

[*In the following essay, Bass discusses the presentation of fear in the poetry of Robert Frost, centering on fears associated with individual experience, including fear of nature, and fears that threaten marriage, including the intrusion of a stranger,*]

Both as a private experience and as an intruder on marriage, fear is a recurring theme in the poetry of Robert Frost. Since it is alien to love, it can threaten marriage through an outside person like the Stranger in "Love and a Question," but his identity varies from poem to poem. Fear is also a private, singly-experienced thing, as in "An Old Man's Winter Night," a poem that sees fear as related to nature. Nature itself is not fear, nor does it know fear (unless, as with the Old Man, it is shocked at him), but fear can grow out of man's relationship with it. A variant is the awe/fear response of human beings in the presence of nature as divinity ("Going for Water"), or it may be the threat of nature to reclaim human institutions—in various Frost poems nature fills in vacated cellar holes and abandoned roads. But in these matters human neglect is at fault, and the resulting fear is an unrealized expression of that fault.

"A Brook in the City" is about urban neuroses, but we shall consider fear that relates to Frost's "country things." This may be as it is experienced by persons together, or alone. An example of the former, "Going for Water," tells the love-shared experience of nature as deity. On a cool autumn evening, a couple whose well has gone dry seek a brook in their woods. They run to meet the moonlight coming up out of the trees, but then pause within the shadow: "And in the hush we joined to make / We heard, we knew we heard the brook."[1] The poem depicts a shared awe in the presence of the stream nymph. The couple were playing with the moon until they entered the darkness, which makes them listen for the brook before they look for it. They do so reverently, the mood in which one should meet nature. Failing in the proper encounter unbalances the awe and turns it into fear.

Something close to such fear is experienced alone in "The Demiurge's Laugh." Though glossed as being "about science,"[2] this poem is also about nature because it takes place "far in the sameness of the wood" and in failing light. ("Going for Water" is set just within the wood, with the expected moonlight waning.) "I was running with joy on the Demon's trail, / Though I knew what I hunted was no true god." The Demon rises from behind the speaker, however, and with a sleepy, half-mocking laugh, catches him by surprise. The "I" feels foolish at being caught, pretends to have been looking for something else, but then sits unnerved against a tree: the quarry catches the hunter in his full but false confidence. The "science" of the poem is the speaker's false certainty that he could track down the Demon-Demiurge, which itself is a false creator.

Both single and dual encounters with fear occur in another poem, "Snow." The Fred Coles, a calm-minded couple, face it differently from the way of Meserve, also married, who seeks out challenges that are at odds with his role as a family man. Mrs. Cole chides Meserve, a preacher, for his weird description of snow piled against the Coles' window, "looking in." Seen by the heroics-seeking male, nature is a horrid, threatening stranger. But Mrs. Cole does not fear Meserve's pulpit rhetoric. He will have to face his demon. "Snow" speaks for the husband Fred as well as for his wife. He jokes about her possessiveness; he wants to encourage Meserve to make the dangerous trip with his team of horses back through the snow to his home, rather than safely staying the night with the Coles. Fred sides with Meserve and male bravado, which means facing competitive danger—"Let the man freeze an ear or two, I say." Meserve should be free to prove himself against the snow, which is nature sought out as an enemy. Yet in the language of "Stopping by Woods on a Snowy Evening," his "promises to keep" ought to be to keep alive for his family's sake, not to seek out an adventure. The delayed news of Meserve's safe arrival finds Fred less sympathetic with the male quest at the end of the poem than he was at the outset; he pretty much accepts his wife's remark, "What spoiled our night was to him just his fun." Meserve came to tell of the snow's danger, which he must go out to meet. He answers a call resisted by the speaker in another poem, "Storm Fear": in it the snowy wind, whispering and beast-like, calls "Come out! Come out!" And the man fears that he and his family, snowed in the next morning, won't be able to save themselves "unaided."

Male questing that runs counter to marriage also appears in a minor but unusual way, in "An Encounter." All but lost in a cedar swamp, the speaker finds an unexpected telegraph pole; then he wonders whether there is anywhere these days where one doesn't find poles and wires. He asks where it's "off for," and what news it carries ("if it knows"). Matching wits with its instant alert, Frost's "I" says he is not "off to" anywhere: "Sometimes I wander out of beaten ways / Half looking for the orchid Calypso." A nymph so-named kept Odysseus on an island for seven years, despite faithful, waiting Penelope, who was "keeper" in another sense. Frost's "I" seeks a wood nymph rather than one of the sea.[3] The omnipresent telegraph takes away the glamor of his quest, however, just as in "Snow" the certainty of the telephone connection between the Coles' house and Meserve's obviates Meserve's snow mission, his challenge to fear.

Ideally, Frost says that love, for all its denial of freedom and gesture, provides safety that in itself is liberating. In philosopher's terms this is shown in "Bond and Free." A crux between the poem's opening and closing, the closing settles (tentatively) in favor of love. "Love" and "Thought" (the latter the abstract of wandering male enterprise) are set off at the outset as alternatives, with Thought as the preference:

> Love has earth to which she clings
> With hills and circling arms about—
> Wall within wall to shut fear out.
> But Thought has need of no such things. . . .

If the poem opens in favor of Thought, rhetoric turns the closing toward Love. The terms are still options, however, paired together somewhat like Frost's famous "fire and ice" alternatives.

> Yet some say Love by being thrall
> And simply staying possesses all
>
> In several beauty that Thought fares far
> To find fused in another star.

Philosophically true, perhaps, this is not so clear-cut in human situations. Although the gloss originally furnished for "A Dream Pang" describes a happily married couple ("He is shown by a dream how really well it is with him"), most of the poem tells of the fear in the dream. The man's beloved follows him to the forest edge, but will not enter, because, "I dare not—too far in his footsteps stray— / He must seek me would he undo the wrong." He dreams that hearing her he wanted to call back to her, and suffered a pang for not doing so. The poem ends with the wood waking, and the man's discovery that she is with him after all. Still, the dream imagery suggests Young Goodman Brown's dilemma, of penetrating too far into the wood, despite his wife's entreaty that he not go there. The fear is that the speaker as a loner is at odds with his other role as husband and lover. This dream situation becomes reality in another poem called "The Thatch," to be discussed below.

The private fear of the speaker in "Desert Places" is not his alarm at interstellar space; "I have it in me so much nearer home / To scare myself with my own desert places." Frost does not, however, mistake his own loneliness for humanity's. The "desert" of "Desert Places" is his own personal fear. In a cognate poem, "On the Heart's Beginning to Cloud the Mind," he is riding on a train at night crossing Utah. But he decides that this desert is not personal to him. True, the flickering light he sees from some distant home seems to be kept "by the people there, / With a Godforsaken brute despair." Then he can tell that intervening trees cause the wavering, that the light is in fact steadfast, that "Matter of fact has made them brave." Other lights have spoken to theirs, even if theirs is the last one kept burning.

Frost's abstracted fear in "Desert Places" is personalized in "An Old Man's Winter Night." The old man lumbers noisily and late through empty rooms, forgetting what he is looking for. He scares the house with his thumping, at last even the outer night. Since human loneliness is a shock to nature, fear possesses it, not him. Whereas in "On the Heart's Beginning to Cloud the Mind" Frost reassures himself that the cedar trees outside the one lighted farmhouse are not marshaling under a leader against it, his "Old Man" seems to hold the outdoors at bay. The frightening thing about him is that he can not remember what it is he is "keeping." "One aged man—one man—can't keep a house, / A farm, a countryside. . . ."

The fear-related role of trees in the preceding poems is central to "Tree at my Window." Here, both the tree and the speaker are tempest-tossed. Nature's "fear" and the man's stand opposed like mirror images, each the seeming reflection of the other, yet each with its own cause. "Your head so much concerned with outer, / Mine with inner, weather." The speaker will not draw a curtain over the closed sash between him and the window tree. Thus the tree has seen him taken and tossed as he slept, just as he has seen it, like him, all but lost in its outer weather. One of the "Hill Wife" poems also describes a tree close outside, but this one seems to be trying to get in. Her plight is close to the shock-incident in Henry James's "The Turn of the Screw," when the governess, seeing Peter Quint peering through the dining room window, rushes outside to apprehend him and stands in the same spot to peer in in turn and frighten the housekeeper, Mrs. Grose. The first stage of such fear is in Frost's "Old Man," who cannot "keep a house, a farm, a countryside," and it is his forgetfulness and vacancy which prevent this and shock the outdoors. James's governess typifies the second phase, of fear having doubled about and become its own mirror image, a reversal that mocks at its former self. Frost is careful, however, to keep the opposites at the window-mirror on their proper sides. Thus in "Tree at My Window," Fate is said to have put the heads of the tree and of the speaker "together"—but on opposite sides of the window; i.e., with "her imagination about her," Fate made the tree outer and the speaker inner.

Outer and inner play a larger role in many of Frost's domestic poems about fear. For example, married love is wrenched into a separated outer and inner in "The Thatch." The speaker is outside and alone "in the winter rain / Intent on giving and taking pain." An assault on the inner is shown by the man's saying, "I would not go in till the light went out; / It would not go out till I came in." Finally, he returns to the proper side of the window after he accidentally unsettles the birds from their nests in the roof thatch and worries about their too being frightened and dislodged into an "outer" place. The poem ends in a way that gives another, post-dated pain to the inner side of the window. The speaker has heard that after he moved away the roof thatch decayed, "letting the rain I knew outdoors / In onto the upper chamber floors." In another "outer" poem which is less painful, "Waiting: Afield at Dusk," Frost writes to "greet her eye" who is "absent most"—that is, the "she" of domestic love who is by nature the inner, keeping creature. True, she goes with him to meet the "outer" in the poem "Going for Water," but she is mainly the "bond" of "Bond and Free," and she is the light protected by the thatch roof. The male needs to keep his touch with the threatening outer more than does the female, who by nature shuns it. When the inner "keeping" does indeed fail, all becomes outer, as in the poem "Ghost House." Things go back to being wild; nature reclaims everything. Woods come back into neglected mowing fields, and although Frost appears to be joking in "Mending Wall" when he attributes a Birnam Wood maneuver to the pines and apple trees on opposite sides of the wall, nevertheless his poems often tell a dream fear of woods "coming across" or "closing in." "Ghost House" describes a vacant cellar hole kept now by nature, just as the road nearby is overgrown. Despite this poem's sweet-sad Georgian manner, there is a ghost in the title, and ghosts are uneasy spirits: uneasy in the terms of other Frost poems, because the inner is not being kept, of its all going wild into the outer.

Several poems show the man as outer by instinct, but tied to the "inner" wife by love. The misunderstanding in "Home Burial" has to do with what the wife saw through the window on the stairway: how her husband, with seeming indifference, lustily dug the grave for their child. Only after pressing the issue does he "see" the reason for her fear and depression when he notices her furtive looks through the window.[4] But so far as she is concerned, he is still outer and does not see; he only looks; in fact, she almost seems to be wilfully preventing his attempts at seeing. She will not forget her grief, nor will she grant that he can know anything of it. Trying to reconcile her after she finally breaks into tears, he thinks this release will make her easier, and (in what seems only a casual note), invokes the outer: "The heart's gone out of it: why keep it up? / Amy! There's someone coming down the road!" That someone is alien to their attempt at domestic, inner life; therefore Amy is not, in her emotional outburst, to be allowed to rush from the house. The poem ends with her present escape and his vow to bring her back by force, if necessary. His "outer" threatens by force to become inner, whereupon her "inner" becomes hysterical and reverses into an outer force (the mocking mirror image) somewhat after the fashion of James's governess when she rushes to the outside of the dining room window. What requires the husband to become inner is his wish to keep domestic troubles at home, and he has the moral advantage, seemingly, in that the wife has not allowed him on her side of the window, has not helped him to be, defies his wish to be, denies his ability to be.

The only casually mentioned threat of an outer "someone" in "Home Burial" becomes more serious in several other poems. The woman in "The Hill Wife" series is younger than the one in "Home Burial," and she has not had children, but the two would understand each other. "The Smile: Her Word" of the Hill Wife is in some ways also like the strange ballad-poem "Love and a Question." "The Smile," however, is from the wife's point of view. Troubled by a beggar who seemed to mock at her young marriage, she wonders "how far down the road he's got.

/ He's watching from the woods as like as not." The stranger who interrupts love, as the wife's fear, continues to threaten from his hiding place. She senses his real but veiled malice, which in another sense is her fear that her love for her husband will not be sufficient to make their marriage last. "Love and a Question" is a related poem, but told from the young bridegroom's point of view, and his fear is different from that of the Hill Wife. The Stranger of "Love and a Question" (Frost personified him with a capital S in a revision) asks a newlywed couple for shelter for the night. He has no visible belongings, only "for all burden, care." The bridegroom thinks it is not enough to give him "a dole of bread, a purse, / A heartfelt prayer," but then again he pauses at whether he should offer anything more. Should he "mar the love of two / By harboring woe in the bridal house"? He does not fear a lack in his own love (the fear of the Hill Wife), but is touched by the loneliness of the "outer" male who craves for inner, domestic security even while by instinct he is also a wanderer, an outer person. The Stranger is the bridegroom's surrogate, while for the Hill Wife he can be only a demon lover luring her away from her hearth.

Like the windows that keep inner from outer in several of the fear poems, Frost's doors fill comparable roles. In the poem "Snow," which as we have seen contrasts male bravado with domestic security, the neglect of a door left open chances the outer threat to the inner. The telephone, also left "open" by neglect or haste, causes fear of the same danger. Hours after the venturesome Meserve left their home on his way back through the snow, the Coles receive a call from his wife asking whether he has gone yet. On learning that he has several hours ago, the wife pauses and leaves the telephone line open. The Coles are kept listening, and Fred's wife asks, "You can't hear whether she has left the door / Wide open . . . the fire's died and the room's dark and cold?" Fear of an open door (letting in what should be kept out) communicates itself over the telephone line, also left fearfully open. After some tense waiting, the Coles learn that Meserve has indeed made it home. Still, the fear of an untended door remains strongly in mind.

Fear of what may lurk outside a closed door, especially at night, appears in a quite different poem, "Locked Out: As Told to a Child." An outsider, a stranger, is assumed to be seeking entrance. This is only a dream, however, and the idea of locking the flowers outside at night where they will be with the unknown makes the fear seem less serious than it may really be. The fear is the speaker's own, but "told to a child." "The time I dreamed the door was tried / And brushed with buttons upon sleeves. . . ." Outside, the next morning, he finds a nasturtium with a "bitten stem"; otherwise, the imaginary stranger did no harm. "I may have been to blame for that." The line in its present revised form[5] leaves an air of mystery, to enhance the quality of fear itself. The original identity of the fear is more transparent: it is the speaker as he is when *he* is outside the door, and his outer identity arouses some alarm in his inner, keeping self.[6] "Inner" and "outer" are being used here in the sense of "Tree at My Window," with the additional possibility as in other poems of the self's partaking of either existence, but at some risk or danger when it does so. The same opposites, differently resolved, are seen from the Hill Wife's point of view in "The Oft-Repeated Dream." In this poem the branch of a dark pine tree brushes against her bedroom window. To her eyes, the tree is the stranger who threatens domestic love.

> It never had been inside the room,
> And only one of the two
> Was afraid in an oft-repeated dream
> Of what the tree might do.

The earlier version of this poem refers to the dark pine as "he," more closely identifying it with the stranger lurking in the wood who (so the wife thought) had previously mocked at her young marriage. In the final poem of her series, "The Impulse," she wanders off "to break a bough / Of black alder" (an echo and acceptance of the dark pine's beckoning from outside her window). She never returns. She scarcely hears her husband calling for her, and rather than going back, only hides "in the fern." Although no demon lover is mentioned, her vanishing into the wood does complete the urge that lurks behind her fear in "The Smile," a poem about the compelling expression on the face of the outsider, which "never came of being gay."

The stranger is a bit more explicit, although still enigmatic, in a longer poem, "The Fear." This work has important ties with a shorter one, "The Draft Horse," although that poem is a parable, whereas "The Fear" is one of Frost's characteristic folk narratives, replete with dialogue. It tells of a farm couple who have returned home late at night in a horse-drawn buggy. Having arrived at the barn, the wife insists she saw a man's face close to the roadside in the bushes. The presumed stranger is part of that "outer" danger which can be avoided by the proper ritual of unlocking a dark house at night: one must rattle the key in the lock in order to warn "someone to be getting out / At one door as we entered at another." In her little poem "House Fear" the Hill Wife has a similar custom: to rattle lock and key, and to "leave the house-door wide / Until they had lit the lamp inside." In "The Fear," however, the woman is braver, more decisive, than the young Hill Wife: she insists on taking the lantern by herself and seeking out the man she has seen. She does not want her husband to come; she will settle with the other man, alone; and she must settle things now, or she will always be afraid of his lurking about. She means to avoid the dilemma of the Hill Wife, who is doomed to feel watched from the wood by the smiling stranger. The brave wife of "The Fear" indeed finds the lurking man and calls him within the circuit of the lantern. Approaching, he says there is a boy with him, his son; therefore, he could not be a robber. He explains that they are stopping at a neighbor's, although he does not tell why they walk so late, in the dark. The wife calls on her husband Joel to understand; he does not reply; she drops the lantern and it goes out. Joel's failure to speak at the grimmest moment of his wife's self-doubt is ominous.[7] His the name of a minor Hebrew prophet, he judges his wife by his silence.

Even more melodramatic is the stranger from the "outer" in "The Witch of Coös." In reprisal for his threat to a marriage, he is killed by the outraged husband, Toffile Lajway, and buried in the cellar of the farmhouse with the aid of the erring wife. Years later, the bones get restless and ascend the cellar stairs trying to get out. "The uncommonly deep snow has made him think / Of his old song, 'The Wild Colonial Boy,'" says the wife to Toffile, on the evening of the bones' attempted escape. The luring snow, opposed to security and domestic ties (as we have seen in "Snow" and "Stopping by Woods on a Snowy Evening"), speaks to the remains of the demon lover, just as the woman who counters him by a trick and turns him upstairs to the attic and traps him behind the attic door is known for her "inner" witchcraft. The function shown above of the door as barrier between inner and outer is neatly and ironically transposed in this poem. The dry, chalky rubbing of the bones behind the attic door at night is an obverse to the buttons imagined to be brushed against the door in the child's poem "Locked Out." The lover's bones are locked forever in, escaped from the damp cellar but tricked into the dry attic.

Whereas many of Frost's poems use domestic images to dramatize inner and outer impulses hidden behind fear, others do so by picturing fear through a trip and a destination. "On a Tree Fallen Across the Road" shows nature interfering with man's directed route. A subtitle undercuts competence (and confidence) to reach its goals, but the poem ends with determination, even certainty, that man will meet and overcome obstacles. The speaker says the fallen tree is not meant to bar our passage to "our journey's end for good" but just to ask us "who we think we are" and to remind us of who we really are. The tree's "Making us get down" anticipates the dilemma of that darker poem "The Draft Horse," in which the couple are made to walk the rest of their night journey. Although that poem is more violent than "Tree Fallen," both show that man's will is accomplished only when he overcomes obstacles meant to humble his pride. To lose that sense of sufficiency induces fear, the mental counterpart to the obstacles themselves.

Another trip / destination poem, "The Times Table," alludes to the farmer's wife in a manner that makes one think of "The Draft Horse." In "The Times Table," the farmer rebukes his mare because she always wants to stop at a drinking place halfway uphill.

> "A sigh for every so many breath,
> And for every so many sigh a death.
> That's what I always tell my wife
> Is the multiplication table of life."

The saying may be true, notes Frost in ending the poem, but it is also a malediction—it will close roads, cause the abandoning of farms, reduce humanity, and "bring back nature in people's place." To measure out life is to diminish it. To measure the sigh of the mare (who after all has a star on her forehead) is an affront to the spirit of life.

In "The Draft Horse" the "we" who drove in "too frail a buggy" are a man and wife, if we take that poem as a parable on fear drawn from the narrative poem "The Fear." In the longer work, a buggy ride at night is guided only by a weak carriage lamp, and the wife is frightened by a man's face at the side of the road in the bushes. In the shorter poem, these details are intensified. The "man who came out of the trees" is the white-faced figure the wife sees in "The Fear." He is abrupt and drastic in the short poem, however, not merely a suggested threat: he seizes the head of the horse "And reaching back to his ribs / Deliberately stabbed him dead." A fatal wound must follow the farmer's remark in "The Times Table" because that remark measures out breath. Cynicism kills life, the spirit of which is breathed into us. Though the mare shows the star on her forehead as she turns her head back to the farmer ("straining her ribs for a monster sigh"), he only thinks of life-breath as measurable. Lack of faith in other circumstances (at night) becomes fear, personified in the deliberate stabbing at breath. A draft horse draws heavy loads—his work is accomplished in a flow of energy that costs heavy breathing. Thus when the heavy beast falls, breaking the shaft of the buggy, "the night drew through the trees / In one long invidious draft." This is the only echo of "draft" from the title, and the word "invidious" suggests a jealous rivalry at work in the darkness. Fear (that grows out of doubt, cynicism) does violence to breath and life, then mocks it with a breath of ill will after it has killed it.

Unlike the couple in "The Fear," the "we" of "The Draft Horse" remain together through the end of the poem, whereas Joel does not answer his wife's distressed cry, even when she drops the lantern that disclosed the face of the stranger. As in "On a Tree Fallen," the "we" have to get down from their vehicle; but to make matters worse, the night couple will have to "walk the rest of the way." "Tree Fallen" describes a simpler more casual impediment. True, the speaker has no ax in the sleigh with him to chop away the tree, but the tree is merely a reminder, not a grim disaster. And the speaker's concluding optimism in "Tree Fallen," though an attempt is made to restate it in "The Draft Horse," sounds naively idealistic in the night poem:

> The most unquestioning pair
> That ever accepted fate
> And the least disposed to ascribe
> Any more than we had to hate.

A draft is after all (in terms of "The Times Table") a drain which may exhaust the supply. Perhaps the spirited optimism of "Tree Fallen" is too much for dark fate to allow (or for the darker fears of Frost to tolerate)—hence the stranger (fear personified) out of the wood, who destroys the "too heavy a horse"—too much draft or spirited breath to be drawing so frail a buggy. Because the couple in the buggy were unquestioning, gave as little credence as they could to hate (a universe ruled by evil), fate makes them suffer for accepting things too easily.

The stranger, then, whether in Frost's domestic or travel poems, is hostile to marriage. He is the most common equivalent of fear. As a demon lover he tries to lure the wife away ("The Hill Wife," "The Witch of Coös"), or with the lure of adventure he tries to make the husband risk his life foolishly ("Snow"). Also, the tension we have noted in Frost's poems between inner and outer is in fact a contest between two halves of the self, which are only partly aware of each other, and whatever mutual awareness exists is competitive. In addressing this dilemma the Wakefield complex is a possible way out, but Frost's fear of this cold sort of answer is his worst fear. At all possible cost, the door / window must keep these halves separate and in balance. They can also be known in the sense of the Fire and Ice opposites, which are Love and Hate, but in some sense they are also Female and Male, Love and Thought. These forces are the most terrifying when they get on the wrong side of things, and Frost uses all his power and control to keep them where they belong. The husband's final threat to Amy in "Home Burial" is not merely brutal and sexual; it states an essential rule for keeping the inner from getting lost in the outer.

[1] All quotations are from Edward Connery Lathem, ed., *The Poetry of Robert Frost* (New York, 1969).

[2] In *A Boy's Will* (London, 1913). All glosses cited in this paper are from the 1913 edition; they are reprinted in Lathem.

[3] In "Flower Gathering" the man has left his lady in the morning, to wander in the fields and woods. At evening he returns, the only excuse for his absence being some gay but faded flowers. She is cool to him, and he asks whether she is "dumb because you know me not, / Or dumb because you know?" The flowers are a renewal of courtship, but the day-long absence with no other excuse is a kind of Calypso venture.

[4] Randall Jarrell, in *The Moment of Poetry,* ed. Don Cameron Allen (Baltimore, 1962), notes that the wife's habitual, furtive glance out of the stair window not only accuses her husband's gross indifference, but is also self-accusing. The husband's family burial plot, which he likens to the size of a bedroom, subconsciously reminds her of the bedroom in which the dead child was conceived; and his grossly digging in the outer clay of the graveyard reminds her subconsciously of his impregnating her inner clay.

[5] It originally read, "I always blamed myself for that"; cited by Lathem.

[6] Frost's poem "The Lockless Door" is a spoof on fear involving both a door and a window. When the fear of someone "outer" knocking at his lockless door gets the best of him, the speaker himself climbs out the open window. Then he climbs back in, to summon in the "whatever" was outside. He's amused at having "emptied my cage" in order to "hide in the world." There is a bit of Hawthorne's Wakefield in this, except that Frost makes his speaker promptly return and open the door from the inside.

7 The wives to whom a stranger beckons in these poems apparently grow out of Frost's own marital possessiveness. According to Lawrance Thompson, Frost never forgave his wife Elinor for letting him think that she still cared for someone else. See *Robert Frost, The Early Years, 1874-1915* (New York, 1966).

Laurence Perrine

SOURCE: "Frost's 'The Fear': Unfinished Sentences, Unanswered Questions," in *College Literature,* Vol. XV, No. 3, 1988, pp. 199-207.

[*In the following essay, Perrine explicates Robert Frost's "The Fear," drawing attention to its "syntax of mystery"—its mood of tension and anxiety, its numerous unfinished sentences, and its undefined relationships among central characters in the poem.*]

I

Amy Lowell's notorious misinterpretation of Robert Frost's poem "The Fear,"[1] in which (she tells us) the protagonist comes face to face with her first husband at the end of the poem and is possibly killed by him,[2] had always seemed to me simply a bizarre critical aberration until I assigned the poem for study in a graduate seminar and found my brightest students as confused about its ending as Lowell. This led me to review the criticism of the poem, where I found that, although Lowell had been firmly put in her place (most particularly by Louis Untermeyer),[3] there remained sufficient disagreement among commentators about various aspects of the poem as to justify a fuller examination than has previously been given it.

Of all Frost's "New England eclogues," none probes more deeply or renders more sharply a single human emotion than "The Fear." The poem's sharp emotional definition is derived, however, from a syntax of mystery. From a single briefly presented incident, the reader must infer a large set of relationships: psychological, emotional, and factual.

The mystery of the poem arises principally from four sources. First, the poem concerns a woman's relationship with two men—Joel, with whom she is currently living, and an unnamed man with whom she had been earlier involved. The exact nature of neither relationship is ever spelled out. Second, the poem has a quadruple *in medias res* beginning. The woman's entrance into her relationship with each of the two men, the specific incident that gives rise to the dialogue and action of the poem, and the beginning of the dialogue itself, all occur before the beginning of the poem. Third, "The Fear" is notably a poem of uncompleted sentences. In the sixty-nine lines of the poem devoted to dialogue, eleven sentences are cut off or left unfinished. In no other poem by Frost, of whatever length, is the reader left so many times to infer what a character would have said had he been allowed or able to finish his thought. Fourth, the ending of the poem, though vividly rendered, calls again upon the reader to infer exactly what has happened.

My procedure will be, first, simply to go through the poem making those inferences which for me best explain the data presented, then to discuss the poem more generally, concentrating on those issues about which there has been critical disagreement.

For ease of discussion I must state a major inference at the onset. The unnamed man in the woman's life, whose vengeance she so fears, is the husband she has deserted; she is not married to Joel. I shall try to justify this inference later.

II

The action of the poem begins with a restive horse in a barn and the lurching shadows of a man and woman thrown larger than life on a nearby farmhouse. The scene at once establishes a mood of nervous tension which will increase until the poem's climax. We do not learn the reason for the horse's uneasiness until line 73, three-quarters deep into the poem. The woman, driving herself and Joel home in their gig, frightened by something seen by the road, had whipped the horse up just before turning into the barnyard.

The woman's first words to Joel—as shown by their unreferenced "it"—continue a dialogue already begun. "I saw it just as plain as a white plate . . . Along the bushes by the roadside." Joel had asked why she whipped up the horses, and this continues her reply. Her tenseness is betrayed when she interrupts Joel's next question, "Are you sure—[it was a face?"] before he has finished it. Her reply to the completed question reveals a lack of sureness. "I can't [go in], and leave a thing like that unsettled." Unless she settles the matter now, irrational fears will control her life. Her remarks about returning to the dark house after an absence betray a similar conflict between rationality and irrationality. Previously she had rejected as fancy her feeling that their loudly rattled key "Seemed to warn someone to be getting out / At one door" as they entered at another, but this new terror seems suddenly to validate it. In the poem's first unfinished sentence, she asks, "What if I'm right, and someone all the time—" "Someone all the time" has been doing what? Spying on them? Watching them? Yes; but for what purpose? And why so often? And how had "someone" gained entrance? She breaks off without posing such unanswerable questions to protest Joel's having taken her arm to hold her back. She is determined to settle the matter.

Joel says reasonably, "I say it's someone passing." She is unpersuaded. Why would anyone be out on foot on this lonely road at such an hour of night, and "What was he standing still for in the bushes?" This last circumstance seems especially sinister to her, though a foot traveler on a narrow unlit road with a horse-and-gig bearing down on him would have little place else to go. Joel, now fully aware that her fear is extraordinary, observes, "There's more in it than you're inclined to say. / Did he look like—" Joel is about to name the husband, but she cuts him short. "He looked like anyone. / I'll never rest tonight until I know. / Give me the lantern."

Terror makes her bold. Unless she settles the matter now, she will begin seeing her husband's face everywhere, looking out of trees and bushes. She gets the lantern for herself. She is determined, moreover, to face her husband alone, and orders Joel inside. "This is my business. / If the time's come to face it, I'm the one / To put it the right way." Put what the right way?—her reasons for having run off with Joel. She can place them in a more favorable light, she thinks, than Joel—and can do so more effectively without the embodiment of her betrayal standing by her side. (In both assumptions she is probably correct.) "He'd never dare—" she resumes, but leaves her thought unfinished on hearing a sound from the road. "He'd never dare attack me" is her meaning, but she is saying so more to reassure herself than Joel, for she clearly believes he might. Joel tries to reason with her: "In the first place you can't make me believe it's—" Again she cuts him short before he can name the dreaded name. "It is—or someone else he's sent to watch." The extraordinary swiftness with which uncertainty about *what* she saw has towered into conviction about *whom* she saw is the measure of her panic. Her comparison of what she saw to a white plate is striking in that a white plate suggests something entirely featureless; yet her imagination has already put features into it—and not only the features of a man's face, but of her husband's face. Yet her response to Joel's asking whether she was sure it was a face—"I can't leave a thing like that unsettled"— betrays a lingering uncertainty, and her response to his first query as to whether it looked like her husband is "He might have been anyone." But now her conviction is complete; even her reservation that it might be "someone else he's sent to watch" is immediately abandoned, for she no longer thinks of her expedition into the dark as one to settle what or whom she saw, but only as one to "have it out with him / While we know definitely where he is."

Joel's next words, "But it's nonsense to think he'd care enough," are meant to be reassuring. But he phrases the remark badly, and the woman's sharp reply indicates that her relationship with Joel has not been all she'd hoped for. "You mean you couldn't understand his caring." But the outburst is momentary. She follows it quickly with an attempt at explanation and then with an urgent plea. The explanation contains two unfinished sentences. Her husband, she says, "hadn't had enough—" Enough of what? Enough of her. And then, "Joel, I won't—I won't—I promise you." Won't what? Won't let him take her back. She wants her relationship with Joel to be stable. "We mustn't say hard things," she says, indirectly apologizing for her angry outburst, and adds, "You mustn't either," showing she is nevertheless still provoked by his remark.

Joel attempts to play the man's rôle—that of protector. "I'll be the one, if anybody goes." But he still sees no reason for either of them to go. Caught up now himself

in the intensity of her conviction, he rationally points out that the lantern makes them an easy target, and that, if the husband only wants confirmation of their being together, he's already had it. The woman ignores his logic and advances, Joel following half-heartedly.

Confronting the night boldly, she cries out—*not* "Who's there?"—but "What do you want?" Her terror is betrayed by her unawareness of the hot lantern against her skirt. Still convinced that someone is there, though no answer comes, she cries out a second time, and is startled when answered. Reaching a hand to Joel for support, made faint by the smell of her scorching skirt, she challenges the voice. It offers to come forward into the lantern light. She bids it do so, once more commanding Joel to "go back!"—a command he once more ignores. The steps advance; she "stands her ground," but her body rocks with fear. She is now so utterly obsessed with the idea that the man advancing is her husband that she cannot accept the meaning of what she sees when a stranger appears with a small boy. "What's a child doing at this time of night—" She cannot finish the sentence, but her meaning is "up and out on the open road." The stranger explains. She still cannot adjust to the reality. "Then I should think you'd try to find / Somewhere to walk—" "Somewhere more suitable" is what she means. The stranger gently reminds her that this country road, lonely as it is, is still the "highway"—the main road between two villages.

"But if that's all—" The "if" implies a lingering inability to admit that this *is* all, but the conclusion dawning in her mind is, "then I've made a spectacular fool of myself." But she can't say that aloud. Leaving her thought unfinished, covered with confusion, she tries to justify herself to both men at once. She first calls on Joel, says, "you realize"—which could be addressed to either man or both—then provides the stranger with a rationalization of her behavior. Again she calls on Joel, this time for support. Her legs suddenly watery, she is unable to turn around. With the sudden release of tension, her bravado whistles out of her like air from a punctured balloon. She faints. The lantern goes out simultaneously with her loss of consciousness.

III

A few words about the woman. She is not a coward, not a weakling. She faces her fear with resolute determination. Her most characteristic mode of speech is the imperative—whether addressing the horse, Joel, or the stranger. In her relationship with Joel she is the dominant partner. It is she who drives the gig, she who gives commands. Joel may stubbornly or gallantly refuse to obey those commands, but it is nevertheless she who leads and he who follows. She is not paranoid. Unlike the protagonist in "The Hill Wife" or the speaker in "Bereft," she does not think that nature or people in general are in conspiracy against her; her fear is sharply focussed on one man: her husband. Nevertheless, her fear far exceeds the bounds of reason. It amounts to hysterical terror, unjustified by the facts of the situation. It breaks out too suddenly, grows too rapidly. She remains only rational enough to foresee that, unless she achieves some resolution, her fear will grow utterly uncontrollable.

How do we explain this excessive fear? First, it may have had some real justification in the character of her husband. A dominating person herself, she would hardly experience such terror had her husband been a man like Joel. We can imagine the husband as a man capable of physical violence. Second, she has left him without explanation, without having had it "out" with him, and yet believing that he still desired her. To the burden of fear she has added the burden of guilt. Her guilt and fear have rubbed up against each other for so long that they are ready to blaze forth in near-panic when provided with the slightest bit of tinder. The face glimpsed by the road is the tinder.

It should now be apparent why I believe the earlier man, not Joel, to be her husband. Though she cannot be proved to have married either, her extreme fear of retaliation is more explicable under the supposition that the first man has a legal claim upon her, and the extreme burden of her guilt is more explicable under the supposition that she has broken marriage vows.[4]

There *may* be one additional element in this combustible combination of emotions—a lingering physical passion for her husband. This suggestion rests on slender evidence, and I will not push it. But her insistence that she can best deal with the husband alone, plus her repeated commands to Joel to "Go back" may indicate an unrecognized *desire* to be alone with him. Her "promise" to Joel that she will not go back to her husband, shows that the possibility of doing so has at least crossed her mind. Her conviction that her husband "hadn't had enough" of her *may* be taken as an unconscious confession that *she* has not "had enough" of him. We may hypothesize a stormy marriage, characterized by continuous conflict, but punctuated by bouts of passion gratifying to both. The grounds for such a conjecture are tenuous. Yet such a combination of fear, guilt, and unrecognized desire would indeed explain the explosion of irrational terror so vividly depicted in Frost's poem.

There are four reasons for thinking that the woman faints at the end of the poem.[5] First, line 69—"The smell of scorching woolen made her faint"—is anticipatory. Though "faint" is here an adjective, not a verb, the line predicts the conclusion both in its account of her mental state and in its language. Second, the lantern does not fall vertically and crash, as it would had she dropped it. It swings (from the rocking of her body); it lengthens (as her body crumples); then touches; then strikes, clatters, and goes out. She has been gripping it tightly. Were she still standing upright, it would not reach the ground. Third, a common human response to danger is to feel suddenly weak and trembly *after* the danger has passed. The woman's more intense response corresponds to the extraordinary pitch of terror she has wrought herself up to. Fourth, the extinction of the lantern simultaneous with her loss of consciousness provides the lantern with the symbolic

function that its prominence in the poem seems to demand. First mentioned in the first two words of the poem, it is extinguished in the last two.[6]

Three critics (two of whom believe the woman married to Joel) read the poem as focusing on a deteriorating relationship between the woman and Joel, and find great significance in the failure of Joel to respond to her final cry.[7] But Joel fails to respond simply because the poem is over. She calls out to him.—She faints.—End of poem. Frost could, of course, have told us the reactions of all three males—the stranger, his son, and Joel—as the woman's body crumpled to the ground. No doubt each made motions and uttered exclamations of surprise or dismay; but Frost knew better than to spoil a good ending. One critic, commenting on her unanswered call, writes, "Possibly, though we cannot know, he has impatiently turned round and gone home."[8] This would be inconsistent with Joel's previous behavior throughout the poem. He has stayed by her—loyally, gallantly, or out of male pride—throughout, even though his judgment does not endorse her action.[9] If we want to speculate about what Joel is up to after her final cry, he is probably stepping forward to break her fall. But Frost knew when his poem was over.

Joel, emotionally low-keyed, is a foil to the woman throughout the poem. Where she is quick to see offense in his well-meant remark about the husband's not caring enough, he simply ignores her stinging rebuke, "You mean you couldn't understand his caring." His next words are that he'll be the one to go out to face the intruder if anyone goes. His behavior nowhere in the poem suggests that this episode will cause a rupture in their relationship.

Except for the brief moments when the woman's conviction almost persuades him that her husband might be out there, Joel is the embodiment of common sense. His rationality contrasts with her irrationality. Even his remark about the husband that "it's nonsense to think he'd care enough," except for his unfortunate choice of words, is logical enough. Though technically not an unfinished sentence (for it ends with a period), its sense needs completion. "Care enough" for what? Care enough, after all this time, to spend the time, effort, and expense which would be required to search for her, perhaps through several states.—How long have the woman and Joel lived together? Long enough for them to have become accustomed to each other and for the initial glow of their romance to have worn off; not long enough for him to have outgrown a certain gallant protectiveness toward her nor long enough for her not to feel a real need of him. How long is that? Three months? Three years? Somewhere between these extremes would be my guess, but to pretend to any exactitude would be foolhardy. Where do she and Joel live? In a remote rural district of New England, far enough from her husband's place of residence as to render negligible any risk that they might meet him or a mutual acquaintance on a day's journey into town. (We do not know whether Joel has ever met the husband. What we do know is that she insists it's *her* business to have it out with the husband.)

Is it still necessary to refute Amy Lowell's interpretation? Perhaps one should leave no base untouched. The principal objection to it is that it transforms a psychodrama into a melodrama, and Frost was always interested in the former rather than the latter. He is interested in the psychology of guilt and irrational fear that begins with the woman's feeling that whenever she and Joel return home after a long absence, the rattle of their key warns someone inside to leave at one door while they enter at another, and develops into an intense conviction that a vague blur she has seen by the side of the road is, out of the thousands of possibilities, the face of her estranged husband. But the details of the poem conclusively disprove Lowell's interpretation. If it *were* her husband, he would not be lurking in the dark beside the road but would be awaiting their return in the barn or on the front steps of the house. When the woman cries out, "What do you want?" the husband, presumably seeking this encounter, would not first remain silent and then reply "Nothing" from a point "well along the road," and then return. This behavior fits a stranger walking along the road who, after stepping aside to let the carriage pass, has resumed his walk and then, recognizing the full terror in the woman's voice, returns to reassure her. If it were the husband, she would recognize him when he steps into the light. If it were the husband, he would not have brought a child along (whom she also does not recognize) to witness his act of revenge. Nor would the husband produce the child, as the stranger does (not knowing the cause of her fear), as proof that he is not a "robber." The woman, were it her husband, would not say, "But if that's all—" and then attempt to explain away her fright. In brief, Lowell's interpretation has more holes in it than a colander.

In the first volume of his biography of Frost, Lawrance Thompson gives a full account of the incident which provided the materials for this poem. Though I would not advance this account as "proof" of my interpretation (I did not discover it, in fact, until after I had formed my conclusions and written the first draft of this paper; and Frost, in any case, often changed his "materials" considerably when transforming them into poetry), the account does generally confirm the interpretation I have given. The woman was a New Hampshire girl who "trained as a nurse in Boston, married there, later fell in love with one of her patients, and ran away from her Boston husband to live in hiding with her lover on a small farm" back in New Hampshire. The stranger and the boy in the poem were Frost himself and his son Carol, then five years old.[10]

NOTES

[1] *The Poetry of Robert Frost,* ed. Edward Connery Lathem (New York: Holt, 1969), pp. 89-92. All references are to this edition.

[2] Amy Lowell, *Tendencies in Modern American Poetry* (New York: Macmillan, 1917), p. 122.

[3] Louis Untermeyer, *The New Era in American Poetry* (New York: Holt, 1919), pp. 26-28.

[4] Reuben A. Brower, *The Poetry of Robert Frost* (New York: Oxford Univ. Press, 1965), p.165; Richard Poirier, *Robert Frost: The Work of Knowing* (New York: Oxford Univ. Press, 1977), pp. 119-123; James K. Bowen, "Propositional and Emotional Language in Robert Frost's 'The Death of the Hired Man,' 'The Fear,' and 'Home Burial,'" *CLA Journal,* 12 (Dec. 1968), 157-158; and Eben Bass, "Frost's Poetry of Fear," *American Literature,* 43 (Jan. 1972), 611-612, all assume that the protagonist is married to Joel.—Amy Lowell; Louis Untermeyer; George W. Nitche, *Human Values in the Poetry of Robert Frost* (Durham, N.C.: Duke Univ. Press, 1960), p. 167; Frank Lentricchia, *Robert Frost: Modern Poetics and the Landscape of Self* (Durham, N.C.: Duke Univ. Press, 1975), p. 70; Elaine Barry, *Robert Frost* (New York: Frederick Ungar, 1973), pp. 71-75; and Floyd C. Watkins, "The Poetry of the Unsaid—Robert Frost's Narrative and Dramatic Poems," *Texas Quarterly,* 15 (Winter 1972), 90, agree with me in seeing the earlier man as the husband.

[5] Frank Lentricchia, p. 73, says, "The lantern accidentally hits the ground and goes out. The woman is left alone with darkness, frozen with objectless fear"; Eben Bass says, "She drops the lantern"; Lawrance Thompson, *Fire and Ice: The Art and Thought of Robert Frost* (New York: Russell & Russell, 1942), p. 110, says that "the relieved woman almost faints, while the lantern drops from her hand to the ground"; Amy Lowell writes, "She comes face to face with her first husband. . . . Does he kill her, or does she merely think that he is going to do so? Which one is crazed, he or she? Either way, Nature has taken her toll."—Louis Untermeyer and Elaine Barry agree with me that she faints.

[6] Frost first intended to call the poem "The Lantern" but was apparently dissuaded by Mrs. Frost, who thought the title not "a fit." *Selected Letters of Robert Frost,* ed. Lawrance Thompson (New York: Holt, 1964), p. 89.

[7] Richard Poirier; Eben Bass; Floyd Watkins.

[8] Richard Poirier.

[9] Amy Lowell and Lawrance Thompson, *Fire and Ice,* state or imply that the woman goes out to face the unknown man "alone"—an obvious misunderstanding.

[10] Lawrance Thompson, *Robert Frost: The Early Years* (New York: Holt, 1966), pp. 344-345.

Sidney D. Braun

SOURCE: "Source and Psychology of Sartre's Le Mur," in *Criticism,* Vol. VII, No. 1, Winter, 1965, pp. 45-51.

[*In the following essay, Braun traces the psychological basis of Jean-Paul Sartre's presentation of fear in "Le Mur" in the* Traité de Psychologie *of Georges Dumas.*]

Finding a number of similarities between Sartre's short story "le Mur" and Andreyev's "The Seven Who Were

Hanged," this writer wrote Sartre some time ago to ask whether, in fact, he had been inspired by the Russian writer. Sartre, much too occupied with more important literary duties, did not have time to reply; but Simone de Beauvoir, who has often acted as his secretary, answered for him. In her courteous but direct reply, in which she denied the influence of Andreyev, she wrote: "En fait il a été inspiré pour le *Mur* par . . . le Traité de psychologie de Dumas au chapitre des émotions: la peur."[1]

The clue supplied to the elusive search revealed two important bits of information: the name of an important psychologist who, during Sartre's stay as a student at the Ecole Normale Supérieure,[2] was the latter's professor of psychology and, secondly, the fact that fear was the principal theme and framework of reference for this short story, first published in the *Nouvelle Revue Française* (July 1937, pp. 38-62). This information did raise, however, in the mind of the present writer several questions. Why, for one thing, was the indicated source not common knowledge? Why, too, in the several psychological studies on Sartre,[3] studies which include the names of those psychologists who had influenced him, was the name of Georges Dumas never referred to? Finally, why did Simone de Beauvoir, who, in her *La Force de l'Age*,[4] scrupulously indicated (even in footnotes) the sources of Sartre's works, including those of the other short stories in the volume *Le Mur*,[5] not shed any light on the genesis of the short story we are presently considering?

1.

These are indeed interesting questions. More important, however, than finding the answers to these questions are the problems relating, first, to Sartre's psychology—since his almost exclusive preoccupation prior to 1938 was with psychology—and, second, to the way in which Dumas' notion of fear influenced Sartre. An examination of the latter problem is basic, of course, for a proper evaluation and explication of Sartre's "Le Mur."

Simone de Beauvoir sheds some biographical light in *La Force de l'Age* on Sartre's intellectual formation. He had read Freud, Adler, and Jung at a time when, in the late Twenties, his generation was being drawn to psychoanalysis; but he was opposed to the psychoanalytic view which "decomposed" man instead of understanding him, and to the theory of the unconscious which, according to him, crushed human liberty. If, therefore, he was more drawn in 1927 to Jaspers (whose treatise on Psychopathology, written in 1913, had just been translated), it was because the latter "saisit des relations singulières, par des intuitions, plus affectives que rationnelles." (p. 47) With regard to Georges Dumas, it is interesting, to say the least, that Simone de Beauvoir, referring to his psychology and to his theory of the "monisme endocrinien" (associated by him with a "dualisme cartésien"), calls it "inacceptable"! (p. 25)[6] As she sees it, then, Sartre viewed the individual as a "totalité synthétique et indivisible," whose conduct was to be judged "globalement." (p. 47) Expressed

differently, "l'individualisme est une prise de position par rapport à la totalité du monde." (p. 144)

On the plane of emotions, therefore, Sartre tried to prove that they do not determine our actions but rather that they constitute a certain *way* in which we *choose* to live these relations. This is the significance of his early psychological studies as well as of his basic *Esquisse d'une théorie des emotions* (1939). As an "experiment in phenomenological psychology," the latter work is a psychological interpretation of emotions, which are a form of existence of consciousness. To recapitulate, then, Sartre's existential psychoanalysis rejects the theory of the unconscious and believes that man is conscious of all his acts. Of course, what Sartre has in mind is that an emotional (i.e. non-reflective) consciousness is a certain way of apprehending the world; but a non-reflective action is not an unconscious one.

Dumas' position on emotions, though stated less clearly, is not basically different from that of Sartre. In his *Traité de Psychologie,* he says, in part: " . . . notre état affectif est à chaque instant déterminé par les rapports du donné matériel, sensoriel ou représentatif *avec nos tendances et nos inclinations.*" (p. 459; italics mine)

On fear, as one of the emotions, Dumas leaves no doubt as to his interpretation. Although he distinguishes between active and passive fear, he finds that the depressive form of fear is characterized "par une dépression subite de l'appareil neuro-musculaire *volontaire.*" (p. 622; italics mine) And the only positive reactions he finds associated with this type of fear are "less spasmes des muscles de la vie organique, muscles intestinaux, muscles vésicaux, muscles vaso-moteurs, d'ù évacuations fécales et urinaires." (*Ibid.*) Such acts, then, if we interpret them correctly, are, even when the subject is immobile and incapable of fleeing, conscious on the non-reflective level.

Sartre, too, sees the body as using a form of incantation when it wishes to free itself of fear; in other words, it transforms itself in order to transform the object of fear. This act, too, is a conscious one on the non-reflective level, since the body is directed by the emotional consciousness to change its relationship to the world so that the qualities brought on by the world be changed. Fear *is* the individual's freedom and so is his choice of "flight."

2.

It is well to remember, then, that, prior to World War II, Sartre published studies in psychological theory[7] and that, at least with regard to the emotion of fear, he gave evidence of having been influenced by his psychology teacher. When, then, he gave up these studies in order to write "Le Mur," the subject of this investigation, as well as the subsequent stories that were to appear in the volume *Le Mur* (1939), his interest in and unique approach to psychology were to be their main source. This is true, of course, even of his *La Nausée*. In a word, what we hope to underline is the fact that critics have often missed the point that Sartre's existential psychoanalysis is important as a psychology, in theory and, especially, in its application to his stories.

"Le Mur"[8] contains a wealth of psychological observations, and its real subject is that of fear. The physical reactions to fear are presented within an existential framework as the narrator describes his own experiences as well as those of his two comrades who, like himself, have been taken captive and are waiting to die. Juan's trembling lips and nostrils, Pablo's (the narrator's) perspiring in the cold, his shirt sticking to his skin, while he feels nothing, Tom's incessant talking, his urinating in his pants without apparently being aware of it; later, when the lieutenant comes for him and Juan who are to be shot, his spontaneous jumping and the tears rolling down the cheeks of Juan—all this is presented as banal physical disorders provoked immediately by a non-reflective—in Sartrean terms—emotional consciousness. These reactions, on this plane, are those of fear of something on the outside that is not controlled by the self, and follow pretty closely the theory of Dumas, who states that fear can assert itself "devant un danger possible, avec un minimum de représentations, et son expression physiologique . . . peut être cependant très accusée." (p. 474) In other words, the body uses its own incantation to free itself of fear. But Sartre views these reactions, in the words of Simone de Beauvoir, as those of "la complaisance," the equivalent, for him, of "bad faith." (*La Force de l'Age*, p. 135)

More important for Sartre, as Simone de Beauvoir puts it, is "la signification d'un visage." (p. 44) The fact that he regarded seriously the interpretation of physiognomy is clearly seen in "Le Mur" when the narrator, referring to Juan, describes the latter's fear in the following manner: "il avait un visage trop fin et la peur, la souffrance l'avaient défiguré, elles avaient tordu tous ses traits . . . Il . . . était devenu gris: son visage et ses mains étaient gris." (p. 15) And the narrator himself wonders about his own facial expression and whether Tom is afraid to see him as he was, "gris et suant." (p. 20)

Following Sartre's phenomenological psychology, fear, then, is not, at first, consciousness *of* being afraid, but rather a physical or non-reflective emotional consciousness. Only when passing from this stage to that of awareness does fear become a reflective emotional consciousness, as can clearly be seen in "Le Mur." This, of course, involves the play of consciousness upon consciousness, of mind upon mind, the relationship between the "en-soi," "pour-soi," "autrui"—the whole interplay effected by the Look, and the role of the human body as flesh which loses its transcendency before death, end of all "projects."

Not ever having been faced with death before, the narrator declares he had never before thought of it. There is, in other words, no previous memory of such an experience which could induce fear in him. It is only when he begins to observe Tom's bundle of flesh, a "masse de chair tendre comme dans une motte de beurre," (p. 14)

and to imagine gunshots or the bayonet going through it, that Tom's body becomes an Object ("en-soi") for him.

It is well to recall, in this connection, that the body itself is at first revealed to us in its immanence by the Other, its possibilities being replaced by probabilities, and that only in the subsequent process of reflection, resulting from the Look of others, do we discover the "en-soi" dimension of our own body.

Hence, the consciousness of Tom's body is then associated with that of his own body—or lack of it since, as he puts it, "je ne sentais plus mes épaules ni mes bras . . . j'avais l'impression qu'il me manquait quelque chose." (p. 14) Not yet fully "aware" of the situation, he wonders whether one suffers a great deal in dying and, bringing imagination rather than memory into play, pictures to himself the "grêle brûlante" (p. 16) of the bullets going through his body. What he wishes, however, is "to understand"—that is, what Death does to the body. Only when the doctor appears on the scene, and when he realizes that he is being observed by him, does the narrator begin to feel crushed by an enormous weight; neither the thought of death nor fear accounts for this feeling; rather, as he puts it, "c'était anonyme. Les pommettes me brûlaient et j'avais mal au crâne." (p. 18) Looking at Tom, with his head now buried in his hands, and at Juan, whose arm the doctor takes, slyly running his hand down to the wrist to get his pulse, he reacts with anger. Sensing, moreover, that he is being looked at, he returns the look. The more conscious he becomes of being the Object of the doctor's fixed gaze, of being watched as drops of perspiration, in spite of the cold, roll down his cheeks, and, at the same time, of feeling nothing while the doctor appears proud just because he feels cold, the more does his anger rise and the more humiliated does he feel.[9] To the doctor, he is an Object, a piece of flesh manifesting a quasi-pathological state of terror; but, apparently assuming a rôle, he tries to convince himself that "ce n'était pas la crainte de souffrir qui me faisait transpirer." (p. 19) Unlike his comrades Juan and Tom, both of whom are obsessed with the fear of suffering which, to them, is associated with death, the narrator watches them both. Juan is asking the doctor whether the pain lasts for a long time, and Tom keeps speaking incessantly, without daring to lift his eyes toward Pablo (the narrator), for fear of seeing him "gris et suant." The play of consciousness upon consciousness—the "pour-soi" having become an "en-soi"—is clearly brought out when the narrator, echoing the Sartrean theme of "l'enfer, c'est les autres," says: "nous étions pareils et pires que des miroirs l'un pour l'autre." (p. 20) As the awareness grows on all that the doctor "était venu regarder nos corps, des corps qui agonisaient tout vifs" (p. 21), Tom, trying desperately to understand the meaning of death, sees his own facticity with eyes that view his body as a corpse. Listening to the latter's *visual* articulation of the body's disintegration, the narrator now sees him, for the first time, as something strange: "il portait sa mort sur sa figure." (p. 23) Death begins, in effect, to take on a dimension of reflective awareness as the three now look at the doctor who, representationally speaking, *is* life. "Il avait les gestes d'un vivant, les soucis d'un vivant; il grelottait dans cette cave, comme devaient grelotter les vivants; il avait un corps obéissant et bien nourri. Nous autres nous ne sentions plus guére nos corps—plus de la même façon en tout cas." (pp. 23-24) The fact that consciousness of fear takes hold of the hitherto "brave" narrator is now brought out in another contrast—between his imagination and memory, his future and past. Not wanting to die "comme une bête," but wishing to "understand," he tries to dismiss from his mind the thought of what would happen the following dawn, with death; he has in his imagination a vivid picture of the cannon shots, sees himself being dragged to the wall and resisting. And he suddenly remembers, very much like Camus's "L'Etranger" how he ran "après le bonheur, après les femmes, après la liberté." (p. 25) Previously he has also recollected his joys on the beach, in the sun and shade, at the bar. Death now begins to appear to him through objects which he sees as "moins denses qu'à l'ordinaire"; and his own body he now observes as that of an Other, as "une espèce de pesanteur." (p. 27) The thought of his own perspiring and "grey" body leaves him with a feeling of horror—a realization of his being cut off, even from the Look of the Other that has hitherto sustained his existence.

3.

At the heart of this story, then, fear exists by virtue of concrete facts of consciousness. This consciousness, as depicted by Sartre, is dependent upon the Look, through which conflict in human relationships and the domination of the Object are also brought out in bold reilef. Death as a theme has always been one of Sartre's concerns, witness his *Huis-Clos, Les Mains sales,* and *Les Morts sans sépulture.* But the fear of death, which is the central theme in "Le Mur," is the fear of physical pain on the more immediate level; in the final analysis, however, it is, as Jolivet[10] reminds us, "de tomber sans rémission 'sous un insupportable regard.'" And since fear of death is also fear of the unknown, the reflective emotional awareness of it is brilliantly dramatized in this story thanks to the Sartrean psychology of the Look or of consciousness. In so doing, Sartre, bearing the initial stamp of Dumas' influence, has succeeded in adding to it his own approach and originality.

NOTES

[1] Georges Dumas, *Traité de Psychologie* (Paris, 1923), I, 473-474.

[2] 1924-1928.

[3] See Peter J. R. Dempsey, *The Psychology of Sartre* (Cork, 1950); Alfred Stern, *Sartre, His Philosophy and Psychoanalysis* (New York, 1953); Arland Usher, *Journey Through Dread* (London, 1955).

[4] Paris, 1960.

[5] For example: "Intimité" (p. 335), "La Chambre" (p. 335), "L'Enfance d'un chef" (p. 337).

[6] A communication to me from Simone de Beauvoir, in reply to a letter I wrote her to indicate the apparent contradiction in her two statements concerning Dumas, reads in part: "Ne pas accepter 'le numisme endocrinien,' ça ne veut pas dire rejeter tout ce qu'il a apporté . . ."

[7] Prior to the publication of *Le Mur* (Paris, 1939), he was the author of *L'Imagination* (Paris, 1936), "La Transcendance de l'Êgo," *Recherches Philosophiques,* VI (1936-37), and *Esquisse d'une théorie des émotions* (Paris, 1939).

[8] All quotations are from the Gallimard edition of 1939.

[9] Stern, *op. cit.,* p. 93, points to self-consciousness as "'acknowledgment' by another person," adding that "our being-for-others is a necessary condition for the development of our self-consciousness, our being-for-ourselves."

[10] Régis Jolivet, *Le Problème de la mort chez M. Heidegger et J.-P. Sartre* (Paris, 1950), p. 95.

Steven H. Gale

SOURCE: "John Osborne: Look Forward in Fear," in *Essays on Contemporary British Drama,* edited by Hedwig Bock and Albert Wertheim, Max Hueber Verlag, 1981, pp. 5-30.

[*In the following essay, Gale identifies fear of the future as the emotional center of John Osborne's* West of Suez, Watch It Come Down, *and other plays of the 1970s.*]

In 1956 John Osborne's *Look Back in Anger* exploded across the English stage with intense anger in a bitter indictment of modern British life. A mixture of despair and black humor were contained in the attacks on humanity, social classes, politics, economics, and the educational system leveled by Jimmy Porter, the drama's main character. Jimmy's expressions of wrath were frequently indiscriminate and overwhelming. While he attempted to expose his wife to the realities and meanings of life so that she would be moved out of her complacency, the underlying hurt which motivated Jimmy's actions was so massive that it controlled him as often as he controlled it.

For a quarter of a century critics have classified *Look Back in Anger* as one of the turning points in the history of twentieth-century English theatre. They have pointed to Osborne's choice of topics, his working-class characters, the realistic language, setting and situations which characterize the play, and which have influenced a generation of playwrights. *Look Back in Anger* is both a good play and an important one. In spite of all the acclaim, however, it is not great, nor is it as thoroughly innovative as has been claimed. What does raise it above its predecessors is its emotional power, an emotional power that is so strong that it almost serves as a substructure. And it is clear that this emotion surges forth out of Osborne's own experiences and being.

Between 1956 and 1965, when *A Patriot for Me* was produced, Osborne wrote seven dramas, a teleplay, and three filmscripts. Many of the topics found in *Look Back in Anger* are dealt with in these works, but the quality, power, and vigor of the anger steadily declines. The studied seriousness of the themes in *A Patriot for Me* and their treatment suggest a cool detachment in Osborne's approach to his material by this time.

A PATRIOT FOR ME

A Patriot for Me was first produced at the Royal Court Theatre in London on June 30, 1965. For five years the Lord Chamberlain had refused to license the play for public performance unless certain cuts and alterations were made and Osborne refused, so the play was staged by the English Stage Society "by arrangement" with the English Stage Company as a club production which placed it outside the Lord Chamberlain's jurisdiction.[1] The question of censorship is important, for once again Osborne explores territory heretofore avoided in the British theatre: homosexuality. Whether this topic is really what the play is about, or whether it is used as a means of expressing a more significant theme is another question.

The plot is simple, though Osborne's revelation of his main theme is so distended that the audience feels that they are caught in the midst of a film co-directed by Antonioni and Fellini in which no one is quite sure what is going on (and they are not involved enough to care to find out). In Act I Alfred Redl's homosexuality is gradually exposed. In Act II he is faced with the consequences of his sexual preference and he is seen trying to function in several social situations. In Act III society forces him to commit suicide.

Despite this simple plot, critics have not come to a consensus of opinion, other than the common complaint that the play is vaguely "unsatisfactory."[2] But when looking at the play in retrospect and in the context of Osborne's later works, certain meanings do become clear. For example, the lengthy exposition of the homosexuality theme allows the dramatist to demonstrate who is involved in such activities, and how they are involved, and it permits him to point out how difficult it is to tell who is homosexual. At the same time that all levels of society are presented, the importance of the establishment is emphasized throughout Act I so that when the Baron's drag ball is presented in Act II, Osborne is striking at the very heart of society.

The first clue of Redl's homosexuality appears when he serves as Siczynski's second at the duel with von Kupper, who has called Siczynski "Fräulein Rothschild."[3] The theme of the death of characters who do not fit into society in Osborne's later works is established early in this play when von Kupper kills his homosexual opponent easily and mercilessly. Similarly, there is a forewarning of Redl's end implied in Siczynski's observation "you're not what they call sociable" (p. 18) by the juxtaposition of these elements. Later, Redl will admit to the Countess

Delyanoff that he has never confided in anyone, that the only ones he might have trusted "were killed" (p. 58). Since von Kupper has accused Siczinski of homosexuality, and since the implication is that Siczinski, having died in Redl's arms, is one with whom Redl could have discussed his problem, it may be assumed that homosexuality is the secret which Redl is trying to hide. Ironically, Redl's inclinations are so obvious that even a stranger in a café recognizes them: "I know what *you're* looking for" (p. 67). It has been suggested that Redl's "failure is one of self-awareness," and that he does not know of his homosexual nature until the climax of Act I,[4] but this seems unlikely. The point of the play does not revolve around Redl's "self-discovery" so much as it does around his attempts to avoid exposure. After all, half of the drama takes place after the revelation occurs. Moreover, there is very little feeling of inner conflict over his sexuality. Instead, what dominates is his fear of being found out as a homosexual, a spy, or both, as he acknowledges to Oblensky (p. 114). Redl's *"stricken"* look in the café confrontation is a result of his realization that he can no longer hide, and the audience becomes privy to what has been bothering him in the very next scene.

In *A Patriot for Me* Osborne's concern is more with society than, as in his earlier plays, with an individual's plight. Redl is an individual, certainly, but his problem is symptomatic of a larger set of circumstances that have a broad, impersonal application. This determines and simultaneously grows out of the dramatist's techniques. Osborne states in a program note for the play's premiere that "The story . . . is true." The drama's historical basis limits the author. As with his literary adaptations, the result is not as forceful as when he works with his own premises. The locale and time of the play (Austria and Hungary between 1890 and 1913) create a distancing effect which produces less emotional content than in his preceding plays. This is reinforced by the sense of a detached observer, perhaps a carry-over of the technique employed in *Inadmissable Evidence* (performed the previous year). The audience is not presented with the protagonist's point of view, as was the case with Jimmy; Redl is characterized through other people's eyes. And it is not the prototypical Osborne hero who emerges. In some ways *A Patriot for Me* is a one-man play, but Redl is not another Jimmy. Dashing, attractive, sometimes warm, he is described by Colonel von Möhl as overpowering and forceful because of his disciplined character (pp. 51-52), though members of the Baron's party and Oblensky (p. 97) have different opinions. Like Jimmy, Redl comes from the working class: he is the eighth of eleven children, and his father was a second grade railway clerk. Unlike Jimmy, he tries to escape his heritage and/or his sexuality through hard work. He is extremely successful at the War College, and the Baron and Kunz comment that he throws himself into his work in order to change his circumstances (p. 82), which may apply to both situations. His sister's death does not move him (he thought about it for ten minutes). He is naturally reticent, and instead of imposing his personality on those around him, à la Jimmy, he tries to hide his true self. Still, his willingness to commit suicide with the pistol given him by his superiors is not to avoid the issue of being a traitor in the service of the Russians, but as the ultimate expression of his individualism.

Redl finally does make Jimmy-like statements, but they do not come until his Act III monologs when he berates his ex-lover's wife, his current lover, and Spanish society. The monolog technique is not utilized in the first two acts because Osborne is too involved in establishing the character of the society to explore his protagonist's character. A combination of other techniques and the play's meaning prevent a clearer picture of Redl from developing. The *coup de théâtre* ball scene, the humor ("Queen Victoria was quite clearly a man"—p. 83), the parallel between the scientific gobbledygook of the pseudo-Freudian, anti-homosexual Dr. Schoepfer (Act II, scene 2) and the crazy Mischa's ramblings (Act III, scene 3) contribute little to an understanding of Redl, for instance. The abundant sensory images (the smell of peppermints, the foul tasting mouths, the sounds of different characters walking, of music, of crowd noises, and of love-making) keep the audience physically aware, yet except for Redl's moans and his reactions to light during sexual activity, they provide scant information that will lead to insights into his character. Further complicating the issue are the inordinate number of parts (92), and the swift movement through twenty-three scenes. Osborne may have improved his techniques for dealing with peripheral characters and creating realistic social milieux, but the delineation of Redl suffers. Shakespeare was able to impart an immense amount of information about his characters by quickly shifting from scene to scene (as with Hal and Hotspur); Osborne's episodic treatment seems to be an experimental attempt to recreate the effect of cinematic structure through rapid jump cuts between public and private scenes. Unfortunately, his talent for strong portrayals of his protagonists is diluted in the process.

In spite of the critics' consternation over this turn of events, it is obvious that Osborne has chosen this path purposefully, and that he has accomplished what he set out to do. Because his concern is for society in *A Patriot for Me* (by definition "patriot" refers to society), his attention to the individual must perforce be diminished. In fact, too fully-developed a protagonist would destroy the drama's effectiveness because homosexuality is not the subject of this play; it merely serves as a metaphor. The protagonist's personal troubles are symbolically interlocked with a diseased society. Actually, homosexuality becomes equated with more than just a corrupt society; it is also related to power and to the decay of civilization. Osborne's presentation leads to the conclusion that Redl's world picture is not of a "deviant subculture"—it *is* the world.[5] Two characters in the play make observations that support this thesis. First, Kunz replies to the Countess' ironic "I can't think of anything more admirable than not having to play a part" by saying, "We all play parts" (p. 49). Second, the Baron interprets the gay life at his ball (and presumably of the world) with the prophetic announcement "We are none of us safe" (p.

77), an early sounding of the themes of uncertainty and frustration that dominate the later plays.

Oblensky's role is a key to understanding the play, for it is through him that the audience becomes aware of certain things. For instance, he reads aloud the love letter to the Countess in which Redl complains, "This is a difficult time" (p. 62). A commentary on the faltering love affair, this also reflects the general *Angst* suffered by a goalless, decadent society. In the third act meeting during which Redl is reprimanded for initiating the arrest of one of Oblensky's best agents, the espionage officer states, "It isn't any fun having no clear idea of the future is it? And you can't re-make your past" (p. 114).

Many critics have been unsure how the title and the drama are related, even though Osborne explains the title in the program note mentioned above. His explanation is straightforward and enlightening: "It was the Emperor Francis II who first used the term 'A Patriot For Me'. One day, when a distinguished servant of the Empire was recommended to him for special notice, his sponsor remarked that he was a staunch and loyal patriot. The old Emperor looked up sharply: 'Ah! But is he a patriot for me?' The Hapsburgs . . . were not interested in German patriotism . . . they were interested only in Imperial patriotism." As with many of Osborne's allusions, there seems to be no direct application of this story to the play. But the words, with the emphasis on "me," suit Redl perfectly. His loyalty is not to a society into which he does not fit, his friends, his fellow-officers, his religion, or his country—his loyalty is to himself. He is his own patriot and object of patriotism. The social element in Redl's death is underscored by the fact that representatives of society supply him with the instrument of death, and the final scene, in which Oblensky examines Dr. Schoepfer's dossier in the same way that he did Redl's in Act I, indicates that everything will continue as before. Society is willing to exploit both sides to gain its own ends.

There is a paradox in the need to use an individual to show the workings of society. When an individual places loyalty to self above loyalty to society, society destroys the individual in an automatic self-protective response. That Redl dies because he does not fit looks forward to *West of Suez* and *Watch It Come Down*.

Between the premiere of *A Patriot for Me* and today, Osborne has continued his prolific output. Eleven new stage dramas, including adaptations of Lope de Vega's *La Fianza Satisfecha* (as *A Bond Honoured*), Henrik Ibsen's *Hedda Gabler*, and Oscar Wilde's novel *The Picture of Dorian Gray*, a "reworking" of Shakespeare's *Coriolanus* (as *A Place Calling Itself Rome*), six teleplays, two filmscripts, and numerous newspaper and journal articles have appeared.

The two most notable features of this list are the increased number of plays written for television, and Osborne's interest in literary subjects. As might be expected, this interest is reflected in the themes of the plays he wrote during the same period. Moreover, his characters typically are involved in filmmaking, television, or writing, and literary allusions are abundant. Interestingly, as these elements become more important in Osborne's writing, there is a corresponding diminishment in emotional impact and in his characters' vitality. It is as though he has adopted the nonchalance and emotional sterility of *Look Back in Anger*'s Helena. Gratification has replaced antagonism as the operative motivation.

In two of Osborne's more recent major plays, though— *West of Suez* and *Watch It Come Down*—a new ingredient is apparent, and it is clear that there has been another shift in the perspective out of which Osborne writes, as fear for the future evolves as his main concern. This shift is especially significant when the emotion that underlies *Look Back in Anger* is compared with these two dramas, for the emotions are opposites. Two minor dramas which signal this transition both opened at the Royal Court Theatre in 1968. *Time Present* (first performed on May 23) and *The Hotel in in Amsterdam* (first performed on July 3) stand between *A Patriot for Me* and *West of Suez* in terms of both content and technique.

TIME PRESENT and THE HOTEL IN AMSTERDAM

Time Present is really not much more than an extended character sketch. Pamela is in some ways just another Jimmy. She can be cruel, telling Constance that "perhaps" she meant to upset her,[6] and announcing that she has turned down "better" people, but she is not as vital as Jimmy is. Possibly this is because her posturing precedes her father's death.

Pamela, whose long-lasting love affair ended the previous year, has moved into Constance's apartment. The differences between the two roommates' furnishings provide the first clues to Pamela's character. Constance, a Member of Parliament, has decorated the apartment with modern, straight-lined Scandinavian furniture. In contrast with Constance's neatness, the untidy Pamela has cluttered the room with relics from her actor father's past: a wall poster features him in the role of Macbeth and a faded production photograph of him in Shakespearean costume stands on the table.

In an awkward exposition, the kind that a Harold Pinter avoids at all costs, Osborne provides more information about Pamela through dialogs between her mother, Edith, and her younger sister, Pauline, before his protagonist appears on stage. Physically, while Pamela is attractive, she is not pretty; like her father, she is a talented performer; her relationship with her mother is not close (they are not even "friends"), but she and her father are quite close. Further details evolve out of the contrasts between Pamela and Constance or Pauline.

The theme of the play is simple, too simple perhaps. Pamela needs, but is unable to respond to others. "I believe in love," she says, "Just because I don't know how

to doesn't mean I don't" (p. 28). Constance, too, observes that "You need love more than anyone I've ever known" (p. 72). But Pamela rejects her closest friends. "Look after Murray," she tells Constance, and Murray, Constance's lover and the father of Pamela's unborn child, is dismissed in favor of an abortionist's services.

Pamela is unable to accept her friends' love because she is living in time present. Osborne includes an excerpt from *Ecclesiastes* as an epigraph in the printed version of the play: "A time to embrace and a time to refrain from embracing. A time to get and a time to lose: a time to keep and a time to cast away." Unfortunately, Pamela is not capable of moving from time to time. More appropriate for her are the opening lines of T. S. Eliot's "Burnt Norton": "Time present and time past/ Are both perhaps present in time future,/ and time future contained in time past." Clearly, Pamela is not an existential heroine. In some ways a familiar Osborne character, isolated and antagonistic, she chooses not to adjust to a changing world. Pauline, who is involved in the drug culture, hippie mentality of the mid-1960's, states, "Your scene is really out" (p. 25). Pamela, noting that she and her sister are not close and know very little about one another (which she sees as "no loss"—p. 22), replies, "Just like my father." And this is the key to the play, of course. Pamela is not trapped so much in her own past as she is influenced by her father's past. Her relationship with her father is symbolized in his chosen name. Born Tristram Prosser, Pamela's father, unlike Pamela, tried to escape his past and his Welsh heritage by adopting the name Giddeon Orme.[7] For Pamela the significance of the surname may lie in the components *or/me*—which complete her identification with her father. In Pamela's vision, Sir Giddeon's prime was during an era of class and taste, and she finds herself unfit to compromise with the vulgar, modern world that surrounds her. As a rejoinder to her sister's criticism she says, "It's impossible to argue with someone wearing such cheap clothes" (p. 25).

Time is important in this play. Constance asserts, "Time is in short supply in the present" (p. 33). Pamela suggests that "we should keep it in its place. Whenever we can. Just because we can't win." But in fact she is paralyzed by time. It is significant that while she is thirty-four, she contradictorily admits to being both twenty-six and twenty-nine. The great irony is that the present in which she is trying to live is actually already past.

Time Present is the first of Osborne's plays which look back not in anger but nostalgically. In an interview Osborne has said "the theatre as I know it . . . has probably got a limited life . . . the literate theatre of words and rounded psychological characterization is a decadent art form." He goes on to say, however, that he intends to continue writing for the stage, and it may be herein lie the seeds of his lack of success with this drama. Pamela's world is much narrowed from Redl's; hers is a stage, and she speaks of it in terms of "timing." Her concern is with a style of life. She is not motivated by a workingclass consciousness, economics, or politics, and her resultant calm detachment is the reverse of Jimmy's. This is true of the supporting characters in the play, too. Pamela speaks bitingly and bitterly about a competing actress, Abigail, but when Abigail appears, the confrontation is anything but dramatic. Pamela's foils are not fully realized as characters; they are straw men, and consequently Pamela herself never quite comes to life as a character. The play lacks the energy and enthusiasm of *Look Back in Anger*. It is too cerebral. Redl is less abrasive and less funny than Jimmy, and the characters in *Time Present* are still further removed from life. Indeed, one of the most important presences in the play never appears on stage. In Act I Sir Giddeon is already in the hospital dying; in Act III he has been dead for several weeks.

Even the generation gap is not seriously considered. Pauline is a caricature. Her philosophy of life is not meant to be taken as an alternative to Pamela's lifestyle. She is too foolish, and the slang which fills her speech and delineates her as a representative of time future was going out of date when the play was mounted in 1968.[8] Of course, this may be part of Osborne's point: even the future is becoming the past. Ultimately, the audience does not feel for Pamela, though the problem of how to avoid her fate has been raised.

Osborne's style interferes with the effectiveness of the drama, too. His writing has become more ostentatious and obvious, and the repetitive pattern in his phrasing seems artificial. For example, "He is, he is dying" (p. 19) and "my own, my own walls" (p. 59) probably do not carry the intensity of emotion intended. So, also, is it with the use of literary and political allusions. Although there is some reflection of the characters in their names and their references to Addison (p. 43) and Vietnam (p. 27), the allusions lend as much to building a cultural milieu as they do to an understanding of the immediate situation. Actually, at times it appears that the inclusion of a reference for its own sake is at least as important as the associations connected with it.

As Osborne proceeds from this point, death, the arts, homosexuality, and related topics become more and more central in his writing. In relation to these subjects the past becomes increasingly important. The plays are set in the past, or the characters are linked to a past in such a way that they are somehow out of joint with the present. And this lack of connection with the present is reenforced by the foreign element: the characters were born abroad (Pamela in India) or the play takes place in a foreign setting as though to reiterate that Osborne's protagonists are not at home in today's England.

In *The Hotel in Amsterdam* the characters are again greatly influenced by an off-stage presence, and while they are a part of the art world of modern London, they have tried to escape both, in this case by fleeing to a foreign locale. This play is a little more thematically complex than *Time Present*, though, and it is also more entertaining. In large part this is due to Osborne's better handling of his characters.

The situation is minimal. A group of three married couples takes a long weekend vacation together in Amsterdam as a means of escaping their boss, the movie producer referred to only by his initials, K. L. These characters are different from Osborne's earlier ones. Stylish, well-to-do, fortyish intelligentsia, they come together for a chance to reaffirm what is valuable in their lives—the need for and the enjoyment of the others in their small group. As Laurie, the most articulate, witty, and vocal member of the gathering notes, "it's not natural. It's bloody unnatural. How often do you get people so different as we all are still all together all friends and who all love each other" (p. 98). This sentiment is immediately undercut by Annie's parody of a Barbra Streisand song ("people who need people are the ghastliest people in the world"), but this is done in a Noel Cowardish manner which looks forward to *West of Suez*. In fact, these characters are relatively well-adjusted, and while Laurie, Osborne's new hero, contains some of Jimmy's self-pity, he is also affectionate and able to express his feelings for his friends. The invective is missing.

Almost no dramatic action takes place on stage; this is because the group is a collection of talkers, and their topics do not lend themselves to action. As Annie comments, "I can tell you what everyone will do—just talk. About what to do, where to go, what we should wear" (p. 114). Even if the social commentary and class consciousness of *Look Back in Anger* were present, these people would not do anything about them. Their targets are comparatively insignificant: the Welsh, Japanese, and Americans, travel, mothers, homosexuality, sex (with a Freudian linking of mothers and rape), sleep, the generation gap, the pill. When class differences are mentioned, it is only in passing (p. 90). The characters are too concerned with having escaped their "monster" of a boss for several days and with congratulating themselves for having done so.

The combination of escape and congratulatory motifs is an interesting one. Very early in Act I it is made clear that the characters are, indeed, escaping (p. 89), and this theme is repeated throughout the drama. They are sure that K. L. will be amazed at their "naughtiness" (p. 93). Yet Margaret's contention that "Here we are congratulating ourselves on escaping from him and we've hardly stopped talking about him" (p. 94) is so obvious that it really does not need to be stated. And in Act II, after having been in Amsterdam for two days, Gus's "we really have had quite a time" (p. 121) has a hollow ring. The continual restatement sounds too much as though everyone is trying to confirm or to convince everyone else that this is true. There is an amusing and revealing parallel in Laurie's joke that only an annual notice of one's birthday in the London *Times* is confirmation of one's existence (p. 102).

The Hotel in Amsterdam is a slice of life. A very special kind of life, to be sure, but a slice of life nonetheless, and it is the differences between the characters and their interactions that make this so. In general each has a personality (perhaps the mixture represents civilized society: e. g., Dan is from a working-class background, Gus is slow but solid). At the same time, the group dynamics, the give and take, the supportiveness are elements which flesh out the play and simultaneously demonstrate Osborne's advance in characterization. The reality of their situation and their exchanges are more vital than the posturing in *Time Present*. These people do not play roles when they are together in the way that they do for K. L., according to Gus (p. 93), and thus they come closer to self-knowledge and to knowing each other than do any characters in Osborne's work since *Inadmissable Evidence*. This extends so far as the perceptive Gus' recognizing that K. L. may be an indispensable linkage in their relationships (p. 117). The irony is that the group is defined by its exclusion of K. L. The double irony is that K. L. apparently needed them. "Where would K. L. be" without his writer and editor, Laurie asks facetiously (p. 100). Apparently the answer is that without his friends he is dead. When K. L. commits suicide, it is with the knowledge that the group is gone and cannot save him, unlike the sham suicide staged by Margaret's younger sister, Gillian.

The ending is melodramatic; the climax does not fit. There have been vague comments about K. L.'s vulnerability and reliance on the group, but they have been countered by the group's words and actions. The tragedy at the end of the drama seems tacked on, separate from the rest of the play. One critic suggests that the conclusion serves as a warning rather than a prophecy of disintegration, now that there is an open recognition of need,[9] yet this has been admitted throughout. Another critic discusses the unconsummated love avowed by Annie and Laurie as a potential for renewal which is undercut by the ending.[10] But what if Osborne's point is that K. L. died because he was not supported? In the final analysis, however, K. L.'s death may be nothing more than exposing the audience to the senseless violence that marks *West of Suez* and *Watch It Come Down*. It may also be an indication that Osborne did not know how to end this play effectively.

Stylistically *The Hotel in Amsterdam* does incorporate some interesting developments. The monologs are shorter, wittier, and less vindictive than previously. More important, though, is Osborne's use of language. Words themselves are important, as evidenced by the characters' concern with Dutch and Laurie's "Italian." Osborne's attempts to reproduce banal, everyday conversation, with some wit thrown in for characterization (in spite of Laurie's sophomoric humor—El Fag Airlines and the Golden Sanitary Towel Presentation), emphasizes the slice of life surface of the play. A limited optimism may be found in the presence of Constance, a successful representative of modern society, on stage as *Time Present* closes, and Laurie's curtain line that the group probably will not return to Amsterdam, "But I expect we might go somewhere else" (p. 143), offers the possibility of a similar gathering. But there is a touch of sinister irony in the fact that these extremely verbal characters frequently resort to vulgarities. This use of vulgar language in the mouths of cultured and sophisticated people is more than an example of the liberating effect of the ending of the Licensing Act; it is an early psychological signal of the evolving fear which will permeate *West of Suez*.

A SENSE OF DETACHMENT

A Sense of Detachment, first staged at the Royal Court Theatre on December 4, 1972, has largely been ignored by the critics, and rightly so. Osborne's use of language for its shock value as an attention-getter, like Henry Miller's, has overwhelmed his content. An anomaly in Osborne's canon, and possibly an attempted parody of 1960's happenings, psycho-drama, and plays like *Hair*, the drama comes across as nasty and dirty, the sort of thing that might be expected of an undergraduate Beyond the Fringe or Goodies revue.

Osborne focuses on a diversity of subjects normally touched only in passing in his other dramas (sex, the generation gap, politics, religion, the battle of the sexes), and in part this may account for the work's failure. It affects a purposeful formlessness, and the stage directions call for improvisation, but within the limits of insult and bad taste.[11] The sense of unstructured happening produces moments of low-brow fun, yet the overall result is something like a Godard film, a lack of connection mixed with stridency, because of the author's aggressive attack on his audience.

The employment of theatrical devices—music, records, film projection, characters seated in the audience, references directed at the audience, literary and theatrically based jokes—are simultaneously used to deride these same devices and to involve the audience as though, in Grand-father's words, "all life is a theatre" (p. 13). This curious mixture is emphasized by the apparent detachment of the actors, and the playwright for that matter. There may be general agreement with the criticism of the two actors placed in the audience, however. Osborne's low opinion of his audience parallels that stated in his non-dramatic writing and interviews, and the playwright may well intend to drive the play-goers away. Given the coarse, vulgar language and the raunchy topics expounded upon in Act I, there is little wonder that the post-intermission stage directions begin *"As the audience returns, if it does"* (p. 27). For those who do return, the second act is more of the same, reenforced by the juxtaposition of pornography and quotations from a variety of poems and songs on miscellaneous subjects, though commonly revolving around love. Does this mean that pornography and love are equatable? The play ends on its most positive note as the Chap and the Girl embrace in preparation for sexual activity.

The social satire incorporated in this non-play is hardly redeeming. It seems that Osborne has momentarily slipped a cog; but *A Sense of Detachment* surely exemplifies the psychological set that drives the dramatist to express his frustrations and fears more seriously in other plays during this period.

WEST OF SUEZ, THE END OF ME OLD CIGAR, and WATCH IT COME DOWN

Osborne's next two major plays have dark endings. While they are separated in time by a very minor work, *West of Suez* and *Watch It Come Down* represent the dramatist's new view of life. There is an extension of certain themes that began to be developed in *Time Present* and *The Hotel in Amsterdam,* and their tone reflects Osborne's concern with the implications of the new world that he sees.

West of Suez was first performed at the Royal Court Theatre on August 17, 1971. Like *The Hotel in Amsterdam,* the drama is about a small group of sophisticated English men and women who are in a foreign locale, but the earlier play's seeds of anxiety become portents of fear for the future as they blend with nostalgia for the past and the combination is overpoweringly significant in Osborne's development. The movement from anger to fear is now complete.

The action takes place at the villa "Mesopotamia" on a sub-tropical island which is *"neither Africa nor Europe, but some of both, also less than both."*[12] Like the settings in Graham Greene's novels, it is a place conducive to deterioration. As Frederica notes, "Nothing heals, everything goes rotten or mildewed. Slimy" (p. 39). That the Tigris and Euphrates valley was the cradle of western civilization, that there are no longer British military posts in Mesopotamia, and that the island setting is between two worlds, literally and figuratively, has more than coincidental bearing on the play's meaning.

The characters also reflect a way of life that is on the wane. When Frederica says "Ah—home to England" (p. 61), she is speaking ironically, for all of the major characters are foreign born. Wyatt, his four daughters, the Brigadier, and Lamb were born in exotic former Empire outposts in the East: Srinigar, Ceylon, Singapore, Mesopotamia, Rangoon, Kuala Lumpur. As the play unfolds, it will be seen that many of their professions are passive. Wyatt and Lamb are writers (with writer's names); Patrick, Robin's husband, is a retired brigadier who is "happy pottering around" (p. 18) and serving as a leftover representative of Colonel Redfern's Edwardian world; Edward, Frederica's husband, is in pathology, a field of medicine "Somewhat inhuman and requiring a detachment that's almost unscientific" (p. 15); Robert, Mary's husband, is a teacher; Wyatt's secretary lives on what his employer does; and Alastair is a homosexual hairdresser. There are also several Americans on the scene: Harry seems to be a beachcomber, the cruise ship tourists are "Helpless and hopeless" (p. 31), and Jed is a special case, a professional student. More about Jed later.

The opening dialog between Frederica and Edward seems to be setting up a Noel Cowardish atmosphere as the couple wittily discusses servants, sleep, relatives, and similar shallow subjects. Their talk is at cross-purposes, for they are not truly listening to each other. Ironically, Edward tells his wife to "Listen to those birds" (p. 12).

Later Wyatt will observe pompously, "Birds chatter and *that* is their mortal flaw. Chatter sins against language, and when we sin against the word, we sin against God" (p. 57). Despite Wyatt's pronouncement, like the characters in *The Hotel in Amsterdam,* these people are talkers, and anyone who talks so much does not have time to listen, which will cost them dearly when their civilized battle of the sexes is pushed aside by more critical events.

Actually, language assumes the importance of a character in this drama. Frederica and Edward consciously play with words in their extended opening dialog. They talk about Miss Nomers (p. 13), joke about bird lovers ("If one can still use [the term] in the feathered sense"—p. 14), refer to Edward's medical specialty as "Blood and shit" (p. 15), and comment on the "syntactical swing" of their sentences (p. 16). When Wyatt speaks, it is in a consciously abbreviated style filled with counterbalancing italics (e.g., pp. 38-41). In contrast, long-haired Jed is almost speechless until his diatribe at the end of the play. Asked where he is going, his answer is simply "Wherever" (p. 50). Apparently a rootless student, his subsequent comment that "Anyplace is home for me" (p. 69) seems to be an extension of his "Wherever," but, as his later outburst reveals, the fact that he feels at home everywhere is especially chilling in its implications.

Language is important to Wyatt and his sophisticated companions because it is a badge of their culture. The dark-skinned servant Leroi's sole words are an announcement that Mrs. James has arrived (p. 69), and Frederica complains that none of the servants listen to orders. One of the characteristics of the ex-patriot British is their propensity for working around native cultures by transporting English social elements wherever they go, and this often includes listening to the BBC. The pseudo-economic, pseudo-sociological jargon of the program descriptions which Robert reads in Act II are not from the real world. In fact, in tone they are suspiciously similar to the pornographic descriptions recited in *A Sense of Detachment.*

The literary allusions that self-consciously lard the dialog are further cultural indicators. There are references to St. Paul (p. 18), King Lear (p. 34), George Moore (p. 38), Yeats (p. 38), Rupert Brooke (p. 41), Cranmer's *Book of Common Prayer* (p. 44), "Papa" Hemingway (p. 68), Samuel Johnson (p. 72), St. Augustine (p. 72), and the King James Bible (p. 73). Wyatt even has a hat that belonged to George Moore, a self-revelatory Irish novelist. This is fitting, given Wyatt's self-centered nature.

The most amusing allusion is to Osborne's own *Look Back in Anger* when Robin repeats Jimmy's words ("as someone said"): "if you've no world of your own, it's rather pleasant to regret the passing of someone else's" (p. 35). Jimmy is speaking almost sentimentally about Colonel Redfern's world, a world that no longer exists, but which was solid and secure and comfortable. By referring to his own earlier work Osborne recognizes his personal alienation from the contemporary world, recognizes that the source of his alienation has changed (his literary, artificial insertion suggests that he has lost the intensity and the ability to create strong emotional impacts based on sincere feelings which characterized that play—instead of creating anew, now he must rely on quoting from his past). He is also clearly stating the theme of cultural decline.

Having established the above in an almost Shavian fashion, Osborne introduces an interview format to express Wyatt's apolitical nature. This apolitical stance is obviously related to the cultural element, and ultimately it is the cause of what happens, for it is nothing more than a form of blindfolding. Mrs. James begins by asking Wyatt, "What do you think of as being Utopia?" to which he answers, "A place without pain, passion or nobility. Where there is no hatred, boredom or imperfection" (p. 71). She then asks, "What do you think of man?" and he replies, "As a defect, striving for excellence." This is the context within which all of Wyatt's answers must be considered. He desires a comfortable world and he is living as though such a world is real. For example, in a world that has a servant class he can answer the query, "In these changing times, do you still believe that words in themselves have any meaning, value or validity?" by saying "I still cling pathetically to the old bardic belief that 'words alone are certain good'" (p. 74).

Wyatt cannot see because of his love of words, or he loves words because he cannot see—the result is the same. "What are your feelings about the island and the people," Mrs. James asks. "All the good things I've seen of the island seem to be legacies of the British, the Spanish and the Dutch. . . . As for the people, they seem to me to be a very unappealing mixture of hysteria and lethargy, brutality and sentimentality" (p. 75), Wyatt replies.

The colonial mind set is appealing because it is easy to live at the expense of others—if there is no sensitivity to the plight of those others. Mrs. James wants to know "What do you think about the class situation in England?" Wyatt answers, "Like many of the upper class, I've liked the sound of broken glass" (pp. 75-76). Throwing champagne glasses into the fireplace following a toast is fine, so long as there is no worry about the expense of replacing the glasses and there is someone to clean up the mess.

The two most important questions come near the end of the interview. Mrs. James asks "How would you describe yourself politically?" and Wyatt states "I wouldn't attempt to." In spite of this, the play's ending is foreshadowed when Mrs. James asks, "What do you dread most at this stage of your life?" Wyatt's answer is ironic in its foreshadowing and in its perceptiveness: "Not death. But ludicrous death. And I also feel it is in the air" (p. 78). It is too bad that he is not as perceptive anywhere else in the play.

A final language/culture connection is seen in the way that the natives are described. Frederica's contention that they are an odd ethnic mixture of "Lethargy and hysteria" and "Brutality and sentimentality" (p. 12) is obviously contradictory (and probably a repetition of her father's stereotyping). In Act II she demonstrates her lack of sensitivity when she comments on the islander's music: "I suppose they think it has a simple, brooding native charm and intensity. Which is about the last thing any of them have got. Anyway, they never stop playing it" (p. 81). This is the kind of insensitivity that Jimmy railed against, and it may be founded in the same class basis. Edward is more insightful. He finds the natives "Perched between one civilization and the next."

When armed islanders step out of the bush and shoot down Wyatt, everything comes together. The ending is shocking, not because the native uprising is barely expected, but because the senseless violence has not been prepared for. That it is Wyatt who dies, though, is fitting, for he represents the attitudes and values against which the natives are rebelling. He claims that "Protest is easy. But grief must be lived" (p. 73), yet he mouths the words without understanding them. Edward and Frederica's combined "We can't be—/ Responsible for others" (p. 19) is ironic as applied to doctors, but actions in the play demonstrate the results of generalized applicability in political and social terms.

Colonial types in an imperialistic setting create a cultural metaphor in *West of Suez*. Osborne demonstrates that both colonialism and culture are things of the past. They are not viable in the modern world. This is not his main point, however. For one thing, he does not appear to be especially fond of his characters. Wyatt, the most engaging, does not come on stage until a third of the way into the drama, and in spite of his wit, he is pompous and shallow. Collectively his family are non-productive aesthetes whose main delight is in the sound of their own idle verbosity and bickering. With the exception of Jed, the killers are not developed. There hardly can be sympathy for a group which is invisible and unknown until it steps out of the darkness for a few moments of butchery. And Jed's tirade destroys his credibility because it is filled with meaningless revolutionary rhetoric and clichés: "Fuck all your *shit.* . . . You're pigs, babies" (pp. 82-84). Critics point out that this most forceful dialog in the play strikingly resembles Osborne's "Damn you England" letter to the *Tribune,* and one wonders if the dramatist "created the chatter only to destroy it."[13] Perhaps this should be taken a step farther. Wyatt spoke about chatter previously, and it may be that Jed is chattering just as the sophisticated characters do, but in a different idiom.

Again, language provides the key to the play. American revolutionaries may help shoot down seventy-year-old men, and American tourists may overcome civilization with litter, cartons, beer cans, cokes, and more hotels (pp. 23, 32), but these are merely symptoms of the disease before which Osborne cringes. The use of four-letter words by cultured characters is too facile to be part of their stereotyping, or to be a means of devaluing the language with which they play, so the words represent more than Osborne's rejection of the characters or their words;

they represent insecurities and fears that psychologically can be manifested only in this way. Jed's alternative forms of expression are dismissable. So what is left? Frustration and despair.

The play's title reenforces Osborne's theme. It is a perverted allusion to Somerset Maugham's fifty-year-old drama, *East of Suez.* Maugham's play has little relevance to this work other than that it is about problems Englishmen face when they do not understand a native population. Possibly more important is the simple reference to an earlier, grander, more civilized time. The focus on Suez is interesting, of course, since the Suez Crisis in 1956 was devastating evidence of the Empire's decline. By placing his drama west of Suez, Osborne moves beyond the Edwardian period into contemporary times, and he draws attention to the symbolic setting sun of the Empire.

The final lines sum up the play's meaning. Standing over the murdered Wyatt, Edward recalls an old English saying: "My God—they've shot the fox" (p. 85). Fox hunting is the prototypical English upper-class sporting activity (expensive, complex, rigid, meaningless activity). Shooting a fox, therefore, is the grossest conduct imaginable. It is contrary to the social code and is done only by outcasts and enemies of society.[14] It is proper that this interpretation is uttered by a pathologist who has diagnosed the situation to someone whose background is lacking the elements which would give the saying any meaning. And this explicitly expresses the theme of *West of Suez:* culture and the members of cultured society can be destroyed without reason and without warning by those who neither know nor care what they are destroying. There have been numerous examples of this throughout history, from the Thugees to the Boxers to the Mau Maus, but Osborne must have felt horribly like a prophet when barely a year after the play opened eight people were massacred by natives with submachine guns on a golf course on the island of St. Croix.

The End of Me Old Cigar, first performed at the Greenwich Theatre on January 16, 1975, is the slightest piece that Osborne has written for the stage. It is on a par with some of his lesser television scripts, like *Jill and Jack* (fittingly published in the same volume), and like *A Sense of Detachment,* it seems something of an anomaly.

In Act I of this social satire Lady Regina Frimley and her female friends are established as fighters for women's liberation who are trying to gain control of Great Britain by having "enticed almost every man in England"[15] to a large country house where the men have been filmed, without their knowledge, while being seduced. The film is to be used to embarrass the men into giving up their role of running the world's affairs. The characters are pure stereotype. Aggressive, plain, unwashed man-haters mingle with shy, downtrodden housewives in working for this common cause, and they speak in clichés befitting their stereotypes.

The upshot is that the women's plans break down under the pressure of good old romantic love and masculine superiority (the housewife finds her appointed conquest more attractive than her assignment, and Lady Regina's male consort tells the victims everything and provides them with a key to the film vault). The battlers for women's rights degenerate into ineffectual recriminations and name calling, and the play ends with the quotation, "A WOMAN IS A WOMAN BUT A GOOD CIGAR IS A *SMOKE!*" (p. 56).

Patently anti-feminist, the play is a male chauvinist's view of women at their worst. While funny at times in its obvious play on spoken and conceptual clichés, it has none of the power of Osborne's previous works, and he seems to be trying to get by on vulgarities and superficial stylishness. Osborne may realize what has happened to his style and technique and be trying to move from the depressive negatism that has characterized his latest dramas. Perhaps *The End of Me Old Cigar* is self-parody. It may be amusing, but it is not good drama.

Watch It Come Down, first performed at the Old Vic on February 24, 1975, may be the culmination of thematic lines that began appearing in *Time Present.* The overriding fear and frustration that underlie Osborne's latest dramas and break through so violently in *West of Suez* are present, perhaps even in greater intensity, yet Osborne's statements are clearer and his style is more controlled than previously.

The movement from *A Patriot for Me*'s European past to the present in *West of Suez*'s former colonial setting terminates in today's rural England in this play. Having established his concern for a kind of character in *West of Suez,* Osborne brings his fears home to his British audience by placing *Watch It Come Down* in a familiar locale. As a metaphor, the converted country railway station presents the image of a faded past, but more significantly, it says that what happened on an anonymous, foreign, sub-tropical island can just as easily happen to native-born Britons in merry old England. The parallels between the two plays are devastatingly significant; *Watch It Come Down* corroborates the theme of a culture under attack.

The characters are typical of those in Osborne's plays during this period. Some of them are admirable; all of them are cultured, bright, and artistically sophisticated. As a film director, Ben Prosser represents the new "plastic" arts. He is successful, with Oscars and awards at Cannes, but he does not like "people," and he is weak.[16] Friends, however, are important, and his sexual desire for his ex-wife, his wife's painter sister, and Jo seems to be stimulated more by his liking them as human beings than by attacks of satyriasis (e.g., pp. 38-39); there is a sense of the comradeship that is present between Laurie and Annie in *The Hotel in Amsterdam.* He also loves his daughter and his dog.

Ben's wife Sally, a writer, is cruel. She is ready to inflict pain at a moment's notice, as when she derides Marion and Ben's daughter (p. 18), yet her cruelty is a defensive reaction to situations that might expose her vulnerability.

As Ben says, she "can't face the future" (p. 28), a conclusion that she repeats in despair later.

Ray, a homosexual in the "rag trade," is a sophisticated version of *Look Back in Anger*'s Cliff. He is pleasant; he is sensitive; he likes those around him; and he is either helpful or used by them, or both. This latter aspect of his personality is important thematically. Ben and Sally are game players. They are as witty and bitter as Edward Albee's George and Martha:

> *SALLY:* . . . The only joke you don't see is yourself.
>
> *BEN:* You should have been a writer. (p. 29)

Like George and Martha, they go too far occasionally. When Sally assails Ben's relationship with Marion and his daughter, his response is indicative of his pain: "Will you . . . for one minute, just stop that fucking pile of shit spewing out of your fucking mouth!" (p. 19). When they go too far, they are sorry (pp. 19, 31), but they are incapable of forcing themselves to comfort one another, even though they want to, so Ray's role is to provide sympathy and understanding. He also serves as their tool; he is used to inform Glen, Jo, and Shirley that Ben and Sally are separating. Although the couple does not intend to separate and is only pretending in order to evoke their friends' reactions, ironically they admit that a separation is possible, and Ray explains to Glen that it is almost as though they want their friends to make a decision for them (p. 49).

The game playing is symptomatic; Ray's analysis is that they "Didn't know what they were doing" (p. 50). Ben "had heavy moral scruples" about testing his friends (p. 13), but play with them he does. He also states that the "one thing" that he has not been able to do is tell Sally the truth (p. 33). Her response is "I'm tired of this." The game gets on their nerves, yet they cannot separate games from reality, as is evident when she interrupts Ben's call to Marion and when Ben retaliates by tearing the new outfit that he has brought Sally (p. 34). This is apropos of Osborne's theme of degeneration of the artistic/aristocratic class, involved with game playing because they are no longer vital, certainly not in a Shavian sense. The world from which they sprang, the world of Sally's dead father, who was in "The Colonial Service" (p. 15), is no longer in effect and it has been replaced by play. When Sally recognizes this ("All the days are long the way we live"), Ben cannot help her escape the trap in which they are both caught: "Oh, knock it off for five minutes. Do your cabaret somewhere else" (p. 14). There is a lack of communication. Ben says, "I don't think you really. . . . Have feelings for anyone. Except dogs. . . . How *little* you know." Sally answers, "How little *you* know" (p. 55). Yet there is feeling. When Ben is shot, Sally cries, "Oh Ben, don't go. Don't leave me" (p. 57). Her personal grief becomes a class lament, though, when she continues, "We all, *the few of us,* need one another."

Glen and Jo contrast with Ben and Sally. Throughout the play Ben and Sally's outbursts of bitterness and violence are followed immediately by tender moments between the second couple, as when the opening confrontation over Ben's family is juxtaposed with Jo's affirmation that Glen "really [is] so very gentle" (p. 20), and Ben's ripping of Sally's present is followed by a quietly affectionate scene. Ben and Sally are emotional, irrational, and noisy, and the action of the play centers on them. Glen and Jo are the intellectual center of the drama, and they articulate the thematic meaning for which Ben and Sally supply the practical examples. Glen is dying. Admirable in a washed-out way, a remnant of an earlier era, he is a homosexual novelist who has come to the last page of his latest book (p. 20). His spectacles are broken (p. 40), but he is the most perceptive character. Glen delivers the play's intellectual commentary throughout. His first statement focusing on Osborne's theme details contemporary England: "Suspicion, cupidity, complacency, hostility, profiteering, small, greedy passions, tweedy romance. . . . Beef barons, pig and veal concentration camps. . . . The Country. It's the last of England for them, the one last, surviving colony. This is England. . . . The fuzzy wuzzies from Durham and the Rhondda are at the last gate" (p. 21). The country is explicitly representational for all of England, and the appellation "fuzzy wuzzies," traditionally applied derogatorily to pagans in foreign countries, is ironically used to label residents of rural and lower working class Britain. Furthermore, Ben and Sally become symbolic representatives of their class when Glen continues in words that appear to be an extension of the above thoughts, but that refer to his friends: "How *did* it happen? They needed one another. But no more. Who's going? . . . Is this really *it* this time?"

The theme of transition, of people caught between dying and emerging cultures, is called up by Glen's allusion to Yeats' "The Second Coming." "So," he says, "it *does* all fall apart" (p. 22). His perceptiveness is further demonstrated when he continues, "We've seen the future *and it doesn't work.*" And he offers a reason for what he sees happening. Books, his culture symbol, are declared "an outmoded form of communication" (p. 23). Later he expands on this when he explains that he became a writer to "show us what we are yesterday and today. They're starting to wonder. But too late. My book's no good. It's too late. The century pulled the carpet out from me" (p. 40). One of Ben's moments of insight corroborates Glen's view: "How can you be a romantic in a world that despises imagination and only gives instruction in orgasms?" Ben also sums up Glen's role as a representative of bygone times: "I loved him because . . . he made his own life out of the twentieth century and what a bad one *it* was. The century, I mean" (p. 52). As Sally notes, "What isn't broken? Dead? Disappearing?" (p. 43).

Jo lends credibility to Glen's perceptions because of her own character and her linking with him. Jo loves Glen, and she needs love. Her nature is so immersed in love, in fact, that she sees herself as love (p. 37), and interpersonal relationships, the love that she simultaneously requires and symbolizes, may be a source of salvation— "It's like religion without pain" (p. 39). Her mode of escape is couched in similar terms: "Release us from ourselves and give us each our other." Thus, when she says that "Glen is the life. If he goes. It all. Goes" (p. 43), she reenforces the impression that Glen is the key, and his pronouncements thereby gain additional substance. Her suicide underscores her contention that "it all goes" if Glen dies, and ironically conceals her sense of love as a source of salvation.

Jo unifies several other threads of plot and theme, too. In various guises the characters seek escape. Ben, for instance, looks to hide in women's arms. Actually, they all share a need for physical contact, for touching, from Jo's tender stroking of Glen's hand (p. 20) to Ben's wanting to hold her (p. 47). But there is no escape, for time has run out. Jo sees the end approaching: "The time is short and all our heads are sore and our hearts sick, oh, into this world, this century we've been born into and made and been made by" (p. 39). Even before events prove her right, Jo's words are confirmed by Sally (" . . . it *is* the time. Because it's running out, and we should be running away"—p. 45), and by Marion ("There's been a lot of time. A wasteland of it"—p. 53).[17]

The group gathered at the railway station hearkens back to those who stayed at the hotel in Amsterdam. In the earlier play the problems stemmed from the personalities involved. But in this play the problems are proof that the world is "all so bad, so brutish, so devilish, so sneering" (p. 51). This is the England described by Glen, and by Sally, who catalogs the "nasty, brutish issue of English Country Life" with armies of Japs and Texans who "slaughter" a "Wildlife Vietnam": "No, there's not much in the land. Fish and animals, yes; and the pigs who *own* it and *run* it" (p. 17).

With the violence and corruption implied in these descriptions, Osborne has come back to the islanders of *West of Suez.* Although the natives are not seen in *Watch It Come Down,* the confrontation between alien cultures is as destructive as it was in the previous drama (though the "muddied, grasping, well-off peasants from public schools and merchant banks" (p. 17) are more cruel and uncivilized in their actions than were the untutored natives). The conflict is epitomized by two events: the murder of Ben's dog and the assault on the railway station. The appalling incident of the dog's death and the characters' reaction to it are foreshadowed when Ben reports that "Major Bluenose" has offered £5 to any of his men who shoot Ben's dogs. The Major has also complained about Ben's cats worrying his sheep (!), and the "layabouts lolling about" (p. 16). Unable to accept those who do not belong, the local residents attack them in a senseless, lawless, violent way. As Sally describes it, "We saw them from the top of the hill, helpless. They tied [Ben's dog] to a tree and set all the male dogs on her. And then they shot her . . . In front of us" (pp. 41-42). In a frenzy of uncontrolled fury and frustration over their loss and their impotence, Ben and Sally fly at one another, smashing, kicking, and tearing as the curtain falls on Act I. Striking out at each other in their grief is

a reflection of the inner turmoil inherent in Osborne's world view.

The assault which brings down the final curtain in a flurry of anti-intellectual destruction is prepared for in the scene that foreshadows the dog's death when Ray accuses the Major of arranging the "smashing up the windows here last month." With Glen's death, Jo's suicide, and Ben's murder, the most talented, likeable, civilized, and social characters are removed. They may be homosexuals or effete literati who were never at the "center" and whose passion and primary success was in insignificant word play, but they would never shoot at the body of a dead woman. Dr. Ashton, the one outsider who appears, is an educated man, a professional who should heal and relieve suffering, yet his response is to blame the victims for not being "popular" with the "yobbos" (p. 56).[18] His lack of emotion may be stereotypically British stiff upper lip; his complete lack of sympathy and continuing condemnation of the sufferers is something else. "You've brought this on yourselves," he says reprovingly to a group who has done nothing more than move into a neighborhood, an action so sinister for the locals that they must destroy what they do not like or understand. The doctor's statement, "you do lead odd sorts of lives, don't you," again blames the victims and sums up the attitude of the yobbos (an attitude graphically portrayed in Sam Peckinpah's 1971 film *Straw Dogs).* He is not understated; he is coldly alien. Sally's reply has the ring of Osborne's truth to it: "Yes. . . . We do. Most of us. You must be glad."

The title of the play combines concepts from Eliot's "Journey of the Magi" and Yeats' "The Second Coming" in a modern idiom. A revolution is taking place in the twentieth century. This is a barbaric age; the old order is falling. The significance of the title also is revealed in Glen's anecdote: "I saw two signs. . . . One was a little triangle of green with a hedge and a bench. And a sign read: 'This is a temporary open space' . . . the other was a site of rubble near the Crystal Palace . . . where bank managers and cashiers fled at the beginning of our . . . century. It said 'Blenkinsop—Demolitionists. We *do* it. You *watch* it. *Come down'*" (p. 50). The linking of open spaces and demolition (near a cultural center) is obviously another reference to Osborne's primary theme.

Once more his theme is reflected in his stylistic elements. There is still pretentiousness in some of his constructions ("They're: splitting up"—p. 21), as though he is flaunting self-conscious, artificial literary techniques in the faces of those he despises and fears. More important, however, are his use of language and literary allusions to augment his themes. In general he is hardly more subtle in expressing his themes through dialog than he was in previous plays—indeed, Glen openly states them. Sex is an important metaphor, and the language reflects a preoccupation with sex. On the one hand, the outburst by Ben ("stop that fucking pile of shit") is neither civilized nor sophisticated. On the other hand, there are times when language and meaning combine perfectly. When Sally talks to Ben about his visit with Marion, she asks "Did you fuck her?" (p. 19). Not did you sleep with her, or make love, but the harsh, shocking, even brutal "Did you fuck her?" Sally is striking at Ben, trying to hurt him by degrading his relationship through these terms, but there is simultaneously a masochistic, self-inflicted punishment aimed at herself. By using these words she is exacerbating the pain which she feels that she deserves because of the nature of her own relationship with Ben.

Similarly, the playwright's allusions are better integrated, too. While there are relatively few literary references, they tend to be associated with death (Leo Tolstoy, p. 10; *Hamlet*, pp. 15, 19; Armageddon, p. 22; Christ's cross, p. 41) or cultures in upheaval (Yeats, p. 22; the Theatre of the Absurd, p. 41). Appropriately, the allusion to *The Death of Iván Ilyich* goes beyond the novel's theme, for Tolstoy died at a remote railway junction.

Overall, the combined effect of Osborne's tightly packed style, witty, real characters, and integration of language, allusions, and themes is to make good drama. *Watch It Come Down* is the best written of his latest plays—in spite of the disturbing, unsettling events depicted. His control makes his statement all the more powerful.

With the performance of *West of Suez,* Osborne's new concern for the future emerges fullblown; *Watch It Come Down* confirms and reenforces this theme. When he wrote *Look Back in Anger*, Osborne was indeed looking back in anger at an insensitive world and time. He was filled with rage. Now he is looking at another insensitive world and time, but he is looking forward and with fear. Where once he was aggressive and sought to goad his contemporaries into a life of feeling, he is now desperate in his fear of a world which is attacking him, and which will crush him and his way of life.

NOTES

[1] The cuts demanded are published at the end of the Faber edition. Interestingly, the Lord Chamberlain's office was abolished in 1968, a fact which may be significant in Osborne's later work.

[2] Mary McCarthy and Kenneth Tynan engaged in a celebrated literary feud over its meaning in *The Observer* (London), July 4 and 18, 1965, and Ronald Hayman concedes to being mystified *(John Osborne.* New York: Ungar, 1972).

[3] *A Patriot for Me* (London: Faber and Faber, 1965), p. 17. All subsequent page references to this play refer to this edition.

[4] Simon Trussler, *The Plays of John Osborne: An Assessment* (London: Gollancz, 1969), pp. 139-40.

[5] This is pointed out by Harold Ferrar in *John Osborne* (New York: Columbia University Press, Columbia Essays on Modern Writers series, 1973), p. 36.

[6] *Time Present and The Hotel in Amsterdam* (London: Faber and Faber, 1968), p. 36. All subsequent page references to these plays refer to this edition.

[7] This leads to several levels of irony, since the name Orme is of Celtic derivation, too. Interestingly, the name Prosser recurs in *Watch It Come Down*.

[8] For example, "turned on and dropping out" (p. 21) and "trip" (p. 23).

[9] Trussler, p. 195.

[10] Ferrar, p. 41.

[11] *A Sense of Detachment* (London: Faber and Faber, 1973), see pp. 14-15. All subsequent page references to this play will refer to this edition.

[12] *West of Suez* (London: Faber and Faber, 1971), p. 11. All subsequent page references to this play refer to this edition.

[13] Hayman, pp. 135-36.

[14] There are also some interesting reverberations with the character of Volpone here.

[15] *The End of Me Old Cigar and Jill and Jack* (London: Faber and Faber, 1975), p. 20. All subsequent page references to this play refer to this edition.

[16] *Watch It Come Down* (London: Faber and Faber, 1975), p. 10. All subsequent page references to this play refer to this edition.

[17] Marion's agonized reference to Eliot is filled with irony, for they have had time and yet they have accomplished nothing, and will accomplish nothing with more time. At the same time, her wasteland allusion resounds with double irony because of its statement about what that time holds in store.

[18] Yobbos is derived from the children's game which reverses the spelling of words. It has come to mean oaffish, violent, Teddy-boy types.

Djelal Kadir

SOURCE: "Intimations of Terror in Borges' Metaphysics," in *Symposium,* Vol. 31, No. 3, Fall, 1977, pp. 196-211.

[*In the following essay, Kadir uses concepts of metaphysics and theology to examine the nature and aesthetic value of terror in the works of Jorge Luis Borges.*]

The paths to Borges' work through theology and philosophy, as implied by the title of this essay, are indicated by

Borges himself: "I am merely a man who has tried to explore the literary possibilities of metaphysics and of religion."[1] My purpose here is to illuminate the concept of terror in Borges' work by referring to these cognate disciplines.

In the unlikely event that evidence other than Borges' "Tlön, Uqbar, Orbis Tertius" were not within reach, the evocation of this work alone would justify the claim, so often intimated by the writer, that theology and philosophy are branches of fantastic literature. Conversely, an equally justifiable claim could be ventured: theology and philosophy constitute an integral part of the epistemology of Borges' literature. His work furnishes ample justification for such a supposition. I refer to the "Epilogue" of *Otras inquisiciones* where, in retrospect, he discerns the first penchant of his work as a tendency "a estimar las ideas religiosas o filosóficas por su valor estético y aun por lo que encierran de singular y de maravilloso."[2] While the observation refers particularly to this collection of essays, these are the theoretical coordinates of his imaginative *oeuvre*. There are no valid grounds for divorcing Borges' essays from his other imaginative writing. His work is unitary, knit by its author's intentional paucity, and composed of many facets which inform and elucidate each other.

In the same collection Borges reveals his own characterization of "aesthetic worth." That suggestive disclosure occurs at the conclusion of the first essay and reads: "esta inminencia de una revelación, que no se produce, es quizá, el hecho estético." With this description of the aesthetic experience, I believe, Borges furnishes a key to the nature of terror in his work.

The following discussion will treat metaphysics and theology in the light of their "aesthetic worth" and of "what is singular and marvelous about them." I use the term metaphysics in accord with its etymons: *meta* meaning *beyond* and *physics* meaning *natural*. By theology I mean that constellation of experiences which gives the discipline its *raison d'être*: what the German theologian Rudolf Otto has delineated so succinctly as the *numinous*. "Terror," as the term appears in my title, forms an integral part of this constellation and its singularly marvelous quality.

Borges' observations on the nature of aesthetic experience and its "objective correlatives" (the forms into which these observations evolve within the author's work) have led to a number of critical studies through a sort of *via negationis*. Most notably, three such studies come to mind: Ana María Barrenechea's, Ronald Christ's, and Manuel Ferrer's.[3] Each of these critical studies appears to be engendered by a literal metaphysics in Borges' work which suggests the existence of a world beyond, a "reality" that can only be alluded to, a perception which, in Kant's terms, is "not un-folded." Perhaps this metaphysical realm is none other than the one Goethe would have us surmise, the one he characterizes in *An den Mona* as:

What beyond our conscious knowing
Or our thought's extremest span
Threads by night the labyrinthene
Pathways of the breast of man.[4]

The potential aesthetic value of the ineffable, of that which lies on the fringes of apprehension, has been recognized as one of the most powerful elements in art. Its requirements border on a religiosity which would have each of us become *homo vates,* visionaries engaged in divination, seers exercising what Coleridge explicitly asked of the reader: "poetic faith." There is a crossroads where literature and metaphysics converge. That point, I believe, rests where we must surmise or divine a reality out of vacuity and silence, and, where the metaphysician comprehends that the boundaries of metaphysics lie within the abstract, noumenal, ideal limits of apprehension. Borges' work would appear to emanate from this point of convergence: "Hay una hora de la tarde en que la llanura está por decir algo; nunca lo dice o tal vez lo dice infinitamente y no lo entendemos, o lo entendemos pero es intraducible como una música."[5] On another occasion, Borges offers the following self-description: "I am . . . simply a man of letters who turns his own perplexities and the respected system of perplexities we call philosophy into forms of literature."[6] In the "Prologue" to his *Obra poética 1923-1966* he indicates the spirit in which his poems should be read: "Este prólogo podría denominarse la estética de Berkeley, no porque la haya profesado el metafísico irlandés . . . , sino porque aplica a las letras el argumento que éste aplicó a la realidad."[7] Borges' understanding of metaphysics bespeaks a comprehension tainted with mystery ("vague," "perplexities"), and an element of fear, a fear of the abstract, of irreality, of a silence which, like the reality of Berkeley and the Idealists, must find its articulation in us: "Me sentí muerto, me sentí percibidor abstracto del mundo; indefinido temor imbuído de ciencia que es la mejor claridad de la metafísica. No creí, no, haber remontado las presuntivas aguas del Tiempo; más bien me sospeché poseedor del sentido reticente o ausente de la inconcebible palabra *eternidad*."[8]

Such states of apprehension and awareness, which have also found articulation in aestheticians like Edmund Burke, writers like Ann Radcliffe, and theologians like Rudolf Otto, emerge as constants in Borges' work. I should like to proceed by interrelating those constants that structure Borges' literature with these articulations which would appear to be the theoretical correlatives to his praxis as poet, essayist, and author of stories. I do not mean to imply that Borges uses the postulates articulated by these writers as blueprint for his work. My intention is far from converting Borges into an ephebe or establishing positive *rapports de fait*. Such attempts would not only prove unfruitful, they would contradict the spirit of authorship so frequently depicted by Borges as nonindividualistic and timeless. The purview of this study is not influence but *confluence,* a congruous simultaneity not necessarily in time but in ideas and forms of expression.[9]

Epistemologically Borges' works reveal him to be a gnostic. His occasional assertions to the contrary notwithstanding, Borges distrusts material reality. Ronald Christ's assertion on this point is more categorical: "the primary tenet of Borges' metaphysic: a denial of objective, external reality."[10] Knowledge for the Argentine author emerges as the object of abstract, ideational apprehension—the Platonic apprehension of Schopenhauer and the Idealists who inexorably permeate his work. In a 1967 interview Borges asserted: "I think I'm Aristotelian, *but I wish it were the other way.* I think it's the English strain that makes me think of particular things and persons being real rather than general ideas being real."[11] It would appear that Borges' statement belies itself. In view of his often cited claim that, like Joseph Conrad, he believes reality to be more fantastic than literature,[12] there appears to be an ironic quality to his confession. The irony, however, does not remain an insoluble paradox. Borges the intellectual and Borges the imaginative author have been in disagreement before, as the short vignette "Borges y yo" attests. Harold Bloom phrases the apparent duality thus: "Borges is imaginatively a gnostic, but intellectually a skeptical humanist."[13] The *oeuvre* of the imaginative Borges would indicate that he has acceded to his wish to be, as he put it, "the other way." By traditional criteria Borges is as much a Platonist, for whom "particular things and persons" emerge as less than perfect incarnations of forms and ideas that vaguely persist in recollection, as he is an Aristotelian, but an Aristotelian who qualifies the reticent generality of the particular by affirming, "si no es verdadera como hecho, lo será como símbolo."[14]

Borges' gnosticism and its ambivalences, the tendency of the particular and of the individual to disintegrate in time and space (the propensity of the concrete for dissolution) in his work provide a link between Borges and the metaphysical terror delineated by Edmund Burke, Ann Radcliffe, and Rudolf Otto. It is the suggestion of a greater order than individual instance and personality, the intimation that a covert cosmos may coexist with our reality, infusing it with awe, that confer upon Borges an affinity with the work and ideas of these writers.

In formulating an aesthetic theory of the sublime, Edmund Burke relied on an implied metaphysics of space and time that attenuates the individual in the face of grandeur. *A Philosophical Enquiry into the Origins of Our Ideas of the Sublime and the Beautiful* (1757) is an empirical treatise, Burke claimed, attempting to establish common principles in making aesthetic judgments and is based on sensation and induction. Burke followed closely the empirical tradition of Bacon, Hobbes, and Locke, English thinkers whom the Anglophile Borges frequently evokes so that, more often than not, he may refute them. As for Burke's idea of sublimity, however, there are clear indications that its principles are operative in the Argentine's work.

"The passions which belong to self-preservation," Burke tells us, "turn on pain and danger; they are simply painful when their causes immediately affect us; they are delightful when we have an idea of pain and danger, without being actually in such circumstances."[15] Aesthetic distance seems to be the key to this "delight," as Burke terms it. "Whatever excites this delight, I call *sublime*" (p. 95). Burke goes on to delineate certain instances which produce sublimity. Perhaps the most significant source of the sublime for subsequent aesthetic theories lies in what Burke calls "All general privations." These privations, he tells us, "are great, because they are terrible: *vacuity, darkness, solitude, silence*" (p. 10). Burke considers the highest degree of sublimity to be astonishment, which he defines as "that state of the soul in which all its motions are suspended with some degree of horror. In this case the mind is so entirely filled with its object, that it cannot entertain any other, nor by consequence reason on that object which employs it" (p. 100). Other causes of the sublime are magnificence, greatness of dimension, and infinity. "However, it may not be amiss to add to these remarks upon magnitude," Burke continues, "that as the great extreme of dimension is sublime, so the last extreme of littleness is in some measure sublime likewise; when we attend to the infinite divisibility of matter . . . ; for division must be infinite as well as addition" (p. 102).

In 1802 Ann Radcliffe began the composition of her final Gothic romance, *Gaston de Blondeville,* which was not to appear for nearly a quarter of a century. The "Introduction" to that work has attained greater notereity than the novel itself. The work's publisher, Colburn, is chiefly responsible for this. In 1826 he excerpted Mrs. Radcliffe's "Introduction" and published the passages in his *New Monthly Magazine* under the title "On the Supernatural in Poetry. By the Late Mrs. Radcliffe."[16] The "essay" has been read and misread ever since. More than the formulation of an aesthetic theory, Ann Radcliffe's motive appears to have been an *apologia* for Gothic romances and the conferal of respectability upon that genre through the establishment of a link to the most respectable of all bulwarks, William Shakespeare. Accordingly, Mrs. Radcliffe presented the reader with two wayfarers in Shakespeare country on a journey from Coventry to Warwick, deeply engaged in a discussion of things terrible and supernatural in the words of Warwickshire's famous native son.

For the purposes of this study, the most interesting part of the dialogue deals with the idea of *terror.* Edmund Burke and the sublime form part of Radcliffe's discussion and in formulating a definition of terror there is a reference to the sublimity of what Burke called "general privations" (vacuity, darkness, solitude, silence). Terror, according to Mrs. Radcliffe, "expands the soul," and "awakens the faculties to a high degree." To use Thompson's succinct paraphrase, "Terror . . . may be seen as coming upon us from without, engulfing us with an aweful sense of the sublime in which sense of self is swallowed in immensity."[17]

From his earlier works on, Borges describes experiences of aesthetic value analogous to Bruke's sublime and its terrible grandeur of vacuity, astonishment, and delightful horror. In the 1954 "Prologue" to his *Historia universal de la infamia* (1935) he writes, "Los doctores del Gran Vehículo enseñan que lo esencial del universo es la vacuidad. Tienen plena razón en lo referente a esa mínima parte del universo que es este libro."[18] The scaffolds, pirates, and their infamy as indicated by the word in the book's title may perturb or horrify ("la palabra infamia aturde en el título"), observes Borges, but, he continues, behind it all there is nothing; "for that very reason perchance it can delight" the reader. Recalling the amusement of the unhappy man who wrote the book, Borges expresses the wish that some of that pleasure may reach the reader. However cavalierly and ironically as Borges may refer to the vacuity and "delightful horror" underlying his work, his perhaps unknowing nod to the principles of sublimity is clearly evident. Nor is this to be the only instance of coincidence.

Grandeur, so basic to the sublime, Burke asserts, derives from greatness of dimension. However, the other extreme, that of attenuated magnitude, "the infinite divisibility of matter," is equally evocative of sublime grandeur. Ana María Barrenechea perceptively has observed this dimensional oxymoron in Borges' work. The immensities that exalt in Borges are mentioned by Barrenechea in her second chapter on "The Infinite," as are Borges' unique Eleatic professions of infinite multiplication and divisibility in the venerable tradition of Zeno of Elea and his mathematical paradoxes. Reviewing a number of Borges' stories, essays, and poems, Barrenechea accumulates an adjectival lexicon of terms that heighten and expand our sense of time and space: "vast, remote, infinite, enormous, outrageous, perpetuated, immortal, grandiose, dilapidated, dilated, incessant, inexhaustable, insatiable, interminable, deep, concave, aggravated, intense, final, farthest, penultimate, lateral, lost, banished, misplaced, tired, exhausted, vertiginous, everlasting."[19] As for the vertigo of infinite subdivisibility and Borges' Eleatic professions, the reader may refer to stories like "El jardín de sonderos que se bifurcan," "La muerte y la brújula," "Funes el memorioso," "El milagro secreto," "La Biblioteca de Babel," "La lotería de Babilonia;" to essays like "Avatares de la tortuga," "Magias parciales del *Quijote*," "Del culto de los libros," "Formas de una leyenda," and "Sobre el *Vathek* de William Beckford."

The idea of the sublime delineated by Burke, and its attendant terror as defined by Ann Radcliffe refer to aesthetic experience. In his study on *The Idea of the Holy*[20] Rudolf Otto presents a category of consciousness correlative to aesthetic sensibility. The field of precognition put forth by Otto may very well underlie the affective discernment in aesthetic experience, particularly in the type of experience articulated by Burke and Radcliffe, and evoked by the work of Borges.[21]

The sensibility posited by Otto, like the aesthetic experience described by Borges, is fundamentally "not-unfolded." It remains, to use Kant's terminology once again, an "unexplicated concept," to be apprehended through nonrational faculties. As the title of Otto's work indicates, its concern is with religious experience, with the divination of the holy. To avoid the moral and ethical overtones of "holy" Otto uses the Roman term *numen* (the power ascribed to objects or beings regarded with awe). From *numen* he derives *numinous* and *numinosity*. This, he tells us, refers to the holy *minus* its moral and rational aspects. Otto uses the Hebrew term *qadôsh,* the Greek ãéoò, and the Latin *sanctus* (*sacer*) to illustrate this particular nuance of holy. The subtitle of Otto's book makes the meaning of his terminology, as well as his objectives, clearer: "An Inquiry Into the Non-Rational Factor in the Idea of the Divine and Its Relation to the Rational." The import of "rationality" for Otto is closely aligned with the work of Immanuel Kant, one of the most significant junctures of confluence where Otto and Borges converge. By "rational" then, Otto means "analytic," or "conceptual." Through the careful choice of "non-rational" over "irrational," Otto has circumvented the charge of being labeled *dialectical* by the Kantians, in whose technical terminology the charge amounts to the accusation of professing vain and empty knowledge. The term Otto opts for, "non-rational," alludes to another type of knowledge which in itself may rightfully be termed a metaphysics, for its object is supersensible, noumenal reality—the "old metaphysics" that Kant's *Critique of Pure Reason* (1781), with its "metaphysics of science" and systematic concepts, aimed to destroy. Nonetheless, Rudolf Otto seeks (and finds) reinforcement in the very heart of the opposition—the opening words of Kant's *Critique of Pure Reason:* "That all our knowledge begins with experience there can be no doubt. For how is it possible that the faculty of cognition should be awakened into exercise otherwise than by means of objects which affect our senses? . . . But, though all our knowledge begins *with* experience, it by no means follows that all arises out of experience."[22] In his qualification of empirical knowledge Kant aligns himself with a Platonic metaphysics of *a priori* cognition from which cognitive elements surface so that, on the occasion of empirical experience, we may "know." According to Otto, the *numinous* belongs to this *a priori* category, which also would appear to define the aesthetic reality as described by Borges. These elements of *a priori* cognition could be said to stand for those Platonic forms so eminently present in Borges' world of irreality, ideas, and transpersonal (supra-individual) dreams.

To suggest the meaning of the irreducible datum he calls *numen* or *numinous*, Otto employs a triadic ideogram: *Mysterium, tremendum, et fascinans.* The various principles of aesthetic experience cited thus far seem to converge in a meaningful way within Otto's Latin phrase.

Mysterium is a negative concept. It connotes absence, abstractness, and inscrutibility. "But," says Otto, "though what is enunciated in the word is negative, what is meant is something absolutely and intensely positive" (p. 13). Otto's use of the term suggests something fundamental to aesthetic experience which, I believe, can be related to the prescience of "poetic faith" demanded by Coleridge and characterized by Borges as "La momentánea fe que exige de nosotros el arte."[23] It can be likened also to the "general privations" of "vacuity, darkness, solitude, and silence," that is to say, the sources of sublimity. More specifically for our purposes, however, the concept of *mysterium* manifests a kinship to Borges definition of aesthetic reality and its *via negationis:* the perpetual futurity of a revelation that retains the quality of unending promise by continually postponing its fulfillment.

"The qualitative *content* of the numinous experience, to which 'the mysterium' stands as *form,* is in one of its aspects the element of daunting 'awefulness' and 'majesty'," says Otto (p. 31). This aspect stands for *tremendum,* the second element in his triad. *Tremendum,* he says, is more than the "fear proper" implied by *tremor.* It comprises three interrelated moments: awefulness, majesty, and energy. Otto attempts to define his term of analogy. Some languages have special expressions which denote this "fear." He offers the Hebrew term *hiqdish* (hallow) and the Greek ἅγιος as examples: "Here we have a terror fraught with inward shuddering such as not even the most menacing and overpowering created thing can instil. It has something spectral in it" (p. 14). This sense of *awe* or "ineffable something which holds the mind" is intensified by "absolute overpoweringness" or *majestas,* characterized by a cowering of the individual which borders on total self-nullification—a displacement of individual existence by a "plenitude of power" which "becomes transmuted into 'plenitude of being'" (p. 21). An urgency or "energy" in the numinous object lends this aweful majesty added impetus. This "charge" can be perceived vividly, according to Otto, in üñã or "wrath," a force which ranges from the "daemonic level up to the idea of the 'living God'" (p. 23).

Tremendum, then, emerges as homologous to the daunting grandeur of Burke's sublime which attenuates the self, suspends all motions of the soul with some degree of horror, and fills the mind entirely with its object. It would certainly appear that *terror* as depicted by Ann Radcliffe, that sense of the sublime in which sense of self is swallowed in immensity, falls within the category of *tremendum.* These homologues bring to mind Borges' rabbi of Prague, Judá León, who gazed fondly on his creature "Y con algún horror" in that cabalistic poem called "El Golem"[24]; and the fey, gnostic dreamer-creator of "The Circular Ruins" who, in the hour of his demise, with terror and humiliation, suddenly comprehends that he, too, is a projection of someone else's dream. Of the many other appropriate instances in Borges work that Otto's *tremendum* brings to mind I cite one more: the aweful terror which the King of Babylonia must have experienced as he found himself lost in the intricate and quintessentially metaphysical labyrinth of infinite desert, without galleries or walls, with which the Arab King compensated the hospitality of his Babylonian counterpart ("Los dos reyes y los dos laberintos").

There are moments in the work of Borges when the *homo vates* yields to the *homo ludens,* when, utterly cowed

before the presence of the *"omnipotentia dei,"* the waning seer gives way to the player, to the *decipherer.* These are the instances in which dread gives way to fascination, when overwhelming circumstances are suddenly perceived as aesthetic symmetries which attain perfection by virtue of the characters' participation and our own; as, for example, when a Faustian hero about to be executed requests a more perfect stratagem of his antagonist in a future incarnation—the labyrinth of the Eleatic straight line, rather than the cabalistic Tetragramaton ("La muerte y la brújula"), or when Borges the poet reveals in "Ajedrez" that

> También el jugador es prisionero
> (La sentencia es de Omar) de otro tablero
> De negras noches y de blancos días.[25]

This captivation, while a contrast to the daunting awe in the numinous, in fact completes Otto's triadic ideogram and is designated as *fascinans*—"something that allures with potent charm" (p. 31).

The result of this simultaneity of dread and fascination is a "harmony of contrasts," says Otto, who notes the parallel between the *fascinosum* of the numinous and the delight so crucial to sublimity. Otto views Burke's sublime as "an authentic schema of the holy" (p. 46). Accordingly, he observes, "the sublime exhibits the same peculiar dual character as the numinous; it is at once daunting, and yet again singularly attracting in its impress upon the mind. It humbles and at the same time exalts us, circumscribes and extends us beyond ourselves" (p. 42).

Like the concepts of the numinous and the sublime, Borges' aesthetics is predicated on a metaphysics of denial. Burke's sublime is founded on "general privations." Otto's numinous finds its consummate representation in sublimity: "In the arts nearly everywhere the most effective means of representing the numinous is 'the sublime'" (p. 65). Aesthetic reality, presented by Borges as the imminence of a revelation which never occurs, bears a striking resemblance to the manifestation of the numinous in the arts. The coincidence between Borges' aesthetics of abnegation and Otto's view that in Western art the most direct methods of representing the numinous "are in a noteworthy way *negative,* viz. *darkness* and *silence*" (p. 68) speaks for itself. Oriental art, argues Otto, has taught us another way to express numinosity: "emptiness; empty distances" which he calls "the sublime of the horizontal" (p. 69). These are undeniably methods most frequently articulated in Borges' discursive affirmations, postulates which serve as theoretical coordinates to his praxis as artist. It might be observed parenthetically that while Oriental influences are clearly present in Borges, "the sublime of the horizontal," the magical quality of the empty, boundless plain is something Borges' own Argentine literary tradition has richly endowed upon him through writers like José Hernández, Leopoldo Lugones, and Ricardo Güiraldes.

As for the vacuities of darkness and silence, their *prima facie* existence in Borges' work is readily apparent. He has written a book of verses to the first (*Elogio de la sombra*, [1969]) and the vacuity of the second permeates in his stories and poems, from the still, poignant contemplation of the Southern plain or the Buenos Aires sunset, to the anonymous silence of a malarial jungle in the East, punctuated by "the disconsolate cry of a bird" at midnight ("Las ruinas circulares"), to the muteness of "the troglodytes, who devour serpents and are ignorant of verbal commerce" ("El inmortal"), and the taciturnity of his heroes—the Dreamer of "Las ruinas circulares," Funes, Jaromir Hladik, Alejandro Villari, Ts'ui Pên, Pedro Salvadores.

More haunting than these readily observable instances of "general privations" in Borges, however, are the generic, the infinitely grander, more awesome, and more "marvelous" correlatives of vacuity which the Argentine has elaborated: the silence, darkness, solitude, vast emptiness which span cosmic space and eternity. Mary Kinzie in her essay on Borges has articulated well the cosmic void which emanates from a symbolic elaboration of the absence of voices, lucidity, and communion that no longer fill the ominous vacuities in Borges' works.[26] The "latency" of thought (and, therefore, of the cosmos; for Borges the Idealist and student of Schopenhauer the world is nothing more than will and idea) ceases, she writes, "to be an implement with Borges and becomes an enigma, a force, a grail. It is as if the idea of thought had been lost or culturally vitiated, while the recollection of its value still persisted in some genetic trace" (p. 7). When one considers works like "El inmortal" and its nefarious city of troglodytes, "El informe de Brodie" and its Yahoos, who for all their backwardness, are not primitive but a degenerate nation no longer capable of deciphering the inscriptions of its past, the true meaning of Kinzie's observation becomes apparent: latency which equals vacuity by its forgotten or unrealized "potentiality" transcends its value as aesthetic "implement," as in Burke's sublime, and becomes a normative, substantiated attribute of a spectral race: "La certidumbre de que todo está escrito nos anula o nos afantasma. Yo conozco distritos en que los jóvenes se prosternan ante los libros y besan con barbarie las páginas, pero no saben descifrar una sola letra." And,

> Y, hecho de consonantes y vocales,
> Habrá un terrible Nombre, que la esencia
> Cifre de Dios y que la Omnipotencia
> Guarde en letras y sílabas cabales.
> Adán y las estrellas lo supieron
> En el Jardín. La herrumbre del pecado
> (Dicen los cabalistas) lo ha borrado
> Y las generaciones lo perdieron.
> ("El Golem")

In his "Prologue" to *Antología personal* Borges alludes to the paucity of his work which, he says, does not dishearten him since it provides an illusion of continuity. The "continuity" he refers to consists of a lyric compression from short story to the intensified terseness of poetry—from "Las ruinas circulares" to "El Golem" or to "Ajedrez." Concision is a function of a program in

Borges' literary aesthetics to reduce "expression" to a *cipher,* to a type of "aleph" whose transparency has somehow been tarnished but whose perturbing and vague intensity cryptically heightens.

"Croce," Borges continues, "juzgó que el arte es expresión; a esta exigencia, o a una deformación de esta exigencia, debemos la peor literatura de nuestro tiempo." He then concludes: "Alguna vez yo también busqué la expresión; ahora sé que mis dioses no me conceden más que la alusión o mención." And, Borges no doubt, would consider them to be benevolent gods for *their* "paucity" and concision. He observes in an essay on "El primer Wells" that "el escritor no debe invalidar con razones humanas la momentánea fe que exige de nosotros el arte."[27] This reaffirmation of the primacy of the suggestive force in literature has led some observers to articulate Borges' kinship to Imagist poets like Wallace Stevens whose "song / That will not declare itself" bespeaks so clearly the "imminence of a revelation that does not take place."[28]

Metaphysics refers to a realm of the abstract, ideal, and the noumenal. Our apprehension of aesthetic reality in literature consists of such an ideational, metaphysical apperception. From this plane, Borges' definition of aesthetic reality as the imminence and unfulfilled promise of a revelation transforms the metaphysical reality of aesthetic experience to yet a second degree of ideal abstraction, not conceived or apprehended, but eternally awaited. At this meta-metaphysical plane, since no potential has cancelled out any possibilities through its own realization, the most perfect totality exists unperturbed. Since nothing is as yet anything, it is everything (see the author's prose poem entitled "The Unending Gift").[29]

A large segment of Borges' literary *œuvre* constantly and unremittingly strives to transform all realized and, therefore, finite entities to this pristine state of perfection. All that has been delineated must be returned to eternal mystery (the intimated *content* of the suggestive *form* we call literature): differentiated time, space, individuality, and all delimiting attributes. Yeats's famed Platonic proclamation, which serves Borges as epigraph for his story "Biografía de Tadeo Isidoro Cruz (1829-1874)," bespeaks the return Borges seeks to accomplish: "I am looking for the face I had before the world was made."

Borges' metaphysics of denial contains within it a duality which I do not think can properly be called a dialectic or a paradox. These terms would imply antinomies or antagonistic counterpostures. More appropriately, Otto's phrase "harmony of contrasts" could be applied to this contiguity. Like the twofold character of the sublime and the numinous, the duality in Borges' metaphysics exalts the individual through the promise of integration with a cosmic fountainhead on the one hand, while, on the other, the individual and individuality become consumed and nullified: Exaltation is coupled with terror—the terror in which "sense of self is swallowed in immensity." Beyond the energy and urgency of this binary animation which emanates from sublimity and numinousity, Borges interjects a "profane" gesture which takes on various forms and serves to intensify the intimated feeling of dread. These aberrants emerge as doubt, vertigo, Faustian obsession with gnosis, violence, heresy, atrocious deed. The result of these gestures, whose psychological implications Borges never elaborates (through a conscious effort),[30] could be seen as a series of predicaments or, more accurately, "statements of predicament" in the face of devouring immensity and its inexorable plenitude. These "statements" find their correlative characterization in a number of protagonists who reflect the varied types of fated, archetypal heroes: Prometheus, Faust, Frankenstein, Cain, Ahab, Judas, the Wandering Jew, and, Borges would add, the being whose variously differentiated manifestations result in each of these protagonists as momentary facets of a grand and timeless scheme.

Borges approaches numinosity and sublimity in the aesthetic experience with ambivalence—the ambivalence so inherent to all gnosticism. The feeling of awe or "hallow" quality of *mysterium* becomes contaminated by an intellectual interrogatory containing an intrinsic element of doubt and skepticism. Thus, Borges' naturalistic humanism reduces the numinosity of vatic experience to a conceptual scheme. The result is a transgression of faith intimating a devastating nihilism in the perpetually promised revelation and its mystery. While Borges refines differentiated reality into pre-existence, simultaneously, he suggests an aweful suspicion of nullity. What furnishes the greatest terror in Borges' work, then, may not necessarily be what Otto called "plenitude of being," but the intimation of a contiguous "plenitude of nothingness."

Another work of literature may help explain this intimated terror, immanent in the trials and travails of gnosis, Friedrich Schiller's poem "The Veiled Image of Sais" (1795). Schiller's hero is a young man, dissatisfied with truths that provide no more than fragmentary knowledge. He travels to Sais in Egypt, the ancient seat of priestly learning, in search of wisdom and comprehension of *the* truth. Before the image of Isis, he is told he must not lift the Goddess' veil behind which truth lies concealed. Whoever lifts the veil, he is warned, will *see* the *truth*. The fervor of his pursuit keeps him from heeding the warning. The next day he is found unconscious before the image. He finally manages to warn others not to let their search lead them into iniquity. He never reveals what he saw. Unable to live with the dread of his experience, he soon dies.

Schiller's poem offers a literary analogy to Borges' suspicion about the unknowable. In the realm of metaphysics the Argentine furnishes a more discursive key to his skepticism—a key which may also explain the nature of his claim to be an Aristotelian. The following passage appears in two different essays of *Otras inquisiciones,* "El ruiseñor de Keats" and "De las alegorias a las novelas":

> Observa Coleridge que todos los hombres nacen aristotélicos o platónicos. Los últimos sienten que las clases, los órdenes y los géneros son realidades; los primeros, que son generalizaciones; para éstos, el lenguaje no es otra cosa que un aproximativo juego de símbolos; para aquéllos es el mapa del universo. El platónico sabe que el universo es de algún modo un cosmos, un orden; ese orden, para el aristotélico, puede ser un error o una ficción de nuestro conocimiento parcial. A través de las latitudes y de las épocas, los dos antagonistas inmortales cambian de dialecto y de nombre: uno es Parménides, Platón, Spinoza, Kant, Francis Bradley; el otro, Heráclito, Aristóteles, Locke, Hume, William James. En las arduas escuelas de la Edad Media, todos invocan a Aristóteles, maestro de la humana razón (*Convivio,* IV, 2), pero los nominalistas son Aristóteles; los realistas, Platón.[31]

Borges' conclusion gives an unusual twist to philosophy's classical confrontation. His rendition of the two antithetical threads in the history of metaphysics, more accurately, the conclusion of this rendition, controverts the traditional representation of Plato and Aristotle. We are taught that Plato's syllogystic idealism is anything but "realist" and that the empiricist, inductive scientism of the Aristotelians one would only consign to outright "nominalism" out of reductionist ebullience, a tendency that ensues from the aftermath of Thomist Scholasticism. While, by traditional criteria, Borges would fall into Platonist ranks, we cannot deny that the Argentine is no less an Aristotelian, if we accept his exegesis of the timeless dialectic. Since Borges operates under the principles of his own rendition, we are obliged to view his work accordingly.

In the light of this philosophical posture, that binary quality, the "harmony of contrasts," the coexistence of cosmic exaltation and of nihilum in the Argentine's work acquires added significance. This duality cannot be called paradoxical, for its existence does not imply antinomy or paradox. Nor can it be called pratactic for the duality involves more than parallel contiguity. More properly, the elements of this twofold relationship should be considered hypotactic by virtue of their interdependence, by virtue of the fact that they acquire added significance through mutual allusion. Thus, the hypotaxis of cosmic totality and nothingness (of exaltation and the implicit terror of nullity) resides in the mutual intensification each of the parts of this duality bestows upon the other. The end result is a literary *oeuvre* whose vatic content is thrown into doubt. At the heart of this ontological skepticism is Borges' own unique synthesis of the epistemological problems implied by Platonic and Aristotelian metaphysics. This synthesis furnishes the *form* to an allusive, suggestive, and intimating world whose *contents* remains ineffable, immaterial, unexplicated, unknowable, or irretrievably lost to generic memory. Thus, for the Platonist in Borges "language is nothing but an approximative set of symbols." For the Aristotelian in him language "is the map of the universe." Nonetheless, while this universe is "an order, a cosmos" for the Platonist, for the Aristotelian it "can be an error or a fiction of our partial knowledge." Since Borges aligns himself so closely with the nineteenth century English Idealists (who, by the way, derive from Aristotle and not from Plato, according to Borges), the universe and its order are none other than the contents of "our partial knowledge;" *esse rerum est percipi,* as Bishop Berkeley's familiar thesis, so vital to Borges, would have it.[32] The implication, of course, is that the universe, the cosmos, may very well be "an error or a fiction." In that case the ineffable content, the *mysterium* of the numinous and the sublime, the contents of the cipher, the promised revelation of aesthetic reality may very well be equally erroneous, fictive, illusory, and inexistent. In the possible likelihood of this eventuality, the differentiated time, space and personality that suffer attenuation and denial so they may become reintegrated with a pre-existent Order may be subjected to nullification literally for nought. It becomes quite clear that Borges' interpretation of Plato and Aristotle makes both equally patrilineal to his metaphysics of denial.

The "aesthetic worth" or "what is singular and marvelous" in this metaphysics has infused Borges' work with a certain disquietude not unlike the immanent terror of the sublime and the numinous. Ronald Christ's discernment of a fundamentally disturbing vision in Borges which he describes as a "metaphysical vision antagonistic to our very selves" (p. 200) seems to allude to this very immanence and its "vague fear infused with knowledge." Behind such a conclusion, which more than one devout observer has gleaned from Borges' *oeuvre,* lies a radical dualism endemic to all Gnostic literature: the synchrony of Genesis and Apocalypse in *gnosis,* the supreme act of knowing that simultaneously is unity and nullity, actualization and dissolution. Borges' gnosticism and affinity with the concepts of sublimity and numinosity may be explained in part through one of his unmistakable precursors, Edgar Allan Poe—the American beneficiary and embodiment of the dark Romanticism that was Edmund Burke's and Ann Radcliffe's inadvertent bequest to the Nineteenth Century. In his "Prose Poem," *Eureka,* Poe illuminates the ominous duality that besets all gnostic endeavors and infuses Borges' "aesthetic reality" with terror. He describes an "Absolute Unity" not unlike the pristine state of perfection and eternal mystery whose imminent revelation in Borges' work promises cosmic plenitude and *nihilum* at the same time: "a novel Universe swelling into existence, and then subsiding into nothingness, at every throb of the Heart Divine." With an "irreverence" more evocative of the sectarians of the *Agnostos Theos* (the Alien God of the Gnostics) than of the Christian mystics, Poe concludes, "And now—this Heart Divine—what is it? *It is our own.*"[33]

NOTES

1 "Foreword" to his *Selected Poems 1923-1967,* Norman Thomas di Giovanni, ed. (New York: Delacourt Press, 1972), p. xv.

2 *Otras inquisiciones,* (Buenos Aires: Emecé Editores, 1960), p. 259.

3 Ana María Barrenechea, *La expresión de irrealidad en la obra de Jorge Luis Borges* (México: El Colegio de México, 1957); Ronald Christ, *The Narrow Act: Borges' Art of Allusion* (New York: New York University Press, 1969); Manuel Ferrer, *Borges y la nada* (London: Tamesis Books, 1971).

4 Cited by Rudolf Otto, *The Idea of the Holy,* trans. John W. Harvey (London: Oxford University Press, 1923), p. 148.

5 "El fin," in *Ficciones,* (Buenos Aires: Emecé Editores, 1956), p. 186-87.

6 "Foreword" to Ronald Christ's *The Narrow Act: Borges' Art of Allusion,* p. ix.

7 *Obra poética 1923-1966* (Buenos Aires: Emecé Editores, 1966), p. i.

8 This key passage is referred to and appears three times in the author's *oeuvre:* "Sentirse en muerte," in his *El idioma de los argentinos* (Buenos Aires: Manuel Gleizer, Editor [Colección Indice], 1928); in the title essay of his *Historia de la eternidad* (Buenos Aires: Editorial Viau y Zona, 1936); in his 1947 essay "Nueva refutación del tiempo," *Otras inquisiciones* (Buenos Aires: Editorial Sur, 1952). I cite from the last of these works, p. 247.

9 In an informal conversation I had with Borges on March 13, 1976 in Bloomington, Indiana, the author denied having any acquaintance with the works of Ann Radcliffe or Rudolph Otto. His familiarity with Edmund Burke's work, on the other hand, was evident.

10 Christ, p. 19.

11 Ronald Christ, "Interview," *Paris Review* (Winter-Spring, 1967), p. 62.

12 See Christ, "Interview," *Paris Review,* p. 40, and Borges' *Otras inquisiciones,* p. 65.

13 Harold Bloom, "Poetic Misprision: Three Cases," in his *The Ringers in the Tower: Studies in Romantic Tradition* (Chicago: University of Chicago Press, 1971), p. 211.

14 "Historia del guerrero y de la cautiva," in *El Aleph* (Buenos Aires: Emecé Editores, 1957), p. 49.

15 I am citing from Peyton E. Richter, ed., *Perspectives in Aesthetics* (New York: The Odyssey Press, Inc., 1967), p. 95.

16 For a more complete account of the vicissitudes of Mrs. Radcliffe's "essay" see Alan D. McKillop, "Mrs. Radcliffe on the Supernatural in Poetry," *The Journal of English and Germanic Philology,* 31 (1932), 352-59.

17 G. Richard Thompson, ed., *The Gothic Imagination: Essays in Dark Romanticism* (Pullman: Washington State University Press, 1974), pp. 3-4.

[18] *Historia universal de la infamia* (Buenos Aires: Emecé Editores, 1954), p. 10.

[19] Barrenechea, *Borges The Labyrinth Maker*, pp. 24-25.

[20] Rudolf Otto, *The Idea of the Holy*, trans. John W. Harvey (London: Oxford University Press, 1923). The work first appeared in German as *Das Heilige,* in 1917.

[21] There is some precedent for the use of Otto's work and terminology in elucidating literary problems. See, for instance, Maud Bodkin, *Archetypal Patterns in Poetry* (London: Oxford University Press, 1934), pp. 223, 241; Walter Kaufman, *From Shakespeare to Existentialism* (Boston: Beacon Press, 1949), p. 37; G. Wilson Knight, *The Crown of Life* (London: Methuen, 1947), p. 128; S. L. Varnado, "The Idea of the Numinous in Gothic Literature," in *The Gothic Imagination: Essays in Dark Romanticism,* G. R. Thompson, ed., pp. 11-21.

[22] Cited by Otto, pp. 113-114.

[23] *Otras inquisiciones,* p. 127.

[24] In *El otro, el mismo* (Buenos Aires: Emecé Editores, 1969), p. 47.

[25] *El otro, y el mismo,* p. 62.

[26] Mary Kinzie, "Recursive Prose," *TriQuarterly 25. Prose for Borges,* C. Newman and M. Kinzie, editors (Evanston: Northwestern University Press, 1972), 5-45.

[27] *Otras inquisiciones,* p. 127.

[28] For an interesting study of Borges and Wallace Stevens, particularly a discussion of the latter's "Metaphors of a Magnifico" with reference to Borges, see Robert Alter, "Borges and Stevens: a note on post-Symbolist writing," in *Triquarterly 25. Prose for Borges,* 275-85.

[29] In *Elogio de la sombra* (Buenos Aires: Emecé Editores, 1969), p. 39.

[30] See Ronald Christ, *The Narrow Act: Borges' Art of Allusion,* Chapter 3, particularly pp. 122 and ff.

[31] *Otras inquisiciones,* pp. 167-68 and 213-14.

[32] See Borges' "La encrucijada de Berkeley," in his first book of essays, *Inquisiciones* (Buenos Aires: Editorial Proa, 1925).

[33] For a discussion of Poe and Gnosticism see Barton Levi St. Armand, "Usher Unveiled: Poe and the Metaphysic of Gnosticism," *Poe Studies,* 5 (1972), 1-8.

Ben P. Indick

SOURCE: "What Makes Him So Scary," in *Discovering Stephen King,* edited by Darrell Schweitzer, Starmont House, Inc., 1985, pp. 9-14.

[In the following essay, Indick surveys techniques used by Stephen King to create fear in such novels as Carrie, Pet Sematary, *and* The Shining.*]*

There are stories of suspense, shock, mystery, and, combining all, fear. Ken Follett and Alistair MacLean are masters of suspense: one reads in a whirlwind of action and intrigue, involved for the safety and victory of the hero. Trevanian and Robert Ludlum add the fillip of shock, the hero placed in a paranoid and violent world. The practitioners of mystery are legion, with as many styles, but their content by definition is a puzzle to unravel. Fear is usually achieved as an amalgamation, together with its own particular quality as an emotion, and is associated by most readers with the writing of Stephen King.

If a story of fear is to succeed, the characters and situations must be such as offer ready association for the reader; the dangers must be of a vitally important and basic nature, whether to the ego or to life itself. Any novel offers a reader an opportunity to share vicariously in the action; fear demands more. While one may believe, sympathize and worry for heroes, only when their danger is perceived as germane, intimate and, finally inimical to the reader's own concerns, can sustained fear be the surmounting, driving force of the story. It is a technique of which King is a master, and is the spine of many of his effective books.

The basic groundwork of these stories is their intense realism, rooted in genuine small towns as a rule, and quite average individuals, with all the familiar ingredients of their lives—their jobs, recreation, quibblings, virtues, infidelities, ambitions, the patchwork quilt of ordinary community and individual life. The prose is terse and idiosyncratic, spiked with obscenities more common to speech than print, but honest to the characters. Into this setting he introduces the abnormal, whether a personal faculty possessed by the protagonist, or a fantastic situation. King's methods vary in his novels, but ever-heightening fear is their strength.

Fear is such a potent element in his second and third novels, *'Salem's Lot* and *The Shining,* that in retrospect it is surprising how small a part it plays in *Carrie,* his first published novel. Since nearly all the characters are unsympathetic, including Carrie herself, reader identification is difficult. She is a high school student described as physically unattractive, "a frog among swans," pimpled, fat, colorless and clumsy. It is in fact the ugly duckling aspect of the story which makes it work, watching Carrie plod along through the indignities piled upon her, adding up the clues King offers in interpolations from future texts on her case, waiting for the explosion.

Fear is nevertheless a basic element, achieved three-fold. First, the reader's sense that something terrible and beyond the ordinary will happen, and, even worse, that such a thing may be possible. Second, the leitmotif King employs, blood, upsetting and even terrifying to many readers. Carrie manages to be drenched in it, first when "the first dark drops of menstrual blood struck the floor in dime-sized drops," later when her classmates humiliate her by pouring volumes of pig's blood over her at a prom, and finally in her stabbing by her fanatical mother and her own death while the menstrual bleeding is renewed.

If these elements of fear are contrived, the third and most basic has nothing at all to do with fantasy, but underlies the entire book. It is the self-conscious real and imagined fears of the young (which do not vanish even in adulthood) of inadequacy, physical changes, need for love and attention, and are evoked in jealousy and hatred, and a desire to sublimate such fear in the castigation of theirs. Their violence in language and action resonates in the sensitive reader and the resultant sense of fear is personally experienced as the expression of suppressed doubts and emotions.

To nail down such inner feelings, King employs shock-expletives. He writes: "The ultimate shit-on, gross-out, put-down, long searched for, was found." The girls write graffiti: "Carrie White eats shit." And, when her mother, fanatic with fundamentalist religiosity, curses Carrie for her menstruation, "You SUCK!" the girl screams, and, again, "You FUCK!" It is not the demonstration of Carrie's psychic powers which terrify, but their use in the service of these dark subconscious doubts.

In *'Salem's Lot,* King employs an external agent, the legendary vampire, to move his story. However, although the machinations of the dread Barlow and his menacing assistant Straker offer traditionally derived chills enough, the source of fear is the danger confronted by ordinary individuals, with whom the reader empathizes. The small New England town offers a wide and varied cross-section of characters, admirable and otherwise, but all very real in the context of the town, and none free of susceptibility to the corruption which gradually overtakes them. That *all* may be corrupted is a very contemporary emendation of Bram Stoker's vampire and his aristocratic tastes. As they become victims, they are no less real to the reader, who recalls them as yesterday's neighbor or friend, and too possibly ourselves. If, finally, the author must complete his story with the customary paraphernalia of the wooden stake, holy water, sunset and such, it offers release from fear in the triumph of yet another ordinary man and a boy.

King offers a powerful postscript in his short story, "One For the Road," wherein that most innocent of creatures, a seven-year old child, apparently helpless in a blinding snowstorm, is revealed as a vampire. A fortuitous Bible stops her advance, but the message of terror at any hand is no less menacing: "There's a little girl somewhere out there. And I think she's still waiting for her good-night kiss."

The Shining, in its complexity, perhaps King's most frightening novel, offers an aged hotel haunted by its past, a child with remarkable powers, and a man who will succumb to the living evil of the atmosphere and his own weakness. Danny's prescience vaguely foresees future terrors; the mounting, uncontrollable rages of his father complement these visions. Danny has such a vision of a shadowy shape cursing and swinging a mallet; he is restored to reality when his father drives up, but the boy suddenly sees on the front seat "a short-handled mallet, its head clotted with blood and hair." Although it is immediately replaced by the bag of groceries which is actually there, the terror is registered. It cannot be dispelled. Something terrible may happen, and when the family of three settles into the vast, empty hotel, it *must* happen. King has by now created a mini-universe beyond rationality, much tighter than the small cosmos of *Salem's Lot.* Very quickly the verity of Danny's vision of violence is confirmed; locked together almost claustrophobically in the hotel with the characters, the reader is by now one of them, fearful of what Danny will see, cowering before Jack's irrationality, while the tension between these poles tightens. Fantasy and reality merge uneasily, in the scenes of the suggestively hating topiary, the ghostly figures and the knowledge of past murders.

When a future offers options, there can be hope; when that future is already limited by the certainty of menace and horror, the atmosphere has to be one of desperation and foreboding for the inevitable outcome. Not until the publication of his *Pet Sematary* would Stephen King again achieve so deadly frightening a situation.

Ours is a paranoid age, living without need of fantasy in daily threat both to the individual and to the world. Kafka and Camus delineated the helplessness of a person in a blind universe; many of Alfred Hitchcock's films and Robert Ludlum's novels are concerned with innocent men who are abruptly thrown into situations of whose nature they are ignorant and in which their lives are endangered.

It is sensibility used by King in several works. In the first part of *The Stand,* a secret government laboratory blunders and set loose upon the helpless, unknowing world a deadly menace. In his short novel, *The Mist,* the fear of an unknown menace creates a nearly unbearable tension for a group of people huddled for safety within the otherwise mundane confines of a supermarket. It becomes a more tangible fear when monstrous creatures are seen as their enemy, but, at the end, when the latter seems to have vanished, the paranoid fear of the unseen remains.

Likewise, viewed abstractly, *Cujo,* with the heroine and her child trapped within the insufferably small confines of their compact car by an unthinkingly vicious animal, may be seen as an existentialist application of a blind, uncaring universe purposelessly destroying. The climax is less victory than release.

It is in *Firestarter,* however, that King achieves his paranoid novel at its best. Pursuit by shadowy but real figures places the reader on the run, and the feeling of helplessness is cemented later by incarceration within the cells of a powerful and sinister governmental organization. It is exacerbated by our knowledge that the young heroine has within her mind the potential for destruction but appears unable to summon it.

Fear for Charlie, fear for ourselves in a situation we cannot control, are the sources of the novel's tension. Demonstrating this essentially paranoid view, the final chapter, even after Charlie's bitter triumph over her captors, is titled "Charlie Alone." Charlie, still hunted, hiding with friends, confides that "they"—that anonymous, concealed, patient, pursuing threat, "they," had killed her father and still seek to kill her. She gives her story to an anti-establishment paper which will, presumably, press for the ignored rights of the individual.

In *Christine,* King has his fun with that most beloved of youth's icons, the automobile, and here it is purely physical destructiveness which is the source of fear. After all, who is unaware of the power of a great machine, especially such a demon-car as that dreadful and unstoppable 1958 Plymouth! Christine is at least as bad and far more directly frightening than a blind, inimical universe, but, at the end, like that abstract enemy, she too appears to be immortal, and immortally dangerous. (The spouse of the author of this examination can attest to this. Having, perhaps foolishly, completed the novel at midnight, she spent the next several hours smoking most of a pack of True Blue 100s and consuming generous draughts of Remy Martin cognac!)

If philosophy and sardonic humor took King's attention for a space, and novelistic impulses other than engendering fear occupied the very estimable pages of *The Dead Zone, Different Seasons, The Dark Tower* and *The Talisman,* the author returned with a vengeance to the Province of Fright in *Pet Sematary.* Perhaps because he had written most of it several years before publishing it, at the time when Fear was his forte, it proved to be his most unnerving novel since *The Shining.*

It is a peculiar mixture King brews, in which Love and Death are commingled, resulting in a terrifying travesty of each. The death of a loved one is one of our greatest pains. It is irrevocable, and not even memory can make up for the loss; it is also a fear and dread we all live with. King posits the possibility of restoration, which, ironically, is itself frightening. If Death is final, what can a revived dead person be like?

Such a disquieting thought is evoked when Louis Creed, a young doctor, who with his family are protagonists, learns that, however fantastic it might seem, it is possible in a mysterious and ancient cemetery to revive the dead. He has the opportunity to do so when the family's pet cat is killed. However, the cat, returned, is not quite the same as it had been. "There was something fundamentally different, fundamentally *wrong* about him." What might have been a joyous miracle is shadowed by this perception.

King plays on innate thoughts of the corruption and decay associated with the interred dead, and as Creed stares

with disgust at the animal, exuding hatred of him, incapable of receiving or giving love, he is uncomfortable and uncertain. Something in Creed must also be changed now. "Keep me in mind, Dr. Creed," he imagines the animal saying, " . . . I'm here to tell you that a man grows what he can and tends it . . . I'm part of what your heart will grow now . . ." The reader's emotions, already conditioned by prior conceptions and fears of death are now twisted uneasily by this new experience and its inherent uncertainties. One suspects the cat will not be the last subject.

Time passes, and because death is never absent, other deaths are noted. Creed's wife recalls with horror her sister's death when both were children, a terrible memory lurking forever in the back of her mind. Death is accompanied by sickness, ugliness, revulsion, and in the litany of dread there is a developing loss of the simple love which had held the small family happy, despite religious differences and the relentless dislike of his wife's parents for him.

In this house of unrest, burdened by the doctor's secret knowledge, the reader waits in fearful anticipation of what may come, and the suspicion is realized when the young son is killed in an accident. The doctor is determined to exercise again the process of revival, whatever the price.

The pace has already been quickening. Emotions are taut as families argue bitterly, nightmares of indescribable horror burden sleep, horror piles upon horror, his tired wife is forced to drive between family and home, reckless with fear and dread, all culminating well beyond Creed's worst expectations, and a devastating final page of altogether chilling irony.

It is the ability of King to understand—and to calculate—the limits of human sensibilities which makes such a scene possible, and to leave in the reader a residue of fear which remains long after the final page is turned.

Fernando Ainsa

SOURCE: "Journal to Luisa Valenzuela's Land of Fear," in *World Literature Today,* Vol. 69, No. 4, Autumn, 1995, pp. 683-90.

[*In the following essay, Ainsa considers the transformation in Luisa Valenzuela's work from individual to collective fear and discusses her attempt to overcome fear through writing.*]

Child psychiatrists utilize a test called "The Land of Fear," developed on a principle using short phrases and drawings, which allows them to measure anxiety in children. The test is arranged into four categories: aggression, insecurity, abandonment, and death. The symbols that embody this "land of fear" are of a cosmic nature (natural disasters such as earthquakes, fires, floods, and volcanic eruptions) and represent a terrifying bestiary (dragons, monsters, wolves, and other malevolent animals) as well as violent or wicked beings (hangmen, devils, witches, torturers, skeletons, ghosts, and apparitions). The landscape of this realm is made up of dismal forests, cemeteries, impenetrable castles, dark dungeons, and a vast arsenal of instruments of torture. Coffins and masks are objects of daily life. Children have no difficulty in identifying with this "land," where, beyond their personal anguish, they recognize the symbols and images that represent what is regarded as the iconography of traditional fear.

This childhood land of fear may be, nevertheless, the faint reflection or dramatic foreboding of a real country where individual fear has turned into collective panic. A land shrouded in secretive silence, with latent and deep-seated fears, wrapped in complicit cowardices, one directed by parodic autocrats and ruled by a system that is legitimized by its own terror, founded with torturers capable of falling in love with their victims or of crying over their victims' bodies,[1] and with homes that are transformed into prisons—a land, sadly, where the borders of anxiety and anguish dissipate into an uncertain urban landscape that could well be Buenos Aires or New York.

This subtle transition from individual fear (forged from archetypal childhood fears, vacillating, ambiguously, between fear and cowardice) to collective terror, lived out like a nightmare, perhaps best sums up the allegory of fear which serves as the theme and leitmotiv of Luisa Valenzuela's work. It is to this inquiry, the exploration of this "land of fear"—as literarily evident as it is skillfully and ironically invoked—that the following pages are dedicated.

FROM NATURAL FEAR TO "IMAGINATIVE" FEAR. Fear, one must recall, is one of the fundamental human emotions. Omnipresent and subtle, its varied expressions have spanned centuries, manifesting themselves as much in the fear of the unknown as in reactions to danger, as much in individual visions as in collective fear (if not panic). Every civilization is the product of "a protracted struggle against fear" (G. Ferrero), since fear is born with man in the darkest ages of his history. In any case, fear "is in us" (George Delpierre), for "all men are afraid" (Jean-Paul Sartre). Nevertheless, if fright or anxiety can be diffuse, fear is always determined by some cause and obeys and reflects a concrete and immediate situation. Fear has a precise object which confers its specificity and identifies a situation that must be confronted. Fear is manifest in those "moments of greatest awe" ("momentos de máximo asombro"), surprise, or coincidence, that "sudden fear" ("de golpe se asusta" [AP, 12]), that "sheer cowardice" ("cobardía pura"), or that sensation by which "Pedro's legs shake because it's too much of a coincidence" (ST, 5; "a Pedro le tiemblan las piernas por demasiada coincidencia"), to which Valenzuela alludes in her short stories.

One is always "afraid of something." When one is afraid, one believes one knows what one is afraid of and acts according to that cause, generally, concealing it out of so much shame at confessing that one is afraid. It is not unusual, therefore, that there should be as many fears as there are objects of fear, including the fear of being afraid. Nevertheless, thanks to this *objectification*, one can externalize danger, identifying it so that one may better fend against it, whether by submission, flight, or direct confrontation. In this regard, Valenzuela suggests:

> Huir no siempre es cobardía, a veces se requiere un gran coraje para apoyar un pie después del otro e ir hacia adelante. Nadie huye de espaldas como debiera huirse, por lo tanto nadie sabe lo que es la retirada, el innoble placer del retroceso, disparar hacia atrás en el tiempo para no tener que enfrentar lo que se ignora. (*GE*, 37)

> (Fleeing is not always cowardly; at times it requires great courage to put one foot before the other and go forward. No one flees with one's back turned, as one should flee; therefore no one knows what retreat is, that ignoble pleasure of withdrawing, leaping back in time to keep from having to face what is unknown.)

This includes the idea of getting used to living with fear, a protective device that Bella, the protagonist of "Cuarta versión" (Eng. "Fourth Version"), assumes when "slowly she forgot the dangers" (*OW*, 46; "poco a poco fue olvidando los peligros" [*CA*, 48]), or that Chiquita, the protagonist of "De noche soy tu caballo" (Eng. "I'm Your Horse at Night"), adopts in choosing to drown herself in happiness, "trying to keep calm" ("tratando de no inquietarse"). Theirs is a daily fear that turns to indifference in cities like New York.

> Este *cool* neoyorquino, de dónde le habrá crecido a ella. Qué contagiosas son las ciudades, se comenta, heme aquí ahora asumiendo esta información como si tal cosa, con aire indiferente, tragándome mi horror, mi espanto. (*CA*, 71-72)

> (Where did she get her New York cool? Cities are so contagious, she thinks. Here I am now, taking in all this information without batting an eyelash, looking indifferent, swallowing the horror, the shock. [*OW*, 67])

Such is a fear that can, moreover, arouse itself or "nourish itself," as Valenzuela explains in *Donde viven las águilas* (1983; Eng. "Up Among the Eagles").

> . . . voy como al descuido alimentando mi miedo, algo callado y propio. Ellos me ven pasar con el palo sobre los hombros y los dos baldes que cuelgan del palo, acarreando agua, y me gustaría saber que nada sospechan de mi miedo. Es un miedo doble faz, bifronte, pero nada hermano de aquel que me impidío bajar una vez que hube escalado la montaña. Este no es un miedo simple, éste refleja otros miedos y se vuelve voraz. (*DV*, 21)

> (. . . almost nonchalantly nourishing my fear. They watch me go by carrying water, the pole across my shoulders and the two pails dangling from it, and

I would like to think they do not suspect my fear. This fear has two faces, not at all like the one that kept me from returning after I had climbed the mountain. No, this is not a simple fear; it reflects others, and becomes voracious. [*C*, 225])

In all cases, fear of the dark, fear of great depths, fear of heights, fear of great speeds or of instability, childhood fears whose recurrence is triggered by any fright with which they are associated (fear of being alone, of getting lost, nighttime fears), and the inevitable fear of death are accepted as *natural fears*. All render deep primordial emotions that are layered in the depths of humankind through generations, for they are collective ancient fabulations that are particularly open to superstitious or magical interpretations. All are vital feelings and emotions that are linked to intense, imaginary situations: the fear of being violated, the fear of punishment, the fear or anxious desire of a violent act. The acute and profound fear of death, the fear of something (dying) that no one can avoid—as J. C. Barker[2] reminds us—since no one escapes death, although this mysterious experience that is "so special, uniquely inexplicable, this fear of something that will never be known," can never be related to others (Paul Tillich). This Valenzuela herself notes in describing that "day-to-day part of me that fears suffering and death, the part that is astonished—the part, perhaps, that is alive out of cowardice" ("parte cotidiana de mí misma que teme al sufrimiento y a la muerte. La parte que se asombra, quizá la que más vive por cobarde" [*GE*, 37]), since fear can also disguise itself as "prudence": "It wasn't that I was afraid; I was just being prudent, as they say: threatening cliffs, beyond imagination—impossible even to consider returning" (*C*, 221; "No fue miedo, fue prudencia como dice la gente: precisamente demasiado hoscos nunca imaginados, imposibles de enfrentar en un descenso" [*DV*, 19]).

If in some cases objective dangers can justify fear, it is the process of the *subjectivization of risk* that brings about a transformation of the nature of such dangers and alters their intensity, according to the degree of the anxiety or emotivity of the subject. It is this subtle passage from fear *in* darkness to fear *of* darkness—of which Jean Delumeau[3] speaks—that marks a qualitative difference between animal fear in facing danger and man's capacity "to imagine," to dream fear. As Bachelard has emphasized, "The dream can be more intense than experience," whereby the dreamer becomes trapped in the deception of his own dream and of the ghosts he creates. That same imagination which lies at the root of creative, artistic, and scientific activity intensifies, exaggerates, and favors what Victor Hugo poetically summarized thus: "Voici le moment ou flottent dans l'aire / tous ces bruits confus que l'ombre exagere" ("Here the moment in which floats through the air / all the confused noises exaggerated by shadows").

Fear qualitatively produced, thanks to its imaginative complement, is a fear one lives much like "a situation," a condition that extends from an initial suggestion to a slower development and, subsequently, more important duration, carrying with it not only the emotional, physi-

ological reaction from the initial sudden fear but also giving shape to real mental representations by precipitating the heightened stimulation of the imagination. Moreover, because the imagination dreads the void, it invents what it does not know, even though it might lose itself in the consequences of its representations. These are the "demands of the mysterious" and of the enigmatic, as Roger Caillois would have it, that create the exaggeration which fear and the supernatural invite.

THE SWEET FRIEND FEAR. Luisa Valenzuela plays with both recourses. An "imaginative" fear is "objectively" established in her portrayal of such cities as Buenos Aires in "Aquí pasan cosas raras" (1975; Eng. "Strange Things Happen Here," 1979) and *Realidad nacional desde la cama* (1990; Eng. *Bedside Manners,* 1994) or New York, "the city that offered me all that is other: the perception of shallow fears" ("la que me dio todo lo otro: la percepción de los miedos a flor de piel"), in *El gato eficaz* (1972) and in *Novela negra con argentinos* (1990; Eng. *Black Novel [with Argentines],* 1992).

In Buenos Aires, where so many "strange things are happening," to be afraid can presuppose that one cannot know "if something is true or a lie" and that one can feel surrounded by "some sort of" trap or by "dark motives." Just as seemingly "out of place" is the kind of fear one suspects is "imaginary," inasmuch as Buenos Aires cannot permit itself—cannot permit one—the luxury of a "conscious hallucination," although one might add that "we who have known him for some time can be sure his fear has nothing to do with the imaginative" (*OD*, 19; "nosotros que venimos tratando desde hace un rato podemos asegurar que su miedo nada tiene de imaginativo" [*DV*, 65]). On the contrary, fear in New York "is a sweet friend fear that's good for the gut, a fear that subsumes me by forcing a trembling from within—a fear that I miss, I need" ("es un dulce miedo amigo bueno para las tripas, miedo cercándome a mí misma forzándose a temblar para adentro. Miedo que echo de menos, que me falta" [*GE*, 15]).

Nevertheless, if fear generally has an object and a cause, anxiety is, on the contrary, a feeling of undefined insecurity, a permanent uneasiness that confuses behavior. Weariness without apparent cause, a feeling of failure, and an inability to react give rise to this vaguely defined fear, although ironically, the censor who tries to "spare" Mariana of "anxieties" in the short story "Los censores" (*DV*, 89; Eng. "The Censors") succumbs to his own preoccupation.

Beyond anxiety lies anguish. Anguish is born from one's perspective and from the anticipation of danger, even when such danger is unknown. In this latent predisposition of the individual, the threat feels indefinite, uncontrollable, like an empty form anticipating its contents. The indefinite wait in the face of an indeterminate danger condemns one to an exhausting yet painful, disorienting state of individual behavior, a permanent feeling of drowning. Therefore, when Bella tells herself in "Cuarta versión" (Eng. "Fourth Version"), "But suffering is never quite placated: when the lovers are together, it runs down other paths and can only be expressed when they are able to freeze it in anecdote" [*OW,* 47; "La angustia no se aplaca nunca: están juntos y la angustia corre por otros canales que sólo logran verbalizar cuando consiguen congelarlos en anécdotas" [*CA,* 48]), she is in truth seeking to define her state of anguish, to give it form in order better to control it, like "a bridge stretching between two alien and cruel worlds of pain" (*OW,* 49; "un puente lanzado entre dos angustias ajenas y atenaceantes" [*CD,* 51]). Bella objectifies this "condition itself of a temporal and finite existence" ("condición misma de una existencia temporal y finita")—referring to Heidegger—and seeks to transcend it by extending a path "to cross over the horror and reach that salvation called asylum" (*OW,* 49; "para atravesar y llegar a esa salvación llamada asilo" [*CA,* 51]) and take action to avert fear.

The restlessness and the underlying fear that exist deep inside all human beings, to which Bella could not be an exception in the particular moment of history she lives, are "distracted"[4] with a specific goal: to help others escape by seeking refuge in a foreign embassy. The anguish is made specific: "The ones outside are desperate to get in; it's a matter of life and death" (*OW,* 50; "Los que están fuera desesperadamente necesitan entrar, cuestión de vida o muerte" [*CA,* 52]).

All fear, including the fear of natural phenomena—even if these are catastrophic, like earthquakes, fires, and floods—exhausts itself, or rather, is exhausted in the duration of the unexpected emotion that gives rise to fear and leaves no other trace than at the moment of initial stimulus (increased heart-beat, cold sweats, and "goose bumps"—all of which stereotypically typify fear).

Whatever the case may be, in the face of threats, of danger (real or imaginary), man externalizes antagonistic feelings: he believes he can confront the threat and defend himself by turning his fear to anger and aggression; or he avoids confronting it and gives in to its dictates, or simply flees from its presence, an indispensable reflex that can save him from death. Herein lies a great deal of ambiguity comprising the signs of fear. "I would have liked to have stayed in order to clarify things, to demonstrate to him my good intentions" ("Hubiera querido quedarme para aclarar las cosas, para demostrarle mis buenas intenciones"), confesses the assaulted protagonist of Valenzuela's "Julia C.," "but the blood that began to run down my arm and the blood I read in his eyes forced me to flee" ("pero la sangre que empezó a correr por mi brazo y la sangre que adiviné en sus ojos me obligaron a huir" [*H*]).

As the philosophers say without irony, there is a time to resist and a time to give in. Beyond the fear in the heart of man, in his soul, wherein he exercises the fullness of his powers and produces affective changes and physiological disturbances, there is a fear that establishes itself in collective space. When fear ceases to be individual and gives free rein to its suggestive nature, it becomes epidemic; it expands and penetrates the social collective body in its entirety and provokes vertigo in the group or in an entire people, inasmuch as "everything is degraded under the influence of fear" ("todo se degrada bajo la influencia del miedo").[5]

Luisa Valenzuela's narrative is centered on the "tiempos de miedo" (times of fear), as she sums up:

> Bella sobre la cama acariciando una sensación inesperada: el miedo. Algo que va a olvidar muy pronto y va a entrever nuevamente y va a dejar sumergir como las distintas ondas de una serpiente marina. Un tiempo de miedo arqueado sobre la superficie consciente, un tiempo de miedo subacuático. (*CA,* 13)

> (Bella is lying on her bed entertaining an unexpected feeling: fear. A feeling she'll forget quite soon and then sense and allow to sink under again, like the curves of a sea-snake. A time of fear arching up from a conscious surface, a time of subaquatic fear. [*OW,* 12])

It is these violent times of which Hegel spoke, where "the fury of destruction" sets in, and in which a ringing doorbell unleashes panic in the night: "Sonaron tres timbrazos cortos y uno largo. Era la señal, y me levanté con disgusto y con un poco de miedo: podían ser ellos o no ser, podría tratarse de una trampa, a estas malditas horas de la noche" (*CA,* 105; "The doorbell rang: three short rings and one long one. That was the signal, and I got up, annoyed and a little frightened; it could be them, and then again, maybe not; at these ungodly hours of the night it could be a trap" [*OW,* 97]).

FEAR AS AN INSTRUMENT OF POWER. It is well known, but also good to recall, that one of the sources of fear is insecurity. The signs that affect contemporary man's need for security lead to the consideration of all marginal or unorthodox behavior as potentially dangerous and terrifying, if not criminal. "Seditious" and "subversive" are appellations in whose name have been justified all kinds of repressive excesses and the acceptance of norms and procedures practiced with impunity to guarantee the "stability" of society. "Her judgments are awfully subversive. Do you think she may be involved in some seditious group?" (*OW,* 48; "Es tan subversiva en sus juicios, ¿no pertenecerá a algún grupo sedicioso?" [*CA,* 50]), it is inquisitorially asked with regard to Bella. With a premonition of what was to come in Argentina's reality, an element of augury that characterizes much of her work, Valenzuela had, by 1967, published a collection of short stories entitled *Los heréticos* (The Heretics) in which, on the one hand, situations that invite transgression abound, yet on the other there is fear induced by insecurity.

All theoreticians of power and those who have examined violence as theory and practice know that power legitimizes itself in the exercise of violence that systematizes the omnipresent State, grinding down with subtle perversity the daily life of citizens who are subject to its laws. The State reclaims for itself such tools of physical violence as the police, the army, and prisons to justify instituted order. In the delegating of individual violence to a repressive administrative system, the basic feelings of security of "one-dimensional man," who is threatened by aggression and reigning tension, are upheld. A great deal of what is modern is built upon the underlying violence of productive industrial and bureaucratic systems that squelch all individual expression.

Violence thus legitimized rationally controls the contemporary world, avoiding excesses and any possible "collective upsurge" by "freezing" the spontaneous and occasional expressions of violence. Individual acts of traditional violence that have always existed are supplanted by "constants," "coordinates," "structures," and true "systems" of violence. If in the past fear was the explainable, direct reflection of all violent acts, present-day violence, devised as a system, as the diffuse expression of technocratic power, engenders a fear that is also diffuse—that is, a "network of fears" and not a fear identified by a specific cause. This idea is expressed by the narrator of *Cola de lagartija* (1983; Eng. *The Lizard's Tail*, 1983).

> Esta red de miedos, este diseño tan geométrico también yo voy tejiendo sin querer, sin darme cuenta, pero no logro comprenderlo . . . una telaraña que me atrapa . . . algo tejido por montones de arañas negras, agazapadas a la espera de su presa, extensísima, kilométrica red y nosotros las presas y también las arañas. (*CL*, 217)

> (This net of fears, this geometric pattern, I go on weaving it too without knowing why, without understanding it. . . . [a spiderweb] woven by clusters of black spiders, crouching in wait for their prey, a broad, mile-wide web with us as the prey, and the spiders too. [*LT*, 198])

In this novel Valenzuela writes a kind of double allegory on the obsessive, egocentric empire of José López Rega, the influential welfare minister of Isabel Perón's government. On the one hand, Valenzuela yields the word to López Rega, whose story she intended to relate "inside and out, living it and telling it, justifying it and/or modifying it" (*LT*, 105; "por dentro y por fuera, viviéndola y narrándola, justificándola y/o modificándola" [*CL*, 105]). This version is written in the imperious first-person narrative of the Sorcerer, who retraces his autobiography, proudly juxtaposed to Scripture. Master of the power machine of language, the narrator permits himself the "incomparable luxury" of "turning dreams into reality, passing from word to deed with complete impunity" ("hacer realidad los sueños o pasar del dicho al hecho"). A power that within the Argentine historical reality of the 1970s was synonymous with violence, López Rega resorts to pathological means in its exercise with divine and maleficent skills, practices which earned him the nickname "El Brujo" (The Sorcerer). Thus he predicted that in his country there would be "un río de sangre" ("a river

of blood"), an image the reader takes to be a certainty, given the historical perspective with which he inevitably reads the novel, for so much blood has been shed in Argentina since 1976. The narrative point of view of "The Sorcerer," however, is not the only one in the novel. Valenzuela writes, in parallel fashion, *another* biography, one which is also narrated in the first person and with which she "deconstructs" the first discourse, exploding it through its own means of exaggeration, though admitting that "he [The Sorcerer] will always have an advantage over me, for he's not only more knowing but also more inventive" (*LT;* "él siempre me llevará ventaja porque no sólo sabe más sino que inventa mejor" [*CL*, 166]). This *other* biography is the deconstruction of "a hegemonic male discourse," as Lucía Guerra Cunningham[6] has pointed out, the sharp refutation of the indiscriminate praise of fantasy. Megalomania and exaggerated willfulness derive from the dramatic union of fantasy and the exercise of unlimited power. The dialectic of violence and fear, which are inextricably linked, are its inevitable result. The sinister process that López Rega inaugurated in Argentina is the best proof of this. If fear is lived individually, tortured or not by self-blame, it is violence that usually establishes fear as a collective phenomenon, where "the shame of being afraid" turns to complicitous silence, as suggested in the short story "El don de la palabra" (Eng. "The Gift of Words"), inasmuch as, "when the Leader speaks, the silence in the trenches is tomblike, to the point that fear of the coming of the rainy season is postponed until the next silence" (*ST*, 24; "cuando el Líder habla del silencio sepulcral dentro de los socavones, al punto de que el temor por la llegada de las lluvias queda postergado hasta nuevo silencio" [*AP*, 31]).

This subtle transition from externalized fear to surreptitious fear is described by Valenzuela in her brief work *Aquí pasan cosas raras* (1975; Eng. *Strange Things Happen Here*, 1979). The setting is a city where "legendary calm has been disrupted" ("se había roto la legendaria calma"), shattered by "the dark forces of violence" ("las oscuras fuerzas de la violencia"), where "everything had gone more underground, become secretive, and terrifying because we were falling down the slide of mutedness" ("todo se había vuelto más subterráneo, solapado y aterrador porque íbamos cayendo en el tobogán del silenciamiento" [*AP*, 6]). Although the author has returned voluntarily to Buenos Aires, and "to return means seeing oneself as forced to try to understand" ("volver significa verse forzada a tratar de entender" [*AP*, 6]), she must keep quiet, because "at times, when everything is clear, all sorts of questions can be asked, but in moments like this the mere fact of still being alive condenses everything that is askable and diminishes its value" (*ST*, 9; "en épocas de claridad pueden hacerse todo tipo de preguntas, pero en momentos como éste el solo hecho de seguir vivo ya condensa todo lo preguntable y lo desvirtúa" [*AP*, 13]). Silence can mean also the appearance of ignorance or forgetfulness, a way of "not wanting to know."

RECUPERATION OF MEMORY FOR OVERCOMING FEAR. Walter Benjamin, in a kind of "philosophical theology of remembering" made of evocation and memory as proposed in "Zur Kritik der Gewalt" ("Toward a Critique of Violence"), affirms that humanity will survive only if it permanently expands the breadth of its memories and gives it a privileged place among "the discards of history." Pleading "in support of a suppressed past," he recoups those discards which belong solely to a modernity that has confused the values of progress and humanity. Benjamin laments that progress has become an end in itself, a progress achieved at any expense and which has forgotten that humanity should be its sole end. In the development of that notion of progress attained through efficiency and calculation, the discards are many, flung onto the trash heap of history and its continuum. A "culture of remembering" should vindicate its place in memory as a way of reaffirming that "we have not been given hope except by the hopeless."

Within the generalization of "forgetful ideologies," in the "lite" culture of the contemporary world that touts forgetfulness as a healthy measure, in this scurrying on "to something else" when someone succumbs to defeat, an exegete of Benjamin's work, Manuel Fraijó, asks with concern if it is possible nowadays for a voice to rise up, "a voice that would pack so much pain and evoke with dignity those who are sacrificed with no dignity whatsoever," as the author of *Discursos interrumpidos* (*Interrupted Discourses*) did with such exemplary intensity.

Therefore, more than combating fear with forgetfulness, one must learn to "stop forgetting," must know how to recoup and assume memory itself, must know history in order better to combat violence. A good example is provided by Valenzuela's short story "Cambio de armas" (Eng. "Other Weapons").

In principle, the space within one's home, far from street violence, offers security. The troubled characters Mario and Pedro said as much to themselves in *Aquí pasan cosas raras:* "Finally they open the door of the apartment without fear, and go to bed without fear, without money, and without illusions." (*ST,* 12; "Por fin abren la puerta del apartamento sin miedo, sin plata y sin ilusiones" [*AP,* 17]). Within the four walls of one's own home it is easy to believe that one is protected from the collective fear that one breathes in the streets, where "so many strange things are happening." Laura makes the same claim in "Cambio de armas," as she faces the door and the latches of the apartment in which she lives in isolation and repeats the phrase to herself with "some sense of security" ("cierta seguridad"), but also with "somewhat of a chill" ("un cierto escalofrío") when she confirms that on the other side of the door are two guards. Are they protecting her or are they keeping her under surveillance? Little by little she suspects that the "multiple locks" on her door do not protect her but instead isolate her. Her house is not a refuge but a prison.

Laura cannot be afraid, however, for she has no memory. She lives in an "absolute present" from which all memory has been erased. Forgetfulness prevents her from turning

a diffuse anguish into a fear with its own cause and object. Nevertheless, although lacking the desire to recover her memory, with difficulty she starts reconstructing fragments of memory in the reflections of mirrors: "It's an inexplicable multiplication, a multiplication of herself in the mirrors and a multiplication of mirrors—the most disconcerting" (*OW,* 113-14; "Se trata de una multiplicación inexplicable, multiplicación de ella misma en los espejos y multiplicación de espejos—la más desconcertante" [*CA,* 122]). In her quick glance before the mirror, in that looking at herself and "failing to recognize herself," in her attempt "to sail all the seas in search of one and the same thing, which certainly does not mean seeing yourself in reflections" (*OW,* 4; "navegar todas las aguas en busca de una misma cosa que no significa en absoluto encontrarse en los reflejos" [*CA,* 4]), scenes are superimposed, scenes in which she is humiliated through sadomasochistic possession where the rituals of torture are unmistakable. Mirrors that reflect her image from the ceiling, forcing her to look at herself as she surrenders to the vulgar insults showered upon her while an experienced, moist tongue licks her body. Mirrors that probably extend through the peephole through which "the guard dogs" ("los perros guardianes") watch her avidly when Roque "dives into her again furiously" ("la penetra con saña"). Around the repeated insult *bitch* a "thick web of stares" ("la densa telaraña de miradas") is woven.

An ambiguous violence whose causes are unknown rules in this home/prison. In this alliance of pain and pleasure, Laura goes about discovering the signs that memory requires to restore the fragmented conscience of an identity that cannot recognize itself in mirrors beyond the moment in which it exists. Moreover, in integrating its fragments, in recognizing in the husband who keeps her locked up the torturer who beat and raped her in the past, she surmises the possible space of her freedom that had been suffocated by the submission to fear.

> ¿Qué será lo prohibido (reprimido)? ¿Dónde terminará el miedo y empezará la necesidad de saber o viceversa? El conocimiento del secreto se paga con la muerte, ¿qué será ese algo tan oculto, esa carga de profundidad tan honda que mejor sería ni sospechar que existe? (*CA,* 134)

> (What is being forbidden? Where does fear end, where does the need to know begin, or viceversa? The price of knowing the secret is death; what is hiding, what is that depth-charge waiting so deep down that it would be better not to even suspect it existed? [*OW,* 125])

. . . she says to herself, sensing that such freedom can only be conquered by rebelling against the order that represses freedom. She suspects it, when, on top of the waves of horror of "an indefinite, milder form of terror" (*OW,* 129), she discovers that "these sudden rebellious bouts" ("estos accesos de rebeldía") "are closely related to another feeling called fear" ("una estrecha relación con el otro sentimiento llamado miedo").

The power, the courage, to rise up against fear, emerges from the knowledge and the recovery of memory: "She suspects—although she doesn't want to question it too much—that something that shouldn't be known is about to be revealed. For a long time, she's feared the existence of those secrets, so deeply entrenched that they no longer belong to her; they're altogether inaccessible" (*OW*, 131; "Ella sospecha—sin querer formulárselo demasiado—que algo está por saberse y no debería saberse. Hace tiempo que teme la existencia de esos secretos tan profundamente arraigados que ya ni le pertenecen de puro inaccesibles" [*CA*, 140]). Only the final "revelation" will provide her the impetus to be free. Laura affirms, however, "I don't want to know anything. Leave me alone" (*OW*, 132; "No quiero saber nada, dejame [*sic*]" [*CA*, 142]), for which she is reproached: "Nothing can be perfect if you stay out there, on the other side of things, if you refuse to know. . . . So listen to me, and maybe you'll pop out of your sweet little dream" (*OW*, 133-34; "Nada puede ser perfecto si te quedas del otro lado de las cosas, si te negás a saber. . . . Así que escuchame, a ver si salís un poco de tu lindo sueño [*sic*]" [*CA*, 143]). To come out of a dream, to know how to grab hold of the past, is nothing more than to consummate an initial act that had been thwarted: to pick up a revolver, raise it, and aim it between the shoulders of one who had given her so much pleasure as he gave her reasons for hating him. Fear has been defeated, thanks to regained memory.

What can one do, however, so that memory does not disappear with life itself? How can one make it "stick" and last, so that it becomes a testimony that is transmitted and remembered years later? There is only one answer, and it seems clear: in order to last, memories must be fixed in the written word. The text is memory's best keeper. Hence the importance of writing as a gesture for eliminating fear, as a weapon to exorcise fears and anxieties.

Valenzuela suspects as much when she posits the question, and she responds: "They were finally free to feel at ease, with Madame off visiting her parents' homeland. . . . Now that they're finally together, the flow of their narration runs dry. Can only times of suffering be recorded?" (*OW*, 46-47; "Porque libres estaban para encontrarse, pero totalmente amordazados en materia narrativa. . . . Ahora que por fin están juntos de la libertad de narrar se les agota. ¿Sólo podrán escribirse los tiempos de angustia?" [*CA*, 48]). However, "suffering is never quite placated: when the lovers are together, it runs down other paths and can only be expressed when they are able to freeze it in anecdote" (*OW*, 47; "la angustia no se aplaca nunca: están juntos y la angustia corre por otros canales que sólo logran verbalizar cuando consiguen congelarlos en anécdotas" [*CA*, 48]).

Valenzuela herself confirms this when she declares, "I knew then that the only way for me to take over my reality—in the minimal space allotted us—was through writing" (*ST;* "Supe entonces que la única manera de apropiarse de mi realidad—en el mínimo espacio que nos es concedido—era a través de la escritura" [*AP*]).

In other cases, when confronting a story that "can't be told because it's too real, too stifling" (*OW*, 3; "nunca puede ser narrada por demasiado real, asfixiante y agobiadora" [*CA*, 3]), the narrator doubts, reads, and rereads the multiple beginnings, wanting to reconstruct at all costs a story that she discards as impossible—a writing that is more responsibility than mission, inasmuch as "our sole mission, a responsibility more than a mission, is to undo the metaphor of power in order to understand it, to try to see how power is so insidious it enters into our lives and into the lives of those who have no voice" ("Nuestra única misión, responsabilidad más que misión, es ir desarmando la metáfora del poder para entenderla, tratar de ver cómo el poder está tan insidioso, se mete en nuestras vidas y en las vidas de aquellos que no tienen voz").

Still, what appears to be a clear metaphor is really not so. If fear is exorcised by the written word and the text is capable of denouncing and undermining the discourse of power which makes it possible, one cannot forget that literature, for its part, "is a fear, a slow fear that secretly finds its way into the meticulous body of language, and from there it begins to speak" ("es un miedo, un lento miedo que se desplaza secretamente en el cuerpo meticuloso de la lengua y desde allí comienza a hablar)," as Juan Carlos Santaella points out in *La literatura y el miedo* (Literature and Fear). The recovery of images forever lost in memory needs fear to transform "stumbling language" ("atropellantes palabras") into a tense writing that includes at once "life and death," because "to write from fear, *with* fear, implies enacting an ethical condition of writing" ("escribir desde el miedo, *con* miedo, implica estatuir una condición ética de la escritura").[7]

Thus, if literature requires fear, this is because it is not possible to write without fear, or because all memory is forever made up of those fragments that will not succumb to definitive silence. It is with this contradictory tension that we can complete this initial foray into Luisa Valenzuela's "land of fear." One thing of which we can be certain is that her work, written as the recovery of a memory that does not capitulate to forgetting, can no longer be silenced by any power.

NOTES

[1] In the short story "Cambio de armas," which is analyzed later in this essay, a military torturer ends up marrying his victim, although he continues humiliating her. On the other hand, in *Donde viven las águilas* it is declared: "Pozo seco de lágrimas se nos vuelve inhumano. Si hasta el torturador llora sobre el cuerpo atormentado de su víctima. Le moja las heridas y el cuerpo en carne viva sufre el ardor salino de las lágrimas y la víctima sabe—a pesar de que sus ojos están vendados, si es que le han dejado ojos—que el torturador llora" (33).

[2] J. C. Barker, *La peur et la mort,* Paris, Stock, 1969.

[3] Jean Delumeau, *La peur en Occident,* Paris, Fayard, 1978.

[4] Heidegger believes that man has a permanent essence of anguish that is consubstantial to his nature, except when he finds himself "distracted" among things.

[5] George Delpierre, *La peur et l'être*, Toulouse, Privat, 1974, p. 55.

[6] *Splintering Darkness: Latin American Women Writers in Search of Themselves,* ed. Lucía Guerra Cunningham, Pittsburgh, Latin American Literary Review Press, 1990, p. 11. See especially Sharon Magnarelli's essay "Framing Power in Luisa Valenzuela's *Cola de lagartija (The Lizard's Tail)* and Isabel Allende's *Casa de los espíritus (House of the Spirits),*" pp. 43-63.

[7] Juan Carlos Santaella, *La literatura y el miedo y otros ensayos,* Caracas, Fundarte, 1990, pp. 7, 8.

WORKS BY LUISA VALENZUELA CITED

Los heréticos. Buenos Aires. Paidós. 1967. References use the abbreviation *H.* Translations are by David Draper Clark.

El gato eficaz. Mexico City. Mortiz. 1972. References use the abbreviation *GE.* Translations are by David Draper Clark.

Aqui pasan cosas raras. Buenos Aires. La Flor. 1975. References use the abbreviation *AP.*

Strange Things Happen Here: Twenty-Six Stories and a Novel. Helen Lane, tr. Harcourt Brace Jovanovich. 1979. References use the abbreviation *ST.*

Cambio de armas. Hanover, N.H. Ediciones del Norte. 1982. References use the abbreviation *CA.*

Other Weapons. Deborah Bonner, tr. Hanover, N.H. Ediciones del Norte. 1985. References use the abbreviation *OW.*

Donde viven las águilas. Buenos Aires. Celtia. 1983. References use the abbreviation *DV.* Translations are by David Draper Clark.

Realidad nacional desde la cama. Buenos Aires. Grupo Editor Latinoamericano. 1993. References use the abbreviation *RN.*

The Censors: A Bilingual Selection of Stories. Willimantic, Ct. Curbstone. 1992. References use the abbreviation *C.*

Donald J. Greiner

SOURCE: "Death, Sleep & the Traveler: John Hawkes' Return to Terror," in *Critique,* Vol. XVII, No. 3, April, 1976, pp. 26-38.

[*In the following essay, Greiner offers a close analysis of terror in John Hawkes's* Death, Sleep & the Traveler, *noting that the "pure terror" of the novel represents Hawkes's movement away from the comic horror that characterized his earlier works.*]

John Hawkes has spent most of his adult life probing the "psychic sores" of his grotesque characters. Beginning with *Charivari* and *The Cannibal* in 1949, he has combined experimental technique with narratives of extraordinary pain and violence to expose the murky interiors of what many people call "reality." Yet despite the shocking images, the revelations of pain, and the investigations of ugliness and failure, Hawkes has always considered himself a comic novelist. Many readers will recall a 1966 interview in which he insisted that "I have always thought that my fictions, no matter how diabolical, were comic. I wanted to be very comic—but they have not been treated as comedy. They have been called 'black, obscene visions of the horror of life' and sometimes rejected as such, sometimes highly praised as such."[1]

The comic treatment of diabolical urges directs his novels through *The Blood Oranges* (1971). Yet in that novel, the humor seems noticeably darker when compared to Skipper's comic bumbling which reaches lyrical heights in *Second Skin* (1964). Cyril, the narrator of *The Blood Oranges,* finds that his tapestry of love not only purges him, the self-styled sex-singer, but also results in Hugh's hanging, Catherine's breakdown, and Fiona's departure. The comedy is a long way from Skipper's "naked history" and his serene celebration of "love at last."

Apparently directing the more recent novels away from the comic terror associated with his work, Hawkes has written in *Death, Sleep & the Traveler* (1974) a truly terrifying book. One of his own statements seems especially pertinent here: "I might add that I'm no longer interested in writing comic novels, that I'm wary now of the 'safety' inherent in the comic form, that from now on I want to come still closer to terror, which I think I'm doing in the short novel I'm trying to write at the moment."[2] The novel he refers to remains unnamed, but it seems likely to be *Death, Sleep & the Traveler,* published almost simultaneously with his remarks. If so, Hawkes correctly describes his latest fiction, for in it the relatively few comic scenes are dwarfed by the exposure of Allert's horrifying dreams.

Most reviewers of the novel failed to take such change of emphasis into account; the publication of *Death, Sleep & the Traveler* elicited the wildly varied reviews which readers of Hawkes have come to expect. One consistently penetrating critic of Hawkes' fiction finds the novel too accessible and laments that it disconcerts him "far too little."[3] Another Hawkes fan believes that the novel is too easy, "a book that is virtually all narrative line and little else."[4] Another reviewer, however, condemns both *Death, Sleep & the Traveler* and Hawkes, and for some reason he also attacks Hawkes' admirers; those who praise Hawkes' artifice are as intolerable as those who create it: "artifice is the good currency which, for those who will accept it, eliminates any need for the best."[5] Finally, another's disapproval is a bit more balanced; Hawkes is granted the stature of a major novelist, but the latest two novels are "rather wispy works," having "the air of dazzling exercises performed on the edge of nothing."[6]

Death, Sleep & the Traveler is not as difficult nor as compelling as *The Cannibal* (1949), *The Beetle Leg* (1951), or *The Lime Twig* (1961), but it is far from a wispy exercise. Hawkes may be turning away from the comic delights of parody and strange laughter, but his latest novel is not a completely new departure. Rather than divorce himself from his earlier work, he has re-entered the dream world of Michael and Margaret Banks in *The Lime Twig*. In that generally acclaimed novel, the Bankses cross the line between reality and dream in search of sexual fulfillment, only to be smashed within the dream following an orgy beyond their wildest fantasies. Yet that violently comic novel ends affirmatively, for with his sacrificial death, Michael Banks redeems his life and brings down the dream world. In *Death, Sleep & the Traveler,* Allert Vanderveenan similarly pursues sexual fulfillment to the netherworld of dreams. Rather than emulate Michael, who realizes his error and tries to surface, Allert elects to remain within the dream where sex and death unite. His prospects—and the novel itself—are especially grim.

Commenting on novels in general, Hawkes argues that "the true sources of fiction—interesting fiction—no doubt lie buried in some inaccessible depth of the psyche."[7] The sea, with all of its traditional suggestions of psychological depth and eternity, plays a crucial role in *Death, Sleep & the Traveler.* Water is everywhere: Allert drinking glass after glass of cold water, Allert struggling to reach the very bottom of the ship's pool, Allert participating in erotic saunas. The sea itself is the central fact of Allert's psyche. Unlike Skipper in *Second Skin* and Cyril in *The Blood Oranges* who bathe in tropical waters, Allert crosses the ocean aboard a ship going nowhere. Hawkes notes the association between sea and psyche in his own fiction: "By now it's obvious that I'm obsessed among other things with the sea and with islands, and whereas Donne says that 'no man is an island,' I myself believe that we're all islands—inaccessible, drifting apart, thirsting to be explored, magical."[8] Hawkes' comment is echoed by Allert himself: "Every man is an island. . . . I am like the rest."[9] Inaccessible to all but himself, unapproachable from the fictional convention of verisimilitude, Allert finds that his psyche is a nameless sea on which he drifts. The novel he narrates invites us to explore the magical atmosphere of his "island."

Allert boards an ocean liner for an adventure to the island of his unconscious. Hawkes, recalling from his childhood the image of a great house ("dead house with beams like great bones"), explains that the abandoned house explored with an older female cousin remains the source of three related images which continue to "obsess" him: the abandoned lighthouse, the abandoned ocean liner, and the fishing village on an island. The village appears in *Charivari,* the lighthouse in *Second Skin,* the liner in *Death, Sleep & the Traveler.* He describes the ship as part of a "waking dream in which I stand alone at the edge of a straight empty shore at low tide and gaze with both fear and longing at an enormous black derelict or damaged ocean liner that looms in awful silence in knee-deep water about a mile from shore." Compelled to explore it, Hawkes remembers how in the waking dream he wades slowly through the shallow water to the ship, convinced that he must investigate its "vast world" until he finds either childhood hopes or emptiness or floating corpses.[10]

In *Death, Sleep & the Traveler* he finds the corpses. The dark ship which Skipper sees on the horizon in *Second Skin* becomes another metaphor for Allert's psyche. Reading Hawkes' latest novel, we are at sea within Allert's grotesque visions, wading with Hawkes himself as we navigate the shallow water to climb aboard and plunge into the terrifying immensity of the narrator's wayward ocean liner.

Allert provides the clue to his own tale. Detailing a scene aboard the ship, he notes his awareness of "concreteness rotating toward illusion" (52). The drift toward illusion describes both the hazy atmosphere of the novel and our inability to pin down anything for precise definition. For on opening *Death, Sleep & the Traveler* we enter the dream world of Allert's subconscious and pursue the illusions of a man who admits to loving psyche's "slime." The novel is framed at beginning and end by his wife's departure, but even the reality of this apparently "concrete" event is suspect. Allert's description of it rotates toward illusion, for he cannot settle upon a definition of Ursula's attire as she walks out the door. His first account suggests that she wears her entire wardrobe: "Dressed in her severe gray suit, her gardening hat, her girdle, her negligee, her sullen silk dress, her black blouse, her stockings, her red pumps, and carrying a carefully packed straw suitcase in either hand, thus she is leaving me" (1). As if his description were not confused enough, Allert confounds us even more when at the end of the novel he insists that she is carrying not straw suitcases but a handbag and a lambskin case while wearing white slacks and a red knit top.

What do we do with such a narrator? The point is that Ursula, Peter (her lover), Ariane (Allert's shipboard mistress), and Olaf (the ship's radio operator who shares Ariane) may all be projections of Allert's mind, complications in his personality which he cannot control until he describes the series of dreams which is *Death, Sleep & the Traveler.* Or perhaps Ursula has had Allert committed to the nearby mental hospital, Acres Wild, leaving him to his sexual fantasies and to his illusions called Ariane and Olaf (he explains several times that he is reluctant to depart on the cruise and that Ursula wants him to enjoy her body and stop dreaming). The novel invites both interpretations. A schizophrenic in the layman's sense of the word, Allert plunges deeper into the violent depths of his dream until he purges himself of all four characters: Ursula leaves; Peter dies of a heart attack; Ariane disappears from the ship, supposedly murdered by Allert; and the radio operator is relieved of duty.

Although difficult to trust, Allert drops enough hints to suggest that the mysterious ocean liner is the dreamer himself, while the sea is his dream world. He describes himself, for example, as "the alerted sleeper" and as "alert yet immobilized," and while immobilized he identifies with the unmoving ship (7, 111). Struggling unsuccessfully to understand a fear he has never known before, he suspects that his problem concerns "two cosmic entities": "the sea, which was incomprehensible, and the ship, which was also incomprehensible in a mechanical fashion but which, further, was suddenly purposeless and hence meaningless in the potentially destructive night" (7). Conscious of his "total identification with the dead ship" and aware of the propeller vibrations inside him, Allert watches the ship point toward "the unmoving fictional horizon" (8), a destination which may become the novel.

Trapped within his vision, Allert is an alerted sleeper dreaming to discover who he is. He notes that even though his life has been uncensored, he cannot explain the meanings of his experiences because each stands before him like an overexposed piece of film. His fantasies control him to such an extent that he has no life outside of the dream-narrative which he hopes to explain to us. Indeed, Ursula taunts him several times with the accusations that he is not real, that he is a "psychic invalid," and that he has "emotionally annihilated himself" (8, 46). In conventional terms, she is correct. Allert has no reality beyond the "cosmic entities" of the ship and the sea, and he is afraid when he feels "the stasis of the ship" in his large body (7). His merger of sex, the ship, and himself is surely clarified when he reveals that he is guided by a compass known as the "rare North Penis" (16).

Allert, of course, defends himself against Ursula's taunts. Arguing that he is not a "psychic casualty," he explains that all he wants is to exist, to believe in "the set and characters on the stage" (9). Yet he also longs to be the director of what he calls his "secret stage," casting all of the characters out of his dreams as projections of himself. Little wonder that he has no answer when Ursula insists that he is incapable of distinguishing between his life and his dreams. His idea of a cast of characters involves the two love triangles of the novel: one with Ursula and Peter, the other with Ariane and Olaf. Each person is the contrast of the other. Suave, sophisticated Peter is the opposite of coarse, dissheveled Olaf; large, sultry Ursula contrasts with tiny, boyish Ariane; and the cold, white, snow-bound scenes of the first triangle are the inversion of the hot, white, ocean-bound locales of the second. In its evocation of sexuality, *Death, Sleep & the Traveler* is Hawkes' most erotic novel. One reviewer calls it "steamy,"[11] and certain scenes—Peter's sauna, the voyeurism, the bats engaged in autofellatio—seem designed to stimulate fantasy without resorting to explicit description. Yet unlike the union of sex and regeneration which is found in *Second Skin* and attempted in *The Blood Oranges*, Allert's sexual fantasies veer toward derangement, exposing his onanism and culminating in death.

His dream of the grapes containing tiny red fetuses wriggling like worms before being crushed suggests his compulsion to negate the union of regeneration and sex.

Ursula later tells him that he dreams rather than lives because he has the face of a fetus. Allert is also fond of using such similes as burning logs as large as the bodies of children. Perhaps the most grotesque images of his onanism and destructive sexuality are the acrobatic bats engaged in autofellatio, their "sickening faces as large as an infant's fist" (123). Recalling the references to crushed fetuses, the bats are also an illuminating reference to Allert's memories of the childhood dreams which produced his first orgasms. In one dream he is a boy eager to know what a nude woman looks like. Dressing as his mother in order to strip, he finds that his most urgent desire is not to see the female body but to "love and relish" himself. When he removes the female panties to expose femininity, he experiences instead a "spectacular ejaculation" (140-1). A similar orgasm occurs in another dream from his boyhood when he views the photograph of a nude woman while sitting in a barber's chair (49-51). Hearing of these dreams, Ursula laughingly replies that the childhood delight in self-induced orgasms accounts for his current fascination with pornography and for what she calls the "psychic siphoning" of his adult "nocturnal emissions" (51). Although she laughs, Allert's predicament is not funny.

Rather than extend the association of lyricism and life which Skipper finds in sex, Allert expands the equation of sterility and sex which Cyril and Hugh suffer.[12] His pornography collection and onanistic dreams make Hugh's nude photographs and masturbation seem like child's play, and his erotic descriptions of dreams while "drenched in sex" leave Cyril's fantasies far behind. Cyril's visions of sexual harmony may accidentally lead to death, but Allert openly courts death as his final mistress. He is so caught up in the problem of self-definition that he seems unreal. Stuck in a dream which lures him to the depths of the ocean liner's pool, he trembles with the realization that he alone is the only "access" to what he wants to know. He becomes, in effect, his own mother when he dresses in her clothes in order to peer at nudity, and the orgastic experience of seeing himself beneath the woman's undergarments suggests that he is incapable of enjoying sex except with his own fantasies. He likes to believe that he willingly shares Ursula with Peter, that he even encourages the triangle, but his repressed dislike of Peter is reflected in his jealousy of the radio operator with whom he shares Ariane. Indeed, Ursula is no more than a symbol for him, one woman and every woman, as his interpretation of her name shows: "uterine, ugly, odorous, earthen, vulval, convolvulaceous, saline, mutable, seductive" (61). If she is only a projection of his psyche, so much the better, for he finds the most satisfactory sex to be not heterosexual but autoerotic. Given the choice between the bats' experience or sex with women, he would choose the bats. Thus all he must do to complete his immersion in the visions of his private fetishes is to eliminate the other "characters," and he dispatches them with ease: two die, one leaves, and one is relieved of duty.

Such visions, of course, are the stuff of madness. Allert is deranged only in the sense that he is cut off from commonplace definitions of reality, an alert sleeper sailing through a sea of dreams, content to stay submerged within the ship. The potential for violence is endless, for he hopes to free himself from all restrictions. Peter the psychiatrist asks him the key question: "What do you think of my theory that a man remains a virgin until he has committed murder?" (26). The equation of sex and death is unmistakable in Peter's question, and the novel chronicles Allert's determination to prove its validity and live the equation. Finding in his own name "paranoia curled in the shape of a child's skeleton," refusing to eat grapes because they might contain fetuses, and incapable of maintaining the sexual triangles which he so erotically describes, Allert encourages the relationship between his onanism and the merger of sex and death. His most spectacular orgasm will occur not during another peeping scene with his "mother" but when he successfully encloses himself within his dream, murdering the "real" Allert and thus shedding his virginity. He has apparently neared his goal by the end of the novel: "I now think without doubt that I, the old Dutchman dispossessed of the helm, am the living proof of all of Peter's theories. Or almost all" (167). His dead or totally insane body will be his final mistress.

When Peter explains that Allert believes normality to be a perversion, he hints at the reversal of standards which motivates the dreamer. Even Ursula interprets one of his visions—in which he drags a narrow tin coffin—as "the telltale dream of an only son," for she knows that the coffin contains a woman, perhaps Ursula, perhaps his mother (111). A few pages later Ariane and Allert ride in a hearselike carriage, and we know that his equation of sex and death is complete. The final thrill will be the murder of his companions, which means either his own death or his complete loss of rationality, since his friends are but images of himself. Allert comments, for example, that the identification he feels with Peter has been achieved by "certain psychic ties" (31). The tin coffin which carries the female corpse is a reference to his "vision of Peter sealed at last in his lead box but with his penis bursting through the roof of the box like an angry asphodel" (31). The union of Allert, Ursula, Peter, sex, and death is perhaps best illustrated when the three lovers join for a sauna.

Walking to the bathhouse, Allert interprets his footsteps as those of a "lurching murderer." He comments on the tension between the white snow and the black water, and he decides that the rocks surrounding the windowless sauna have the "texture of a man's skull." The searing, dry heat "stimulates visions," and Allert admits that the heat is high enough to bring death. Luxuriating in the nudity and in the excitement of Ursula's penchant for oral sex, he wonders if the heat will kill them. Later, when climbing from the bath to the house, he has the vision of Peter dead in the lead coffin. Although Allert claims that their sexual sojourn amid the searing heat, the nudity, and the oil of eucalyptus has the "clarity of a peaceful dream," the only clarity we can be sure of is that he equates sex and death.

Allert undergoes a parallel experience aboard the imaginary ocean liner. Ship and pool replace bathhouse and sauna, Ursula and Peter become Ariane and Olaf, and death again is the result. Hinting that the ocean liner is another vision from his dream world, Allert admits that once aboard the ship he expects monsters and bad dreams. He gets them: "A clear day was no guarantee against the diving and rising monsters of the deep. The length of the corridor was spanned underfoot by a thin rubber mat. . . . Through the thickly-smoked lenses of my dark glasses the details of the corridor were so darkly obliterated that it might have been leading me through some unfamiliar hotel or through the severe structure of a bad dream" (28). In addition to paralleling the sauna, the experience in the pool is a metaphor for Allert's plunge into his own psyche. While swimming, he likes to submerge as deeply as possible, struggling to achieve the bottom, to propitiate the god of "all those in fear of drowning at sea" before prolonging the "ritualized agony of the return to the surface" (33). He enjoys the shadows lurking at the bottom, and on another occasion he wonders if he were "wearing the rubber suit of the skin diver beneath my clothes. In the grip of the steam whistle my body was drowning in its own breath. Inside the rubber skin I was a person generating his own unwanted lubricant of poisoned grease" (79). All of the water imagery, the references to rubber suits and mats, and the explorations of the unconscious finally meet in his recollection of yet another dream experience. Waking, he finds himself wet in bed and bound in double thick sheets which engulf him like "some enormous scab," surely a reference to a psychiatric cure known as the rubber-sheet treatment. The moment baffles him, and he wonders where sleep has taken him and what he has dreamed (128). The only answers to these crucial questions are that he has entered his unconscious—the one place where he truly lives—and that he has dreamed a novel titled *Death, Sleep & the Traveler*.

Unable to believe in what he calls "the reality of the human self," he knows that he is inexplicable except, perhaps, when he dreams. For Allert, the alert sleeper, is a sick man, surely schizophrenic, perhaps murderously insane.[13] Obsessed since childhood with sex, he finds that he does not want to repudiate his onanism nor his mania that sex leads to death, even though Peter tells him that at the nearby asylum, Acres Wild, sexual affairs are often part of the cure. Allert never says so explicitly, but he is likely a patient at Acres Wild suffering a series of psychic shocks while wrapped in rubber sheets. Peter argues that the treatment is barbaric and dangerous. Note his references to white, sex, sea, water, sexual agony, death, and other images consistently used throughout the novel as he describes the cure in terms reminiscent of the sauna, the ocean voyage, and Allert's plunge into the pool:

> by subjecting the patient to deeper and deeper states of coma we brought him increasingly close to death's door. The patient descended within himself and, while we, the worried staff, hovered at his side, always waiting to administer the antidote or undertake the rescue mission, so to speak, the patient was traveling inside himself and in a kind

of sexual agony was sinking into the depths of psychic darkness, drowning in the sea of the self, submerging into the long slow chaos of the dreamer on the edge of extinction. The closer such a patient came to death the greater his cure. The whiter and wetter he became in his grave of rubber sheets, my friend, and the deeper his breathing, the slower his pulse, the more he felt himself consumed as in liquid lead, the greater the agony with which he approached oblivion, then the greater and more profound and more joyous his recovery, his rebirth. (143)

The terror is that Allert is never reborn. He remains, as it were, at the bottom of the pool, free to explore fantasies of sex and death, eager to probe the darkness of his unconscious being. For him, the great joy is not the recovery from but the approach to oblivion. Listening to Peter's description of the rubber-sheet cure, Allert imagines "some hostile patient who, in a mad stroke of understanding, snatches from the pocket of Peter's long white coat a cheap paperbound work of fiction concerning a pair of young nurses who set about using their sexuality as a cure for maniacs" (143).

Perhaps he is that maniac, Peter the doctor, Ursula and Ariane the pair of young nurses, and *Death, Sleep & the Traveler* the paperback book of fiction. More likely, however, only the first of these possibilities is true, that Allert is a patient who at times imagines himself a ship traveling on the sea of his erotic, death-filled dreams. Coma and myth are one, Peter tells him, a fact which he discovers during his incarceration in the rubber sheets: "has it ever occurred to you that your life is a coma? That you live your entire life in a coma? Sometimes I cannot help but think that you never entirely emerge from your flickering cave" (144). Filtering his life through fantasy, Allert prefers the cave with its bats. Ursula is correct when she argues that a man without a memory is a man without an identity and thus unreal. Allert is that man.

At the end of the novel, he wonders if he should commit himself to Acres Wild, forgetting that he is probably already there. Rejecting a return to what we would call "reality," he opts for his dreams: "Instead I shall simply think and dream, think and dream. I shall dream of she who guided me to the end of the journey, whoever she is, and I shall think of porridge, leeks, tobacco, white clay, and water coursing through a Roman aqueduct" (179). We never learn the answers to the questions which he raises early in the novel, queries which ponder if he is free, lost, exhilarated, or "flushed with grief." All we can do is accept his intuition that he is now "more youthful and yet closer to death" than ever before (38). He seems confident. At the end of the novel, he rushes toward death and his greatest sexual experience.

Though the creator of dozens of grotesque, violence-prone characters, Hawkes has always encouraged the reader's sympathy for psychically maimed, often bewildered people. In most of his novels, the identification of victim and victimizer is so complete that the reader sympathizes with both simultaneously. Indeed, Hawkes argues that "this special sympathy for decay, deterioration, destruction (and for the maimed, the victimized) is one of the essential qualities of the imagination."[14] In the past, he has used what he calls "extreme fictive detachment," reader identification with the prevailing point of view, and comedy to generate such sympathy.

Death, Sleep & the Traveler is an unusual addition to his canon because it does not have the often outrageous tone of humor usually associated with novels as violent as *The Cannibal* and *Second Skin*. Though Hawkes remains completely detached from the wanderings of Allert's psyche, and though he again uses the first-person point of view to narrow the distance between reader and narrator and thus encourage sympathy, he has turned from comic terror to terror in his latest fiction. Sympathy is maintained, despite the reader's revulsion at witnessing Allert's violent dreams, because one naturally feels for a character so completely unable to determine his identity. Yet terror tempered by comedy is somehow less stark than terror standing alone. Since pure terror finally denies us the humanizing gesture of laughter, *Death, Sleep & the Traveler* is closer to *The Blood Oranges* than to *Second Skin*, and probably closest of all to the grim, though funny, earlier *The Beetle Leg* and *The Owl* (1954). Its relative accessibility, perhaps the result of Hawkes' desire for a wider public, may be a flaw. True Hawkes fans like their novels tough. Yet comparative ease does not always undermine impact. In *Death, Sleep & the Traveler*, Hawkes has set aside the affirmative lyricism of his more recent novels to explore once again the dark recesses of terror.

NOTES

[1] "John Hawkes on His Novels: An Interview with John Graham," *Massachusetts Review,* 7 (Summer 1966), 459.

[2] John Hawkes, "Notes on Writing a Novel," *Tri-Quarterly,* 30 (Spring 1974), 111.

[3] W. M. Frohock, "How Hawkes's Humor Works," *Southwest Review,* 59 (Summer 1974), 331.

[4] Stephen Koch, "Circling Hawkes," *Saturday Review / World,* 1 June 1974, p. 22.

[5] David Bromwich, review of *Death, Sleep & the Traveler, New York Times Book Review,* 21 April 1974, p. 6.

[6] Michael Wood, "O Tempora! O Moors!" *New York Review of Books,* 8 August 1974, p. 41. See also the following reviews: Walter Sublette, "To the World of the Rusty Dead," *Oui,* May 1974, pp. 31-2; Rust Hills, "Writing," *Esquire,* July 1974, pp. 42-9; Phillip Corwin, "Brief Appraisal of Recent Fiction," *National Observer,* 20 July 1974, p. 21.

[7] Hawkes, "Notes," p. 112.

[8] Hawkes, "Notes," p. 113.

[9] John Hawkes, *Death, Sleep & the Traveler* (New York: New Directions, 1974), p. 104. Subsequent references are to this edition.

[10] Hawkes, "Notes," pp. 114-5.

[11] Rust Hills, "Writing," *Esquire,* July 1974, pp. 42-9.

[12] Apparently Hawkes hopes to encourage allusions to his other novels: the phrase "second skin" is used (p. 138), and the description of the grapes (p. 14) recalls the erotic grape-tasting game in *The Blood Oranges.*

[13] There is even a hint that he is "imperfectly lobotomized" (p. 135).

[14] Hawkes, "Notes," p. 119.

Michael J. Shapiro

SOURCE: "The Politics of Fear: DeLillo's Postmodern Burrow," in *Reading the Postmodern Polity: Political Theory as Textual Practice,* University of Minnesota Press, 1992, pp. 122-39.

[*In the following essay, Shapiro discusses the textual framework provided in Don DeLillo's* White Noise *for experiencing fears that are typically obscured in modern life by a complex of social codes and distanced by the prevalence of electronic media.*]

> *Video is a weapon that takes over consciousness itself.*
>
> —Paul Virilio

KAFKA'S BURROW

By the time Franz Kafka wrote his story "The Burrow" (early in this century), the age of merchandising had arrived, and people in industrial societies were beginning to experience a saturation of private, commercially oriented appeals, along with all the publicly disseminated codes aimed at producing docile, officially approved forms of citizen consciousness. Our "postmodern condition" experiences a density of messages and images, a cacophony of codes, competing for pieces of contemporary consciousness on a scale that far exceeds the situation in which Kafka wrote. It represents a qualitative shift in the relationship between the cultural and the social that perhaps justifies the concept "postmodern." Nevertheless, Kafka had already realized as keenly as anyone ever has that a simple notion of enlightenment, the idea that our condition can be clarified by enlightened contemplation, is misguided. He recognized that, especially in our century, consciousness can be more of an enemy than an ally.

Of course, this recognition is predicated on a Nietzschean view of consciousness, the view that there is no intelligible world to be known, for "the world" is fundamentally disordered; it is a container of opposing forces.

Insofar as there is intelligibility, it is a result of intelligibility systems that humans impose. Within such a view, the domain of the nonintelligible is an agonistic arena of alternative possible systems of intelligibility.

If intelligibility is a human practice rather than an independent feature of the world, consciousness must confront a dilemma. Thus, the creature in the burrow, who is digging a complicated maze as protection from the predators it imagines to be operating both outside the burrow and under it, is represented as one who cannot distinguish the extent to which the "dangers" impinging on the inner space it has created are from the "outside" or are produced by its own (interpretive) activity. At the outset, the creature tries to control its fear:

> But you do not know me if you think I am afraid, or that I built my burrow simply out of fear. At a distance of some thousand paces from this hole lies, covered by a movable layer of moss, the real entrance to the burrow; it is secured as safely as anything in this world can be secured; yet someone could step on the moss or break through it, and then my burrow would lie open, and anyone who liked—please note, however, that quite uncommon abilities would also be required—could make his way in and destroy everything for good. I know that very well, and even now, at the zenith of my life, I can scarcely pass an hour in complete tranquility; at least at one point in the dark moss I am vulnerable, and in my dreams I often see a greedy muzzle sniffing around it persistently.[1]

Eventually, the creature becomes aware that the sole evidence of the existence of its enemies is noise. Beginning in a romanticized state of silence and tranquility, as its efforts to create an impregnable burrow proceed, the creature draws disparate conclusions about the whistling it begins to hear in the walls. Its inability to determine whether the noises are produced by its own burrowing or by a predator can be read allegorically as pertaining to interpretation in general. Interpretation of the object world, which is required for the creature's rational planning for its defense, encounters the dilemma of intelligibility: how to discover how what is known can be reliably separated from the ideational enactments of the knower, how, in short, to distinguish the perception of objects from the object effects of perceptual acts.

It becomes evident, finally, that the shattering of the creature's tranquility bears on the issue of consciousness itself. The creature's consciousness turns out to be constitutive of the "danger." The mind, in its contemplative mode, cannot offer tools for coping with the world inasmuch as it is implicated in the enactment of that world.

While there is no definitive solution to the dilemma of intelligibility and its implications for creating a rational order to contain and channel one's fears in nonobsessive, effective ways, Kafka's solution was constitutive of his work; he wrote in a style designed to provide escape routes out of the mazes produced by the prevailing systems of intelligibility, the objectifying intellectual structures that immure us within prevailing danger codes. Kafka did not want to be the "old architect" that the creature in his burrow had become when, in its old age, it was resigned to the insecurities its own consciousness had created:

> Between that day and this lie my years of maturity, but is it not as if there were no interval at all between them? I still take long rests from my labors and listen at the wall, and the burrower has changed his intention anew, he has turned back, he is returning from his journey, thinking he has given me ample time in the interval to prepare for his reception. But on my side everything is worse prepared for than it was then; the great burrow stands defenseless, and I am no longer a young apprentice but an old architect.[2]

In short, rather than an old architect, one who simply reproduces the danger codes contained in the prevailing systems of intelligibility, Kafka was a wily and cunning writer, who identified with his version of Ulysses. . . .

THE POSTMODERN BURROW

The more radical postmodernist modes of theorizing and writing are also designed to provide escape routes, and, arguably, the textual strategies must now be more radical because the postmodern burrow is a more densely articulated maze. Kafka anticipated these forms of writing by exploring the inner space of consciousness and demonstrating its ambiguities and uncanny relationships with the spaces outside of consciousness. But where postmodernist fiction departs from Kafka's ambiguities and enigmas is in its representations of the tangle of codes that represents modernity's spaces. It draws its impetus from the postindustrial age of esoteric structures of communication and information, positing an extreme breakdown in the legibility of modern society and its spatial practices (the complex sets of boundary practices that carve up and administer activities) and representing the extreme difficulties one has in locating the self in history, in the modern city, and in the complex sets of codes that bear on issues of survival. Like Kafka, postmodernist writers recognize the dilemma of consciousness. What they add is the recognition that the modern consciousness is organized less on the basis of one or more dominant, universalistic codes, such as the spiritual or scientific, and more by a jumble of representational practices, a variety of film and television images along with vocalized and written scripts that have colonized modern thinking. Thus, for example, novelist Manuel Puig represents a young Argentinian boy's musings about sexuality and romance with an imagined interaction he has with the Hollywood film star Rita Hayworth.[3]

At a minimum, the postmodernist writer is not driven by the old notion of consciousness raising, working instead within the conceptual space opened by Kafka's suspicions about the complicity between consciousness and the objects it represents. But in order to appreciate the contribution of postmodernist fiction to locating the self in the postmodern order, it is necessary to map certain aspects of that order, to isolate the historical situation within which such writing can register important effects. For example, one cannot understand the contemporary, fear-driven issue of "national security" outside of the context of what is thought to be at stake, of "who" it is that must be made secure from various internationally inspired forms of danger. Therefore, before turning to an exemplary postmodernist writer, Don DeLillo, who has been termed, among other things, a "connoisseur of fear,"[4] it is necessary to elucidate both the present and the radical postmodernist mode of theorizing it. This has been provided in Foucault's genealogically oriented investigations, which are designed to denaturalize and politicize the present by showing how remarkable its structures and techniques of power and authority are when placed in historical perspective.

GENEALOGIES OF THE PRESENT

Historically, the democratization of safety or protection has been a mixed blessing. One dominant political narrative, in which the development of civil society has led to an increasing protection of persons from arbitrary state power, tends to read wholly favorably. The sovereign and other representatives of the state have been increasingly limited, and their power has been displaced by a broad process of deliberation, which extends to policies that can put populations at risk in peace or war. However, there are other scenarios that emerge from this displacement in the collective identity of a society. It can be shown, for example, that the historical displacement of sovereign power has not meant that representations of safety are now deposited in the hands of individuals who can locate themselves unambiguously within fields of local and remote forms of danger. Although it is no longer an individual sovereign who can exercise power over life and death, the modern defense of the society as a whole carries with it imperatives that distribute dangers and risks that must now be read within an ideational terrain that is more dense than ever. Death remains effectively if not officially on the policy agenda. What has changed, as Foucault has pointed out, is that what is at risk is no longer the safety of the sovereign but the existence of the social body as a whole. What is to be protected is the "population," which is a relatively recent form of collective identity, inherited from the eighteenth century and now an integral part of the grammar of modern "security" policy.

> One of the great innovations in the techniques of power in the eighteenth century was the emergence of "population" as an economic and political problem: population as wealth, population as manpower or labor capacity, population balanced between its own growth and the resources it commanded. Governments perceived that they were not dealing simply with subjects, or even with a "people," but with a "population."[5]

This aspect of modernity, which Foucault has helped to isolate, is not clearly encoded in policy talk, in the discourses with which we construct problems related both to sudden annihilation or to a more gradual debilitation from the effects of the toxicities used, ironically, in the name of more vitality (energy, defense, etc.). This is because that talk is aimed outward at constructions of the world rather than inward at what we have become such that we can have such a world. Although within various forms of official discourse there is only a dim recognition of the relevance of our cultural condition, of both what and who we are and of the forces constructing our imagination of what is to be feared in the postnuclear age, in which a politics of exterminism is possible, our intellectual and artistic discourses are increasingly aimed at alerting us to the consequences of the unprecedented capacity for the destruction of human life.

AN EXEMPLARY MODERN CONVERSATION ABOUT FEAR

More of the implications of how "we" in the contemporary age have fear emerge in a conversation, reported and analyzed by Barry Lopez, that occurred between a Danish anthropologist and an Eskimo shaman in 1924. What is most evident in Lopez's treatment of the conversation is that Eskimos use fear rather than belief as an epistemological category. This is the case, Lopez implies, because their experience of their surroundings is more intimate or less mediated than that of the citizen of modern, industrial societies.

> Eskimos do not maintain this intimacy with nature without paying a certain price. When I have thought about the ways in which they differ from people in my own culture, I have realized that they are more afraid than we are. On a day-to-day basis, they have more fear. Not of being dumped into cold water from an umiak, not a debilitating fear. They are afraid because they accept fully what is violent and tragic in nature. It is a fear tied to their knowledge that sudden cataclysmic events are as much a part of life, of really living, as are the moments when one pauses to look at something beautiful. A Central Eskimo shaman named Aua, queried by Knud Rasmussen about Eskimo beliefs, answered, We do not believe, we fear.[6]

Some might file this interaction under the simple notion of misunderstanding, but, if read appropriately, the shaman was supplying the beginnings of a very powerful interpretive reflection. In offering a less-than-obvious translation, he was also both contrasting two cultures and supplying a penetrating reading of modernity. The response turns the questioner back on himself, encouraging reflection on the ontological conditions and premises of the question. What, one must now ask, has made the concept of belief so central to social sciences such as anthropology, and what are the social, cultural, and historical contexts of such questioning disciplines? In short, Aua has provoked a phenomenological moment in the conduct of an inquiry. He has encouraged a questioning of the complex interrelations between a practice of inquiry and the historical practices out of which it emerges. With such a questioning, we are set on a track that helps to disclose the contemporary politics of fear.

The effective distance that the shaman's remark provides us is similar to that which Foucault's revision of the traditional Kantian questions has provided. Shifting the ground of knowing from the "what"—Kant's "What can I know?"— Foucault sought to situate knowing within the reigning practices of subjectivity within which "knowing" is practiced. This construal of knowing as a practice is linked, for Foucault, to particular times and places, to the subject's situation rather than merely its formal structures of apprehension (Kant's exclusive focus). Thus, the question emerges in Foucault's version as, "How have my questions been produced?"[7] Moreover, this "how" has considerable historical, ontological, and social depth, for it is meant to evoke, at once, both the peculiar set of practices that constitute the present human condition and the process by which that condition has evolved through a complex process of interactions between chance occurrences and political, social, and administrative tendencies.

What is therefore most revelatory about the question posed to the Eskimo shaman along with his response is the remarkable difference between an epistemology of fear and an epistemology of belief. At a simple level, Aua was saying that for Eskimos beliefs are an extravagance rather than a mode of knowing and appraising. The daily survival demands within which the Eskimo operates render fear as the appropriate knowledge vehicle, because it implies a high degree of alertness to immediate danger. By contrast, in the modern, postindustrial condition shared by Rasmussen and us, "danger" is bureaucratized. There is an extremely dense layer of mediation between what one might be advised to fear (i.e., fearing is as elliptical as my advisory metaphor) and what one's moment-to-moment experience appears to be. That is not to say that fear ought not to be an effective epistemological category for us. It is to say, simply, that for complex reasons, it isn't. Part of this complexity has to do with how we sequester death rather than confront it. But this is an issue to be treated later.

What remains to be discussed in connection with this exemplary conversation between Rasmussen and Aua is "belief." Without attempting an extensive genealogical treatment of this modern (cognitive) attribute, it should suffice to note that "belief" has become an increasingly important dimension of the modern, psychologized self because of the extent to which "we" in modernity have a complex, institutionalized relationship to both individual and collective aspects of survival and protection. The process of creating, administrating, and legitimating "security," "protection," "safety," and the like rarely involves face-to-face, reciprocal relationships. Because both individual and reciprocal approaches to treating danger have been displaced, and because there are competing meaning frames, as well as institutionalized "policies" involving media such as print, visual signs, and voice-at-a-distance, we have "beliefs." "Beliefs," in short, are phenomena that are intimately connected to a variety of institutionalized interests and procedures involved in indirect influence.

This scenario about the cultural and political foundations of interest in "beliefs" is predicated on the modern gap between experience and knowledge. For example, in the case of whatever health hazards may arise from various electronic emissions, one must rely on various knowledge agents, who are nominated within a complex web of medical, scientific, and public policy discourses, all having varying degrees of authority over the representation of the potential dangers. Living in a world in which danger is mediated, persons interested in focusing their fears effectively must become consumers of representations, hence the displacement of an epistemology of fear by an epistemology of belief. For a variety of reasons, agents on both sides of dangers—the potential victims as well as the representers and explicators—tend to occult as often as they disclose them. But doubtless what is chiefly implicated on both sides is mortal danger's status in modern representational practices. It would be less appropriate to say that such danger has a "bad press" than to say that it lacks an effective press. This allows whatever/whoever has authority over life and death and the processes by which mortal fear becomes focused on real or imagined objects to escape contentiousness, to operate in an atmosphere in which fear is depoliticized. As Jack Gladney, the narrator and "main character" in *White Noise* says, while scanning the television to get the news after having fled from an "airborne toxic event,"

> Everything we love and have worked for is under serious threat. But we have looked around and see no response from the official organs of the media. The airborne toxic event is a horrifying thing. Our fear is enormous. Even if there hasn't been a great loss of life, don't we deserve some attention for our suffering, our human worry, our terror? Isn't fear news?[8]

DON DELILLO AND THE REPOLITICIZATION OF FEAR

In *White Noise,* DeLillo produces a powerful thematization of fear and death. But this is not a traditional consciousness-raising novel aimed at alerting people either to imminent dangers or their dire consequences, as is the case, for example, with Nevil Shute's *On The Beach,* a bestselling depiction of the death of the human race as a result of nuclear war.[9] In Shute's book the reader learns, among other things, that even Australia is not safe from the radiation fallout of a nuclear war, and such themes were popular enough to produce both a follow-up film and comic strip. The media history of Shute's story is more of a DeLillo-type theme than the dangers toward which it gestures. DeLillo's novel does its work not by raising consciousness but by revealing the dilemmas and aporias of consciousness, by showing in general the extent to which consciousness is owned and operated by modern, media scripts—for example, Gladney hears one of his children mumbling "Toyota Celica" in her sleep—and in particular by showing the way modern fear remains ineffectively focused because, in a fundamental way, our epoch has rendered "real" danger illegible. Its signs are softened and commodified. Advertising, modern consumer society's most pervasive and energetic emitter of signs, forms danger into merchandising. In an analysis of the events surrounding the assassination of President Kennedy (and other similar events) DeLillo discusses this softening and commodifying of danger in a passage that anticipates much of the thematic in his *White Noise:*

> One of advertising's unspoken rules is to absorb social disruptions and dangers into the molded jell of mass-brand production. This is the philosophy of total consumerism. Black rage becomes the tacit subject of commercials for Lite beer. The ex-athletes who appear in such commercials, large black men tutored in snarls, intense stares, various intimidating gestures and expressions, serve the consumer culture by debasing righteous anger. They allow it to be incorporated into the living-room world of sitcoms and game shows. The mean looks and gestures they are asked to supply in a given commercial's scenario are ways by which the culture softens the texture of real danger, changes real things to fantasies, undercuts meaning and purpose. We consume social threats and problems as if they were breakfast food.[10]

DeLillo is aware that the America he is thematizing is a postmodern culture inasmuch as he recognizes the "radical structural difference" (as Jameson has put it) involved in the change from earlier stages of capitalism to the modern, information/consumer stage.[11] What DeLillo adds to this recognition is a postmodernist style. America, for DeLillo, is not a *thing* to be depicted; it is a system of "codes" in the two important senses of that term. In the first instance, the codes are the set of messages emerging from the electronically communicated images on which he dwells in *Americana* (his first novel) or the noises and advertising slogans that populate people's consciousness throughout *White Noise.* And, according to DeLillo, the more sophisticated the technology becomes, the more controlling and determining the codes become. "Sophisticated devices," he states, "cause people to lose convictions. We are more easily shaped, swayed, influenced."[12] He elaborates this perspective by updating, into our present technologically sophisticated surveillance situation, the Kafkaesque condition of one who is subject to criminal investigation. Mudger, the investigator/security agent in *Running Dog,* puts the case clearly:

> When technology reaches a certain level, people begin to feel like criminals . . . someone is after you, the computers maybe, the machine-police. You can't escape investigation. The facts about you and your whole existence have been collected or are being collected. Banks, insurance companies, credit organizations, tax examiners, passport offices, reporting services, police agencies, intelligence gatherers, devices make us pliant.[13]

There is, of course, a normative force to "codes," which is the second sense of the term, that emphasizes a code as an authoritative rule (as in "the penal code"). Technologically assisted information systems of codes seem to have a more powerful regulatory force, and modern reality, for DeLillo, is an overlapping set of information systems. We live in a postmodernist burrow, a maze constructed by the codes—at once informational and regulatory—that emerge from intelligence organizations, media messages and consumer products, banking and commercial systems, and so forth. For example, as Jack Gladney is in midnarration in *White Noise,* we get this message:

> PLEASE NOTE. In several days, your new automated banking card will arrive in the mail. If it is a red card with a silver stripe, your secret code will be the same as it is now. If it is a green card with a gray stripe, you must appear at your branch, with your card, to devise a new secret code. Codes based on birthdays are popular. WARNING. Do not write down your code. Do not carry your code on your person. REMEMBER. You cannot access your account unless your code is entered properly. Know your code. Reveal your code to no one. Only your code allows you to enter the system.[14]

This is more than a message for the characters in *White Noise;* it is the condition against which DeLillo writes. Like Kafka, his writing is aimed at escaping from closed systems, from the web of codes that remain unread because they are confused with the "real."[15] What DeLillo's recent fiction, particularly his *White Noise,* seems designed to do is to deconstruct the maze, a deconstruction effected not with simple, unreflective statements about the maze but with a variety of narrative, grammatical, and rhetorical strategies that first construct it and then deconstruct it.

One of the first and most essential textual strategies is DeLillo's construction of characters. For example, in a discussion of his *Players,* he refers to his work as "pure fiction" in that his characters "have been momentarily separated from the story telling apparatus; they're still ideas, vague shapes."[16] And the characters lack a consistent, coherent personality, operating more as linguistic vehicles than self-contained and controlled identities. What DeLillo says of his characters in *End Zone* is a persistent pattern in his *White Noise,* as well. "Some of the characters have a made up nature. They are pieces of jargon. They engage in wars of jargon with each other. There is a mechanical element, a kind of fragmented self-consciousness."[17]

In *White Noise,* this strategy is enhanced by creating separate voices for various media, as well as for persons. One reviewer mistakes this textual strategy, which represents postindustrial society's fragmentation and difficult-to-discern codes, for poor character development, complaining that DeLillo does not "render as faithfully as possible, the feelings his characters would be likely to have in the situation he has them in."[18]

DeLillo is not after pure feelings (whatever those might be) but is pursuing the delirium one experiences in trying to focus feelings in a world of names and codes that prevent feelings, especially fear and dread, from effectively situating themselves in systems of self-interpretation that connect with practical experience and likely consequences. In *White Noise,* as in other novels, even though characters narrate, they do not control the flow of discourse. Committed to a view that "style and language reflect the landscape," DeLillo interweaves his character's musings with the media voices that construct modern meaning systems. To deconstruct such systems, one must first represent them. The seemingly bland and impenetrable facticity of the world must be placed in a centrifuge to separate out the many layers of codes, the maze constructing that facticity. Kinnear, an anarchist in *Players,* recognizes the layers of complex codes constituting intelligence/surveillance relations, financial relations, and so on. "It's everywhere . . . mazes . . ." And, a moment later, "Behind every stark fact we encounter layers of ambiguity."[19]

In *Players,* DeLillo gives us a glimpse of some of the layers underlying what appears as the simple fact of money by representing the gap between the direct, tactile experience of holding it and the complex modes for assembling and transmitting financial holdings. DeLillo has Lyle's gaze, in *Players,* pierce the "paper existence" of money:

> He'd seen the encoding rooms, the microfilming of checks, money moving, shrinking as it moved, beginning to elude visualization, to pass from paper existence to electronic sequences, its meaning increasingly complex, harder to name. It was condensation, the whole process, a paring away of money's accidental properties, of money's touch.[20]

Here is how DeLillo works, dissolving objectivities into the processes—particularly the contemporary electronic processes—that constitute them. And, recognizing that the modern world is populated less by things than by simulacra, DeLillo has the action in *White Noise* hover ambiguously across television and face-to-face relations as the distinction between the real and representation breaks down. DeLillo decodes modernity in both important senses. He displays the informational and communications systems, the mediating structures that produce meanings, and he challenges their authority. It is his style, his way of playing with the codes constructing modernity that is his functional vehicle.

Confronting the dilemma of codes—mastering them without being mastered by them—DeLillo's rhetorical moves, some of which are very spare gestures, provoke powerful reflection on modernity's closed system of codes, which, among other things, are complicit in obscuring danger and death. His analyses are delivered less in the form of conventional plots and more in revealing linguistic fragments, which reflect the fragmented nature of modern subjectivity. For example, in *White Noise,* there is a reference to two women who are reunited on television—they had been "twin sisters in the lost city of Atlantis 50,000 years ago"—and are now "food stylists for NASA."[21]

This fictional but highly plausible vocation conveys the general level of merchandising mediation for even such basic human functions as eating. That NASA is the venue for this new profession conveys the banality and bureaucratized collective inattention of systems for hastening danger and death. It implies, moreover, that this banal commodification of food services, mixed with a death machine, constructs our postmodern defense system (our burrow) as an intricate web of complicit practices that diffuse rather than focus danger and death.

DeLillo is showing, with a seemingly trivial aside here, that even our agencies directly implicated in creating potential for mass destruction are "agencies" in a highly dispersed, cultural sense. People whose vocations seem very distant from death are part of a penumbra of banal practices that, though not as effective as the main agents of death and destruction, all contribute to the phenomenon. The ritual space within which societies used to cope with death, making it intimate by confronting it and delimiting its meaning from all that is nondeath, is displaced by processes producing radical nonintimacy. Discursive and nondiscursive practices serve to defer attention to death-related services by making them quotidian rather than decisive and extraordinary.

DeLillo also conveys an image of postmodern society with a postmodernist grammar. Individual subjects are not responsible for apprehending objects or creating actions. What are objectified or enacted throughout *White Noise* are vague tendencies produced out of the same milieu that produces the fragmented and ambiguous system of subjectivities, of which each character is a representative.

There is, nevertheless, a rough plot to *White Noise,* which is meant to reflect modernity's most powerful plot, the production of death. As Gladney puts it early in the novel, "All plots tend to move deathward," but even this seemingly ideationally committed pronouncement turns out to have been ventriloquized through an unwary speaker who, reflecting on it six lines later, says, "Is this true? Why did I say it? What does it mean?"[22] This desultory and unfocused relation to death pervades the story, as almost every banal activity seems to have a contrived, oblique relation to death—for example, there are elderly students in a posture class, about whom the narrator remarks, "We seem to believe it is possible to ward off death by following rules of good grooming."[23]

At its most general level, the novel centers around the Gladney family. Jack Gladney is the head of the Department of Hitler Studies (a discipline he has founded) at College-on-the-Hill. While his three former wives are all connected with the intelligence community and are described as lean and angular, Gladney's current wife, Babette, is a plump, earth-mother type who teaches a posture class and conspires with Gladney to hold death at arm's length by sinking into a structure of self-indulgent, preoccupied domesticity. But ironically, the very family that provides a retreat from the realities of danger and death also provides openings for its presence. For example, Jack and Babette's son Heinrich remains preoccupied with danger and death and therefore resists the house epistemology, the avoidance and distraction practiced by his parents. The ever-present television set produces news of dangers within its continuous stream of simulated experiences, dangers that present themselves through the vocalizations of the children as well as through the TV's more direct interventions into the house conversations.

Thus Jack's displacement strategies, burying himself in domesticity and in academic abstractions—adopting a keen interest in Hitler, an arch purveyor of death who had become a killer in order to deal with his preoccupation with death—do not avail him. He is assailed by dangers through the chinks in his domestic, defensive burrow by the interaction of his children with the electronic simulations produced by the commodified information order surrounding his household.

Gladney's studied inattention is further frustrated by his friend Murray, whose sophistication—"I'm from New York," he keeps saying to explain it—continually summons Gladney out of his inattention and urges him to decode modernity. "You have to learn how to look," he says, urging Gladney to find the "codes and messages."[24] In contrast with Gladney's lexical simplicity—Gladney speaks in brief fragments, expressing wonder and confusion—Murray theorizes culture, waxing eloquent, for example, on television as myth, while Gladney and Babette wonder how to insulate their children from the cultural flotsam and jetsam of TV. Meanwhile, the television monologue continues: "Dacron, Orlon, Lycra spandex" intrudes into the conversation.[25]

While Gladney and Babette press continually to burrow into family life to ward off the fear of death, their friend Murray and all the intruding cultural signs provoke confrontations with them. And, most important for the structure of the novel, "events" intrude as well. Once family and college life and their cultural contents have been portrayed in Part I, "the airborne toxic event" occurs, and the family runs from the danger, only to encounter it as Gladney is exposed to the toxicity while stepping out of his car to fill his gas tank during the exodus.

The novel then moves to the last part, the "Dylarama" where the family learns that Babette has been taking a privately produced drug, dylar, designed to overcome the fear of death. Once apprised of this, Gladney sets out to kill Babette's supplier, with whom she has been engaging in sexual encounters in return for being an experimental subject for the drug (in a TV-dominated motel room). In effect, Gladney's preoccupation with killing as a way of coping with the fear of death (represented with his Hitler obsession) comes close to actualization, although he fails both to kill the dylar man, Mr. Gray, and ultimately to push away the fear of death.

In the end, DeLillo has shown the inefficacy of all "fear-of-death inhibitors,"[26] and one character, Winnie Richards, expresses the need to incorporate fear of death into life:

> I think it's a mistake to lose one's sense of death, even one's fear of death. Isn't death the boundary

we need? Doesn't it give a precious texture to life, a sense of definition? You have to ask yourself whether anything you do in this life would have beauty and meaning without the knowledge that you carry of a final line, a border or limit.[27]

And, in the same dialogue, DeLillo expresses the importance of preserving an epistemology of fear with imagery that recalls vividly the Eskimo shaman scenario developed above. Speaking of her "spacey theory about human fear," Winnie says to Gladney, as she draws him imaginatively out of his home/burrow:

> Picture yourself, Jack, a confirmed homebody, a sedentary fellow who finds himself walking in a deep wood. You spot something out of the corner of your eye. Before you know anything else, you know that this thing is very large and that it has no place in your ordinary frame of reference, a flaw in the world picture. Either it shouldn't be here or you shouldn't. Now the thing comes into full view. It is a grizzly bear, enormous, shiny brown, dripping with slime from its bared fangs. Jack, you have never seen a large animal in the wild. The sight of this grizzer is so electrifyingly strange that it gives you a renewed sense of yourself, a fresh awareness of the self—the self in terms of a unique, horrific situation. You see yourself in a new and intense way. You rediscover yourself. You are lit up for your own imminent dismemberment. The beast on hind legs has enabled you to see who you are as if for the first time, outside familiar surroundings, alone, distinct, whole. The name we give to this complicated process is fear.[28]

This is the most important insight at which *White Noise* arrives. But *White Noise* is a novel, not a treatise on the importance of fear, and the structure of the novel, its narrative journey, its rhetorical motions, the grammars of its characters, deploy modernity's repressive politics of fear. They map the various mediating structures whose authority ("codes") inhibit both individual recognition of the place of death in identity formation and the development of public, discursive modes for problematizing danger in a way that allows people to connect everyday experience to vital questions. It is these inhibiting structures, then, that DeLillo's textual practices as well as his thematics bring into recognition.

With his style as well as with his character's remarks, DeLillo elaborates the mediating linguistic systems that drown out significant connection between danger and efficacious forms of apprehension. All that unfocused fear can discern is the noise of linguistic evasions. At one point, Babette, in the grip of fear, wonders if death is merely that estranging linguistic mediation.

"What if death is nothing but sound?"

"Electrical noise."

"You hear it forever. Sound all around. How awful."

"Uniform, white."[29]

And DeLillo proliferates the white noise with his writing. The main narrators are often interrupted, just as we expect coherence, by emissions from the postindustrial, consumer culture. One chapter's action ends with, "A woman passing on the street said, 'A decongestant, an antihistamine, a cough suppressant, a pain reliever,'" and another with the word, "Panasonic."

While DeLillo's subjectivities, in the form of linguistic fragments, reproduce the noise that drowns out self-awareness or the ability of those in modernity to locate the sources of production of the modern self, his rhetoric conveys the displacements with which the self is shielded from significant problematics connecting death and danger to life. For example, he employs a metaphor of physical bulk to show how Gladney is caught in ineffective surmises about how to ward off death. Gladney's preoccupation with Hitler is decoded by Murray, who says, "Some people are larger than life. Hitler is larger than death. You thought he would protect you. I understand completely."[30] This interpretation makes coherent the size imagery DeLillo introduces near the beginning where we learn that Gladney is comforted by his bulk; he is carrying 230 pounds on a six-foot, three-inch frame and has big hands and feet.[31] And later, Gladney is amazed that his very large colleague, Cotsakis, described as a "monolith of thick and wadded flesh,"[32] could be dead (from drowning). Gladney is incredulous and questions Murray about the death: "Poor Cotsakis, lost in the surf . . . that enormous man. . . . Dead. A big man like that . . . to be so enormous, then to die."[33]

It is also the overall structure of DeLillo's narrative that contributes to his mapping of modernity's fear and sense of death inhibitors. The story in *White Noise* is in the shape of a loop, in that it begins and ends representing quotidian family existence in the midst of the commodified, consumer culture, its characters suspended in a commercial zone saturated with consumer messages. On the very first page, as the students arrive at College-on-the-Hill, DeLillo describes the objects inside the caravan of station wagons carrying parents and students.

> As the cars slowed to a crawl and stopped, students sprang out and raced to the rear doors to begin removing the objects inside; the stereo sets, radios, personal computers; small refrigerators and table ranges; the cartons of phonograph records and cassettes; the hair dryers and styling irons; the tennis rackets, soccer balls, hockey and lacrosse sticks, bows and arrows; the controlled substances; the birth control pills and devices; the junk food still in shopping bags—onion-and-garlic chips, nacho thins, peanut cream patties, Waffelos and Kabooms, fruit chews and toffee popcorn; the Dum-Dum pops, the Mystic mints.[34]

After the narrative journey from domesticity to calamity and rash actions, the story is drawn back to the mundane venues of family life. At the very end, people are in a supermarket with a slightly altered relation to products. They are more anxious as a result of the "airborne toxic event," but their fear is not directed at environmental, life-threatening dangers; they are simply slightly less able to negotiate movement through the aisles, and their buying behavior is somewhat disoriented and suspicious.

> They turn into the wrong aisle, peer along shelves, sometimes stop abruptly, causing other carts to run into them. . . . They scrutinize the small print on packages, wary of a second level of betrayal. The men scan for stamped dates, the women for ingredients.[35]

With his narrative, DeLillo has informed us about the powerful delegating effects of modern, commercial/consumer-oriented space. Although the residents of the town have been forced out of their domestic routines by an event that should alter their relationships to themselves and life in general, they are summoned back into their old shopping haunts, and the new unease they experience remains quarantined within their relationship to consumer products.[36]

In addition to the connection with products, which absorbs much of the ideational energy of his characters, DeLillo, with his writing as well as with his thematics, presents the mediating and productive effects of television on what, for the modern person, is the "real," and, more important, what is to be feared. The TV is his window in the postmodern burrow, bringing near dangers and generating fears as well as desires. As Gladney puts it:

> Blacksmith is nowhere near a large city. We don't feel threatened in quite the same way as other towns do. We're not smack in the path of history and its contaminations. If our complaints have a focal point, it would have to be the TV set, where the outer torment lurks, causing fear and secret desires.[37]

DeLillo represents the TV role by giving it a voice throughout the novel. The narrator is often interrupted by the TV, and, at the level of thematics, DeLillo has identified here a radical entanglement between TV as informational technology and the modern constitution of danger. For example, much of the anxiety that characters in *White Noise* manifest is connected to TV weather forecasts. In a sequence about shoppers crowding the roads to avoid being out later when snow is forecast, Gladney narrates:

> Older people in particular were susceptible to news of impending calamity as it was forecast on TV by grave men standing before digital radar maps or pulsing photographs of the planet.[38]

DeLillo expresses this about TV weather with an ironic reversal. Earlier, we learn that Gladney's German teacher—tutoring Gladney who knows no German and must lead an upcoming conference on Hitler studies—is fascinated by meteorology. As a German teacher who also teaches meteorology, his strategy is to approach danger and death rather than to simply fear them. When asked how his interest in meteorology came about, he responds, "My mother's death had a terrible impact on me," and then he adds that after seeing a weather report on TV, "I turned to meteorology for comfort."[39]

DeLillo is attuned here to an important aspect of the popular culture of fear and its relationship to media. Recently, Andrew Ross has pointed out that there have been large-scale cultural transformations in weather forecasting. For example, the old "weather folklore," which was based on an "everyday cult of 'experience,'" has been replaced by a "professional ethos of 'expertise,'" and that expertise, produced on TV weather forecasts, has turned increasingly toward a representation of global dangers. The modern weather report, Ross says, is danger-oriented, albeit in a displaced, commodified sense; it represents "the almost complete commodification of bodily maintenance in the face of year-round weather threats and assaults."[40]

The inhibiting effects of TV on locating danger and death, however, is the major role it plays in *White Noise*. Mr. Gray, the inventor of the death-fear inhibitor, dylar, is represented as one who speaks with a TV-like babble and is encountered in a motel room dominated by a TV, and the "airborne toxic event" is presented on TV with various fear-deflecting modes of representation, for example, "They're calling it a black billowing cloud"[41] (after having called it an "airborne toxic event"). This gap between the danger and its representation is also reflected in Gladney's conversation with a technician running a "simuvac" machine, which is another piece of forecasting technology designed to predict his life expectancy after his exposure to the toxicity.

"Am I going to die?" he asks the technician. "Not as such," is the response. "What do you mean?" asks Gladney. "Not in so many words," comes the response. "How many words does it take?" asks Gladney. The technician again: "It's not a question of words; it's a question of years. We'll know more in fifteen years. In the meantime we definitely have a situation."[42]

It is not surprising that in a modern culture with death-distancing representational practices, one cannot effect an epistemology of fear. Recognizing this, DeLillo dwells from time to time on the issue of epistemologies of belief and their inefficacy in our postmodern, anxiety-ridden burrow. We rely not on experience but "data," Gladney says. "Terrifying data is now an industry in itself."[43] "Knowledge," DeLillo recognizes, is temporarily reassuring but largely ineffective, and modern people are simply consumers of representations of danger—especially now, says Babette, who explains why her pedagogy extends to teaching a course on "Eating and Drinking: Basic Parameters":

> Knowledge changes every day. People like to have their beliefs reinforced. Don't lie down after eating a heavy meal. Don't drink liquor on an empty stomach. If you must swim, wait at least an hour after eating. The world is more complicated for adults than it is for children. We didn't grow up with all these shifting facts and attitudes. One day they just started appearing. So people need to be reassured by someone in a position of authority that a certain way to do something is the right way or the wrong way, at least for the time being. I'm the closest they could find, that's all.[44]

CONCLUSION

If this were a treatise that lived up to Jürgen Habermas's demand for a way to theorize the present, it would be appropriate to conclude by explicitly recognizing "the necessity of gleaning normatively substantive principles from modern experience."[45] But whatever normative force this chapter has is immanent in its style, particularly its juxtapositions of themes and thinkers, and the politics of fear I have attempted to present is not connected to the failure of the modern state to steer society in ways that retain a rational basis for policy deliberation (to paraphrase the Habermasian, somewhat state-centric problematic).

My aim has been, rather, to create a frame within which certain thinkers, through their textual practices as much as through their thematics, help us to think themes that are rarely accessible because of modernity's modes of problematizing and often obscuring danger and death. Moreover, my concern is with the recovery of *politics,* not rational steering mechanisms, where politics is understood as a recognition that we are always involved in a struggle to, as Paul Virilio has put it, "extract life from death."[46] And "life" is seen not simply as a matter of duration and "policy," thereby a matter of protection— for the "burrow" is as much a prison as it is a shelter— but an intense encounter with death; it is a living with danger rather than merely a consuming of frightening data. *White Noise* ends with neither a hopeful sign nor a lament but with Gladney in line at the supermarket, scanning the tabloid versions of the fear industry.

> Everything we need that is not food or love is here in the tabloid racks. The tales of the supernatural and the extraterrestrial, the miracle vitamins, the cures for cancer, the remedies for obesity, the cults of the famous and the dead.[47]

To end in DeLillo's spirit, then, we can look around with his kind of discernment. For example, recently there was a report of a new fear in the *Wall Street Journal.* The story begins:

> If anything can make '80s-style strivers take action, it's fear. Afraid of flab, they join health clubs. Afraid of being lonely, they deluge magazines with personal ads.
>
> Now there's a new fear making the rounds—the fear of forgetfulness.[48]

It is Alzheimer's that people often suspect is implicated in their memory lapses, and although "very few middle-aged worriers are actually suffering from troubles so serious" (doctors call such lapses "age-associated memory impairment"), there is a small industry developing to supply products for the worriers. As the writer puts it, "where there is fear, there are people trying to capitalize on taming that fear," and she goes on to elaborate the growing industry in adult education courses, memory-training manuals, cassette tapes, and the like.

A Harvard doctor sums up the aim of the product seekers:

> They want to eat a certain kind of food, do a certain kind of exercise to prevent mortality. . . . But the average life expectancy is still three score plus 10, which is what's written in the Bible.[49]

NOTES

[1] Franz Kafka, "The Burrow," trans. Willa and Edwin Muir, in *The Complete Stories, ed. Nahum N. Glatzer (New York: Schocken, 1971),* p. 325.

[2] Ibid., p. 357.

[3] Manuel Puig, *Betrayed by Rita Hayworth,* trans. Suzanne Jill Levine (New York: Dutton, 1971).

[4] The expression comes from a review of DeLillo's *White Noise.* See Pico Iyer, "A Connoisseur of Fear," *Partisan Review* 53 (1986), pp. 292-97.

[5] Michel Foucault, *The History of Sexuality,* trans. Robert Hurley (New York: Pantheon, 1978), p. 25.

[6] Barry Lopez, *Arctic Dreams: Desire and Imagination in a Northern Landscape* (New York: Scribners, 1986), p. 201.

[7] This particular formulation of the Foucauldian question is suggested in James W. Bernauer, "Michel Foucault's Ecstatic Thinking," in *The Final Foucault,* ed. James Bernauer and David Rasmussen (Cambridge: MIT Press, 1988), p. 46.

[8] Don DeLillo, *White Noise* (New York: Viking-Penguin, 1985), p. 162.

[9] Nevil Shute, *On The Beach* (New York: Morrow, 1957).

[10] Don DeLillo, "American Blood: A Journey through the Labyrinth of Dallas and JFK," *Rolling Stone,* December 8, 1983, p. 27.

[11] Fredric Jameson, "The Politics of Theory: Ideological Positions in the Postmodernist Debate," *New German Critique,* no. 33 (Fall 1984), p. 53.

[12] DeLillo, "American Blood," p. 27.

[13] Don DeLillo, *Running Dog* (New York: Vintage, 1978), p. 93.

[14] DeLillo, *White Noise,* pp. 294-95.

[15] For a detailed exegesis of DeLillo's fiction based on systems theory and the general argument that DeLillo's writing attacks closed systems, see Tom LeClair's extensive study, *In the Loop: Don DeLillo and the Systems Novel* (Urbana: University of Illinois Press, 1987).

[16] Tom LeClair, "An Interview with Don DeLillo," in *Anything Can Happen: Interviews with Contemporary American Novelists,* ed. Tom LeClair and Larry McCaffery (Urbana: University of Illinois Press, 1983), p. 83.

[17] Ibid., p. 81.

[18] Bruce Bawer, "Don DeLillo's America," *New Criterion* 3 (April 1985), p. 37.

[19] Don DeLillo, *Players* (New York: Vintage, 1984), p. 104.

[20] Ibid., p. 110.

[21] DeLillo, *White Noise,* p. 143.

[22] Ibid., p. 26.

[23] Ibid., p. 27.

[24] Ibid., p. 51.

[25] Ibid., p. 52.

[26] Ibid., p. 228.

[27] Ibid., pp. 228-29.

[28] Ibid.

[29] Ibid., p. 198.

[30] Ibid., p. 287.

[31] Ibid., p. 32.

[32] Ibid., p. 69.

[33] Ibid., p. 168.

[34] Ibid., p. 3.

[35] Ibid., p. 326.

[36] The idea that narrations or stories exemplify spatial practices is developed by Michel de Certeau. See "Spatial Stories," chapter 9 in *The Practice of Everyday Life,* trans. Steven F. Rendell (Berkeley: University of California Press, 1984), pp. 115-30.

[37] DeLillo, *White Noise,* p. 85.

[38] Ibid., p. 167.

[39] Ibid., p. 55.

[40] Andrew Ross, "The Work of Nature in the Age of Electronic Emission," *Social Text,* Winter/Spring 1987/88, p. 120.

[41] DeLillo, *White Noise,* p. 115.

[42] Ibid., p. 140.

[43] Ibid., p. 319.

[44] Ibid., pp. 171-72.

[45] Jürgen Habermas, "The New Obscurity: The Crisis of the Welfare State and the Exhaustion of Utopian Energies," trans. Phillip Jacobs, *Philosophy and Social Criticism* 11 (Winter 1986), p. 1.

[46] Paul Virilio and Sylvere Lotringer, *Pure War,* trans. Mark Polizotti (New York: Semiotext[e], 1983), p. 139.

[47] DeLillo, *White Noise,* p. 326.

[48] Pamela Sebastian, "As Baby Boomers Age, Many Become Forgetful—and Often Assume the Worst," *Wall Street Journal,* June 22, 1988, sec. 2, p. 27.

[49] Ibid.

FURTHER READING

Butts, Richard. "The Analogical Mere: Landscape and Terror in *Beowulf.*" *English Studies* 68, No. 2 (April 1987): 113-21.
>   Maintains that Hrothgar's description of Grendel's mere in *Beowulf* is "an extended metaphor for terror" rather than a realistic evocation of landscape.

Cixous, Hélène. "Fiction and Its Phantoms: A Reading of Freud's *Das Unheimliche* ("The 'Uncanny')." *New Literary History* VII, No. 3 (Spring 1976): 525-48.
>   Contends that Sigmund Freud's essay *Das Unheimliche* functions as a work of fiction with Freud as its hesitant narrator.

Freud, Sigmund. "The 'Uncanny.'" *New Literary History* VII, No. 3 (Spring 1976): 619-45.
>   Translated reprint of Freud's *Das Unheimliche,* a study of fear and anxiety as it manifests itself in psychology and in literature.

Grimes, Larry. "Night Terror and Morning Calm: A Reading of Hemingway's 'Indian Camp' as Sequel to 'Three Shots.'" *Studies in Short Fiction* XII, No. 4 (Fall 1975): 413-15.
>   Interpretation of two Ernest Hemingway short stories in sequence that emphasizes a child's fear of, and confrontation with, death.

Heller, Terry. *The Delights of Terror: An Aesthetics of the Tale of Terror.* Urbana: University of Illinois Press, 1987, 218 p.
>   Survey of the workings of terror in literature that offers analyses of Edgar Allan Poe's short stories, Bram Stoker's *Dracula,* and other works of horror fiction.

Jaeger, C. Stephen. "The Barons' Intrigue in Gottfried's *Tristan*: Notes Toward a Sociology of Fear in Court Society." *Journal of English and Germanic Philology* LXXXIII, No. 1 (January 1984): 46-66.

> Studies the sociological implications of Gottfried's use of fear—an ignoble emotion by the standards of courtly romance—as motivation for his hero in *Tristan*.

Linkfield, Thomas P. "The Evil in Michigan's Northern Forests." *Midwestern Miscellany* 11 (1983): 40-48.

> Distinguishes between terror and horror—the latter implying a supernatural element lacking in the former—using the examples of David Osborn's *Open Season* and Robert C. Wilson's *Crooked Tree*.

Tropp, Martin. *Images of Fear: How Horror Stories Helped Shape Modern Culture (1818-1918)*. Jefferson, N. C.: McFarland & Company, 1990, 235 p.

> Examines the effects that five well-known works of Victorian fiction—Mary Shelley's *Frankenstein*, Robert Louis Stevenson's *Dr. Jekyll and Mr. Hyde*, Bram Stoker's *Dracula*, Jane Austen's *Northanger Abbey*, and Charles Dickens's *Bleak House*—have had on the modern consciousness.

Vanderbilt, Kermit and Daniel Weiss. "From Rifleman to Flagbearer: Henry Fleming's Separate Peace in *The Red Badge of Courage*." *Modern Fiction Studies* XI, No. 4 (Winter 1965-66): 371-80.

> Argues that, in realizing its aim to present "a psychological portrayal of fear," Stephen Crane's *The Red Badge of Courage* achieves "structural and psychological unity."

Imagism

INTRODUCTION

Imagism was a short-lived but influential movement in English and American poetry that flourished during the years 1912 to 1917. Self-consciously modernist in their aesthetic outlook, the Imagists sought to dislodge the diction, sentimentality, moralizing tone, and conventional forms of Victorian poetry, and instead to concentrate on the precise rendering of images in free verse. Influenced by the ideas of the poet and philosopher T. E. Hulme, Ezra Pound and F. S. Flint first documented the theory of Imagism in London early in the second decade of the twentieth century. Their ideals for the new movement appeared in Flint's "Imagisme," printed in the periodical *Poetry* in March of 1913, which became the manifesto of the fledgling group. Together Flint and Pound devised the three primary precepts of Imagism, calling for conciseness, musical rhythm, and "the direct treatment of the 'thing' whether subjective or objective." These theories were soon after put into practice in the first Imagist anthology, edited by Pound and entitled *Des Imagistes* (1914). The collection featured poems by Pound, Richard Aldington, and H.D. (Hilda Doolittle)—all members of the coterie—as well as verse by several young poets whose writing bore affinities to that of the Imagists, including Amy Lowell, John Gould Fletcher, James Joyce, and William Carlos Williams.

Tensions led to Pound's break with the Imagists less than a year after the publication of *Des Imagistes* to form a related movement called Vorticism. Meanwhile, the American Amy Lowell had arrived in England and become the group's de facto head after Pound's departure. She successfully endeavored to bring more poets into the fold—including D. H. Lawrence—and to popularize Imagism across the Atlantic. Each year between 1915 and 1917 Lowell edited a volume of the anthology *Some Imagist Poets*. After a period of considerable interest, the Imagist movement, as such, had run its course by 1917. Many members of the group, however, continued to write in accordance with Imagist precepts. A final *Imagist Anthology*, edited by Aldington, appeared in 1930, and despite its tardiness attests to certain enduring qualities among the writings of these early modernists. In the ensuing decades, critics have attempted to assess the overall impact of the Imagists and see in their typically spare poems a prefiguring of the high modernist verse of T. S. Eliot's *The Waste Land* and Pound's *Cantos*, as well as an influence on the poetry of William Carlos Williams, Wallace Stevens, Marianne Moore, E. E. Cummings, and others.

REPRESENTATIVE WORKS

Richard Aldington
Images (poetry) 1915
Images of Desire (poetry) 1919
Images of War (poetry) 1919
War and Love (poetry) 1919
Exile, and Other Poems (poetry) 1923
A Fool i' the Forest (poetry) 1925
The Love of Myrrhine and Konallis, followed by Nineteen Prose Poems (poetry) 1926
Collected Poems (poetry) 1928
The Eaten Heart (poetry) 1929
A Dream in the Luxembourg [also published as *Love and the Luxembourg*] (poetry) 1930

H. D.
Sea Garden (poetry) 1916
Hymen (poetry) 1921
Helidora, and Other Poems (poetry) 1924
Collected Poems (poetry) 1925
Hippolytus Temporizes (drama) 1927

John Gould Fletcher
The Book of Nature (poetry) 1913
The Dominant City (poetry) 1913
Fire and Wine (poetry) 1913
Fool's Gold (poetry) 1913
Visions of the Evening (poetry) 1913
Irradiations—Sand and Spray (poetry) 1915
Goblins and Pagodas (poetry) 1916
Japanese Prints (poetry) 1918
The Tree of Life (poetry) 1918
Breakers and Granite (poetry) 1921
Preludes and Symphonies (poetry) 1922
Parables (poetry) 1925
Branches of Adam (poetry) 1926
The Black Rock (poetry) 1928

F. S. Flint
In the Net of the Stars (poetry) 1909
Cadences (poetry) 1915
Otherworld: Cadences (poetry) 1920

D. H. Lawrence
Love Poems, and Others (poetry) 1913
Amores (poetry) 1916
Look! We Have Come Through! (poetry) 1917
New Poems (poetry) 1918
Bay: A Book of Poems (poetry) 1919
Tortoises (poetry) 1921
Birds, Beasts, and Flowers (poetry) 1923
Collected Poems (poetry) 1928

Pansies (poetry) 1929
Nettles (poetry) 1930

Amy Lowell
    A Dome of Many-Coloured Glass (poetry) 1912
    Sword Blades and Poppy Seed (poetry) 1914
    Some Imagist Poets [editor] (poetry) 1915
    Men, Women, and Ghosts (poetry) 1916
    Some Imagist Poets, 1916 [editor] (poetry) 1916
    Some Imagist Poets, 1917 [editor] (poetry) 1917
    Can Grande's Castle (poetry) 1918
    Pictures of the Floating World (poetry) 1919
    Legends (poetry) 1921
    What's O'Clock? (poetry) 1925
    East Wind (poetry) 1926
    Ballads for Sale (poetry) 1927
    Selected Poems (poetry) 1928

Ezra Pound
    A Lume Spento (poetry) 1908
    A Quinzaine for This Yule (poetry) 1908
    Exultations (poetry) 1909
    Personæ (poetry) 1909
    Provença (poetry) 1910
    Canzoni (poetry) 1911
    Ripostes (poetry) 1912
    Des Imagistes: An Anthology [editor] (poetry) 1914
    Lustra (poetry) 1916
    Quia Pauper Amavi (poetry) 1919
    Umbra: The Early Poems of Ezra Pound (poetry) 1920
    Poems 1918-21 (poetry) 1921
    A Draft of XVI Cantos of Ezra Pound for the Beginning of a Poem of Some Length (poetry) 1925
    Personæ: The Collected Poems of Ezra Pound (poetry) 1926
    A Draft of the Cantos XVII to XXVII of Ezra Pound (poetry) 1928
    Selected Poems of Ezra Pound (poetry) 1928

HISTORY AND DEVELOPMENT

Richard Aldington and Amy Lowell

[*In the following essay, Aldington and Lowell outline the central tenets of Imagism.*]

SOURCE: Preface to *Some Imagist Poets, 1915: An Anthology,* Houghton Mifflin Company, 1915, pp. v-viii.

In March, 1914, a volume appeared entitled *Des Imagistes.* It was a collection of the work of various young poets, presented together as a school. This school has been widely discussed by those interested in new movements in the arts, and has already become a household word. Differences of taste and judgment, however, have arisen among the contributors to that book; growing tendencies are forcing them along different paths. Those of us whose work appears in this volume have therefore decided to publish our collection under a new title, and we have been joined by two or three poets who did not contribute to the first volume, our wider scope making this possible.

In this new book we have followed a slightly different arrangement to that of the former Anthology. Instead of an arbitrary selection by an editor, each poet has been permitted to represent himself by the work he considers his best, the only stipulation being that it should not yet have appeared in book form. A sort of informal committee—consisting of more than half the authors here represented—have arranged the book and decided what should be printed and what omitted, but, as a general rule, the poets have been allowed absolute freedom in this direction, limitations of space only being imposed upon them. Also, to avoid any appearance of precedence, they have been put in alphabetical order.

As it has been suggested that much of the misunderstanding of the former volume was due to the fact that we did not explain ourselves in a preface, we have thought it wise to tell the public what our aims are, and why we are banded together between one set of covers.

The poets in this volume do not represent a clique. Several of them are personally unknown to the others, but they are united by certain common principles, arrived at independently. These principles are not new; they have fallen into desuetude. They are the essentials of all great poetry, indeed of all great literature, and they are simply these:—

1. To use the language of common speech, but to employ always the *exact* word, not the nearly-exact, nor the merely decorative word.

2. To create new rhythms—as the expression of new moods—and not to copy old rhythms, which merely echo old moods. We do not insist upon "free-verse" as the only method of writing poetry. We fight for it as for a principle of liberty. We believe that the individuality of a poet may often be better expressed in free-verse than in conventional forms. In poetry, a new cadence means a new idea.

3. To allow absolute freedom in the choice of subject. It is not good art to write badly about aeroplanes and automobiles; nor is it necessarily bad art to write well about the past. We believe passionately in the artistic value of modern life, but we wish to point out that there is nothing so uninspiring nor so old-fashioned as an aeroplane of the year 1911.

4. To present an image (hence the name: "Imagist"). We are not a school of painters, but we believe that poetry should render particulars exactly and not deal in vague generalities, however magnificent and sonorous. It is for this reason that we oppose the cosmic poet, who seems to us to shirk the real difficulties of his art.

5. To produce poetry that is hard and clear, never blurred nor indefinite.

6. Finally, most of us believe that concentration is of the very essence of poetry.

The subject of free-verse is too complicated to be discussed here. We may say briefly, that we attach the term to all that increasing amount of writing whose cadence is more marked, more definite, and closer knit than that of prose, but which is not so violently nor so obviously accented as the so-called "regular verse." We refer those interested in the question to the Greek Melic poets, and to the many excellent French studies on the subject by such distinguished and well-equipped authors as Remy de Gourmont, Gustave Kahn, Georges Duhamel, Charles Vildrac, Henri Ghéon, Robert de Souza, André Spire, etc.

We wish it to be clearly understood that we do not represent an exclusive artistic sect; we publish our work together because of mutual artistic sympathy, and we propose to bring out our coöperative volume each year for a short term of years, until we have made a place for ourselves and our principles such as we desire.

Amy Lowell

[In the following essay, Lowell identifies Imagism as a descendant of French Symbolism and clarifies the aims of Imagist poetry.]

SOURCE: Preface to *Some Imagist Poets, 1916: An Annual Anthology,* Houghton Mifflin Company, 1916, pp. v-xii.

In bringing the second volume of *Some Imagist Poets* before the public, the authors wish to express their gratitude for the interest which the 1915 volume aroused. The discussion of it was widespread, and even those critics out of sympathy with Imagist tenets accorded it much space. In the Preface to that book, we endeavoured to present those tenets in a succinct form. But the very brevity we employed has lead to a great deal of misunderstanding. We have decided, therefore, to explain the laws which govern us a little more fully. A few people may understand, and the rest can merely misunderstand again, a result to which we are quite accustomed.

In the first place "Imagism" does not mean merely the presentation of pictures. "Imagism" refers to the manner of representation, not to the subject. It means a clear presentation of whatever the author wishes to convey. Now he may wish to convey a mood of indecision, in which case the poem should be indecisive; he may wish to bring before his reader the constantly shifting and changing lights over a landscape, or the varying attitudes of mind of a person under strong emotion, then his poem must shift and change to present this clearly. The "exact" word does not mean the word which exactly describes the object in itself, it means the "exact" word which brings the effect of that object before the reader as it presented itself to the poet's mind at the time of writing the poem. Imagists deal but little with similes, although much of

their poetry is metaphorical. The reason for this is that while acknowledging the figure to be an integral part of all poetry, they feel that the constant imposing of one figure upon another in the same poem blurs the central effect.

The great French critic, Remy de Gourmont, wrote last Summer in *La France* that the Imagists were the descendants of the French *Symbolistes.* In the Preface to his *Livre des Masques,* M. de Gourmont has thus described *Symbolisme:* "Individualism in literature, liberty of art, abandonment of existing forms . . . The sole excuse which a man can have for writing is to write down himself, to unveil for others the sort of world which mirrors itself in his individual glass . . . He should create his own aesthetics—and we should admit as many aesthetics as there are original minds, and judge them for what they are and not what they are not." In this sense the Imagists are descendants of the *Symbolistes;* they are Individualists.

The only reason that Imagism has seemed so anarchaic and strange to English and American reviewers is that their minds do not easily and quickly suggest the steps by which modern art has arrived at its present position. Its immediate prototype cannot be found in English or American literature, we must turn to Europe for it. With Debussy and Stravinsky in music, and Gauguin and Matisse in painting, it should have been evident to every one that art was entering upon an era of change. But music and painting are universal languages, so we have become accustomed to new idioms in them, while we still find it hard to recognize a changed idiom in literature.

The crux of the situation is just here. It is in the idiom employed. Imagism asks to be judged by different standards from those employed in Nineteenth-Century art. It is small wonder that Imagist poetry should be incomprehensible to men whose sole touchstone for art is the literature of one country for a period of four centuries. And it is an illuminating fact that among poets and men conversant with many poetic idioms, Imagism is rarely misconceived. They may not agree with us, but they do not misunderstand us.

This must not be misconstrued into the desire to belittle our forerunners. On the contrary, the Imagists have the greatest admiration for the past, and humility towards it. But they have been caught in the throes of a new birth. The exterior world is changing, and with it men's feelings, and every age must express its feelings in its own individual way. No art is any more "egoistic" than another; all art is an attempt to express the feelings of the artist, whether it be couched in narrative form or employ a more personal expression.

It is not what Imagists write about which makes them hard of comprehension; it is the way they write it. All nations have laws of prosody, which undergo changes from time to time. The laws of English metrical prosody are well known to every one concerned with the subject. But that is only one form of prosody. Other nations have had different ones: Anglo-Saxon poetry was founded upon alliteration, Greek and Roman was built upon quantity, the Oriental was formed out of repetition, and the Japanese Hokku got its effects by an exact and never-to-be-added-to series of single syllables. So it is evident that poetry can be written in many modes. That the Imagists base much of their poetry upon cadence and not upon metre makes them neither good nor bad. And no one realizes more than they that no theories nor rules make poetry. They claim for their work only that it is sincere.

It is this very fact of "cadence" which has misled so many reviewers, until some have been betrayed into saying that the Imagists discard rhythm, when rhythm is the most important quality in their technique. The definition of *vers libre* is—a verse-form based upon cadence. Now cadence in music is one thing, cadence in poetry quite another, since we are not dealing with tone but with rhythm. It is the sense of perfect balance of flow and rhythm. Not only must the syllables so fall as to increase and continue the movement, but the whole poem must be as rounded and recurring as the circular swing of a balanced pendulum. It can be fast or slow, it may even jerk, but this perfect swing it must have, even its jerks must follow the central movement. To illustrate: Suppose a person were given the task of walking, or running, round a large circle, with two minutes given to do it in. Two minutes which he would just consume if he walked round the circle quietly. But in order to make the task easier for him, or harder, as the case might be, he was required to complete each half of the circle in exactly a minute. No other restrictions were placed upon him. He might dawdle in the beginning, and run madly to reach the half-circle mark on time, and then complete his task by walking steadily round the second half to goal. Or he might leap, and run, and skip, and linger in all sorts of ways, making up for slow going by fast, and for extra haste by pauses, and varying these movements on either lap of the circle as the humour seized him, only so that he were just one minute in traversing the first half-circle, and just one minute in traversing the second. Another illustration which may be employed is that of a Japanese wood-carving where a toad in one corner is balanced by a spray of blown flowers in the opposite upper one. The flowers are not the same shape as the toad, neither are they the same size, but the balance is preserved.

The unit in *vers libre* is not the foot, the number of the syllables, the quantity, or the line. The unit is the strophe, which may be the whole poem, or may be only a part. Each strophe is a complete circle: in fact, the meaning of the Greek word "strophe" is simply that part of the poem which was recited while the chorus were making a turn round the altar set up in the centre of the theatre. The simile of the circle is more than a simile, therefore; it is a fact. Of course the circle need not always be the same size, nor need the times allowed to negotiate it be always the same. There is room here for an infinite number of variations. Also, circles can be added to circles, movement upon move-

ment, to the poem, provided each movement completes itself, and ramifies naturally into the next. But one thing must be borne in mind: a cadenced poem is written to be read aloud, in this way only will its rhythm be felt. Poetry is a spoken and not a written art.

The *vers libristes* are often accused of declaring that they have discovered a new thing. Where such an idea started, it is impossible to say, certainly none of the better *vers libristes* was ever guilty of so ridiculous a statement. The name *vers libre* is new, the thing, most emphatically, is not. Not new in English poetry, at any rate. You will find something very much like it in Dryden's *Threnodia Augustalis;* a great deal of Milton's *Samson Agonistes* is written in it; and Matthew Arnold's *Philomela* is a shining example of it. Practically all of Henley's *London Voluntaries* are written in it, and (so potent are names) until it was christened *vers libre,* no one thought of objecting to it. But the oldest reference to *vers libre* is to be found in Chaucer's *House of Fame,* where the Eagle addresses the Poet in these words:

> And nevertheless hast set thy wyt
> Although that in thy heed full lyte is
> To make bookes, songes, or dytees
> In rhyme or elles in cadence.

Commentators have wasted reams of paper in an endeavour to determine what Chaucer meant by this. But is it not possible that he meant a verse based upon rhythm, but which did not follow the strict metrical prosody of his usual practice?

One of the charges frequently brought against the Imagists is that they write, not poetry, but "shredded prose." This misconception springs from the almost complete ignorance of the public in regard to the laws of cadenced verse. But, in fact, what is prose and what is poetry? Is it merely a matter of typographical arrangement? Must everything which is printed in equal lines, with rhymes at the ends, be called poetry, and everything which is printed in a block be called prose? Aristotle, who certainly knew more about this subject than any one else, declares in his *Rhetoric* that prose is rhythmical without being metrical (that is to say, without insistence on any single rhythm), and then goes on to state the feet that are employed in prose, making, incidentally, the remark that the iambic prevailed in ordinary conversation. The fact is, that there is no hard and fast dividing line between prose and poetry. As a French poet of distinction, Paul Fort, has said: "Prose and poetry are but one instrument, graduated." It is not a question of typography; it is not even a question of rules and forms. Poetry is the vision in a man's soul which he translates as best he can with the means at his disposal.

We are young, we are experimentalists, but we ask to be judged by our own standards, not by those which have governed other men at other times.

P. E. Firchow

[In the following essay, Firchow locates the poetics of Imagism as advanced by Ezra Pound within the classical tradition in poetry.]

SOURCE: "Ezra Pound's Imagism and the Tradition," in *Comparative Literature Studies,* XVIII, September, 1981, pp. 379-85.

> Only from about the year 1926 did the features of the post-war world begin clearly to emerge—and not only in the sphere of politics. From about that date one began slowly to realize that the intellectual and artistic output of the previous seven years had been rather the last efforts of an old world, than the struggles of a new."
>
> —T. S. Eliot, "Last Words" (1939)

> In some ways, I can think of no one whom he resembled more than Irving Babbitt—a comparison neither man would have relished. Perhaps the backgrounds were not unlike; perhaps if Pound had stopped at home, and become, as he might have become, a professor of comparative literature, the resemblance might have been closer still.
>
> —T. S. Eliot, "Ezra Pound" (1946)

Of all major English or American poets of the early decades of this century, Ezra Pound is the one who most closely approximates the conventional model of the "revolutionary" avant-garde poet—a poet like Apollinaire, for instance, or Marinetti or Vicente Huidobro. Pound's urgent appeal to his contemporaries to "make it new" has a definite and by no means accidentally futurist ring about it, as does his continual denigration of those who fail to keep up with the times, especially Americans. Of his alter-ego, Hugh Selwyn Mauberley, he writes that "he had been born/In a half-savage country, out of date;" and in the same poem he denounces as "an old bitch gone in the teeth" the civilization which has sent a myriad of its best citizens to their deaths in Flanders fields "for two gross of broken statues,/For a few thousand battered books."[1] As the literary histories never tire of telling us, it was Ezra Pound who transformed Yeats into a modern poet and who assisted substantially (despite his own disavowal) in a similar transformation of T. S. Eliot. He made them, as it were, "new."

It would seem reasonable to conclude from all this that Pound had little sympathy for the preservation of honored traditions or for the veneration of great literary monuments of the past. This is reasonable certainly, but it is also dead wrong. For with Pound the making of the new always consists of a remaking of the old. He remakes or modernizes, for instance, not merely Yeats the poet of the nineties—or describes the remaking of himself in "Hugh Selwyn Mauberley"—but he also remakes Sextus Propertius, along with a "myriad" of Provençal, Greek, Italian, Chinese and Anglo-Saxon poets. History for Pound is never bunk, though some of his remakings

of history, both literary and political, have struck academic commentators as bunk. The individual collections of Pound's poetry are often deliberately marked with "old" elements: *A Lume Spento* (1908), his first book; or *Personae* (1909), his second; or later ones like *Ripostes* (1912), *Lustra* (1915), or even *A Draft of XVI Cantos* (1925). Hence it should not be surprising that in late 1912 Pound was asked by Edward March to join the Georgians, a group he later affected to despise; or that in the same year Arthur Quiller-Couch approached him with the request to include two of his poems in the *Oxford Book of Victorian Verse.* Pound agreed, observing that "this is no small honour—at least I count it a recognition."[2] As J. B. Harmer writes in his study of the Imagist movement, "when 1912 opened Pound was a more reactionary poet than H.D. or even Aldington; a less accurate scholar than Flint, and a man curiously unaware of much that was happening in European literature."[3] He read Flaubert, for instance, for the first time in 1912—that very same author who was later to become Mauberley's "true Penelope."[4]

Both before and after 1912, the virtual signature of a Pound poem was the transformation/translation of old and traditional materials (European or Oriental) into a new work of art. This is true even of poems like "Les Millwin" or "The Temperaments" (both from *Lustra*) which are full of contemporary colloquialism, a trick that originates in Pound's compounding Juvenal with Whitman. It is true of the sort of Romantic braggadoccio with which "Tenzone" (also from *Lustra*) concludes:

> I mate with my free kind upon the crags;
> the hidden recesses
> Have heard the echo of my heels,
> in the cool light,
> in the darkness (91).

It is especially true of the *Cantos,* from which the broken statues and the few thousand battered books are never far distant.

It is also true of the literary movement with which Pound is most often and inextricably identified: Imagism.[5] Imagism, despite its revolutionary trappings and publicity as a movement of the Anglo-British avant-garde, is old-fashioned in a number of basic respects. H.D., the poet who was seen by Pound as most characteristic of Imagism, writes lyrical poems on conventional themes like flowers and Greek mythology. Indeed, her first appearance in print—in *Poetry* (Chicago)—was under the rubric of "Verses, Translations and Reflections from 'The Anthology'" (that is, the classical *Greek Anthology*). There is very little new about her poems except for their medium: free verse.[6] And even in this respect, as Pound was well aware, it was not revolutionary. The *Psalms* had used free verse long before the Imagists, as had Milton, Whitman, and Rimbaud.

More than any other feature of Pound's supposed revolution in modern poetry, it was the emphasis on free verse that attracted attention. It seemed as if Pound meant to break the chains with which the muse had always been bound. That is what may have happened, but if so, it was not a result of Pound's intention. Writing on "The Tradition" in 1913, Pound adduced the example of Euripedes as a great writer of free verse, and associated free verse with the Melic poets who "composed to the feel of the thing, to the cadence, as have all good poets since."[7] And René Taupin, in his classic study of the influence of French symbolist poetry on modernist American poetry, maintains that all of Pound's experiments aimed at "unretour à la poésie soit quantitative, soit musicale, et le vers libre luimême n'est pour lui que 'the sense of quantity reasserting itself in poetry.'"[8] Pound, in other words, was seeking not so much a revolution as a renewal, a revivification of an old tradition; or, to use his own word, he was seeking a rennaissance, an American renaissance. The constituent elements for such a renaissance, according to Pound's series, "America: Chances and Remedies" (May-June 1913), were the very traditional as well as non-literary ones of "an indiscriminate enthusiasm" and "a propaganda."[9]

Pound's Imagism was born in 1912 and was directly based on H.D.'s early poems, though the name Pound chose for his movement clearly indicates that he also had in mind T. E. Hulme's imagist *cénacle,* as well as French symbolism. Its principles, Pound wrote in a note accompanying Hulme's "Complete Poetical Works" in *Ripostes,* might not be as interesting as those of the "inherent dynamists," or *Les Unanimistes,* but they were sounder than those of the Impressionists or post-Impressionists. In another note—this one attached to Aldington's and Imagism's first appearance in *Poetry*—Pound described the group as consisting of ardent Hellenists who were also *vers libristes* and who were seeking to attain subtle cadences in their poetry similar to those of "Mallarmé and his followers."[10]

The French influence is made even more explicit in Pound's first relatively detailed account of the new school in *Poetry* (January 1913), where he pronounces that "the important work of the last twenty-five years has been done in Paris." In this essay he also makes clear that he is no rigid dogmatist or revolutionary: "To belong to a school does not in the least mean that one writes poetry to a theory. One writes poetry when, where, because, and as one feels like writing it. A school exists when two or three young men [sic] agree, more or less, to call certain things good; when they prefer such of their verses as have certain qualities to such of their verses as do not have them."[11] This pragmatic aspect of Pound's imagism makes it quite different from its more programmatic Hulmean predecessor, as Pound was quite aware when he wrote to F. S. Flint in 1915: ". . . . when on a certain evening in, I think 1912, I coined the word *Imagisme,* I certainly intended it to mean something which was the poetry of H.D. and most emphatically NOT the poetry of friend [Edward] Storer" who had been (along with Pound) a member of the Hulme circle.[12]

In the essay on Imagism that Flint "wrote"—he actually rewrote a draft by Pound—for the March 1913 issue of

Poetry, the *Imagistes* are explicitly described as "not a revolutionary school" whose "only endeavour was to write in accordance with the best tradition, as they found it in the best writers of all time,—in Sappho, Catullus, Villon." Even this tradition, Pound was later to argue in another contribution to *Poetry,* was not sacred, but merely "a beauty which we preserve and not a set of fetters to bind us." The Imagists had rules, to be sure, but as Pound warned us in his follow-up essay ("A Few Don'ts by an Imagiste"), "consider the rules recorded by Mr. Flint, not as dogma—never consider anything dogma—but as the result of long contemplation, which . . . may be worth consideration." These rules were: "1. Direct treatment of the 'thing', whether subjective or objective. 2. To use absolutely no word that did not contribute to the presentation. 3. As regarding rhythm: to compose in sequence of the musical phrase, not in sequence of a metronome."[13] Except possibly for the last rule enjoining free verse, this program contains nothing revolutionary and little that might be called new. It could have been subscribed to by almost any one of the Georgian poets, and in fact was by at least one—who was also to become a famous Imagist/Amygist—D. H. Lawrence. Not surprisingly, therefore, Harold Monro—the first non-imagist poet to discuss the new movement in detail—noted as early as 1915 that imagism was really not new. Coleridge, he said, "mentions the points emphasized in the Imagist principles." And if this was the case, then the rather puzzled Monro felt safe in concluding that "it has never become very clear in what particular respects they [the Imagists] may be considered innovators."[14]

It is clear then—or should be—that Pound and the first Imagists were not writing in conformity with, or in illustration of, a fixed program. They were writing the kind of poetry they liked to write; and they recognized that this poetry had certain affinities that might—more for practical reasons than anything else—be advertised as a kind of school. This is precisely why Pound objected to Amy Lowell's edging him out of the movement, as appears from a letter to her in August 1914: ". . . . that would deprive me of my machinery for gathering stray good poems and presenting them to the public in more or less permanent form and of discovering new talent . . . or poems which could not be presented to the public in other ways, poems that would be lost in the magazines."[15] It was this machinery of Pound's that, for instance, had also gathered Joyce's poem, "I Hear an Army," into the Imagist fold, at a time (December 1913) when Pound knew nothing of Joyce except what little Yeats had told him.[16] And this is how Allen Upward reacted poetically to the Poundean machine:

> After many years I sent them [his poems] to
>   Chicago, and they were printed
> by Harriet Monroe. (They also were printed in
>   *The Egoist.*)
> Thereupon Ezra Pound the generous rose up and
>   called me an Imagist. (I had no idea what he

meant).
And he included me in an anthology of Imagists.

And thou unborn literary historian (if you ever
    mention my name)
Write me down as an imitator of Po Li and
    Shakespeare
As well as of Edward Storer and T. E. Hulme.[17]

The anthology to which Upward refers here was the oddly named *Des Imagistes* (1914), an inspired but highly eclectic collection of poems put together by Pound's machine. It was to become one of the most important and influential collections in the history of modern English and American poetry; but influential, I think, more for what it seemed to be—and for the poets it gathered under one cover—than for what it was. Of the thirty-seven poems in *Des Imagistes,* fully eighteen (or nearly half) were either translations or imitations of classical models, and often marked by archaic language or style: e.g., "Hermes/who awaiteth" (H.D., "Hermes of the Ways"); "Πότια, Πότια, / Thou hearest me not" (Aldington, "To a Greek Marble"); "O prayers in the dark! / O incense to Poseidon!" (Williams, "Postlude"); "The shadowy flowers of Orcus / Remember Thee" (Pound, "Δώρια").[18] Here was a group of ardent Hellenists indeed; and not only ardent Hellenists, but also ardent Sinologists. At least five of the poems are recognizable translations or pastiches of classical Chinese poems. Echoes of the French symbolists are also frequent—as, for instance, in F. S. Flint's "The Swan"—though, surprisingly, only one poem (by Aldington) is written in direct imitation of them. Even the "English" poems are often marked either by non-modern subject matter—for instance, Ford Madox Hueffer's "In the Little Old Market-Place"—or by definitely ninety-ish tone and diction, as in Skipwith Cannell's fifth "Nocturne":

I am weary with love, and thy lips
Are night-born poppies.
Give me therefore thy lips
That I may know sleep.[19]

Virtually the only really "new" poems in the collection are the three so-called "Documents" at the end of the volume. But these are highly personal, in-groupish and discursive—hardly Imagist, in other words. Hueffer's "Fragments," for example, is an English poem transliterated into Greek, which refers, among other things, to Ezra's whiskers and which anticipates *The Waste Land* with its ironically scholarly footnotes. This is just the sort of thing the young Auden was to pick up a decade and a half later.

What then is the specifically Imagist significance of *Des Imagistes?* Undoubtedly, in the first place, its commitment to free verse. Secondly, the attention it gave and attracted to H.D.'s work. Thirdly, as a piece of propaganda, which led readers to other, more genuinely Imagist poems, such as Pound's "In a Station of the Metro." And finally as a work which prepared the ground for understanding poets like T. S. Eliot—or the later Pound himself—who would incorporate Imagist principles and techniques into poems that went beyond those principles.

To make larger claims for Imagism, as Graham Hough does in *Reflections on a Literary Revolution,* in which he argues that Imagism is to be equated with modernism generally, is to claim too much.[20] Imagism is an undoubted and essential part of the modernist movement in Britain and America, but it is only a part. And a part, moreover, with strong links to the past. The Imagist image, Frank Kermode is surely right in saying, is merely a subspecies of the Romantic Image.[21] Or as Pound was to remark in "A Retrospect" (1918), Imagism and *vers libre* had been forces for the good but not overwhelming forces: "Perhaps a few good poems have come from the new method, and if so it is justified."[22] T. S. Eliot summed it up some thirty years later: "Imagism produced a few good poems—notably those of H.D.—but it was quickly absorbed into more comprehensive influences, including Pound's."[23]

NOTES

[1] Ezra Pound, *Collected Shorter Poems* (London: Faber & Faber, 1952), p. 108. All further references to this collection will be contained in the text, by page number enclosed in parentheses.

[2] Noel Stock, *The Life of Ezra Pound* (New York: Pantheon, 1970), pp. 123-24.

[3] J. B. Harmer, *Victory in Limbo: Imagism, 1908-1917* (London: Secker & Warburg, 1975), p. 76.

[4] Stock, *Life,* p. 119.

[5] Aside from works cited elsewhere in this essay, useful discussions of the Imagist movement include: Luigi Berti, *Imagismo* (Padua: Cedam, 1944); Douglas Bush, *Mythology and the Romantic Tradition in English Poetry* (Cambridge, Mass.: Harvard University Press, 1937); Stanley K. Coffman, *Imagism* (Norman: University of Oklahoma Press, 1951); Glenn Hughes, *Imagism and the Imagists: A Study in Modern Poetry* (Stanford: Stanford University Press, 1931); Hugh Kenner, *The Pound Era* (Berkeley: University of California Press, 1971).

[6] For a more extended treatment of H.D. as an imagist poet, see my essay on her in *American Writers,* Supplement I, ed. Leonard Unger (New York: Scribner's, 1979).

[7] Ezra Pound, "The Tradition," in *Literary Essays,* ed. T. S. Eliot (Norfolk, Conn.: New Directions, 1954), pp. 92-93.

[8] René Taupin, *L'Influence du symbolisme francais sur la poésie américaine de 1910 à 1920* (Paris: Librairie Ancienne Honoré Champion, 1929), p. 135.

[9] Quoted in Stock, *Life,* p. 115.

[10] *Poetry* (Chicago), I (November 1912), 65.

[11] *Ibid.,* I (Jan. 1913), 123-25.

[12] Quoted in Harmer, *Victory,* p. 45.

[13] F. S. Flint, "Imagisme," *Poetry* (Chicago), I (March 1913), 199; and Ezra Pound, "A Few Don'ts by an Imagiste," *Poetry* (Chicago), I (March 1913), 201.

[14] Harold Monro, "The Imagists Discussed," *The Egoist,* V (May 1, 1915), 77-78.

[15] Ezra Pound, *Letters,* ed. D. D. Paige (London: Faber & Faber, 1961), p. 77.

[16] A little later, when Pound entered on his "vorticist" phase, he even claimed Dante for imagism. Writing in the *Fortnightly Review* in 1914, Pound asserted that "Dante's *Paradiso* is the most wonderful *image*. By that I do not mean that it is a perseveringly imagistic performance. The permanent part is Imagisme, the rest, the discourses with the calendar of saints and the discussions about the nature of the moon, are philology." Reprinted in *Ezra Pound, A Critical Anthology,* edited by J. P. Sullivan (Harmondsworth: Penguin, 1970), p. 51.

[17] Allen Upward, "The Discarded Imagist," *Poetry* (Chicago), VI (September 1915), 318.

[18] *Des Imagistes, An Anthology* (New York: Boni, 1914), p. 21; p. 10; p. 39; p. 41.

[19] *Ibid.,* p. 37.

[20] Graham Hough, *Reflections on a Literary Revolution* (Washington: Catholic University of America, 1960), p. 10.

[21] Frank Kermode, *Romantic Image* (London: Routledge & Kegan Paul, 1957), p. 136.

[22] Ezra Pound, "A Retrospect," in *Literary Essays,* p. 3.

[23] T. S. Eliot, "Ezra Pound," in *Ezra Pound, A Collection of Critical Essays* (Englewood Cliffs: Prentice-Hall, 1963), p. 20. This essay was originally published in *Poetry* (Chicago) in 1946.

David Perkins

[*In the following essay, Perkins discusses the development of the Imagist movement, offers examples of poetry embodying Imagist principles, and discusses the works of Richard Aldington, H.D., John Gould Fletcher, Amy Lowell, and Herbert Read in relation to Imagism.*]

SOURCE: "Imagism," in *A History of Modern Poetry: From the 1890s to the High Modernist Mode,* The Belknap Press of the Harvard University Press, 1976, pp. 329-47.

Imagism has been described as the grammar school of modern poetry, the instruction and drill in basic principles. The metaphor greatly exaggerates—neither Yeats nor Eliot were ever Imagists, for example, though both were occasionally claimed for the group—but among the several modern movements in English and American poetry just before World War I, the Imagists probably had a more distinct impact than any other group on the style of American poets. The reasons for this were partly the shrewdness with which first Pound and then Amy Lowell promoted the movement, partly the clear doctrine and practical tips offered by the Imagist manifestos and other bulletins, and partly because the Imagist program merged with other, already influential tendencies: Impressionist exact notation; interest in Chinese and Japanese poetry, in which poets now remarked a spare, suggestive, visual imagery in terse forms such as haiku; the orientation of poetry in the 1890s to painting, sculpture, and other "spatial" arts; the special attention symbolist poetry directed to imagery; Hulme's plea that poetry must be precisely phrased and that the essential means to precision is metaphor; the development of free verse; the rejection of poetic diction and "rhetoric"; the cultivation of the idiomatic and the colloquial. Imagist poems were not difficult to read, and after 1914, when Pound could no longer impose his standards on the movement, they were not very difficult to write. Like Georgian poetry in England or the "realism" of Masters and Sandburg in America, Imagism became a relatively accessible way to be in on the "new" and the "modern."

THE IMAGIST MOVEMENT

Imagism was conceived in the spring of 1912 in a tea shop in Kensington, where, over buns, Pound informed two young poets, H.D. and Richard Aldington, that they were *Imagistes.* What the term then meant to him can only be guessed, but by October he was spreading the news—half-seriously and half as a publicity stunt—of a school of *Imagisme.* "Isms" were in the air. The August 1912 *Poetry Review* included an article by F. S. Flint on "Contemporary French Poetry," in which one could read up on Unanisme, Impulsionnisme, Paroxysme, and so forth. Marinetti had long since caused a stir with Futurism, and before Marinetti there had been the "symbolist movement" of Yeats and Symons. England had its home-grown movement in the Georgian poets.

In October, Pound's *Ripostes* appeared, including as an appendix "The Complete Poetical Works of T. E. Hulme," five short poems. There was also a prefatory note by Pound. "*Les Imagistes,*" he said (typically he used French for literary movements), have the future "in their keeping." They descended from the forgotten "School of Images" of 1909. (He was thinking of the small group of poets who used to meet with T. E. Hulme at The Eiffel Tower restaurant in Soho.) At about the same time Pound used the new term in letters to Harriet Monroe, who mentioned the new school in her November 1912 issue of *Poetry.* The January 1913 issue printed five poems by H.D., which were signed (at Pound's insistence) "H.D. Imagiste." There was also a note by Pound: "The youngest school" in London "is that of the Imagistes

. . . one of their watchwords is Precision." In March 1913 *Poetry* printed the famous brief statement of Imagiste principles and the list of tips Pound had originally composed as a rejection slip for *Poetry*. With these statements, and with Imagiste poems by H.D. and Aldington to serve as examples, the "movement" was successfully planted in America.

Pound decided to put together an Imagiste anthology. By the summer of 1913 he had selected poems by Aldington, H.D., Flint, and himself to make up the bulk of the book and had also accepted for it one poem each from Skipwith Cannell, Amy Lowell, William Carlos Williams, Joyce, Hueffer, Allen Upward, and John Cournos. This collection was sent to Alfred Kreymborg in New York and published as *Des Imagistes: An Anthology* (1914).

Meanwhile, in Boston, Amy Lowell was intrigued. As Harriet Monroe tells it, Miss Lowell read in the January 1913 issue of *Poetry*, "some poems signed 'H.D. Imagiste'; and suddenly it came over her: 'Why, I too am an Imagiste!'" She sailed for London that June armed with a letter of introduction from Miss Monroe. Pound corrected her poetry ("He could *make* you write," she later conceded), and found her "ALL RIGHT." The next summer she returned to London, but her state of mind was less docile and more self-confident. For the April issue of *Poetry* had started off with eight of her poems (mostly in free verse) and her second volume, *Sword Blades and Poppy Seed,* was in proof. She thought the success of the Georgian anthologies might be emulated and proposed to the Imagistes that their anthology be brought out annually for five years. She promised to pay for publication if that proved necessary. But she was miffed that the first anthology had included only one of her poems. Subsequent anthologies, she said, should be "democratic": they should allow each contributor approximately the same amount of space. To Pound the notion was absurd. The arts were not a "democratic beergarden." Miss Lowell's suggestion was very welcome to the other Imagistes, however, and in 1915 *Some Imagist Poets* (the term now Anglicized—or Americanized) appeared, containing poems of Aldington, H.D., Flint, Amy Lowell, John Gould Fletcher, and D. H. Lawrence. (Pound had formally seceded from the movement.)

Even though Miss Lowell had gone ahead with her "democratic" anthology, she and Pound had managed to part cordially at the end of the summer. But poisons were working. She knew Pound thought her lacking in standards and she was critical of him. During the fall Macmillan's advertised her *Sword Blades and Poppy Seed* by explaining that, "Of the poets who to-day are doing the interesting and original work, there is no more striking and unique figure than Amy Lowell. The foremost member of the 'Imagists'—a group of poets that includes William Butler Yeats, Ezra Pound, Ford Maddox Hueffer. . . ." Such "charlatanism" was too much for Pound. His letter of protest was firm; he advised her to "cease referring to yourself as an Imagiste." Miss Lowell made light of the advertisement: "The names," she replied, "were simply put in to boom the book, a thing that is constantly done over here." ("Your knowledge of how to 'get yourself over,'" she later wrote him, "is *nil*.") As time passed, Pound felt that the poetry of the Imagists (he now called them "Amygists") was becoming undisciplined, sloppy, and diluted. In Miss Lowell's opinion there were now "bitterest enmities" between herself and Pound. As for Pound, he thought her verse "putrid" but liked her personally—at least until 1922, when she refused to contribute to his scheme of financial support for Eliot. "Aw shucks! dearie," he then wrote her, "ain't you the hell-roarer, ain't you the kuss." In 1928, in a letter to Taupin, he summed up the Imagists as a "bunch of goups."

After 1914 the Imagist movement was captained by Miss Lowell. Richard Aldington, as editor of *The Egoist,* provided auxiliary aid in the form of an Imagist number (May 1, 1915). In the same year Miss Lowell praised the new school at a meeting of the conservative Poetry Society in New York, and was henceforth embattled. She held readings, gave lectures, and cultivated editors, reviewers, and anthologists. Hostile articles on Imagism in the *New Republic,* Chicago *Evening Post, Nation,* and *Atlantic Monthly* raised her blood pressure, but were not otherwise unwelcome. "Well?—Clap or hiss," Miss Lowell used to tell audiences at her readings, "I don't care which; but do something!" Critical attack provoked defense, and the Imagists were more widely heard of than any movement since. Imagist anthologies were issued in 1916 and 1917; thereafter there were no more. But whenever critics discussed modern poetry, the school continued to be noticed as an important phase or tendency. Poems of the Imagist kind continued to be written, though it became increasingly difficult to say precisely what this kind was.

THE IMAGIST DOCTRINE

The first public statement of Imagist principles was that printed by *Poetry* in March 1913. Written by Pound, the statement was signed by Flint, who said he had obtained the three-fold program by interviewing an Imagiste:

> 1. Direct treatment of the "thing," whether subjective or objective.

> 2. To use absolutely no word that did not contribute to the presentation.

> 3. As regarding rhythm: to compose in sequence of the musical phrase, not in sequence of a metronome.

The list illustrates that so far as doctrine was concerned, Imagisme, as Pound conceived it, was not so much a special type of poetry as a name for whatever he had learned (from Hulme, Hueffer, Yeats, and others . . .) about "HOW TO WRITE" since coming to London in 1908. He was in the habit of scribbling such recipes. In 1916, for example, "the whole art" of poetry was divided (with no reference to Imagisme) into:

a. concision, or style, or saying what you mean in the fewest and clearest words.

b. the actual necessity for creating or constructing something; of presenting an image, or enough images of concrete things arranged to stir the reader.

The historical importance of Imagism, in other words, does not lie in the formulation of a poetic doctrine, for Pound had developed his ideas with no reference to Imagism and continued to hold them after he disowned the movement. The importance was, rather, the extent to which the name, movement, and attendant controversies caused these values to be effectively disseminated.

So far as Pound endowed Imagism with a program distinct from his principles of effective writing in general, it must be sought in the special role assigned to the "image." Pound defined his key term only vaguely. An image is, he said in the same issue of *Poetry*, "that which presents an intellectual and emotional complex in an instant of time. . . . It is better to present one Image in a lifetime than to produce voluminous works." Whatever else the "doctrine of the image" might include was not to be published, readers were told, for "it does not concern the public and would provoke useless discussion."

The March 1913 issue contained further admonishments from Pound, "A Few Don'ts by an Imagiste," which helped interpret the program: for example, "Use no superfluous word, no adjective, which does not reveal something"; "Go in fear of abstractions"; "Let the candidate fill his mind with the finest cadences he can discover, preferably in a foreign language so that the meaning of the words may be less likely to divert his attention from the movement"; "Don't be 'viewy'—leave that to the writers of pretty little philosophic essays"; "Don't chop your stuff into separate *iambs*." Such tips were admirably practical, and the offhand phrasing enhanced their authority.

In June 1914 in *The Egoist* Aldington again explained what Imagism was, but the most influential single statement produced in the whole course of the movement was his Preface to the Imagist anthology for 1915. It listed six points, "the essentials of all great poetry, indeed of all great literature":

1. To use the language of common speech, but to employ always the *exact* word, not the nearly exact, nor the merely decorative word.

2. To create new rhythms—as the expression of new moods—and not to copy old rhythms, which merely echo old moods. We do not insist upon "free-verse" as the only method of writing poetry. We fight for it as a principle of liberty. We believe that the individuality of a poet may often be better expressed in free-verse than in conventional forms. In poetry, a new cadence means a new idea.

3. To allow absolute freedom in the choice of subject. It is not good art to write badly about aeroplanes and automobiles; nor is it necessarily bad art to write about the past. We believe passionately in the artistic value of modern life, but we wish to point out that there is nothing so uninspiring nor so old-fashioned as an aeroplane of the year 1911.

4. To present an image (hence the name: "Imagist"). We are not a school of painters, but we believe that poetry should render particulars exactly and not deal in vague generalities, however magnificent and sonorous. It is for this reason that we oppose the cosmic poet, who seems to us to shirk the real difficulties of his art.

5. To produce poetry that is hard and clear, never blurred nor indefinite.

6. Finally, most of us believe that concentration is of the very essence of poetry.

The statement was directed against undemanding techniques and against conventional, though not necessarily conservative attitudes. Instead of many adjectives and statements, there would be an image rendered in concentrated, exact, idiomatic speech. Instead, for example, of the looseness of Masefield's "The West Wind"—

It's a warm wind, the west wind, full of bird's cries;
I never hear the west wind but tears are in my eyes.
For it comes from the west lands, the old brown hills,
And April's in the west wind, and daffodils—

there would be Aldington's "New Love":

She has new leaves
After her dead flowers,
Like the little almond-tree
Which the frost hurt.

As opposed to frequent demands at this time for a specifically contemporary subject matter, Aldington implicitly defended the "Hellenism" of himself and H.D. by invoking the poet's right to "absolute freedom in the choice of subject," a principle to which all would-be Modernists subscribed. Against the expectation that poetry would be metrical, he adopted a point of view that legitimized free verse without decrying meters. Whether verse was traditional or free, there should be "new rhythms" as the expression of "new" and individual moods.

Against the poets and poetic habits Aldington implicitly criticized, his points were effectively made. On the other hand, though this Preface was so strongly influenced by Pound that it seemed mainly a restatement of his views, one finds, if one compares it with Pound's earlier statement, that a vulgarization has set in. "Concentration," the "*exact* word," and "hard and clear" style do not impose quite so severe a standard as Pound's second article, "To use absolutely no word that did not contribute to the presentation" (and this was the essential article in

Pound's opinion). Moreover, although Pound was probably not quite sure what he meant by an "Image," he thought of it as a "complex" concretely presented. In Aldington's Preface the concept of the Image is wavering toward a much simpler notion, that of a clear, quick rendering of particulars without commentary. Imagist poems of this kind would of course be much easier to write.

The attacks on Imagism that followed in 1915 raised only two important issues. The controversy over free verse—is it poetry?—was discussed in Chapter 14. Secondly, it was immediately pointed out that Imagist successes could only be small-scale. As Conrad Aiken put it, the Imagists

> give us frail pictures—whiffs of windy beaches, marshes, meadows, city streets, disheveled leaves; pictures pleasant and suggestive enough. But seldom is any of them more than a nice description, coolly sensuous, a rustle to the ear, a ripple to the eye. Of organic movement there is practically none.

One could not write a long Imagist poem. Quite apart from particular issues, however, controversy gradually caused the doctrine of Imagism to become less definite. For the battle on behalf of Imagism was fought by Amy Lowell. Since her temperament was not ideological but political, she compromised doctrine, like many another politician, in order to prevail in the field. In *Tendencies in Modern American Poetry* she characterized the Imagist principles as "Simplicity and directness of speech; subtlety and beauty of rhythms; individualistic freedom of idea; clearness and vividness of presentation; and concentration." With such generalities no one could quarrel, but neither could anyone be arrested by them, as poets had been by Pound's statement in *Poetry* four years before.

THE IMAGIST POEM

Once the Imagist poem was established as a type, it was written occasionally by many poets who were not members of the original Imagist group. Familiar instances are Sandburg's "Fog" and Williams' "El Hombre." Many other poets, such as Marianne Moore, e.e. cummings, and Archibald MacLeish, were strongly influenced by Imagist principles and style, even though they did not write specifically Imagist poems. Because the poems of T. E. Hulme were the first examples of Imagism offered to the world (by Pound in October 1912), his "Autumn" may be used to exemplify the mode:

> A touch of cold in the Autumn night—
> I walked abroad,
> And saw the ruddy moon lean over a hedge
> Like a red-faced farmer.
> I did not stop to speak, but nodded,
> And round about were the wistful stars
> With white faces like town children.

The poem was probably written in conscious contrast with Shelley's famous "To the Moon," for Shelley's poem also contrasts the moon to the stars and thinks about companionability or the lack of it:

> Art thou pale for weariness
> Of climbing heaven, and gazing on the earth,
>   Wandering companionless
> Among the stars that have a different birth,—
> And ever-changing, like a joyless eye
> That finds no object worth its constancy?

Whether or not Hulme recalled Shelley, his verses are anti-Romantic. Within the Romantic tradition to view the cold and starry heavens in autumn would predictably evoke feelings of melancholy, loneliness, and death. If such feelings are present here, it is only in a complex, indirect, and controlled way. Hulme's "red-faced farmer," unlike Shelley's pale moon, seems well fed, healthy, comfortable, and neighborly, and is humorously regarded. What is conveyed by the poem is not, as with Shelley, a comparison that projects the poet's "moan" (as Hulme would have put it) into the moon but a comparison in altogether unexpected terms. If we ask what is communicated in Shelley's poem, "the poet's feeling of loneliness" would be an inadequate, though not incorrect generalization. In the case of Hulme's poem, the "meaning" cannot be conveyed by a generalization.

Another modal poem, often cited, was H.D.'s "Oread":

> Whirl up, sea—
> Whirl your pointed pines,
> Splash your great pines
> On our rocks,
> Hurl your green over us,
> Cover us with your pools of fir.

The perception of the sea as a pine and fir forest is fresh and apt; the cadenced lines enact an emotional transition; the effect is complex, immediate, and made wholly by concrete means; the poet avoids discursive or generalizing comment. As a final example we may turn to MacLeish's "Ars Poetica," which illustrates much that the Imagist movement taught other poets. A poem, MacLeish writes, should be "palpable and mute"; it should not tell a "history of grief" at length but should evoke it through concrete particulars:

> For all the history of grief
> An empty doorway and a maple leaf
>
> For love
> The leaning grasses and two lights above the
>   sea—
>
> A poem should not mean
> But be.

SOME IMAGIST POETS

None of the poets published in the Imagist anthologies remained an Imagist in later life, and some from the outset were Imagists only occasionally. We may here touch on the careers of five poets—Aldington, H.D., Fletcher, Amy Lowell, and Herbert Read—who were closely identified with the Imagist movement. Pound was, of course, the most important of the Imagists, but his

Imagist phase is described in Chapter 20. D. H. Lawrence was included in the anthologies mainly for reasons of good fellowship; he wrote no poems of the Imagist kind, and is discussed in Chapter 19. Of the poets to be taken up here, Aldington, H.D., Fletcher, and Lowell were prominent in the Imagist anthologies; Herbert Read came to the movement slightly later, was strongly influenced by it, and continued there-after to be a spokesman for the Imagist ideals. In fact, after the mid-1920s he was their most important contemporary spokesman.

Poems by Richard Aldington (1892-1962) were first published in 1909. Labeled "Imagiste" and trumpeted by Pound, the eighteen-year-old Aldington attended Yeats's Monday evenings, knew Hulme, Ford, Lawrence, Amy Lowell, married H.D., became literary editor of *Egoist,* and was in the thick of literary goings-on in avant-garde London. The poems he wrote at this time were often mythopoeic, evoking a Mediterranean landscape. They were composed in free verse and presented "images"— mostly sensuously appealing ones. Aldington's poems were often said to be "hellenic," though their attitudes and scenery descended more immediately from Swinburne and the Pre-Raphaelites. During and after World War I he departed steadily further from the Imagist style; in *Exile and Other Poems* (1923) he wrote the directly personal and talky type of poem that in the nineteenth century was often called an "effusion." "I abandon, cast off, utterly deny the virtue of 'extreme compression and essential significance of every word,'" he wrote Herbert Read in 1924. "I say that is the narrow path that leadeth to sterility. . . . Pound, Flint, both went down on that; I saw them go; and I shall live to see you and Tom [Eliot] go the same way." After *A Fool i' the Forest* (1925) he published mostly prose. His chief success was with his novel of the war, *Death of a Hero* (1929).

According to his occasional private explanations, Pound invented the Imagist movement to obtain attention for the work of Hilda Doolittle (1886-1961), who published under her initials "H.D." She grew up in Philadelphia, where she was acquainted with Pound and William Carlos Williams. She went to Europe in 1911 and spent the rest of her life there. She and Richard Aldington were married in 1912; they separated after the war. Pound, Amy Lowell, Louis Untermeyer, and others frequently mentioned her poems as the purest examples of Imagism. Her phrasing was usually idiomatic and economical. The units of syntax were short and there were few subordinate clauses. Abstract generalizations were infrequent. The poems were made of simple statements juxtaposed, as in "The Pool":

> Are you alive?
> I touch you.
> You quiver like a sea-fish.
> I cover you with my net.
> What are you—banded onc?

Such writing struck many readers as clear, swift, and uncluttered.

H.D. translated from classical Greek—Euripides, Sappho, Homer, the Greek anthology. Her original verses also brought Greece to mind, for the light, color, and landscape might be Mediterranean and she usually alluded to Greek myth or re-created it in the poem. Because her landscape, subject, and sensibility seemed "Greek," so did her style. Richard Eberhart summarized a common opinion when he said in 1958, she "gives us the best glimpse we have today of classic poetry, an English poetry . . . nearly Greek in concept and execution . . . crystal-bright, hard and pure, clean and fine." Those more deeply versed in English and Greek poetry recognized that her "Greece" was typically Romantic and literary, a Hellenic world distilled from Shelley, Keats, Byron, Arnold, Swinburne, and many another English poet of the nineteenth century. To such readers her Imagist "hardness" of style was not impressively "Greek," neither was it especially "modern," for except that the diction was idiosyncratic and the verse was free, it recalled the familiar "sculpture of rhyme" of the 1890s. It was obvious that her art, like that of the aesthetes, had limited itself by retreating from the world of actual experience. Moreover, the feelings it expressed were often strained and unreal, as when the speaker in the much-admired "Orchard" falls prostrate before a pear,

> crying:
> you have flayed us
> with your blossoms,
> spare us the beauty
> of fruit-trees.

Like other Imagists, H.D. gradually abandoned the mode. *The Walls Do Not Fall* (1944) inaugurated a remarkable poetic self-renewal. This sequence of poems is meditative and also mythical and archetypal, showing the influence of both Freud (whose patient she was) and Jung. The symbols are taken from diverse traditions—Christian, Egyptian, cabalistic, astrological—for she assumed that these different symbolisms evoked the same underlying realities. The poem was written in London during World War II and was followed by two long sequences of a similar kind, *Tribute to the Angels* (1945) and *The Flowering of the Rod* (1946).

John Gould Fletcher (1886-1950) was only occasionally an Imagist, but because he was one of the six poets in Miss Lowell's Imagist anthologies, he was, throughout most of his life, presumed to be an Imagist by a literary public that could hardly have been paying close attention to his works. In fact, he began as an aggressively experimentalist, Modernist poet and ended as a regional one. In 1908 (one year later than Pound) he sailed for Italy, for, as he later explained, he was disgusted with the "mediocrity, the optimism, the worldliness" of the United States, and regarded Europe as the place to "acquire an education." Again like Pound, in 1909 he moved to London. He studied Impressionist and post-Impressionist painting, oriental poetry (in translation), and the French symbolist poets (he claimed to have introduced Pound to them). He read, it was said, a book of French poetry every day.

In 1913 he was briefly at the center of avant-garde affairs. He published five books of poetry at his own expense. He agreed to back Pound financially (Fletcher had inherited money) in taking over the suffragette *New Freewoman*, which eventually became *The Egoist*. When Amy Lowell came to London that summer he told her his plan to write a poem on a modern city by objectively recording just what one sees. Quarreling with Pound, he refused to appear in *Des Imagistes,* and proposed to Miss Lowell that they jointly edit and finance a rival anthology. He was determined "to risk everything in order to become a modern artist." His notions of what constituted modernism were strangely external and confused but for this very reason they were typical of many writers at the beginning of what Pound called "le mouvement." To be a modern artist, as Fletcher saw it, involved "a determination to make and accept every kind of experiment." If one "aroused the hatred of the mob," so had Cezanne, Gauguin, Van Gogh, and Stravinski. There was "but one lesson the modern artist must learn," which was (quoting Synge) that "to be human again, we must learn first to be brutal." Having just seen Stravinski's *Rite of Spring,* he felt that artists everywhere "were turning back to the primitively ugly, knowing that in primitiveness alone lay strength."

Fletcher's verse of this period may be illustrated by his "Irradiations" and Color Symphonies. His purpose in these poems was to evoke and orchestrate moods, while excluding any more definite content. Some of the "Irradiations" were recognizably symbolist:

> Far trumpets like a vague rout of faded roses
> Burst 'gainst the wet green silence of distant
>   forests:
> A clash of cymbals—then the swift swaying
>   footsteps
> Of the wind that undulates along the languid
>   terraces.

Some however, were Imagist:

> Flickering of incessant rain
> On flashing pavements:
> Sudden scurry of umbrellas:
> Bending, recurved blossoms of the storm.

And in other instances the mood he sought to evoke required an emulation of Whitman, whom Fletcher had also been reading:

> I saw that all the women—although their bodies
>   were dexterously concealed—
> Were thinking with all their might what the men
>   were like.

The Color Symphonies, he later explained, attempted to render "certain predominant moods in the terms of things happening. Thus one gets expectancy described as a traveler looking at blue mountains in the distance." The "prevailing mood" was indicated by a color, as in the "Blue Symphony," in which images of blue objects recur. In this symphony the setting, decor, and suggestive spareness in description produce a vaguely "oriental" feeling, as in the lines evoking an autumnal garden:

> Sombre wreck—autumnal leaves;
> Shadowy roofs
> In the blue mist,
> And a willow-branch that is broken.
>
> Oh, old pagodas of my soul, how you glittered
>   across green trees.

Becoming dissatisfied with these shimmerings, Fletcher wished to articulate ideas. In the 1920s and 1930s he composed meditative, often religiously questing lyrics and effusions of a kind that used frequently to be called "cosmic." Gradually, he became a regional poet of his native Arkansas, where he was now living, for he felt the poetic appeal of American landscape and regional life. He sympathized with the social values of Allen Tate, John Crowe Ransom, and other Fugitive writers, for he shared their idealization of Southern agrarian traditionalism as opposed to urban, industrialized rootlessness in the North. The most important product of this late, regional phase was *South Star* (1941). The volume includes a poetic history of the state of Arkansas, more impressive as regional piety than as poetry, as well as shorter lyrics which effectively combine his Imagist-Impressionist methods of presentation, his search for general, ultimate meanings, and his imaginative response to local objects and scenes.

Amy Lowell (1874-1925) was one of the distinguished and wealthy Lowells of Boston. The family tree included generals, judges, historians, and the poet, James Russell Lowell; Robert Lowell is of the same family. Her brother Abbott Lawrence Lowell, who became President of Harvard, made no public comment on the avant-garde writings and other eccentricities of his sister. She was enormously overweight because of a glandular disturbance, smoked cigars, slept with sixteen pillows, and worked from midnight to dawn, sleeping by day. These and other oddities contributed to her reputation, but what contributed more were her energy, shrewdness, determination, and pluck. By these virtues she thrust herself into prominence among the poets of the time, but her position was precarious. Her poetry, though often written with sensitivity and intelligence, could not justify the importance that seemed to be hers—that was hers if we think only of her leadership in promoting the new art.

Her first volume, *A Dome of Many-Coloured Glass* (1912), was conventionally derivative from the English Romantic tradition. Her next one, *Sword Blades and Poppy Seed* (1914), showed the impact of her contact with the Imagist and experimentalist avant-garde in London in the summer of 1913. Along with its ballads, dramatic monologues, and rhymed, stanzaic lyrics, it included poems in free verse. There were also three examples of what she called "polyphonic prose," a way of writing, she explained, that uses cadence, assonance, alliteration, rhyme, echo effects, and even "perhaps true metre for a few minutes," but handles them in a more varying and flexible way than is possible in traditional verse:

> The inkstand is full of ink, and the paper lies white and unspotted, in the round of light thrown by a candle. Puffs of darkness sweep into the corners, and keep rolling through the room behind his chair. The air is silver and pearl, for the night is liquid with moonlight.

Men, Women and Ghosts (1916) was a collection of narratives in meters, free verse, and polyphonic prose. Among them was the much-anthologized dramatic monologue, "Patterns" and a block ("The Overgrown Pasture") of four dramatic monologues by rural New England speakers. In these she was deliberately challenging Robert Frost and wrote in dialect, as she considered he ought to have done. *Can Grande's Castle* (1918) was a volume of polyphonic prose, and in *Pictures of a Floating World* (1919) Miss Lowell, who felt that volumes of poetry should have a unified character and effect, published the short lyrics she had written and stored up since 1914.

These free-verse lyrics display the qualities for which her work was exemplary at this time. Her diction and syntax are relatively simple, straightforward, and idiomatic. She renders sensations with exact impression. The poems adhere closely to the concrete, avoiding generalization and "rhetoric." "November" is an example:

> The vine leaves against the brick walls of my
> house
> Are rusty and broken.
> Dead leaves gather under the pine-trees,
> The brittle boughs of lilac-bushes
> Sweep against the stars.
> And I sit under a lamp
> Trying to write down the emptiness of my heart.
> Even the cat will not stay with me,
> But prefers the rain
> Under the meagre shelter of a cellar window.

Despite its virtues the poem illustrates how Miss Lowell, like Sandburg, H.D., Aldington, and many other "new" poets, was "modern" only in some aspects of form and style. In sensibility and imagination she was safely within the fold of familiar Romantic convention.

In 1921 she published *Fir-Flower Tablets,* a volume of translations from ancient Chinese poetry. She knew no Chinese and used English versions supplied by Florence Ayscough, a friend who lived in Shanghai. "The great poets of the T'ang Dynasty," she felt, "are without doubt among the finest poets that the world has ever seen". (Such a judgment on poets she could not read tells much about Miss Lowell.) Her translations would "knock a hole" in Pound's *Cathay.* In 1922 her *A Critical Fable* appeared. Imitating a poem of the same name by James Russell Lowell, it contained doggerel criticisms of contemporary poets, including herself (her authorship was concealed at first), excited much interest, and shows how the poetic scene was viewed from one influential and representative perspective in the year of *The Waste Land.*

By this time Miss Lowell was heavily engaged in her massive biography of Keats. She was ill and unused to close and detailed scholarship ("Keats is killing me"); but she was indomitable, and the work was published in 1925, four months before she died. The three volumes of poetry published posthumously show no change in the direction of her talent, and include two of her better-known poems, "Lilacs" and "Meeting-House Hill."

A distinguished essayist, novelist, lecturer, and critic of art and literature, Sir Herbert Read (1893-1968) was also an autobiographer. His account of his early poetic career (*The Innocent Eye,* 1933) reveals much about the feelings and aspirations of the first young writers formed by the Modernist revolution. Read's situation differed from that of Hulme, Pound, Eliot, or Lawrence in the crucial respect that he did not participate in creating an avant-garde poetry but adopted one created by others. His interest in poetry was awakened by a schoolteacher, but for a long time the only audience, patron, and encourager of his verse was a Quaker tailor in Leeds, where Read was working as a bank clerk. The seventeen-year-old poet delighted in Tennyson; Blake descended on him "like an apocalypse"; he was entranced with Yeats and Ralph Hodgson, Donne and Browning. It was apparently in the Imagist anthology for 1915 that Read first encountered Imagist verse and doctrine. Now twenty-two or twenty-three, he had found, he felt, the essence of the avant-garde or modern movement in poetry. As an officer in the trenches he composed Imagist poems of war experience; for example, "Movement of Troops":

> We entrain in open trucks
> and soon glide away
>   from the plains of Artois.
>
> With a wake of white smoke
> we plunge
> down dark avenues of silent trees.
>
> A watcher sees
> our red light gleam
> occasionally.

To the end of his life Read was likely to identify the "new poetic awareness" of the twentieth century as Imagism and to restate some of the leading premises of the Imagist manifestos as his own poetic creed: "A poem is not a statement, but a . . . manifestation of *being*"; "The rhythmical pattern corresponds . . . with the inner feeling."

War experience caused him to question his Imagist procedures, for he was trying, he later said, "to maintain an abstract aesthetic ideal in the midst of terrorful and inhuman events." He wished to achieve a more direct expression of what he was feeling and undergoing; he therefore composed longer narrative and meditative poems, which turned out to be diffuse and uncontrolled. Toward the end of the war, on leave in London, he became acquainted with Flint, Aldington, Pound, and Eliot (who became a lifelong friend), and learned, he said, to write in a more self-disciplined way: "Poetry was reduced to an instrument of precision"; "Criticism had become innate.")

If we mean by Imagism only the sort of poem exemplified in "Movement of Troops," Read rarely wrote Imagist poems after 1919. He sometimes emulated the Metaphysical Poets in the 1920s and Auden in the 1930s, and practiced diverse styles through his long career. He called himself a Romantic, wrote several books on the English Romantic poets, and turned for inspiration to their work as much as to that of his twentieth-century contemporaries. His lacks of intensity and control were usually less apparent in his lyrics than in his longer meditative or "philosophic" utterances. But in a general sense of the term Imagist, Read may be said to have remained true to his first phase, for images are the especially striking and valuable element of his poetry. He had a gift for seeing freshly and for imaginatively transforming what he saw.

To represent the many, minor American poets who, though not among the original Imagist or "Amygist" groups, adopted the mode as a consequence of the publicity it received, we may mention Henry Bellamann (1882-1945). Although known mainly for his novel *King's Row* (1940), he published poetry in the 1920s. Applied to poets such as Bellamann, the term Imagist suggests short, free-verse impressions of objects, places, or human encounters, with a reticent evocation of emotion and deeper significance. Such poems are more concrete and succinct than the conventional poems of the previous generation. Their subjects are less likely to be beauty, death, love, and God, but, instead, such poems focus on "Hedges," "Goose Creek," "Leaf Prints," or "Wind in the Sycamores"—often with a touch of humor. Bellamann tried the notes of many poets, including Adelaide Crapsey and H.D., but the general model for all this poetry in America was Amy Lowell.

B. Rajan

[*In the following essay, Rajan presents a negative assessment of Imagist aims, techniques, and achievement.*]

SOURCE: "Imagism: A Reconsideration," in *Modern American Poetry*, Dennis Dobson, Ltd., 1950, pp. 81-94.

An article on Imagism can claim to be doubly justified in any symposium on modern American poetry. The movement assembled, particularly in its criticism, many of the tendencies which went to make up the 'Poetic Renaissance' and is consequently often discussed in detail in academic histories of the period. But it is also notable for a different reason; it is perhaps the only movement with a wide American influence, to have had English practitioners and an English following. Having said this much one is compelled to add, that the intrinsic importance of Imagism cannot now be considered very great. It produced a small amount of competent minor poetry, engaged the interests of Ezra Pound for a few years and helped to disseminate some ideas of T. E. Hulme. But it

had nothing positive to say which was not said far better in the early poetry of Eliot. And the mannerisms of the school, its restricted range, its decorative monotony, its failure to utilize the resources of language make it difficult to realize that it was once radical and *avant garde* and a cause for consternation in academic America.

Some such movement of technical innovation as Imagism however, seems necessary at the beginning of a new literary period. The reformation of style has usually to precede the deeper reformation of the sensibilities which create style. 'Every revolution' in poetry says Eliot 'is apt to be and sometimes to announce itself as, a return to common speech. That is the revolution which Wordsworth announced in his prefaces and he was right: but the same revolution had been carried out a century before by Oldham, Waller, Denham and Dryden; and the same revolution was due over again something over a century later.'[1] After the excesses of poetic diction in the late nineteenth century and the early years of the twentieth it was certainly necessary for the good health of poetry to advocate a return to common speech. But there are many ways of achieving this return and the way Imagism proposes is unfortunately not the right one. It is necessary to insist on this criticism because of the prevalent superstition that the theories of Imagism were sound but their execution inadequate and that the failure of the movement can be attributed almost entirely to the lack of genius among the poets who composed it. Edwin Muir claims for instance that the theory of Imagism was 'insufficient though salutary' and goes on to contrast its practice as 'constricting'.[2] Herbert Read argues that 'though attempts have been made to create an "imagist" poetry directly under the influence of Hulme's theories, and though these attempts have been of great value in the introduction of a clearer tone into poetic expression, they have remained comparatively obscure because they have not been the vehicle of any momentous intelligence. That does not alter the validity of the ideas or the possibility of their general application'.[3] I hope this essay will succeed in demonstrating that doctrines as barren as those of Imagism could not have been the vehicle of any 'momentous intelligence' and that the failure of the movement is consequently one of teaching as well as of talent. A reconsideration of Imagism is nevertheless justified because by uncovering its critical shortcomings, and the effect of those shortcomings on its poetic practice, one is able to define one's own position by dissent and to give that dissent an historical validity. A movement may be important to the literary critic for the negative but still significant reason that it has led to important and influential mistakes.

The history of Imagism has been conveniently summarized by F. S. Flint.[4] Hulme is apparently to be regarded as its father though his poems appeared in no Imagist anthology. His meeting with Flint early in 1909 led to the formation of a 'dining-and-talking society' which held its first meeting on March 25th. Pound joined the society in April, a week after the publication of *Personae*, and was the first to attach the label *Imagisme* to the poetic theories of the group. The society dissolved in 1911 but 1912 saw the publication of Hulme's 'Collected Poems'—all five of them—as a supplement to Ezra Pound's *Ripostes*. In January of the same year Harold Monro opened the Poetry Bookshop in London, and in October Harriet Monroe published the first issue of *Poetry* in Chicago. Three poems by Aldington appeared in the November number, and three by H.D. in the following January. The March issue included the first public statement of Imagist principles by Pound, over the signature of F. S. Flint. Pound also contributed 'A Few Don'ts by an Imagiste'. Publication in England proved more difficult but the founding of *Poetry and Drama* by Harold Monro in March 1913 provided limited facilities. The magazine only survived till December 1914 but eleven months earlier *The New Freewoman* had been transformed into *The Egoist,* and, Aldington installed as an associate editor. *The Egoist* was to be the chief organ of Imagism in England, a similar service being performed in America by *Poetry* and by *The Little Review*. With the publication of the first Imagist anthology in March 1914 Imagism began to be respectable and Pound's interest in it began, characteristically, to wane. 'Imagism', he told Glenn Hughes 'was a point on the curve of my development. Some people remained at that point. I moved on.'[5] He moved on to Vorticism and the violences of *Blast*. Meanwhile Imagism had discovered a fairy godmother in the ample person of Miss Amy Lowell, a writer whose poetic talents were inconsiderable but whose entrepreneurial abilities were immense. On July 17th, 1914, Miss Lowell invited her dazzled associates to what is reverentially known as the 'Imagist Dinner'. The menu, preserved for us by the devotion of Professor Hughes, is far more impressive than any Imagist poem.[6] The result of this ceremony was the appearance in 1915 of *Some Imagist Poets* the first of three Imagist anthologies issued annually up to 1917. A fourth anthology, published in 1930, was little more than a nonstalgic retrospect. The 1915 collection is the most important for our purposes since it is prefaced by that celebrated manifesto from which all discussions of the movement begin. It is a manifesto which has been misunderstood and mangled often enough to deserve the courtesy of extensive quotation.

> The poets in this volume do not represent a clique. Several of them are personally unknown to the others, but they are united by certain common principles arrived at independently. These principles are not new; they have fallen into desuetude. They are the essentials of all great poetry, indeed of all great literature, and they are simply these:

> 1. To use the language of common speech, but to employ always the *exact* word, not the nearly exact, nor the merely decorative word.[7]

> 2. To create new rhythms—as the expression of new moods—and not to copy old rhythms which merely echo old moods. We do not insist on 'free verse' as the only method of writing poetry. We fight for it as for a principle of liberty. We believe that the individuality of a poet may often be better expressed in free-verse than in conventional forms. In poetry, a new cadence means a new idea.

> 3. To allow absolute freedom in the choice of subject. It is not good art to write badly about aeroplanes and automobiles; nor is it necessarily bad art to write well about the past. We believe passionately in the artistic value of modern life, but we wish to point out that there is nothing so uninspiring or old-fashioned as an aeroplane of the year 1911.

> 4. To present an image (hence the name: 'Imagist'). We are not a school of painters, but we believe that poetry should render particulars exactly and not deal in vague generalities, however magnificent and sonorous. It is for this reason that we oppose the cosmic poet, who seems to us to shirk the real difficulties of his art.

> 5. To produce poetry that is hard and clear, never blurred nor indefinite.

> 6. Finally most of us believe that concentration is of the very essence of poetry.[8]

Succeeding anthologies help to annotate the vocabulary employed. We are told for instance that 'the "exact word" does not mean the word which exactly describes the object in itself, it means the "exact" word which brings the effect of that object before the reader as it presented itself to the poet's mind at the time of writing the poem'.[9] Our interest then, is not in the object itself, but in the poet's reaction to the object. So far, so good; but unfortunately nothing is said about the all-important nature of this reaction. Our only clues are in the words 'effect' and 'presented' and these, if they suggest anything, suggest that the reaction is passive, a mere registering and assembling of sense impressions.[10] The annotation therefore does little to remedy the most serious weakness of the manifesto, its tacit assumption that the best of poetry is imitative rather than creative. The operative words are 'hard', 'clear', 'exact' and 'render', words which are appropriate to the description of something seen, not to the communication of something that is experienced. This insistence on poetry as accurate imitation can be seen even more clearly in the epigrams of Hulme:

> It is essential to prove that beauty may be in *small, dry* things.

> A period of *hard, dry* classical verse is coming.

> The great aim is *accurate, precise and definite description* . . . the poet is forced to use new analogies *and especially to construct a plaster model of a thing* to express his emotion at the sight of the vision he sees, his wonder and ecstasy.[11]

The emphasis is always on outline, size and texture. There is never any recognition of the kind of experience through language, the experience defined and made permanent by language of which all enduring poetry consists. And it follows from this conception of poetry as the presentation of something seen that you are forced to label as rhetoric any comment on the thing seen. Description and evaluation become separable acts and the business of poetry is to describe and not to evaluate. Its aim is 'precise and definite description', never the transformation of description by its agent, the rebirth of the known through the experience of knowing. If the language of poetry differs from that of prose it differs only because it is more accurate, because it matches more exactly the contours of the real. 'Plain speech' says Hulme 'is essentially inaccurate. It is only by new metaphors . . . that it can be made more precise.' Such a conception of poetry is catastrophically misleading and not the less so for being put forward by Bergson.[12] It may be wholly admirable in analysis to separate reality from our judgements on reality. But because poetry rests on the experience of synthesis, every fact in its universe must demand the valuation of the whole poem for its context. The situation must embody its own comment. The image itself, every nuance and colour of its landscape, must be pervaded by the conclusions it is helping to establish. Imagism seldom supplies us with this unity. It is never much more than a form of poetic draughtsmanship. Its style is accordingly an exterior device, a means of recording something felt or perceived, not the living power and operative agent through which that perception or emotion comes into being. The criticism can perhaps be better defined by considering the last stanza of Aldington's *Choricos:*

> For silently
> Brushing the field with red-shod feet,
> With purple robe
> Searing the grass as with a sudden flame,
> Death,
> Thou hast come upon us.
> And of all the ancient songs
> Passing to the swallow-blue halls
> By the dark streams of Persephone,
> This only remains—
> That in the end we turn to thee,
> Death,
> We turn to thee, singing
> One last song.

The passage has grace and a certain languid unity but it is a unity of gesture not of being. At the end of it we have really learned nothing about death except that it is fashionable to sing when we confront it. Contrast any Elizabethan comment in the same mood (the great scene from *Antony and Cleopatra,* for instance, or that between Isabella and Claudia in the third act of *Measure for Measure*) and it will be plain that the coherence achieved there is of an entirely different and superior order. Even in lines so apparently artless as 'Give me my robe, put on my crown; I have/Immortal longings in me' a universe of values is suggested. The crown is the imperial crown of Egypt; but it is also death, the consummation of life. The double function of 'immortal' ('immortal longings' and 'longings for immortality') is accordingly essential as a comment. One has to be arrested by the ambiguity in order to realize that it does not exist, since the 'crown', the reward of an immortal longing, can never be less than immortality. It is of course platitudinous to assert that Aldington's poems do not achieve this richness and I

shall have lived unnecessarily on the public goodwill if I go on to suggest that Aldington is not Shakespeare. These differences are worth insisting on only because they exemplify an inherent deficiency in the best of Imagist writing. If the 'great aim' of poetry is restricted to description then it follows that the language of the poet must remain neutral to the objects it is describing. It can light up its subject with certain preconceptions, or bring to it the colouring of a given emotional mood. But the mood remains unqualified and static. It is asserted rather than created; the poem can stabilize but it cannot change it. Such limitations are the natural consequence of regarding the thing represented as something external to the act of representation. They are therefore to be expected not only in Imagist theory but also, to a greater or less extent, in all those 'representational' theories of poetry which descend from Aristotle and from classical criticism to Bergson. But in Greek tragedy or even Miltonic epic— forms in which the thing said is freely separable from the way of saying it—the limitation is not unfair to its material and the theory provides the appropriate apparatus for the poetic facts which it was designed to interpret. The difficulty arises with reflective and lyric poetry, where the language is the form, not the vehicle of its content, and where the thing said is inseparable from the way of saying it. To discuss such material adequately we need a theory of poetic activity in which, to quote Coleridge, 'the act of contemplation makes the thing contemplated'. The mind, in such experience, is united to its object in order to create the reality which it knows. This unity, in my opinion, is characteristic of the best lyric and reflective poetry; a theory like Imagism which can make no provision for it is bound to approach such writing in the wrong way. Its consequence can only be that the poet, compelled to represent rather than to experience, is forced to expel from his imagination all generalizations, all moral imperatives, and all evaluations or syntheses of fact which must be lived through to acquire their poetic validity. But a universe so simplified is necessarily devoid of any significant structure or of any sense of movement to an inclusive unity. The order it provides is formalized and lifeless and the images it initiates never extend into or demand the context and completion of the poem. These deficiencies are evident in several of H.D.'s lyrics:

> I saw the first pear
> as it fell—
> the honey seeking, golden-banded,
> the yellow swarm
> was not more fleet than I,
> (Spare us from loveliness)
> and I fell prostrate
> crying:
> you have flayed us
> with your blossoms.
> spare us the beauty
> of fruit trees.
>
> The honey-seeking
> paused not,
> The air thundered their song
> and I alone was prostrate
> O rough-hewn

god of the orchard
I bring you an offering—
do you, alone unbeautiful,
son of the god
spare us from loveliness

these fallen hazel-nuts,
stripped late of their green sheaths,
grapes, red-purple,
their berries
dripping with wine,
pomegranates already broken,
and shrunken figs
and quinces untouched,
I bring you as offering.

It will be noted that if the particular images in this poem possess any force, it is only because of the repeated (and 'cosmic') supplication. But the poem merely circles round this supplication; the decorative catalogue of fruits with which it ends is evidence that no progression has been achieved or attempted. There is not, as in the well-known lines which follow, a completion of the abstract by the concrete, a demand by each for the presence of the other:

Dust as we are, the immortal spirit grows
Like harmony in music; there is a dark
Inscrutable workmanship that reconciles
Discordant elements, makes them cling together
In one society.

The effect here depends on two contrasted sets of associations. 'Harmony' and 'Workmanship' suggest a pre-ordained pattern based on eternal law; 'reconciles' and 'cling' with their suppressed image of separated lovers suggest the tension and conflicts of actual existence and the sense of order it progressively achieves. But the immortal spirit 'grows like harmony', reconciling discords; the 'dark, inscrutable' workmanship cannot be separated from its concrete and human realization. The passage therefore does not merely declare certain abstract and cosmic principles of order; it also defines through its distinctive imagery the way in which that order is established in human reality. The concrete lives 'in one society' with the general in Wordsworth's metaphors as well as in his philosophy; speculative truths are made vital by their functioning in an accurate, precise and definite experience. If the Imagists had followed Pound's condescending advice ('read as much of Wordsworth as does not seem too unutterably dull"[13]) they might perhaps have understood from such passages that no isolation of the local from the cosmic can be effected, and that an image is poetically justifiable only when its own implicit valuation completes a whole system of metaphor and comment. The requirement is well illustrated by this 'abstraction' from *Troilus and Cressida*:

Time hath, my lord, a wallet at his back
Wherein he puts alms for oblivion.

Even the casual 'my lord' is indispensable. It is 'in character' for Ulysses, but in character also for the life of the image. It is part of the picture which the image proposes

(the generous lord helping the impoverished beggar) but it also succeeds in commenting on that picture since, by suggesting that time lives on our charity, it makes us more conscious that we can afford to yield nothing to time. Ulysses' ironical courtesy moreover stimulates the recognition that the negligent 'lord' is really time's servant. After this one cannot help seeing that time's 'wallet' is really bottomless and that all that remains of the grandeur of Achilles is his helpless and destructive reliance on his past. The manner in which the second line fades away (the last foot of the pentameter can barely be sounded) perfectly captures this self-defeating negligence. The personification is thus intensely dramatic, and dramatic not only because it occurs in a drama. Like every poetic image it possesses its own life; but that life is made more particular and vivid by its incorporation in the context of the whole. Similarly when Ulysses talks of 'this chaos where degree is suffocate', 'degree' and 'chaos' are presumably two of the cosmic abstractions which the well-dressed Imagist is advised to abhor. But like the mendicant 'time', they acquire their local reality. The image of 'suffocation', of 'chaos' stifling 'degree' suggests far more forcibly than any direct assertion the inherent will of the universe to order. That suggestion is weighted by the theme of Ulysses' homily, the progressive collapse of each stage of being into the stage below it till everything returns to that murderous impotence from which the creation of order first began.

Without needing to press illustration further, it should be plain that no vigorous tradition of poetic writing can afford to separate description from comment or the abstract from the concrete. When the eighteenth century did so its powers of observation became atrophied and abstract, and when the nineteenth did so, its powers of generalization became standardized and lifeless. The concern of any new movement in poetry should be to reconcile these separated elements, and to bring them together in the wholeness of poetic experience. All that Imagism seems to propose, however, is a new version of an ancient mistake. The dissociation of sensibility it inherits is strengthened and not corrected by its doctrines, its implicit separation of the object described from the language of describing. Its fear of 'sonorous' generalities thus leads, not to a fusion of the general with the particular, but to a microcosmic obsession with the minute and concrete. The elements of the poetic synthesis are driven further apart instead of being unified. The world of description becomes flat, characterless, and devoid of moral shading but those who like Aldington find its climate unhealthy can only desert it for the kind of cosmic statement which Imagism has ostensibly been designed to repudiate:

And even if the release takes place
And the dialogue of the two natures is perfect
Still, the end must be tragic. It is easy to see that,
Though the fundamental essential tragedy perhaps
(Some say 'of course')
Is not death but birth.

And here is another sample of 'accurate, precise and definite description' taken from Aldington's poem on his childhood:

> The town was dull;
> The front was dull;
> The High Street and the other street were dull—
> And there was a public park, I remember,
> And that was damned dull too.

The two worlds exclude, instead of completing each other. Generalities in these poems are uncompromisingly general just as the images in other Imagist poems are husks of sensation emptied of all comment. And when as in Fletcher's *The Attainment,* the two elements are mingled, the relationships between them remain static and external:

> Daring in my humility
> I tore the veil aside and there lay truth
> Outstretched and shining like a sleeping bride
> Beyond the grasp of genius or of youth.
> Long I gazed lovingly on her; she slept still;
> And in her naked glory all the earth
> Dwindled down to a narrow speck, until
> I rose and, ere I passed the gates of birth,
> I prayed that as Isaiah's lips with fire
> Were purged, so on my lips the fire might be.
> And then I merged with that eternity
> Which is beyond the world and its desire.

Professor Hughes informs us that this reversion to nineteenth century rhetoric was dictated by Fletcher's 'inner needs'.[14] But it is surprising how often the needs of Imagist poets either prevent them from writing poetry at all or else make them write poems which are the very reverse of Imagist. Thus Pound left the movement soon after it began and Flint after 1920 devoted himself increasingly to translation and reviewing. Fletcher's return to 'cosmicism' has already been discussed. Lawrence's appearance in the Imagist anthologies was not much more than an entertaining accident. Aldington whose early poems rank as Imagist classics drifted more and more towards philosophical rhetoric. Only H.D. has remained faithful to the Imagist manifesto and H.D.'s development, as Professor Hughes admits, 'has been chiefly from the short lyric to the long, or rather, from the lyric to the narrative and dramatic poem. Certainly she has not perceptibly widened her art and it is questionable how much she has deepened it; what she has done is to lengthen it'.[15] The sterility of Imagism could not be better brought out than in a comment of this kind on the perfect Imagist, and it is a barrenness which unfortunately extends to something more than a local failure of doctrine or procedure. The conception of poetry as a form of description, rather than as a mode of experience, is one which corrupts not only Imagism but many of the alternatives which criticism sets against it. It limits our use of the resources of language since not all the evocations of language are descriptive. It compels us to distinguish the technique of a poem from the perceptions which that technique has been devised to express. It separates imagery from its kernel of comment and generalities from

their concrete validation. Because of these simplifications it is also unhistorical; it can see the past only as an external prescription, not as a power of meaning in the present. Finally these partitions and exclusions, even if they do not make poetic experience impossible, must interfere seriously with its range and effectiveness. They are therefore bitterly hostile to that personally experienced yet representative synthesis from which the poetry of each generation requires to be created.

Having discussed the failings of Imagism one is in a better position to assess its historical significance. Critics have usually seen in the movement the first premonitions of a new order in poetry, an order whose interests are dramatically opposed to the traditional standards of nineteenth century writing. One's doubts about such credentials are natural; they are strengthened by Livingstone Lowes's discovery that admirable Imagist poems can be made by putting Meredith's novels into free verse.[16] Since similar results can be secured by rearranging Pater (see, for example, the passage from *The Renaissance* which Yeats puts at the beginning of the Oxford Book) one is forced to conclude that the Imagists are really less modern than they are made to be. The manifestoes apparently deny this—'we believe passionately in the artistic value of modern life'[17]—but despite this brave show of up-to-dateness the preferences of Imagism seem rooted in the past and its reaction to the present essentially defensive: 'It is not good art to write badly about aeroplanes and automobiles; nor is it necessarily bad art to write well about the past'. Far from being a credo of modernity this is almost an apology for not being modern enough. One would expect the people who devised this formula to be far more interested in Sapphics than in aeroplanes. So it is not surprising that when Aldington thinks of Dover, he uses it exclusively as material for disgust, and that when Flint writes of London, his poem is not about city life at all but about green skies, moonlight, and the climbing of a birch tree. This repudiation of the present (or what is only a stage better, the cultivation of simplified and static emotions about it) culminates in these remarks of H.D.'s:

> . . . the inner world of imagination, the ivory tower, where poets presumably do live, in memory, does stand stark with the sun-lit isles around it, while battle and din of battle and the whole dreary, tragic spectacle of our time seems blurred and sodden and not to be recalled, save in moments of repudiation, historical necessity. . . . Miss Monroe was one of the first to print and recognize my talent. But how strangely, farcically blind to our predicament.[18] The letter suggested with really staggeringly inept solicitude that H.D. would do so well—maybe, finally, if she could get into 'life', into the rhythm of our time, in touch with events, and so on and so on and so on. I don't know what else she said. I was laughing too much.

It may be true, as her critics have frequently argued, that H.D.'s talents were born out of their time. That in itself is no condemnation of them. Anachronisms have their place in poetry and the language and values of a different civilization may well speak significantly of the age in which we live. But to do so they must be regulated by an emotion more complex and civilized than one of dainty disgust. Since the doctrines of Imagism, and the temperaments of many of its poets are hostile to the development of this complex reaction the movement fails to be vitally representative either of the traditional or the new. It is therefore unable, as the best of poetry is able, to discover and regenerate tradition as an element in the meaning of the new. The technical changes it initiates merely preserve the sensibility of the nineties by providing it with an up-to-date exterior. One must turn to other and more critical talents for the deeper changes of sentiment and insight which should inform and justify these outer innovations.

1 'The Music of Poetry', *Partisan Review,* Nov.-Dec. 1942, p. 457.

2 'The Present Age', *Introductions to English Literature,* ed. Bonamy Dobrée (London, 1939), Vol. V, p. 51.

3 Intro. to T. E. Hulme's 'Notes on Language and Style', *The Criterion,* July 1925.

4 'The History of Imagism', *The Egoist,* May 1st, 1915.

5 Glenn Hughes, *Imagism and the Imagists* (Stanford University, 1931), p. 38.

6 Hughes, *op. cit.,* p. 36.

7 Presumably an allusion to a remark of Hulme's: 'Plain speech is essentially inaccurate. It is only by new metaphors . . . that it can be made more precise.'

8 *Some Imagist Poets* (London, 1915), pp. vi-vii.

9 *Some Imagist Poets* 1916 (London, 1916), p. vi.

10 Pound, who on occasion is wiser than his brethren, defines the image as presenting 'an intellectual and emotional complex in an instant of time'. He adds that 'it is the presentation of such a "complex" simultaneously which gives that sense of sudden liberation: that sense of freedom from time limits and space limits; that sense of sudden growth, which we experience in the presence of the greatest works of art'. (*Pavannes and Divisions,* New York, 1918.) A poetic image however does not merely 'present' but compels through language a response to the thing presented.

11 Quotations from T. E. Hulme throughout this essay are from *Speculations,* ed. H. Read (London, 1925) and from Michael Roberts's *T. E. Hulme* (London, 1938), pp. 258-303.

12 T. E. Hulme, 'Bergson's Theory of Art', *Speculations,* pp. 143-69.

13 'A Few Don'ts by an Imagist', *Poetry* (Chicago), Jan. 1913.

14 Hughes, *op. cit.,* p. 149.

15 *Ibid.,* p. 111.

16 'An Unacknowledged Imagist', *Nation,* February 24, 1916; *Convention and Revolt in Poetry* (London, 1930), pp. 178-84.

17 The claim is more fervent a year later: 'Imagism asks to be judged by different standards from those employed in nineteenth-century art. . . . This must not be construed into the desire to belittle our forerunners. On the contrary, the Imagists have the greatest admiration for the past and humility towards it. But they have been caught in the throes of a new birth. The exterior world is changing, and with it men's feelings, and every age must express its feelings in its own individual way.' *Some Imagist Poets 1916* (London, 1916), Preface, pp. vii-viii.

18 'A Note on Poetry', *The Oxford Anthology of American Literature* (New York, 1938), p. 1287.

A. R. Jones

[*In the following essay, Jones examines sources for establishing a factual history of Imagism.*]

SOURCE: "Notes towards a History of Imagism," in *The South Atlantic Quarterly,* Vol. 60, Summer, 1961, pp. 262-85.

"Imagism is a faded legend," wrote J. Isaacs in 1951, "and its history has been misrepresented by interested parties."[1] If Imagism was ever a faded legend, recent criticism and research has quickened interest in the period to which it belongs until it has begun to take on brighter, even blatant, coloring. The interest of the modern critic in the early years of this century has now little or nothing to do with any nostalgia for the good old Edwardian days, which was the case with much of the earlier writings on the period; nor have most of the recent critics any personal axe to grind in their telling of the history of the time. It is not, for most of them, a period that they themselves lived through and in which they buried their own youth and aspirations. Indeed, this period has at last taken on the same kind of distance as any other and yet at the same time is both rich in interest and diversity and pertinently related to the contemporary scene. The period has been taken out of the field of autobiography and memoir and handed over to the biographer and the literary historian whose work is now to establish the facts.

If J. Isaacs' first proposition now seems untrue, there can, at least, be no doubt whatsoever about the truth of his second. Imagism certainly has been "misrepresented by interested parties." Indeed, we might point out by way of illustration that J. Isaacs himself has to some extent contributed to this misrepresentation.[2] Moreover, in 1954 he reported, without comment, that Robert Frost had told him that "Flint was responsible for the imagist movement in poetry, not Ezra Pound, nor T. E. Hulme."[3] This, as he must have realized, conflicts with his own account of the movement's genesis published three years before.

A more interesting misrepresentation is that of Ford Madox (Hueffer) Ford, whose foreword to the *Imagist Anthology 1930* [4] takes the form of a rhetorical reminiscence which he gives the nostalgic title, "Those Were the Days." In that foreword he confuses the history of Imagism to an extent that does credit to his imaginative powers;

> It is difficult to disentangle Futurism from Cubism and Vorticism and Imagism . . . and, indeed, even from Impressionism and Post-Impressionism and Dadaism and Hyper-realism. At least it isn't now. But in those days it was bewildering. You have to remember that by 1913 Futurism was really a world movement. . . . But by 1913 there had come divisions. A strong group in France, Germany and London began to call themselves CUBISTS. . . . Mr Ezra Pound and the at present ubiquitous Mr. Wyndham Lewis with the assistance of Mr Richard Aldington and my bewildered and not unpleasantly titillated self—evolved VORTICISM, which was, like CUBISM, a step toward some sort of constructive aesthetics. . . . What exactly VORTICISM was— though its most loyal champion—I never knew. . . . And as a by-product of VORTICISM there evolved itself . . . *Imagism*.

Ford's flirting among the isms of the period is, to say the least, cavalier, and his idea that Imagism emerged light-heartedly from a meaningless chaos of artistic and poetic movements sometime after the break-up of Futurism in 1913 is, as he says, "bewildering," even now. Ford shows himself to be hopelessly out of touch with a period in which these isms were felt to be irreconcilably divergent by those who believed in them with such passionate conviction. Vorticism, for example, was felt to be not "like Cubism" in any way, but directly opposed to it and was "evolved" by Gaudier-Brzeska. Anyway, it had nothing to do with Imagism except perhaps that Ezra Pound was somehow involved with both movements and Imagism certainly predates Vorticism and cannot have been evolved from it, not even as a by-product.

Yet Ezra Pound clearly asks us to take Ford seriously. On numerous occasions Pound has persisted in his contention that "during the years immediately pre-war in London," Ford was preeminently "the critical LIGHT." In fairness to Ford we should point out that he makes no such claim for himself though no one would claim that Ford was a retiring or modest man or anything but a boastful and arrogant one. As far as Imagism is concerned, Ford confesses to *not* knowing any of the contributors to the *Imagist Anthology 1930* for which he wrote his foreword. Or rather, he puts the matter the other way round by saying that, "No doubt every contributor in this volume will . . . protest to its editor that till now they have never heard of me. And that would be Proper . . . because at that date I died." The contributors to that anthology—

Richard Aldington, John Cournos, H.D., J. G. Fletcher, F. S. Flint, James Joyce, D. H. Lawrence, William Carlos Williams—must be considered as forming a significant nucleus of Imagist poets, and yet, as Ford admits, none of them was likely to have even heard of him. Ezra Pound alone of the Imagist poets, it seems, knew Ford. If Ford's influence did not reach these poets, then we can only remark how dimly "the critical LIGHT" must have been burning.

By saying that he "died" at the birth of Imagism, Ford means to tell us that he retired at that time from the literary scene: "I wrote a farewell to Literature . . . and, Fate taking me at my word," he says, "it was ten years before I wrote another book. (I except Propaganda which falls into the category of *biblia abiblia*.)" In fact, for the sake of precision, between 1913 and 1924, inclusive, Ford published no less than sixteen volumes of one kind or another, including *The Good Soldier* (1915), and collaborated in three others, as well as translating Pierre Loti's *The Trail of the Barbarians*. We can only wonder what he would have done more had he not taken a farewell to literature. However, as a reason for his "retirement" from the world of letters he says that the young Imagist poets of the time were beginning to practice what he had always preached and therefore he felt justified in leaving the further development of the English language in their safe-keeping.

> If I then went underground, it was quite sincerely because I considered that in this group of young people were writers perfectly calculated to carry on the work that I had, not so much begun, as tried to foster in others. I desired to see English become at once more colloquial and more exact, verse more fluid and more exacting of its practitioners . . . and above all . . . that it should be realized that poetry, as it were dynamically, is a matter of rendering, not comment. You must not say: "I am so happy"; you must behave as if you were happy. . . . And perhaps above all I was anxious that Anglo-Saxondom should realize that all creative prose like all imaginative verse is Poetry . . . emotions have their own peculiar cadences and . . . poetic ideas are best expressed by the renderings of concrete objects. . . .

Ford says nothing here about poetry that had not been said, and said much more precisely, many times before by the young experimental poets who grouped themselves around T. E. Hulme from 1908 onwards. There is little or no evidence of Ford's having any direct influence on poetry, either on its practice or on its theory, and little or nothing, so far as objective evidence is concerned, to justify Pound's insistence that Ford "did the WORK for English writing"—apart, that is, from Pound's insistence.

With so many luminaries to choose from at that time in London, we wonder what exactly Pound saw in Ford that made him single him out in this way. In spite of the achievement of Ford's much overpraised novel, *The Good Soldier,* neither his critical work nor his poetry nor his novels seem to support such extravagant claims for him. The force of personal influence is, of course, extremely elusive and not easily measured but we can say that in the case of Ford it does not seem to have been very distinctly felt except by Pound. Perhaps it was Ford's qualities as an editor that attracted Pound for he said, "The EVENT of 1909-10 was Ford Madox (Hueffer) Ford's 'English Review,' and no greater condemnation of the utter filth of the whole social system of that time can be dug up than the fact of that review's passing out of his hands." First of all, it is worth noting that the reason it passed "out of his hands" was because under Ford's management the review was losing, according to Violet Hunt, about £120 a month. Moreover, during the twelve issues of the review which Ford published from December, 1908, he printed work mainly by established writers such as Thomas Hardy, Henry James, Joseph Conrad, John Galsworthy, and W. H. Hudson. It is well to recall Pound's attack on what he called London's "respectable / and middle generation" of this period which he derided as "stew like Wells, nickle cash register Bennett. All degrading the values. Chesterton meaning also slosh at least then and TO me. Belloc pathetic in that he had MEANT to do the fine thing. . . ." Pound seems to have overlooked the fact that Ford published in the *English Review* work by H. G. Wells, Arnold Bennett, G. K. Chesterton, and Hilaire Belloc and thus furthered, presumably, the degradation of the values. In fact Ford's review on the whole stood for the literary establishment and published the work of accepted writers. It cannot really be said to have been revolutionary or even experimental and avant-garde. In poetry, for instance, apart from printing D. G. Rossetti's "The Ballad of Jan Van Hunks," Ford also published poems by Rupert Brooke and Walter de la Mare. He was persuaded to publish three poems by W. B. Yeats out of respect for his established reputation, but he did not really appreciate his poetry until he had been converted by Pound's instruction. Ford's "discovery" of D. H. Lawrence, his publication of poems by Flint and Pound, do not look very daring, or even surprising, when set into the context of the review as a whole. Ford had too great a respect for the established figures of literature, was too much of the literary and social snob, ever to have offended the accepted conventions and tastes of his time by turning the *English Review* into a platform for the new, experimental writing. Pound introduced him to some of London's younger and livelier poets and authors and managed to broaden his taste and outlook. Indeed, there is evidence that Pound effected a considerable and, in some ways, decisive influence on Ford and also managed to exercise some little influence on the *English Review*.

Pound is the chief propagandist for the Ford myth. He is also one of the main sources of information about the genesis and development of the Imagist movement. Both René Taupin, when writing his book, *L'Influence du symbolism français sur la poésie américaine (de 1910 à 1920)*, and Glenn Hughes, when writing *Imagism and Imagists,* wrote to Pound for information which he freely gave.

Pound's letter to Taupin[5] is of the greatest importance to the history of Imagism because, in the first place, he takes credit for beginning the Imagist movement, al-

though dissociating himself from its later development, and, in the second place, he asserts that the movement had begun *before* the poets involved had become familiar with the work of the French Symbolist poets. He says that the influence of the French Symbolist poets on the formation of the new English poetry was tenuous and indirect, "Comme le pain doit quelquechose au vanneur de blé, etc. Tant d'opérations intermédiaires." He goes on to stress this point:

> Réforme métrique plus profonde—date de 1905 on commence avant de connaître Fr. modernes. J'ai "lancé" les Imagistes (anthologie *Des Imagistes*: mais on doit me dissocier de la décadence des Imagistes, qui commence avec leurs anthologies postérieures [même la première de ces anthologies]).

There is no telling why Pound chose the date 1905 as the beginning of metrical reform; otherwise his position is clearly stated. In this letter he also makes an interesting reference to the earlier group associated with T. E. Hulme:

> En 1908-9 à Londres (avant le début de H.D.): cénacle T. E. Hulme, Flint, D. Fitzgerald, moi, etc. Flint, beaucoup français-ifié, jamais arrivé à condensation
>
> concentration
>
> avoir centre
>
> Symbolistes français> les "90's" à Londres. . . .
>
> Fort[e] diffèrence entre Flint: (*tolérance* pour *toutes* les fautes et imbécilités des poètes françaises). Moi—examen très sévère—et intolérance.

Although Pound includes Hulme, with himself, in the *cénacle* of 1908-9, he does not single him out as the leader of the group and furthermore he confuses the unity of the group by including the name of Fitzgerald. Nevertheless, he does single out F. S. Flint as an enthusiastic (although, compared with himself, indiscriminate) admirer of French poetry, but he associates that admiration with the decadents of the 1890's and with Arthur Symons. He reiterates his belief that the vogue in England for French Symbolist poetry came about through his advocacy and came after the Imagist movement had already got under way: "Mais ma connaissance des poètes fr. mod. et ma propagande pour ces poètes en Amérique (1912-17-23) venait en sens genéral *après* l'inception de l'Imagisme à Londres (1908-13-14)." Taupin's interest was, of course, in the influence of French Symbolist poetry during the decade 1910-1920 and although he launches into generalization that spread over the period 1890-1923 we can take it that he was in fact answering a letter which asked for information about a specific period and sought to clarify the part played by Pound as regards the influence of the Symbolists during that period. A curious point to note is that although Pound takes credit for launching the Imagists with *Des Imagistes,* which was published in the spring of 1914, he nonetheless dates the inception of the movement somewhat vaguely as "1908-13-14."

In reply to Glenn Hughes's enquiry regarding Imagism and the Imagists, Pound is rather more lucid but only a little less vague.

> Lawrence was never an Imagist. He was an *Amygist.* Ford dug him up and boomed him in *Eng. Rev.* before Imagism was launched. Neither he nor Fletcher accepted the Imagist program. When the prospect of Amy's yearly outcroppings was by her assured, they agreed to something different. . . . The name was invented to launch H.D. and Aldington before either had enough stuff for a volume. Also to establish a critical demarcation long since knocked to hell.
>
> T. E. Hulme was an original or pre-[.] Bill Williams was as "original" as cd. be managed by writing from London to N.J. Flint was the next acquisition, tho' really impressionist. He and Ford and one or two others shd. by careful cataloguing have been in another group, but in those far days there weren't enough non-symmetricals to have each a farm to themselves.[6]

The main point that emerges from this letter is that Pound launched Imagism in order to establish a particular critical doctrine and to push the work of H.D. and Richard Aldington. He does not consider that D. H. Lawrence, J. G. Fletcher, Ford, Flint, and "one or two others" were genuine Imagist poets. William Carlos Williams he classes as "original." The original members of the anthology, *Des Imagistes,* number eleven in all and were, apart from Pound himself, Richard Aldington, H.D., F. S. Flint, Skipworth Cannell, Amy Lowell, William Carlos Williams, James Joyce, Ford Madox Ford, Allen Upward, and John Cournos. If we eliminate those poets who Pound considers were *not* really Imagist poets at all, we are left with only four Imagist poets proper including Pound himself. Also we may note that although Pound gives Hughes the impression that he was responsible for organizing the movement—and, indeed, he was both editor and contributor—he is not very helpful in volunteering information about his own relations with Imagism and the Imagists or about his own attitude towards the critical doctrines by which they wrote and for which he has been credited. He does on this occasion single out T. E. Hulme as "an original or pre-" but does not commit himself any farther.

In spite of Pound's assurances to the contrary, René Taupin, after exhaustive research, managed to determine a vital connection between the French Symbolists and the Imagist poets. He traced the influence of Rèmy de Gourmont and, to a lesser extent, Jules de Gaultier on the Imagist aesthetic and also isolated the influence of specific French poets on the work of individual Imagist writers. He found that Pound had read widely in French poetry and was indebted mainly to Gautier, Rimbaud, Corbière, and Laforgue, but also to Tailhade and Jammes; F. S. Flint was strongly influenced in his work by Verhaeren and de Bosschère; Amy Lowell by de Requier and Paul Fort; J. G. Fletcher by a succession of French poets, particularly by Rimbaud, Corbière, and Laforgue, and more consistently by Verhaeren. In the

case of H.D. and Richard Aldington, Taupin found difficulty in tracing specific influences and concludes that they were mainly indebted to the work of classical writers. Taupin's exacting study demonstrated that the Imagist poets as a whole had a thorough knowledge of French Symbolist poetry and were, at least after 1910, decisively influenced by their work and example.

Pound's unreliability as a source of the history of literary London before the 1914-1918 war is further illustrated by his replies to Michael Roberts' inquiries. In 1937 Michael Roberts was engaged in writing his book on T. E. Hulme[7] and he wrote to Ezra Pound asking for information. Pound's replies are of interest in themselves but, again, his answers to specific questions are evasive, vague, and impatient in what is now recognizably the Pound epistolary manner. He gives little away on the question that interested Roberts particularly, which was that of Pound's relations with Hulme and the Hulme circle. Such information, if it had been forthcoming, might well have shed invaluable light on the history of Imagism as well as giving important and in some respects crucial insight into his own poetic development. Only one of these replies has been previously published, and then in an expurgated form.[8] They are all addressed from "EZRA POUND / Via Marsala 12-15/ RAPALLO / Italy" and have the heading "A tax is not a share/ A nation need not and / should not pay rent for / its own credit./ 1937 anno XV."

> [Postcard dated 1st May]
>
> Have you decided whether FIVE poems are ONE poem?
>
> Are you paying any attention to relation of Hulme's ideas to those functioning or lying fallow in London in 1908?
>
> and or to dates of printing. also N. Age stuff our pseudonym?
>
> Naturally I cd. do a month's work on yr/book . . . and who wd/ thank me even impolitely for doing it?
>
> Yrs E.P.
>
> [Letter dated 9th May]
>
> Re/Hulme What are you doing the book *FOR*????
>
> Preface by Eliot wd. sell the book. but he wasn't in London then.
>
> I mean do YOU want to prove or DO something, or are you out to harmonize with the shit which is Squire's england, and to use retrospect to blanket and damp down the active thought (what tiny particle there is) of the time?
>
> In any case can't learn anything about it from me short of coming here and talking.
>
> Balzac comedie humaine needed to convey the London of then to young men of now. I haven't the time.

If Hulme has anything CONstructive for tomorrow/ Fire away. But if you are merely out to maintain bloomsbuggy yatter . . . .

Personally I have no use for any man who is distracting attention from vital question at this time.

Yrs.
E.P.

[Letter dated 15th May]

Waaaal, yng/man lemme remind you ONE thing. I mean I can help you if you have the sense to be helped. and it won't take long.

What do think ARE Hulme's ideas?

Hulme said that all any man ever THOUGHT wd/ go on the back of an envelope.

What he said about the rest of one's scribblings you can prob/ discover from his "graphic remains."

Shall be interested in the "back of the envelope" when you have succeeded in digging it out and reconstructing it.

Yrs.
E.P.

[Postcard dated 14th July]

do you want to warm up possible public by printing poem or foretaste of Hulme book in magazine Ronald Duncan/co /Lloyds, 6 Pall Mall, says he will go to press by Aug/6.

(last day for ms/)

Lecture probably to QUEST society (G.R.S. Mead's) W. Lewis, I, and, I am fairly sure, T.E.H. lectured to Quest/ I suppose trace is left in Quest (the quarterly or monthly mag/edt/ by Mead).

I take it you mean "we shd/establish hierarc/ of val/" Bother of T.E.H. inverting his word order in sentence//. As nearly as I recall someone took me to Tour Eifel for group dinner after publication of Personae or at least while it was in the press/ I think . . in fact yes, sure, Personae was out. Flint in press/ and I read Altaforte/ No means of metting 'em till I had been pubd/

Fitzgerald, occasionally or once or twice Colum/ Jo. Cambell, Flint, Tancred. First talk I remember H. talking of Upward's "New Word." H "useful" mainly re/ sculpture.

"cinders" attitude NOT american—good deal later. Problem for writers in 1909 was OF language, word order. H's slopping round with Bergson a BORE.

[Letter dated 20th July]

Dear R/

what I am trying to get into yr/ head is the

PROPORTION of ole T.E.H. to London 1908 to 1910, '12, '14.

Hulme wasn't hated and loathed by the ole bastards because they didn't know he was there.

The man who did the WORK for English writing was Ford Mx Hueffer (now Ford).

The old crusted lice and advocates of corpse language knew that the *English Review* existed.

You ought for the sake of perspective to read THROUGH the whole of the Eng. Rev. files for the first two years/ I mean for as long as Ford had it.

Until you have done that you will be prey to superstition/

You won't know what WAS. and you will consider that Hulme or any of the chaps of my generation invented the moon and preceded Galileo's use of the telescope.

Don't think that I read the Eng/ Rev/ *then*. I did NOT lie down with Wells, or read "Tono Bungay." Nothing to be proud of, but so was it.

I was learning how Yeats did it. I believe that T.E.H. (if you dig up ms/ you can verify) referred in verse to "the pavement grey" or gray, don't remember his spelling.

He had read Upward's new word. I didn't till I knew Upward about 1912-16 and I suppose I am sole reader of all Upward's books now surviving.

I spose there is a set in Brit/Mus/ and it might be poss/ for you to borrow my set, if you are in London.

I believe Hulme made mrs K/ and Flint do a good deal of the sweating over the actual translations of Bergson and Sorel/ having got his slice on the options.

I remember Flint glumpily talking about Hulme as a "dangerous Man" Wich I take to mean that he colluded Frankie into doing something useful

TO T.E.H. at least.

Frankie is another study

You ought also to remember who were still alive in those years/ and on whom young eyes were bent. Hulme's weren't that was part of his value. The respectable/ and the middle generation, illustrious punks and messers/ fakes like Shaw/ stew like Wells, nickle cash register Bennett. All degrading the values. Chesterton meaning also slosh at least then and TO me. Belloc pathetic in that he had MEANT to do the fine thing and been jockeyed into serving, at least to some extent, a shitten order of a pewked society. but NOT, as I felt, liking the owners of the shit pile.

Of course for those years london was Strand Magazine romance to young foreigner/

Dare say Mike Arlen Kilyumjian was the last rrromantic in Aladin's cave. Ansum kebs/ décolété ladies etCet and SETera.

ALL vurry pleasant oh mahrrrvelous.

War prob/ bitched most of that for you fledglings. or mebbe youth iz yewth.

Wonder what Doc/ Johnson wd/ have done about cubism?

Apart ça do you see any change from Hume's england to Hulme's?

I mean the england INside his head?

Yrs.
E.P.

The subject of Hulme clearly continued to worry Pound after this exchange with Michael Roberts. Although Roberts never took up Pound's suggestion to publish a poem or an article in Ronald Duncan's magazine, *Townsman,* in January, 1939, Pound published in that magazine two poems, "Song of Empire" and "Slice of Life," and an article called "This Hulme Business"[9] in which he tries to put Hulme in his place once and for all. In this article he repeats much that he had said before in his letters to Roberts. He emphasizes the relative insignificance of Hulme compared to the total intellectual picture of London at that time; and he stresses the importance of Ford Madox Ford and the *English Review.* Altogether Pound ignores Hulme's role as a decisive, influential leader among London's avant-garde, a role adequately substantiated by the testimonies of F. S. Flint, J. G. Fletcher, Richard Aldington, Wyndham Lewis, J. C. Squire, Edward Marsh, and many other writers and artists of the period who agree that Hulme's influence on London's intellectual life was profound and enduring. Moreover, all these contemporaries agree that Hulme was the prime mover in establishing a changed attitude towards, and new methods in, poetry and aesthetics. Pound's insistence that the critic should keep a proper sense of proportion and should place his subject in the right perspective of his time is a most salutary reminder as a corrective to the excesses that biographers are given to committing. Nevertheless, Pound's idea of proportion might also represent an essential distortion of fact particularly when it neglects the force of certain personalities and ideas which might well be out of all proportion to relative numbers or reputations. A literary historian of the period is bound to give considerable weight to what Pound has to say not only because his remarks are important in assessing his own biography and development as a poet, but also because he himself figured so large in the intellectual life of London at the time. In his letters to René Taupin and Glenn Hughes, as in his correspondence with Michael Roberts, we might well be impressed by the fact that Pound was generous enough with his time to trouble to answer at all, but in assessing the actual documentary worth of these answers we cannot overlook certain curious and significant "misrepresentations."

Glenn Hughes's account of the history of Imagism is indebted to Pound although he owes much more to F. S. Flint's history of the movement which he published in the *Egoist.*[10] J. Isaacs also uses this article by Flint. Although neither Hughes nor Isaacs is agreed in detail, they are both broadly similar in their accounts. Glenn Hughes[11] sees French Symbolism as being "the principal forerunner of imagism" and he gives an elaborate account of the development of Symbolist poetry from the time of the Parnassians' revolt against Romanticism in 1860 to the emergence of Symbolism proper under Jean Moréas down to the classicists of the "Ecole Romane," the Cubists, the Fantasists, the Unanimists, the Dadaists, and the Surrealists. He allows T. E. Hulme the title "father of imagism" and starts his account with Hulme's founding of the Poets' Club in 1908. Though none of the members of the Poets' Club were themselves poets, Hughes tells us, they discussed experimental, Imagist poems (we wonder where Hughes thinks they got them from). Early in 1909, says Hughes, Hulme met F. S. Flint and thereafter a new dining and talking society was founded. This society met in Soho on Thursday evenings, the first meeting being held on March 25th, 1909. On April 22nd, 1909, Ezra Pound joined the group, says Hughes, and thereafter Pound became the leader of the Imagist poets at least until he was displaced by Amy Lowell.

J. Isaacs' account of the movement is briefer and more lucid:

> The movement began . . . in 1908 when T. E. Hulme founded a Poets' Club which met in Soho every Wednesday to dine and to read poetry. A small pamphlet was issued For Christmas 1908 which contained Hulme's *Autumn,* the first and most famous of the Imagist poems. . . . Early in 1909 T. E. Hulme met F. S. Flint and from 25th March a new group was formed. . . . On 22nd April 1909 there was introduced an American poet, Ezra Pound . . . so ended the first phases, the softer phase, the 90'sh phase of the "School of the Image". . . . The next phase is the invention of the label "Imagist" and the reign of Ezra Pound. . . . Ezra Pound became the impressario of the movement.[12]

Clearly both Glenn Hughes's and J. Isaacs' accounts rely heavily on Flint's article, "The History of Imagism," and should be compared with it as well as with each other:

> Somewhere in the gloom of the year 1908, Mr. T. E. Hulme . . . proposed to a companion that they should found a Poets' Club. The thing was done there and then. The Club began to dine; and its members to read their verses. At the end of the year they published a small plaquette of them, called "For Christmas MDCCCCVIIII." In this plaquette was printed one of the first "Imagist" poems by T. E. Hulme; *Autumn.*

> I think what brought the real nucleus of this group (1909 group) together was a dissatisfaction with English poetry as it was then (and still is alas!) being written. We proposed at various times to

replace it by pure *vers libre;* by the Japanese *tanka* and *haikai*. . . . In all this Hulme was ringleader. He insisted too on absolutely accurate presentation and no verbiage. . . . There was also a lot of talk and practice among us . . . of what we called the Image. We were very much influenced by modern French symbolist poetry. . . .

Pound collected together a number of poems of different writers . . . and in February-March 1914 they were published in America and England as "Des Imagistes; an Anthology" which though it did not set the Thames seems to have set America on fire. . . . There is no difference, except that which springs from difference of temperament and talent, between an imagist poem of today and those written by Edward Storer and T. E. Hulme."[13]

Glenn Hughes and J. Isaacs both document, with varying success, the rather bare account of Imagism given by F. S. Flint. All the accounts agree that there were two groups to which T. E. Hulme belonged, the 1908 Poets' Club and a new group which was formed in 1909 and joined first by Flint and later by Pound. Hughes rather surprisingly says that the members of the 1908 Poets' Club were not themselves poets although they discussed poetry. J. Isaacs says that the Poets' Club met in Soho on Wednesday and Hughes says the 1909 group met in Soho on Thursdays. The plaquette which Flint says was produced by the 1908 Poets' Club and called *For Christmas MDCCCCVII* is ignored by Hughes and described by Isaacs as a "pamphlet" called "For Christmas 1908." The difficulty that both writers face is that using Flint as their "source" they are unclear as to how the 1908 Poets' Club became what Flint calls merely the "1909 group." Moreover, of course, neither Flint nor Pound was an original member of the 1908 Poets' Club and yet Flint, Isaacs, and Hughes are agreed that Imagism was born in that club and that it was T. E. Hulme who gave it birth.

In July, 1906, T. E. Hulme, having been sent down from Cambridge and having broken the ties with his family, took a passage on a cargo boat to Montreal, Canada. He traveled widely over the vast prairie lands of the middle west, working only in order to provide himself with enough money to enable him to move on to the next town or province. It was during this period that he began to concern himself seriously with aesthetics and with poetry and it was during this period that he came, quite independently, to certain conclusions concerning the nature of poetic language and the supremacy of the image. "The first time I ever felt the necessity or inevitableness of verse," he said, "was in the desire to reproduce the peculiar quality of feeling which is induced by the flat spaces and wide horizons of the virgin prairie of Western Canada."[14] At that time he wrote to Miss A. M. Pattison to say, "I have got lots of ideas and experiences and am very glad I came, even if it were only for a suitable image I thought of one day working in the railway."[15] He began to write a number of poems centered on the ideas and feelings aroused by his experience of the vast space, the huge sky, and the flat, rolling grass lands of Canada. "The flats of Canada," he wrote, "are incomprehensible

on any single theory."[16] He sought to encompass this incomprehensibility by containing it within the image:

> Somewhere the gods (the blanket-makers in the
> 　　prairie of cold)
> 　　　　Sleep in their blankets.

Or again,

> Brand of the obscene gods
> 　On their flying cattle,
> 　Roaming the sky prairie.

He later worked some of the images he had conceived in Canada into his poetry. The important point to stress is that by the time that he had returned from Canada in the spring of 1907 he had already conceived the salient features of the theory and practice of what came to be called Imagism. What Pound calls his "slopping round with Bergson" enabled Hulme to lend his theory at least the trappings of philosophical respectability. He found that he could use (or rather misuse) Bergson's philosophical ideas in order to provide himself with a suitable language in which to order and propagate his conception of poetry and poetic language. Bergson had said that there are two distinct ways of "knowing" reality; intellectually by means of the analytic method, and instinctively by means of the intuition. Hulme assumes that there are two distinct kinds of language; prose which is a counter language, a practical but essentially blunt instrument of communication, and poetry which is, or can be, a sensitive and individual instrument for communicating the unique, imaginative experience of the poet. Prose is the language of the intellect, a concept language; poetry is the language of intuition, an imagistic language. Only the language of poetry can communicate our intuitions of the intensive, real nature of experience. "No image," says Bergson, "can replace the intuition of duration" but

> many diverse images, borrowed from very different orders of things, may, by the convergence of their action, direct consciousness to the precise point where there is a certain intuition to be seized. By choosing images as dissimilar as possible, we shall prevent any one of them from usurping the place of the intuition it is intended to call up, since it would then be driven away at once by its rivals. By providing that, in spite of their differences of aspect, they all require from the mind the same kind of attention, and in some sort the same degree of tension, we shall gradually accustom consciousness to a particular and clearly defined disposition— that precisely which it must adopt in order to appear to itself as it really is, without any veil.[17]

Moreover, as Bergson points out, "the image has at least this advantage, that it keeps us in the concrete." It is not, of course, necessary to understand Bergsonian metaphysics in order to understand Hulme's theory and practice of Imagism, but in Bergson Hulme found a congenial language in which to clothe his theory of creative imagination as well as justification for asserting the paramount importance in poetry of the image or conceit. Indeed,

Bergson himself was surprised at the way Hulme was applying in aesthetics what to him were philosophical ideas and enthusiastically testified to the brilliance of Hulme's ideas;

> Ou je me trompe beaucoup, ou il est destiné à produire des oeuvres intéressantes et importantes dans le domaine de la philosophie en général, et plus particulièrement peut-être dans celui de la philosophie de l'art.[18]

Hulme's conception of Imagism was individually conceived under the pressure of his own personal experiences in Canada; he looked to Bergson to provide a language in which he could frame an appropriate aesthetic and to the practice of Japanese poets to furnish a hard, concise illustration as to the handling of the conceit in a pithy, condensed form.

When he returned to London, Hulme vigorously publicized his views about poetry in the literary clubs and meetings. He became friendly with a number of poets, particularly Selwyn Image, Edward Storer, and the remnants of the Rhymers' Club. Early in 1908 he founded, together with Henry Simpson, the "Poets' Club" and became its first secretary. The rules of the club show that it was a club for poets, that it met monthly, not weekly, and that it met in St. James' Street and not in Soho. The club consisted of not more than fifty members with a committee of five. The club met once a month, July, August, and September excepted, at the United Arts Club (above Rumpelmayer's), 10, St. James' Street, S.W., where the members dined and after dinner read original verse compositions and papers on some subject connected with poetry which were then discussed by the members. Rule 7 of the club proposed that "The Club shall endeavour to promote the publication of the poems of such of its members as shall be deemed to possess exceptional merit." and it was in accordance with this rule that, somewhat belatedly, in January, 1909, in fact, there appeared a volume of poetry, printed under the Club's auspices, entitled *For Christmas MDCCCCVIII*. This was certainly something more than a pamphlet and contained poems by Selwyn Image, Lady Margaret Sackville, Henry Simpson, Mrs. Marion Cran, F. W. Tancred, and Dermot Freyer. Hulme contributed two poems, "A City Sunset" and "Autumn," both of which demonstrate the maturity to which he had brought his practice of Imagism.

Hulme's interest in the Poets' Club did not sustain itself very long and the members were soon complaining of his inefficiency. However, in spite of this, the Club had established itself as a center of fresh poetic activity and by February, 1909, it was at least prominent enough to be singled out for attack in the *New Age,* curiously by F. S. Flint;

> I think of this club and its after dinner ratiocinations, its tea-parties in suave South Audley Street; and then of Verlaine at the Hôtel de Ville, with his hat on the peg, as a proof of his presence, but he himself in a café hard by with other poets, conning feverishly and excitedly the mysteries of their craft—and I laugh.[19]

F. S. Flint's attack is really directed against the upper class, dilettante character of the Poets' Club. As secretary, Hulme replied to this attack on the Club's behalf.[20] He pointed out, reasonably enough, that there is no necessary correlation between obscure cafés and good poetry, neither is there any reason to suppose that good poets must be addicted to Circean excesses and discoloured linen. Flint's nostalgia for the Bohemian life and French poetry gave Hulme his excuse for attacking him as a "belated Romantic," and thus demonstrating that at this early stage not only his Imagism but also his anti-Romanticism was fully developed. Hulme continued to regard the elegant meetings of the Poets' Club as essentially classical and civilized and the verses that the Club nourished as cultivated exercises in the new classicism which he was ushering in. This clash with Flint led very quickly to a firm friendship between them from which Hulme at least profited in a number of ways. The most important contribution which Flint made was to introduce Hulme to French Symbolist poetry. It was through Flint that Hulme was brought into contact with the contemporary French poetry and Hulme was quick to see how their example could help him and his fellow poets achieve that hardness, clarity, and restraint that he had already made the keystone of his Imagism. Hulme ceased to act as secretary to the Poets' Club but never ceased to attend their meetings as an ordinary member. He gathered about him his own friends and admirers and although it was never formalized into a club this group met fairly regularly in the Eiffel Tower, a Soho restaurant. Hulme was very much the center of these informal gatherings, the first of which is recorded as being held on 25th March, 1909. He dominated the discussions and argued endlessly and dogmatically about poetic tradition and poetic form and tirelessly impressed upon the meetings his idea of the new Imagism. Poems were read at the meetings and the points raised were passionately argued, but Hulme himself dictated the terms of the meetings and even insisted that only Imagistic poems were to be written by the members at all. The nucleus of this group, apart from Hulme himself and F. S. Flint, were Francis Tancred, Edward Storer, Florence Farr, and Joseph Campbell. Hulme's continued close association with the original Poets' Club is testified to by the fact that he proposed both F. S. Flint and Ezra Pound to election as members and that at Christmas, 1909, he published two further poems in their volume, *The Book of the Poets' Club*. Both F. S. Flint and Ezra Pound also contributed to that volume.

Pound did not arrive upon London's literary scene until the late summer of 1908 and did not really become part of it until after the publication of *Personae* in April of the following year. As late as May, 1909, the bewildered and enthusiastic Pound wrote to William Carlos Williams lavishly recommending the London literary world and criticizing his own shortcomings as a poet:

> I have sinned in nearly every possible way, even the ways I most condemn. . . . There is no town like London to make one feel the vanity of all art except the highest. To make one disbelieve in all but the most careful and conservative presentation of one's stuff. . . .

If you'll read Yeats and Browning and Francis Thompson and Swinburne and Rossetti you'll learn something about the progress of English poetry in the last century. And if you'll read Margaret Sackville, Rosamund Watson, Ernest Rhys, Jim G. Fairfax, you'll learn what the people of second rank can do, and what damn good work it is.[21]

This letter indicates the limitations of Pound's attitude towards English poetry before his meeting with Hulme. He was very quick to change his attitude and to adapt himself to the general tone of dissatisfaction with English poetry which prevailed at the Hulme gatherings. He soon lost this uncritical enthusiasm for English poetry as it then was and, taking Hulme's lead, he adopted with evangelical fervor, the cause of English poetry as it ought to be. Indeed, his enthusiasm for "the progress of English poetry in the last century" hardly outlasted the posting of this letter for on 22nd April, 1909, he was introduced into the Eiffel Tower gathering.

Pound's introduction to the group was characteristically dramatic. Dressed like the hero of Italian grand opera with his bright carroty beard waving, he read aloud his poem *Sestina: Altaforte* standing on a café table. He gave this dramatic monologue the full Browning Society treatment, roaring it out until the restaurant trembled and the waiters discreetly placed screens round the tables occupied by Hulme and his friends. Pound could hardly have been aware that this kind of behavior was calculated to arouse antagonism among a group of poets dedicated to restraint in poetry. Under the influence of Hulme and of the Eiffel Tower discussions, Pound soon abandoned the rhetorical and declamatory stylisms of his early poetry and began to experiment with epigrams and short lyrics and altogether to write in a more modest and retiring tone of voice. He also applied his enormous energy to the task of disseminating the ideas and views conceived and adopted by Hulme and his friends and, in the process, made them his own. Pound exercised his considerable talent for publicity on behalf of the group and very soon Hulme's theories of poetry were being distributed in London and America under the banner of Imagism. Pound both formalized and organized the Imagist movement; he issued the so-called Imagist Manifesto and recruited new poets, in particular H.D. and Richard Aldington, to its ranks. Hulme and his friends tolerated Pound because of his obvious poetic ability and perhaps more important, because of his immense goodheartedness, but they all felt that Pound had taken over Hulme's poetic theories without sufficiently acknowledging their source, as, indeed, they felt he had taken over F. S. Flint's views of French Symbolism without acknowledging his indebtedness. So far as poetry is concerned, there is no reason to suppose that the theory and practice of Imagism as directed by Pound and as exported to America is essentially any different from that conceived by Hulme and hammered out in argument and discussion over the tables of the Eiffel Tower or in the more select atmosphere of the Poets' Club. However much Pound says he owes to Ford or to Guido or to Fenellosa, he owes the ideas behind the Imagist movement to Hulme.

In an essay on his poetry, Richard Aldington pointed out that Pound's real gift as a poet was "the power of becoming absorbed in another personality long enough to produce from this stimulus one or several lyrics"[22] and this chameleon-like gift also allowed him to take on other men's theories and attitudes and make them his own.

In January, 1912, Hulme published five of his short poems in the *New Age,* under the title "The Complete Poetical Works of T. E. Hulme,"[23] and these poems were reprinted as an appendix to Pound's volume of poetry *Ripostes*[24] with a short preface by Pound in which the word *Imagisme* is first officially associated with the new poetry. In 1913, Pound followed this up by publishing "A Few Don'ts by an Imagiste" in *Poetry* (Chicago)[25] by which time he had joined several American poets in the movement, including H.D., J. G. Fletcher, and William Carlos Williams.

In December, 1912, Edward Marsh published the first volume of *Georgian Poetry* with immense success. He had invited Pound to contribute two of his poems, "The Goodly Fere" and "Portrait d'une Femme," to the Georgian anthology but Pound replied that he was just bringing the latter poems out in a volume of his own and could not let him have the "Portrait d'une Femme," and that "The Goodly Fere" did not illustrate any modern tendency in poetry.[26] By the time the second anthology was being collected, Marsh had decided to exclude American poets so that there was no question of including Pound. By that time, anyway, Pound and Marsh had quarrelled over the principles of the new system of quantitative verse and Marsh has recorded that "this planted in me a lasting suspicion of his artistic seriousness." In June, 1913, Marsh learnt from Wilfrid Gibson that "there's a movement for a 'Post-Georgian' anthology, of the Pound-Flint-Hulme school, who don't like being out of G. P. but I don't think it will come off."[27] Clearly, Marsh saw the Imagist anthology as an answer to *Georgian Poetry* by those poets who had been left out by Marsh. Pound himself says he published the anthology in order to launch H.D. and Richard Aldington. Yet Aldington confesses that what he calls "Ezra's 'Imagism'" was "forced on H.D. and me against our wills" and that neither he nor Hilda Doolittle was fully aware that it was "simply advertising bull-dust."[28] He also confirms that Hulme did not take Pound, or his attempts to publicize Imagism as his own, at all seriously but, in fact, treated both as a joke. Whatever Pound's motive was, he edited *Des Imagistes* in 1914 and closed rather than opened an epoch in English poetry. In 1915 Pound was responsible for publishing the *Catholic Anthology,* which virtually introduced T. S. Eliot to English poetry and also introduced a new epoch in modern poetry.

Pound had no intention of turning *Des Imagistes* into an annual anthology on the lines of *Georgian Poetry,* but this *was* the intention of Amy Lowell, one of the contributors to Pound's volume. At first Pound welcomed Amy Lowell's plan although he made it clear that he would not contribute and also that he would rather she did not publish under the flag of Imagism;

I think your idea most excellent, only I think your annual anthology should be called *Vers Libre* or something of that sort. Obviously it will consist in great part of the work of people who have not taken the trouble to find out what I mean by "Imagisme." I should, as I have said, like to keep the term associated with a certain clarity and intensity.

A number of your contributors object to being labelled. Vers libre seems to be their one common bond. Also if you use such a title (or anything similar) there need be no bothersome explanation of my absence. . . .

If you want to drag in the word Imagisme you can use a sub-title "an anthology devoted to Imagisme, vers libre and modern movements in verse" or something of that sort.[29]

Amy Lowell had just published a volume of poems entitled *Sword Blades and Poppy Seed*, the advertisement for which read:

Of the poets who today are doing the interesting and original work, there is no more striking and unique figure than Amy Lowell. The foremost member of the "Imagists"—a group of poets that includes William Butler Yeats, Ezra Pound, Ford Madox Hueffer—she has won wide recognition for her writing in new and free forms of poetical expression.

Pound was naturally outraged at what he calls "arrant charlatanism" on the part of the publishers and he reports W. B. Yeats as "more amused than delighted"[30] at being numbered among the Imagists. Pound's relations with Amy Lowell cooled perceptibly after this and when the anthology appeared in 1916, it was called *Some Imagist Poets*. Clearly she had ignored Pound's plea not to call it Imagist, thinking that the success of Pound's original anthology was too good not to be followed up. In fact, Amy Lowell in the anthologies she published in 1915, 1916, and 1917 introduced only two poets whose work was not represented in the original anthology: J. G. Fletcher and D. H. Lawrence. Pound had already taken Fletcher under his wing and had already grouped his work with that of the Imagists. D. H. Lawrence, however, appeared regularly as a contributor to *Georgian Poetry*. Pound was right to object that he "never was an Imagist" and certainly his inclusion alone is enough to establish that Amy Lowell never really understood the "critical demarcation" which Pound had inherited from Hulme, had developed and modified into a program of poetic reform, and had assiduously worked to uphold for the six years between 1908 and 1914. Imagism is a pioneer movement in poetry that, more than anything else, opened up the ground on which modern poetry has been built; it is the movement that led poetry from the romantic decadence of the nineteenth century into the twentieth. The history of Imagism has yet properly to be written but a start cannot be made until the misconceptions surrounding it have been examined and swept away.

NOTES

[1] *The Background of Modern Poetry* (London, 1951), chap. iii.

[2] *Ibid.*

[3] B.B.C. talk printed in the *Listener,* April 1, 1954.

[4] London, 1930.

[5] *The Letters of Ezra Pound,* ed. D. D. Paige (London, 1951), pp. 292-95.

[6] *Ibid.,* p. 288.

[7] *T. E. Hulme* (London, 1938).

[8] Pound to Roberts, 20th July 1937, *The Letters of Ezra Pound,* pp. 388-89. This transcription should be compared to the version printed by D. D. Paige.

[9] *Townsman,* II, no. 5 (January, 1939).

[10] "The History of Imagism," *Egoist,* II, no. 5 (May 1, 1915).

[11] *Imagism and Imagists* (Stanford, 1931).

[12] *The Background of Modern Poetry,* chap. iii.

[13] *Egoist,* II, no. 5 (May 1, 1915).

[14] "A Lecture on Modern Poetry," *T. E. Hulme,* Appendix II.

[15] Herbert Read, *The True Voice of Feeling* (London, 1953), p. 52.

[16] *Speculations,* ed. H. Read (London, 1924), p. 223.

[17] H. Bergson, *An Introduction to Metaphysics,* trans. T. E. Hulme (London, 1913), p. 14.

[18] *Speculations,* p. x.

[19] *New Age,* IV, February 11, 1909.

[20] *New Age,* IV, February 18, 1909.

[21] *The Letters of Ezra Pound,* pp. 41-42.

[22] *Egoist,* II, no. 5 (May 1, 1915).

[23] *New Age,* X, January 23, 1912.

[24] *Ripostes* (London, 1912).

[25] *Poetry* (Chicago), March, 1913.

[26] Christopher Hassall, *Edward Marsh* (London, 1959), p. 193.

[27] *Ibid.*, p. 229.

[28] Letter dated April 30, 1954.

[29] *The Letters of Ezra Pound,* pp. 78-79.

[30] Ibid., pp. 84-85.

MAJOR FIGURES

Cyrena N. Pondrom

[*In the following essay, Pondrom discusses the contributions of H.D. to the theory and practice of Imagism.*]

SOURCE: "H.D. and the Origins of Imagism," in *Sagetrieb: A Journal Devoted to Poets,* Vol. 4, Spring, 1985, pp. 73-97.

At the conclusion of his book, Noel Stock, the biographer of Ezra Pound, summarized: "With Yeats, Joyce, Lewis and Eliot dead he was the last survivor among the leading men of the formative years of the 'modern movement' in English literature—the movement in which he himself had played an important part, not only as innovator and renewer of language, but as impresario and publicity-agent, fund-raiser and office boy."[1] One could easily conclude from Stock's summation that modernism was a movement which owed its foundation and its characteristics to men alone. His emphasis is hardly atypical, even today, when a rapidly swelling scholarship on women writers makes only the least informed unaware that modernism possessed important women members.

The honor role of modernists who wrote in English must include, of course, Gertrude Stein, Hilda Doolittle, Dorothy Richardson, Marianne Moore, Virginia Woolf, and Edith Sitwell, to name only those leaders whose innovative work began within the period Stock calls "the formative years" of the modern movement. To those must be added the women whose genius lay more in the arenas of "impresario . . . publicity-agent [and] fund-raiser"—Amy Lowell, of course, and the great editors and publishers, without whom the shape and probably even the scope and influence of modernism would surely have been different: Harriet Monroe. Dora Marsden. Harriet Shaw Weaver. Margaret Anderson. Sylvia Beach.

Several of these women—among them Hilda Doolittle and Gertrude Stein—were not merely important participants in the modernist movement, but can claim priority in the creation of some of the literary models from which modernism developed. What is more, a systematic examination of the characteristics of major women modernists would prompt a revision in conventional descriptions of modernist political tendencies, use of myth, and attitudes toward a transcendental ideal, and even in the theory of

the nature of the modernist movement itself. Thus in very important ways the literary history of modernism is an account that remains to be written.[2] An appropriate place to begin that reconsideration lies in the origins of imagism.

Most thoughtful students of the origins of modern poetry now recognize that important roots of modern poetry lie in imagism. Although Ezra Pound after 1914 made a number of statements intended to minimize public valuation of the importance of imagism, his own poetry and his theories of poetic form and structure which undergird the modernist long poem grow directly out of it.[3] Consequently, it is of considerable significance to consider how the fundamental elements of the theory of the image and the nature and structure of the imagist poem came into being. A close comparison of the early "theory" of imagism with the actual practice of Ezra Pound, Richard Aldington, and H.D. strongly supports the inference that H.D.'s early poems were models which enabled the precepts of imagism to be defined. To evaluate the evidence for this proposition we must review again the oft-told tale of the beginnings of imagism.

When Hilda Doolittle arrived in London in the fall of 1911, Ezra Pound had already been in Europe three years. He had published six slim volumes of poetry—*A Lume Spento* (Venice, 1908), *A Quinzaine for this Yule* (London, 1908), *Personae* (London, 1909), *Exultations* (London, 1909), *Provença* (Boston, 1910), and *Canzoni* (London, 1911). With this he could claim a volume of comparative scholarship, *The Spirit of Romance* (London, 1910), and a volume of translations of the poetry of Guido Cavalcanti. H.D. at this time had written (for Frances Gregg) and published, apparently in New York commercial papers in 1910, only a few poems, which she has said were inspired by those in the volume of Theocritus Pound had given her.[4] Probably it was predictable that critics focused attention primarily on Pound as the originator of imagism.

At the end of 1911 and in the spring of 1912, H.D., Pound, and Richard Aldington lived in adjacent flats in Church Walk, Kensington, and met frequently, along with F. S. Flint, to discuss modern poetry.[5] Flint introduced them to the work of contemporary French poets,[6] and by May H.D., Aldington, and Pound were all three in Paris,[7] then ablaze with groups of poets issuing manifestoes and promulgating "rules" for the revitalization of modern poetry. Typical were the *fantaisistes,* the *unanimistes,* the *Whitmanistes,* the *futuristes,* the *paroxystes*—and so on, almost *ad infinitum.*[8] A complete report on this ferment appeared in the August, 1912, issue of *The Poetry Review,* in F. S. Flint's monograph, "Contemporary French Poetry."

It was during this exposure to the animated French coteries that the group decided to form a movement themselves: *imagisme.* "In the spring or early summer of 1912, 'H.D.,' Richard Aldington and myself decided that we were agreed upon . . . three principles," Pound wrote later, " . . . agreeing upon these three positions we thought we had as much right to a group name as a number of French 'schools' proclaimed by Mr. Flint in the August number of Harold Munro's [sic] magazine. . . . "[9]

On August 18, 1912, Pound first used the term *imagiste* in writing, in a letter to Harriet Monroe. He agreed to send *Poetry* interesting new work from London and Paris, and he included as a first installment two poems of his own for the magazine: "To Whistler: American" and "Middle-Aged." He called the latter "an over-elaborate post-Browning 'Imagiste' affair."[10] It was probably a month or six weeks later that Pound discovered that H.D. was a poet of real merit. The tale is told in H.D.'s own inimitable words:

> "But Dryad," (in the Museum tea room), "this is poetry." He slashed with a pencil. "Cut this out, shorten this line. 'Hermes of the Ways' is a good title. I'll send this to Harriet Monroe of *Poetry*. Have you a copy? Yes? Then we can send this, or I'll type it when I get back. Will this do?" And he scrawled "H.D. Imagiste" at the bottom of the page.[11]

Pound sent the poems in a letter dated only October [1912]. Pound's letter, like H.D.'s account of the event, clearly implies that little time elapsed between his discovery of her poems and his actually sending them to Monroe. In the letter to her he says, "I've had luck again, and am sending you some *modern* stuff by an American. . . ." A few days later, in a letter dated 13 October, he sent some more of his own poems to Monroe with the comment: "You must use your own discretion about printing this batch of verses. At any rate, don't use them until you've used 'H.D.' and Aldington. . . ."[12] He referred to this "batch" of poems as "Contemporania." (Pound continued to send poems to Monroe in small batches throughout the fall, and from them she eventually selected a dozen which appeared in the April, 1913, issue of *Poetry* under the heading "Contemporania."[13] We know, thus, that between August 18, 1912, when he first agreed to send material to *Poetry,* and October 13, Pound had sent Monroe poems by H.D. and Aldington, followed by a few of the poems of his own intended for the series "Contemporania."

Pound's own "imagiste affair," "Middle-Aged," appeared in the first issue of *Poetry,* in October, 1912, and the Aldington poems, "Au Vieux Jardin," "To a Greek Marble," and "Choricos" in November, 1912. H.D.'s poems—"Priapus" ["Orchard"], "Hermes of the Ways" and "Epigram"—appeared in January, 1913. True to Pound's request, Monroe did not publish more of his poems until April, 1913, after the poems by H.D. and Aldington had appeared.

In March, 1913, however, she published the now famous brief essays by Flint and Pound explaining the principles of imagism. It was there that Pound first defined the "image" as "that which presents an intellectual and emotional complex in an instant of time," and directed his fellow poets—if they would learn from imagism—to

Use no superfluous word, no adjective, which does not reveal something.

Don't use such an expression as "dim lands *of peace*." It dulls the image. It mixes an abstraction with the concrete. It comes from the writer's not realizing that the natural object is always the *adequate* symbol.

Go in fear of abstractions. . . . [14]

In the same issue, F. S. Flint, always self-effacing, represented himself as the interviewer of an imagist, and summarized as a result of his conversation the familiar "rules" of imagism:

> 1. Direct treatment of the "thing," whether subjective or objective.
>
> 2. To use absolutely no word that does not contribute to the presentation.
>
> 3. . . . to compose in sequence of the musical phrase, not in sequence of a metronome.[15]

During the formative months between Pound's first recorded use of the name *imagisme* and the date of the publication of the first descriptions of the movement in March, 1913, there were, then, only a handful of poems which Pound had explicitly advanced under the label *imagiste* as the evidence of a new movement: his own "Middle-Aged," the three poems by Aldington, and the three by H.D. A comparison of them offers interesting evidence of the significance of H.D. in creating the models that were to make imagism the foundation of the modern movement in English and American poetry.

Of particular interest is the first poem that Pound labelled *imagiste*. The poem begins with a poeticism of the type imagism rejected, and continues with an explicit comparison which is distinctly not the "super-position" of images, without explanation, that Pound later extolled in writing about his own imagist poem "In a Station of the Metro."[16] The first lines are

> 'Tis but a vague, invarious delight
> As gold that rains about some buried king.[17]

The first line is simple assertion, which equates an unspecified "it" (*'Tis*) with a descriptive complement (*vague, invarious delight*) so intangible that the mind can conjure no clear image. There is an attempt to be more graphic in the next line, with the simile comparing the "delight" to the "gold that rains about some buried king." Such a simile, with the abstract emotion stated first, and then discursively compared by means of "as" to an exotic unrelated object, is almost the antithesis of the technique which Pound himself endorsed as a hallmark of imagism and source of technical renewal for modern poetry.

"The point of Imagisme is that it does not use images *as ornaments*. The image is itself the speech," Pound wrote in 1914.[18] Applying such a prescription to the poem itself, the critic would expect the concrete image to precede the general statement of feeling and to generate in the reader an emotion which the poet wished to communicate. Only then, if at all, would one expect the poet to use a simile linking his specific image to an abstractly labelled state, such as "the vague invarious delight" of middle-aged desire. (Indeed, if the image "worked," the explanatory simile would be superfluous.) The progress in "Middle-Aged" is the reverse.

The next two stanzas develop two sustained similes which elaborate the scene which produces the "gold which rains about some buried king" and explicitly make the comparison with the "I" of the poem:

> As the fine flakes,
> When tourists frolicking
> Stamp on his roof or in the glazing light
> Try photographs, wolf down their ale and cakes
> And start to inspect some further pyramid;
>
> As the fine dust, in the hid cell
> Beneath their transitory step and merriment,
> Drifts through the air, and the sarcophagus
> Gains yet another crust
> Of useless riches for the occupant,
> So I, the fires that lit once dreams
> Now over and spent,
> Lie dead within four walls . . .

Although these lines present a vivid objective scene, the exact nature of the comparison remains abstract and equivocal: the syntax establishes a comparison between the I-figure and the falling gilt or dust of the Pharoah's tomb, but the sense insists upon a comparison between the (presumably newly middle-aged) persona and the dead king.[19] Eventually the elaborate similes emerge. The speaker is like the dead king, and love seems to him now no more than the dust or gilt which sifts down upon the mummy in his case as the living play above. Love now elicits only "precious metaphors" rather than more robust action, and even these are futile, for the dark (of middle-age) hides their beauty even from those with a cat's eyes.

This technique is quite unlike that urged by Pound in his famous explication of his "In a Station of the Metro" as a paradigm imagist poem. There two vivid and explicit images are juxtaposed without syntactical connection explaining the significance of their relationship. The emotion in the poem is perceived by the reader as the product of the interaction of the two images, with their respective emotional weights. Such a perception is, as Pound argued, instantaneous. "Middle-Aged," in contrast, is analytic, reader-response slower, and perhaps more cognitive than emotive. In addition, the cadence of the language, although cast in *vers libre,* is not that of ordinary speech (another precept of imagism), and the poem contains several "poetic" inversions like "the fires that lit once dreams" of the preceding stanza.

Pound, in his cover letter to Monroe, called the poem a "post-Browning" as well as an "imagiste" affair; and in fact the traces of Browning are rather more clear than the imagist tendencies. The poem has some affinities with "Cino," another rather interesting poem that anticipates

some of the tendencies of the imagist movement but is clearly in the pre-imagist mode.

Three other poems appeared in *Poetry* under the description "imagist" prior to the publication of the three by H.D.—the Aldington poems Pound apparently sent just before he was shown H.D.'s work. These lyrics are even further from the hard, clear autonomous images of H.D.'s "Hermes of the Ways" or "Priapus." A good illustration is "Au Vieux Jardin":

> I have sat here happy in the gardens,
> Watching the still pool and the reeds
> And the dark clouds
> Which the wind of the upper air
> Tore like the green leafy boughs
> Of the divers-hued trees of late summer;
> But though I greatly delight
> In these and the water lilies,
> That which sets me nighest to weeping
> Is the rose and white colour of the smooth flag-
>   stones,
> And the pale yellow grasses
> Among them.[20]

In this poem the emotion to be conveyed is asserted in a simple declarative sentence in line one; the images which follow explain the source of the speaker's happiness. As in Pound's "Middle-Aged," the abstract generalization precedes the concrete image, rather than arising from it. The speaker's pleasure in the scene is complex, and reaches an intensity difficult to distinguish from misery. These shifts in emotion are conveyed strictly by declarative statements; an examination of the images alone ("the rose and white colour of the smooth flag-stones") would not lead the reader to a similar affective response.

The language of the poem, although dominated by simple description of natural objects in the manner imagists prized, also exhibits elevated and artificial diction of the kind they sought to discourage. The phrases "green leafy boughs," "divers-hued trees," and "That which sets me nighest to weeping" are all examples. In its choice of a homely and everyday theme, this poem, like Pound's, does reflect a post-symbolist emphasis on the empirical world; but it nevertheless remains a pre-imagist poem.

The other two poems by Aldington published in the same issue in November, 1912, use more esoteric settings for more abstract laments. The first, "Choricos," which Charles Norman identified as the poem Aldington began in 1911 in imitation of Euripides,[21] is an address to Death. The poem begins as follows:

> The ancient songs
> Pass deathward mournfully.
>
> Cold lips that sing no more, and withered wreaths,
> Regretful eyes, and drooping breasts and wings—
> Symbols of ancient songs
> Mournfully passing
> Down to the great white surges. . . . [22]

The major characteristic that this poem shares with imagist poetry is its use of free verse. That connection is not insignificant. The battle to free poetry from the demands of an obligatory regular metric was at times a strident one, and it was being aggressively waged by the founders of modernism (and others, like Robert Bridges and Maurice Hewlett) between the years 1908 and 1912. But in other respects, this poem might better be described as a degradation of symbolism. Even though Pound presented it as an example of imagism, it better illustrates his instructions about what not to do enunciated in "A Few Don'ts by an Imagiste" in March, 1913.

The poem continues as a song to death, asserting an equation between that abstraction and various natural experiences, as in the sixth stanza:

> O Death,
> Thou art an healing wind
> That blowest over white flowers
> A-tremble with dew;
> Thou art a wind flowing
> Over dark leagues of lonely sea;
> Thou art the dusk and the fragrance;
> Thou art the lips of love mournfully smiling;
> Thou art the pale peace of one
> Satiate with old desires; . . . [23]

One of the most distinctive things about these lines is the absence of clear images. One can imagine a white flower bearing dew, but no visual image readily arises for "a wind flowing/Over dark leagues of lonely sea." Similarly, "the dusk and the fragrance" and "the lips of love mournfully smiling" have insufficient detail for the reader to be moved by a concrete vision, and Aldington's "pale peace" seems almost to anticipate the "dim lands of peace" that Pound was so shortly to use as an illustration of what not to do.[24] These examples are not isolated ones. The poem uses *thou, thee* or *thy* seventeen times, and *thou* is accompanied by the archaic form of the verb: *art, blowest, layest, sealest.* Flowers are "a-tremble," and the poem is generally beset by "pallid chaplets" and "illimitable quietude."

"To a Greek Marble," the third of the Aldington poems published in November, 1912, "presents/no adjunct to the Muses' diadem." The poem is a direct invocation of a statue of a Greek goddess, undoubtedly like those among the marbles in the British Museum where Aldington, H.D. and Pound spent so much time in these years. The poem is a lament that the figure remains silent and unhearing despite the speaker's persistent whispers of past trysts:

> I have whispered thee in thy solitudes
> Of our loves in Phrygia,
> The far ecstasy of burning noons
> When the fragile pipes
> Ceased in the cypress shade,
> And the brown fingers of the shepherd
> Moved over slim shoulders . . . [25]

As in the previous poem, the majority of phrases combine an abstraction with the concrete, with the result that the visual image is imprecise and the intensity of the lines reduced. A "far" ecstasy is no more vivid than an ecstasy, and even, by the expression of distance, perhaps somewhat attenuated in imagined clarity. "Burning noons" approaches cliché, and "pipes" gain very little in visible characteristics by being "fragile." The effect of the poem depends more upon the emotive strength of nouns describing states of being than it does upon the reader's reaction to concrete, vividly imagined objects or scenes.

There is an unstated comparison, however, which is very much in keeping with imagist techniques—comparison of the unresponsive marble goddess with a real woman. Either the "White grave goddess" (line 2) is literally the Greek marble of the title and the "loves in Phrygia" metaphoric, or the goddess is metaphor for a woman who remains oblivious to the speaker's pleas, notwithstanding past intimacies. If the first reading is chosen, the poem deals with the completeness and autonomy of the work of art, which elicits ecstasy and longing from its human beholder, who can have neither completeness nor autonomy. If the second reading is selected, the poem is part of a long tradition of male literary invocations to the beautiful but cruelly unresponsive woman, one who, in this case, is placed quite explicitly on a pedestal. The poem is enriched by the co-existence of these two patterns of meaning, as the suggestion that the words might express human sexual longing intensifies the sense of the observer's longing before the work of art. Conversely, a systematic reading of the poem as revealing the absolute dichotomy between the work of art and the human observer strengthens the apprehension of the remoteness of the human woman to which the marble seems to refer.

The imagist poems of H.D. stand in sharp contrast to these early poems of Pound and Aldington in clarity, sharpness, precision, objectivity, and use of a presentational rather than a discursive style. All three poems that she published in January, 1913, use figures drawn from Greek mythology (as does Aldington's "Choricos"), but in a fashion as concrete as the original epics or stories. The poem entitled "Priapus" and subtitled "Keeper of Orchards," for example, begins:

> I saw the first pear
> As it fell.
> The honey-seeking, golden-banded,
> The yellow swarm
> Was not more fleet than I,
> (Spare us from loveliness!)
> And I fell prostrate,
> Crying,
> Thou hast flayed us with thy blossoms;
> Spare us the beauty
> Of fruit-trees![26]

The prayer is to Priapus, the son of Dionysus and Aphrodite, and thus offspring of revelry and love. He is the god of fruitfulness, the protector of the bees, the vine, the garden. He was represented in sculpture as the phallus or as a small garden god with twisted body and huge penis. The poem presents a moment in the orchard at harvest time, a moment fraught with intense and conflicting emotions.

It is the inevitable instant at which the ripeness of the maturing fruit passes from the conclusion of growth to the beginning of decay. It is the moment at which the fruit is at its sweetest. This swelling, fecund fruit is primal—it is the *first* pear—and its fall is primal too. Its uterine shape invokes the female gift for reproduction as the phallic god of the garden invokes the male. The speaker in the poem speeds by sight to the place of fall with the swiftness of the bees ("The honey-seeking, golden-banded,/The yellow swarm"), whom Priapus protects, who come to make honey from the fruit. The very act of seeing is an expression of passionate desire to apprehend that moment—its beauty, its meaning, its fruit. Made analogous to the bees by the identity of action, the speaker too seems about to recreate that moment into something sweet, something with the power to nourish and please. At that very moment of apprehension there is another apprehension, the recognition of the intense experience of plenitude, ripeness (perhaps, in a subtext, even of birth itself) as threat: ("Spare us from loveliness!")

Like the pear, the speaker falls—"prostrate,/Crying." The possible meanings of the fall and tears are many, and all are a part of the exegesis of that moment. The loveliness may be too great, the experience too intense, so that at the moment of its apprehension the ecstasy cannot be distinguished from pain. The moment of fruition may contain the recognition of destruction, and the experience of the greatest loveliness may make the inevitability of its loss through decay unbearable. The fall may be complete submission to the beauty perceived, and the tears the tears of joyous apprehension. Again, the fall may be the primal human fall, brought about by eating of the fruit of the tree of the knowledge of good and evil; the act of seeing the beauty and death in the moment of the pear's fall may be the modern counterpart to that ancient myth of overreaching. The fall may be a sexual fall, and the tears the reflection both of joy at that moment and anguish at its power to flay and to consume. The structure of the poem invites all these suggestions, and the poem derives its significance from the complicated sum of all of these endlessly interacting meanings.

The second stanza identifies this paradoxical moment of conflicting emotions as the peculiar triumph or affliction of the human speaker:

> The honey-seeking
> Paused not,
> The air thundered their song,
> And I alone was prostrate.

The speaker next renews the petition to the "God of the orchard" to "Spare us from loveliness" and pledges an offering. That offering is enumerated in the fourth and final stanza:

> The fallen hazel-nuts,
> Stripped late of their green sheaths,
> The grapes, red-purple,
> Their berries
> Dripping with wine,

> Pomegranates already broken,
> And shrunken fig,
> And quinces untouched,
> I bring thee as offering.

These offerings are of fruits past their prime; the grapes have begun to ferment, the pomegranates are broken, and the womb-like fig has lost its ripe fullness. These fruits, like the untouched quinces, were not consumed in their ripeness. They are an appropriate gift from one praying to be spared the moment of consuming intensity.

The implication that the cost of escape from that moment is to die without being savoured again suggests a sexual subtext; the experiences that loveliness brings are anguishing, but the cost of escaping them is barrenness or inutility. In early fall, 1912, when H.D. showed this poem to Pound, her own life was fraught with just such anguishing conflicts. Engaged to Pound before he left for Europe in 1908, H.D. in 1910 had become seriously involved with Frances Gregg. It was with Frances and her mother that H.D. had made the journey to Europe in 1911, from which H.D. was never permanently to return to the United States. Pound himself apparently also became involved with Gregg—one friend recalled him as "engaged" to her.[27] Throughout 1912, H.D. was constantly in the company of Pound and Aldington, whom she would not marry until 1913. It seems clear that in 1911 and 1912 H.D. was torn, both between heterosexual and homosexual attractions and between personal poetic creativity and the role of handmaiden and muse which she felt Pound thrust upon her.[28] Each sexual alternative must have seemed to offer anguish which could be escaped only at the cost of physical or poetic barrenness. The intensity of experience which this poem captures, then, has its correlative in H.D.'s own life, but the control she gains through the embodiment of the experience in juxtaposed images epitomizes the "objectivity" which came to be identified as a hallmark of modernism.[29]

Indeed, one of the striking aspects of this poem is the total absence of words which describe an emotion or state of being. Instead H.D. presents an action which embodies a mood. Contrast, for example, Aldington's

> I have sat here happy . . .
> ("Au Vieux Jardin")
> Pity my sadness, . . .
> ("To a Greek Marble")

or Pound's "vague invarious delight" ("Middle-Aged") with H.D.'s

> I fell prostrate,
> Crying.

The lines from H.D. are laden with all the ambiguity and radiance of observed experience; the mind returns to them again and again, reinterpreting as the feelings they elicit change with each added detail from the poem. The Aldington lines are simple assertion; if the speaker is not an authority upon whether he is happy or sad, who is?

Thus the images that follow are simply elaboration upon the causes of the emotion named. The contrast illuminates with clarity the difference between the image as ornament and the image as speech.

In all three examples from Aldington and Pound, the abstraction precedes the images and controls the way they are understood. In "Priapus" the image, whether object or act, precedes any statement of mood and gives rise to the reader's apprehension of it. This difference has implications for the depth, intensity and economy of the poem. Because the meaning of the event or image is not constrained by prior abstractions, the poem's interpretations are multiple and paradoxical. In some ways the poem's images and actions are much like a non-literary event about which we have similar amounts of information. Our experience of the poem is intensified because we identify the emotion by a reflective awareness of our response to our own imaginative enactment of the scene.[30] We grasp the mood not by cognition of an external abstraction but by reflexive inspection of feeling. The poem is economical because each image is itself speech, not ornament; if we were to eliminate a set of images, the meaning of the poem would change. In contrast, in Pound's "Middle-Aged," for example, each of the comparisons which begin stanzas two and three ("As the fine flakes, . ."; "As the fine dust, . . .") is essentially an expansion upon the meaning of the first simile, "'Tis but a vague, invarious delight/As gold that rains about some buried king."

The same economy, the same precedence of image over abstraction, characterizes the second of the poems by H.D. which appeared in *Poetry* in January, 1913. In this poem the crystalline structure of the poem is anticipated by the imagery itself. The first part begins:

> The hard sand breaks,
> And the grains of it
> Are clear as wine.
>
> Far off over the leagues of it,
> The wind,
> Playing on the wide shore,
> Piles little ridges,
> And the great waves
> Break over it.[31]

These lines match sound to scene almost to the point of being onomatopoetic. Consider: it/wine/it/wind/wide/piles/little/ridges/it: the i's squeak like sand under foot; the single syllable words keep time like footsteps. (Pound said, "I believe that every emotion and every phase of emotion has some toneless phrase, some rhythm-phrase to express it."[32])

The poem is the first of a powerful series of poems by H.D. that present the speaker buffeted at the boundaries of two colliding worlds. (One thinks, as well, of "Oread," "Evening," "Sea Rose.") At this boundary there is a no man's land that seems both land and sea. The wind which tosses the ceaselessly moving sea tosses the sand into small replicas of the waves which break over it. The

speaker belongs to this boundary area. The fluid, restless sea, Great Mother, with its "leagues" of distance and depth, its fearsome power, its associations with creativity and psyche, and all the possibilities of its "many-foamed ways," draws her to its edge. The land behind is the sea's reciprocal: stable, sheltering, and safe, but it does not draw the speaker from the shore. Here the speaker finds "him/Of the triple path-ways,/Hermes,/Who awaiteth."

Hermes Trismegistus is the name given by Neo-Platonists to the Egyptian god Thoth, whom the Greek Hermes closely resembled. Hermes the thrice great, believed to be the author of books of occult wisdom, was the god of writing, learning, and wisdom ("the triple-pathways"). In Greek mythology he was the inventor of the lyre, the alphabet, numbers and music. He was both god of eloquence and protector of travellers, and small statues of his figure were set up along the roads. This is the figure who waits for the speaker. Whatever route may bring travellers to this boundary ("Facing three ways,/Welcoming wayfarers"), Hermes proffers the skills by which they may stay. The loneliness of this place, its link to what is primal in experience, its threat, are the speech of the images with which Part I of the poem ends:

> Wind rushes
> Over the dunes,
> And the coarse, salt-crusted grass
> Answers.
>
> Heu,
> It whips round my ankles!

In the second part of the poem, the speaker looks inland from this boundary instead of toward the sea: "Small is/This white stream,/Flowing below ground/from the poplar-shaded hill,/But the water is sweet." Unlike the salt water of the sea, the land water can sustain life, even though its flow is small in this boundary place. The "sea-orchard" of the first part here bears small, hard fruits, and "The boughs of the trees/Are twisted/By many bafflings." This is no ordinary beauty, for that which lives and grows shows the stress of its place on a boundary. Nonetheless, it stands on a stable place, and the sea does not destroy it:

> Twisted are
> The small-leafed boughs.
> But the shadow of them
> Is not the shadow of the mast head
> Nor of the torn sails.

The poem concludes with an invocation to Hermes, whose protection continues here at this place where the sea meets the land:

> Hermes, Hermes,
> The great sea foamed,
> Gnashed its teeth about me;
> But you have waited,
> Where sea-grass tangles with
> Shore-grass.

There is not a single direct statement of emotion in the poem. No word lays claim to desperation, struggle, fear, courage or fortitude. Yet the poem communicates all these things and offers a spare and elegant vision of resolve before a challenge that almost overwhelms, and of will that refuses to relinquish two mutually exclusive worlds. Because it does not intrude the personal details of the poet's life, it elicits an intense response from any who have experienced deep conflicts. It is the relationship of the images, the form, which presents the structure of a primal human experience. Pound understood, in 1914, this power of poetry. He wrote:

> The statements of [analytic geometry] . . . are "lords" over fact. They are the thrones and dominations that rule over form and recurrence. And in like manner are great works of art lords over fact, over race-long recurrent moods, and over to-morrow.

> Great works of art contain this fourth sort of equation. They cause form to come into being. By the "image" I mean such an equation; not an equation of mathematics, not something about *a, b,* and *c,* having something to do with form, but about *sea, cliffs, night,* having something to do with mood.[33]

One can enrich one's understanding of H.D.'s "Hermes" by noting the elements of her own experience which may have given rise to it. An expatriate for only a year's length, H.D. surely stood on the boundary between two cultures. The "sea-orchard" which "shelters from the west" recalls the American heritage which she never relinquished, though she spent most of her adult life abroad. She stood on the boundary between two definitions of her sexual identity, and was shaping with pain an identity which relinquished neither role. She stood poised between a traditional childhood as the daughter of a distinguished professor and the unstable life of the expatriate writer abroad, and she again preserved elements of her heritage in her life and art. She faced the unfathomable depths of her psyche and her creativity, and she drew strength to confront them from her craft as a writer, from her study, and in time from her exploration of the wisdom of the occult. The myth of Hermes embodies those skills to which she turned for the strength to remain at the boundaries of her life.

These biographical details are unnecessary for an accurate reading of the poem, and would even narrow the meaning and intensity of the poem were they present. As it stands, the poem provides the form which readers fill with the comparable intense experiences of their own. In doing so, the poem anticipates more than the prescriptions of imagism. Its method is more fully described by the discussions of poetic form in Pound's essay on "Vorticism" than by the early imagist documents, which focus chiefly on metric, economy, the use of ordinary language, the preference for metaphor over simile, and the avoidance of imprecision and abstraction. The way form (or the relationship of the elements of a poem) itself becomes an image is not explicitly considered in the first

explanations of imagism in March, 1913. Thus these poems do more than offer models for the description of imagism. They actually provide early poetic models for the important transformation of the static form of imagist doctrine into vorticism.

And it was vorticism which offered a description of a dynamic form which itself made a statement; form which could support the long poem with its efforts to offer comprehensive order for experience; form which enabled the poem to make an absolute statement because it imposed the same relationship among the "values" of the poem's "equation" even though readers drew the specific equivalence for each "value" from their own diverse experience; form which supported the multiple simultaneous meanings necessary to present the complexity of the modern world and the relativity of its truth. Thus, H.D. is far more than that relatively "minor" poet offered us by so many literary historians: the most talented imagist in the years of the beginnings of modernism, but a poet whose work remained within what Pound reviled as the creative cul de sac of "Amygism." Instead we must view her poems as important not only to the founding but also to the development of the dynamic current of modernism which shaped the nature of a literary generation and beyond.

But the writings about imagism and vorticism are Pound's. What credit is due a poet who does not explain her method or expound its benefits? The record compels one to argue that Pound's own understandings of what modern poetry should be trying to do significantly depended upon the models which H.D.'s poems offered him. The evidence may be summarized as follows.

On August 18, 1912, Pound was prepared to send to Harriet Monroe as "imagist" a poem of his own that met few of the criteria outlined for the imagist poem in "Imagisme" and "A Few Don'ts by an Imagiste" in March, 1913. In September, 1912, he sent three poems by Richard Aldington which similarly violated many of the precepts laid down six months later. Two of these first four poems, his own "Middle-Aged" and Aldington's "Choricos," he himself excluded from the anthology *Des Imagistes,* which was assembled in the summer of 1913, although it first appeared in February, 1914.[34] In their stead he included two poems of his own which had appeared before an imagist school was established: "The Return," published in *The English Review* in June, 1912, and "Doria," which first appeared in *The Poetry Review* in February, 1912. Of these, the one that genuinely meets the more profound requirements of imagism is "The Return."

Between Pound's application of the word imagism to poems only distantly related to what became that movement's precepts and his enunciation of the characteristics of imagism came his reading of H.D.'s poems "Priapus" and "Hermes of the Ways." That reading led him, the record intimates, to re-examine his own work to find examples that approximated that standard. The result was the exclusion of "Middle-Aged" and the inclusion of "The Return," when he assembled the poems for *Des Imagistes* in spring and summer, 1913. The result was also the description in March, 1913, of the process by which imagism worked. Whether or not those precepts had been discussed in the spring or early summer of 1912, Pound clearly did not envision fully how they applied to actual poems when he sent "Middle-Aged" and "Choricos" to *Poetry*.

Pound very quickly grasped the first implications of H.D.'s poems—he had an almost unerring eye for poetic brilliance—but what he first saw was more technical than structural. As he reconsidered her work, and similar poems among his own, between spring, 1913, and summer, 1914, he saw more clearly the dynamic formal, structural principles which underlay such poems. The result of that understanding appears in the significant advance in poetic theory that characterizes the essay, "Vorticism," which appeared in *The Fortnightly Review* on September 1, 1914. Preceding the composition of that essay Pound had been exposed to the theories of Bergson[35] and the drive toward abstraction of the cubists, futurists and abstract expressionists in painting and of Gaudier-Brzeska in sculpture—as well as to the poetry of H.D. In "Vorticism," he stressed the nature of the image as a conception of the mind (with the capacity to be absolute which Bergson attributed to acts of intuition), and sought to explain the formal function of juxtaposed images in the poem as analogous to the "planes in relation" of post-impressionist art. He stressed the concrete and objective nature of the poetic image, even when it expressed a subjective state of mind, and he turned to the language of the geometers of the fourth dimension (then the subject of considerable attention in the popular scientific press[36] in an attempt to explain how the images of a poem can combine to create a concrete form which cannot be visually represented in two planes. (Like the attempts to represent the fourth dimension by a succession of three-dimensional projections, the total form of the poem emerges from the superposition of a succession of coherent patterns implicit in the relationship of images in the poem and recreated in the mind of the reader.)

The most significant development in this essay is Pound's effort to develop a theory of poetic form and function which accommodates the simultaneously visual and dynamically conceptual character of poetry. He had developed by February, 1912, before he encountered H.D.'s poems and described the precepts of imagism, the idea of an absolute rhythm in poetry which makes its statement without interpretation. As Hugh Kenner has argued, it is on this, fundamentally musical, idea that the excellence of "The Return" (June, 1912) was based.[37] Now he sought to broaden and expand his theory to reflect in a more sophisticated way than the early precepts of imagism did the visual and conceptual character of poetry as well. In an early version of the essay Pound made explicit the fact that the poems which had prompted these efforts were those of H.D.

The essay "Vorticism," which is widely discussed by Pound critics as central to his mature concepts of poetic

form, is an elaboration and expansion of "Vortex. Pound." which appeared in *Blast,* 1 (June 20, 1914). Pound concluded that essay thus:

POETRY

The vorticist will use only the primary media of his art.

The primary pigment of poetry is the IMAGE.

The vorticist will not allow the primary expression of any concept or emotion to drag itself out into mimicry.

In painting Kandinski, Picasso.

In poetry this by, "H.D."

Whirl up sea—
Whirl your pointed pines,
Splash your great pines
On our rocks,
Hurl your green over us,
Cover us with your pools of fir.[38]

The poem, of course, is "Oread," which had appeared in *The Egoist* in February, 1914. Significantly, Pound ranges H.D. beside Kandinsky and Picasso as innovators of the modernist form he sought to describe. Clearly the poems of H.D. continued to be examples which served Pound as a basis for the elaboration of his own ideas of poetry.

Pound's poems, as well as his critical writings, changed in the months immediately after his discovery of H.D.'s work. The evidence lies in the poems published as "Contemporania" in the April, 1913, issue of *Poetry*. These poems were sent to Monroe in several batches between October, 1912, and their appearance.[39] Pound's letter to Monroe on October 13, 1912, appears to be a cover note for the first group of poems; in it he comments specifically on "The Epilogue" and "The Dance" (which may be "Dance Figure") and alludes with some comments about "the 'Yawp'" to "A Pact," a poem addressed to Walt Whitman. These three poems, assembled a few days after he sent H.D.'s poems to Monroe, clearly have not yet made the transition to an imagist method. Pound explicitly is uneasy about them.

One, "A Pact"—a narrative poem with a few telling images—is a pledge to use Walt Whitman's poetic innovations, presumably his everyday diction and free verse, both of which were inspiring Pound's French contemporaries:

I make a pact with you, Walt Whitman—
I have detested you long enough.

. . . . .

It was you that broke the new wood,
Now is a time for carving.[40]

Given the date of its submission, the poem is a fascinating declaration of a decision to adopt a new language. (It also anticipates Yeats' analogous declaration in "A Coat," which appeared first in *Poetry,* in 1914.) Although more direct and colloquial, it does not itself fully illustrate the new style, since the fundamental statements of the poem are made by direct assertion rather than by image.

Of the other two poems listed in this first batch, "The Epilogue" was never published (the poem by that name in *Collected Shorter Poems* is a different one[41]); and "'The Dance,'" Pound wrote, "has little but its rhythm to recommend it."[42] If the reference is to "Dance Figure," the judgment was too harsh, and he let the poem appear. In any case, Pound seems to be measuring his poems against a style he could not yet quite command. During the next two months, however, he developed his own version of the directness, the clarity, the economy of imagist statement, which he so much admired in the poetry of H.D.

The most important evidence of this achievement is "In a Station of the Metro," a poem which he used in "Vorticism" to explain his evolution from his pre-imagist to his imagist phase. In the essay, Pound dates that progress as eighteen months earlier. Since "Vorticism" was published September 1, 1914, a year and a half earlier would be March, 1913, a month before the poem appeared. (Such a late dating for the poem might be supported by Pound's casual remark in "How I Began" in *T. P.'s Weekly* of June 6, 1913, that he had been trying to write the poem for "well over a year" and had composed its final version "only the other night."[43]) If, on the other hand, Pound meant to date his composition of "Metro" as eighteen months before the time of writing (rather than publishing) the "Vorticism" essay, the poem would have been composed in November or December of 1912, since the publishing history of *Blast* shows that the essay could not realistically have been written earlier than May 1.[44] This would place the writing of "Metro" just before the time Pound sent in the second batch of poems for the "Contemporania" sequence. The poem is commonly associated with the beginnings of imagism and hence is usually treated as if it were prior to H.D.'s poems, or at least simultaneous. In fact, though, it must have been written in the two months after he had sent H.D.'s poems to *Poetry.*

Evidence that Pound sought to develop a more direct, economical style, free from archaism and more reliant on the image, in the three months following his discovery of H.D.'s poems also exists in the language and printing history of "Contemporania." In addition to "Dance Figure," "A Pact," and "In a Station of the Metro," nine other poems made up the "Contemporania": "Tenzone," "The Condolence," "The Garret," "The Garden," "Ortus," "Salutation," "Salutation the Second," "Pax Saturni," and "Commission." Of these, "Pax Saturni" was not reprinted until the 1960s, when it appeared under the title "Reflection and Advice."

Four others were omitted when the sequence was reprinted August 15, 1913, in *The New Freewoman,* accompanying an essay by Rebecca West which summarized key excerpts from "Imagisme" and "A Few Don'ts." She introduced the sequence with the words: "The following poems are written by Mr Ezra Pound since he became an *imagiste*."[45] Interestingly, the poems which were omitted—"A Pact," "The Condolence," "Ortus," and "Commission"—are poems with only limited claim to imagist style. Whether because he no longer thought them excellent or was pressed for space, Pound clearly selected for omission the transitional poems which most resembled his earlier work and least resembled the imagism for which, as we have seen, H.D. set the standard. The other poems of "Contemporania" show a new hardness, a new avoidance of abstraction, and a new commitment toward making the image the speech—as well as a satiric thrust which cannot be linked to H.D.'s models at all.

Pound himself described what had happened to his style between October, 1912, and early 1913, with these lines from "Salutation the Second" in "Contemporania":

> Here they stand without quaint devices,
> Here they are with nothing archaic about them.
>
>   . . . . .
>
> Go, little naked and impudent songs,
>
>   . . . . .
>
> Go! rejuvenate things![46]

Finally, there remains the difficult question of the nature of H.D.'s debt to Pound. With respect to this, practically everyone has taken Pound at his own estimation. He had claimed that he invented imagism to get H.D. started.[47] Indeed, the whole circumstances of the fall of 1912 suggest that Pound's "Ortus," written along with the other poems of "Contemporania," should be read as an address to H.D.—and as a claim to have made her:

> How have I laboured?
> How have I not laboured
> To bring her soul to brith,
> To give these elements a name and a centre!
> She is beautiful as the sunlight, and as fluid.
> She has no name, and no place.
> How have I laboured to bring her soul into
>   separation;
> To give her a name and her being!
>
> Surely you are bound and entwined,
> You are mingled with the elements unborn;
> I have loved a stream and a shadow.
>
> I beseech you enter your life.
> I beseech you learn to say "I,"
> When I question you;
> For you are no part, but a whole,
> No portion, but a being.[48]

H.D. was a woman Pound "named," with the initials H.D., and she lived behind them so completely that some reviewers of *Sea Garden* spoke of the author as a man. She herself said, in 1958, "The significance of 'first love' can not be overestimated."[49] But she was also developing a life and identity separate from the powerful personality of a man to whom she had once been engaged. Some of her poems themselves testify to what sort of stress was involved for this woman, in 1913, to become, "no part, but a whole."

Nevertheless, as we have seen, the dates of his own actions belie Pound's claim that imagism was invented to publicize H.D.'s poetry, and the very self-absorption which could lead Pound repeatedly to claim responsibility for her career, and more, was a danger H.D. recognized and from which she withdrew. At some time in London, before his marriage, Pound again proposed to H.D. "Let's be engaged"; when her child was born, Pound appeared, to declare, "'My only real criticism is that this is not my child.'"[50] But H.D. would not resume the relationship on Pound's terms. Years later she explained:

> . . . my poetry . . . was built on or around the crater of an extinct volcano. . . . The vines grow more abundantly on those volcanic slopes. Ezra would have destroyed me and the center they call "Air and Crystal" of my poetry.[51]

There can be no doubt that the relationship with Pound is important to H.D.'s decision to write poetry, and the whole question of H.D.'s debt to Pound is one which merits further attention. But treating H.D. as a poet Pound molded ignores the critical facts that she began her poetic career in the years just after her engagement to Pound ended, and that her first poems—which we do not have—were written for the woman who filled "like a blue flame" the "vacuum" Pound left.[52] (One may wonder if H.D. read "Ortus" with irony, and why indeed Pound chose not to reprint it in England in 1913.)

We cannot know what we would have seen of H.D.'s work without the admiration and encouragement of Pound's astonished, "But, Dryad, this is poetry." Her motivation may have been more than a little the determination to demonstrate her independent skill. But we do know that what she showed Pound was already poetry. That he proposed editorial changes should surprise none; many agree that both Yeats and Eliot profited from Pound's editorial hand, but few would argue that they would have been substantially poorer poets without it. The facts are: that H.D. wrote powerful poems which support Pound's definitions of the image and the vortex—*before* he formulated these ideas and before his own poetry showed any consistent effort to achieve these goals. And, in addition, that in the months immediately after H.D.'s poems came into his hands, Pound's practice and his theory rapidly changed in an effort to define and demonstrate these ideas of poetic form. Without minimizing the significance of other figures or the tumultuous intellectual currents of the day, we can surely say: H.D. appears to have been the catalyst and her poems the model which set modern poetry on its now familiar way.

NOTES

[1] Noel Stock, *The Life of Ezra Pound* (New York: Random House, 1970), p. 460.

[2] I am now at work on a study entitled *Women and the Rise of Modernism* that will consider the contributions of H.D., Stein, Moore, Sitwell, Woolf and Richardson to modernism, and the revisions in literary history and theory of the movement which their achievements imply.

[3] Hugh Kenner discusses at length the significance of the doctrine of the image and notes that "Imagist propaganda merged into the Vorticist." He refers to Pound's transfer of attention from imagism to vorticism as a "change in terminology" through which Pound continued to elaborate the basic ideas which had been apparent in the essential elements of imagism. See *The Pound Era* (Berkeley: University of California Press, 1971), pp. 180-186, 191. Kenner does not, however, acknowledge the importance of H.D.'s work at critical moments in the development of the theory of the image. Kenner also takes at face value Pound's self-aggrandizing claim that the origin of imagism was a moment of casual generosity intended to get H.D.'s poems published, when the record is clear that he was trying to form a literary movement under the label of "imagism" before he had seen her poems. [See *The Pound Era*, p. 177.] For other recent critics giving due weight to the significance of imagist ideas in the rise of poetic modernism, see John T. Gage, *In the Arresting Eye: The Rhetoric of Imagism* (Baton Rouge: LSU Press, 1981), p. 7 and *passim,* and Peter Jones, "Introduction" in *Imagist Poetry* (London: Penguin, 1972).

[4] H.D., "Autobiographical Notes," unpublished, cited in Susan Stanford Friedman, "H.D.," *Dictionary of Literary Biography: Modern American Poetry* (B.C. Research, forthcoming).

[5] Cyrena N. Pondrom, *The Road from Paris: French Influence on English Poetry, 1900-1920* (Cambridge: Cambridge University Press, 1974), p. 20.

[6] Unpublished letter, Pound to Isabel W. Pound, 21 February, 1912, cited in Pondrom, *Road,* p. 19.

[7] Postcard, 9 May 1912, in "Selected Letters from H.D. to F. S. Flint," ed. Cyrena N. Pondrom, *Contemporary Literature,* 11:4 (Fall, 1969), p. 559. See also Stock, p. 116.

[8] Pondrom, *Road,* pp. 22-23, 82-83.

[9] Ezra Pound, "A Stray Document," *Make It New* (London, 1934), p. 335.

[10] Letter, Pound to Harriet Monroe, [18] August, 1912, *The Letters of Ezra Pound,* ed. D. D. Paige (London: Faber, 1951), p. 44.

[11] H.D., *End to Torment: A Memoir of Ezra Pound,* ed. Norman Holmes Pearson and Michael King (New York: New Directions, 1979), p. 18.

[12] Pound, *Letters,* ed. Paige, p. 46.

[13] Ellen Williams, *Harriet Monroe and the Poetry Renaissance: The First Ten Years of "Poetry" 1912-22* (Urbana: University of Illinois Press, 1977), p. 43.

[14] Ezra Pound, "A Few Don'ts by an Imagiste," *Poetry,* 1:6 (March, 1913). Rep. in Pound, *Literary Essays,* ed. T. S. Eliot (London: Faber, 1954), pp. 4-5.

[15] F. S. Flint, "Imagisme," *Poetry,* 1:6 (March, 1913). Rep. in Pound, *Literary Essays,* p. 3. These two brief articles were the first printed explanations of the imagist movement.

[16] "Vorticism," *The Fortnightly Review,* September, 1914, reprinted in *Gaudier-Brzeska* (New York: New Directions, 1970), p. 89.

[17] Ezra Pound, *Collected Shorter Poems,* 2nd ed. (London: Faber, 1968), p. 252.

[18] Pound, "Vorticism," p. 88.

[19] Janice S. Robinson, in *H.D.: The Life and Work of an American Poet* (Boston: Houghton Mifflin, 1982), pp. 45-46, asserts that Pound's "Middle-Aged" was written in response to H.D.'s "Priapus" and "Hermes of the Ways," which he recognized as superior to his own poems. Such homage might be refreshing, but in this case must be untrue, since Pound sent "Middle-Aged" to Monroe on August 18, 1912 (see note 8, above). H.D. indicated in her unpublished "Autobiographical Notes" that Pound's reading of the two poems occurred in autumn, and internal evidence in Pound's letters suggests a date between the third week in September and the first week of October [Pound, *Letters,* pp. 44-45]. Thus one must conclude that Pound had not seen the poems by H.D. at the time he composed "Middle-Aged."

[20] *Poetry,* 1:2 (November, 1912). Reprinted in *Des Imagistes,* ed. Ezra Pound (1914, rep. New York: Frank Shay, 1917), p. 11.

[21] Charles Norman, *Ezra Pound* (New York: Macmillan, 1960), p. 89.

[22] *Des Imagistes,* p. 7.

[23] *Des Imagistes,* pp. 7-8.

[24] As N. Christoph de Nagy has pointed out, the phrase "dim lands of peace" which Pound cited as a negative example actually may be found in "On a Marsh Road," a poem in the Ford Madox Ford (nee Hueffer) volume *The Fear of the Night* (1904). See de Nagy, *Ezra Pound's Poetics and Literary Tradition: The Critical Decade* (Berne: Francke Verlag, 1966), pp. 58, 116. He acknowledges the reference in the midst of an argument insisting that it was Ford whose critical (as opposed to poetic) writings "freed Pound from the stilted archaic language of his early volumes." De Nagy attributes the influence particularly to the ideas contained in the preface to Ford's *Collected Poems,* an essay for which an early draft appeared as "Impressionism—Some Speculations" in *Poetry* in August and September, 1913. Pound wrote Harriet Monroe announcing his discovery of the piece in May, 1913 [see *Selected Letters,* ed. Paige, pp. 56-57], a month after the appearance of the two essays describing imagism and nearly eight months after his discovery of H.D.'s poetry. De Nagy treats H.D. largely as Pound's creation, and seeks to justify the priority he ascribes to Ford's influence by asserting the significance of "'man to man' discussion" [p. 13].

[25] *Poetry,* 1:2 (November, 1912). Reprinted in *Des Imagistes,* p. 10.

[26] *Poetry,* 1:4 (January, 1913). Reprinted in *Des Imagistes,* pp. 24-25. In later printings, the title is "Orchard."

[27] Charles Norman cites an interview with Margaret Widdemer. See his *Ezra Pound,* p. 6. For other discussion of the ambiguities and internal conflict of this period see H.D., *End to Torment,* pp. 17-19; Friedman, "H.D."; Barbara Guest, *Herself Defined* (New York: Doubleday, 1984), pp. 32-39.

[28] H.D., *End to Torment,* p. 35.

[29] Pound called for a verse "free from emotional slither" as early as February, 1912, in *The Poetry Review* (Rep. *Literary Essays,* p. 12), and T. S. Eliot made the idea of objectivity a touchstone of modern poetry for the next few years with his doctrine of the "objective correlative" in "Hamlet and His Problems" in 1919.

[30] Put in the language of Bergson, we know the feeling directly and absolutely, for we enter it and grasp it from within, by intuition. The assertion *about* feeling, the abstraction, we know only relatively, for it is external to our mind, and we approach it only through the succession of points of view given to us by analysis. See Henri Bergson, "Introduction to Metaphysics," in *The Creative Mind* (Totawa, N.J.: Philosophical Library, 1965), pp. 159-162. This classic essay, translated by fellow imagists T. E. Hulme and F. S. Flint in England in 1912, provides a philosophical rationale for many of the important goals and techniques of imagism. The fact that the poets did not use the philosophy systematically or acknowledge its significance openly does not undercut its importance in understanding the rise of modernism.

[31] "Hermes of the Ways," *Poetry,* 1:4 (January, 1913). Reprinted in *Des Imagistes,* pp. 21-23.

[32] Pound, "Vorticism," p. 84. Pound made comparable assertions as early as the beginning of 1912.

[33] Pound, "Vorticism," pp. 91-92.

[34] Alfred Kreymborg says he received the poems for *Des Imagistes* before the end of the summer, 1913. See

Troubadour: An American Autobiography (New York: Sagamore Press, 1957), p. 158. Stock says word of the anthology was circulating in London by June 22 [Stock, p. 139]. Definite plans for publication were forthcoming by November, but Pound added at least one more poem—Joyce's "I hear an Army Charging"—in early January, 1914.

[35] Stock [p. 106] says Pound attended a series of lectures on Bergson given by T. E. Hulme in November and December, 1911, which probably included "Bergson's Theory of Art" and "the Philosophy of Intensive Manifolds."

[36] Linda Dalrymple Henderson, "A New Facet of Cubism: 'The Fourth Dimension' and 'Non-Euclidean Geometry' Reinterpreted," *The Art Quarterly,* 34:4 (Winter, 1971), p. 42. *Scientific American* actually held a contest in 1909 for submission of the best description of the fourth dimension. The author presents diagrams of mathematicians' efforts to represent the fourth dimension by a series of projections in three-dimensional space. I am grateful to Professor Barbara Buenger, Department of Art History, UW-Madison, for calling this reference to my attention.

[37] Kenner, pp. 189-191.

[38] *Blast,* 1 (June 20, 1914), p. 154. (Rep. Santa Barbara: Black Sparrow Press, 1981).

[39] Stock [p. 134] says the poems were sent "in two lots in October and December 1912." Williams [p. 43] says, "The group was selected out of a number of poems that Pound sent in several batches in 1912."

[40] Ezra Pound, *Collected Shorter Poems,* p. 98.

[41] K. K. Ruthven, *A Guide to Ezra Pound's Personae (1926)* (Berkeley: University of California Press, 1969), p. 266.

[42] Pound to Harriet Monroe, October 13, 1912, in *Letters,* ed. Paige, p. 45.

[43] Ezra Pound, "How I Began," *T.P.'s Weekly,* June 6, 1913, p. 707.

[44] The first plans for *Blast* did not use the label "vorticism." As late as April 15, 1914, *The Egoist* carried an advertisement for the first number, announced for April, which said the journal would discuss imagisme in verse, as well as cubism and futurism in art, but made no reference to vorticism. Kenner [p. 238] says it was Pound who coined the phrase, and "held up [the review] some weeks" so that pages containing the vorticism manifesto could be added to those already printed. The first number did not come out until June 20. Clearly, Pound would not have drafted the essay for *Fortnightly* explaining vorticism before he had written the pages for *Blast.* Thus, May 1 is a practical earliest date at which the essay could have been drafted, a date which would place the composition of "Metro" in November. The likelihood is that Pound wrote the essay for *Fortnightly* after the appearance of

Blast had caused so much fuss, and thus that "Metro" should be dated slightly later.

[45] Rebecca West, *The New Freewoman,* 1:5 (August 15, 1913), 87.

[46] "Salutation the Second," *Poetry,* 2:1 (April, 1913). Rep. in *Collected Shorter Poems,* pp. 94-95.

[47] For example, Pound to Glenn Hughes, September 26, 1927, in *Letters,* ed. Paige, p. 288. The same assertion, repeated in *Ezra Pound: Dichtung und Prosa,* figures in H.D.'s memoir of Pound, *End to Torment, e.g.* see p. 4.

[48] *Collected Shorter Poems,* pp. 93-94.

[49] H.D., *End to Torment,* p. 19.

[50] H.D., *End to Torment,* p. 30.

[51] H.D., *End to Torment,* p. 35.

[52] H.D., *End to Torment,* p. 8. I am very grateful to my colleague, Professor Susan Stanford Friedman, for urging me to examine the significance of Gregg in this connection, as well as for her thoughtful reading of this manuscript and her other very helpful comments on it. I am also indebted to her for permitting me to cite [note 4] her unpublished essay on H.D.'s life.

William Pratt

[In the following essay, Pratt focuses on the Imagist and ironic qualities of Ezra Pound's works as seminal to defining the Modern Age in English poetry.]

SOURCE: "Imagination and Irony: The Shaping of International Style," in *The South Atlantic Quarterly,* Vol. 83, No. 1, Winter, 1984, pp. 91-102.

"Two basic literary qualities," Charles Baudelaire noted in his journals, "super-realism and irony. An individual way of seeing things . . . also a satanic turn of mind."[1] The French poets who followed him translated these qualities into Symbolism, the first movement in modern poetry, and Ezra Pound made a further translation into Imagism, which was the second movement. Imagism certainly was "an individual way of seeing things," though of course it was a good deal more. In an effort to define the characteristics of the Imagist poem that are basic to Modernism, I once listed what might be called the "Five I's of Modernism":

    I Instantaneity (of Time)

    II Impersonality (of Viewpoint)

    III Intensity (of Feeling)

    IV Irregularity, or Asymmetry (of Form)

V Immanence, or Incarnation (of Truth, Reality, Being)[2]

and I contended that if we take the Imagist poem in its fullest potentiality, "it is possible to identify Imagism with Modernism."

The other quality Baudelaire noted was "a satanic turn of mind," which for him was the essence of laughter, an awareness of the duality of hu⸳ ⸳n nature that was the source of irony. Having made the case that Pound the Imagist was opening up new possibilities for poetic expression, I would now like to make the case for Pound the Ironist, believing that together they make Pound the Internationalist, the Father of Modernism in English poetry, as Baudelaire was the Father of Modernism in French poetry. I would emphasize again that Imagism was Pound's primary intuition, the rallying point for the revolution in poetic style that occurred between 1910 and 1920, and I fully agree with Stephen Spender that "the aims of the Imagist movement in poetry provide the archetype of a modern creative procedure."[3] Imagism released English verse from the necessity of regular meter and at the same time focussed poetic meaning on the concrete immediacy of the Image, which in Pound's definition was nothing simple, but "an intellectual and emotional complex in an instant of time." The invention of Imagism was indispensable to Modernism, no matter how arbitrary or fortuitous it may seem,[4] but there is another indispensable element which requires that we dot one more *I* to have the full effect of modern poetic style.

For Pound, as we know, Imagism was only the beginning; from the highly suggestive simplicity of the Imagist poem, he went on to develop the fuller complexity and maturity of style evident in his longer poems, especially in *Homage to Sextus Propertius, Hugh Selwyn Mauberley,* and ultimately the *Cantos*. He progressed poetically, to use his own terms in *The ABC of Reading,* from the class of "inventors" to the class of "masters," and the key to his growth as a major poet is not to be found as much in his passage from Imagism to Vorticism, I think, as in his more and more frequent use of irony in his poetry. If Imagism contains five I's essential to Modernism, Irony is the sixth I. If we look for a thread connecting the enormous diversity of styles in Pound's poetry, I think we will see that as he infused more and more irony into his images, he attained that ultimate degree of sophistication we know as characteristically Poundian, and at the same time, characteristically Modern. Pound, as R. P. Blackmur once put it, was one of those rare poets who are "the executive artists of their generation," and if we agree with Hugh Kenner that the whole modern period can be called The Pound Era, we might also be justified in calling it, more broadly, The Age of Irony.

Irony was not a conspicuous ingredient in the early poetry of Pound, any more than it was conspicuous in the early poetry of his first master, Yeats. Both poets were inheritors of a late-Romantic style that favored the pathetic rather than the ironic mode of expression. Yeats

brought this style to its last fruition in his Celtic Twilight poems of the nineties, and Pound began as an imitator of that side of Yeats—as any reader of *The Collected Early Poems of Ezra Pound* can readily see. But Yeats, at the time Pound met him in London in 1908, was emerging from the mists of the Celtic Twilight into a harsher light and was in the process of adapting his poetic style to his changing experience, especially his personal disappointments in love and in the Irish nationalist movement, seeking to turn away from "the quarrel with others," out of which, in his view, rhetoric is made, to the "quarrel with ourselves," out of which poetry is made. "Technique is the test of sincerity," Pound affirmed, and he credited Yeats with having been the first of his contemporaries to meet that test poetically: "I went to London because I thought Yeats knew more about poetry than any body else," he said, explaining that "Yeats by 1908 had written simple lyrics in which there were no departures from the natural order of words."[5] As Yeats's "private secretary" in 1913 and 1914, Pound remembered little of the feverish activity at Stone Cottage in Sussex except "mostly reading aloud. Doughty's *Dawn in Britain* and so on. And wrangling, you see. The Irish like contradiction. He tried to learn fencing at forty-five, which was amusing. He would thrash around with the foils like a whale. He sometimes gave the impression of being even worse an idiot than I am."[6] What Pound did not seem to remember was that Yeats had by 1908 not only learned to write in a more natural poetic syntax but was also working out his theory of the Mask, or Opposing Self, which enabled him to speak in a different voice, that is, self-critically, in his poetry, a definite departure from the often self-pitying voice of his Celtic Twilight poetry. The soulful laments of *The Wind Among the Reeds,* in 1899, such as "He Bids His Beloved Be at Peace," had been ably echoed by Pound (see especially "He Speaks to the Moonlight Concerning the Beloved," a poem that might almost have been written by Yeats), but Yeats had moved to the more austere love poems of *In the Seven Woods* in 1904, one of which, "The Folly of Being Comforted," was an early favorite of Pound's:

'Because of that great nobleness of hers
The fire that stirs about her, when she stirs,
Burns but more clearly. O she had not these ways
When all the wild summer was in her gaze.'

O heart! O heart! If she'd but turn her head,
You'd know the folly of being comforted.[7]

Yeats's "folly" was his salvation as a poet, for by self-dramatization he achieved a greater realism and objectivity; he was able to give personal disillusionment a tragic eloquence. No matter how much Pound later forgot of what he learned from Yeats, I think it would be safe to say that he had detected the emerging tone of self-irony in Yeats's poetry very early, and that it led him to make experiments of a similar kind in his own poetry, based on his theory of the Persona, his special word for the Mask. Pound's use of the Persona, like Yeats's use of the Mask, became increasingly ironic as his poetry matured, reaching its fullest expression in *Propertius* and *Mauberley* at the end of the Imagist decade in 1920 and carrying on into the *Cantos* that would take him the rest of his life to complete. If we look for the principal differences between Yeats's Mask and Pound's Persona, we discover that Yeats generated his Mask out of conflicts within himself, whereas Pound generated his Personae out of creative interaction with poets much like himself. For Yeats, the Self came first and then the Mask; for Pound, the Personae came first, and the self was somehow projected out of them.

To trace the development of irony in Pound's poetry is somewhat more challenging than to trace it in Yeats, because there is a greater diversity of styles to compare and many more masks, or personae, to try to see behind. We know from what Pound says of his experiments with poetic style, in his book on Gaudier-Brzeska in 1916, that it was always his own consciousness he was seeking to express, through all the various personae he projected:

> In the "search for oneself," in the search for "sincere self-expression" one gropes, one finds some seeming verity. One says "I am" this, that, or the other, and with the words scarcely uttered one ceases to be that thing.

> I began this search for the real in a book called *Personae,* casting off, as it were, complete masks of the self in each poem. I continued in a long series of translations, which were but more elaborate masks.[8]

Thinking of this statement as we leaf through the *Collected Early Poems* may cause us to wonder what "sincere self-expression" could have meant to a poet who spoke so often in the manner of other poets. There is not only the recurrent voice of the early Yeats but also the voices of Swinburne and Rossetti and Browning, and of who knows what forgotten Victorian poets. Where Pound is not imitating, he is translating, and his versions of poets from other languages—the French of Villon, the Provençal of Bertrand de Born, the Anglo-Saxon of the "Seafarer"—are more original than his imitations of English poets. Translating and imitating were the means by which Pound had to discover himself, but his first efforts often sound more like impersonations than personae. Where his own voice can first be heard is in those verses where he was not mimicking but parodying another poet; until *Ripostes,* in 1912, which marked the beginning of his Imagist period, only a few parodies scattered through the early volumes give any hint of what his real poetic gifts might be.

That Pound was an unusually gifted parodist is to be seen throughout his work, to the very last *Cantos;* his first notable success appeared in the *Canzoni* of 1911, the "Song in the Manner of Housman" (later called "Mr. Housman's Message"), where he tellingly echoed *A Shropshire Lad* in such lines as

> London is a woeful place,
> Shropshire is much pleasanter.
> Then let us smile a little space
> Upon fond nature's morbid grace
>   Oh, Woe, woe, woe, etcetera . . .

This parody of Housman was good enough to survive Pound's later cuttings, but another and longer parody of Tennyson did not. It appears in the *Collected Early Poems* as "Redondillas, or Something of that Sort," but a note tells us that in the first proofs it was called "Locksley Hall, forty years further." It consists of random reflections on the age, circa 1910, and anticipates some of the themes that would appear later in *Mauberley:*

> I sing the gaudy to-day and cosmopolite
>   civilization
> Of my hatred of crudities, of my weariness of
>   banalities,
> I sing of the ways that I love, of Beauty and
>   delicate savours

Though Pound knew that his poem lacked subtlety:

> I don't like this hobbledy metre
>   but find it easy to write in,

he did manage to score on some large targets:

> I would sing the American people,
>   God send them some civilization;
> I would sing of the nations of Europe,
>   God grant them some method of cleansing
> The fetid extent of their evils.

There is not only a hint of *Mauberley,* but of the *Cantos* as well, in this loose and rollicking parody, which is uneven, but at times prophetic in a serious way of the later Pound:

> They tell me to "Mirror My Age,"
>   God pity the age if I do do it,
> Perhaps I myself would prefer
>   to sing of the dead and the buried. . . .
> We ever live in the now
>   it is better to live in than sing of.

Beneath the light-hearted banter, we can discern a more than mild discontent with the age he was then seeking, somewhat falteringly, to portray, and at a time well before the First World War had come along to dash any confidence in progress and to cause a general disillusionment with modern civilization that we know so well from the postwar poetry of Pound and Yeats and Eliot.

A few more glimmers of light can be gathered from the gloom of Pound's early poems, if we look at two parodies that appear in the "Poems from Miscellaneous Manuscripts" section of the *Collected Early Poems.* They display some of that extravagant humor which in the later *Cantos* Pound would label *hilaritas.* The first is titled, "'It is a Shame'—with Apologies to the Modern Celtic School, or P'ti'cru—a Ballad," and it begins:

> I have heard the yap of the fairy dog
>   P'ti'cru
> Of the pearl white pup
>   P'ti'cru
> His hide is an incandescent light
> His every whisker gloweth bright
>   P'ti'cru

In a note to this wild piece of mockery, Pound explains with tongue in cheek: "In the impassioned rehash of the mystically beautiful celtic mythology, I find one touching figure neglected. My Lords: justice for the fairy dog. He came from Avalon. The olde frenche booke says one could not tell his qualities or his beauty, and his color was historically as I have described it."[9] Clearly, if Pound thought of Yeats as the only poet writing in English from whom other poets could learn, he was able to parody as well as to imitate him. We know, of course, from the later, more urbane parody he wrote, called "The Lake Isle," that Pound was eventually able to overcome his infatuation with the dreamy melancholy of the early Yeats, but this playful earlier parody establishes a prior point of departure between Pound and Yeats. If Pound had not been able to laugh at Yeats's more sombre moods, it is unlikely the two poets would have learned as much as they did from each other during the course of their enormously productive friendship.

Another poem from the manuscripts left unpublished by Pound that reveals his gift for more than mere imitation is a parody of a poet he might have been thought only to scorn: Rudyard Kipling. Kipling's verse was even more popular than Housman's in the early decades of the twentieth century, and one of the most widely quoted of all Kipling's poems was "When Earth's Last Picture is Painted." It may be described as an apotheosis of the artist, who is portrayed as reaching a state of perfection in heaven, where at last "He will paint the thing as he sees it / For the God of things as they are." Pound's take-off on the sentimental piety of Kipling is worth quoting in full:

THE LOGICAL CONCLUSION

When earth's last thesis is copied
From the theses that went before,
When idea from fact has departed
And bare-boned factlets shall bore,
When all joy shall have fled from study
And scholarship reign supreme;
When truth shall "baaa" on the hill crests
And no one shall dare to dream;

When all the good poems have been buried
With comment annoted in full
And art shall bow down in homage
To scholarship's zinc-plated bull,
When there shall be nothing to research
But the notes of annoted notes,
And Baalam's ass shall inquire
The price of imported oats;

Then no one shall tell him the answer
For each shall know the one fact
That lies in the special ass-ignment
From which he is making his tract.
So the ass shall sigh uninstructed
While each in his separate book
Shall grind for the love of grinding
And only the devil shall look.

Hilarious as it is, this parody effectively mocks not only the pretensions of Kipling but also the pretensions of those earnest scholars who were doing then what so many do now: smothering live poetry with pages of dull commentary. From his college days on, Pound railed against the kind of academic scholarship that stultifies imagination with fact, and we know that even Eliot did not escape censure, at least privately, for what Pound called "the 'English Department' universitaire attitude: literature not something enjoyable, but something which your blasted New England conscience makes you feel you *ought* to enjoy."[10] Pound's position as a critic of poetry was always farther from Eliot than from Yeats, who in "The Scholars," wrote of the "Old learned, respectable bald heads" who "Edit and annotate the lines / That young men, tossing in their beds, / Rhymed out in love's despair" and asked:

Lord, what would they say
Did their Catullus walk that way?

In *The Spirit of Romance,* published in 1910, at about the same time as he must have written his parody of Kipling, Pound tried to set an example of what lively learning could do for the appreciation of poetry, and in the preface to that volume, he argued: "Art is a joyous thing. Its happiness antedates even Whistler; apropos of which I would in all seriousness plead for a greater levity, a more befitting levity, in our study of the arts."

If Pound first began speaking with his own voice through parody, he went on cultivating it through satire, as we see in many of the poems that appeared in *Ripostes* in 1912 and *Lustra* in 1915, at the same time that he was actively promoting Imagism. The quality of poetic style he was advocating most vigorously at this crucial stage was what he called *hardness,* and it is possible to see some convergence between Imagism and Irony in his definitions of what constituted hardness in poetry. His reviews of Yeats's *Responsibilities* and of Joyce's *Dubliners* in 1914 praised both Irish writers for their hardness of style. Speaking of the "manifestly new note in his later work," he says of Yeats that "one has felt his work becoming gaunter, seeking greater hardness of outline," while he says of Joyce (one of whose poems he included in *Des Imagistes* in 1914): "Mr. Joyce writes a clear hard prose." Hardness was also the quality he found in the French writers he most admired, Gautier and Flaubert. "Gautier is intent on being hard," he wrote approvingly in his essay on "The Hard and Soft in French Poetry," and in another essay, "The Serious Artist," he praised Flaubert as a satirist to be read for his "diagnosis," since "satire is surgery" good for the health of language. While hardness connoted for Pound concreteness of imagery, or what in the Imagist doctrine he called "Direct treatment of the thing," it also connoted a critical realism very close to satire. It has often been said that Imagism was as much a critical as a creative movement, and there is at least one of Pound's Imagist poems which is hard in both senses, of the concrete and the satirical:

L'ART, 1910

Green arsenic smeared on an egg-white cloth,
Crushed strawberries! Come, let us feast our eyes.

Here, the combination of descriptive imagery, in the garishly clashing colors of "Green arsenic," "egg-white cloth," and "Crushed strawberries," is combined with the sardonic twist of an invitation to "feast our eyes" on a stomach-turning omelette made of arsenic, egg, and strawberries.

There are more fully developed satires in *Ripostes* and *Lustra*, of course, including the well-known "Portrait de'une Femme" (a foreshadowing, in the lady's effete cultivation, of the Lady Valentine in *Mauberley*), and the various "Salutations" that are sarcastic apologies for Pound's new style, e.g., "Salutation the Second," which says in mock-sympathy, "Poor Dear! He has lost his illusions," and "Further Instructions," which jokes about the change from politeness to effrontery in his manners: "You are very idle, my songs. / I fear you will come to a bad end." Both the Imagist and satirical poems are minor works, and some, like the series of "Mœurs Contemporaines," are in the class of light verse, sketches of manners, dialogues of the pseudo-sophisticated, more *vers de société* than searching social criticism, but they do display sharp observation and an ear for conversational speech that distinguishes them from Pound's earlier imitative lyrics. They can be seen as experiments pointing toward more ambitious works, or in Pound's terms "a preparation of the palette," and they had the effect of ridding his style of archaisms and mannerisms; in his later view, "Honestly I think *Lustra* has done a work of purgation of minds."[11]

Lustra, with its series of short satirical poems, marks the most definite shift toward the ironic mode in Pound's poetry; there is also one longer poem of this period worth examining, since it is a sort of verse setting of his prose polemic on American culture, *Patria Mia*. It is "L'Homme Moyen Sensuel," published in the *Little Review* in 1917. In form, it is a broad burlesque of Byron's *Don Juan*, but it is an improvement over the earlier parody of Tennyson's "Locksley Hall" in having a more unified subject, the state of American culture.

> 'Tis of my country that I would endite,
> In hopes to set some misconceptions right,

it begins, and it goes on to describe the history of a fictitious young American named Radway:

> Radway? My hero, for it will be more inspiring
> If I set forth a bawdy plot like Byron
> Than if I treat the nation as a whole.

This "average man" gets his education from the newspapers and popular magazines of the day, goes to the city, gets a job writing for mass circulation periodicals, has his fling with "pretty Irish girls in Chinese laundries," and, in short, becomes very much a man of the world, who looks and acts like every other American:

> Still we look toward that day when man, with
>   unction,
> Will long only to be a *social function,*

> And even Zeus' wild lightning fear to strike
> Lest it should fail to treat all men alike.

Eventually, Radway attains respectability and becomes "a pillar in / An organization for the suppression of sin," having learned that there is profit in being morally upright:

> For as Ben Franklin said, with such urbanity:
> "Nothing will pay thee, friend, like Christianity."

The career of Radway, the common man, ends in success, both social and financial, and Pound leaves him with a quatrain almost good enough for *Mauberley* (except for the rhymes):

> 'Twas as a business asset *pure an' simple*
> That Radway joined the Baptist Broadway
>   Temple.
>
> I find no moral for a peroration,
> He is the prototype of half the nation.

As social satire, "L'Homme Moyen Sensuel" is broad rather than deep, but it pokes fun at the crassness, smugness, and conventionality of American civilization, which formed a hostile environment for artists and forced many intelligent Americans, like Pound, into exile, and it is a step in the direction of the much more complex treatment of the conflict between the artist and his society which he would soon portray in *Propertius* and *Mauberley*.

To reach that more sophisticated plane of criticism, Pound needed to exchange his single-edged weapons of parody and satire for the double-edged axe of irony, and in that transaction the influence of Eliot must be counted as a factor. Whether Pound would have developed the full complexity of his mature style if he had never met Eliot may be questionable, but taking Eliot's indebtedness to Pound so much for granted, we must at least wonder whether Pound's debt to Eliot in mid-career was not as great as his debt to Yeats in his early career. It is not a question of imitation but of assimilation: no one would accuse Pound of borrowing directly from "The Love-Song of J. Alfred Prufrock" when he wrote *Hugh Selwyn Mauberley,* but different as they are, the two poems have much in common, in their personae of the cultivated intellectual failure, in their self-ironic and allusive styles, even in their criticism of the superficial, materialistic society around them; and knowing that "Prufrock" came before *Mauberley,* we can draw our own conclusions about the direction of influence. We know that Pound and Eliot first met in 1914 and that Pound immediately recognized the originality of "The Love-Song of J. Alfred Prufrock" (which had seemed unpublishable up to that time), sending it off to Harriet Monroe in Chicago with the opinion that it was "the best poem I have yet had or seen from an American" and continuing to hound her ("Do get on with that Eliot") until she printed it in *Poetry* magazine in 1915. By 1917, when he financed the publishing of Eliot's first collection, *Prufrock and Other Observations,* out of his own meagre pocket, Pound was crediting Eliot with being the most innovative poet around: "Anyhow Eliot has thought of things I had not thought of, and damned if many of the others have done so. Inventive, creative, or what not."[12] Pound reviewed Eliot's book for *Poetry,* noting with enthusiasm "how complete is Mr. Eliot's depiction of our contemporary civilization," and praising his skill in combining "two sorts of metaphor: his wholly unrealizable, always apt, half ironic suggestion, and his precise realizable picture."[13] In other words, Pound recognized both Imagism and Irony in Eliot's poetry when he first read it, and he was quick to discern the strong influence of Laforgue, which led him to take a new interest in the French Symbolist poet, as we know from the essay he wrote in 1917 on "Irony, Laforgue, and Some Satire." He called Laforgue "the most sophisticated of all the French poets," and spoke of his "delicate irony, the citadel of the intelligent," saying that "the ironist is one who suggests that the reader should think." He praised Laforgue as "an incomparable artist" who was "nine-tenths of him, critic," and who wrote "not the popular language of any country but an international tongue common to the excessively cultivated."[14] In short, the qualities which Eliot's poetry shared with Laforgue's brought Pound to a new understanding of the possibilities for developing a poetic style cosmopolitan and critical enough to suit the age, with a complex irony as its chief instrument. The early *Cantos,* as well as *Propertius* and *Mauberley,* undoubtedly owe something to Pound's reading of Eliot and Laforgue, for their use of irony was different from anything that can be seen in his poetry up to that time—it was double-edged, cutting with one stroke the poet and his age. In becoming self-ironic like Eliot and Laforgue, Pound increased the subtlety of his poetry, leveling criticism at himself as well as his society, and so was able to emerge as one of the masters, as well as one of the inventors, of modern poetry in English.

The *Homage to Sextus Propertius,* in 1917, was Pound's real breakthrough to the new style, his first major long poem; and some critics, notably R. P. Blackmur, regarded it in time as his finest poem, simply because it was so close to the viewpoint of the Latin poet he was translating that his poetry gained a consistency and firmness which it lacked when he was writing only from his own perspective. Similar praise might have been given to his translations from Li Po (or Rihaku) in *Cathay* in 1915, but such acclaim would hardly do justice to Pound's achievement. However much we may admire *Cathay,* we can see that *Propertius* is a more sophisticated poem, and the difference is chiefly in the greater audibility of Pound's voice speaking from within the persona. The distinction of *Propertius* is the duality of the voice: it speaks both with the tongue of the Latin poet of the Silver Age of Imperial Rome and with the tongue of the American poet of the Ironic Age of the later Imperial West. Pound had to insist that "my *Homage to Sextus Propertius* is *not* a translation of Propertius," because there were many readers who insisted that it was (and one very discerning reader, Thomas Hardy, even suggested to Pound that he give the poem a different title,

"Sextus Propertius Soliloquizes," so that readers would not go on making that mistake). As late as 1931, Pound felt the need to explain what *Propertius* was really about, to clear up the confusion that still surrounded it:

> I may perhaps avoid charges of further mystification and wilful obscurity by saying that it presents certain emotions as vital to me in 1917, faced with the infinite and ineffable imbecility of the British Empire, as they were to Propertius some centuries earlier, when faced with the infinite and ineffable imbecility of the Roman Empire. These emotions are defined largely, but not entirely, in Propertius' own terms. If the reader does not find relation to life defined in the poem, he may conclude that I have been unsuccessful in my endeavors.[15]

Pound's clarification serves to verify that the poem speaks for two poets, and two different ages, at once; it establishes a historical parallel that is meant to criticize ancient Roman and modern Western (not simply "British") civilization simultaneously, and a personal parallel that brackets Pound and Propertius as fellow poets. Pound did not point out, however, the further subtlety in the poem, which causes the two poets to be self-critics as well as critics of their ages. Propertius was a translator of his predecessors, the Greek poets, just as Pound was a translator of the Latin poet. Those "shades of Callimachus, Coan ghosts of Philetas," with which the poem begins, are speaking through Propertius as Propertius' shade is speaking through Pound, and both poets concede that they are too literary and allusive ever to be popular, except with a small and highly literate audience; they know that public recognition will be belated and grudging:

> I ask a wreath which will not crush my head,
> and there is no hurry about it.
> I shall have, doubtless, a boom after my funeral,
> Seeing that long standing increases all things
> regardless of quality.

Pound and Propertius criticize their respective ages for lacking a taste for high art, but they also criticize themselves for failing to produce it; instead of writing heroic poems about conquest and worldly glory, they prefer to write unfashionably personal and private love poems:

> Yet you ask on what account I write so many
> love-lyrics
> And whence this soft book comes into my mouth.
> Neither Calliope nor Apollo sang these things into
> my ear,
> My genius is no more than a girl.

The irony here is both defensive and accusative; one cannot escape the sense that Pound as Propertius is not only publicly condemned but self-condemned. If the age is to be blamed for its ambitions for wealth and power, its pomposity and delusions of grandeur, the poet who disdains such ambitions risks another kind of blame, for being merely selfish and pleasure-loving, intent on praising the beauty of women when he knows well that "There are enough women in hell, / quite enough beautiful women," and that "Death has his tooth in the lot / Avernus lusts for the lot of them." If Pound and Propertius sing of exalted moments of passion ("Me happy, night, night full of brightness"), some of their most poignant lines are those that express the mutability of life and the inevitability of death:

> In vain, you call back the shade,
> In vain, Cynthia. Vain call to unanswering
>   shadow,
>   Small talk comes from small bones.

We remember that Propertius was ranked not among the major epic and dramatic poets, like Virgil and Ovid, but among the minor class of lyric and elegiac poets; and Pound places himself in that company, too, but with a further twist of irony, in that he comprehends two ages and two poetic voices in his poem. Pound with the mask of Propertius is a greater poet than Propertius himself, since the distance between the two poets is as important as the resemblance between them, and we are justified in saying that what Pound added to Propertius is what makes a major poet out of a minor one—just as we can say that what Eliot added to Laforgue made a major poet out of a minor one. The historical as well as the personal irony is deepened by the gulf of time separating Pound from Propertius, giving the theme of poetic immortality a wider frame of reference:

> Flame burns, rain sinks into the cracks
> And they all go to rack ruin beneath the thud of
>   the years.
> Stands genius a deathless adornment,
>   a name not to be worn out with the years.

When we turn from *Homage to Sextus Propertius* to *Hugh Selwyn Mauberley,* we are bound to be aware of the parallels between these two long poems of Pound's middle period and to remember that Pound himself raised the question, "I wonder how far *Mauberley* is merely a translation of the *Homage to S.P.,* for such as couldn't understand the latter?"[16] Yet to regard it as a translation of a translation would hardly account for the originality of *Mauberley,* or the fact that it remains central to Pound's whole work—being both retrospective and prospective, it is the most ambitious of Pound's persona poems, and a masterly criticism of the age as well as of himself. Perhaps the best way to distinguish them is to say that Mauberley is the poet Pound discovered in himself while he was writing *Propertius:* a poet too refined for his age, "out of key with his time," who

>   had been born
> In a half savage country, out of date;
> Bent resolutely on wringing lilies from the acorn. . . .

The indictment of himself, as well as of what "the age demanded," is once again doubly ironic, but whereas in *Propertius* the persona was a real poet who wrote of a civilization and a language long dead, in *Mauberley* the persona is an imaginary poet of Pound's own time and language who is so much like himself that he knows the same people Pound knew in London and writes poetry— the superb "Envoi"—as good as Pound could write at his best, but all to no avail, since his "final exclusion from the world of letters" is inevitable. Mauberley is closer to Pound than Propertius was, and in the near-identity of poet and persona, there is an even greater delicacy of irony, for one is never quite sure when Pound is speaking as Pound and when he is speaking as Mauberley. Readers have long found it a fascinating game, trying to distinguish poet from persona in *Mauberley,* and most have probably agreed with F. R. Leavis that "throughout there is a subtlety of tone, a complexity of attitude, such as we associate with seventeenth-century wit."[17]

No explication of the poem, however exhaustive, can remove this subtlety, nor indeed would one want it removed, for that would be to take away the very quality that makes it one of the masterpieces of modernism. *Mauberley* is Pound's ironic self-portrait of the artist, and as such stands as a poetic companion to Joyce's novel, for the artist is as autobiographical in Pound's poem as in Joyce's *Portrait of the Artist as a Young Man*—a work which, like "Prufrock," Pound was the first to applaud in manuscript and then see into publication, and which therefore lurks in the background of *Mauberley* as Eliot's poem does. Mauberley is a more mature artist than Stephen Dedalus, and to compare them is simply to recognize how complementary they are—as Pound liked to say, "there is no competition among the best." Joyce is as intermeshed with Stephen as Pound is with Mauberley, and it is about equally difficult to distinguish them, no matter how hard we try: like identical twins, they can only be distinguished by those who live with them. And yet every reader does know that the author and the persona, of the novel as well as the poem, are different human beings; the irony is always present, effectively keeping Joyce and Stephen, Pound and Mauberley, from ever merging into a single consciousness. The distinction increases at the end, in both cases, for Stephen Dedalus shows the naive optimism of youth as he leaves Dublin for Paris, hoping that there he can "forge in the smithy of my soul the uncreated conscience of my race," while Mauberley acts with weary resignation as he leaves London for the remote South Seas, having given up the struggle "to resuscitate the dead art / Of poetry," and having failed to present the age what it demanded, "an accelerated image / Of its own grimace," and composing his epitaph in a gesture of rejection:

> I was
> And I no more exist;
> Here drifted
> An hedonist.

We know that Joyce the artist was never as callow as Stephen the artist, and we know that Pound the poet was never as defeated as Mauberley the poet; the author and his persona part company at the end; however, in each case it is hard to say where the separation occurs, and we realize that the author's criticism of his character is also a criticism of himself: the self-irony holds, even at the end.

Mauberley is the most complex of Pound's ironic poems, because the author and persona are most closely identified; it is also a development of his technique of Imagism, since each section of the poem is a separate Imagist poem in itself. It is therefore a culmination of his modernism, unsurpassed by anything he wrote later. The *Cantos* continue much of the time in the mode of *Mauberley,* with ironic uses of image and persona, though the *Pisan Cantos* introduce a new kind of self-irony into the context, since from there to the end, the poet speaks for himself more directly:

> as a lone ant from a broken ant-hill
> from the wreckage of Europe, ego scriptor.
>
> (Canto LXXVI)[18]

The later *Cantos* have much in common with *Mauberley,* too; the poet is clearly criticizing himself as he criticizes his age; but the irony becomes more tragic: he no longer wears a mask, but stands naked to his enemies, like Lear in his madness, seeing his world destroyed and himself with it, like the tragic hero in the last act of a play, after the recognition of his tragic flaw has been expressed, but still able to sing nobly of beauty among the ruins:

> First came the seen, then thus the palpable
> Elysium, though it were in the halls of hell,
> What thou lovest well is thy true heritage.
>
> (Canto LXXXI)

The techniques of Imagism and Irony are generally constant in Pound at his best, as they are usually lacking at his worst, when he becomes didactic and prosaic. Together, they give his poetry its peculiarly modern character, enabling him to express himself as he criticizes himself, to express his age as he criticizes it. Many of the *Cantos* are brought into focus and made memorable by a single ironic image:

> Being more live than they, more full of flames and
> voices.
>
> (Canto VII)

> In the gloom, the gold gathers the light against it.
>
> (Canto XI)

> Who even dead, yet hath his mind entire!
>
> (Canto XLVII)

> Tching prayed on the mountain and
> wrote MAKE IT NEW
> on his bath tub.
>
> (Canto LIII)

and finally, and most touchingly:

> That I lost my center
> fighting the world
> The dreams clash
> and are shattered—
> and that I tried to make a paradiso
> terrestre.
>
> (Notes for Canto CXVII)

As Pound utters his swan song in the *Cantos* and the voice fades into oblivion, he is still asserting his heroic aspiration but admitting his failure to achieve it. We can hear the voices of Propertius and Mauberley speaking again, but this time without the masks: there is no other ancient or modern poet beside him; it is Pound himself, the lone survivor of his age, the poet who more than any other gave it its style and thereby its measure of immortality, forced to recognize at the end that he is as mortal as his age. The poet cannot save himself or his world from the destruction of time, though his poetry can and does endure to tell later generations what visions of paradise were possible within the halls of hell. The last irony of Ezra Pound's poetry is inevitably tragic; the images that he made to mirror his age are even truer than he might have wished: "I cannot make it cohere" is more than a merely personal lament: it partakes of the disintegration of the age. The very brilliance of Pound's images reflects a paradise lost even as it is found, dissolving into the chaos around and within him. His paradise was, as he said repeatedly, "not artificial"—it was real, but as momentary as his world; he could create the images, with an amazing fecundity that is one of the proofs of his poetic genius, but he could not unify or give continuity to them. "They tell me to 'Mirror My Age,'" as he wrote early in his career, "God pity the age if I do do it." Pound was true to his prophecy, and the modern, international style of poetry which he fathered and mastered endures as one of the artistic monuments of an otherwise all too materialistic and destructive period of civilization—an ironic tribute which shows the age both its glory and its damnation.[19] As Pound said in 1965, when he was struggling with the last fragmentary *Cantos,* "It is difficult to write a paradise when all the superficial indications are that you ought to write an apocalypse."[20] As he moved with increasing skill from parody to satire, then to a self-irony that deepened into a tragic irony, Pound demonstrated that a poet is truest to himself and his age when he is most critical of both, for by making images that reveal the always mortal imperfections of man, he expresses the constantly immortal longings in man for perfection:

> a blown husk that is finished
> but the light sings eternal
> a pale flare over marshes
> where the salt hay whispers to tide's
> change
>
> (Canto CXV)

In the last Drafts and Fragments of Cantos, the irony has grown darker, the images more fleeting, but the voice of one of the master poets of the modern age is still to be heard, as distinguishable, and as distinguished, as ever.

NOTES

[1] *The Essence of Laughter and Other Essays, Journals and Letters,* ed. Peter Quennell, Meridian Books (New York, 1956), p. 167.

[2] "Ezra Pound and the Image," in *Ezra Pound: The London Years, 1908-20,* ed. Philip Grover (New York, 1978), p. 27.

[3] "The Seminal Image," in *The Struggle of the Modern* (Berkeley, Calif., 1963), p. 110.

[4] The shortest account of the birth of Imagism is to be found in *End to Torment: A Memoir of Ezra Pound* (New York, 1979) p. 18, where H.D. recalls how suddenly she became the first "Imagiste" when she showed Pound a few of her poems in the British Museum Tea Room, one afternoon in 1912. He edited them, signed them "H.D., 'Imagiste'" and sent them off to be published in *Poetry*.

[5] *Writers at Work: The Paris Review Interviews*, 2d ser. (New York, 1965), p. 39.

[6] Ibid. 43.

[7] Reprinted by permission of Michael and Anne Yeats.

[8] *Gaudier-Brzeska: A Memoir* (1916; New York, 1960), p. 85.

[9] *The Collected Early Poems of Ezra Pound*, ed. Michael John King (New York, 1976), p. 273. [Pound's poems are reprinted by permission of New Directions Publishing Corporation.]

[10] *The Letters of Ezra Pound*, 1907-1941, ed. D. D. Paige (New York, 1950), p. 151.

[11] Ibid. 181-82.

[12] Ibid. 114.

[13] *Literary Essays of Ezra Pound* (New York, 1954), p. 419.

[14] Ibid. 283.

[15] *Letters of Ezra Pound*, p. 231.

[16] Ibid. 239.

[17] *New Bearings in English Poetry* (London, 1932), p. 141.

[18] Lines of the *Cantos* are reprinted by permission of New Directions Publishing Corporation. Ezra Pound, *The Cantos of Ezra Pound*. Copyright 1934, 1940, 1948, 1972 by the Estate of Ezra Pound; and Ezra Pound, *Personae*. Copyright 1926 by Ezra Pound.

[19] In 1859 Baudelaire asked, with astonishing foresight: "But what are we to say of the modern artist who has risen to the heights *in spite of* his century, unless it be things which this age will not accept, and which we must leave to future ages to utter?" *The Mirror of Art*, trans. Jonathan Mayne (New York, 1956), p. 249.

[20] *Writers at Work*, p. 56.

Brendan Jackson

[In the following essay, Jackson focuses on "Hermes of the Ways" in an examination of the extent to which H.D.'s poetry adheres to the principles of Imagism.]

SOURCE: "The Fulsomeness of Her Prolixity": Reflections on "H.D., 'Imagiste'," in *The South Atlantic Quarterly*, Vol. 83, No. 1, Winter, 1984, pp. 91-102.

From its inception the Imagist movement was associated with the ideal of concision. The second of the three precepts announced in F. S. Flint's note "Imagisme" was "To use absolutely no word that did not contribute to the presentation." Pound's "A Few Don'ts by an Imagiste" repeatedly returns to this principle: "Use no superfluous word," "Use either no ornament or good ornament," "the natural object is always the *adequate* symbol." Even later, when Imagism had been appropriated by Amy Lowell, we find the same emphasis, in theory if not always in practice: "most of us believe that concentration is of the very essence of poetry."[1]

It is not, therefore, surprising to find that H.D., who was—and is—regularly acknowledged as the prime exemplar of Imagism,[2] is conventionally credited with a demanding, even a ruthless economy. When Pound sent H.D.'s poems to Harriet Monroe in October 1912 he claimed enthusiastically that they were "in the laconic speech of the Imagistes."[3] The word "laconic," with its allusion to the legendary terseness of the ancient Spartans, is suggestive of Pound's own austere poem, "Δώρια" published, in the same month as this letter was written, in *Riposta*. And it anticipates the epigraph of Pound's 1914 anthology, *Des Imagistes*: "And she also was of Sikilia and was gay in the valleys of Aetna, and knew the Doric singing."[4]

When Harriet Monroe announced the Imagists in *Poetry* in November 1912, she described them as "a group of ardent Hellenists," and although this was an inadequate phrase, Pound, Richard Aldington, and H.D. did regard the Greek lyric poets as their literary ancestors. Pound was to trace the phanopoeic poetic mode back to the Greek lyrist Ibycus as well as to Liu Ch'e, and Aldington regarded the Greek lyric poets as the first to have used free verse.[5]

Des Imagistes was published without a preface, or any explanatory material. In accordance with Imagist principle the poems are simply presented, without comment or description, and the anthology was immediately criticized as being merely a heterogeneous collection, with no real unity. The epigraph does, however, offer an important indication of the underlying theme. The quotation is taken from Moschus' "Lament for Bion." In this poem the dead Bion is presented as a master of the Doric melic tradition, and Moschus prophesies that he will, by the power of his song, win his own resurrection. Thus not only is the classical motif in Imagism reaffirmed, appropriately enough since the purpose of the anthology was primarily to publish the original "ardent Hellenists," H.D. and Richard Aldington, but the epigraph has a more specific aptness. The "Lament for Bion" is both an elegy for a lost voice in poetry and a promise of renewal. The "she" referred to in the epigraph to *Des Imagistes* is Koré, the Maiden: Persephone, who cyclically dies, but is always reborn. So with the true tradition of poetry. Furthermore, the translation used in *Des Imagistes* is from Richard Aldington's version, first published in the *New Freewoman* on 15 September 1913; and in this version Aldington makes an extraordinary error. (Pound was not alone in making howlers in classical translation.) According to Aldington it is Moschus, the elegist, who claims the power to recall Bion to life. If Pound did not consult the Greek original (or the Loeb translation, published in 1912) he may well have thought of the Imagists as assuming the role of Moschus in renewing the "Dorian mood." *Des Imagistes* included Pound's "The Return," that remarkable poem which is itself part elegy and part promise. This poem had been first published in June 1912 and appeared in *Ripostes*. Its reappearance in an *avant-garde* anthology two years later is unexpected. But the poem has, according to this interpretation, a peculiar appropriateness to the concealed theme of *Des Imagistes*. Pound is not seeking, as Aldington might have done, wistfully to disinter the old gods, but to resurrect, as it were, "the Doric singing." Pound's "Δώρια" too is retrieved for this anthology from its first appearance in February 1912, and from *Ripostes*.

The equation "H.D.'s Imagism = Greek economy" has become a cliché of criticism, endorsed by H.D. herself in the "Epitaph" published in the belated 1930 Imagist anthology:[6]

> Greek flower; Greek ecstasy
> reclaims for ever
>
> one who died
> following
> intricate songs' lost measure.

And yet, although it is true that H.D. sought inspiration in the myths and legends and in the poetry of ancient Greece, her response to experience is far from the classical spirit.

The first of her poems signed "H.D., 'Imagiste'" in *Poetry* for January 1913 is the well-known "Hermes of the Ways." Just over a year after its first publication Aldington was to select the first fifteen lines of this poem as an ideal "specimen of Imagism," praising it in these terms: "Hard, direct treatment, absolutely personal rhythm, few and expressive adjectives, no inversions, and a keen emotion presented objectively."[7] The praise seems just, although later in the poem we do find inversions, and Aldington ignores the archaic "awaiteth." More important, the hardness and the objectivity which Aldington discerns are relative qualities, as will shortly be argued. Nonetheless, the poem is impressive, in its detail and in its overall structure, which sustains a balance between the arduous challenge of the sea and the austere security of a coastal orchard. It is divided into two numbered sec-

tions in which the two images are juxtaposed, and this juxtaposition is maintained to the very end of the poem:

> The boughs of the trees
> Are twisted
> By many bafflings;
> Twisted are
> The small-leafed boughs.
> But the shadow of them
> Is not the shadow of the mast-head
> Nor of the torn sails.
> Hermes, Hermes,
> The great sea foamed,
> Gnashed its teeth about me;
> But you have waited,
> Where sea-grass tangles with
> Shore-grass.

The tortured, stunted trees of the sea-orchard are closely observed, but there is no pictorial indulgence; their image is presented as witness to the inner truth of the situation, and to introduce the contrasting memory of sea voyaging, which is also made present by an image: the shadow of the masthead and of torn sails. The gratitude for the sanctuary provided by Hermes does not admit sentimental elaboration: the god's gift is a refuge, but a severe one.

This poem, however, does not simply depend in a general sense on Greece for its classical atmosphere, but derives directly from a poem in the Greek Anthology. Its seed is to be found in the work of another woman poet, Anyte of Tegea, who lived in Arcadia in the third century BC. A reading of Anyte's brief poem illuminates H.D.'s method, and provides a helpful gloss on Harriet Monroe's note on H.D.: "Her sketches from the Greek are not offered as exact translations."[8] It also furnishes a corrective to the popular legend of H.D.'s unrelenting drive toward concision.

Anyte's poem consists of a single quatrain. A literal prose translation by Richard Aldington, which he also entitled "Hermes of the Ways," runs as follows:

> I, Hermes, stand here at the cross-roads by the wind-beaten
> orchard, near the hoary-grey coast;
> And I keep a resting-place for weary men. And the cool stainless spring gushes out.[9]

H.D.'s elaboration of this short original runs to fifty-four lines, and we have her own testimony that her draft was subjected to excisions by Pound: the poem was, therefore, originally even longer.[10] The additional material consists of a far more developed visualization of the scene. It is true that this is achieved by an accumulation of detail, not by an indulgence in adjectival description; nonetheless, although H.D.'s speech is indeed "laconic," her selection of detail is far less rigorous than that of her Greek inspiration.

It is interesting too that H.D. has chosen a different persona, and again the effect of this change is to render her poem less austere than the Greek original. Anyte speaks for the god Hermes: the poem is, in fact or in fancy, an inscription on the base of the god's statue. The bald statement is benign, but epitomizes the Olympian *apathein*. H.D., by contrast, speaks as the wayfarer, one of the "weary men," mortal, knowing fear and exhaustion. Her work has been repeatedly characterized as "hard" and "chiselled," but in comparison with the severity of the Greek this poem is expansive and rooted in human travail. In the context of Edwardian and even of Georgian poetry, H.D.'s poem is indeed "hard" in both sentiment and technique. Anyte corrects our perspective.

It is curious that H.D. did not acknowledge her debt in this poem. In the *Collected Poems* it appears even without the enigmatic caption which introduced it in *Poetry:* "Verses, Translations and Reflections from 'The Anthology.'"[11] Yet she was frequently to use this method of expanding or "reflecting on" classical originals. Her reconstructions of the dramatic context of six of the Sapphic fragments are perhaps the best-known examples. In each case she takes a phrase of a few words from Sappho and writes a poem of from 42 to 109 lines. At least three of the six are in their published form reductions of yet longer poems.[12] H.D.'s espousal in these poems of a confessional use of the dramatic monologue, in which the status of the persona is uncertain, is one symptom of her drift from Imagist asceticism to the expansiveness of her novels, with their failure adequately to distance character from creator. Most significant in relation to H.D.'s Imagism is, again, her apparent lack of sympathy with Sappho's "hardness." Maurice Bowra has defined the qualities of Sappho's poetry in terms which are uncannily suggestive of Imagist ideals:

> her melodious words . . . seem to be absolutely natural, the speech of every day raised to an almost unprecedented purity and power. She seldom uses metaphor and relies for her most impressive effects on simple statements like: "I loved you, Atthis, a time ago." . . . This is an art, which hardly needs images to enrich it, because it has passed beyond them and moves in a world where everything is seen and felt so clearly that it needs no ornament or explanation. . . . We feel no gap and no conflict between her matter and its presentation, and it is hard to imagine how she composed poems, which at once look effortlessly simple and yet make every word do its task with uncommon strength and flawless truth.[13]

The diction of exalted speech identified here was one of the aims of Imagism. Pound continually reiterated the lesson he had learnt from Ford Madox Hueffer. The language of poetry, he insisted, must depart "in no way from speech save by a heightened intensity (i.e. simplicity)." The sparing use of metaphor characterizes Pound's own practice, as Professor Max Nänny has pointed out; and this is true despite Pound's fondness for quoting Aristotle's dictum on metaphor as the hallmark of genius. The more or less rigorous eschewing of all images is, oddly enough, central to the Imagist ideal. The freedom from ornament and the taut excision of every otiose word which Bowra found in Sappho, and the fusion of "matter" with "presentation" (a typically Imagist word) are at the heart of Imagist propaganda, as is the poetry of statement: "Direct treatment of the 'thing.' . . . To use absolutely no word that did not contribute to the presentation."[14]

Many of these features are to be found in H.D.'s poetry: it is not without reason that her fellow poets and critics, both contemporary and later, have acknowledged her as "the perfect Imagist."[15] But even in her early verse, repetition threatens to become a mannerism, and Bernard Engel has justly noted that "excess reliance upon rhetorical devices, especially repetition, unfortunately becomes characteristic of H.D.'s later work."[16]

Longinus in his essay *On the Sublime* isolates a further quality of Sappho's poetry: the selection and combination of the most striking details in the thing presented. This is fundamental to Pound's mature style and originates in his Imagist / Vorticist ideal: "Take a chisel and cut away all the stone you don't want." Pound praised Joyce, even at the expense of Hueffer, for Joyce's "more rigorous selection of the presented detail." It is perhaps with precisely this in mind that E. P., Pound tells us in *Mauberley,*

> strove to resuscitate the dead art
> Of poetry; to maintain 'the sublime'
> In the old sense.

"All art," Walter Pater emphasized, "does but consist in the removal of surplusage," and Pater like Pound uses the example of Flaubert and the analogy of the sculptor. But not only do H.D.'s expansions of Greek originals furnish many examples of repetition; each poem taken as a whole betrays a profligate supererogation.[17]

One further instance will suffice. "Lais" is based on a four-line epigram by Plato. H.D.'s poem has 57 lines. (The coefficient of expansion is approximately the same as in "Hermes of the Ways.") At the end, she takes nine lines (containing sixty words) to translate the thirty words of Plato's quatrain. Thomas Burnett Swann in his monograph on H.D. argues, or rather asserts, that in H.D.'s poem "Plato's epigram has become a full-scale lyric which forcefully illustrates Lais's tragedy as well as stating it."[18] But the "characterization" which he praises evokes no more than a sentimentalized stereotype; the dramatization consists of superfluous embellishment of Plato's bald presentation. There is nothing in H.D.'s poem which is not present, with eloquent brevity, in Plato's: H.D. suffers through diffuseness.

"DICHTEN = CONDENSARE."[19] Pound's four-word poem "Papyrus" is said to have been composed as a "satire on H.D. and her Sapphics."[20] Certainly Pound was concise. He had the Greek economy. Poem after poem in *Lustra* exemplifies the poetry of statement. There are innumerable stories of his condensing the poems of others, most notoriously *The Waste Land*. He has himself told us how a thirty-line poem was first halved in length and ultimately reduced to the two-line "haiku-like sentence" of "In a Station of the Metro."[21] Despite the length of the

Cantos, their difficulty is due rather to what Pound omits than to what he includes. By contrast, and in defiance of the legend, one is tempted to say that H.D.'s standard method is to expand, to dilate; and, too often, to dilute.

Yet Pound was as impressed as Aldington by "Hermes of the Ways": "But, Dryad, this is poetry."[22] (Is it possible that he was not aware of its origin in Anyte's laconic quatrain?) Pound was to insist that Vorticism was an "intensive" art and told the story of the progressive compression of the "Metro poem" to illustrate the point; and yet he affirmed that Imagism was, simply, Vorticist poetry and gave as his paradigm H.D.'s "Oread." To identify the pervasive diffuseness of H.D.'s work is to offer a corrective to her popular reputation, but only approaches the really interesting question: Whence, if not from pure economy, derives that intensive quality which we still find in much of her early poetry, and which has prompted Pound and many others to "place" her as the essential Imagist?

The least known (and by far the shortest) of the three poems of H.D. which Harriet Monroe published in January 1913 is the four-line "Epigram":

> The golden one is gone from the banquets;
> She, beloved of Atimetus,
> The swallow, the bright Homonoea;
> Gone the dear chatterer.

Interestingly, although it appeared in *Des Imagistes* in 1914, H.D. omitted this model of terseness from her *Collected Poems.* The poem consists solely of the statement of loss and five different epithets for Homonoea. The effect derives from the contrasting impact of the final epithet, "the dear chatterer." The poem ends, as is appropriate for an epigram, with a punch-line. The contrast is most extreme between the opening and the close: "The golden one" and "the dear chatterer." The intervening images mediate the transition, "swallow" in particular anticipating "chatterer" while being perfectly adapted to its immediate context through its associations with romance and with migration. The poem is not, therefore, simply a contraposition of two incompatible evaluations of Homonoea. "Dear" in the last line indicates that the poet does not dissociate herself from the generous epithets that have gone before: rather, "chatterer" adds one further dimension, a more objective assessment, and so "places" the girl without contradicting the earlier praise.

The poem is pure image: the interaction of the five epithets creates a composite, rounded image without any supervention of comment. As a result, the elegiac force of "gone" in the first line is modified when the word is repeated in the fourth; the final tone is of realistic acceptance of Homonoea, humorously recognized, and valued, for what she is—or rather was. It may be worth observing that the repetition of "gone" contributes to this modulation of tone, and so the repetition is in this case not inert. The poem is small, but it is certainly intensive; and it displays most of the merits that Maurice Bowra found in Sappho.

It is time to consider the poem Pound selected as the exemplar of Vorticist poetry. "In painting Kandinsky, Picasso," he wrote, in the first issue of *Blast.* "In poetry this by 'H.D.'":

> Whirl up sea—
> Whirl your pointed pines,
> Splash your great pines
> On our rocks,
> Hurl your green over us,
> Cover us with your pools of fir.

In *Blast* the poem is untitled. When it appeared in *Some Imagist Poets 1915* it was called "Oread," and this is the title which appears in the *Collected Poems.* F. S. Flint in the *Egoist* referred to the poem as "PINES," clearly believing that it speaks of pines, imaged as a green sea. May Sinclair took the same view, and the accepted title, "Oread," would seem to confirm this reading. Pound, however, appears to have read the poem differently: he recalled only a little later, in 1917, "'H.D.'s' waves like pine tops"; and, although he was perhaps speaking casually, it is odd to misremember the subject of a poem— and certainly of a poem which Pound is claiming still rings in his head! More recently critics have tended, curiously, to follow Pound's reading: of the poem as about the sea, imaged as a pine forest.[23] This confusion is, paradoxically, illuminating, for all such formulations misrepresent the poem. The poem is not about pines or sea. It is perhaps slight, but it functions in a non-discursive mode and cannot be "unfolded" or explained; for "the Image is more than an idea. It is a vortex or cluster of fused ideas and is endowed with energy."[24]

And indeed the most immediately striking quality of "Oread" is perhaps its projection of a contained energy: it is vibrant, yet reaches stasis. The stasis is achieved in part by the poet's refusal to extend her compass. The poem presents a moment's mood, without evaluation or analysis. H.D. does not deal here in work of secondary intensity. The interpenetration of the images of pines and sea also contributes to the poem's stability, through the creation of a perfectly equipoised dynamic tension. The energy is a product of the intensity of the poet's vision. It is bodied forth in the centering of the poem on forceful verbs. In six short lines we find five violent verbs: "whirl" (twice), "splash," "hurl" (strengthened by the assonantal relationship with "whirl"), and "cover." All are in the imperative mood; each is placed at the beginning of a line; and only commas are allowed to articulate this avalanche of energy. Thus we have a movement of breathless crescendo, or rather of repeated climax, suggestive of the surging of sea and forest alike. And thus the poem is a worthy model of authentic imagism, of Pound's vorticist ideal. We may note, however, that even in this poem H.D. does not forsake repetition. "Whirl" is repeated, as is "pines." More notably, the five clauses really offer alternative expressions of a single idea.

The exploitation of powerful verbs which is the major source of the vibrancy in "Oread" is not unique in H.D.'s poetry. The importance of what we may call the *verbe juste* may be seen in her "Priapus," another of the first "Imagiste" poems published in *Poetry* in January 1913. Here once again the imperative is used to introduce tension ("Spare us from loveliness!"), which is then increased by the extraordinary "Thou hast *flayed* us with thy blossoms" before the imperative is repeated:

> Spare us the beauty
> Of fruit trees!

The humming of the bees in this poem is expressed in a verb which conveys exquisitely the neurasthenic hyperaesthesia of the hearer: "The air *thundered* their song."[25] Less obvious, perhaps, but no less effective, is the use of forceful verbs even in the presentation of a rose:

> I could scrape the colour
> from the petal
> like split dye from a rock.

And this poem continues, in an address to the rose:

> If I could break you
> I could break a tree.[26]

In "The Pool," a short poem which appeared in *Some Imagist Poets 1915,* the verbs are not in themselves startling, but it is the way in which they are deployed which energizes the poem:

> Are you alive?
> I touch you.
> You quiver like a sea-fish.
> I cover you with my net.
> What are you—banded one?

Here "sea-fish" and "net" are the only nouns, and "alive" and "banded" the only adjectives ("banded" is of course a verbal adjective; and "alive" also has a verbal quality). Apart from the verbs these are the only lexical words in the poem: all other words are pronouns or grammatical particles. The mystery is created by the avoidance of nouns. The poem is framed by two interrogative uses of the copula. Within this frame are the three simple sentences, which rely almost entirely for their meaning and effect on the choice of verbs; and there is an intricate relation of sound between these verbs, with "touch" echoed by the assonance of "cover," which also provides a half-rhyme with "quiver." But particularly noteworthy in this poem is the grammatical counterpoint. Each line forms a complete sentence, and the subjects of these sentences are, in order: you: I: you: I: you. In this way is evoked the sense of interaction between the poet and the "thing," and so this poem also quivers into mysterious life.

Two poems published in *Poetry* in March 1915 further illustrate H.D.'s sense of the value of strong verbs. "Storm," in which the imagery associates forest and sea, is suggestive of a less fully realized version of "Oread." "You crash over the trees," she apostrophizes the storm, and "a weighted leaf . . . sinks, / A green stone." "The Wind Sleepers," too, gains power from forceful verbs, use of the imperative mood, and exploitation of verbal

adjectives, although in this case the effect is vitiated by recurrent weaknesses in H.D.'s poetry: mannered repetition and a precious recourse to classical machinery.

Finally, the importance of verbs (and especially verbs in the imperative mood) and the almost complete eschewing of adjectives (which Pound repeatedly recommended) are well illustrated in the second section of "The Garden," which I give entire:

> O wind,
> rend open the heat,
> cut apart the heat,
> rend it sideways.
>
> Fruit can not drop
> through this thick air:
> fruit can not fall into heat
> that presses up and blunts
> the points of pears
> and rounds the grapes.
>
> Cut the heat,
> plough through it,
> turning it on either side
> of your path.

This reliance on the force of verbs is perfectly in accordance with the arguments of Ernest Fenollosa in "The Chinese Written Character as a Medium for Poetry," which Pound was to characterize in 1916 as "Fenollosa's big essay on verbs, mostly on verbs." Fenollosa, as Pound summarizes him, "inveighs against 'IS', wants transitive verbs."[27] But Pound, although he attached lasting importance to the awareness of process, of the tireless action in nature, did not adopt Fenollosa's technical program based on transitive verbs in the subject-verb-object model of the simple sentence. Pound's verse displays a disregard for formal syntax (which John Berryman has suggested may account for his dislike of Milton[28]) and is characteristically based on the dynamic juxtaposition of nouns and nominal groups, as well as of larger units. And H.D., although she does use a high concentration of forceful verbs and retains orthodox sentence structure, and occasionally, as has been shown, exploits it for special purposes, confines herself to short syntactical units, imaged in the halting movement of her short lines.

The intensity of presentation achieved in this way, at whatever cost, the focussing on perception, the "direct treatment of the 'thing,'" even when the "thing" is subjective, and the bodying forth of the transactional nature of experience are sufficient to explain the central position in the Imagist movement assigned to H.D. by her peers. But Imagism is, oddly, open to the two contradictory charges of being too impersonal and too self-indulgent. F. S. Flint, writing about H.D. in 1915, noted that "an artist cannot be inhuman and be understood," and continued with a remark which hindsight invests with a sad irony: "I think I have detected in one or two of H.D.'s later poems a tendency to pare and cut too far."[29] The expansive subjectivity manifested in H.D.'s rhapsodies on the Sapphic fragments, and in her "Lais," "Nossis," and "Heliodora," was no doubt fostered by her allegiance to Amygism: to the Imagist group of the official anthologies organized by Amy Lowell after Pound's defection, or deposition. Pound himself noted as much. But the seeds were there. One recalls that it was H.D.'s poems in *Poetry* which persuaded the far from laconic Amy Lowell that she, too, was an "Imagiste."[30] A comparison of one of those first Imagist poems, "Hermes of the Ways," with Anyte's brief original forces a revaluation of H.D.'s reputation for ascêsis, for ruthless pruning, for a relentless artistic conscience.[31]

NOTES

[1] F. S. Flint, "Imagisme," *Poetry* 1 (March 1913): 199; Pound, "A Few Don'ts by an Imagiste," ibid. 201-2; Preface, *Some Imagist Poets: An Anthology* (London, 1915), p. vii.

[2] See, e.g., Harold Monro, "The Imagists Discussed," *Egoist* 2 (1 May 1915): 79; Richard Aldington, *Life for Life's Sake* (London, 1968), p. 124; Glenn Hughes, *Imagism and the Imagists: A Study in Modern Poetry* (London, 1960), pp. 110 ff.

[3] Pound to Harriet Monroe, London, Oct. 1912: *The Letters of Ezra Pound 1907-1941*, ed. D. D. Paige (London, 1951), p. 45.

[4] *Des Imagistes* (London, 1914).

[5] Harriet Monroe, *Poetry* 1 (1913): 65; Pound, "Vorticism" (1914), reprinted in *Gaudier-Brzeska: A Memoir* (London, 1916): the relevant passage appears on p. 95; Aldington, "A Playntyve Ballade," *Egoist* 2 (1 Oct. 1915): 161: "When Sappho sang 'In the Isles of Greece,' / When Ibycus founded a new free verse. . . ." See also Preface, *Some Imagist Poets 1915*, pp. vii-viii.

[6] Verses of H.D. are reprinted by permission of New Directions Publishing Corporation. Hilda Doolittle, *Collected Poems of H.D.* Copyright 1929, 1953 by Norman Holmes Pearson.

[7] "Modern Poetry and the Imagists," *Egoist* 1 (1 June 1914): 202-3.

[8] *Poetry* 1 (Jan. 1913): 135.

[9] *Egoist* 2 (1 Sept. 1915): 139; I give the text of Anyte's poem from *The Greek Anthology*, ed. (and trans) W. R. Paton, Loeb Classical Library (London, 1917), III, 169:

> Here stand I, Hermes, in the cross-roads by the wind-swept belt of trees near the grey beach, giving rest to weary travellers, and cold and stainless is the water that the fountain sheds.

The Greek text reads:

> Ἑρμᾶς τάδ' ἕστακα παρ' ὄρχατον ἠνεμόεντα
> ἐν τριόδοις, πολιᾶς ἐγγύθεν ἀϊόνος,

> ἀνδράσι κεκμηῶσιν ἔχων ἄμπαυσιν ὁδοῖο
> ψυχρὸν δ' ἀχραὲς κράνα ὑποϊάχει.

[10] H.D., *End to Torment.*

[11] *Poetry* 1 (Jan. 1913): 118.

[12] See "A Selection of Poetry and Prose," introduced by Norman Holmes Pearson, *Contemporary Literature* 10 (Autumn 1969): 587-626. This selection includes three unpublished poems of H.D., dating from 1916: "Amaranth," "Eros," and "Envy." The Sapphic "Fragment Forty-One" (H.D., *Collected Poems*, New York, 1925, pp. 267-71) consists, with slight alterations, of the first three sections of the five-section "Amaranth." "Fragment Forty" (*Collected Poems*, pp. 255-58) is the final five sections of the seven-section "Eros." "Fragment Sixty-Eight" (*Collected Poems*, pp. 276-79) is "Envy" with the third of its four sections omitted.

[13] C. M. Bowra, *Landmarks in Greek Literature* (London, 1966), p. 93.

[14] Pound to Harriet Monroe, Coleman's Hatch, Jan. 1915: *Letters*, p. 91; Max Nänny, "Ezra Pound, Master of Metonymy: Context, Contiguity and Contact in His 'Personae'": paper delivered to the Fifth International Ezra Pound Conference, University of Durham, April 1979; Aristotle, *Poetics*, 1459a: for Pound's allusions see *The Spirit of Romance* (1910) (London, 1953), p. 158; "The Divine Mystery," *New Freewoman* 1 (15 Nov. 1913): 207-8; Ernest Fenollosa, *The Chinese Written Character as a Medium for Poetry* (London, 1936), p. 26 (footnote by Ezra Pound); "D'Artagnan Twenty Years After," *Criterion* 16: 606-17. The final quotation is taken from Flint's "Imagisme," *Poetry* 1 (March 1913): 199.

[15] Glenn Hughes, *Imagism and the Imagists*, p. 110; some supporting references are given above, note 2.

[16] Bernard F. Engel, "Poems That Matter and Dilutations," *Contemporary Literature* 10 (Autumn 1969): 513.

[17] Pseudo-Longinus, *De Sublimitate*, X: a translation by H. L. Havell is available in *Aristotle: Poetics*, trans. John Warrington, Everyman (London, 1963), pp. 150-52; Pound to Iris Barry, London, 27 July 1916: *Letters*, p. 142; Pound, "Dubliners and Mr. James Joyce," *Egoist* 1 (15 July 1914): 267; "E. P. Ode pour L'Election de son Sepulchre," *Hugh Selwyn Mauberley*, I: Ezra Pound, *Collected Shorter Poems*, 2d ed. (1952; London, 1968), p. 205; Walter Pater, "Style," in Ian Small, ed., *The Aesthetes: A Sourcebook* (London, 1979), pp. 30 ff.

[18] *The Classical World of H.D.* (Lincoln Neb., 1962), p. 73.

[19] Ezra Pound, *ABC of Reading* (London, 1934), p. 77; see also p. 20.

[20] Glenn Hughes, *Imagism and the Imagists*, p. 123.

[21] "Vorticism," in *Gaudier-Brzeska*, pp. 100-103.

[22] H.D., *End to Torment*, p. 18.

[23] "VORTEX. POUND," *Blast* no. 1, p. 154; Flint, "The Poetry of H.D.," *Egoist* 2 (1 May 1915): 73; May Sinclair, "Two Notes," *Egoist* 2 (1 June 1915): 88; Pound, "A Retrospect," *Literary Essays of Ezra Pound*, ed. T. S. Eliot (London, 1954), p. 14; Bernard Engel "Poems That Matter," p. 511. Swann includes the poem under "Sea Poems" rather than "Mountain Poems," commenting with judicious solemnity that it is best read as about the sea, although he acknowledges the possibility of the converse interpretation (*The Classical World of H.D.*, pp. 24-25).

[24] Ezra Pound, "Affirmations, IV: As for Imagisme," *New Age* 16 (28 Jan. 1915): 149.

[25] My emphases.

[26] "The Garden" (*Some Imagist Poets 1915*).

[27] Ezra Pound to Iris Barry, London, June 1916: *Letters*, p. 131.

[28] *The Freedom of the Poet* (New York, 1976), p. 264.

[29] "The Poetry of H.D.", *Egoist* 2 (1 May 1915): 73.

[30] The story is told by S. Foster Damon, *Amy Lowell: A Chronicle* (Boston, 1935), p. 192.

[31] The final phrases are adapted from Richard Aldington, *Life for Life's Sake*, p. 126: "Version after version of a poem was discarded by H.D. in the search for perfection, and the pruning was ruthless. I had thought I was fairly exacting, but I was staggered by this relentless artistic conscience."

Vivian de Sola Pinto

[*In the following essay, de Sola Pinto summarizes the contributions of T. E. Hulme, Ezra Pound, and D. H. Lawrence to the development of modern English poetry.*]

SOURCE: "Trench Poets, Imagists and D. H. Lawrence," in *Crisis in English Poetry: 1880-1940*, Hutchinson's University Library, 1951, pp. 151-157.

In the years immediately preceding the First World War there was a group of poets in London working on principles almost diametrically opposed to those of the Georgians. The Georgians had assumed that there was still an upper middle class with a living poetic culture, and that it was possible by means of a few minor reforms to achieve a renewal of the classic English poetic tradition comparable with that effected by Dryden in the sixteen-sixties, by Wordsworth in the seventeen-nineties or by Tennyson in the eighteen-forties. The Imagists, although they were only minor poets, had the merit of perceiving and declaring that this was no longer possible. They were the first true "modernist" group in the sense that they no longer attempted to communicate with a general public of poetry lovers which had ceased to exist, but concentrated on searching for a means of expressing the modern consciousness for their own satisfaction and that of their friends. The pretence that humanity was steadily progressing towards the millennium was to be abandoned and the poets had to recognize that they were living in a new dark age of barbarism and vulgarity where the arts could only survive in small islands of culture, which was no longer the possession of a securely established social class but which had to be fashioned anew by a self-chosen *élite* that managed to escape the spiritual degradation of a commercialized world. This attitude seems at first sight very much like that of the Tragic Generation of the 'nineties, with whom indeed the Imagists had definite connections, but actually it was different. The aesthetes of the 'nineties withdrew into their ivory tower, because they hated the vulgarity of the contemporary world and wanted to lose themselves among beautiful fantasies. The Imagists, on the contrary, wanted to create a very precise and concentrated expression of a new sort of consciousness for which the traditional techniques were inadequate.

Their philosopher was Thomas Edward Hulme (1883-1917), who was killed while serving in the artillery on the Western Front. Hulme's essays and notes (with six short poems) were published under the title of *Speculations* in 1924, but in the years preceding the war he had influenced the Imagists through his articles in periodicals and his friendship with Ezra Pound. Hulme was the first English thinker to make a frontal attack on the liberal humanism which had been the foundation of English middle-class culture since the Renaissance. His main contention was that the humanist tradition was now moribund, and that art and philosophy in Europe had to make a new start. Philosophy was to revert to something like scholasticism and art to something like the hieratic and geometrical art of Ancient Egypt and Byzantium. This art was to be based on the idea of original sin, the conception of man as a very imperfect creature "intrinsically limited but disciplined by order" as opposed to the romantic view of man as "an infinite reservoir of possibilities". The world was no longer to be regarded as a glorious place with which man was naturally in harmony but "a landscape with occasional oases. . . . But mainly deserts of dirt, ash-pits of the cosmos, grass on ashpits". This is a remarkable foreshadowing of Eliot's vision of the Waste Land. Hulme contended that there was "no universal ego but a few definite persons gradually built up". He clearly looked forward to a period like the Dark Ages when the values of ethics and religion and art would be the property of a small *élite* in a barbarous world. In his essay on *Romanticism and Classicism* he pleads for a classical poetry founded on fancy rather than imagination and foretells the coming of such a poetry: "I prophesy that a period of dry, hard, classical verse is coming". "I think there is an increasing proportion of people who simply can't stand Swinburne".

Hulme's ideas are a good deal more interesting than the poems of his Imagist disciples. The chief of these was the

American Ezra Pound (1885-) who had settled in London and published a series of volumes of verse beginning with *Personae* (1909). Pound is a poet of real originality but his talent was overlaid by masses of rather ill-digested learning. He started as a disciple of Browning and Swinburne and some of his early poems even show the influence of Kipling. Then he passed to study the Provençal trobadors from whose works he produced a series of free translations. In the years immediately preceding 1914 he was translating or rather adapting Anglo-Saxon, Latin, Chinese and Japanese poetry. He was a bold and tireless experimenter in metre and his most important contribution to the poetry of the crisis is perhaps to be found in his development of an unrhymed "free verse" which was neither the sprawling quality of Whitman's metre nor the flatness of Arnold's unrhymed lyrics. He probably owed something to Henley and his experiments certainly had an important effect on the work of T. S. Eliot.

Pound was the presiding spirit of the group which produced the anthology called *Des Imagistes* in 1914. This rather dilettante and precious collection includes work by the English poets F. S. Flint, Richard Aldington and F. M. Hueffer, the Irishman James Joyce and the Americans Ezra Pound, Allen Upward, H.D. (Hilda Doolittle), Amy Lowell and William Carlos Williams. The strong American element in the Imagist group is significant. The tradition of middle-class culture was much weaker in America than in England and was being swamped by the great influx of immigrants. It was therefore natural that American poets should reject it sooner than their English counterparts.

Instead of imitating the English romantics like the Georgians, the Imagists attempted to reproduce the qualities of Ancient Greek and Chinese poetry. They aimed at hard, clear, brilliant effects instead of the soft, dreamy vagueness or the hollow Miltonic rhetoric of the English nineteenth-century tradition. Their aims as expressed in *Some Imagist Poets* (1915) can be summarized as follows:

> (1) To use the language of common speech, but to employ always the exact word, not the nearly exact, nor the merely decorative word.
>
> (2) To produce poetry that is hard and clear, and not to deal in vague generalities, however magnificent and sonorous.
>
> (3) To create new rhythms and not to copy old rhythms, which merely echo old moods.

These aims, though inadequate, were salutary as a protest against the hollow wordiness of much contemporary English poetry, its reliance on the jingle of rhyme and the mechanical quality of its metre. The Imagists, however, lived too much among books, were too self-consciously Bohemian, and lacked both fundamental brainwork and contact with contemporary actualities. They aimed at the clarity and concentration of the classic Chinese lyric and the Greek epigram but did not realize that these forms grew out of highly civilized societies in conditions which

did not exist in early twentieth-century England. The result is that the neo-hellenism and *chinoiserie* of the Imagist anthologies now seem as faded and affected as the neo-romanticism of the Georgians. However, the Imagists are to be commended for showing that English poetry needed a new technique and, as Edwin Muir has written, for "removing unnecessary rules and a burdensome mass of dead associations". Imagism was only one phase in Pound's career. He passed on to a direct satire on the modern world in *Hugh Selwyn Mauberley* (1920), perhaps his best poem, which suffers, however, by comparison with T. S. Eliot's early writing, by which it is probably influenced. His *Draft of XXX Cantos* designed to be the first instalment of his masterpiece is a vast jumbled mass, in which Social Credit, the Renaissance, Ancient Greece and China jostle each other without any apparent coherence. Unlike Yeats and Eliot, with both of whom he was intimate, Pound yielded to the attractions of fascism and became Mussolini's American mouthpiece in the Second World War.

The most notable writer directly connected with the Imagists is certainly David Herbert Lawrence (1885-1930). Lawrence, like Blake with whom he has often been compared, is difficult to fit into any historical perspective. He contributed both to Georgian Poetry and the later Imagist anthologies, but he was neither a Georgian nor an Imagist. He was singularly unfortunate in his life and the period in which his genius developed. The son of a Nottinghamshire miner and an ambitious mother, he turned his back on his working-class world and became first a teacher and then a novelist and the husband of a divorced German baroness. Had he been born twenty or thirty years earlier in a period when Victorian society was still stable and possessed a really solid culture, Lawrence might have become a great regional author like Hardy in contact with the world of letters and scholarship and at the same time drawing strength from a local folk tradition. Unfortunately he grew up in a period of confusion when the old class structure of English life was collapsing in the years immediately preceding the First World War. The war turned him into a kind of pariah, and he suffered bitter humiliation on account of his German wife and because he was rejected as physically unfit for military service. At the same time his passionate and frank (but never ignoble) treatment of sexual themes in a series of magnificent works of prose fiction exposed him to a stupid puritanical outcry, and caused several of his books to be banned, thus turning him into an isolated and embittered man.

He described himself as a "passionately religious man"; he had lost his belief in the puritan Christianity of his ancestors in his youth, but he made a kind of religion for himself which he imagined to have been the primitive religion of mankind. This was a belief in "dark gods" who were the representatives of the "blood" as opposed to the intellect. In his later years he was haunted by a notion of finding remains of this primitive religion and culture, and also of building up a community which should be free from the ugliness and spiritual degradation of commercialized "civilization". The quest for this ideal "natural" life drove him on a series of pilgrimages to Ceylon, Australia and finally California and Mexico.

In the Preface to his *Collected Poems* Lawrence wrote that most of his early verses "in their fragmentary fashion . . . make up a biography of an emotional and inner life". They represent a long, difficult Voyage Within undertaken with the courage and determination of a poet who was one of the great life-adventurers of his age. He started by writing verse in the rhyming forms of the Georgians, but, unlike theirs, his early Nature poems are full of sharp personal sensations, almost painful in their intensity. The transition from this beautiful but essentially minor poetry of his youth to his major achievements in verse is seen in the memorable sequence of lyrics called *Look We Have Come Through* (1917). The complexity of Lawrence's earlier emotional experience is now simplified into a kind of duel of sex, a "conflict of love and hate" between man and wife. The sequence is a true voyage of discovery in the world of the spirit leading to an exciting culmination in a group of poems that express an annihilation of the ego and a sort of mystical rebirth or regeneration. The remarkable poem *Manifesto* ends with a vision of a universe where all human beings have completely realized their individualities, where

> all men detach themselves and become unique
>
> . . . . .
>
> Every human being will then be like a flower,
>   untrammelled,
> Every movement will be direct.
> Only to be will be such delight, we cover our
>   faces when we think of it
> Lest our faces betray us to some untimely fiend.

Lawrence had now developed a peculiar kind of free verse which owes something to Whitman and probably also the Old Testament poetry in which he had been steeped in his youth. In this form he wrote the collection of poems called *Birds, Beasts and Flowers* (1923) which represents the full flowering of his poetic genius freed from the autobiographical preoccupation. Here he gives notable expression to that awareness of "unknown modes of being" which is, perhaps, his most signal contribution to English poetry. His *Snake* in this collection is both a spiritual exploration of a life different from that of a humanity and a profound criticism of the world of "civilization":

> He lifted his head from his drinking, as cattle do,
> And looked at me vaguely, as drinking cattle do,
> And flickered his two-forked tongue from his lips,
>   and mused a moment
> And stooped and drank a little more,
> Being earth-brown, earth-golden from the burning
>   bowels of the earth
> . . . he seemed to me again like a king,
> Like a king in exile, uncrowned in the
>   underworld,
> Now due to be crowned again.

When Lawrence was dying of consumption in the South of France in the Spring of 1930, he wrote a handful of poems which deal with the themes of death and eternity. Fragmentary as they are, these last words of Lawrence, notably *Bavarian Gentians, Shadows* and *The Ship of Death* have an intensity of vision and a tranquil majesty of imagery and rhythm which give them a unique place in modern English poetry, and suggest that, if Lawrence had lived longer, he might have become a religious poet of a very high order. Some of his poetry, like some of his fiction, suffers because he was, in his own words "torn off from the body of mankind" and lacked a social background and a tradition. Apart from his considerable contribution to the rebuilding of English poetry, the importance of which is perhaps only beginning to be fully realized, he played a notable part as a critic in clearing away the lumber of dead traditions, and setting before English poets that salutary ideal which he described in a famous letter [dated 11th June 1916.]:

> The essence of poetry with us in this age of stark and unlovely actualities is a stark directness, without a shadow of a lie, or a shadow of deflection anywhere. Everything can go, but this stark, bare, rocky directness of statement, this alone makes poetry, to-day.

Stanley K. Coffman, Jr.

[In the following essay, Coffman examines aesthetic theories developed by T. E. Hulme.]

SOURCE: "T. E. Hulme as Imagist," in *Imagism: A Chapter for the History of Modern Poetry,* University of Oklahoma Press, 1951, pp. 47-73.

Hulme has been called the first Imagist poet and the movement's theorist. The Imagists themselves were the first so to describe him. Pound started it in *Ripostes* and (obliquely) in *Des Imagistes* and the *Catholic Anthology* by associating Imagism with the discussion of the image carried on in Hulme's 1909 club. Flint, in his "History of Imagism," not only confirmed the rather vague assertions of Pound, but went on to deny Imagism any originality other than the originality of Hulme, and most literary histories have accepted his word.

The argument is not completely convincing. Pound was never specific in acknowledging his debt to Hulme; Flint's "History" was not impartial or disinterested—he was annoyed that Pound should take credit for ideas he thought were not his own, and said as much in a letter to Amy Lowell. Both he and Aldington, who requested the "History," intended that it should deflate Pound's expansive pride as the founder of a new school of poetry. And while the parallels between certain theories of the Imagist manifestoes and passages from Hulme's notes are inescapable, they are not clear and conclusive enough to support the indebtedness usually claimed. More detailed study of Hulme's aesthetic and his experimental poems and comparison of these with the Imagism of the anthologies make it by no means certain that Imagism is simply a watered-down version of the *Speculations,* or, if one wishes, a reduction of their principles to essentials.

Before 1913, Hulme seems to have been primarily interested in poetry. He did not remain long with the Poets' Club of 1908, but the group organized in 1909 was certainly exposed to his poetic theory: Flint attended regularly, Pound occasionally. The *salon* which grew out of these meetings attracted a much larger circle, but for that reason probably limited the effectiveness of Hulme's proselyting. Flint, Aldington, and Pound were present frequently, though Pound has stated that it was an unsatisfactory place to discuss poetry. Probably their attendance was due more to a desire for general conversation than to the hope of hearing Hulme elaborate his ideas.

Hulme published no articles exclusively concerned with poetics, and did little lecturing. He spoke before an audience at the Poetry Bookshop in the summer of 1912 on "The New Philosophy of Art as Illustrated in Poetry"; and in 1914 he was one of a series of lecturers in Kensington Town Hall on new developments in art and literature, reading a paper on modern poetry. On this occasion, Wyndham Lewis also appeared in support of Hulme, and Pound illustrated the points of both speakers by reciting some of his and Hulme's poems. Michael Roberts quotes one of the audience:

> Hulme was not a good lecturer, and Wyndham Lewis read a paper supporting Hulme and came off pretty badly himself, mumbling in a husky voice, with his head buried in his manuscript. The audience felt as if they could snatch the papers from the poets and read them for themselves—there was so obviously something very worthwhile buried in all their abstract mumbling. To end it all, Ezra Pound stood up, all self-possessed, complete in velvet coat, flowing tie, pointed beard and halo of fiery hair. Lolling against the stage, he became very witty and fluent, and with his Yankee voice snarled out some of his and Hulme's poems. Somehow, such a voice rather clowned verse.[1]

It seems probable that many of his contemporaries knew of Hulme as a theorist, but that few of them knew much about his theory. They must have been acquainted with fragments of it, but he did not have the opportunity to publicize it frequently or systematically enough to root it firmly in their minds. On the other hand, the Imagists Flint, Aldington, and Pound must have known Hulme's theories better than did most of his contemporaries; they were interested in poetry and, especially Flint and Pound, had many opportunities to discuss the subject with him.

The second poets' club developed into the *salon* of 1913-14 as Hulme's interest was turning to modern art, and the salon reflects this trend. The impression of contemporaries is that Hulme was more concerned with the visual arts than with poetry: his friends were principally painters and sculptors, and probably his closest friend was the sculptor Jacob Epstein. The *salon* was preceded by a regular dinner with several of the artists, and topics of interest to them dominated the Frith Street evenings. He defended Epstein against the violent criticism occasioned by his work for the British Medical Association Building and for the Wilde Memorial in Paris, and in a brief series of *New Age* articles upheld the modern, geometrical, non-representative art.

> I am attempting in this new series of articles to define the characteristics of a new constructive geometric art which seems to me to be emerging at the present moment.[2]

He further publicized the cause by persuading Orage to reproduce in *The New Age* some of the drawings of Epstein, Gaudier, Nevinson, Roberts, and David Bomberg. However, Michael Roberts has pointed to what was probably the only tangible result of all this enthusiasm: that Epstein's drawing, "The Rock Drill," as well as his carvings in flenite, and some of the early sculpture of Gaudier-Brzeska might be taken to show the influence of Hulme's theories.

Hulme became known, then, less through the poetry clubs and his poetic theory than through the Frith Street *salon* and his theories on the new art; and it was not until 1914 that he found some demand for his lectures. At this time he was forced to drop out of the circles where his theories were gaining respect; England entered the war in the summer, and Hulme joined the service toward the close of the year. Not only were most minds turned to matters other than aesthetics, but Hulme was not able to be in London for periods long enough to consolidate what position he had established for himself, even had he so desired. While he cannot be considered a prominent critic and theorist of the years 1908-17, neither can he be dismissed as a thinker of no significance for the artists of the period; and although his poetic theory had only a limited circulation, it is hardly possible that at least two of the Imagists, Flint and Pound, should have failed to become familiar with it. Imagism *could* have had its source in Hulme.

Hulme analyzed in some detail what he considered the two main problems of the artist. One involves perception, or what he sees; the other involves expression, or how he communicates what he sees. The ordinary man, he said, perceives only with reference to present or future action; that is, he sees not *the* table, but *a* table, classifying objects with reference to immediate or potential use. The artist, however, sees not stock types, but individuals. His problem is to see things as they really are, apart from any conventional way of seeing them. Literature, in fact, may be defined as "entirely the deliberate standing still, hovering and thinking oneself into an artificial view, for the moment, and not effecting any real actions at all."

The literary artist has next to "bend" language to express his unconventional vision. It must be bent to his use because words are designed to serve an essentially practical purpose. They are tags or labels which we give to objects of perception and their function is primarily to classify. By its nature, the process leads to compromise and to conventional expression, because it abstracts from an object the characteristics it has in common with other objects and classifies it on this basis. Consequently, a word tends to give a lowest common denominator of meaning. Its meaning is further conditioned by the fact that it serves not only in perception but in communication, where a similar process takes place. A word is a medium for exchange of information between men, and the extent of the information it conveys is determined by a general agreement that a word means this or that. It circulates at a fixed value, though to individuals it may have other values outside the agreed area. Both the perceptual and communicative uses of words emphasize the abstract rather than the individual; words tend to assume the characteristics of counters that can be moved about upon a chess board.

The artist's second problem, then, is to break the stiff, general patterns which make language incapable of expressing an individual, personal reaction. Instead of conveying only part of an emotion, the part representing the agreed area of meaning, he seeks to convey the full range of his own individual feeling; he endeavors to express what lies outside the circle represented by the word as a counter. His success depends directly upon his ability to use metaphor, because by revealing new analogies to the reader he can convey the freshness and individuality of new vision.

The function of analogy in poetry may be summed up as follows: "to enable one to dwell and linger upon a point of excitement":

> The inner psychology of a poet at such a creative moment is like that of a drunkard who pushes his hand forward along a table, with an important gesture, and remains there pondering over it. In that relaxing gesture of pushing comes the inner psychology of all these moments.[3]

Two characteristics of analogy not only permit but force the reader to linger over points significant to the poet. One is the concrete, visual quality of the imagery used in the comparison. "Each word must be an image *seen,* not a counter."[4] The image is a representation of a physical object, and the reader reacts to it in the same way he would to a physical object. A direct, personal reaction eliminates the need for poet and reader to communicate through the leveling medium of ordinary counter words. Further, the physical thing evokes in the reader an emotion he feels as his own, and he is therefore inclined to linger over it with more pleasure. A poetry of images "endeavors to arrest you, and to make you continuously see a physical thing, to prevent you gliding through an abstract process."[5]

Concreteness of imagery insures freshness, but so does the novelty of an original juxtaposition of images, the second source of the analogy's strength. It produces a shock of recognition that also brings the reader to an abrupt stop. The effect Hulme wanted was one that would set poetry apart from the practical and dully reasonable attitudes of normal life. "Never, never, never a simple statement. It has no effect. Always must have analogies, which make an other-world through-the-glass effect, which is what I want."[6] The theory sets art squarely to the task of creating, not imitating; "beauty does not exist by itself in nature, waiting to be copied, only organized pieces of cinders."[7]

Hulme hoped to give his faith in analogy a sound basis by arguing that thought is "the simultaneous presentation to the mind of two different images . . . merely the discovery of new analogies, when useful and sincere, and not mere paradoxes."[8] His argument oversimplifies for the sake of staying on "easily defined routes"; doubtless he would not have insisted upon the unqualified statement that one thinks solely in terms of images. But he certainly would have given up only a part of his proposition. He was convinced that the imaging process must be present in good writing. "A man cannot write without seeing at the same time a visual signification before his eyes. It is this image which precedes the writing and makes it firm."[9]

Hulme has asserted a debt to Henri Bergson for certain points in his aesthetic; and as one studies the aesthetic, he finds an approach and a subsequent, hasty retreat from Bergson which is characteristic of Hulme's philosophy as a whole. Hulme began by adopting certain conclusions as a point of departure for an analysis of what one feels in art; he cited two aspects of Bergsonism which he considered important for aesthetics. One is the conception of reality as a flux of interpenetrated elements unseizable by the intellect; the other is the orientation of the mind toward action and the significance of this orientation for the normal habits of operation which the human mind has developed. The mind or intellect apprehends external phenomena in such a way that man can act on them, not so that he can know them; it places a veil between man and reality. It is the artist who, emancipated from the necessity for action, can lift the veil and expose reality. He does not ask, "How can I put this to my own use?" but, "How does this reveal the inner life of things?" While normal perception sees the features of a living being as "assembled, not as mutually organized," and misses the intention of life that runs through them and gives them significance, this "intention is just what the artist tries to regain . . . in breaking down . . . the barrier that space puts up between him and his model."[10] This is the basis for Hulme's statement of the artist's problem of perception.

Bergson also provided Hulme with an analysis of language which revealed the limitations imposed upon it by its service to the intellect and its consequent inability to express what the artist sees. He admitted that language has contributed generously to intelligence. Without it, intellect would have remained fixed on the external objects with which it deals, and would never have been freed for more complex processes of thought. Yet its service has seriously restricted its power to express what is beyond the confines of intellect. It cannot, for example, adequately express a reality like consciousness, because consciousness is made up of interpenetrated states. Language, conditioned by the analytical habits of intellect, spreads out in space what depends for its identity upon an interpenetration. It can express reality only in non-real terms.

Finally Bergson had also solved the problem of communication in terms of the image or analogy. Faced with the difficulty of expressing the "unique" and "inexpressible," his philosophy relied heavily upon striking analogies. He did not believe that images can express reality fully or even partially, but he was convinced that they provide the only means by which man can approach the point where he will be forced to surrender to it.

> No image can replace the intuition of duration, but many diverse images, borrowed from very different orders of things, may, by the convergence of their action, direct consciousness to the precise point where there is a certain intuition to be seized.[11]

The artist prepares the way for intuition by lulling the active and resistant powers of intellect and creating a state of mind receptive to suggestion. For example, a poet employs both imagery and rhythm to gain his effect.

> The poet is he with whom feelings develop into images, and the images themselves into words which translate them while obeying the laws of rhythm.[12]

Through the rhythms of his words, he can subdue the intellect and prepare the way for an intuition. He not only has the command of the image, he can create conditions which increase its effectiveness.

One is still on ground of agreement between Hulme and Bergson. A passage from Hulme's "Lecture on Modern Poetry" is clearly an echo of Bergson on the poet's method:

> Say the poet is moved by a certain landscape, he selects from that certain images which, put into juxtaposition in separate lines, serve to suggest and evoke the state he feels. To this piling-up and juxtaposition of distinct images in different lines, one can find a fanciful analogy in music. A great revolution in music when, for the melody that is one-dimensional music, was substituted harmony which moves in two. Two visual images form what one may call a visual chord. They unite to suggest an image which is different to both.[13]

The parallels bear out Hulme's statement that he was indebted to Bergson for providing his roughly formulated aesthetic with an efficient vocabulary. Both theorists insisted that the poet's vision is an unconventional one, adjudged language incompetent to express it, and relied upon metaphor and analogy to bring the reader into range of the vision's effectiveness. But Hulme's debt is limited to Bergson's lucid argument of these related ideas; beyond this the theories of the two men are at wide variance.

According to Bergson, the artist sees reality. He escapes the mind's normal orientation toward action and turns instead to the search for pure knowledge; he has learned that intuition serves where intellect fails. Through intuition, he discerns in the face of a living being, for example, the

> intention of life, the simple movement that runs through the lines, that binds them together and gives them significance. This intention is just what the artist tries to regain, in placing himself back within the object by a kind of sympathy, in breaking down, by an effort of intuition, the barrier that space puts up between him and his model.

Bergson was so certain of the existence of intuition in aesthetics that he relied upon it to explain what he meant by his metaphysical use of the term, pointing to the phenomenon which frequently occurs when one has gathered all of his materials and is prepared for writing. Before one can begin effectively, there must be an intuition which suddenly forces the work forward in a specific direction, the words falling into place as he proceeds. Bergson even cited the aesthetic in *proof* of the possibility that the metaphysical exists: "That an effort of this kind is not impossible, is proved by the existence in man of an aesthetic faculty along with normal perception."[14]

Hulme's philosophy is marked by a consistent refusal to grant to intuition the powers Bergson gave it, and he defined literature as the "hovering and thinking oneself into an *artificial view*," hardly a phrase one would apply to reality.[15] Recall for a moment his defense of analogy: it evokes a physical and thus an individual reaction, and it startles the reader out of his normal habits of thought by presenting relations unseen before. It avoids the abstract and makes language a sharp instrument with which to probe human feelings. Although he wrote, "Images in verse are not mere decoration, but the very essence of an intuitive language,"[16] there is no evidence that the artist knows or puts his audience in touch with any reality except that which can be defined in the relative terms of a sense of existence newly freshened and recharged with immediacy by the sudden apprehension of unexpected likeness.

Hulme described literature as either *romantic* or *classic*. The terms carry into his aesthetic the same meaning they had in his philosophy, and represent opposing views of what the artist sees, what constitutes his vision. The romantic assumes that the human mind can apprehend the realities of religion as well as those of the external world; he is the humanist, who, assuming a continuity between the world of absolute truths and the world of intellect, tends to explain the religious in human terms and reduce God to the level of man. He believes in man as a measure of all things and consequently in the doctrines of individualism, progress, and perfectibility. The classicist refuses to view man so optimistically; he assumes a discontinuity between the areas of religious, absolute truth and of mind or intellect. He argues that the "gaps" can be bridged not by the intellect, but by intuition, and is unwilling to grant intuition any but occasional efficacy. He believes God the absolute measure of all things, man subordinate and rigidly limited in his power to apprehend reality.

As romantics, he pointed to Keats, Coleridge, Byron, Shelley, and Swinburne. Characteristically, he neglected to analyze the work of each poet to support his classification, proceeding instead to speak in general terms, and leaving the reader to perform the detailed criticism for himself. Of the romantics, he wrote:

> Verse to them always means a bringing in of some of the emotions that are grouped round the word infinite . . . I object to the sloppiness which doesn't consider that a poem is a poem unless it is moaning or whining about something or other.[17]

Believing that man reflects and can comprehend the divine, the romantic poet likes to treat ideas and emotions that he thinks representative of divinity or at least of the mysterious forces of the universe. He likes to talk of the soul and of the realities above those of practical, everyday life, suggesting easy comprehension where there is none.

> If I use the word soul, or speak of higher realities, . . . you will know that at that precise point I didn't know of any real reason and was trying to bluff you.[18]

Attempting to convey an idea of the infinite, which man is theoretically capable of understanding, the romantic crashes headlong into the fact that not language but comprehension fails him, and he takes refuge in a technique which depends upon the impressiveness of mystery and evasion. Instead of admitting the absolute, inscrutable mystery of reality, he makes a fetish of the mystery and believes that he is thus dealing with reality itself.

> Escapes to the infinite:
>   (i) Art. Blur, Strangeness, music.
>   (ii) Sentimentality.[19]

Sentimentality is another characteristic of romantic verse. Individualism encourages an abnormal care for one's own feelings; personal emotions are given an importance, a significance and sanctity, which they do not deserve. Further, the tendency of the romantic is toward the more lugubrious emotions: he "moans" about the way man is oppressed by society, he "whines" about his inability to use himself to the full extent consistent with his divine nature. "The thing has got so bad now that a poem which is all dry and hard . . . would not be considered poetry at all. Poetry that isn't damp isn't poetry at all."[20] The romantic attitude, in short, makes literature a falsehood.

> The literary man deliberately perpetrates a hypocrisy, in that he fits together his own isolated moments of ecstasy (and generally deliberate use of big words without personal meaning attached) and presents them as pictures of higher life, thereby giving old maids a sense of superiority to other people and giving mandarins the opportunity to talk of "ideals." Then makes attempt to justify himself by inventing the soul and saying that occasionally the lower world gets glimpses of this, and that inferentially he is the medium. As a matter of fact, being certain moments of ecstasy perhaps brought on by drink.[21]

The classicists include Horace, most of the Elizabethans, and the Augustans. Hulme described classical verse in terms of the philosophical attitude from which he drew the name:

> even in the most imaginative flights there is always a holding back, a reservation. The classical poet never forgets this finiteness, this limit of man. He remembers always that he is mixed up with earth. He may jump, but he always returns back; he never flies away into the circumambient gas.[22]

In order to encompass poets of such diverse techniques as the Elizabethans and the Augustans, Hulme found it necessary to distinguish between static and dynamic classicism. The dynamic includes the Elizabethans and, in particular, Shakespeare—even his most imaginative and logically preposterous metaphors are presented with a flourish and an amused detachment.

The distinction between romantic and classical verse was not an academic point with Hulme. It was his way of distinguishing in poetic theory between the foolish overestimation of man's potentialities which extends his vision to include reality, and the wise foreshortening of his vision which also accepts the foreshortening with good grace. It represented a plea and a prophecy. The terms in which he described the two types of verse eloquently argued his belief that the poet should reject the romantic and turn to the classic, and he confidently predicted that a reform was about to take place.

> I want to maintain that after a hundred years of romanticism, we are in for a classical revival. . . . I prophesy that a period of dry, hard, classical verse is coming.[23]

He made specific suggestions for the guidance of poets who wished to achieve the "cheerful, dry and sophisticated" tone of the new verse, and even wrote a handful of poems to demonstrate his theories.

Perhaps Hulme's most sweeping recommendation restricted the subject matter of poetry. As man is a limited creature who cannot know reality, it is vain to insist that his art reveal the truths of the universe. Since "we no longer believe in perfection, either in verse or in thought, we frankly acknowledge the relative."[24] Instead of trying to communicate perfection, the classicist attempts to communicate an individual, personal mood. Hulme excluded as inappropriate and romantic the vast, vague emotions loosely grouped under the adjective *inspirational*: poetry, he said, is not religion, nor have the two any aims in common; it is not designed to impel men toward Progress. The aim is to express the vivid patches, the "sudden lifts" in life, "cf. love, fighting, dancing. The moments of ecstasy."[25]

> Speaking of personal matters, the first time I ever felt the necessity or inevitableness of verse, was in the desire to reproduce the peculiar quality of feeling which is induced by the flat spaces and wide horizons of the virgin prairie of western Canada.[26]

It would be a mistake to interpret the "sudden lift" or the emotion evoked by the Canadian landscape as in any way associated with the ecstasy of the romantic poets. The feelings that Hulme wanted poetry to express were the minor, transient, almost trivial ones which result from seeing physical things in an unconventional way. And although poetry is most intense when dealing with the vivid patches inspired by love and fighting, it does not have to wait for their appearance. Any new way of seeing objects of routine existence is worth expression.

> The effort of the literary man to find subtle analogies for the ordinary street feelings he experiences leads to the differentiation and importance of those feelings. What would be unnoticed by others, and is nothing when not labelled, becomes an important emotion. A transitory artificial impression is deliberately cultivated into an emotion and written about. Reason here creates and modifies an emotion, *e.g.* standing at street corners. Hence the sudden joy these produce in the reader when he remembers a half-forgotten impression, "How true!"[27]

Hulme tends to reduce poetry almost to the creation of sophisticated *bons mots*. Convinced of man's ineffectiveness as a seer who can reveal the mystery of the universe, Hulme insisted that he turn his eyes from searching the horizon to examining a limited area around his feet. There is nothing "new under the sun," and all literature is an

> accident, a happy escape from platitude. . . . Literature like pitching, how to throw phrases about, to satisfy a demand. An exercise for the time being, no eternal body to be added to.[28]

After all, poetry is "for the amusement of bankers and other sedentary armchair people in after-dinner moods. No other." The following comprises its range of usefulness:

> (i) amuse banker
>
> (ii) for use of clerks in love to send to sweethearts
>
> (iii) temporary moods (in theatres) of cultivated people
>
> (iv) songs of war.[29]

If the classical poet's art consists of making the phenomena of everyday life poetic by presenting them in an unusual way, he will have to rely on analogy. A single original comparison sharpens interest where the most colorful and concentrated description fails. The distinctive characteristic of Hulme's conception of analogy is his obsession with the solid physical sensations it can convey. "*It is the physical analogies that hold me, . . . *not the *vain* decorative and verbal images of the ordinary poets. . . . The process of invention is that of gradually making solid the castles in the air."[30]

In "Cinders" he had made some effort to give his preoccupation with the physical a philosophical basis. He expressed a belief that the soul is "undifferentiated," that it

is given personality through the body. One's being, so far as he knows, is simply the accumulation of feelings produced by reactions of the body to various stimuli. Emotion is physical in nature and depends "on real solid vision or sound." Consequently the poet will express himself in terms of physical sensations, the kind of knowledge that affects men most deeply and directly. "All poetry is an affair of the body—that is, to be real it must affect the body."[31] Of course, the sensations conveyed by poetry cannot equal in intensity those experienced directly, because feeling is filtered through language; but poetry can be an effective "compromise for a language of intuition which would hand over sensations bodily."

> With perfect style, the solid leather for reading, each sentence should be a lump, a piece of clay, a vision seen; rather, a wall touched with soft fingers. Never should one feel light vaporous bridges between one solid sense and another. No bridges—all solid; then never exasperated. . . . Always seek the hard, definite, personal word.[32]

The primary weapon of the classical poet in the invention of new analogies is fancy. Dealing with "finite things," it can produce the kind of imagery which Hulme felt essential to effective verse. He insisted upon a clearly defined distinction between fancy and imagination, with which it is sometimes confused: "where you get the [creative or artistic impulse] exhibited in the realm of emotions you get imagination, and . . . where you get this quality exhibited in the contemplation of finite things you get fancy."[33] Originally, he said, the words *fancy* and *imagination* had been synonymous, but they had been differentiated by eighteenth-century German writers on aesthetics. Thereafter imagination had become the shibboleth of the poets he described as romantic and had become associated with the characteristics of their work. Its connotations of emotionalism as well as of social and artistic lawlessness made it a word extremely unpleasant to Hulme's ear; fancy, on the other hand, seemed to suggest the control and precision which Hulme wanted in poetry. The distinction was a convenient way to justify his own poetic tastes.

Convenient though it may have been, it was not very effective because Hulme did not offer a detailed exposition of what he meant by the words. His references to them leave some question whether he really meant to draw so clear a line between them and dismiss imagination as a faculty detrimental to poetry. On one occasion he contrasted intellect, which can deal with complexities of the mechanical kind, can produce intricate diagrams and patterns, with fancy, which can create from its material an organic product whose nature cannot be explained simply by analysis of its parts. The contrast, of course, applies to aesthetics the manifolds theory Hulme had found so useful in philosophy. As in metaphysics it had allowed for the appearance of phenomena unpredictable in the mechanistic terms of cause and effect, so in aesthetics it allowed for the existence of a truly creative element above the mere organization of materials. Hulme believed that art is creative, that its value derives from more than mechanical arrangement of form; he had therefore to attribute some such ability to fancy since he had categorically condemned imagination. As Michael Roberts has pointed out, the result is that Hulme's fancy is similar to the romantic definition of imagination made by Coleridge. Fancy appears to be imagination with its egotism deflated, its emotion held in check by reason, and, one suspects, its attitude tempered by a sense of humor.

Hulme established a reasonable standard for evaluating the new verse. If its function is to communicate a personal feeling or physical sensation, its measure as good or bad verse must reside in the effectiveness with which it conveys this feeling. One can define art as "a passionate desire for accuracy, and the essentially aesthetic emotion as the excitement which is generated by direct communication."[34] Verse is not an occult art, exempt from the demands of clarity. It is "simply and solely the means of expression . . . just as prose is, and if you can't justify it from that point of view it's not worth preserving."[35] In fact, its difference from prose is only a matter of degree. It is more efficient than prose because it is the advance guard which creates the images that give language its freshness and directness. Poetry

> chooses fresh epithets and fresh metaphors, not so much because they are new and we are tired of the old, but because the old cease to convey a physical thing and become abstract counters.[36]

Prose, in Hulme's vocabulary, was simply a word to describe language whose imagery has gone stale. "Prose is . . . the museum where the dead images of verse are preserved."[37] Bad poetry is prose no matter how perfect it may be metrically.

But he did not think the question of metrics irrelevant. He recommended that the classical poet seek a new verse form and pointed to specific defects in the old which encouraged a verse that appealed to the ear and frequently had no effect other than to lull the faculties of the mind into a mild condition of hypnosis. Even more serious, it restricted the poet's choice of the most accurate language in which to clothe his metaphor. The new verse, depending as it does upon images which strike the eye and arrest the mind, demands a free and elastic metrical pattern. "I contend that this method of recording impressions by visual images in distinct lines does not require the old metric system."[38] The implication is that what the new method does require is a form similar to the French *vers libre*, and the two of its principles which Hulme chose to mention were those that would best suit Imagism: denial of a regular number of syllables as the basis for versification; determination of line length by the requirements of the imagery, the contours of the poet's thought.

Although his emphasis upon imagery suggested an argument against traditional metrical patterns, this was not the ostensible reason offered for rejecting them. "The principle on which I rely in this paper is that there is an intimate connection between the verse form and the state of poetry at any period."[39] It is usually true but seldom recognized that an efflorescence of verse in a given pe-

riod can be traced to the invention or introduction of a new verse form. Hulme attributed the lively interest in poetry among the Elizabethans to their discovery of blank verse and the contemporary renaissance in French poetry to Kahn's statement of the principles of *vers libre*. He believed in the value of a new form per se.

> One might sum it all up in this way: a shell is a very suitable covering for the egg at a certain period of its career, but very unsuitable at a later age. . . . I will conclude, ladies and gentlemen, by saying, the shell must be broken.[40]

Hulme's poems are not merely unimaginative exercises written to the specifications of a blueprint. While they are clearly meant to demonstrate his theory, they do not need the theory to justify their appearance in print; and while they conform to his recommendations, they place them in a perspective that suggests their relative importance, and in at least one case they reveal clearly a significant point which would probably be overlooked on the strength of his theory alone.

The poems deal with the subjects of everyday perception:

> *Above the quiet dock in midnight,*
> *Tangled in the tall mast's corded height,*
> *Hangs the moon. What seemed so far away*
> *Is but a child's balloon, forgotten after play.*[41]

or:

> *Alluring, earth-seducing, with high conceits*
> *is the sunset that coquettes*
> *at the end of westward streets.*
>
> *A sudden flaring sky*
> *troubling strangely the passer-by*
> *with vision, alien to long streets, of Cytherea,*
> *or the smooth flesh of Lady Castlemaine. . . .*
> *A frolic of crimson*
> *is the spreading glory of the sky*
> *heaven's wanton*
> *flaunting a trailed red robe*
> *along the fretted city roofs*
> *about the time of homeward-going crowds*
> *—a vain maid, lingering, loth to go. . . .* [42]

The subjects are not only conventional perceptually, but are "standard" material for poetry. Perhaps Hulme selected them for both characteristics, because his intent was to force the reader to see an object apart from a normal, or practical, and a stylized, or literary, way of seeing it. In any case, the poems show him following literally his own advice on the choice of subject matter. He deals not with vast emotions or with the problems of the universe, but with the very personal feelings that result from viewing a physical object in an unusual way.

The originality and freshness of feeling are conveyed by analogy. The poems make no pretense of demanding more attention than the analogies on which they are based seem to warrant. Success or failure depends wholly upon effectiveness of imagery. The imagery is, however, slightly different from what one would have expected. While Hulme emphasizes the importance of the purely physical aspects of the image and its effect upon the reader's feelings, and while his theory thus seems to argue for a richly sensuous verse, he uses the physical object in such a way that its "hardness" is only one consideration. His plea for a poetry that would appeal to the senses was not intended to encourage what is ordinarily understood as sensuous poetry, and the poems show that the object is important not only because it is physical, but because its peculiar nature completes a contrast. One finds the moon compared to a child's balloon, a sunset compared to a coquettish girl, the stars to the white faces of town children, and the sky described in these lines:

> *Oh, God, make small*
> *The old star-eaten blanket of the sky,*
> *That I may fold it round me and in comfort lie.*[43]

The comparison in each case reduces a normally "poetic" and impressive perception to the level of the trivia of everyday life. The reduction, of course, works to the advantage of both: the poetic loses its conventional stiffness and artificiality and the trivial becomes suddenly worthy of notice.

The total effect conveys a freshness, which was what Hulme admittedly sought, mingled with a feeling of amusement and usually irony, of which he made little in his theory. He did say on one occasion: "Analogies in poetry, like the likenesses of babies, to be taken half seriously, with a smile,"[44] but this is the only reference to an aspect of analogy that shows up in his poems and is fundamental to his aesthetic as far as it pertains to poetry. His philosophy, wavering between admission and denial of man's ability to know reality, never wholly entered the area of admission; the section of *Speculations* entitled "Cinders" almost flatly refused to grant him the power. His poems accept the tragic nature of man's limitations with an ironic amusement that shows most clearly in the kind of contrast he expected analogy to make. The physical object not only insures a concise reaction, but, being trivial, reduces the lofty to insignificance and produces an effect of amused irony appropriate to the classical attitude and the pessimistic view of "Cinders."

Finally, the poems suggest that Hulme's argument for a new verse form reflects more accurately the requirements of imagism than it does his belief in the value of a new form per se. The poems have no regular metrical pattern. The rhythm is iambic where one can define a pattern, but the metre is ignored where an analogy seems to require it. Line lengths are adjustable to the linguistic demands of the image. Michael Roberts has said that Hulme was not unaware of the importance of sound values in poetry and that in one of his manuscript poems he had carefully marked the accents. Nevertheless, his poems are free of the traditional patterns: imagism seems to be inextricably related, at least in Hulme's practice, to a free verse.

Beyond its immediate interest as a forerunner of Imagism, Hulme's theory of poetry has a more general signifi-

cance. His defense of an imagist verse (and the statements of the Imagists who followed him), represent a surrender of certain claims—at once a withdrawal from fields of knowledge and communication in which the poet had competed with the scientist and the philosopher and an effort, within narrow and more clearly defined limits, to make the poetic medium more exact and scientific. Hulme and the Imagists mark the beginning of this effort, which culminates in the more complex and elaborate theories of certain contemporary critics, to delineate for poetry an area, distinct and inviolate, in which it can operate without fear of encroachment from other forms of knowledge—to establish a place for poetry in a scientific, machine world. And while Imagism was only a first stage, its assumptions (whether metaphysical—as with Hulme—or aesthetic—as with Pound) have not been wholly replaced; poetry still has some difficulty, for example, in countering satisfactorily its reasons for insisting that the brief lyric is the form most suitable to the contemporary artist.

NOTES

[1] Michael Roberts, *T. E. Hulme* (London, 1938), 21-22.

[2] "Modern Art—I," *The New Age,* Vol. XIV, No. 11 (January 15, 1914), 341.

[3] "Notes on Language and Style," 292; I have used the notes published by Michael Roberts as Appendix III in *T. E. Hulme.*

[4] *Ibid.,* 274.

[5] *Speculations* (New York, 1924), 134.

[6] "Notes on Language and Style," 285-86.

[7] *Ibid.,* 299.

[8] *Ibid.,* 281.

[9] *Ibid.*

[10] *Creative Evolution* (New York, 1911), 177.

[11] *An Introduction to Metaphysics* (New York, 1912), 16.

[12] *Time and Free Will* (New York, 1910), 15.

[13] Roberts, *T. E. Hulme,* 266 (Appendix II).

[14] *Creative Evolution,* 176-77.

[15] "Notes on Languages and Style," 296.

[16] *Speculations,* 135.

[17] *Ibid.,* 126-27.

[18] "Lecture on Modern Poetry," in Roberts, *T. E. Hulme,* 258-59.

[19] *Speculations,* 232.

[20] *Ibid.,* 126-27.

[21] "Notes on Language and Style," 303.

[22] *Speculations,* 120.

[23] *Ibid.,* 113, 137.

[24] "Lecture on Modern Poetry," 264.

[25] "Notes on Language and Style," 302.

[26] "Lecture on Modern Poetry," 266.

[27] "Notes on Language and Style," 295.

[28] *Ibid.,* 283.

[29] *Ibid.,* 293.

[30] *Ibid.,* 276.

[31] *Speculations,* 242.

[32] "Notes on Language and Style," 275; *Speculations,* 231.

[33] *Speculations,* 134.

[34] *Ibid.,* 162.

[35] "Lecture on Modern Poetry," 258.

[36] "Searchers After Reality," *The New Age,* Vol. V, No. 17 (August 19, 1909), 315.

[37] *Ibid.*

[38] "Lecture on Modern Poetry," 267.

[39] *Ibid.,* 259-60.

[40] *Ibid.,* 270.

[41] "Above the Dock," *Speculations,* 266.

[42] "A City Sunset," *T. E. Hulme,* 257.

[43] "The Embankment," *Speculations,* 267.

[44] "Notes on Language and Style," 283.

Edmund S. de Chasca

[*In the following essay, de Chasca examines Fletcher's works of the mid-1910s, noting his philosophical alignment with Imagism but citing technical departures from Imagist precepts.*]

SOURCE: "Fletcher's Poetry—1916-1918," in *John Gould Fletcher and Imagism,* University of Missouri Press, 1978, pp. 179-222.

Prior to his association with the imagists, Fletcher was able to manage only derivative verse, and after 1916 his production fell off sharply for several years, but from the spring of 1913 to the fall of 1916 he turned out a surprising amount of mature work.[1] Imagism was at least partly responsible for this remarkable output; certainly an atmosphere of friendly (and not so friendly) competition encouraged him to write poems. In any case, Fletcher's participation in the imagist movement coincided with the most fecund and brilliant period of his artistic life.

While most of the poems Fletcher wrote during these three and a half years are in free verse and deal with nature, they reflect the poet's constant need to experiment and reorient himself. From the "Irradiations" of 1913 he moved to the more abstract and extended color "Symphonies" of 1914; the following year he wrote a number of poems based on American settings and locales, many of them in polyphonic prose; and in 1916, beginning with "Lincoln," he addressed himself to that unimagistic abstraction, "humanity." During each of these phases, moreover, Fletcher experimented with forms and styles. At the same time he was turning out the American poems in the winter and spring of 1915, for example, he was composing the terse "Ghosts of an Old House," the haiku-like *Japanese Prints,* and some love poems that would later appear under the title, *The Tree of Life.*

The purpose here is to determine how many of these works, if any, may rightly be termed "imagistic" and in the process to introduce the unfamiliar reader to the most important and characteristic specimens of poetry written by Fletcher during these years. Since discrepancies frequently exist between composition and publication dates—the American poems of 1915, for example, were not published until 1921—I will proceed chronologically according to when the poems actually were written.

Irradiations

In this group of thirty-six poems, the speaker "irradiates" outward his joy in nature, expressing pagan delight in the sensual world:

> I drink of the red bowl of the sunlight:
> I swim through seas of rain:
> I dig my toes into earth:
> I taste the smack of the wind:
> I am myself:
> I live.[2]

While approximately half of the poems relate the speaker to nature through the Whitman-like use of the personal pronoun, some offer quite objective description:

> The clouds pass
> Over the polished mirror of the sky:
> The clouds pass, puffs of grey,
> There is no star
>
> (p. 21)

Others show a strong French symbolist influence:

> Slowly along the lamp-emblazoned street,
> Amid the last sad drifting crowds of midnight
>
> (p. 28)

A few have nothing to do with nature but are about people (XXI, XXV) or abstractions (XXVIII). These poems, as well as ones in which the mood is too vague or not fully realized, or ones in which the poet makes personal, prosaic statements about the ideas connected with the mood, are among the weakest of the group. The best are those that contrast an initial elation with a subsequent depression or, as in the following example, bare a tension between nature and the inner longings of the speaker:

> O SEEDED grass, you army of little men
> Crawling up the long slope with quivering, quick
>   blades of steel:
> You who storm millions of graves, tiny green
>   tentacles of Earth,
> Interlace yourselves tightly over my heart,
> And do not let me go:
> Fcr I would lie here forever and watch with one
>   eye
> The pilgrimaging ants in your dull, savage
>   jungles,
> The while with the other I see the stiff lines of the
>   slope
> Break in mid-air, a wave surprisingly arrested,
> And above them, wavering, dancing, bodiless,
>   colourless, unreal,
> The long thin lazy fingers of the heat.
>
> (p. 17)

The note of sadness in this piece—we know the poet cannot lie among the grass blades forever—combined with a joy and desire for complete immersion in nature give the poem a special poignancy.

A number of "Irradiations" reflect Fletcher's enthusiasm for modern painting, dance, and contemporary music. He is adept at portraying movement and color and at seeing shapes within natural phenomena. One of the best known of the series might well have been inspired by a painting of Leon Bakst or a prélude by Claude Debussy:

> Over the roof-tops race the shadows of clouds;
> Like horses the shadows of clouds charge down
>   the street.
> Whirlpools of purple and gold,
> Winds from the mountains of cinnabar,
> Lacquered mandarin moments, palanquins
>   swaying and balancing
> Amid the vermilion pavilions, against the jade
>   balustrades.
> Glint of the glittering wings of dragon-flies in the
>   light:
> Silver filaments, golden flakes settling
>   downwards,
> Rippling, quivering flutters, repulse and
>   surrender,
> The sun broidered upon the rain,
> the rain rustling with the sun.

> Over the roof-tops race the shadows of clouds;
> Like horses the shadows of clouds charge down
>   the street.
>
> (p. 7)

These lines caused quite a stir in their time, especially the "vermilion pavilions" phrase. Fletcher's method is to select words as much for their sound as for their meaning, often intensely colorful, and to pile them together in swiftly moving, rhythmical lines. We do not focus on individual elements but on assonance clusters such as "Glint of the glittering wings." The result is a great richness of sound and color. Admirers of "Irradiations" often praise them for their brilliance of verbal texture, exquisite diction, and unusual images—the quality of being "gorgeous." Detractors say that they overuse color and sound effects and heap so many sensations one upon another that we lose a definite impression of the whole. If every poem in the group were like "Over the roof-tops" these criticisms might be just, but the majority are not so "gorgeous." Fletcher avoids satiation by mixing in somber and austere entries with the more heavily assonated and highly colored pieces. The poem following "Irradiation V," for instance, strikes a more subdued note. This suite of thirty-six pieces in its entirety balances itself with shifts in tone and mood that relieve, anticipate, and harmonize with each other.

Irradiations has traditionally been regarded as a collection of imagistic productions, probably in the beginning because it was in free verse and was distributed at the same time as *Some Imagist Poems, 1915*. Later anthologists and critics, for the most part, have both tacitly and explicitly sustained this judgment. William Pratt includes two "Irradiations" in his collection,[3] *The Imagist Poem,* and Louis Untermeyer features some of the briefer, more colorful poems of the group in his widely circulated *Modern American Poetry and Modern British Poetry* anthology. Edna Stephens writes in a 1968 study of Fletcher that "some of the poems in the book [*Irradiations*] fit well under the Imagist banner."[4]

Indeed, there are features in *Irradiations* that are consistent with imagist credo. Some of the poems, like number IV ("The iridescent vibrations of midsummer night"), are quite objective; it reminds one of a scientist studying light waves. Others, such as number XV, "O seeded grass," focus closely on individual concrete details. Also, Fletcher often "sees his image" clearly, as in the opening lines of "Irradiation III": "In the grey skirts of the fog seamews skirl desolately, / And flick like bits of paper propelled by a wind." Pound labeled these lines "obvious" in his criticisms of the manuscript, but they do illustrate direct treatment. Finally, the rhythms of *Irradiations* are not conventionally patterned. Except for a few unsuccessfully rhymed pieces, the cadence follows the "ebb and flow of the emotion."

At the same time, however, the poems display many nonimagistic characteristics. Some show a fondness for vast panoramas coupled with a tendency to evoke the infinite: "Blue, brown, blue: sky, sand, sea: / I swell to your immensity" (p. 5). Direct statements abound in others, often taking the form of platitude ("Here upon earth there is life, and then death," [p. 31]), or of speculation on cosmic questions ("But why should I not remember that my night is dawn in / another part of the world" [p. 31]). In "Irradiation XXII," which has its admirers, the speaker utters a heroic sentiment not unlike that expressed in Tennyson's "Ulysses": "God willing, we shall this day meet that old enemy" (p. 24). Lastly, Pound's loathed abstractions may be found throughout the volume. Number VI is practically drowned in them:

> All is silent under the steep cone of afternoon:
> The sky is imperturbably profound.
> The ultimate divine union seems about to be
>   accomplished,
> All is troubled at the attainment
> Of the inexhaustible infinite.
>
> (p. 8)

Nor is this passage exceptional in its lack of concreteness. Throughout the series, Fletcher employs words like *love, joy, death, glory,* and *lust.*

Let us look at two individual poems that are generally considered good examples of imagism. The first gives the effect of a spring rain:

> Flickering of incessant rain
> On flashing pavements:
> Sudden scurry of umbrellas:
> Bending, recurved blossoms of the storm.
>
> The winds came clanging and clattering
> From long white highroads whipping in ribbons
>   up summits:
> They strew upon the city gusty wafts of apple-
>   blossom,
> And the rustling of innumerable translucent
>   leaves.
>
> Uneven tinkling, the lazy rain
> Dripping from the eaves.
>
> (p. 9)

"Irradiation VII" is concrete, in free verse, and yields several striking images ("recurved blossoms of the storm," "whipping in ribbons up summits"). Nevertheless, it is not imagism. The effect is vague. Phrases like "rustling of innumerable translucent leaves" and "uneven tinkling, the lazy rain" suggest the muted, soft quality of an afternoon rain, but they do so by insinuating themselves into the ear, not by striking the eye. The pleasant backwash of sound created by the consistent onomatopoeia blurs rather than delineates. Nor does the poem, in any sense, "present an Image." Ideas and emotions are not fused into a single metaphorical structure and endowed with energy but are spread out over a surface. The effect is not sudden but cumulative. Imagery, as in the "blossoms" comparison, adds to or qualifies the central impression; it is an essential element, but the poem is not built around any single metaphor. It is an effective por-

trayal of mood, displaying the delicate, wavering sense of light and sound that is characteristic of Fletcher, but it is neither "hard" nor does it present an image.

Perhaps the "Irradiation" that comes closest to satisfying Pound's definition of an Image is number X:

> The trees, like great jade elephants,
> Chained, stamp and shake 'neath the gadflies of
>   the breeze;
> The trees lunge and plunge, unruly elephants:
> The clouds are their crimson howdah-canopies,
> The sunlight glints like the golden robe of a Shah.
> Would I were tossed on the wrinkled backs of
>   those trees
>
> (p. 12).

René Taupin contends that this poem is unimagistic because it represents a "play of the fancy" rather than the deeper creative-inventive faculty. He also states that it is not "clarified" as are the images created by Pound, H.D., and Aldington. In comparing it to H.D.'s "Oread," he declares: "There is in H.D.'s image an inevitability and a rapidity which carry one as close to sensation as language can. In the Fletcher poem, the spirit and imagination work to 'suggest' by a rather long detour."[5] Taupin, whose study contains many incisive insights, seems too bent here on proving out his thesis that the modern American poetry movement merely represents a diluted continuation of French symbolism. Fletcher's comparison does not work "by a rather long detour," but is appropriate and immediate. We do not mull over whether the trees are like great jade elephants, but accept (or reject) the likeness right away. "Irradiation X" satisfies Pound's definition of an image in other respects, as well. Sustained by an unusual yet apt comparison, the poem is its image. Moreover, each element of the metaphor takes on a higher life by being yoked with the other. The comparison between the elephants, with their naked, wrinkled hides, and the verdent, leafy trees, sets off a chain of associations that amounts to a third reality, greater than the component parts. Finally, the image has movement and energy. Using active verbs to gain motion and power, it works in a short space of time, and the reader must put forth some mental effort to unite the two unlike elements. The poem is germinal; it moves.

Two aspects of "Irradiation X," nevertheless, are not imagistic. First, phrases like "crimson howdah-canopies" and "golden robe of a Shah," together with the internal rhyme, "lunge and plunge," make for a richness of color and sound that the pure imagist would prefer to avoid. Second, the sudden injection of personal emotion at the end ("Would I were tossed on the wrinkled backs of those trees") violates the imagist's dedication to impersonality. The poem would be more objective if this line were expunged but also, most of us would agree, weaker.

The Color "Symphonies"

In the preamble to *Goblins and Pagodas,* Fletcher explains that his purpose in the eleven "Symphonies" is to "narrate certain important phases of the emotional and intellectual development—in short, the life—of an artist." He goes on to say: "I have tried to state each phase in the terms of a certain colour, or combination of colours, which is emotionally akin to that phase. This colour, and the imaginative phantasmagoria of landscape which it evokes, thereby creates, in a definite and tangible form, the dominant mood of each poem."[6] He then arbitrarily assigns certain colors to certain moods: for example, blue suggests "depth, mystery, and distance," green the "self-sufficing pagan worship of nature," and violet tokens "regret and remembrance."

The key to understanding Fletcher's technique in the "Symphonies" is the indefinite basis of communication. Since the imagery often is summoned by color associations rather than by external items of experience, objects take on "the 'impossible' behavior of dreams."[7] Sometimes the speaker seems to be in an actual place, at other times he walks in an imaginary land. The following passage from the "White Symphony," for instance, is fantasy:

> Downwards through the blue abyss it slides,
> The white snow-water of my dreams,
> Downwards crashing from slippery rock
> Into the boiling chasm:
> In which no eye dare look, for it is the chasm of
>   death.
>
> (p. 55)

Later, however, when the speaker says: "As evening came on, I climbed the tower, / To gaze upon the city far beneath" (p. 56), we feel the situation is grounded in external reality, a judgment confirmed by Fletcher's statement in his memoirs that he wrote the section shortly after climbing "the tower of the Crystal Palace" and "looking at the vast valley of the Thames and the far heights of Hampstead below" (*Life Is My Song*, p. 142). Due to the abstract and changing foundation of the imagery in these "Symphonies," it is easy to become confused.

The multisectional structure of the "Symphonies" adds to their difficulty. They are each divided into three to six parts, with each section usually involving a shift in point of view, mood, or scene. Although the degree of cohesion of these parts varies from poem to poem, it is best to think of them as thematically and tonally related, but not consecutive. One critic suggested that the "Blue Symphony" consisted of five separate poems,[8] an exaggerated judgment but indicative of the distinctness of its "movements." Nevertheless, these poems, are synthetic, the parts arriving at a whole much the way the divisions of a panel painting do; one thinks particularly of the "White Symphony" with its three, easily visualized "scenes," or the "Blue Symphony," which unfolds like a Chinese roll picture. Although Fletcher failed to reproduce musical "symphonic" structure in these poems, he did use both colors and free-verse rhythms as motifs. Mostly, the title reflects Fletcher's desire for interdependency of the arts. He wished to imitate what he took to be the free-

dom and irregularity of musical form, not its strictness; he wished to borrow its license for extravagant and improvised utterance.

Individually, the eleven "Symphonies" vary greatly in character and artistic merit, although they share the romantic themes of frustration, futility, solitary wandering, mystic longing and aspiration. Best known are the "Blue," "Green," and "White Symphonies." The "Blue Symphony," along with the "Golden," is one of two pieces with a distinctly Oriental flavor. It opens on a note of disappointment and loneliness:

> Palely the dawn
> Leaves me facing timidly
> Old gardens sunken:
> And in the gardens is water.
>
> (p. 25)

In the remainder of the poem, the speaker pursues not only beauty, which the Sennin sprites of Taoist belief have hidden from him,[9] but sexual fulfillment and the vision of the "Jagged unwrinkled mountains, ranges of death." At the end, he resignedly makes his way "Towards those blue death-mountains / I have forgot so long." This poem is the most tonally perfect of the series—the effect is of blue lava cooling—and accomplishes the difficult task of conveying a mood of dignified sorrow.

The "Green Symphony," with its rhapsodic descriptions of springtime, is the most popular of the group:

> Like scampering rabbits,
> Flashes of sunlight sweep the lawn;
> They fling in passing
> Patterns of shadow,
> Golden and green.
>
> (p. 39)

Much less abstract than the "Blue Symphony," the poem has many passages of delightful, pure description ("The trees lash the sky with their leaves, / Uneasily shaking their dark manes" [p. 42]). The dominant color, moreover, is obviously appropriate to its subject, something that cannot be said for many of these long poems. "Green Symphony," however, is tonally imperfect, the last section especially being marred by such gaffes as "For I have unveiled naked beauty" (p. 44). Nor is the poem as ambitious in its overall aims as the majority of the "Symphonies"; lacking philosophical import, it is not truly representative of the group. In this respect, it is unfortunate that Untermeyer chose the "Green Symphony" for his *Modern American Poetry and Modern British Poetry* anthology.

The "White Symphony," on the other hand, sets for itself the mighty task of expressing the artist's unending quest for perfection . . . the pursuit of the impossible."[10] The dominant color stands generally for what we want but cannot have. The poem contains a good deal of abstract statement ("Towards the ultimate, / Towards the silence" [p. 55]), interspersed with wild, hallucinatory imagery.

"Whiteness" is both attractive and repellent throughout the poem. In Part II, for instance, the speaker walks at midnight in a garden, intoxicated by the scent of white flowers, only to find that daylight brings disenchantment:

> In the morning, at the dayspring,
> I wakened, shivering; lo,
> The white garden that blossomed at my feet
> Was a garden hidden in snow.
>
> (p. 58)

At the close, "whiteness" takes on a weary, deathlike quality with the poem ending, according to Fletcher, "in a cry for earthly imperfection": "O that the white scroll of heaven might be rolled up / And the naked red lighting thrust at the smouldering earth!" (p. 61). While the "White Symphony" has its admirers, among them its author, the work fails to mix effectively the specific with the infinite. There is an irritating sense of nothing being pinned down. The words do not crystallize about a sharp central impression but fly off to nowhere. Infinity can rapidly become boring when the boundaries of the finite are not marked. Furthermore, the poem seems contrived, a flaw that is common to many of these "Symphonies," as though the author had been contracted to complete a series. Self-conscious and hyperaesthetic attempts to imitate the effects of painting and music, they exemplify Fletcher's belief at the time that "the more suggestion, the more art; the more arrangement of rhythm, symbol, analogy, the more poetry."[11] This criterion may be acceptable for judging a certain type of poetic art, but it is a dangerous basis on which to build specific poems. We can readily admire Fletcher for undertaking such an ambitious program but, with the exception of the "Blue Symphony," not appreciate its outcome.

Obviously, the overall aims and characteristic effects of the "Symphonies" are distantly removed from imagist goals. One could list the many and obvious specific violations of imagist credo—abstractions, frequent lapses into direct statement, a failure to maintain concentration over the entire length of the poem—but more important is the difference in approach. The "Symphonies" do not treat physical objects in terms of solid sensation but deal with grand, far-removed themes. They do not aim at a "precise" effect, but are loose, vague, and abstract. The strict imagist gives up sharp outlines, easily perceived wholes, but in the "Symphonies" we do not see things, we do not visualize wholes. True, the imagists characteristically use color, and Fletcher bases his imagery on color, but he handles it differently. H.D.'s sharp and pale colors delineate, but the colors that Fletcher splashes—in these poems at least—are thick and turgid, as in the postimpressionist paintings he admired. His purpose is to smear or spread a quality over a surface, resulting in the very blurring and obscuring of outline that the imagists tried to avoid. Furthermore, even when not clogged by color, Fletcher's images in the "Symphonies" do not behave like, say, H.D.'s. One need only compare the first lines of "Helen":

> All Greece hates
> the still eyes in the white face,
> the lustre as of olives

> where she stands
> and the white hands.

with this passage from the "White Symphony":

> Like spraying rockets
> My peonies shower
> Their glories on the night.
>
> . . . . .
>
> Soar, crash, and sparkle,
> Shoal of stars drifting
> Like silver fishes,
> Through the black sluggish boughs.
>
> (pp. 54, 55)

H.D.'s even monosyllables create a static effect, as though white blocks, one by one, were being placed before us. Each rhythmic impulse gives a separate picture of eyes, face, complexion, and hands. Fletcher's images, on the other hand, flash, move, and dart about like fireworks. The unmistakable sound effect of "crash" and the implied explosive sounds of "spraying rockets" and of the verb "sparkle" reinforce the meaning and contribute to an overall "softness" and fluidity of presentation. A phrase like "Shoal of stars" is effective because it is indeterminate—the night here is the "great, dark soft thing" that Carl Sandburg saw from his railroad car window. In the "Symphonies" and in many of his other poems as well, Fletcher favors a wavering, fluctuating treatment of his material, the imagery following the impulses of his mind. Pound summed up this quality when he wrote to Harriet Monroe: "Fletcher is sputter, bright flash, sputter. Impressionist temperament, made intense at half-seconds."[12]

There are features in the "Symphonies" that are not inconsistent with imagism: the use, for the most part, of free verse; the absence of a tendency to preach; the concrete statement of mood. Readers in 1916 most likely considered the "Shoal of stars" passage or the following lines from the "Grey Symphony," to be "imagistic":

> Of my long nights afar in alien cities
> I have remembered only this:
> They were black scarves all dusted over with
>   silver,
> In which I wrapped my dreams;
> They were black screens on which I made those
>   pictures
> That faded out the next day.
>
> (p. 91)

Exquisite pictures like this may be found throughout the "Symphonies," but they are imagery, not imagism. Such passages function as decorative, pleasant interludes that dot the larger poem; they are cosmetic, not essential. Most certainly they do not "present an image." Since readers were confused as to what the word actually meant, though, often what was merely pictorial was considered to be "imagistic."

The entire "Blue Symphony" has been regarded as an imagist work, probably because it was one of Fletcher's entries in the 1915 anthology. Harold Monro focused on this poem in his attack on the group and later, Glenn Hughes wrote in his *Imagism and the Imagists:* "Because of its almost flawless imagery, its subtle cadence, and its remarkable unity of effect, this poem will very likely stand, along with two or three of the other "Symphonies,' as one of the finest examples of sustained imagistic writing."[13] One can readily agree that this first of the "Symphonies" has a singleness of tone, an inevitability of phrasing, and a certain clarity and measure. Moreover, the poem fits scene to mood throughout, there are no letups in "concentration," and the relatively short free-verse lines enforce a conciseness of effect. To classify the "Blue Symphony" as imagism, however, is to ignore the most important element in all of Pound's definitions of the "image"—that it should be "endowed with energy." Fletcher's calm and motionless poem sustains only a mild intensity, working quietly throughout. Certainly the "Blue Symphony" does not contain a "VORTEX, from which, and through which, and into which, ideas are constantly rushing." Pound did declare, in a footnote to his "Vorticism" article, that he could see nothing against a long imagist poem and that the best Japanese Noh plays were gathered about one image. But even if we grant the possibility of an extended imagist poem—and in order to do so Pound's one-sentence definitions of the "image" would have to be revised—the "Blue Symphony" still lacks the definiteness and high level of motion of the Noh plays or of "whole sections from Dante." Notwithstanding its unity of effect, the "Blue Symphony" is too passive to be imagistic.

We might also remark here on Fletcher's other long entry in *Some Imagist Poets, 1915,* entitled "London Excursion." One of three experimental poems written in June 1914, this work illustrates the "unrelated method," a term that refers not, as has been suggested, to the manner of progression, but to the poet's relation to his material. Fletcher, who long had harbored the ambition of writing about a modern city, now decided to approach the task by simply grasping his environment as a series of detached objects, withholding commentary on how these objects related to him. He would look intently at things, recording images as they presented themselves to his consciousness, no matter how farfetched. In this way, he believed, the material would take on an existence of its own, "unrelated" to the poet. Actually, the nine sketches that comprise "London Excursion" produce the opposite effect: they tell us as much about the observer as about the scenes they represent. They are a series of highly subjective and impressionistic pictures of a day spent in the metropolis, beginning with a bus-top ride from an adjoining suburb and ending with the nighttime return:

'BUS-TOP

Black shapes bending,
Taxicabs crush in the crowd.
The tops are each a shining square
Shuttles that steadily press through woolly fabric.

Drooping blossom,
Gas-standards over

Spray out jingling tumult
Of white-hot rays.

Monotonous domes of bowler-hats
Vibrate in the heat.

Silently, easily we sway through braying traffic,
Down the crowded street.
The tumult crouches over us,
Or suddenly drifts to one side.[14]

The influence of the second-generation French symbolists is apparent in the "drooping blossom" of the gas lamps and the herdlike behavior of the crowd, but the first and third stanzas strike a fresh note. In particular, the "Monotonous domes of bowler hats / Vibrate in the heat," with its train of assonances and wavering movement, is uniquely Fletcherian. Most of the other poems in the series, however, are not as impressive as "'Bus-top." Some, like "Arrival," are so impressionistic as to be amorphous; others are strained to the point of hysteria: "My soul / Shrieking / Is jolted forwards by a long hot bar—/ Into direct distances. / It pierces the small of my back" (p. 41). Reading these lines, we wonder if the poet is seriously injured and can picture him holding his back in pain. Indeed, "London Excursion" suffers from Fletcher's violent and continual effort to be new and experimental. He exerts his sensibility to the utmost, with the result that both it and the reader's attention are overtaxed. Still, the series contains many fine touches and makes stimulating, if not memorable, reading. "London Excursion," of course, with its intense subjectivity and "softness" of treatment, is the very opposite of imagism. Pound criticized the series for its "general diffuseness and lack of a central vortex," as well as for its "rhetorical flourishes."[15] The group of poems passed as "imagistic" among readers of the 1915 anthology, however, because of their novel subject matter, free-verse treatment, and nondidactic attitude.

American Poems

The poems based on American settings and locales, which Fletcher wrote during his visit to the United States from November 1915 to June 1916, represent an effort to rediscover his native roots after an absence of more than six years. Most of them are based on scenes encountered during two journeys, the first to Chicago and Arkansas, the second a steamboat journey down the Mississippi followed by a train trip through Texas, New Mexico, and Arizona. With the exception of "The Ghosts of an Old House," the poems that resulted from these travels were collected in *Breakers and Granite* (1921) where, along with some verses composed in 1920, they were arranged geographically to constitute a panorama of America.

The first significant poems to result from Fletcher's travels were "The Ghosts of an Old House," published as the "Goblins" part of *Goblins and Pagodas* (1916). These twenty-four short vers libres were inspired by Fletcher's stay in his boyhood home in Little Rock, Arkansas, and, as he explains in the preface, represented an attempt "to relate my childish terror concerning this house—a terror not uncommon among children, as I can testify—to the aspects that called it forth" (p. xviii). Fletcher's method is to take some object that reminds him of the past and use it as the basis for a meditation or flight of fantasy.[16] The environment is forbidding: old Indian skulls stare out of glass cases, footsteps shuffle on secretive back staircases, owls flap and rats scurry, trees hold their branches as though a man had been hanged from them. Themes of morbid brooding and death interweave with objects as the speaker, observing signs of the futile lives that were once led in the house, wonders what awaits him. The best section is "The Attic," which concludes with the following poem:

The Yardstick

Yardstick that measured out so many miles of
   cloth,
Yardstick that covered me,
I wonder do you hop of nights
Out to the still hill-cemetery,
And up and down go measuring
A clayey grave for me?

(p. 16)

The whimsicality of this piece is characteristic of a certain gnomelike quality of the entire series. Fletcher wisely understood that an effective presentation of ghostly subjects must include an occasional lightness of touch. He also varies the point of view. Here a child is speaking:

I cannot go to this room,
Without feeling something big and angry
Waiting for me
To throw me on the bed,
And press its thumbs in my throat.

(p. 5)

But in the following poem the viewpoint is that of a mature adult, looking over the shoulder of the child from the vantage point of time:

The Toy Cabinet

By the old toy cabinet,
I stand and turn over dusty things:
Chessmen—card games—hoops and balls—
Toy rifles, helmets, swords,
In the far corner
A doll's tea-set in a box.

Where are you, golden child,
Who gave tea to your dolls and me?
The golden child is growing old,
Further than Rome or Babylon
From you have passed those foolish years.
She lives—she suffers—she forgets.

(p. 15)

The blunt, direct, free verse of the first stanza, with its simple enumeration of various toys, takes us back to childhood, when all objects seemed large, but in the second stanza the mature adult speaks with an awareness of the passage of time and death as evoked by vanished civilizations. Throughout the series, Fletcher mingles a

reserved pleasure of rediscovery with childish fear, overlaying both with a sense of the futility of life. These poems are more than "haunted house" exercises, therefore, or pieces of easy nostalgia. Through careful adjustments of tone, Fletcher manages to convey the complexity of the emotions he feels regarding his boyhood.

The style employed in "The Ghosts of an Old House" is deliberately bare and plainspoken. Several critics, indeed, considered them to be little more than chopped-up prose. Fletcher has this to say about them in *Life Is My Song:*

> These poems . . . were far more imagistic, in the narrowest and strictest sense—the sense of H.D. and Pound—than anything I had yet written. . . . Their poignancy resided not in any rhetorical elaboration of detail nor in the working up of analogy between the object and myself—as in the case of the 'symphonies'—but in bald, stark directness of statement. Thus I may claim for them that they are the only imagistic poems which are also purely southern poems.
>
> (p. 196)

According to these remarks, Fletcher seems to have believed that imagism consisted merely of the superficial characteristics of shortness, terseness, and the use of vers libre. Of course, this was a mistaken notion. Following its logic, even abstractions would be imagism if they were uttered in a "bald, stark" manner. Pound, Aldington, and H.D. wrote many poems that were succinct and austere in tone, but these qualities in themselves did not make their work imagistic.

To be sure, the "Old House" verses do exhibit characteristics that are in accord with imagist credo: they are concise, compressed, and austere in tone; they avoid sentimentality; the diction is simple and the language is used economically, maintaining the line of the rhythm throughout. One of them even creates the kind of precise, visual effects that we associate with imagism:

Old Nursery

In the tired face of the mirror
There is a blue curtain reflected.
If I could lift the reflection,
Peer a little beyond, I would see
A boy crying
Because his sister is ill in another room
And he has no one to play with:
A boy listlessly scattering building blocks,
And crying,
Because no one will build for him the palace of
   Fairy Morgana.
I cannot lift the curtain:
It is stiff and frozen.

(p. 7)

If every poem in the series were like this one, they might be considered imagistic productions, but "Old Nursery" is an exception. Moreover, many of the other poems in "The Ghosts of an Old House" display distinctly non-imagistic qualities: they try to evoke a mood, not deliver an emotion; they are personal, not objective; they use abstractions ("Some worn-out story of broken effort and desire"); they frequently resort to direct statement instead of trying to maintain a line of visual signification; and, finally, they make frequent use of anthropomorphism and pathetic fallacy, devices that the strict imagist shunned since they tended to emphasize the poet rather than what he was portraying. Regardless of Fletcher's intent, "The Ghosts of an Old House" is not imagistic.

During this first trip to the West Fletcher also wrote a series of quasi-Indian poems, a group of Japanese poems, and a few lyrics, but the greater portion of his energies that winter and spring was devoted to polyphonic prose. No less than forty-nine pages of *Breakers and Granite,* in fact, consist of pieces in this hybrid form. It has already been noted that the richly decorative effects realized by polyphonic prose are the very opposite of imagism. Let us briefly now look at some general characteristics of Fletcher's work in this style.

Unlike Amy Lowell's efforts in the medium, many of which are fictitious, exotic narratives, Fletcher's polyphonics describe American subjects. His typical works in this form attempt to portray an entire historical epoch or a whole city or region. In "The Passing of the South," "Clipper Ships," and "The Passing of the West," for example, Fletcher tried to synthesize the South's defeat in the Civil War, the clipper-ship era (1830-1854), and the frontier West. More limited in scope, "The Building of Chicago" treats that energetic city as the meeting place of the four directional winds, while "The Old South" is a sultry evocation of New Orleans and the delta.

A recurrent theme in the polyphonic prose pieces is the ruing of the past:

> Passing is the wild free life of the desert—the open
> air, the chaparral, the boundless waste, the blue
> sky over all! . . . The last great stretch of sunlight,
> of loneliness, of silence, is forever gone.[17]

Mankind appears in these works, not as individuals but collectively, as teeming multitudes, scurrying and unimportant ("They creep, black, greasy masses out of the earth like ants," p. 146), or blend indistinguishably with their surroundings:

> It is noon and the carnival, king of fools, rules the
> city. A beautiful woman, her face cold, haughty,
> expressionless, the fire in her eyes half hidden,
> goes dancing down the street with a man whose
> shape is like an ape. (p. 59)

Fletcher depicts America as mighty and involved in ceaseless change, but civilization not as necessarily progressing; the manswarm that inhabits the continent does not understand the symbols of desire it creates but passes through life in a kind of dream.

The polyphonics rely heavily on dramatic contrast. Fletcher frequently juxtaposes slow and static passages with those describing rapid movement and action, as in "The Passing of the South," where a funeral procession is followed by the crackling description of a battle. The cadenced prose pieces also tell a kind of story, albeit one that deals with places and facts rather than people, each with a clearly defined beginning and ending. Even a piece comprised of motionless description, like "New England Sunset," draws to a vivid close as the sky turns totally dark. Finally, each composition is usually held together by a recurring phrase, dominant thought, or image. In "Clipper-Ships," the motif is "Beautiful as a tiered cloud" (p. 35); in "The Passing of the South" it is the sentence "On a catafalque, draped in black, under bronze cannon, forlorn and white, rigid in death, the corpse of the South is borne to its tomb" (p. 90). Fletcher's use of refrain gives weight and dignity to the more epical pieces and stabilizes a swift-moving portrait like "Clipper-Ships."

The polyphonics are written in a kind of oratorical prose, formal, at times perfervid, often wildly emotional and enthusiastic. Rhetorical questions, parallel constructions, and exclamation points abound, as do printed sound effects in obvious imitation of Amy Lowell: "Gurgle, boom, surge," goes the surf, "Tinkle-tinkle-drop," the rain (p. 62). At its worst, the writing is artificial, strained, and hysterical. In one sentence, for example, Fletcher characterizes the wind as "flickering, licking dry wavelets, screaming, fighting, tingling, tossing, clanging, prowling, growling, howling, rasping, soaring, crashing and ebbing away" (p. 114).

Elsewhere, he indulges in a different kind of extravagance:

> The sky, blue of metal, through which the sun
> blows in passing many a hammered petal of gold,
> rose, vermilion, from its frozen lips. The water
> deepest blue of sapphires, glancing flint-shaped
> play of wavelets out of which the sun strikes
> coppery fires. . . . The trees brittle coral, blue and
> silver, birch and maple, crackling, shaking thinner
> than coral ever grew. (p. 26)

Fletcher here is deliberately striving for a "hard," gemlike quality in imitation of Amy Lowell's "externality." The result, as in much of Miss Lowell's poetry, is not a picture of something we can see, but a devitalized and fatiguing display of colored words.

Fletcher's polyphonic style works best on fantastic subjects that fit the artificiality of the form, when the words portray rapid, constant motion:

> Beautiful as a tiered cloud, a ghostly clipper-ship
> emerges from the surges that keep running away
> before day on the low Pacific Shore. . . . Swimming
> like a duck, steering like a fish, easy yet dry, lively
> yet stiff, she lifts cloud on cloud of crowded stainless
> sail. She creeps abeam, within hail, she dips, she
> chases, she outpaces like a mettlesome racer the
> lumbering tea-kettle that keeps her company. (pp.
> 40-41)

One is reminded of William Carlos Williams's well-heeled yachts that stand for everything "fleckless, free and / naturally to be desired." With its spontaneity and effective imitation of the yachts' bobbing movement, "Clipper-Ships" is the best of his polyphonics and one of the few in which the method fits the subject matter.

Fletcher eventually came to realize that the polyphonic pieces were really not verse but prose, stating in 1919: "As for 'spaced prose,' 'polyphonic prose,' 'mosaics,' 'blend'—and all the other more or less experimental forms which I and others have attempted—they are not and should not be called verse at all."[18] Even so, he included "Clipper-Ships," "The Old South," and "The Passing of the South," in *Selected Poems* (1938). The form appealed to him and Amy Lowell because its flexibility, freedom, and richness of sound enabled them to display their virtuosity with words; certainly polyphonic prose was well suited to Miss Lowell's dramatic readings. So far as I know, no one has continued this abortive experiment. Quite justly, the rhymed prose poem has gone the way of the clipper ships it once celebrated.

The most important verses to result from Fletcher's productive second trip to the West were the two series entitled "Down the Mississippi" and "Arizona Poems." The first is an attempt to evoke the spirit of the big river, the second various scenes in San Antonio, New Mexico, and Arizona. Both groups illustrate Fletcher's "Oriental" method of rendering nature and allow him to indulge his liking for large vistas and the infinite. In his description of the Grand Canyon, for example, Fletcher resorts to using five adjectives, which would have been anathema to Pound:

> I have seen that which is mysterious,
> Aloof, divided, silent;
> Something not of this earth.[19]

He repeatedly uses the words *mystery, silence,* and *stillness* in these southern and western settings to invoke some inscrutable will or spirit that hovers over the land. His attitude toward nature, in this respect, is not unlike Robinson Jeffers's: both poets see a grand, mystical significance in its more rugged aspects, and humankind appears small in comparison. Fletcher, however, does not share the California poet's belief in a "pitiless God," nor does he emphasize violence.

Some incidental quotations will suggest the texture and quality of these two groups. The first of the "Mississippi" poems, "Embarkation," describes the river as an inscrutable force, moving slowly and hypnotically through the gloomy forest:

> Dull masses of dense green,
> The forests range their sombre platforms;
> Between them silently, like a spirit,
> The river finds its own mysterious path.
>
> (p. 49)

The atmosphere is reminiscent of Joseph Conrad's Congo River. Fletcher also successfully conveys the stifling humidity of the river valley: "Heat pressing upon earth with irresistible langour, / Turns all the solid forest into half-liquid smudge" (p. 51).

The six "Arizona Poems" are less bound as a geographical sequence than the "Mississippi" poems and are more a series of independent but related impressions. Tauter and more dramatic, they sometimes blend human types with the natural description. The following excerpt portrays Mexican low-life in a section of San Antonio:

> By an alley lined with tumble-down shacks,
> And street-lamps askew, half sputtering,
> Feebly glimmering on gutters choked with filth
>   and dogs
> Scratching their mangy backs:
> Half-naked children are running about,
> Women puff cigarettes in black doorways,
> Crickets are crying.
>
> (p. 102)

Elsewhere, Fletcher imitates his idol Gaugin's technique of interfusing life and landscape. The Indian in "The Well in the Desert," for example, whom the speaker in a reverie imagines to be Christ, seems to belong in the desert and has that savage quality that Gauguin's Tahitians possess:

> An Indian with a red sash, flannel shirt and blue
>   trousers,
> And a red band about his coarse black hair.
> Eyes dark as an antelope's
> Looked up at me:
>
> (p. 101)

Likewise, the fuel vendor of the fifth poem seems a part of the desert scenery that he endlessly patrols. The final poem of the series, one of Amy Lowell's favorites, compares some distantly seen rain showers with an Indian dance:

> And now the showers
> Surround the mesa like a troop of silver dancers:
> Shaking their rattles, stamping, chanting, roaring,
> Whirling, extinguishing the last red wisp of light.
>
> (p. 113)

The "Arizona Poems" are more varied and animated than the "Mississippi" series, but neither group is high-powered. They do not overwhelm us like "Irradiations" but exploit mild effects, sustaining a calm, pleasant intensity. Nevertheless, such imaginative description is difficult to create, and Fletcher is to be admired for the skill and apparent ease with which he can evoke a region and its atmosphere.

In spite of their vagueness and "softness" of treatment, both the "Mississippi" and "Arizona" poems were regarded as imagistic productions, probably because three of the "Arizona" group appeared as part of Fletcher's entry in *Some Imagist Poets, 1916,* and also because of their brilliant color effects: "The sun throws soft shafts of golden light / Over rose-buttressed palisades" (p. 40). During these months both Fletcher and Amy Lowell made frequent use of what they believed to be an imagistic technique, which they referred to in their letters as the "color technique"—not to be confused with Fletcher's programmatic use of color in the "Symphonies." The following passage is characteristic of Amy Lowell:

> I am a woman, sick for passion,
> Gazing at a white moon hanging over tall lilies.
> The lilies sway and darken,
> And a wind ruffles my hair.
> There is a scrape of gravel behind me,
> A red coat crashes scarlet against the lilies.[20]

Miss Lowell's influence was so predominant that critics like O. W. Firkins considered writing of this kind to be "normal Imagism." As we have seen, though, the use of color in itself does not make for imagism. H.D.'s colors are brittle:

> I could scrape the colour
> From the petals
> like split dye from a rock.[21]

But Fletcher's colors often "run" and are subordinate to an overall vagueness, as in this example from "Mississippi":

> Like an enormous serpent, dialating, uncoiling,
> Displaying a broad scaly back of earth-smeared
> 　　gold;
> Swaying out sinuously between the dull
> 　　motionless forests,
> As molten metal might glide down the lip of a
> 　　vase of dark bronze.
>
> 　　　　　　　　　　　　　　　　(p. 49)

The "molten metal" line represents a quasi-imagistic technique, but the differences between Fletcher's passage and H.D.'s are significant: H.D. focuses on the small petals of a rose, while Fletcher views the river from a distance; H.D.'s comparison is one of four related metaphors, each of which tries to convey the sharp, brittle quality of the rose, whereas Fletcher's "molten metal" line is one of several decorative and casually introduced similes; lastly, H.D.'s overall treatment is "hard" and static, while Fletcher's is "soft" and fluid. The "color technique," therefore, was exactly that, a technique of using color that emphasized visuality, but it was not imagism.

One of Fletcher's entries in the 1916 anthology, to be sure, does come close to being imagism:

> The Skaters
>
> Black swallows swooping or gliding
> In a flurry of entangled loops and curves;
> The skaters skim over the frozen river.
> And the grinding click of their skates as they
> 　　impinge upon the surface,
> Is like the brushing together of thin wing-tips of
> 　　silver.
>
> 　　　　　　　　　　　　　　　　(p. 48)

Edna B. Stephens comments that this poem is "justly famous as an example of an Imagist poem" and avers that "no one would quarrel" with this classification.[22] I would not dispute her judgment very strenuously—certainly we see a definite, if not a precise picture in the poem, and the last four lines superimpose one image upon another. Nevertheless, as Fletcher himself points out in his memoirs, the effectiveness of this poem depends a great deal on sound ("Black swallows swooping," "skim," "click"); furthermore, the picture we are asked to visualize in the first two lines is really impressionistically indeterminate and vague in outline. What is precise in this poem is not the seen image but the sound of the "grinding click of the skates." I agree with Stephens as to the merits of the piece, but rather than calling it strict imagism, let us say that it is composed in the imagist manner.

Japanese Prints

The majority of the sixty-six short poems that make up *Japanese Prints* (1918) were written during a week in February 1915, when Fletcher visited the Clarence Buckingham Collection of ukiyoe prints at the Art Institute of Chicago as part of his first western trip.[23] Already keenly interested in Oriental art, Fletcher was moved by these seventeenth- and eighteenth-century masterpieces to write a series of epigrammatic poems, each based on an individual picture. He chose not to follow strict Japanese metrical patterns, believing that "Good hokkus cannot be written in English," but tried to "illustrate something of the charm"[24] of both Japanese poetry and art.

Many of the verses do capture the spirit of the Far East inasmuch as they are brief, concentrated, and veil a delicate emotion behind universal natural facts. The following poem, as Edna Stephens points out,[25] is very much like a haiku:

> Moods
> A poet's moods:
> Fluttering butterflies in the rain.
>
> 　　　　　　　　　　　　　　　　(p. 85)

Many of the most successful *Japanese Prints* are more personal in tone, however, and therefore are not strictly Japanese:

> Memory and Forgetting
>
> I have forgotten how many times he kissed me,
> But I cannot forget
> A swaying branch—a leaf that fell
> To earth.
>
> 　　　　　　　　　　　　　　　　(p. 41)

In these four concise lines Fletcher suggests an entire state of mind. Through a central antithesis ("I have forgotten," "I cannot forget") and a few well-chosen details, he conveys a sense of loss as muted by time into perpetual sorrow. Throughout the volume, Fletcher is at his best when dealing with controlled regret or sadness. Here is another in this key:

> Despair
>
> Despair hangs in the broken folds of my garments;
> It clogs my footsteps,
> Like snow in the cherry bloom.

In my heart is the sorrow
Of years like red leaves buried in the snow.

(p. 74)

Once again we have an internal rightness, an aptness of phrasing, and a fragile quality that is irresistible. The "despair" is not traceable to a specific event but is a "sorrow / Of years" which, as well as being painful, possesses the fascination and glimmer of "red leaves buried in the snow." Several critics have regarded *Japanese Prints* as a sort of literary bric-a-brac, poems of slight intention, but while they are small and fragile, the finest of them are not lacking in substance.

Although a good number—perhaps one-third—of these poems portray a mood with exactness and charm, many of the others fall short of their desired effect. One common fault is wordiness. When, Fletcher loses sight of the goals of brevity and clarity, he fails:

Lovers Embracing

Force and yielding meet together:
An attack is half repulsed.
Shafts of broken sunlight dissolving
Convolutions of torpid cloud.

(p. 21)

As Amy Lowell states, this poem "is in Fletcher's most personal idiom, but it is not in the least in the idiom of Japan."[26] Elsewhere, he makes appropriate gestures but the words lack import. Here is a poem that wears the Oriental mask but fails to move us:

A Woman Standing by a Gate with an Umbrella

Late summer changes to autumn:
Chrysanthemums are scattered
Behind the palings.

Gold and vermilion
The afternoon.

I wait here dreaming of vermilion sunsets:
In my heart is a half fear of the chill autumn rain.

(p. 32)

While the last line is effective, the poem as a whole does not ring true. The details are not sharp; instead we find Fletcher relying on his old trick of letting colors do his work for him: the "Gold and vermilion / The afternoon" phrase simply applies color without contributing to the mood, and the repeat of "vermilion" in the next line smacks of mannerism, recalling "vermilion pavilions" in "Irradiation V." Certainly a good number of *Japanese Prints* are mechanical and posed, products of an oversimplified formula. This is not surprising, considering how quickly Fletcher wrote them. What is remarkable is that he produced so many good poems in the short space of a week.

In his memoirs, Fletcher compares these poems to Edgar Lee Masters's *Spoon River Anthology,* saying: "What I intended by Japanese Prints was a brief commentary on life and on manners, a kind of 'Spoon River' *à la Japonaise,* more compressed indeed, and more decorative, but not less valid and direct" (*Life Is My Song,* p. 200). When read in this light, a number of *Prints* taken on a new dimension. We can see a Mastersian blighted quality, for example, in "Spring Love," as the lovers become ill-suited for each other in the natural course of the relationship. The hand of Masters is also visible in "A Life":

Her life was like a swiftly rushing stream
Green and scarlet,
Falling into darkness.

The seasons passed for her,
Like pale iris wilting,
Or peonies flying to ribbons before the storm-
gusts.
The sombre pine-tops waited until the seasons had
passed.

Then in her heart they grew
The snows of changeless winter
Stirred by the bitter winds of unsatisfied desire.

(p. 70)

As in so many of the *Spoon River* epitaphs, a frustrated, bitter life is here compassed within a few lines. Actually, though, Fletcher's portraits have little in common with Masters's character studies, as a look at one of the poems from *Spoon River Anthology* will reveal:

Lucius Atherton

When my moustache curled,
And my hair was black,
And I wore tight trousers
And a diamond stud,
I was an excellent knave of hearts and took many
a trick.
But when the gray hairs began to appear—
Lo! a new generation of girls
Laughed at me, not fearing me,
And I had no more exciting adventures
Wherein I was all but shot for a heartless devil,
But only drabby affairs, warmed-over affairs
Of other days and other men.
And time went on until I lived at Mayer's
restaurant,
Partaking of short-orders, a gray, untidy,
Toothless, discarded, rural Don Juan. . . .
There is a mighty shade here who sings
Of one named Beatrice;
And I see now that the force that made him great
Drove me to the dregs of life.

The secret of this portrait lies in its use of realistic detail. Lucius [Lucifer?] Atherton is as genuine as his diamond stud and moves in the sordid but recognizable world of "Mayer's restaurant." The psychology of the worn-out Lothario, moreover, is thoroughly believable, even if we do not now accept the oversimplified Freudian lesson of the last four lines. Unlike Lucius Atherton, Fletcher's characters in *Japanese Prints* do not resemble real people. The details and milieu do not point up individual character, but are decorative and standardized paraphernalia with both the charm and the inaccessibility of the exotic. Japanese fans, lanterns, robes, swords, lotus gardens (Chinese), and Yoshiwara festivals, amidst which move young Daimyo's and geishas, provide nice window dressing but do not make us feel close to the lives which are lived in them. The characters, furthermore, do not utter individualized emotions but repeat the same sentiments of disappointment or wistful longing. Phrases like "Alas, the torn lantern of my hope / Trembles and sputters in the rain" strike a chord when first encountered, but after repetition become mere gesture. *Japanese Prints* is made up of charming and sometimes memorable productions, but Fletcher makes a mistake when he invites comparison with Masters's epitaphs.

Fletcher's enthusiasm for Oriental poetry and art was typical of the American Poetry Renaissance. Various translations of Far Eastern verse, in both French and English, were available for poets to read, imitate, paraphrase, and modify for their own uses. Pound's own adaptations of Ernest Fenellosa's translations of the Chinese poet, Li Po (*Cathay,* 1915) and his versions of the Noh plays (*Certain Noble Plays of Japan,* 1916) did much toward fostering an interest in Oriental verse. Amy Lowell, in collaboration with Florence Ayscough, also translated some Chinese poems (*Fir-Flower Tablets,* 1921). As for original work, Adelaide Crapsey attempted to render the Japanese tanka in English with her "Cinquain" form:

> Triad
>
> These be
> Three silent things:
> The falling snow . . . the hour
> Before the dawn . . . the mouth of one
> Just dead.[27]

Among the imagists, H.D. and Aldington were drawn to Greek verse and Flint was a confirmed Francophile, but both Amy Lowell and Pound, as well as Fletcher, wrote original poems in the Oriental manner. Miss Lowell's "Lacquer Prints" section from *Pictures of the Floating World* (1919), for example, possibly inspired by Fletcher's *Japanese Prints,* entirely consists of Chinese and Japanese pieces. As for Pound his contributions to *Des Imagistes* (1914) were nearly all in the Chinese mode and the famous "Metro" was inspired by what he called the Japanese "one image poem,"[28] that is, the haiku.

This is not to imply that imagism received its chief impetus from the Orient; its main sources were in Greek and French verse and in Pound's Provençal poets. Certain of the imagists, however, did feel a kinship between their own attitude and that of the Chinese and Japanese poets. Fletcher himself stated the reason for this affinity in his February 1919 *Poetry* review of Arthur Waley's *Chinese Poems.* "The one quality," he said, "that is common to all these Chinese singers is their absolute sincerity, their refusal to accept any make-believes about life. . . . A great modesty before Nature is the Chinese poet's chief characteristic. This refusal to see anything especially fine or important or heroic about man and his destiny, is the

elementary principle of the Chinese character." Once again we have the old touchstone of "sincerity," or what Pound called "contestation." Fletcher, Lowell, and Pound admired Far Eastern poets because they wrote sincerely about what moved them without inflating the experience or making it assume an undue importance. They liked their reticence, their way of looking outward to nature in "a spirit of intense observation, of patient surrender to truth."[29] The imagists and Far Eastern poets held other obvious points in common as well. Both believed that thoughts and emotions should be expressed concretely in images rather than literally stated; both believed that a certain kind of egotistically exuberant poetic emotion should be held in check, restrained behind a seemingly objective outward gaze; lastly, both subscribed to a reductionist aesthetic, believing that poetic expression should be as concise as possible—Matsuo Bash , the greatest Japanese haiku poet, would sometimes refine a single poem over a period of years. Therefore, in spite of some differences in form, subject matter, and total effect—Japanese haikus do not "explode" like H.D.'s "Oread"—the imagists could feel that they shared with the Orient similar poetic values. Consequently, insofar as they attempt to maintain a brevity, concentration, and clarity of image, *Japanese Prints* are among Fletcher's most imagistic productions. Along with "The Ghosts of an Old House" they represent one of his few consistent efforts to pare down, to hone, to restrict his expression to a short compass. Usually Fletcher was an exuberant poet, a free spender of words. *Japanese Prints* demonstrates that he could master the epigram when necessary; when he chose, Fletcher could practice the imagist virtues of spareness and concision. His failure to do so more often shows his fundamental lack of sympathy with those values. Significantly, Fletcher called his Japanese poems "very slight things"[30] and wrote Miss Lowell that he lost all interest in them even before they were published.[31]

The Tree of Life

Originally entitled "Love's Tragedy," *The Tree of Life* (1918) consists of five groups of autobiographical love poems written sporadically between the fall of 1913 and the winter of 1916.[32] Introduced by a group of "Preludes," and concluded by "Postludes," and an "Epilogue," the fifty-six poems in between record Fletcher's love affair with Daisy Arbuthnot.

The five sections in *The Tree of Life* correspond to the progression of his relationship with Daisy. Poems in the first section such as "The Walk in the Garden," "The Offering," and "November Days," commemorate that heady but apprehensive first meeting between Fletcher and Mrs. Arbuthnot in Kew Gardens during the fall of 1913. The foreboding tone is due to Fletcher's sexual inexperience and his realization that he was becoming enmeshed with the wife of another man. Section two, "Fruit of Flame," with its scenes of contented suburban living, recalls the months Fletcher spent with Daisy at her home in Sydenham during the spring and summer of 1914. The separation that takes place in the middle of the book refers to Fletcher's return to America, necessitated by the outbreak of World War I. The rest of the poems reflect the poet's uncertainty over whether he would ever return to England and Mrs. Arbuthnot, and his increasing loneliness and disillusionment in America. Book V, in particular, reveals the severe depression and isolation that Fletcher endured in Boston during the winter of 1915-1916 when his career was at a standstill and his relationship with Amy Lowell was deteriorating. These last poems are really more about Fletcher's personal problems than a love relationship.

The theme of *The Tree of Life* is that love is inherently tragic, that the ideal of perfect love, as symbolized by the "tree of life," can never be attained. Unfortunately, Fletcher fails to give concrete instances of the cause of his disillusionment. Is he disenchanted because love stales or cannot endure separation? Because love can achieve a transcendency, a divine power, only on rare occasions? These ideas linger in the background of certain poems but are never put forward with any consistency or degree of definition. One explanation for "love's tragedy" may be found in the destructive impulses of the speaker, both toward himself and his loved one ("Till the harsh feet of hatred trampled it in the dust" [pp. 60-61]). Another possible reason for the speaker's disenchantment is that the actuality of love can never match his extravagant visions of it ("Who made of love an image and who worshipped it at night" [pp. 93-94]). Whatever message Fletcher intended, it is lost amid two general an outpouring of feelings. He does not body forth a theme in *The Tree of Life* but only gives us a number of half-realized ideas.

Although the volume lacks coherence as a whole, some of the individual poems strike a fresh note. Most successful are mood pieces like "The Walk in the Garden," "On the Verandah," or "The Offering," which commemorate a specific event or moment in the lovers' relationship. These two- to three-page episodes place the lovers in a natural setting and then draw parallels between their emotional state and the surroundings. The speaker and his loved one enjoy moments of rare peace as they lie on gently sensual beaches or wander like lost primitives through luxuriant gardens. In the following lines, autumnal lushness reflects the lovers' wistful melancholy:

> Still and windless was the day,
> Tho great green trees dreamed and gloomed
> And drooped over each alleyway
> Silent cascades of weary leaves;
> They yellowed slowly,
> Some of them blazed like orange suns.
> The asters, violet and melancholy,
> Would have dropt their petals had breezes come.
>
> (p. 16)

Fletcher adeptly portrays trees, flowers, and pools of water. Phrases like "cold colonnades," "evergreen fronds," and "glassy glaucous pools" stay in the mind. He is also good at conveying pale and delicate lighting effects. Many of the poems have a faded out or bleached quality, as though they were products of memory.

Also worthy of mention in *The Tree of Life* are a handful of verses that consist of bitter and acidulous direct statement. Some offer strange insights into love:

> The Conflict
>
> I have fled away into deserts,
> I have hidden myself from you,
> Lo, you always at my side!
> I cannot shake myself free.
> In the evening stillness
> With your cold eyes you sit watching,
> Longing, hungering still for me;
> I will open my heart and give you
> All my blood, at last.
>
> (p. 26)

Like Stephen Crane's epigrams, this poem depends on a stark concision, a tart, pointed quality for its effect, as though the speaker had bitten on iron filings. "The Conflict" and "The Ordeal" also are similar to Crane's poems in that they express fascination with guilt and self-destruction. The speaker has lost the blood from his heart in giving his love, but derives a peculiar satisfaction from his sacrifice. One of the virtues of *The Tree of Life* is that Fletcher deals with cruel and harsh feelings which, for him anyway, accompany love—hatred, scorn, a sense of unbearable closeness—rather than offering the niceties of sentiment that were prevalent at the time.

Many of the rest of the poems in *The Tree of Life,* are of embarrassingly low quality and display all of the qualities the imagists were trying to escape: abstractions, trite sentiments, and sing-song rhythms. Particularly in the last half of the volume, the verses contain atrocious lapses in style, tyroisms that show an amazing disregard for poetic craftsmanship. Here are a few examples of what one critic calls "awkward spontaneities":[33]

> I am blinded, I am weak, sad, hurt, afraid,
> O love, keep back some little love for me,
>
> . . . . .
>
> I know well you are all the world to me,
> You know well I am all the world to you.
>
> . . . . .
>
> We are parting, parting forever:—
> We can never meet again, never, never, never;[34]

Not only do such prosaicisms appear without warning to mar what might be an otherwise beautiful passage, sometimes entire stanzas or whole poems consist solely of such flat remarks. To make matters worse, the sentiment often has no dignity but carries a whining, self-pitying tone. The style is ludicrous; in one poem the speaker refers to his "heart-break," and in another asks, "What does it matter whether I go on or not?"

Fletcher's unevenness often has been discussed by his critics. Even, Amy Lowell found it necessary to write in *Tendencies in Modern American Poetry* that his "fecundity of creation naturally leads to the production of much that is below the level of his best, and one of his marked traits is the uncritical, unselective habit of mind." Another contemporary friend, Conrad Aiken, tries to explain "the astonishing unequalness which alone would constitute a sort of distinction in the work of Mr. Fletcher" by arguing that he is an "unconscious" poet who writes best when surrendering himself to "verbal reflexes." He adds that for Fletcher it is "a great handicap, to have to adhere too closely, throughout a longish poem, to a fixed and unalterable idea."[35] Aiken's hypothesis might account for the failure of much of Fletcher's later work, a great deal of which was written according to conscious plan, but it backfires when applied to *The Tree of Life* which, as Fletcher himself states in a letter to R. N. Linscott, was "purely subconscious . . . practically improvised, with very little rewriting, and without any definite plan." Miss Lowell's "fecundity of creation" theory is more convincing: Fletcher would write poems and even whole volumes in spurts as they came to him and publish them with little revision. If the original inspiration was of a high order, as in "Irradiations," then fine, but if not, as in *The Tree of Life,* the results were embarrassing.

The question remains, why could Fletcher not take these improvisations and make them better by eliminating the dross from gold? Several explanations may be put forward. In the first place, between 1913 and 1916 Fletcher seems to have had little idea of what constituted his best and worst work. He lacked confidence in his poetry, was diffident in putting it forward, and relied on others, namely Pound and Miss Lowell, to decide for him what was good and what was bad. In 1913, for instance, he said in a letter to Harriet Monroe that he did not know whether "Irradiations" was an improvement over his earlier work or not; in 1914 he could not make up his mind whether the group of love poems he had just completed were the best or worst he had written, telling Amy Lowell, "that is for you to decide"; and, in 1915 he left out the brilliant "Mississippi" and "Arizona" poems from the list of "five good things" he had done that year.[36] When Fletcher did pass judgment on his work, furthermore, it was according to his own very personal set of standards. He repeatedly judged the poems in the "Love's Tragedy" manuscript "the best I have ever done,"[37] because of their "control over verbal technique, versatility of rhythm, architectural unity—the high qualities of art."[38] In other words, he thought highly of his love poems because they were the result of techniques similar to those he had employed in his "Symphonies." Because Fletcher was most concerned with the larger shape his improvisations took, he may have been less sensitive to the harmful effect of clichés, flat prosaic statements, and other matters of style. Finally, the many dead spots in some of Fletcher's volumes can be explained by his personality. He was stubborn, proud, and in some ways lacked self-awareness. His feelings were too close to him, particularly where love and personal suffering were concerned. In the case of *The Tree of Life,* no one could convince him that the transmission of those feelings raw onto paper was not good poetry.

Certainly the "Symphonies" and *Breakers and Granite,* as well as *The Tree of Life,* could be greatly improved if some of the weaker poems had been deleted or shortened. Nevertheless, the many failures printed by Fletcher both during his tenure with the imagists and throughout his career, should not detract from his achievement. Unfortunately, he left out most of his best verse from the Pulitzer-Prize-winning *selected Poems* (1938) and included much that is mediocre. The best of Fletcher's poems, in a single, accessible volume, would reveal him to be a fresh and talented writer.

Fletcher and Imagism

We are now in a position to ask, with William James, "What has been concluded, that we should conclude anything at all concerning it?"

To begin with, a survey of Fletcher's poetry from 1913 to 1916 reveals that very little of his large and varied output was, strictly speaking, imagistic. Certainly the "Symphonies," "London Excursion," polyphonic prose pieces, "Mississippi" and "Arizona" poems, and most of *The Tree of Life,* in their length, frequent abstraction, and courting of the infinite, do not even remotely approach imagist ideals. As for the many short, objective, free-verse poems that Fletcher composed—*Irradiations,* "The Ghosts of an Old House," *Japanese Prints,* "The Skaters," and other 1916 and 1917 anthology pieces—these have often passed for being imagistic, but they do not consistently possess the qualities of precision and "hardness" so crucial to the imagist aesthetic; nor do they aim at the sudden, intense release of energy that Pound associated with his image. At no time did Fletcher wholeheartedly adopt or try to realize imagist goals, i.e., to write poetry of a plastic nature or to "present an Image." Indeed, that he could produce the glaringly non-imagistic love poems that comprise *The Tree of Life* throughout the period of his association with the movement indicates that he was indifferent to some of the central tenets of imagism.

Fletcher's own beliefs in regard to the function of poetry as compared to those of the early imagists may be summarized as follows. He did not favor a maximum of visual content but felt that poetic style should be an attempt to develop the musical quality of literature. As a result, his poems cultivate not a sharpness of outline, but a richness of sound. Furthermore, while the early imagists focused on concrete objects and small pieces of reality, Fletcher tried to bring out the underlying essence of a scene. His most common way of doing this was through his "symphonic" method, which led to the quiet prolongation of effect rather than to the forceful "hit" or impact Pound tried to attain in his "image." It also resulted in the writing of many long poems, something the imagists were not known for. Lastly, Fletcher's manner of composition was different from that of the early imagists. They prided themselves on paring down their utterances to the fewest words possible and strove, through careful pruning, to give their compositions a finished, "made" quality. Fletcher customarily dashed off his poems in improvisational bursts and left them essentially unrevised. His work, characteristically, is not restrained and severe in tone, but has an exuberant and overflowing quality.

In spite of these differences, Fletcher was a bona fide participant in the movement, strongly involved in its intrigues, active in helping to write its prefaces, and a vocal defender of some of its tenets. How do we account for this paradox? The explanation is that Fletcher and his fellow imagists had a very broad concept of what constituted a literary school. Imagism, like the French "-isms" from which it took its cue, did not demand from its members rigid adherence to a specific doctrine, but only required that they agree to follow loose guidelines in writing poetry and share a common attitude toward life. It was this undefinable but real "attitude toward life" that Fletcher held in common with his imagist colleagues. Much more important than the flexible principles in the various manifestoes was their belief that they could rely on each other to write directly and "sincerely" about whatever moved them. Something was in the air, a new attitude toward experience which the principles of the manifestoes could only intimate, but which was, above all, their reason for banding together. Fletcher, by expressing his distaste for the mannerisms of recent poetry and by committing himself to metric freedom and definite treatment of a subject—indeed, by his whole artistic demeanor—showed that he shared this attitude toward experience and as a result could unhesitatingly be accepted as a peer.

John Gould Fletcher, imagist, fought many battles for Amy Lowell and the movement, but he was much more than one of her troopers: he was a gifted poet and intelligent man of letters whose work deserves a better fate than it has received. Now that the story of Fletcher's role in the imagist movement has been told, let us hope attention may shift to his verse.

NOTES

[1] See Appendix [not here reprinted].

[2] John Gould Fletcher, *Irradiations: Sand and Spray*, p. 33.

[3] William Pratt, ed., *The Imagist Poem*, p. 94.

[4] Edna B. Stephens, *John Gould Fletcher*, p. 30.

[5] René Taupin, *L'Influence du Symbolisme Français sur la Poésie Americaine (de 1910 à 1920)*, pp. 197-98.

[6] John Gould Fletcher, *Goblins and Pagodas*, p. xviii.

[7] Stanley Coffman, *Imagism*, p. 177.

[8] Ferris Greenslet, "The Poetry of John Gould Fletcher," p. 73.

[9] For a discussion of the Chinese influences in this poem, see Stephens, *John Gould Fletcher*, pp. 33-42.

[10] John Gould Fletcher, *Life Is My Song*, p. 139.

[11] Ibid., p. 143.

[12] Ezra Pound, *The Letters of Ezra Pound*, ed. D. D. Paige, p. 49.

[13] Glenn Hughes, *Imagism and the Imagists*, pp. 140-41.

[14] *Some Imagist Poets, 1915*, pp. 43-44.

[15] Fletcher, *Life*, p. 144.

[16] Ibid., p. 196.

[17] John Gould Fletcher, *Breakers and Granite*, p. 125.

[18] John Gould Fletcher, "A Rational Explanation of Vers Libre," p. 13.

[19] Fletcher, *Breakers and Granite*, p. 95.

[20] Amy Lowell, *The Complete Poetical Works*, p. 234.

[21] Hilda Doolittle (H.D.), *Collected Poems*, p. 34.

[22] Stephens, *John Gould Fletcher*, p. 29.

[23] John Gould Fletcher, "The Orient and Contemporary Poetry," pp. 160-61.

[24] John Gould Fletcher, *Japanese Prints*, pp. 16-17.

[25] Stephens, *John Gould Fletcher*, p. 63.

[26] Amy Lowell, *Tendencies in Modern American Poetry*, p. 341.

[27] Pratt, *The Imagist Poem*, p. 122.

[28] Ezra Pound, "Vorticism," p. 167.

[29] Fletcher, "The Orient and Contemporary Poetry," p. 172.

[30] Fletcher to R. N. Linscott, 26 September 1916, University of Arkansas Library, John Gould Fletcher Papers.

[31] Fletcher to Amy Lowell, 6 March 1918, Fletcher Papers.

[32] John Gould Fletcher, *The Tree of Life*. "The Aster Flower" was composed during the autumn of 1913, "Fruit of Flame" during the spring and summer of 1914, "From Empty Days" during the winter of 1914-1915, and "Dreams in the Night" and "Toward the Darkness" during the spring of 1915 and the winter of 1915-1916.

[33] Hughes, *Imagism and the Imagists*, p. 142.

[34] Fletcher, *The Tree of Life*, pp. 23, 33, 49.

[35] Conrad Aiken, *Scepticisms*, pp. 106-9.

[36] Fletcher to Amy Lowell, 16 April 1914, Harvard University Library, John Gould Fletcher-Amy Lowell Correspondence.

[37] Fletcher to Amy Lowell, 7 December 1916, Fletcher-Lowell Correspondence.

[38] Fletcher to R. N. Linscott, 24 February 1919, Fletcher Papers.

A. R. C. Finch

[*In the following essay, Finch theorizes that H.D.'s poetic style antedates and extends beyond the formulation of the Imagist principles most closely associated with her works.*]

SOURCE: "H.D., "Imagiste?" in *Cumberland Poetry Review*, Vol. VII, No. 1, Fall, 1987, pp. 36-45.

Although Ezra Pound intended his term *Imagisme* to mean specifically "something which was the poetry of H.D.,"[1] and although H.D.'s early work is frequently thought to be the quintessential Imagiste poetry, her connection with the movement that has come to be almost synonymous with her name has many problematic aspects. H.D. developed her unique style uniquely. Even the poems by her which gave the Imagiste movement its name can be easily distinguished from the work of later, avowed Imagistes through H.D.'s use of specifically *non*-Imagistic techniques, particularly her fundamental attention to words as words.

H.D.'s connection with the Imagiste group was consistent. H.D. was one of the original three poets in Pound's group, and she stayed with the movement after Pound was supplanted by Amy Lowell as its leader. But H.D.'s desire to associate herself publicly with Imagism was never completely wholehearted. In 1913 she requested that the word *Imagiste* not appear after her name in *Poetry* magazine. If J. B. Harmer's characterization of the Imagiste group under Amy Lowell as "little more than a publishing consortium" is correct (41), and if Pound did indeed coin the term *Imagisme* around H.D.'s already developed poetic style, then there is no reason to suspect that H.D. identified herself with the movement *per se* except insofar as its tenets coincided with her own aims.

In 1913, Pound named the following principles as the guiding tenets of *Imagisme:*

Direct treatment of the "thing," whether objective or subjective

To use absolutely no word that does not contribute to the presentation

As regards rhythm, to compose in the sequence of the musical phrase, not of the metronome

To conform to the "doctrine of the image"

His *don'ts* included the advice to avoid abstractions, to emphasize cadences, to use rhyme well—with a slight element of surprise—and to be aware of the image as presenting an "intellectual and emotional complex in an instant of time."[2] The following year, Richard Aldington added more guidelines: to use as few adjectives as possible, to use the exact word, and to avoid sentimentality and slop in favor of "harshness."[3] Finally, Pound in 1916 defined *Imagisme* as a manner of presentation, rather than as merely pictures, and as "the clear representation of what the author wishes to convey."[4]

To some extent, H.D.'s early poetry acknowledges these principles, but her poems follow them with such fluidity and flexibility that they seem to use the principles in the service of their lyricism rather than concentrating on the illustration of either an image or the Imagistic principles. This may be the very reason she is called the perfect *Imagiste*. Compared with works written specifically to embody the Imagistic principles, H.D.'s poems are strikingly different; they avoid the limitations on mood and focus imposed by strict adherence to the theory of "direct treatment of the thing":

> Over the green cold leaves
> and the rippled silver
> and the tarnished copper
> of its neck and beak,
> toward the deep black water
> beneath the arches,
> the swan floats slowly.
> —F. S. Flint, "The Swan"

> The vast dark trees
> flow like blue veils
> of tears
> Into the water
> —J. S. Fletcher, "Blue Symphony"

> A rose-yellow moon in a pale sky
> When the sunset is faint vermilion
> On the mist among the tree-boughs
> Are you to me.
> —Richard Aldington, "Images" (III)

Even some of the less evocative passages from *Sea Garden*, H.D.'s first book, show an emotional expressiveness far beyond such direct presentation of images:

> The light of her face falls from its flower,
> as a hyacinth,
> hidden in a far valley,
> perishes upon burnt grass.
> —"Acon"

> Stunted, with small leaf,
> You are flung on the sand,
> You are lifted
> in the crisp sand
> that drives in the wind.
> —"Sea Rose"

The allusive language in these poems ("hyacinth," with its classical connotations, and the archaic-sounding "perishes"); the use of repetition and parallelism ("You are flung/You are lifted"; "far valley/burnt grass"); the chiastic metaphorical play in the first ("falls from its flower, as a hyacinth . . . perishes"); and the attention to verbal music ("perishes"/"hidden"; "stunted"/"flung") work on levels other than the imagistic, and even the images evoke so much more than the "thing itself" that these poems might almost be seen as misusing Imagistic principles. With their preponderance of anapests ("of her face," "from its flower," "you are flung on the sand," etc.), these poems demonstrate H.D.'s emphasis on verbal music. Their rhythms contrast dramatically with the descriptive-phrase rhythms of the other *Imagiste* poems quoted—poems that, when scanned, display a flattening abundance of spondees.

The lyrics of *Sea Garden* belie, or question, even the central Imagistic idea of an image as the expression of intellectual and emotional qualities. The "complex" of qualities never inheres straightforwardly in one particular image in these lyrics. The image in Pound's "In a Station of the Metro," often cited as an Imagistic model, presents a good contrast to H.D.'s early use of images:

> The apparition of these faces in the crowd;
> Petals on a wet, black bough.

This poem evokes images and sentiments far removed from the original image of the faces in the crowd. The evoked images are employed, however, to render this original image as completely and accurately as possible. The poem begins and ends with the concrete image it attempts to render. Even the ironic reverse image that can be read as an undercurrent in the poem, because of its direct opposition to the core image, serves to concentrate energy back onto the original emotional and intellectual complex: the contrast with the harmonious quietness of nature only focusses more power on the emotionally ambiguous scene of urban alienation. That such double meanings can be read in this little poem shows that Pound was a more skillful and subtle *Imagiste* than either Aldington or Fletcher (whose pun on "vail of tears" is anything but subtle), but not that he was any less of an *Imagiste* than they. All of these poets use emotions only to give primacy to the power of the one image; the poignancy they evoke is always visually grounded and centered.

H.D. works in the opposite direction. Her apparent concentration on concrete images is almost sneaky because it is just in this process that she is able to focus the poem on metaphysical or emotional realities that she could never present directly without bogging the poem down in abstraction:

> The shrivelled seeds
> are spilt on the path—
> the grass bends with dust,
> the grass slips
> under its cracked leaf;
> yet far beyond the spent seed-pods,
> and the blackened stalks of mint,
> the poplar is bright on the hill.
>   —"Mid-Day"

> Amber husk,
> fluted with gold,
> fruit on the sand,
> marked with a rich grain.
>   —"Sea Poppies"

In the first poem, the subjectively logical judgment "yet" orders and emphasizes the contrast between the scene described with the emotionally loaded past participles "shrivelled," "cracked," "spent," and "blackened" and the final image of the bright tree on the hill. Neither image is the ultimate point of the poem in the *Imagiste* sense; nor could it be, even if the scenes were described more starkly. The contrast between the two images, and the implied emotional state of the speaker who notices that contrast, is the poem's real subject. In "Sea Poppies," again, the repetitive, passionate, subjective metaphors that describe the flowers focus attention on the speaker's feelings much more than on the image of the flowers, or possibly the speaker's feelings and the speaker's perceptions of the flowers are inseparable. Unlike the singular, self-conscious metaphors in Fletcher's "Blue Symphony" or Aldington's "Images," the metaphors of fruit, grain, and gold in "Sea Poppies" are engrained in the description and cannot be separated from the description, objectified, and regarded almost as images in themselves.

In several poems, H.D. even uses images in the service of a stated metaphysical idea:

> Each of us like you
> has died once,
> each of us has crossed an old wood-path
> and found winter-leaves
> so golden in the sun-fire
> that even the live wood-flowers
> were dark.
>   —"Adonis"

While in "Adonis" the idea of death is stated explicitly, before it is described allusively, the subtle evocation of the abstract without any use of abstractions will appear as strong negativistic trend in H.D.'s later poetry. The denial of everything that the vision of Mary is not in "Tribute to the Angels" is a late example. A fascinating early use of the technique in reference to a concrete object is found in *Sea Garden*'s "The Helmsman." This poem is about the sea and evokes the sea at every point, but the word *sea* never appears, and the only word referring to it before the last stanza is *tang*. The word *bees* is treated similarly in the first two stanzas of "The Orchard." H.D. shows the importance of an image to a poem in these cases by writing the poem around the image. We become aware of the size and shape of the gap left in "The Helmsman" by the omission of the word *sea* and are thus tantalized into a recognition of the sea's importance to the poem. This is a very sophisticated and almost subversive alteration of the Imagistic ideal of "direct treatment of the thing."

> The flash of sun on the snow,
> the fringe of light and the drift,
> the crest and the hill-shadow—
> ah, surely now I forget,

Ah, splendour, my goddess turns:
or was it the sudden heat
beneath quivering of molten flesh,
of veins, purple as violets?
—"Hippolytus Temporizes"

The repetitive musicality of the first three lines of "Hippolytus Temporizes," whose three-beat swing might have almost been thought by Pound to hold a slight echo of the metronome, demonstrates H.D.'s sense of the power of words-as-words—not just as tools for capturing an image—as much as does her technique of structuring a poem around an omitted word. In many of her poems, words gain a ritualistic power through repetition that has nothing to do with the principles of *Imagisme*. In "Sea Heroes" and "The Islands" the poet chants Greek names as if they were a spell. She often recites, in a similar way, the names of flowers so unusual that they have little imagistic value. Other poems repeat a simple word continually in such a way that a new dimension is added to the word in each context, the result being that the word has participated in many images and accumulated their power, finally embodying connotatively a sense of the whole poem. This process occurs with the word *gold* in "Adonis," with *silver* in "Pear Tree," and in a condensed form in "Sea Poppies":

. . . flung by the sea
and grated shells
and split conch shells.
Beautiful; wide-spread,
fire upon leaf,
what meadow yields
so fragrant a leaf
as your bright leaf?

Perhaps the most striking use of repetition is in "Sea Gods":

We bring violets,
great masses—single, sweet,
wood-violets, stream violets,
violets from a wet marsh . . .
yellow violets, gold,
burnt with a rare tint—
violets like red ash
among tufts of grass—

Repetition in these passages adds power and concreteness to words which are at first quite general. In a way H.D. creates her own "exact words" by this method. In the poem's verbal world, words gain verbal evocative power during the course of the poem, rather than borrowing power because of a relation to images external to the poem.

H.D.'s cadence can be seen at times as beautifully true to the *Imagiste* idea of original rhythms which grow out of the poem rather than imposing themselves on it. In the first stanza of "At Ithaca," each line carries over into the beginning of the next, in a movement which can be thought of as growing out of the movement of the loom and that of waves:

Over and back,
the long waves crawl
and track the sand with foam;
night darkens and the sea

takes on that desperate tone
of dark that wives put on
when all their love is done.

Alternately, however, the two- and three-beat lines in this stanza can be seen as metrically influenced if not determined, and the rhyme and rhythm in the last lines combine into a distinctive musicality completely different from the flatness of consciously *Imagiste* poems and more like the tone of relatively early Yeats. Like all the other *Imagiste* principles that can be traced in H.D.'s work, this one receives problematic treatment.

The *Imagiste* principles were well suited to H.D.'s purposes. She used concrete imagery, flexible rhythms, and economy in language to create a highly idiosyncratic, mystical reality. When some of H.D.'s aesthetic principles were carried to their extreme by poets whose major commitment was to such "Imagiste" techniques, the result was poems that are often superficial and clumsy in comparison with her controlled complexity. That H.D. is considered the greatest of the *Imagistes* may lead one to conclude that the *Imagiste* tenets were better suited to be the tools of a poet who already had her own musical and metaphysical preoccupations than to be goals in themselves.

NOTES

[1] Pound in a letter to Flint, 7 July 1915, unpublished; quoted in Harmer 59.

[2] Pound in *Poetry,* January 1913, quoted in Hughes 26-8.

[3] Aldington in *The Egoist,* 1914, quoted in Harmer 45.

[4] Pound in the preface to *Some Imagist Poets,* 1916, quoted in Harmer 46.

WORKS CITED

Collins, H. P. *Modern Poetry.* London: Jonathan Cape, 1925.

H.D. *Sea Garden: Imagist Poems.* Boston: Houghton Mifflin, 1917.

H.D. *Selected Poems.* New York: Grove Press, 1957.

Harmer, J. B. *Victory in Limbo.* London: Becker and Warburg, 1975.

Hughes, Glenn. *Imagism and the Imagists.* New York: Biblo and Tanner, 1975.

Neil Roberts

[*In the following essay, Roberts focuses on D. H. Lawrence's long poem sequences in a discussion of his poetry in relation to Imagism and the development of modern English poetry.*]

SOURCE: "Lawrence, Imagism and Beyond," in *British Poetry, 1900-50: Aspects of Tradition,* edited by Gary Day and Brian Docherty, St. Martin's Press, 1995, pp. 81-93.

The importance of Lawrence's association with the Imagist movement—which meant for him, above all, the personality and poetic example of H.D.—tends to be underestimated, probably because of a stereotyped idea of the Imagist poem as something small, static and precious. If, however, we think not of set-pieces like 'In the Station of the Metro' but of what Imagism made possible, of what the major Imagists went on to do, Lawrence's association with them seems less incongruous.

What the most important of the Imagists—Pound and H.D.—went on to do was, of course, to write long poems, or sequences. Lawrence, too, habitually wrote in sequences, from *Look! We Have Come Through!* on, and critics have of course noticed this fact, but rarely is it given proper critical weight. His reputation is that of a poet who wrote, or published, too much. It is assumed that he is a very uneven poet, that his successes form a small proportion of his total *oeuvre,* that reading through the whole of *Birds, Beasts and Flowers,* still less, God forbid, *Pansies,* is a tedious and unrewarding exercise. The fact that he wrote some poems, such as 'Snake' and 'Bavarian Gentians', that read very well in selections and anthologies, confirms the prejudice: these poems stand for Lawrence's achievement.

'Snake' and 'Bavarian Gentians' are great poems, but appreciation of them in isolation misrepresents the nature of Lawrence's poetry. Evaluation of poetry is still in the grip of New Critical criteria, despite all that has happened since. But Lawrence, in his famous Introduction to the American edition of *New Poems,* written in 1919, entitled 'Poetry of the Present', wrote a proleptic challenge to New Criticism. In the Introduction he rejects perfection, completeness and finality. 'In the immediate present there is no perfection, no consummation, nothing finished. The strands are all flying, quivering, intermingling into the web, the waters are shaking the moon.'[1] There is some affinity between Lawrence's idea in this essay and Pound's 'intellectual and emotional complex in an instant of time',[2] but Lawrence's argument—or rather, perhaps, his characteristic idiom—makes the break with the well-made poem more inevitable. It can be argued that the instantaneousness of the image presupposes other instants, so that the Imagist poet could not rest in the small complete poem. But Lawrence's metaphor of the strands 'intermingling into the web' makes the consequence inevitable.

It is surprising that Lawrence does not refer to the importance of sequences in the essay; perhaps the campaign for free verse, which turns out to be the main theme, was more urgent. The relationship of the essay to the actual poetry is curious and complicated. The poems that it introduces, though called 'New', mostly antedate *Look! We Have Come Through!,* which had been published two years before. At the end of it he actually writes 'All this should have come as a preface to *Look! We Have Come Through!*'[3] However, I think Tom Marshall is right in saying (though he doesn't explain the comment) that the Introduction 'has most relevance not to *Look! We Have Come Through!* but to his achievement in *Birds, Beasts and Flowers*'[4] (and, I would add, in *Pansies*). In other words, the essay anticipates what Lawrence was to achieve in poetry in the next ten years, rather than describes what he had already done.

Sandra Gilbert suggestively remarks that 'the dialectic or repetitive essay-poems in *Birds, Beasts and Flowers* preserve the gestures of their composition in the way that action-painting retains the movements of the artist'.[5] This analogy is in the spirit of 'Poetry of the Present'. Lawrence employs a rhetoric of incompleteness and of process; the present is by definition incomplete, it cannot reflect upon and judge itself. The present of the poem is necessarily that of its own composition, so that the act of composition is partly its own theme. This does not mean that the poems are self-reflexive in a post-modernist sense (which would surely have been anathema to Lawrence) but that the poems are, in an important sense, unedited (by which I don't mean unrevised) or, in Gilbert's terms, 'preserve the gestures of their composition':

> Fig-trees, weird fig-trees
> Made of thick smooth silver,
> Made of sweet, untarnished silver in the sea-
>   southern air—
> I say untarnished, but I mean opaque—
>   ('Bare Fig Trees', *CP,* p. 298)

Of course, when Lawrence wrote 'untarnished' he *did* mean that; now, a line later, he means something else, and both moments of meaning are preserved. There is a limit of course to how much of this kind of thing a poet can do without it becoming a mannerism, and Lawrence does not make a habit of correcting himself.[6] But the subtle difference, here, between the connotations of 'untarnished' and 'opaque' is a microcosm of the much larger and more significant shifts of thought and feeling that occur, very often, *between* poems.

Sandra Gilbert, having proposed the interesting parallel with 'action-painting', is disappointingly conventional when she comes to criticise certain aspects of Lawrence's poetry that, understandably, she dislikes. Here, for example, she compares the notorious 'Figs' with 'Pomegranate':

> The terms in which Lawrence views the fate of the fig . . . 'the secret is laid bare / And rottenness soon sets in. . . . Ripe figs won't keep'—almost directly contradict the judgement with which he concludes 'Pomegranate': 'I prefer my heart to be broken. / It is so lovely, dawn-kaleidoscopic, within the crack.' In 'Pomegranate' the poet sees the process of nature as a positive good because he is writing of it for its own sake: the flowering, the fruiting, the ripening and the rupture are natural, inevitable. Lawrence knows, attending to the reality rather than intending morality, that it would be

absurd to object on some human ground to so mysterious and uncontrollable a process . . .

In 'Figs' however, the rupture of the fig becomes an obscenity because the writer is not attending to his real subject, the fig as it is in nature, but rather imposing a puritanical, human horror on nature.[7]

There is some sloppy thinking about 'reality' here, as well as presumption in decreeing what is the poet's 'real subject', which would be unimportant if they had not been contradicted by Gilbert's intuition about the nature of Lawrence's poetry. Lawrence never writes about 'the process of nature . . . for its own sake'. The present out of which the poem is written is always governed by a particular feeling or complex of feelings. Sometimes, as in 'Figs', some of these feelings may be ugly. But it is inconsistent to praise the poems for preserving the gestures of their composition, and then in specific instances to object to those gestures.

The problem is that to examine 'Figs' as a discrete poem, and compare it with another discrete poem, 'Pomegranate', is inappropriate to Lawrence's method. It is to consider 'Figs' as something whole, complete, final and would-be perfect: in other words to consider it according to, essentially, New Critical criteria. The presence of such criteria is evident in Gilbert's assertion that Lawrence's 'real subject' is 'the fig as it is in nature' rather than the 'puritanical, human horror'. What happens is that the subject shifts within the poem. To assert that the first subject is real and the second imposed is a strategy for translating an ideological objection into formalist terms.

The 'complete' poem is so by virtue of being closed to any possible objection the reader might make against it. Its implied author (or 'subject' in another sense) is completely in command of the relevant experience. This is the ideal poem of much twentieth-century criticism. In Lawrence's terms, it is the poetry of the past or the future. But if we step outside the charmed circle of literary criticism, it is evident that no such command of experience is possible. Lawrence's offence, in a poem such as 'Figs', is that the command is so blatantly absent. The second half of the poem is repetitive, assertive and linguistically thin. The mood has changed utterly from the amusing, slyly sexy opening. However, it is clearly not legitimate to condemn Lawrence for having these feelings: nor, if we take his poetics seriously, for expressing them so nakedly. What is objectionable is the arrogant complacency of embodying these feelings in a 'poem', with all the authority that has been invested in that word. 'Figs' so evidently fails to be a poem in this sense that the reader feels insulted.

All this is the consequence of reading 'Figs' in the traditional way. And, as long as it is read as a discrete poem, this will be the consequence. But it is not a discrete poem. Sandra Gilbert points out the contradiction of 'Figs' in 'Pomegranate': 'I prefer my heart to be broken. / It is so lovely, dawn-kaleidoscopic, within the crack.'[8] Her conclusion is that 'Pomegranate' is a good poem, and 'Figs' a bad one. But what we actually have here is a practical demonstration of Lawrence's poetic. 'Pomegranate',

'Peach', 'Figs', 'Medlars and Sorb-Apples' and 'Grapes' follow each other in sequence, the first five poems in the volume. With varying emphases and considerable contrasts of feeling these poems circle around a number of related themes: the body, sexuality, corruption, secrecy and 'candid revelation'. They are open to each other, though they do not subvert Lawrence's poetic by forming a 'poetic whole' together; one poem is not supplanted by another, and there is no teleological development. Rather, Lawrence's own metaphors apply: 'The strands are all flying, quivering, intermingling into the web, the waters are shaking the moon. There is no round, consummate moon on the face of running water, nor on the face of the unfinished tide. There are no gems of the living plasm.'[9] The strident anti-feminist sentiments in 'Figs' are flying strands, as are the lines from 'Pomegranate' or these from 'Peach':

> Why the ripple down the sphere?
> Why the suggestion of incision?
>
>   *(CP*, p. 279)

Birds, Beasts and Flowers consists, substantially, of a series of 'sequences' such as this one: the 'Trees' 'Flowers', 'Evangelic Beasts', 'Creatures' and 'Reptiles' sections each consist mainly of a group of poems that form a thematic 'web'. Only the last three sections, 'Birds', 'Animals' and 'Ghosts' are collections of largely unrelated individual poems, though odd unrelated poems occur in the other sections as well—for example, the celebrated 'Snake' is tucked in with the sequence of tortoise poems, the most unified group in the volume. If, as I have said above, the act of composition is partly the theme of these sequences, but they are not self-reflexive in the post-modernist sense, it does not follow that they need to be completed by some kind of biographical reference to the circumstances in which they were written. This is how *Birds, Beasts and Flowers* (and *Pansies*) differ from *Look! We Have Come Through!* This collection is presented as a sequence; Lawrence prints a ponderous Foreword and Argument to instruct us to read the poems in this way.[10] But, despite, the quasi-narrative biographical foundation, the connections are not made in the poems themselves. There is no 'web' of discourse in which the flyings 'strands' of the poems meet. This is, perhaps, reflected in the notorious fact that despite their subsequent classification as 'Unrhyming Poems', most of them are in rhyme and metre, and so make gestures towards the 'static perfection' that Lawrence associates with these devices. Even the famous 'Song of a Man who has Come Through', one of the most successful poems in the volume, which is in free verse, claims in its idiom and its title a finality that few of the later poems claim. The more naked, often courageously confessional poems, such as 'First Morning', 'Mutilation' and 'Humiliation' are remarkable in their way, but they connect up through Lawrence's biography, not through the poetics of the sequence.

The two essays that Lawrence wrote to introduce the two editions of *Pansies* in 1929 are more self-deprecating than the introduction to *New Poems*, but they offer similar guidance to the reader:

It suits the modern temper better to have its state of mind made up of apparently irrelevant thoughts that scurry in different directions yet belong to the same nest: each thought trotting down the page like an independent creature, each with its own small head and tail, trotting its own little way, then curling up to sleep. We prefer it, at least the young seem to prefer it to those solid blocks of mental pabulum packed like bales in the pages of a proper heavy book. Even we prefer it to those slightly didactic opinions and slices of wisdom which are laid horizontally across the pages of Pascal's *Pensées* or La Bruyère's *Caractères*, separated only by *pattes de mouches*, like faint sprigs of parsley.[11]

The delightfully apt and satirical touch of the *pattes de mouches* alerts us to the great importance of presentation, and comes to mind when I consider the comparison of at least one extreme of the *Pansies* with Imagist poetry. David Ellis has recently published a good essay contributing to the rescue of *Pansies* from the contemptuous or at best apologetic manner in which they are commonly treated—and makes, though he does not develop, an important point about sequences within the volume—but seems to me to betray prejudice when, in discussing 'Sea-Weed', he refers to 'the mistaken belief that [Lawrence] was an Imagist'.[12] Here is the poem in question.

> Sea-weed sways and sways and swirls
> as if swaying were its form of stillness;
> and if it flushes against fierce rock
> it slips over it as shadows do, without hurting itself.
>   (*CP*, p. 467)

And here is an extract from a representative early poem by H.D., one of the ones on which Lawrence based his high opinion of her.

> They say you are twisted by the sea,
> you are cut apart
> by wave-break upon wave-break,
> that you are misshapen by the sharp rocks,
> broken by the rasp and after-rasp.[13]

There are evident differences, which it is tempting to call differences of temperament. Lawrence's longer line suggests a more relaxed voice, and in 'without hurting itself' he permits himself a looser, more colloquial diction. And yet the similarities, against the general background of the kinds of poetry being written in the second and third decades of the twentieth century, are very striking. Would either of them be very obviously out of place in a volume that included the other? Among the reasons why we might think so is the difference in the ways we have become conventionally accustomed to read H.D.'s *Sea-Garden* and Lawrence's *Pansies*. I don't know whether H.D.'s poems have ever been printed with *pattes de mouches*, but it would be no surprise to find that they had. They have accrued an aura of preciosity. Yet there is nothing precious about 'Sea-Rose', even if it is a little more self-consciously poised and considered than Lawrence's poem. Reading it with the more brisk attention that we give to *Pansies* might bring out an energy that is stifled by the *pattes de mouches*—actual or meta-

phorical—that surround it. Lawrence's admiration of H.D. was real and based on a sense of affinity if not indebtedness that is still evident more than ten years after he broke his friendship with her.

However, even if we were to read *Sea-Garden* in the way we read (or should read) *Pansies*, we should undoubtedly miss one of the characteristics that David Ellis rightly considers 'a crucial feature' of Lawrence's volume: variety.[14] With or without *pattes de mouches*, the reader of *Sea-Garden* is bound to feel that a particular way of writing is being privileged, even if the moment of the individual poem is not. Ellis has demonstrated the variety of the kinds of poem that might be defined as 'pansies', drawing on poems from *More Pansies, Last Poems* and even *Birds, Beasts and Flowers*. I want to show that the experience of this variety, of contrasting but related themes and modes, is built into the structure of the volume, at least its first two thirds: the later part of the book is more monotonous, consisting predominantly of the kind of didactic poems often wrongly thought to be typical of the book as a whole. My argument is not that Lawrence's poems cannot be criticised, but that criticism should attend to the sequence, not just to the isolated poem.

Pansies is, as much as *Birds, Beasts and Flowers,* a structured volume—more systematically so than Ellis implies—though its structure is not signalled like that of the earlier book. Most of it consists of a series of mini-sequences of poems 'clustered together in coherent groups',[15] as Sandra Gilbert says. Gilbert itemises several of these groups, but I prefer not to do so formally because I think this would misrepresent their character. They are like pulses, or series of pulses, of thought, feeling, and sometimes form, that often merge into each other, so that while all readers would recognise their existence, they might place the divisions differently. 'Sea-Weed', for example, belongs to a small sequence of short poems about the natural world. It is immediately preceded by two other 'imagistic' poems, 'Spray' and 'New Moon', though neither of these has the H.D.-like intensity of 'Sea-Weed', and 'New Moon' is, unfortunately, more reminiscent of T. E. Hulme. More interesting is the relation of 'Sea-Weed' to the other four poems of the group, which, though equally short, are not predominantly imagistic. For example, 'Little Fish':

> The tiny fish enjoy themselves
> in the sea.
> Quick little splinters of life,
> their little lives are fun to them
> in the sea.
>   (*CP*, p. 466)

This is as slight, or slight-seeming, as *Pansies* gets. The language of four of its five lines is almost provocatively casual and childish—perhaps the language in which adults address(ed) children rather than that of children themselves. One might go so far as to suggest that it is an early twentieth-century equivalent of a 'Song of Innocence', in which this kind of language functions as the language of conventional children's poetry functioned for

Blake. At the same time, the poem is hinged on a middle line that *is* imagistic, or (perhaps the same thing) comes from a particularly attentive and imaginative adult addressing a child. It is the quality of this line that justifies foregrounding the style of the other lines as I have done: it would be naive to call it the only poetic line in the poem, but perhaps it makes the others poetic. This poem's thematic relation to 'Sea-Weed' is obvious, but what is interesting is the stylistic relationship. The Imagist poem encapsulates what Hopkins might have called the instress of the sea-weed through a (for Lawrence) unusually intense sound patterning and something between a Yeatsian resolved paradox and a Blakean clash of contraries, of violence and stillness. This piling up of poets' names is deliberate. 'Little Fish' looks at the self-delight of the creatures in a language that is almost innocent of poetic precedent, as if its sub-text were that this is, or ought to be, all that need be said, it ought to be as simple as this. But it doesn't, of course, supplant the other poem; the support of the context is needed to be able to read it like this. 'Fun', for example, is a word commonly associated with cocktails, jazz and triviality, in Lawrence. Here it is redeemed by the proximity of 'Sea-Weed', and perhaps even even more by the immediately preceding poem, 'The Gazelle Calf':

> The gazelle calf, O my children,
> goes behind its mother across the desert,
> goes behind its mother on blithe bare foot
> requiring no shoes, O my children!
>
> > (*CP,* p. 466)

(This obviously also influences my reading of a very different way of addressing children in 'Little Fish'.)

Two poems after 'Little Fish', we have Lawrence in more didactic mood, in 'Self-Pity':

> I never saw a wild thing
> sorry for itself.
> A small bird will drop frozen dead from a bough
> without ever having felt sorry for itself.
>
> > (*CP,* p. 467)

This works on its own as something between a proverb and a short homily, but it works better for picking up the 'blithe bare foot' of the gazelle calf, the 'fun' of the fish and the stillness-in-motion of the sea-weed. Finally, 'The Mosquito Knows—is the most aphoristic of the group:

> The mosquito knows full well, small as he is
> he's a beast of prey.
> But after all
> he only takes his bellyful,
> he doesn't put my blood in the bank.
>
> > (*CP,* p. 466)

This also works perfectly well on its own but, like all the poems, it interacts with the sequence. This gives us, within a broad thematic consistency, a sharp and rapid alteration of mode—imagism, satire, homily, innocent-eye, mock-oratory—corresponding to shifts of focus within the thematic field.

Most importantly, this thematic field does not produce a tight sequence isolated from the rest of the volume. 'Self-Pity' encapsulates the message of the series of longer homilies, a few pages earlier, about 'fighting'; and 'The Mosquito Knows—' obviously relates to the sequence of poems about money. A reader might with some justice point out that I have made this little sequence artificially tight, and point out that 'The Gazelle Calf' is preceded by 'Sex and Trust':

> If you want to have sex, you've got to trust
> at the core of your heart, the other creature.
> The other creature, the other creature
> not merely the personal upstart;
> but the creature there, that has come to meet you
> trust it you must, you must
> or the experience amounts to nothing,
> mere evacuation-lust.
>
> > (*CP,* p. 466)

This is probably more typical of *Pansies* than any of the other poems I have quoted, all of which could hold their own in an anthology (in the case of 'Little Fish', perhaps a children's anthology). 'Sex and Trust' is decidedly not anthologisable. The repeated words 'trust' and 'creature' insist on a significance that the poem does not supply. Even more obviously than 'Figs' it is, considered as a discrete poem, unsuccessful. But the various evocations of creature-liness in the following poems *do* supply a context of significance for that word, while the blitheness, self-delight, sufficiency, lack of self-pity, and stillness of the various creatures supply a penumbra of connotations for 'trust'. At the same time 'Sex and Trust' provides a framework of human meaning for the nature-poems, both by itself and by linking this sequence with the one that precedes it, which includes 'The Risen Lord', 'Beware, O My Dear Young Men—' and 'Sex Isn't Sin—'. These are all longer didactic poems, Lawrence's most notorious kind: these poems particularly gain from being read not as complacently self-sufficient monuments but as strands 'flying' to connect with other very different poems in a web that is itself not complete.

It would be inconsistent with the way of reading *Pansies* I am describing to suggest that there is a pattern or a central controlling idea. There are, however, repeated expressions of a particular feeling that I want to privilege here because it has an important bearing on so much else in the book, and so much else in Lawrence. This is the feeling expressed in what I imagine all readers would agree to be the beautiful short poem, 'Desire is Dead':

> Desire may be dead
> and still a man can be
> a meeting place for sun and rain,
> wonder outwaiting pain
> as in a wintry tree.
>
> > (*CP,* p. 504)

This poem needs no context or sequence. It is not 'poetry of the present': it returns upon itself and completes itself with the best of them.[16] But many poems of various kinds, and on various ostensible themes, are touched by this exquisite expression of acceptance—meet momentarily at this still point. 'Self-Pity' takes on a different shade of meaning, the poems about old age assume a more personal note, the didactic poems about sex in the head seem less like obsessional ranting, the references to the phallus seem more impersonal, and any accusation of wish-fulfilment in them has to test itself against this and other confessions of the death of desire. In the larger and troubled arena of Lawrence and sexuality, this group of poems, and their pervasive echoes throughout *Pansies,* may contribute to an argument that Lawrence explores a large range of sexual perspectives, among which his fantasies about virility and male dominance are not definitive.

The history of modernism has always found Lawrence an awkward figure to deal with. His poems look out of place in a movement defined by the work of Eliot and Pound, just as his novels look out of place in a movement defined by the work of Joyce, Woolf and Faulkner. So he looks increasingly marginal and, as a poet, amateurish. But any concept of modernism worthy of the name has to embrace all the innovative work that was being done during the relevant period. To call Lawrence a modernist is not to measure his work by standards derived from other writers, but to assert that it is part of the defining body of modernist texts. At least as early as 1916, when he was working on the main draft of *Women in Love,* he was incorporating Imagist techniques into the novel,[17] and he consistently praised the work of H.D.,[18] with which, as I have briefly shown, certain of his poems have affinities, not only during the period of their friendship but many years later. Most importantly, for the purpose of this chapter, Lawrence made a significant and, though not unnoticed, as yet critically unassimilated contribution to the most distinctive genre of modern poetry: the long poem/sequence. That this may have come about almost by accident, a by-product of Lawrence's habits of writing and even (in the case of *Pansies*) state of health, with only the most casual theoretical foundation, does not detract from its importance.

I have tried to show that *Birds, Beasts and Flowers* and *Pansies* are more similar than they are usually considered to be: that the appreciation of a few 'perfected' poems in the one, and the dismissal of the other for its comparative lack of such poems, alike miss the point. Both volumes are open and informal sequences, with numerous interconnections of 'strands', in which poems in a large variety of modes, often individually incomplete, representing various thoughts, moods and feelings, form a 'web' whose pattern, always provisional, will be different for every reader, and every reading. As such they are eminently *scriptible* texts, but with their predominantly conversational tone, their concern with the present moment of experience, the absence of provocatively deliberate fragmentation, they are also, in the older but I hope not entirely discredited sense, eminently readable. They should be read whole, and more rapidly than one normally reads a volume of poetry. Only when a number of readers have reported on the results of such readings will a proper debate on their importance be possible.

Notes

[1] D. H. Lawrence, 'Poetry of the Present', in V. de Sola Pinto and W. Roberts (eds), *The Complete Poems of D. H. Lawrence,* vol. 1 (London: Heinemann, 1964) p. 182; hereafter referred to as *CP* with page numbers given in the text.

[2] E. Pound, 'A Retrospect', in T. S. Eliot (ed.), *Literary Essays of Ezra Pound* (London: Faber, 1954) p. 4.

[3] D. H. Lawrence, 'Poetry of the Present', *Complete Poems,* p. 186.

[4] T. Marshall, *The Psychic Mariner, A Reading of the Poems of D. H. Lawrence* (London: Heinemann, 1970) p. 5. See also, D. Ellis, 'The Place of "Pansies" in Lawrence's Poetry', in D. Ellis and H. Mills, *D. H. Lawrence's Non-fiction* (Cambridge: Cambridge University Press, 1988) p. 147. Ellis refers to the greater use of free verse in *Birds, Beasts and Flowers.*

[5] S. Gilbert, *Acts of Attention, The Poems of D. H. Lawrence* (New York: Cornell University Press, 1972) p. 141.

[6] Another pertinent example is when the 'He is dumb' of 'Lui et Elle', in the Tortoise sequence (*Complete Poems,* vol. 1, p. 362), is corrected by 'I thought he was dumb / I said he was dumb, / Yet I've heard him cry', in 'Tortoise Shout' (ibid., p. 363).

[7] S. Gilbert, op. cit., pp. 144-5.

[8] D. H. Lawrence, 'Pomegranate', *Complete Poems,* vol. 1, p. 279; cited by Gilbert, op. cit., p. 144.

[9] D. H. Lawrence, 'Poetry of the Present', *Complete Poems,* vol. 1, p. 182.

[10] D. H. Lawrence, *Complete Poems,* vol. 1, p. 191.

[11] D. H. Lawrence, 'Introduction to *Pansies*', *Complete Poems,* vol. 1, p. 417.

[12] D. Ellis, op. cit., p. 159.

[13] H.D., 'Sea Gods', in *Collected Poems 1912-1944,* ed. L. L. Martz (Manchester: Carcanet, 1984) pp. 29-30.

[14] D. Ellis, op. cit., p. 164.

[15] S. Gilbert, op. cit., p. 256.

[16] There are numerous poems in *Pansies* (though not as high a proportion as in *Look! We Have Come Through!*) in rhyme and metre. However, most of these—such as 'Red Herring' and 'The Little Wowser'—are in a rough metre deriving from street-ballads that Lawrence uses, mainly, to find a voice for the working-class environment in which he grew up. They evoke a completely different

tradition, popular, oral and improvisatory, from that conjured by the beautiful cadences of 'Desire is Dead'. Such poems neither achieve nor aspire to the 'perfected' state; their rhyme and metre are as open and 'present' as free verse.

[17] I have discussed the importance of Imagism for Lawrence's development as a novelist in a paper, 'Lawrence and Imagism', to be published in W. Pratt and R. Richardson (eds), *Homage to Imagism* (New York: AMS Press) forthcoming.

[18] See letters to A. W. Macleod and Edward Marsh, in *The Letters of D. H. Lawrence,* vol. 3 (Cambridge: Cambridge University Press, 1984) pp. 61, and 84.

Bernard Duffey

[*In the following essay, Duffey traces the development of Pound's Imagist aesthetics through an examination of his early critical writings.*]

SOURCE: "Ezra Pound and the Attainment of Imagism," in *Toward a New American Literary History: Essays in Honor of Arlin Turner,* edited by Louis J. Budd, Edwin H. Cady, and Carl L. Anderson, Duke University Press, 1980, pp. 181-94.

There is evidence that when Ezra Pound arrived in London in the fall of 1908 he was ready to inaugurate a poetic career. During the three months or so in Venice which had intervened between his discharge from the faculty of Wabash College and his appearance in the English capital, he had employed a Venetian printer to put together the seventy-two-page volume, *A Lume Spento* (he translated the phrase, "With Torches Quenched"), which would be his first book of poems. He promptly dispatched some forty copies to his father in Philadelphia with instructions to begin a campaign toward securing American publication for the book. "The American reprint," he urged, "has got to be worked by kicking up such a hell of a row with genuine and faked reviews that Scribner or somebody can be brought to see the sense of making a reprint. I shall write a few myself and get someone to sign 'em."[1] A copy of *A Lume Spento* had gone to William Carlos Williams for his reaction, and Pound's friend seems to have felt the work to be dangerously idiosyncratic. Pound had replied, "But, mon cher, would a collection of mild, pretty verses convince any publisher or critic that *I* happen to be a genius and deserve audience?"[2] And he proceeded to outline his idea of his work.

> To me, the short so-called dramatic lyric—at any rate the sort of thing I do—is the poetic part of a drama the rest of which (to me the prose part) is left to the reader's imagination or set in a short note. I catch the character I happen to be interested in at the moment he interests me, usually a moment of song, self-awareness, or sudden understanding or revelation. And the rest of the play would bore

me and presumably the reader. I paint my man as I *conceive* him. Et Voila tout! (pp. 3-4)

The letter contained one other emphasis. "Then again you must remember I don't try to write for the public. I can't. I haven't that kind of intelligence" (p. 6). Such a letter leaves little doubt that, despite his Browningesque inclination toward dramatic monologue, Pound had set out to be an independent, self-defining poet from the beginning.

The letter also suggested that at least some part of *A Lume Spento* had been written during his months at Wabash where the flamboyance of his personality had roused a distrust capped by his befriending a stranded actress, and so had resulted in his dismissal. "If anybody stuck *you* in Indiana for four months," he said to Williams, "and you didn't at least *write* some unconstrained something or other, I'd give up hope for your salvation" (p. 5). Beyond such generalized rebelliousness, however, Pound's letter had begun to outline a specific sense of his writing, one I will be arguing here that culminated in the definitions of Imagism he arrived at in 1913 and, in doing so, formulated in short compass a highly complex sense of his own poetic ends and means.

Pound himself would often speak slightingly of Imagism in later years, and some of his critics, notably Hugh Kenner in *The Pound Era,*[3] have been inclined to dismiss the matter as essentially a side issue in the story of his evolution. Kenner himself proposed a centering of Pound's poetic impulses in his association with the Vorticist activity of 1914-1915. Donald Davie, arguing in a related direction, also characterized Pound's involvement with Imagism as "spectacular, brief, and tangential."[4] It seems, however, that Pound's own disavowals may have been more forcibly affected by his anger at the misuse he felt Amy Lowell and others had made of his program than by any basic alteration in his own thinking, and that perpetuation of them is misleading. Toward supporting this conclusion, my present purpose will be to read Pound's early critical writing in some detail and to urge that Imagist ideas were present from its beginning. During its course they ramified toward an overall view of the nature and value of poetry, and at a certain moment, they were put together to make a clear, consistent, and durable formulation of Pound's most basic poetic commitment.

That formulation appeared in the famous "manifesto" in *Poetry* magazine[5] consisting of a short letter Pound had largely prepared for his friend F. S. Flint to sign urging "direct treatment of the 'thing,' whether subjective or objective" along with the exclusion of any language "that did not contribute to the presentation," and rhythmical composition "in sequence of the musical phrase, not in sequence of a metronome." To these stipulations, Pound, in his own name, added a longer list of recommendations headed off by his definition of an image as " . . . that which presents an intellectual and emotional complex in an instant of time." He referred his meaning of "complex" to the "newer psychologists such as Hart," and, after this rather casual gloss, went on to more particular definition giving the image independent and sufficient existence in its own right: "It is the presentation of such a 'complex' instantaneously which gives that sense of sudden liberation; that sense of freedom from time limits and space limits; that sense of sudden growth, which we experience in the presence of the greatest works of art" (p. 205).

To come back to beginnings, the London of 1908 in which Pound arrived was itself showing some signs of readiness for a degree of poetic innovation, or even of program. The general literary scene had been subject to larger or smaller shock waves as early as the advent of Rossetti and Swinburne in poetry, Hardy in fiction, and Shaw in the drama. In an editorial in his *Poetry Review* of 1912 Harold Monro continued the story by noting that, after Swinburne in poetry, came the generation of the nineties, "John Davidson, Francis Thompson, W. E. Henley, W. B. Yeats, William Watson, Lionel Johnson, and Ernest Dowson."[6] But, his judgment ran, "Our impression of the period is one of a poetry stunned by fact" (p. 248). The root cause of such paralysis he located in a radically new element in English awareness. "In 1871 *The Descent of Man* was published, and henceforward the Victorian manner of thought, the honest doubt, and mild groping toward infinity, became, in the face of new revelation, harmlessly ridiculous" (p. 247). Finally, such dispersal of established convention, followed by the failure of the fin de siècle to establish a new mode, meant that "poetry entered virginal upon the twentieth century, and the poets of today find themselves suddenly emerging from a transition period, a strange world about them, a broken tradition behind, and a new one in the future to create" (p. 248).

There were other signs of enlarging awareness besides Monro's. "The revolution of the word began, so far as it affected the men who were of my age in London in 1908, with the LONE whimper of Ford Madox Hueffer,"[7] Pound always insisted, and Hueffer's moral was that poetry must be at least as well written as prose. It is true that the *English Review* which Hueffer (later, Ford Madox Ford) was to begin editing in 1908 would briefly become a center for vitality and discipline in English writing, but also T. E. Hulme would assemble the Poets' Club in 1908 which met for a year or two to hear Hulme call attention, among other things, to what he called "the image." Hulme had been commenting on William James, Henri Bergson, and Remy de Gourmont in the *New Age* as early as 1909 and following with particular interest the revolt they bespoke against any rationalistic domination of thought. His concept of the image was especially linked with Bergson's argument for the reality of time as "duration," and for "intuition" as the faculty by which such reality could be apprehended. The connection would be made explicit, and public, by 1911 as in that year Hulme commented in print on a book of poetic theory by Tancrède de Visan, a follower of Mallarmé, applying Bergsonian thought to symbolism: "Life is a continuous and unanalysable curve which cannot be seized clearly. It can only be got at by a kind of central vision as opposed to analytic description. This central vision expresses itself by means of symbols. M. Visan would then define Symbolism as an attempt by means of successive and accumulated images to express and exteriorize such a central lyric intuition."[8] In still another quarter, and in the literary column he called "Books and Persons" and signed as "Jacob Tonson," Arnold Bennett opined in 1908 that Robert Bridges and W. B. Yeats were the two best among contemporary poets,[9] and in the words of Osbert Burdett both were noted for their innovation, Bridges in "metrics" and Yeats as a "Symbolist."[10]

The idea of poetic "symbolism" added a real but somewhat unaccountable seasoning to the English poetic air. In opening his own "Recent Verse" column in the *New Age* in 1908, F. S. Flint began with an epigraph from Mallarmé. "In truth, there is no prose; there is the alphabet, and there are verses more or less compact, more or less diffuse." Flint went on to pose his own avant-garde standards by citing Poe's charge against the reality of the long poem and urging that conventional poetic form did "not sustain anyone who is not a genius." He concluded that "a poet should listen to the instinctual rhythm within him."[11] Flint was to reiterate his sense of needed innovation as his column proceeded on through the two years-odd of its duration to argue that "the only common relationship of the new writers is to the anarchy of their times, out of which they have sprung and which they reflect" (p. 449), and that the pressing need of English poetry was for "a revaluation of all poetical values."[12] In February of 1909 he gave condescending notice to "a little plaquette of verse by members of the Poets' Club" (p. 327). The following week he was chided by T. E. Hulme for his judgment, but he was also invited to inspect the club at first hand and to join it if he wished. This Flint proceeded to do, entering the group at about the same time that Pound was to be drawn into it.

Pound's earliest critical writing was not immediately affected by such lines of thought, however. It was, instead, to begin drawing together a complex innovative position of its own. He had given a set of lectures at the Regent Street Polytechnic in London on "The Development of Literature in Southern Europe," and, following the same path toward quick publication blazed by his poetry, he had this material in book form in the summer of 1910 as *The Spirit of Romance,* published by Dent. His task as lecturer had been largely expository and descriptive, a tracing of poetic expression in the languages of Provence, Tuscany, northern France, Spain, and Portugal, with a chapter on medieval Latin lyric, the general subject in which he had specialized both as undergraduate and graduate student. Through this process, however, his account also kept a critical argument in view which, concluding his chapter on Villon, he applied in summary to the main line of the verse he had been describing, one he rooted in the pervasive "realism" of romance expression. "Dante's vision is real, because he saw it. Villon's verse is real, because he lived it; as Bertran de Born, as Arnaut Marvoil, as that mad poseur Vidal, he lived it. For these men life is in the press. No brew of books, no distillation of sources will match the tang of them."[13] Such argument in fact drew on two shaping ideas: those of the "Romance" tradition as a path leading to the discovery of literary vigor and a notion of literary vigor, in turn, made dependent on the act of intensely felt and recorded life.

Such thinking was to be a controlling power throughout the book. In an opening comment on Ovid, Pound noted that the *Metamorphoses* "has the clarity of French scientific prose" (p. 15). Ovid's art, "before Browning, raises the dead and dissects their mental processes" (p. 16). His chapter on Arnaut Daniel praised the troubadour who had been honored by Dante as a poet "not content with conventional phrase, or with words which do not convey his exact meaning," (p. 25) and one, consequently, whom Dante had esteemed for "maestria" (p. 133). Following his subject into its Tuscan flowering in Guido Cavalcanti and Dante himself, Pound noted a change from Provençal origins. "The cult of Provence had been a cult of the emotions; and with it there had been some, hardly conscious, study of emotional psychology. In Tuscany the cult is a cult of the harmonies of the mind." But it was still the qualities of directness and presence which had prevailed; ". . . this virtue it ever has, it is not rhetorical, it aims to be what it is, and never pretends to be something it is not" (p. 116).

Pound's long chapter on Dante clung persistently to the same critical theme. He characterized the *Commedia* as "the journey of Dante's intelligence through the states of mind wherein dwell all sorts and conditions of men before death," and the Italian's journey became a symbol of "mankind's struggle upward out of ignorance into the clear light of philosophy" (p. 127). Likening the famous fourfold range of Dante's meaning to the complexity of a mathematical synthesis of particulars into a single logical unity, Pound used an extended comparison he was later to salvage and repeat in his "Vorticism" essay of 1914, but he also went on to more particular specification. Beauty in Dante was like that of Whistler's painting, less the source of immediate impact on the reader than of a power by which, after absorbing it, "one finds new beauty in natural things" and so is admitted "to a deeper knowledge, to a finer perception of beauty" (p. 154). Like Wordsworth, Dante had feeling for nature, but "he describes the actual sensation with more intensity," and Dante stood in sharp contrast to Whitman's "catalogues and flounderings" (p. 155). In language, Shakespeare was "more beautifully suggestive," Dante "more beautifully definite" (p. 158). Like Arnaut Daniel's, Dante's "vividness" depended greatly on comparison to a "particular phenomenon." Underlying all was "the great sub-surge of his truth and his sincerity" (p. 163).

The Spirit of Romance could be surveyed at greater length, but its insistence on vivid and sharply felt experience and expression would only repeat itself the further. Villon, thus, was a poet who "never lies to himself; he does not know much, but what he knows he knows; man is an animal, certain things he can feel" (p. 169). The simplicity and realism of the Spanish *Poema del Cid* was

superior to the more ornate and conventional *Song of Roland*. Even the philosophy of Richard of St. Victor attained a state of poetry; "not because of its floridity, but because of its intensity" (p. 116). Finally, Pound concluded, poetry by its vividness might well be more closely related to "the best of music, of painting, and of sculpture, than to any part of literature which is not true poetry." Matthew Arnold's standard for poetry as a "criticism of life" was blasphemy against both poetry and life itself. "Poetry," to the contrary, "is about as much a criticism of life as a red-hot iron is a criticism of fire" (p. 122).

The Spirit of Romance was a study in literary history rather than a program for poetic composition, but it clearly gathered itself around a sense of the responsibility primary for composition. Its repeated insistence on directness and intensity was a plainly delineated move, this early, toward establishing what would become the first principle of Imagism.

Pound's critical and theoretical writing burgeoned in the years between 1910 and 1913. He contributed a growing number of short pieces to the literary press and in addition published three more substantial items following *The Spirit of Romance*. In 1911 he made his own debut in the *New Age*, the vigorously independent socialist weekly whose purchase by A. R. Orage in 1907 had created the review of "politics, literature and the arts" where Hulme and Flint, along with other innovating notables on the London scene, had already appeared. In a series of articles called "I Gather the Limbs of Osiris" and published between November, 1911, and February, 1912, Pound returned to poetry of the past, particularly to Arnaut Daniel this time, but now to fashion a more explicitly stated critical position out of it.[14] Also in 1912 he printed in *The Quest* magazine of London an essay to be called "Psychology and the Troubadours" which in 1932 and afterwards, appeared as a new fifth chapter in *The Spirit of Romance*. Late in the year a second series of essays, "Patria Mia," also appeared in the *New Age*.

Since 1908, he had brought out five small volumes of verse.[15] Much writing had in fact been carried forward from one book to the next, and the whole was strongly marked by Pound's sense of the literary past. It may well have seemed that his poetry was growing repetitious of the note he had first struck in *A Lume Spento*. As sympathetic a reviewer of *Exultations* in 1909 as F. S. Flint could complain that "if Mr. Pound could only forget his literature he would exult to more purpose."[16] *Canzoni* drew even sharper criticism in 1911 and, particularly, a pointed personal objection from Ford Madox Hueffer against its sometimes elaborate archaism.[17]

The "Osiris" essays, however, did not wholly preempt new ground. Much of their content, like that of *The Spirit of Romance*, was given over to translating and commenting on older poetry, but in the process a number of critical points emerged. Chief among these was the need Pound now expressed for revision of current poetry in a twofold direction. On the one hand lay the familiar argument, " . . . we must have a simplicity and directness of utterance." But this position was now expanded to advocate an utterance which also "is different from the simplicity and directness of daily speech, which is more 'curial,' more dignified." There were few fallacies, Pound thought, "more common than the opinion that poetry should mimic daily speech."[18] He was to provide a friendly review of Hueffer's volume of verse, *High Germany,* in the *Poetry Review,* but in it he also took exception. "Mr. Hueffer is so obsessed with the idea that the language of poetry should not be a dead language, that he forgets it must be the speech of to-day dignified, more intense, more dynamic, than to-day's speech as spoken."[19]

The argument of the "Osiris" series dwelt further on points that suggested how a poetically "curial" speech might best be sought. In treating Daniel's work, as in his consideration of the Anglo-Saxon "Seafarer" which opened the series, Pound announced that he was seeking "a new method in scholarship," an emphasis on the "luminous detail in history," one that generated "a sudden insight into circumjacent conditions, into their causes, their effects, into sequence, and law," and the essay was not long in converting such "luminous detail" from a historical to a poetic context. In addition to the historian, Pound argued, "the artist seeks out the luminous detail and presents it. He does not comment. . . . As scholarship has erred in presenting all detail as of equal import, so also in literature, in a present school of writing, we see a similar tendency" (p. 130). The sense of reality he sought was not that of orthodox realism. Just as the language of mere daily life diminished the force of poetry, so a literature that aspired only to the experience of daily life would find its force spent, its "curial" resonance and suggestion occluded.

As the decade proceeded, this concept would turn out to have large consequences for Pound's sense of poetry. The idea of the "luminous detail" is clearly a first effort at defining what he would later call the "image," as it indeed called for an "intellectual and emotional complex" and one implying freedom "from time limits and space limits; that sense of sudden growth, which we experience in the greatest works of art." And one need not press the concept too hard to see in it also a beginning of the very sense of history that would be emerging in *The Cantos* by the decade's end as an aestheticizing of Pound's loyalties and antagonisms into moments intensely if not always clearly suggestive of special meaning, an argument that would seek to alter history by Imagist methods from the recording and interpreting of fact to make of it something more like high drama, one suddenly revealing the nature of the forces animating it. The process had found echo as far back as Pound's 1908 letter to Williams affirming the "moment of song, self-awareness, or sudden understanding or revelation" by which a dramatic character or, now, a dramatic situation, made itself resonant with implication.

The sense of image toward which Pound was moving was one, again, seeking "intellectual and emotional complex"

as its substance. Good writing was always what he called "efficient" writing. But this did not mean that good writing was sparse in meaning. Imagist "efficiency," rather, and in contrast to the flatness and "dailiness" of realism, sought "revelation" or luminous moment. This had been the drift of argument throughout the "Osiris" essays, and in their course it was developed into a number of other particulars.

Later in 1912, Pound's essay on "Psychology and the Troubadours" carried the argument to greater length. His subject was the familiar preoccupation with the langue d'oc and its poetry, but for the first time the question now drew him to the obsessive subject of troubadour poetry, that of chivalric love and its celebration. Such seeming conventionality was in fact now to reveal unsuspected thrusts toward the sense of "liberation" and "sudden growth" that Imagism also would seek.

Troubadour poetry, he held, shared with Greek myth a participation in what he proposed "as a sort of permanent basis in humanity,"[20] an act that in his summary would sound much like the direct and intuitive participation in the Bergsonian flux which Hulme had been advocating for poetry and one, further, that Hulme identified with the advent of symbolism. Hulme's interest in symbolism, however, appeared to be something rather different from the linguistic and transcendental emphasis of chief concern to Mallarmé and his circle. Hulme had been particularly taken with Visan's book applying Bergson to symbolist theory, and during the same month he reviewed that work he also supplied a second review to the *New Age* treating the later and still living French symbolist author, Remy de Gourmont. Delior, the work's author, particularly stressed the philosophic materialism implicit in Gourmont's thought, its emphasis on human life as a biological phenomenon existing wholly in its physical processes and one for which "ideas" or intimations of a mental or spiritual realm were never more than secondary manifestations of physical being. The emotions of love, in particular, were biological and, within those limits alone, psychological. Hulme, nevertheless, saw Gourmont as a spokesman also for symbolism, but such symbolism, now, was necessarily a phenomenon contained within the Bergsonian realm of duration as it was likewise wholly contained within a physical universe. In particular, said Hulme, Gourmont "sees life essentially, as the necessity to procreation, try to disguise it how we may, and art is one of the forms of the sexual instinct."[21]

Pound too sought a common ground for the mixture of physical and spiritual he identified in troubadour poetry, and, with a more traditional imagination than Hulme but with no less emphasis, he too drove toward a sense of physical ambience by resorting to an ancient doctrine he imputed to Greek myth and to troubadour poetry alike, that of the correspondence of microcosm and macrocosm. As microcosm, man contained in himself what Pound called both "sun" and "moon," the light both of the ordinary and the extraordinary. The saint or seer was one who in fact and in flesh experienced the sacred, a union of force between physical and spiritual poles. As one example, the monk "develops at infinite trouble and expense the secondary pole within himself" and so "produces his charged surface, which registers the beauties, celestial or otherwise, by contemplation." In a second case, that of the lover, "which I must say seems more in accord with 'mens sana in corpore sano,' the charged surface is produced between the predominant natural poles of two human mechanisms. Sex is, that is to say, of a double function and purpose, reproductive and educational."[22] To write imaginatively and out of the truth of awareness would be to apprehend the macrocosm by vivid apprehension of the microcosm. Intuitive seizure of the part could provide intuitive illumination of the whole. "We have about us the universe of fluid force, and below us the germinal universe of wood alive, of stone alive. Man is—the sensitive part of him—a mechanism, for the purpose of our further discussion a mechanism rather like an electric appliance, switches, wires, etc." (p. 92). Hulme had also emphasized Gourmont's claim that one should never hesitate "to introduce science into literature or literature into science,"[23] and Pound's description of man as "mechanism" here seemed more akin to Hulme's feeling for the living texture of "durée" than to any more rationalistic scheme. Wood was "alive," stone was "alive," and man's openness to such life was like that of a conductor of electrical impulse.[24]

If Hulme had found such "symbolist" poetry to be a potentially liberating and validating power in modern writing, its force thus was a supra-rationalistic but still wholly natural one, and Pound shared in that line of argument. The center of consciousness, he urged, lay in what "Greek psychologists" had called "the *phantistikon*," the image-making faculty. One kind of mind "is like soap-bubbles reflecting sundry patches of the macrocosmos," and such accidental and superficial reflection of reality was unimportant. With others, however, consciousness might be "germinal." "Their thoughts are in them as the thought of the tree is in the seed, or in the grass, or the grain, or the blossom. And these minds are the more poetic, and they affect mind about them, and transmute it as the seed the earth. And this latter sort of mind is close on the vital universe. . . ."[25]

Pound thus had arrived at an agreement with what may be called a natural symbolism and, in doing so, had defined the reality within which Imagist perceptions could claim substantive, intuitive worth. He shared ground with Hulme's feeling for Bergson and Gourmont. The Imagist aim in poetry would not be only for "efficiency," for "luminous detail" as such, it would also include mind's knowing such event as revelation *within* the flux of experience. "There is," Pound argued, "in what I have called 'the natural course of events' the exalted moment, the vision unsought or at least the vision gained without machination" (p. 97). Richard of St. Victor had suggested that "by naming over all the most beautiful things we know we may draw back upon our minds some vestige of the heavenly splendor" (p. 96). Dante had done something of the sort by preceding the movement of the *Divine Comedy* into the *Paradiso* with his six cantos of

vivid and moving description of the earthly paradise (p. 140). In Pound's view of the matter, to succeed in such effort was to make all there was of heavenly revelation available to the earthly eye. The goal of poetry must be the attainment of the most pointed, most illuminating revelation available to human sight.

If, in all this, "Psychology and the Troubadours" seemed to run beyond Imagist definitions, the link between them, that of hewing to a universe of vital meaning, may be suggested from a brief essay entitled, in odd spelling, "Prologomena," appearing in the February, 1912, *Poetry Review*. In its compass, Pound was once again seeking to justify his continued absorption in the past. To this end, he epitomized his argument in a four-point "credo" within the essay that in itself repeated four times over the "naturalness" of the virtue he sought for, its relation to living force, just as in his troubadour essay he had come down so strongly on the sensitivity of that poetry to the implications of its naturally supernatural world.

The "credo" first professed belief in "an absolute rhythm," one which corresponded "exactly to the emotion or shade of emotion to be expressed," an intimate union, that is, between poetic means and substance and so between form and implication. The second heading was that of "Symbols." Repeating here his feeling for a naturalness paralleling Dante's harmony of idea with precise natural fact, Pound announced, "I believe that the proper and perfect symbol is the natural object." If a secondary suggestion was present, it should appear "so that a sense, and the poetic quality of the passage, is not lost to those who do not understand the symbol as such, to whom for example a hawk is a hawk." Revelation lay more in particulars than in transcendental gesture. Technique, in turn, was "the test of a man's sincerity," without which any claim to revelation must be hollow, and the "trampling down of every convention that impedes or obscures the determination of the law, or the precise rendering of the impulse." Finally, "some poems may have form as a tree has form, some as water poured into a vase." Form might be symmetrical or not, but it must accurately apprehend and shape its subject.[26] The drift of the whole argument was summed up, finally, near the conclusion of the "Osiris" series itself, to which Pound referred in "Prologomena," and which was appearing during the same time in the *New Age*. "For it is not until poetry is 'close to the thing' that it will be a vital part of contemporary life. As long as the poet says not what he, at the very crux of clarified conception, means but is content to say something ornate and approximate, just so long will serious people, intently alive, consider poetry as balderdash."[27]

In September of 1912 Pound's "Patria Mia" series began appearing in the *New Age*. Its chief concern, of course, was the state of American writing, along with implications for American art in general. What appeared in it was considerably briefer and differently pointed from the content of the small book Pound would seek to make under the same title by conflating this material with a later set of *New Age* essays,[28] and the "Patria Mia" of the

New Age particularly emphasized the importance of freedom, culture, and discipline to American expression. Its concluding argument gathered up much of the force of the whole eleven articles as it moved toward establishing Whitman as representative of an American character in poetry possessed of great potential achievement. "It is, as nearly as I can define it, a certain generosity; a certain carelessness, or looseness, if you will; a hatred of the sordid, an ability to forget the part for the whole, a desire for largeness; a willingness to stand exposed."[29] In displaying such spirit, Pound argued, Whitman spoke for a certain venturesomeness and devotion to freedom, which were the most admirable and useful of American traits. "One may not need him at home," Pound cautioned, "but if one is abroad; if one is ever likely to forget one's birthright . . . one can find in Whitman the reassurance."

But the Poundian and Imagist drive for a parallel sort of freedom needed complement, one figured forth in this case by a second American, the painter Whistler. His message was essential. "It was, in substance, that being born an American is no excuse for being content with a parochial standard" (p. 36), a view that Pound would seek tirelessly to impose on Harriet Monroe's eclectic hospitality in *Poetry*. Whistler was the "martinet" of American art, especially, needed, and the Imagist manifesto in *Poetry* was in effect a redaction of his lesson for emerging American expression.

By the end of 1912, thus, I would argue, a broad ground had been prepared from which the Imagist prescriptions would take their character, and from which Pound could develop his argument of "The Serious Artist" later in 1913[30] that artists constituted "the antennae of the race." The value of direct and vivid expression had been described in a major current of poetry flowing from the late Latin to Villon. The force of that stream had been summed up in the doctrine of "the luminous detail." Such luminosity had been related to a combined physical and mythological doctrine of intuition which itself roughly agreed with aspects of both Bergson's and Gourmont's thinking as linked to the needs of contemporary expression by T. E. Hulme. The statement of the program itself was drawn up for and published in a new, hopeful American literary venture. In all this, Pound had prepared a prescription for authenticity in poetry related to past and present both, and one finding force and value where, he would hold, life revealed itself most tellingly.

The formalizing of Imagism in March of 1913 was a focussing of the whole development of Pound's thinking over a period of five years, one clearly the opposite of accidental or trivial in its relation to his concerns and one difficult to dislodge from a position at the center of his thought about his own art. The formulation had hardly been arrived at, however, before dissension from his program began to manifest itself. His anthology, *Des Imagistes,* appeared in 1914. Its publication had been more a lucky accident, however, than the result of dependable circumstances, and when Amy Lowell appealed to certain of Pound's associates to allow her to assume responsibility for continuing the anthology, and coupled her offer of support with freedom from Pound's stringent taskmastering, a number of them turned against what they now saw as an overbearing narrowness in his program. Pound's efforts in behalf of his cause had not flagged. He had assembled its first volume and had secured its publication. He had, furthermore, prepared a much larger statement of Imagist aims and ideas than could be fitted into *Poetry*'s limited space. In August of 1914, however, Pound and the original Imagist group had parted, and, he wrote Harriet Monroe, he was retitling the Imagist essay as "Vorticism."[31] It would appear the next month in the *Fortnightly Review.*

The event was Pound's first plain avowal of his abandonment of the Imagist cause. What "Vorticism" was to mean to him is too complex a subject to more than glance at here, but it was not easy to separate from the central Imagist principles he was to repeat in defining it. It is worth noting that his adoption of the new label would be announced in an essay still holding to his term *Imagisme* and still centered in the same emphases that had marked his earlier critical writing. At its end, he proposed a definition for what he now wanted to call a "vortex," but that definition itself began by identifying the old and new language. "The image is not an idea. It is a radiant node or cluster; it is what I can, must perforce, call a VORTEX, from which, and through which, and into which, ideas are continually rushing."[32]

The term Pound had originally coined had been seized upon by a group hostile to him, and it became necessary to find a new term. In the place of "Image," consequently, there would be "Vortex." There would be no change, however, in his concept of the poetic unit, a "primary pigment" that was still the rendering of an "intellectual and emotional complex in an instant of time." Most notably, Pound the Vorticist would now reach out for a better sense of his poetry's relation to other arts (a concern, however, that had been noted as early as 1910 in *The Spirit of Romance*) just as Imagism had been concerned with the relation of it to a literary complex. That new effort, an Imagism writ larger, would dominate the Vorticist program.

NOTES

[1] Quoted from Donald Gallup, *A Bibliography of Ezra Pound* (London, 1963), p. 21.

[2] *The Letters of Ezra Pound,* ed. D. D. Paige (New York, 1950), p. 4. Page references following in parentheses are to this volume.

[3] Berkeley and Los Angeles, 1971. See especially the chapter on "Imagism," pp. 173-192.

[4] *Ezra Pound, Poet as Sculptor* (New York, 1964), p. 36.

[5] F. S. Flint, "Imagisme," and Ezra Pound, "A Few Don'ts By An Imagiste," *Poetry,* I (March, 1913), 198-206. The page reference following in parentheses is to this volume.

[6] "The Nineties," *Poetry Review,* I (June, 1912), 247. Page references following in parentheses are to this volume.

[7] *Polite Essays* (Norfolk, Conn., [1939]), p. 50.

[8] "Book of the Week," *New Age,* IX (Aug. 24, 1911), 401.

[9] *New Age,* IV (Dec. 3, 1908), 112.

[10] "The Last Ten Years in English Literature," *New Age,* III (June 13, 1908), 136 and (July 4, 1908), 191.

[11] "Recent Verse," *New Age,* III (Aug. 15, 1908), 312. The page reference following in parentheses is to this volume.

[12] "Recent Verse," *New Age,* IV (Nov. 26, 1908), 96. The page reference following in parentheses is to this volume.

[13] *The Spirit of Romance* (Norfolk, Conn., [1953]), p. 178. Page references following in parentheses are to this volume.

[14] Reprinted in Ezra Pound, *Selected Prose 1908-1965,* ed. William Cookson (New York, 1973), pp. 19-43.

[15] *A Lume Spento* (1908); *A Quinzaine for This Yule* (1908); *Personae of Ezra Pound* (1909); *Exultations of Ezra Pound* (1909); *Canzoni of Ezra Pound* (1911).

[16] "Verse," *New Age,* VI (Jan. 6, 1910), 234.

[17] See Noel Stock, *The Life of Ezra Pound* (New York, 1970), p. 103.

[18] *New Age,* X (Feb. 15, 1912), 369. The page reference following in parentheses is to this volume.

[19] *Poetry Review,* I (March, 1912), 133.

[20] *The Spirit of Romance,* p. 92.

[21] *New Age,* V (July 8, 1909), 219.

[22] *The Spirit of Romance,* p. 94. The page reference following in parentheses is to this volume.

[23] *New Age,* V (July 8, 1909), 219.

[24] There are signs indicating that Pound's attachment to this line of thought remained with him for several years at the least. *A Lume Spento* had contained such poems as "The Tree" or "La Fraisne" recording the poet's sense of union with living trees leading to supra-rational intuition. Several years later Pound would record of his first meeting with Arnold Dolmetsch, the musician and maker of musical instruments, his sense that he had, in metamorphosed fact, encountered the figure of Pan. "The undeniable tradition of metamorphosis teaches us that things do not remain always the same, they become other things by

swift, unanalysable processes" ("Affirmations I: Arnold Dolmetsch," *New Age,* XVI [Jan. 7, 1915], 246). Pound's phrase here echoes Hulme's rendering of Bergson's sense of flux as "a continuous and unanalysable curve." . . .

[25] *The Spirit of Romance,* pp. 92-93. Page references following in parentheses are to this volume.

[26] *Poetry Review,* I (Feb. 2, 1912), 75.

[27] *New Age,* X (Feb. 15, 1912), 369.

[28] The volume, *Patria Mia,* was not to be published until much later. Its manuscript had been sent to a small Chicago publisher, Ralph Fletcher Seymour, but was lost during a reorganization of his business. It was eventually recovered by Seymour and appeared in 1950. The Seymour text is reprinted in Pound, *Selected Prose 1909-1965,* pp. 101-146.

[29] *New Age,* XI (Nov. 14, 1912), 36. The page reference following in parentheses is to this volume.

[30] *New Freewoman,* I (Oct. 15, 1913), 162.

[31] See Ellen Williams, *Harriet Monroe and the Poetry Renaissance* (Urbana, Ill., 1977), pp. 132-133.

[32] Quoted from Richard Ellmann and Charles Feidelson (eds.), *The Modern Tradition* (New York, 1965), p. 152.

SOURCES AND INFLUENCES

Wallace Martin

[*In the following essay, Martin locates sources of Imagist aesthetics in theories of philosophy and psychology that were current in the early twentieth century.*]

SOURCE: "The Sources of the Imagist Aesthetic," in *PMLA,* Vol. 84, No. 2, March, 1970, pp. 196-204.

When subjected to scholarly scrutiny, literary revolutions usually prove less novel than they appear to be. We now know that the twentieth-century reaction against Romanticism was largely based on Romantic principles, and a number of writers have argued that Aestheticism, Symbolism, Imagism, and Surrealism are essentially extensions of the literary revolution that began in the eighteenth century. At the same time, these movements do embody distinctive features that cannot be explained by reference to their literary tradition. For an understanding of innovation in aesthetic theory, we often must turn to intellectual history. The influence of Schopenhauer and Hartmann on Symbolism, and that of Bergson and Freud on Surrealism, did not determine the character of these movements. But knowledge of such influences helps us understand the origin and process of literary change, as well as the historical process of which literature is a part.

The purpose of this paper is to show that the aesthetic tenets of Imagism were based upon philosophic and psychological theories of the early twentieth century, and that as a result Imagism did constitute a significant departure from the Romantic tradition. The origins of the Imagist aesthetic have been discussed for five decades and the conclusion that Imagism is a lineal descendent of Symbolism has seldom been questioned. Starting from this historical view of the relationship between the two movements, critics have argued that neither the theory nor the practice of the Imagist poets is inherently different from that of the Symbolists. An examination of the evidence on which these conclusions are based must precede discussion of alternative sources for the aesthetic of Hulme and Pound.

The Imagists themselves were proud to acknowledge their indebtedness to Symbolism, as witnessed by their frequent citation of Rémy de Gourmont's statement that "les imagistes anglais procèdent évidemment des symbolistes français."[1] Pound's capsule history of the genealogy of the image, recorded in a letter to René Taupin dated May 1928, corroborates Gourmont's view: "L'idée de l'image doit 'quelque chose' aux symbolistes français via T. E. Hulme, via Yeat[s] <Symons<Mallarmé."[2] Considerable scholarly effort has been expended in attempts to substantiate this assertion. In *L'Influence du symbolisme français sur la poésie américaine,* Taupin examined the relationship between Symbolism and Imagism in detail. He found that the influence of Symbolism on Hulme and Pound was less apparent (and hence presumably less direct) than it was on the minor Imagists. Pursuing Herbert Read's suggestion that Hulme derived many of his ideas from Gourmont, Taupin concluded that *Le Problème du style* was the primary source of Hulme's aesthetic; if further evidence of Hulme's indebtedness to Symbolism was needed, it was provided, Taupin said, by Hulme's assertion that his theories were partially vitiated by his preoccupation with the theory and practice of modern art, "'et en particulier du symbolisme'."[3] The influence of the Symbolists on Pound, in Taupin's view, was probably mediated by Hulme. The partisan quarrel regarding Pound's indebtedness to Hulme, which began in 1915, need not detain us here, since it flourished only while untrammeled by scholarship. N. Christoph de Nagy has recently discovered that Pound read Gourmont before writing the Imagist manifesto; hence insofar as Hulme reiterated Gourmont, Pound may have been doing the same thing independently.[4]

Following the publication of Taupin's book in 1929, a curious divergence developed between scholarly and critical treatments of the relationship between Symbolism and Imagism. Stanley K. Coffman, whose *Imagism: A Chapter for the History of Modern Poetry* is the best scholarly study of the problem, concluded that there was less evidence of a close relationship between the two movements than Taupin had suggested. Frank Kermode

and Graham Hough, on the other hand, transporting the problem from the realm of scholarship to that of aesthetic theory, imply that the relationship was closer than any earlier writer had suggested it was. The thesis of Hough's *Image and Experience* is that "we shall find the roots of English Imagist poetry in the French Symbolist area, the area that is bounded by Mallarmé and Rimbaud."[5] Frank Kermode concludes that "Hulme hands over to the English tradition a modernized, but essentially traditional, aesthetic of Symbolism," and that "Pound's own aesthetic is not fundamentally different from Hulme's, though he is quite right to insist that it was available to him without Hulme's mediation."[6] An analysis of their position will show that it is untenable. Pound's conception of the image is quite different from Hulme's; and neither is historically derived from or theoretically similar to the aesthetic of the Symbolists.

It is ironic that efforts to discredit the intentional fallacy have not resulted in more skepticism with respect to the statements of creative writers concerning literary history. Thus Gourmont's remark about the historical continuity of Symbolism and Imagism has not been discussed in relation to Gourmont's conception of Symbolism;[7] thus the meanings of *symbolisme* for Hulme and Pound, dependent upon the use of that word by French authors and critics between 1900 and 1912, have not been investigated; and thus the evidence that Pound had no knowledge of what the term meant to its proponents has been unduly neglected. "Symbole??" wrote Pound in the letter of 1928 quoted above, "Je n'ai jamais lu 'les idées des symbolistes' sur ce sujet."[8] Corroboration is provided by an article he wrote in 1914: "One can be grossly 'symbolic,' for example, by using the term 'cross' to mean 'trial.' The symbolist's *symbols* have a fixed value, like numbers in arithmetic, like 1, 2, and 7. . . . Moreover, one does not want to be called a symbolist, because symbolism has usually been associated with mushy technique."[9] This passage can hardly be explained as an imperfect account of something that Hulme told Pound; it is based either on misinformation or no information at all. Citing this passage, Donald Davie justifiably concludes that critics go astray in attempting to relate Pound to the Symbolist tradition.[10]

The problem of Hulme's knowledge of Symbolism has been complicated by excessive conjecture resulting from a lack of information. Pound's placement of Hulme as a link in the chain of Symbolist influence, quoted above, is vitiated by his own ignorance of that movement; and the quotation from Hulme in which, according to Taupin, he acknowledges his debt to the Symbolists, is in fact a remark that Hulme made concerning French aesthetics, not his own.[11] Hulme never refers to Mallarmé or his theories; nowhere does he mention Gourmont, the generally accepted "source" of his aesthetic. As Coffman notes, absence of such reference is curious, since Hulme "was not usually reticent about such matters" (*Imagism*, p. 83). The most important evidence concerning what Hulme knew about Symbolism is contained in his review of Tancrède de Visan's *L'Attitude du lyrisme contemporain.*

In this review, which has escaped the attention of his critics, Hulme says that he was introduced to contemporary French poetry by André Beaunier's *La Poésie nouvelle* (Paris, 1902), which he read in 1905 or 1906.[12] Hulme's conception of Symbolism was based upon these two books and was therefore quite different from Symbolism as conceived today.

In *La Poésie nouvelle,* Beaunier identifies Rimbaud, Laforgue, Jammes, Merrill, Fort, and Elskamp as Symbolists and defines the symbol as "une image que l'on peut employer pour la représentation d'une idée" (p. 45). This is not the symbol of Mallarmé, nor is it the symbol of Symbolism as generally understood today. But the symbol is of secondary importance in Beaunier's discussion of Symbolism. Two-thirds of his introduction is devoted to versification, in particular free verse, which at that time was considered the major contribution of the Symbolists to poetic theory.[13] The definition of Symbolism in Visan's *L'Attitude du lyrisme contemporain* (1911) likewise involves reference to *l'image* and discusses Symbolism as if it were a contemporaneous movement. Reference to *l'image* in both of the definitions of Symbolism read by Hulme was in a sense anomalous, for the word was of little theoretical significance either to Mallarmé (who emphasized *l'idée*) or to most of the poets discussed by Beaunier and Visan. Symbolism, as Hulme understood it, was what scholars today refer to as Post-Symbolism. Since its most significant innovation, according to many French critics, was free verse, it is understandable that he and his contemporaries turned to French poetry for information about the theory and practice of versification, rather than for a new aesthetic.

If Pound and Hulme did not derive the aesthetic of the image from the Symbolists, they must have either discovered it elsewhere or invented it through an unmediated act of imagination. The latter hypothesis is unlikely, in view of the wealth of sources available to them. In the late nineteenth century, *l'image* was an important theoretical term in the empiricist-associationist tradition of French psychology. Bergson, in *Matière et mémoire* (1896), redefined *image* in terms of an organicist theory of psychology. Pound's conception of the image was based upon the former tradition, Hulme's (after 1908) upon the latter. French critics and aestheticians also made use of the psychological conception of the image, but Hulme and Pound were not directly indebted to them in the formulation of the Imagist aesthetic. Gourmont derived his theory of the image from a French psychologist whose works were also read by Hulme, and such similarities as exist in the writings of Hulme and Gourmont result from their indebtedness to the same sources. Evidence to support these conclusions is provided by a consideration of the importance of *l'image* in French psychology and philosophy.

A meeting of the Société Française de la Philosophie in 1908 was devoted to discussion of *l'image* as part of the society's project to publish a philosophical dictionary. The resultant definition provides a history of the word in French philosophy and a survey of its contemporaneous applications. The primary meanings recorded were: "A. Reproduction, soit concrète, soit mentale, de ce qui a été perçu par la vue. . . . B. Répétition mentale, généralement affaiblie, d'une *sensation* (ou plus exactement d'une *perception*) précédemment éprouvée. . . . C. On a souvent étendu le mot *image* à toute présentation ou représentation sensible."[14] Meanings "B" and "C" were rare before 1870; in the following decade their use became so common and indiscriminate that in 1882 the French philosopher Renouvier was moved to say: "Si j'avais à voter sur cette question de terminologie dans un congrès de philosophes (dont je ne demande pas la réunion), je voudrais exclure ici le mot image."[15]

In extending the use of *image* to describe a variety of mental phenomena, French psychology reflected a trend evident in other countries. British and German psychologists (and philosophers—there was no clear demarcation between the disciplines) were using comparable terms loosely; when their works were translated into French, precise terminological equivalence was not always possible. In the dictionary published by the Société Française de la Philosophie, "Bild" and "Vorstellung" are given as German equivalents of *image,* and the only English equivalent listed is "image." In practice, however, *image* was employed to render such varied English words as "impression," "picture," "recept," and "portrait"; and in one French work on psychology that was translated into English and read by Hulme, the "impressions," "recepts," and "portraits" of English psychologists returned to their native language as "images."[16] Of these terminological mutations, the most significant involves the word "impression," a central term in British empiricism. Translated into French as *image* and retranslated into English as "image," the "impression" of Locke and Hume, retaining its associationist implications, left unmistakable traces of its influence in the aesthetic of Hulme and Pound.

During a century and a half that witnessed the transformation of most sciences, Hume's theory of psychology was generally accepted by academic psychologists with only minor modifications. Hippolyte Taine's *De l'intelligence* (1870), in France considered a standard work on psychology for at least three decades, testifies to the persistence of Hume's theory. Taine begins his book with a discussion of signs (language and other forms of symbolism) which, as the concrete manifestations of thought, are the basis of the psychologist's analysis of ideas. Book I concludes with the statement that "since our ideas may be reduced to images, their laws may be reduced to laws of images; images then are what we must study."[17] The second book is devoted to an explanation of how signs originate in images; the third treats the origin of images in sensations. Comparison of Taine's theory with Part I, Section I, of Hume's *Treatise of Human Nature* reveals no significant differences (Taine's image has precisely the meaning of Hume's impression). Ideas are less vivid and precise than images, since the details of particular images are lost when superimposed to form ideas. Even the simplest ideas possess some ambiguity; thus they give rise to confusions that can be eliminated only by reducing them to their constituent images. To summarize the relationship between impression/image and idea, as discussed by Hume and Taine, in the words of T. E. Hulme: "Thought is prior to language and consists in the simultaneous presentation to the mind of two different images. Language is only a more or less feeble way of doing this."[18]

Like T. E. Hulme, Taine associates the clear recollection of images with the "precise, intense, colored representations attained by the imaginations of great artists." Hulme's debt to the psychological tradition represented by Taine is quite obvious: Hulme refers to Taine's writings on psychology, and two of his "notes" employ examples also used by Taine. Taine says that in the process of reducing images to ideas, we gradually strip away visual elements until nothing is left but a word. "This word so reduced is not however a lifeless symbol, without traces of signification; it is more like the trunk of a tree, stripped of its leaves and branches."[19] In the "Notes on Language and Style," Hulme wrote: "Regard each word as a picture, then a succession of pictures. Only the dead skeleton remains. We cut the leaves off. When the tree becomes a mast, the leaves become unnecessary" (*FS*, p. 83).[20] Hulme uses another example to describe the process: "Picture gallery (a) recognition of names. (b) progress to recognition of characteristics" (*FS*, p. 89). In the first chapter of his book, Taine employs a similar analogy. In an art gallery arranged by schools, he says, after we have spent an hour or two looking at pictures, we sit down and reflect on what we have seen. Many qualities come to mind as images are mentally evoked; if we attempt to define certain of these qualities, we will disengage words appropriate to them. This, in essence, is how images are combined to form an abstract characteristic symbolized by a word.

Although the argument that Hulme read Taine's *De l'intelligence* is largely inferential, there is indisputable evidence that he read the works of Théodule Ribot, a French psychologist and philosopher who was, like Taine, a product of the empiricist tradition.[21] Ribot is scarcely known today; in the history of ideas, however, he deserves to be remembered as one of the most influential writers of his time. Schopenhauer's "Idée" was absorbed into the aesthetic of Symbolism either directly or mediately through Ribot's *La Philosophie de Schopenhauer;*[22] Gourmont's *Le Problème du style* is essentially an elaboration of two books by Ribot, as even those sympathetic to Gourmont are willing to admit;[23] and in coining the word "dissociation," which Gourmont transmitted to Eliot, Ribot's influence extended into English literary history.

Ribot introduced the concept of dissociation in *L'Evolution des idées générales* (Paris, 1897), which elaborates the psychological theory upon which his later study of the creative imagination is based. While his account of the process through which images become

ideas is essentially the same as that presented by Taine, he posits a motor base for all mental activity and makes use of the experimental data provided by the German psychologist Wundt to refine the simplistic hypotheses of the associationist tradition. Sensations are selectively registered as images. Similar images are united to form a generic image, and abstraction occurs when the manifold features of the generic image are dissociated from it, leaving one abstract characteristic. This process presupposes and may be succeeded by association (a term, he says, that other psychologists have used incorrectly), whereby characteristics are generalized through synthesis and fusion.

This thesis is supported by experimental evidence showing how inferior forms of abstraction, manifested in animals and children, have evolved through primitive societies to the highly developed conceptual systems of civilized man. Animals, which display the lowest form of recognizable mental activity, think by means of a "logique des images," based on generic images; as T. E. Hulme later put it, "animals are in the same state that men were before symbolic language was invented."[24] Their mental state is not so undesirable as it might seem, however, since increasing degrees of abstraction lead ultimately toward impoverished simplifications. The problem is posed clearly in Ribot's summary of his argument: "Nous avons vu l'abstraction, à mesure qu'elle monte et s'affermit, se séparer de plus en plus nettement de l'image et finalement, au moment du symbolisme pur, la séparation devient un antagonisme. C'est que, au fond, il y a entre les deux, dès le début, opposition de nature et de procédé. L'idéal de l'image est une complexité toujours croissante, l'idéal de l'abstraction est un simplification toujours croissante: parce que l'une se former par addition et l'autre par soustraction" (*EIG*, p. 151).[25] Insofar as abstraction results in simplification of the rich imagistic complexity of experience, Hulme's statement that "we must judge the world from the status of animals, leaving out 'truth,' etc." is understandable.[26]

Ribot does not consider thinking in general ideas superior to modes of thought employing images. Men can be classified psychologically as imaginative or abstract thinkers. The former, which include novelists, poets, and painters, think imagistically and "rêvent une œuvre organique, vivante, donc *complexe,*" whereas the latter (scientists and philosophers, for example) seek simple, abstract solutions and find complex, concrete realities distasteful. "Donc, au fond, l'antagonisme de l'image et de l'idée, c'est celui du tout et de la partie" (*EIG*, p. 151). In this recrudescence of a doctrine originating in British empiricism—the doctrine that immediate impressions or images are closer to reality and therefore more distinct, more reliable than ideas—early twentieth-century writers found a scientific sanction for an aesthetic of the image.

In his *Essai sur l'imagination créatrice* (1900; English edition, 1906), Ribot devotes his attention exclusively to the image, implying that ideas are of little consequence in the creative process. Earlier discussions of the imagination erred, he argues, in not distinguishing between its passive and active states. The former is "the purely *representative* faculty"; the latter is "the faculty of creating by means of the intermediation of images" (*ECI*, p. 8).[27] In cases of vivid, active imagination, "the motor element of the image"—that element which incites one toward action—"tends to cause it to lose its purely 'inner' character, to objectify it, to externalize it, to project it outside ourselves" in some form of creation (*FCI*, p. 5). Having based his view of the imaginative faculty on a mechanistic hypothesis, Ribot never evokes this hypothesis for the purposes of causal explanation in the succeeding discussion. Like many of his contemporaries, Ribot proves his psychological orthodoxy with a genuflection toward mechanistic materialism; but it is important to remember that the most rigorously materialistic psychologists could themselves offer nothing more than such a gesture as evidence that thought and imagination were the result of incipient motor actions (an assumption that survives in the early writings of I. A. Richards). Ribot was an orthodox and respected psychologist. If, in the following discussion, aspects of his theory seem "romantic" or "antirational," as does the Imagist theory to some critics, then one must in all justice apply these terms to a major segment of early twentieth-century science, as well as to literary theory.

Two of the three sections of Ribot's book are relevant to the Imagist aesthetic: the first, which deals with the intellectual, emotional, unconscious, and integrating principles of the creative imagination; and the last, which treats the main types of imagination. Intellectually, images are combined through "objective" or "subjective" causality. In subjective association, "the revived image of a face, a monument, a landscape, an occurrence, is, most often, only partial. It depends on various conditions that revive the essential part and drop minor details, and this 'essential' which survives dissociation depends on subjective causes" (*ECI*, p. 20). There is an apposite passage in Pound's description of one type of image: "Emotion seizing upon some external scene or action carries it intact to the mind; and that vortex purges it of all save the essential or dominant or dramatic qualities, and it emerges like the external original" ("AI," p. 349).[28] The emotional element is even more important to creation than the intellectual, according to Ribot, since it leads to the fusion of disparate images with similar emotive stimuli. More important, it is the very source of creation: "In order that a creative act occur, there is required, first, a need; then, that it arouse a combination of images; and lastly, that it objectify and *realize* itself in an appropriate form" (*ECI*, pp. 43-44). The emotional element leads us to realize that "every image is comparable to a force" (p. 62); as Pound said, "emotional force gives the image" ("AI," p. 349). The unconscious factor adds to the creative process an element of unpredictability. All of these elements distinguished for analytic purposes should not, however, be allowed to obscure the fact that creation is fundamentally a synthesizing process: "The ideal is a construction of images that should become a reality" (*ECI*, p. 80).

In the last section of the book, Ribot distinguishes between two types of artistic imagination, the plastic and the diffluent, in a passage that may have influenced Pound's discussions of symbolism. "By 'plastic imagination' I understand that which has for its special characters clearness and precision of form; more explicitly those forms whose materials are clear images (whatever be their nature) . . . giving the impression of reality. . . . The plastic imagination could be summed up in the expression, *clearness in complexity*" (*ECI*, p. 184; pp. 192-193). This is of course the type of imagination displayed in the visual arts; in poetry, it is exemplified in the works of the Parnassians and particularly in Gautier (whom Ribot quotes). The diffluent imagination, on the other hand, "consists of vaguely-outlined, indistinct images that are evoked and joined according to the least rigorous modes of association," usually as a result of an interior emotional state ("the romantic turn of mind") unable to objectify itself. "The images of this class have an 'impressionist' mark. . . . They act less through a direct influence than by evoking, suggesting, whispering. . . . We may justly call them crepuscular or twilight ideas."[29]

Ribot illustrates the diffluent imagination in literature through a discussion of Symbolism:

> This form of art despises the clear and exact representation of the outer world: it erases it by a sort of music that aspires to express the changing and fleeting inwardness of the human soul. . . . It makes use of a natural or artificial lack of precision: everything floats as in a dream, men as well as things, often without mark in time and space. . . . The word is the sign *par excellence*. As, according to the symbolists, it should give us emotions rather than representations, it is necessary that it lose, partially, its intellectual function and undergo a new adaption.
>
> A principal process consists of employing usual words and changing their ordinary acceptation, or rather, associating them in such a way that they lose their precise meaning, and appear vague and mysterious. (pp. 202-203).

Pound, in his article on "Vorticism" (1914), says that the Symbolists "dealt in 'association'," that "they degraded the symbol to the status of a word." The latter statement is enigmatic, in that the symbol, in poetry, is of necessity a word. The interpretation suggested by the assumption that Pound was indebted to Ribot (one of the few writers of his time who attacked Symbolist procedures) is that the symbol was degraded to the status of a *sign*—a word lacking precise imagistic reference.

The possibility that Pound, like Hulme, was indebted specifically to Ribot is incidental to the argument regarding the relationship of Hulme and Pound to French psychological theory. Emphasis on the image was pervasive during this period. To cite only two instances: Hulme read works by Jules de Gaultier and Gabriel Séailles.[30] The latter's *Essai sur le génie dans l'art* (1897) begins, as do Taine and Ribot, with the image as the fundamental element of mental processes and aesthetic creation, and then explains the creative process as one involving the organization of images. The application of the psychological theory of images to language as a medium of communication is discussed in Gaultier's *Le Bovarysme*. His thesis is that because of the attrition of the imagistic associations of words, most of them have lost their precise descriptive and denotative value, thus becoming mere "notions." In aesthetics and stylistics, the concept of the image was as pervasive as it was in psychology and philosophy. And during the first decade of the twentieth century, the distinction between image and idea was of increasing importance in French literary criticism, as witnessed by the definition of Symbolism cited earlier in this paper. *L'idée* was frequently identified with reductive abstractionism and lost the efficacy as an aesthetic term with which Mallarmé had invested it; *l'image*, having evolved from mental picture to the richest element of the psychic life, appeared with increasing frequency in discussions of poetry.[31]

Earlier writers have discussed the parallels between *l'image* as defined by Gourmont and the "image" of Hulme and Pound. In view of the lack of evidence that either Hulme or Pound read *Le Problème du style* during the period preceding or immediately following the latter's formulation of Imagism, and in view of Gourmont's reliance on Ribot (whom Hulme did read), there is no reason to assume that Gourmont influenced the aesthetic of the image.[32] In the first flush of his enthusiasm for Gourmont (1913), Pound discussed his works in articles appearing in *Poetry* and *The New Age*. Neither article makes any reference to *Le Problème du style* or to Gourmont's discussion of the image in *Esthétique de la langue française*. Attempts to prove that it was Gourmont, rather than Ribot, who influenced the "image" of Hulme and Pound are likely to prove unsuccessful.

Hulme and Pound were heirs to the empiricist psychological tradition represented by Ribot; the significant differences in their conceptions of the image resulted from Hulme's interest in an organicist psychology in which the image was endowed with even greater importance. For Ribot and his predecessors, idea and image were both aspects of mental representation, as opposed to reality, in the mind-matter antithesis. For Bergson this antithesis and the resultant antinomy between Idealism and Realism were the crucial philosophic problems of the age. In the introduction to *Matière et mémoire* (1896), he appeals to that judicious arbiter of philosophic disputes, the man in the street, in order to show that Idealism and Realism are equally ludicrous. What then is the truth of the matter? At this point the man in the street begins to sound disquietingly like a Bergsonian in bourgeois disguise: "Such a mind would naturally believe that matter exists just as it is perceived; and, since it is perceived as an image, the mind would make of it, in itself, an image. . . . Matter, in our view, is an aggregate of 'images.' And by 'image'

we mean a certain existence which is more than that which the idealist calls a *representation*, but less than that which the realist calls a *thing*—an existence placed half-way between the 'thing' and the 'representation.'"[33]

In this view, images are not only logically prior to mental processes; they are the organic unity that obviates the analytic impasse inevitably resulting from Descartes's "ghost in the machine." The central importance of the image in Bergson's psychological theory is indicated by its prominence in *Matière et mémoire*, the four sections of which treat the selection of images, the recollection of images, the persistence or survival of images, and the delimitation and fixation of images respectively. As Lydie Adolphe has shown in *La Dialectique des images chez Bergson*, Bergson's concept of the image is one of the most important elements of his philosophy. For the image is the expressive embodiment of the intuition.

Images, for Bergson, are the medium of communication in poetry and embody the central insights of philosophy. In his *Essai sur les données immédiates de la conscience* (a work which Hulme read in 1907), Bergson described poetic creation as follows: "D'où vient le charme de la poésie? Le poète est celui chez qui les sentiments se développent en images, et les images elles-mêmes en paroles, dociles au rythme, pour les traduire. En voyant repasser devant nos yeux ces images, nous éprouverons à notre tour le sentiment qui en était pour ainsi dire l'équivalent émotionnel."[34] The relationship between image and intuition is defined in Bergson's "Introduction à la métaphysique," a work which Hulme translated: "Many diverse images, borrowed from very different orders of things, may, by the convergence of their action, direct consciousness to the precise point where there is a certain intuition to be seized."[35] Hence poetry, which Hulme refers to as "a compromise for a language of intuition," is inevitably based on images.

"Bergson," says Hulme, "represents a reaction against the atomic and rational psychology of Taine and Spencer, against the idea that states of mind can be arrived at by the summation of more elementary states." The Parnassians, he says, like the psychologists of their time, "employed always clear and precise descriptions of external things"—a method advocated by Hulme in his pre-Bergsonian writings—"and strove by combinations of such 'atoms of the beautiful' to manufacture a living beauty." But "life is a continuous and unanalyzable curve which cannot be seized clearly, but can only be felt as a kind of intuition. It can only be got at by a kind of central vision," the vision sought by the Post-Symbolists and philosophically articulated by Bergson.[36]

Hulme was not the only critic to make use of Bergson's philosophy in discussing poetry. In *L'Attitude du lyrisme contemporain* (Paris, 1911), Tancrède de Visan attempted to relate Bergson's philosophy to the practices of contemporary French poets. Visan defined the poetry of his time as follows: "Le symbolisme ou attitude poétique contemporaine se sert d'images successives ou accumulées pour extérioriser une intuition lyrique" (pp. 459-460). This definition was noted in Hulme's review of the book ("M. Visan would then define Symbolism as an attempt by means of successive and accumulated images to express and exteriorize such a central lyric intuition"); it was repeated by F. S. Flint in his renowned essay on "Contemporary French Poetry": "[Symbolism is] an attempt to evoke the subconscious element of life, to set vibrating the infinite within us, by the exquisite juxtaposition of images. Its philosophy, in fact . . . was the philosophy of intuitiveness: it has been formulated by Bergson."[37] Hulme and Flint seem to have accepted Visan's identification of Symbolism as a contemporaneous movement; they gave currency in England to a Bergsonian and "imagistic" conception of French poetry that was more a product of Visan's theorizing than of an inductive survey of French poetic practice.

There is no evidence that Bergson or Visan exercised any direct influence on Pound, whose rationalism led him to theorize about poetry in terms of an empiricist rather than an organicist psychology. His interest in the literary implications of psychological theory is most strikingly illustrated in his allusion to the Freudian "complex" in defining the image as "that which presents an intellectual and emotional complex in an instant of time."[38] His distinction between Imagism and Impressionism, and his discussion of the objective and subjective image, both of which are based on a subject-object dichotomy, parallel theoretical distinctions in the works of Ribot. Impressionism, Pound says, corresponds to the conception of man as a being toward whom "perception moves, as a plastic substance *receiving* impressions"; Imagism, a subclass of expressionism, comes about when man directs "a certain fluid force against substance . . . *conceiving* instead of merely reflecting and observing."[39] This distinction is essentially the same as that made by Ribot in his discussion of the passive and active imagination, referred to earlier in this paper.[40]

In his most complete exposition of the aesthetic of Imagism, Pound says that the image may be either objective or subjective, depending upon whether it re-creates a single experience or transforms and fuses elements of disparate experiences ("AI," p. 349); his distinction parallels Ribot's between the subjective and objective modes of imaginative association. Ribot assumes that the interaction of images in creation "rests on a physiological basis: the existence of several [electric] currents diffusing themselves through the brain and the possibility of receiving simultaneous excitations" (*ECI*, p. 62). Ribot's view suggests that the following quotation from Pound may be intended as physiological rather than metaphoric: "The best artist is the man whose machinery can stand the highest voltage. The better the machinery, the more precise, the stronger; the more exact will be the record of the voltage and of the various currents that have passed through it" ("AI," p. 350).

But the psychologistic emphasis in Pound's aesthetic has a significance beyond any correspondences to particular sources. His frequent use of scientific analogies in his early criticism, his partiality toward mechanistic explanations of mental phenomena,[41] and his deduction of the types of poetry from psychological dispositions, together constitute an aspect of his thought deserving detailed investigation.

Pound's development as a poet is reflected in his critical writings but cannot be understood on the basis of those writings alone. His distinctions between Imagism and Symbolism as poetic theories should not be allowed to obscure the continuous evolution of poetic practice through which his early poetry (1908-12) is related to its symbolist antecedents. If one accepts Anna Balakian's persuasive argument that Verlaine, not Mallarmé, is the typical poet of "Symbolism," and that "symbolism" (uncapitalized) is the appropriate name for an international poetic movement characterized by "ambiguity of indirect communication, affiliation with music, and the 'decadent' spirit,"[42] Pound's early poetry can be seen in its proper perspective. Through Arthur Symons, Dowson, and the early Yeats, Pound assimilated the symbolist conventions that pervade his pre-*Ripostes* volumes—probably without being aware of the ultimate sources of these conventions.[43] In certain poems published in 1912 (notably "The Return," "Apparuit," and "Άþñéá"), a quintessential symbolism, freed from decadent trappings and aestheticist overtones, seems at the same time to embody the basic precepts of Imagism, as enunciated nearly a year later.

Recognition of the stylistic continuity that links Pound's early poetry to symbolism contributes to an understanding of the historical significance of Imagism. If symbolism was part of a poetic milieu that early twentieth-century poets could absorb without being conscious of its origins, the Imagist manifesto can be seen as an attempt, on Pound's part, to become conscious of both theory and practice in order to separate himself from the mannerisms of his early poetry. The Imagist manifesto was primarily a statement of intent rather than analysis of an accomplishment; but because such statements reflect intentions and influence those of other poets, it is possible to discuss their importance as one of several forces shaping the development of poetry.

Any attempt to discover the sources of the "image" as discussed by Hulme and Pound leads from particular works to intellectual history. The appearance of an Imagist aesthetic, here considered as involving a psychology of creation and a philosophy of poetic communication, seems to follow naturally from an interest in contemporary philosophy and psychology. Undoubtedly Hulme and Pound, like the Symbolists, emphasize a mode of creation that eschews explicit conceptual content. In these circumstances, it is tempting, and even revealing, to treat Symbolism and Imagism as interrelated extensions of the Romantic tradition. However, so long as conceptual clarity is not conceived as the defining characteristic of poetic expression, one cannot absorb Imagism into the Romantic tradition without at the same time implicating considerable portions of Renaissance and even Classic poetics.

Once the fundamental distinctions between Symbolism and Imagism are recognized, endless discriminations follow. The broader issue involved in these discriminations is the extent to which, creatively and critically, Imagism, rather than transmitting an etiolated Romanticism, initiated a new movement toward objectification, toward "presentation" as an alternative to the elaborate stratagems whereby earlier writers accommodated to the irremediable disjunction of subject and object.

The early writings of Hulme and Pound show that they were seeking not objects to correlate with their emotional states, but a means of presenting objects that in some sense embodied emotion. The empiricist tradition and even the organicism of Bergson could not entirely eliminate the separation of subject and object. But by hypothesizing a mental "object"—the image—which through its "Dinglichkeit" (as Ransom called it) served as simulacrum of reality, psychology provided the basis for an objective aesthetic. In a larger historical perspective, Objectivism, as its proponents indicate, is a logical culmination of ideas originating in Imagism. And the "image" that is so important in post-Behaviorist psychology (exemplified in such works as *Plans and the Structure of Behavior* and Kenneth E. Boulding's *The Image*) is related to Objectivism much as Ribot and his contemporaries were related to Imagism.[44]

The Symbolists, according to A. G. Lehmann, were attempting "to find an autonomous field for art, distinct from science or history, and without interference from their intellectual criteria of truth."[45] Hulme and Pound, on the other hand, based their theories of poetry on the philosophy and psychology of their time, seeking rational solutions to aesthetic problems. If their theories are Romantic, a major segment of twentieth-century science is likewise implicated. And if theory led Pound to practices that fail to satisfy our demand for intelligibility, we can profit from an understanding of how, in his desire to escape both subjective and metaphysical irrelevance, he placed his faith in a scientific reductionism that has, despite reason, survived in our time.[46]

[1] "Revue du mois," *Mercure de France,* CXI (1915), 355; Stanley K. Coffman, *Imagism: A Chapter for the History of Modern Poetry* (Norman, Okla., 1951), p. 89.

[2] *The Letters of Ezra Pound, 1907-1941,* ed. D. D. Paige (New York, 1950), p. 218.

[3] "The Example of Rémy de Gourmont," *Criterion,* X (1931), 619; *L'Influence du symbolisme français sur la poésie américaine* (Paris, 1929), p. 85.

[4] *Ezra Pound's Poetics and Literary Tradition* (Bern, 1966), pp. 70-72.

[5] London, 1960, p. 51.

[6] *Romantic Image* (New York, 1964), p. 121.

[7] "Le Symbolisme pourra (et même devra) être considéré par nous comme le libre et personnel développement de l'individu esthétique." *L'Idéalisme* (Paris, 1893), p. 12. Gourmont employed substantially the same definition of Symbolism in his later writings. In discussing the Imagists (see n. 1), he cited their "horreur du cliché . . . de la rhétorique et du grandiose" as evidence of their indebtedness to Symbolism; but such similarities hardly entail any specific indebtedness.

[8] *Letters,* p. 218.

[9] "Vorticism," *Fortnightly Review,* XCVI (1914), 463.

[10] *The Poet as Sculptor* (London, 1965), p. 66.

[11] "The Plan for a Book," *Speculations,* ed. Herbert Read (London, 1924), p. 263.

[12] *New Age,* IX (1911), 400.

[13] Kenneth Cornell, *The Post-Symbolist Period* (New Haven, Conn., 1958), p. 51.

[14] André Lalande, et al., *Vocabulaire technique et critique de la philosophie* (Paris, 1926), I, 339. This definition was first published in the *Bulletin de la Société Française de Philosophie,* "séance du 2 juillet 1908."

[15] Quoted in Lalande, I, 340.

[16] These examples are taken from Théodule Ribot's *Essay on the Creative Imagination,* trans. A. H. Baron (London, 1906).

[17] *On Intelligence,* trans. T. D. Haye (London, 1871), p. 34. English translations of French works are quoted when there is no reason to suppose that Hulme or Pound read the French edition.

[18] "Notes on Language and Style," *Further Speculations,* ed. Sam Hynes (Lincoln, Neb., 1962), p. 84. Elsewhere, I have argued that "Notes on Language and Style" and "Cinders" represent the first phase of Hulme's thought, antedating his discovery of Bergson. Later in this paper, I discuss the importance of Bergson in Hulme's subsequent writings.

[19] *On Intelligence,* p. 3.

[20] *FS* designates *Further Speculations.*

[21] A letter from Hulme to Edward Marsh indicates that Hulme read Ribot's *Essai sur l'imagination créatrice* before Nov. 1912. See A. R. Jones, *The Life and Opinions of Thomas Ernest Hulme* (London, 1960), p. 209. Hulme alludes to Ribot in *Speculations,* p. 263. On the importance of Taine and Ribot in French psychology, see Edwin G. Boring, *A History of Experimental Psychology* (New York, 1929), pp. 606-607, 667-668.

[22] A. G. Lehmann, *The Symbolist Aesthetic in France, 1885-1895* (Oxford, 1950), pp. 60-67; Karl-D. Utti, *La*

Passion littéraire de Rémy de Gourmont (Paris, 1962), p. 65.

[23] Utti, pp. 78-97; p. 272. While Utti acknowledges Gourmont's debt to Ribot, he does not indicate the extent to which Gourmont simply paraphrases Ribot in long passages of *Le Probléme du style.*

[24] "Cinders," *Speculations,* p. 229.

[25] *EIG* designates *L'Evolution des idées générales.*

[26] "Cinders," *Speculations,* p. 229.

[27] *ECI* designates *Essay on the Creative Imagination,* trans. A. H. Baron (London, 1906).

[28] "AI" designates Pound's "As for Imagisme," *New Age,* XVI (1915).

[29] *ECI,* pp. 195-196. Pound wrote a poem entitled "Revolt against the Crepuscular Spirit in Modern Poetry," in which he proposed to substitute "shapes of power" and "men" for the vague "shadows" and "dreams" in the poetry of his contemporaries.

[30] An article that Hulme wrote on Gaultier is reprinted in *FS;* Séailles is mentioned in *Speculations,* p. 263.

[31] Elsewhere, I have discussed the distinction between *l'image* and *l'idée,* and that between "la littérature des images" and "la littérature des idées," in nineteenth-century French criticism: "'The Forgotten School of 1909' and the Origins of Imagism," *A Catalogue of the Imagist Poets* (New York, 1966), pp. 27-28. Georges Renard and (through him) Gourmont reinterpreted these distinctions, which Renard discovered in the writings of Balzac; for a discussion of Balzac's use of the terms, see Marc Eigeldinger, *La Philosophie de l'art chez Balzac* (Geneva, 1957), pp. 127-141.

[32] Glen S. Burne, in *Rémy de Gourmont* (Carbondale, Ill., 1963), and Karl-D. Utti discuss Gourmont's conception of *l'image* and touch on its relevance to Pound and Hulme; Donald Davie and N. Christoph de Nagy, in their books on Pound, treat Gourmont's influence on his thought. Taupin's assertion that Gourmont influenced Hulme is cited without comment by Burne and Utti. In "Imagism: A Unity of Gesture," which appears in *American Poetry,* ed. Irvin Ehrenpreis (London, 1965), Alun R. Jones asserts that Hulme read Gourmont in 1907 (p. 116). Jones has apparently come to this conclusion since writing his book on Hulme, but he does not note the evidence on which it is based.

[33] *Matter and Memory* (London, 1911), pp. vii-viii. Hulme may have read this work in French.

[34] Paris, 1989, p. 11. The information concerning when Hulme read this work is from an interview with F. S. Flint.

[35] *An Introduction to Metaphysics,* trans. T. E. Hulme (London, 1913), p. 14.

[36] *New Age,* IX (1911), 400-401.

[37] *Poetry Review,* I (1912), 355.

[38] See my "Freud and Imagism," *N&Q,* VIII (1961), 470-471, 474. Walter Sutton discovered the source of Pound's "complex" independently; see his discussion in *Modern American Criticism* (Englewood Cliffs, N. J., 1963), pp. 4-5. I am grateful to Prof. Sutton for many helpful suggestions regarding this paper.

[39] "Vorticism," p. 467.

[40] In *Subconscious Phenomena,* ed. Hugo Münsterberg (London, 1911)—a work which Pound alludes to in the Imagist manifesto—Ribot makes a similar distinction between the static and dynamic subconscious.

[41] In "The New Therapy," *New Age,* XXX (1922), to cite only one instance, Pound discusses Louis Bernan's thesis that the glands are the primary determinants of human behavior and concludes that this theory "offers us a comforting relief from Freudian excess" (pp. 259-260).

[42] *The Symbolist Movement* (New York, 1967), p. 101.

[43] The influence of Symons, Dowson, and Yeats on Pound's early poetry and its resultant symbolism are discussed in detail by de Nagy, *The Poetry of Ezra Pound: The Pre-Imagist Stage* (Bern, 1960), pp. 27-53; pp. 85-104. Neither de Nagy nor Thomas H. Jackson—*The Early Poetry of Ezra Pound* (Cambridge, Mass., 1968)—suggests that any French poet influenced the symbolism of Pound's early poetry.

[44] The thesis that the Imagists and their successors inaugurated a new tradition that leads to Objectivism is brilliantly presented in J. Hillis Miller's *Poets of Reality* (Cambridge, Mass., 1965) and L. S. Dembo's *Conceptions of Reality in Modern American Poetry* (Berkeley, Calif., 1966).

[45] *The Symbolist Aesthetic,* p. 72.

[46] Behaviorism has been undermined by rigorous application of the very logical premises upon which it is based. See Sigmund Koch's demolition of Behaviorist theory, and B. F. Skinner's melancholy reply, in *Behaviorism and Phenomenology,* ed. T. W. Wann (Chicago, 1965), pp. 1-45.

Ian Fletcher

[In the following essay, Fletcher discusses sources of Imagism within the English literary tradition.]

SOURCE: "Some Anticipations of Imagism," in *A Catalogue of the Imagist Poets,* J. Howard Woolmer, 1966, pp. 39-53.

Sing we a song
To the Blessed Gods
By the dusky olives,

By the green figs
And the violet grapes,
By the water-casks.

Cry to the Gods,
To the Gods that gave us
Heavy harvest.

Hurtful harvest,
Venomous vintage.

In slant sunlight
Fruit by fruit
Of the Earth-Mother.

In grey twilight
Shaft on shaft
Of the Archer-Goddess.

In thick grasses
Sudden gold
Of the glowing crocus.

In dewy gardens
Multitudinous
Sleepy roses.

They have given us corn
And the lurid blood-hued
Dog-star.

Humid woods
And the terror of moist woods
African.

It reads like an imitation of H.D. Clearly it is touched by Imagist influence: verbs are suppressed; verse is free, leaning on musical phrase in sequence rather than on metronome; there is a sensuous verification of objects, accumulating to an emotional climax in the final stanza. The constructions 'fruit by fruit' and 'shaft on shaft' recall similar terse expressions of process in H.D.

The poem was in fact published in the year 1900. It appeared anonymously in an Oxford undergraduate magazine the *X*, which ran for two years from 1898. The content of the *X* runs the narrow gamut of subject-matter and attitude typical of its time. Beginning with a somewhat colourless devotion to several arts in a mutedly *symboliste* vein, it becomes jingoist in 1899, the year when the Boer War was declared, and returns to 'decadent' themes in 1900. The final issue prints an obituary of Wilde, celebrating his genius and deploring the treatment he received from his fellow-countrymen. It is perhaps the last sparkle of the anti-bourgeois virulence of the 1890's and on the episode the Proctors doubtless had the last word, for there were no further issues. The point is, however, that all roads and sewers lead down to the 1890's, that junction of influences, movements, abortive excellencies and wavering anticipations.

In the standard work on imagism, published in 1931, Glenn Hughes treats the movement as an air-plant in relation to the English tradition. His book possesses both the advantages and disadvantages of fairly immediate literary history. It records actual discussion of some of the major figures involved in the movement, evoking such figures in vivid presence. These discussions no doubt enabled Hughes to clarify the phases through which Imagism passed. But Hughes also discriminates between the pure and less pure exponents of the doctrine and 'places' the achievement of H.D. above, for example, that of Flint, while recalling, without actually treating at length, the work of minor or marginal talents (Storer, Cournos, Tancred).

Yet the defects of the book stem from its immediacy. The sources of the movement are derived from the actual programmatic utterances of the Imagists themselves and, no doubt, from the table-talk of the survivors. After listing the remoter models, Japanese, Chinese, Hebrew, Hughes proceeds to the statement that the modern influence was French and in particular French Symbolism. Such a comment is just, but too exclusive. On the other hand, it may be that the insistence on Hulme and De Gourmont was misplaced: their importance lies rather in their influence on Eliot and Pound, while the poems of Hulme which Hughes quotes have little in common with Imagism.

The poet, in the twentieth century, is forced into the role of man of letters, particularly if he is advanced in technique and subject: his audience must be first startled, then subdued. He is forced to propagandize indeed, not merely for his own art, but for the dignity of art in an alien world. In propagandizing for his own art, his version of literary history is certain to be slanted: we may think of Yeats' Preface to the *Oxford Book of Modern Verse* or Graves' judgments in his recent Oxford and Cambridge lectures. This role requires no defence: apart from the actual achievement of these two poets, although literary tradition remains continuous and enveloping, upon the moment of precipitation, of illumination of one sensibility by another, only the poet himself can pronounce. A poet's canon tends to be formed either from poets to whom he owes everything or those to whom he owes nothing; never from those figures against whom he reacts, however fruitfully, or those whose work in any way stands to muffle the impact of his own. As with propagandists for the 'modern movement' in general, the Imagists in their pronouncements tended for polemical reasons to bracket off the English sources of Imagism. Indeed, much of the literary history of the years 1870 to 1920 is having to be re-written, so brilliant and persuasive have been the arguments for a 'modern movement' virtually autonomous, though Wyndham Lewis' judgment that its revolution consisted rather in the distance it went back than in the leap it took forward, is only faintly overstated. It is ironic that a similar occultation should be imposed by the figures of the 1890's, to whom the poets of the 'modern movement' owed much. Both the poets of that decade and the writers of naturalist and psychological short stories insisted on French allegiances to an extent that blurred their dependence on purely English sources. It is common to hear these figures discussed exclusively in terms of French sources, while the Pre-Raphaelite influence, for example, is rarely touched on.

Two attempts have recently been made to re-write the literary history of the period immediately prior to the 'modern movement' of which Imagism forms an early phase. Frank Kermode's *Romantic Image* seems a brilliant sortie in several directions, ambitions impossible to fulfill within the compass of a protracted essay. One objective is to assert a continuity within the English tradition from Romanticism to Symbolism with some suggestive gestures towards the 'modern movement'. Partly polemical, this involved combating Eliot's version of a 'dissociated sensibility' intensifying in the nineteenth century English tradition. Yet another objective seemed to be towards a reorientation of our attitudes towards present-day poetry. These Kermode seems to suggest are limited still by the noxious *symboliste* aesthetic which influenced Eliot. Polemical perhaps is the wrong word for *Romantic Image* since much of the book consists in an exploration of the dancer image as a hieroglyph of associated sensibility. 'Provocative' does more justice to its effect. The polemics are half-hearted, which may explain the odd omission of the Joycean 'epiphany' from the record, with its clear descent from Pater's 'will as vision' and the relation between the doctrine of the essay on *Style* and the 'images' of the *Renaissance*.

The relation of Imagism to the 'modern movement' as a whole, considered as a 'general part of the European mind' is discussed in Thomas Parkinson's 'Intimate and Impersonal: An Aspect of Modern Poetic,' (*Journal of Aesthetics and Art History*, 16, 373-383). For Parkinson, the disjunction between Imagism and the poets of the 1890's and the Symbolists is sharper than it is for Kermode. More positively than Kermode, Parkinson is concerned with the aesthetics of the 'modern movement'. The impersonality of Imagism, the insistence on the artist as creator of artifacts, as formulated by Flint and Pound, Parkinson relates to broadly contemporary and broadly similar notions: Ortega y Gasset's 'dehumanization of art' and Eliot's 'objective correlative'. Eliot's re-statement of the role that tradition plays, that the completely original art-work is either a false concept or involves an unreadable work, Parkinson reminds us, points to the highly polemical nature of Eliot's early essays with their deliberate denial of the Romantic and late-Romantic cult of 'sincerity' and of Pater's unique individual (in the essay on *Style*) with his unique sense of the world. It is the essay on *Style* which, for Parkinson, provides the basis for the aesthetic of the poets of the 1890's. In terms of Aesthetic, it might seem, the sole continuity between the poets of the *fin de siècle* and those of Imagism remains one of conscious antithesis.

It is still curious that in Flint's manifesto the three poets who represent the 'best tradition' are Sappho, Catullus and Villon, all of them concrete and direct perhaps, but apparently confessional, and very much the heroic mod-

els for the lyric poets of the 1890's. 'De-humanization' is one aspect merely of Imagist theory and that aspect which appears to distinguish most radically the Imagists from their English predecessors. The constant attempt to direct attention away from the artist towards the artifact can be found in an admittedly obscure sonnet of Mallarmé, *Don du Poème* where the aim of the poet is to produce an artifact which, perfected, belongs to everyone but the poet himself.

It is pertinent to recall some elements in Imagist doctrine. "An Image" Pound observes is "that which presents an intellectual and emotional complex in an instant of time . . . it is the presentation of such a 'complex' instantaneously which gives that sense of sudden liberation: that sense of freedom from time limits and space limits; that sense of sudden growth, which we experience in the presence of the greatest works of art." And again: "the natural object is always the *adequate* symbol," unadorned, unqualified. The object should be 'presented' rather than 'described' and should be allowed its own identity in presentation through a music which so far as possible flows; "let the beginning of the next line, catch the rise of the rhythm wave, unless you want a definite longish pause." The poet should work like the musician in stresses and syllables, studying coldly the rhythms of masters, preferably in other languages, so as not to be distracted by discursive meanings (like Hughes, I ignore Pound's Vorticist re-statements).

What this suggests is Symbolism with its 'magical' assumptions discounted: a renewed attempt to subdue a familiar nineteenth century antinomy between subject and object. Symbolism attempted to maintain the authority of the ego and to invest the object with a sacramental life; to return, though in a purely private manner, to the 'correspondences' of the Renaissance before the duality of subject and object had been painfully surrendered to, which accounts for Pound's accusation that it degrades the symbol to a form of metonymy. In Pater's criticism, it would seem that the antinomy is resolved by dropping the object as far as possible, so that in that sense Parkinson's analysis is valid. However, 'complex' is clearly, in spite of Pound's hints about the 'newer psychologists', a version of 'epiphany' or 'will as vision'. In Pound's imagist poems, if not in W. C. Williams', the mere presentation of the object is not enough. Moreover, theory apart, the actual texts of the Imagist poets are anticipated in several ways by Pater. Pater frequently describes a secular 'epiphany', the moment when a landscape or a townscape so arranges itself, or is patient of arrangement by the spectator into the 'significant forms' hinted at in the essay on Giorgione.

> In its primary aspect, a great picture has no more definite message for us than an accidental play of sunlight and shadow for a few moments on a wall or floor: is itself, in truth, a space of such fallen light, caught as the colours are in an Eastern carpet, but refined upon and dealt with more subtly and exquisitely than by Nature herself.

In describing Du Bellay, Pater speaks of his best-known poem as "a composition in which the matter is almost nothing, the form almost everything"—his own criterion for lyric, and in Pater's usual manner we are given not abstract statement but concrete presentation, in which the object becomes all, the subject nothing, if momentarily only.

> A sudden light transfigures some trivial thing, a weather-vane, a windmill, a winnowing fan, the dust in the barn-door. A moment—and the thing itself has vanished, because it was pure effect; but it leaves a relish behind it, a longing that the accident may happen again.

Symbolism and impressionism, whether in painting (the Rose Croix, the Synthetists) or in literature, are a culmination of that close relation between the arts that distinguishes the nineteenth century. Pound by resisting the 'viewy' reacts against nineteenth century attempts at total art; he sees, for example, a line running from impressionism to futurism and relates the anti-rhetorical movement of the English 1890's with Whistler and the cubists' extrusion of literary matter from painting. Such phenomena 'move together' but 'they do not, of course, move in step.' The painter, Pound observes, can 'describe' natural detail more effectively than the poet.

Pound's references to 'impressionism' must clearly refer to the later stages of that movement. Monet's impressionism of light is based on the unique, individual sensation; so too is Pisarro's. Later impressionism becomes more interested in the poetry of urban life, the dynamic chaos of surging forms and lights: cafes, theatres, night life, musicians, washerwomen; and Degas' dancers, with their colour, form, movement, light, through whom the essence of life itself might be captured. Art becomes free of the social rhetoric of realism, (as through symbolism and the English *fin de siècle* poetry attempts to free itself of the discursive) even though it requires little distortion to turn the moment of insight (Lautrec's psychological curiosity about the 'moment of life,' for example) into literary anecdote. Degas' *Au Café,* for example, was moralized as 'The Absinthe Drinkers' when that picture was exhibited in England in 1893. However, for the later Impressionists, the object is re-affirmed and the artist retains freedom to find poetry alive even in the most painful and prosaic details of the modern, urban world. (The documentation is in the propaganda of the New English Art Club). Sensuous, mobile, in love with light, the feeling eye, the personal 'impression' the Paterian and the painterly senses of the word are not so embarrassingly disjunct, for Pater, in spite of his subjectivism and moralizing submits to his epiphanies as *sui generis.*

Free verse, organically determined from within, 'every emotion and every phase of emotion has some toneless phrase, some rhythm phrase to express it,' is one of the marks of Imagism, and the subtler prose rhythmists of the nineteenth century, a Meredith or a Pater, write often in a species of free verse. This was recognized by W. B. Yeats when he prefaced his selections in the *Oxford Book of Modern Verse* with the famous Mona Lisa passage, typographically arranged as free-verse. The passage was at one time dismissed as 'a purple panel' of the grossest sort, but the analysis of Sr. Giorgio Melchiori and a recent broadcast talk by W. A. Ward make that view untenable. In the simplest sense, Pater gathers up in the passage, insights scattered through his whole essay on Leonardo, but the passage is important for other reasons. As Ward puts it 'Pater plainly attributes much more to the painting of the Mona Lisa than is, strictly speaking, legible upon it.' Pater's contemporary, J. A. Symonds, remarked that he "attributes to the painter a far greater degree of sceptical self-consciousness than he was at all likely to have possessed." Another Victorian critic suggested that Pater was projecting into Leonardo's image "a meaning oddly characteristic of the conventional over-refinement of the present day" and Pater himself admits: "Certainly the Lady Lisa might stand as the symbol of the modern idea." In place of earlier images of Leonardo as great artificer, true to natural appearance (Vasari), as mage, the discoverer and expounder of the secrets of nature (the German romantics), Pater presents Leonardo as victim of the 'Fatal Woman' and yet by presenting the 'Fatal Woman' as image, Leonardo becomes master as well as victim. Pater himself rediscovers his own sense of freedom in creating *his* image via Leonardo's Lisa; in creating a model which would enable him to continue writing in 'the determinist nightmare' of the Post-Darwinian nineteenth century world. The Mona Lisa image is the first example of Symbolist thaumaturgy. Darwin's authoritative (so it seemed) mechanistic analysis had destroyed in man 'his every illusion of divinity', Pater's phrase, and Pater's aesthetic philosophy and practice were essentially an attempt to restore to man his sense of freedom. Ward reminds us that the explicit statement of how this thaumaturgic activity operates can be found in the essay on *Style* of 1888. In that essay, Pater makes a distinction between 'masculine' and 'feminine' in art; the 'masculine' Pater defines as the 'controlling, rational, forming, power' of the artist, exerted on 'the feminine' which is the brute mass of the artist's experience. It is 'soul' as opposed to 'mind', a further and related distinction. Art is born out of the work in organization achieved by mind. It is the design made on 'the web' of the artist's experience. The 'web', the feminine part of Pater's experience is his expectation of reality as taught to him by Darwin: perpetual flux, the context of 'determinist nightmare', existing under the influence of natural law or in Pater's despairing term 'necessity'. And, finally, as Ward puts it:

> although man's consciousness and being were fragmented into moments which changed even as they were formed, those fragments bore in them 'the central forces' of the world.

For Pater, organic development meant that although the organism constantly changed, it contained vestigially legible upon it the synoptic history of that development.

There are three particulars of the feminine part of Pater's experience, 'the web' on which the design must be projected; all 'that is actual' in his knowledge of the world.

It is the business of art to reflect these in a male manner, submitting them to the rational, controlling, organizing power of design. By reducing as far as may be, the incoherent flux of experience to design, the artist will be able to emancipate himself from that experience. To the extent that the power of design affects the artist's own response to the incoherence and determinism of the nightmare it will establish his freedom from it. And the type of such a design is the Mona Lisa. In that image:

> we may see Pater struggling to evolve the myth, or artistic model, which would locate and give expression to that material. He was intent on transmuting those ideas of reality which have been described, into an image—intent on rendering the impalpable, of making the ideas he wished to express 'saturate and become identical with' the vessel made to contain them. He wishes to define the image on the female 'fabric' of his dreams. And he wishes the fabric of dreams to be legible upon the image.

> In the Daughters of Herodias, Leonardo's picture, the characters, Pater says, are: "clairvoyants, through whom, as through delicate instruments, one becomes aware of the subtler forces of nature, all that is magnetic in it." They are 'significant examples' in which we actually see those forces at work on the human flesh. . . . Pater was trying to create an image or model, or design, into which he could pour all the female fluid matter of his understanding of the world so as to locate it there and make it legible.

The 'forces of nature' and the 'magic web' are what he wishes to express. The Mona Lisa contains all the three particulars Ward defines and at the same time the masculine demands Pater is making in that she reduces the particulars to a design. She satisfies what the spirit needs in the face of modern life 'the sense of freedom'. In its free rhythms, not necessarily in Yeats' precise arrangement, the opening lines run:

> The presence that rose thus so strangely beside the
>   waters
> Is expressive of what in the ways of a thousand
>   years:
> Man had come to desire.

To desire at the historical moment, when Pater was writing: the Lady Lisa being expressive of what *he* desires. 'The ways of a thousand years' is both properly liturgical and attempts to give, as Ward notes, universality and authority to the image.

> Hers is the head
> Upon which all 'the ends of the world' are come and
> The eyelids are a little weary.

The ends of the world is also both liturgical and an attempt to invest the image with universality but the phrase contains also the explicit statement of Pater's aims, expressed concretely as always. Mona Lisa is 'a head', a single entity, 'upon which all the ends of the world are come,' concentrating in a single, finite image, all the

fluid matter of man's apprehension of the world, his sense of relation to the objects about, and of their 'tyranny' over him. Lisa's beauty is

> Wrought out from within upon the flesh,
> The deposit, little cell by cell,
> Of strange thoughts
> And fantastic reveries
> And exquisite passions.

The image is organic, but changes, developing as it is conceived: 'cell by cell' shows knowledge of the doctrine of organic development in the biological no less than the aesthetic sense. The Lady Lisa, Pater tells us, the image, defined itself on 'the fabric of his dreams.' All history is vestigially legible in the moment of our apprehension of her face:

> All the thought and experience of the world
> Have etched and moulded there.

She contains, still following Ward's account, a synoptic history of the development of civilization.

> The animalism of Greece,
> The lust of Rome,
> The mysticism of the Middle Ages
> With its spiritual ambition and imaginative loves,
> The return of the Pagan world,
> The sins of the Borgias.

This subserves Pater's notion of the conflict between the Hellenic and the Christian elements in Western culture and his cyclic theory of civilizations passing through the stages of Saint, Artist and Philosopher. But in a deeper sense evolution has introduced a new conception of time into the English consciousness. In a moment there are concentrated 'a thousand experiences:' just as the notion of carbon contains both the notions of coal and of the diamond. The artist's business, Ward continues,

> was thus to collapse the growth of a thing into one of his moments of vision, and to contradict temporal development. He was to make the moment 'wholly concrete'. The moment becomes 'wholly concrete,' Pater maintains, when, in his own words, 'all the interests and effects of a long history, have condensed themselves, and. . . . seem to absorb past and future in the intense consciousness of the present. Thus are created 'exquisite pauses in time. . . . in which we seem to be spectators of all the fullness of existence, and which are like some consummate extract or quintessence of life.'

And the Mona Lisa is one such 'exquisite pause,' part of her function being to resist this evanescence and decay. With the world 'melting under our feet', in this post-Darwinian moment, Pater felt the need of security, which was to be achieved by constructing stasis, and art was the means of construction. A man could dwell in one of the 'exquisite pauses' art created and so become freed, emancipated from the deliquescence of the world. Part of the Lady Lisa's function then is to help us 'expand our moments a little beyond their allotted span,' and in a late book, *Plato and Platonism,* Pater speaks of 'certain pregnant types' who will present in an instant something like 'the accumulated history of mankind'. So we proceed to the passage Yeats quotes at the beginning of his anthology:

> She is older than the rocks,
> Among which she sits;
> Like the vampire she has been dead many times,
> And learned the secrets of the grave;
> And has been a diver in deep seas
> And keeps their fallen day about her;
> And trafficked for strange webs
> With Eastern Merchants:
> And as Leda,
> Was the mother of Helen of Troy,
> And, as Saint Anne,
> The mother of Mary.

Like the Fatal Woman, she is constantly born into time, but older than time. The image picks up all the attempts to interpret Lisa's smile—it was the Germans of the Romantic period, who had first attempted to interpret the background of rock and water. She is 'spectator of all the fullness', ideally detached, passive, like all Fatal Women, for

> All this has been to her
> But as the sound of lyres and flutes.

The lyres and flutes refer probably to another contemporary interpretation of the Fatal Woman, Swinburne's *Laus Veneris,* and to Vasari's account of how Leonardo arranged for musicians to play to La Gioconda while she was sitting, to dispel the melancholy that so often afflicts the faces of sitters. Ward's analysis continues by pointing out that though she is detached from her experience, she has organized it into her design and so is able to free herself from it. But at the same time as she frees herself from the experience, that experience cannot be denied, and must be suffered.

> It lives in the delicacy,
> With which it has moulded the changing
>   lineaments
> And tinged the eyelids
> And the hands.

We understand, says Pater, that any construction we make 'shows the clear, perpetual outline of face or limb' is but an image of ours—a design in a web, for nothing in our experience of the world is 'perpetual' or 'clear.' But we must, none the less, make the design contradict the reality of our experience, formulate and organize it, or the world will degenerate into total incomprehensibility. The *Mona Lisa* is Pater's suggested design. The male and female parts of man's experience and desire are reconciled there. She at once resists and gives expression to the 'magnetic nightmare.' In so far as she is eternal, and in so far as she imposed 'a clear, definite outline' on 'all the thought and experience of the world' she succeeds in her resistance. She shows the action of mind on soul, shows man dealing masterfully with his experience so as to control it, thus, gives him back his sense of freedom. She is at once the realisation and the suggestion of an artistic ideal.

As Pater himself puts it:

> modern philosophy has conceived the idea of humanity as wrought upon and summing up in itself all modes of thought and life. Certainly the Lady Lisa might stand as the embodiment of the old fancy, the symbol of the modern idea.

I have dealt at great length with this passage, because it seems, both in itself and in the doctrine which accompanies it and is crystallized within it, to anticipate aspects of Imagist theory. The repeated 'and' is a trick of syntax used by, for example, H.D.; and Pater uses many auxiliary verbs which have an effect of unobtrusiveness.

According to Ford Madox Ford, it was Arthur Symons who provided the model in free-verse for the Imagists. Symons, however, wrote little in this mode, though as we shall see he has his own importance as precursor. In his introduction to the poems of Lionel Johnson of 1915, Pound seizes on a few lines here and there where Johnson's swift and accurate phrasing seems to foreshadow Imagism, as well as recall Gautier and Chinese verse. However, Symons is more important both from the point of view of 'organic' verse-structure and the creation of 'images.' Much of his verse is concerned with the glittering patina, the bright surface truths of urban life: the streets by night; the half-world of the ballet and the music-hall. The ideal objectivity of the Imagist is rarely achieved. Landscapes and townscapes remain creations of the observer's mood: the old duality persists. A good example is *Dieppe: Grey and Green:*

> The grey-green stretch of sandy grass,
> Indefinitely desolate.
> A sea of lead, a sky of slate;
> Already autumn in the air, alas!
>
> One stark monotony of stone,
> The long hotel, acutely white,
> Against the after-sunset light
> Withers grey-green, and takes the grass's tone.
>
> Listless and endless it outlies
> And means, to you and me, no more
> Than any pebble on the shore,
> Or this indifferent moment as it dies.

Here, we encounter broken and rugged lines, melting detail, a hazy harmony such as a Monet might relish, and a final evocation of a sad 'epiphany' in Pater's mode. The title is Whistlerian. The scene is analyzed methodically rather as an art-critic might analyse a painting. The hotel for example is described in painterly terms as 'long', all detail evaporated and 'acutely' suggests both painfully and vividly white, the glowing negation of colour. Shape, then, is definite, but defined emotively in terms of colour. The first seven lines are all images: grey-green of sandy grass; sky of slate; stark monotony of stone; long hotel; sea of lead, and so forth. The verse itself, with its careful play of monosyllables, the bare fact, against the subjective polysyllables, moves freely without metronome. It is not until the eighth line that a verb appears and the word 'takes' is satisfyingly ambiguous. The final stanza deviates from Imagist and returns to Impressionist technique. *Dieppe: Grey and Green* is lyrical in form, as Pater had recommended, for in the lyric, matter and form are as far as possible, fused. Listless, endless, formless, passing, a wavering fugitive moment becomes a sensation worthy of poetic existence because of the 'epiphany' of sky, grass, sea and the ennui of colour in the hotel, almost, we are tempted to say, by the moment's very existence.

In other poems also, imagist lines tend to be embedded in impressionist and 'decadent' detail. In *Nocturne,* for example, London resolves itself into disparate images: 'the dome of cloud'; 'The long embankment with its lights/ The pavement glittering with fallen rain.' while the river 'shakes with wavering gleams/ That softly plunged through depths that lay/ Impenetrable . . .' and most notably:

> A bright train flashed with all its squares
> Of warm light where the bridge lay mistily.

though once again the poem is tugged back to the subject, the observer.

White Heliotrope similarly opens with a stanza without verbs and with the same irregularities of rhythm and play of monosyllables that characterize *At Dieppe: Grey and Green,* though in that poem, the scene passes from a Renoir to the psychological curiosity of Lautrec. In Symons' prose impressions of Dieppe, published in the *Savoy* of 1896, we find again the same primary diction, economy in the use of the verb in order to give an instantaneous impression of the town: line fades, colour shimmers. The life of Dieppe is captured through colour as though it lived in a painting: the bright yellow and blue dresses of the fashionable women with their huge, floating hats; the shadowy grey mass of the Eglise Saint-Jacques; Dieppe's sea and sky whose thousand shifts of luminosity and colour Symons studies from twilight to sunrise. And the same procedure is adopted in his numerous 'impressionistic travel pieces.'

Dieppe deals with that typical impressionistic subject—the sea (Jongkind, Monet, Boudin); in other poems Symons touches on another impressionist and *symboliste* subject, the dancer; and there are no doubt obscure connexions between the living and moving *Symboliste* Image and Pound's reaction from Amygisme towards the 'Vortex', but this is not the place for discussing those. Folded away in magazines, without doubt, are other poems which anticipate Imagism in its earlier phases. Such will only alter the received version of literary history very mildly, but they serve as a reminder that tradition is not built on ruptures.

Lorelei Cederstrom

[In the following essay, Cederstrom identifies Whitman as "a powerful and pervasive force" on Imagist theory and practice.]

SOURCE: "Walt Whitman and the Imagists," in *Walt Whitman of Mickle Street: A Centennial Collection,* edited by Geoffrey M. Sill, The University of Tennessee Press/Knoxville, 1994, pp. 205-23.

The influence of Walt Whitman upon the Imagist poets is a complex issue. Although several recent studies have clarified Whitman's relationship to certain Imagists like Ezra Pound, Whitman's influence upon the poetic theory of Imagism has been less clearly defined.[1] A major difficulty in addressing this question is that many of the Imagists considered their poetic practice to be directly opposed to Whitman's. This essay will demonstrate that, notwithstanding the pleas of Imagists to the contrary, Walt Whitman's poetry was a powerful and pervasive force on their practice and technique.

The most vociferous denial of Whitman's influence came from the Imagists' self-styled spokesperson, Amy Lowell. She found fault with every aspect of Whitman's style and technique, beginning with his point of view, which she felt to be confining: "He had a curiously limited way of viewing life principally from the outside," she noted. She felt that Whitman's form was the result of this superficial viewpoint; his form sprang, she wrote, "not from a positive desire to give substance to a new conception of beauty, but from a negative one not to incorporate in his work any existing beauties, whatsoever. Here at once is a cleavage with the moderns" ("Walt Whitman and the New Poetry" 507). She viewed his use of free verse, an element so vital to the Imagists, with an equally skeptical eye, claiming that Whitman did not write in *vers libre* at all, but in a "highly emotional prose." She found him guilty of "inversion . . . clichés . . . wrong use of foreign words," and that catch-all of modern disparagement, "bad taste." Moreover, Lowell prefaced her first Imagist anthology, *Some Imagist Poets* (1915), with the Imagist "Credo," which contains a denial of "cosmic" poetry and all it represents: "We are not a school of painters, but we believe that poetry should render particulars exactly and not deal in vague generalities, however magnificent and sonorous. It is for this reason that we oppose the cosmic poet, who seems to us to shirk the real difficulties of his art." In spite of these and other similar denials, a case can be made for a connection between Whitman and the Imagist poets John Gould Fletcher, Richard Aldington, and F. S. Flint; indeed, it can be demonstrated that Whitman had some influence on Lowell herself.

Before exploring the dynamics of these specific relationships, it should be emphasized that there is little doubt that Whitman himself wrote poems that can be called Imagist. This has been noted by several critics—Waskow, Asselineau, and others—and need only be re-emphasized here. An early poem, "Pictures," rejected for the 1855 edition of *Leaves of Grass,* leaned strongly in the direction of Imagism. Such poems as "A Farm Picture," "The Runner," "The Dalliance of the Eagles," "Cavalry Crossing a Ford," "Bivouac on a Mountain Side," and others are Imagist poems in the purest sense. However, these "Imagist" poems of Whitman's can be dismissed as accidental unless it can be determined that Whitman's aesthetic principles are in agreement with Imagist theory. A comparison of Whitman's poetic theory with the Imagist "Credo" set out by Lowell will demonstrate the accord in their ideas about the nature of poetry.

The first principle of the Imagists, as described by Lowell, is to "use the exact word," the word that most precisely describes the object, but in the language of common speech. We can find no contradiction of this principle in Whitman's 1855 preface to *Leaves of Grass,* where he states: "The art of art, the glory of expression and the sunshine of the light of letters is simplicity. Nothing is better than simplicity. . . . nothing can make up for excess or for lack of definiteness" (*LG* 717).

Second, the Imagists emphasize the importance of the use of new rhythms in poetry, and in spite of Lowell's condemnation of Whitman's use of free verse, the continuing influence of his poems stands as a testament to the fecundity of the verse from which has come to be associated with his name. Whitman emphasizes the organic development of rhythm from thought, noting: "The rhyme and uniformity of perfect poems show the free growth of metrical laws and bud from them as unerringly and loosely as lilacs or roses on a bush, and take shapes as compact as the shapes of chestnuts and oranges and melons and pears, and shed the perfume impalpable to form" (*LG* 714). The concept of form in Imagist theory emphasizes the same freedom: "In poetry," Lowell writes, "a new cadence means a new idea." Whitman also encourages the organic development of form: "The cleanest expression is that which finds no sphere worthy of itself and makes one" (*LG* 717).

The third principle of the Imagists is absolute freedom in the choice of subject. Neither objects nor ideas of the past or present should predominate, for good art may be about either age. Subjects drawn from the modern age must, however, be used with caution, since, as Lowell warned in 1915, "There is nothing so uninspiring nor so old-fashioned as an aeroplane of the year 1911." Whitman, too, asserts the need for durability in the choice of subjects. He emphasizes the necessity of speaking to the modern world, but at the same time notes that the "prescient" poet "projects himself centuries ahead and judges performer or performance after the changes of time." Whitman's statements recall Lowell's about the aeroplane, for he warns the poet to ask himself whether a "new discovery in science or arrival at superior planes of thought and judgment and behavior fixed him or his so that either can be looked down upon" (*LG* 726).

The most critical area of comparison occurs with the fourth statement of the Imagist credo. Here the Imagists state their rejection of the cosmic poet and their own dedication to the portrayal of an image. As noted earlier, there is evidence within the body of Whitman's work that he found the simple portrayal of an image to be a worthwhile artistic pursuit, and there is evidence of this belief in his artistic creed as well. He notes, "In these Leaves

everything is literally photographed. Nothing is poeticized, no divergence, not a step, not an inch, nothing for beauty's sake, no euphemism, no rhyme" (Whitman, *Complete Writings* 6: 71). Whitman agrees most heartily that the poet should not deal in vague generalities. Things and their description are the lifestream of the poet. In "Song of Myself" he writes: "I accept Reality and dare not question it. / Materialism first and last imbuing" (*LG* 51). For Whitman all ideas, all metaphysics, are inherent in things. The thoughts of the poet "are the hymns of the praise of things. In the talk on the soul and eternity and God off of his equal plane he is silent. . . . he sees eternity in men and women" (*LG* 713). Whitman departs from the Imagists in that he goes beyond them; he begins with things, and, from things shown clearly, the poet points the way to the soul. In Whitman's words, "folks expect of the poet to indicate more than the beauty and dignity which always attach to dumb real objects. . . . they expect him to indicate the path between reality and their souls" (*LG* 714). This is not to say that the way to the soul should be described in vague abstractions. It should, rather, grow out of the life of the things described. The great poet, by careful choice of image, creates a cosmic awareness, a consciousness of the life which illuminates the simplest picture. The great poet is not to speak of the soul directly, although Whitman himself often does this, but refer to it by precise, definite pictures.

Whitman's remarks about definiteness seem to contradict another of his statements, namely, his demand for "indirection." He writes: "For such the expression of the American poet is to be transcendent and new. It is to be indirect and not direct or descriptive or epic" (*LG* 712). It is necessary to understand what Whitman means by "indirect" here, for it appears to contradict his earlier statements regarding the presentation of a definite thing, a rendering of particulars. Whitman is referring here to the role of the poet as one who "points the way to the soul." The way to cosmic consciousness is by indirection; through image, the soul enters the poem secretly, indirectly. The poet, for Whitman, does more than describe. He describes, photographs, excluding nothing for beauty's sake, and by this presentation of direct image, transcendence occurs, cosmic values enter. It is because the Imagist poets value the image not for its own sake but, in Pound's words, for the "intellectual and emotional complex" which surrounds it, that Imagist theory can be said to be in agreement with Whitman. When the Imagists speak of their disagreement with cosmic poetry, they voice disapproval of the very vague abstract discussions of God and the universe which Whitman himself deplores. Whitman writes, "The poetic quality is not marshaled in rhyme or uniformity or abstract addresses to things nor in melancholy complaints or good precepts, but is the life of these and much else and is in the soul" (*LG* 714). E. H. Eby, in a study of Whitman's use of the word "indirection," points out also that indirection transcends simple image-making: "Indirection, then, involves but is more than image-making, more than an analogy, more than myth, more than symbolism. It goes beyond all that because it must be free and fluid and illimitable in its suggestiveness" (9). Although it is plain that Whitman's verse transcends image-making, it does not transcend the principles of the Imagist poet, for Pound also writes of the ability of the great poet to "liberate," to set the reader free from time limits and space limits," and infuse the reader with a "sense of sudden growth" (Hughes 28-29).

An image may thus be both definite and suggestive. To return to the Imagist doctrine, the fifth statement can be presented here without comment, as it touches on the last statements. Lowell notes that the Imagist wishes to "produce poetry that is hard and clear, never blurred or indefinite." Whitman has written as well that "nothing can make up for excess or for the lack of definiteness" (*LG* 717). The final statement of the Imagist theory reads, "Finally, most of us believe that concentration is of the very essence of poetry." Whitman similarly compares the poet to a stone-cutter who carves "solid and beautiful forms . . . where there are now no solid forms" (*LG* 712). The poet is "the arbiter of the diverse and he is the key." Although Whitman is aware of the need for concentration in image-making, in his theories of method he advocates neither the narrow compactness found in Pound, nor the extreme vagueness of the Symbolists or cosmic poets. "The greatest poet," he writes, "has less a marked style and is more the channel of thoughts and things without increase or diminution, and is the free channel of himself" (*LG* 717). The self is the measure, and the self both expands and contracts, concentrates and diversifies. Whitman's poetry is often extremely concentrated; the catalogs are an obvious testament to this concentration. It is his soul that is expansive, but his expansive soul finds expression in earthbound, physical imagery. Thus, point for point, there is a consistent similarity between Whitman's poetics and the Imagist theories set out by Lowell.

Let us now examine in some detail Whitman's influence on the early Imagist writers. Amy Lowell has stated that Whitman gave to the Imagists no more than an attitude, a vision of the poet as a seer which she and the other modern poets could accept. She was aware of the several short Imagist poems to be found within *Leaves of Grass,* but in the end disavowed their influence on her or the others. In her 1927 article in the *Yale Review,* she writes: "It would be utter folly to consider that the vignettes in modern work derive from Whitman when Emily Dickinson did the same thing better" (515). But it is possible, nonetheless, to trace an example in which her own poetic practice derived directly from Whitman. In his autobiography, John Gould Fletcher mentioned a circumstance wherein Whitman inspired him and he, in turn, had some influence upon Lowell's method. While on a visit to London, Fletcher was seized by the desire to present London in a series of images of the kind Whitman used in his city catalogs. "I was carried away by Whitman's robust realism, by his masterly grasp of the details and contrasts of life to be found in just such a city as I was now visiting" (*Life Is My Song* 42). In a discussion of the poems they both were working on, Fletcher described to Miss Lowell his desire to capture London life in a poem.

Miss Lowell asked about this method. Looking out a window, Fletcher said:

> I would sit and look at every object in just such a view as this is. . . . I would try and describe all these objects without in any way identifying myself with them. I would try and put down their essence, their moods . . . by finding words and color sounds that would orchestrate them, make them speak to the reader by means of such combinations. I would thus try and get at the dominant moods of the city; the moods of early morning, the moods of evening, the mood of midnight. Then I would take in other objects. For example, the banks, the hospitals, the churches, the hotels, the clubs, the theaters, the stores, the street traffic, the railway stations, the restaurants, the parks, the public houses, the street corners. Thus the whole city would become recreated in my mind by grasping the objects in it simply as objects and nothing more. . . . The trouble with them [the Imagists] is that they cultivate too much the fragment. They haven't tackled yet, in perfectly free form, a whole city full of people. It has always been my ambition to do so. (*Life Is My Song* 92)

Fletcher quotes Lowell as describing his idea as "fascinating" and "perfectly original." She suggested that he call this idea the "unrelated method." "Not quite unrelated," Fletcher replied, "I simply want to be able to look at everything frankly as if for the first time. For that reason, I want to feel detached from it, as if it had a life of its own, which is my business to see and describe." Finally, Fletcher confessed, to the reader but not to Lowell, the origin of his "new" method:

> I was not aware how much Miss Lowell could understand of this; but at any rate, I felt, as I sat there, that she understood and sympathized far more than Pound would have done. I had never mentioned this particular desire of mine to him, nor to any of his friends. . . . Moreover, the idea itself was derivable remotely from Whitman's realistic "catalogue passages" interspersed throughout *Leaves of Grass* and from Blake's "seeing through, not with the eye," and I already knew what he thought of Blake and Whitman. (*Life Is My Song* 93)

Amy Lowell later confessed to Fletcher that her poem "A London Thoroughfare" had been written as a direct result of the method she heard him describe (*Life Is My Song* 102).

In addition to this direct influence, Whitman's influence is obvious in other poems of Miss Lowell's as well. She was probably unaware that she was using Whitman's techniques, but she freely admitted that she admired his attitudes and his visions, and they appear in her work. She uses images in "In Excelsis" which are highly reminiscent of "Song of Myself" and "Children of Adam":

> I drink your lips,
> I eat the whiteness of your hands and feet.
> My mouth is open,
> As a new jar I am empty and open.
>
> (Untermeyer 170)

Her long poem "Lilacs" bears a resemblance to Whitman's "When Lilacs Last At The Dooryard Bloom'd":

> Lilacs in dooryards,
> Holding quiet conversations with an early moon;
> Lilacs watching a deserted house
> Settling sideways into the grass of an old road;
> Lilacs, wind-beaten, staggering under a lopsided
>   shock of bloom
> Above a cellar dug into a hill.
> You are everywhere.
> You are everywhere.
>
> (Untermeyer 172)

The ending of Lowell's poem refers to Whitman's last thought in "When Lilacs." Whitman's poem concludes with an image of "Lilac and star and bird twined with the chant of my soul." Lowell's ends with the self as well: "Lilac in me because I am New England." Also, in "Solitaire," Lowell describes the wandering exploration of the mind through a sleeping city, in a poem that could be called a miniature of Whitman's "The Sleepers." The opening lines suggest the comparison immediately:

> When night drifts along the streets of the city,
> And sifts down between the uneven roofs,
> My mind begins to peek and peer. . . .
>
> (Untermeyer 161)

Lowell's prose poems such as "Midday and Afternoon" are reincarnations of Whitman's catalogs and use the method that Fletcher described. The very conception of a prose poem may have come from Whitman, for Lowell called his poetry "a highly emotional prose." Lowell accepted this "prose" as having poetic value because of its "approach and return." She defines return as "some device by which a poem is brought back to its starting place," or some "dominant emotional symbol" ("Walt Whitman and the New Poetry" 509). For Whitman, this dominant emotional symbol was the self, which unites the profusion of life. In "Midday and Afternoon," Lowell, too, finds a center in the "I": "Swirl of crowded streets. Shock and recoil of traffic. The stock-still brick facade of an old church, against which the waves of people lurch and withdraw. . . . I am a place of the town, a bit of blown dust, thrust along with the crowd. Proud to feel the pavement under me, reeling with feet" (*Some Imagist Poets* 1916, 84-85). Thus, in spite of her denials of Whitman's influence, it is present in the theme, the vision, the images, and even the method which Amy Lowell consistently employs in her own work.

It is not surprising that John Gould Fletcher should have explained a Whitmanian technique to Amy Lowell, for, of all the Imagists, Fletcher, spiritually, is most indebted to Whitman. Fletcher loved and admired Whitman greatly. In a poem called "Whitman," he describes him as a "mountain" of poetic vision which no single man can quarry. The influence of Whitman on Fletcher has been mentioned by other critics, including Lowell: "He became an ardent Whitmanite and his own writing reflected this devotion," she writes ("Walt Whitman and the New Poetry" 511). Fletcher shares Whitman's mysticism, his peculiar kind of patriotism, his method of intuiting the inner life and essential being of things, his poetic freedom, and many of his themes. In Fletcher's first book, *Irradiations—Sand and Spray,* there are passages that could be inserted directly into "Song of Myself," so close are they in theme and style to Whitman's own, albeit lacking in Whitman's power:

> O seeded grass, you army of little men
> Crawling up the long slope with quivering quick
>   blades of steel,
> You who storm millions of graves, tiny green
>   tentacles of earth,
> Interlace yourselves tightly over my heart,
> And do not let me go!
> For I would be here forever and watch with one
>   eye
> The pilgrimaging ants in your dull, savage
>   jungles,
> The while with the other I see the stiff lines of the
>   slope,
> Break in mid-air, a wave surprisingly arrested, and
>   above it, wavering, dancing, bodiless,
>   colourless, unreal,
> The long, thin, lazy fingers of the heat. . . .
>
> (*Selected Poems* 6)

Fletcher's early "Symphonies," from *Goblins and Pagodas,* the Green, the White, the Blue, and the Scarlet, all bear clear evidence of Whitman's brand of mystical vision. "Oh, old pagodas of my soul, how you glittered across green trees!" is the cry of the "Symphonies," a vision of the soul in flight, absorbing, transcending, dreaming. Like Whitman, he becomes one with the cosmos in his mystical visions:

> I am a glittering raindrop
> Hugged close by the cool rhododendron.
> I am a daisy starring
> The exquisite corners of the close-cropped turf. . . .
>
> (*Selected Poems* 21)

> I will abide in this forest of pines;
> For I have unveiled naked beauty,
> And the things that she whispered to me in the
>   darkness
> Are buried deep in my heart.
>
> (*Selected Poems* 25)

Throughout these poems, Fletcher describes the flight of what Whitman terms the "fluid and swallowing soul":

> Towards the impossible
> Towards the inaccessible
> Towards the ultimate,
> Towards the silence,
> Towards the eternal
> These blossoms go.
>
> The peonies spring like rockets in the twilight,
> And out of them all, I rise.
>
> (*Selected Poems* 27)

Glenn Hughes, in his study of the Imagists, has noted other relationships between Fletcher and Whitman. "The

Return to Life" in Fletcher's *The Sea of Life,* he notes, is straight out of Whitman. He calls *Breakers and Granite* "Fletcher's salute to America"—"a Whitmanesque book, overflowing with rich impressions"—and states that Fletcher's "Lincoln" has already taken its place beside Whitman's "When Lilacs" as "one of the greatest eulogies inspired by the best-loved American" (Hughes 147). Whitman's voice can be found throughout Fletcher's poems. The latter writer's long poem "Autobiography" contains many elements of "Song of Myself," including catalog passages, a traveling point of view, and an attempt at identification with universal values. Fletcher's poem "To Columbus" refers persistently to Whitman's "A Thought of Columbus"; each emphasizes the "cumulus" of life, the years and people that have gone in and out of existence in the centuries since Columbus set forth. Both point out the relationship between the journey of the soul through life and Columbus's journey to the new world. Both poems end with a juxtaposition of Columbus's dreams and modern perspectives. Fletcher states:

> And we bring with us the old seed ripened to a
>   fruit, the proud will grow bitter and silent. . . .
> You who once guided us westward, here on this
>   eastward shore will not look down and
>   understand.
>
> (*Selected Poems* 155)

Whitman's poem ends with a similar, though less bitter, testament to Columbus as progenitor of the present:

> O'er the long backward path to thee—one vast
>   consensus, north, south, east, west,
> Soul plaudits! acclamation! reverent echoes!
> One manifold, huge memory to thee! oceans and
>   lands!
> The modern world to thee and thought of thee!
>
> (*LG* 582)

In spite of the many resemblances to Whitman, Fletcher seems to have missed many of Whitman's methodic innovations and, with the exception of his new use of Whitman's city imagery, he used very few of the dynamic techniques which Whitman anticipated. He did, however, inherit Whitman's concerns, and the cosmic awareness that shaped Whitman's poetry was very much a part of Fletcher's perception. Fletcher proves that a cosmic view need not bar a poet from the Imagist movement, of which he was very much an accepted member.

In opposition to Fletcher, Richard Aldington, of all the Imagists, is the least obviously indebted to Walt Whitman. His poetic vision lacks Whitman's love and Whitman's joy. Aldington, like his close friend D. H. Lawrence, rejected Whitman's desire to merge with every aspect of humanity. Aldington rejected much of society, appalled by its cruelty, hurt by its indifference, and disgusted by its ugliness. This rejection found its way into his poetry. A poem called "People," later titled "Resentment," strongly suggests Whitman's influence in its negation of Whitman's merging self:

> Why should you try to crush me?
> Am I so Christlike?
> You beat against me,
> Immense waves, filthy with refuse.
> I am the last upright of a smashed break water.
> But you shall not crush me
> Though you bury me in foaming slime
> And hiss your hatred about me.
> You break over me, cover me; I shudder at the
>   contact;
> Yet I pierce through you
> And stand up, torn, dripping, shaken,
> But whole and fierce.
>
> (116)

Aldington achieves wholeness by resisting others, Whitman by accepting them.

Whitman and Aldington approach each other more directly in their war poetry, for both lived through war, were closely connected to it, and revealed in their poetry that they were affected by it. Whitman in "Drum Taps" and Aldington in "Images of War" share an ability to transcend the horrors of the battlefield. In "Bivouac on a Mountain Side," Whitman, in pure Imagist terms, describes a "traveling army halting"; then, without moralizing, he turns his attention overhead: "And over all the sky—the sky! far, far out of reach, studded, breaking out, the eternal stars" (*LG* 300). Aldington's "In the Trenches" makes the same kind of transcendental leap. From the weary soldier the poet turns his eyes upward:

> Impotent,
> How impotent is all this clamour,
> This destruction and contest . . .
> Night after night the Pleiades sing
> And Orion swings his belt across the sky. . . .

But Aldington moralizes, preaches, and ends with the bitter question:

> Can you stay them with your noise
> Then kill Winter with your cannon,
> Hold back Orion with your bayonets
> And crush the spring leaf with your armies!
>
> (82-83)

Here we have one example of Whitman writing a more nearly perfect Imagist poem than a writer commonly associated with the Imagist tradition. This becomes ironic in light of Aldington's comments about Whitman:

> If you feel you are too rhetorical or too didactic, you
> must have a tendency to write like old Walt Whitman,
> whom I have just been reading, and who might have
> been a jolly fine poet, if he hadn't been spoilt with
> the ideal that all poets should mouth platitudes in
> pompous language, and so draw a highly moral lesson
> from what they saw. Like every American, Whitman
> had to be cosmic. Bah! what is cosmic? (Fletcher
> quoting Aldington, *Life Is My Song* 79)

It is safe to answer that Aldington was as cosmic as Whitman in the two poems discussed above and certainly more didactic, rhetorical, and pompous.

A cosmic point of view derives from the ability to transcend actuality, no matter how grim. In their poems of war, both Whitman and Aldington were able to transcend death and attain a vision of beauty. Aldington describes a dead soldier as abstractly beautiful:

> More beautiful than one can tell,
> More subtly colored than a perfect Goya,
> And more austere and lovely in repose
> Than Angelo's hand could ever carve in stone.
>
> (96)

Whitman finds the beauty of the soul present in the face of a dead youth:

> O the bullet could never kill what you really are,
>   dear friend,
> Nor the bayonet stab what you really are;
> The soul! yourself I see, great as any, good as the
>   best,
> Waiting secure and content, which the bullet
>   could never kill,
> Nor the bayonet stab O friend
>
> (*LG* 322)

The climax of "Drum Taps" occurs when Whitman sees in the face of a dead boy that "this face is the face of the Christ himself. / Dead and divine and the brother of all, and here again he lies" (*LG* 307). Aldington's ability to transcend never goes beyond the visual appreciation of the dead in repose and the evidence of recurring life found in nature. Aldington was too horrified by war and death ever to achieve the acceptance and transcendence that Whitman did. Whitman's sympathies always reached beyond the bounds of individuality, so much so that he could write of a soldier, "poor boy! I never knew you, / Yet I think I could not refuse this moment to die for you, if that would save you" (*LG* 310).

Apart from Aldington's direct denials of Whitman, it is only in their war poetry that the two poets reveal any similarities. After his early work, Aldington's poetry became bitter and ironic, its sensuality earthbound rather than transcendental. It was only the soul-shattering experience of war that forced Aldington to search for universal or cosmic realities. In his writings about his poetry, particularly in his preface to *The Complete Poems,* Aldington gives us a clue to the areas of similarity he has with Whitman, as well as to their fundamental differences. He writes:

> This brings me to two other elements of poetry about which I feel great diffidence in speaking— I mean reverence and the sense of mystery. By "reverence" I understand no false or affected humility, but an intimate and spontaneous conviction that what is not me, what is outside of me, is far greater and more interesting than I am, although the only account I can give of it is how it appears to me and through me.

Thus, by his own admission, Aldington never achieves the pure union of the Me and the Not-Me that Whitman did, even though he does share with Whitman a genuine humility and the awareness that the Me and the Not-Me can only be united in the self. Yet, in his next statement, which follows the one above, he demonstrates that he was aware of the cosmic powers which hold everything together:

> By the sense of mystery I understand the experience of certain places and times when one's whole nature seems to be in touch with a presence, a *genius loci,* a potency. I won't go into the psychology of this or even attempt to argue that it may not be a self-induced delusion. I shall only say that the experience seems to have occurred to many other people in many ages, and add that when I use the word "god" or "gods" or the name of some Hellenic deity, I am not indulging in a mythological flourish but refer to the actual experience of some "potency." (16)

Because Aldington never achieves any true union of Me and Not-Me, his poems remain spiritually on a lower level than Whitman's. Clouded by *maya,* his transcendence never more than momentary, he could not free the self from bitterness. It might have benefited Aldington's poetic vision if he had not confused Whitman's cosmic spirit with platitude, but had grasped it as Whitman's relationship with the "potency" he so greatly respected.

Finally, some brief mention should be made of F. S. Flint, as certain of Whitman's tendencies found their way into his work. In the title poem of *Otherworld,* for example, Flint has written what has almost come to be a pattern poem for the Imagist writers, a description of the workaday London world and a transcendental view of that world. We have seen how this method can be traced back to Whitman. Each of the Imagist poets seems to draw back from Whitman's idea of merging, and Flint is no exception. His poem called "Easter" describes both a brand of camaraderie very like Whitman's own and a revulsion at the notion of a union with mankind in multitude. The poem begins with words right out of Whitman:

> We lurch on, and, stumbling,
> touch each other.
> You do not shrink, friend,
> There you, and I here,
> Side by side, we go, jesting.
> We do not seek, we do not avoid, contact.

But Flint then sets up a separation between him and his friend and the rest of humanity:

> The flags of the stone steps are hollowed;
> and you and I must strive to remain two
> and not to merge in the multitude.
> It impinges on us; it separates us;
> we shrink from it; we brave through it;
> we laugh; we jest; we jeer;
> and we save fragments of our souls.
>
> (*Some Imagist Poets* 1916, 51)

By their constant assault on Whitman's idea of merging, the Imagist writers reveal how very much he remains in their thoughts. However, Flint reveals that he shares many of Whitman's attitudes. In "Give Me the Splendid

Silent Sun," Whitman describes a dichotomy in his desires. The first half of the poem describes his love of, his yearning for, "solitude" and the "primal sanities of Nature" (*LG* 312). In the latter half of the poem, he rejects these visions of peace for the bustling and confusion of Manhattan streets in wartime, for "the endless and noisy chorus, the rustle and clank of muskets, (even the sight of the wounded)" (*LG* 314). In a poem on the same theme, "War-Time," Flint rejects the road that leads "past the bovine quiet of houses," the "tranquillity of . . . gardens." The road he would take is the one to the city with its "swift-rattling of motor buses, and the dust and the tattered paper." He wants the place

> where amid the din . . .
> the news is shouted,
> and soldiers gather, off duty.
>
> There I can feel the heat of Europe's fever;
> and I can make,
> as each man makes the beauty of the woman he
>   loves,
> no spring and no woman's beauty,
> while that is burning.

Present throughout Whitman's work is his vision of the poet. Every experience for Whitman is good because it becomes a part of his poetry; he transforms everything he sees, every incident into art. Even in the midst of war he could write, "I have nourish'd the wounded and sooth'd many a dying soldier, / And at intervals waiting or in the midst of camp, / Composed these songs" (*LG* 319). Flint is capable as well of transcending experience by writing a poem about it. Flint transforms and transcends actuality by a series of Platonic steps which Whitman often utilized. The path from the locked-up ego, to sympathy for another person, to transcendence of the painful experience, to cosmic realization, to art, is a course both Whitman and Flint describe in their poetry. In "Gloom," Flint describes the loneliness of the self without transcendental view:

> I sat there in the dark
> of the room and of my mind . . .
> Then
> I gathered up within me all my powers
> until outside of me was nothing:
> I was all—
> All stubborn, fighting, sadness and revulsion.
>   (*Some Imagist Poets* 1916, 51)

A woman touches him, but he is closed against her until he intuits her pain: "Then I thought: she has gone away; she is hurt." His intuition gives him grace; by sympathy with another being, by rising above his selfish ego, Flint is able to move above the "gloom," release the flow of his cosmic spirit, become creative soul and write a poem:

> . . . and I felt the presence of the fields we had
>   walked over, the roads we
>   had followed,
> the flowers we had watched together,

> before it [gloom] came.
> . . . And I came away,
> full of the sweet and bitter juices of life;
> and I lit the lamp in my room,
> and made this poem.
>   (*Some Imagist Poets* 1916, 64)

This process, though on a scale smaller than Whitman's, is a central aspect of his method. Implicit here is a step that goes beyond Plato's final stage of identification with universal values. For Flint and Whitman, this awareness leads to the release of the creative energies. Thus, awareness of the universal serves a Bergsonian function, intuiting for the purpose of art.

In conclusion, it can be seen that, in spite of their denials, the Imagists learned a great deal about poetic technique from Whitman's *Leaves of Grass*. Ezra Pound was later to see himself and Imagism as "an encrustation of the ages" (59) upon the rock of Whitman's power, for all of the basic elements of Imagist technique are present in Whitman's theoretical writings as well as his poetry. Whitman believed that poetry should be particular; he incorporated within his method the juxtapositions and tensions between the real and the ideal that are so much a part of the Imagist method. He felt that common objects had their place in poetry, yet enveloped these objects with his own "intellectual and emotional complex."[2] Whitman was an Imagist in the way that Pound was later to be an Imagist; each used Imagist techniques to write cosmic poetry. Whitman anticipated every essential aspect of Imagist theory and technique; his own words best summarize his influence: "I am an acme of things accomplish'd, and an encloser of things to be" (*LG* 80).

NOTES

[1] Cf. James E. Miller, *American Quest,* and Erkkila, *Walt Whitman among the French.* Miller, in his chapter on "Ezra Pound's Cantos," explores Whitman's "presence in both the form and content of *The Cantos*" (69-98). Erkkila, similarly, in the epilogue to her book, discusses the indirect path by which Whitman influenced such American authors as Pound and Eliot through French authors. She notes: "Pound consistently proposed Whitman's French followers and admirers as models for literary America" (234). In spite of the excellence of these studies and their clarification of the relationship between Whitman and the later Imagists, Whitman's influence on the early Imagists requires some explication.

[2] Pound, of course, defined the image as "an intellectual and emotional complex in an instant of time." However, Pound's definition is frequently clipped at this point, and it is the next sentence that looks directly toward Whitman. Pound continues: "It is the presentation of such a complex instantaneously which gives that sense of sudden liberation; that sense of freedom from time limits and space limits; that sense of sudden growth which we experience in the greatest works of art."

WORKS CITED

Aldington, Richard. *The Complete Poems.* London: A. Wingate, 1948.

Asselineau, Roger. "Whitman's Style: From Mysticism to Art." *Whitman.* Ed. Roy Harvey Pearce. Englewood Cliffs, N.J.: Prentice, 1962. 89-106.

Eby, E. H. "Walt Whitman's Indirections." *Walt Whitman Review* 12 (1966): 5-16.

Erkkila, Betsy. *Walt Whitman among the French.* Princeton: Princeton UP, 1980.

Fletcher, John Gould. *Selected Poems.* Boston: Houghton, 1938.

Flint, F. S. "Otherworld." *Some Imagist Poets.* Ed. Amy Lowell. Boston: Houghton, 1916.

Hughes, Glen. *Imagism and the Imagists.* Stanford, Calif.: Stanford UP, 1931.

Lowell, Amy, ed. *Some Imagist Poets.* Boston: Houghton, 1915. 2d ed. 1916. 3d ed. 1917.

———. "Walt Whitman and the New Poetry." *Yale Review* 16 (Apr. 1927): 502-19. Rpt. *Poetry and Poets: Essays.* Boston: Houghton, 1930. 61-87.

Miller, James E., Jr., ed. *The American Quest for a Supreme Fiction.* Chicago: U of Chicago P, 1979.

Pound, Ezra. "Walt Whitman." In "Walt Whitman and Ezra Pound." By Herbert Bergman. *American Literature* 27 (1955): 59.

Untermeyer, Louis, ed. *Modern American Poetry.* New York: Harcourt Brace, 1950.

Waskow, Howard J. *Whitman: Explorations in Form.* Chicago: U of Chicago P, 1966.

Whitman, Walt. *The Complete Writings.* Ed. R. M. Bucke et al. New York: Putnam's, 1902.

———. *Leaves of Grass: Comprehensive Reader's Edition.* Ed. Harold W. Blodgett and Sculley Bradley. New York: New York UP, 1965. Abbreviated as *LG.*

Daniel Stempel

[*In the following essay, Stempel asserts that translations by Lafcadio Hearn served as an important source of Japanese style and technique for writers of the Imagist movement.*]

SOURCE: "Lafcadio Hearn's Translations and the Origins of Imagist Aesthetics," in *Comparative Literature*

East and West: Traditions and Trends, edited by Cornelia N. Moore and Raymond A. Moody, The College of Languages, Linguistics and Literature, University of Hawaii and the East-West Center, 1989, pp. 31-7.

Lafcadio Hearn is a minor figure in American literary history, a transplanted exotic who flourished in the hothouse atmosphere of late nineteenth century aesthetic impressionism. But literary history, like political history or economic history, too often ignores what lies outside its self-defined limits. It constructs what it imagines is a temporal narrative of authors and works when it is, in fact, deciding in advance just which texts can be admitted into the canon of so-called "literary" documents. It ignores those which may lie in the border regions of journalism and travel literature, for example. There are times when literary historians must be reminded that there is a broader history outside their discipline and that it cannot be isolated from that history without becoming a victim of its own myopic methods. Poets do not spend their lives reading only poetry, novelists do not read only the novels of their predecessors. Literature, like every other human activity, interacts with society, past and present.

As a specific example, we search in vain for any mention of Lafcadio Hearn in the histories of the Imagist movement of the first two decades of this century. The Imagists claimed to have derived their principles of economy of diction and sharp visual focus from the poetry and art of Japan, among other sources, but the literary historians seem to be unaware of the contribution of the Japanese poems and songs which Hearn collected, translated, and explicated in the articles and books which he published between 1894 and 1904.

Yet there is ample evidence that anyone interested in Japan at that time would have turned to Hearn as the most popular and most readable expert on Japan. Richard Aldington, who was in the movement from the time that it was named and founded by Ezra Pound in 1912 in a Kensington tea-shop to its gradual demise a decade later, wrote that he had read Lafcadio Hearn when he was a schoolboy, in the aftermath of the Russo-Japanese war of 1904-5.[1] We do not know when Pound himself read Hearn, but in 1916 and 1917 he urged James Joyce to read George Gould's 1908 biography of Hearn. Gould was a Philadelphia ophthalmologist who had treated Hearn for failing vision with some degree of success. It is significant, I think, that Pound did not have to explain to Joyce who Hearn was.[2] John Gould Fletcher recalled that he had read Hearn's translations of Japanese poetry, among others, when he was associated with the Imagists.[3] In 1915 Amy Lowell delivered a lecture on "The New Manner in Modern Poetry" and illustrated it by reading poems by Ezra Pound, Richard Aldington, H.D., and translations of Japanese poems by Lafcadio Hearn.[4]

But perhaps more important was the fact that two influential men of letters in America and England, Ferris Greenslet, Hearn's editor at Houghton Mifflin, and Edward Thomas, critic and poet, were actively campaigning for recognition of the value of Hearn's writings. Greenslet contributed an article on John Gould Fletcher to the special issue on Imagism of *The Egoist* (May 1915) and published a collection of some of Hearn's translations in the same year. His prefatory Publisher's Note observes: "In their limitation of a poem to the presentation of a single impression and in their ability to present that impression with the utmost vividness and with the sternest economy of words, these Japanese poets are strangely akin to the Imagists, the youngest of the modern schools."[5] Edward Thomas, already respected and admired by poets like the young Robert Frost, published a short biography of Hearn in 1912, at about the same time that the Imagist movement officially began. Rather than asking if any Imagists had read Hearn's translations, perhaps we should ask if there were any who had not.

J. B. Harmer's history of Imagism and the Imagists, *Victory in Limbo: Imagism 1908-17* (1975), is the latest and most thoroughly researched of the three standard histories. Harmer devotes ten pages to the Japanese influence on the Imagists without once mentioning Hearn's work. Why not? I suspect that the answer lies in the unfortunate practice of writing literary history by relying on other literary histories rather than by checking the original texts. Harmer's major source is Earl Miner's *The Japanese Tradition in British and American Literature,* published in 1958 and based on his 1955 doctoral dissertation. Miner recognizes Hearn's "enormous popular appeal"[6] and attempts to distinguish between what was mere romantic journalism and what was of lasting literary value in Hearn's work, but he has very little to say about Hearn's translations of Japanese poetry and what little there is, is incorrect.

Miner notes that Hearn "recognized himself that he had no poetic genius." But he goes on to make questionable literary judgments: "He did have a talent approaching genius for that rhythmical prose which is frequently and mistakenly called poetic, but it is easy to see that concentrated and brief poems like the Japanese forms cannot be adequately translated by a writer of periodic prose. . . . Hearn did adapt the translations of his acquaintances, but only to flavor his prose or for short chapters on special subjects such as poems about insects or folk songs, and with no aim to set himself up as a translator. All of his translations of Japanese poetry, culled from here and there, have made up only one small, posthumous volume."[7] This is a reference to Greenslet's collection which does *not* contain all of Hearn's translations of Japanese poetry. It is, in fact, composed almost entirely of translations into prose, but much of his work was in verse, not prose.

Miner is forced to confess at one point that Hearn's translations had some influence on American poets. Conrad Aiken wrote him: "Of course [Japanese poetry] was all in the air—at Harvard [and everyone] around the Harvard Advocate was already aware of Hearn's hokku, and we all had shots at them. So when Fletcher and I dived into Japanese and Chinese poetry and art [in the

years between 1915 and 1917] it was already old stuff for me."[8] Miner seems to be taken aback by this statement: "The intermingling of talk about Hearn and haiku makes more sense than it at first seems to, because the section indebted to Hearn [in Aiken's *The House of Dust*] offers examples of Pound's super-repository technique which recur in Aiken's work of this period. . . . "[9]

Miner refuses to accept his own evidence that Aiken could have learned "Pound's super-repository technique" from Hearn's translations, which he had read at Harvard before Basil Hall Chamberlain's *Japanese Poetry* (1911) appeared and certainly before Pound began to devise his program for the Imagists. Perhaps Miner was too quick in dismissing the influence of Hearn's translations on modern poetry.

Let us take a look at the translations which Miner excludes from consideration. Anyone who has read Hearn's essays and his correspondence soon realizes that he had thought deeply about the problems of translation and that he would never have dashed off a sloppy rendering of an original merely to supply some romantic atmosphere for his travel sketches. The fact that he did not think of himself as a poet was a point in his favor as a translator. Instead of Pound's "creative misprision," to use contemporary critical jargon, he sought accuracy in translation. Translation, Hearn believed, begins with total fidelity to the original, although the best translations—which are very rare—do not halt there.

Hearn was not a novice in the art of translation when he came to Japan in 1890. In 1882 he published a book of translations of Théophile Gautier's short stories, a task which he had begun when he went to New Orleans in 1877 to work as a journalist. He had no illusions about his work, remarking wryly, "Verily the path of the translator is hard."[10] Perhaps even more rare in translators, he had a generous appreciation of the work of his rivals. In a letter to Jerome A. Hart of San Francisco, commenting on Hart's review of his book, Hearn corrected a rather free rendering of a line from Gautier's epitaph for Clarimonde (in the story of that name) which Hart had offered as a substitute for Hearn's original rendering. He added apologetically, "But I think your second line is a masterpiece of faithfulness; and, as you justly remark, my hobby is literalism."[11] He carried this hobby to its logical extreme in his first translations from Japanese, which tried to capture for Western readers the peculiarities of Japanese syntax. These translations of prose, not poetry, follow exactly the form of the interlinear translations in Chamberlain's *A Handbook of Colloquial Japanese* (1888). Chamberlain was trying to convey in English the levels of honorific usage in Japanese:

> Otottsan wa, d de gozaimasu?
> Honourable-father-Mr. as-for, how is?
> Or, more politely
> Go shimpu wa, ikaga de irasshaimasu?
> August real-father as-for, how deigns-to-be?[12]

When Hearn tried to capture the language of an innkeeper chasing away the curious villagers from his foreign guests, he used the same technique: "Now august-to-eat-time-is; to-look-at *evil* matter is. *Honorable-return-ing-time-in*-to-look-at-as-for-is-good."[13]

For his translations of Japanese poetry Hearn used a variety of methods, ranging from literal word by word renderings to paraphrases in English metrical forms. For the purposes of this paper, however, the most interesting translations are those for which Hearn chose an unrhymed couplet, either metrical or in free verse. He often used the couplet form for different Japanese verse forms, without regard for the number of lines in the originals, which might vary from three for the haiku to four for the *dodoitsu*, a folk song form, and five for the tanka. One of his most successful efforts is this translation of a *dodoitsu*, a street song:

> Kamiyo konokata
> Kawaranu mono wa
> Midzu no nagare to
>   Koi no michi.
>
> Things never changed since the Time of the Gods:
> The flowing of water, the Way of Love.[14]

Although Hearn had to shift the word order to fit English patterns, he did not add anything which was not in the original. Moreover he succeeded in reproducing the effect of the short five-syllable final line. This was rarely possible, Hearn believed, without confusing the Western reader who lacked the background to understand the elliptical references of Japanese verse. "So the term 'ittakkiri'—meaning 'all gone,' or 'entirely vanished' is contemptuously applied to verses in which the versemaker has uttered his whole thought;—praise being reserved for compositions that leave in the mind the thrilling of a something unsaid." He warned, "The impossibility of preserving the inner quality of such poems in a literal rendering will now be obvious. Whatever I attempt in this direction must of necessity be ittakkiri; for the unspoken has to be expressed; and what the Japanese poet is able to say in seventeen or twenty-one syllables may need in English more than double that number of words."[15] So, for example, Hearn translates a haiku on the *higurashi*, a species of cicada, whose name signifies that its cry heralds the coming of twilight:

> Already, O Higurashi, your call announces the
>   evening! Alas, for the passing
> day, with its duties left undone![16]

The first line of his couplet expands and explains the meaning of the simple apostrophe "Higurashi ya!" which is the first line of the haiku. The second and third lines "Ky no ketai wo / Omou toki", literally translated, mean simply: "Time to think of today's unfinished work."

This juxtaposition of an explanatory or descriptive line and a line containing a personal image or impression can be found throughout Hearn's translations. In one instance he even supplied an explanatory line which is not found in the original:

> However fickle I seem, my heart is never
>   unfaithful: Out of the slime itself,
> spotless the lotus grows.[17]

The original, the song of a prostitute, is simply: "In muddy water / Though it is raised / With roots growing here and there / The lotus blossoms / As a beautiful flower." Hearn's couplet pairs the image in the second line, which needs no explanation for a Japanese audience, with a preceding line that gives its significance for the Western reader.

These are not isolated examples, although someone acquainted only with Greenslet's collection might think so. Of course, he also translated many haiku into prose, but there is one characteristic of his translations, prose or poetry, which one does not find in Chamberlain's essay on "Bash and the Poetical Epigram," which first appeared in the *Transactions of the Asiatic Society of Japan* in 1902 and was reprinted in *Japanese Poetry* (1911).[18] Hearn sensed the division between thematic statement and specific impression and arranged his translations to mirror that contrast. Chamberlain used shorter couplets with run-on lines that compress the haiku into a single English sentence that ignores the dual structure.

This brings us back to Miner's discussion of Pound's "super-pository technique." Describing his efforts to crystallize in as short a form as possible the experience of seeing beautiful faces as he got out of a train in the Paris métro, Pound writes:

> The 'one image' poem is a form of super-position, that is to say, it is one idea set on top of another. I found it useful in getting out of the impasse in which I had been left by my métro emotion. I wrote a thirty-line poem, and destroyed it because it was what we call work 'of second intensity.' Six months later I made a poem half that length; a year later I made the following *hokku*-like sentence:
>
> The apparition of these faces in the crowd: Petals, on a wet black bough.
>
> I dare say it is meaningless unless one has drifted into a certain vein of thought. In a poem of this sort one is trying to record the precise instant when a thing outward and objective transforms itself, or darts into a thing inward and subjective.[19]

Miner describes this poem, "In a Station of the Métro," as a *"discordia concors,"* a combination of a line which is "a relatively straightforward, unmetaphorical statement" and a line which is a "sharply defined metaphorical image. . . ." He praises Pound for being the first to discover and define this technique: "The discovery of this technique in a poetic form written in a language he did not know is one of the insights of Pound's genius."[20] Miner then goes on to trace its use throughout Pound's writings, including the *Cantos*.

As I have shown in a few examples, one of Hearn's techniques of translation was to provide an explanatory line combined with the image in the Japanese original and this is exactly what Pound did in his "In a Station of the Métro." It is not a haiku—only the thematic subject simply named or announced, as in Japanese, combined with the image or impression can create a true haiku. Perhaps if Pound had written "Métro Station—/ Petals on a wet black bough" that would have been a haiku. As it is, he imitated Hearn's practice of going beyond the limits of the literal in order to guide the Western reader to the proper interpretation, thinking that this was a Japanese technique. So Pound's "super-pository method" turns out to be based on the translations of that minor exotic, Lafcadio Hearn.

Miner pokes fun at the popular conception of Hearn as the romanticizer of all things Japanese: "It is this view of Japan replacing Loti's harsher one, which probably helped give currency to the stage and fictional types of the refined and intrepid Japanese, which makes dowagers gush and gruff men sigh, and which the mature reader can only feel is an impairment of the spirit called Lafcadio Hearnia."[21] That view of both Hearn and Japan has long since disappeared and we no longer romanticize either. Unfortunately, one cannot say the same about the critical adulation of Ezra Pound which (uncritically) credits him with something between papal infallibility and divine omniscience. I think it is time that we began to ask for another view of Ezra Pound—one that goes beyond the ideal image of Pound as the only begetter of all that is new in modern poetry to an understanding of his faults as well as his virtues. For Pound, who spent a long life playing the *enfant terrible* in a world he never understood, was human, all-too-human. I am merely asking for a Pound of flesh.

NOTES

[1] Alister Kershaw and Frédéric-Jacques Temple, eds., *Richard Aldington: An Intimate Portrait* (Carbondale and Edwardsville: Southern Illinois UP, 1965) 74.

[2] Forrest Reid, ed., *Pound/Joyce* (New York: New Directions, 1967) 85, 96, 97.

[3] Earl Miner, *The Japanese Tradition in British and American Literature* (Princeton: Princeton UP, 1958) 91.

[4] S. Foster Damon, *Amy Lowell* (Boston: Houghton Mifflin, 1935) 301.

[5] Lafcadio Hearn, trans., *Japanese Lyrics* (Boston: Houghton Mifflin, 1915) n.p.

[6] Miner 62-63.

[7] Miner 90-91.

[8] Miner 183.

[9] Miner 183-184.

[10] Elizabeth Bisland, *The Life and Letters of Lafcadio Hearn*, vol. 1 (Boston: Houghton Mifflin, 1906) 250.

[11] Bisland 244.

[12] Basil Hall Chamberlain, *A Handbook of Colloquial Japanese* (London: Trubner, 1888) 4.

[13] Lafcadio Hearn, *Glimpses of Unfamiliar Japan*, vol. 5 of *The Writings of Lafcadio Hearn*, Koizumi edition (Boston and New York: Houghton Mifflin, 1923) 263.

[14] Lafcadio Hearn, *Gleanings in Buddha-Fields*, vol. 8 of *The Writings of Lafcadio Hearn* 24-27.

[15] Lafcadio Hearn, *In Ghostly Japan*, vol. 9 of *The Writings of Lafcadio Hearn* 313-316.

[16] Lafcadio Hearn, *Shadowings*, vol. 10 of *The Writings of Lafcadio Hearn* 55.

[17] The original, which Hearn does not supply, is: "Doro mizu ni / Sodaterarete mo / Ne wa shosho ni / Saite kirena / Hasu no hana." See John F. Embree, *Japanese Peasant Songs. Memoirs of the American Folklore Society* 38 (Philadelphia: American Folklore Society, 1943) 28.

[18] In a note appended to this essay, Chamberlain writes, "Since the present essay was completed, the writer's attention has been drawn to Mr. Hearn's two latest works, 'Shadowings,' pp. 69-100 (1901), and 'A Japanese Miscellany,' pp. 92-118 (1901), containing respectively collections of epigrams on the curious subjects of cicadae and dragon-flies,—no less than 107 in all, or more, if those are counted of which not the original text, but only the translation is given. Some of the renderings are in the metre of the elegiac distich, which, owing to the far larger number of syllables of that form of verse, necessitates more or less expansion of the originals. Others, rendered literally, though less attractive as English—or Anglicized—poems, possess superior value for the scientific inquirer. All well exhibit the endless dexterity with which the Japanese epigrammatist can modulate the trilling of his tiny pipe" ("Bash and the Japanese Poetical Epigram," *Transactions of the Asiatic Society of Japan*, vol. XXX [Tokyo: Rikkyo Gakuin Press, 1902] 362).

[19] Ezra Pound, "Vorticism," *Fortnightly Review* 96 (1914): 467.

[20] Miner 115.

[21] Miner 61-62.

Yoshinobu Hakutani

[*In the following essay, Hakutani focuses on the poetry, essays, and correspondence of Yone Noguchi as sources of Japanese poetics in the Imagist techniques of Ezra Pound.*]

SOURCE: "Ezra Pound, Yone Noguchi and Imagism," in *Modern Philology*, Vol. 90, August, 1992, pp. 46-69.

I

It is commonplace to say that imagism played a crucial role in poetic modernism and that Ezra Pound, more than anyone else, put this poetics to practice in the 1910s. Yet imagism still remains a somewhat cloudy topic. Many discussions content themselves with restatements of Pound's celebrated essay on vorticism, published in September 1914.[1] Even Hugh Kenner, the most eminent critic of Pound, says, "The history of the Imagist Movement is a red herring." He admonishes one "to keep one's eyes on Pound's texts, and avoid generalities about Imagism."[2]

In that "Vorticism" essay, Pound acknowledged for the first time in his career his indebtedness to the spirit of Japanese poetry in general and the technique of hokku in particular. Among the Poundians, and there have been many in the East and in the West, who have tried to reconstruct the historical set of circumstances in which Pound moved, Earl Miner gives the best account of the profound influences Japanese poetry had upon the early Pound. It is Miner who offers the best annotated evidence that the sources for Pound's interest in Japanese poetics were partly provided by Pound's fellow imagists such as T. E. Hulme, F. S. Flint, and Richard Aldington.[3]

It is Miner as well who most frequently comments on the role Yone Noguchi played in the introduction and interpretation of Japanese poetry to an English audience during the early decades of the twentieth century.[4] Noguchi was indeed a well-known bilingual Japanese and American poet, who by 1915 had published not only books of criticism widely read in England and America (*The Spirit of Japanese Poetry* and *The Spirit of Japanese Art*), but also several collections of his own English poems. By this date, moreover, his poems had been praised by Willa Cather, Joaquin Miller, and Gelett Burgess in America, by Bliss Carman in Canada, and by George Meredith, William Rossetti, Thomas Hardy, and others in England. What is surprising, therefore, is Miner's dismissive treatment of Noguchi's English writings as having had little to do with the imagist movement and with Pound in particular.

II

As Pound explained in his essay, the image is not a static, rational idea: "It is a radiant node or cluster; it is what I can, and must perforce, call a VORTEX, from which, and through which, and into which, ideas are constantly rushing. In decency one can only call it a VORTEX. And from this necessity came the name 'vorticism'" ("Vorticism," pp. 469-70). A year later Pound defined the form of an image by stating that the image "may be a sketch, a vignette, a criticism, an epigram or anything else you like. It may be impressionism, it may even be very good prose." An image, he argued, does not constitute simply a picture of something. As a vortex, the image must be "endowed with energy."[5] Imagism, in turn, is likened to the painter's use of pigment. "The painter," Pound wrote, "should use his colour because he sees it or feels it. I don't much care whether he is representative or non-rep-resentative. . . . It is the same in writing poems, the author must use his *image* . . . *not* because he thinks he can use it to back up some creed or some system of ethics or economics" ("Vorticism," p. 464).

To demonstrate his poetic theory, Pound thought of an image not as a decorative emblem or symbol but as a seed capable of germinating and developing into another organism. As an illustration he presented what he called "a *hokku*-like sentence" he had written:

> The apparition of these faces in the crowd:
>   Petals, on a wet, black bough.

"In a poem of this sort," he explained, "one is trying to record the precise instant when a thing outward and objective transforms itself, or darts into a thing inward and subjective" ("Vorticism," p. 467). The image of the faces in the crowd is based in immediate experience at a metro station in Paris; it was "a thing outward and objective." Not only did Pound actually see the "thing," but it generated such a sensation that he could not shake it out of his mind. This image, he emphasizes, "transforms itself, or darts into a thing inward and subjective," that is, the image of the "Petals, on a wet, black bough." Imagism is further contrasted to symbolism: "The symbolist's *symbols* have a fixed value, like numbers in arithmetic, like 1, 2, and 7. The imagiste's images have a variable significance, like the signs *a, b,* and *x* in algebra" ("Vorticism," p. 463).

Although Pound's definition is clear enough, the sources for his ideas are hard to determine. Most discussions about the genesis of the imagist movement are speculative at best. Pound's insistence that an image in poetry must be active rather than passive suggests that a poem is not a description of something, but, as Aristotle had said of tragedy, an action. Pound approaches Aristotelianism in his insistence that the image of the faces in the crowd in his metro poem was not simply a description of his sensation at the station but an active entity capable of dynamic development. According to his experience, this particular image instantly transformed itself into another image, the image of the petals on a wet, black bough. To Pound the success of this poem resulted from his instantaneous perception of the relatedness between the two entirely different objects.

But Pound's note on the genesis of "In a Station of the Metro" in the "Vorticism" essay makes it clear that there was nothing instantaneous about the composition of this poem. It was in 1911 that Pound, having seen those "beautiful faces" at La Concorde, wrote a thirty-line poem "and destroyed it because it was what we call work 'of second intensity'" ("Vorticism," p. 467). Six months later he reduced the longer text to a poem half the length, and still a year later he wrote the final version, a two-line poem. Pound's insistence on the instantaneous perception of the metro images drove him to repeated attempts at recreating the instantaneous images he had perceived a year-and-a-half earlier. Traditionally, the principles of instantaneity and spontaneity are as fundamental for the composition of hokku as when applied to Zen-inspired painting and calligraphy. In any event, his discovery of hokku in 1913-14 was, as he says, "useful in getting out of the impasse in which I had been left by my metro emotion" ("Vorticism," p. 467). To Pound, the most important thing he learned about hokku was "this particular sort of consciousness," which he was unable to identify with any version of impressionist art.[6]

Another equally important tenet of imagism calls for directness in expression. The immediate model for this principle was nineteenth-century French prose. Pound did not mention specific English poets but seemed adamantly opposed to Victorian poetry, which he characterized as wordy and rhetorical. Instead he urged his fellow poets "to bring poetry up to the level of prose." "Flaubert and De Maupassant," he believed, "lifted prose to the rank of a finer art, and one has no patience with contemporary poets who escape from all the difficulties of the infinitely difficult art of good prose by pouring themselves into loose verses" ("Vorticism," p. 462).

If Pound's ideal poetry has the directness and clarity of good prose as opposed to the suggestiveness and vagueness of symbolist poetry, then his sources certainly did not include W. B. Yeats. Even though Yeats dedicated the noh play *At the Hawk's Well* to Pound, Yeats was not enthusiastic about Pound's poetics. "My own theory of poetical or legendary drama," Yeats wrote to Fiona Macleod, "is that it should have no realistic, or elaborate, but only a symbolic and decorative setting. A forest, for instance, should be represented by a forest pattern and not by a forest painting."[7] The difference between Pound and Yeats reveals itself in the two poets' differing views of the Japanese noh play. A symbolist and spiritualist poet, Yeats was fascinated by the noh play. By contrast, Pound was interested not in particular images and symbols but in the unifying effect a noh play produces on the stage.

This disagreement between Pound and Yeats over whether poetic images should be suggestive or active also involves what Noguchi, a poet and critic well acquainted with both poets, felt compelled to write in "What Is a Hokku Poem?" published in London.[8] In that essay, Noguchi first defined hokku as an expression of Japanese poets' "understanding of Nature" or, better put, as a song or chant of "their longing or wonder or adoration toward Mother Nature" that is "never mystified by any cloud or mist like Truth or Beauty of Keats' understanding." Noguchi differentiated between the "suggestive" and subjective coloration of English poetry and the Japanese hokku, "distinctly clear-cut like a diamond or star." "I say," he argued, "that the star itself has almost no share in the creation of a condition even when your dream or vision is gained through its beauty. . . . I value the 'hokku' poem, at least some of them, because of its own truth and humanity simple and plain." Noguchi then analyzed the aim of hokku: the hokku poet expresses the spirit of nature rather than the will of man or woman. Noguchi would agree that hokku is "suggestive" only if the word 'suggestive' means that "truth and humanity are suggestive." He added, "But I can say myself as a poet . . . that your poem would certainly end in artificiality if you start out to be suggestive from the beginning."[9]

Finally, Noguchi based his definition and analysis of aim in Zen philosophy, understood as discipline of the mind: one should not allow one's individuality to control action. Zen does not, indeed, recognize human reality, the existence of good and evil, because this reality is but the creation of man's will rather than the spirit of nature. Noguchi thus observed that "there is no word in so common use by Western critics as suggestive, which makes more mischief than enlightenment." Although Western critics "mean it quite simply . . . to be a new force of salvation, . . . I say that no critic is necessary for this world of poetry."[10]

By 1918 Pound's vorticist theory had extended to his discussion of Chinese characters. As the correspondence between Pound and Mary Fenollosa, widow of Ernest Fenollosa, indicates, Pound began to receive Fenollosa's manuscripts as early as 1913.[11] Fenollosa's essay "The Chinese Written Character as a Medium of Poetry," posthumously published by Pound in *The Little Review* in 1918, attempted to show that Chinese characters, which Pound called ideograms, derive from visual rather than aural experiences. A Chinese character, Fenollosa noted, signifies an observable action instead of an abstract notion. Unlike a Western word, a phonetic sign, it denotes a concrete, natural phenomenon. The Chinese character, Fenollosa wrote, "is based upon a vivid shorthand picture of the operations of nature. In the algebraic figure and in the spoken word there is no natural connection between thing and sign: all depends upon sheer convention. But the Chinese method follows natural suggestion."[12]

Pound's attempt to verify Fenollosa's thoery involved not only his contemporaries, poets and critics living in London in the 1910s, but his own effort to search for ideas in other sources. One of these sources was the Japanese noh play, in which Pound became interested through Fenollosa's notes. It is generally understood that Pound's interest in Japanese poetry, especially hokku, grew partly through his acquaintance with Fenollosa's writings. None of Fenollosa's writings, however, directly concerns Japanese poetry, let alone hokku. Having lived many years in Japan as an art critic, Fenollosa became well versed in Japanese art and literature, but his actual knowledge of the Japanese language was not profound.[13] It is, therefore, inconceivable that Pound became well acquainted with hokku through Fenollosa. It is also unlikely that English contemporaries such as T. E. Hulme and F. S. Flint, who are said to have introduced hokku to Pound, served his purpose. Pound would not have been able to learn from them the subtle elements of Japanese poetry because they had no firsthand knowledge of the Japanese language.[14]

III

Pound's most likely source of information was Noguchi. He first corresponded with Pound and then met Pound, along with Yeats, when he gave a series of lectures on Japanese poetry in England in early 1914. The relationship between Pound and Noguchi began in 1911, when Noguchi sent his fifth collection of English poems, *The Pilgrimage* (1908 and 1909) in two volumes, to Pound with a note: "As I am not yet acquainted with your work, I wish you [would] send your books or books which you like to have me read. This little note may sound quite businesslike, but I can promise you that I can do better in my next letter to you." Noguchi also wrote as a postscript: "I am anxious to read not only your poetical work but also your criticism."[15] Pound acknowledged receipt of the books and note in a letter postmarked September 2, 1911.

> c/o Elkin Mathews
> Vigo St. London.
>
> Dear Yone Noguchi:
>
> I want to thank you very much for your lovely books & for your kindness in sending them to me.
>
> I had, of course, known of you, but I am much occupied with my mediaeval studies & had neglected to read your books altho' they lie with my own in Mathews Shop & I am very familiar with the appearance of their covers.
>
> I am reading those you sent me but I do not yet know what to say of them except that they have delighted me. Besides it is very hard to write to you until I know more about you, you are older than I am—I gather from the dates of the poems—you have been to New York. You are giving us the spirit of Japan, is it not? very much as I am trying to deliver from obscurity certain forgotten odours of Provence & Tuscany (my works on Guido Cavalcanti, & Arnaut Daniel, are, the one in press, the other ready to be printed.)
>
> I have sent you two volumes of poems. I do not know whether to send you "The Spirit of Romance" or not: It treats of mediaeval poetry in southern Europe but has many flaws of workmanship. . . .
>
> Of your country I know almost nothing—surely if the east & the west are ever to understand each other that understanding must come slowly & come first through the arts.
>
> You ask about my "criticism". There is some criticism in the "Spirit of Romance" & there will be some in the prefaces to the "Guido" & the "Arnaut". But I might be more to the point if we who are artists should discuss the matters of technique & motive between ourselves. Also if you should write about these matters I would discuss your letters with Mr. Yeats & likewise my answers. . . .
>
> Yours very sincerely
> Ezra Pound[16]

Although Noguchi did not write again as Pound had suggested, Noguchi published his essay "What Is a Hokku Poem?" in London in January 1913, as noted earlier. In

the meantime three books of criticism by Noguchi appeared during this period: *The Spirit of Japanese Poetry* (London, 1914; cited hereafter in the text), *Through the Torii* (London, 1914), and *The Spirit of Japanese Art* (London, 1915). Noguchi was also invited to contribute "The Everlasting Sorrow: A Japanese Noh Play" in 1917 and an article, "The Japanese Noh Play," in 1918 to *The Egoist*.[17] Pound's encouragement was perhaps responsible for the publication of some of Noguchi's own hokku poems in *The Egoist* and in *Poetry*.[18]

Because his essays and lectures during this period also dealt with Japanese art, Yeats, who was interested in Japanese painting and the noh play, became interested in Noguchi's work as well.[19] As Pound's and Yeats's letters to Noguchi indicate, Pound and Yeats not only were close associates themselves but also were both well acquainted with Noguchi. Despite the active dialogues that occurred between Pound and Noguchi, critics have not seriously considered their relationship. The only critic who has mentioned Noguchi in discussing the imagist movement regarded him not as a poet and critic from whose ideas Pound might have benefited but as one of the poets whom Pound himself influenced.[20] Such a preposterous connection is undermined by the simple fact that most of Noguchi's English poems, as Pound noted in his letter to Noguchi, had been published in America and England long before the early 1910s, when Pound and his fellow poets began to discuss imagism among themselves. It is more accurate historically to say that Noguchi influenced Pound rather than the other way around.

Pound had apparently known little about Japanese poetry before he attended the April 1909 meeting of the Poet's Club. This group, headed by T. E. Hulme, was succeeded by another group called "Les Imagistes," or "Des Imagistes," which Pound led from 1912 to 1914.[21] Although Pound in fact joined the Poets' Club, its sessions did not prove of much inspiration to him. Richard Aldington, who joined in 1911, was more interested in the color prints of Utamaro, Hokusai, and others found in the British Museum than in Japanese poetry.[22] The fact that Pound was more seriously interested than Aldington was in Japanese poetry is indicated by Aldington's parody of Pound's metro poem that appeared in the January 1915 issue of *The Egoist*.[23] Allen Upward, another member of "Les Imagistes" whom Pound had met in 1911, had some importance for Pound because Upward used the term "whirl-swirl" in his book *The New Word* (New York, 1908). Upward, a self-styled intellectual and a poet, had "a powerful and original mind clearly and trenchantly concerned with matters that bear directly on what Pound meant by 'vortex.'"[24] But Upward, who was well read in Confucius and perhaps familiar with Chinese poetry, did not have sufficient knowledge of Japanese poetry, let alone of hokku, to influence Pound.[25]

The degree of Pound's initial interest in hokku, therefore, was not entirely clear, for he was much occupied with Provençal poetry and criticism, as his letter to Noguchi indicates. It is quite possible that Pound learned about hokku from T. E. Hulme and F. S. Flint, who were experimenting with hokku and tanka, the thirty-one-syllable Japanese poetic form.[26] The difficulty with this assumption, however, is that Hulme and Flint studied hokku through French translators and critics who used the terms 'haiku' and 'haikai', more modern words, rather than 'hokku'. Most strikingly, neither Pound nor Noguchi referred to the Japanese poem as 'haiku' or 'haikai'; both consistently called it 'hokku' in their writings.

However coincidental this might have been, there are two more pieces of evidence suggesting that Pound might have learned about hokku in Noguchi's work. First, as I have already observed, the essay "What Is a Hokku Poem?"—in which Noguchi declared that poetic images must be active instead of suggestive, direct instead of symbolic, and that the aim of a hokku is to understand the spirit of nature rather than to express the will of man—was published in *Rhythm* (London) in January 1913, almost two years before Pound's essay "Vorticism." Even Pound's essay "A Few Don'ts," the earliest manifesto on imagism, appeared in the March 1913 issue of *Poetry* (Chicago) two months after Noguchi's essay. Second, Noguchi's book of criticism, *The Spirit of Japanese Poetry,* was published in London by John Murray in March 1914, half a year before Pound's "Vorticism" essay.[27]

Moreover, the key chapter of Noguchi's book, entitled "The Japanese Hokku Poetry," was a lecture delivered in the Hall of Magdalen College, Oxford, on January 28, 1914, at the invitation of Robert Bridges, the poet laureate, and T. H. Warren, president of the college and professor of poetry in the university. The first chapter, "Japanese Poetry," was also based on a lecture Noguchi gave at the Japan Society of London on January 14. The rest of the book had been presented as other lectures to such audiences as the Royal Asiatic Society and the Quest Society in England before April 1914, when Noguchi left London for Tokyo by way of Paris, Berlin, and Moscow. It is altogether possible that Pound heard Noguchi lecture at the Quest Society since Pound, Wyndham Lewis, and T. E. Hulme all lectured there in 1914.[28] During this stay in England, *Through the Torii,* another collection of essays that included a variety of commentary on William Rossetti, James Whistler, W. B. Yeats, and Oscar Wilde, and his autobiography, *The Story of Yone Noguchi Told by Himself,* also appeared in print.

Interestingly enough, Pound's "Vorticism" essay quoted a famous hokku by Moritake (1452-1540) just before discussing the often-quoted metro poem:

> The fallen blossom flies back to its branch:
> A butterfly.

> ["Vorticism," p. 467]

This hokku in Japanese has three lines:

> Rak-ka eda ni
> Kaeru to mireba
> Kocho-o kana

Noguchi translated this poem in three lines:

> I thought I saw the fallen leaves
> Returning to their branches:
> Alas, butterflies were they.

> [*Spirit of Japanese Poetry,* p. 50]

Pound must have reconstructed the hokku in two lines simply because he had in mind "a form of super-position" in which his metro poem was to be composed. The similarities between Pound's and Noguchi's versions of the poem in question do not seem coincidental, because the superpository division is indicated by a colon in both constructions. Both translations have identical key words: "fallen," "branch," and "butterfly." The only difference in diction is between Pound's "blossom" (*ka* in Japanese) and Noguchi's "leaves." In syntax, however, these translations are different: Noguchi's version is subjective from the start and ends objectively; the reverse is true in Pound's rendering. Syntactically, Noguchi's version is closer to the Japanese original than Pound's. A literal translation of Moritake's first two lines, "Rak-ka eda ni / Kaeru to mireba," would read: "The fallen blossom appears to come back to its branch."

What appealed to Pound was the terseness and intensity of imagery in a hokku. Irked by the decorative and superfluous style of much Victorian poetry, he urged his fellow poets to eliminate words that do not contribute to the central meaning of the poem. "All poetic language," Pound insisted, "is the language of exploration. Since the beginning of bad writing, writers have used images as ornaments" ("Vorticism," p. 466). By saying, "Great literature is simply language charged with meaning to the utmost possible degree," he meant to elaborate the imagist principle that using fewer words maximizes and intensifies meaning.[29] In "What Is a Hokku Poem?" Noguchi wrote, "I always thought that the most beautiful flowers grow close to the ground, and they need no hundred petals for expressing their own beauty; how can you call it real poetry if you cannot tell it by a few words?"[30]

Pound, furthermore, applied the principle of terseness and intensity to the construction of a single image in his poetry. "The 'one image poem,'" Pound noted, "is a form of super-position, that is to say it is one idea set on top of another. I found it useful in getting out of the impasse in which I had been left by my metro emotion" ("Vorticism," p. 467). Noguchi pointed out the same technique: "*Hokku* means literally a single utterance or the utterance of a single verse; that utterance should be like a 'moth light playing on reality's dusk,' or 'an art hung, as a web, in the air of perfume,' swinging soft in music of a moment" (*Spirit of Japanese Poetry,* p. 39). To illustrate his point, Noguchi quoted a hokku by Buson:

> The night of the Spring,—
> Oh, between the eve
> And the dawn.

This hokku was placed against the opening passage of *Makura Zoshi* (Pillow Sketches) by Sei Shonagon, a celebrated prose writer in medieval Japan: "I love to watch the dawn grow gradually white and whiter, till a faint rosy tinge crowns the mountain's crest, while slender streaks of purple cloud extend themselves above." Noguchi considered Buson's image far more vivid and intensive than Sei Shonagon's, remarking, "Buson is pleased to introduce the night of the Spring which should be beautiful without questioning, since it lies between those two beautiful things, the eve and the dawn" (*Spirit of Japanese Poetry,* pp. 48-49).

IV

Not only was Noguchi an interpreter of hokku poems for the English reader, but he tried his hand at writing hokku poems in English as well. He later collected them in the volume *Japanese Hokkus* (Boston, 1920), which he dedicated to Yeats.[31] One of Noguchi's earliest hokku is reminiscent of Buson's, quoted above:

Tell me the street to Heaven.
This? Or that? Oh, which?
What webs of streets!

He wrote this hokku in England, he says, "when I most abruptly awoke in 1902 to the noise of Charing Cross. . . . And it was by Westminster Bridge where I heard the evening chime that I wrote again in 'hokku' which appears, when translated, as follows":

Is it, Oh, list:
The great voice of Judgment Day?
So runs Thames and my Life.[32]

Noguchi wrote many such hokku-like poems in imitation of the Japanese hokku, as did Pound. The superpository technique, which Pound said he had discovered in Japanese hokku, resembles that of Noguchi. For instance, Pound's "Alba," typical of his many hokku-like poems, reads:

As cool as the pale wet leaves
of lily-of-the-valley
She lay beside me in the dawn.[33]

Most of Noguchi's hokku, as the two poems quoted above show, do have a form of superposition. Like Pound's, Noguchi's hokku constitutes one image poem which has two separate ideas set on top of one another. In the first poem by Noguchi, an idea of "the street to Heaven" is set on top of an idea of "webs," despite a close similarity between the two images. In the second, an idea of the flow of the Thames is set on top of an idea of the course of "my Life."

But there are some differences between Noguchi's and Pound's hokku. Noguchi does not as closely adhere to the well-established Japanese syllabic measure of five or seven as does Pound. Noguchi's two hokku above have 7-5-4 and 4-7-6 measures; Pound's "Alba," "Fan-Piece, for Her Imperial Lord," and "Ts'ai Chi'h" have those of

7-7-8, 7-5-7, and 8-7-7, respectively. If the first line of Pound's metro poem had been reconstructed as two lines, the poem would have had a measure of 5-7-7 (The apparition / Of these faces in the crowd: / Petals, on a wet, black bough) much like a Japanese hokku. Noguchi, moreover, tends to ignore the long-established poetic tradition in which a Japanese hokku has an explicit reference to a season. Pound, on the other hand, consciously adheres to this tradition as seen in many of his hokku-like poems and somewhat longer pieces such as "Heather" and "Society."[34]

What a Japanese hokku and Pound's image share besides their brevity and intensity is the poet's ability to escape the confinement of the poem. The sense of liberation in hokku is usually accomplished through references to time and space. A Japanese hokku contains not only a reference to a season, an indication of time, but also an image of nature, that of space. Pound's hokku-like poems, such as "In a Station of the Metro" and "Alba," indeed have references to time and space. Pound called the metro emotion, which came from the image of the faces in the crowd, "a thing outward and objective" and the image of the "petals, on a wet, black bough" "a thing inward and subjective." The image of the petals, nevertheless, is a natural object in contrast to that of the faces in the crowded station, a human object.

In Pound's mind—in the realm of subjective perception—the image of the faces, an objective image, transforms into the image of the petals, a subjective image. This perception also means that the image of the faces, an image of man, transforms into that of the petals, an image of nature. The shifting of objective and subjective images in Pound's poem is depicted in terms of a vortex, in which an image is not only active in itself but capable of merging into another image that appears in its wake. Because Pound's image has this tendency, it is often as difficult to separate the mental vision from the external as it is to separate mind from matter, the perceiver from the perceived, in Japanese hokku.

In *The Spirit of Japanese Poetry,* Noguchi is as critical as Pound of the Western poet's tendency to wordiness. Noguchi's emphasis on the Japanese hokku as "the real poetry of action" entails that a hokku aim to narrow the distance between man and nature, the perceiver and the perceived. The narrower the distance, the better the hokku becomes. Based upon "Lao Tze's canon of spiritual anarchism" and Zen's principle of controlling the mind, Noguchi declares:

To attach too closely to the subject matter in literary expression is never a way to complete the real saturation; the real infinite significance will only be accomplished at such a consummate moment when the end and means are least noticeable, and the subject and expression never fluctuate from each other, being in perfect collocation; it is the partial loss of the birthright of each that gains an artistic triumph. . . . I do never mean that the *Hokku* poems are lyrical poetry in the general

Western understanding; but the Japanese mind gets the effect before perceiving the fact of their brevity, its sensibility resounding to their single note, as if the calm bosom of river water to the song of a bird. [*Spirit of Japanese Poetry,* p. 34]

To illustrate what he calls "the sense of mystical affinity between the life of Nature and the life of man, between the beauty of flowers and the beauty of love," he quotes his own poem:

It's accident to exist as a flower or a poet;
A mere twist of evolution but from the same force:
I see no form in them but only beauty in evidence;
It's the single touch of their imagination to get the
  embodiment of a poet or a flower:
To be a poet is to be a flower,
To be the dancer is to make the singer sing.

[*Spirit of Japanese Poetry,* p. 37]

Pound, on the other hand, views the affinity between man and nature differently. What Pound calls "a thing inward and subjective" does not necessarily correspond to a vision of man; nor is "a thing outward and objective" the same thing as a vision of nature.

To explain the transformation of images between man and nature, the perceiver and the perceived, in Japanese hokku, Noguchi quoted Basho's "The Old Pond," perhaps the most celebrated hokku ever written:

The old pond!
A frog leapt into—
List, the water sound!

One may think a frog an absurd poetic subject, but Basho focused his vision on a scene of autumnal desolation, an image of nature. The pond was perhaps situated on the premises of an ancient temple whose silence was suddenly broken by a frog plunging into the deep water. As Noguchi conceived the experience, Basho, a Zen Buddhist, was "supposed to awaken into enlightenment now when he heard the voice bursting out of voicelessness, and the conception that life and death were mere change of condition was deepened into faith" (*Spirit of Japanese Poetry,* pp. 45-46). Basho was not suggesting that the tranquility of the pond meant death or that the frog symbolized life. Just as Pound had the sensation of seeing the beautiful faces in the metro station, Basho here had the sensation of hearing the sound bursting out of soundlessness. A hokku is not a representation of goodness, truth, or beauty; there is nothing particularly good, true, or beautiful about a frog's jumping into the water.

It seems as though Basho, in writing the poem, carried nature within him and brought himself to the deepest level of nature where all sounds lapse into the world of silence and infinity. Though his vision is based upon reality, it transcends time and space. What a Zen poet like Basho is showing is that man can do enough naturally, enjoy doing it, and achieve his peace of mind. This fusion of man and nature is called spontaneity in Zen.

The best hokku poems, because of their linguistic limitations, are inwardly extensive and outwardly infinite. A severe constraint imposed on one aspect of hokku must be balanced by a spontaneous, boundless freedom on the other.

From a Zen point of view, such a vision is devoid of thought and emotion. Since Zen is the most important philosophical tradition influencing Japanese hokku, the hokku poet aims at understanding the spirit of nature. Basho thus recognizes little division between man and nature, the subjective and the objective; he is never concerned with the problems of good and evil. Placed against this tradition, Pound's poetics in its philosophical aspect considerably differs from Basho's. Pound cannot be called a Zen poet because he declared: "An 'Image' is that which presents an intellectual and emotional complex in an instant of time."[35] A Zen poet seeks satori, an enlightenment that transcends time and place, and even the consciousness of self. This enlightenment is defined as a state of mu, nothingness, which is absolutely free of any thought or emotion; it is so completely free that such a state corresponds to that of nature. For a Zen-inspired poet, nature is a mirror of the enlightened self; one must see and hear things as they really are by making one's consciousness pure and clear. Pound seems to be able to appreciate this state of mind, but obviously he does not necessarily try to seek it in his own work.

In fact, Japanese hokku seldom take physical love, war, beasts, earthquakes, floods, and the like for their subjects. And while Pound's poetry does express good and evil, love and hatred, individual feeling and collective myth, Basho's shuns such sentiments and emotions altogether. Pound and a Zen poet, however, do agree that their poetic vision is spontaneous and capable of attaining enlightenment. Pound maintained, "It is the presentation of such a 'complex' instantaneously which gives that sense of sudden liberation; that sense of freedom from time and space limits; that sense of sudden growth, which we experience in the presence of the greatest works of art."[36] Pound's observation, however, is very much a Western formulation of an experience familiar to Zen-inspired artists.

This sense of liberation suggests an impersonal conception of poetry, for it focuses attention not upon the poet but upon the image. T. S. Eliot, whom most observers agree Pound influenced, held the same view.[37] Japanese poets such as Basho and Buson held the same principle. Their poetry seldom dealt with dreams, fantasies, or concepts of heaven and hell; it was strictly concerned with the portrayal of nature—mountains, trees, birds, waterfalls, nights, days, seasons. For the Japanese hokku poet, nature is a mirror of the enlightened self; the poet must see and hear things as they really are by making his or her consciousness pure, natural, and unemotional. "Japanese poets," Noguchi wrote, "go to Nature to make life more meaningful, sing of flowers and birds to make humanity more intensive" (*Spirit of Japanese Poetry,* p. 37).

As opposed to his later poetry, Pound's early poetry, and his hokku-like poems in particular, have little to do with his personal emotion or thought. In such poetry, Pound is not really concerned with thought and emotion. If Pound's hokku sounded intellectual or emotional, it did so only to an English reader who was still Arnoldian in his or her taste and unfamiliar with the imagist movement of the 1910s, not to mention with "the spirit of Japanese poetry" Noguchi tried to introduce to the English audience. Japanese poetry shuns symbols and metaphors because figurative language might lessen the intensity and spontaneity of a newly experienced sensation. Such expressions would not only undermine originality in the poet's sensibility but resort to intellectualization—as well as what Noguchi, perhaps echoing Matthew Arnold, called "a criticism of life," which traditionally Japanese poetry was not.[38]

The hokku poet may not only aim at expressing sensation but also at generalizing and hence depersonalizing it. This characteristic can be shown even by one of Basho's lesser-known hokku:

> How cool it is,
> Putting the feet on the wall:
> An afternoon nap.[39]

Basho was interested in expressing how his feet, anyone's feet, would feel when placed on a wall inside a house on a warm summer afternoon. His subject was none other than this direct sensation. He did not want to convey any emotion, any thought, any beauty; there remained only poetry, only nature.

In "Alba" what Pound expressed was not the personal feeling he had about the woman lying beside him at dawn but his spontaneous sensation of the coolness of "the pale wet leaves / of lily-of-the-valley." Likewise, the sensation of slowly cooling hot water was Pound's subject in "The Bath Tub," as the title suggests, rather than his feelings about the woman.[40] The image of a "fan of white silk, / clear as frost on the grass-blade" is central in "Fan-Piece, for Her Imperial Lord," where a minimal image of the lord's concubine is evoked by a one-word reference to her: "You also are laid aside."[41] Such subtleties could not have been learned from Pound's fellow imagists like Flint and Aldington, who remained labored, superficial imitators of Japanese hokku. Pound and Noguchi, by contrast, showed themselves far more capable of understanding the spirit of Japanese poetry.

V

As partly suggested in the remarks on superposition quoted above, the hokku also provided a structural model for Pound's version of imagism. Acknowledging that the Japanese had evolved this short form of poetry, Pound seized upon the unique form of "super-position" which, he observed, constitutes a hokku. To him, the hokku often consists of two disparate images in juxtaposition, and yet it appears as a single image. Lacking the copula 'is' or the preposition 'like', the image cannot be metaphoric or analogical. As Pound's account of the composition of the metro poem shows, he had no intention of likening the image of the beautiful faces in the crowd to the image of petals on a wet, black bough or of making one image suggestive or representative of the other.[42] If one image is used to suggest another or to represent another, both images would be weakened. But if one image is used to generate or intensify another, and the other image, in turn, intensifies the first one, then the whole poem as one image would be intensified.

The key to the superpository structure of Pound's image is a coalescence of two unlike images. Such an image must be generated "in an instant of time," as Pound cautions in his essay "A Few Don'ts."[43] Creating such an image needs no preparations, no explanations, no qualifications; Pound calls "the 'natural course of events' the exalted moment, the vision unsought or at least the vision gained without machination."[44] In *The Spirit of Japanese Poetry* and *The Spirit of Romance* Noguchi and Pound respectively emphasized this revelatory moment when high poetry must be written. But such a parallel in their poetics does not necessitate that one's ideas came from the other's. Pound's observations might have been made independently.

It is quite possible that Pound became acquainted through other sources with many of the superpository hokku which Noguchi cited as examples in *The Spirit of Japanese Poetry*. In addition to Moritake's "I Thought I Saw the Fallen Leaves" and Basho's "The Old Pond," quoted earlier, Noguchi translated the following in *The Spirit of Japanese Poetry*: Buson's "Oh, How Cool—" (p. 47) and "Prince Young, Gallant" (p. 36), Basho's "Lying Ill on Journey" (p. 38), and Hokushi's "It Has Burned Down" (p. 27). It may be significant, however, that in another collection of critical essays Noguchi cited several of his own numerous hokku in English along with those by ancient masters. Many of Noguchi's English hokku, moreover, had been published in *The Pilgrimage* (1908, 1909). Pound might have acquainted himself with Noguchi's published hokku before he experimented with his version.

As Pound would account for the circumstances of his metro poem in Paris in 1912, Noguchi also narrated the experience he had had in London in 1903:

> I myself was a *hokku* student since I was fifteen or sixteen years old; during many years of my Western life, now amid the California forest, then by the skyscrapers of New York, again in the London 'bus, I often tried to translate the *hokku* of our old masters but I gave up my hope when I had written the following in English:
>
> My Love's lengthened hair
> Swings o'er me from Heaven's gate:
> Lo, Evening's shadow!

It was in London, to say more particularly, Hyde Park, that I wrote the above *hokku* in English, where I walked slowly, my mind being filled with the thought of the long hair of Rossetti's woman as I perhaps had visited Tate's Gallery that afternoon. . . . I exclaimed then: "What use to try the impossibility in translation, when I have a moment to feel a *hokku* feeling and write about it in English?"[45]

Structurally, Pound's metro poem resembles Noguchi's Hyde Park hokku. As in Pound's poem where the outward image of the faces in the crowd is set on top of the inward image of petals on a wet, black bough, so the actual vision of an evening shadow in Noguchi's poem is juxtaposed to an envisioning of a woman's long hair. In each poem a pair of images, similar in form but different in content, coalesces into another autonomous image, which generates different meaning. The superposition of the paired images transforms into a different image in form and content, what Pound calls "the 'one image' poem" ("Vorticism," p. 467). This transformation of images retains the sensation of each separate object perceived, but it also conveys a greater sensation by uniting the two experiences.[46] For both poets, such a transformation is optimal, for they believe that images in poetry cannot and should not be divided as external and internal, physical and mental, objective and subjective.[47]

To illustrate the energy latent in this transformation of images, Pound provided an anecdote: "I once saw a small child go to an electric light switch and say, 'Mamma, can I *open* the light?' She was using the age-old language of exploration, the language of art" ("Vorticism," p. 466). Although he later became interested in Fenollosa's explanation that written Chinese characters denote action, he was first attracted to the poetics of the hokku, what he called "the sense of exploration . . . the beauty of this sort of knowing" ("Vorticism," pp. 466-67). Noguchi expounded this poetics in terms of an intensive art by referring to Kikaku's celebrated hokku:

> Autumn's full moon:
> Lo, the shadows of a pine-tree
> Upon the mats!

The beauty of the harvest moon is not only humanized but intensified by the shadow of a tree Kikaku saw on the tatami mats. "Really," Noguchi wrote, "it was my first opportunity to observe the full beauty of the light and shadow, more the beauty of the shadow in fact, far more luminous than the light itself, with such a decorativeness, particularly when it stamped the dustless mats as a dragon-shaped ageless pine-tree."[48] The situation here, shared by Pound and Noguchi, is one of finding, discovering, and hence of inventing the new.

As if to bear out Pound's vorticist thinking in poetry, Noguchi made a modest proposal for English poets. "I think," he wrote, "it is time for them to live more of the passive side of Life and Nature, so as to make the meaning of the whole of them perfect and clear, to value the beauty of inaction so as to emphasise action, to think of Death so as to make Life more attractive." To the Japanese mind, an intensive art can be created not from action but from inaction. Noguchi thus argued that the larger part of life "is builded upon the unreality by the strength of which the reality becomes intensified; when we sing of the beauty of night, that is to glorify, through the attitude of reverse, in the way of silence, the vigour and wonder of the day" (*Spirit of Japanese Poetry,* pp. 24-25).

Noguchi's paradox was echoed in Pound's statement about vorticism. To Pound, an intensive art is not an emphatic art. By an intensive art, Pound meant "one . . . concerned with the relative intensity, or relative significance, of different sorts of expression. . . . They are more dynamic. I do not mean they are more emphatic, or that they are yelled louder" ("Vorticism," p. 468).

Pound illustrated this intensive art with a hokku-like sentence in his essay "Affirmations," first published in the *New Age* in 1915:

> The pine-tree in mist upon the far hill looks like
> a fragment of Japanese armour.

The images appear in simile form, but Pound has no intention of intensifying the beauty of either image by comparison to the other. "In either case," he points out, "the beauty, in so far as it is beauty of form, is the result of 'planes in relation.' . . . The tree and the armour are beautiful because their diverse planes overlie in a certain manner." Unlike the sculptor or the painter, the poet, who must use words to intensify his art, Pound says, "may cast on the reader's mind a more vivid image of either the armour or the pine by mentioning them close together . . . for he works not with planes or with colours but with the names of objects and of properties. It is his business so to use, so to arrange, these names as to cast a more definite image than the layman can cast."[49]

Critics have shown over the years that Pound's idea of vorticism underlies not only his short imagistic poems but also his longer pieces such as the *Cantos, Cathay,* and his translations of noh plays. Noguchi, on the other hand, attempted to intensify an image in a poem longer than the hokku by endowing it with action and autonomy. "The Passing of Summer" (1909), for instance, reads:

> An empty cup whence the light of passion is
> drunk!—
> To-day a sad rumour passes through the trees,
> A chill wind is borne by the stream,
> The waves shiver in pain;
> Where now the cicada's song long and hot?[50]

Such visual images as an empty cup, the chilly wind blowing over the stream, and the shivering waves do not simply denote the passing of summer; they constitute its action. Similarly, experiences or memories of experiences like drinking "the light of passion" and hearing "the cicada's song long and hot" do not merely express the poet's nostalgia or sentiment about the summer; these images, rather than being metonymies, recreate the actions of the summer.[51] In Noguchi's poetry, as in the hokku, poetry and sensation are spontaneously conjoined and intensified, to leave no room for rationalism or moralism.

VI

Numerous parallels between Pound's poetics and Noguchi's do not entail the conclusion that both poets held the same principles throughout their respective careers. Much of Noguchi's art and literary criticism shows great enthusiasm at times for Yeats's mysticism and Whitman's transcendentalism.[52] Noguchi had a taste for certain styles of poetry that Pound obviously did not. But their writings as a whole suggest that both writers, as poets and critics, agreed on the ideas of imagism during the period between 1908—when *The Pilgrimage,* Noguchi's fifth collection of English poems, appeared in Tokyo and London—and 1914, when Noguchi's *The Spirit of Japanese Poetry* was published in London. For Noguchi, this period came in the middle of his career as it coincided with Pound's early career and interest in imagism. This agreement on imagism constituted an interpenetrating relationship of Japanese poetics and Western intentions in early modernism. Pound's launching of "Imagism" in London in 1912 and 1913 with the support of T. E. Hulme, F. S. Flint, H.D., Richard Aldington, and others has become a legend of sorts. And much of the imagist work by various hands began to appear in Chicago in *Poetry* and in London in *Des Imagistes* and *The Freewoman* (later *The Egoist*). But the sources that Noguchi brought to Western attention as early as 1903, when *From the Eastern Sea,* the third collection of his English poems, was published in London, have become not only obscure but neglected.

In March 1913 Pound and his associates collectively drew up and published the three principles of their "faith." The first was "direct treatment of the 'thing,' whether subjective or objective." Noguchi would wholeheartedly have endorsed the formulation. The second principle called for using "absolutely no word that does not contribute to the presentation," and Noguchi had documented the practice of this tenet in the hokku by Japanese masters as well as in his own work. The third principle was "to compose in sequence of the musical phrase, not in sequence of the metronome" ("Vorticism," p. 462). Because the Japanese language radically differs from a Western language in rhythm, rhyme, stress, or tone, Noguchi would readily have assented to the proposal.

Much of Pound's early work and Noguchi's clearly reflects this accord between the imagists and Noguchi. It is true that while Pound was fascinated by Japanese poetics, he was also interested in vorticism as applied to visual arts, as his commentary on such artists as Gaudier-Brzeska, Brancusi, and Picasso indicates. Through the Poets' Club, Pound was also closely associated with Hulme, Flint, Aldington, Upward, and others, some of whom were initially attracted to Japanese color prints by such painters as Utamaro and Hokusai exhibited in the British Museum. There is clear evidence that Pound's associates also tried their hand at hokku with various degrees of seriousness and success. By the mid 1910s, imagism had indeed become the literary zeitgeist, and any poet living in London would have received some influence from the Japanese sources.

To sum up, then, Noguchi's English poems had been widely circulated in London well before September 1914, when Pound's "Vorticism" essay appeared, and Noguchi's

essay on hokku in *Rhythm* and his book *The Spirit of Japanese Poetry* were published in January 1913 and March 1914, respectively. The material in the essay and the book was delivered as a series of lectures during his stay in England from December 1913 to April 1914. In these circumstances, it is hardly conceivable that the imagists did not acquaint themselves with Noguchi's ideas. Even though Pound's modernist theory might partly have derived from other sources, one can scarcely overlook the direct link between Japanese poetics and Pound's imagism through Noguchi.

NOTES

[1] Ezra Pound, "Vorticism," *Fortnightly Review,* n.s., no. 573 (September 1, 1914): 461-71; hereafter cited as "Vorticism."

[2] Hugh Kenner, *The Poetry of Ezra Pound* (Millwood, N.Y., 1947), p. 58.

[3] Earl Miner, "Pound, *Haiku* and the Image," *Hudson Review* 9 (Winter 1957): 570-84, and *The Japanese Tradition in British and American Literature* (Princeton, N.J., 1958). There is some ambiguity in Miner's chronology since, in his article, the date of Pound's joining the Poets' Club is said to be "just before the first World War," which means perhaps between 1913 and 1914 (Miner, "Pound," p. 572). There is also another ambiguity with respect to the time and circumstance of Pound's learning about "the usefulness of Japanese poetry from Flint." Flint's interest in Japanese poetry is indicated in his own account of the matter, published in *The Egoist* for May 1, 1915: "I had been advocating in the course of a series of articles on recent books of verse a poetry in *vers libre,* akin in spirit to the Japanese" (Miner, *Japanese Tradition,* p. 100).

[4] For Noguchi's life and work, see Yoshinobu Hakutani, ed., *Selected English Writings of Yone Noguchi: An East-West Literary Assimilation,* vol. 1, *Poetry* (Cranbury, N.J., 1990), and vol. 2, *Prose* (Cranbury, N.J., 1992). For the most recent study of Noguchi's life, including an interview with his son, the late American sculptor Isamu Noguchi, see Hakutani, "Father and Son: A Conversation with Isamu Noguchi," *Journal of Modern Literature* (in press). For a discussion of Noguchi's English poetry and literary criticism, see Hakutani, "Yone Noguchi's Poetry: From Whitman to Zen," *Comparative Literature Studies* 22 (Spring 1985): 67-79.

[5] Ezra Pound, "As for Imagisme," *New Age* 14 (1915): 349.

[6] The impact of hokku on Pound was apparently greater and more beneficial than that on his fellow imagists. Regarding the form of superposition as ideal for expressing instantaneous perception, Pound wrote in a footnote: "Mr. Flint and Mr. Rodker have made longer poems depending on a similar presentation of matter. So also have Richard Aldington, in his *In Via Sestina,* and 'H.D.' in

her *Oread,* which latter poems express much stronger emotions than that in my lines here given" ("Vorticism," p. 467). Pound's argument here suggests that hokku and Pound's hokku-like poems can express instantaneous and spontaneous perception better than can the longer poems and the poems with stronger emotions.

[7] E. A. Sharp, *William Sharp* [Fiona Macleod]: *A Memoir* (London, 1910), pp. 280-81.

[8] Yone Noguchi, "What Is a Hokku Poem?" *Rhythm* 11 (1913): 354-59. The essay was reprinted in Noguchi's *Through the Torii* (London, 1914; Boston, 1922), pp. 126-39. The page numbers cited hereafter refer to the *Rhythm* version.

[9] Noguchi, "What Is a Hokku Poem?" p. 355.

[10] Ibid.

[11] In a November 24, 1913, letter to Pound, Mary Fenollosa wrote: "I am beginning with [sic] right now, to send you material." On the following day she wrote again: "Please don't get discouraged at the ragged way this manuscript is coming to you. As I said yesterday, it will all get there in time,—which is the most important thing." See *Ezra Pound and Japan: Letters and Essays,* ed. Sanehide Kodama (Redding Ridge, Conn., 1987), p. 6.

[12] Ernest Fenollosa, *The Chinese Written Character as a Medium for Poetry,* ed. Ezra Pound (New York, 1936), p. 8.

[13] One of Pound's critics who acknowledge this fact, Roy E. Teele, demonstrates Fenollosa's failure to understand the Japanese language, particularly the essential rhythm of the noh text Fenollosa translated. See Roy E. Teele, "The Japanese Translations," *Texas Quarterly* 10 (1967): 61-66.

[14] Earl Miner, who states that Pound knew nothing about Japanese poetry before 1913 or 1914, believes that Pound later learned about hokku in the writings of the French translators (Miner, "Pound," pp. 572-73).

[15] *Ezra Pound and Japan,* p. 4.

[16] Yone Noguchi, *Collected English Letters,* ed. Ikuko Atsumi (Tokyo, 1975), pp. 210-11.

[17] See Yone Noguchi, "The Everlasting Sorrow: A Japanese Noh Play," *The Egoist* 4 (October 1917): 141-43, and "The Japanese Noh Play," *The Egoist* 5 (August 1918): 99.

[18] See K. L. Goodwin, *The Influence of Ezra Pound* (London, 1966), p. 32.

[19] Noguchi first met Yeats in 1903 as indicated in a letter Noguchi wrote to Leonie Gilmour, his first wife: "I made many a nice young, lovely, kind friend among literary *genius* (attention!) W. B. Yeats or Laurence Binyon, Moore and Bridges. They are so good; they invite me almost every day" (Noguchi, *Collected English Letters,* p. 106). In 1921, Yeats in Oxford wrote to Noguchi in Tokyo: "Though I have been so long in writing[,] your 'Hiroshige' has given me the greatest pleasure. I take more and more pleasure from oriental art; find more and more that it accords with what I aim at in my own work. The European painter of the last two or three hundred years grows strange to me as I grow older, begins to speak as with a foreign tongue.... The old French poets were simple as the modern are not, & I find in Francois Villon the same thoughts, with more intellectual power, that I find in the Gaelic poet [Raftery]. I would be simple myself but I do not know how. I am always turning over pages like those you have sent me, hoping that in my old age I may discover how.... A form of beauty scarcely lasts a generation with us, but it lasts with you for centuries. You no more want to change it than a pious man wants to change the Lord's Prayer, or the Crucifix on the wall [blurred] at least not unless we have infected you with our egotism" (Noguchi, *Collected English Letters,* pp. 220-21).

[20] Goodwin, p. 32.

[21] See William Pratt, *The Imagist Poem* (New York, 1963), pp. 14-15; J. B. Harmer, *Victory in Limbo: Imagism 1908-1917* (New York, 1975), p. 17; Humphrey Carpenter, *A Serious Character: The Life of Ezra Pound* (Boston, 1988), p. 115.

[22] It is speculative, of course, but quite possible that Aldington, fascinated by Japanese visual arts, might have read the three articles Noguchi published about the subject in this period: "Utamaro," *Rhythm* 11, no. 10 (1912): 257-60, "Koyetsu," *Rhythm* 11, no. 11 (1912): 302-5, "The Last Master [Yoshitoshi] of the Ukiyoye School," *Transactions of the Japan Society of London* 12 (1914): 144-56. Moreover, Yone Noguchi, *The Spirit of Japanese Art* (London, 1915) includes chapters on major Japanese painters such as Koyetsu, Kenzan, Kyosai, and Busho Hara, besides Utamaro and Hiroshige. If Aldington had read these essays, he would very well have been acquainted with Noguchi's writings about Japanese poetics.

[23] Aldington's poem reads:

> The apparition of these poems in a crowd:
> White faces in a black dead faint.

See Aldington, "Penultimate Poetry," *The Egoist* (January 15, 1915). This poem sounds more like senryu, a humorous haiku, than the hokku Pound was advocating.

[24] Donald Davie, *Ezra Pound* (New York, 1975), p. 42; Carpenter, p. 247.

[25] Compare Harmer, p. 38.

[26] Miner, "Pound" (n. 3 above), p. 572.

[27] See Usaburo Toyama, ed., *Essays on Yone Noguchi* (Tokyo, 1975), 1:327. (The text is mostly in Japanese.) Toyama, an art historian, was married to Noguchi's daughter Hifumi.

[28] A. R. Jones, *The Life and Opinions of Thomas Ernest Hulme* (Boston, 1960), p. 122. Neither Noel Stock, in *Poet in Exile: Ezra Pound* (Manchester, 1964), nor Humphrey Carpenter in *A Serious Character* mentions Pound's activities at the Quest Society, let alone Pound's possible interactions with Noguchi.

[29] See T. S. Eliot, ed. and introduction, *Literary Essays of Ezra Pound* (Norfolk, Conn., 1954), p. 23.

[30] Noguchi, "What Is a Hokku Poem?" (n. 8 above), p. 355.

[31] About this time Noguchi also wrote an essay entitled "A Japanese Note on Yeats," included in *Through the Torii* (n. 8 above), pp. 110-17.

[32] Noguchi's "Tell Me the Street to Heaven" was first published in his essay, "What Is a Hokku Poem?" (p. 358) and reprinted in *Through the Torii*. "Is It, Oh, List" was also included in the same issue and reprinted in *Through the Torii* with a change in the third line: "So runs Thames, so runs my Life" (p. 136).

[33] Ezra Pound, *Personae* (New York, 1926), p. 109.

[34] Ibid., pp. 109-11.

[35] Eliot, ed., p. 4.

[36] Ibid.

[37] See T. S. Eliot, *Selected Essays, 1917-1932* (New York, 1932), pp. 8-10.

[38] Noguchi, *Through the Torii,* p. 159.

[39] The original in Japanese reads "Hiya hiya to / Kabe wo fumaete / Hirune kana." See Harold G. Henderson, *An Introduction to Haiku* (Garden City, N.Y., 1958), p. 49. The English translation of this hokku is mine.

[40] Pound, *Personae,* p. 100.

[41] Ibid., p. 108.

[42] Alan Durant tries to show that Pound's metro poem contains a number of metaphors and associations, and that it is not as imagistic as critics say. While Durant's interpretation holds insofar as the various elements in the poem appear to the reader as metaphors and associations, Pound's intention does differ from the emphases of such an interpretation. The same thing may occur in the interpretation of a Japanese hokku, but traditionally the language of the hokku, as Noguchi demonstrates throughout *The Spirit of Japanese Poetry* (London, 1914), shuns metaphor and symbolism. See Alan Durant, "Pound, Modernism and Literary Criticism: A Reply to Donald Davie," *Critical Quarterly* 28 (1986): 154-66.

[43] Eliot, ed. (n. 29 above), p. 4.

[44] Ezra Pound, *The Spirit of Romance* (London, 1910; reprint, New York, 1968), p. 97.

[45] Noguchi, "Again on *Hokku,*" in *Through the Torii* (n. 8 above), pp. 140-46. A verbatim account is given in the introduction to his *Japanese Hokkus* (Boston, 1920), pp. 22-23. For Noguchi's London experiences, see "My First London Experience (1903)," and "Again in London (1913-14)," in *The Story of Yone Noguchi Told by Himself* (London, 1914), pp. 119-65.

[46] The union of different experiences is reminiscent of T. S. Eliot's statement about an amalgamation. In reference to John Donne's poetry, Eliot writes, "When a poet's mind is perfectly equipped for its work, it is constantly amalgamating disparate experience; the ordinary man's experience is chaotic, irregular, fragmentary. The latter falls in love, or reads Spinoza, and these two experiences have nothing to do with each other, or with the noise of the typewriter or the smell of cooking; in the mind of the poet these experiences are always forming new wholes" (*Selected Essays,* p. 247).

[47] In *The Spirit of Japanese Poetry,* Noguchi wrote, "As the so-called literary expression is a secondary matter in the realm of poetry, there is no strict boundary between the domains generally called subjective and objective; while some *Hokku* poems appear to be objective, those poems are again by turns quite subjective through the great virtue of the writers having the fullest identification with the matter written on. You might call such collation poetical trespassing; but it is the very point whence the Japanese poetry gains unusual freedom; that freedom makes us join at once with the soul of Nature" (pp. 43-44).

[48] Noguchi, "What Is a Hokku Poem?" p. 357.

[49] Ezra Pound, *Gaudier-Brzeska: A Memoir* (London, 1916; reprint, New York, 1970), pp. 120-21.

[50] Yone Noguchi, *The Pilgrimage* (London, 1908), 1:68.

[51] To the Japanese, such expressions as "the light of passion" and "the cicada's song" immediately evoke images of hot summer. These phrases in Japanese are attributed to or closely associated with summer.

[52] For Whitman's influence on Noguchi, see Hakutani, "Yone Noguchi's Poetry: From Whitman to Zen" (n. 4 above): "Like Whitman, Noguchi believes in monism, and his ultimate goal in writing poetry is to achieve the ecstasies of the self in nature. . . . Though he became a different kind of nature poet after he returned to Japan, his later poems still bear out Whitman's influence" (p. 69).

Milton A. Cohen

[*In the following essay, Cohen draws parallels between Pound's "A Few Don'ts by an Imagiste" (1913) and the principles outlined by the Austrian-born American composer Arnold Schoenberg in* Theory of Harmony *(1911), placing both in the destructive phase of the development of new art forms.*]

SOURCE: "Subversive Pedagogies: Schoenberg's Theory of Harmony and Pound's 'A Few Don'ts by an Imagiste'," in *Mosaic,* Vol. 24, No. 1, Winter, 1988, pp. 49-65.

"The urge for destruction is also a creative urge!"

—Mikhail Bakunin, 1842

"To destroy is always the first step in any creation."

—E.E. Cummings, 1922

The quotations above bracket eighty years of almost continuous upheaval in the arts—battles in which innovative artists challenged the repositories of stifling tradition: the academies, the conservative critics, the bourgeois public. Seen from a historical perspective that has vindicated the avant-garde, these struggles acquire the trappings of heroic myth. Indeed, popular histories of Modernism invest these struggles with a "moral" sanctity, as witness John Russell's use of the term to describe Impressionist painting (18).

"Moral" or not, the struggle *against* prevailing tradition defines the discourse of both general survey and specialized study alike. "There is . . . almost no avant-garde manifestation," writes Renato Poggioli, "which is not a new variation on the attitude defined by Apollinaire as 'antitradition'" (53). The precise nature of this oppositional stance, however, is problematic. For one thing, there is the cheerful paradox that artists destroy by creating. An artist's weapon, after all, is his art: even the most calculated slap at academic tradition and bourgeois propriety—say, the urinal that Duchamp submitted to the 1917 Exhibition of the Society of Independent Artists as a "Fountain" by "R. Mutt"—acquires, willy-nilly, the privileged status (and price tag) of *objet d'art.* How much more so with "serious" compositions that scandalized the public and subverted the traditions. Historians and critics celebrate a *Le Déjeuner sur l'Herbe* or *Le Sacre du Printemps* not merely as the torpedo that sank an outworn tradition, but as the birth-cry of a *new* esthetics, "a beginning from ground zero," as Rosalind Krauss observes (157). Perhaps the German Expressionist painter Franz Marc expressed as well as anyone the intertwined acts of destroying and creating: "In this time of great struggle for a new art, we fight like disorganized 'savages' against an old, established power. The battle seems to be unequal, but spiritual matters are never decided by numbers, only by the power of ideas. The dreaded weapons of the 'savages' are their *new ideas.* New ideas kill better than steel and destroy what was thought to be indestructible" (61).

"New ideas," however, may not always suffice. The dominance of the "old, established power" may be so pervasive and entrenched as to require a direct attack on the sources of its legitimacy—its theoretical underpinnings, its conventions, its prestige—so as to clear the way for constructive innovation or to legitimize innovations already present. Thus, if artists destroy by creating, they must also at times create by destroying.

Two forms of destructive attack are well known: the satire or caricature and the manifesto. Although the Modernist period is not especially known for its satire, a sizable number of painters and writers earned their bread this way (Shapiro 32-35). The avant-garde's preferred form of assault, the manifesto, interwines constructive and destructive ends as it declares a movement's *programme* while it condemns prevailing ideas. The Futurist painters, for example, aimed much of their "Technical Manifesto" at imitation, harmony, good taste, art critics, "bituminous tints," archaicism, and especially the nude: "We demand for ten years, the total suppression of the nude in painting" (Taylor 126-27).

A third mode of attack, however, has gone virtually unnoticed: pedagogy. Where it is considered, teaching is typically treated as a conservative act—what "schools" do to maintain the old ways. Thus Poggioli: "The school does not aim to discuss; it intends to teach. In place of proclamations and programs, manifestos and reviews . . . the school prefers to create new variants of traditional poetics and rhetoric, normative or didactic simply by nature" (24). Poggioli's contrast quickly falls apart, however, when one considers that two prime movers of Modernism, Ezra Pound and Arnold Schoenberg, were both committed teachers who put their pedagogy in the service of their radical esthetics. Schoenberg's teaching, especially of his two famous disciples Berg and Webern, is well known. Pound, though stymied in an academic career, was nontheless a born teacher—a "village explainer" in Stein's unkind phrase.

Although spread over a lifetime, Pound's and Schoenberg's influence as teachers arguably reached its zenith in two contemporaneous works: Schoenberg's *Theory of Harmony* (1911),[1] often ranked among the two or three major treatises on music theory in the twentieth century, and Pound's "A Few Don'ts by an Imagiste" (1913), which, with its companion-piece, "Imagisme," formally launched the Imagist movement in *Poetry* magazine. On first glance, the two tracts seem scarcely comparable. Pound's "Don'ts," clearly intended as part of a propaganda blitz, runs to six short pages of aphoristic advice to the prospective poet. Schoenberg's massive textbook weighs in at over 400 densely-packed pages, footnoted and profusely illustrated with musical examples. Its style is more discursive and "teacherly" than the terse "Don'ts": Schoenberg analyzes, discusses, illustrates, repeats himself, and above all seeks to persuade his student-reader; Pound commands and virtually browbeats his reader to obey. The two tracts are also separate in lacking any personal or intellectual discourse between their authors:

Pound and Schoenberg never met in those years, and although Pound may have been familiar with *Theory of Harmony* and may have attended the London premiere of Schoenberg's *Five Pieces for Orchestra* in 1912, he does not mention Schoenberg's theories until several years later and then without enthusiasm (Schafer 506-07, 33).

Yet, for all their differences in size, scope and provenance, *Theory of Harmony* and "A Few Don'ts" play such similar roles within their respective arts as to merit a comparative study of their ideas and influence. Contrary to Poggioli, these tracts were penned not by conservative pedagogues but by teacher-artists as they were restructuring music and poetry. Each author, moreover, was the galvanizing force of a small group of like-minded artists—the Schoenberg-Berg-Webern triad and "Les Imagistes" (Pound, Aldington and H.D.)—who were then evolving a new style: Pantonal Expressionism and Imagism, respectively.[2] Within these emerging styles *Theory of Harmony* and "A Few Don'ts" play several overlapping roles: as theoretical rationales for the innovative work of their authors, as stated or implied manifestos of two burgeoning styles, as destroyers of established esthetics and conventional practice, and as pedagogies that promote their ideas by teaching future composers and poets. These tracts thus occupy parallel positions within the destructive phase of two avant-garde movements and achieve their subversions through pedagogy. Their comparison, in turn, reveals congruent strengths and weaknesses in the styles they influenced.

Published amidst a welter of artistic movements, creeds and manifestos, these two tracts owe at least part of their inspiration to the declamatory *Zeitgeist* of pre-war Europe. The author of "Imagisme" acknowledges this militant milieu even as he tries to distinguish Imagism from it: "The *imagistes* admitted that they were contemporaries of the Post Impressionists and the Futurists; but they had nothing in common with these schools. They had not published a manifesto. They were not a revolutionary school" (199). Pound's disclaimer, however, is disingenuous, for his two articles, following so soon after the Futurist exhibition, manifesto and lectures in London, *are* Imagism's first manifesto; and the practices advocated in "A Few Don'ts" are indeed "revolutionary." Schoenberg's bulky textbook certainly does not *look* like an incendiary manifesto: it offers no program and speaks, explicitly at least, for no group. Indeed, its ostensible purpose is to instruct students in the "handicraft of harmony," the conventions "necessary for complying with the major-minor system" (396, 48). Yet, interlaced with its dry, orderly presentation of harmonic combinations is a subversive subtext: commentaries in which Schoenberg switches hats from upholder of the rules to intelligent skeptic who asks "whether they need be so"—questions, that is, their very authority (Carter xiv). Similarly, although Schoenberg writes in the singular, his questions, like Pound's "Don'ts," reflect the current thinking and most recent innovations of an avant-garde group.

By 1913, Pound had associated with the Hulme circle for four years, absorbing those aspects of Hulme's poetics that corresponded with his own reformist ideas, and sharing in the group's experiments in proto-Imagist and Haiku poems (Stock 63-64). Schoenberg and his two student-disciples had achieved comparatively more when *Theory* appeared, composing major works in the Pantonal-Expressionist style since about 1908. As Schoenberg acknowledges, the ideas that his text advances by questioning assumptions of the prevailing system reflect "that which the art has already achieved" (386) and thus provide a theoretical rationale for techniques that had come to him through "musical intuition" rather than through "deliberation" (410).

If these tracts rationalize what their authors were achieving in practice and formalize the ideas of a group—function, that is, as either open or implied manifestos—they also promulgate their ideas by *teaching* their student-readers which esthetic theories are no longer valid, which artistic practices are outworn, and which models are still worth emulating. This pedagogic intent is self-evident and primary in *Theory of Harmony*. In the Imagist articles, however, pedagogy at first seems only a narrative stratagem, as the author of "Imagisme" adopts the persona of an "approaching poetaster" taken in hand by the new movement. Yet in "A Few Don'ts" Pound is emphatically pedagogic in reversing the perspective and addressing his readers *as* students: "The immediate necessity is to tabulate A LIST OF DON'TS for those beginning to write verses" (201). What *Theory* and "Don'ts" offer their student-readers is a decidedly negative attack on the prevailing esthetics of their day, Schoenberg by deflating "false theories," by identifying "inadequacies of the tonal system" (12, 330) and Pound by proscribing outworn practices of Victorian poetics. Both writers, interestingly, acknowledge their negativism. Pound refers sardonically to the "Mosaic negatives" of his "Don'ts"; Schoenberg concedes that his ideas "even if they are negative, even if they do not themselves lay any foundations, are all the same no less fruitful than positive principles . . . they have at least cleared the ground for a foundation" (386). Such clearing, however, amounts here to nothing less than an esthetic *coup d'état*.

That these subversions should come from two artists who understood and respected their artistic forbears as well as did Pound and Schoenberg is more than ironic, and their complex attitudes toward tradition should be distinguished from the generalized hostility that Poggioli describes above. Pound's complete and simultaneous immersion in several poetic traditions virtually defines his early work and fueled his rancor against what he considered the flaccid poetics of his age. His Imagist principles thus embody the other meaning of "revolutionary": a circular return to the great epochs of the past to rejuvenate a desiccated present. The Imagists sought "to write in accordance with the best tradition, as they found it in the best writers of all time—in Sappho, Catullus, Villon" (Flint 199). To "break with tradition" meant for Pound to "desert the more obvious imbecilities of one's immediate elders" ("Notes" 227).

Schoenberg, too, revered his tradition, as the breadth of his citations in *Theory of Harmony* and his essays on and transcriptions of Bach and Brahms amply testify. "No one," he writes, "loves his predecessors more deeply, more fervently, more respectfully, than the artist who gives us something truly new" (*Theory* 401). Uneasy about being branded a radical, he claims that his ideas are *evolutionary*, that the older music "is not at all under attack" (*Theory* 408). He is correct in the sense that the principles he questions—central tonality, resolved dissonances and "non-harmonic tones"—had in practice steadily eroded through the nineteenth century and into the first years of the twentieth with his own post-romantic compositions. "Tonality," he recalls later, "was already dethroned in practice, if not in theory" ("Composition" 216-17). As his questioning in *Theory* formalizes these tendencies and extends them to their logical conclusions, however, the tottering tonal system collapses. Put another way, his critique so expands the harmonic possibilities within the tonal system as to remove its last distinguishing features *as* a system.

Having shorn music and poetry of outworn or insupportable principles of organization, both tracts are reluctant to posit new ones—another major parallel linking them. Schoenberg concedes that his critique does not "lay any [new] foundation" in the sense of offering a new "system" or specific, *con*structive procedures. Pound's "Don'ts" are similarly bereft of new organizing principles: even the affirmative rules of "Imagisme" touch on form only glancingly when they tie composition to "the sequence of the musical phrase" rather than to that of the metronome.

This absence of new structures to replace the discredited ones produces in Imagist and Pantonal-Expressionist works a curious kind of esthetic entropy, in which potential energy (possibilities of direction and force) that once inhered in the formal conventions of diatonic tonality and regularly rhymed and metered verse now devolve to what both artists considered the irreducible denominator of their arts, the tone and image. The resulting structures of these works, determined only by the artist's emotion and sense of organicism, were tightly compressed and highly charged juxtapositions of these tones and images. Indeed, so truncated is the typical structure of these works that both Pound and Schoenberg tend to describe them in the spatial terminology of painting as much as in the temporal diction of literature and music. Perhaps more than any other cause, the formal instabilities of these compressed structures—their inability to support long, complex works and (in Pound's subsequent view) Imagism's tendency toward rhythmic flabbiness—led both artists in a very few years to take similar corrective measures: to assert the constructive organizing principles that are so notably absent in *Theory of Harmony* and "A Few Don'ts," principles codified in Schoenberg's Twelve-Tone Method and Pound's "rhyme and regular strophes."

. . . . .

The neophytes who read Pound's "A Few Don'ts by an Imagiste" in 1913 were no doubt startled (as they were intended to be) not only by Pound's dictatorial tone but

also by his highly negative advice. For "A Few Don'ts" is far more definite about what new poets should avoid than about what they should embrace. Indeed, two of the three "rules" in "Imagisme" are couched at least partly in the negative:

> 2. To use absolutely no word that did not contribute to the presentation.

> 3. As regarding rhythm to compose in sequence of the musical phrase, *not* in sequence of a metronome.

(199, emphasis mine)

Moreover, apart from the demand for concision in rule two, the "constructive" rules and definition of the image in the *Poetry* articles are notoriously vague. What constitutes a "direct" treatment of the thing? How large is a "complex": as small as a petal? As large as *Paradiso?*[3] What is "the sequence of the musical phrase"? Although Pound would later clarify some of these ambiguities, his student-readers would likely have looked to the more specific "Don'ts" article for immediate answers—and there find a barrage of proscriptions.

Some of the "Don'ts" simply restate the second rule about avoiding prolixity (201, 202, 205). Other "Don'ts" fan out over several aspects of poetry. They caution against using synesthesia and sloppy diction (206), against using abstractions (201), against philosophizing and against describing as opposed to presenting (203).

Certain practices Pound does not ban outright, but he carefully qualifies their use. A rhyme, for example, "must have in it some slight element of surprise if it is to give pleasure; it need not be bizarre or curious, but it must be used well if used at all" (205). His advice about rhythm and meter is particularly noteworthy in its failure to explain what "the sequence of the musical phrase" means. Instead, it attacks the regularity of metrical verse and of end-stopped lines. Once again, his advice is essentially negative and general: "Your rhythmic structure should not destroy the shape of your words, or their natural sound, or their meaning" (204).

The broadest "Don'ts" address the craft and profession of poetry. They urge a dedication and seriousness comparable to those of the composer, the scientist, the prose stylist. Even these, however, are couched in the negative: "Don't imagine that the art of poetry is any simpler than the art of music . . ." (203). So pervasive is Pound's urge to proscribe that it carries even to the disclaimer prefacing the "Don'ts"—"never consider anything as dogma"—a statement that self-destructs with "never."

Against this fearsome array of negatives, Pound's *pre*scriptions are vague—commonplace, really—and decidedly conservative. They fall into roughly two categories: models to emulate (Dante, Sappho, Catullus, Villon, etc.) and techniques to master. The latter amount to little more than variations on the theme "learn your craft": the novice should learn "the finest cadences" (202); should master "assonance and alliteration, rhyme immediate and delayed, simple and polyphonic" (203); should practice translating and writing good prose for their salutary discipline (203, 205). About the only two declarative statements that a neophyte could apply directly are: "Let the beginning of the next line catch the rise of the rhythm wave" ([204], i.e., enjambement is acceptable) and "the natural object is always the adequate symbol" (201)—a variant of "Direct treatment of the thing itself."

The striking contrast between Pound's specific "Don'ts" and his vague, general "Do's" leaves little doubt about his esthetic purposes. First, of course, he wants to purge poetry of "poetic dilettantism" (200)—thus, his comparisons to the professional rigors of music and science. It is significant, however, that of the models he cites as worthy, not one comes from the Victorians and only one (heavily qualified) from the English Romantics. The omissions are not accidental, for the practices that Pound forbids are a laundry list of Victorian esthetics: Tennysonian prolixity, philosophizing and abstractions; narrative description; fixed patterns of rhythm and structure; and images used as "ornaments" (à la Swinburne) rather than as "the speech itself." If Pound's "Don'ts" subvert the substance and structure of Victorian poetry, they offer the novice precious few *constructive* practices. From his other essays ("Prolegomena" 9; "Affirmations" 375; "Status" 39), it is clear that Pound felt that the "musical phrase" should correspond organically to a particular emotion. Lacking such glosses, however, the *Poetry* credo simply frees the novice of metronomic dependence and opens the way to free verse—without providing a road map.

Schoenberg's attack on nineteenth-century esthetics differs from Pound's in that the composer attacks principles and, with one exception, does not bother to forbid practices resulting from those principles. His targets are the very pillars of the major-minor system, the first of which is central tonality as an organizing force. Tonality, he declares often, "is no natural law of music, eternally valid" (9, 127-28, 369) because "nothing is definitive in culture; everything is only a preparation for a higher stage of development" (97). The diatonic scale, therefore, is "not . . . the ultimate goal of music but rather a provisional stopping place. The overtone series which led the ear to it, still contains many problems that will have to be faced . . . and the ear will have to attack the problems *because it is so disposed*" (25). This evolutionary view itself justifies studying the tonal system to understand both how it evolved and how it must be superseded: "Let the pupil learn the laws and effect of tonality just as if they still prevailed, but let him know of the tendencies that are leading to their annulment. Let him know that the conditions leading to the dissolution of the system are inherent in the conditions upon which it is established" (29).

Of the "tendencies" and "conditions" that guarantee the dissolution of tonality, the principle of modulation encompasses them all: "Every chord that is set beside the principal tone has at least as much tendency to lead away from it [modulation] as to return to it [cadence]. And if

. . . a work of art is to emerge we must have this movement-generating conflict. The tonality must be placed in danger of losing its sovereignty; the modulation's appetites for independence and the tendencies toward mutiny must be given opportunities to activate themselves" (151). The "danger" arises when the excursions outward become so extensive as to weaken the pull of the tonic center and ultimately to efface its existence. As the tonic atrophies and distant keys acquire increasing independence, the very hierarchy that *subordinates* remote keys to a central tonic itself begins to crumble. What replaces this tonal hierarchy is an egalitarian concept of interchangeability, in which "each degree of the scale governing a work can become a fundamental or at least . . . gain a more significant position in another district" (151). Freed of subservience to a tonic, "every chord can be connected with every other" (241); "all chords can be vagrant" (387); and "any triad can follow any other triad" (165).

Given this inevitable civil strife between the tonic and its outlying keys, Schoenberg foresees two possible outcomes: either the tonic is made to prevail via cadences at crucial junctures, or it is "superceded" (370). He leaves no doubt about which solution he rejects: "that one *can* create tonality, I consider possible. Only, whether one *must* still work for it, indeed whether one *ought* to work for it any more at all, I doubt" (394n)—particularly when maintaining the tonal center seems more a traditional obeisance than a "structural necessity" (28).

Schoenberg's second target was the traditional distinction between dissonance and consonance and the practice of requiring that a dissonance be preceded by and resolved into a consonance. He argues that "the distinction between them is only a matter of degree, not of kind." Because dissonances appear in the "remote overtones" of the fundamental (while consonances appear in closer overtones), dissonances are therefore nothing more than "remote consonances" (21). Just as his finely-honed sense of tonal relationships permits him to see that "even excursions into the most remote regions of tonality may be organic to the fundamental" and are thus permissible, so Schoenberg's encompassing concept that dissonance is organically related to the fundamental leads him to conclude that "any simultaneous combination of sounds, any progression is possible" (70). Rather than carefully resolve a dissonance into a consonance, a composer may simply "skip away from the dissonance" (140)—a freedom Schoenberg calls "the emancipation of the dissonance." Noting how the parameters of consonance have constantly expanded, he confidently predicts that "what today is harmonically remote can tomorrow be close at hand. . . . It all simply depends on the growing ability of the analyzing ear to familiarize itself with remote overtones, thereby expanding the conception of what is euphonious, suitable for art, so that it embraces the whole natural phenomenon" (21). His critique of non-harmonic tones is similar: "There are . . . no non-harmonic tones, no tones foreign to harmony, but merely tones foreign to the harmonic system" (317, 321).

Just as Pound's "Don'ts" defer all constructive decisions to the poet's sensibility, so Schoenberg's compositional conclusions theoretically give the novice virtual *carte blanche*: "There are no limits to the possibilities of tones sounding together, to harmonic possibilities; [the limits are] at most the possibilities of fitting the harmonies into a system that will establish their esthetic value" (322, Carter's interpolation). Without a "system" to judge admissibility, "any material can be suitable for art" (26). Similarly, just as Pound's constructive "Do's" are vague, so Schoenberg becomes evasive and at times even contradictory about new structures to accommodate the compositional freedom resulting from his critiques. He disclaims any intent to "formulate" a new system or "to set up new eternal laws" (12). Logically, he cannot do so, since he argues that all man-made "systems" are inherently flawed. Anticipating the criticism that this reluctance leaves the student to face "without preparation a freedom he cannot cope with" (328), he simply ducks the issue:

> Only a pedagogical consideration keeps me from giving the pupil a completely free hand with these chords. Up to now I have told him exactly when he can rely upon this or that harmony to be effective according to traditional experience; and I should like to continue that way. But there are no traditional experiences upon which to base the free use of these chords.... Consequently, I will take the ... position that the master is free; but the pupil stays under restriction until he has become free." (331)

And when will the pupil become free? Why, when he is no longer a pupil: "One does not give freedom; the other takes it. And only the master can take it: one, that is, who has it anyhow" (329). Still less satisfying to the pupil is Schoenberg's guidance in using "non-harmonic" tones: "the simplest way is the one patterned after the historical evolution, but the as yet non-historical future will bring something different" (331).

If he skirts the "errors" of past theorists—those of systematizing and of composing rules based on that system—Schoenberg still cannot resist one proscriptive caution. Discussing how the chromatic scale "justifies" dissonant progressions, he notes that "tone doublings, octaves, seldom appear [in these chromatic progressions]. The explanation for that is, perhaps, that the tone doubled would acquire a predominance over the others and would thereby turn into a kind of root, *which it should scarcely be*" (420, emphasis mine). These roots are undesirable, he concludes, because the "traditional chords" they form are out of place ("too cold, too dry, expressionless") in a dissonant, chromatic environment. Without quite forbidding tone doubling—a basic method of establishing a central tonality—he emphasizes its inappropriateness to the chromatic scale. Young composers could thus draw their own conclusions about using *any* means to establish a tonal center.

Schoenberg is similarly teasing in predicting what the "something different" will be that supplants the major-minor system. Without developing or defending his ideas, he casually considers fluctuating or suspended tonality, the chromatic scale, the whole-tone scale, quartal harmonies, and a "new epoch of polyphonic style" (389). Except for the whole-tone scale, he finds them all attractive possibilities. Suspended tonality can be as "intelligible" as central tonality: "nothing is lost from the impression of completeness if the tonality is merely hinted at, yes, even if it is erased" (128). "Anarchy would not ensue under these conditions but rather a new form of order" because "the discarding of the tonal bond could favor the self-directed functioning of other bonds" (152). Quartal harmonies can accommodate "all phenomena of harmony" (407). As for basing "our thought, not on the seven tones of the major scale, but rather on the twelve tones of the chromatic scale," Schoenberg predicts in his 1911 edition: "A future theory will undoubtedly follow that course; it would thereby reach the only correct solution to this otherwise difficult problem" (387n). Twelve years would pass before he fulfilled this prophecy with his "Twelve-Tone Method."

About the only new constructive ideas Schoenberg proffers assertively are *Klangfarbenmelodie* (tone-color melodies) and expression as a guide through uncharted terrain. To end a 400-page book on harmony with paean to a different tonal property, timbre, is provocative. Still more so is the assertion that

> the tone becomes perceptible by virtue of tone color, of which one dimension is pitch. Tone color is, thus, the main topic, pitch a subdivision. . . . Now, if it is possible to create patterns out of tone colors that are differentiated according to pitch, patterns we call "melodies" . . . then it must also be possible to make such progressions out of the tone colors of the other dimensions, out of that which we call simply "tone color," progressions whose relations to one another work with a kind of logic entirely equivalent to that logic which satisfies us in the melody of pitches." (421)

Acknowledging that such speculations may be no more than a "futuristic fantasy," he nevertheless devotes his closing sentences to predicting their realization and promise: "Tone-color melodies! How acute the senses that would be able to perceive them! How high the development of spirit that could find pleasure in such subtle things" (422). Just as Pound observes that expressive emotion is the generating force in Imagist poetry, so Schoenberg notes that "in composing I make decisions only according to feeling, according to the feeling for form. . . . Every chord I put down corresponds to a necessity . . . o f my urge to expression" (417). While the object of this expression is formal, its workings are "instinctive. Consciousness has little influence on it" (416). Tracing the creative urge to subliminal feeling may seem surprising coming from one so analytical as Schoenberg, until we recall that he comes out of the Austro-German romantic tradition and that when he wrote *Theory of Harmony* he was painting and associating with the German Expressionist painters of The Blue Rider.

Schoenberg's two affirmative ideas—*Klangfarbenmelodie* and expression as creative impetus—imply structural consequences parallel to Pound's constructive ideas in the Imagist articles. Tone-color melodies direct the composer's attention away from large, abstract structures and toward the timbre and texture of the individual tone as a self-sufficient unit of meaning. A microcosmic structure, tone-color melody tends to be aphoristically short and to change, chameleon-like, as instrumentation changes. Expression and instinct are appropriate guides to form if older organizing principles no longer obtain and all combinations are possible: "Only the ear may take the lead, the ear, sensitivity to tone, the creative urge, the imagination, nothing else; never mathematics, calculation, aesthetics" (331). Analogously, Pound's dismantling of Victorian rhetoric and his emphasis on the image concentrate poetic structure in the microcosmic "one-image poem." As both writers negate the organizing principles of nineteenth-century form, they come to rely on the individual emotion, the "urge for expression" to generate form. Moreover, in scaling down the formal denominator to the individual tone and image, both artists gravitate away from a sequential concept of music and poetry *unfolding* in time and toward a spatial, painterly one of the tone and image *existing* in self-sufficient instantaneity. Although not a painter himself like Schoenberg (though he associated with them), Pound spoke in painterly terms about composing his most famous Imagist poem, "In a Station of the Metro": "I found suddenly the expression. I do not mean that I found words, but there came an equation . . . not in speech, but in little splotches of colour. It was just that—a 'pattern', or hardly a pattern, if by 'pattern' you mean something with a 'repeat' in it. But it was a word, the beginning for me of language in colour" (*Gaudier-Brzeska* 87). To see *how* these processes work, however, we must look at two representative works of Pantonal-Expressionism and Imagism.

. . . . .

Composed two years before *Theory of Harmony,* Schoenberg's *Five Pieces for Orchestra* (1909) was undoubtedly one of the works that occasioned the textbook's theoretical rationale—"that which the art has already achieved." Like so many other "Pieces" written in the Pantonal-Expressionist style, this title accurately conveys the work's brevity and fragmentation. The score runs to 416 measures and requires about fifteen minutes to perform. Of the five pieces, the fourth (which Schoenberg entitled "Peripetia") is the shortest, lasting less than two minutes.

Within its scant 65 measures, however, "Peripetia" shifts its meter seven times among 3/4, 2/4 and 4/4; it changes tempo five times, from agitated *molto allegro* to moody *meno mosso,* and closes with a steadily accelerating crescendo that trails off "pp" in the winds and horns. Within a given tempo, moreover, the dynamics oscillate abruptly between extremes of *molto piano* and *fortissimo.* For example, in the 15 bars marked *meno mosso* (bars 308-23), the dynamics lurch between "pp" and "fff" five times, sometimes over a single measure (e.g., bars 312-

13). These abrupt shifts of meter, tempo and dynamics result in a disjointed, agitated forward motion.

The aphoristic motifs of this movement intensify its fragmentation. The primary motif opens the piece "f" on a rising crescendo. It recurs often in different guises, e.g., as an expressive clarinet passage (274-77), as a Scriabinesque condensation for trumpets (284-85), and later as an inverted *expressivo* passage for cellos (309-10). Although Schoenberg identifies a "secondary voice" in bar 293, the motif is barely audible amidst a thick-textured counterpoint. Finally, two other discernible motifs should be noted: an ostinato rhythm in the horns that immediately follows the opening statement (267-69) and recurs several times thereafter, and an emphatic descending figure in the tuba that occurs near the close of the "ff" middle section (296-97) and again as the culminating and most discernible motif of the final crescendo (327).

The interwoven repetition of these motifs may suggest—on paper—a discernible structure to "Peripetia": a rough sonata form, in which the themes expand contrapuntally in the "ff" development (283-98) and, following a slow recapitulation (beginning at bars 299-301), accelerate again for the coda (323-30). Several factors, however, impede the listener from hearing this form. First, the motifs are so brief and vanish so quickly that they do not establish themselves as easily recognizable components of a fixed structure. Rather, they seem discrete and autonomous fragments that follow in a simple sequence of contrasts (fast and slow, loud and soft). Second, just as Schoenberg later predicts in *Theory of Harmony,* he develops these motifs contrapuntally rather than harmonically. Thus, several "principal" motifs, each lasting no more than a measure or two, interweave and overlap, as in bars 287-91 of the *Tempo Imo* section. Following the thread of one motif, therefore, is virtually impossible; one can only *sense* the fragments of several.

Tonality provides no help in finding the "center," since the piece bears no key signature, and the opening motif spans two octaves (from low D in the tenor clef to high B in the treble clef). Dissonances abound; for example, in the concluding chord of the first motif, A in the clarinets clashes with A# in the bass clarinet, while G in the cellos rubs against A♭ in the basses. In sum, the motifs of this short piece flare up suddenly, crunch against each other in jarring juxtapositions and dissonant harmonies, and fade evanescently, leaving the listener with a recollection of seemingly disconnected episodes, fragmentary moments, clashing tone-colors.

Juxtaposed colors are also the subject of the Imagist poem that Pound published in *Lustra* (1916), though he obviously wrote it much earlier:

> L'ART, 1910
> Green arsenic smeared on an egg-white cloth,
> Crushed strawberries! Come, let us feast our eyes.

As his title reveals immediately, the "art" of 1910 for Pound is Modernist. 1910 was the year of London's first taste of Modernist painting, via Roger Fry's Post-Impressionist Exhibition in November. Although Pound was not around to see it, he doubtless learned of its impact from his London friends. Moreover, he was briefly in Paris in late March of 1910 and may well have feasted his own eyes at the spring *Salon des Independents* or Bernheim-Jeune.

If critical comments on this poem are reliable, Pound did not much like what he saw and satirized it—a reading based on the ugly images of the first line and the potentially ironic hyperbole of the exclamation mark and "feast." Yet several features of the poem work against this satirical reading, even apart from the biographical fact that Pound strongly sympathized with Modernist painting at this time. Certainly, the first line, riding on the ugly verb "smeared," evokes multiple unpleasantries. Arsenic, the pigment base of emerald (or "Paris") green, also denotes its more deadly meaning, as it poisons the "egg-white" canvas cloth; "smeared" is doubly nauseating, since it can adhere to egg-white, as well as to "arsenic." Yet the line closes with a comma—not with the original colon (or in later editions semi-colon) of "In a Station of the Metro"—which suggests that "Crushed strawberries" is not an ironic metaphor for the entire first line, but rather an imagistic metaphor for the *next* major color the speaker sees. And what a contrast! The bright red juice of those crushed berries exactly complements the emerald green, just as its life-sustaining sweetness provides the antidote to the bitter, deadly arsenic. The exclamation mark thus suggests the speaker's surprise and sensuous delight, not simply in the strawberry red itself, but in its jarring juxtaposition to emerald green. "Feast" intensifies his gormandizing joy, until "eyes" returns the image to metaphor (albeit a clichéd one), inviting us to *see* as deeply as we would taste the piquant savor of these opposites. If the art of 1910 thus dares to juxtapose bright complementary colors—a technique that intensifies each color and exactly corresponds to the strident dissonances Schoenberg was then legitimizing—so Pound strives for the same intensity of perceptual experience in his two-line structure by juxtaposing bright green and red, bitterness and sweetness, poison and sustenance, nausea and feasting—a structure, in short, that objectifies the intense pleasure-pain the speaker *feels* standing before "L'ART, 1910."

The parallel relations of "Peripetia" and "L'ART, 1910" to the pedagogical subversions of *Theory of Harmony* and "A Few Don'ts by an Imagiste" should now be clear. As the tracts undermine key features of nineteenth-century structure (a theme clearly centered and extensively developed via smooth transitions into a regular pattern), so the works reflecting these subversions are marked by the antitheses of these features: motifs that are highly compressed and fragmented to convey a sense of instantaneity and flickering change; contrasting elements that are abruptly juxtaposed (complementary images, dissonant harmonies, etc.) to produce a heightened intensity of expression.

As the styles reflecting the negative esthetics of *Theory of Harmony* and "A Few Don'ts" continued into the war

years, they testify to the potency of these tracts in "clearing the ground" of nineteenth-century music theory and poetic practice. Increasingly, however, Schoenberg and Pound chafed under the structural deficiencies of these "negativist" styles and set about to rectify them.

. . . . .

Almost as soon as "A Few Don'ts" appeared, Pound recognized flaws in Imagist theory and practice that impelled him—fully as much as did his personal feud with Amy Lowell—to move beyond the *Poetry* statements. As he later acknowledged, these flaws stemmed from the laconic vagueness of the *Poetry* doctrine—misconstrued and abused by *vers libre* poets: "The defect of earlier imagist propaganda was not in misstatement but in incomplete statement. The diluters took the handiest and easiest meaning, and thought only of the STATIONARY image. If you can't think of imagism or phanopoeia as including the moving image, you will have to make a really needless division of fixed image and praxis or action" (*ABC* 52). As numerous critics have observed, the static Imagist poem skimps on verbs; indeed, Pound's famous "In a Station of the Metro" lacks them altogether. His move into Vorticism in 1914-15 aimed to restore this dynamism by redefining the image: "The image is not an idea. It is a radiant node or cluster; it is . . . a VORTEX, from which, and through which, and into which, ideas are constantly rushing" (*Gaudier-Brzeska* 89).

This more dynamic conception of the image addresses a second problem of the *Poetry* statements. In scaling Imagist presentation to "an instant of time," Pound constricts the poem's essential structure to a single juxtaposition; as he describes it in *Gaudier-Brzeska*: "the 'one-image' poem is a form of superposition, that is to say, it is one image set on top of another" (89). This spatial conception, as John Gage argues, precludes a temporal basis for developing the image sequentially into a significant order. Longer Imagist poems simply amplify the core structure in "accumulative" strings that lack transitions and thus lack "a sense of necessity compelling a conclusion" (108-14).

A dynamic conception of the image, by contrast, permitted Pound to see it (in Herbert Schneidau's phrase) as "a body of potentialities" that can metamorphose and develop (88). In 1915, Pound writes: "The undeniable tradition of metamorphoses teaches us that things do not remain always the same. They become other things by swift and unanalysable process." In the same essay, his definition of myth as "a work of art" virtually restates Imagist process: "an impersonal or objective story woven out of [the myth-maker's] own emotion, as the nearest equation that he was capable of putting into words" ("Dolmetsch" 431). Pound's promotion of Joyce and Eliot in 1916-18 doubtless intensified his interest in the metamorphic image within a mythic structure. As Schneidau argues, he applied his concept of the "luminous detail" to the "Joycean lesson that great art consisted of the universal in the particular, here, the permanence in the detail" (117). Pound's 1917 review-essay on Eliot—a major statement of his revised esthetics—corroborates this view: "Art does not avoid universals, it strikes at them all the harder in that it strikes through particulars" (420). Having once defined poetic structure, the image now functions as "luminous detail," metamorphosing and developing to evoke universals of space and time in an evolving structure sufficiently large and loose to accommodate an "endless poem of no known category. . . . all about everything" that Pound was then writing: the *Cantos* (qtd. in Schneidau 145n).

As he drifted from an exclusively visual and spatial conception of the image, embodied in *phanopoeia*, Pound moved toward two other kinds of poetry that he later defined as *logopoeia*, "the dance of the intellect among words," and *melopoeia*, the "musical property which directs the bearing or trend of meaning" ("How" 25). The ironic word-play of *logopoeia*, he concludes in 1917, is not especially suited for free verse, for it "demands a *set form* used with irreproachable skill. Satire needs, usually, the form of cutting *rhymes* to drive it home" ("Irony" 283, emphasis mine). *Melopoeia* always occupied a high niche in Pound's poetics, but his writings from 1915-18 show that his increasing concern about its abuse in free verse led him to the same structural conclusions that he reached regarding *logopoeia*. The source of this abuse can be traced directly to the vague injunctions in the *Poetry* articles to "compose in the sequence of the musical phrase" and to "behave as . . . a good musician." Pound's other statements then and later show that, far from advocating rhythmic anarchy, he called for a flexible and organic relation between rhythm and the individual "creative emotion" (as opposed to the mechanical measure) that generates it: "I do not believe that Chopin wrote to a metronome. There is undoubtedly a sense of music that takes count of the 'shape' of the rhythm in a melody, rather than of bar division. . . . The creation of such shapes is part of thematic invention. Some musicians have the faculty of invention, rhythmic, melodic. Likewise, some poets" ("Eliot" 421).

Some poets, however, lack this faculty: namely, the *vers libre* poets who misconstrued Pound's advice in *Poetry*, to his steadily increasing vexation. In 1915, he complains that "bad free verse" is "made by those who have not sufficient skill to make words move in rhythm of the creative emotion" ("Affirmations" 376). A year later, he rails at the Imagist's "sloppiness" ("Status" 39), at their "looseness, lack of rhythmical construction and intensity" ("Correspondence" 323). Still later, he fumes to Harriet Monroe that "the *vers libre* public are probably by now as stone blind to the vocal or oral properties of a poem as the 'sonnet' public was five or seven years ago to the actual language" (*Letters* 127). Finally, in his 1917 essay on the musical theorist, Arnold Dolmetsch, he concludes: "Poets who are not interested in music are, or become, bad poets. . . . *Vers libre* has become a pest. . . . It is too late to prevent it. It is here. There is too much of it. One might, conceivably, improve it. . . . and one stop at

least a little of the idiotic and narrow discussion based on an ignorance of music" ("Verse" 42).

In fact, Pound was working then to "improve" contemporary verse by restoring its musical vigor. Yet his rhythmic and formal prescriptions drastically curtail and even reverse his earlier support of free verse: "Unless a man can put some thematic invention into *vers libre,* he would do well to stick to 'regular' metres, which have certain chances of being musical from their form, and certain other chances of being musical through his failure of fitting the form" ("Eliot" 422). Recalling his (and Eliot's) reformist efforts in this period, he summarized: "at a particular date in a particular room, two authors . . . decided that the dilutation of *vers libre,* Amygism, Lee Masterism, general floppiness had gone too far and that some counter-current must be set going. . . . Remedy prescribed. . . . Rhyme and regular strophes" ("Monroe" 14). In his own verse, he took a healthy dose of his medicine, not only by seeking "to resurrect the art of the lyric, I mean words to be sung," but also in pursuing the structural implications of his renewed interest in *logopoeia* and *melopoeia:* the "rhyme and regular strophes" of *Hugh Selwyn Mauberley* (*Letters* 128).

In the same year that Pound published his revised views of rhyme and metrics in "T.S. Eliot," Schoenberg was working on his own structural reforms in the large oratorio, *Jacob's Ladder.* His impetus paralleled Pound's in two respects. First, Schoenberg perceived serious structural limitations of the Pantonal-Expressionist style—limitations implicit in the theoretical subversions of *Theory of Harmony.* Like Pound's call for "rhyme and regular strophes," Schoenberg strove to rationalize, unify and systematize structural decisions that had been largely "subconscious" and disconnected in Pantonal works by prescribing a specific method of composition.

In "Composition with Twelve Tones (1)," Schoenberg recalls that the foremost characteristics of these Pantonal pieces were "their extreme expressiveness and their extraordinary brevity. At that time [1908-11], neither I nor my pupils were conscious of the reasons for these features. . . . Thus, subconsciously, consequences were drawn from an innovation which, like every innovation, destroys while it produces. New colourful harmony was offered; but much was lost" (217). Chief among those losses was a harmonic structure sufficient for mounting large, complex works. As Schoenberg notes, the structural function of harmony—its role in "distinguishing the features of form. . . . comparable to the effect of punctuation in the construction of sentences, of subdivision into paragraphs, and of fusion into chapters—could scarcely be assured with chords whose constructive values had not as yet been explored. Hence, it seemed impossible to compose pieces of complicated organization or of great length" (217).

For a time, Schoenberg sidestepped the problem of size by following a text in larger Pantonal works such as *Pierrot Lunaire* and *Erwartung*. Yet the need remained for a "comprehensible" method of unifying horizontal and vertical space to sustain large works. Likewise, "the desire for a conscious control of the new means and forms will arise in every artist's mind; and he will wish to know *consciously* the laws and rules which govern the form which he has conceived 'as in a dream'" ("Composition" 218). In *Jacob's Ladder,* this control began to take shape, both thematically and structurally, in a principle Schoenberg later formulated: "the unity of musical space demands an absolute and unitary perception. In this space . . . there is no absolute down, no right or left, forward or backward. Every musical configuration, every movement of tones has to be comprehended primarily as a mutual relation of sounds . . . appearing at different places and times" ("Composition" 223).

It would take Schoenberg another four years to realize this principle in a set of compositional procedures that restore to the composer "conscious control" over his material and the structural means to sustain large-scale works: the "Method of Composing with Twelve Tones Which are Related Only with One Another."

The constructive "rules" that Pound and Schoenberg devised in these years point up the structural shortcomings of their major theoretical statements, *Theory of Harmony* and "A Few Don'ts by an Imagiste"—deficiencies that resulted from their predominantly negative orientation, from their subversive intent. Yet, measured *by* that intent, each tract was remarkably successful. *Theory of Harmony* provided young composers a theoretical rationale for abandoning central tonality and for leaving dissonances unresolved. "A Few Don'ts" offered "poetasters" tips to rid their work of Victorian prolixity, sentimentality and prosody and to concentrate their expression into potent images. In their ability to influence young Turks of the next generation—Anton Webern and Alban Berg, E.E. Cummings and William Carlos Williams—and at the same time to represent major statements of Modernist innovators and avant-garde movements, these tracts demonstrate the contribution of pedagogy to the avant-garde's ascendence and remind us that for a new esthetics to be established, an old one must be destroyed.

NOTES

[1] The Carter translation of *Harmonielehre* is based on the third edition (1922), but it clearly indicates where and how this edition diverges from the original 1911 version that I shall consider.

[2] In deference to Schoenberg, who objected to the term "atonal" as nonsensical, I use "Pantonal" (the term he preferred) to indicate compositions not organized around a single tonal center.

[3] The problem of scale appears in *Gaudier-Brzeska* where Pound refers to Dante's *Paradiso* as "the most wonderful image" and to the whole Japanese *Noh* play as "one image" in a chapter that stresses, the painterly instantaneity of the "one-image poem" (86-94).

WORKS CITED

Carter, Roy E. Preface. *Theory of Harmony.* By Schoenberg.

"Futurist Painting: Technical Manifesto" 1910. Taylor 125-27.

Gage, John. *In the Arresting Eye: The Rhetoric of Imagism.* Baton Rouge: Louisiana State UP, 1981.

Krauss, Rosalind. *The Originality of the Avant-Garde and Other Modernist Myths.* Cambridge: MIT, 1985.

Marc, Franz. "The Savages of Germany." *The Blaue Reiter Almanac.* 1912. Documents of 20th-Century Art. New York: Viking, 1974.

Poggioli, Renato. *The Theory of the Avant-Garde.* New York: Harper, 1971.

Pound, Ezra. *ABC of Reading.* 1934. New York: New Directions, 1960.

———. "Affirmations: As for Imagisme" (1915). *Ezra Pound: Selected Prose.* Ed. and Intro. William Cookson. New York: New Directions, 1973. 344-47.

———. "Arnold Dolmetsch" (1915). Rpt. in *Literary Essays,* 431-36.

———. "L'ART, 1910." *Lustra* (1916). Rpt. in *Personnae: The Collected Poems of Ezra Pound* (1926). New York: New Directions, 1950. 113.

———. "Correspondence." *Poetry* (March 1916): 323.

———. *Ezra Pound: Selected Letters 1907-1941.* Ed. D.D. Paige. New York: New Directions, 1971.

———. "A Few Don'ts by an Imagiste." *Poetry* (March 1913): 200-06.

———. *Gaudier-Brzeska: A Memoir.* 1916. New York: New Directions, 1970.

———. "Harold Monro" (1933). Rpt. in *Ezra Pound: Polite Essays.* Plainview, NY: Books for Libraries, 1966. 14.

———. "How to Read" (1919). Rpt. in *Literary Essays.* 15-40.

———. "Imagisme," *Poetry* (March 1913): 198-200.

———. "In a Station of the Metro." *Poetry* (April 1913): 12.

———. "Irony, Laforgue, and Some Satire" (1917). Rpt. in *Literary Essays.* 280-84.

———. *Literary Essays of Ezra Pound.* Ed. & Intro. T.S. Eliot. New York: New Directions, 1954.

————. "Notes on Elizabethan Classicists" (1917). Rpt. in *Literary Essays*. 227-48.

————. "Prolegomena" (1912). Rpt. in *Literary Essays*. 8-14.

————. "Status Rerum, —the Second," *Poetry* (April 1916): 38-43.

————. "T.S. Eliot" (1917). Rpt. in *Literary Essays*. 418-22.

————. "Verse Libre and Arnold Dolmetsch" (1917). Rpt. in Schafer, 42-45.

Russell, John. *The Meanings of Modern Art*. New York: MOMA, 1981.

Schafer, R. Murray, ed. *Ezra Pound and Music: The Complete Criticism*. New York: New Directions, 1977.

Schneidau, Herbert. *Ezra Pound: The Image and the Real*. Baton Rouge: Louisiana UP, 1969.

Schoenberg, Arnold. "Composition with Twelve Tones (1)." 1941. Rpt. in *Style and Idea: Selected Writings of Arnold Schoenberg*. Ed. Leonard Stein. New York: St. Martins, 1975. 214-45.

————. *Five Pieces for Orchestra*, op. 16. Peters ed. no 6061 (1952).

————. *Theory of Harmony*. 3rd ed. 1922. Trans. with Preface Roy E. Carter. Berkeley: U of California P, 1978.

Shapiro, Theda. *Painters and Politics: The European Avant-Garde and Society 1900-1925*. New York: Elsevier, 1976.

Stock, Noel. *The Life of Ezra Pound*. Expanded ed. San Francisco: North Point, 1982.

Taylor, Joshua. *Futurism*. New York: MOMA, 1961.

IMAGISM AND OTHER MOVEMENTS

William Skaff

[*In the following essay, Skaff focuses on the importance of metaphor and the unconscious in the poetic theories advanced by Ezra Pound and the Surrealists.*]

SOURCE: "Pound's Imagism and the Surreal," in *Journal of Modern Literature*, Vol. 12, July, 1985, pp. 185-210.

I

In an essay of 1937, "D'Artagnan Twenty Years After," in which Ezra Pound reminisces of the few years when Imagism came to maturity, soon to be subsumed by Vorticism, two topics continually recur: Surrealism and metaphor. Since *Blast*, 1914, and in particular, *The Little Review*, 1917/19, Pound finds "very little news intervening between that date and the present on the literary frontier." He then mentions what might possibly have been considered innovative: "1923 winter of the same periodical showed a fair list of surrealists with all the subsequent features of that little coterie."[1] But Pound proceeds to assert that the Surrealist program was not new: "so unmoving was the air in the French parlour and dining room that Aragon's generation doesn't yet know that at given date the French were missing a train already gone from the Ormond St. and Kensington junction,"[2] an imaginary depot that represents the collaboration of Pound and the activities of the Rebel Art Centre.[3] That "train" left in the year in which Pound codified the Imagist movement: "by 1912 it was established, at least in Ormond St. . . ."[4] With a characteristic boldness Pound is implying, in fact, that the principles of Imagism are so similar to those of Surrealism that the former should be considered not the precursor, but the founder of the aesthetic mode that we usually associate with the latter: "I should reiterate the sentence on a great deal of Paris being chronologically later than the London of 1914, . . . and so far as I can make out from incipient London 1936-37 there is ten years of time lag still in your city."[5] Ten years after 1914 is 1924, the year in which the first "Manifesto of Surrealism" appeared.

Significantly, not only is Surrealism on Pound's mind in relation to Imagism, but also metaphor itself in relation to both movements, as Pound resorts to what had become by that time a customary allusion: "Aristotle spoke the true word about metaphor, the apt use whereof is the true hall-mark of genius; . . . the writer's blood test is his swift contraposition of objects."[6] That the surreal could exist before 1924 is not surprising when we note that the definition of the Surreal image that André Breton provides in the "Manifesto" is a prophetic quotation from Pierre Reverdy that was originally published in 1918 and that, incidentally, specifies the metaphoric: "the image is a pure creation of the mind. It cannot be born from a comparison but from a juxtaposition of two more or less distant realities. The more the relationship between the two juxtaposed realities is distant and true, the stronger the image will be—the greater its emotional power and poetic reality."[7]

Pound gave further indication in 1930 in "Epstein, Belgion and Meaning" of the relationship between Surrealism and the concerns, in addition to metaphor, of the early formative period of his poetic: "anyone who has for a quarter of a century held to an admiration for thirteenth-century poetry and fifteenth-century painting has very little difficulty in adjusting himself to surrealism"; and we observe that Pound is using the term generically, not historically: "surrealism that comes after a period of aesthetic purism." The variety of mysticism in Provençal and Tuscan poetry, especially Cavalcanti, through which Pound viewed his own profoundest psychic experiences he finds present in Surrealist verse: "one could, I think, consider Guido [Cavalcanti] surrealist, in a sense that Bertrand de Born was not." Mysticism is then associated with the unconscious mind: "the mystics have always annoyed the enchaired professors. There is no reason why MM. Breton, Péret, Aragon should have their subconsciousness decorated with the universe of Avicenna." Pound continues to relate the surreal and the mystic with a favorite allusion: "the surrealists are making a fresh start with a hitherto undigested content. 'I saw three angels,' wrote Swedenborg, 'they had hats on their heads.'"[8] Breton will quote this same statement of Swedenborg's as an example of the Surreal.[9] Significantly, the topic of Surrealism itself reminds Pound of the relationship between poetry and science as well, a theoretical correspondence also present since *The Spirit of Romance*. Issues related to a "scientific poetic" then emerge, such as an approval of the Surrealists' acknowledgment of "an external reality," and a demand for the overthrowing of the logic of "monolinear sentence structure,"[10] as Pound proceeds to laud two French poets, Apollinaire and Cocteau, whose Surrealist tendencies Breton would later praise.[11]

Pound's assertion of the affinity between-Imagism and Surrealism comes as no surprise when we recall that Pound originally defined the Image in terms of the neopsychoanalytic psychology of Bertrand Hart. The immediate technical characteristics of Imagist theory—metaphor, objectivism (simple, concrete statement), and visuality—are found to be integrally related when illuminated by a comparison with Surrealist theory and technique.[12] Further, the relationship of Imagism to Pound's perpetual quest for a poetic at once mystical and scientific is clarified by a consideration of the role of the unconscious in the poetic process as he perceived it.[13] And finally, a consideration of Imagism in terms of Surrealism will help to illuminate the similarities and differences between the Image and the poetic figure into which it evolved, the Ideogram.[14]

II

Through their poems and paintings the Surrealists sought to express or stir the unconscious region of the mind, which they considered to be the source of true knowledge about the world. From Freud they learned that the mind's powers far exceed its customary logical, deductive operations, though they reversed the direction of his therapeutic program from repression to liberation, rejecting his assumption that the subliminal was harmful to conscious, everyday life. From Hegel they acquired the concept of a dialectic process that would reconcile the antinomies of this world through a theory of knowledge that posited the synthesis of subject and object, and mind and matter, though they rejected the theory of a transcendental Idea realizing itself through man and his world in a manner in accord with conceptual reasoning.[15] The unconscious for

the Surrealists becomes, then, by implication, a force through which all of the discrete objects and experiences of the phenomenal world are fused into a state of unity. As Ferdinand Alquié explains, Surrealism

> presupposes the kinship of the powers which construct the Universe and the principles that direct our thoughts; it calls for the liberation of forces common to man and Nature. . . . Surrealism is not a flight into the unreal or into dream, but an attempt to penetrate into what has more reality than the logical and objective universe[,] . . . an immanent beyond. . . . [F]or surrealism is a question not of giving free rein to a fantasy void of sense but of unveiling the nature of things and of man.[16]

The unconscious, however, can never be perceived directly; we experience only its manifestations: in sleep, the dream, and, in a waking state, the poetic. Thus the surreal state sought by Surrealist art is simultaneously conscious and unconscious, a synthesis of the psychological and the concrete, as primal motivational forces dislocate the ordinary course of events, expressing a truth about reality through the fusion of the previously separate: a fundamental relationship operative in the world but previously unavailable to deductive processes is thus revealed.

The basic Surrealist image is, as a result, the metaphor itself, through which two ordinarily incongruent or disparate experiences are wrenched out of their customary context in the phenomenal world and fused into a new combination, or two usually separate and isolated objects are either juxtaposed or metamorphose into each other. As Breton indicates, the ability to reach the unconscious consists essentially of the power to create metaphor: "it is the marvellous faculty of attaining two widely separate realities without departing from the realm of our experience; of bringing them together and drawing a spark from their contact."[17] When the reader encounters such an image presented concretely in the poem and attempts to imagine it, he will be jarred at first by its seeming unnaturalness and his customary logical preconception of the relationships between objects and events in the everyday world will be destroyed. Once liberated from the purely conscious, empirical world, these previously isolated components of reality form a new whole which, revealing an essential, unsuspected relation between certain elements of reality, stirs his unconscious and provides him with an experience of that unifying, subliminal region. In this way, the Surrealists emphasize the essence of metaphor, unification, in their work through the disparateness of the elements being united. Significantly, the metaphoric implies that the marvelous, the mystical, is present in this world, and has been unavailable only because man has limited his perception of phenomenal reality. This poetic is to be distinguished from that of the Symbolists, whose mysticism sought a transcendent realm, separate from the phenomenal world, to which its symbols beckoned.[18]

When joining the apparently dissimilar, Surrealist poets often base the metaphorical union upon the coincidental similarity of visual properties. Paul Eluard's "je descends dans mon miroir / Comme un mort dans sa tombe ouverte,"[19] for instance, relies upon the similarity of the actual depth of a grave and the visual depth of a rectangular mirror. Benjamin Péret's "un petit lampion froid / doré comme un oeuf sur le plat"[20] depends upon the visual resemblance of an egg yolk in the middle of its white to a lamp and the glow that surrounds it. In these images, one object metamorphoses into the other in the reader's imagination because of the coincidental similarity of visual form.

The metaphor of coincidental visual similarity, in fact, may very well be the archetypal Surrealist image. A visual relationship defies the assumed course of nature by dislocating reality and joining together ordinarily disparate objects. Yet a coincidental similarity has no basis in deductive logic, providing a nonlogical means of uniting otherwise disparate experience. The metaphor of coincidental visual similarity will thus be both startling and unifying, the two characteristics of unconscious experience for the Surrealists, as it reveals a new relationship between objects in reality. Significantly, Breton often depicts coincidental visual similarities in his metaphors: he wishes to achieve both the shock of incongruity and a sense of relationship at the same time. For instance, in the metaphor "Ma femme à la chevelure de feu de bois,"[21] the reader pictures a head of hair as a fire. Again, in the metaphor "peupliers / Dont les premières feuilles perdues beurrent les roses morceaux de pain de l'air,"[22] the reader notices the visual similarity that is being implied between random pats of butter on a slice of bread and falling leaves in the air. He feels the incongruence of the elements at the same time that he experiences unification. For Breton, these unexpected visual superpositions achieve absolute metaphor, "the spontaneous, extralucid, insolent rapport which establishes itself under certain conditions between one thing and another,"[23] the synthesis of the unconscious and the real world. Breton implies that the physical transformation that takes place in the reader's mind is made possible by the visual: "I demand that he who still refuses, for instance, to *see* a horse galloping on a tomato should be looked on as a cretin."[24]

Breton's emphasis on visual metaphor may account for why Surrealism could be both a literary and an artistic movement with no change of aesthetic principles. Surrealist painting often portrays metaphors of coincidental visual similarity by superimposing objects in the painted environment on the basis of their shape or configuration. Max Ernst's *The Elephant of Celebes* (1921), for instance, transforms the inanimate into the animate by depicting a piece of mechanical equipment so that it suggests an elephant. The foreground is dominated by a round dark green tank resting on the ground upon two stubby columns that look like an elephant's fat legs. A flexible tube protruding from the front of the tank in a semicircle suggests a trunk. In René Magritte's *The Red Model* (1935), the inanimate metamorphoses into the human again through visual resemblance. The upper half of a pair of shoes is laces and leather, the bottom half the flesh and toes of the foot that usually wears them. Salvador Dali's *Mae West* (1934-36) merges the face of the movie star with a drawing room. Her hair is simultaneously the drapery of the entry; her chin and neck are portrayed as the steps into the room; her lips are converted into a sofa; her nose is located where the fireplace should be and has a clock on top of it; and her eyes are blended with paintings inside of gold frames hung on the wall.

III

What the Surrealists sought through metaphor as the marvelous, an immanent rather than transcendent mysticism, Pound terms "delightful psychic experience"[25] during that phase of his development between 1910 and 1912 when he was preoccupied with medieval romance. Pound was always to insist on mysticism's material, and thus external, empirical, basis in order to emphasize its origin in reality itself: "it is a spiritual chemistry, and modern science and modern mysticism are both set to confirm it."[26] Likewise, Breton would come to posit a similar confluence to iterate that the Surreal occurs in the phenomenal world: "recent discoveries in physics have shown that the opposition between idealism and materialism is one of pure form."[27] Just as the Surrealists will associate the process of metaphor with the transmutational doctrine of alchemy in its uniting of the psychic and the material world,[28] so does Pound: in order to understand Cavalcanti's use of *virtù* "one must have in mind the connotations alchemical, astrological, metaphysical, which Swedenborg would have called correspondences." On the basis of alchemy Pound asserts, in turn, that a romantic-erotic love can provide the impetus for the fusion of the internal and external, the spiritual and physical:

> The equations of alchemy were apt to be written as women's names and the women so named endowed with the magical powers of the compounds. *La virtù* is the potency, the efficient property of a substance or person. Thus modern science shows us radium with a noble virtue of energy. Each thing or person was held to send forth magnetisms of certain effect; in Sonnet XXXV, the image of his [Cavalcanti's] lady has these powers.[29]

The Surrealists also will believe in a cult of love that would function as a source of insight into and union with the universe. As Alquié explains,

> love (read passion-love) immediately takes first place in Surrealist preoccupations. In it are found once more all the prodigies of the Universe, all the powers of consciousness, all the agitation of feeling. It effects the supreme synthesis of subjective and objective. . . . It is from love that the surrealists expect the great revelation. . . . [30]

Pound finds the origin of alchemy in the everpresent capacity of primitive man for this essential metaphoric mystical experience that unifies the individual and the cosmos, the expression of which is subsequently attenuated in myth: "Greek myth arose when someone having passed through delightful psychic experience tried to communicate it to others."[31] As Pound elaborates elsewhere, "the undeniable tradition of metamorphosis teaches us that things do not always remain the same. They become other things by swift and unanalysable process. . . . The first myths arose when a man walked into sheer 'nonsense,' that is to say, when some very vivid and undeniable adventure befell him . . . ; perceiving that no one could understand what he meant when he said that he 'turned into a tree' he made a myth."[32] Breton will assert the same link between primitive mentality, metamorphosis, and immanent mysticism; there exists, he observes, "profound affinities between surrealism and 'primitive' thought. Both envision the abolition of the hegemony of the conscious and the everyday, leading to the conquest of *revelatory emotion*."[33]

The medieval cult of erotico-mysticism that Pound explored during this romance period particularly through Cavalcanti held that celestial light would pass from God through the lady to her lover. Even her visual image alone would be sufficient for this insight into the truth of the cosmos to occur, but the heat generated by sexual intercourse was thought to be in essence the energy of light, of divine illumination. At the beginning of the 1930s Pound identified the origin of this love cult to be a specific primitive ritual, the rite of Eleusis, during which he believed that a priest and priestess engaged in sexual intercourse that resulted in a celestial revelation.[34] Pound believed that Cavalcanti's erotico-mysticism was based on Robert Grosseteste's theory of light, an idea, as Pound understood it, with both metaphysical and scientific implications. The passage from Etienne Gilson's *Philosophie du Moyen Age* that Pound quotes in "Cavalcanti" as an explanation of Grosseteste's theory implies a correlation between the light that is the basis of material forms and the mystical light of divine illumination that provides insight into the nature of the universe.[35] In 1938 Pound draws a telling correspondence:

> Grosseteste on Light may or may not be scientific but at least his mind gives us a structure. He throws onto our spectrum a beauty comparable to a work by Max Ernst. The mind making forms can verbally transmit them when the mental voltage is high enough. It is not absolutely necessary that the imagination be registered either by sound or on painted canvas.[36]

Thus, Pound came to associate the Surreal with the immanent mysticism of troubadour and Tuscan poetry through which he interpreted his own intensest psychological experiences, and for the expression of which he was in the process of seeking an adequate poetic technique. Furthermore, he came to associate a particular style of painting, Ernst's Surrealism, with the kind of poetry that he wished to write, at least at the time that he was preoccupied with medieval romance.

Although Pound does not specify which Ernst paintings he has in mind, those painted just before and while both men were in Paris between 1922 and 1924,[37] like *The Elephant of Celebes,* display properties of visual metaphor, of metamorphosis: for instance, in *Woman, Old Man, and Flower II* (1923), the dominant foreground figure is composed of a nude human being from the waist down and a human neck, but the torso is a leather and metal vest with transparent panels and the head is a fanpiece of the same materials; *Ubu Imperator* (1924) consists of a spinning top of wood with human hands and holes signifying eyes and mouth. Even the works in the Surrealist number of *The Little Review* that Pound certainly did see, though they are not paintings but collages (altered engravings), depict transformations and incongruent juxtapositions.[38]

Aristotle's definition of poetic genius as the ability to create metaphor had been with Pound since *The Spirit of Romance,* and the doctrine of luminous detail was simply a uniting of metaphoric technique with the theory of physical-psychic light as found in Cavalcanti and Grosseteste. Luminous details result in metaphoric knowledge: "certain facts give one a sudden insight into circumjacent conditions," that is, into relations between objects, "sequence," "law,"[39] that are not visible to one in an ordinary psychological state. The immanent mystical state must be one of clarity in order to see the new arrangement of reality dictated by the insight: "the ecstacy is not a whirl or madness of the senses, but a glow arising from the exact nature of the perception."[40] At the same time, however, Pound, like the Surrealists, advises that this clear perception of relations involves a dislocation of our ordinary experience of the phenomenal world: of Aristotle's remark on metaphor Pound explains that "by 'apt use,' I should say it were well to understand, a swiftness, almost a violence, and certainly a vividness," and definitely "not elaboration or complication."[41] Pound's instructions for attaining this ability to perceive clearly in order for the metaphoric immanent mystical to occur is precisely what the Surrealists would specify for attainment of the surreal vision: "the function of an art is to strengthen the perceptive faculties and free them from encumbrance, such encumbrances, for instance, as set moods, set ideas, conventions; from the results of experience which is common but unnecessary, experience induced by the stupidity of the experiencer and not by the inevitable laws of nature" that will be revealed through the mystical or surreal experience. Thus, "poetry is identified with the other arts in this main purpose, that is, of liberation."[42]

IV

By the time that Pound codified his Imagist movement in mid-1912, he had begun to think of his immanent mysticism—his "radiant world where one thought cuts through another with lean edge, a world of moving energies"[43]—not only in terms of the medieval love cult and the modern physics of light waves, magnetism, electricity, and atomic radiation,[44] but also in terms of modern psychology: the poet's "work remains the permanent basis of psychology and metaphysics";[45] "he is the advance guard of the psychologist on the watch for new emotions, new vibrations sensible to faculties as yet ill understood."[46] Bernard Hart's observation that his psychology "is the analogue of that underlying all the great conceptual constructions of physical science—the atomic theory, the wave theory of light, the law of gravity, and the modern theory of mendelian heredity"[47] may have helped Pound to see its relevance to his developing poetic. Above all, Hart's description of the function of the unconscious reinforced for Pound the importance of the metaphoric in the poetic process as he began to perceive that the unconscious mind played a central role in his immanent mystical experiences, and thus in the creation of the poetic figure that would communicate them.

Pound did employ a nonliterary concept in order to clarify his poetic theory when he came to supply a definition of the Image, and the discipline of thought from which that concept came betrays the creative origin and affective function of this kind of poetic figure: "an 'Image' is that which presents an intellectual and emotional complex in an instant of time. I use the term 'complex' rather in the technical sense employed by the newer psychologists, such as Hart, though we might not agree absolutely in our application."[48] Pound's recourse to a contemporary psychologist to explain the origin and function of the Image already suggests the surreal nature of his poetic, for Hart was a neopsychoanalyst: his was a dynamic psychology, based upon motivation, and a depth psychology, postulating the unconscious as a functioning region of the mind. In 1910 Hart characterizes "in our own terminology" that fundamental tenet of psychoanalytic psychology that he chooses to adopt:

> The unconscious (*unbewusstsein*) is regarded as a sea of unconscious ideas and emotions, upon whose surface plays the phenomenal consciousness of which we are personally aware. These unconscious ideas are agglomerated into groups with accompanying affects, the systems thus formed being termed "complexes." These complexes are regarded as possessing both potential and kinetic energy, and thus are capable of influencing the flow of phenomenal consciousness according to certain definite laws.[49]

Thus, Hart was not, strictly speaking, an orthodox Freudian, but in 1912 saw himself as presenting a "systematic"[50] exposition of psychoanalysis with what he felt were appropriate changes of emphasis in certain aspects of the theory, such as diminishing the significance of the sexual instinct in complex formation, and with certain modifications based on other schools of depth psychology, as with his definition of complex, which he adopted from Jung.

Complexes for Hart, then, are not a symptom of a pathological psyche resulting from the repression of normal or perverted sexuality, but rather constitute the operating mechanisms of the ordinary healthy mind. Hart finds an appropriate analogy for the complex in the physical sciences: "complexes, then, are causes which determine the behaviour of the conscious stream, and the action which they exert upon consciousness may be regarded as the psychological analogue of the conception of 'force' in physics."[51] As Hart explains elsewhere,

> Strictly speaking, it can never itself become a fact of experience, a portion of phenomenal consciousness.

> Certain ideas, affects, and conative tendencies belonging to the complex may become facts of experience, we may become aware that we possess the complex—but the complex as a whole and as a directing force can never be actually experienced.[52]

Pound appears to have Hart's analogy of unconscious impulses as forces in mind when he explains, in relation to Imagism, that an artist "can, within limits, not only record but create. At least he can move as a force; he can produce 'order-giving vibrations'; by which one may mean merely, he can departmentalise such part of the life-force as flows through him."[53]

Neither Hart nor Freud, however, had in 1912 read an Imagist poem or seen a Surrealist painting. Both deny the possibility of representing a complex through the content of sensory experience, a stipulation that probably accounts for Pound's suspicion that Hart would not entirely agree with the "application" of the concept to a work of art, despite Pound's use of the term in its "technical" sense. As Hart observes, "the lack of a perceptual equivalent to many of Freud's conceptions is very striking when we peruse such a work as the *Traumdeutung*." Yet in Hart's very denial of the possibility lies the key to the surreal: "here the individual dream image is conceived as being constellated by a large number of unconscious complexes—as a result of the *combination* and *interaction* of these complexes the single image emerges into consciousness" (my emphasis). So, in turn, does the quotation from Freud that Hart offers for support: "how can one picture to oneself the psychical condition during sleep? Do all the dream thoughts (subsequently elicited by analysis) actually *exist together,* or after one another, or do they constitute different *contemporaneous* streams finally *coalescing*"[54] (my emphasis). We must remember that the engagement of a work of art takes place in the mind; thus we must, above all, focus our attention on the effect of the poem or painting rather than on its literal, concrete state on the paper or canvas. Once a poet realizes that, according to Hart, "a single idea or *image* in consciousness may be conditioned (constellated) by a *multiplicity* of unconscious complexes" (my emphasis), then all he has to do is produce a work of art that does not "picture," but rather reproduces psychologically in the reader "what a mass of *simultaneous* unconscious ideas may be like"[55] (my emphasis), exactly Hart's definition of a complex. Pound believed that such a poem capturing the momentary eruption of an unconscious impulse was possible: "energy, or emotion, expresses itself in form. . . . When an energy or emotion 'presents an image,' this may find adequate expression in words";[56] hence, the Image.

For Pound, therefore, the Image is a metaphor, and its effect is surreal: "it is the presentation of such a 'complex' instantaneously which gives the sense of sudden liberation; that sense of freedom from time limits and space limits; that sense of sudden growth, which we experience in the presence of a great work of art."[57] The effect of "sudden liberation" occurs when objects are no longer discrete entities bounded by time and space, but rather coalesce. In essence, an Image gives the reader a sense of unity by dislocating phenomenal reality, just like a Surreal image. In Pound's own words, "Imagisme" *is* "absolute metaphor."[58] Pound's definition of the one-Image poem actually specifies a surreal fusion of two disparate objects: "the 'one image poem' is a form of superposition, that is to say, it is one idea set on top of another." Significantly, Pound's justification for creating these Images is the same as the purpose Breton gave for the Surreal metaphor: both theoreticians wish to depict the union of unconscious and conscious, of the mystical and the real. As Pound observes, "in a poem of this sort one is trying to record the precise instant when a thing outward and objective transforms itself, or darts into a thing inward and subjective."[59] The terms of Pound's explanation conform exactly to Breton's account of the Surreal image: "we have attempted to present interior reality and exterior reality as two elements in the process of unification, of finally becoming *one*,"[60] approaching the "point where the distinction between subjective and objective ceases to be necessary or useful."[61]

Technically, Pound, like Breton through Reverdy, prefers juxtaposition as the appropriate verbal form for the metaphoric experience the poet wishes to convey.[62] Like simile, pure metaphor (employing copula), and verbal, adjectival, adverbial, and prepositional metaphor, juxtaposition is also a metaphoric figure. Metaphoric action is initiated linguistically, but the superposition of elements occurs psychologically in the mind, where the event of reading actually takes place. Thus, in terms of Hart's psychology, when two concrete objects are juxtaposed by a poem, the psychic energy or force of the complex is transferred from one mental image to another in the writer's mind when the poem is created and in the reader's when it is read. All metaphors expressed in Indo-European languages must occur cerebrally: they do not exist on the printed page. Only in certain Chinese ideograms does superposition of two verbal elements occur, an attribute which initially attracted Pound to them.

Juxtaposition is, in fact, an ideal verbal method of presenting a metaphor depicting the visual similarity of ordinarily incongruent objects. Each element is presented independently, and the reader is not directed by the logic of the syntax to imagine any definite, nonvisual aspect of the objects, such as the specific activity of a verbal metaphor, or the specific property of an adjectival metaphor. Consequently, the reader is given a chance to encounter the first object by itself and unmodified—in its full integrity as an object—and thus tends to read it as a complete visual image. When he encounters the second object, also separate and whole, he is inclined to superimpose its visual image onto the previous visual image, and a metaphoric fusion occurs based on visual similarity that implies a relationship more profound than one arrived at by deductive logic. With verbal or adjectival metaphors, on the other hand, the reader may be able to visualize the noun, but he has no chance to visualize, alone and in its entirety, the object implied by the verb or adjective. Thus he tends to conceive of the relationship between the two

elements in terms other than, or in addition to, visual properties, such as the laws of logic or the customary course of nature, when he attempts to imagine the noun performing the activity of the verb or displaying the property of the adjective.

The archetypal Imagist poem is, according to Pound, "In a Station of the Metro":

> The apparition of these faces in the crowd:
> Petals, on a wet, black bough.[63]

This poem is actually a surrealistic metaphor delivered in two lines by means of juxtaposition: a number of faces standing out from the dark business suits and shadows of a dimly lit subway station metamorphose into petals gleaming with rain on a dark tree limb on the basis of the coincidental visual similarity of their teardrop outlines and the bright contrast with their surroundings. The word "apparition" itself suggests a mental event based on a congruity of visual image, and as we read, we understand: the *appearance* of these faces looks the same as (becomes) petals. The two objects to be visually superimposed are each contained within a single line of poetry, entirely separated from one another, so that their metamorphosis in the reader's mind can be sudden and complete. No overt syntactic structure joins the two lines, eliminating any possible suggestion of logical connection or subordination. The reader can only assume that apposition is implied, a relationship of equality, identity. His only recourse is to visualize, and he is subsequently shocked by the fusion of disparate objects that suggests a heretofore unsuspected relation in the world.[64]

Similarly, H.D.'s "Oread," which Pound once cited as the definitive Imagist poem,[65] relies upon verbal metaphor to achieve its surreal visual transformation. The waves of the ocean and the wind-swept pine trees of a forest are completely fused when verbs usually describing turbulent water are applied to the forest. Snow-capped peaks of trees merge with white-capped ocean waves:

> Whirl up, sea—
> whirl your pointed pines,
> splash your great pines
> on our rocks,
> hurl your green over us,
> cover us with your pools of fir.

By imagining his beloved as literally occupying his body, Eluard achieves a similar fusion of different objects in "L'Amoureuse." Words that refer to her simultaneously refer to him: "Elle a toujours les yeux ouverts / Et ne me laisse pas dormir" (7-8).[66]

Not surprisingly, Pound's explanation of the aesthetic quality of a visual metaphor describes the effect of these poems, and of Surrealist painting. Pound observes of the statement, "the pine tree in mist upon the far hill looks like a fragment of Japanese armour," that "the beauty, in so far as it is a beauty of form, is a result of 'planes in relation.' The tree and the armour are beautiful because their diverse planes overlie in a certain manner."[67] This visual superposition of objects forms the basis of much Surrealist art, and of much of Pound's verse from the Imagist period. Pound's images are often actually quite similar to those found in both Surrealist poetry and painting. To consider "A Girl," for example, the first stanza consists of a surreal transformation in process, a girl metamorphosing into a tree. These lines portray that inclination to identify with one's surroundings characteristic of the unifying childhood imagination:

> The tree has entered my hands,
> The sap has ascended my arms,
> The tree has grown into my breast—
> Downward,
> The branches grow out of me, like arms.
>
> (1-5)

By the second stanza, the metamorphosis has already been completed:

> Tree you are,
> Moss you are,
> You are violets with wind about them.
> A child—*so* high—you are,
> And all this is folly to the world.
>
> (6-10)[68]

The transformation depicted in Pound's poem, according to which a child thinks that she is both a girl and a tree at the same time, is similar to the metamorphoses portrayed in two Surrealist works of art. Magritte's painting *Discovery* (1927) is a half-length portrait of a nude young woman who is at once flesh and wood: her left cheek, arm, and thigh, and her right shoulder, breast, and hip are a light brown wood grain, while the rest of her body is in tan flesh tones. Eluard's poem "L'Amoureuse," in which the beloved merges with the body and consciousness of the poet, depicts the process of transformation in a way similar to Pound's first stanza. Each successive line presents another part of the body becoming the woman:

> Elle est debout sur mes paupières
> Et ses cheveux sont dans les miens,
> Elle a la forme de mes mains,
> Elle a la couleur de mes yeux,
> Elle s'engloutit dans mon ombre
> Comme une pierre sur le ceil.
>
> (1-6)[69]

Again, in a passage from "Dance Figure," a series of surreal transformations based upon visual similarity occur:

> Thine arms are as a young sapling under the bark;
> Thy face as a river with lights.
>
> White as an almond are thy shoulders;
> As new almonds stripped from the husk.
>
> (10-17)[70]

In the first image, Pound juxtaposes a woman's pale, bare shoulder and a white, husked almond, and, in the second, the naked arm under her clothing and the raw wood of a branch without its bark. In either case the two objects are

related by a coincidental similarity in shape and color: shoulders and almonds are oval, and arms and branches are long, thin, cylindrical, and crooked, bending at the elbow or joint. Breton's metaphors "Ma femme aux hanches de nacelle" (44) and "Ma femme aux fesses de dos de cygne" (49) from "L'Union libre"[71] are similarly based upon the coincidental visual resemblance between a hip and a skiff, or a buttock and a swan's back, enabling a surreal transformation to occur.

Thus, although Imagism is notorious for promulgating a spare style employing concrete language and avoiding the abstract, the Image was never to function as a purely objective recording of reality. As Pound exhorts, "don't be descriptive; remember that a painter can describe a landscape much better than you can."[72] Why then does Pound demand verse that is "harder and saner," eschewing "rhetorical din" and "painted adjectives"?[73] Pound solves the conundrum immediately after advising against the descriptive. He proceeds to offer a metaphor of Shakespeare's as the proto-Imagist alternative and draws a telling distinction: "when Shakespeare talks of the 'Dawn in russet mantle clad' he presents something which the painter does not present. There is in this line of his nothing that one can call description; he *presents*"[74] (my emphasis). The same distinction is implicit in two of the three original Imagist principles: "1. *Direct* treatment of the 'thing' whether subjective or objective" and "2. To use absolutely no word that does not contribute to the *presentation*"[75] (my emphasis), as well as in Pound's definition: "an Image is that which *presents* . . ." (my emphasis). For Pound, to describe is simply to record the phenomenal world as it is experienced consciously and rationally by the mind; to present an Image concretely, to treat the "thing" directly, on the other hand, is to offer to the reader the metaphoric transformation of reality with no unnecessary language that would obstruct its effectiveness to instill a surreal shock, a mystical revelation, in the reader.

In turn, Pound's dictum to present directly, to engage only in the concrete and avoid abstractions, covertly demands the creation of visual Images. Pound speaks of the metaphoric as "that part of your poetry which strikes upon the imaginative eye of the reader."[76] Pound's preference for the visual originates philosophically, of course, in the medieval cult of mystical love associated with Cavalcanti. The visual as an artistic strategy to stir the unconscious is, however, as important to Imagism itself as it is to Surrealism. Granting that the unconscious functions to unify fragments of our conscious, rational experience, that is, metaphorically, visual metaphor is desired because the comparison will be registered by the reader initially in a nonrational way. If a juxtaposition is employed, the lack of overt syntactic structure will further forestall the logical analysis of the imagery. Simple denotative description is preferred to one charged with emotional or intellectual connotations so that both objects will be registered as concretely as possible, rather than abstractly, just as Dali, for instance, employs a hyperreal style for his Surreal paintings, avoiding the rhetoric of turbulent brushstroke or flamboyant, unnatural color. Thus, the reader is instantaneously shocked by the unexpected unity of a visual superposition, only to analyze rationally and construct a meaning upon subsequent readings.

This unique way that an Imagist or Surrealist work of art functions actually parallels the ordinary course of our mental activity according to Hart's analysis of the human psyche. Hart is particularly insistent upon "the unconscious origin of beliefs and actions," in fact, of most of our ideas and feelings, as opposed to "the subsequent process of rationalization to which they are subjected." As he proceeds to explain,

> The prevalence of "rationalisation" is responsible for the erroneous belief that reason, taken in the sense of logical deduction from given premises, plays the dominating role in the formation of human thought and conduct. In most cases the thought or action makes its appearance without any such antecedent process, moulded by the various complexes resulting from our instinct and experience. The "reason" is evolved subsequently, to satisfy our craving for rationality.[77]

Being metaphoric in nature, the Imagist or Surreal poem simply replaces the complex, the unconscious force, as the origin of the mental event being encountered by the mind. Rationalization, the "meaning of the poem," only occurs after the initial subliminal shock, when the conscious, rational mind, presented with an unconscious, and thus unnatural and illogical, visual image, is momentarily paralyzed. Only after the reader recovers from the initial unconscious shock of enlightenment does he proceed to analyze rationally, seeking the abstract in the concrete in order to formulate a thematic statement. For Pound and the Surrealists, however, the concrete embodiment of the mystical insight as an image in the poem would be its most truthful form of expression.[78]

V

The relationship between Imagism and Surrealism can help to bring into focus the subtle, complex evolution of the Image into the Ideogram, Pound's final definition of the poetic figure that would govern the composition of *The Cantos*. Pound distinguishes between the two in the same essay that he associates Imagism and Surrealism, "D'Artagnan Twenty Years After": "from dead thesis, metaphor is distinct. Any thesis is dead in itself. Life comes in metaphor and metaphor starts TOWARD ideogram."[79] The catalyst for the Image's metamorphosis into the Ideogram was Pound's encounter with the notebooks of the Sinologist Ernest Fenollosa,[80] presented to Pound by Fenollosa's widow for editing in late 1913.[81] Perhaps by the close of 1914,[82] and certainly by the beginning of 1915, Pound began to view the Image in terms of the Chinese ideogram, precipitating a gradual theoretical shift: "it is quite true that we have sought the force of Chinese ideographs *without knowing it*.[83]

An Imagist theory defined through Hart's psychology easily accommodated the doctrines of Pound's Vorticist

stage during 1914. The movement inherent in the image as a Vortex, "a radiant node or cluster . . . from which, through which, and into which, ideas are constantly rushing"[84] is the movement of psychic energy or force generated by the complex. Certain changes of emphasis, however, are already perceptible. The immanent mysticism from the medieval-romance period that found a psychological definition through Hart in terms of the unconscious is still present, but the rational is now given a greater role in its operation and the use to which it is put. What had been called a mystical light is now referred to as both "spontaneity" and "intuition" in terms of "their function in art": "I passed my last exam. in mathematics on sheer intuition. I saw where the line *had* to go, as clearly as I ever saw an image, or felt *caelestem intus vigorem*." This increased emphasis on the rational is coupled with a more pronounced preoccupation with the operations of the external world. Whereas for the Imagist the poetic figure liberated one from the limits of space and time because of its metaphoric dislocation of the phenomenal world, now for the Vorticist the poetic figure, as an analogue to the equation of analytical geometry governing the circle, is liberating because of the universality of its law: "it is the circle free of space and time limits. It is universal, existing in perfection, in freedom from space and time."[85]

With Fenollosa the change of emphasis is complete; Fenollosa's continual assertion of the presence of energy in nature, in the external world, shifted Pound's focus away from Hart's internal energy of the mind. The Ideogram at that point became a more ambitious figure than the Image. A change in the specificity and complexity of relations to be depicted, of subject matter to be treated, necessitated a shift in the degree to which the various components of the mind would participate in the generation of the poetic figure. In order to seek truths in the more practical everyday fabric of life—political, social, economic—the conscious and rational would have to play a greater role than the unconscious in image formation. This broadening of the expressive content of what Pound conceived as the fundamental poetic figure coincided with, and was perhaps inspired by, the codification in his mind of the social role of the poet.[86]

To be sure, the Ideogram is still to remain a result of mystical, or intuitive, insight, a combination of the unconscious and the conscious, the emotional and the rational, and not a product of pure reason. Pound not only objects to the scholastic logic castigated by Fenollosa,[87] but also to inductive reasoning, the more commonly held notion of scientific cognition: just as Pound had contrasted "imperfect inductions" with "luminous details,"[88] so in his final Ideogrammatic phase he will observe that "an idea is only an imperfect induction from fact."[89] Thus, in structure the Ideogram remains metaphoric, based upon an analogical operation of the mind that would perceive "identity of structure,"[90] as Fenollosa characterizes the goal of metaphor, among apparent anomalies. The ordinary course of the phenomenal world would still have to be dislocated in order to discover these affinities, just as the grammar of language reflecting the customary course of reality would have to be violated through juxtaposition if the metaphoric insight is to be expressed. As Fenollosa observes that "nature herself has no grammar,"[91] so Pound notes that "in a city the visual impressions succeed each other, overlap, overcross, they are 'cinematographic,' but they are not a linear sequence. They are often a flood of nouns without verbal relations"; "we no longer think or need to think in terms of monolinear logic, the sentence structure, subject, predicate, object, etc."[92] The subject matter that the Ideogram must treat has, however, become more specific and more complex than that of the Image. Previously Pound cautioned simply against the use of "abstractions" in the creation of the poetic figure, for the concrete, the "natural object," is always "adequate." He was referring to a general feeling, "*peace*." Now Pound tellingly specifies the abstractions that are not to appear directly in the poem: the poet is not to use an image "to back up some creed or some system of ethics or economics."[93]

The "Affirmations" essays appearing at the beginning of 1915 are transitional pieces in which we see the Image gradually becoming the Ideogram. Realizing this himself, Pound advises, in "Affirmations—As for Imagisme," that "I cannot guarantee that my thoughts about it [Imagism] will remain absolutely stationary." He proceeds to define "two sorts" of Image; firstly,

> It can arise within the mind. It is then "subjective." External causes play upon the mind, perhaps; if so, they are drawn into the mind, fused, transmitted, and emerge in an Image unlike themselves. Secondly, the Image can be objective. Emotion seizing upon some external scene or action carries it intact to the mind; and that vortex purges it of all save the essential or dominant or dramatic qualities, and it emerges like the external original.

Pound makes clear that the function of neither of these two kinds of "Image" is mimetic representation: "in either case the Image is more than an idea. It is a vortex or cluster of fused ideas and is endowed with energy. If it does not fulfill these specifications, it is not what I mean by an Image. It may be a sketch, a vignette, a criticism, an epigram," or an instance of "impressionism,"[94] Pound's term for description.

At first glance, Pound's distinction between the two psychological origins of the Image, triggered by either subjective mental processes or objective sense perception, seems as if it might be paralleling Hart's distinction between the two kinds of "stimulus" activating a "complex": "whenever one or more of the ideas belonging to a complex is roused to activity, either by some external event, or by processes of association occurring in the mind itself."[95] Pound's account of the origin of the first kind of "Image," however, entails *both* of these stimuli, for "external causes" are said to set off the train of association that results in their eventually being "fused" according to the complex that they stirred. Thus, the second kind of "Image," although conceived of as a metaphor, is

not really an Image, but an Ideogram. The metaphoric action now takes place on a more rational, conscious level, as the mind deals more directly with the phenomenal world, for the resulting poetic figure, metaphysically considered, is "like the external original." Instead of a simple object, the more historically or motivationally complicated "external scene or action" is now said to initiate creativity. The poetic process still involves the unconscious mind, the source, as Hart contends, of social and ethical values, but now to a lesser degree than the conscious rational mind that can process more complex or more conceptual data and recognize universal laws. A complex in its conscious state will strip the scene or action to its essential features, producing none other than a reflection of that very governing universal that the mind had originally sensed to be present in the scene or action from the beginning. Thus, the "vortex" that "purges" and "fuses" is no longer simply the unconscious that amalgamates. The relations that are discovered will be more ideational in character, although they still result from the metaphoric perception of the external world and are expressed through the juxtaposition of the concrete.[96]

Pound has now made possible *The Cantos,* a poem that can analogically treat rich and complicated, yet specific and detailed, subject matter. Interestingly, Pound greatly admired Aragon's "The Red Front," despite its Communist orientation, a Surrealist poem that deals concretely and specifically with contemporary politics and economics.[97] But Aragon's poem, though characteristic of Surrealist verse in its method of juxtaposing the seemingly incongruent, is atypical in its specificity. Thus Pound parts company with the Surrealists in seeking relations that are less mysterious, more clearly defined and readily applicable to the phenomenal world. Such a preference originally moved Pound from a more unconscious Imagist poetic to the more conscious and intellectual Ideogrammatic. We can understand, then, why Pound feels constrained in "Affirmations—Vorticism" to distinguish between automatic painting and Vorticist art. He once again calls upon the image of the rose in magnetized iron filings as an example of the kind of pattern-forming energy behind nature that a poet is to express.[98] Whereas the Imagist was simply to express the "life-force" within him through its form-giving capacity, now, however, a broader, more varied subject-matter is implicitly recommended when Pound observes that "there are, of course, various sorts or various subdivisions of energy," which he proceeds to distinguish for the first time: "these forces may be the 'love of God,' the 'life-force,' emotions, passions, what you will." Automatic painting simply expressed "exclusive *organic*" energy, "a state of cell memory, a vegetable or visceral energy," whereas the Vorticist wishes to express "his complex consciousness," "instinct and intellect together." The cause of automatic painting's unsatisfactoriness, according to Pound, reveals his new Ideogrammatic poetic: "the softness and the ultimate failure of interest in automatic painting are caused by a complete lack of conscious intellect."[99] For Pound, as for the Surrealists, automatism only gives access to the unconscious; once the subliminal reaches consciousness, it must be utilized through an integration into the real world, for Pound more directly and more specifically than for the Surrealists.

NOTES

[1] *Selected Prose, 1909-1965,* ed. William Cookson (New Directions, 1973), p. 452.

[2] *Selected Prose,* p. 456.

[3] Patricia Hutchins characterizes Pound's London residence in *Ezra Pound's Kensington: An Exploration, 1885-1913* (Henry Regnery, 1965). Jeffrey Meyers, *The Enemy: A Biography of Wyndham Lewis* (London: Routledge and Kegan Paul, 1980), p. 52, notes that the Rebel Art Centre was located at 38 Great Ormond Street, near Queen Square. See also Pound, "Vorticism" (September 1914), *Gaudier-Brzeska: A Memoir,* 2nd ed. (New Directions, 1970), p. 81.

[4] *Selected Prose,* p. 453. Significantly, Pound mistakes the date of the Rebel Art Centre here, placing it in his Imagist phase, when it opened in March 1914, and closed by June of the same year (Meyers, 52-54). Pound conceived the existence of the Imagist school some time between April and August of 1912, according to Noel Stock, *The Life of Ezra Pound,* 2nd ed. (Avon, 1974), p. 162.

[5] *Selected Prose,* p. 457.

[6] *Selected Prose,* p. 452. See also, for instance, *The Spirit of Romance* (1910), 2nd ed. (New Directions, 1929), p. 158; "The Serious Artist" (1913), *Literary Essays,* ed. T. S. Eliot (New Directions, 1954), p. 52; and Ernest Fenollosa, *The Chinese Written Character as a Medium for Poetry* (1919), ed. Ezra Pound (rpt. City Lights, 1964), p. 22, Pound's footnote.

[7] *Manifestoes of Surrealism,* trans. Richard Seaver and Helen R. Lane (University of Michigan Press, 1969), p. 20. Reverdy's statement first appeared in *Nord-Sud* (March 1918).

[8] *Ezra Pound and the Visual Arts,* ed. Harriet Zinnes (New Directions, 1980), p. 165. Pound discusses the relationship between Cavalcanti and Avicenna in "Cavalcanti" (1910-1931), *Literary Essays,* pp. 149-200 passim. The Swedenborg quotation appears again in *Guide to Kulchur* (1938), 2nd ed. (New Directions, 1952), p. 73.

[9] "Rising Sign" (1947), *What is Surrealism?: Selected Writings,* ed. Franklin Rosemont (Monad Press, 1978), p. 282.

[10] *Visual Arts,* p. 166.

[11] "Rising Sign," *What is Surrealism?,* pp. 282-83.

[12] Commentary on Pound frequently subsumes the Image under the Ideogram, and as a result, a critical consensus still does not exist regarding what for Pound was the linguistic structure of the Image, its psychological origin in the writer, and its intended effect upon the reader. Walter Sutton, "The Literary Image and the Reader: A Consideration of the Theory of Spatial Form," *Journal of Aesthetics and Art Criticism,* XVI (September 1957), believes that the call for both the objective and the metaphoric simply "points to a source of confusion in Pound's own theory" (13), while John T. Gage, *In the Arresting Eye: The Rhetoric of Imagism* (Louisiana State University Press, 1981), having noted "the condition of simultaneity which the imagists desire," concludes that "by metaphor the imagists did not mean metaphor," but rather "a literal statement of reality" (58, 111, 162).

Laszlo K. Gefin, *Ideogram: History of a Poetic Method* (University of Texas Press, 1982), minimizes the role of the visual in the Image, drawing a distinction between the physical properties of language transcription with the cerebral functioning of language proper:" 'superposition' is physically impossible in writing; only juxtaposition is available to the poet." Although he admits that "superposition can come about in the mind of the reader," Gefin at the same time denies the possibility of visual metaphor, observing of "In a Station of the Metro" that "the poem is *not* a metaphor" (9, 11, 12). Gage, having posited that a comparison in poetry is experienced "cognitively" rather than through "visualization," proceeds to offer a *visual,* physical example—a picture of the vase-faces optical illusion from Gestalt psychology, which the viewer can only see as one or the other at a time—as proof in itself that a metaphor superimposing objects visually cannot be experienced by the reader, rather than considering the *psychological* cognitive effect of the visual metaphor upon the reader (60-61). Yet, Anne Cluysenaar, *Aspects of Literary Stylistics: A Discussion of Dominant Structures in Verse and Prose* (St. Martin's Press, 1976), with regard to the same Gestalt optical illusion, had previously noted that the simultaneity is nevertheless experienced "in the perceptual mind's eye" (59-61).

[13] Previous considerations of the relationship between Hart's version of the unconscious and Imagist theory have not been entirely satisfactory. J. B. Harmer, *Victory in Limbo: Imagism 1908-1917* (St. Martin's Press, 1975), summarily dismisses the psychological description with which Pound accompanies his linguistic prescriptions for the Image: "how far he understood Hart is questionable" (165). Hugh Witemeyer, *The Poetry of Ezra Pound: Forms of Renewal 1908-1920* (University of California Press, 1969), decides that Pound's "reference to Hart is little more than a pseudoscientific smokescreen" (33). Wallace Martin, "Freud and Imagism," *Notes and Queries,* N.S. VIII (December 1961), 470-71, attempts to trace Pound's remarks to Freud when Hart repeatedly stated that he employed the term "complex" according to Jung's usage. See Hart's "The Relation of Complex and Sentiment," *British Journal of Psychology,* XIII (1922), 142; *Psychopathology, Its Development and Its Place in Medicine* (Cambridge: Cambridge University Press,

1927), p. 102; and *The Psychology of Insanity*, 4th ed. (Cambridge: Cambridge University Press, 1931), p. 78. Also assuming that Hart "used the term 'complex' in an orthodox Freudian sense," Witemeyer wrongly implies that for Hart the presence of a complex would automatically "lead to irrational behavior" since his "chief concern is with obsessive and insane actions that may be caused by the complex" (33). As Hart explains in his chapter "Complexes," however, "the ascertaining of the causes determining the flow of our consciousness is the ultimate aim of psychology. We shall expect, of course, that the laws discovered will be identical in the sane and insane" (*The Psychology of Insanity*, 1st ed. [1912], pp. 60-61).

More fruitful is Martin A. Kayman, "A Context for Hart's 'Complex': A Contribution to a Study of Pound and Science," *Paideuma*, XII (Fall/Winter, 1983), 23-35. While Kayman offers a "scientific," that is, psychological, parapsychological, and occult, context for Pound's use of the term "complex," this study will focus extensively on Hart's thought and the use Pound made of it in the formulation of Imagist theory and practice.

[14] The relationship between Surrealism and Imagism, or Pound in general, has not been explored in any detail. Paul Ray, *The Surrealist Movement in England* (Cornell University Press, 1971), asserts that Imagism, with its emphasis on the image "replacing statement and description," simply prepared the ground for the later Surrealist group in England that avowed ties with the original French movement. Imagism is erroneously said to be "reinforced by Freud's analysis of dream-imagery and the doctrines of French symbolism" (262). Andrew Clearfield, "Pound, Paris, and Dada," *Paideuma*, VII (1978), 113-40, claims that Pound "never took much interest in or had much sympathy for the new movement, Surrealism," and that "of Breton he says nothing" (124-25). Yet Breton's *Nadja* (1928) is mentioned in an approving context in "Cavalcanti," *Literary Essays*, pp. 194-95. In fact, by 1921, when Pound moved to Paris to stay until 1924 (Stock, 311-36), the so-called French Dadaists were already displaying Surrealist tendencies in theory and practice before the movement was officially codified with the first "Manifesto" of 1924. Gefin is astute to observe in passing that the principles governing ideogrammatic poetry are also operative in the collage compositions of Max Ernst (xvii).

[15] See "Second Manifesto of Surrealism" (1930), p. 123, and "Surrealist Situation of the Object" (1935), pp. 258-60, in *Manifestoes of Surrealism*, and "Situation of Surrealism Between the Two Wars" (1943), *What is Surrealism?*, p. 246. The combined use of Freud and Hegel in Surrealist theory is discussed by Ferdinand Alquié, *The Philosophy of Surrealism*, trans. Bernard Waldrop (University of Michigan Press, 1965), pp. 34, 71, 110; Anna Balakian, *Surrealism: The Road to the Absolute*, 2nd ed. (Dutton, 1970), pp. 125, 131-32, 137-38; and Michel Carrouges, *André Breton and the Basic Concepts of Surrealism*, trans. Maura Prendergast (University of Alabama Press, 1974), passim.

[16] Alquié, pp. 33-34, 84, 98. See also J. H. Matthews, *An Introduction to Surrealism* (Pennsylvania State University Press, 1965), pp. 62-80.

[17] "Max Ernst" (1920), *What is Surrealism?*, p. 8.

[18] For the difference between Surrealism and Symbolism see Anna Balakian, "Metaphor and Metamorphosis in André Breton's Poetics," *French Studies*, XIX (1965), 34-35; and Jean Pierrot, *The Decadent Imagination, 1880-1900*, trans. Derek Coltman (University of Chicago Press, 1981), pp. 256-64.

[19] From "Mourir," quoted by Mary Ann Caws, *The Poetry of Dada and Surrealism: Aragon, Breton, Tzara, Eluard, and Desnos* (Princeton University Press, 1970), p. 161.

[20] From "Au Bout du monde," quoted by Balakian, *Surrealism*, p. 156.

[21] From "L'Union libre," *Young Cherry Trees Secured Against Hares / Jeunes cerisiers garantis les lièvres*, trans. Elouard Roditi (1946; University of Michigan Press, 1969), n.p.

[22] From "L'Air de l'eau," *Young Cherry Trees*, n.p.

[23] "Rising Sign," *What is Surrealism?*, p. 280.

[24] "Exhibition X . . . Y . . ." (1929), *What is Surrealism?*, p. 43.

[25] "Psychology and Troubadours" (1912), *The Spirit of Romance*, p. 92. Witemeyer provides an extended discussion of this concept (23-43).

[26] "Introduction" (1910) to Cavalcanti poems, *Ezra Pound: Translations*, ed. Hugh Kenner, 2nd ed. (New Directions, 1963), p. 18.

[27] Quoted by Inez Hedges, *Languages of Revolt: Dada and Surrealist Literature and Film* (Duke University Press, 1983), p. 4.

[28] See Carrouges, pp. 48-66, and Hedges, pp. 3-33.

[29] "Introduction" to Cavalcanti, *Translations*, p. 18.

[30] Alquié, pp. 84-85. Both Aragon, the Surrealist with whom Pound was most friendly during his Paris years, and Breton in *Nadja*, which Pound read, and in other writings, were vehement on the surreal efficacy of love, as well as Eluard and others.

[31] "Psychology and Troubadours," *The Spirit of Romance*, p. 92.

[32] "Arnold Dolmetsch" (1915), *Literary Essays*, p. 431. See also "Allen Upward Serious" (1914), *Selected Prose*, pp. 407-12. For Allen Upward's contribution to Pound's thought on myth, see Donald Davie, *Ezra Pound* (Pen-

guin, 1975), pp. 63-72 et passim; Ronald Bush, *The Genesis of Ezra Pound's Cantos* (Princeton University Press, 1976), pp. 91-102; and Richard Godden, "Icons, Etymologies, Origins and Monkey Puzzles in the Languages of Upward and Fenollosa," in Ian F. A. Bell, ed., *Ezra Pound: Tactics for Reading* (Barnes and Noble, 1982), pp. 221-44, who asserts, further, a confluence between the thought of Upward and Fenollosa.

[33] "Interview with René Balance" (1945), *What is Surrealism?*, p. 256.

[34] Peter Makin, *Provence and Pound* (University of California Press, 1978), pp. 244-47; Leon Surette, *A Light from Eleusis: A Study of Ezra Pound's Cantos* (Oxford: Clarendon Press, 1979), pp. 67-80. See "Psychology and Troubadours," *The Spirit of Romance*, pp. 92-100, and "Terra Italica" (1931-32), *Selected Prose*, pp. 55-56.

[35] "Cavalcanti," *Literary Essays*, p. 160. See Stuart Y. McDougal, *Ezra Pound and the Troubadour Tradition* (Princeton University Press, 1972), p. 75.

[36] *Guide to Kulchur*, p. 77.

[37] During 1921 Breton organized Ernst's first one-man exhibition in Paris, consisting of collages, at the Gallerie Au Sans Pareil, which Pound may have seen on one of his trips to France. Ernst moved to Paris in 1922. See Diane Waldman, *Max Ernst: A Retrospective* (Solomon R. Guggenheim Museum, 1975), p. 253.

[38] *The Little Review*, IX:4 (Autumn/Winter, 1923-24), pp. 9, 12, 13, 14.

[39] "I Gather the Limbs of Osiris" (1911-12), *Selected Prose*, p. 22.

[40] "Psychology and Troubadours," *The Spirit of Romance*, p. 91.

[41] "The Serious Artist," *Literary Essays*, p. 52.

[42] "The Wisdom of Poetry" (1912), *Selected Prose*, p. 360.

[43] "Cavalcanti," *Literary Essays*, p. 154.

[44] For the scientific background of Pound's poetic and its correspondence with his mystical theory, see Ian F. A. Bell, *Critic as Scientist: The Modernist Poetics of Ezra Pound* (London: Methuen, 1981); and Martin A. Kayman, "A Model for Pound's Use of 'Science,'" *Ezra Pound: Tactics for Reading*, pp. 79-102.

[45] "I Gather the Limbs of Osiris," *Selected Prose*, p. 23.

[46] "The Wisdom of Poetry," *Selected Prose*, p. 361.

[47] "The Conception of the Subconscious," in Hugo Münsterberg, et. al., *Subconscious Phenomena* (Richard G. Badger, 1910), p. 131.

[48] "A Few Don'ts," *Poetry*, I (March 1913), 200-06; *Literary Essays*, p. 4.

[49] "The Conception of the Subconscious," *Subconscious Phenomena*, pp. 129-30. Years later in his "Introduction to the Fourth Edition" of *The Psychology of Insanity*, Hart advises that in his work "Freud's topographical differentiation of the mind into conscious, preconscious, and unconscious regions has not been adopted. The existence of unconscious processes has been assumed as a conception necessary for the adequate explanation of the phenomena of consciousness, but these processes are regarded from a functional rather than a topographical standpoint, and they have not the precise and peculiar character which Freud ascribes to his 'Unconscious'" (14-15). Yet, Hart is misconstruing the topographical as the static, for Freud's unconscious is unquestionably composed of dynamic impulses, and conversely, Hart is diminishing the topographical aspect of his own complexes, which remain in the mind in a latent state when not actively influencing consciousness.

[50] *Psychology of Insanity*, 1st ed., p. v.

[51] *The Psychology of Insanity*, p. 62.

[52] "The Conception of the Subconscious," *Subconscious Phenomena*, p. 133.

[53] "Affirmations—As For Imagisme" (28 January 1915), *Selected Prose*, p. 376.

[54] "The Conception of the Subconscious," *Subconscious Phenomena*, pp. 134-35.

[55] "The Conception of the Subconscious," *Subconscious Phenomena*, pp. 130, 136.

[56] "Affirmations—As for Imagisme," *Selected Prose*, p. 376.

[57] "A Few Don'ts," *Literary Essays*, p. 4.

[58] "Vorticism," *Gaudier-Brzeska*, p. 85.

[59] "Vorticism," *Gaudier-Brzeska*, p. 89.

[60] "What is Surrealism?" (1934), *What is Surrealism?*, p. 116.

[61] "The Automatic Message" (1933), *What is Surrealism?*, p. 109.

[62] In addition to Gefin, pp. xi-xviii, on juxtaposition as a modern artistic technique, see Roger Shattuck, "The Mode of Juxtaposition," in Mary Ann Caws, ed., *About French Poetry from Dada to "Tel Quel": Text and Theory* (Wayne State University Press, 1974), pp. 19-22.

[63] "Vorticism," *Gaudier-Brzeska*, p. 89.

[64] The *haiku* that inspired this one-Image poem also consists of a metaphor based on a coincidental visual similarity:

> The fallen blossom flies back to its branch:
> A butterfly.

The petals of the flower fluttering through the air to settle on a branch resemble a butterfly in both shape and color, as well as behavior. This resemblance suggests the verbal metaphor of the first line, and then the complete transformation effected by the second. However, the visual superposition of two natural objects in the *haiku* follows the Oriental sense of the unity and harmony of nature. Such an image is more shocking to the modern Western mind, which has less faith in such a unity. Also, Pound's poem is more disturbing, and more unifying, because the human is being transformed into the natural. See "Vorticism," *Gaudier-Brzeska*, pp. 88-89. Earl Miner studies the relationship between the *haiku* and Pound's Image in *The Japanese Tradition in British and American Literature* (Princeton University Press, 1958), Chapter V.

[65] "Vortex. Pound.," *Blast*, No. 1 (20 June 1914) p. 154: "the primary pigment of poetry is the Image. . . . In painting Kandinski, Picasso. In poetry this by, 'H. D.'" "Oread" originally appeared in *The Egoist* in 1914 and was reprinted in *Collected Poems* (Boni and Liveright, 1925).

[66] *Uninterrupted Poetry: Selected Writings*, trans. Lloyd Alexander (New Directions, 1975), p. 4.

[67] *Gaudier-Brzeska* (1916), *Gaudier-Brzeska*, pp. 120-21.

[68] *Ripostes* (1912); *Personae: The Collected Shorter Poems*, 2nd ed. (New Directions, 1949), p. 62.

[69] *Uninterrupted Poetry*, p. 4.

[70] *Poetry*, 2 (April 1913); *Personae*, p. 91.

[71] *Young Cherry Trees*, n.p.

[72] "A Few Don'ts," *Literary Essays*, p. 6.

[73] "Prolegomena," *Poetry Review*, 1:2 (February 1912), 72-76; *Literary Essays*, p. 12.

[74] "A Few Don'ts," *Literary Essays*, p. 6.

[75] "A Retrospect," *Literary Essays*, p. 3. These principles originally appeared in F. S. Flint, "Imagisme," *Poetry*, I (January 1913), 198-200.

[76] "A Few Don'ts," *Literary Essays*, p. 7.

[77] *The Psychology of Insanity*, 1st ed., pp. 65, 66-67.

[78] Despite Gage's analytical confusions, his own sensitive, accurate accounts of his experience of the Imagist verse that he discusses support this account of the affective dynamics of the Image. Regarding short Imagist poems, he notes the "poet's suppression of explicit comparison, rendering the two terms of the comparison interchangeable" (66). Likewise, he observes that the "effect" of the lack of syntactical connection in John Gould Fletcher's "The Skaters" is to "render the subject of the comparison momentarily ambiguous, . . . creating an equilibrium between the parts of the comparison, . . . allowing the reader momentarily to view either swallows or skaters in terms of the other" (64). Regarding longer Imagist poems, he admits that "the temporal activity of reading may be manipulated in such a way as to give the reader the illusion of instantaneity" (107), "giving the reader the sensation that his attention has been 'arrested,' *as if* by a visual scene" (107-08), the stanzas of the poem experienced "*as if* they had been simultaneous" (111). Similarly, just before he denies the label "metaphor" to "In a Station of the Metro," Gefin observes that "the second line is the 'inward' 'natural picture,' coalescing for an instant with the superimposed external image, so that 'faces in the crowd' and 'petals on a wet black bough' are *one*" (12).

[79] *Selected Prose*, p. 453.

[80] Herbert N. Schneidau, *Ezra Pound: The Image and the Real* (Louisiana State University Press, 1969), pp. 56-73, sees this event as decisive.

[81] Stock, pp. 201-02.

[82] In "Vorticism" Pound says, "Ibycus and Lui Ch'e presented the 'Image'" (*Gaudier-Brzeska*, p. 83).

[83] "Imagisme and England: A Vindication and an Anthology," *T.P.'s Weekly*, XXV (20 February 1915), 185. Pound began, in fact, to perceive the Image in retrospect as if it had been defined as the Ideogram all along: "the ideogrammatic method did not wait for Fenollosa's treatise to become current in book form. We didn't wait to know of Fenollosa's existence" (*Selected Prose*, p. 453).

[84] "Vorticism," *Gaudier-Brzeska*, p. 92.

[85] "Vorticism," *Gaudier-Brzeska*, p. 91.

[86] See "Allen Upward Serious," *Selected Prose*, pp. 407-12.

[87] Fenollosa, pp. 25-27.

[88] "I Gather the Limbs of Osiris," *Selected Prose*, p. 23.

[89] "Translators of Greek: Early Translators of Homer; Translation of Aeschylus" (1919), *Literary Essays*, p. 267.

[90] Fenollosa, p. 22.

[91] Fenollosa, p. 16.

[92] Review of Jean Cocteau, *Poesies 1917-1920*, *Dial*, LXX (January 1921), 110; "Epstein, Belgion and Mean-

ing," *Visual Arts,* p. 166. Herbert Schneidau, "Wisdom Past Metaphor: Another View of Pound, Fenollosa, and Objective Verse," *Paideuma,* V (1976), 15-29, has suggested that the Ideogram is essentially metonymic rather than metaphoric, following Roman Jakobson's distinction between the two modes. The difficulty with this distinction is that, as Paul Ricoeur points out in *The Rule of Metaphor: Multi-Disciplinary Studies of the Creation of Meaning in Language,* trans. Robert Czerny (Toronto: University of Toronto Press, 1977), pp. 174-87, Jakobson may be oversimplifying the metaphoric process itself. Randa Dubnick, "Visible Poetry: Metaphor and Metonymy in the Paintings of René Magritte," *Contemporary Literature,* XXI (1980), 407-19, finds both modes present in Magritte's Surrealist work.

93 "A Few Don'ts," *Literary Essays,* p. 5; "Vorticism," *Gaudier-Brzeska,* p. 86.

94 "Affirmations—As for Imagisme," *Selected Prose,* pp. 374-75. N. Christoph de Nagy, *Ezra Pound's Poetics and Literary Tradition: The Critical Decade* (Bern: A. Franke Verlag, 1966), pp. 77-80, offers this passage, incorrectly I believe, as a definition of the original Image.

95 *The Psychology of Insanity,* 1st ed., p. 63.

96 As Christine Brooke-Rose, *A ZBC of Ezra Pound* (University of California Press, 1971), observes of the ideogrammatic method, "it is the juxtaposition that creates the idea, by metaphoric replacement" (114). Schneidau's analysis of the Image applies more aptly to the Ideogram: "Imagism's merging of essentiality and definiteness, of conceptual and perceptual images, is in fact the determinative form of the particular containing the universal" (*The Image and the Real,* 97). Hugh Kenner's discussion of the Ideogram in *The Poetry of Ezra Pound* (London: Faber and Faber, 1951), pp. 76-105, is incisive.

97 Pound asked E. E. Cummings if he could include Cummings' translation of Aragon's poem in an upcoming anthology in a letter of 6 April 1933, *Selected Letters, 1907-1941,* ed. D. D. Paige (Harcourt Brace, 1950), p. 244. The translation is extant in E. E. Cummings, *Complete Poems, 1910-1962,* 2nd ed., ed. George James. Firmage (London: Granada, 1981), II. 881-97.

98 See "Cavalcanti," *Literary Essays,* p. 154.

99 "Affirmations—Vorticism" (14 January 1915), *Visual Arts,* pp. 7-8.

Warren Ramsey

[*In the following essay, Ramsey discusses such qualities as immediacy and precise imagery in an examination of common traits shared by Imagist poetry and the works of nineteenth-century literary Symbolists.*]

SOURCE: "Uses of the Visible: American Imagism, French Symbolism," in *Comparative Literature Studies,* Vol. IV, Nos. 1-2, 1967, pp. 177-91.

> The actual landscape with its actual horns
> Of butcher and baker blowing, as if to hear,
> Hear hard, gets at an essential integrity.
> —Wallace Stevens

What were the common qualities, if any, of literary symbolism of the later nineteenth century and Imagism—meaning by the latter an idea of a contemporary rightness in English verse that began to come clear around T. E. Hulme, F. S. Flint, and Ezra Pound about 1910? The question is not easy to answer. If one begins with Flint's recollection, "We were very much influenced by modern French symbolist poetry,"[1] that was shortly before Pound's first appearance at the Poets' Club. Among members of the original "School of Images," loosely grouped since 1908, only Flint and Hulme wrote verse that would now be described as Imagist. Pound was to become familiar with recent French poetry only while he was enunciating the principles of *Imagisme* and discovering illustrative examples in the writings of Hulme and others. In the modern French poetry which he came to like, sharpness of contour was the rule. But he liked little or nothing that can be called symbolist—if we mean by that an idea of rightness which prevailed around Mallarmé about 1885 and for a while thereafter. The same might be said of Amy Lowell. Qualities common to Imagism and symbolism are not to be sought along the usual lines of appreciation and influence.

"Pound and Eliot had dipped, selectively," writes Henry May, "into the reservoir of recent French poetry. Believers in direct, concrete statement, they were not symbolists. They were not concerned with the paradoxes of Baudelaire or the difficult nuances of Mallarmé and Verlaine. What they found in France was novelty and daring, precise new images, Corbière's irony, Remy de Gourmont's insistence on sensation and dislike of theory. The French, Pound tirelessly insisted, could teach us to be craftsmen and not moralists."[2]

Flint may or may not have been concerned with the "paradoxes" of Baudelaire, but certain poems from *Les Fleurs du mal* are hardly disguised by the English cast he gave them in works more or less his own. The "difficult nuances" of Mallarmé and Verlaine are so dissimilar that little purpose is served by mentioning them together, or by pointing to the "novelty and daring" of writers in a tradition essentially far more conservative than the English one— writers whose sense of rhetoric contributed largely to the growth of, particularly, Wallace Stevens. And the chief contribution of one of the nimblest of theorists, Remy de Gourmont—the verse and prose tales that bemused Aldington and Pound being so strangely forgotten now— was his method of dissociating ideas too readily associated.

Apart from these objections, however, the obstinate truth remains that the Imagists were in fact "believers in direct, concrete statement." Thus René Taupin, in his *L'Influence du symbolisme français sur la poésie américaine (de 1910 à 1920),* could indicate relatively few resemblances between Imagism and symbolism, though he could suggest parallels between Imagists and Parnassians, who also strove for precision and sought to correct certain Romantic excesses by looking to Gautier and L'Art pour l'Art. More recently, William Pratt has written: "If 'Imagisme is not symbolism,' as Pound insisted, it is a direct descendant: given the different native traditions and the different historical moments, the 'Image' and the 'Symbol' are at their best aesthetic equivalents, the difference being, as Taupin admirably stated it, 'a difference only of precision.'"[3] But this difference is crucial; and Taupin had made it clear that in his judgment the less precise image of the symbolist poem differs from that of the *imagiste* work in its power to yield before an immaterial reality of which it is the sign.[4]

"In their interest in the clearly delineated object," says Don Geiger, "some of the [Imagists'] verse seemed to be sealed in a hard varnish. Many of their poems tended to be pictorial and non-dramatic in character, a kind of imaginative reporting of objects, so that for a time it appeared that they had made a compact to split the world of poetic possibilities with another famous school, the Symbolist poets—with Imagists caring little about how they or anyone else might feel about a carefully described outer world and the Symbolists caring little about describing an outer world which they felt so intensely."[5]

The present study begins with a glance at such main principles as may be discernible in a divided world of poetic possibilities. It will then proceed to the question of immediacy—not a particularly symbolist term, perhaps, but one that will serve to indicate a desideratum of certain poets writing early in the twentieth century, and to poems in which this quality was sought.

As formulated by Pound, Flint, Aldington, and Amy Lowell, the Imagist programme was explicit with regard to three objectives. These were "direct treatment of the 'thing,' whether subjective or objective," rigorous economy in use of words, and composition "in sequence of the musical phrase, not in sequence of a metronome." To these principles Aldington added good literary counsel of a cheerful but somewhat general nature, and Pound his now celebrated definition of the image as "that which presents an intellectual or emotional complex in an instant of time." Flint, who had participated in "the Imagist movement" from the beginning and whose knowledge of French poetry remains impressive to this day, was singularly unpretentious in his comments, which include his two-page "History of Imagism." There were four cardinal principles of 'Imagisme' as he stated them. The fourth was "the 'doctrine of the Image'—not for publication."[6]

Prefacing her anthology, *Some Imagist Poets,* in 1915, Amy Lowell enlarged on the first of the above points. The Imagist, she believed, must endeavor "to use the language of common speech, but to employ always the *exact* word, not the nearly-exact, nor the merely decorative word." Though "Amygism" was shortly to become a term by which writers could disavow whatever might have been over-rigid in their own theory and practice, only Amy Lowell, among professed Imagists, hinted at a helpful distinction between universals and particulars. "To present an image . . ." reads her fourth point. "We are not a school of painters, but we believe that poets should render particulars exactly and not deal in vague generalities. . . ." And she states as a fifth and kindred aim: "To produce poetry that is hard and clear, never blurred or indefinite."

Finally, Miss Lowell recommended concision, as earlier statements of Imagist purpose had done: " . . . Most of us believe that concentration is of the very essence of poetry."

"Concentration"—"no superfluous word"—"as few adjectives as possible"—the theme is persistent. Hardly less so is that of composition with new freedom of phrase. As Pound and Flint had urged poets to avoid metronomic regularity, so Miss Lowell advised them "to create new rhythms—as the expression of new moods—and not to copy old rhythms, which merely echo old moods. We do not insist upon 'free-verse' as the only method of writing poetry. We fight for it as a principle of liberty. We believe that the individuality of a poet may often be better expressed in free-verse than in conventional forms. In poetry, a new cadence means a new idea."

At this distance, no aspect of the Imagist writers is more arresting than the contrast between their pronouncements on style and the organization of language, consisting largely of admonishments, of negatives, and positions of their undeveloped aesthetics. Flint had his intimation, and then said no more, of "a form of expression, like the Japanese, in which an image is the resonant heart of an exquisite moment." Along with his "Don'ts" Pound had said that "it is the presentation of such a complex [intellectual or emotional in an instant of time] which gives that sense of sudden liberation; that sense of freedom from time limits and space limits; that sense of sudden growth, which we experience in the presence of great works of art." Like a Proustian *moment privilégié,* in the elucidation of which Proust used language very similar to Flint's, the moment of awareness perpetuated in a fine Imagist poem illuminated the author's work as a whole. Hedged about by the negatives of the Imagist poetics, it was an aesthetic affirmation.

French symbolist theory, either as crystallized around Mallarmé or renewed by Albert Thibaudet's reading of Mallarmé and the writers of *La Phalange* at approximately the time of *imagisme,* could offer nothing as elegantly prescriptive as the latter movement's "Don'ts." It is, however, possible to point out certain characteristics of symbolist poetry of which Flint and Aldington must have been thoroughly aware. There was, for example, the symbolist passion for order. Nourished by nineteenth-century Hellenism as well as by long tradition, it gave intensity to the search for realities beyond the immediate ones. The symbol was no longer that cipher in the pre-conceived hieroglyph which it had been even for Diderot and for Goethe. It was, instead, embodied in the tautly organized reflexive work: the thing discovered as well as the agent of discovery. There is no better appreciation of the new kind of symbolic order, always precarious and secured afresh by each separate poem, than Wallace Stevens' lines from "The Idea of Order at Key West":

> Ramon Fernandez, tell me, if you know,
> Why, when the singing ended and we turned
> Toward the town, tell why the glassy lights,
> As the night descended, tilting in the air,
> Mastered the night and portioned out the sea,
> Fixing emblazoned zones and fiery poles,
> Arranging, deepening, enchanting night.
>
> Oh! Blessed rage for order, pale Ramon,
> The maker's rage to order words of the sea,
> Words of the fragrant portals, dimly starred,
> And of ourselves and of our origins,
> In ghostlier demarcations, keener sounds.

The order in question here is imposed upon, rather than revealed within, the objective world. And the order is of a classicist kind. Almost entirely concerned with questions of style though the Imagists were, their conclusions regarding the beauties of omission, the virtues of concentration, are essentially the same as those which Mallarmé and Stefan George had rediscovered before them, in old grammars and rhetorics, if any book was needed, rather than in old *grimoires*.

Apropos of that peculiar energy of conviction which the Imagists brought to their search for order, their rejection of what they termed Romantic, it is well to remember that Hulme was an admirer of Georges Sorel as well as of Bergson. Human nature is something to which violence must be done. And the late nineteenth-century poets, those who had sought to make *le dandysme* heroic, a way of life, would not have been surprised by this point of view. As long as that "discipline" or "ascesis" of which Hulme and Eliot speak often did not paralyze the form-making impulse, it was a means of combatting "Romantic vagueness" and discovering beauty in the smallest of small dry things. Suppose, however, that an Imagist ideal of control should, in the mind of a young poet from the "dark occidental continent" (as a writer for the London *Egoist* called North America) become confused with a latent Puritanism fundamentally intolerant of any aesthetic expression at all? Then that parsimony in use of adjectives, presentation inste ad of representation, Doric simplicity—negative virtues successfully recommended by Aldington to young poets of temperament sufficiently like his own, could turn to flatness, slightly perverse and self-defeating. Recent French verse could suggest means of ellipsis and emphasis to some. To others, especially to Stevens, it suggested just the opposite, the art of language in its richness and variety, sustained and natural styles owing something to sound pedagogical negatives like those of *imagisme* but never defined or exhausted by them.

And what of a common concern with music on the part of Imagists and symbolists? When Pound urged composition "in sequence of the musical phrase, not in sequence of the metronome," this was to jostle the sovereignty of the iambic pentameter, to invite greater freedom of foot and line. He was advocating *vers libéré* and *vers libre,* thinking of French poets who had practiced both, and preparing the way for a great many free verse poems in American magazines. Whitman came back sharpened through Laforguian lenses; the best of American free verse was to owe directly or indirectly to French examples or at least to have been tested by them—to be the work of poets who were deliberately setting out to do something else. In either case, the primary unity was that of the line, of no set length, the secondary unity that of the group of lines, marked off from other groups. A free-verse poem, with its apparent waverings, might be the more faithful to fluctuations of attention, and even to "certain rhythms of life and breathing more central to man than his inmost sentiments, since they are the living law, variable with each individual, of his depression and his exaltation, his regrets and his hopes."[7] For the effort of the *vers-libristes* had not only been roughly parallel to that of the Impressionist painters, whom they admired. It had also sought to free an inner music, as Bergson understood that term. From such inner music rises the image, more revealing than the abstract product of dialectical or conceptual thought. And music thus understood and much neglected by the Imagists, even by Hulme, the translator of Bergson, is in the immediate background of the movement.

Pound's predilection for musical scores, settings, even composition (including jazz composition) is reasonably well known. Many of his briefer pieces, delicately transparent as they are, and at just the time when *imagiste* theory was calling for greater density of concrete detail, might have been written with some tentative musical setting in mind. They are words for music perhaps. In this direction lies "the initiative yielded to the Word," as Thibaudet was rediscovering it in Mallarmé at this time—a freeing of language toward forms less encumbered by discourse which had characterized the nineteenth century and accelerated toward the end. Like those defenders of pure poetry who derived from symbolism, Pound makes more explicit claims for the music of verse than did Mallarmé. It was rather the principal taks of the symbolist, at a time when Wagner's presence was somewhat overpowering, to keep clear the border-line between two arts.

If, like Max Jacob's *poèmes-phrases,*[8] some of the more rigorously Imagist poems are lacking in inner music, the fact is not to be attributed to their brevity. Take, for example, John Gould Fletcher's

> It is evening, and the earth
> Wraps her shoulders in an old blue shawl.

This miniature yet complete poem can be appreciated without attention to the fact that it has exactly seventeen syllables, or that it ends in one of those spondees which the Japanese *haiku* does not require but which Imagist adapters of the form usually did. Fletcher's little poem is neither taut nor angular, neither too short nor too long, because exactly proportionate to the poetic action it presents, and it possesses its own kind of music for the same reason.

Perhaps, as in the case of Jacob's brief poems, the trouble with certain Imagist efforts is simply that two kinds of imagery cannot be dominant at once. Writers who had learned that the visual image is the most effective way of bringing a work, particularly a short work, alive, could not attach equal importance to the more hidden forms of imagery. Except in a few of Mallarmé's transitional poems, reconciliation of Parnassian and symbolist modes is rare.

Judith Gautier's *Le Livre de jade* had been well read; the Goncourts had aroused fresh interest in things Oriental; painters and poets alike had seen some of their most secret hopes realized in Japanese prints. An idea of Oriental art had been formative in turn-of-the-century Paris as in the London of 1908-12. Certain of Mallarmé's poems, and some of the Imagists', are composed with a deft minimum of strokes, reminiscent of a Japanese drawing. And another underlying assumption shared by Imagists and symbolists was that of negation as a force. One can turn to Stevens almost as readily as to Mallarmé for examples of the poetry of "pure absence":

> One must have a mind of winter
> To regard the frost and the boughs
> Of the pine trees crusted with snow,
>
> And have been cold a long time
> To behold the junipers shagged with ice,
> And spruces rough in the distant glitter
>
> Of the January sun; and not to think
> Of any misery in the sound of the land
> Full of the same wind
> That is blowing in the same bare place
>
> For the listener, who listens in the snow;
> And, nothing himself, beholds
> Nothing that is not there and nothing that is.
>   —"The Snow Man"

The last line, like another of Stevens', "Bring down from nowhere nothing's wax-like blooms" ("Mr. Burnshaw and the Statue"), was in all likelihood influenced by Mallarmé's use of the word *rien,* which gives to the term some of its etymologically positive meaning. In a more general yet unmistakable way, Stevens' use of imagery of whiteness owes to Mallarmé's. And there is a similar willingness to dispense with the leverage of the subject in Mallarmé's "Eventails" and in Stevens' "Infanta Marina":

> And thus she roamed
> In the roamings of her fan
> Partaking of the sea
> And of the evening,
> And they flowed around
> And uttered their subsiding sound.

The slight gesture is allowed to stand for the universal rhythm.

An essentially classicist desire for interlocking, monad-like forms; a checking of inner dynamism by containing rhythms finding their equivalents in lines of varying length; an appreciation of music as another art presenting, like poetry, a more inclusive action than a picture can—these characteristics are shared in varying degree by symbolists and Imagists.

Coming to the question of precision (understood here as the quality lent to a work by its particulars), we must start with the fact that, characteristically, Mallarmé abstracts details from a given arrangement of objects. An early draft can be fairly direct:

> Toujours plus souriant au désastre plus beau,
> Soupirs de sang, or meurtrier, pamoison, fête!
> Une millième fois avec ardeur s'apprête
> Mon solitaire amour à vaincre le tombeau.
>
> Quoi! de tout ce coucher pas même un cher
>   lambeau
> Ne reste. . . .

In the revised form of the above, an ablative absolute thrusts more of the implied action into the poem's already long foreground, concentrating the remainder:

> Victorieusement fui le suicide beau
> Tison de gloire, sang par écume, or, tempête!
> O rire si là-bas une pourpre s'apprête
> A ne tendre royal que mon absent tombeau
>
> Quoi! de tout cet éclat pas même le lambeau
> S'attarde. . . .

Lines 2-4 have lost adjectives and gained vivid substantives. But any vestiges of a Romantic sunset piece are lost with the word *coucher* of the earlier line 5. The more or less direct representation of the first draft has been replaced by a symbolism of general decline and fall.

From the definitive form of Mallarmé's poem to William Carlos Williams' "El Hombre," the distance is little short of interplanetary:

> It's a strange courage
> You give me, ancient star:
>
> Shine alone in the sunrise
> Toward which you lend no part!

This poem presents a set of objects from which particulars have not been abstracted; perhaps even, in keeping with the early vision of what an Imagist poem might be, the heart of a *moment privilégié.* The feeling expressed is of a stoical kind, but the poet remains close to it and to his poem.

After quoting the above lines as his theme, Wallace Stevens continues:

I

Shine alone, shine nakedly, shine like bronze,
That reflects neither my face nor any inner part
Of my being, shine like fire, that mirrors nothing.

II

Lend no part to any humanity that suffuses
You in its own light.
Be not chimera of morning,
Half-man, half-star.
Be not an intelligence,
Like a widow's bird
Or an old horse.
   —"Nuances on a Theme by Williams"

This is lean, precise, shunning abstractions. Reconciliation of subject with object, a main tendency of poetic expression ever since the later eighteenth century, affirmed by Baudelaire's theory of correspondences and refined by symbolist theory and practice, is expressly repudiated. Though subject and object are in fact associated by negative statement, "Nuances" does nothing to diminish the distance between symbolist and Imagist modes. The American poet cherishes the particularities of a set of objects; the French poet suppresses them.

Earlier in this article it was noted that certain recognizably classicist traits are common to symbolist and Imagist verse. One classicist principle, however, could hardly have been shared by an Imagist fully cognizant of Hulme's definition of art as passionate desire for accuracy, by one who had felt the impact of this conception in his own creative process. This was the classical view that aesthetic verisimilitude involved fidelity to an inner model as well as to an external object. The other and more "modern" kind of verisimilitude, which holds the artist responsible for particularizing details of an external object, is not to be sought in Mallarmé's major poems. Inheritor of a sense of the poet's task sometimes very classical indeed, Mallarmé worked toward an essential rather than an existent object. Only in certain poems incidental to his main effort can his conception of the true-seeming be compared to the Imagists'.

"We introduce into human beings the *Perfection* that properly belongs only to the divine," wrote Hulme, "and thus confuse both human and divine things by not clearly separating them."[9] Many would try to avoid such confusion. Since about 1910, most poetic practice has tended to show how complex, how disparate and imperfect are the data somehow reconciled in the moment of insight. Mallarmé spoke admiringly of what might be called the "impure poetry" of his time, of poetic styles which have been regarded as models since. But he himself introduced perfection into human beings, and has been chided for "angelism" in words almost identical to Hulme's.

With all the vigor of a new-found conviction that aesthetic ideas are born with flesh upon their bones, Hulme searched the past for examples of the precision he urged. Of the many lines in Keats's "Isabella, or the Pot of Basil," he singled out one for approval:

  And she forgot the blue above the trees.

Why, Hulme wondered, did the poet put 'blue above the trees' and not 'sky'? 'Sky' is just as attractive an expression. Simply for the reason, that he instinctively felt that the word 'sky' would not convey over the actual vividness of the feeling he wanted to express. The choice of the right detail, the blue above the trees, forces the vividness on you. . . ."[10]

Mallarmé and his abstraction toward analogue and archetype stand apart. French criticism and aesthetics had helped to formulate the new notion of verisimilitude, and had acknowledged the life-giving power of the right detail. Such details turn up even in long-maligned poetry of the eighteenth century. And Sainte-Beuve read the Lake Poets with an attention that he did not give to epistles and satires of the classical periods. He caught a tone new for his time and place, and the vibrations were to be far-reaching:

 Je ne suis pas de ceux pour qui les causeries,
 Au coin du feu, l'hiver, ont de grandes douceurs;
 Car j'ai pour tous voisins d'intrépides chasseurs,
 Rêvant de chiens dressés, de meutes aguerries,

 Et des fermiers causant jachères et prairies,
 Et le juge de paix avec ses vieilles soeurs,
 Deux revêches beautés parlant de ravisseurs,
 Portraits comme on en voit sur les tapisseries. . . .
   —"Sonnet, Imité de Wordsworth"

Why was it that Sainte-Beuve, attempting much less here than in some other poems, such as "Les Rayons jaunes" and "Ma Muse," actually accomplished more? No answer is likely to be complete. With reference to some other poems as well, one may be hazarded.

The most versatile of French critics argued effectively in favor of precision, for *bocage vert* instead of *bocage romantique,* for *lac bleu* rather than *lac mélancolique,* and even for particular shades of green or blue. " . . . Il semble par trop aisé et par trop simple de dire que les feuilles sont vertes et les flots bleus. En cela peut-être les adversaires du pittoresque se trompent. Les feuilles, en effet, ne sont pas toujours vertes, les flots ne sont pas toujours bleus; ou plutôt il n'y a dans la nature, à parler rigoureusement, ni vert, ni bleu, ni rouge proprement dit; les couleurs naturelles des choses sont des couleurs sans nom; mais, selon la disposition d'âme du spectateur, selon la saison de l'année, l'heure du jour, le jeu de la lumière, ces couleurs ondulent à l'infini, et permettent au poète et au peintre d'inventer ainsi à l'infini, tout en paraissant copier."[11] Such anticipation of Impressionist theory illuminates the only way in which such a "passionate desire for accuracy"[12] as Hulme's can become a viable aesthetic position. The artist can conceivably be content with accuracy as he reacts to swiftly changing appearances, like the water-colorist—whether painter or poet—of 1880, on the eve of the symbolist revelation.

Only so can the artist avoid *du beau vert, du beau bleu,* colors too much like those of *la belle nature* of a neo-classical world-view, wherein nature can have only a counter-existence because not freshly apprehended.

Pursuit of verisimilitude-as-accuracy had continued with glances at George Crabbe ("Cities and towns, the various haunts of men / Require the pencil; they defy the pen"), with further lessons from the Lake Poets. The difficulties and dangers of the search were amply justified by Baudelaire's *Tableaux parisiens.* The representational but far from static poetry of 1880 is explained in great part by this conception of what constitutes aesthetic likeness. Rilke, in whose early writings a struggle between a rather brutal naturalism and a somewhat diaphanous immaterialism was waged, learned partly from Rodin to give necessary density to his thing-poems. Malte, and the generation for which he stood, learned to see.

More than one literary movement was buoyed up by new understanding of the rôle of the active imagination and of the visual image as evidence of the creative imagination. An emphasis on visual imagery in several literary traditions led to poems of marked concentration and immediacy, turning, many of them, around a single visual image. Despite some degeneration into self-parody, inevitable in a body of verse that wavered between artificial concision and splendid freedom of form, some of the best poets writing in English were submitted to an Imagist tempering. Certain guiding principles found expression in Imagist theory. Others, more important, relating to the nature of the image, were expressed sketchily or not at all—and required no further elucidation because sensed by the creatively inclined.

Hulme is least satisfying, and other Anglo-American Imagists with him, in his failure to give due place to the non-imitative arts, to music and architecture. Time and again, he insists on the slipperiness of the non-mimetic. "Readers of poetry," he says, characteristically, "may attach more importance to the other things, but this is the quality the poets recognize among each other. If one wants to fix it down then one can describe it as a kind of instinctive feeling which is conveyed over to one, that the poet is describing something which is actually present to him, which he realises visually at first hand."[13] This is not good enough as far as it goes, because it goes too far and sets the perspective for well-known depreciation of Milton. It is stimulating atelier criticism, however, speaking in a plain blunt no-nonsense way to a generation. Valéry's Eupalinos, seeing in the temple he had built the mathematical image of a physical reality, went much deeper. But many young writers learned from Hulme, directly or indirectly, to face objects without flinching.

If a *petite voie* of real interest to modern writers can be traced from eighteenth-century passages to whole twentieth-century poems, what characteristic is most likely to pass unnoticed along this way? Taking as a first example Sainte-Beuve's adaptation, quoted above, there is no lack of the small dry things in which, Hulme and the Imagists believed, beauty must be discovered.[14] Substantives are vivid, and for the time and place, unexpected. Adjectives are few and telling. A genre scene is poetically presented, rather than prosaically represented. Very much a part of the effect, too, are the singing alexandrines, touching with a kind of candid lyricism a complex of images which most of Sainte-Beuve's contemporary readers, used to rarer Romantic altitudes, found unpoetic. Then, of course, there is "tapisseries," suddenly transforming homely objects and circumstances.

Théophile Gautier, seeking to delineate the character and bustling movement of a Flemish market-town, bringing in snatches of conversation along with the conversational tone—writing, in short, very much the kind of verse Sainte-Beuve had in mind and possibly thinking of *Joseph Delorme* as he did so—also relied ultimately on the refracting power of a work of graphic art:

> Sur le bord d'un canal profond dont les eaux
>   vertes
> Dorment, de nénuphars et de bateaux couvertes,
> Avec ses toits aigus, ses immenses greniers,
> Les tours au front d'ardoise où nichent les
>   cigognes,
> Les cabarets bruyants qui regorgent d'ivrognes,
> Est un vieux bourg flamand tel que le peint
>   Teniers. . . .
>
>   —"Albertus"

Though something of greater consequence occurs in *Tableaux parisiens,* that section of his book which Baudelaire had not meant to write at first, which took possession of him and became the most interesting section of *Les Fleurs du mal,* the poetic means are similar. Not quite submerged by the genre detail of Baudelaire's poem are its plaster deities:

> Je n'ai pas oublié, voisine de la ville,
> Notre blanche maison, petite mais tranquille;
> Sa Pomone de plâtre et sa vieille Vénus
> Dans un bosquet chétif cachant leurs membres
>   nus. . . .

More or less hidden, too, is the timelessness of the imagery in Baudelaire's as in Sainte-Beuve's poem: an imagery of works and days, domestic or pastoral, dealing with pasture or plowland, farmers and village notables. The quiet beginning and equally quiet end of Baudelaire's poem enclose universals.

A number of poems and groups of poems deserve consideration here, among them a whole series composed by Mallarmé as legends for a set of pictures by the realistic painter Raffaelli. Like its companion-pieces, "Le Savetier" deals with the dismay of the idealist faced by the world of appearances. For lavender-vendor, road-mender, garlic-and-onion seller, for workingman's spouse, glazier, newsboy, and haberdasher, Mallarmé sketches not another picture but a definitive trait, a gesture. The jottings are as impromptu as the same poet's letters in verse, and more revealing of a scene, an epoch, and an author than his symbolist poems. To notice only the lines about the cobbler:

> Hors de la poix rien à faire,
> Le lys naît blanc, comme odeur
> Simplement je le préfère
> A ce bon raccommodeur.
>
> Il va de cuir à ma paire
> Adjoindre plus que je n'eus
> Jamais, cela désespère
> Un besoin de talons nus.
>
> Son marteau qui ne dévie
> Fixe de clous gouailleurs
> Sur la semelle l'envie
> Toujours conduisant ailleurs.
>
> Il recréerait des souliers,
> O pieds! si vous le vouliez!

Away from the cobbler's wax, the poet comments sadly, there isn't much doing. The lily is born white, and it only so happens that he prefers it to this excellent cobbler. Bent on half-soling the poet's shoes, the fellow will make them more of the earth earthy than ever before, and the relentless hammer never misses. This is picturesque poetry with a difference: like an Imagist poem, it isolates a single moment, a single revealing gesture, in this case the unswerving hammer upraised above the mocking nails.

Francis Jammes, who said, "Le poète arrive à un âge où quand il dit: le ciel est bleu, cette expression lui suffit,"[15] must be neglected here. For reasons that should be rather obvious after this much discussion of *imagiste* aims and ideas, he was not thus passed over by Pound. But the aspect of Jammes's work which drew Pound's best superlatives, the small town "Spoon-Rivered," as he said, in *Existences,* is not the one of most interest today. It is, rather, "la vie des choses," the way in which objects either homely or exotic are allowed to carry with them their suggestions of a unique, rather than an individual and private symbolism, as was the case before about 1885.

Another poet relevant to the Imagist effort must be hurried over. The *persona* in *Les Poésies et le Journal Intime de A. O. Barnabooth* has the effect of setting Valery Larbaud's verse at about the same distance from its author as the one in Sainte-Beuve's *La Vie, poésies et pensées de Joseph Delorme.* There would be other reasons, too, for drawing a parallel between the exponent of the Lake Poets and the particular sponsor of James Joyce—two students of things English whose verse is a prolongation of acute critical faculties. No doubt Barnabooth, with his vision of someone rattling long in a cab, someone who hums for his own benefit

> Au long de Brompton Road, Marylebone ou Holborn
> Et regarde en songeant à la littérature
> Les hauts monuments noirs dans l'air épais et jaune

was more of a poet than Delorme. His verse-postcards from various points of interest (the best of them from

London, however) are bright and clear or properly murky. But the question here is not that of relative merit but rather of a kind of verse.

Hulme's notebooks can bring us close to the center of the Imagist *prise de conscience.* In them we find, for one thing, signs of sympathy with that Flemish vision of primary reality which, ever since the seventeenth century, has fascinated those whose thoughts have strayed toward a kind of art that would remain close to life:

> Town sky-line
>
> On a summer day, in Town,
> Where chimneys fret the cumuli,
> Flora passing in disdain
> Lifts her flounced blue gown, the sky.
> So see I, her white cloud petticoat,
> Clear Valenciennes, meshed by twisted cowls,
> Rent by tall chimneys, torn lace, frayed and
>   fissured,
> Slowly died along the scented way.

Meticulously rendered detail, something not unlike that well-known mirror of realistic fiction borne along the path, the whole suddenly touched by mention of a goddess (even a Roman one!)—surely Hulme must have remembered, as he trudged into Flanders, Baudelaire's "Je n'ai pas oublié. . . ." A very different kind of feeling is in question in the following:

> As a fowl in the tall grass lies
> Beneath the terror of the hawk,
> The tressed white light crept
> Whispering with hand on mouth mysterious
> Hunting the leaping shadows in straight streets
> By the white houses of old Flemish towns.

The use of slowing monosyllables in the final line is somewhat less powerful than in line 3. Perhaps it is the fact that a single word is not a monosyllable, and this word having associations reaching far beyond the primary reality which gives the fine grave beauty to this line.

Then there are the fragments along the way toward one of the best known of Hulme's distinguished handful of poems:

> Here stand I on the pavement hard
> From love's warm paradise debarred.
>
> . . . . .
>
> Oh God, narrow the sky,
> The old star-eaten blanket,
> Till it fold me round in warmth.
>
> . . . . .
>
> Down the long desolate streets of stars
>
> . . . . .
>
> No blanket is the sky to keep warm the little stars
>
> . . . . .

Somewhere the gods (the blanket-makers in the
    prairie of cold)
Sleep in their blankets.
["Religion is the expansive lie of temporary
    warmth."][16]

The poem using something from all these fragments illustrates many of the qualities and some of limitations of Imagist verse:

The Embankment

(The fantasia of a fallen gentleman on a cold,
    bitter night)

Once, in finesse of fiddles found I ecstasy,
In a flash of gold heels on the hard pavement.
Now see I
That warmth's the very stuff of poesy.
Oh, God, make small
The old star-eaten blanket of the sky,
That I may fold it round me and in comfort lie.

The subtitle is merely descriptive. The first two lines are highly contrived. Despite the change from "pavement hard" to "hard pavement," for which Pound claimed responsibility, the opening of the poem tends to confirm one's suspicion that Hulme's anti-"Romanticism" was no simple unequivocal sentiment. And the Imagist has his usual difficulty in passing from the crisp *haiku*-like record of a moment of insight to the more sustained work: the earlier past of "The Embankment" only serves to prepare, more or less artificially, the last three lines. These, however, invite comparison, if not with symbolist poetry, at least with that *poésie sans mensonge* which Rimbaud desired so ardently. It allows the glimpse of beauty or suggestion of grandeur in combination with that commonplace detail which seems to be necessary to satisfy our modern sense of what is plausible, real.

To that unobtrusive revelation of universals beneath particulars which had characterized a modern epistolary genre for almost a century, the Imagists added their conviction, shared by contemporary poets of other traditions, that the images of things, clear and immediate on the limits of consciousness, stand revealed in the only possible light. To those who, like Malte, have learned to see, they give up their secret: that strict minimum of traits, that inner reality subject to time, without which something would not have been what for a moment it was. What Imagist verse lacked in mystery, in shadow and relief, it sometimes made up in poignancy, because of the fragility of its forms, the inevitable narrowness of the limits within which a vision can remain entirely sharp and clear.

NOTES

[1] In "A History of Imagism," *The Egoist,* II (May 1, 1915), 71.

[2] *The End of American Innocence* (New York, 1960), p. 273.

[3] *The Imagist Poem,* edited and with an introduction by William Pratt (New York, 1963), p. 35.

[4] René Taupin, "L'Imagisme et le réel," in his *L'Influence du symbolisme français sur la poésie américaine* (*de 1910 à 1920*) (Paris, 1929), pp. 104-106.

[5] "Imagism; the New Poetry Forty Years After," *Prairie Schooner,* XXX, No. 2 (Summer 1956), 139-40.

[6] Ezra Pound's "A Few Don'ts by an Imagiste" was published in *Poetry* for March 1913; it was included in "A Retrospect," *Pavannes and Divisions* (New York, 1918), pp. 95-111; and in "A Stray Document," *Make It New* (London, 1934), pp. 335-41. F. S. Flint's essay, "Imagisme," was published in *Poetry,* March 1913; his "A History of Imagism," in *The Egoist* (1915), has been mentioned above. See also Richard Aldington's "Modern Poetry and the Imagists," *The Egoist,* I (June 1, 1914), 201-203; and Amy Lowell's preface to *Some Imagist Poets* (Boston, 1915).

[7] "... certains rythmes de vie et de respiration qui sont plus intérieurs à l'homme que ses sentiments les plus intérieurs, étant la loi vivante, variable avec chaque personne, de sa dépression et de son exaltation, de ses regrets et de ses espérances." Bergson, *Le Rire.*

[8] For a discussion of Jacob's *haiku*-like poems and their possible debt to Imagist verse, see S. J. Collier, "Max Jacob's *Le Cornet à dés:* A Critical Analysis," *French Studies,* XI, No. 2 (April 1957), 164.

[9] Quoted by Glenn Hughes, *Imagism and the Imagists: A Study in Modern Poetry* (Stanford, 1931), p. 14.

[10] "Bergson's Theory of Art," *Speculations,* ed. Herbert Read, 2nd ed. (London, reprinted 1954), pp. 163-64.

[11] Sainte-Beuve, *Poésies complètes* (Paris, 1840), pp. 137-38.

[12] "You could define art, then, as a passionate desire for accuracy, and the essentially aesthetic emotion as the excitement which is generated by direct communication. Ordinary language communicates nothing of the individuality and freshness of things." "Bergson's Theory of Art," *Speculations,* pp. 162-163.

[13] *Ibid.,* p. 167. Again: "Now any tendency towards counter language of this kind has to be carefully avoided by poetry. It always endeavors, on the contrary, to arrest you and to make you continuously see a physical thing." *Ibid.,* p. 166.

[14] "It is essential to prove that beauty may be in small, dry things." "Romanticism and Classicism," *Speculations,* p. 131. "I prophesy that a period of dry, hard, classical verse is coming." *Ibid.,* p. 133.

[15] In the preface to his *Premier Livre des quatrains.* Quoted by Taupin, *op. cit.,* p. 104.

[16] Fragments published in *Further Speculations,* ed. Sam Hynes (Minneapolis, 1955), pp. 216-217.

James Naremore

[*In the following essay, Naremore discusses the influence of contemporary French poetry on the poetics of Imagism, emphasizing particularly the role of the English critic F. S. Flint in informing English writers of recent developments in French literature.*]

SOURCE: "The Imagists and the French 'Generation of 1900'," in *Contemporary Literature*, Vol. 11, No. 3, Summer, 1970, pp. 354-74.

In the August 1912 issue of *The Poetry Review*, F. S. Flint wrote a lengthy essay entitled "Contemporary French Poetry." The essay—monograph might be a better term for it, since it occupies virtually the entire issue— is an encyclopedic review of modern French poetry, with copious quotations and an account of the rapid proliferation of new French "schools," including *Neo-Mallarmisme*, the Abbey Group, *Unanimisme, Futurisme, L'Impulsionisme, Les Paroxystes, Les Fantasistes*, etc. Scattered among the writings of the Imagist poets, and in the histories of the Imagist movement as well, one can find testimony to the considerable importance of Flint's project. Ezra Pound, for example, wrote that it was something "everybody had to get; it was the first large article on contemporary stuff"; and René Taupin has called it "the most informed and important [discussion of new French poetry] in England."[1]

The essay had an immediate effect on Pound, who appears at that time to have known relatively little about French poetry.[2] His memory of the article is inaccurate in some details, but he is quite clear about his reaction: "In the spring or early summer of 1912," he writes, he, Aldington, and H.D. "thought we had as much right to a group name, at least as much right, as a number of French 'schools' proclaimed by Mr. Flint in the August number of Harold Monro's magazine for 1911."[3] Pound is wrong about the year of Flint's essay and about the magazine where it appeared. His reference to "spring or early summer" may be wrong, too; he could not have responded when he says he did unless he had read the survey prior to publication (something which was quite possible). In any case, Pound credits the review of new French poetry with at least one important result: it prompted him to announce a new school, the *Imagistes,* complete with a French title.

In the years that followed the appearance of Flint's essay, the Imagist interest in contemporary French verse was obvious, and it has been well documented. Pound, Aldington, Amy Lowell, and Fletcher all made references to new French poetry. In 1913, Pound began his series of articles, "The Approach to Paris," in *The New Age,* where he praised not only Rimbaud and Gourmont, but also the younger poets like Romains and Vildrac; he also suggested to Harriet Monroe that she establish a permanent column in *Poetry* devoted to French verse. At times he was caustic toward those who knew nothing of the French moderns. "There is no culture that is not at least bilingual," he wrote. "Yet in 1912 or 1913 we find an American editor who writes of Henri de Régnier and M. Remy de Gourmont as 'these young men.' . . . He has no desire to add to his presumably superabundant knowledge."[4] In *The Egoist* between 1914 and 1915 virtually everyone talked about French poetry; a number of young French poets were published in the magazine, and Nicholas Beauduin discussed new work from France. Meanwhile Aldington wrote about French poetry for *The Little Review,* and the prefaces to the Imagist anthologies contained references to younger men like Vildrac, Duhamel, and Spire. Through all this, Flint continued to be the best informed exponent of the French, writing "The French Chronicle" for *Poetry and Drama,* where he reviewed poets like André Salmon and Apollinaire, and commented again on the futurist movement. In 1919, he wrote a comprehensive survey of recent French verse for *The Chapbook,* a survey rather like his earlier *Poetry Review* article, but this time devoted to postwar poetry.

All this is more or less a matter of record. But in spite of the obvious interest the Imagists had in new French poetry, very little has been said about the influence this poetry might have had on Imagist practice. Everybody knows that several of the Imagists were Francophiles, but until recently the French influence on Imagist poetics has been explained largely in terms of French symbolism. I say "until recently" because the latest historian of the Imagist movement, Stanley Coffman, persuasively argues that the importance of the symbolists to Imagism has been exaggerated.[5]

There remains, however, very little in the histories to indicate what, if anything, the Imagists might have absorbed from the poets who were roughly their contemporaries, the post-symbolist, neo-symbolist generation in France, the "generation of 1900," as Flint called them in his essay. The importance of Flint's and later Pound's discussions of modern French poetry has not yet been examined in detail. M. Taupin has documented the relationship between the Imagists and the symbolists, but on the subject of the younger French poets he has only a few remarks. He says at one point that movements like futurism and *Unanimisme* had a "real but very vague, imprecise and paradoxical influence" on the Imagists; the French and the English were both seeking to rid poetry of sentimentality, he notes, and in their mutual desire to attack the abuse of adjectives and abstractions, they were no doubt in sympathy.[6] Of Flint's *Poetry Review* survey, he says that it gave the English a sense of "clear intentions which are affirmed in the manner of manifestos," and of the "souci de la technique."[7] He indicates as well that such essays by Flint had much to do with the popularity of the *vers libre* in England, but he does not make the relevance of the younger poets much more precise. Flint himself once commented, "The Imagists admitted that they were contemporaries of the Post-Impressionists and the Futurists, but they had nothing in common with these schools."[8] The critics who have discussed Imagism have generally taken such remarks at something near to face value, so that we hear much about French symbolism, haiku, and the eclecticism of Pound, but almost nothing about the generation of 1900 in France and their importance.

In a way, this lack of commentary on the younger French poets is understandable. One major Imagist poet, H.D., spoke relatively little about modern French experiments, even when a knowledge of them was most in vogue, and she arrived at her manner before she learned about the French. Few of the Imagists wrote about French poetry as well as Pound, and none of them with as much knowledge and care as Flint. But Flint and Pound were both important as aestheticians for the movement, and they both did enough proselytizing for the French to enable us to talk about a possible modern French influence.

In point of fact, if one reviews the contemporary French poets Flint and later Pound introduced in the little magazines during the Imagist years, one can find the evidence for such an influence. Certainly the young French poets were not the sole inspiration for Imagism; the seeds of the English movement and many of its characteristic styles were there before there was widespread interest in new French poetry. But if they did not find in France a pantheon or a revelation, the Imagists discovered a literary scene which they felt was vital, alive to experimentation, and worth emulating. It may be true that as a "school" the Imagists had relatively little in common with the manifestos of *Unanimisme* or futurism or any of the other French movements, just as they had little in common with the stated aims of the symbolists. One has only to look at Pound's letters or the Imagist anthologies to see that the Imagists did not have so terribly much in common even with one another. Nevertheless the connection between the work of Arcos, Romains, Duhamel, Vildrac, Ghéon, Apollinaire, Marinetti, and others, and the work of several of the Imagists, is often quite noticeable, enough so for us to talk about influences or sometimes rapports between the French and the English during the first two decades of the century. In some cases, the relationship seems much more direct, the influence more tangible, than that between the Imagists and the French symbolists.

The younger generation of French poets, like the Imagists after them, elaborated some of the suggestions offered by the symbolists. Generally, they saw themselves as a development from symbolism rather than as a reaction against it. They charged symbolism with certain unfortunate mannerisms and extravagances, but many of them also clearly acknowledged a debt to the symbolists. For the younger French poets, and for Flint at least among the English, the "heritage" of symbolism was twofold: it had left behind the notion of free verse, and it had experimented with "the exquisite juxtaposition of images."[9] Flint regarded the older generation—Laforgue, Kahn, de Regnier, Viele-Griffin, Verhaeren, Fort, Claudel, and Jammes—as men who had "retested the capabilities of language."[10] He praised them because they sought to "strip poetry of rhetoric"; because they used "images" to evoke "intuitions" (his Bergsonian explanation of sym-

bolist poetry may show a debt to Hulme, though the French themselves had been using Bergson this way); and because they began experimentation with a "new manner," the *vers libre*. Their aim had been to break the tyranny of the alexandrine, to subordinate rhyme to "the general music of the verse," and to make rhyme give way to assonance "where the music demanded it."[11]

The symbolists had been the first theorists of a new technique; the generation of 1900, who were Flint's subject in the *Poetry Review* survey, had revived the method and passionately advocated it. As Pound once pointed out, the Imagists owed to the symbolists "comme le pain doit quelque chose au vanneur de blé";[12] the technical experiments of the younger French poets, on the other hand, were a more immediate source of education for the English and Americans. Vildrac and Duhamel, for example, had suggested that rhyme be abandoned entirely, except perhaps for an occasional charming or witty adornment. And the younger generation as a whole advocated experimentation; they wanted not a form, but "a free spirit, capable of finding expression in an infinite variety of forms."[13] The cult of sincerity, of organic form, was being exhorted with a new intensity.

As this might suggest, the younger French poets were important to Imagist versification. Pound, for example, repeatedly emphasized the economy of the new French poetry: "I, personally, happen to be tired of verses which are left full of blank spaces for interchangeable adjectives. In the more or less related systems of versification which have been adopted by Romains, Chennevière, Vildrac, Duhamel, and their friends, I do not find such an excessive allowance of blank spaces, and this seems to me a healthy tendency."[14] Beyond this general value, however, the French moderns had more specific contributions to make. Nearly all the poets Flint writes of in the 1912 *Poetry Review* article advocate some sort of verse experimentation, so that the essay becomes a virtual survey of ideas about free verse. Flint's own interest in the subject may come from Robert De Souza, whose book, *Du Rythme en Français,* had just been published. In any case, one can make a good argument that Flint's discussion of the new French poets in 1912 was a major source of encouragement for *vers libre* in England. Symons, Henley, Ford, and the members of the "School of Images" had all made experiments with free verse, but before the period 1912 to 1917, as both Aldington and T. S. Eliot have testified, it was almost impossible to speak of *vers libre* outside France. During that time, however, the term, along with Flint's "cadence," became a part of everyone's literary baggage.

Of the younger French poets who influenced the Imagists' practice, or who had close affinities with it, mention has often been made of Charles Vildrac and Georges Duhamel and their book, *Notes sur la technique poétique,* which Flint and Pound seem both to have read with great interest. Before discussing the *Notes,* however, I want to mention one poet who has received no attention at all from the historians: he is Henri Ghéon, whose idea of the "analytical strophe" Flint wrote about at length. Taupin has contended that Ghéon appears in Flint's survey of 1912 almost by way of contrast with Vildrac and Duhamel, and that his theories had little effect. But while Flint does point out some of the objections of De Souza and others to Ghéon's method, the treatment he himself gives is more sympathetic; and whether Ghéon became a direct influence or not, his versification is strikingly like what we can find in a number of Imagist poems.

Ghéon was a leading experimenter with the "new manner." In a speech that Flint once translated for *Poetry and Drama,* Ghéon had said: "for a poem to exist, it will never suffice for it to have a harmony of sentiments, of images and of ideas; harmony is as though void, if before all there is no harmony of sounds. The most intimate poem is something sonorous. Even hushed, it speaks to the ear before speaking to the mind."[15] Ghéon's concern with the rhythms and sounds of poetry led him to advocate that the term "verse" be done away with altogether, to be replaced by the "rhythmic unit," or hemistich, which would contribute to the basic unit of composition, the strophe. As Flint summarizes the theory, "the rhythmic units . . . though each is given a line to itself, only count by their groupings, proportions, and reciprocal relations in the strophe-organism uniting them."[16] Here, as Flint quoted it, is an example from Ghéon's practice:

> Saine ivresse quotidienne
> si connue
> que le coeur ne s'en d'éfie point
> jour après jour
> je l'aurais bue
> comme sans amour
> —et mon coeur est plein:
> plus d'autre soif
> plus d'autre faim
> quand le vent passe![17]

This style, with its repetitions and carefully modulated phrases that vary in length, is the characteristic manner in the short early poems of Aldington and H.D., arrived at by reading Greek poetry, and before they had any knowledge of Ghéon. It is little wonder that Pound, reading this, decided he was entitled to found a school of his own. Here, cited by Flint for instructive comparison, is a more extreme instance of Ghéon's method:

> C'est Alger
> ou tout germe
> ou tout fleure
> ou tout fleurit
> murit:
> voici
> toutes les graines
> tous les fruits
> d'ici
> d'ailleurs
> semez!
> cueillez![18]

Not all of Ghéon's poems took this form, and Ghéon was not the only poet of the period who designed his work by piling up successive short rhythmic units of irregular length. But Ghéon theorized that this manner was ideal, and it became, for a time, identified with him. De Souza, Vildrac, and Duhamel had objected that "analytical strophe" was as inadequate a term as *vers libre,* that the natural tendency to pronounce successive groups of rhythmic feet in a single breath ought to be an indication of something called a verse, and that some ideas are not suited to the shortening of the breath that they felt Ghéon's form caused. Duhamel and Vildrac were condescending; they remarked: "cela doit rester une technique d'exception."[19] Flint, however, had a more positive reaction. Speaking of the poem above, he observed: "if you discount a slight staccato effect, which is either involuntarily felt by the reader or forced on the poet by his form, you will find that these lines have a very cunning rhythm."[20]

The Imagists never adopted the term "analytical strophe," but on the whole they were less cautious than Duhamel and Vildrac about ordering the poem as a column of rather short units. As I have said, Aldington and H.D. came upon a similar manner before they knew modern French literature, and they were quite probably an influence on Lowell, Fletcher, and Williams. In any case, a large number of Imagist poems use a form like the one Ghéon had recommended. Consider, for example, the way Amy Lowell imitates the waves in "Venus Transiens":

> Tell me,
> Was Venus more beautiful
> Than you are,
> When she topped
> The crinkled waves,
> Drifting shoreward
> On her plaited shell?[21]

In terms of his emphasis on the strophe as the basic unit of composition, as opposed to the verse, Ghéon was closer in spirit to many Imagist poems than were Vildrac and Duhamel. However, because the Imagists had already made a few experiments in this manner before they came upon Ghéon, his work may represent nothing more than a striking affinity with their practice. The *Notes* of Vildrac and Duhamel, on the other hand, were a clearly acknowledged influence.

Flint described the Duhamel-Vildrac theories in the *Poetry Review* essay, and allusions to them appear in the later public and private statements of both Pound and Flint, and in the prefaces to the Imagist anthologies. Duhamel and Vildrac had recommended a verse that was partly free and partly controlled by some rhythmic pattern; they argued that in most of the good verse by their contemporaries, the strophe was held in order by what they called a "rhythmic constant." In this technique, each verse contains a fixed number of syllables plus a variable part of the line. These lines by Duhamel, for example, are said to have a four-syllable constant, which I have capitalized:

> PENSEZ-VOUS PAS a ce tison dont la course
> CINGLE LE NOIR d'un long regret qui ne veut
>   pas perir?

AH! DEVINEZ comment je regne ou je demeure
ET QUE JE VIS entre ici et la, longuement.[22]

Actually, the first eight syllables in each of these lines form a regular unit, and one can feel the pressure of the alexandrine behind the verses. There is the sense that a traditional form is there but that it is being subtly departed from. Such an effect is perhaps analogous to T. S. Eliot's notions that free verse cannot really be free, and to his experiments in the early poems like "Prufrock," where there is the pressure of blank verse behind the apparently irregular form.

Duhamel and Vildrac described several other means of imposing a sense of design on the poem, including one technique that the historians of Imagism seem to have overlooked: the *équilibre rythmique,* in which a certain mathematical relationship could be established between the hemistiches. For example, these lines by André Salmon:

> Cette rose / à ton corsage,
> Cette fleur rouge / à ton col entr'ouvert . . . [23]

I have marked off the hemistiches so that the relationship can be seen clearly: the first is related to the second in the same way as the third is related to the fourth; the first is related to the third in the same way as the second is related to the fourth; and so on, through all the possible combinations.

Richard Aldington claimed to have used the rhythmic constant, and though his measure is not as regular as the one described in the *Notes,* the habit that he and the other Imagists made of repeating words or phrases at the opening of each verse has the effect of a constant. Likewise, Pound never copied directly the effects Duhamel and Vildrac had described, but he does at times seem to have learned a lesson from them. Take this passage from "Dance Figure," for example:

> I have not found thee in the tents,
> In the broken darkness.
> I have not found thee at the well-head
> Among the women with pitchers.[24]

These lines are not, strictly speaking, *équilibre rythmique,* but the principle is the same. Thus the relation of the first line to the second is the same as the relation of the third to the fourth, and so on.

In general, what Pound and the other Imagists seem to have adopted from Duhamel and Vildrac was not so much their specific applications of metric—obviously French and English are different languages with different metrical traditions and different problems for the poet— as their aim, which was to attack rhyme and make the verse conform to the meaning of the poet while still retaining some sense of form. Duhamel and Vildrac were also important to the Imagists because of their effective attack on "dishonesty." Vildrac especially seems to have interested Pound by his ability to write clearly and without affectation. In "The Approach to Paris," Pound wrote, "Those who are interested in ritual and . . . invocation may have been interested in M. de Gourmont's litanies, those who are interested in a certain purging of the poetic idiom may be interested in the work of such men as Vildrac."[25] Some of the best known proclamations of the Imagists are in fact drawn from the *Notes.* I do not think that anyone has ever noticed that Flint's famous description of Imagist verse, "in the sequence of the musical phrase, not in sequence of a metronome,"[26] later repeated by Pound in *Pavannes and Divisions,* is an echo of a remark by Duhamel and Vildrac: "nous pouvons chanter sans metronome."[27] Indeed, Flint's term, "cadence," probably also comes from the *Notes,* where it is used quite often.

Marinetti and the futurists also offered suggestions that the Imagists found attractive, although the relationship between futurism and Imagism is in many ways a tenuous one. The Imagists did not seek to reject the past, and they avoided the eccentricities that were associated with Marinetti and his followers. On the whole, their attitude toward futurism was ambivalent. Flint was one of the first to discuss the futurists, in the 1912 *Poetry Review* essay, and the next year he somewhat reluctantly talked about futurism in "The French Chronicle" for *Poetry and Drama.* In 1912 he could write: "Read the futuristic programme again, and then ask yourself whether English poetry, too, has not need of the greater part of it."[28] But the part of the program the Imagists felt the need of, at least where versification was concerned, was not much more than what they found in a number of young French poets who were not futurists.

There was rather little specific contribution by the futurists to Imagist versification, which never became "words at liberty." In 1913 Flint seemed intrigued by Marinetti's attack on the "typographical harmony of the page, which is contrary to the flux and reflux of the language,"[29] but in succeeding years neither he nor any of the inner circle of Imagists carried on this attack, unless one considers *vers libre* itself an instance. Not until E. E. Cummings, so far as I can tell, does a poet in English make any concentrated and effective attack on traditional typography. There were, however, some suggestions by Marinetti that had greater effect. "What is the use," Flint wrote in *Poetry and Drama,* "of logical syntax in poetry? Why should we have so absolute a respect for the integrity of words?" Pondering the futurist manifesto, Flint saw that poetry might become "a series of emotional ejaculations, cunningly modulated, and coloured by a swift play of subtle and far-reaching analogies."[30] Certainly many of the Imagist experiments in later years correspond roughly to this description. Parts of J. G. Fletcher's "London Excursion," and a number of Amy Lowell's poems in *Pictures of a Floating World* (1919), poems like "Dolphins in Blue Water" or "Motor Lights on a Hill Road," are not much more than verbs, participles, images, and analogies in a very loose syntactical arrangement. In general, however, the futurists do not seem to have done much more than reinforce certain convictions about versification that the Imagists obtained from many sources, including their own innovations. Coffman, I think, quite accurately sums up the relationship between futurism and Imagism: "Both rigidly restricted the use of the adjective. . . . Both proclaimed the need of the modern poet for a free form of verse. Both condemned rhetoric. Both (the Futurist more aggressively than the Imagist) asserted the importance of complete freedom for the play of images and analogies. Futurism's vigor and energy . . . and its concentration on its own times had an undeniable appeal to the Imagism of the early years."[31]

Coffman's last sentence serves to remind us that if the younger poets in France had an effect on Imagist versification, they also had an influence on the choice of subject. Generally speaking, before 1912 the English poets had no obvious modernity of subject matter. In this regard, a group of French poets, including André Spire, René Arcos, Jules Romains, and the Italian Marinetti, had a significant effect in the way they were able to deal poetically with the atmosphere of contemporary life. Flint, for example, wrote with what now seems an almost naive admiration of Spire's ability to create poetry out of mundane affairs: "He wanders through the cities watching men and women at work; he is not afraid to write of a servant dusting and the gritty loathsomeness to her of the dust."[32] And in 1913 Pound wrote that he could not see about him "any young man whose work is as refreshing as Romains'." On *Un Être en Marche,* he made these comments: "The author has achieved a form which fully conveys the sense of modern life. He is able to mention any familiar thing . . . without its seeming incongruous, and the result is undeniably poetic."[33]

A year before Pound's remarks were written, Flint had quoted Romains' poetry at great length in *The Poetry Review,* with this description of it: "M. Romains is a great creator of images. He is the epic poet of modern life. . . . What other poet would dare . . . to celebrate with fervor the underground railway (*Deux Poèmes*)? . . . Imagine a man who wanders through a large town, brooding over the everchanging spectacle . . . alternately exalted and depressed, but always rendering his vision and his sensations by words that reproduce exactly what he has seen, except that it has become intensified and serried in passing through his imagination."[34] The last sentence would be a fairly good description of a number of later Imagist poems. The work of Aldington is a case in point. His earliest poems, "Choricos," "To a Greek Marble," "Argyria," "Stele," "Lesbia," have an unorthodox versification, but their subject matter is classicism; the settings, the images, the entire paraphernalia of the poems are designed to suggest the ambiance of Greek antiquity. The languorous vowel sounds and the use of color and decor in a poem like "Choricos" are very like the early Tennyson. But most of the poems Aldington wrote after Flint and Pound had discussed the French moderns are quite different. Compare "Cinema Exit," for example, or "In the Tube":

> A row of advertisements,
> A row of windows,

> Set in brown woodwork pitted with brass nails,
> A row of hard faces,
> Immobile,
> In the swaying train,
> Rush across the flickering background of
>   fluted dingy tunnel;
> A row of eyes,
> Eyes of greed, of pitiful blankness, of
>   plethoric complacency,
> Immobile,
> Gaze, stare at one point,
> At my eyes.[35]

I have already discussed this style of versification in regard to Henri Ghéon; notice the repetitions and the way the line lengths are determined by the speaker's voice, by what he wants to emphasize. This style, however, was with Aldington from the start. What is new here is the series of images of the modern city, of man in relation to the crowd and the machine. One cannot argue that the poem was directly influenced by Romains or any other poet, but there is good reason to believe that Aldington had drawn the lessons of the French moderns. He has none of the acceptance of the city that we feel in Romains or Apollinaire, but he does give us vivid images of the city; and he renders "his vision and his sensations by words that reproduce exactly what he has seen, except that it has become intensified and serried in passing through his . . . imagination."

Flint also began to show around 1912 an interest in urban visions, and in poems like "The Beggar" and "Eau-Forte" he made conscious use of ugliness. His poems of this sort are often very like Aldington's; Flint's "Tube," for instance, is virtually the same poem as Aldington's "In the Tube." He was more and more preoccupied with the relationship of the sensitive individual to the crowd, and in this respect his work approximates the description Pound gave to the poetry of Vildrac: "the Nietzschean, pre-unanimist type," he called it, in which the poet "tries to impress his personality on the crowd and is disillusioned."[36] The closest Flint comes to the crowd-spirit is in these lines:

> All I meet are shabby, all go one way,
> Drawn by the same magnet, urged by the
>   same demon.
> We are the respectable; and behind us,
>   though we do not see him,
> Driving us with his goad, is hunger—the
>   first law of our land . . .
>
>   . . . . .
>
> For him we shove each other at the tramcars,
> Crowd elbow to elbow in the tubes, through
>   which we are hurled.
> Packed and swaying.

But the problem described here is more personal than social. "Hunger" is the necessity that makes a poet hold a job, that forces him to join a crowd of which he wants no part:

To-morrow I shall spend the best hours
  of my day
Pent up with people who do not speak the
  language I seek,
And who would not understand it if it were
  found.[37]

Pound was perhaps the least influenced by the subject matter and social philosophy of the French schools, in spite of his great admiration for Romains. After 1912, his versification is sometimes reminiscent of the French, and once he had read Duhamel and others he was prompted to make a "pact" with Walt Whitman. (Ghéon had wanted to call the *Unanimistes* "Whitmanistes.") But the poems of *Ripostes* and after do not show any special interest in the city; the reference to "a million people surly with traffic" in "N. Y." is about as close as Pound comes to the subject. By contrast, J. G. Fletcher, who perhaps next to Flint knew the French poets better than any of the Imagists, made use of both the *Unanimistes* and futurists. His "America, 1915," for example, sounds a good deal like both Whitman and the French: "Immense machines are clamoring, rattling, battling, wheeling, screaming, heaving, weaving.... Between the cities, over plain and hill, reel double paths of shining steel, where screaming locomotives pass like black shuttles ... strong black bird machines [bear] men on their backs. Purring autos squawk and squeal, and spray and flutter, pale flashes through the rack."[38] The weight and frequency of verbals, the attempt to endow mechanical objects with animal characteristics, the celebration of autos, trains, and airplanes—all this can be found in French experimentation around 1912.

"London Excursion" is a far more successful example of Fletcher's poetry, and it shows the French influence even more strikingly. The poem describes a man going into London by bus, spending the day walking the streets, and returning home at night. Here are the impressions of the protagonist as he stands at a bus stop:

Black shapes bending
Taxicabs crush in the crowd.

The tops are each a shining square
Shuttles that steadily press through woolly
  fabric.

Drooping blossom,
Gas standards over
Spray out jingling tumult
Of white-hot rays.

Monotonous domes of bowler-hats
Vibrate in the heat.
Silently, easily we sway through braying
  traffic,
Down the crowded street.
The tumult crouches over us,
Or suddenly drifts to one side.[39]

A contemporary reviewer noted, "If 'London Excursion' follows any lead, it is the lead of the new schools of poetry and painting in France."[40] The poem is indeed redolent of French experiment. The syntax and imagery,

as I have already indicated, have something in common with the uses Flint had suggested might be made of futurism. To see just how French the poem is, compare it with Apollinaire's "Zone," written in 1912:

Bergère ô tour Eiffel le troupeau des ponts
  bêle ce matin

    . . . . .

J'ai vu ce matin une jolie rue dont j'ai
  oublié le nom
Neuve et propre du soleil elle était le
  clairon
Les directeurs les ouvriers et les belles
  sténo-dactylographes
Du lundi matin au samedi soir quatre fois
  par jour y passent
Le matin par trois fois la sirène y gémit
Une cloche rageuse y aboie vers midi

    . . . . .

Maintenant tu marches dans Paris tout seul
  parmi la foule
Des troupeaux d'autobus mugissants près de
  toi roulent.[41]

I do not know if Fletcher had "Zone" in mind when he wrote "London Excursion." Certainly the two poems are different in several ways, but they also have some marked similarities: both have protagonists who are walking the streets of large cities, both have a time span of a single day, both have an unusual syntax and a very free play of images and analogies. Even details in the poems are alike: Fletcher's "braying traffic" is strikingly reminiscent of "le troupeau des ponts bêle" or of the "troupeaux d'autobus mugissants près de toi roulent" in Apollinaire. Whether Fletcher used "Zone" or not (he had, by the way, read Apollinaire), the comparison should indicate how real was the influence of the French moderns on his poetry.

This discussion of Fletcher's poem leads to the subject of what influence contemporary French poets may have had on the quality of the image itself. In this case, the doctrine of the English poets seems to have been sufficiently codified during the discussions of the earlier "School of Images" and through Pound's intense devotion to a Parnassian clarity. In this respect, however, we should note that while Pound said little about the images of the new French poets, he made clarity of language one of their distinguishing virtues: "There would seem to be a certain agreement between the styles of Romains, Duhamel, Vildrac, Jouve, Arcos, . . . and a few others, though Romains may have been the prime mover for their sort of clarification of the speech."[42] And even if the notion of the primacy of the image did not come from the generation of 1900, the Imagists did sometimes find in their contemporaries a use of the image to which they could respond with approval. Reference to the image and praise of effective imagery occur everywhere in Flint's *Poetry Review* survey. He praises, for example, the "illumination of vivid imagery" in Paul Castiaux:

Au ras dunes,
Classiquement importune
A ce soir parfumé d'essences recueillies
La pleine lune
Caresse d'inutile ivoire le ciel vert.[43]

But these particular lines smack too much of the *symbolistes* to have earned Pound's approval. In fact, he largely passes over the younger poets' use of images and reserves most of his praise in that respect for Gautier's *Emaux et Camées,* for the "presentative method" of Laurent de Tailhade, and for Francis Jammes. One contemporary French poet who could produce Pound's hard, clear image was Jean de Bosschère. Neither Flint nor Pound mentions his work in the 1912-13 period, but Flint wrote a translation of *The Closed Door* in 1917, and Bosschère himself wrote an appreciation of Pound in *The Egoist.* May Sinclair, who introduced Flint's translation, described Bosschère's images as having "Sharpness, precision, purity, the cold clearness of crystal."[44] Bosschère, however, is hardly an influence; his work in this vein comes a bit late, and he, like the other French poets who were praised for their images, seems only to have produced the kind of effects the Imagists were already creating and arguing for.

The question of influences on the concept of the image is a difficult one in any case, since it is by no means clear that the Imagists had the same notion of what the image was. Flint and Pound, for example, had very different ideas in this respect. The difference is indicated in May Sinclair's translation of Bosschère, where she points out that there is a marked difference between Bosschère's poetry and Flint's; it is also shown in Pound's remark that Flint "and Ford and one or two others shd. by careful cataloging have been in another group, but in those far days there weren't enough non-symmetricals to have each a farm to themselves."[45] Pound had wanted to emphasize a radical difference between the Imagists and the French symbolists, but Flint felt no such compulsion. Pound's comment on "permanent metaphor," a metaphor that corresponds exactly to the poetic emotion and that "is, as I understand it, 'symbolism' in its profounder sense,"[46] is as close as he comes to acknowledging any *arrière-plan* for the image. Flint, and perhaps Hulme before him, was more impressed by the symbolists and Bergson. As a result, he was more inclined to use terms like "symbol" and "image" interchangeably. Here, for example, is his explanation of the poetic image, which, he says, the younger French poets inherited from the previous generation:

> A symbol is a sign used in place of reality, as in algebra; but the symbolist poet attempts to give you an *intuition* of the reality itself, and of the forces, vague to us, behind it, by a series of *images* which the imagination seizes and brings together in its effort to *insert* itself and express that reality, and to evoke at the same time the *infinity* of which it is the culminating point in the present.[47]

I have emphasized some of the words here to indicate the relationship between symbolism, Henri Bergson, and the poetic image. One of the more striking things about this passage, at least if we contrast it with Pound's ideas, is that it contends "image" is a better term for what the French symbolists were seeking than "symbol." Flint was, one notices, inclined to use the term "infinity" in relation to the image, but to explain the working of the image in the language of Bergson, with terms like "intuition" and "insert."

It was in part because of his interest in Bergson that Flint admired the modern French poet René Arcos. It is probably Bergson (whom Flint had helped T. E. Hulme translate), and perhaps Arcos as well, who is somewhere behind this poem by Flint:

> O golden-red and tall chrysanthemums,
> you are the graceful soul of the china vase
> wherein you stand
> amid your leaves.
>
> O quiet room,
> you are the symbol of my patient heart.
>
> O flowers of flame, O tall chrysanthemums,
> my love who comes
> will wave wide ripples of disquiet there,
> and a great tide of the eternal sea
> will rise at her approach,
> and surge to song.
>
> O quiet room, O flame chrysanthemums,
> images of my heart and its proud love,
> you have no presage of the power that comes
> to fill with anguish the essential calm.
>
> O calm wrought face, O sphinx behind the door,
> her hand is on the latch![48]

One may notice the feeling of real duration that is evoked by the overwrought atmosphere, the speaker's hypersensitivity to minutiae. Also, notice the way expressions like "soul," "symbol," and "images" are used interchangeably. The poem records an instance of what Arcos called "paroxysm," an especially intense variety of the pathetic fallacy in which, as Flint had described the effect in Arcos' poetry, the objects are infused with a "glowing sensation" that unifies and embodies the "scrap-metal of experience."[49]

This, again, is not to say that Arcos was a direct influence, though he could well have been. Where the doctrine of the image is concerned, the French moderns and the Imagists often came upon the same effects separately, though sometimes by the same paths. The relationship between the new French poets and the Imagists in this respect can be described in most cases by Pound's remark on Rimbaud's "Tête de Faune": "I am not sure that we would notice the poem if we had not come, by our own route, to this precise desire."[50] While the *Effort Libre* was a very real influence on Imagist versification, and while the younger French poets helped to transform the subject matter of Imagist poetry, the French moderns might be said to have affirmed the doctrine of the image in their own ways, so that France and England and America sometimes seemed to be parts of the same school.

This paper began with a reference to F. S. Flint, and it is appropriate that it should end with him. For if Flint did not single-handedly account for the interest in modern French literature during the period, he was always the first and best informed exponent of that literature. His importance to his contemporaries in this regard is roughly like the importance of Arthur Symons to the generation before. I want to emphasize that importance because Flint is usually portrayed as a minor character in the Imagist movement. In America he is an especially obscure figure, even in comparison with Amy Lowell or J. G. Fletcher—this in spite of the fact that Robert Frost several times claimed that Flint was the originator of Imagism.[51] In the histories, he is often characterized as T. E. Hulme's adjutant, as a latecomer to the movement, and as a man so in love with French literature that he was a less discriminating critic than Pound.[52]

One can trace what may well be the source of the last of these notions. It is first voiced by Pound himself, in a letter to René Taupin: "Fort difference entre Flint: (*tolérance* pour *tous* les fautes et imbécillités des poètes français.) Moi—examen très sévère—et intolérance."[53] Pound is talking about Flint's *Poetry Review* survey, but he is both inaccurate and somewhat unfair. That particular essay has a clearly defined descriptive intent. It aims to provide a complete landscape of modern French experimentation, and it constantly defers to that aim, even though it often expresses pleasure with some poets and dissatisfaction or disagreement with others. There are, in fact, relatively few poets about whom Flint does not express some intellectual or aesthetic reservations; and it is clear that he thinks poets like Nicolas Beauduin or Henri Martin-Barzun are minor compared to Arcos, Spire, Vildrac, Duhamel, and Romains. Flint was a gentler, more self-effacing personality than Pound; his temperament was not suited to the manifesto, and that may be why he has received comparatively little attention from the historians. But even though he had what Glenn Hughes calls a "tendency toward self-disparagement" and what Richard Aldington termed "an almost imbecile modesty,"[54] that does not mean he was undiscriminating. Flint, for example, did not overpraise Jules Romains, as Pound did. Nor did he dismiss Apollinaire's *Alcools* by saying that it was "a clever book," as Pound did. On the contrary, Flint's judgment of Apollinaire—"a curious, fantastic, keen, supple poet, expert in subtle and piercing notations"[55]—is a good deal more acute than Pound's.

But all this is not so much intended to lower Pound's reputation as to raise Flint's. If he had done nothing more than write the *Poetry Review* survey, his importance to the Imagist movement would still be considerable. As a matter of fact, he did do more. As Pound himself once cryptically remarked, "Frankie is *another* study,"[56] a study that remains largely undone.

NOTES

[1] Letter to Harriet Monroe, *The Letters of Ezra Pound*, ed. D. D. Paige (New York, 1950), p. 35; René Taupin, *L'Influence du symbolisme français sur la poésie americaine (de 1910 à 1920)* (Paris, 1929), p. 91; my translation of Taupin.

I am deeply grateful to Mrs. Cyrena N. Pondrom, from whom I received much helpful advice in the preparation of this article. Her examination of the transmission of post-symbolist French influence to English poetry, 1900-1920, *The Road from Paris,* is forthcoming.

[2] See, for example, N. Christoph de Nagy, *The Poetry of Ezra Pound: The Pre-Imagist Stage* (Bern, 1960); see also Pound's letter to René Taupin, *Letters,* p. 217.

[3] *Pavannes and Divisions* (New York, 1918), p. 95. Pound's remark on p. 96 should also be noted: "The first use of the word 'Imagiste' was in my note to T. E. Hulme's five poems, printed at the end of my 'Ripostes' in the autumn of 1912." In other words, Pound began using the word immediately after the appearance of Flint's essay.

[4] *Ibid.,* p. 243.

[5] *Imagism: A Chapter in the History of Modern Poetry* (Norman, 1951), pp. 74-103.

[6] Taupin, p. 119.

[7] *Ibid.,* p. 91.

[8] Quoted by Jacob Isaacs, *The Background of Modern Poetry* (New York, 1952), p. 35.

[9] F. S. Flint, "Contemporary French Poetry," *The Poetry Review* (New York, 1952), p. 35.

[10] *Ibid.,* p. 57.

[11] *Ibid.,* p. 360.

[12] Letter to Taupin, *Letters,* p. 218.

[13] "Contemporary French Poetry," p. 361.

[14] "The Approach to Paris," *The New Age,* XIII (September 25, 1913), pp. 632-633.

[15] *Poetry and Drama,* II (March 1914), 43.

[16] "Contemporary French Poetry," p. 363.

[17] Quoted by Flint, "Contemporary French Poetry," p. 363.

[18] *Ibid.*

[19] Georges Duhamel and Charles Vildrac, *Notes sur la technique poétique* (Paris, 1925), p. 27.

[20] "Contemporary French Poetry," p. 364.

[21] *The Poems of Amy Lowell* (Boston, 1955), p. 210.

[22] Duhamel and Vildrac, p. 13.

[23] Quoted by Duhamel and Vildrac, p. 23.

[24] *Ezra Pound: Selected Poems* (London, 1928), p. 98.

[25] "The Approach to Paris," p. 632.

[26] "Imagisme," *Poetry: A Magazine of Verse*, I (March 1913), 199.

[27] Duhamel and Vildrac, p. 13.

[28] "Contemporary French Poetry," p. 411.

[29] "The French Chronicle," *Poetry and Drama*, I (September 1913), 360.

[30] *Ibid.*

[31] Coffman, pp. 196-197.

[32] "Contemporary French Poetry," p. 367.

[33] "The Approach to Paris," *The New Age*, XIII (September 18, 1913), 608.

[34] "Contemporary French Poetry," p. 383.

[35] *The Poems of Richard Aldington* (New York, 1934), p. 39.

[36] "The Approach to Paris" (September 25, 1913), p. 631.

[37] *Otherworld: Cadences* (London, 1920), pp. 6-7.

[38] *The Little Review*, II (May 1915), 23-25.

[39] As quoted in *The Little Review*, p. 31.

[40] George Lane, "Some Imagist Poets," *The Little Review*, II (May 1915), 31.

[41] *Alcools* (Garden City, N.Y., 1965), pp. 3-7.

[42] "The Approach to Paris" (September 18, 1913), p. 607.

[43] Quoted by Flint, "Contemporary French Poetry," p. 378.

[44] *The Closed Door* (London, 1917), p. 6.

[45] Letter to Glenn Hughes, *Letters*, p. 213.

[46] "Vorticism," *Fortnightly Review*, XCVI (September 1, 1914), 463.

[47] "Contemporary French Poetry," p. 357.

[48] *Cadences* (London, 1915), p. 4.

[49] "Contemporary French Poetry," p. 385.

[50] "The Approach to Paris," *The New Age*, XIII (October 16, 1913), 726.

[51] Jacob Isaacs, "Best Loved of American Poets," *The Listener*, April 1, 1954, pp. 565-566.

[52] See Herbert Read, *The True Voice of Feeling* (New York, 1953), p. 105; Coffman, pp. 106-113; Taupin, p. 91.

[53] Letter to Taupin, *Letters*, p. 216.

[54] Glenn Hughes, *Imagism and the Imagists: A Study in Modern Poetry* (Stanford, 1931), p. 165.

[55] "Contemporary French Poetry," p. 362.

[56] Letter to Michael Roberts, *Letters*, p. 296.

Elaine Rusinko

[*In the following essay, which was based on a paper presented at the National Conference of the American Association for the Advancement of Slavic Studies, Rusinko identifies similarities between Imagism and Russian Acmeism.*]

SOURCE: "Russian Acmeism and Anglo-American Imagism," in *Ulbandus Review*, Vol. 1, No. 2, Spring, 1978, pp. 37-49.

In his introduction to *The Spirit of Romance*, Ezra Pound described the history of literary criticism as "a vain struggle to find a terminology which will define something."[1] In inventing the term "Imagism," (if not the entire movement), Pound contributed to the frustration of subsequent literary critics and historians, who have vainly attempted to define this poetic school, which encompassed, at one time or another in the decade of its existence, the work of Richard Aldington, F. S. Flint, William Carlos Williams, Amy Lowell, D. H. Lawrence, T. S. Eliot, and Ezra Pound himself, among others. Described, at the one extreme, as "the starting point of modern poetry" (T. S. Eliot), and at the other as "a few points in agreement on a small number of principles for a few weeks" (René Taupin),[2] the term "Imagism" continues to defy simple definition. In Russian literary history, Acmeism has suffered much the same fate. Associated with certain clichés, no simple definition has been able to describe the work of even the movement's three outstanding representatives, Gumilev, Akhmatova, and Mandelshtam, not to mention their numerous followers and imitators.[3]

What then is to be gained from juxtaposing these two amorphous terms and analyzing the comparison? Of course, both movements deserve attention if only because they directed the early talents of what were to become outstanding poets. However, they also occupy a crucial stage in the development of modern poetry, and perhaps the study of Imagism and Acmeism is more valuable for the insight it provides into the process of literary development, a process which, especially in the early years of the twentieth century, paid little attention to national boundaries. By now it is generally recognized that Russian Symbolism was a facet of a broader, international movement, but the international scope of the movement which succeeded Symbolism is not so well known.[4] And because, within their respective literary histories, each movement has become encumbered by clichés and catch-words, perhaps the comparative approach may not be unprofitable.

However, this is not the introduction to an influence study. Though recent research has shown that Gumilev was, in fact, acquainted with certain British literary figures,[5] and that Akhmatova's later poetry demonstrates a familiarity with Eliot's work,[6] this occurred long after the creation of the principles of Acmeism, which are so similar to those expressed about the same time by the Imagists. Apparently neither group was aware of the other before about 1915.[7] Rather, each group absorbed what was in the international poetic air and reacted independently along similar lines—thus providing a much more interesting problem for the literary historian than a case of direct influence. The question then becomes, what was in that international poetic atmosphere that prompted the simultaneous spontaneous generation of Acmeism and Imagism?

This question is an illustration of how the comparative method can illuminate some of the dark spots in Russian literary history. Traditionally, Acmeism has been seen as a reaction to Symbolism. This oversimplification has, for the most part, given way to a more subtle description of Acmeism, as a continuation and reform of Symbolism. This generalization, though accurate, has outlived its usefulness. The British example suggests another approach to the question of the sources of inspiration and origins of Acmeism. Gumilev, in his manifesto "Acmeism and the Heritage of Symbolism," acknowledges only the highest sort of influence—Shakespeare, Villon, Rabelais, Gautier.[8] Though he pays homage elsewhere to Annensky and Bryusov, one gets the feeling that Gumilev was reluctant to lessen the originality of the new movement by acknowledging the influence of contemporaries. The Imagists were more candid about their models. In Pound's words, "The history of English poetic glory is a history of successful steals from the French."[9] It now becomes clear that Acmeism also owes much to French poetry, not only to the heritage of French Symbolism as filtered through Bryusov's aesthetic brand of Symbolism, but directly as well.

By the first decade of the twentieth century, the older generation of French Symbolists had ceded their positions to a new generation of poets, and these were introducing reforms in the Symbolist tradition. This younger group of poets—Remy de Gourmont, Henri de Régnier, Francis Jammes, Paul Claudel, Charles Vildrac and Georges Duhamel—objected to the excessive vagueness of their predecessors, and introduced a note of precision into their poetry. This was to be the decisive influence on both Acmeism and Imagism.[10] Though Gumilev was certainly aware of the new developments in French poetry and probably even met some of the practitioners during his stay in Paris in 1907-1908, he acknowledges them as models only in 1917, in a recently discovered article in an English journal,[11] where he singles out Jammes, Claudel, Vildrac, and Duhamel as models for Russian poets. To be sure, the 1912 Acmeist manifesto had expressed preference for Romanic light over Germanic mistiness, but nowhere is Gumilev as explicit as Pound about "going to school to the French" until after he has "singlehandedly invented," so to speak, Acmeism. No doubt a further exploration of this French influence would prove fruitful.

Despite the similarities of their origin, however, Acmeism and Imagism were not in exactly analogous starting positions. Much of the innovative groundwork already accomplished by the Symbolists in Russia—the modernization of poetic diction, experimentation with rhyme and meter—had to be done initially in England by Imagism. This accounts for the fact that Imagism is often considered the starting point of modern English poetry, whereas in Russian literary history, Acmeism is overshadowed by the more revolutionary accomplishments of both its predecessor, Symbolism, and its contemporary rival, Futurism. The Imagists were reacting against the conventionalism of the Victorian poetic tradition; the Acmeists, against the "abstractionism" of the Symbolists. The result, however, amounted to the same thing—a turn away from conventionality, banality, and vagueness to concreteness, freshness of language and perspective, and emphasis on technique. Both Acmeists and Imagists saw their purpose as therapeutic, to bring poetry out of the "blurry" nineteenth century into the "hardness" of the twentieth, to use Pound's terms.

However, considering the times and the prevalence of literary polemic, this common sense approach to technique seemed an insufficient basis for a literary school. It was necessary to have a movement complete with manifesto and ideology in order to substantiate the seriousness of the cause.[12] In fact, neither movement was as revolutionary as it liked to appear; among the modernists, both Acmeists and Imagists were traditionalists. However, a philosophy was necessary, and, in each case, the ideology proved to be the weak spot in their defenses. Gumilev's theoretical statements were deliberately provocative, and subsequent criticism of Acmeism was often aimed at the rather weak theory rather than at the poetry itself. Gumilev's counterpart as theoretician in the Imagist movement was T. E. Hulme. Hulme's writings, particularly his essay "Romanticism and Classicism,"[13] reveal a cultural conservatism and classical orientation which is not unlike that expressed by Gumilev in his Acmeist manifesto.

Writing around 1912, Hulme predicted a "classical revival" in poetry, which was to refute the romantic confusion of poetry and religion. (He calls romanticism "spilt religion" [118]). His rather idiosyncratic definition of romanticism and classicism has caused some critical confusion, but, in fact, it provides a useful framework for the understanding of post-Symbolism—Russian, as well as English. The romantic, says Hulme, "must always be talking of the infinite," always "flying off into the circumambient gas," while in classical verse, the poet never forgets the finiteness of man, "he remembers always that he is mixed up with earth." (120) This recalls Gumilev's emphasis on the distinctness of the spheres of human experience, of poetry and religion, and his insistence that poetry concern itself with the real world, instead of mystical and spiritual matters.

In opposition to romanticism's "sloppiness," Hulme proposes what he calls a "dry and hard, properly classical poetry." (126) He explains what he means by this:

> The essence of poetry to most people is that it must lead them to a beyond of some kind. Verse strictly confined to the earthly and the definite . . . might seem to them to be excellent writing, excellent craftsmanship, but not poetry. So much has romanticism debauched us, that, without some form of vagueness, we deny the highest. (127) . . . It is essential to prove that beauty may be in small, dry things. (131)

Of course, Acmeism also represented a reconsideration of aesthetic values. Gumilev complains that mystical Symbolism, that strain in which Blok and Vyacheslav Ivanov persisted, ignored the true value and beauty of material objects in favor of what they represent of the other world. Acmeism, he said, insisted on the "specific gravity" of objects. Half a year earlier, Pound had used the same metaphor to describe the attitude of Imagism: "Poetry is in some odd way concerned with the specific gravity of things."[14]

Both Hulme and Gumilev had set up their programs primarily to counter the prevailing poetic ideology and, secondarily, to support their proposals for technical reform, which, perhaps, were not really in need of ideological support. In the Russian example, the aesthetic position advocated by Gumilev could not compete successfully on the same grounds with the more sophisticated mystical philosophy of the Symbolists, and Acmeism was hampered, rather than helped, by its pseudo-philosophical backing. In the Imagist movement, however, Hulme the philosopher early gave way to Pound the poet, and the emphasis shifted from abstract theory to questions of poetic technique. Nonetheless, when we isolate the aesthetic ideals of the Acmeist-Imagist ideology—an emphasis on the earthly, the beauty of "small dry things," hardness—we find that they correspond nicely to the technical principles demonstrated by the poetry itself. These principles were never clearly formulated by the Acmeists, but Pound provides a guide for the aspiring poet in his list of rules entitled "A Few Don'ts by an Imagist."[15]

Perhaps the most fundamental "don't" warns against effortless, inspired poetry and emphasizes the importance of craftsmanship and technique. "Don't imagine that you can please the expert before you have spent at least as much effort on the art of verse as the average piano teacher spends on the art of music." (202) Again, Gumilev uses the same metaphor: "One must study to write poems, just as long and as diligently as to play the piano. After all, it wouldn't occur to anyone to play the piano, not having studied it."[16] Pound defined "technique" as "doing what one sets out to do, in the most efficient manner."[17] Technique implies control, and good writing, says Pound, is writing that is perfectly controlled, where the writer says just what he means.

This emphasis on control, on technique, was sure to antagonize those poets who considered poetry a mystery, divinely inspired. Pound anticipated criticism: "It is not uncommon to hear practicing 'poets' speak of 'technique' as if it were a thing antipathetic to poetry,"[18] and one is reminded of Hulme's prediction that the new "classicism" will not be recognized as poetry by those who have been "debauched" by romanticism. And this, in fact, is exactly how Acmeism and Imagism were received by their rivals. As late as 1921, for example, Blok objected to Gumilev's analytical article on poetic theory, "This is terrible. Up to now we have thought completely differently, . . . that for a poet, inspiration is necessary."[19] In fact, neither Acmeism nor Imagism denied the poet the possibility of genuine inspiration; indeed, if one looks past the "classical" trappings, it is apparent that both movements rest upon certain underlying romantic principles. Hulme allowed inspiration to creep into his theory under the name of "fancy." Gumilev, despite his emphasis on teaching the craft of poetry, recognized that no amount of technical knowledge can make up for the spark of talent necessary to the genuine poet, and throughout his work, he insists on the privileged and superior nature of the poet. And Pound concludes his list of rules with a quotation from Vildrac and Duhamel's *Notes sur la technique poètique:* "Mais d'abord il faut être un poète." ("Don'ts," 206)

Why then this emphasis on technique, if in the end it all comes down to being a poet? In this apparent contradiction lies an important contribution of the post-Symbolists at the expense, perhaps, of ideological consistency. Both Acmeism and Imagism were concerned not only with producing great art, but with revitalizing tradition, and for this revitalization, a "back to basics" approach was required. "Through technique alone," said Pound, "has the *art,* as distinct from the work of the accidentally inspired genius, any chance for resurrection."[29] Similarly, Gumilev praised Vyacheslav Ivanov's "great distinctive individuality," but warned that for those who do not possess his genius, to follow him would be futile. He noted the gap between "this individual solitary development" of Ivanov and "that balance of all the capacities of the spirit" which is Acmeism. (IV, 315) Whereas Symbolism had "completed its circle of development and was in decline," according to Gumilev, Acmeism represented a foundation for future poetic development.[21]

In order to foster this development, and being dedicated to the proposition that poetry is a craft that can be learned, Acmeism and Imagism went about the business of teaching it. Both Pound and Gumilev demonstrate a pedagogical approach in their theoretical writings,[22] and each was involved in actual studio work with aspiring poets.[23] Their approaches were similar. The first step in becoming a poet is to master the rules of the craft. Pound's "Don'ts" demand, "Let the neophyte know assonance and alliteration, rhyme immediate and delayed, simple and polyphonic, as a musician would expect to know harmony and counterpoint and all the minutiae of his craft. No time is too great to give to these matters . . . , even if the artist seldom have need of them." (203) Gumilev advised his students, "When you have mastered all the rules and have done innumerable poetic exercises, then you will be able to discard them and write according to inspiration, regardless of everything. As Calderon said, then you can lock the rules in a box and throw the key into the sea." (Odoevtseva, 41)

The poetry of both Pound and Gumilev, the primary teachers in their respective schools, demonstrates that they practiced what they preached. They each experimented with difficult and unusual forms—ballades, ghazals, the Japanese haiku and tanka, the Malaysian pantoum. And Imagism became identified with the innovative form "free verse," *vers libre,* which Pound insisted was at least as difficult as the conventional forms. He quotes Eliot, "No *vers* is *libre* for the man who wants to do a good job." (*Literary Essays,* 12)

Pound further advised the aspiring Imagist, in his inimitable, half-ironic manner, "Be influenced by as many great artists as you can, but have the decency either to acknowledge the debt outright, or to try to conceal it." ("Don'ts," 202) Pound readily acknowledged his own debt to the French Symbolists and the Provençal tradition of the troubadours. Gumilev's work also shows the effect of his study of troubadour poetry, as well as his debt to the French Parnassians. Other Acmeists and Imagists frankly pattern their verse after classical Greek models. In contrast to their Futurist rivals, Acmeists and Imagists were not revolutionaries; their only endeavor, as F. S. Flint put it, was "to write in accordance with the best tradition, as they found it in the best writers of all time,"[24] and Mandelshtam's definition of Acmeism (*"toska po mirovoi kul'ture"*) applies as well to the Imagists.

Going beyond mere imitation of great artists, both Imagists and Acmeists practiced the craft of poetry by doing translations. Pound advised, "Translation is . . . good training, if you find that your original matter 'wobbles' when you try to rewrite it. The meaning of the poem to be translated can not 'wobble'." ("Don'ts," 205) And Gumilev, in a theoretical article on translation, stressed the necessity of "expressing the spirit of the original through the form." (IV, 190) Both Pound and Gumilev did translations from Oriental poetry, Gumilev translated Coleridge and Gautier, Pound and the other Imagists put the Provençal poets and classical Greek poetry into English. The influence of this translation work is felt in their own poetry, where one finds numerous examples of poems whose form and imagery were inspired by the classics or by Oriental masters. The latter especially provided a model for the kind of primitivism, or fresh perspective, sought by the post-Symbolists.

Pound's well-known haiku-style poem "In a Station of the Metro" is as good an example as any of the result of Imagist craftsmanship:

> The apparition of these faces in the crowd;
> Petals on a wet, black bough.[25]

It illustrates Pound's concept of the "image,"—"that which presents an intellectual and emotional complex in an instant of time."[26] Another formulation of this doctrine of the image became the first rule of Imagism, "direct treatment of the 'thing'." (Flint, 199) Richard Aldington explained, with tongue in cheek, precisely what this meant:

> To convey emotion by presenting the object and circumstance of the emotion without comment. For example, we do not say, 'Oh how I admire that exquisite, that beautiful, that—25 more adjectives—woman' or 'o exquisite, o beautiful, o 25 more adjectives woman, you are cosmic, let us spoon for ever,' but we present that woman, we make an 'image' of her, we make the scene convey the emotion.[27]

And he uses the stanza from H.D.'s poetry as illustration: "The hard sand breaks,/ And the grains of it/ Are clear as wine."

Pound was so struck by the clarity and intensity of H.D.'s poems that he later declared that he invented Imagism in order to publicize them. However, this style of simple and vivid imagery goes back to T. E. Hulme, who insisted that poetry must always be a "solid thing," and that "each word must be an image seen, not a counter."[28] Hulme's images create "solid things" from abstract and distant objects, revitalizing motifs which had grown stale in conventional poetic usage. He sees "the ruddy moon lean over a hedge/ Like a red-faced farmer," or "tangled in the tall mast's corded height" like a "child's balloon forgotten after play."[29] Very similar is what Gumilev noted as Mandelshtam's "first Acmeism image": *"Net, ne luna a svetlyi tsiferblat/ siyaet mine."* ("No, not the moon, but a bright clock-face/ shines at me." IV, 364) In this sort of "solid imagery," the object is diminished in the interests of clarity, economy and simplicity. Gorodetsky called this device "reverse hyperbole," and claimed it as an Acmeist invention. (Timenchik, 28) Gumilev's poetry provides many examples: "the sunset like a cracked melon" (I, 249), or the "eye of the sun . . . like the heart of a pomegranate" (II, 79). And of course, Akhmatova's "concrete imagery" is too well known to require comment. This return to the "modesty" of the concrete image was a significant part of the revitalization of the art. As Pound put it,

> It is not until poetry lives again 'close to the thing' that it will be a vital part of contemporary life. As long as the poet says not what he . . . means, but

is content to say something ornate and approximate, just so long will serious people, intently alive, consider poetry as balderdash—a sort of embroidery for dilletantes and women.[30]

The second Imagist rule, to use absolutely no word that does not contribute to the presentation, accounts for the terseness of much of Imagist, and similarly, Acmeist verse. Resembling Pound's haiku-style "Metro" poem is Gumilev's short poem, written in the style of the Oriental tanka:

Vot devushka s gazelimi glazami
Vykhodit zamuzh za amerikantsa—
Zachem Kolumb Ameriku otkryl?

The girl with eyes like a gazelle
Is marrying an American—
Why did Columbus discover America?

(II, 166)

Pound called this technique the "presentative method" as opposed to the "representational method" of Symbolism: "It means constatation of fact. It presents. It does not comment. The presentative method is equity. It fights for a sane valuation. It cannot bring fine things into ridicule. It will not pervert a thing from its true use by trying to ascribe to it alien uses."[31] This formulation is strikingly similar to Mandelshtam's wonder at the law of identity, A = A,[32] and his description of the chaos that reigned in Symbolism, where every pot and broom refused to accept its true earthly function and demanded a higher, absolute, symbolic significance.[33] Again this principle, essential to Acmeism and Imagism, can be traced to the French. Francis Jammes writes, "The poet arrives at an age where, when he says, the sky is blue, this expression is sufficient." (Quoted in Taupin, 104) With Acmeism and Imagism, not only the individual poet, but poetry as a whole reached this paradoxical stage of sophisticated primitivism.

The creative moment of modern poetry represented by Acmeism and Imagism foundered upon the destructive reality of war and revolution. The movements were short-lived, and their contributions to poetic theory and ideology were sparse and diffuse. However, if Acmeism and Imagism did not bring a new metaphysic or system of ideas to modern poetry, they did contribute to a renewed aesthetic taste, an attitude toward the nature and function of poetry, which has characterized the mainstream of modern poetry to the present day. As Mandelshtam noted, literary schools live not by ideas, but by tastes. ("On the Nature of the Word," 299) The taste for simplicity, clarity, economy, and craftsmanship is the heritage of Acmeism and Imagism, which is still alive in modern Russian and English poetry.[34]

NOTES

[1] Ezra Pound, *The Spirit of Romance* (Norfolk, Conn.: New Directions, 1952), p. 13.

[2] Quoted by W. C. Pratt in the introduction to *The Imagist Poem: Modern Poetry in Miniature* (New York: Dutton, 1963), pp. 12, 14.

[3] See "Toward a Definition of Acmeism," a supplementary issue of *Russian Language Journal* (Spring 1975).

[4] The primary treatment of the international aspects of Russian Symbolism is Georgette Donchin's *The Influence of French Symbolism on Russian Poetry* (The Hague: Mouton, 1958). René Taupin's study, *L'Influence du symbolisme français sur la poèsie américaine* (Paris: Champion, 1929), deals with Anglo-American post-Symbolism in the international context. Russian Acmeism has not been treated as part of an international movement, except for Ryszard Przybylski's comparison of the ideas of Mandelshtam and T. E. Hulme, cited in N. S. Gumilev, *Sobranie sochinenii v chetyrekh tomakh*, ed. G. P. Struve and B. A. Filippov (Washington: Kamkin, 1962-1968), Vol. IV, p. 631.

[5] See my article, "Gumilev in London: An Unknown Interview," *Russian Literature Triquarterly*, No. 16 (Winter 1978).

[6] V. N. Toporov, "K otzvukam zapadnoevropeiskoi poezii u Akhmatovoi." *Slavic Poetics*, ed. Roman Jakobson, et al. (The Hague: Mouton, 1973).

[7] The first article on Imagism in a Russian journal seems to be Z. Vengerova's "Angliiskie futuristy," *Strelets*, No. 1 (1915), pp. 93-104.

[8] N. S. Gumilev, "Nasledie simvolizma i akmeizm," *Sobranie sochinenii v chetyrekh tomakh*, Vol. IV, pp. 171-176. Subsequent references to this edition will be cited in the text by volume and page number.

[9] *The New Age,* September 11, 1913, p. 577.

[10] The French influence was introduced into England in 1911 by Ford Maddox Hueffer and F. S. Flint; in 1913, Pound wrote a series of articles for the British journal *The New Age* where he reviewed the merits of contemporary French poetry and held up the new generation of Symbolists as models. In Russia, it was a French poet and correspondent to the Symbolist journal *Vesy,* and later to *Apollon,* René Ghil, who introduced the new French poets.

[11] C. R. Bechhofer, "An Interview with Nicholas Gumileff," *The New Age,* June 28, 1918. Reprinted in *Russian Literature Triquarterly,* No. 16 (Winter 1978).

[12] There is evidence that the Acmeist manifesto was prompted by the rivalry of the Futurists. (R. D. Timenchik, "Zametki ob akmeizme," *Russian Literature,* No. 7-8 [1974], p. 25.) Stanley Coffman, a scholar of Imagism, suggests that Pound recognized that his program might profit by being presented as a militant aesthetic movement similar to those which were attracting attention at the time. (*Imagism: A Chapter for the History of Modern Poetry* [Folcroft, Pa.: Folcroft Press, 1970], p. 138.)

[13] Included in *Speculations: Essays on Humanism and the Philosophy of Art,* ed. by Herbert Read (New York: Harcourt, Brace and Company, 1924), pp. 113-140.

[14] *Poetry Review,* Vol. I, No. 3 (March 1912), p. 134.

[15] *Poetry,* Vol. I, No. 6 (March 1913), pp. 200-206.

[16] Quoted in Irina Odoevtseva, *Na beregakh Nevy* (Washington: Kamkin, 1967), p. 41.

[17] "The Serious Artist," in *Literary Essays of Ezra Pound,* ed. T. S. Eliot (Norfolk, Conn.: New Directions, 1954), p. 54.

[18] *The New Age,* January 25, 1912, p. 297.

[19] "Bez bozhestva, bez vdokhnoveniya," *Sobranie sochinenii* (Moscow and Leningrad, 1962), Vol. VI, p. 182.

[20] *The New Age,* February 15, 1912, p. 370.

[21] It is ironic, of course, that Acmeism, the movement, has been largely overshadowed by the "great distinctive individualities" of Akhmatova and Mandelshtam, a development which Gumilcv, apparently, did not foresee.

[22] Note, for example, the titles of their articles: Pound, "The ABC of Reading," "How to Read"; Gumilev, "Chitatel'."

[23] "Arts should be taught by artists, not sterile professors." Pound, quoted in Coffman, *Imagism,* p. 90.

[24] F.S. Flint, "Imagisme," *Poetry,* Vol. I, No. 6 (March 1913), p. 199.

[25] "In a Station of the Metro" appeared first in *Poetry,* Vol. 2, No. 1. (April 1913), and was subsequently included in the collection *Lustra,* and in *Personae: The Collected Shorter Poems of Ezra Pound* (New York: New Directions, 1926), p. 109.

[26] The emphasis on images was to come up in a subsequent poetic movement in Russia, Imaginism, and had no exact parallel in Acmeism. In the case of the later movement, there is evidence of direct influence of the English group on the Russian poets, in the notes of a British foreign correspondent. (*Times Literary Supplement,* October 13, 1921, p. 661.) See also Nils Åke Nilsson, *The Russian Imaginists* (Stockholm: Almquist and Wiksell, 1970).

[27] Richard Aldington, "Modern Poetry and the Imagists," *The Egoist,* Vol. 1, No. 11 (June 1914), p. 202.

[28] *Notes on Language and Style,* ed. Herbert Read (1929; rpt. Folcroft, Pa.: Folcroft Press, 1970), p. 11.

[29] From "Above the dock" and "Autumn." The "Complete Poetical Works of T. E. Hulme" is included as an appendix in *Speculations,* pp. 265-267.

[30] *The New Age,* February 15, 1912, p. 370.

[31] *The New Age,* October 2, 1913, p. 662.

[32] "Utro akmeizma," *Sobranie sochinenii,* ed. G. P. Struve and B. A. Filippov (Munich: Inter-Language Literary Associates, 1966), Vol. II, p. 366.

[33] "O prirode slova," *Sobranie sochinenii,* Vol. II, p. 297.

[34] A preliminary version of this article was presented at the National Conference of the American Association for the Advancement of Slavic Studies in Columbus, October 1978.

INFLUENCE AND LEGACY

Terry Whalen

[*In the following essay, Whalen identifies Imagist qualities in the poetry of Philip Larkin.*]

SOURCE: "Philip Larkin's Imagist Bias: His Poetry of Observation," in *Critical Quarterly,* Vol. 23, No. 2, Summer, 1981, pp. 29-46.

Larkin's use of traditional poetic forms and his openly expressed contempt for Modernism have gained for him a reputation as a relatively provincial poet. Many see his admiration for such minor poets as John Betjeman, for instance, as being in step with the narrow taste he exhibits in the selections which make up his edition of *The Oxford Book of Twentieth-Century Verse* (1973). Evaluating the technical cleverness of Modernist jazz musicians, Larkin has remarked that 'I dislike such things not because they are new, but because they are irresponsible exploitations of technique in contradiction of life as we know it. This is my essential criticism of modernism, whether perpetuated by Parker, Pound or Picasso: it helps us neither to enjoy nor endure'.[1] Modernist art is given to obscurity without profundity, is inclined to pretentiousness. In an interview with Ian Hamilton, Larkin has expressed his impatience this way:

> What I do feel a bit rebellious about is that poetry seems to have got into the hands of a critical industry which is concerned with culture in the abstract, and this I do rather lay at the door of Eliot and Pound . . . I think a lot of this 'myth-kitty' business has grown out of that, because first of all you have to be terribly educated, you have to read everything to know these things, and secondly you've got somehow to work them in to show that you are working them in. But to me . . . the whole of classical and biblical mythology means very little, and I think that using them today not only fills poems full of dead spots but dodges the writer's duty to be original. (*London Magazine,* 4 (Nov. 1964), pp. 71-2)

On the basis of these kinds of reservations, it therefore makes sense that Larkin's critics have acquired the habit of discussing his poetry away from the Modernists and next to the work of such figures as Edward Thomas and Thomas Hardy, or discuss it in the context of the more close-up tradition of the Movement poets. But Larkin's poetry is not as alien to the work of the Modernists as first thoughts tend to assume.

An overlooked impulse in Larkin's poetry is its Imagist bias; Larkin is a poet of observation *par excellence,* and his own literary criticism is punctuated with comments which have an Imagist ring to them. It is arguable that his rejection of the Modernists is really no more than a healthy cynicism about their more pedantic and cryptic gestures, and that his own poetry and his views on poetry are in rhythm with an Imagist kind of wisdom. Robert Conquest once said that Movement poetry is 'empirical in its attitude to all that comes',[2] a statement which provokes one to notice that Larkin is essentially a poet of sensation and impression, a craftsman who enacts the levity of Wallace Stevens's claim that 'The greatest poverty is not to live / In the physical world'.[3] Larkin is exceptionally alert to the surface suggestions of the immediate physical world, and he is also a poet of delicate epiphany. In this basically Imagist bias of his art we can recognize some of his finest poetic effects. Additionally, the anti-romantic nature of much Imagist theory is in almost exact consonance with his disposition as a poet of restraint.

Larkin's is a poetry of visual participation in the observable physical world. His speakers often beckon the reader into a beholding process. 'Look', says the speaker in 'Home is so sad', at 'the pictures and the cutlery. / The music in the piano stool. That vase'.[4] This kind of invitation to witness is not simply an accident of form in Larkin's work, it is the result of an epistemological conviction that the truth—as Larkin sees it—is inseparable from an empirical alertness of mind ('When I see a couple of kids', begins the speaker in 'High windows'). In an important and central way, Larkin's speakers are like the people on the train in 'The Whitsun weddings'; they are 'loaded with the sum of all they saw'. What we, as readers, see is the product of the engagement of an empirical intelligence and a sensitive poetic personality with the physical fact of the world. We are involved in the process by proxy, join the perceptual journey in accordance with the degree of our own willingness to respond to the substance and the suggestiveness of the world as he presents it. The reader ventures little distance in the world of Larkin's poetry unless he participates in the speaker's empirical glance. Any concentrated experience of Larkin's poetry includes the visual process of looking, noticing, gazing, even staring at the world, as it is carefully recreated in its curious detail. The most trivial sorting of Larkin's lines in this regard gives evidence of at least *his* insistence on the importance of the process:

> For the moment, wait,
> Look down at the yard. Outside seems old
>   enough:
> Red brick, lagged pipes, and someone walking by
>   it
> Out to the car park, free.
>
> ('The building')

> One sees, with a sharp tender shock,
> His hand withdrawn, holding her hand.
>
> ('An Arundel tomb')

> My swivel eye hungers from pose to pose—
> ('Lines on a young lady's photograph album')

> The eye can hardly pick them out
> From the cold shade they shelter in,
> Till the wind distresses tail and mane
>
> ('At grass')

> The eye sees you
> Simplified by distance
> Into an origin
>
> ('Solar')

> Latest face, so effortless
> Your great arrival at my eyes
>
> ('Latest face')

> One shivers slightly, looking up there.
>
> ('Sad steps')

In what amounts to a habit of beholding visual sensitivity, Larkin aligns his art with an honoured tradition of empirically oriented poetry, one which reaches backward throughout most of the great poetry of the English speaking tradition. The centre of gravity in Larkin's poetry is the physical world as it suggestively manifests itself on the stage of his sensitive and personal imagination. The Imagists attempted to retrieve that empirical tradition in the early part of this century, and briefly to survey anew some of their comments in the context of Larkin's own reviews and his poetry is to recognise their legacy in the midst of his attitude to craft.

In an assembled shower of phrases from Larkin's critical work which follows, there is a kinship between Larkin's pencilling of empirical graces and the similarly pictorial bias of the Imagist theorists. In a recent comment on 'the poet' Larkin has stressed the need for the poet 'to recreate the familiar'.[5] And particularly of Barnes, he has said that his 'view of nature is clear . . . and shining, full of exquisite pictorial natures'.[6] His empirical bias is shown, in a negative context, in his comments on Auden's *Homage to Clio* (1960). In a review of that volume, he regretted the intrusion of a new 'abstract windiness' into Auden's style, censoriously noting that Auden's poetry needed to find 'root again in the life surrounding him rather than in his reading'.[7] He praises the fact that in Betjeman 'the eye leads the spirit',[8] and we can add to his lauding of this talent his claim that Betjeman holds a 'belief that a poem's meaning should be communicated directly and not by symbol',[9] and his notice of Betjeman's 'astonishing command of detail, both visual and circumstantial'.[10]

Appropriately, one concludes the shower with Larkin's tribute to Hardy's ability to 'often be extremely direct'[11] in his treatment of the physical world. In his recognition of Hardy's talent for 'a kind of telescoping of a couple of images',[12] he points to a quality of Hardy's craft which makes us realise—or perhaps simply to remember—that Hardy is a major figure in the maintenance of the imagistic base of English poetry. On such evidence we recognise in Larkin's concerns, and in his phrasing of them, a connection with the language of T. E. Hulme, and Ezra Pound. Phrases such as 'extremely direct', or 'exquisite pictorial natures', and the 'telescoping of a couple of images', are consonant with—if not in echo of—the terminology of the Imagist theorists.

If we go back to the Imagist theorists, we recall their desire to animate again the empirical basis of thought and art, and in that aim we can recognise many of Larkin's similar concerns. Thus, in a language which is in kinship with Larkin's own critical standards, there is Hulme's comment that: 'Poetry . . . is not a counter language, but a *visual concrete one*. It is a compromise for a language of intuition which would hand over sensations bodily. It always endeavours to arrest you, and to *make you continuously see a physical thing,* to prevent you gliding through an abstract process'[13] (my emphasis). For Hulme, this is not a mere matter of contriving a concrete metaphor in the work, but rather has to do with the empirical authenticity of the thought process which the poem embodies. The poem is conceived as a re-creation of the physical world as perceived in a moment of unusually alert attention to the meaning of its face. Hulme was therefore to say that 'Whenever you get an extraordinary interest in a thing, a great zest in its contemplation . . . you have justification for poetry' ('Romanticism and classicism", p. 102). And when he tried to create a critical litmus test for the authenticity of any given poem in this regard, he said that a quality of 'freshness' is visible, a freshness which is difficult to sham: 'Freshness convinces you, you feel at once that the artist was in an actual physical state. You feel that for a minute' (*ibid.,* p. 103). It is a comment which is in step with Pound's directive that the poet must 'use his *image* because he sees or feels it, *not* because he thinks he can use it to back up some system of ethics or economics',[14] a comment which somewhat ironically sounds like an early version of Larkin's scorn of 'myth-kitty'. Much of Larkin's poetry even centrally and exclusively contains a good deal of that 'zest' and that 'freshness' of which Hulme speaks. It is there, for instance, in the virtual tumble of detail from the physical world, which is at the living base of his poem, 'Show Saturday'. It is a poem which has a crowded life of its own, a Breughel-like grasp of the immediacy of life's plural detail:

> In the main arena, more judges meet by a jeep;
> The jumping's on next. Announcement,
>   splutteringly loud.
>
> Clash with the quack of a man with pound notes
>   round his hat
> And a lit-up board. There's more than just
>   animals:
> Bead-stalls, balloon-men, a Bank; a beer-marquee
>   that
> Half-screens a canvas Gents; a tent selling tweed,
> And another, jackets. Folks sit about on bales

> Like great straw dice. For each scene is linked by
>   spaces
> Not given to anything much, where kids scrap,
>   freed,
> While their owners stare different ways with
>   incurious faces.
> The wrestling starts, late; a wide ring of people;
>   then cars;
> Then trees; then pale sky. Two young men in
>   acrobats' tights
> And embroidered trunks hug each other; rock over
>   the grass,
> Stiff-legged, in a two-man scrum. One falls: they
>   shake hands.
> Two more start, one gray-haired: he wins, though.
>   They're not so much fights
>
> As long immobile strainings that end in unbalance
> With one on his back, unharmed, while the other
>   stands
> Smoothing his hair. But there are other talents—

The 'zest' continues in a celebratory rendering of a freshly animated imagery of objects, people, and their gestures. In its observation of the plural tumble of life it is reminiscent of what Randall Jarrell has termed the 'empirical gaiety'[15] of William Carlos Williams's art. And it is an effect which Larkin also manages in 'The Whitsun weddings' and 'To the sea' and it is attributable to his empirical curiosity of mind and his kinship with the Imagists' view of the poem as the act of the mind in close contact with the physical world.

But it is neither the conviction of the Imagist theorists nor of Larkin that poetry is only the act of the empirical imagination in continual representation of the world's plenitude. The mistake of many of the Imagist poets was that they mistook simple selection of objects for actually saying something profound. The quality of freshness is there as part of Larkin's authenticating reality, but the expressive dimension of his poetry transforms the empirical glance into something much larger, more interesting and coherent. For Larkin, an impression of the world is at the stimulating base of the work, but there is also a process of thought regarding the impression which he also conveys. In this sense, he can be said to take the Imagist theorists more seriously than did many of the Imagist practitioners.

Larkin's Imagist impulse is visible in the process of empirical thought which is embodied in each of his works separately. Each poem evokes the world and ponders it without leaving it behind. It is for this reason that his symbolic effects are natural, and seem to rise inevitably from within the context of the poem's individual setting. This strategy of form is at work in the exploratory empiricism of 'Church going', 'The old fools', and 'High windows', for example. Interestingly, the symbolism which this kind of poetry embodies is that which Pound described as the 'perfect symbol'. Pound describes it: '*Symbols.*—I believe that the proper and perfect symbol is the natural object, that if a man uses "symbols" he must so use them that their symbolic function does not obtrude; so that *a* sense, and the poetic quality of the passage, is not lost to those who do not understand the symbol as such, to whom, for instance, a hawk is a hawk' ('A few don'ts', 1913; reprinted in Shapiro, p. 105). Larkin is a master of exactly this kind of effect, and it is one which he admires in the work of Hardy and Betjeman. The physical visage of the church in 'Church going', for instance, is empirically rendered as evidence of the speaker's thematic point about the decline of traditional belief. A survey of its details shows it to be a living index of the decline of all the values which it once more vigorously embodied. And in Larkin's evocation of the physical fact of the hospital in 'The building', the empirical imagination registers it as a naturally symbolic expression of the human desire to build it physically and spiritually into a substitute cathedral:

> Higher than the handsomest hotel
> The lucent comb shows up for miles, but see,
> All round it close-ribbed streets rise and fall
> Like a great sigh out of the last century.
> The porters are scruffy; what keep drawing up
> At the entrance are not taxis, and in the hall
> As well as creepers hangs a frightening smell.

The circumstantial contemplation of the poem proceeds from here through another ten stanzas. As the speaker wanders through the hospital's sights, he gathers images of the fearful faces of the entering patients. The gestures of the patients accumulate into a powerful imaginative logic, one in which the stock natural symbolism of the hospital as substitute church is finally questioned. On the basis of the speaker's witness of the setting, he deduces that the proper metaphor for the hospital is that of a prison. 'O world', says the speaker in the sixth stanza, 'Your loves, your chances, are beyond the stretch / Of any hand from here!' And as the cumulative impression of the hospital reaches a cohering moment of integrity, he expresses the meaning of the building in a manner of saddened empirical discovery. The hospital is a natural symbol, not of healing, but of the undeniable existential fact of death. In keeping with its consistent use of natural symbolism, the speaker concludes his experiential journey through the physical details of the place, by saying of the patients that:

> All know they are going to die.
> Not yet, perhaps not here, but in the end,
> And somewhere like this. This is what it means,
> This clean-sliced cliff; a struggle to transcend
> The thought of dying, for unless its powers
> Outbuild cathedrals nothing contravenes
> The coming dark, though crowds each evening try

> With wasteful, weak, propitiatory flowers.

Thematically, the poem deals with the inadequacy of modern man's attempt to outbuild death with a new faith in medicine and technology. Ironically, the very attempt to defeat death is seen as an evasion of its presence. All of the appearance of control is an illusion. And yet the fix we are in is that religious illusions are seen as even less adequate. Up the street from the hospital is a 'locked

church'. The natural symbolism of that fact is compelling evidence for the speaker's case. Hence, in a contemplation in which the physical world is intimately involved in the process of thought, the speaker accumulates the empirical evidence into a dismally accurate conclusion, given the circumstances. To use a phrase from 'Lines on a young lady's photograph album', what is 'In every sense empirically true' about the hospital is its visible testimony of our pathetic weakness in the face of the mortality which it tries to outbuild. The 'wasteful, weak, propitiatory flowers' complete the foray into reality as an embodied epiphany, the discovery of a telling clue. The flowers, in their naturally symbolic effect, indicate the fragility of the human being, its sad beauty. They project a sadly ironic truth. For all their smallness, there is more meaning in their failure than in the illusion of the longevity which the 'clean-sliced cliff' unsuccessfully projects.

It was Stevens who said that 'Much of the world of fact is the equivalent of the world of imagination',[16] which is an empirical conviction that is at the centre of this poem, and it can also be said to underline a good deal of Larkin's poetry as a whole. None the less, the world of fact is uninteresting unless sifted and rearranged into meaning by the unifying intelligence of the poet. Additionally, the poet's colouring of the fact of the world by his poetic personality gives it a dimension which takes it still further past a mere suspension of objects.

Neither Larkin nor Stevens claims that the poem of reality, the poem of empirical fact, is an objectively verifiable medium of truth. Stevens has said that 'Poetry is an unofficial view of being' ('Imagination as value', p. 222), and Larkin, I think, would agree. But it is worth noticing that the poetry of this order does mimic the inductive method, can be said to be more directly experiential than more confidently mythic poetry. On the basis of that distinction, it is given to an openness to experience, an intelligence of the senses which more traditionally mythic poetry will tend to lack. Grounded in actual observation, each poem becomes—as Larkin once described it—its 'own sole freshly-created universe',[17] and has an integrity in the recognisable world of experience.

The subjective dimension of the poem lies in the fact that it is precisely the personality of the poet which enables him to realise a meaning in what he sees. It is the emotional colouring of the personae which gives a uniqueness to the particular vision of the physical world. Thus, it is the familiar ironic persona of Larkin's 'Mr Bleaney' which colours the world which that poem embodies. The world perceived in the poem is one which that particular persona has an inclination to recognise. Paradoxically, the persona's limitation of perception is his very qualification *for* the uniqueness of his moment of vision.

Larkin finds the reality of the sub-heroic Mr Bleaney indexed in the physical details of his room. The prosaic quality of Bleaney's existence is captured in the speaker's beholding empirical consciousness. His eye collects impressions in a journey toward comprehension:

Flowered curtains, thin and frayed,
Fall to within five inches of the sill,

Whose window shows a strip of building land,
Tussocky, littered. 'Mr Bleaney took
My bit of garden properly in hand.'
Bed, upright chair, sixty-watt bulb, no hook

Behind the door, no room for books or bags—
'I'll take it.' So it happens that I lie
Where Mr Bleaney lay, and stub my fags
On the same saucer-souvenir . . .

The objects which are selected to compromise the contemplation have all the freshness and realistic presence which Hulme stated as necessary to the image. But the ordering of the images, the connecting of the spaces between them, is the cohering process which gives the poem its true brilliance. And the poem beckons us to participate in that process. There is a unifying quality in all of the central images, an essence which is recognised and abstracted. At the same time the process of thought is stated in the natural symbolism of the objects just as they are also collected into a perceptible whole. We notice the dearth of aesthetic demeanour in Bleaney's room, and how the 'Tussocky, littered' strip of building land shares with the equally tussocky curtains, light bulb, and minimally functional furniture, an unkempt, unfinished quality which physically represents Mr Bleaney's life. All of these images have an analogous form; they quite naturally represent the protean quality of Bleaney's life. Significantly, it is because the speaker detects a similarly tossed clumsiness in the sky that the somewhat glib persona can consent to an existential respect for Bleaney's unambitious and awkwardly low-keyed existence:

But if he stood and watched the frigid wind
Tousling the clouds, lay on the fusty bed
Telling himself that this was home, and grinned,
And shivered, without shaking off the dread

That how we live measures our own nature,
And at his age having no more to show
Than one hired box should make him pretty sure
He warranted no better, I don't know.

The 'frigid wind / Tousling the clouds', bears an analogous relation to the 'strip of land / Tussocky, littered'. Even the sounds are analogous to the similar visage of pictures. Because of this ragged quality which is noticed in all selected details of the scene, Bleaney's life is perceived as having a kind of sanction for its prosiness which is noticed as somehow written into the scheme of things. There are people like Bleaney, says the speaker, just as there are days and settings like the one here evoked. In the poet's foray into reality in this particular 'sole freshly-created universe', there is a realised recognition of this truth. And in terms of Imagist theory, the poem passes the test; there is the illusion that, in Hulme's words, 'the artist was in an actual physical state', and in the participating experience of reading the poem, 'You feel that for a minute'.

This physical orientation of thought and expression in Larkin's work is one of the major grounds on which we recognise a consonance of his craft—and of brilliance—with the Imagists. Both Hulmè and Larkin seem to agree that, as Stevens aptly puts it, 'Accuracy of observation is the equivalent of accuracy of thinking'.[18] Stevens also once said that 'The real is the only base. But it is the base' (*Adagia*, p. 160). The real is the stimulus, and is an integral part of the thinking process of the poem. And the poet's personality plays a central part in the colouring of the real, just as the real often challenges the colour of his view, altering its shade. The Imagist impulse in Larkin's work is always part of a larger interest in personal expression, usually of new personal discovery in the complex conversation of thinking and feeling which takes place between the poet and his world. We see this in the process of thought which 'Mr Bleaney' expresses. Further, Larkin quite typically completes the empirical journey with a qualifying agnostic gesture. The speaker finally says, 'I don't know', indicating that the epiphany of existential raggedness in the poem is not meant as a controlling perception in the world of his imagination. There is often a final scepticism in Larkin's poems. His speakers continually undercut themselves in gestures of doubt, express an urbane negative capability, an unwillingness to nail down their ponderings into dogmatic conclusions. Additionally, Larkin is a poet capable of adopting radically different postures and personae. He once said that 'What I should like to write is different kinds of poems that might be by different people',[19] a comment which exists as caveat for a legion of critics who have tried to find a singularity of tone (usually a bleak one) in his work. Some of Larkin's personae are humorous and sarcastic ones, others are deeply sad, while still others are impressed by beauty, have an instinct for praise, and a sense of the mystical profound. And because of the temporary, circumstantial nature of his individual poems, no single poem can comfortably be said to represent his complete view; he resists conclusiveness with as much energy as many of his critics pursue it.

Larkin is a poet who writes from a versatile poetic personality, and, as in 'Mr Bleaney', the persona which he adopts is the one which he finds most appropriate to the setting which he confronts. And his settings are not always especially chosen to be dreary ones, just as the epiphany which rises from the setting does not always match the visage of the setting as we are at first led to view it. If, for instance, we turn to 'Dublinesque', the 'freshly-created universe' is, as the poet requires, *'freshly . . . created'*. The speaker in the poem wears the familiar persona of poignant sadness, and also embodies Larkin's much overlooked instinct for praise. In its registration of a complex moment of epiphany, it reminds us of the subtlety of the Imagists' view in this regard. Its brilliant achievement characterises the Imagist requirement that the poem represent a moment of highly suggestive illumination or epiphany out of the context of the immediate physical world:

Down stucco sidestreets,
Where light is pewter
And afternoon mist
Brings lights on in shops

Above race-guides and rosaries,
A funeral passes.

The hearse is ahead,
But after there follows
A troop of streetwalkers
In wide flowered hats,
Leg-of-mutton sleeves,
And ankle-length dresses.

There is an air of great friendliness,
As if they were honouring
One they were fond of;
Some caper a few steps,
Skirts held skilfully
(Someone claps time),

And of a great sadness also.
As they wend away
A voice is heard singing
Of Kitty, or Katy,
As if the name meant once
All love, all beauty.

Wallace Stevens has said that 'Poetry increases the feeling for reality' (*Adagia,* p. 162), and in this poem it takes the shape of a feeling for an entire culture. There is an essentially Imagist pictorial visibility to the scene, and the speaker's empirical imagination searches out, and *real*ises the living reality of its physical world. The juxtaposition of the 'race-guides and rosaries' telescopes two contradictory images between which blossoms an empirically shrewd comment about the life and culture of Dublin. Larkin is here in effortless company with Joyce, giving us an immediate sense of the culture, its physical-spiritual reality. The poem as a whole embodies a moment of epiphany, one in which the ostensible contradictions in the scene are blended musically into an illumination. The illumination is based on a perception of a quality which pervades life in Dublin like the 'afternoon mist' which so evanescently suggests its surface. Hence, while the fact of the funeral initially appears in odd contradiction to the gaiety of the funeral party, a gaiety which is caught in the speaker's participation in the liveliness of its visage in the middle stanzas, the empirical intelligence accumulates the particulars of the scene into something more profound. At its centre is the recognition of a sadly beautiful quality in the life which is witnessed. As in "Home is so sad', there is a recognition of a spirited courage in the energy of the people, one which saves the speaker from a simply pathetic conclusion. The sound of the voice 'singing / Of Kitty, or Katy', rises from the scene as audibly appropriate to the imagery. In that sound, and in the sight of the physical world of the poem, it rises as a very Irish version of a Wordsworthian 'still, sad music of humanity', one which is as poignantly beautiful as it is also energetic. Larkin's respect for it shows in a rising tone of praise which turns the epiphany to song.

Stevens has said that 'Reality is the spirit's true center' (*Adagia,* p. 162) and we can add that the spirit is also the true centre of reality in Larkin's world. The close interplay, the conversation, between spirit and the physical world is the fulcrum on which the empirical poise of his poetry rests. His personae, each of which is governed by an astute empirical intelligence, show a willingness to move exploratively into the living detail of actually felt or imagined physical worlds. Larkin himself sees the act of recreating the experience from which the poem takes its inception to be an act of victory over time, and his statement on the matter sounds very like an essentially Imagist conviction about the work of art as the expression of life's rarest moments of realization, the poet's moments of epiphany. With the experience of 'Dublinesque' present as example, one recognises the more specifically that the following comment by Larkin has an Imagist ring to it:

> I write poems to preserve things I have seen/thought/felt (if I may so indicate a composite and complex experience) both for myself and for others, though I feel that my prime responsibility is to the experience itself, which I am trying to keep from oblivion for its own sake. Why I should do this I have no idea, but I think the impulse to preserve lies at the bottom of all art.

(*Poets of the 1950's,* pp. 77-8)

Significantly, Larkin emphasises a close connection between seeing, thinking, and feeling. In his view, each poem recreates a real perception, moves it upward into the kind of transcendence from time which the work of art, in its qualified way, can assure. In his statement of his preservative instinct, Larkin echoes the Imagist notion, once expressed by Hulme, that 'Literature, like memory, selects only the vivid patches of life', and that in a sense 'Life is composed of exquisite moments and the rest is only shadows of them'.[20] Larkin's comment on his motivation to preserve not only underlines the accomplishment of 'Dublinesque', it brings to mind Pound's famous description of the 'Image' and his description of its epiphanic effect of managing a victory over time and place. When the writer successfully conveys the complexity of the experience which Larkin has termed a 'seen/thought/felt' one, he approximates the 'Image' which Pound had described as: 'that which represents an intellectual and emotional complex in an instant of time . . . It is the presentation of such a "complex" instantaneously which gives the sense of a sudden liberation; that sense of freedom from time limits and space limits; that sense of sudden growth, which we experience in the presence of the greatest works of art' ('A few don'ts', 1913; reprinted in Shapiro, 105). Both Pound and Larkin, in strikingly similar terminology, express a view of art which is concerned with the registration of a moment of perception in time that seems to transcend our more ordinary awareness of life. Of course, it is a classic definition of the artist that he is the one who sees/thinks/feels more than the people around him, and is able to articulate the complexity of his insights. The artist is the person who makes public his diary of perceptive moments. 'Dublinesque' and a whole series of Larkin's poems carefully enact the process involved in the selection of the 'vivid patches of life' which he has deemed worth transforming into public statement. 'Dublinesque' is the act of preservation of a thing which is 'seen/thought/felt'. In the empirical sharpness of its Imagist base, and the characteristic sensitivity of its triumph, it is the registration of a moment of deeply felt connection of the poet with his world.

Moments of epiphany are of central importance in Larkin's work. The complexity and delicacy of his art lies precisely in the carefully recreated difficulty of perception which these moments embody. In especially his longer poems, he registers transcending epiphanies which heighten inevitably as his speakers' observations accumulate into vision. The lengthy observations of the speaker in 'The Whitsun weddings', for instance, gather into a concluding statement of praise and celebration which transcends ordinary limits of awareness and moves to that 'lift off the ground' (to borrow Larkin's own locution for the effect)[21] which we associate with the poetry of vision:

> There we were aimed. And as we raced across
>   Bright knots of rail
> Past standing Pullmans, walls of blackened moss
> Came close, and it was nearly done, this frail
> Travelling coincidence; and what it held
> Stood ready to be loosed with all the power
> That being changed can give. We slowed again,
> And as the tightened brakes took hold, there
>   swelled
> A sense of falling, like an arrow-shower
> Sent out of sight, somewhere becoming rain.

The image travels safely past easy analysis. The effect is a vorticistic one in that it recalls Pound's claim that the 'VORTEX' is a 'radiant node or cluster' of imagery, a complex 'from which and through which, and into which, ideas are constantly rushing' ('Vorticism', p. 469). Larkin's strategy of imagery captures all of the beauty, pathos, hope, anxiety, and deep sense of community which the 'frail/Travelling coincidence' finally represents for the speaker. The vorticistic design of the imagery moves triumphantly past mere idea and arrives at the rich suggestivity of Imagist art.

In other poems, Larkin uses the suggestive dimension of images to further his more religious speculations. He quite often knocks at those doors of eternity which, at the same time, he tends to think lead nowhere. As the speaker in 'The old fools' contemplates a calmness in the old people, he momently cheers himself with the thought that their minds have distilled images from experience which linger in a deeply intimating way:

> Perhaps being old is having lighted rooms
> Inside your head, and people in them, acting.
> People you know, yet can't quite name; each
>   looms
> Like a deep loss restored, from known doors
>   turning,
> Setting down a lamp, smiling from a stair,
>   extracting
> A known book from the shelves; or sometimes
>   only
> The rooms themselves, chairs and a fire burning,
> The blown bush at the window, or the sun's
> Faint friendliness on the wall some lonely

> Rain-ceased midsummer evening. That is where
>   they live:
> Not here and now, but where all happened once.

Each image is both slight and very suggestive at the same time; each one embodies that hint of meaning which Stevens once claimed is the miracle of logic or 'pheasant disappearing in the brush' (*Adagia*, p. 173) that characterises poetry at its most expressive. Larkin refuses to build the suggestions into a mythic conviction. There is the potential here for a Platonic view of being, or one which entertains notions about a collective consciousness, but characteristically, the speaker in the poem concludes his long contemplation about age and death with the agnostic conclusion that 'Well, / We shall find out'. Gestures toward the eternal are always held back by Larkin's tentative cast of mind. As a poet living in a post-Christian world, he has, like the speaker in 'Church going', a 'hunger in himself to be more serious', but that hunger is disappointed by the conviction that established religion is presently no more than, as he named it in 'Aubade', a 'vast moth-eaten musical brocade / Created to pretend we never die'. None the less, many of Larkin's poems move toward an imaginative dimension of transcendence in a highly personal and uniquely cautious way. He is a very sceptical poet, but his scepticism does not completely erase a more romantic impulse in his poetry, a thirst for a mystical dimension to existence which is visible in his religious poems.

Interestingly, Hulme's views on the work of classical art as being religiously inconclusive now read, in retrospect, as centrally appropriate to Larkin's kind of tentativeness in such matters. In Hulme's seminal definition of the 'classic motion' he made a statement which can both sanction and focus Larkin's kind of restraint; it defines a kind of control which is restrained without being simply inhibited:

> What I mean by classical in verse, then, is this. That even in the most imaginative flights there is always a holding back, a reservation. The classical poet never forgets his finiteness, his limit of man. *He remembers always that he is mixed up with earth. He may jump, but he always returns back; he never flies away into the circumambient gas.*
>
> You might say if you wished that the whole of the romantic attitude seems to crystallise in verse round metaphors of flight. Hugo is always flying, flying over abysses, flying up into the eternal gases. The word infinite in every other line.
>
> *In the classical attitude you never seem to swing right along to the infinite nothing.* If you say an extravagant thing which does exceed the limits inside which you know man to be fastened, yet there is always conveyed in some way at the end of an impression of yourself standing outside it, and not quite believing it, or consciously putting it forward as a flourish. *You never go blindly into an atmosphere more than the truth, an atmosphere too rarefied for man to breathe for long. You are always faithful to the conception of a limit.*
>
> ('Romanticism and classicism',
>   Shapiro, p. 103—my emphasis)

Hulme's definition unwittingly provides us with a pre-dated description of Larkin's carefully measured moments of epiphany in some of his more mystical poems. Larkin's tendency is to record the moment of flight and at the same time to hold back from the 'swing right along to the infinite nothing'. Thus, the speaker at the end of 'Church going' for instance, remembers that he is 'mixed up with earth' even though he is also gesturing toward an eternal land of the mind. His classical (or new classical) attitude holds him back from the conclusiveness of faith:

> For, though I've no idea
> What this accoutred frowsty barn is worth,
> It pleases me to stand in silence here;
>
> A serious house on serious earth it is,
> In whose blent air all our compulsions meet,
> Are recognised, and robed as destinies.
> And that much can never be obsolete,
> Since someone will forever be surprising
> A hunger in himself to be more serious,
> And gravitating with it to this ground,
> Which he once heard, was proper to grow wise in,
> If only that so many dead lie round.

We have moved successfully into a rarefied 'atmosphere', but are returned to 'the conception of a limit'. Significantly, the ironic turning back leaves us seriously facing the graveyard, a perspective which underlines the need to be 'serious' just as it also prevents us from 'flying away into circumambient gas'. The flight is romantic, but romantic in the order of the difficult realism which Hulme is speaking of.

In the concluding epiphany of 'High windows', there is the same reining in of the flight, the same recognition of the power of the 'atmosphere', and the same corresponding recognition that it is 'too rarefied for man to breathe for long':

> Rather than words comes the thought of high
>   windows:
> The sun-comprehending glass,
> And beyond it, the deep blue air, that shows
> Nothing, and is nowhere, and is endless.

The speaker is both given to a flight into an epiphany of wonder, and into an epiphany of void. The precarious poise of the moment, its designed ambiguity, is as delicate as anything which is conceivable in art. The image is crafted carefully to embody a gracefulness of vorticistic motion. There is the suggestiveness of Pound's 'VORTEX' at work in the dramatic quality of the moment, and there is also the recognition of limit which Hulme has defined as the hallmark of the 'classic of motion'. A sense of the boundless mystery of the universe is momently captured as an instance of beautification suggested by the high windows, but there is also the recognition of the vacancy of the sky and its counter-suggestion of void. The wonder is definitely there but it is passing and it is also diminished by ambiguity. It is not, in other words, as confidently and mythically based as Shelley's otherwise very similar sense of wonder in these famous analogous lines:

> The One remains, the many change and pass;
> Heaven's light forever shines, Earth's shadows
>   fly;
> Life, like a dome of many-coloured glass,
> Stains the white radiance of Eternity.
>
> (*Adonais*, LII)

Larkin's kind of wonder is more contemporary, it is not underpinned by a Platonic mythic conviction. Hulme had said that 'Wonder can only be an attitude of man passing from one stage to another, it can never be a permanently fixed thing' (*Rom. & Cl.,* p. 104). Wonder was once encouraged by myths which became stale, and that is why 'A romantic movement must have an end of the very nature of the thing' ('Romanticism and classicism', pp. 103-4). While many twentieth-century poets have attempted to revitalise the myths, others have settled for a passing wonder which is suggested by the physical world in those moments of rare perception which are poetry of another order. In the context, one thinks of the Imagist practitioners, the poetry of Wallace Stevens, and even of D. H. Lawrence, a poet whose influence on Larkin has yet to be noticed as a profound one. Larkin writes in this tradition of incidental wonder, and it has caused a great deal of confusion (and annoyance) in his more myth-hungry critics. But the poet must write from his own lights, so it is pointless to lecture him on his perspective, especially given that its shade can shift so radically from poem to poem.

Larkin's moments of epiphany are varied; he turns up epiphanies of both light and of void. In particularly negative poems such as 'Ambulances', 'Absences', and 'Aubade' (to make only a short list), the epiphanies are of bleakness; these are representative poems which discover an emptiness just beneath the surface of existence. They are poems which seem to have had more effect on Larkin's critics than is called for, given that he has so many other poems which turn up epiphanies of light. In short, there is even a kind of balance in Larkin's view, a balance which comes from the basically dualistic view of existence that accumulates in the evidence of all of his poetry to date. He is a poet who—in a metaphorical sense only—knows a great deal about heaven and a great deal about hell. So it is very ironic, I think, that the consistently more hellish wasteland and Confessional poetry of the century is not recognised for the all but terminal despair which it embodies, and that Larkin's work is not perceived as an unillusioned and yet relatively hopeful alternative to that tradition. Again ironic is the fact that Larkin has been handed a reputation for being an extremely bleak writer who suffers from a kind of existential ill will, an inability to get on with sharing a few wholesale illusions with the rest of humanity. But he has gone as far as his honesty and his imagination will allow him, and it is a distance which is further than is commonly assumed. Its extent is gestured at in 'Water', where his speaker says that if he 'were called in / To construct a religion', he would,

> . . . raise in the east
> A glass of water
> Where any-angled light
> Would congregate endlessly.

There is an approximate religious experience, an agnostic wonder, which is suggested to the receptive empirical imagination as it sparkles out of the fact of the physical world. It will not very readily atone one to the reality of human failure, suffering, and death, but it beckons the imagination in a hopeful way. It is elusive and it does not suggest a myth. None the less, it is evidence of a hope, and evidence that the metaphor of the wasteland is a very abstract metaphor indeed—so abstract that it overlooks the persistence of beautification even in the midst of decay. Subjectivism, that bane of the modern intellectual which turns toward insanity in most of its manifestations, is unaware of this truth at its peril. That Larkin is a poet who continues to resist its fashionable call is a measure of his vitality and originality as a poet. That he could absorb the healthier aspects of Modernism in the form of an Imagist bias, without being absorbed by Modernism's more cryptic and solipsistic gestures, is a feat which has too long gone unnoticed.

It is unfortunate, I think, that the nature of the Modernist revolution has not yet been fully seen for the mixed, even contradictory, movement that it was. While it is usual to mark off its identity in the subjectively allusive and sometimes bookish poetry of Eliot and Pound, the more empirical poetry of the Imagists stands, in a sense, in opposition to that very aspect of their achievement. Interestingly, Thom Gunn, speaking of the relationship between the contemporary poet and the Modernists, has said:

> The only assumption shared by the poets who have emerged in the last ten or fifteen years is that they do not want to continue the revolution inaugurated by Pound and finally made respectable by learned commentaries on the *Four Quartets*. Yet nobody has pretended that, once the revolution was abandoned, it was possible simply to take up where Hardy left off, as if the experiments of Pound and Eliot had never taken place. Clearly we must, without embodying the revolution, attempt to benefit from it, to understand its causes and study its mistakes. ('Modes of control', *Yale Review,* 80 (1964), p. 447)

Gunn claims that contemporary poets have much to learn from the Imagist aspect of the revolution, and he admires the Imagists' ability for 'exact delineation of the external world' (p. 449), noting that in the poetry of observation there is often the discovery of a momentary spiritual health which transcends confinement in the self. And to highlight a phrase from one of Gunn's own poems, this attention to 'the world's bare surface'[22] is an especially emphatic one in his most recent volumes. Ted Hughes and R. S. Thomas are also poets who are remarkable in their empirical bias, their desire to connect freshly with the mystery of the physical world. All three of these poets are radically different from Larkin (on several grounds), but they nonetheless would appear to share with Larkin a rudimentary conviction that 'The greatest poverty / Is not to live in the physical world'. Interestingly, Gunn, Hughes, Larkin, and Thomas are all poets of crisp observation and epiphany, and they are also poets of doubt and wonder at the same time. Their works constitute one of the most vital emerging traditions of English poetry today, and a good deal of its poetic is a neo-Imagist one.

NOTES

[1] *All What Jazz: A Record Diary 1961-68* (London, 1970), p. 17.

[2] *New Lines,* (1956 rpt. New York 1967), p. xv.

[3] 'Esthetique Du Mal', in *The Collected Poems of Wallace Stevens* (New York, 1957), p. 325.

[4] With the exception of 'Aubade', which appeared in *TLS* (23 Dec. 1977, p. 1491), all quotes from Larkin's poetry are from the following editions: *The Less Deceived* (1955; rpt. London, 1966); *The Whitsun Weddings* (1964; rpt. London, 1968); *High Windows* (London, 1974).

[5] 'Subsidies and side effects', *TLS* (18 Feb. 1977), p. 183.

[6] 'The poetry of William Barnes', *Listener* (16 Aug. 1962), p. 257.

[7] 'What's become of Wystan?', *Spectator* (15 July 1960), p. 104.

[8] Introduction to *John Betjeman: Collected Poems* (London, 1971), p. xxiii.

[9] 'Betjeman en bloc', *Listen,* 3 (spring 1959), p. 15.

[10] 'The blending of Betjeman', *Spectator* (2 Dec. 1960), p. 913.

[11] 'Philip Larkin praises the poetry of Thomas Hardy', *Listener* (25 July 1968), p. 111.

[12] *Ibid.,* p. 111.

[13] 'Romanticism and classicism', 1924; rpt. in *Prose Keys to Modern poetry,* ed. Karl Shapiro (New York, 1961), p. 101.

[14] 'Vorticism', *Fortnighty Review,* 96, (1914), p. 464.

[15] 'An introduction to the selected poems of William Carlos Williams', 1948; rpt. in *Poetry and The Age* (New York, 1955), p. 217.

[16] 'Imagination as value', 1949; rpt. in *The Modern Tradition,* ed. Richard Ellman and Charles Feidelson Jr. (New York, 1965), p. 223.

[17] Quoted by John Press in *A Map of Modern English Verse* (London, 1969), p. 258. His source: *Poets of the 1950's,* ed. D. J. Enright (Tokyo, 1955), pp. 77-8.

[18] 'Adagia', in *Opus Posthumous,* ed. and Introd. by Samuel French Morse (New York, 1966), p. 158.

[19] 'Not like Larkin' (transcription from BBC Radio 3), *Listener,* 88 (1972), p. 209.

[20] 'Notes on language and style', 1925; rpt. in *Further Speculations,* ed. Sam Hynes (Minneapolis, 1955), p. 99.

[21] Thwaite tells us that Larkin once said to him that in the reading of 'The Whitsun weddings', as the voice comes to the close, it should 'lift off the ground'. See 'The poetry of Philip Larkin' in *The Survival of Poetry,* ed. Martin Dodsworth (London, 1970), p. 48.

[22] 'A snow vision', in *Poems 1950-1966: A Selection* (London, 1969), p. 43.

Linda W. Wagner

[*In the following essay, Wagner discusses the influence of Ezra Pound's Imagist aesthetics on the early works of Ernest Hemingway, in particular his novel* The Sun Also Rises *(1926).*]

SOURCE: "The Sun Also Rises: One Debt to Imagism," in *The Journal of Narrative Technique,* Vol. 2, No. 2, May, 1972, pp. 88-98.

Ernest Hemingway's appreciation for Ezra Pound is widely known—his constant praise for Pound during a life marred by broken friendships and bitter words; his 1956 check for $1000, sent to Pound seemingly in lieu of the Nobel Prize medal. Yet Hemingway's fiction is rarely read as having benefited from his intense relationship with the older writer in the early 1920's. We know the legends of the young Hemingway in Paris, apprentice to Stein, Joyce, and Pound, but we have never known what happened to Hemingway's early work. John Peale Bishop remembers, however, that the early manuscripts went to Pound and "came back to him blue penciled, most of the adjectives gone. The comments were unsparing."[1] Whereas Stein's influence was mainly general, it would seem that Pound's dicta were substantiated with practical suggestions.

By the early 1920's, Pound had enriched his earlier Imagist and Vorticist theories with precepts directed toward prose. From 1916 to 1918 he had read all of Henry James' writing, in the process of editing the James issue of *The Little Review;* and his long friendship with Ford Madox Ford was finally bearing conscious fruit. So that by the time of his meeting with Hemingway, Pound was deeply interested in prose; in fact, in 1923, he helped William Bird bring out the six books of "new prose" that were to reform prose in the same way Imagism had revitalized poetry a decade before. Among those six books were Williams' *The Great American Novel,* Pound's *Indiscretions,* and Hemingway's first book, *3 Stories & 10 Poems.*

Pound's excitement over Hemingway's writing (judging it the best prose he had read in forty years) probably allowed the presence of those ten poems in a series dedicated to prose. By 1922, Hemingway had written more poems than stories,[2] poems easily marked as Imagist. Among others, "Along with Youth" and "Oklahoma" illustrate well the chary use of words, the reliance on free verse, and the emphasis on the observable detail of an "Image."

During the years following 1913, when the essays about Imagism first appeared, the trademark of that poetic movement was concentration. One of the primary aims was "To use absolutely no word that does not contribute to the presentation,"[3] a directive aimed at eliminating from poetry its weak phrases and lines of filler. "Use either no ornament or good ornament," Pound warned; "Don't be descriptive. . . . Go in fear of abstractions." Such axioms demanded that the poet employ his craft consciously, a word at a time, and that he give his impression the sharp focus of the image.

Pound also defined the image as "that which presents an intellectual and emotional complex in an instant of time." By stressing the wide inclusive powers of the image, he greatly strengthened the Imagist concept; and his emphasis on *speed* gave new life to the post-Victorian poem that was nearly buried in expected details. As he continued, "It is the presentation of such a 'complex' instantaneously which gives the sense of sudden liberation . . . that sense of sudden growth which we experience in the presence of the greatest works of art"—epiphany, if you will.

The Imagists usually worked in free verse forms because they could thus more easily attain organic form, a shape consistent with the mood and subject of the poem being written. Concentration, speed, and the use of the writer's own conversational language—these were the chief means the Imagists chose to present those objects or experiences which would convey the "white light" of full meaning. Concentration, speed, and the use of the writer's own conversational language—these are certainly trademarks of the famous Hemingway style.

Influence studies are impractical unless intrinsic evidence exists in quantity. The montage effect of the highly compressed stories and vignettes of Hemingway's 1924 *In Our Time* is the young writer's most obvious tribute to Imagism itself, and has been noted by several critics. But perhaps the most sustained example of the Imagist method transferred to prose is that maligned novel, *The Sun Also Rises,* 1926. In using the methods of suggestion, compression, and speed within the outlines of traditional novel form, Hemingway achieved a lyric evocation of one segment of life in the 1920's.

Perhaps we should remember that Hemingway was disappointed throughout his life because *SAR* was the novel most often misread; it was the "naturalistic" Hemingway, or at any rate, the "realistic" novel. As he recalled much later, "I sometimes think my style is suggestive rather than direct. The reader must often use his imagination or lose the most subtle part of my thought."[4]

The Sun Also Rises is not, of course, a picture of the "lost generation." Hemingway's poetic method of telling the reader that has caused some confusion. His epigraphs to the book and his final title (the book was called *Fiesta* in its European publication) prove that to him Stein's comment is indeed only "splendid bombast."[5] He uses Stein's comment as the first epigraph for the novel, but the second—the quotation from *Ecclesiastes*—follows it, as if in contradiction:

> One generation passeth away, and another generation cometh; but the earth abideth forever. . . . The sun also ariseth, and the sun goeth down, and hasteth to the place where he arose. . . . All the rivers run into the sea; yet the sea is not full; unto the place from whence the rivers come, thither they return again.

By choosing an affirmative phrase as title, Hemingway further reinforces his view, that these characters are not "lost," but merely "beat up." More important, they still have the strength to act against worn out social forms and find truth for themselves. Jake does, when he gives Brett to Romero in order to make her happy; and Brett does when she sends Romero away. But, because society's arbitrary evaluations of these acts would be unsympathetic, Hemingway has to create the organic whole of the novel so that the acts in themselves convey the proper nobility. It is a difficult task, bucking conventional morality; but Hemingway made it even more difficult by using techniques that could easily be called "poetic," at least in relation to Pound's terminology.

One of the most troublesome of Hemingway's techniques was the strict first person narration. Jake Barnes, with his self-effacing terseness, gives the readers of *SAR* only skeletons of action and characterization. We know very little about Bill and Mike, for example, though everything Hemingway tells us about Bill is positive. But in Mike's scenes, interpreting his remarks is sometimes hard. The same kind of ambivalence surrounds both Brett and Jake. Obviously they are the protagonists, but some of the circumstances surrounding them could stand a more sympathetic explanation—or at least a fuller one—than Jake with his assumed stoicism can realistically give them. Hemingway tried rewriting this novel in third person, so that his 1926 audience would have help with the somewhat unconventional characters, but he evidently liked that effect less well. So he returned to the strictly "objective" presentation of Jake's telling his own story, as it occurred, rather than in a past tense, which would at least have allowed for more reflection. This turning loose a character on an audience, reminiscent as it was of Pirandello, was also a manifestation of Pound's principle, "Direct treatment of the 'thing' concerned," with little ostensible interference from the author. How different Jake Barnes' version of his story was from Carrie Meeber's account of hers.

When Pound directed writers to "Use absolutely no word that does not contribute to the presentation," he was implying a sharp selection of detail. Because Hemingway's selection of detail was so accurate, even skeletal presentations are usually convincing. Brett's bowed head as Mike and Robert argue shows well her tired submission to the present situation, just as Jake's drinking too much after Brett leaves with Romero tells us clearly his emotional state. The repetition of mealtime and drinking scenes in the novel is particularly good for showing the slight but telling changes in a few recurring details. It is of course these changes in the existing relationships that are the real center of the novel, rather than any linear plot.

Following the sometimes minute vacillations in a friendship, or the subtle shadings in a conversation, admittedly demands close attention from the reader. As T.S. Eliot was to point out, reading the modern novel requires concentration as intense as reading poetry—as well as training in that kind of skill. "A prose that is altogether alive demands something that the ordinary novel-reader is not prepared to give."[6]

Hemingway also used a somewhat oblique characterization of his protagonists. Jake and Brett are not always present. Jake as narrator usually speaks about others rather than himself, and when he does think about his own dilemma, it is again in the laconic phrases that leave much to the reader's own empathy. Even though Hemingway introduces Jake in the opening chapter, his focus seemingly falls on Robert Cohn. He tells us innocently enough that Cohn was a college boxing champ, although "he cared nothing for boxing, in fact he disliked it." Then Hemingway begins to accumulate related details: later we see that Romero loves his bullfighting, just as Bill and Jake love fishing. We must then be suspicious of a man who devotes himself to something he dislikes. Subsequent chapters continue the parallel descriptions of Jake and Cohn, and less apparently of Frances Clyne with Brett. It is a stroke of genius that Hemingway waits until we have clearly seen what Jake and Brett are not to present them for what they are—sad but honest people— together, in a would-be love scene.

The Sun Also Rises is also filled with passages that could easily be considered images if they were isolated from their context. An image to Pound was to be more than just a pictorial representation: "an image presents an intellectual and emotional complex in an instant of time." The brief moment when Brett enters the café in the company of homosexuals combines a good set of graphic details with the evocation of Jake's sad excitement and anger as he sees her:

> A crowd of young men, some in jerseys and some in their shirt-sleeves, got out. I could see their hands and newly washed, wavy hair in the light from the door. The policeman standing by the door looked at me and smiled. They came in. As they went in, under the light I saw white hands, wavy hair, white faces, grimacing, gesturing, talking. With them was Brett. She looked very lovely and she was very much with them.

> One of them saw Georgette and said: "I do declare. There is an actual harlot. I'm going to dance with her, Lett. You watch me."

The tall dark one, called Lett, said: "Don't you be rash."

The wavy blond one answered: "Don't you worry, dear." And with them was Brett.[7]

The policeman's smile, the grimacing, the dancing—Hemingway often worked through actions to reveal character and specific mood. But the touchstone here, as often throughout the book, is Jake's own mood, his astonished sadness, caught in the simple refrain line, "And with them was Brett."

Not only does Hemingway use concentrated descriptive passages, he also moves quickly from one passage to another, sometimes without logical transition. This use of juxtaposition to achieve speed in impressions is another poetic technique, enabling a short piece of writing to encompass many disparate meanings. Near the end of the novel, when the reader's attention should be on Brett and Romero as lovers, or on Jake as sacrificial figure, Hemingway instead moves to the account of a young man killed in the morning bull run. "A big horn wound. All for fun. Just for fun," says the surly bartender, picking up one of the repeated key words in the book—*fun, luck, values*. The bartender's emphasis on the unreasoning fun ends with Hemingway's objective report of the younger man's death, his funeral, and the subsequent death of the bull.

The coffin was loaded into the baggage-car of the train, and the widow and the two children rode, sitting, all three together, in an open third-class railway-carriage. The train started with a jerk, and then ran smoothly, going down grade around the edge of the plateau and out into the fields of grain that blew in the wind on the plain on the way to Tafalla.

The bull who killed Vicente Girones was named Bocanegra, was Number 118 of the bull-breeding establishment of Sanchez Taberno, and was killed by Pedro Romero as the third bull of that same afternoon. His ear was cut by popular acclamation and given to Pedro Romero, who, in turn, gave it to Brett, who wrapped it in a handkerchief belonging to myself, and left both ear and handkerchief, along with a number of Muratti cigarette-stubs, shoved far back in the drawer of the bed-table that stood beside her bed in the Hotel Montoya, in Pamplona (198-99).

Hemingway follows this already wide-reaching image with the suggestion of Cohn's "death" as Brett leaves with Romero. This brief descriptive sequence, then, has established the deaths of man, bull, man—all at the whim of the fiesta and its larger-than-life hero, the matador.[8]

Another device used frequently in the book is Hemingway's re-creation of natural idiom—in both dialogue and introspective passages—and perhaps more importantly his use of prose rhythms appropriate to the effect of the writing desired. Although the Imagist axiom, "Compose in the sequence of the musical phrase, not that of the metronome," was more liberating to poetry than it was to prose, it also spoke for a kind of freedom in prose—

sentences unrestricted in tone, diction, or length because of formal English standards. In passages like this opening to Part III, Hemingway arranges sentences of varying lengths and compositions to create the tone he wants (here, a melancholic nostalgia), a tone which may be at odds with the ostensible facts of such a passage.

In the morning it was all over. The fiesta was finished. I woke about nine o'clock, had a bath, dressed, and went down-stairs. The square was empty and there were no people on the streets. A few children were picking up rocket-sticks in the square. The cafés were just opening and the waiters were carrying out the comfortable white wicker chairs and arranging them around the marble-topped tables in the shade of the arcade. They were sweeping the streets and sprinkling them with a hose.

I sat in one of the wicker chairs and leaned back comfortably. The waiter was in no hurry to come. The white-paper announcements of the unloading of the bulls and the big schedules of special trains were still up on the pillars of the arcade. A waiter wearing a blue apron came out with a bucket of water and a cloth, and commenced to tear down the notices, pulling the paper off in strips and washing and rubbing away the paper that stuck to the stone. The fiesta was over (277).

In these two paragraphs Hemingway moves from an emphasis on Jake's feelings and actions to the specific details of his locale, using those details to complete his sketch of Jake—alone, and now numbly realizing only that "it was all over." To open the second section with more description of Jake helps the reader keep his focus on the protagonist. The observable details are significant to the story (here and usually throughout the novel) primarily because they help identify an emotional state. Even the movement within this passage, building from the short rhythms of the opening to the longer phrases of the penultimate sentence, and coming back to the restrained "refrain," suggests a crescendo in feeling.

"The fiesta was over," repeated as it is in varying contexts, is an example of Pound's *organ base,* which term he described as "a sort of residue of sound which remains in the ear" and acts to establish mood.[9] That Hemingway was cognizant of the effects single repeated words or phrases might have is evident not only in his fictional techniques but in his comments about this repetition. Lillian Ross, for one, quotes his saying, "In the first paragraph of *Farewell,* I used the word *and* consciously over and over the way Mr. Johann Sebastian Bach used a note in music when he was emitting counterpoint."[10] It seems unlikely that Hemingway would have missed Pound's later enthusiasms about the "prose tradition in verse." As Pound explained,

Good writing is writing that is perfectly controlled, the writer says just what he means. He says it with complete clarity and simplicity. He uses the smallest number of words. . . . Also there are various kinds of clarity. There is the clarity of the request: Send me four pounds of ten-penny nails. And there is the syntactical simplicity of the request: Buy me the kind of Rembrandt I like. This last is an utter cryptogram. It presupposes a more complex and intimate understanding of the speaker than most of us ever acquire of anyone. It has as many meanings, almost, as there are persons who might speak it. . . .

It is the almost constant labour of the prose artist to translate this latter kind of clarity into the former; to say "Send me the kind of Rembrandt I like" in the terms of "Send me four pounds of ten-penny nails."[11]

Hemingway's emphasis on clarity and seemingly simple diction certainly reflects these kinds of distinctions.

The passage describing the fiesta also provides a good example of Hemingway's failure to use overt symbols (a failure which troubled many critics enough that they began inventing parallels between bulls, steers, and men). In repeating "The fiesta was over," Hemingway suggests broader implications for "fiesta"—a natural expectation of gaiety and freedom, here ironically doomed because of the circumstances of the characters. Through the description, we easily feel Jake's nostalgia, but not because fiesta is a true symbol; it never assumes any existence other than its apparent one. As Pound, again, had phrased the definition, "the natural object is always the adequate symbol. . . . if a man use 'symbols' he must use them that their symbolic function does not obtrude."[12] In one sense, in *The Sun Also Rises,* the amount of liquor a person drinks is symbolic—of both the kind of person he is, and the emotional condition he is in. So too is anger, and various stages of it. But the purely literary symbol—which the unsuccessful fireworks exhibition might suggest—is rare. Even the fireworks sequence is used more to show various characters' reaction to the failure than it is to represent another object or state of being *per se.* That Brett does not want to watch the failure is as significant for her character as the fact that she enjoys the artistry of the bullfights.

A corollary to the principle about symbolism is Pound's warning that the writer "Go in fear of abstractions." Love, hate, grief, religion, death, fear—these are the prime movers of the novel, yet the words scarcely appear. *SAR* is essentially a study of various kinds of love, yet no character ever discusses that passion. We are forewarned of Hemingway's definition to come in *Death in the Afternoon,* that "obscenity" is "unsoundness in abstract conversation or, indeed, any other metaphysical tendency in speech" (95). As Floyd Watkins has capably pointed out, Hemingway characters are nearly always to be mistrusted when they speak in abstract terms, whereas Hemingway heroes identify themselves by their preference for the concrete.[13]

Perhaps more than being a study of kinds of love, *SAR* is the paradigm of Jake's initiation into the fullest kind of that emotion. Jake's self-abnegation is not martyrdom; he knows he can not benefit from Brett's affair with Romero. But his education throughout the book consists in learning just how much his love—and hers—can bear.

In Part I, it is Jake who wishes they could marry. By Part III he has learned that any fulfillment of their relationship is impossible. There is no question that he still loves Brett, perhaps even more in her new-found and convincing nobility.[14]

The novel in its three-part division is also the story of Brett's coming to maturity. Although in Part I she considers herself one with the Count and Jake, the men share satisfactions she does not understand. By the end of the novel she has lost the coy femininity that makes her somewhat cloying. She has thought of someone else—Romero—and she continues thinking, of Mike and—always—of Jake. Stanley Edgar Hyman suggests, "The key action of the book is Brett's renunciation of Romero for the boy's own good, the first truly unselfish act of her life."[15] It could well be that her separation from the church is suggested throughout the novel to help build toward the ending, with her turn to Jake. Brett has no suprahuman comforts; she must call Jake, and the reader must see her telegram to him, as he does, as completely natural.

In his first novel, Hemingway appears to have drawn a little on a Hamlet-like situation. The many male characters act as either complements or foils to Jake, and the inevitable comparisons serve to keep Jake before us at all times, whether he is or not. By making him physically less than a competitor, however, Hemingway allows Jake *as person* rather than as male to occupy the center of these relationships, even the peripheral ones with Krum and Woolsey, the Britisher Harris, and the Basques. All of these masculine ties help to substantiate Jake's real if injured manliness (see Hemingway's *Paris Review* comments), and add pathos to his love affair with Brett. Jake's wound is his ironic gift from life, and he has no choice but to live with it—gracefully. Never again will Hemingway create such a sensational wound for a protagonist, even in the more obviously war-oriented novels, but it does serve a powerfully dramatic function in keeping the otherwise normal Jake out of the normal rivalry for Brett's affections.

Yet, for all his anguish, what does Jake say? Hemingway's choice of idiom for his hero could well have been autobiographical, but it also bears the trace of Pound's ideal character, who speaks in his own unliterary voice, speaks in cryptic suggestion, and speaks with truth. "I've got a rotten headache," when he can no longer bear seeing Brett; "I wanted to get home." The leave-taking scene with Brett after the dialogue with Count Mippipopolous has Jake vacillating between "Don't be sentimental" and then, after a kiss, "You don't have to go." But after Brett does go, Hemingway gives us some brief introspection so that we understand the depth of Jake's feelings. When he comes to the more important good-byes at the end of Part I, as Brett is going to San Sebastian, Hemingway relies on our earlier knowledge, and gives us Jake as an objective sketch: "The door opened and I went upstairs and went to bed." We can presumably re-create the rest for ourselves.

Hemingway relies on Jake's silence or near-silence frequently, not only in the love scenes. Jake says only

"Wasn't the town nice at night?" trying to reach Cohn through his own foggy bombast. (Jake's method here is Imagist also, bringing Cohn back to one specific experience, one night, one town; and having Cohn react like the most literal-minded of men.) Instead of dialectics, Hemingway here gives us suggestion.

Even Jake's wound is given in a simple declarative sentence, the poignancy of its terseness aided by the opening modifier: "Undressing, I looked at myself in the mirror of the big armoire beside the bed." The only adjective in the sentence describes a piece of furniture; the situation itself needs no description. Hemingway is, graphically, and in mirror image, "presenting," as Pound had edicted. The mention of bed also adds pathos to the brief line. The concentration on the furniture offers a moment of deflection also, before Hemingway brings us back to more understatement:

> Undressing, I looked at myself in the mirror of the big armoire beside the bed. That was a typically French way to furnish a room. Practical, too, I suppose. Of all the ways to be wounded. I suppose it was funny (30).

The climactic act of the novel, for Jake, his giving Brett to Romero, is another model of suggestive gesture instead of speech: "He looked at me. It was a final look to ask if it were understood. It was understood all right."

The chief danger in reading Hemingway is, I think, to overlook this rather apparent origin of many of his stylistic traits. Simplicity has too often become simple-mindedness, just as Williams' "No ideas but in things" has become "No ideas." For instance, a recent essay by Ihab Hassan equates Hemingway's style with the character of Jake Barnes. I agree with Hassan's summary of Hemingway's remarkable tightness in writing, "Its rigor, terseness, and repetitions, its intractable concreteness and vast omissions, resist rhetoric, resist even statement, and discourage the mind from habitual closure." We cannot read Hemingway with any sense of complacence because we are thrown too much on our own, and the old patterns of expectation do not work. But Hassan goes on to move from seeing style, somehow separated, to seeing style as the only possible means of re-creating any Hemingway hero, any Hemingway theme, because he finds Hemingway very close to a contemporary "blankness and rage. . . . Indeed, Hemingway's fiction makes for itself a place in the tradition of silence that extends from Sade, through Kafka, Genet, and Beckett, to the inverted literary imagination of our day."[16] He continues,

> the ethic of Hemingway's characters is not only reductive but also solitary. What they endure, they can never share with others. Existentially, they remain alone; they find momentary communion only in a dangerous ritual. Always they disengage themselves from the complexities of human relations, and simplify their social existence to the primary functions of the body. "The only thing that could spoil a day was people . . ." Hemingway writes. "People were always the limiters of happiness except for the very few that were as good as spring itself"(91).

While Hassan's thesis in the complete essay is almost convincing, I am bothered by his tendency to overstate—just as Hemingway's use of *always* in the above excerpt is quickly disproved, so can Hassan's be a few lines before. There is a tone of pride here that is misleading; an attitude of "my-knowledge-is-so-dreadful-that-I-cannot-communicate-it." Perhaps the Hemingway protagonist is "alone" in that he is usually limited to a few confidants rather than a menage. But he does have intimates—Bill Gorton, the Count, Montoya, in a sense Romero, and in another sense, Brett. In fact, Jake seems much less isolated than the miserable Cohn, who has literally no one to talk with. And yes, the kind of idiom Hemingway uses is terse and cryptic, but primarily because the emotions are too big to handle in abstract words, not because no emotions exist, or because there is no desire to communicate. *The Sun Also Rises* gives evidence, in its various set scenes, of a great deal of communication. Jake understands perfectly what he must do for Brett, and Brett knows how little she has to say to reach him (in contrast to Frances Clyne who takes an entire chapter to do what Brett can do in three lines). "Let's not talk," Brett tells him. "Talking's all bilge" (25).

The tacit understanding that exists here is better evidence of the author's interest in love, it seems to me, than of his obsession with death. The too-facile equation between death and silence need not shadow every cryptic idiom in American literature. Neither is the prevalent mood in this novel one of terror, as Mr. Hassan later states. (Terror of what? In Jake's eyes, the worst has already happened.) It seems to be rather one of sorrow, of sorrow growing from the unfulfilled love of Jake and Brett which acts in turn as a graphic image for the loves of the many other characters—men with men as well as men with women—which come so seldom to fruition. For those few relationships that had the warmth of the sun in his title, Hemingway was only too grateful. In fact, most of his fiction stands in tribute to just such slight moments.

In his eagerness to present rather than to tell (to render rather than report), Hemingway erred only in following the Imagist doctrines perhaps too closely. *The Sun Also Rises* is a difficult book to read correctly, until the reader understands the way it works; then it becomes a masterpiece of concentration, with every detail conveying multiple impressions, and every speech creating both single character and complex interrelationships. It also takes us back to Pound's 1923 description of the best modern prose, which should "tell the truth about *moeurs contemporaines* without fake, melodrama, conventional ending."[17] There is nothing fake about anything in *The Sun Also Rises,* least of all the writing. And to read it as a masterpiece of suggestion makes one compliment Mark Schorer for his statement that Hemingway had in his career written "the very finest prose of our time. And most of it is poetry."[18]

NOTES

[1] Quoted by George Wickes in *Americans in Paris* (Garden City, New York, 1969), 162.

[2] Throughout his life, Hemingway considered himself a poet, and occasionally talked of bringing out a collection of poems.

[3] "Imagism" and "A Few Don'ts by an Imagiste," *Poetry,* I, No. 6 (March 1913), 199-201.

[4] "The Great Writer's Last Reflections on Himself, His Craft, Love, and Life," *Playboy,* X, No. 1 (January 1963), 120ff.

[5] Carlos Baker, *Ernest Hemingway, A Life Story* (New York, 1969), 179.

[6] Introduction to *Nightwood, The Selected Works of Djuna Barnes* (New York, 1962), 228.

[7] *The Sun Also Rises* (New York, 1954), 20. Later page references to this edition are given in parentheses in the text.

[8] As Hemingway's columns on bullfighting substantiate, the lure of the matador is irresistible, for both sexes. See pp. 90-108, *By-Line: Ernest Hemingway,* ed. William White (New York, 1967).

[9] *Poetry,* 205.

[10] Lillian Ross, "Ernest Hemingway," *The New Yorker* (May 13, 1950), 60.

[11] "The Serious Artist," *Literary Essays of Ezra Pound* (Norfolk, Conn., 1935), 50.

[12] *Poetry,* 205.

[13] See *The Flesh and the Word* (Nashville, Tenn., 1971).

[14] Hemingway's interest in Brett as character—much like his later fascination with Pilar—seems genuine. As he wrote in a 1956 column (*By-Line,* 461): "I have always considered that it was easy to be a man compared to being a woman who lives by as rigid standards as men live by. No one of us lives by as rigid standards nor has a good ethics as we planned but an attempt is made."

[15] Stanley Edgar Hyman, *Standards: A Chronical of Books for Our Time* (New York, 1966), 31.

[16] Ihab Hassan, "Hemingway: Valor Against the Void" in *The Dismemberment of Orpheus* (New York, 1971), 80 ff.

[17] Pound, *Pavannes and Divagations* (Norfolk, Conn., 1958), 50-51.

[18] "With Grace Under Pressure," *New Republic,* 127 (October 6, 1952), 19.

Ethan Lewis

[In the following essay, Lewis interprets Wallace Stevens's "Thirteen Ways of Looking at a Blackbird" utilizing Imagist poetic theory.]

SOURCE: "Thirteen Ways of Looking at Imagism," in *South Dakota Review,* Vol. 30, No. 4, Winter, 1992, pp. 66-86.

"Not all objects are equal. The vice of imagism was that it did not recognize this."[11] Despite, or perhaps on account of this critique, Wallace Stevens wrote a work that rivals any for its imagism. "Thirteen Ways of Looking at a Blackbird" (PM, 20-22) was written in the year Amy Lowell published her third (and final) installment of *Some Imagist Poets.* "Ways" is itself another, better imagist anthology—better, but also different. Like most of the poems in Lowell's collection, each "Way" treats things of no ostensible importance. In the process, however, each is a study of a mode—a "Way"—of perceiving, which for Stevens, is "the Thing Itself," while the objects perceived are but "Ideas about the Thing" (PM, 387).

This shift in focus differentiates Stevens not only from the Imagist school, but from Ezra Pound as well. Much of this essay is cast as an implicit dialogue between Stevens and Pound, the major innovator, arguably the founder of imagist poetry. Pound and Stevens of course transcended the narrow limits of this form. Indeed, to call "Ways" and some other Stevens works "Imagist" requires that we look at him in Pound's terms. I must stress from the outset that this approach is, simply, *an* approach. Its utility lies in what it reveals. As Marjorie Perloff points out, Stevens critics tend not to explore his structures, but rather his ideas.[2] A "Poundian/Imagist" approach to Stevens works because his structures are so rich. Furthermore, the use of Pound's critical vocabulary enables us to look at Stevens' own criticism in a more technical light. My aim is less to read Stevens as Pound might (and never did); but to add another dimension to Stevens' gloss upon himself, which in Harold Bloom's words, "is more advanced as *interpretation* than our criticism as yet has gotten to be."[3] With this in mind, let us look at the "Ways of Looking at a Blackbird" as thirteen imagist poems.

I

Among twenty snowy mountains,
The only moving thing
Was the eye of the blackbird.

Pound described "The 'one image poem'" as "a form of super-position, . . . it is one idea set on top of another." Such juxtapositions were intended to convey "the precise instant when a thing outward and objective transforms itself . . . into a thing inward and subjective."[4] "Way I" is a different type of image, joining two "ideas" by description rather than super-position. "Among" and "only" suggest that the "twenty snowy mountains" and the "eye of the blackbird" compose a single natural scene. We might well impose one image on another *in thought,* as it is almost physically impossible to behold twenty mountains and a blackbird's eye in one sighting, and we are not invited to visualize them sequentially. Still, one is not definitely forced into this cognitive response, because the syntactic structure of the poem implies that the images may be understood to follow upon each other, viz.: We scan our eyes across a snowy, mountainous landscape. Suddenly, our gaze falls upon a blackbird, as still as his surroundings except for his twitching eye.

II

> I was of three minds,
> Like a tree
> In which there are three blackbirds.

Here, the thing seen is literally in the mind's eye—or rather there is no thing seen, only a thing considered (the fact that "I was of three minds"), to which an impression ("a tree in which there are three blackbirds") is appended *via* simile. Moreover, this impression, Pound might protest, "is used as an ornament" (GB, 88), i.e. as something that lends grace or beauty, but is accessory to the thing itself. For Stevens, however, this accessory nature might be an attraction. As an ornament, the simile is *analogous* to 'being of three minds.' II is therefore a poem in which "The thing stated has been accompanied by a restatement and the restatement has illustrated and given definition to the thing stated. . . . the fundamental books of the human spirit are vast collections of such analogies and it is the analogies that have helped to make these books what they are" (NA, 129). Stevens, in other words, revels in analogy, where Pound tries to efface it—either by replacing "like" or "as" with a colon (as in the famous "In a Station of the Metro"); or by using a figure "there with purpose . . . to interpret a definite meaning"[5]—a figure so essential to the presentation as to be no less a thing than that for which it is an analogue. For Pound, there is, ideally, no "restatement;" only "interpret [ation]," which by definition differs from what it interprets.

Another way to look at II in Pound's terms is as a superposition of perceptual modes—one *type* of idea (reflection [here specifically, reflection on reflection]) set upon another type (vision).

III

> The blackbird whirled in the autumn winds.
> It was a small part of the pantomime.

> (*Cf.:* The apparition of these faces in the crowd:
>   Petals on a wet, black bough.)

I and "In a Station of the Metro" are two different forms of "one image poem." III also differs from Pound's image, though perceived one way, III shares "Metro'"'s principle of construction. I, as was mentioned, forms a single natural image. The single image in Pound's work comes from the "super-position [of] one idea set on top

of another" (GB, 89). III arguably presents a single image in the first line and a commentary on this image in the second. But III then also "sets one idea on top of another": an idea in the form of a vision atop an idea in the form of a comment. Is III an instance of "super-position"? Cognitively, yes; visually, no—unless for "pantomime" one substitutes a picture of what one imagines a pantomime to look like (e.g. Marcel Marceau in performance). Even then, there might not be super-position if the blackbird's role as a "part of the pantomime" were considered. (One might then imagine a single impression: Marceau and hovering blackbird together on an outdoor stage in October).

IV

> A man and a woman
> Are one.
> A man and a woman and a blackbird
> Are one.

IV and V do not present images of any particular things seen at all. This fact of course does not preclude their being imagist poems, by either Pound's standards or what are apparently Stevens' (which, Stevens never having written a treatise on the image, must be inferred from his other writings). According to Pound, an image needn't be seen, only felt. An image is defined not by its appearance, but by the fact that, as poetic expression, it is irreducible. "The image is the poet's pigment."

> The painter should use his color because he sees it or feels it. I don't much care whether he is representative or non-representative. He should *depend,* of course, on the creative, not upon the mimetic or representational part in his work. It is the same in writing poems, the author must use his *image* because he sees it or feels it, *not* because he thinks he can use it to back up some creed or some system of ethics or economics. (GB, 86)

The fourth of the "Thirteen Ways" is an abstraction—and there is nothing Stevens appears to have felt more intensely. "The imagination is the only genius. It is intrepid and eager and *the extreme of its achievement lies in abstraction*" (NA, 139; emphasis added). It is worth considering this highly unusual facet of Stevens' intellect in relation to Pound and Williams, whose poetics are explicitly opposed to abstraction. Pound concurs with Ernest Fenollosa, in linking poetry with science and abstraction with pedantic "philosophical discussion." Williams is even more directly antithetical to Stevens than is Pound in this regard, for Williams sets *imagination* against abstraction. "[T]he thing that stands eternally in the way of really good writing is always one: the virtual impossibility of lifting to the imagination those things which lie under the direct scrutiny of the senses . . . It is this difficulty that sets a value upon all works of art and makes them a necessity."[6] The image for Williams and Pound is concrete and particular—it is never the abstract "man," "woman" and "blackbird" who together form a more abstract "one." It is "the *apparition* of *these* faces in the crowd;" a "*red* wheelbarrow *beside* the *white* chickens on which *so much depends.*"

One hesitates to push this point too far—"so much depends" is a somewhat abstract expression; so are "a," rather than *the* "red wheelbarrow" and "the" instead of *a particular* crowd. Then again, Williams and Pound might counter that such descriptions were superfluous to the idea being presented and would actually detract from the specificity of the images. Stevens, on the other hand, might defend such vagueness as intrinsic to the image and perhaps even support this defense by citing Pound, *viz.: the image, being irreducible, must mark the extreme of the poet's achievement. The image must therefore be abstract.* Yet whether the abstract or concrete is least reducible is itself matter for "philosophical discussion." It is the old Many vs. One, Aristotelian vs. Platonic confrontation: do we derive the idea from particulars, or are particulars emanations of one idea? The answer depends on the way one looks at things, and since for Stevens, "Things seen are things as seen" (OP, 162), his "primary pigment" is abstract.

V

I do not know which to prefer,
The beauty of inflections
Or the beauty of innuendoes,
The blackbird whistling
Or just after.

Way V is chiefly an auditory image. It is comparable to what Robert Frost called an "image to the ear,"[7] the effect of which emerges from how the poem is spoken. But one might protest that V is merely *about* images to the ear—"The beauty of inflections," "the beauty of innuendoes," "The blackbird whistling," the sound or silence "just after" the blackbird whistles—that it does not present these things despite its sonorousness. Yet what constitutes "an image to the ear," Robert Kern observes in his essay on "Frost and Modernism," is not the sound *per se,* but the manipulation of tone. Such an image allows a reader to "encounter, through his speech, the inwardness of a person, rather than just objects in the world, no matter how emotionally evocative. . . . The effect is not the imagist avoidance of 'rhetoric,' the virtual displacement of linguistic conventions by sharply observed concrete particulars (or what Hulme refers to as the bodily handing-over of sensations), but a conscious indulgence in rhetoric, understood as the careful fashioning (or capturing and preserving) of speech-sounds."[8] Kern's words apply to Frost' s "A Patch of Old Snow," but are readily transferable to "Way V" and other Stevens' poems, such as "Le Monocle de Mon Oncle," "To a High-Toned Old Christian Woman," or "The Emperor of Ice Cream," in which "a conscious indulgence in rhetoric is so important. Stevens actually says of rhetoric that "there is nothing more congenial . . . to the imagination" (NA, 145). And indeed, in these poems, rhetoric seems as *generative* of the speaker as it is indicative of him:

"Mother of heaven, regina of the clouds,
O sceptre of the sun, crown of the moon,

There is not nothing, no, no, never nothing,
Like the clashed edges of two words that kill."
And so I mocked her in magnificent measure.
Or was it that I mocked myself alone?
(PM, 39)

VI

Icicles filled the long window
With barbaric glass.
The shadow of the blackbird
Crossed it, to and fro.
The mood
Traced in the shadow
An indecipherable cause.

VI resists super-position in several ways. In a manner similar to I, lines 1-4 comprise a single image: a window covered by icicles behind which the shadow of a blackbird crosses "to and fro." Unlike I, we needn't even superimpose *in thought* one image (11. 1-2, or 3-4) upon another (11. 3-4, or 1-2) because they may both be readily encompassed in one view. As a gloss on 1-4, lines 5-7 seem to invite the possibility that two different kinds of ideas may be superimposed (as was the case in II, and possibly in III): an objective presentation of an image (1-4) set upon a subjective reinterpretation of a portion of that image (5-7). But this possibility is negated upon closer inspection of line 2: "barbaric glass" serves notice that the imagination works subjectively upon the image from the moment of visual contact with the thing seen.

Must such images necessarily be given emotional or causal motives appended to their surface forms? Stevens implies that they must in order for poetry to be a truly (and perhaps true) imaginative act:

The bare image and the image as a symbol are the contrast: the image without meaning and the image as meaning. When the image is used to suggest something else, it is secondary. Poetry as an imaginative thing consists of more than lies [sic] on the surface. . . . Not all objects are equal. The vice of imagism was that it did not recognize this. (OP, 161, 168)

For Stevens, then, a work of the first intensity cannot be the "bare" presentation of a form. Pound essentially agrees:

By the "image" I mean . . . an equation; not an equation of mathematics, not something about *a, b,* and *c,* having something to do with form, but about *sea, cliffs, night,* having something to do with mood. (GB, 92).

Where Stevens and Pound differ is in their notions of what the image is about. The Pound image primarily concerns *sea, cliffs,* and *night* (or "faces" and "petals," or whatever the poem apparently presents)." [I]f a man use 'symbols,'" Pound writes elsewhere, "he must so use them that their symbolic function does not obtrude" (LE, 9). Stevens' case is quite different. VI, for instance, might be described as 'an equation about *mood* having something to do with *icicles, shadow,* and *blackbird.*'

Compared with Ways I-V, one could see how unsatisfactory VI would be had it ended on line 4, "barbaric glass" not-withstanding. By themselves, lines 1-4 come as close to comprising a "bare image" as Stevens would allow. (Cf. "The Snow Man" in which even "the nothing that is" is subjected to imaginative appraisal, such that "junipers [are] *shagged* with ice" and "spruces [are] *rough* in *the distant glitter*" [PM, 54]). The preceding poems all chiefly concern "Ways of Looking" (or Thinking) rather than the object of sight (or thought). Each implies a mind-set: the search for movement ("Among twenty snowy mountains, / The *only* moving thing . . ."); being "of three minds;" musing on life's "pantomime," on unity, on "which to prefer, . . ." VI joins this list with the addition of lines 5-7:

> The mood
> Traced in the shadow
> An indecipherable cause.

By themselves, *these* lines would compose an image in the Stevensian sense, for we need not know what the shadow is *of*. If as Pound insisted, an image "direct[ly] treat[] the 'thing'" (GB, 83; LE, 3), the thing "directly treated" by the Stevens image is the manner of thought.

Hence, Stevens' images are often *symbolic* in the sense that their meaning is extrinsic to what they ostensibly depict. Since meaning inheres in the perception of the image, the image itself must generally be "secondary." The exceptions would be passages like this from VI, or from Stevens' longer meditative poems like "Description without Place":

> There might be, too, a change immenser than
> A poet's metaphors in which being would
>
> Come true, a point in the fire of the music where
> Dazzle yields to a clarity and we observe,
>
> And observing is completing and we are content,
>
> . . . . .
>
> (PM, 272)

Yet pure images of thought like this are difficult to attain, harder still to sustain for any duration. Even here, the image-content is expressed metaphorically, as "a point in the fire of the music." Often in his meditative verses, Stevens attaches the concept of perception to a thing perceived. The same poem begins:

> It is possible that to seem—it is to be, As the sun
>   is something
> seeming and it is.
>
> The sun is an example. What it seems It is, and in
>   such seeming
> all things are.
>
> Thus things are like a seeming of the sun Or like a
>   seeming of
> the moon or night . . .
>
> (PM, 270)

But though one's focus is directed to the concrete "sun," the "sun" itself is not the thing 'treated directly,' rather it is a symbol for the concept of 'seeming as being.' Only "the image as a symbol" is for Stevens, "the image as meaning."

VII

> O thin men of Haddam,
> Why do you imagine golden birds?
> Do you not see how the blackbird
> Walks around the feet
> Of the women about you?

VIII

> I know noble accents
> And lucid inescapable rhythms;
> But I know, too,
> That the blackbird is involved
> In what I know.

These poems may be jointly explored as more explicit statements of Stevens' dictum mentioned in relation to VI: i.e. that the image must also be a symbol, "Poetry as an imaginative thing consist [ing] of more than lies upon the surface" (OP, 161). In VII and VIII, the blackbird is 'looked at' as the symbolic embodiment of the intrinsic relation between reality and the imagination. As is put so eloquently in "The Noble Rider and the Sound of Words," for Stevens, "the nature of poetry . . . is an interdependence of the imagination and reality as equals" (NA, 27). An imaginative construct that does not adhere to reality is impossible to believe in; on its part, the imagination brought in contact with reality through the poetic medium "enhances the sense of reality, heightens it, intensifies it," "gives to everything it touches . . . a[n] inherent nobility" (NA, 77, 33). The speaker in VII implores a mystical society, presumably of poets (the "thin men of Haddam" are "imagine [rs]" or perhaps "imag [e-ineers]"), to think not of "golden birds" unconnected to their Haddamite environs, but of "the blackbird / Walk[ing] around the feet / Of the women about you." That the verbs "imagine" and "see" are opposed in this context, and that "imagine" refers to "golden birds" and "see" to the blackbird, actually supports this reading. One can "imagine" anything so long as the components of the thing-imagined (here "gold" and "birds") are of the material world. (Stevens wrote, "the imagination creates nothing. We are able to romanticize and to give blue jays fifteen toes, but if there was no such thing as a bird we could not create it" [LWS, 465]). One can, then, imagine something one has never seen and in which one cannot believe. Things seen, however, are also things imagined, for "Things seen are things as seen" (OP, 162); and what is visible and imagined forms the basis of belief:

> There is, in fact, a world of poetry indistinguishable from the world in which we live, or, I ought to say, no doubt, from the world in which we shall come to live, since what makes the poet the potent figure that he is, or was, or ought to be, is that he creates the world to which we turn incessantly and

without knowing it and that he gives to life the supreme fictions without which we are unable to conceive of it. (NA, 31)

It is therefore beyond question that "the blackbird is involved / In what I know." What may be questioned is whether VII and VIII constitute images, even in the Stevensian sense, which as we have seen includes (in fact prefers) abstract images of thought. I suppose that within this definition, VII and VIII are included. Yet they seem less vivid than the other Ways, less examples of "direct presentation" than rhetorical statements. The thoughts are not expressed with the precision of IV, the other exclusively cognitive image in the collection. Perhaps it is just that, that VII and VIII do not direct us to *see* (i.e. see or feel) much at all. They read like short (free) verse essays. If they do not contradict Stevens' sanction of rhetoric as "congenial to the imagination," they yet reinforce Pound's insistence that the image be at "the farthest remove from rhetoric" (GB, 83). What saves VIII for me is its music, specifically the onamatopoeia of lines 1-2, which are what they describe: "Nobl [y] accented" with rhythms "loose" though "inescapable." Like V, VIII is mainly an image for the ear. VII, though instructive, is in my view the weakest of the Ways.

> IX
> When the blackbird flew out of sight,
> It marked the edge
> Of one of many circles.

Way IX is as *impressive* as Way VII is weak. I have chosen that term to convey what is most striking about IX: the form the image impresses upon the reader's mind. If "the form of sphere above sphere" in the *Paradiso* comprises part of "the most wonderful *image*," as Pound claims (GB, 86), IX replicates that "part" in little. "Marked" and "edge" refine the form of "many circles;" so too does the reference to the blackbird's *departure*. With the bird "out of sight" what remains in the image is *solely* a form—hence, a form heightened, enhanced. The importance of form in imagism is therefore dramatized by this absence. In theory, the imagist poet seeks to capture the form of something more so than the thing itself; that is, "direct treatment of the thing" means delineation of its form. Pound lauded vorticism for having made him "see form[s]. . . . new chords, new keys of design," like "the appearance of the sky where it juts down between houses," or "the great 'V's' of light that dart through the chinks over the curtain rings" (GB, 126). T.E. Hulme, similarly, wrote that modern poetry "attempts to fix an impression," and his biographer describes Hulme's own poetic efforts in terms of "bend[ing] his language to the exact curve of his thought."[9] For Stevens, it is in form where the real and imaginary coincide. "Art, broadly, is the form of life, or the sound or color of life. Considered as form (in the abstract) it is often indistinguishable from life itself" (OP, 158)

> X
> At the sight of blackbirds
> Flying in a green light,

Even the bawds of euphony
Would cry out sharply.

Like V and VI, X is a complex image of multiple superpositions: black upon ("in") green, euphony upon cacophony ("cry . . . sharply"), vision ("the sight of blackbirds / Flying in a green light") upon sound (the bawds of euphony / Would cry out sharply").

Stevens is the most colorful of Imagists. Although Pound, Williams, and Hulme include colors in some images, they do not treat colors as images. Mention of "a red wheel / barrow // beside the white / chickens," of "the figure 5 / in gold / on a red / firetruck," or of "Petals on a wet, black bow," "Pale carnage beneath bright mist," or "the ruddy moon . . . like a red-faced farmer" do not invite the reader to abstract the color from the object of which it is a part, thus to think of the color as a "thing" treated.[10]

The line from "April" illustrates particularly well the difficulty of abstracting color from the colored object in Pound. The colors are too integrated with their objects to be "solid"—i.e. white, gray, or gray-green (olive boughs are being described); they are instead "pale" and "bright." Notice too that were these colors solid, they would be achromatic, capable of setting a mood (of thus being essential *to* the image), but less able in themselves to project memorable color-forms. (The same can be said of "black" in "Metro," "white" in "The Jewel Stairs' Grievance," and "grey" in "Gentildonna"). The colors in the Williams and Hulme images here cited stand out more than Pound's colors, but are clearly subordinate to other forms.

"Black" is of course subordinate to "blackbird" in Stevens' "Ways," yet it is possible to abstract "black" from "bird" because the object that blackness is superimposed upon is, first and foremost, a color. "Green" turns "green light" into a perceptible form. Thus, the super-position of objects is fundamentally a super-position of colors—there is no "wheelbarrow," "chickens," "moon" or "farmer" to share what is here, literally *limelight*.[11]

In "Disillusionment of Ten O'Clock" (PM, 11), color may be said to inhere in the poem itself:

> The houses are haunted
> By white night-gowns.
> None are green,
> Or purple with green rings,
> Or green with yellow rings,
> Or yellow with blue rings.

The colors (note their vibrancy, hence their potential to stand as images by themselves) do not belong to the night-gowns ("None are green, . . ."). Deprived of an object (indeed, objectively nonexistent), the colors subsist solely in the poem, a thing not to be seen so much as read. What we are meant to *see* are colors. Like a poem or natural light, weather is invisible unless there is something in it—like rain, or "red." And so, at the end of "Disillusionment" ("Only, here and there, an old sailor, . . . Catches tigers / In red weather"), we see red.[12]

Stevens' most effective color-image is "Sea-Surface Full of Clouds" (PM, 89-92). Unlike "Disillusionment," this poem does not simply invite us to see colors divorced from objects; nor to abstract a color-pattern, as does "Way X"; but rather, to take color as a primary component of both reality and imagination—as an instance of "fact as we want it to be" (PM, 206). But along with stating Stevens' thesis on the interdependence of real and imagined, it is also an extended commentary on Pound's dictum that an imagist poem tries "to record the precise instant when a thing outward and objective transforms itself into a thing inward and subjective" (GB, 89). The consistent structure of the work (five six tercet sections, with each line corresponding to those lines in parallel position in the other four sections) mimes the frame of mind in which the speaker holds one seascape at five separate moments. As in Pound's and Williams' poems, colors and objects are inseparably joined in images; and yet like Stevens' other color-studies, colors as images are also foregrounded. This double-vision emerges partially from a tension between our knowledge of what the poem represents, and the syntactic representation of color as an object in itself:

> . . . Paradisal green
> Gave suavity to the perplexed machine
>
> Of ocean, which like limpid water lay.
>
> (I. 5-7)

The reference to "Paradisal green," we know from the context, is to the color of the ocean. And yet, "green" is the subject of the sentence in which "ocean" appears merely as the possessive modifier for a metaphor.

Syntactic structures at the close of sections I, III-V create a similar impression.

> . . . And sometimes the sea
> poured brilliant iris on the glistening blue.
>
> (I. 17-18)

> The shrouding shadows, . . .
>
> . . . . .
>
> Deluged the ocean with a sapphire blue.
>
> (III. 14, 18)

> . . .—But more suddenly the heaven rolled
>
> Its bluest sea-clouds in the thinking green,
>
> . . . . .
>
> (IV. 15-16)

> . . . Then the sea
> And heaven rolled as one and from the two
> Came fresh transfigurings of freshest blue.
>
> (V. 16-18)

Color in these lines becomes the object of the verb, or prepositional phrase. Though the color subsists in the ocean and in the reflection of the clouds upon the ocean, mention of "glistening blue," "sapphire blue," "thinking green," "freshest blue," and (most striking, I think) "brilliant iris"—each without a referent, and preceded each time by an adjective *referring to* the color, evokes a double-vision of a colorful scene, and of the color itself.

The repeated effect of the color allusions at corresponding loci in each section, also accounts for this double-vision. "[I]t is not too extravagant to think of . . . the repetitions of resemblances as a source of the ideal," Stevens wrote (NA, 81); and here indeed repetitions-of the shade of green at line five, of the variant of blue within the last four lines-create *ideals* (understood Platonically in this context as *ideas*) in the reader's consciousness. Because the resemblances repeated are primarily *of color* ("Paradisal green," "sham-like green," "uncertain green," "too-fluent green," "motley green;" "glistening blue," "blue heaven," "sapphire blue," "bluest sea-clouds," "freshest blue"), ideals of "green" and "blue" are engendered along with ideals of green and blue 'things' (sea, sky, clouds).

> XI
> He rode over Connecticut
> In a glass coach.
> Once, a fear pierced him,
> In that he mistook the shadow of his equipage
> For blackbirds.

This is a very abstract image—though we are asked to perceive events, an ostensibly easier task than the perception of concepts that Ways II and IV required. The protagonist of this image-drama "rode over Connecticut / In a glass coach" (first event). He then "mistook / The shadow of his equipage / For blackbirds." Yet the incidents in XI are in fact more difficult to see than are the earlier conceptual forms. To the experience of being "of three minds" in II was attached the concrete symbol of "a tree / In which there are three blackbirds." To the abstract notion of "one"ness in IV were appended three abstractions, which despite their generality, are readily conceptualized. "Man," "woman," and "blackbird" are each specific enough to have their own form—*contrast* "human," "bird," or "Connecticut." What does it mean to "ride over Connecticut," or, while we are on this subject, to "place a jar in Tennessee"? Neither state is very large, though each is diverse enough to foster uncertainty. In "Anecdote of a Jar" (PM, 46), we are at least informed that the jar is in the Tennessee wilderness—but to "r[i]de over Connecticut" might refer to a Hartford street, a path in Old Saybrook, the interstate, or some other course. It may even allude to all of the above—because "He rode" (i.e. *was riding*) no one time is necessarily referred to.

With this opening, Stevens achieves "that sense of freedom from time limits and space limits" which, according to Pound, is an effect produced by the image (LE, 4). But rather than doing so by Pound's means of "super-position"—"which presents an intellectual and emotional complex in an instant of time"—he relies on a technique more consistent with his own tenets. He engages imaginatively with the reality of space and time (the state of

Connecticut at plausibly more than one time) to create an image free from spatial and temporal exactitude. The superposition that follows is likewise mediated by Stevensian propensities:

> Once, a fear pierced him,
> In that he mistook
> The shadow of his equipage
> For blackbirds.

That "Once" threatens to inject the moment described into a particular historical moment. Yet if the prologue works as intended, the reader is sufficiently removed from time so that that "Once" merely delineates *an* "instant" in which the image occurs. Moreover, as we have seen, Stevens is less intent on capturing what he perceives than he is on recording the "Way" that he perceives—whether this be expressed in the study of a working mind (II, VI), a comment on the perceived (I, III, X), an abstract concept (IV), a personal reflection (V, VIII), or a rhetorical statement (VII).

Thus, where Pound might make an image of this instant by compressing details to produce "that sense of freedom from time and space"—

> The shadow of his equipage:
> Blackbirds.

—Stevens presents another image at a further remove, or rather, at two removes. For his image is not of "the shadow of his equipage" seen as blackbirds; nor *of* this seeing, i.e. the "mist[aking]" of the shadow for blackbirds; but of the "fear" occasioned by this mistaking: "Once, a fear pierced him, / *In that* he mistook / The shadow of his equipage / For blackbirds."

Yet Stevens can present a Poundlike "sense" of instantaneousness:

> XII
>
> The river is moving.
> The blackbird must be flying.

XII may be understood discursively, as a premise with the minor following upon the major: Since "The river is moving," "The blackbird must [then] be flying." Yet since 'Since' must be assumed, one may read XII as a superposition of two unrelated statements—as an attempt, possibly, to depict two different times and places *at once* and *in the same place*. The punctuation somewhat impedes this reading, hence the impression is less powerful than what Pound achieves in "Metro," where the colon between "ideas" implies their fusion into a single time and place. That fusion is impossible,[13] but Pound, and to a lesser extent Stevens in Way XII, create an illusion of this effect and thus a *"sense of"* (one can never have more than a "sense of") "freedom from time limits and space limits."

> XIII
>
> It was evening all afternoon.
> It was snowing.

> And it was going to snow.
> The blackbird sat
> In the cedar-limbs.

Of XIII, one might say what Pound did about a line of Lionel Johnson's (LE, 362): that "no one has written purer Imagisme than [Stevens] has in the[se] line[s]." The subject is treated extraordinarily directly. Each word is essential to the presentation. The first two of Pound's famed Imagist tenets are thus fulfilled. With respect to the third: "compose in the sequence of the musical phrase, not in sequence of a metronome" (LE, 3)—it is difficult to imagine the sequence of this musical phrase assuming a different form than it does here. Arguably, the tenet "regarding rhythm" is least conducive to empirical proof. Way IV would seem a rare exception; there, the sequence of the first two lines appears to dictate that the verbal equation can only be extended in line three, in order for the new equation to still equal "one." Had Stevens written:

> A man and a woman
> Are one.
> A man and a woman
> And a blackbird
> Are one.

the equation might then appear imbalanced: "A man and a woman / And a blackbird" are *two* lines. There is an obvious logical fallacy to this 'proof': "one" need not refer to one line. Still, that "one" could have this denotation; and above that, the reader's desire for symmetry in an image *about* equivalence, suggest that the fallacy, though logical, is not experiential.[14]

> A man and a woman and a blackbird
> Are one.

> A man and a woman
> And a blackbird
> Are not.

If we are willing to dispense with logic to the extent that Pound and Stevens are (the former by distinguishing science from logic [ABC, 18], the latter by asserting that "Poetry must be irrational" [OP, 162]), it is clear—indeed, quasi-logical—that XIII is composed in the only musical sequence appropriate to the image. "It was evening all afternoon" is one complete statement, or "phrase." Of course, a phrase need not appear entirely on a single line of poetry (cf.: "so much depends / upon // a red wheel / barrow"); but because this phrase does, and because it is the initial phrase in the image, it determines the musical time signature of XIII. XIII, as it were, begins in the signature "1/1"—one phrase to one line; a complete grammatical statement equaling one phrase (a signature often utilized by Pound).[15] Lineation thus follows accordingly, until the last line:

> It was evening all afternoon=complete
> grammatical statement=musical phrase=line
> It was snowing =complete grammatical
> statement=musical

phrase=line
 And it was going to snow = [complete
 grammatical statement = musical phrase = line]
 The blackbird sat = [complete grammatical
 statement = musical phrase = line]

"In the cedar-limbs" is not a complete statement though it does not disrupt the pattern. Just as a piece of music might end on a partial phrase, or *coda* (literally, a concluding section of a musical, *literary,* or dramatic work that is *formally distinct from the main structure;* something that serves to summarize, *or round out and conclude*), so too might the image. (There can be no coda in the middle of a piece, hence "all afternoon" becomes part of the first phrase.)

This exercise in "scoring" points to the intrinsic relation between imagist and organicist doctrines; to what Frank Kermode views as the hallmark of symbolist and imagist works. Such works "derive their power," writes Kermode, "from internal reference: their quality . . . is dependent upon the organisms to which they belong."[16] Ideally, then, "the sequence of the musical phrase" in an imagist poem is determined by single lines or groups of lines that conform to a particular sequence. Such rules would not always apply, yet would be applicable to a *pure* image like XIII.

EPILOGUE

As we have been looking at Stevens' work from a Poundian slant, and as "Thirteen Ways" is listed in Stevens' *ouevre* as a *single* poem, one wonders: are the "Ways" *altogether* construable as *an* Image? May they (it?) be viewed as 'one idea set atop another set atop another set atop another . . .' so as to comprise a complex "form of super-position" (or "visual chord," in Hulme's words[17]), and thus "a one-image poem"? Theoretically, I suppose "Ways" may, though I confess great difficulty in so interpreting them. Again, the premise of the Ways, and of Stevens' imagism generally, is that we are not invited to see some *thing but* some *way* of seeing the thing. This I perceive to be the fundamental difference between Stevens' work, and Pound's and Williams': where the latter poets are intent on "lifting to the imagination those things which lie under the direct scrutiny of the senses," Stevens seeks to lift the scrutinizing apparatus—i.e. the imagination—up to the senses.

NOTES

1 Stevens, *Opus Posthumous,* ed. Samuel French Morse (New York: Alfred A. Knopff, 1957) 168; subsequently cited in the text as OP. The following works of Stevens' will also be cited in the essay according to the abbreviations with which they are here accompanied: *Letters of Wallace Stevens,* ed. Holly. Stevens (New York: Alfred A. Knopf, 1966) LWS; *The Necessary Angel: Essays on Reality and the Imagination* (New York: Alfred A. Knopf, 1951) NA; *The Palm at the End of the Mind: Selected Poems and a Play,* ed. Holly Stevens (New York: Knopff-Vintage, 1972) PM.

2 Perloff neatly delineates the debate between Pound and Stevens critics as to "whose era" modernist poetry really is. Stevens criticism frequently subordinates matters of technique to those of content; essays on Pound are often inversely disproportional. (*See* "Pound/Stevens: Whose Era?", *The Dance of the Intellect* [Cambridge: Cambridge UP, 1985] 1-32. It is hoped that this essay moves toward redressing the first of these imbalances by focusing on Stevens' technique, on his syntax especially.

3 *Wallace Stevens: The Poems of Our Climate* (Ithaca: Cornell UP, 1977) 168.

4 "Vorticism," in Pound, *Gaudier-Brzeska: A Memoir* (1916; New York: New Directions, 1970) 89; subsequently cited in the text as GB. "Vorticism" premiered in the *Fortnightly Review,* XCVI (1914) 461-71.

5 Pound, *Literary Essays* (New York: New Directions, 1935) 154; subsequently cited in the text as LE.

6 Pound, *ABC of Reading* (London: Faber and Faber, 1951) 20; subsequently cited in the text as ABC; *see also* Fenollosa's treatise on "The Chinese Written Character as a Medium for Poetry," edited by Pound (1936; San Francisco: City Lights Books, 1968) 28. Williams, *Selected Essays* (New York: Random House, 1954) 11.

7 *Selected Prose of Robert Frost,* ed. Hyde Cox and Edward Connery Lathem (New York: Holt, Rinehart and Winston, 1966) 60.

8 Robert Kern, "Frost and Modernism," *American Literature,* 60: 1 (1988) 11.

9 T.E. Hulme, *Further Speculations,* ed. Sam Hynes (Minneapolis: U of Minnesota P, 1955) 72; Alun R. Jones, *The Life and Opinions of T.E. Hulme* (Boston: Beacon Press, 1960) 50.

10 These lines are excerpted from Williams' "The Red Wheelbarrow" and "The Great Figure"; Pound's "In a Station of the Metro" and "April"; and Hulme's "Autumn." The extreme example of an Imagist using color as a pretext for presenting something else is John Gould Fletcher, whose series of color "Symphonies" (more symbolist than they are imagist) describe emotions to which colors are subjectively assigned. Only H.D. approximates Stevens' method of abstracting color from the object in which it inheres, so as to directly treat color. (*Vide* "Oread": "Whirl up, sea— . . . Hurl your green over us"; or "Evening": "black creeps from root to root"). Yet she does not employ colors as frequently as does Stevens, nor is her color-range as wide as his.

11 When light is presented as a perceived form, that is a form *in itself,* it is then divine or supernatural, and so without color reference. Eliot and Pound are masters of depicting such light. *Vide* Eliot's Tenth Chorus from "The Rock," Pound's late *Cantos* (especially the fragment titled "From Canto CXV"), and such early Pound

lyrics as "The House of Splendour" and "'Blandula, Tenella, Vagula'." In "'Blandula'," color is a medium in which light inheres. In Way X, light is the medium in which color inheres. Pound and Eliot are unquestionably the great Imagists of light but the great Imagist of color is Stevens.

[12] Could Stevens have intended the pun: that at the end of disillusionment, one "sees red," i.e. is angry. The old sailor catching tigers seems to be having an exciting time, but the speaker's tone is rather combative ("None are green, . . . None of them are strange, . . . People are not going / To dream of baboons and periwinkles"), and what he is protesting against is the failure of imagination, the failure to create illusions. The pun would be consistent with Stevens' train of thought. Of course, for the pun to work we must understand the "end of disillusionment" negatively, not as signaling the dawn of new illusions.

[13] John T. Gage explains this impossibility in some detail in his remarkable study, *In the Arresting Eye: The Rhetoric of Imagism* (Baton Rouge: Louisiana State UP, 1981) 60-63.

[14] Gage describes this effect as follows: "the feeling which results from the experience of the figure is not the same as the emotion being described. . . . [A]nalogy communicates a feeling which is distinct from the experience of the poem, yet which is fundamental to its communication because morphologically like it" (*In the Arresting Eye*, 78-79).

[15] The best account of Pound's lineation comes in Donald Davie's comments on "South-Folk in Cold Country": "The poem establishes a convention by which the gauge of a poetic line is not the number of syllables or of stressed syllables, or of metrical feet, but the fulfillment of the simple grammatical unit, the sentence." Davie develops this remark in *Ezra Pound: Poet as Sculptor* (New York: Oxford UP, 1964) 41-47; 60-63.

[16] Frank Kermode, "Romantic Image" (London: Routledge and Kegan Paul, 1957) 102.

[17] Hulme, *Further Speculations,* 73. Though the concepts of "visual chord" and "super-position" can be linked, as they are here, they cannot truly be identified. The visual chord implies a union of images "to suggest an image which is different to both" (73). Super-position, on the other hand, implies the paradoxical separation of images conjoined, such that, in Fenollosa's words, "two things added together do not produce a third thing but suggest some fundamental relation between the two" ("The Chinese Written Character," 10). The product of super-position is indeed "a third thing"—what Pound calls an "image" as distinct from the "ideas" superposed—though its existence is predicated on *"relation"* rather than *coalescence.* Even the so-called "fusion" of ideas into a single time and space does not negate the individuality of each superposed idea. For a more detailed discussion of super-position, *see* Chapter 1 of my "Modernist Image: Imagist Technique in the Work of Pound, Eliot, and Williams," diss., Boston College, 1991.

FURTHER READING

Anthologies

Aldington, Richard, ed. *Imagist Anthology, 1930.* London: Chatto & Windus, 1930, 154 p.
Contains poems by Pound, Lowell, Flint, Hulme, and others associated with the Imagist movement.

Jones, Peter, ed. *Imagist Poetry.* Harmondsworth: Penguin, 1972, 188 p.
Includes an introduction outlining the development of Imagism.

Pratt, William, ed. *The Imagist Poem: Modern Poetry in Miniature.* New York: Dutton, 1963, 128 p.
Includes an introduction surveying the major writers and themes of the Imagist movement.

Secondary Sources

Aldington, Richard. "Chapter IX." In *Life for Life's Sake: A Book of Reminiscences*, pp. 133-59. New York: The Viking Press, 1941.
Personal recollection of the Imagist movement by one of the group's founding members.

Clements, Patricia. "The Imagists." In *Baudelaire & The English Tradition*, pp. 260-99. Princeton, N.J.: Princeton University Press, 1985.
Recounts the development of Imagism in theory and practice, as a self-consciously modern and at times self-contradictory movement spawned from the innovations of the French Symbolists, particularly Charles Baudelaire.

Dembo, L. S. "H.D. *Imagiste* and Her Octopus Intelligence." In *H.D. Woman and Poet*, edited by Michael King, pp. 209-25. Orono: University of Maine at Orono, 1986.
Reveals indications of H.D.'s transcendence of Ezra Pound's early influence in her autobiographical *Her* and in her novel *Hermione.*

Durrell, Lawrence. "Georgians and Imagists." In *A Key to Modern British Poetry*, pp. 119-42. Norman: University of Oklahoma Press, 1952.
Includes a survey of the Imagist movement which notes its influences and early theoreticians. Durrell sees Ezra Pound and T. S. Eliot as the major figures to arise from the movement and separates their work from that of the "lesser" Imagists, whose poetry he finds marred by "English sentimentality."

Gage, John T. *In the Arresting Eye: The Rhetoric of Imagism.* Baton Rouge: Louisiana State University Press, 1981, 186 p.
Attempts to liberate Imagist poetry from "the inadequacies of Imagist theory," which may be said to hamper an aesthetic appreciation of these works.

Gould, Jean. *Amy: The World of Amy Lowell and the Imagist Movement*. New York: Dodd, Mead & Company, 1975, 372 p.

> Biography of Lowell that focuses on her dedication to the development of Imagism.

Gross, Harvey. "Imagism and Visual Prosody." In *Sound and Form in Modern Poetry: A Study of Prosody from Thomas Hardy to Robert Lowell*, pp. 100-29. Ann Arbor: University of Michigan Press, 1964.

> Considers the theory and verse of the Imagists T. E. Hulme, Ezra Pound, Amy Lowell, and H.D. as well as the influence of these on the poetic form of such poets as Marianne Moore, William Carlos Williams, and E. E. Cummings.

Guimond, James. "After Imagism." *Ohio Review* 15, No. 1 (Fall 1973): 5-28.

> Studies "the cultural significance of one particularly American branch of the Imagist movement—the kind of Imagism, exemplified in William Carlos Williams' 'red wheelbarrow' poem, which is characterized by its extremely stark presentation of commonplace objects."

Harmer, J. B. *Victory in Limbo: Imagism 1908-1917*. London: Secker & Warburg, 1975, 238 p.

> Describes Imagism as "the one literary movement in Britain and America that reflected the energies of modernism" otherwise neglected in the arts of these two nations.

Hasbany, Richard. "The Shock of Vision: An Imagist Reading of *In Our Time*." In *Ernest Hemingway: Five Decades of Criticism*, edited by Linda Welshimer Wagner, pp. 224-40. East Lansing: Michigan State University Press, 1974.

> Investigates the possible influence of T. E. Hulme and Ezra Pound on Hemingway's early collection of short stories *In Our Time*.

Healey, Claire. "Some Imagist Essays: Amy Lowell." *The New England Quarterly* 43, No. 1 (March 1970): 134-38.

> Details Lowell's predominance over the Imagist movement during the period from 1913 to 1917.

Hughes, Glenn. *Imagism & the Imagists: A Study in Modern Poetry*. Palo Alto, Calif.: Stanford University Press, 1931, 283 p.

> History of the Imagist movement that places particular emphasis on seven key members of the group: Richard Aldington, H.D., John Gould Fletcher, F. S. Flint, D. H. Lawrence, Amy Lowell, and Ezra Pound.

Kenner, Hugh. "Imagism." In *The Pound Era*, pp. 173-91. Berkeley: University of California Press, 1971.

> Probes Ezra Pound's sway over the nascent Imagist movement in 1912.

Moody, A. D. "H.D., *Imagiste*: An Elemental Mind." *Agenda* 25, Nos. 3-4 (Autumn/Winter 1987-88): 77-96.

> Analyzes H.D.'s concept of Imagism as it departs from theories originally articulated by Ezra Pound.

Pondrom, Cyrena N., ed. "Selected Letters from H.D. to F. S. Flint: A Commentary on the Imagist Period." *Contemporary Literature* 10, No. 4 (Autumn 1969): 557-86.

> Collection of letters in which H.D. "clarifies our view of the inner workings of the coterie of Imagism and the ways those associated with it sought to surmount the disruption of the First World War."

Pratt, William, and Robert Richardson, eds. *Homage to Imagism*. New York: AMS Press, 1992, 169 p.

> Includes an introduction on the enduring significance of Imagism by Pratt, reprints of Imagist poems, and essays on D.H. Lawrence, H. D., and others associated with the movement by various contributors.

Schuchard, Ronald. "'As Regarding Rhythm': Yeats and the Imagists." *Yeats: An Annual of Critical and Textual Studies* 2 (1984): 209-26.

> Highlights the neglected importance of W. B. Yeats's concern with poetic rhythm on the work of Ezra Pound in the early formative years of the Imagist movement.

Spender, Stephen. "The Seminal Image." In *The Struggle of the Modern*, pp. 110-15. Berkeley: University of California Press, 1963.

> Briefly summarizes the "essential principles of the famous Imagist manifesto" and the subsequent influence of this work on modern poetry.

Tanner, Tony. "Transcendentalism and Imagism." In *The Reign of Wonder: Naivety and Reality in American Literature*, pp. 87-93. Cambridge: Cambridge University Press, 1965.

> Compares the aesthetic approaches of Transcendentalism and Imagism in order to arrive at a definition of the latter.

Thacker, Andrew. "Imagist Travels in Modernist Space." *Textual Practice* 7, No. 2 (Summer 1993): 224-46.

> Offers readings of Imagist poems about transportation in a postmodern idiom. Thacker observes how many reveal "sites of struggle over gender and sexuality" in the contemporary urban environment.

Twentieth-Century Literary Criticism

Cumulative Indexes
Volumes 1-74

How to Use This Index

The main references

Calvino, Italo
   1923–1985 .... CLC 5, 8, 11, 22, 33, 39,
                              73; SSC 3

list all author entries in the following Gale Literary Criticism series:

BLC = *Black Literature Criticism*
CLC = *Contemporary Literary Criticism*
CLR = *Children's Literature Review*
CMLC = *Classical and Medieval Literature Criticism*
DA = *DISCovering Authors*
DAB = *DISCovering Authors: British*
DAC = *DISCovering Authors: Canadian*
DAM = *DISCovering Authors: Modules*
      DRAM: *Dramatists Module*; *MST*: *Most-Studied Authors Module*;
      MULT: *Multicultural Authors Module*; *NOV*: *Novelists Module*;
      POET: *Poets Module*; *POP*: *Popular Fiction and Genre Authors Module*
DC = *Drama Criticism*
HLC = *Hispanic Literature Criticism*
LC = *Literature Criticism from 1400 to 1800*
NCLC = *Nineteenth-Century Literature Criticism*
PC = *Poetry Criticism*
SSC = *Short Story Criticism*
TCLC = *Twentieth-Century Literary Criticism*
WLC = *World Literature Criticism, 1500 to the Present*

The cross-references

See also CANR 23; CA 85-88;
   obituary CA116

list all author entries in the following Gale biographical and literary sources:

AAYA = *Authors & Artists for Young Adults*
AITN = *Authors in the News*
BEST = *Bestsellers*
BW = *Black Writers*
CA = *Contemporary Authors*
CAAS = *Contemporary Authors Autobiography Series*
CABS = *Contemporary Authors Bibliographical Series*
CANR = *Contemporary Authors New Revision Series*
CAP = *Contemporary Authors Permanent Series*
CDALB = *Concise Dictionary of American Literary Biography*
CDBLB = *Concise Dictionary of British Literary Biography*
DLB = *Dictionary of Literary Biography*
DLBD = *Dictionary of Literary Biography Documentary Series*
DLBY = *Dictionary of Literary Biography Yearbook*
HW = *Hispanic Writers*
JRDA = *Junior DISCovering Authors*
MAICYA = *Major Authors and Illustrators for Children and Young Adults*
MTCW = *Major 20th-Century Writers*
NNAL = *Native North American Literature*
SAAS = *Something about the Author Autobiography Series*
SATA = *Something about the Author*
YABC = *Yesterday's Authors of Books for Children*

Literary Criticism Series
Cumulative Author Index

Bass, Kingsley B., Jr.
See Bullins, Ed
Bass, Rick 1958- .... **CLC 79**
See also CA 126; CANR 53
Bassani, Giorgio 1916- .... **CLC 9**
See also CA 65-68; CANR 33; DLB 128, 177;
MTCW
Bastos, Augusto (Antonio) Roa
See Roa Bastos, Augusto (Antonio)
Bataille, Georges 1897-1962 .... **CLC 29**
See also CA 101; 89-92
Bates, H(erbert) E(rnest) 1905-1974**CLC 46;**
DAB; DAM POP; SSC 10
See also CA 93-96; 45-48; CANR 34; DLB 162;
MTCW
Bauchart
See Camus, Albert
Baudelaire, Charles 1821-1867 .**NCLC 6, 29,**
55; DA; DAB; DAC; DAM MST, POET;
PC 1; SSC 18; WLC
Baudrillard, Jean 1929- .... **CLC 60**
Baum, L(yman) Frank 1856-1919 ...... **TCLC 7**
See also CA 108; 133; CLR 15; DLB 22; JRDA;
MAICYA; MTCW; SATA 18
Baum, Louis F.
See Baum, L(yman) Frank
Baumbach, Jonathan 1933- ....**CLC 6, 23**
See also CA 13-16R; CAAS 5; CANR 12;
DLBY 80; INT CANR-12; MTCW
Bausch, Richard (Carl) 1945- .... **CLC 51**
See also CA 101; CAAS 14; CANR 43, 61; DLB
130
Baxter, Charles 1947-**CLC 45, 78; DAM POP**
See also CA 57-60; CANR 40; DLB 130
Baxter, George Owen
See Faust, Frederick (Schiller)
Baxter, James K(eir) 1926-1972 .... **CLC 14** .
See also CA 77-80
Baxter, John
See Hunt, E(verette) Howard, (Jr.)
Bayer, Sylvia
See Glassco, John
Baynton, Barbara 1857-1929 .... **TCLC 57**
Beagle, Peter S(oyer) 1939- ...... **CLC 7, 104**
See also CA 9-12R; CANR 4, 51; DLBY 80;
INT CANR-4; SATA 60
Bean, Normal
See Burroughs, Edgar Rice
Beard, Charles A(ustin) 1874-1948 **TCLC 15**
See also CA 115; DLB 17; SATA 18
Beardsley, Aubrey 1872-1898 .... **NCLC 6**
Beattie, Ann 1947-**CLC 8, 13, 18, 40, 63; DAM**
NOV, POP; SSC 11
See also BEST 90:2; CA 81-84; CANR 53;
DLBY 82; MTCW
Beattie, James 1735-1803 .... **NCLC 25**
See also DLB 109
Beauchamp, Kathleen Mansfield 1888-1923
See Mansfield, Katherine
See also CA 104; 134; DA; DAC; DAM MST
Beaumarchais, Pierre-Augustin Caron de 1732-
1799 ....**DC 4**
See also DAM DRAM
Beaumont, Francis 1584(?)-1616**LC 33; DC 6**
See also CDBLB Before 1660; DLB 58, 121
Beauvoir, Simone (Lucie Ernestine Marie
Bertrand) de 1908-1986**CLC 1, 2, 4, 8, 14,**
31, 44, 50, 71; DA; DAB; DAC; DAM MST,
NOV; WLC
See also CA 9-12R; 118; CANR 28, 61; DLB
72; DLBY 86; MTCW
Becker, Carl (Lotus) 1873-1945 ..... **TCLC 63**
See also CA 157; DLB 17
Becker, Jurek 1937-1997 ....**CLC 7, 19**
See also CA 85-88; 157; CANR 60; DLB 75
Becker, Walter 1950- .... **CLC 26**
Beckett, Samuel (Barclay) 1906-1989 **CLC 1,**

2, 3, 4, 6, 9, 10, 11, 14, 18, 29, 57, 59, 83;
DA; DAB; DAC; DAM DRAM, MST,
NOV; SSC 16; WLC
See also CA 5-8R; 130; CANR 33, 61; CDBLB
1945-1960; DLB 13, 15; DLBY 90; MTCW
Beckford, William 1760-1844 .... **NCLC 16**
See also DLB 39
Beckman, Gunnel 1910- .... **CLC 26**
See also CA 33-36R; CANR 15; CLR 25;
MAICYA; SAAS 9; SATA 6
Becque, Henri 1837-1899 .... **NCLC 3**
Beddoes, Thomas Lovell 1803-1849 **NCLC 3**
See also DLB 96
Bede c. 673-735 .... **CMLC 20**
See also DLB 146
Bedford, Donald F.
See Fearing, Kenneth (Flexner)
Beecher, Catharine Esther 1800-1878 **N C L C**
30
See also DLB 1
Beecher, John 1904-1980 .... **CLC 6**
See also AITN 1; CA 5-8R; 105; CANR 8
Beer, Johann 1655-1700 .... **LC 5**
See also DLB 168
Beer, Patricia 1924- .... **CLC 58**
See also CA 61-64; CANR 13, 46; DLB 40
Beerbohm, Max
See Beerbohm, (Henry) Max(imilian)
Beerbohm, (Henry) Max(imilian) 1872-1956
TCLC 1, 24
See also CA 104; 154; DLB 34, 100
Beer-Hofmann, Richard 1866-1945**TCLC 60**
See also CA 160; DLB 81
Begiebing, Robert J(ohn) 1946- .... **CLC 70**
See also CA 122; CANR 40
Behan, Brendan 1923-1964 **CLC 1, 8, 11, 15,**
79; DAM DRAM
See also CA 73-76; CANR 33; CDBLB 1945-
1960; DLB 13; MTCW
Behn, Aphra 1640(?)-1689**LC 1, 30; DA; DAB;**
DAC; DAM DRAM, MST, NOV, POET;
DC 4; PC 13; WLC
See also DLB 39, 80, 131
Behrman, S(amuel) N(athaniel) 1893-1973
CLC 40
See also CA 13-16; 45-48; CAP 1; DLB 7, 44
Belasco, David 1853-1931 .... **TCLC 3**
See also CA 104; DLB 7
Belcheva, Elisaveta 1893- .... **CLC 10**
See also Bagryana, Elisaveta
Beldone, Phil "Cheech"
See Ellison, Harlan (Jay)
Beleno
See Azuela, Mariano
Belinski, Vissarion Grigoryevich 1811-1848
NCLC 5
Belitt, Ben 1911- .... **CLC 22**
See also CA 13-16R; CAAS 4; CANR 7; DLB
5
Bell, Gertrude 1868-1926 .... **TCLC 67**
See also DLB 174
Bell, James Madison 1826-1902 ...**TCLC 43;**
BLC; DAM MULT
See also BW 1; CA 122; 124; DLB 50
Bell, Madison Smartt 1957- ...... **CLC 41, 102**
See also CA 111; CANR 28, 54
Bell, Marvin (Hartley) 1937-**CLC 8, 31; DAM**
POET
See also CA 21-24R; CAAS 14; CANR 59; DLB
5; MTCW
Bell, W. L. D.
See Mencken, H(enry) L(ouis)
Bellamy, Atwood C.
See Mencken, H(enry) L(ouis)
Bellamy, Edward 1850-1898 .... **NCLC 4**
See also DLB 12
Bellin, Edward J.

See Kuttner, Henry
Belloc, (Joseph) Hilaire (Pierre Sebastien Rene
Swanton) 1870-1953 **TCLC 7, 18; DAM**
POET
See also CA 106; 152; DLB 19, 100, 141, 174;
YABC 1
Belloc, Joseph Peter Rene Hilaire
See Belloc, (Joseph) Hilaire (Pierre Sebastien
Rene Swanton)
Belloc, Joseph Pierre Hilaire
See Belloc, (Joseph) Hilaire (Pierre Sebastien
Rene Swanton)
Belloc, M. A.
See Lowndes, Marie Adelaide (Belloc)
Bellow, Saul 1915-**CLC 1, 2, 3, 6, 8, 10, 13, 15,**
25, 33, 34, 63, 79; DA; DAB; DAC; DAM
MST, NOV, POP; SSC 14; WLC
See also AITN 2; BEST 89:3; CA 5-8R; CABS
1; CANR 29, 53; CDALB 1941-1968; DLB
2, 28; DLBD 3; DLBY 82; MTCW
Belser, Reimond Karel Maria de 1929-
See Ruyslinck, Ward
See also CA 152
Bely, Andrey .... **TCLC 7; PC 11**
See also Bugayev, Boris Nikolayevich
Benary, Margot
See Benary-Isbert, Margot
Benary-Isbert, Margot 1889-1979 .... **CLC 12**
See also CA 5-8R; 89-92; CANR 4; CLR 12;
MAICYA; SATA 2; SATA-Obit 21
Benavente (y Martinez), Jacinto 1866-1954
TCLC 3; DAM DRAM, MULT
See also CA 106; 131; HW; MTCW
Benchley, Peter (Bradford) 1940- **CLC 4, 8;**
DAM NOV, POP
See also AAYA 14; AITN 2; CA 17-20R; CANR
12, 35; MTCW; SATA 3, 89
Benchley, Robert (Charles) 1889-1945**T C L C**
1, 55
See also CA 105; 153; DLB 11
Benda, Julien 1867-1956 .... **TCLC 60**
See also CA 120; 154
Benedict, Ruth (Fulton) 1887-1948 **TCLC 60**
See also CA 158
Benedikt, Michael 1935- ....**CLC 4, 14**
See also CA 13-16R; CANR 7; DLB 5
Benet, Juan 1927- .... **CLC 28**
See also CA 143
Benet, Stephen Vincent 1898-1943 . **TCLC 7;**
DAM POET; SSC 10
See also CA 104; 152; DLB 4, 48, 102; YABC
1
Benet, William Rose 1886-1950 ....**TCLC 28;**
DAM POET
See also CA 118; 152; DLB 45
Benford, Gregory (Albert) 1941- ...... **CLC 52**
See also CA 69-72; CAAS 27; CANR 12, 24,
49; DLBY 82
Bengtsson, Frans (Gunnar) 1894-1954**T C L C**
48
Benjamin, David
See Slavitt, David R(ytman)
Benjamin, Lois
See Gould, Lois
Benjamin, Walter 1892-1940 .... **TCLC 39**
Benn, Gottfried 1886-1956 .... **TCLC 3**
See also CA 106; 153; DLB 56
Bennett, Alan 1934-**CLC 45, 77; DAB; DAM**
MST
See also CA 103; CANR 35, 55; MTCW
Bennett, (Enoch) Arnold 1867-1931**TCLC 5,**
20
See also CA 106; 155; CDBLB 1890-1914;
DLB 10, 34, 98, 135
Bennett, Elizabeth
See Mitchell, Margaret (Munnerlyn)
Bennett, George Harold 1930-

See Bennett, Hal
See also BW 1; CA 97-100
Bennett, Hal .... **CLC 5**
See also Bennett, George Harold
See also DLB 33
Bennett, Jay 1912- .... **CLC 35**
See also AAYA 10; CA 69-72; CANR 11, 42;
JRDA; SAAS 4; SATA 41, 87; SATA-Brief
27
Bennett, Louise (Simone) 1919-**CLC 28; BLC;**
DAM MULT
See also BW 2; CA 151; DLB 117
Benson, E(dward) F(rederic) 1867-1940
TCLC 27
See also CA 114; 157; DLB 135, 153
Benson, Jackson J. 1930- .... **CLC 34**
See also CA 25-28R; DLB 111
Benson, Sally 1900-1972 .... **CLC 17**
See also CA 19-20; 37-40R; CAP 1; SATA 1,
35; SATA-Obit 27
Benson, Stella 1892-1933 .... **TCLC 17**
See also CA 117; 155; DLB 36, 162
Bentham, Jeremy 1748-1832 .... **NCLC 38**
See also DLB 107, 158
Bentley, E(dmund) C(lerihew) 1875-1956
TCLC 12
See also CA 108; DLB 70
Bentley, Eric (Russell) 1916- .... **CLC 24**
See also CA 5-8R; CANR 6; INT CANR-6
Beranger, Pierre Jean de 1780-1857**NCLC 34**
Berdyaev, Nicolas
See Berdyaev, Nikolai (Aleksandrovich)
Berdyaev, Nikolai (Aleksandrovich) 1874-1948
TCLC 67
See also CA 120; 157
Berdyayev, Nikolai (Aleksandrovich)
See Berdyaev, Nikolai (Aleksandrovich)
Berendt, John (Lawrence) 1939- ...... **CLC 86**
See also CA 146
Berger, Colonel
See Malraux, (Georges-)Andre
Berger, John (Peter) 1926- ....**CLC 2, 19**
See also CA 81-84; CANR 51; DLB 14
Berger, Melvin H. 1927-...................... **CLC 12**
See also CA 5-8R; CANR 4; CLR 32; SAAS 2;
SATA 5, 88
Berger, Thomas (Louis) 1924-**CLC 3, 5, 8, 11,**
18, 38; DAM NOV
See also CA 1-4R; CANR 5, 28, 51; DLB 2;
DLBY 80; INT CANR-28; MTCW
Bergman, (Ernst) Ingmar 1918- **CLC 16, 72**
See also CA 81-84; CANR 33
Bergson, Henri 1859-1941 .... **TCLC 32**
Bergstein, Eleanor 1938- .... **CLC 4**
See also CA 53-56; CANR 5
Berkoff, Steven 1937- .... **CLC 56**
See also CA 104
Bermant, Chaim (Icyk) 1929- .... **CLC 40**
See also CA 57-60; CANR 6, 31, 57
Bern, Victoria
See Fisher, M(ary) F(rances) K(ennedy)
Bernanos, (Paul Louis) Georges 1888-1948
TCLC 3
See also CA 104; 130; DLB 72
Bernard, April 1956- .... **CLC 59**
See also CA 131
Berne, Victoria
See Fisher, M(ary) F(rances) K(ennedy)
Bernhard, Thomas 1931-1989 **CLC 3, 32, 61**
See also CA 85-88; 127; CANR 32, 57; DLB
85, 124; MTCW
Bernhardt, Sarah (Henriette Rosine) 1844-1923
TCLC 75
See also CA 157
Berriault, Gina 1926- .... **CLC 54**
See also CA 116; 129; DLB 130
Berrigan, Daniel 1921-......................... **CLC 4**

See also CA 33-36R; CAAS 1; CANR 11, 43;
DLB 5
Berrigan, Edmund Joseph Michael, Jr. 1934-
1983
See Berrigan, Ted
See also CA 61-64; 110; CANR 14
Berrigan, Ted .... **CLC 37**
See also Berrigan, Edmund Joseph Michael, Jr.
See also DLB 5, 169
Berry, Charles Edward Anderson 1931-
See Berry, Chuck
See also CA 115
Berry, Chuck .... **CLC 17**
See also Berry, Charles Edward Anderson
Berry, Jonas
See Ashbery, John (Lawrence)
Berry, Wendell (Erdman) 1934- **CLC 4, 6, 8,**
27, 46; DAM POET
See also AITN 1; CA 73-76; CANR 50; DLB 5,
6
Berryman, John 1914-1972**CLC 1, 2, 3, 4, 6, 8,**
10, 13, 25, 62; DAM POET
See also CA 13-16; 33-36R; CABS 2; CANR
35; CAP 1; CDALB 1941-1968; DLB 48;
MTCW
Bertolucci, Bernardo 1940- .... **CLC 16**
See also CA 106
Berton, Pierre (Francis De Marigny) 1920-
CLC 104
See also CA 1-4R; CANR 2, 56; DLB 68
Bertrand, Aloysius 1807-1841 .... **NCLC 31**
Bertran de Born c. 1140-1215 .... **CMLC 5**
Besant, Annie (Wood) 1847-1933 .... **TCLC 9**
See also CA 105
Bessie, Alvah 1904-1985 .... **CLC 23**
See also CA 5-8R; 116; CANR 2; DLB 26
Bethlen, T. D.
See Silverberg, Robert
Beti, Mongo ...... **CLC 27; BLC; DAM MULT**
See also Biyidi, Alexandre
Betjeman, John 1906-1984 **CLC 2, 6, 10, 34,**
43; DAB; DAM MST, POET
See also CA 9-12R; 112; CANR 33, 56; CDBLB
1945-1960; DLB 20; DLBY 84; MTCW
Bettelheim, Bruno 1903-1990 .... **CLC 79**
See also CA 81-84; 131; CANR 23, 61; MTCW
Betti, Ugo 1892-1953 .... **TCLC 5**
See also CA 104; 155
Betts, Doris (Waugh) 1932- ...... **CLC 3, 6, 28**
See also CA 13-16R; CANR 9; DLBY 82; INT
CANR-9
Bevan, Alistair
See Roberts, Keith (John Kingston)
Bialik, Chaim Nachman 1873-1934**TCLC 25**
Bickerstaff, Isaac
See Swift, Jonathan
Bidart, Frank 1939- .... **CLC 33**
See also CA 140
Bienek, Horst 1930- .... **CLC 7, 11**
See also CA 73-76; DLB 75
Bierce, Ambrose (Gwinett) 1842-1914(?)
TCLC 1, 7, 44; DA; DAC; DAM MST; SSC
9; WLC
See also CA 104; 139; CDALB 1865-1917;
DLB 11, 12, 23, 71, 74
Biggers, Earl Derr 1884-1933 .... **TCLC 65**
See also CA 108; 153
Billings, Josh
See Shaw, Henry Wheeler
Billington, (Lady) Rachel (Mary) 1942- **C L C**
43
See also AITN 2; CA 33-36R; CANR 44
Binyon, T(imothy) J(ohn) 1936- .... **CLC 34**
See also CA 111; CANR 28
Bioy Casares, Adolfo 1914-**CLC 4, 8, 13, 88;**
DAM MULT; HLC; SSC 17
See also CA 29-32R; CANR 19, 43; DLB 113;

HW; MTCW
Bird, Cordwainer
See Ellison, Harlan (Jay)
Bird, Robert Montgomery 1806-1854**NCLC 1**
Birney, (Alfred) Earle 1904- **CLC 1, 4, 6, 11;**
DAC; DAM MST, POET
See also CA 1-4R; CANR 5, 20; DLB 88;
MTCW
Bishop, Elizabeth 1911-1979 **CLC 1, 4, 9, 13,**
15, 32; DA; DAC; DAM MST, POET; PC
3
See also CA 5-8R; 89-92; CABS 2; CANR 26,
61; CDALB 1968-1988; DLB 5, 169;
MTCW; SATA-Obit 24
Bishop, John 1935- .... **CLC 10**
See also CA 105
Bissett, Bill 1939- .... **CLC 18; PC 14**
See also CA 69-72; CAAS 19; CANR 15; DLB
53; MTCW
Bitov, Andrei (Georgievich) 1937- ... **CLC 57**
See also CA 142
Biyidi, Alexandre 1932-
See Beti, Mongo
See also BW 1; CA 114; 124; MTCW
Bjarme, Brynjolf
See Ibsen, Henrik (Johan)
Bjornson, Bjornstjerne (Martinius) 1832-1910
TCLC 7, 37
See also CA 104
Black, Robert
See Holdstock, Robert P.
Blackburn, Paul 1926-1971 .... **CLC 9, 43**
See also CA 81-84; 33-36R; CANR 34; DLB
16; DLBY 81
Black Elk 1863-1950**TCLC 33; DAM MULT**
See also CA 144; NNAL
Black Hobart
See Sanders, (James) Ed(ward)
Blacklin, Malcolm
See Chambers, Aidan
Blackmore, R(ichard) D(oddridge) 1825-1900
TCLC 27
See also CA 120; DLB 18
Blackmur, R(ichard) P(almer) 1904-1965
CLC 2, 24
See also CA 11-12; 25-28R; CAP 1; DLB 63
Black Tarantula
See Acker, Kathy
Blackwood, Algernon (Henry) 1869-1951
TCLC 5
See also CA 105; 150; DLB 153, 156, 178
Blackwood, Caroline 1931-1996**CLC 6, 9, 100**
See also CA 85-88; 151; CANR 32, 61; DLB
14; MTCW
Blade, Alexander
See Hamilton, Edmond; Silverberg, Robert
Blaga, Lucian 1895-1961 .... **CLC 75**
Blair, Eric (Arthur) 1903-1950
See Orwell, George
See also CA 104; 132; DA; DAB; DAC; DAM
MST, NOV; MTCW; SATA 29
Blais, Marie-Claire 1939-**CLC 2, 4, 6, 13, 22;**
DAC; DAM MST
See also CA 21-24R; CAAS 4; CANR 38; DLB
53; MTCW
Blaise, Clark 1940- .... **CLC 29**
See also AITN 2; CA 53-56; CAAS 3; CANR
5; DLB 53
Blake, Fairley
See De Voto, Bernard (Augustine)
Blake, Nicholas
See Day Lewis, C(ecil)
See also DLB 77
Blake, William 1757-1827 . **NCLC 13, 37, 57;**
DA; DAB; DAC; DAM MST, POET; PC
12; WLC
See also CDBLB 1789-1832; DLB 93, 163;

MAICYA; SATA 30

Blake, William J(ames) 1894-1969 ...... **PC 12**
See also CA 5-8R; 25-28R

Blasco Ibanez, Vicente 1867-1928 **TCLC 12; DAM NOV**
See also CA 110; 131; HW; MTCW

Blatty, William Peter 1928-**CLC 2; DAM POP**
See also CA 5-8R; CANR 9

Bleeck, Oliver
See Thomas, Ross (Elmore)

Blessing, Lee 1949- .... **CLC 54**

Blish, James (Benjamin) 1921-1975 . **CLC 14**
See also CA 1-4R; 57-60; CANR 3; DLB 8; MTCW; SATA 66

Bliss, Reginald
See Wells, H(erbert) G(eorge)

Blixen, Karen (Christentze Dinesen) 1885-1962
See Dinesen, Isak
See also CA 25-28; CANR 22, 50; CAP 2; MTCW; SATA 44

Bloch, Robert (Albert) 1917-1994 .... **CLC 33**
See also CA 5-8R; 146; CAAS 20; CANR 5; DLB 44; INT CANR-5; SATA 12; SATA-Obit 82

Blok, Alexander (Alexandrovich) 1880-1921 **TCLC 5**
See also CA 104

Blom, Jan
See Breytenbach, Breyten

Bloom, Harold 1930- .... **CLC 24, 103**
See also CA 13-16R; CANR 39; DLB 67

Bloomfield, Aurelius
See Bourne, Randolph S(illiman)

Blount, Roy (Alton), Jr. 1941- .... **CLC 38**
See also CA 53-56; CANR 10, 28, 61; INT CANR-28; MTCW

Bloy, Leon 1846-1917 .... **TCLC 22**
See also CA 121; DLB 123

Blume, Judy (Sussman) 1938- ... **CLC 12, 30; DAM NOV, POP**
See also AAYA 3; CA 29-32R; CANR 13, 37; CLR 2, 15; DLB 52; JRDA; MAICYA; MTCW; SATA 2, 31, 79

Blunden, Edmund (Charles) 1896-1974 **C L C 2, 56**
See also CA 17-18; 45-48; CANR 54; CAP 2; DLB 20, 100, 155; MTCW

Bly, Robert (Elwood) 1926-**CLC 1, 2, 5, 10, 15, 38; DAM POET**
See also CA 5-8R; CANR 41; DLB 5; MTCW

Boas, Franz 1858-1942 .... **TCLC 56**
See also CA 115

Bobette
See Simenon, Georges (Jacques Christian)

Boccaccio, Giovanni 1313-1375 ... **CMLC 13; SSC 10**

Bochco, Steven 1943- .... **CLC 35**
See also AAYA 11; CA 124; 138

Bodenheim, Maxwell 1892-1954 .... **TCLC 44**
See also CA 110; DLB 9, 45

Bodker, Cecil 1927- .... **CLC 21**
See also CA 73-76; CANR 13, 44; CLR 23; MAICYA; SATA 14

Boell, Heinrich (Theodor) 1917-1985 **CLC 2, 3, 6, 9, 11, 15, 27, 32, 72; DA; DAB; DAC; DAM MST, NOV; SSC 23; WLC**
See also CA 21-24R; 116; CANR 24; DLB 69; DLBY 85; MTCW

Boerne, Alfred
See Doeblin, Alfred

Boethius 480(?)-524(?) .... **CMLC 15**
See also DLB 115

Bogan, Louise 1897-1970 .**CLC 4, 39, 46, 93; DAM POET; PC 12**
See also CA 73-76; 25-28R; CANR 33; DLB 45, 169; MTCW

Bogarde, Dirk .... **CLC 19**

See also Van Den Bogarde, Derek Jules Gaspard Ulric Niven
See also DLB 14

Bogosian, Eric 1953- .... **CLC 45**
See also CA 138

Bograd, Larry 1953- .... **CLC 35**
See also CA 93-96; CANR 57; SAAS 21; SATA 33, 89

Boiardo, Matteo Maria 1441-1494 .... **LC 6**

Boileau-Despreaux, Nicolas 1636-1711 . **LC 3**

Bojer, Johan 1872-1959 .... **TCLC 64**

Boland, Eavan (Aisling) 1944- .. **CLC 40, 67; DAM POET**
See also CA 143; CANR 61; DLB 40

Bolt, Lee
See Faust, Frederick (Schiller)

Bolt, Robert (Oxton) 1924-1995**CLC 14; DAM DRAM**
See also CA 17-20R; 147; CANR 35; DLB 13; MTCW

Bombet, Louis-Alexandre-Cesar
See Stendhal

Bomkauf
See Kaufman, Bob (Garnell)

Bonaventura .... **NCLC 35**
See also DLB 90

Bond, Edward 1934- **CLC 4, 6, 13, 23; DAM DRAM**
See also CA 25-28R; CANR 38; DLB 13; MTCW

Bonham, Frank 1914-1989 .... **CLC 12**
See also AAYA 1; CA 9-12R; CANR 4, 36; JRDA; MAICYA; SAAS 3; SATA 1, 49; SATA-Obit 62

Bonnefoy, Yves 1923-... **CLC 9, 15, 58; DAM MST, POET**
See also CA 85-88; CANR 33; MTCW

Bontemps, Arna(ud Wendell) 1902-1973**C L C 1, 18; BLC; DAM MULT, NOV, POET**
See also BW 1; CA 1-4R; 41-44R; CANR 4, 35; CLR 6; DLB 48, 51; JRDA; MAICYA; MTCW; SATA 2, 44; SATA-Obit 24

Booth, Martin 1944- .... **CLC 13**
See also CA 93-96; CAAS 2

Booth, Philip 1925- .... **CLC 23**
See also CA 5-8R; CANR 5; DLBY 82

Booth, Wayne C(layson) 1921- .... **CLC 24**
See also CA 1-4R; CAAS 5; CANR 3, 43; DLB 67

Borchert, Wolfgang 1921-1947 .... **TCLC 5**
See also CA 104; DLB 69, 124

Borel, Petrus 1809-1859 .... **NCLC 41**

Borges, Jorge Luis 1899-1986**CLC 1, 2, 3, 4, 6, 8, 9, 10, 13, 19, 44, 48, 83; DA; DAB; DAC; DAM MST, MULT; HLC; SSC 4; WLC**
See also AAYA 19; CA 21-24R; CANR 19, 33; DLB 113; DLBY 86; HW; MTCW

Borowski, Tadeusz 1922-1951 .... **TCLC 9**
See also CA 106; 154

Borrow, George (Henry) 1803-1881 **NCLC 9**
See also DLB 21, 55, 166

Bosman, Herman Charles 1905-1951 **T C L C 49**
See also Malan, Herman
See also CA 160

Bosschere, Jean de 1878(?)-1953 ... **TCLC 19**
See also CA 115

Boswell, James 1740-1795 . **LC 4; DA; DAB; DAC; DAM MST; WLC**
See also CDBLB 1660-1789; DLB 104, 142

Bottoms, David 1949- .... **CLC 53**
See also CA 105; CANR 22; DLB 120; DLBY 83

Boucicault, Dion 1820-1890 .... **NCLC 41**

Boucolon, Maryse 1937(?)-
See Conde, Maryse
See also CA 110; CANR 30, 53

Bourget, Paul (Charles Joseph) 1852-1935 **TCLC 12**
See also CA 107; DLB 123

Bourjaily, Vance (Nye) 1922- ....**CLC 8, 62**
See also CA 1-4R; CAAS 1; CANR 2; DLB 2, 143

Bourne, Randolph S(illiman) 1886-1918 **TCLC 16**
See also CA 117; 155; DLB 63

Bova, Ben(jamin William) 1932- ...... **CLC 45**
See also AAYA 16; CA 5-8R; CAAS 18; CANR 11, 56; CLR 3; DLBY 81; INT CANR-11; MAICYA; MTCW; SATA 6, 68

Bowen, Elizabeth (Dorothea Cole) 1899-1973 **CLC 1, 3, 6, 11, 15, 22; DAM NOV; SSC 3, 28**
See also CA 17-18; 41-44R; CANR 35; CAP 2; CDBLB 1945-1960; DLB 15, 162; MTCW

Bowering, George 1935- .... **CLC 15, 47**
See also CA 21-24R; CAAS 16; CANR 10; DLB 53

Bowering, Marilyn R(uthe) 1949- .... **CLC 32**
See also CA 101; CANR 49

Bowers, Edgar 1924- .... **CLC 9**
See also CA 5-8R; CANR 24; DLB 5

Bowie, David .... **CLC 17**
See also Jones, David Robert

Bowles, Jane (Sydney) 1917-1973 **CLC 3, 68**
See also CA 19-20; 41-44R; CAP 2

Bowles, Paul (Frederick) 1910- **CLC 1, 2, 19, 53; SSC 3**
See also CA 1-4R; CAAS 1; CANR 1, 19, 50; DLB 5, 6; MTCW

Box, Edgar
See Vidal, Gore

Boyd, Nancy
See Millay, Edna St. Vincent

Boyd, William 1952- .... **CLC 28, 53, 70**
See also CA 114; 120; CANR 51

Boyle, Kay 1902-1992**CLC 1, 5, 19, 58; SSC 5**
See also CA 13-16R; 140; CAAS 1; CANR 29, 61; DLB 4, 9, 48, 86; DLBY 93; MTCW

Boyle, Mark
See Kienzle, William X(avier)

Boyle, Patrick 1905-1982 .... **CLC 19**
See also CA 127

Boyle, T. C. 1948-
See Boyle, T(homas) Coraghessan

Boyle, T(homas) Coraghessan 1948-**CLC 36, 55, 90; DAM POP; SSC 16**
See also BEST 90:4; CA 120; CANR 44; DLBY 86

Boz
See Dickens, Charles (John Huffam)

Brackenridge, Hugh Henry 1748-1816**N C L C 7**
See also DLB 11, 37

Bradbury, Edward P.
See Moorcock, Michael (John)

Bradbury, Malcolm (Stanley) 1932- **CLC 32, 61; DAM NOV**
See also CA 1-4R; CANR 1, 33; DLB 14; MTCW

Bradbury, Ray (Douglas) 1920-**CLC 1, 3, 10, 15, 42, 98; DA; DAB; DAC; DAM MST, NOV, POP; SSC 29; WLC**
See also AAYA 15; AITN 1, 2; CA 1-4R; CANR 2, 30; CDALB 1968-1988; DLB 2, 8; MTCW; SATA 11, 64

Bradford, Gamaliel 1863-1932 ...... **TCLC 36**
See also CA 160; DLB 17

Bradley, David (Henry, Jr.) 1950- .. **CLC 23; BLC; DAM MULT**
See also BW 1; CA 104; CANR 26; DLB 33

Bradley, John Ed(mund, Jr.) 1958- .. **CLC 55**
See also CA 139

Bradley, Marion Zimmer 1930-**CLC 30; DAM**

See also CA 25-28R; CANR 32; HW; MTCW

Castedo, Elena 1937- .... **CLC 65**
See also CA 132

Castedo-Ellerman, Elena
See Castedo, Elena

Castellanos, Rosario 1925-1974 **CLC 66; DAM MULT; HLC**
See also CA 131; 53-56; CANR 58; DLB 113; HW

Castelvetro, Lodovico 1505-1571 .... **LC 12**

Castiglione, Baldassare 1478-1529 ...... **LC 12**

Castle, Robert
See Hamilton, Edmond

Castro, Guillen de 1569-1631 .... **LC 19**

Castro, Rosalia de 1837-1885 **NCLC 3; DAM MULT**

Cather, Willa
See Cather, Willa Sibert

Cather, Willa Sibert 1873-1947 **TCLC 1, 11, 31; DA; DAB; DAC; DAM MST, NOV; SSC 2; WLC**
See also CA 104; 128; CDALB 1865-1917; DLB 9, 54, 78; DLBD 1; MTCW; SATA 30

Cato, Marcus Porcius 234B.C.-149B.C.
CMLC 21

Catton, (Charles) Bruce 1899-1978 .. **CLC 35**
See also AITN 1; CA 5-8R; 81-84; CANR 7; DLB 17; SATA 2; SATA-Obit 24

Catullus c. 84B.C.-c. 54B.C. .... **CMLC 18**

Cauldwell, Frank
See King, Francis (Henry)

Caunitz, William J. 1933-1996 .... **CLC 34**
See also BEST 89:3; CA 125; 130; 152; INT 130

Causley, Charles (Stanley) 1917- .... **CLC 7**
See also CA 9-12R; CANR 5, 35; CLR 30; DLB 27; MTCW; SATA 3, 66

Caute, David 1936- .... **CLC 29; DAM NOV**
See also CA 1-4R; CAAS 4; CANR 1, 33; DLB 14

Cavafy, C(onstantine) P(eter) 1863-1933
TCLC 2, 7; DAM POET
See also Kavafis, Konstantinos Petrou
See also CA 148

Cavallo, Evelyn
See Spark, Muriel (Sarah)

Cavanna, Betty .... **CLC 12**
See also Harrison, Elizabeth Cavanna
See also JRDA; MAICYA; SAAS 4; SATA 1, 30

Cavendish, Margaret Lucas 1623-1673 **LC 30**
See also DLB 131

Caxton, William 1421(?)-1491(?) .... **LC 17**
See also DLB 170

Cayrol, Jean 1911- .... **CLC 11**
See also CA 89-92; DLB 83

Cela, Camilo Jose 1916- **CLC 4, 13, 59; DAM MULT; HLC**
See also BEST 90:2; CA 21-24R; CAAS 10; CANR 21, 32; DLBY 89; HW; MTCW

Celan, Paul **CLC 10, 19, 53, 82; PC 10**
See also Antschel, Paul
See also DLB 69

Celine, Louis-Ferdinand CLC 1, 3, 4, 7, 9, 15, 47
See also Destouches, Louis-Ferdinand
See also DLB 72

Cellini, Benvenuto 1500-1571 .... **LC 7**

Cendrars, Blaise .... **CLC 18**
See also Sauser-Hall, Frederic

Cernuda (y Bidon), Luis 1902-1963 **CLC 54; DAM POET**
See also CA 131; 89-92; DLB 134; HW

Cervantes (Saavedra), Miguel de 1547-1616
LC 6, 23; DA; DAB; DAC; DAM MST, NOV; SSC 12; WLC

Cesaire, Aime (Fernand) 1913- . **CLC 19, 32;**

BLC; DAM MULT, POET
See also BW 2; CA 65-68; CANR 24, 43; MTCW

Chabon, Michael 1963- .... **CLC 55**
See also CA 139; CANR 57

Chabrol, Claude 1930- .... **CLC 16**
See also CA 110

Challans, Mary 1905-1983
See Renault, Mary
See also CA 81-84; 111; SATA 23; SATA-Obit 36

Challis, George
See Faust, Frederick (Schiller)

Chambers, Aidan 1934- .... **CLC 35**
See also CA 25-28R; CANR 12, 31, 58; JRDA; MAICYA; SAAS 12; SATA 1, 69

Chambers, James 1948-
See Cliff, Jimmy
See also CA 124

Chambers, Jessie
See Lawrence, D(avid) H(erbert Richards)

Chambers, Robert W. 1865-1933 ... **TCLC 41**

Chandler, Raymond (Thornton) 1888-1959
TCLC 1, 7; SSC 23
See also CA 104; 129; CANR 60; CDALB 1929-1941; DLBD 6; MTCW

Chang, Eileen 1920- .... **SSC 28**

Chang, Jung 1952- .... **CLC 71**
See also CA 142

Channing, William Ellery 1780-1842 **NCLC 17**
See also DLB 1, 59

Chaplin, Charles Spencer 1889-1977 **CLC 16**
See also Chaplin, Charlie
See also CA 81-84; 73-76

Chaplin, Charlie
See Chaplin, Charles Spencer
See also DLB 44

Chapman, George 1559(?)-1634 **LC 22; DAM DRAM**
See also DLB 62, 121

Chapman, Graham 1941-1989 .... **CLC 21**
See also Monty Python
See also CA 116; 129; CANR 35

Chapman, John Jay 1862-1933 .... **TCLC 7**
See also CA 104

Chapman, Lee
See Bradley, Marion Zimmer

Chapman, Walker
See Silverberg, Robert

Chappell, Fred (Davis) 1936- ..... **CLC 40, 78**
See also CA 5-8R; CAAS 4; CANR 8, 33; DLB 6, 105

Char, Rene(-Emile) 1907-1988 **CLC 9, 11, 14, 55; DAM POET**
See also CA 13-16R; 124; CANR 32; MTCW

Charby, Jay
See Ellison, Harlan (Jay)

Chardin, Pierre Teilhard de
See Teilhard de Chardin, (Marie Joseph) Pierre

Charles I 1600-1649 .... **LC 13**

Charyn, Jerome 1937- .... **CLC 5, 8, 18**
See also CA 5-8R; CAAS 1; CANR 7, 61; DLBY 83; MTCW

Chase, Mary (Coyle) 1907-1981 .... **DC 1**
See also CA 77-80; 105; SATA 17; SATA-Obit 29

Chase, Mary Ellen 1887-1973 .... **CLC 2**
See also CA 13-16; 41-44R; CAP 1; SATA 10

Chase, Nicholas
See Hyde, Anthony

Chateaubriand, Francois Rene de 1768-1848
NCLC 3
See also DLB 119

Chatterje, Sarat Chandra 1876-1936(?)
See Chatterji, Saratchandra
See also CA 109

Chatterji, Bankim Chandra 1838-1894 **NCLC 19**

Chatterji, Saratchandra .... **TCLC 13**
See also Chatterje, Sarat Chandra

Chatterton, Thomas 1752-1770 . **LC 3; DAM POET**
See also DLB 109

Chatwin, (Charles) Bruce 1940-1989 **CLC 28, 57, 59; DAM POP**
See also AAYA 4; BEST 90:1; CA 85-88; 127

Chaucer, Daniel
See Ford, Ford Madox

Chaucer, Geoffrey 1340(?)-1400 **LC 17; DA; DAB; DAC; DAM MST, POET; PC 19; WLCS**
See also CDBLB Before 1660; DLB 146

Chaviaras, Strates 1935-
See Haviaras, Stratis
See also CA 105

Chayefsky, Paddy .... **CLC 23**
See also Chayefsky, Sidney
See also DLB 7, 44; DLBY 81

Chayefsky, Sidney 1923-1981
See Chayefsky, Paddy
See also CA 9-12R; 104; CANR 18; DAM DRAM

Chedid, Andree 1920- .... **CLC 47**
See also CA 145

Cheever, John 1912-1982 **CLC 3, 7, 8, 11, 15, 25, 64; DA; DAB; DAC; DAM MST, NOV, POP; SSC 1; WLC**
See also CA 5-8R; 106; CABS 1; CANR 5, 27; CDALB 1941-1968; DLB 2, 102; DLBY 80, 82; INT CANR-5; MTCW

Cheever, Susan 1943- .... **CLC 18, 48**
See also CA 103; CANR 27, 51; DLBY 82; INT CANR-27

Chekhonte, Antosha
See Chekhov, Anton (Pavlovich)

Chekhov, Anton (Pavlovich) 1860-1904 **TCLC 3, 10, 31, 55; DA; DAB; DAC; DAM DRAM, MST; SSC 2, 28; WLC**
See also CA 104; 124; SATA 90

Chernyshevsky, Nikolay Gavrilovich 1828-1889
NCLC 1

Cherry, Carolyn Janice 1942-
See Cherryh, C. J.
See also CA 65-68; CANR 10

Cherryh, C. J. .... **CLC 35**
See also Cherry, Carolyn Janice
See also DLBY 80; SATA 93

Chesnutt, Charles W(addell) 1858-1932
TCLC 5, 39; BLC; DAM MULT; SSC 7
See also BW 1; CA 106; 125; DLB 12, 50, 78; MTCW

Chester, Alfred 1929(?)-1971 .... **CLC 49**
See also CA 33-36R; DLB 130

Chesterton, G(ilbert) K(eith) 1874-1936
TCLC 1, 6, 64; DAM NOV, POET; SSC 1
See also CA 104; 132; CDBLB 1914-1945; DLB 10, 19, 34, 70, 98, 149, 178; MTCW; SATA 27

Chiang Pin-chin 1904-1986
See Ding Ling
See also CA 118

Ch'ien Chung-shu 1910- .... **CLC 22**
See also CA 130; MTCW

Child, L. Maria
See Child, Lydia Maria

Child, Lydia Maria 1802-1880 .... **NCLC 6**
See also DLB 1, 74; SATA 67

Child, Mrs.
See Child, Lydia Maria

Child, Philip 1898-1978 .... **CLC 19, 68**
See also CA 13-14; CAP 1; SATA 47

Childers, (Robert) Erskine 1870-1922 **TCLC 65**

60; CLR 3; JRDA; MAICYA; SAAS 21; SATA 8, 70

Collier, Jeremy 1650-1726 .... **LC 6**

Collier, John 1901-1980 .... **SSC 19**
See also CA 65-68; 97-100; CANR 10; DLB 77

Collingwood, R(obin) G(eorge) 1889(?)-1943 **TCLC 67**
See also CA 117; 155

Collins, Hunt
See Hunter, Evan

Collins, Linda 1931- .... **CLC 44**
See also CA 125

Collins, (William) Wilkie 1824-1889**NCLC 1, 18**
See also CDBLB 1832-1890; DLB 18, 70, 159

Collins, William 1721-1759 . **LC 4, 40; DAM POET**
See also DLB 109

Collodi, Carlo 1826-1890 .... **NCLC 54**
See also Lorenzini, Carlo
See also CLR 5

Colman, George
See Glassco, John

Colt, Winchester Remington
See Hubbard, L(afayette) Ron(ald)

Colter, Cyrus 1910- .... **CLC 58**
See also BW 1; CA 65-68; CANR 10; DLB 33

Colton, James
See Hansen, Joseph

Colum, Padraic 1881-1972 .... **CLC 28**
See also CA 73-76; 33-36R; CANR 35; CLR 36; MAICYA; MTCW; SATA 15

Colvin, James
See Moorcock, Michael (John)

Colwin, Laurie (E.) 1944-1992**CLC 5, 13, 23, 84**
See also CA 89-92; 139; CANR 20, 46; DLBY 80; MTCW

Comfort, Alex(ander) 1920-**CLC 7; DAM POP**
See also CA 1-4R; CANR 1, 45

Comfort, Montgomery
See Campbell, (John) Ramsey

Compton-Burnett, I(vy) 1884(?)-1969**CLC 1, 3, 10, 15, 34; DAM NOV**
See also CA 1-4R; 25-28R; CANR 4; DLB 36; MTCW

Comstock, Anthony 1844-1915 ...... **TCLC 13**
See also CA 110

Comte, Auguste 1798-1857 .... **NCLC 54**

Conan Doyle, Arthur
See Doyle, Arthur Conan

Conde, Maryse 1937- ...... **CLC 52, 92; DAM MULT**
See also Boucolon, Maryse
See also BW 2

Condillac, Etienne Bonnot de 1714-1780 **LC 26**

Condon, Richard (Thomas) 1915-1996**CLC 4, 6, 8, 10, 45, 100; DAM NOV**
See also BEST 90:3; CA 1-4R; 151; CAAS 1; CANR 2, 23; INT CANR-23; MTCW

Confucius 551B.C.-479B.C.. **CMLC 19; DA; DAB; DAC; DAM MST; WLCS**

Congreve, William 1670-1729 **LC 5, 21; DA; DAB; DAC; DAM DRAM, MST, POET; DC 2; WLC**
See also CDBLB 1660-1789; DLB 39, 84

Connell, Evan S(helby), Jr. 1924-**CLC 4, 6, 45; DAM NOV**
See also AAYA 7; CA 1-4R; CAAS 2; CANR 2, 39; DLB 2; DLBY 81; MTCW

Connelly, Marc(us Cook) 1890-1980 .. **CLC 7**
See also CA 85-88; 102; CANR 30; DLB 7; DLBY 80; SATA-Obit 25

Connor, Ralph .... **TCLC 31**
See also Gordon, Charles William

See also DLB 92

Conrad, Joseph 1857-1924**TCLC 1, 6, 13, 25, 43, 57; DA; DAB; DAC; DAM MST, NOV; SSC 9; WLC**
See also CA 104; 131; CANR 60; CDBLB 1890-1914; DLB 10, 34, 98, 156; MTCW SATA 27

Conrad, Robert Arnold
See Hart, Moss

Conroy, Donald Pat(rick) 1945- **CLC 30, 74; DAM NOV, POP**
See also AAYA 8; AITN 1; CA 85-88; CANR 24, 53; DLB 6; MTCW

Constant (de Rebecque), (Henri) Benjamin 1767-1830 .... **NCLC 6**
See also DLB 119

Conybeare, Charles Augustus
See Eliot, T(homas) S(tearns)

Cook, Michael 1933-........................... **CLC 58**
See also CA 93-96; DLB 53

Cook, Robin 1940- .... **CLC 14; DAM POP**
See also BEST 90:2; CA 108; 111; CANR 41; INT 111

Cook, Roy
See Silverberg, Robert

Cooke, Elizabeth 1948- .... **CLC 55**
See also CA 129

Cooke, John Esten 1830-1886 .... **NCLC 5**
See also DLB 3

Cooke, John Estes
See Baum, L(yman) Frank

Cooke, M. E.
See Creasey, John

Cooke, Margaret
See Creasey, John

Cook-Lynn, Elizabeth 1930-.. **CLC 93; DAM MULT**
See also CA 133; DLB 175; NNAL

Cooney, Ray .... **CLC 62**

Cooper, Douglas 1960- .... **CLC 86**

Cooper, Henry St. John
See Creasey, John

Cooper, J(oan) California .... **CLC 56; DAM MULT**
See also AAYA 12; BW 1; CA 125; CANR 55

Cooper, James Fenimore 1789-1851**NCLC 1, 27, 54**
See also AAYA 22; CDALB 1640-1865; DLB 3; SATA 19

Coover, Robert (Lowell) 1932- **CLC 3, 7, 15, 32, 46, 87; DAM NOV; SSC 15**
See also CA 45-48; CANR 3, 37, 58; DLB 2; DLBY 81; MTCW

Copeland, Stewart (Armstrong) 1952-**CLC 26**

Coppard, A(lfred) E(dgar) 1878-1957 **TCLC 5; SSC 21**
See also CA 114; DLB 162; YABC 1

Coppee, Francois 1842-1908 .... **TCLC 25**

Coppola, Francis Ford 1939- .... **CLC 16**
See also CA 77-80; CANR 40; DLB 44

Corbiere, Tristan 1845-1875 .... **NCLC 43**

Corcoran, Barbara 1911- .... **CLC 17**
See also AAYA 14; CA 21-24R; CAAS 2; CANR 11, 28, 48; DLB 52; JRDA; SAAS 20; SATA 3, 77

Cordelier, Maurice
See Giraudoux, (Hippolyte) Jean

Corelli, Marie 1855-1924 .... **TCLC 51**
See also Mackay, Mary
See also DLB 34, 156

Corman, Cid .... **CLC 9**
See also Corman, Sidney
See also CAAS 2; DLB 5

Corman, Sidney 1924-
See Corman, Cid
See also CA 85-88; CANR 44; DAM POET

Cormier, Robert (Edmund) 1925-**CLC 12, 30;**

DA; DAB; DAC; DAM MST, NOV
See also AAYA 3, 19; CA 1-4R; CANR 5, 23; CDALB 1968-1988; CLR 12; DLB 52; INT CANR-23; JRDA; MAICYA; MTCW; SATA 10, 45, 83

Corn, Alfred (DeWitt III) 1943- .... **CLC 33**
See also CA 104; CAAS 25; CANR 44; DLB 120; DLBY 80

Corneille, Pierre 1606-1684 .... **LC 28; DAB; DAM MST**

Cornwell, David (John Moore) 1931- **CLC 9, 15; DAM POP**
See also le Carre, John
See also CA 5-8R; CANR 13, 33, 59; MTCW

Corso, (Nunzio) Gregory 1930- .... **CLC 1, 11**
See also CA 5-8R; CANR 41; DLB 5, 16; MTCW

Cortazar, Julio 1914-1984**CLC 2, 3, 5, 10, 13, 15, 33, 34, 92; DAM MULT, NOV; HLC; SSC 7**
See also CA 21-24R; CANR 12, 32; DLB 113; HW; MTCW

CORTES, HERNAN 1484-1547 .... **LC 31**

Corwin, Cecil
See Kornbluth, C(yril) M.

Cosic, Dobrica 1921- .... **CLC 14**
See also CA 122; 138; DLB 181

Costain, Thomas B(ertram) 1885-1965 **C L C 30**
See also CA 5-8R; 25-28R; DLB 9

Costantini, Humberto 1924(?)-1987 . **CLC 49**
See also CA 131; 122; HW

Costello, Elvis 1955- .... **CLC 21**

Cotes, Cecil V.
See Duncan, Sara Jeannette

Cotter, Joseph Seamon Sr. 1861-1949 **T C L C 28; BLC; DAM MULT**
See also BW 1; CA 124; DLB 50

Couch, Arthur Thomas Quiller
See Quiller-Couch, Arthur Thomas

Coulton, James
See Hansen, Joseph

Couperus, Louis (Marie Anne) 1863-1923 **TCLC 15**
See also CA 115

Coupland, Douglas 1961-**CLC 85; DAC; DAM POP**
See also CA 142; CANR 57

Court, Wesli
See Turco, Lewis (Putnam)

Courtenay, Bryce 1933- .... **CLC 59**
See also CA 138

Courtney, Robert
See Ellison, Harlan (Jay)

Cousteau, Jacques-Yves 1910-1997 .. **CLC 30**
See also CA 65-68; 159; CANR 15; MTCW; SATA 38

Cowan, Peter (Walkinshaw) 1914- .... **SSC 28**
See also CA 21-24R; CANR 9, 25, 50

Coward, Noel (Peirce) 1899-1973**CLC 1, 9, 29, 51; DAM DRAM**
See also AITN 1; CA 17-18; 41-44R; CANR 35; CAP 2; CDBLB 1914-1945; DLB 10; MTCW

Cowley, Malcolm 1898-1989 .... **CLC 39**
See also CA 5-8R; 128; CANR 3, 55; DLB 4, 48; DLBY 81, 89; MTCW

Cowper, William 1731-1800 . **NCLC 8; DAM POET**
See also DLB 104, 109

Cox, William Trevor 1928- .... **CLC 9, 14, 71; DAM NOV**
See also Trevor, William
See also CA 9-12R; CANR 4, 37, 55; DLB 14; INT CANR-37; MTCW

Coyne, P. J.
See Masters, Hilary

Cozzens, James Gould 1903-1978**CLC 1, 4, 11, 92**
See also CA 9-12R; 81-84; CANR 19; CDALB 1941-1968; DLB 9; DLBD 2; DLBY 84; MTCW

Crabbe, George 1754-1832 .... **NCLC 26**
See also DLB 93

Craddock, Charles Egbert
See Murfree, Mary Noailles

Craig, A. A.
See Anderson, Poul (William)

Craik, Dinah Maria (Mulock) 1826-1887 **NCLC 38**
See also DLB 35, 163; MAICYA; SATA 34

Cram, Ralph Adams 1863-1942 ..... **TCLC 45**
See also CA 160

Crane, (Harold) Hart 1899-1932 **TCLC 2, 5; DA; DAB; DAC; DAM MST, POET; PC 3; WLC**
See also CA 104; 127; CDALB 1917-1929; DLB 4, 48; MTCW

Crane, R(onald) S(almon) 1886-1967**CLC 27**
See also CA 85-88; DLB 63

Crane, Stephen (Townley) 1871-1900 **TCLC 11, 17, 32; DA; DAB; DAC; DAM MST, NOV, POET; SSC 7; WLC**
See also AAYA 21; CA 109; 140; CDALB 1865-1917; DLB 12, 54, 78; YABC 2

Crase, Douglas 1944- .... **CLC 58**
See also CA 106

Crashaw, Richard 1612(?)-1649 .... **LC 24**
See also DLB 126

Craven, Margaret 1901-1980 . **CLC 17; DAC**
See also CA 103

Crawford, F(rancis) Marion 1854-1909**TCLC 10**
See also CA 107; DLB 71

Crawford, Isabella Valancy 1850-1887**NCLC 12**
See also DLB 92

Crayon, Geoffrey
See Irving, Washington

Creasey, John 1908-1973 .... **CLC 11**
See also CA 5-8R; 41-44R; CANR 8, 59; DLB 77; MTCW

Crebillon, Claude Prosper Jolyot de (fils) 1707-1777 .... **LC 28**

Credo
See Creasey, John

Credo, Alvaro J. de
See Prado (Calvo), Pedro

Creeley, Robert (White) 1926-**CLC 1, 2, 4, 8, 11, 15, 36, 78; DAM POET**
See also CA 1-4R; CAAS 10; CANR 23, 43; DLB 5, 16, 169; MTCW

Crews, Harry (Eugene) 1935- **CLC 6, 23, 49**
See also AITN 1; CA 25-28R; CANR 20, 57; DLB 6, 143; MTCW

Crichton, (John) Michael 1942-**CLC 2, 6, 54, 90; DAM NOV, POP**
See also AAYA 10; AITN 2; CA 25-28R; CANR 13, 40, 54; DLBY 81; INT CANR-13; JRDA; MTCW; SATA 9, 88

Crispin, Edmund .... **CLC 22**
See also Montgomery, (Robert) Bruce
See also DLB 87

Cristofer, Michael 1945(?)- .... **CLC 28; DAM DRAM**
See also CA 110; 152; DLB 7

Croce, Benedetto 1866-1952 .... **TCLC 37**
See also CA 120; 155

Crockett, David 1786-1836 .... **NCLC 8**
See also DLB 3, 11

Crockett, Davy
See Crockett, David

Crofts, Freeman Wills 1879-1957 .. **TCLC 55**
See also CA 115; DLB 77

Croker, John Wilson 1780-1857 .... **NCLC 10**
See also DLB 110

Crommelynck, Fernand 1885-1970 .. **CLC 75**
See also CA 89-92

Cronin, A(rchibald) J(oseph) 1896-1981**CLC 32**
See also CA 1-4R; 102; CANR 5; SATA 47; SATA-Obit 25

Cross, Amanda
See Heilbrun, Carolyn G(old)

Crothers, Rachel 1878(?)-1958 ...... **TCLC 19**
See also CA 113; DLB 7

Croves, Hal
See Traven, B.

Crow Dog, Mary (Ellen) (?)- .... **CLC 93**
See also Brave Bird, Mary
See also CA 154

Crowfield, Christopher
See Stowe, Harriet (Elizabeth) Beecher

Crowley, Aleister .... **TCLC 7**
See also Crowley, Edward Alexander

Crowley, Edward Alexander 1875-1947
See Crowley, Aleister
See also CA 104

Crowley, John 1942- .... **CLC 57**
See also CA 61-64; CANR 43; DLBY 82; SATA 65

Crud
See Crumb, R(obert)

Crumarums
See Crumb, R(obert)

Crumb, R(obert) 1943- .... **CLC 17**
See also CA 106

Crumbum
See Crumb, R(obert)

Crumski
See Crumb, R(obert)

Crum the Bum
See Crumb, R(obert)

Crunk
See Crumb, R(obert)

Crustt
See Crumb, R(obert)

Cryer, Gretchen (Kiger) 1935- .... **CLC 21**
See also CA 114; 123

Csath, Geza 1887-1919 .... **TCLC 13**
See also CA 111

Cudlip, David 1933- .... **CLC 34**

Cullen, Countee 1903-1946**TCLC 4, 37; BLC; DA; DAC; DAM MST, MULT, POET; WLCS**
See also BW 1; CA 108; 124; CDALB 1917-1929; DLB 4, 48, 51; MTCW; SATA 18

Cum, R.
See Crumb, R(obert)

Cummings, Bruce F(rederick) 1889-1919
See Barbellion, W. N. P.
See also CA 123

Cummings, E(dward) E(stlin) 1894-1962**CLC 1, 3, 8, 12, 15, 68; DA; DAB; DAC; DAM MST, POET; PC 5; WLC 2**
See also CA 73-76; CANR 31; CDALB 1929-1941; DLB 4, 48; MTCW

Cunha, Euclides (Rodrigues Pimenta) da 1866-1909 .... **TCLC 24**
See also CA 123

Cunningham, E. V.
See Fast, Howard (Melvin)

Cunningham, J(ames) V(incent) 1911-1985 **CLC 3, 31**
See also CA 1-4R; 115; CANR 1; DLB 5

Cunningham, Julia (Woolfolk) 1916-**CLC 12**
See also CA 9-12R; CANR 4, 19, 36; JRDA; MAICYA; SAAS 2; SATA 1, 26

Cunningham, Michael 1952- .... **CLC 34**
See also CA 136

Cunninghame Graham, R(obert) B(ontine)
1852-1936 .... **TCLC 19**
See also Graham, R(obert) B(ontine) Cunninghame
See also CA 119; DLB 98

Currie, Ellen 19(?)- .... **CLC 44**

Curtin, Philip
See Lowndes, Marie Adelaide (Belloc)

Curtis, Price
See Ellison, Harlan (Jay)

Cutrate, Joe
See Spiegelman, Art

Cynewulf c. 770-c. 840 .... **CMLC 23**

Czaczkes, Shmuel Yosef
See Agnon, S(hmuel) Y(osef Halevi)

Dabrowska, Maria (Szumska) 1889-1965**CLC 15**
See also CA 106

Dabydeen, David 1955- .... **CLC 34**
See also BW 1; CA 125; CANR 56

Dacey, Philip 1939- .... **CLC 51**
See also CA 37-40R; CAAS 17; CANR 14, 32; DLB 105

Dagerman, Stig (Halvard) 1923-1954 **TCLC 17**
See also CA 117; 155

Dahl, Roald 1916-1990**CLC 1, 6, 18, 79; DAB; DAC; DAM MST, NOV, POP**
See also AAYA 15; CA 1-4R; 133; CANR 6, 32, 37, 62; CLR 1, 7, 41; DLB 139; JRDA; MAICYA; MTCW; SATA 1, 26, 73; SATA-Obit 65

Dahlberg, Edward 1900-1977 .. **CLC 1, 7, 14**
See also CA 9-12R; 69-72; CANR 31, 62; DLB 48; MTCW

Daitch, Susan 1954- .... **CLC 103**

Dale, Colin .... **TCLC 18**
See also Lawrence, T(homas) E(dward)

Dale, George E.
See Asimov, Isaac

Daly, Elizabeth 1878-1967 .... **CLC 52**
See also CA 23-24; 25-28R; CANR 60; CAP 2

Daly, Maureen 1921- .... **CLC 17**
See also AAYA 5; CANR 37; JRDA; MAICYA; SAAS 1; SATA 2

Damas, Leon-Gontran 1912-1978 .... **CLC 84**
See also BW 1; CA 125; 73-76

Dana, Richard Henry Sr. 1787-1879**NCLC 53**

Daniel, Samuel 1562(?)-1619 .... **LC 24**
See also DLB 62

Daniels, Brett
See Adler, Renata

Dannay, Frederic 1905-1982 . **CLC 11; DAM POP**
See also Queen, Ellery
See also CA 1-4R; 107; CANR 1, 39; DLB 137; MTCW

D'Annunzio, Gabriele 1863-1938**TCLC 6, 40**
See also CA 104; 155

Danois, N. le
See Gourmont, Remy (-Marie-Charles) de

d'Antibes, Germain
See Simenon, Georges (Jacques Christian)

Danticat, Edwidge 1969- .... **CLC 94**
See also CA 152

Danvers, Dennis 1947- .... **CLC 70**

Danziger, Paula 1944- .... **CLC 21**
See also AAYA 4; CA 112; 115; CANR 37; CLR 20; JRDA; MAICYA; SATA 36, 63; SATA-Brief 30

Da Ponte, Lorenzo 1749-1838 .... **NCLC 50**

Dario, Ruben 1867-1916 .... **TCLC 4; DAM MULT; HLC; PC 15**
See also CA 131; HW; MTCW

Darley, George 1795-1846 .... **NCLC 2**
See also DLB 96

Darwin, Charles 1809-1882 .... **NCLC 57**
See also DLB 57, 166

Author Index

Daryush, Elizabeth 1887-1977 ...... **CLC 6, 19**
 See also CA 49-52; CANR 3; DLB 20
Dashwood, Edmee Elizabeth Monica de la Pasture 1890-1943
 See Delafield, E. M.
 See also CA 119; 154
Daudet, (Louis Marie) Alphonse 1840-1897
 NCLC 1
 See also DLB 123
Daumal, Rene 1908-1944 .... **TCLC 14**
 See also CA 114
Davenport, Guy (Mattison, Jr.) 1927-**CLC 6, 14, 38; SSC 16**
 See also CA 33-36R; CANR 23; DLB 130
Davidson, Avram 1923-
 See Queen, Ellery
 See also CA 101; CANR 26; DLB 8
Davidson, Donald (Grady) 1893-1968**CLC 2, 13, 19**
 See also CA 5-8R; 25-28R; CANR 4; DLB 45
Davidson, Hugh
 See Hamilton, Edmond
Davidson, John 1857-1909 .... **TCLC 24**
 See also CA 118; DLB 19
Davidson, Sara 1943- .... **CLC 9**
 See also CA 81-84; CANR 44
Davie, Donald (Alfred) 1922-1995 . **CLC 5, 8, 10, 31**
 See also CA 1-4R, 149; CAAS 3; CANR 1, 44; DLB 27; MTCW
Davies, Ray(mond Douglas) 1944- ... **CLC 21**
 See also CA 116; 146
Davies, Rhys 1903-1978 .... **CLC 23**
 See also CA 9-12R; 81-84; CANR 4; DLB 139
Davies, (William) Robertson 1913-1995 **C L C 2, 7, 13, 25, 42, 75, 91; DA; DAB; DAC; DAM MST, NOV, POP; WLC**
 See also BEST 89:2; CA 33-36R; 150; CANR 17, 42; DLB 68; INT CANR-17; MTCW
Davies, W(illiam) H(enry) 1871-1940**TCLC 5**
 See also CA 104; DLB 19, 174
Davies, Walter C.
 See Kornbluth, C(yril) M.
Davis, Angela (Yvonne) 1944- **CLC 77; DAM MULT**
 See also BW 2; CA 57-60; CANR 10
Davis, B. Lynch
 See Bioy Casares, Adolfo; Borges, Jorge Luis
Davis, Gordon
 See Hunt, E(verette) Howard, (Jr.)
Davis, Harold Lenoir 1896-1960 ...... **CLC 49**
 See also CA 89-92; DLB 9
Davis, Rebecca (Blaine) Harding 1831-1910
 TCLC 6
 See also CA 104; DLB 74
Davis, Richard Harding 1864-1916**TCLC 24**
 See also CA 114; DLB 12, 23, 78, 79; DLBD 13
Davison, Frank Dalby 1893-1970 ..... **CLC 15**
 See also CA 116
Davison, Lawrence H.
 See Lawrence, D(avid) H(erbert Richards)
Davison, Peter (Hubert) 1928- .... **CLC 28**
 See also CA 9-12R; CAAS 4; CANR 3, 43; DLB 5
Davys, Mary 1674-1732 .... **LC 1**
 See also DLB 39
Dawson, Fielding 1930- .... **CLC 6**
 See also CA 85-88; DLB 130
Dawson, Peter
 See Faust, Frederick (Schiller)
Day, Clarence (Shepard, Jr.) 1874-1935
 TCLC 25
 See also CA 108; DLB 11
Day, Thomas 1748-1789 .... **LC 1**
 See also DLB 39; YABC 1
Day Lewis, C(ecil) 1904-1972 . **CLC 1, 6, 10;**

DAM POET; PC 11
 See also Blake, Nicholas
 See also CA 13-16; 33-36R; CANR 34; CAP 1; DLB 15, 20; MTCW
Dazai, Osamu .... **TCLC 11**
 See also Tsushima, Shuji
 See also DLB 182
de Andrade, Carlos Drummond
 See Drummond de Andrade, Carlos
Deane, Norman
 See Creasey, John
de Beauvoir, Simone (Lucie Ernestine Marie Bertrand)
 See Beauvoir, Simone (Lucie Ernestine Marie Bertrand) de
de Beer, P.
 See Bosman, Herman Charles
de Brissac, Malcolm
 See Dickinson, Peter (Malcolm)
de Chardin, Pierre Teilhard
 See Teilhard de Chardin, (Marie Joseph) Pierre
Dee, John 1527-1608 .... **LC 20**
Deer, Sandra 1940- .... **CLC 45**
De Ferrari, Gabriella 1941- .... **CLC 65**
 See also CA 146
Defoe, Daniel 1660(?)-1731 **LC 1; DA; DAB; DAC; DAM MST, NOV; WLC**
 See also CDBLB 1660-1789; DLB 39, 95, 101; JRDA; MAICYA; SATA 22
de Gourmont, Remy(-Marie-Charles)
 See Gourmont, Remy (-Marie-Charles) de
de Hartog, Jan 1914- .... **CLC 19**
 See also CA 1-4R; CANR 1
de Hostos, E. M.
 See Hostos (y Bonilla), Eugenio Maria de
de Hostos, Eugenio M.
 See Hostos (y Bonilla), Eugenio Maria de
Deighton, Len .... **CLC 4, 7, 22, 46**
 See also Deighton, Leonard Cyril
 See also AAYA 6; BEST 89:2; CDBLB 1960 to Present; DLB 87
Deighton, Leonard Cyril 1929-
 See Deighton, Len
 See also CA 9-12R; CANR 19, 33; DAM NOV, POP; MTCW
Dekker, Thomas 1572(?)-1632 .. **LC 22; DAM DRAM**
 See also CDBLB Before 1660; DLB 62, 172
Delafield, E. M. 1890-1943 .... **TCLC 61**
 See also Dashwood, Edmee Elizabeth Monica de la Pasture
 See also DLB 34
de la Mare, Walter (John) 1873-1956**TCLC 4, 53; DAB; DAC; DAM MST, POET; SSC 14; WLC**
 See also CDBLB 1914-1945; CLR 23; DLB 162; SATA 16
Delaney, Franey
 See O'Hara, John (Henry)
Delaney, Shelagh 1939-**CLC 29; DAM DRAM**
 See also CA 17-20R; CANR 30; CDBLB 1960 to Present; DLB 13; MTCW
Delany, Mary (Granville Pendarves) 1700-1788
 LC 12
Delany, Samuel R(ay, Jr.) 1942-**CLC 8, 14, 38; BLC; DAM MULT**
 See also BW 2; CA 81-84; CANR 27, 43; DLB 8, 33; MTCW
De La Ramee, (Marie) Louise 1839-1908
 See Ouida
 See also SATA 20
de la Roche, Mazo 1879-1961 .... **CLC 14**
 See also CA 85-88; CANR 30; DLB 68; SATA 64
De La Salle, Innocent
 See Hartmann, Sadakichi
Delbanco, Nicholas (Franklin) 1942- **CLC 6,**

13
 See also CA 17-20R; CAAS 2; CANR 29, 55; DLB 6
del Castillo, Michel 1933- .... **CLC 38**
 See also CA 109
Deledda, Grazia (Cosima) 1875(?)-1936
 TCLC 23
 See also CA 123
Delibes, Miguel .... **CLC 8, 18**
 See also Delibes Setien, Miguel
Delibes Setien, Miguel 1920-
 See Delibes, Miguel
 See also CA 45-48; CANR 1, 32; HW; MTCW
DeLillo, Don 1936- **CLC 8, 10, 13, 27, 39, 54, 76; DAM NOV, POP**
 See also BEST 89:1; CA 81-84; CANR 21; DLB 6, 173; MTCW
de Lisser, H. G.
 See De Lisser, H(erbert) G(eorge)
 See also DLB 117
De Lisser, H(erbert) G(eorge) 1878-1944
 TCLC 12
 See also de Lisser, H. G.
 See also BW 2; CA 109; 152
Deloria, Vine (Victor), Jr. 1933- ..... **CLC 21; DAM MULT**
 See also CA 53-56; CANR 5, 20, 48; DLB 175; MTCW; NNAL; SATA 21
Del Vecchio, John M(ichael) 1947- ... **CLC 29**
 See also CA 110; DLBD 9
de Man, Paul (Adolph Michel) 1919-1983
 CLC 55
 See also CA 128; 111; CANR 61; DLB 67; MTCW
De Marinis, Rick 1934- .... **CLC 54**
 See also CA 57-60; CAAS 24; CANR 9, 25, 50
Dembry, R. Emmet
 See Murfree, Mary Noailles
Demby, William 1922- . **CLC 53; BLC; DAM MULT**
 See also BW 1; CA 81-84; DLB 33
de Menton, Francisco
 See Chin, Frank (Chew, Jr.)
Demijohn, Thom
 See Disch, Thomas M(ichael)
de Montherlant, Henry (Milon)
 See Montherlant, Henry (Milon) de
Demosthenes 384B.C.-322B.C. ...... **CMLC 13**
 See also DLB 176
de Natale, Francine
 See Malzberg, Barry N(athaniel)
Denby, Edwin (Orr) 1903-1983 .... **CLC 48**
 See also CA 138; 110
Denis, Julio
 See Cortazar, Julio
Denmark, Harrison
 See Zelazny, Roger (Joseph)
Dennis, John 1658-1734 .... **LC 11**
 See also DLB 101
Dennis, Nigel (Forbes) 1912-1989....... **CLC 8**
 See also CA 25-28R; 129; DLB 13, 15; MTCW
Dent, Lester 1904(?)-1959 .... **TCLC 72**
 See also CA 112
De Palma, Brian (Russell) 1940- .... **CLC 20**
 See also CA 109
De Quincey, Thomas 1785-1859 ...... **NCLC 4**
 See also CDBLB 1789-1832; DLB 110; 144
Deren, Eleanora 1908(?)-1961
 See Deren, Maya
 See also CA 111
Deren, Maya 1917-1961 .... **CLC 16, 102**
 See also Deren, Eleanora
Derleth, August (William) 1909-1971**CLC 31**
 See also CA 1-4R; 29-32R; CANR 4; DLB 9; SATA 5
Der Nister 1884-1950 .... **TCLC 56**
de Routisie, Albert

See also CA 49-52; CANR 2, 53
Epstein, Jacob 1956- .... **CLC 19**
See also CA 114
Epstein, Joseph 1937- .... **CLC 39**
See also CA 112; 119; CANR 50
Epstein, Leslie 1938- .... **CLC 27**
See also CA 73-76; CAAS 12; CANR 23
Equiano, Olaudah 1745(?)-1797 **LC 16; BLC; DAM MULT**
See also DLB 37, 50
ER .... **TCLC 33**
See also CA 160; DLB 85
Erasmus, Desiderius 1469(?)-1536 ...... **LC 16**
Erdman, Paul E(mil) 1932- .... **CLC 25**
See also AITN 1; CA 61-64; CANR 13, 43
Erdrich, Louise 1954- ..... **CLC 39, 54; DAM MULT, NOV, POP**
See also AAYA 10; BEST 89:1; CA 114; CANR 41, 62; DLB 152, 175; MTCW; NNAL; SATA 94
Erenburg, Ilya (Grigoryevich)
See Ehrenburg, Ilya (Grigoryevich)
Erickson, Stephen Michael 1950-
See Erickson, Steve
See also CA 129
Erickson, Steve 1950- .... **CLC 64**
See also Erickson, Stephen Michael
See also CANR 60
Ericson, Walter
See Fast, Howard (Melvin)
Eriksson, Buntel
See Bergman, (Ernst) Ingmar
Ernaux, Annie 1940- .... **CLC 88**
See also CA 147
Eschenbach, Wolfram von
See Wolfram von Eschenbach
Eseki, Bruno
See Mphahlele, Ezekiel
Esenin, Sergei (Alexandrovich) 1895-1925 **TCLC 4**
See also CA 104
Eshleman, Clayton 1935- .... **CLC 7**
See also CA 33-36R; CAAS 6; DLB 5
Espriella, Don Manuel Alvarez
See Southey, Robert
Espriu, Salvador 1913-1985 .... **CLC 9**
See also CA 154; 115; DLB 134
Espronceda, Jose de 1808-1842 ..... **NCLC 39**
Esse, James
See Stephens, James
Esterbrook, Tom
See Hubbard, L(afayette) Ron(ald)
Estleman, Loren D. 1952- **CLC 48; DAM NOV, POP**
See also CA 85-88; CANR 27; INT CANR-27; MTCW
Eugenides, Jeffrey 1960(?)- .... **CLC 81**
See also CA 144
Euripides c. 485B.C.-406B.C.**CMLC 23; DA; DAB; DAC; DAM DRAM, MST; DC 4; WLCS**
See also DLB 176
Evan, Evin
See Faust, Frederick (Schiller)
Evans, Evan
See Faust, Frederick (Schiller)
Evans, Marian
See Eliot, George
Evans, Mary Ann
See Eliot, George
Evarts, Esther
See Benson, Sally
Everett, Percival L. 1956- .... **CLC 57**
See also BW 2; CA 129
Everson, R(onald) G(ilmour) 1903- . **CLC 27**
See also CA 17-20R; DLB 88
Everson, William (Oliver) 1912-1994 **CLC 1,**

5, 14
See also CA 9-12R; 145; CANR 20; DLB 5, 16; MTCW
Evtushenko, Evgenii Aleksandrovich
See Yevtushenko, Yevgeny (Alexandrovich)
Ewart, Gavin (Buchanan) 1916-1995**CLC 13, 46**
See also CA 89-92; 150; CANR 17, 46; DLB 40; MTCW
Ewers, Hanns Heinz 1871-1943 ..... **TCLC 12**
See also CA 109; 149
Ewing, Frederick R.
See Sturgeon, Theodore (Hamilton)
Exley, Frederick (Earl) 1929-1992 **CLC 6, 11**
See also AITN 2; CA 81-84; 138; DLB 143; DLBY 81
Eynhardt, Guillermo
See Quiroga, Horacio (Sylvestre)
Ezekiel, Nissim 1924- .... **CLC 61**
See also CA 61-64
Ezekiel, Tish O'Dowd 1943- .... **CLC 34**
See also CA 129
Fadeyev, A.
See Bulgya, Alexander Alexandrovich
Fadeyev, Alexander .... **TCLC 53**
See also Bulgya, Alexander Alexandrovich
Fagen, Donald 1948- .... **CLC 26**
Fainzilberg, Ilya Arnoldovich 1897-1937
See Ilf, Ilya
See also CA 120
Fair, Ronald L. 1932- .... **CLC 18**
See also BW 1; CA 69-72; CANR 25; DLB 33
Fairbairn, Roger
See Carr, John Dickson
Fairbairns, Zoe (Ann) 1948- .... **CLC 32**
See also CA 103; CANR 21
Falco, Gian
See Papini, Giovanni
Falconer, James
See Kirkup, James
Falconer, Kenneth
See Kornbluth, C(yril) M.
Falkland, Samuel
See Heijermans, Herman
Fallaci, Oriana 1930- .... **CLC 11**
See also CA 77-80; CANR 15, 58; MTCW
Faludy, George 1913- .... **CLC 42**
See also CA 21-24R
Faludy, Gyoergy
See Faludy, George
Fanon, Frantz 1925-1961**CLC 74; BLC; DAM MULT**
See also BW 1; CA 116; 89-92
Fanshawe, Ann 1625-1680 .... **LC 11**
Fante, John (Thomas) 1911-1983 ..... **CLC 60**
See also CA 69-72; 109; CANR 23; DLB 130; DLBY 83
Farah, Nuruddin 1945- **CLC 53; BLC; DAM MULT**
See also BW 2; CA 106; DLB 125
Fargue, Leon-Paul 1876(?)-1947 ... **TCLC 11**
See also CA 109
Farigoule, Louis
See Romains, Jules
Farina, Richard 1936(?)-1966 .... **CLC 9**
See also CA 81-84; 25-28R
Farley, Walter (Lorimer) 1915-1989 **CLC 17**
See also CA 17-20R; CANR 8, 29; DLB 22; JRDA; MAICYA; SATA 2, 43
Farmer, Philip Jose 1918- ....**CLC 1, 19**
See also CA 1-4R; CANR 4, 35; DLB 8; MTCW; SATA 93
Farquhar, George 1677-1707 ...**LC 21; DAM DRAM**
See also DLB 84
Farrell, J(ames) G(ordon) 1935-1979 **CLC 6**
See also CA 73-76; 89-92; CANR 36; DLB 14;

MTCW
Farrell, James T(homas) 1904-1979**CLC 1, 4, 8, 11, 66; SSC 28**
See also CA 5-8R; 89-92; CANR 9, 61; DLB 4, 9, 86; DLBD 2; MTCW
Farren, Richard J.
See Betjeman, John
Farren, Richard M.
See Betjeman, John
Fassbinder, Rainer Werner 1946-1982**CLC 20**
See also CA 93-96; 106; CANR 31
Fast, Howard (Melvin) 1914- **CLC 23; DAM NOV**
See also AAYA 16; CA 1-4R; CAAS 18; CANR 1, 33, 54; DLB 9; INT CANR-33; SATA 7
Faulcon, Robert
See Holdstock, Robert P.
Faulkner, William (Cuthbert) 1897-1962**CLC 1, 3, 6, 8, 9, 11, 14, 18, 28, 52, 68; DA; DAB; DAC; DAM MST, NOV; SSC 1; WLC**
See also AAYA 7; CA 81-84; CANR 33; CDALB 1929-1941; DLB 9, 11, 44, 102; DLBD 2; DLBY 86; MTCW
Fauset, Jessie Redmon 1884(?)-1961**CLC 19, 54; BLC; DAM MULT**
See also BW 1; CA 109; DLB 51
Faust, Frederick (Schiller) 1892-1944(?) **TCLC 49; DAM POP**
See also CA 108; 152
Faust, Irvin 1924- .... **CLC 8**
See also CA 33-36R; CANR 28; DLB 2, 28; DLBY 80
Fawkes, Guy
See Benchley, Robert (Charles)
Fearing, Kenneth (Flexner) 1902-1961 . **C L C 51**
See also CA 93-96; CANR 59; DLB 9
Fecamps, Elise
See Creasey, John
Federman, Raymond 1928- .... **CLC 6, 47**
See also CA 17-20R; CAAS 8; CANR 10, 43; DLBY 80
Federspiel, J(uerg) F. 1931- .... **CLC 42**
See also CA 146
Feiffer, Jules (Ralph) 1929- ..... **CLC 2, 8, 64; DAM DRAM**
See also AAYA 3; CA 17-20R; CANR 30, 59; DLB 7, 44; INT CANR-30; MTCW; SATA 8, 61
Feige, Hermann Albert Otto Maximilian
See Traven, B.
Feinberg, David B. 1956-1994 .... **CLC 59**
See also CA 135; 147
Feinstein, Elaine 1930- .... **CLC 36**
See also CA 69-72; CAAS 1; CANR 31; DLB 14, 40; MTCW
Feldman, Irving (Mordecai) 1928- ..... **CLC 7**
See also CA 1-4R; CANR 1; DLB 169
Felix-Tchicaya, Gerald
See Tchicaya, Gerald Felix
Fellini, Federico 1920-1993 .... **CLC 16, 85**
See also CA 65-68; 143; CANR 33
Felsen, Henry Gregor 1916- .... **CLC 17**
See also CA 1-4R; CANR 1; SAAS 2; SATA 1
Fenton, James Martin 1949- .... **CLC 32**
See also CA 102; DLB 40
Ferber, Edna 1887-1968.............. **CLC 18, 93**
See also AITN 1; CA 5-8R; 25-28R; DLB 9, 28, 86; MTCW; SATA 7
Ferguson, Helen
See Kavan, Anna
Ferguson, Samuel 1810-1886 .... **NCLC 33**
See also DLB 32
Fergusson, Robert 1750-1774 .... **LC 29**
See also DLB 109
Ferling, Lawrence
See Ferlinghetti, Lawrence (Monsanto)

See also Clutha, Janet Paterson Frame
France, Anatole .... **TCLC 9**
  See also Thibault, Jacques Anatole Francois
  See also DLB 123
Francis, Claude 19(?)- .... **CLC 50**
Francis, Dick 1920-**CLC 2, 22, 42, 102; DAM POP**
  See also AAYA 5, 21; BEST 89:3; CA 5-8R;
  CANR 9, 42; CDBLB 1960 to Present; DLB
  87; INT CANR-9; MTCW
Francis, Robert (Churchill) 1901-1987 **C L C 15**
  See also CA 1-4R; 123; CANR 1
Frank, Anne(lies Marie) 1929-1945**TCLC 17; DA; DAB; DAC; DAM MST; WLC**
  See also AAYA 12; CA 113; 133; MTCW; SATA
  87; SATA-Brief 42
Frank, Elizabeth 1945- .... **CLC 39**
  See also CA 121; 126; INT 126
Frankl, Viktor E(mil) 1905- .... **CLC 93**
  See also CA 65-68
Franklin, Benjamin
  See Hasek, Jaroslav (Matej Frantisek)
Franklin, Benjamin 1706-1790 .. **LC 25; DA; DAB; DAC; DAM MST; WLCS**
  See also CDALB 1640-1865; DLB 24, 43, 73
Franklin, (Stella Maraia Sarah) Miles 1879-
  1954 .... **TCLC 7**
  See also CA 104
Fraser, (Lady) Antonia (Pakenham) 1932-
  CLC 32
  See also CA 85-88; CANR 44; MTCW; SATA-
  Brief 32
Fraser, George MacDonald 1925- ...... **CLC 7**
  See also CA 45-48; CANR 2, 48
Fraser, Sylvia 1935- .... **CLC 64**
  See also CA 45-48; CANR 1, 16, 60
Frayn, Michael 1933-**CLC 3, 7, 31, 47; DAM DRAM, NOV**
  See also CA 5-8R; CANR 30; DLB 13, 14;
  MTCW
Fraze, Candida (Merrill) 1945- .... **CLC 50**
  See also CA 126
Frazer, J(ames) G(eorge) 1854-1941**TCLC 32**
  See also CA 118
Frazer, Robert Caine
  See Creasey, John
Frazer, Sir James George
  See Frazer, J(ames) G(eorge)
Frazier, Ian 1951- .... **CLC 46**
  See also CA 130; CANR 54
Frederic, Harold 1856-1898 .... **NCLC 10**
  See also DLB 12, 23; DLBD 13
Frederick, John
  See Faust, Frederick (Schiller)
Frederick the Great 1712-1786 .... **LC 14**
Fredro, Aleksander 1793-1876 .... **NCLC 8**
Freeling, Nicolas 1927- .... **CLC 38**
  See also CA 49-52; CAAS 12; CANR 1, 17,
  50; DLB 87
Freeman, Douglas Southall 1886-1953**T C L C 11**
  See also CA 109; DLB 17
Freeman, Judith 1946- .... **CLC 55**
  See also CA 148
Freeman, Mary Eleanor Wilkins 1852-1930
  TCLC 9; SSC 1
  See also CA 106; DLB 12, 78
Freeman, R(ichard) Austin 1862-1943 **T C L C 21**
  See also CA 113; DLB 70
French, Albert 1943- .... **CLC 86**
French, Marilyn 1929-**CLC 10, 18, 60; DAM DRAM, NOV, POP**
  See also CA 69-72; CANR 3, 31; INT CANR-
  31; MTCW
French, Paul

See Asimov, Isaac
Freneau, Philip Morin 1752-1832 ... **NCLC 1**
  See also DLB 37, 43
Freud, Sigmund 1856-1939 .... **TCLC 52**
  See also CA 115; 133; MTCW
Friedan, Betty (Naomi) 1921- .... **CLC 74**
  See also CA 65-68; CANR 18, 45; MTCW
Friedlander, Saul 1932- .... **CLC 90**
  See also CA 117; 130
Friedman, B(ernard) H(arper) 1926- **CLC 7**
  See also CA 1-4R; CANR 3, 48
Friedman, Bruce Jay 1930- ...... **CLC 3, 5, 56**
  See also CA 9-12R; CANR 25, 52; DLB 2, 28;
  INT CANR-25
Friel, Brian 1929- .... **CLC 5, 42, 59**
  See also CA 21-24R; CANR 33; DLB 13;
  MTCW
Friis-Baastad, Babbis Ellinor 1921-1970**C L C 12**
  See also CA 17-20R; 134; SATA 7
Frisch, Max (Rudolf) 1911-1991**CLC 3, 9, 14, 18, 32, 44; DAM DRAM, NOV**
  See also CA 85-88; 134; CANR 32; DLB 69,
  124; MTCW
Fromentin, Eugene (Samuel Auguste) 1820-
  1876 .... **NCLC 10**
  See also DLB 123
Frost, Frederick
  See Faust, Frederick (Schiller)
Frost, Robert (Lee) 1874-1963**CLC 1, 3, 4, 9, 10, 13, 15, 26, 34, 44; DA; DAB; DAC; DAM MST, POET; PC 1; WLC**
  See also AAYA 21; CA 89-92; CANR 33;
  CDALB 1917-1929; DLB 54; DLBD 7;
  MTCW; SATA 14
Froude, James Anthony 1818-1894**NCLC 43**
  See also DLB 18, 57, 144
Froy, Herald
  See Waterhouse, Keith (Spencer)
Fry, Christopher 1907- **CLC 2, 10, 14; DAM DRAM**
  See also CA 17-20R; CAAS 23; CANR 9, 30;
  DLB 13; MTCW; SATA 66
Frye, (Herman) Northrop 1912-1991**CLC 24, 70**
  See also CA 5-8R; 133; CANR 8, 37; DLB 67,
  68; MTCW
Fuchs, Daniel 1909-1993 ....**CLC 8, 22**
  See also CA 81-84; 142; CAAS 5; CANR 40;
  DLB 9, 26, 28; DLBY 93
Fuchs, Daniel 1934- .... **CLC 34**
  See also CA 37-40R; CANR 14, 48
Fuentes, Carlos 1928-**CLC 3, 8, 10, 13, 22, 41, 60; DA; DAB; DAC; DAM MST, MULT, NOV; HLC; SSC 24; WLC**
  See also AAYA 4; AITN 2; CA 69-72; CANR
  10, 32; DLB 113; HW; MTCW
Fuentes, Gregorio Lopez y
  See Lopez y Fuentes, Gregorio
Fugard, (Harold) Athol 1932-**CLC 5, 9, 14, 25, 40, 80; DAM DRAM; DC 3**
  See also AAYA 17; CA 85-88; CANR 32, 54;
  MTCW
Fugard, Sheila 1932- .... **CLC 48**
  See also CA 125
Fuller, Charles (H., Jr.) 1939-**CLC 25; BLC; DAM DRAM, MULT; DC 1**
  See also BW 2; CA 108; 112; DLB 38; INT 112;
  MTCW
Fuller, John (Leopold) 1937- .... **CLC 62**
  See also CA 21-24R; CANR 9, 44; DLB 40
Fuller, Margaret .... **NCLC 5, 50**
  See also Ossoli, Sarah Margaret (Fuller
  marchesa d')
Fuller, Roy (Broadbent) 1912-1991**CLC 4, 28**
  See also CA 5-8R; 135; CAAS 10; CANR 53;
  DLB 15, 20; SATA 87

Fulton, Alice 1952- .... **CLC 52**
  See also CA 116; CANR 57
Furphy, Joseph 1843-1912.............. **TCLC 25**
Fussell, Paul 1924- .... **CLC 74**
  See also BEST 90:1; CA 17-20R; CANR 8, 21,
  35; INT CANR-21; MTCW
Futabatei, Shimei 1864-1909 .... **TCLC 44**
  See also DLB 180
Futrelle, Jacques 1875-1912 .... **TCLC 19**
  See also CA 113; 155
Gaboriau, Emile 1835-1873 .... **NCLC 14**
Gadda, Carlo Emilio 1893-1973 .... **CLC 11**
  See also CA 89-92; DLB 177
Gaddis, William 1922-**CLC 1, 3, 6, 8, 10, 19, 43, 86**
  See also CA 17-20R; CANR 21, 48; DLB 2;
  MTCW
Gage, Walter
  See Inge, William (Motter)
Gaines, Ernest J(ames) 1933- **CLC 3, 11, 18, 86; BLC; DAM MULT**
  See also AAYA 18; AITN 1; BW 2; CA 9-12R;
  CANR 6, 24, 42; CDALB 1968-1988; DLB
  2, 33, 152; DLBY 80; MTCW; SATA 86
Gaitskill, Mary 1954- .... **CLC 69**
  See also CA 128; CANR 61
Galdos, Benito Perez
  See Perez Galdos, Benito
Gale, Zona 1874-1938**TCLC 7; DAM DRAM**
  See also CA 105; 153; DLB 9, 78
Galeano, Eduardo (Hughes) 1940- ... **CLC 72**
  See also CA 29-32R; CANR 13, 32; HW
Galiano, Juan Valera y Alcala
  See Valera y Alcala-Galiano, Juan
Gallagher, Tess 1943- ...... **CLC 18, 63; DAM POET; PC 9**
  See also CA 106; DLB 120
Gallant, Mavis 1922- ... **CLC 7, 18, 38; DAC; DAM MST; SSC 5**
  See also CA 69-72; CANR 29; DLB 53; MTCW
Gallant, Roy A(rthur) 1924- .... **CLC 17**
  See also CA 5-8R; CANR 4, 29, 54; CLR 30;
  MAICYA; SATA 4, 68
Gallico, Paul (William) 1897-1976 ..... **CLC 2**
  See also AITN 1; CA 5-8R; 69-72; CANR 23;
  DLB 9, 171; MAICYA; SATA 13
Gallo, Max Louis 1932- .... **CLC 95**
  See also CA 85-88
Gallois, Lucien
  See Desnos, Robert
Gallup, Ralph
  See Whitemore, Hugh (John)
Galsworthy, John 1867-1933**TCLC 1, 45; DA; DAB; DAC; DAM DRAM, MST, NOV; SSC 22; WLC 2**
  See also CA 104; 141; CDBLB 1890-1914;
  DLB 10, 34, 98, 162; DLBD 16
Galt, John 1779-1839 .... **NCLC 1**
  See also DLB 99, 116, 159
Galvin, James 1951- .... **CLC 38**
  See also CA 108; CANR 26
Gamboa, Federico 1864-1939 .... **TCLC 36**
Gandhi, M. K.
  See Gandhi, Mohandas Karamchand
Gandhi, Mahatma
  See Gandhi, Mohandas Karamchand
Gandhi, Mohandas Karamchand 1869-1948
  TCLC 59; DAM MULT
  See also CA 121; 132; MTCW
Gann, Ernest Kellogg 1910-1991 ...... **CLC 23**
  See also AITN 1; CA 1-4R; 136; CANR 1
Garcia, Cristina 1958- .... **CLC 76**
  See also CA 141
Garcia Lorca, Federico 1898-1936**TCLC 1, 7, 49; DA; DAB; DAC; DAM DRAM, MST, MULT, POET; DC 2; HLC; PC 3; WLC**
  See also CA 104; 131; DLB 108; HW; MTCW

See also Barker, Harley Granville
See also CA 104
Grass, Guenter (Wilhelm) 1927-CLC **1, 2, 4, 6, 11, 15, 22, 32, 49, 88; DA; DAB; DAC; DAM MST, NOV; WLC**
See also CA 13-16R; CANR 20; DLB 75, 124; MTCW
Gratton, Thomas
See Hulme, T(homas) E(rnest)
Grau, Shirley Ann 1929-.. CLC **4, 9; SSC 15**
See also CA 89-92; CANR 22; DLB 2; INT CANR-22; MTCW
Gravel, Fern
See Hall, James Norman
Graver, Elizabeth 1964- .... CLC **70**
See also CA 135
Graves, Richard Perceval 1945- .... CLC **44**
See also CA 65-68; CANR 9, 26, 51
Graves, Robert (von Ranke) 1895-1985 **C L C 1, 2, 6, 11, 39, 44, 45; DAB; DAC; DAM MST, POET; PC 6**
See also CA 5-8R; 117; CANR 5, 36; CDBLB 1914-1945; DLB 20, 100; DLBY 85; MTCW; SATA 45
Graves, Valerie
See Bradley, Marion Zimmer
Gray, Alasdair (James) 1934- .... CLC **41**
See also CA 126; CANR 47; INT 126; MTCW
Gray, Amlin 1946- .... CLC **29**
See also CA 138
Gray, Francine du Plessix 1930- ..... CLC **22; DAM NOV**
See also BEST 90:3; CA 61-64; CAAS 2; CANR 11, 33; INT CANR-11; MTCW
Gray, John (Henry) 1866-1934 ...... TCLC **19**
See also CA 119
Gray, Simon (James Holliday) 1936- CLC **9, 14, 36**
See also AITN 1; CA 21-24R; CAAS 3; CANR 32; DLB 13; MTCW
Gray, Spalding 1941-CLC **49; DAM POP; DC 7**
See also CA 128
Gray, Thomas 1716-1771LC **4, 40; DA; DAB; DAC; DAM MST; PC 2; WLC**
See also CDBLB 1660-1789; DLB 109
Grayson, David
See Baker, Ray Stannard
Grayson, Richard (A.) 1951- .... CLC **38**
See also CA 85-88; CANR 14, 31, 57
Greeley, Andrew M(oran) 1928-..... CLC **28; DAM POP**
See also CA 5-8R; CAAS 7; CANR 7, 43; MTCW
Green, Anna Katharine 1846-1935 TCLC **63**
See also CA 112; 159
Green, Brian
See Card, Orson Scott
Green, Hannah
See Greenberg, Joanne (Goldenberg)
Green, Hannah 1927(?)-1996 .... CLC **3**
See also CA 73-76; CANR 59
Green, Henry 1905-1973 .... CLC **2, 13, 97**
See also Yorke, Henry Vincent
See also DLB 15
Green, Julian (Hartridge) 1900-
See Green, Julien
See also CA 21-24R; CANR 33; DLB 4, 72; MTCW
Green, Julien .... CLC **3, 11, 77**
See also Green, Julian (Hartridge)
Green, Paul (Eliot) 1894-1981CLC **25; DAM DRAM**
See also AITN 1; CA 5-8R; 103; CANR 3; DLB 7, 9; DLBY 81
Greenberg, Ivan 1908-1973
See Rahv, Philip

See also CA 85-88
Greenberg, Joanne (Goldenberg) 1932- **C L C 7, 30**
See also AAYA 12; CA 5-8R; CANR 14, 32; SATA 25
Greenberg, Richard 1959(?)- .... CLC **57**
See also CA 138
Greene, Bette 1934- .... CLC **30**
See also AAYA 7; CA 53-56; CANR 4; CLR 2; JRDA; MAICYA; SAAS 16; SATA 8
Greene, Gael .... CLC **8**
See also CA 13-16R; CANR 10
Greene, Graham (Henry) 1904-1991CLC **1, 3, 6, 9, 14, 18, 27, 37, 70, 72; DA; DAB; DAC; DAM MST, NOV; SSC 29; WLC**
See also AITN 2; CA 13-16R; 133; CANR 35, 61; CDBLB 1945-1960; DLB 13, 15, 77, 100, 162; DLBY 91; MTCW; SATA 20
Greer, Richard
See Silverberg, Robert
Gregor, Arthur 1923- .... CLC **9**
See also CA 25-28R; CAAS 10; CANR 11; SATA 36
Gregor, Lee
See Pohl, Frederik
Gregory, Isabella Augusta (Persse) 1852-1932 TCLC **1**
See also CA 104; DLB 10
Gregory, J. Dennis
See Williams, John A(lfred)
Grendon, Stephen
See Derleth, August (William)
Grenville, Kate 1950- .... CLC **61**
See also CA 118; CANR 53
Grenville, Pelham
See Wodehouse, P(elham) G(renville)
Greve, Felix Paul (Berthold Friedrich) 1879-1948
See Grove, Frederick Philip
See also CA 104; 141; DAC; DAM MST
Grey, Zane 1872-1939 .. TCLC **6; DAM POP**
See also CA 104; 132; DLB 9; MTCW
Grieg, (Johan) Nordahl (Brun) 1902-1943 TCLC **10**
See also CA 107
Grieve, C(hristopher) M(urray) 1892-1978 CLC **11, 19; DAM POET**
See also MacDiarmid, Hugh; Pteleon
See also CA 5-8R; 85-88; CANR 33; MTCW
Griffin, Gerald 1803-1840 .... NCLC **7**
See also DLB 159
Griffin, John Howard 1920-1980 ..... CLC **68**
See also AITN 1; CA 1-4R; 101; CANR 2
Griffin, Peter 1942- .... CLC **39**
See also CA 136
Griffith, D(avid Lewelyn) W(ark) 1875(?)-1948 TCLC **68**
See also CA 119; 150
Griffith, Lawrence
See Griffith, D(avid Lewelyn) W(ark)
Griffiths, Trevor 1935- .... CLC **13, 52**
See also CA 97-100; CANR 45; DLB 13
Grigson, Geoffrey (Edward Harvey) 1905-1985 CLC **7, 39**
See also CA 25-28R; 118; CANR 20, 33; DLB 27; MTCW
Grillparzer, Franz 1791-1872 .... NCLC **1**
See also DLB 133
Grimble, Reverend Charles James
See Eliot, T(homas) S(tearns)
Grimke, Charlotte L(ottie) Forten 1837(?)-1914
See Forten, Charlotte L.
See also BW 1; CA 117; 124; DAM MULT, POET
Grimm, Jacob Ludwig Karl 1785-1863NCLC **3**
See also DLB 90; MAICYA; SATA 22

Grimm, Wilhelm Karl 1786-1859 .... NCLC **3**
See also DLB 90; MAICYA; SATA 22
Grimmelshausen, Johann Jakob Christoffel von 1621-1676 .... LC **6**
See also DLB 168
Grindel, Eugene 1895-1952
See Eluard, Paul
See also CA 104
Grisham, John 1955- .... CLC **84; DAM POP**
See also AAYA 14; CA 138; CANR 47
Grossman, David 1954- .... CLC **67**
See also CA 138
Grossman, Vasily (Semenovich) 1905-1964 CLC **41**
See also CA 124; 130; MTCW
Grove, Frederick Philip .... TCLC **4**
See also Greve, Felix Paul (Berthold Friedrich)
See also DLB 92
Grubb
See Crumb, R(obert)
Grumbach, Doris (Isaac) 1918-CLC **13, 22, 64**
See also CA 5-8R; CAAS 2; CANR 9, 42; INT CANR-9
Grundtvig, Nicolai Frederik Severin 1783-1872 NCLC **1**
Grunge
See Crumb, R(obert)
Grunwald, Lisa 1959- .... CLC **44**
See also CA 120
Guare, John 1938- . CLC **8, 14, 29, 67; DAM DRAM**
See also CA 73-76; CANR 21; DLB 7; MTCW
Gudjonsson, Halldor Kiljan 1902-
See Laxness, Halldor
See also CA 103
Guenter, Erich
See Eich, Guenter
Guest, Barbara 1920- .... CLC **34**
See also CA 25-28R; CANR 11, 44; DLB 5
Guest, Judith (Ann) 1936- CLC **8, 30; DAM NOV, POP**
See also AAYA 7; CA 77-80; CANR 15; INT CANR-15; MTCW
Guevara, Che .... CLC **87; HLC**
See also Guevara (Serna), Ernesto
Guevara (Serna), Ernesto 1928-1967
See Guevara, Che
See also CA 127; 111; CANR 56; DAM MULT; HW
Guild, Nicholas M. 1944- .... CLC **33**
See also CA 93-96
Guillemin, Jacques
See Sartre, Jean-Paul
Guillen, Jorge 1893-1984 .... CLC **11; DAM MULT, POET**
See also CA 89-92; 112; DLB 108; HW
Guillen, Nicolas (Cristobal) 1902-1989 **C L C 48, 79; BLC; DAM MST, MULT, POET; HLC**
See also BW 2; CA 116; 125; 129; HW
Guillevic, (Eugene) 1907- .... CLC **33**
See also CA 93-96
Guillois
See Desnos, Robert
Guillois, Valentin
See Desnos, Robert
Guiney, Louise Imogen 1861-1920 TCLC **41**
See also CA 160; DLB 54
Guiraldes, Ricardo (Guillermo) 1886-1927 TCLC **39**
See also CA 131; HW; MTCW
Gumilev, Nikolai Stephanovich 1886-1921 TCLC **60**
Gunesekera, Romesh 1954- .... CLC **91**
See also CA 159
Gunn, Bill .... CLC **5**
See also Gunn, William Harrison

See also DLB 38

Gunn, Thom(son William) 1929-**CLC 3, 6, 18, 32, 81; DAM POET**
See also CA 17-20R; CANR 9, 33; CDBLB 1960 to Present; DLB 27; INT CANR-33; MTCW

Gunn, William Harrison 1934(?)-1989
See Gunn, Bill
See also AITN 1; BW 1; CA 13-16R; 128; CANR 12, 25

Gunnars, Kristjana 1948-................. **CLC 69**
See also CA 113; DLB 60

Gurdjieff, G(eorgei) I(vanovich) 1877(?)-1949 **TCLC 71**
See also CA 157

Gurganus, Allan 1947-. **CLC 70; DAM POP**
See also BEST 90:1; CA 135

Gurney, A(lbert) R(amsdell), Jr. 1930-. **C L C 32, 50, 54; DAM DRAM**
See also CA 77-80; CANR 32

Gurney, Ivor (Bertie) 1890-1937 ... **TCLC 33**

Gurney, Peter
See Gurney, A(lbert) R(amsdell), Jr.

Guro, Elena 1877-1913 .... **TCLC 56**

Gustafson, James M(oody) 1925- ... **CLC 100**
See also CA 25-28R; CANR 37

Gustafson, Ralph (Barker) 1909 ..... **CLC 36**
See also CA 21-24R; CANR 8, 45; DLB 88

Gut, Gom
See Simenon, Georges (Jacques Christian)

Guterson, David 1956- .... **CLC 91**
See also CA 132

Guthrie, A(lfred) B(ertram), Jr. 1901-1991 **CLC 23**
See also CA 57-60; 134; CANR 24; DLB 6; SATA 62; SATA-Obit 67

Guthrie, Isobel
See Grieve, C(hristopher) M(urray)

Guthrie, Woodrow Wilson 1912-1967
See Guthrie, Woody
See also CA 113; 93-96

Guthrie, Woody .... **CLC 35**
See also Guthrie, Woodrow Wilson

Guy, Rosa (Cuthbert) 1928- .... **CLC 26**
See also AAYA 4; BW 2; CA 17-20R; CANR 14, 34; CLR 13; DLB 33; JRDA; MAICYA; SATA 14, 62

Gwendolyn
See Bennett, (Enoch) Arnold

H. D. .... **CLC 3, 8, 14, 31, 34, 73; PC 5**
See also Doolittle, Hilda

H. de V.
See Buchan, John

Haavikko, Paavo Juhani 1931- .. **CLC 18, 34**
See also CA 106

Habbema, Koos
See Heijermans, Herman

Habermas, Juergen 1929-................. **CLC 104**
See also CA 109

Habermas, Jurgen
See Habermas, Juergen

Hacker, Marilyn 1942- **CLC 5, 9, 23, 72, 91; DAM POET**
See also CA 77-80; DLB 120

Haggard, H(enry) Rider 1856-1925**TCLC 11**
See also CA 108; 148; DLB 70, 156, 174, 178; SATA 16

Hagiosy, L.
See Larbaud, Valery (Nicolas)

Hagiwara Sakutaro 1886-1942**TCLC 60; PC 18**

Haig, Fenil
See Ford, Ford Madox

Haig-Brown, Roderick (Langmere) 1908-1976 **CLC 21**
See also CA 5-8R; 69-72; CANR 4, 38; CLR 31; DLB 88; MAICYA; SATA 12

Hailey, Arthur 1920-**CLC 5; DAM NOV, POP**
See also AITN 2; BEST 90:3; CA 1-4R; CANR 2, 36; DLB 88; DLBY 82; MTCW

Hailey, Elizabeth Forsythe 1938- ..... **CLC 40**
See also CA 93-96; CAAS 1; CANR 15, 48; INT CANR-15

Haines, John (Meade) 1924-.............. **CLC 58**
See also CA 17-20R; CANR 13, 34; DLB 5

Hakluyt, Richard 1552-1616 ....**LC 31**

Haldeman, Joe (William) 1943- .... **CLC 61**
See also CA 53-56; CAAS 25; CANR 6; DLB 8; INT CANR-6

Haley, Alex(ander Murray Palmer) 1921-1992 **CLC 8, 12, 76; BLC; DA; DAB; DAC; DAM MST, MULT, POP**
See also BW 2; CA 77-80; 136; CANR 61; DLB 38; MTCW

Haliburton, Thomas Chandler 1796-1865 **NCLC 15**
See also DLB 11, 99

Hall, Donald (Andrew, Jr.) 1928- **CLC 1, 13, 37, 59; DAM POET**
See also CA 5-8R; CAAS 7; CANR 2, 44; DLB 5; SATA 23

Hall, Frederic Sauser
See Sauser-Hall, Frederic

Hall, James
See Kuttner, Henry

Hall, James Norman 1887-1951 ..... **TCLC 23**
See also CA 123; SATA 21

Hall, (Marguerite) Radclyffe 1886-1943 **TCLC 12**
See also CA 110; 150

Hall, Rodney 1935- .... **CLC 51**
See also CA 109

Halleck, Fitz-Greene 1790-1867 .... **NCLC 47**
See also DLB 3

Halliday, Michael
See Creasey, John

Halpern, Daniel 1945- .... **CLC 14**
See also CA 33-36R

Hamburger, Michael (Peter Leopold) 1924- **CLC 5, 14**
See also CA 5-8R; CAAS 4; CANR 2, 47; DLB 27

Hamill, Pete 1935- .... **CLC 10**
See also CA 25-28R; CANR 18

Hamilton, Alexander 1755(?)-1804 **NCLC 49**
See also DLB 37

Hamilton, Clive
See Lewis, C(live) S(taples)

Hamilton, Edmond 1904-1977 .... **CLC 1**
See also CA 1-4R; CANR 3; DLB 8

Hamilton, Eugene (Jacob) Lee
See Lee-Hamilton, Eugene (Jacob)

Hamilton, Franklin
See Silverberg, Robert

Hamilton, Gail
See Corcoran, Barbara

Hamilton, Mollie
See Kaye, M(ary) M(argaret)

Hamilton, (Anthony Walter) Patrick 1904-1962 **CLC 51**
See also CA 113; DLB 10

Hamilton, Virginia 1936-....... **CLC 26; DAM MULT**
See also AAYA 2, 21; BW 2; CA 25-28R; CANR 20, 37; CLR 1, 11, 40; DLB 33, 52; INT CANR-20; JRDA; MAICYA; MTCW; SATA 4, 56, 79

Hammett, (Samuel) Dashiell 1894-1961 **C L C 3, 5, 10, 19, 47; SSC 17**
See also AITN 1; CA 81-84; CANR 42; CDALB 1929-1941; DLBD 6; DLBY 96; MTCW

Hammon, Jupiter 1711(?)-1800(?) ..**NCLC 5; BLC; DAM MULT, POET; PC 16**
See also DLB 31, 50

Hammond, Keith
See Kuttner, Henry

Hamner, Earl (Henry), Jr. 1923- ...... **CLC 12**
See also AITN 2; CA 73-76; DLB 6

Hampton, Christopher (James) 1946- **CLC 4**
See also CA 25-28R; DLB 13; MTCW

Hamsun, Knut .... **TCLC 2, 14, 49**
See also Pedersen, Knut

Handke, Peter 1942-**CLC 5, 8, 10, 15, 38; DAM DRAM, NOV**
See also CA 77-80; CANR 33; DLB 85, 124; MTCW

Hanley, James 1901-1985 ..... **CLC 3, 5, 8, 13**
See also CA 73-76; 117; CANR 36; MTCW

Hannah, Barry 1942- .... **CLC 23, 38, 90**
See also CA 108; 110; CANR 43; DLB 6; INT 110; MTCW

Hannon, Ezra
See Hunter, Evan

Hansberry, Lorraine (Vivian) 1930-1965**CLC 17, 62; BLC; DA; DAB; DAC; DAM DRAM, MST, MULT; DC 2**
See also BW 1; CA 109; 25-28R; CABS 3; CANR 58; CDALB 1941-1968; DLB 7, 38; MTCW

Hansen, Joseph 1923-........................., **CLC 38**
See also CA 29-32R; CAAS 17; CANR 16, 44; INT CANR-16

Hansen, Martin A. 1909-1955 .... **TCLC 32**

Hanson, Kenneth O(stlin) 1922- .... **CLC 13**
See also CA 53-56; CANR 7

Hardwick, Elizabeth 1916- .... **CLC 13; DAM NOV**
See also CA 5-8R; CANR 3, 32; DLB 6; MTCW

Hardy, Thomas 1840-1928**TCLC 4, 10, 18, 32, 48, 53, 72; DA; DAB; DAC; DAM MST, NOV, POET; PC 8; SSC 2; WLC**
See also CA 104; 123; CDBLB 1890-1914; DLB 18, 19, 135; MTCW

Hare, David 1947- .... **CLC 29, 58**
See also CA 97-100; CANR 39; DLB 13; MTCW

Harford, Henry
See Hudson, W(illiam) H(enry)

Hargrave, Leonie
See Disch, Thomas M(ichael)

Harjo, Joy 1951- .... **CLC 83; DAM MULT**
See also CA 114; CANR 35; DLB 120, 175; NNAL

Harlan, Louis R(udolph) 1922- .... **CLC 34**
See also CA 21-24R; CANR 25, 55

Harling, Robert 1951(?)- .... **CLC 53**
See also CA 147

Harmon, William (Ruth) 1938-......... **CLC 38**
See also CA 33-36R; CANR 14, 32, 35; SATA 65

Harper, F. E. W.
See Harper, Frances Ellen Watkins

Harper, Frances E. W.
See Harper, Frances Ellen Watkins

Harper, Frances E. Watkins
See Harper, Frances Ellen Watkins

Harper, Frances Ellen
See Harper, Frances Ellen Watkins

Harper, Frances Ellen Watkins 1825-1911 **TCLC 14; BLC; DAM MULT, POET**
See also BW 1; CA 111; 125; DLB 50

Harper, Michael S(teven) 1938-....**CLC 7, 22**
See also BW 1; CA 33-36R; CANR 24; DLB 41

Harper, Mrs. F. E. W.
See Harper, Frances Ellen Watkins

Harris, Christie (Lucy) Irwin 1907- **CLC 12**
See also CA 5-8R; CANR 6; CLR 47; DLB 88; JRDA; MAICYA; SAAS 10; SATA 6, 74

Harris, Frank 1856-1931 .... **TCLC 24**
See also CA 109; 150; DLB 156

Brief 27

Hugo, Richard F(ranklin) 1923-1982 **CLC 6, 18, 32; DAM POET**
See also CA 49-52; 108; CANR 3; DLB 5

Hugo, Victor (Marie) 1802-1885 **NCLC 3, 10, 21; DA; DAB; DAC; DAM DRAM, MST, NOV, POET; PC 17; WLC**
See also DLB 119; SATA 47

Huidobro, Vicente
See Huidobro Fernandez, Vicente Garcia

Huidobro Fernandez, Vicente Garcia 1893-1948 .... **TCLC 31**
See also CA 131; HW

Hulme, Keri 1947- .... **CLC 39**
See also CA 125; INT 125

Hulme, T(homas) E(rnest) 1883-1917 **T C L C 21**
See also CA 117; DLB 19

Hume, David 1711-1776 .... **LC 7**
See also DLB 104

Humphrey, William 1924-1997 .... **CLC 45**
See also CA 77-80; 160; DLB 6

Humphreys, Emyr Owen 1919- .... **CLC 47**
See also CA 5-8R; CANR 3, 24; DLB 15

Humphreys, Josephine 1945- ..... **CLC 34, 57**
See also CA 121; 127; INT 127

Huneker, James Gibbons 1857-1921 **TCLC 65**
See also DLB 71

Hungerford, Pixie
See Brinsmead, H(esba) F(ay)

Hunt, E(verette) Howard, (Jr.) 1918- . **CLC 3**
See also AITN 1; CA 45-48; CANR 2, 47

Hunt, Kyle
See Creasey, John

Hunt, (James Henry) Leigh 1784-1859 **N C L C 1; DAM POET**

Hunt, Marsha 1946- .... **CLC 70**
See also BW 2; CA 143

Hunt, Violet 1866-1942 .... **TCLC 53**
See also DLB 162

Hunter, E. Waldo
See Sturgeon, Theodore (Hamilton)

Hunter, Evan 1926- . **CLC 11, 31; DAM POP**
See also CA 5-8R; CANR 5, 38, 62; DLBY 82; INT CANR-5; MTCW; SATA 25

Hunter, Kristin (Eggleston) 1931- .... **CLC 35**
See also AITN 1; BW 1; CA 13-16R; CANR 13; CLR 3; DLB 33; INT CANR-13; MAICYA; SAAS 10; SATA 12

Hunter, Mollie 1922- .... **CLC 21**
See also McIlwraith, Maureen Mollie Hunter
See also AAYA 13; CANR 37; CLR 25; DLB 161; JRDA; MAICYA; SAAS 7; SATA 54

Hunter, Robert (?)-1734 .... **LC 7**

Hurston, Zora Neale 1903-1960 **CLC 7, 30, 61; BLC; DA; DAC; DAM MST, MULT, NOV; SSC 4; WLCS**
See also AAYA 15; BW 1; CA 85-88; CANR 61; DLB 51, 86; MTCW

Huston, John (Marcellus) 1906-1987 **CLC 20**
See also CA 73-76; 123; CANR 34; DLB 26

Hustvedt, Siri 1955- .... **CLC 76**
See also CA 137

Hutten, Ulrich von 1488-1523 .... **LC 16**
See also DLB 179

Huxley, Aldous (Leonard) 1894-1963 **CLC 1, 3, 4, 5, 8, 11, 18, 35, 79; DA; DAB; DAC; DAM MST, NOV; WLC**
See also AAYA 11; CA 85-88; CANR 44; CDBLB 1914-1945; DLB 36, 100, 162; MTCW; SATA 63

Huysmans, Charles Marie Georges 1848-1907
See Huysmans, Joris-Karl
See also CA 104

Huysmans, Joris-Karl .... **TCLC 7, 69**
See also Huysmans, Charles Marie Georges
See also DLB 123

Hwang, David Henry 1957- ... **CLC 55; DAM DRAM; DC 4**
See also CA 127; 132; INT 132

Hyde, Anthony 1946- .... **CLC 42**
See also CA 136

Hyde, Margaret O(ldroyd) 1917- ..... **CLC 21**
See also CA 1-4R; CANR 1, 36; CLR 23; JRDA; MAICYA; SAAS 8; SATA 1, 42, 76

Hynes, James 1956(?)- .... **CLC 65**

Ian, Janis 1951- .... **CLC 21**
See also CA 105

Ibanez, Vicente Blasco
See Blasco Ibanez, Vicente

Ibarguengoitia, Jorge 1928-1983 ..... **CLC 37**
See also CA 124; 113; HW

Ibsen, Henrik (Johan) 1828-1906 **TCLC 2, 8, 16, 37, 52; DA; DAB; DAC; DAM DRAM, MST; DC 2; WLC**
See also CA 104; 141

Ibuse Masuji 1898-1993 .... **CLC 22**
See also CA 127; 141; DLB 180

Ichikawa, Kon 1915- .... **CLC 20**
See also CA 121

Idle, Eric 1943- .... **CLC 21**
See also Monty Python
See also CA 116; CANR 35

Ignatow, David 1914- .... **CLC 4, 7, 14, 40**
See also CA 9-12R; CAAS 3; CANR 31, 57; DLB 5

Ihimaera, Witi 1944- .... **CLC 46**
See also CA 77-80

Ilf, Ilya .... **TCLC 21**
See also Fainzilberg, Ilya Arnoldovich

Illyes, Gyula 1902-1983 .... **PC 16**
See also CA 114; 109

Immermann, Karl (Lebrecht) 1796-1840 **NCLC 4, 49**
See also DLB 133

Inchbald, Elizabeth 1753-1821 ...... **NCLC 62**
See also DLB 39, 89

Inclan, Ramon (Maria) del Valle
See Valle-Inclan, Ramon (Maria) del

Infante, G(uillermo) Cabrera
See Cabrera Infante, G(uillermo)

Ingalls, Rachel (Holmes) 1940- .... **CLC 42**
See also CA 123; 127

Ingamells, Rex 1913-1955 .... **TCLC 35**

Inge, William (Motter) 1913-1973 . **CLC 1, 8, 19; DAM DRAM**
See also CA 9-12R; CDALB 1941-1968; DLB 7; MTCW

Ingelow, Jean 1820-1897 .... **NCLC 39**
See also DLB 35, 163; SATA 33

Ingram, Willis J.
See Harris, Mark

Innaurato, Albert (F.) 1948(?)- .. **CLC 21, 60**
See also CA 115; 122; INT 122

Innes, Michael
See Stewart, J(ohn) I(nnes) M(ackintosh)

Ionesco, Eugene 1909-1994 **CLC 1, 4, 6, 9, 11, 15, 41, 86; DA; DAB; DAC; DAM DRAM, MST; WLC**
See also CA 9-12R; 144; CANR 55; MTCW; SATA 7; SATA-Obit 79

Iqbal, Muhammad 1873-1938 .... **TCLC 28**

Ireland, Patrick
See O'Doherty, Brian

Iron, Ralph
See Schreiner, Olive (Emilie Albertina)

Irving, John (Winslow) 1942- **CLC 13, 23, 38; DAM NOV, POP**
See also AAYA 8; BEST 89:3; CA 25-28R; CANR 28; DLB 6; DLBY 82; MTCW

Irving, Washington 1783-1859 . **NCLC 2, 19; DA; DAB; DAM MST; SSC 2; WLC**
See also CDALB 1640-1865; DLB 3, 11, 30, 59, 73, 74; YABC 2

Irwin, P. K.
See Page, P(atricia) K(athleen)

Isaacs, Susan 1943- .... **CLC 32; DAM POP**
See also BEST 89:1; CA 89-92; CANR 20, 41; INT CANR-20; MTCW

Isherwood, Christopher (William Bradshaw) 1904-1986 .... **CLC 1, 9, 11, 14, 44; DAM DRAM, NOV**
See also CA 13-16R; 117; CANR 35; DLB 15; DLBY 86; MTCW

Ishiguro, Kazuo 1954- **CLC 27, 56, 59; DAM NOV**
See also BEST 90:2; CA 120; CANR 49; MTCW

Ishikawa, Hakuhin
See Ishikawa, Takuboku

Ishikawa, Takuboku 1886(?)-1912 **TCLC 15; DAM POET; PC 10**
See also CA 113; 153

Iskander, Fazil 1929- .... **CLC 47**
See also CA 102

Isler, Alan (David) 1934- .... **CLC 91**
See also CA 156

Ivan IV 1530-1584 .... **LC 17**

Ivanov, Vyacheslav Ivanovich 1866-1949 **TCLC 33**
See also CA 122

Ivask, Ivar Vidrik 1927-1992 .... **CLC 14**
See also CA 37-40R; 139; CANR 24

Ives, Morgan
See Bradley, Marion Zimmer

J. R. S.
See Gogarty, Oliver St. John

Jabran, Kahlil
See Gibran, Kahlil

Jabran, Khalil
See Gibran, Kahlil

Jackson, Daniel
See Wingrove, David (John)

Jackson, Jesse 1908-1983 .... **CLC 12**
See also BW 1; CA 25-28R; 109; CANR 27; CLR 28; MAICYA; SATA 2, 29; SATA-Obit 48

Jackson, Laura (Riding) 1901-1991
See Riding, Laura
See also CA 65-68; 135; CANR 28; DLB 48

Jackson, Sam
See Trumbo, Dalton

Jackson, Sara
See Wingrove, David (John)

Jackson, Shirley 1919-1965 . **CLC 11, 60, 87; DA; DAC; DAM MST; SSC 9; WLC**
See also AAYA 9; CA 1-4R; 25-28R; CANR 4, 52; CDALB 1941-1968; DLB 6; SATA 2

Jacob, (Cyprien-)Max 1876-1944 .... **TCLC 6**
See also CA 104

Jacobs, Jim 1942- .... **CLC 12**
See also CA 97-100; INT 97-100

Jacobs, W(illiam) W(ymark) 1863-1943 **TCLC 22**
See also CA 121; DLB 135

Jacobsen, Jens Peter 1847-1885 .... **NCLC 34**

Jacobsen, Josephine 1908- .... **CLC 48, 102**
See also CA 33-36R; CAAS 18; CANR 23, 48

Jacobson, Dan 1929- .... **CLC 4, 14**
See also CA 1-4R; CANR 2, 25; DLB 14; MTCW

Jacqueline
See Carpentier (y Valmont), Alejo

Jagger, Mick 1944- .... **CLC 17**

Jakes, John (William) 1932- .. **CLC 29; DAM NOV, POP**
See also BEST 89:4; CA 57-60; CANR 10, 43; DLBY 83; INT CANR-10; MTCW; SATA 62

James, Andrew
See Kirkup, James

James, C(yril) L(ionel) R(obert) 1901-1989

See also CA 101; CAAS 9; CANR 39, 59; MTCW

Koontz, Dean R(ay) 1945- ..... **CLC 78; DAM NOV, POP**
See also AAYA 9; BEST 89:3, 90:2; CA 108; CANR 19, 36, 52; MTCW; SATA 92

Kopit, Arthur (Lee) 1937-**CLC 1, 18, 33; DAM DRAM**
See also AITN 1; CA 81-84; CABS 3; DLB 7; MTCW

Kops, Bernard 1926- .... **CLC 4**
See also CA 5-8R; DLB 13

Kornbluth, C(yril) M. 1923-1958 .... **TCLC 8**
See also CA 105; 160; DLB 8

Korolenko, V. G.
See Korolenko, Vladimir Galaktionovich

Korolenko, Vladimir
See Korolenko, Vladimir Galaktionovich

Korolenko, Vladimir G.
See Korolenko, Vladimir Galaktionovich

Korolenko, Vladimir Galaktionovich 1853-1921 .... **TCLC 22**
See also CA 121

Korzybski, Alfred (Habdank Skarbek) 1879-1950 .... **TCLC 61**
See also CA 123; 160

Kosinski, Jerzy (Nikodem) 1933-1991**CLC 1, 2, 3, 6, 10, 15, 53, 70; DAM NOV**
See also CA 17-20R; 134; CANR 9, 46; DLB 2; DLBY 82; MTCW

Kostelanetz, Richard (Cory) 1940- .. **CLC 28**
See also CA 13-16R; CAAS 8; CANR 38

Kostrowitzki, Wilhelm Apollinaris de 1880-1918
See Apollinaire, Guillaume
See also CA 104

Kotlowitz, Robert 1924- .... **CLC 4**
See also CA 33-36R; CANR 36

Kotzebue, August (Friedrich Ferdinand) von 1761-1819 .... **NCLC 25**
See also DLB 94

Kotzwinkle, William 1938- ..... **CLC 5, 14, 35**
See also CA 45-48; CANR 3, 44; CLR 6; DLB 173; MAICYA; SATA 24, 70

Kowna, Stancy
See Szymborska, Wislawa

Kozol, Jonathan 1936- .... **CLC 17**
See also CA 61-64; CANR 16, 45

Kozoll, Michael 1940(?)- .... **CLC 35**

Kramer, Kathryn 19(?)- .... **CLC 34**

Kramer, Larry 1935- .... **CLC 42; DAM POP**
See also CA 124; 126; CANR 60

Krasicki, Ignacy 1735-1801 .... **NCLC 8**

Krasinski, Zygmunt 1812-1859 .... **NCLC 4**

Kraus, Karl 1874-1936 .... **TCLC 5**
See also CA 104; DLB 118

Kreve (Mickevicius), Vincas 1882-1954**TCLC 27**

Kristeva, Julia 1941- .... **CLC 77**
See also CA 154

Kristofferson, Kris 1936- .... **CLC 26**
See also CA 104

Krizanc, John 1956- .... **CLC 57**

Krleza, Miroslav 1893-1981 .... **CLC 8**
See also CA 97-100; 105; CANR 50; DLB 147

Kroetsch, Robert 1927-**CLC 5, 23, 57; DAC; DAM POET**
See also CA 17-20R; CANR 8, 38; DLB 53; MTCW

Kroetz, Franz
See Kroetz, Franz Xaver

Kroetz, Franz Xaver 1946- .... **CLC 41**
See also CA 130

Kroker, Arthur 1945- .... **CLC 77**

Kropotkin, Peter (Aleksieevich) 1842-1921 **TCLC 36**
See also CA 119

Krotkov, Yuri 1917- .... **CLC 19**
See also CA 102

Krumb
See Crumb, R(obert)

Krumgold, Joseph (Quincy) 1908-1980 **C L C 12**
See also CA 9-12R; 101; CANR 7; MAICYA; SATA 1, 48; SATA-Obit 23

Krumwitz
See Crumb, R(obert)

Krutch, Joseph Wood 1893-1970 ...... **CLC 24**
See also CA 1-4R; 25-28R; CANR 4; DLB 63

Krutzch, Gus
See Eliot, T(homas) S(tearns)

Krylov, Ivan Andreevich 1768(?)-1844**N C L C 1**
See also DLB 150

Kubin, Alfred (Leopold Isidor) 1877-1959 **TCLC 23**
See also CA 112; 149; DLB 81

Kubrick, Stanley 1928- .... **CLC 16**
See also CA 81-84; CANR 33; DLB 26

Kumin, Maxine (Winokur) 1925- **CLC 5, 13, 28; DAM POET; PC 15**
See also AITN 2; CA 1-4R; CAAS 8; CANR 1, 21; DLB 5; MTCW; SATA 12

Kundera, Milan 1929- **CLC 4, 9, 19, 32, 68; DAM NOV; SSC 24**
See also AAYA 2; CA 85-88; CANR 19, 52; MTCW

Kunene, Mazisi (Raymond) 1930- .... **CLC 85**
See also BW 1; CA 125; DLB 117

Kunitz, Stanley (Jasspon) 1905-**CLC 6, 11, 14; PC 19**
See also CA 41-44R; CANR 26, 57; DLB 48; INT CANR-26; MTCW

Kunze, Reiner 1933- .... **CLC 10**
See also CA 93-96; DLB 75

Kuprin, Aleksandr Ivanovich 1870-1938 **TCLC 5**
See also CA 104

Kureishi, Hanif 1954(?)- .... **CLC 64**
See also CA 139

Kurosawa, Akira 1910-**CLC 16; DAM MULT**
See also AAYA 11; CA 101; CANR 46

Kushner, Tony 1957(?)-**CLC 81; DAM DRAM**
See also CA 144

Kuttner, Henry 1915-1958 .... **TCLC 10**
See Vance, Jack
See also CA 107; 157; DLB 8

Kuzma, Greg 1944- .... **CLC 7**
See also CA 33-36R

Kuzmin, Mikhail 1872(?)-1936 ...... **TCLC 40**

Kyd, Thomas 1558-1594**LC 22; DAM DRAM; DC 3**
See also DLB 62

Kyprianos, Iossif
See Samarakis, Antonis

La Bruyere, Jean de 1645-1696 .... **LC 17**

Lacan, Jacques (Marie Emile) 1901-1981 **CLC 75**
See also CA 121; 104

Laclos, Pierre Ambroise Francois Choderlos de 1741-1803 .... **NCLC 4**

La Colere, Francois
See Aragon, Louis

Lacolere, Francois
See Aragon, Louis

La Deshabilleuse
See Simenon, Georges (Jacques Christian)

Lady Gregory
See Gregory, Isabella Augusta (Persse)

Lady of Quality, A
See Bagnold, Enid

La Fayette, Marie (Madelaine Pioche de la Vergne Comtes 1634-1693 .... **LC 2**

Lafayette, Rene

See Hubbard, L(afayette) Ron(ald)

Laforgue, Jules 1860-1887**NCLC 5, 53; PC 14; SSC 20**

Lagerkvist, Paer (Fabian) 1891-1974 **CLC 7, 10, 13, 54; DAM DRAM, NOV**
See also Lagerkvist, Par
See also CA 85-88; 49-52; MTCW

Lagerkvist, Par .... **SSC 12**
See also Lagerkvist, Paer (Fabian)

Lagerloef, Selma (Ottiliana Lovisa) 1858-1940 **TCLC 4, 36**
See also Lagerlof, Selma (Ottiliana Lovisa)
See also CA 108; SATA 15

Lagerlof, Selma (Ottiliana Lovisa)
See Lagerloef, Selma (Ottiliana Lovisa)
See also CLR 7; SATA 15

La Guma, (Justin) Alex(ander) 1925-1985 **CLC 19; DAM NOV**
See also BW 1; CA 49-52; 118; CANR 25; DLB 117; MTCW

Laidlaw, A. K.
See Grieve, C(hristopher) M(urray)

Lainez, Manuel Mujica
See Mujica Lainez, Manuel
See also HW

Laing, R(onald) D(avid) 1927-1989 .. **CLC 95**
See also CA 107; 129; CANR 34; MTCW

Lamartine, Alphonse (Marie Louis Prat) de 1790-1869**NCLC 11; DAM POET; PC 16**

Lamb, Charles 1775-1834 ..... **NCLC 10; DA; DAB; DAC; DAM MST; WLC**
See also CDBLB 1789-1832; DLB 93, 107, 163; SATA 17

Lamb, Lady Caroline 1785-1828 ... **NCLC 38**
See also DLB 116

Lamming, George (William) 1927- **CLC 2, 4, 66; BLC; DAM MULT**
See also BW 2; CA 85-88; CANR 26; DLB 125; MTCW

L'Amour, Louis (Dearborn) 1908-1988 **C L C 25, 55; DAM NOV, POP**
See also AAYA 16; AITN 2; BEST 89:2; CA 1-4R; 125; CANR 3, 25, 40; DLBY 80; MTCW

Lampedusa, Giuseppe (Tomasi) di 1896-1957 **TCLC 13**
See also Tomasi di Lampedusa, Giuseppe
See also DLB 177

Lampman, Archibald 1861-1899 ... **NCLC 25**
See also DLB 92

Lancaster, Bruce 1896-1963 .... **CLC 36**
See also CA 9-10; CAP 1; SATA 9

Lanchester, John .... **CLC 99**

Landau, Mark Alexandrovich
See Aldanov, Mark (Alexandrovich)

Landau-Aldanov, Mark Alexandrovich
See Aldanov, Mark (Alexandrovich)

Landis, Jerry
See Simon, Paul (Frederick)

Landis, John 1950- .... **CLC 26**
See also CA 112; 122

Landolfi, Tommaso 1908-1979 .... **CLC 11, 49**
See also CA 127; 117; DLB 177

Landon, Letitia Elizabeth 1802-1838 **N C L C 15**
See also DLB 96

Landor, Walter Savage 1775-1864 **NCLC 14**
See also DLB 93, 107

Landwirth, Heinz 1927-
See Lind, Jakov
See also CA 9-12R; CANR 7

Lane, Patrick 1939- ... **CLC 25; DAM POET**
See also CA 97-100; CANR 54; DLB 53; INT 97-100

Lang, Andrew 1844-1912 .... **TCLC 16**
See also CA 114; 137; DLB 98, 141, 184; MAICYA; SATA 16

Lang, Fritz 1890-1976 .... **CLC 20, 103**

Lish, Gordon (Jay) 1934- ... **CLC 45; SSC 18**
   See also CA 113; 117; DLB 130; INT 117
Lispector, Clarice 1925-1977 .... **CLC 43**
   See also CA 139; 116; DLB 113
Littell, Robert 1935(?)- .... **CLC 42**
   See also CA 109; 112
Little, Malcolm 1925-1965
   See Malcolm X
   See also BW 1; CA 125; 111; DA; DAB; DAC;
   DAM MST, MULT; MTCW
Littlewit, Humphrey Gent.
   See Lovecraft, H(oward) P(hillips)
Litwos
   See Sienkiewicz, Henryk (Adam Alexander
   Pius)
Liu E 1857-1909 .... **TCLC 15**
   See also CA 115
Lively, Penelope (Margaret) 1933- .. **CLC 32,**
   50; DAM NOV
   See also CA 41-44R; CANR 29; CLR 7; DLB
   14, 161; JRDA; MAICYA; MTCW; SATA 7,
   60
Livesay, Dorothy (Kathleen) 1909-**CLC 4, 15,**
   79; DAC; DAM MST, POET
   See also AITN 2; CA 25-28R; CAAS 8; CANR
   36; DLB 68; MTCW
Livy c. 59B.C.-c. 17 .... **CMLC 11**
Lizardi, Jose Joaquin Fernandez de 1776-1827
   NCLC 30
Llewellyn, Richard
   See Llewellyn Lloyd, Richard Dafydd Vivian
   See also DLB 15
Llewellyn Lloyd, Richard Dafydd Vivian 1906-
   1983 .... **CLC 7, 80**
   See also Llewellyn, Richard
   See also CA 53-56; 111; CANR 7; SATA 11;
   SATA-Obit 37
Llosa, (Jorge) Mario (Pedro) Vargas
   See Vargas Llosa, (Jorge) Mario (Pedro)
Lloyd Webber, Andrew 1948-
   See Webber, Andrew Lloyd
   See also AAYA 1; CA 116; 149; DAM DRAM;
   SATA 56
Llull, Ramon c. 1235-c. 1316 .... **CMLC 12**
Locke, Alain (Le Roy) 1886-1954 .. **TCLC 43**
   See also BW 1; CA 106; 124; DLB 51
Locke, John 1632-1704 .... **LC 7, 35**
   See also DLB 101
Locke-Elliott, Sumner
   See Elliott, Sumner Locke
Lockhart, John Gibson 1794-1854 .. **NCLC 6**
   See also DLB 110, 116, 144
Lodge, David (John) 1935- .... **CLC 36; DAM**
   POP
   See also BEST 90:1; CA 17-20R; CANR 19,
   53; DLB 14; INT CANR-19; MTCW
Loennbohm, Armas Eino Leopold 1878-1926
   See Leino, Eino
   See also CA 123
Loewinsohn, Ron(ald William) 1937-**CLC 52**
   See also CA 25-28R
Logan, Jake
   See Smith, Martin Cruz
Logan, John (Burton) 1923-1987 .... **CLC 5**
   See also CA 77-80; 124; CANR 45; DLB 5
Lo Kuan-chung 1330(?)-1400(?) .... **LC 12**
Lombard, Nap
   See Johnson, Pamela Hansford
London, Jack . TCLC 9, 15, 39; SSC 4; WLC
   See also London, John Griffith
   See also AAYA 13; AITN 2; CDALB 1865-
   1917; DLB 8, 12, 78; SATA 18
London, John Griffith 1876-1916
   See London, Jack
   See also CA 110; 119; DA; DAB; DAC; DAM
   MST, NOV; JRDA; MAICYA; MTCW
Long, Emmett

   See Leonard, Elmore (John, Jr.)
Longbaugh, Harry
   See Goldman, William (W.)
Longfellow, Henry Wadsworth 1807-1882
   NCLC 2, 45; DA; DAB; DAC; DAM MST,
   POET; WLCS
   See also CDALB 1640-1865; DLB 1, 59; SATA
   19
Longley, Michael 1939- .... **CLC 29**
   See also CA 102; DLB 40
Longus fl. c. 2nd cent. - .... **CMLC 7**
Longway, A. Hugh
   See Lang, Andrew
Lonnrot, Elias 1802-1884 .... **NCLC 53**
Lopate, Phillip 1943- .... **CLC 29**
   See also CA 97-100; DLBY 80; INT 97-100
Lopez Portillo (y Pacheco), Jose 1920-**CLC 46**
   See also CA 129; HW
Lopez y Fuentes, Gregorio 1897(?)-1966**CLC**
   32
   See also CA 131; HW
Lorca, Federico Garcia
   See Garcia Lorca, Federico
Lord, Bette Bao 1938- .... **CLC 23**
   See also BEST 90:3; CA 107; CANR 41; INT
   107; SATA 58
Lord Auch
   See Bataille, Georges
Lord Byron
   See Byron, George Gordon (Noel)
Lorde, Audre (Geraldine) 1934-1992**CLC 18,**
   71; BLC; DAM MULT, POET; PC 12
   See also BW 1; CA 25-28R; 142; CANR 16,
   26, 46; DLB 41; MTCW
Lord Houghton
   See Milnes, Richard Monckton
Lord Jeffrey
   See Jeffrey, Francis
Lorenzini, Carlo 1826-1890
   See Collodi, Carlo
   See also MAICYA; SATA 29
Lorenzo, Heberto Padilla
   See Padilla (Lorenzo), Heberto
Loris
   See Hofmannsthal, Hugo von
Loti, Pierre .... **TCLC 11**
   See also Viaud, (Louis Marie) Julien
   See also DLB 123
Louie, David Wong 1954- .... **CLC 70**
   See also CA 139
Louis, Father M.
   See Merton, Thomas
Lovecraft, H(oward) P(hillips) 1890-1937
   TCLC 4, 22; DAM POP; SSC 3
   See also AAYA 14; CA 104; 133; MTCW
Lovelace, Earl 1935- .... **CLC 51**
   See also BW 2; CA 77-80; CANR 41; DLB 125;
   MTCW
Lovelace, Richard 1618-1657 .... **LC 24**
   See also DLB 131
Lowell, Amy 1874-1925 .... **TCLC 1, 8; DAM**
   POET; PC 13
   See also CA 104; 151; DLB 54, 140
Lowell, James Russell 1819-1891 .... **NCLC 2**
   See also CDALB 1640-1865; DLB 1, 11, 64,
   79
Lowell, Robert (Traill Spence, Jr.) 1917-1977
   CLC 1, 2, 3, 4, 5, 8, 9, 11, 15, 37; DA; DAB;
   DAC; DAM MST, NOV; PC 3; WLC
   See also CA 9-12R; 73-76; CABS 2; CANR 26,
   60; DLB 5, 169; MTCW
Lowndes, Marie Adelaide (Belloc) 1868-1947
   TCLC 12
   See also CA 107; DLB 70
Lowry, (Clarence) Malcolm 1909-1957**T C L C**
   6, 40
   See also CA 105; 131; CANR 62; CDBLB

   1945-1960; DLB 15; MTCW
Lowry, Mina Gertrude 1882-1966
   See Loy, Mina
   See also CA 113
Loxsmith, John
   See Brunner, John (Kilian Houston)
Loy, Mina .... **CLC 28; DAM POET; PC 16**
   See also Lowry, Mina Gertrude
   See also DLB 4, 54
Loyson-Bridet
   See Schwob, (Mayer Andre) Marcel
Lucas, Craig 1951- .... **CLC 64**
   See also CA 137
Lucas, E(dward) V(errall) 1868-1938 **T C L C**
   73
   See also DLB 98, 149, 153; SATA 20
Lucas, George 1944- .... **CLC 16**
   See also AAYA 1; CA 77-80; CANR 30; SATA
   56
Lucas, Hans
   See Godard, Jean-Luc
Lucas, Victoria
   See Plath, Sylvia
Ludlam, Charles 1943-1987 .... **CLC 46, 50**
   See also CA 85-88; 122
Ludlum, Robert 1927-**CLC 22, 43; DAM NOV,**
   POP
   See also AAYA 10; BEST 89:1, 90:3; CA 33-
   36R; CANR 25, 41; DLBY 82; MTCW
Ludwig, Ken .... **CLC 60**
Ludwig, Otto 1813-1865 .... **NCLC 4**
   See also DLB 129
Lugones, Leopoldo 1874-1938 .... **TCLC 15**
   See also CA 116; 131; HW
Lu Hsun 1881-1936 .... **TCLC 3; SSC 20**
   See also Shu-Jen, Chou
Lukacs, George .... **CLC 24**
   See also Lukacs, Gyorgy (Szegeny von)
Lukacs, Gyorgy (Szegeny von) 1885-1971
   See Lukacs, George
   See also CA 101; 29-32R; CANR 62
Luke, Peter (Ambrose Cyprian) 1919-1995
   CLC 38
   See also CA 81-84; 147; DLB 13
Lunar, Dennis
   See Mungo, Raymond
Lurie, Alison 1926- .... **CLC 4, 5, 18, 39**
   See also CA 1-4R; CANR 2, 17, 50; DLB 2;
   MTCW; SATA 46
Lustig, Arnost 1926- .... **CLC 56**
   See also AAYA 3; CA 69-72; CANR 47; SATA
   56
Luther, Martin 1483-1546 .... **LC 9, 37**
   See also DLB 179
Luxemburg, Rosa 1870(?)-1919 ..... **TCLC 63**
   See also CA 118
Luzi, Mario 1914- .... **CLC 13**
   See also CA 61-64; CANR 9; DLB 128
Lyly, John 1554(?)-1606 .... **DC 7**
   See also DAM DRAM; DLB 62, 167
L'Ymagier
   See Gourmont, Remy (-Marie-Charles) de
Lynch, B. Suarez
   See Bioy Casares, Adolfo; Borges, Jorge Luis
Lynch, David (K.) 1946- .... **CLC 66**
   See also CA 124; 129
Lynch, James
   See Andreyev, Leonid (Nikolaevich)
Lynch Davis, B.
   See Bioy Casares, Adolfo; Borges, Jorge Luis
Lyndsay, Sir David 1490-1555 .... **LC 20**
Lynn, Kenneth S(chuyler) 1923- .... **CLC 50**
   See also CA 1-4R; CANR 3, 27
Lynx
   See West, Rebecca
Lyons, Marcus
   See Blish, James (Benjamin)

Mander, (Mary) Jane 1877-1949 ... **TCLC 31**
Mandeville, John fl. 1350- .... **CMLC 19**
 See also DLB 146
Mandiargues, Andre Pieyre de .... **CLC 41**
 See also Pieyre de Mandiargues, Andre
 See also DLB 83
Mandrake, Ethel Belle
 See Thurman, Wallace (Henry)
Mangan, James Clarence 1803-1849**NCLC 27**
Maniere, J.-E.
 See Giraudoux, (Hippolyte) Jean
Manley, (Mary) Delariviere 1672(?)-1724**L C 1**
 See also DLB 39, 80
Mann, Abel
 See Creasey, John
Mann, Emily 1952- .... **DC 7**
 See also CA 130; CANR 55
Mann, (Luiz) Heinrich 1871-1950 ... **TCLC 9**
 See also CA 106; DLB 66
Mann, (Paul) Thomas 1875-1955 **TCLC 2, 8, 14, 21, 35, 44, 60; DA; DAB; DAC; DAM MST, NOV; SSC 5; WLC**
 See also CA 104; 128; DLB 66; MTCW
Mannheim, Karl 1893-1947 .... **TCLC 65**
Manning, David
 See Faust, Frederick (Schiller)
Manning, Frederic 1887(?)-1935 ... **TCLC 25**
 See also CA 124
Manning, Olivia 1915-1980 .... **CLC 5, 19**
 See also CA 5-8R; 101; CANR 29; MTCW
Mano, D. Keith 1942- .... **CLC 2, 10**
 See also CA 25-28R; CAAS 6; CANR 26, 57; DLB 6
Mansfield, Katherine**TCLC 2, 8, 39; DAB; SSC 9, 23; WLC**
 See also Beauchamp, Kathleen Mansfield
 See also DLB 162
Manso, Peter 1940- .... **CLC 39**
 See also CA 29-32R; CANR 44
Mantecon, Juan Jimenez
 See Jimenez (Mantecon), Juan Ramon
Manton, Peter
 See Creasey, John
Man Without a Spleen, A
 See Chekhov, Anton (Pavlovich)
Manzoni, Alessandro 1785-1873 .... **NCLC 29**
Mapu, Abraham (ben Jekutiel) 1808-1867 **NCLC 18**
Mara, Sally
 See Queneau, Raymond
Marat, Jean Paul 1743-1793 .... **LC 10**
Marcel, Gabriel Honore 1889-1973 . **CLC 15**
 See also CA 102; 45-48; MTCW
Marchbanks, Samuel
 See Davies, (William) Robertson
Marchi, Giacomo
 See Bassani, Giorgio
Margulies, Donald .... **CLC 76**
Marie de France c. 12th cent. - .... **CMLC 8**
Marie de l'Incarnation 1599-1672 ...... **LC 10**
Marier, Captain Victor
 See Griffith, D(avid Lewelyn) W(ark)
Mariner, Scott
 See Pohl, Frederik
Marinetti, Filippo Tommaso 1876-1944**TCLC 10**
 See also CA 107; DLB 114
Marivaux, Pierre Carlet de Chamblain de 1688-1763 .... **LC 4; DC 7**
Markandaya, Kamala .... **CLC 8, 38**
 See also Taylor, Kamala (Purnaiya)
Markfield, Wallace 1926- .... **CLC 8**
 See also CA 69-72; CAAS 3; DLB 2, 28
Markham, Edwin 1852-1940 .... **TCLC 47**
 See also CA 160; DLB 54
Markham, Robert

 See Amis, Kingsley (William)
Marks, J
 See Highwater, Jamake (Mamake)
Marks-Highwater, J
 See Highwater, Jamake (Mamake)
Markson, David M(errill) 1927- .... **CLC 67**
 See also CA 49-52; CANR 1
Marley, Bob .... **CLC 17**
 See also Marley, Robert Nesta
Marley, Robert Nesta 1945-1981
 See Marley, Bob
 See also CA 107; 103
Marlowe, Christopher 1564-1593**LC 22; DA; DAB; DAC; DAM DRAM, MST; DC 1; WLC**
 See also CDBLB Before 1660; DLB 62
Marlowe, Stephen 1928-
 See Queen, Ellery
 See also CA 13-16R; CANR 6, 55
Marmontel, Jean-Francois 1723-1799 .. **LC 2**
Marquand, John P(hillips) 1893-1960**CLC 2, 10**
 See also CA 85-88; DLB 9, 102
Marques, Rene 1919-1979 ..... **CLC 96; DAM MULT; HLC**
 See also CA 97-100; 85-88; DLB 113; HW
Marquez, Gabriel (Jose) Garcia
 See Garcia Marquez, Gabriel (Jose)
Marquis, Don(ald Robert Perry) 1878-1937 **TCLC 7**
 See also CA 104; DLB 11, 25
Marric, J. J.
 See Creasey, John
Marrow, Bernard
 See Moore, Brian
Marryat, Frederick 1792-1848 .... **NCLC 3**
 See also DLB 21, 163
Marsden, James
 See Creasey, John
Marsh, (Edith) Ngaio 1899-1982 **CLC 7, 53; DAM POP**
 See also CA 9-12R; CANR 6, 58; DLB 77; MTCW
Marshall, Garry 1934- .... **CLC 17**
 See also AAYA 3; CA 111; SATA 60
Marshall, Paule 1929-**CLC 27, 72; BLC; DAM MULT; SSC 3**
 See also BW 2; CA 77-80; CANR 25; DLB 157; MTCW
Marsten, Richard
 See Hunter, Evan
Marston, John 1576-1634**LC 33; DAM DRAM**
 See also DLB 58, 172
Martha, Henry
 See Harris, Mark
Marti, Jose 1853-1895**NCLC 63; DAM MULT; HLC**
Martial c. 40-c. 104 .... **PC 10**
Martin, Ken
 See Hubbard, L(afayette) Ron(ald)
Martin, Richard
 See Creasey, John
Martin, Steve 1945- .... **CLC 30**
 See also CA 97-100; CANR 30; MTCW
Martin, Valerie 1948- .... **CLC 89**
 See also BEST 90:2; CA 85-88; CANR 49
Martin, Violet Florence 1862-1915 **TCLC 51**
Martin, Webber
 See Silverberg, Robert
Martindale, Patrick Victor
 See White, Patrick (Victor Martindale)
Martin du Gard, Roger 1881-1958 **TCLC 24**
 See also CA 118; DLB 65
Martineau, Harriet 1802-1876 .... **NCLC 26**
 See also DLB 21, 55, 159, 163, 166; YABC 2
Martines, Julia
 See O'Faolain, Julia

Martinez, Enrique Gonzalez
 See Gonzalez Martinez, Enrique
Martinez, Jacinto Benavente y
 See Benavente (y Martinez), Jacinto
Martinez Ruiz, Jose 1873-1967
 See Azorin; Ruiz, Jose Martinez
 See also CA 93-96; HW
Martinez Sierra, Gregorio 1881-1947**TCLC 6**
 See also CA 115
Martinez Sierra, Maria (de la O'LeJarraga) 1874-1974 .... **TCLC 6**
 See also CA 115
Martinsen, Martin
 See Follett, Ken(neth Martin)
Martinson, Harry (Edmund) 1904-1978**C L C 14**
 See also CA 77-80; CANR 34
Marut, Ret
 See Traven, B.
Marut, Robert
 See Traven, B.
Marvell, Andrew 1621-1678**LC 4; DA; DAB; DAC; DAM MST, POET; PC 10; WLC**
 See also CDBLB 1660-1789; DLB 131
Marx, Karl (Heinrich) 1818-1883 . **NCLC 17**
 See also DLB 129
Masaoka Shiki .... **TCLC 18**
 See also Masaoka Tsunenori
Masaoka Tsunenori 1867-1902
 See Masaoka Shiki
 See also CA 117
Masefield, John (Edward) 1878-1967**CLC 11, 47; DAM POET**
 See also CA 19-20; 25-28R; CANR 33; CAP 2; CDBLB 1890-1914; DLB 10, 19, 153, 160; MTCW; SATA 19
Maso, Carole 19(?)- .... **CLC 44**
Mason, Bobbie Ann 1940-**CLC 28, 43, 82; SSC 4**
 See also AAYA 5; CA 53-56; CANR 11, 31, 58; DLB 173; DLBY 87; INT CANR-31; MTCW
Mason, Ernst
 See Pohl, Frederik
Mason, Lee W.
 See Malzberg, Barry N(athaniel)
Mason, Nick 1945- .... **CLC 35**
Mason, Tally
 See Derleth, August (William)
Mass, William
 See Gibson, William
Masters, Edgar Lee 1868-1950 **TCLC 2, 25; DA; DAC; DAM MST, POET; PC 1; WLCS**
 See also CA 104; 133; CDALB 1865-1917; DLB 54; MTCW
Masters, Hilary 1928- .... **CLC 48**
 See also CA 25-28R; CANR 13, 47
Mastrosimone, William 19(?)- .... **CLC 36**
Mathe, Albert
 See Camus, Albert
Mather, Cotton 1663-1728 .... **LC 38**
 See also CDALB 1640-1865; DLB 24, 30, 140
Mather, Increase 1639-1723 .... **LC 38**
 See also DLB 24
Matheson, Richard Burton 1926- ..... **CLC 37**
 See also CA 97-100; DLB 8, 44; INT 97-100
Mathews, Harry 1930- .... **CLC 6, 52**
 See also CA 21-24R; CAAS 6; CANR 18, 40
Mathews, John Joseph 1894-1979 .. **CLC 84; DAM MULT**
 See also CA 19-20; 142; CANR 45; CAP 2; DLB 175; NNAL
Mathias, Roland (Glyn) 1915- .... **CLC 45**
 See also CA 97-100; CANR 19, 41; DLB 27
Matsuo Basho 1644-1694 .... **PC 3**
 See also DAM POET

Matheson, Rodney
See Creasey, John
Matthews, Greg 1949- .... **CLC 45**
See also CA 135
Matthews, William 1942- .... **CLC 40**
See also CA 29-32R; CAAS 18; CANR 12, 57;
DLB 5
Matthias, John (Edward) 1941- .... **CLC 9**
See also CA 33-36R; CANR 56
Matthiessen, Peter 1927-**CLC 5, 7, 11, 32, 64;**
DAM NOV
See also AAYA 6; BEST 90:4; CA 9-12R;
CANR 21, 50; DLB 6, 173; MTCW; SATA
27
Maturin, Charles Robert 1780(?)-1824**NCLC**
6
See also DLB 178
Matute (Ausejo), Ana Maria 1925- .. **CLC 11**
See also CA 89-92; MTCW
Maugham, W. S.
See Maugham, W(illiam) Somerset
Maugham, W(illiam) Somerset 1874-1965
CLC 1, 11, 15, 67, 93; DA; DAB; DAC;
DAM DRAM, MST, NOV; SSC 8; WLC
See also CA 5-8R; 25-28R; CANR 40; CDBLB
1914-1945; DLB 10, 36, 77, 100, 162;
MTCW; SATA 54
Maugham, William Somerset
See Maugham, W(illiam) Somerset
Maupassant, (Henri Rene Albert) Guy de 1850-
1893**NCLC 1, 42; DA; DAB; DAC; DAM**
MST; SSC 1; WLC
See also DLB 123
Maupin, Armistead 1944-**CLC 95; DAM POP**
See also CA 125; 130; CANR 58; INT 130
Maurhut, Richard
See Traven, B.
Mauriac, Claude 1914-1996 .... **CLC 9**
See also CA 89-92; 152; DLB 83
Mauriac, Francois (Charles) 1885-1970 **C L C**
4, 9, 56; SSC 24
See also CA 25-28; CAP 2; DLB 65; MTCW
Mavor, Osborne Henry 1888-1951
See Bridie, James
See also CA 104
Maxwell, William (Keepers, Jr.) 1908-**CLC 19**
See also CA 93-96; CANR 54; DLBY 80; INT
93-96
May, Elaine 1932- .... **CLC 16**
See also CA 124; 142; DLB 44
Mayakovski, Vladimir (Vladimirovich) 1893-
1930 .... **TCLC 4, 18**
See also CA 104; 158
Mayhew, Henry 1812-1887 .... **NCLC 31**
See also DLB 18, 55
Mayle, Peter 1939(?)- .... **CLC 89**
See also CA 139
Maynard, Joyce 1953- .... **CLC 23**
See also CA 111; 129
Mayne, William (James Carter) 1928-**CLC 12**
See also AAYA 20; CA 9-12R; CANR 37; CLR
25; JRDA; MAICYA; SAAS 11; SATA 6, 68
Mayo, Jim
See L'Amour, Louis (Dearborn)
Maysles, Albert 1926- .... **CLC 16**
See also CA 29-32R
Maysles, David 1932- .... **CLC 16**
Mazer, Norma Fox 1931- .... **CLC 26**
See also AAYA 5; CA 69-72; CANR 12, 32;
CLR 23; JRDA; MAICYA; SAAS 1; SATA
24, 67
Mazzini, Guiseppe 1805-1872 .... **NCLC 34**
McAuley, James Phillip 1917-1976 .. **CLC 45**
See also CA 97-100
McBain, Ed
See Hunter, Evan
McBrien, William Augustine 1930- .. **CLC 44**

See also CA 107
McCaffrey, Anne (Inez) 1926-**CLC 17; DAM**
NOV, POP
See also AAYA 6; AITN 2; BEST 89:2; CA 25-
28R; CANR 15, 35, 55; DLB 8; JRDA;
MAICYA; MTCW; SAAS 11; SATA 8, 70
McCall, Nathan 1955(?)- .... **CLC 86**
See also CA 146
McCann, Arthur
See Campbell, John W(ood, Jr.)
McCann, Edson
See Pohl, Frederik
McCarthy, Charles, Jr. 1933-
See McCarthy, Cormac
See also CANR 42; DAM POP
McCarthy, Cormac 1933- **CLC 4, 57, 59, 101**
See also McCarthy, Charles, Jr.
See also DLB 6, 143
McCarthy, Mary (Therese) 1912-1989**CLC 1,**
3, 5, 14, 24, 39, 59; SSC 24
See also CA 5-8R; 129; CANR 16, 50; DLB 2;
DLBY 81; INT CANR-16; MTCW
McCartney, (James) Paul 1942- **CLC 12, 35**
See also CA 146
McCauley, Stephen (D.) 1955- .... **CLC 50**
See also CA 141
McClure, Michael (Thomas) 1932-**CLC 6, 10**
See also CA 21-24R; CANR 17, 46; DLB 16
McCorkle, Jill (Collins) 1958- .... **CLC 51**
See also CA 121; DLBY 87
McCourt, James 1941- .... **CLC 5**
See also CA 57-60
McCoy, Horace (Stanley) 1897-1955**TCLC 28**
See also CA 108; 155; DLB 9
McCrae, John 1872-1918 .... **TCLC 12**
See also CA 109; DLB 92
McCreigh, James
See Pohl, Frederik
McCullers, (Lula) Carson (Smith) 1917-1967
CLC 1, 4, 10, 12, 48, 100; DA; DAB; DAC;
DAM MST, NOV; SSC 9, 24; WLC
See also AAYA 21; CA 5-8R; 25-28R; CABS
1, 3; CANR 18; CDALB 1941-1968; DLB
2, 7, 173; MTCW; SATA 27
McCulloch, John Tyler
See Burroughs, Edgar Rice
McCullough, Colleen 1938(?)-**CLC 27; DAM**
NOV, POP
See also CA 81-84; CANR 17, 46; MTCW
McDermott, Alice 1953- .... **CLC 90**
See also CA 109; CANR 40
McElroy, Joseph 1930- .... **CLC 5, 47**
See also CA 17-20R
McEwan, Ian (Russell) 1948- .... **CLC 13, 66;**
DAM NOV
See also BEST 90:4; CA 61-64; CANR 14, 41;
DLB 14; MTCW
McFadden, David 1940- .... **CLC 48**
See also CA 104; DLB 60; INT 104
McFarland, Dennis 1950- .... **CLC 65**
McGahern, John 1934-**CLC 5, 9, 48; SSC 17**
See also CA 17-20R; CANR 29; DLB 14;
MTCW
McGinley, Patrick (Anthony) 1937- . **CLC 41**
See also CA 120; 127; CANR 56; INT 127
McGinley, Phyllis 1905-1978 .... **CLC 14**
See also CA 9-12R; 77-80; CANR 19; DLB 11,
48; SATA 2, 44; SATA-Obit 24
McGinniss, Joe 1942- .... **CLC 32**
See also AITN 2; BEST 89:2; CA 25-28R;
CANR 26; INT CANR-26
McGivern, Maureen Daly
See Daly, Maureen
McGrath, Patrick 1950- .... **CLC 55**
See also CA 136
McGrath, Thomas (Matthew) 1916-1990**CLC**
28, 59; DAM POET

See also CA 9-12R; 132; CANR 6, 33; MTCW;
SATA 41; SATA-Obit 66
McGuane, Thomas (Francis III) 1939-**CLC 3,**
7, 18, 45
See also AITN 2; CA 49-52; CANR 5, 24, 49;
DLB 2; DLBY 80; INT CANR-24; MTCW
McGuckian, Medbh 1950- ..... **CLC 48; DAM**
POET
See also CA 143; DLB 40
McHale, Tom 1942(?)-1982 .... **CLC 3, 5**
See also AITN 1; CA 77-80; 106
McIlvanney, William 1936- .... **CLC 42**
See also CA 25-28R; CANR 61; DLB 14
McIlwraith, Maureen Mollie Hunter
See Hunter, Mollie
See also SATA 2
McInerney, Jay 1955- ... **CLC 34; DAM POP**
See also AAYA 18; CA 116; 123; CANR 45;
INT 123
McIntyre, Vonda N(eel) 1948- .... **CLC 18**
See also CA 81-84; CANR 17, 34; MTCW
McKay, ClaudeTCLC 7, 41; BLC; DAB; PC 2
See also McKay, Festus Claudius
See also DLB 4, 45, 51, 117
McKay, Festus Claudius 1889-1948
See McKay, Claude
See also BW 1; CA 104; 124; DA; DAC; DAM
MST, MULT, NOV, POET; MTCW; WLC
McKuen, Rod 1933- .... **CLC 1, 3**
See also AITN 1; CA 41-44R; CANR 40
McLoughlin, R. B.
See Mencken, H(enry) L(ouis)
McLuhan, (Herbert) Marshall 1911-1980
CLC 37, 83
See also CA 9-12R; 102; CANR 12, 34, 61;
DLB 88; INT CANR-12; MTCW
McMillan, Terry (L.) 1951-**CLC 50, 61; DAM**
MULT, NOV, POP
See also AAYA 21; BW 2; CA 140; CANR 60
McMurtry, Larry (Jeff) 1936-**CLC 2, 3, 7, 11,**
27, 44; DAM NOV, POP
See also AAYA 15; AITN 2; BEST 89:2; CA 5-
8R; CANR 19, 43; CDALB 1968-1988; DLB
2, 143; DLBY 80, 87; MTCW
McNally, T. M. 1961- .... **CLC 82**
McNally, Terrence 1939-....**CLC 4, 7, 41, 91;**
DAM DRAM
See also CA 45-48; CANR 2, 56; DLB 7
McNamer, Deirdre 1950- .... **CLC 70**
McNeile, Herman Cyril 1888-1937
See Sapper
See also DLB 77
McNickle, (William) D'Arcy 1904-1977 **C L C**
89; DAM MULT
See also CA 9-12R; 85-88; CANR 5, 45; DLB
175; NNAL; SATA-Obit 22
McPhee, John (Angus) 1931- .... **CLC 36**
See also BEST 90:1; CA 65-68; CANR 20, 46;
MTCW
McPherson, James Alan 1943- ... **CLC 19, 77**
See also BW 1; CA 25-28R; CAAS 17; CANR
24; DLB 38; MTCW
McPherson, William (Alexander) 1933- **C L C**
34
See also CA 69-72; CANR 28; INT CANR-28
Mead, Margaret 1901-1978 .... **CLC 37**
See also AITN 1; CA 1-4R; 81-84; CANR 4;
MTCW; SATA-Obit 20
Meaker, Marijane (Agnes) 1927-
See Kerr, M. E.
See also CA 107; CANR 37; INT 107; JRDA;
MAICYA; MTCW; SATA 20, 61
Medoff, Mark (Howard) 1940- ... **CLC 6, 23;**
DAM DRAM
See also AITN 1; CA 53-56; CANR 5; DLB 7;
INT CANR-5
Medvedev, P. N.

Pilnyak, Boris .... **TCLC 23**
See also Vogau, Boris Andreyevich
Pincherle, Alberto 1907-1990 ... **CLC 11, 18;**
DAM NOV
See also Moravia, Alberto
See also CA 25-28R; 132; CANR 33; MTCW
Pinckney, Darryl 1953- .... **CLC 76**
See also BW 2; CA 143
Pindar 518B.C.-446B.C. .... **CMLC 12; PC 19**
See also DLB 176
Pineda, Cecile 1942- .... **CLC 39**
See also CA 118
Pinero, Arthur Wing 1855-1934 ... **TCLC 32;**
DAM DRAM
See also CA 110; 153; DLB 10
Pinero, Miguel (Antonio Gomez) 1946-1988
CLC 4, 55
See also CA 61-64; 125; CANR 29; HW
Pinget, Robert 1919-1997 .... **CLC 7, 13, 37**
See also CA 85-88; 160; DLB 83
Pink Floyd
See Barrett, (Roger) Syd; Gilmour, David; Mason, Nick; Waters, Roger; Wright, Rick
Pinkney, Edward 1802-1828 .... **NCLC 31**
Pinkwater, Daniel Manus 1941- .... **CLC 35**
See also Pinkwater, Manus
See also AAYA 1; CA 29-32R; CANR 12, 38;
CLR 4; JRDA; MAICYA; SAAS 3; SATA 46,
76
Pinkwater, Manus
See Pinkwater, Daniel Manus
See also SATA 8
Pinsky, Robert 1940-**CLC 9, 19, 38, 94; DAM**
POET
See also CA 29-32R; CAAS 4; CANR 58;
DLBY 82
Pinta, Harold
See Pinter, Harold
Pinter, Harold 1930-**CLC 1, 3, 6, 9, 11, 15, 27,**
58, 73; DA; DAB; DAC; DAM DRAM,
MST; WLC
See also CA 5-8R; CANR 33; CDBLB 1960 to
Present; DLB 13; MTCW
Piozzi, Hester Lynch (Thrale) 1741-1821
NCLC 57
See also DLB 104, 142
Pirandello, Luigi 1867-1936**TCLC 4, 29; DA;**
DAB; DAC; DAM DRAM, MST; DC 5;
SSC 22; WLC
See also CA 104; 153
Pirsig, Robert M(aynard) 1928-**CLC 4, 6, 73;**
DAM POP
See also CA 53-56; CANR 42; MTCW; SATA
39
Pisarev, Dmitry Ivanovich 1840-1868 **N C L C**
25
Pix, Mary (Griffith) 1666-1709 .... **LC 8**
See also DLB 80
Pixerecourt, Guilbert de 1773-1844**NCLC 39**
Plaatje, Sol(omon) T(shekisho) 1876-1932
TCLC 73
See also BW 2; CA 141
Plaidy, Jean
See Hibbert, Eleanor Alice Burford
Planche, James Robinson 1796-1880**NCLC 42**
Plant, Robert 1948- .... **CLC 12**
Plante, David (Robert) 1940- **CLC 7, 23, 38;**
DAM NOV
See also CA 37-40R; CANR 12, 36, 58; DLBY
83; INT CANR-12; MTCW
Plath, Sylvia 1932-1963 **CLC 1, 2, 3, 5, 9, 11,**
14, 17, 50, 51, 62; DA; DAB; DAC; DAM
MST, POET; PC 1; WLC
See also AAYA 13; CA 19-20; CANR 34; CAP
2; CDALB 1941-1968; DLB 5, 6, 152;
MTCW
Plato 428(?)B.C.-348(?)B.C. .... **CMLC 8; DA;**

DAB; DAC; DAM MST; WLCS
See also DLB 176
Platonov, Andrei .... **TCLC 14**
See also Klimentov, Andrei Platonovich
Platt, Kin 1911- .... **CLC 26**
See also AAYA 11; CA 17-20R; CANR 11;
JRDA; SAAS 17; SATA 21, 86
Plautus c. 251B.C.-184B.C. ....**DC 6**
Plick et Plock
See Simenon, Georges (Jacques Christian)
Plimpton, George (Ames) 1927- .... **CLC 36**
See also AITN 1; CA 21-24R; CANR 32;
MTCW; SATA 10
Pliny the Elder c. 23-79 .... **CMLC 23**
Plomer, William Charles Franklin 1903-1973
CLC 4, 8
See also CA 21-22; CANR 34; CAP 2; DLB
20, 162; MTCW; SATA 24
Plowman, Piers
See Kavanagh, Patrick (Joseph)
Plum, J.
See Wodehouse, P(elham) G(renville)
Plumly, Stanley (Ross) 1939- .... **CLC 33**
See also CA 108; 110; DLB 5; INT 110
Plumpe, Friedrich Wilhelm 1888-1931**T C L C**
53
See also CA 112
Po Chu-i 772-846 .... **CMLC 24**
Poe, Edgar Allan 1809-1849**NCLC 1, 16, 55;**
DA; DAB; DAC; DAM MST, POET; PC
1; SSC 1, 22; WLC
See also AAYA 14; CDALB 1640-1865; DLB
3, 59, 73, 74; SATA 23
Poet of Titchfield Street, The
See Pound, Ezra (Weston Loomis)
Pohl, Frederik 1919- .... **CLC 18; SSC 25**
See also CA 61-64; CAAS 1; CANR 11, 37;
DLB 8; INT CANR-11; MTCW; SATA 24
Poirier, Louis 1910-
See Gracq, Julien
See also CA 122; 126
Poitier, Sidney 1927- .... **CLC 26**
See also BW 1; CA 117
Polanski, Roman 1933- .... **CLC 16**
See also CA 77-80
Poliakoff, Stephen 1952- .... **CLC 38**
See also CA 106; DLB 13
Police, The
See Copeland, Stewart (Armstrong); Summers,
Andrew James; Sumner, Gordon Matthew
Polidori, John William 1795-1821 . **NCLC 51**
See also DLB 116
Pollitt, Katha 1949- .... **CLC 28**
See also CA 120; 122; MTCW
Pollock, (Mary) Sharon 1936-**CLC 50; DAC;**
DAM DRAM, MST
See also CA 141; DLB 60
Polo, Marco 1254-1324 .... **CMLC 15**
Polonsky, Abraham (Lincoln) 1910- **CLC 92**
See also CA 104; DLB 26; INT 104
Polybius c. 200B.C.-c. 118B.C. ...... **CMLC 17**
See also DLB 176
Pomerance, Bernard 1940- .... **CLC 13; DAM**
DRAM
See also CA 101; CANR 49
Ponge, Francis (Jean Gaston Alfred) 1899-1988
CLC 6, 18; DAM POET
See also CA 85-88; 126; CANR 40
Pontoppidan, Henrik 1857-1943 .... **TCLC 29**
Poole, Josephine .... **CLC 17**
See also Helyar, Jane Penelope Josephine
See also SAAS 2; SATA 5
Popa, Vasko 1922-1991 .... **CLC 19**
See also CA 112; 148; DLB 181
Pope, Alexander 1688-1744 **LC 3; DA; DAB;**
DAC; DAM MST, POET; WLC
See also CDBLB 1660-1789; DLB 95, 101

Porter, Connie (Rose) 1959(?)- .... **CLC 70**
See also BW 2; CA 142; SATA 81
Porter, Gene(va Grace) Stratton 1863(?)-1924
TCLC 21
See also CA 112
Porter, Katherine Anne 1890-1980**CLC 1, 3, 7,**
10, 13, 15, 27, 101; DA; DAB; DAC; DAM
MST, NOV; SSC 4
See also AITN 2; CA 1-4R; 101; CANR 1; DLB
4, 9, 102; DLBD 12; DLBY 80; MTCW;
SATA 39; SATA-Obit 23
Porter, Peter (Neville Frederick) 1929-**CLC 5,**
13, 33
See also CA 85-88; DLB 40
Porter, William Sydney 1862-1910
See Henry, O.
See also CA 104; 131; CDALB 1865-1917; DA;
DAB; DAC; DAM MST; DLB 12, 78, 79;
MTCW; YABC 2
Portillo (y Pacheco), Jose Lopez
See Lopez Portillo (y Pacheco), Jose
Post, Melville Davisson 1869-1930 **TCLC 39**
See also CA 110
Potok, Chaim 1929- . **CLC 2, 7, 14, 26; DAM**
NOV
See also AAYA 15; AITN 1, 2; CA 17-20R;
CANR 19, 35; DLB 28, 152; INT CANR-
19; MTCW; SATA 33
Potter, (Helen) Beatrix 1866-1943
See Webb, (Martha) Beatrice (Potter)
See also MAICYA
Potter, Dennis (Christopher George) 1935-1994
CLC 58, 86
See also CA 107; 145; CANR 33, 61; MTCW
Pound, Ezra (Weston Loomis) 1885-1972
CLC 1, 2, 3, 4, 5, 7, 10, 13, 18, 34, 48, 50;
DA; DAB; DAC; DAM MST, POET; PC
4; WLC
See also CA 5-8R; 37-40R; CANR 40; CDALB
1917-1929; DLB 4, 45, 63; DLBD 15;
MTCW
Povod, Reinaldo 1959-1994 .... **CLC 44**
See also CA 136; 146
Powell, Adam Clayton, Jr. 1908-1972**CLC 89;**
BLC; DAM MULT
See also BW 1; CA 102; 33-36R
Powell, Anthony (Dymoke) 1905-**CLC 1, 3, 7,**
9, 10, 31
See also CA 1-4R; CANR 1, 32, 62; CDBLB
1945-1960; DLB 15; MTCW
Powell, Dawn 1897-1965 .... **CLC 66**
See also CA 5-8R
Powell, Padgett 1952- .... **CLC 34**
See also CA 126
Power, Susan 1961- .... **CLC 91**
Powers, J(ames) F(arl) 1917-**CLC 1, 4, 8, 57;**
SSC 4
See also CA 1-4R; CANR 2, 61; DLB 130;
MTCW
Powers, John J(ames) 1945-
See Powers, John R.
See also CA 69-72
Powers, John R. .... **CLC 66**
See also Powers, John J(ames)
Powers, Richard (S.) 1957- .... **CLC 93**
See also CA 148
Pownall, David 1938- .... **CLC 10**
See also CA 89-92; CAAS 18; CANR 49; DLB
14
Powys, John Cowper 1872-1963**CLC 7, 9, 15,**
46
See also CA 85-88; DLB 15; MTCW
Powys, T(heodore) F(rancis) 1875-1953
TCLC 9
See also CA 106; DLB 36, 162
Prado (Calvo), Pedro 1886-1952 ... **TCLC 75**
See also CA 131; HW

Prager, Emily 1952- .... **CLC 56**

Pratt, E(dwin) J(ohn) 1883(?)-1964 **CLC 19;**
　　DAC; DAM POET
　　See also CA 141; 93-96; DLB 92

Premchand .... **TCLC 21**
　　See also Srivastava, Dhanpat Rai

Preussler, Otfried 1923- .... **CLC 17**
　　See also CA 77-80; SATA 24

Prevert, Jacques (Henri Marie) 1900-1977
　　CLC 15
　　See also CA 77-80; 69-72; CANR 29, 61;
　　MTCW; SATA-Obit 30

Prevost, Abbe (Antoine Francois) 1697-1763
　　LC 1

Price, (Edward) Reynolds 1933- **CLC 3, 6, 13,**
　　43, 50, 63; DAM NOV; SSC 22
　　See also CA 1-4R; CANR 1, 37, 57; DLB 2;
　　INT CANR-37

Price, Richard 1949- .... **CLC 6, 12**
　　See also CA 49-52; CANR 3; DLBY 81

Prichard, Katharine Susannah 1883-1969
　　CLC 46
　　See also CA 11-12; CANR 33; CAP 1; MTCW;
　　SATA 66

Priestley, J(ohn) B(oynton) 1894-1984 **CLC 2,**
　　5, 9, 34; DAM DRAM, NOV
　　See also CA 9-12R; 113; CANR 33; CDBLB
　　1914-1945; DLB 10, 34, 77, 100, 139; DLBY
　　84; MTCW

Prince 1958(?)- .... **CLC 35**

Prince, F(rank) T(empleton) 1912- .. **CLC 22**
　　See also CA 101; CANR 43; DLB 20

Prince Kropotkin
　　See Kropotkin, Peter (Aleksieevich)

Prior, Matthew 1664-1721 .... **LC 4**
　　See also DLB 95

Prishvin, Mikhail 1873-1954 .... **TCLC 75**

Pritchard, William H(arrison) 1932- **CLC 34**
　　See also CA 65-68; CANR 23; DLB 111

Pritchett, V(ictor) S(awdon) 1900-1997 **C L C**
　　5, 13, 15, 41; DAM NOV; SSC 14
　　See also CA 61-64; 157; CANR 31; DLB 15,
　　139; MTCW

Private 19022
　　See Manning, Frederic

Probst, Mark 1925- .... **CLC 59**
　　See also CA 130

Prokosch, Frederic 1908-1989 ...... **CLC 4, 48**
　　See also CA 73-76; 128; DLB 48

Prophet, The
　　See Dreiser, Theodore (Herman Albert)

Prose, Francine 1947- .... **CLC 45**
　　See also CA 109; 112; CANR 46

Proudhon
　　See Cunha, Euclides (Rodrigues Pimenta) da

Proulx, E. Annie 1935- .... **CLC 81**

Proust, (Valentin-Louis-George-Eugene-)
　　Marcel 1871-1922 **TCLC 7, 13, 33; DA;**
　　DAB; DAC; DAM MST, NOV; WLC
　　See also CA 104; 120; DLB 65; MTCW

Prowler, Harley
　　See Masters, Edgar Lee

Prus, Boleslaw 1845-1912 .... **TCLC 48**

Pryor, Richard (Franklin Lenox Thomas) 1940-
　　CLC 26
　　See also CA 122

Przybyszewski, Stanislaw 1868-1927 **TCLC 36**
　　See also CA 160; DLB 66

Pteleon
　　See Grieve, C(hristopher) M(urray)
　　See also DAM POET

Puckett, Lute
　　See Masters, Edgar Lee

Puig, Manuel 1932-1990 **CLC 3, 5, 10, 28, 65;**
　　DAM MULT; HLC
　　See also CA 45-48; CANR 2, 32; DLB 113; HW;
　　MTCW

Pulitzer, Joseph 1847-1911 .... **TCLC 76**
　　See also CA 114; DLB 23

Purdy, Al(fred Wellington) 1918- **CLC 3, 6, 14,**
　　50; DAC; DAM MST, POET
　　See also CA 81-84; CAAS 17; CANR 42; DLB
　　88

Purdy, James (Amos) 1923- **CLC 2, 4, 10, 28,**
　　52
　　See also CA 33-36R; CAAS 1; CANR 19, 51;
　　DLB 2; INT CANR-19; MTCW

Pure, Simon
　　See Swinnerton, Frank Arthur

Pushkin, Alexander (Sergeyevich) 1799-1837
　　NCLC 3, 27; DA; DAB; DAC; DAM
　　DRAM, MST, POET; PC 10; SSC 27;
　　WLC
　　See also SATA 61

P'u Sung-ling 1640-1715 .... **LC 3**

Putnam, Arthur Lee
　　See Alger, Horatio, Jr.

Puzo, Mario 1920- **CLC 1, 2, 6, 36; DAM NOV,**
　　POP
　　See also CA 65-68; CANR 4, 42; DLB 6;
　　MTCW

Pygge, Edward
　　See Barnes, Julian (Patrick)

Pyle, Ernest Taylor 1900-1945
　　See Pyle, Ernie
　　See also CA 115; 160

Pyle, Ernie 1900-1945 .... **TCLC 75**
　　See also Pyle, Ernest Taylor
　　See also DLB 29

Pym, Barbara (Mary Crampton) 1913-1980
　　CLC 13, 19, 37
　　See also CA 13-14; 97-100; CANR 13, 34; CAP
　　1; DLB 14; DLBY 87; MTCW

Pynchon, Thomas (Ruggles, Jr.) 1937- **CLC 2,**
　　3, 6, 9, 11, 18, 33, 62, 72; DA; DAB; DAC;
　　DAM MST, NOV, POP; SSC 14; WLC
　　See also BEST 90:2; CA 17-20R; CANR 22,
　　46; DLB 2, 173; MTCW

Pythagoras c. 570B.C.-c. 500B.C. . **CMLC 22**
　　See also DLB 176

Qian Zhongshu
　　See Ch'ien Chung-shu

Qroll
　　See Dagerman, Stig (Halvard)

Quarrington, Paul (Lewis) 1953- ..... **CLC 65**
　　See also CA 129; CANR 62

Quasimodo, Salvatore 1901-1968 ..... **CLC 10**
　　See also CA 13-16; 25-28R; CAP 1; DLB 114;
　　MTCW

Quay, Stephen 1947- .... **CLC 95**

Quay, The Brothers
　　See Quay, Stephen; Quay, Timothy

Quay, Timothy 1947- .... **CLC 95**

Queen, Ellery .... **CLC 3, 11**
　　See also Dannay, Frederic; Davidson, Avram;
　　Lee, Manfred B(ennington); Marlowe,
　　Stephen; Sturgeon, Theodore (Hamilton);
　　Vance, John Holbrook

Queen, Ellery, Jr.
　　See Dannay, Frederic; Lee, Manfred
　　B(ennington)

Queneau, Raymond 1903-1976 **CLC 2, 5, 10,**
　　42
　　See also CA 77-80; 69-72; CANR 32; DLB 72;
　　MTCW

Quevedo, Francisco de 1580-1645 .... **LC 23**

Quiller-Couch, Arthur Thomas 1863-1944
　　TCLC 53
　　See also CA 118; DLB 135, 153

Quin, Ann (Marie) 1936-1973 .... **CLC 6**
　　See also CA 9-12R; 45-48; DLB 14

Quinn, Martin
　　See Smith, Martin Cruz

Quinn, Peter 1947- .... **CLC 91**

Quinn, Simon
　　See Smith, Martin Cruz

Quiroga, Horacio (Sylvestre) 1878-1937
　　TCLC 20; DAM MULT; HLC
　　See also CA 117; 131; HW; MTCW

Quoirez, Francoise 1935- .... **CLC 9**
　　See also Sagan, Francoise
　　See also CA 49-52; CANR 6, 39; MTCW

Raabe, Wilhelm 1831-1910 .... **TCLC 45**
　　See also DLB 129

Rabe, David (William) 1940- ... **CLC 4, 8, 33;**
　　DAM DRAM
　　See also CA 85-88; CABS 3; CANR 59; DLB 7

Rabelais, Francois 1483-1553 **LC 5; DA; DAB;**
　　DAC; DAM MST; WLC

Rabinovitch, Sholem 1859-1916
　　See Aleichem, Sholom
　　See also CA 104

Rachilde 1860-1953 .... **TCLC 67**
　　See also DLB 123

Racine, Jean 1639-1699 . **LC 28; DAB; DAM**
　　MST

Radcliffe, Ann (Ward) 1764-1823 **NCLC 6, 55**
　　See also DLB 39, 178

Radiguet, Raymond 1903-1923 ...... **TCLC 29**
　　See also DLB 65

Radnoti, Miklos 1909-1944 .... **TCLC 16**
　　See also CA 118

Rado, James 1939- .... **CLC 17**
　　See also CA 105

Radvanyi, Netty 1900-1983
　　See Seghers, Anna
　　See also CA 85-88; 110

Rae, Ben
　　See Griffiths, Trevor

Raeburn, John (Hay) 1941- .... **CLC 34**
　　See also CA 57-60

Ragni, Gerome 1942-1991 .... **CLC 17**
　　See also CA 105; 134

Rahv, Philip 1908-1973 .... **CLC 24**
　　See also Greenberg, Ivan
　　See also DLB 137

Raine, Craig 1944- .... **CLC 32, 103**
　　See also CA 108; CANR 29, 51; DLB 40

Raine, Kathleen (Jessie) 1908- ...... **CLC 7, 45**
　　See also CA 85-88; CANR 46; DLB 20; MTCW

Rainis, Janis 1865-1929 .... **TCLC 29**

Rakosi, Carl .... **CLC 47**
　　See also Rawley, Callman
　　See also CAAS 5

Raleigh, Richard
　　See Lovecraft, H(oward) P(hillips)

Raleigh, Sir Walter 1554(?)-1618 . **LC 31, 39**
　　See also CDBLB Before 1660; DLB 172

Rallentando, H. P.
　　See Sayers, Dorothy L(eigh)

Ramal, Walter
　　See de la Mare, Walter (John)

Ramon, Juan
　　See Jimenez (Mantecon), Juan Ramon

Ramos, Graciliano 1892-1953 .... **TCLC 32**

Rampersad, Arnold 1941- .... **CLC 44**
　　See also BW 2; CA 127; 133; DLB 111; INT
　　133

Rampling, Anne
　　See Rice, Anne

Ramsay, Allan 1684(?)-1758 .... **LC 29**
　　See also DLB 95

Ramuz, Charles-Ferdinand 1878-1947 **T C L C**
　　33

Rand, Ayn 1905-1982 **CLC 3, 30, 44, 79; DA;**
　　DAC; DAM MST, NOV, POP; WLC
　　See also AAYA 10; CA 13-16R; 105; CANR
　　27; MTCW

Randall, Dudley (Felker) 1914- **CLC 1; BLC;**
　　DAM MULT
　　See also BW 1; CA 25-28R; CANR 23; DLB

MTCW

Rimbaud, (Jean Nicolas) Arthur 1854-1891
    NCLC 4, 35; DA; DAB; DAC; DAM MST,
    POET; PC 3; WLC
Rinehart, Mary Roberts 1876-1958**TCLC 52**
    See also CA 108
Ringmaster, The
    See Mencken, H(enry) L(ouis)
Ringwood, Gwen(dolyn Margaret) Pharis
    1910-1984 .... **CLC 48**
    See also CA 148; 112; DLB 88
Rio, Michel 19(?)- .... **CLC 43**
Ritsos, Giannes
    See Ritsos, Yannis
Ritsos, Yannis 1909-1990 .... **CLC 6, 13, 31**
    See also CA 77-80; 133; CANR 39, 61; MTCW
Ritter, Erika 1948(?)- .... **CLC 52**
Rivera, Jose Eustasio 1889-1928 ... **TCLC 35**
    See also HW
Rivers, Conrad Kent 1933-1968 .... **CLC 1**
    See also BW 1; CA 85-88; DLB 41
Rivers, Elfrida
    See Bradley, Marion Zimmer
Riverside, John
    See Heinlein, Robert A(nson)
Rizal, Jose 1861-1896 .... **NCLC 27**
Roa Bastos, Augusto (Antonio) 1917-**CLC 45;**
    DAM MULT; HLC
    See also CA 131; DLB 113; HW
Robbe-Grillet, Alain 1922- **CLC 1, 2, 4, 6, 8,**
    10, 14, 43
    See also CA 9-12R; CANR 33; DLB 83; MTCW
Robbins, Harold 1916- ... **CLC 5; DAM NOV**
    See also CA 73-76; CANR 26, 54; MTCW
Robbins, Thomas Eugene 1936-
    See Robbins, Tom
    See also CA 81-84; CANR 29, 59; DAM NOV,
    POP; MTCW
Robbins, Tom .... **CLC 9, 32, 64**
    See also Robbins, Thomas Eugene
    See also BEST 90:3; DLBY 80
Robbins, Trina 1938- .... **CLC 21**
    See also CA 128
Roberts, Charles G(eorge) D(ouglas) 1860-1943
    TCLC 8
    See also CA 105; CLR 33; DLB 92; SATA 88;
    SATA-Brief 29
Roberts, Elizabeth Madox 1886-1941 **TCLC
    68**
    See also CA 111; DLB 9, 54, 102; SATA 33;
    SATA-Brief 27
Roberts, Kate 1891-1985 .... **CLC 15**
    See also CA 107; 116
Roberts, Keith (John Kingston) 1935-**CLC 14**
    See also CA 25-28R; CANR 46
Roberts, Kenneth (Lewis) 1885-1957**TCLC 23**
    See also CA 109; DLB 9
Roberts, Michele (B.) 1949- .... **CLC 48**
    See also CA 115; CANR 58
Robertson, Ellis
    See Ellison, Harlan (Jay); Silverberg, Robert
Robertson, Thomas William 1829-1871**NCLC
    35; DAM DRAM**
Robeson, Kenneth
    See Dent, Lester
Robinson, Edwin Arlington 1869-1935**TCLC
    5; DA; DAC; DAM MST, POET; PC 1**
    See also CA 104; 133; CDALB 1865-1917;
    DLB 54; MTCW
Robinson, Henry Crabb 1775-1867**NCLC 15**
    See also DLB 107
Robinson, Jill 1936- .... **CLC 10**
    See also CA 102; INT 102
Robinson, Kim Stanley 1952- .... **CLC 34**
    See also CA 126
Robinson, Lloyd
    See Silverberg, Robert

Robinson, Marilynne 1944- .... **CLC 25**
    See also CA 116
Robinson, Smokey .... **CLC 21**
    See also Robinson, William, Jr.
Robinson, William, Jr. 1940-
    See Robinson, Smokey
    See also CA 116
Robison, Mary 1949- .... **CLC 42, 98**
    See also CA 113; 116; DLB 130; INT 116
Rod, Edouard 1857-1910 .... **TCLC 52**
Roddenberry, Eugene Wesley 1921-1991
    See Roddenberry, Gene
    See also CA 110; 135; CANR 37; SATA 45;
    SATA-Obit 69
Roddenberry, Gene .... **CLC 17**
    See also Roddenberry, Eugene Wesley
    See also AAYA 5; SATA-Obit 69
Rodgers, Mary 1931- .... **CLC 12**
    See also CA 49-52; CANR 8, 55; CLR 20; INT
    CANR-8; JRDA; MAICYA; SATA 8
Rodgers, W(illiam) R(obert) 1909-1969**CLC 7**
    See also CA 85-88; DLB 20
Rodman, Eric
    See Silverberg, Robert
Rodman, Howard 1920(?)-1985 .... **CLC 65**
    See also CA 118
Rodman, Maia
    See Wojciechowska, Maia (Teresa)
Rodriguez, Claudio 1934- .... **CLC 10**
    See also DLB 134
Roelvaag, O(le) E(dvart) 1876-1931**TCLC 17**
    See also CA 117; DLB 9
Roethke, Theodore (Huebner) 1908-1963**CLC
    1, 3, 8, 11, 19, 46, 101; DAM POET; PC 15**
    See also CA 81-84; CABS 2; CDALB 1941-
    1968; DLB 5; MTCW
Rogers, Thomas Hunton 1927- .... **CLC 57**
    See also CA 89-92; INT 89-92
Rogers, Will(iam Penn Adair) 1879-1935
    TCLC 8, 71; DAM MULT
    See also CA 105; 144; DLB 11; NNAL
Rogin, Gilbert 1929- .... **CLC 18**
    See also CA 65-68; CANR 15
Rohan, Koda .... **TCLC 22**
    See also Koda Shigeyuki
Rohlfs, Anna Katharine Green
    See Green, Anna Katharine
Rohmer, Eric .... **CLC 16**
    See also Scherer, Jean-Marie Maurice
Rohmer, Sax .... **TCLC 28**
    See also Ward, Arthur Henry Sarsfield
    See also DLB 70
Roiphe, Anne (Richardson) 1935- .. **CLC 3, 9**
    See also CA 89-92; CANR 45; DLBY 80; INT
    89-92
Rojas, Fernando de 1465-1541 .... **LC 23**
**Rolfe, Frederick (William Serafino Austin
    Lewis Mary)** 1860-1913 .... **TCLC 12**
    See also CA 107; DLB 34, 156
Rolland, Romain 1866-1944 .... **TCLC 23**
    See also CA 118; DLB 65
Rolle, Richard c. 1300-c. 1349 ...... **CMLC 21**
    See also DLB 146
Rolvaag, O(le) E(dvart)
    See Roelvaag, O(le) E(dvart)
Romain Arnaud, Saint
    See Aragon, Louis
Romains, Jules 1885-1972 .... **CLC 7**
    See also CA 85-88; CANR 34; DLB 65; MTCW
Romero, Jose Ruben 1890-1952 .... **TCLC 14**
    See also CA 114; 131; HW
Ronsard, Pierre de 1524-1585... **LC 6; PC 11**
Rooke, Leon 1934- .. **CLC 25, 34; DAM POP**
    See also CA 25-28R; CANR 23, 53
Roosevelt, Theodore 1858-1919 ..... **TCLC 69**
    See also CA 115; DLB 47
Roper, William 1498-1578 .... **LC 10**

Roquelaure, A. N.
    See Rice, Anne
Rosa, Joao Guimaraes 1908-1967 .... **CLC 23**
    See also CA 89-92; DLB 113
Rose, Wendy 1948-**CLC 85; DAM MULT; PC
    13**
    See also CA 53-56; CANR 5, 51; DLB 175;
    NNAL; SATA 12
Rosen, R. D.
    See Rosen, Richard (Dean)
Rosen, Richard (Dean) 1949- .... **CLC 39**
    See also CA 77-80; CANR 62; INT CANR-30
Rosenberg, Isaac 1890-1918 .... **TCLC 12**
    See also CA 107; DLB 20
Rosenblatt, Joe .... **CLC 15**
    See also Rosenblatt, Joseph
Rosenblatt, Joseph 1933-
    See Rosenblatt, Joe
    See also CA 89-92; INT 89-92
Rosenfeld, Samuel 1896-1963
    See Tzara, Tristan
    See also CA 89-92
Rosenstock, Sami
    See Tzara, Tristan
Rosenstock, Samuel
    See Tzara, Tristan
Rosenthal, M(acha) L(ouis) 1917-1996 . **C L C
    28**
    See also CA 1-4R; 152; CAAS 6; CANR 4, 51;
    DLB 5; SATA 59
Ross, Barnaby
    See Dannay, Frederic
Ross, Bernard L.
    See Follett, Ken(neth Martin)
Ross, J. H.
    See Lawrence, T(homas) E(dward)
Ross, Martin
    See Martin, Violet Florence
    See also DLB 135
Ross, (James) Sinclair 1908- **CLC 13; DAC;
    DAM MST; SSC 24**
    See also CA 73-76; DLB 88
Rossetti, Christina (Georgina) 1830-1894
    **NCLC 2, 50; DA; DAB; DAC; DAM MST,
    POET; PC 7; WLC**
    See also DLB 35, 163; MAICYA; SATA 20
Rossetti, Dante Gabriel 1828-1882. **NCLC 4;
    DA; DAB; DAC; DAM MST, POET; WLC**
    See also CDBLB 1832-1890; DLB 35
Rossner, Judith (Perelman) 1935-**CLC 6, 9, 29**
    See also AITN 2; BEST 90:3; CA 17-20R;
    CANR 18, 51; DLB 6; INT CANR-18;
    MTCW
Rostand, Edmond (Eugene Alexis) 1868-1918
    **TCLC 6, 37; DA; DAB; DAC; DAM
    DRAM, MST**
    See also CA 104; 126; MTCW
Roth, Henry 1906-1995 ..... **CLC 2, 6, 11, 104**
    See also CA 11-12; 149; CANR 38; CAP 1;
    DLB 28; MTCW
Roth, Philip (Milton) 1933-**CLC 1, 2, 3, 4, 6, 9,
    15, 22, 31, 47, 66, 86; DA; DAB; DAC;
    DAM MST, NOV, POP; SSC 26; WLC**
    See also BEST 90:3; CA 1-4R; CANR 1, 22,
    36, 55; CDALB 1968-1988; DLB 2, 28, 173;
    DLBY 82; MTCW
Rothenberg, Jerome 1931- .... **CLC 6, 57**
    See also CA 45-48; CANR 1; DLB 5
Roumain, Jacques (Jean Baptiste) 1907-1944
    TCLC 19; BLC; DAM MULT
    See also BW 1; CA 117; 125
Rourke, Constance (Mayfield) 1885-1941
    TCLC 12
    See also CA 107; YABC 1
Rousseau, Jean-Baptiste 1671-1741 ...... **LC 9**
Rousseau, Jean-Jacques 1712-1778**LC 14, 36;
    DA; DAB; DAC; DAM MST; WLC**

Shue, Larry 1946-1985 **CLC 52; DAM DRAM**
See also CA 145; 117
Shu-Jen, Chou 1881-1936
See Lu Hsun
See also CA 104
Shulman, Alix Kates 1932- .... **CLC 2, 10**
See also CA 29-32R; CANR 43; SATA 7
Shuster, Joe 1914- .... **CLC 21**
Shute, Nevil .... **CLC 30**
See also Norway, Nevil Shute
Shuttle, Penelope (Diane) 1947- .... **CLC 7**
See also CA 93-96; CANR 39; DLB 14, 40
Sidney, Mary 1561-1621 .... **LC 19, 39**
Sidney, Sir Philip 1554-1586 **LC 19, 39; DA;
DAB; DAC; DAM MST, POET**
See also CDBLB Before 1660; DLB 167
Siegel, Jerome 1914-1996 .... **CLC 21**
See also CA 116; 151
Siegel, Jerry
See Siegel, Jerome
Sienkiewicz, Henryk (Adam Alexander Pius)
1846-1916 .... **TCLC 3**
See also CA 104; 134
Sierra, Gregorio Martinez
See Martinez Sierra, Gregorio
Sierra, Maria (de la O'LeJarraga) Martinez
See Martinez Sierra, Maria (de la O'LeJarraga)
Sigal, Clancy 1926- .... **CLC 7**
See also CA 1-4R
Sigourney, Lydia Howard (Huntley) 1791-1865
NCLC 21
See also DLB 1, 42, 73
Siguenza y Gongora, Carlos de 1645-1700 **L C
8**
Sigurjonsson, Johann 1880-1919 ... **TCLC 27**
Sikelianos, Angelos 1884-1951 .... **TCLC 39**
Silkin, Jon 1930- .... **CLC 2, 6, 43**
See also CA 5-8R; CAAS 5; DLB 27
Silko, Leslie (Marmon) 1948- **CLC 23, 74; DA;
DAC; DAM MST, MULT, POP; WLCS**
See also AAYA 14; CA 115; 122; CANR 45;
DLB 143, 175; NNAL
Sillanpaa, Frans Eemil 1888-1964 ... **CLC 19**
See also CA 129; 93-96; MTCW
Sillitoe, Alan 1928- ... **CLC 1, 3, 6, 10, 19, 57**
See also AITN 1; CA 9-12R; CAAS 2; CANR
8, 26, 55; CDBLB 1960 to Present; DLB 14,
139; MTCW; SATA 61
Silone, Ignazio 1900-1978 .... **CLC 4**
See also CA 25-28; 81-84; CANR 34; CAP 2;
MTCW
Silver, Joan Micklin 1935- .... **CLC 20**
See also CA 114; 121; INT 121
Silver, Nicholas
See Faust, Frederick (Schiller)
Silverberg, Robert 1935- **CLC 7; DAM POP**
See also CA 1-4R; CAAS 3; CANR 1, 20, 36;
DLB 8; INT CANR-20; MAICYA; MTCW;
SATA 13, 91
Silverstein, Alvin 1933- .... **CLC 17**
See also CA 49-52; CANR 2; CLR 25; JRDA;
MAICYA; SATA 8, 69
Silverstein, Virginia B(arbara Opshelor) 1937-
CLC 17
See also CA 49-52; CANR 2; CLR 25; JRDA;
MAICYA; SATA 8, 69
Sim, Georges
See Simenon, Georges (Jacques Christian)
Simak, Clifford D(onald) 1904-1988 **CLC 1, 55**
See also CA 1-4R; 125; CANR 1, 35; DLB 8;
MTCW; SATA-Obit 56
Simenon, Georges (Jacques Christian) 1903-
1989 .. **CLC 1, 2, 3, 8, 18, 47; DAM POP**
See also CA 85-88; 129; CANR 35; DLB 72;
DLBY 89; MTCW
Simic, Charles 1938- .... **CLC 6, 9, 22, 49, 68;
DAM POET**

See also CA 29-32R; CAAS 4; CANR 12, 33,
52, 61; DLB 105
Simmel, Georg 1858-1918 .... **TCLC 64**
See also CA 157
Simmons, Charles (Paul) 1924- .... **CLC 57**
See also CA 89-92; INT 89-92
Simmons, Dan 1948- ..... **CLC 44; DAM POP**
See also AAYA 16; CA 138; CANR 53
Simmons, James (Stewart Alexander) 1933-
CLC 43
See also CA 105; CAAS 21; DLB 40
Simms, William Gilmore 1806-1870 **NCLC 3**
See also DLB 3, 30, 59, 73
Simon, Carly 1945- .... **CLC 26**
See also CA 105
Simon, Claude 1913- **CLC 4, 9, 15, 39; DAM
NOV**
See also CA 89-92; CANR 33; DLB 83; MTCW
Simon, (Marvin) Neil 1927- **CLC 6, 11, 31, 39,
70; DAM DRAM**
See also AITN 1; CA 21-24R; CANR 26, 54;
DLB 7; MTCW
Simon, Paul (Frederick) 1941(?)- ..... **CLC 17**
See also CA 116; 153
Simonon, Paul 1956(?)- .... **CLC 30**
Simpson, Harriette
See Arnow, Harriette (Louisa) Simpson
Simpson, Louis (Aston Marantz) 1923- **CLC 4,
7, 9, 32; DAM POET**
See also CA 1-4R; CAAS 4; CANR 1, 61; DLB
5; MTCW
Simpson, Mona (Elizabeth) 1957- .... **CLC 44**
See also CA 122; 135
Simpson, N(orman) F(rederick) 1919- **CLC 29**
See also CA 13-16R; DLB 13
Sinclair, Andrew (Annandale) 1935- . **CLC 2,
14**
See also CA 9-12R; CAAS 5; CANR 14, 38;
DLB 14; MTCW
Sinclair, Emil
See Hesse, Hermann
Sinclair, Iain 1943- .... **CLC 76**
See also CA 132
Sinclair, Iain MacGregor
See Sinclair, Iain
Sinclair, Irene
See Griffith, D(avid Lewelyn) W(ark)
Sinclair, Mary Amelia St. Clair 1865(?)-1946
See Sinclair, May
See also CA 104
Sinclair, May .... **TCLC 3, 11**
See also Sinclair, Mary Amelia St. Clair
See also DLB 36, 135
Sinclair, Roy
See Griffith, D(avid Lewelyn) W(ark)
Sinclair, Upton (Beall) 1878-1968 **CLC 1, 11,
15, 63; DA; DAB; DAC; DAM MST, NOV;
WLC**
See also CA 5-8R; 25-28R; CANR 7; CDALB
1929-1941; DLB 9; INT CANR-7; MTCW;
SATA 9
Singer, Isaac
See Singer, Isaac Bashevis
Singer, Isaac Bashevis 1904-1991 **CLC 1, 3, 6,
9, 11, 15, 23, 38, 69; DA; DAB; DAC; DAM
MST, NOV; SSC 3; WLC**
See also AITN 1, 2; CA 1-4R; 134; CANR 1,
39; CDALB 1941-1968; CLR 1; DLB 6, 28,
52; DLBY 91; JRDA; MAICYA; MTCW;
SATA 3, 27; SATA-Obit 68
Singer, Israel Joshua 1893-1944 .... **TCLC 33**
Singh, Khushwant 1915- .... **CLC 11**
See also CA 9-12R; CAAS 9; CANR 6
Singleton, Ann
See Benedict, Ruth (Fulton)
Sinjohn, John
See Galsworthy, John

Sinyavsky, Andrei (Donatevich) 1925-1997
CLC 8
See also CA 85-88; 159
Sirin, V.
See Nabokov, Vladimir (Vladimirovich)
Sissman, L(ouis) E(dward) 1928-1976 **CLC 9,
18**
See also CA 21-24R; 65-68; CANR 13; DLB 5
Sisson, C(harles) H(ubert) 1914- .... **CLC 8**
See also CA 1-4R; CAAS 3; CANR 3, 48; DLB
27
Sitwell, Dame Edith 1887-1964 **CLC 2, 9, 67;
DAM POET; PC 3**
See also CA 9-12R; CANR 35; CDBLB 1945-
1960; DLB 20; MTCW
Siwaarmill, H. P.
See Sharp, William
Sjoewall, Maj 1935- .... **CLC 7**
See also CA 65-68
Sjowall, Maj
See Sjoewall, Maj
Skelton, Robin 1925-1997 .... **CLC 13**
See also AITN 2; CA 5-8R; 160; CAAS 5;
CANR 28; DLB 27, 53
Skolimowski, Jerzy 1938- .... **CLC 20**
See also CA 128
Skram, Amalie (Bertha) 1847-1905 **TCLC 25**
Skvorecky, Josef (Vaclav) 1924- **CLC 15, 39,
69; DAC; DAM NOV**
See also CA 61-64; CAAS 1; CANR 10, 34;
MTCW
Slade, Bernard .... **CLC 11, 46**
See also Newbound, Bernard Slade
See also CAAS 9; DLB 53
Slaughter, Carolyn 1946- .... **CLC 56**
See also CA 85-88
Slaughter, Frank G(ill) 1908- .... **CLC 29**
See also AITN 2; CA 5-8R; CANR 5; INT
CANR-5
Slavitt, David R(ytman) 1935- ...... **CLC 5, 14**
See also CA 21-24R; CAAS 3; CANR 41; DLB
5, 6
Slesinger, Tess 1905-1945 .... **TCLC 10**
See also CA 107; DLB 102
Slessor, Kenneth 1901-1971 .... **CLC 14**
See also CA 102; 89-92
Slowacki, Juliusz 1809-1849 .... **NCLC 15**
Smart, Christopher 1722-1771 .. **LC 3; DAM
POET; PC 13**
See also DLB 109
Smart, Elizabeth 1913-1986 .... **CLC 54**
See also CA 81-84; 118; DLB 88
Smiley, Jane (Graves) 1949- **CLC 53, 76; DAM
POP**
See also CA 104; CANR 30, 50; INT CANR-
30
Smith, A(rthur) J(ames) M(arshall) 1902-1980
CLC 15; DAC
See also CA 1-4R; 102; CANR 4; DLB 88
Smith, Adam 1723-1790 .... **LC 36**
See also DLB 104
Smith, Alexander 1829-1867 .... **NCLC 59**
See also DLB 32, 55
Smith, Anna Deavere 1950- .... **CLC 86**
See also CA 133
Smith, Betty (Wehner) 1896-1972 .... **CLC 19**
See also CA 5-8R; 33-36R; DLBY 82; SATA 6
Smith, Charlotte (Turner) 1749-1806 **N C L C
23**
See also DLB 39, 109
Smith, Clark Ashton 1893-1961 .... **CLC 43**
See also CA 143
Smith, Dave .... **CLC 22, 42**
See also Smith, David (Jeddie)
See also CAAS 7; DLB 5
Smith, David (Jeddie) 1942-
See Smith, Dave

Stairs, Gordon
  See Austin, Mary (Hunter)
Stannard, Martin 1947- .... **CLC 44**
  See also CA 142; DLB 155
Stanton, Elizabeth Cady 1815-1902**TCLC 73**
  See also DLB 79
Stanton, Maura 1946- .... **CLC 9**
  See also CA 89-92; CANR 15; DLB 120
Stanton, Schuyler
  See Baum, L(yman) Frank
Stapledon, (William) Olaf 1886-1950 **T C L C 22**
  See also CA 111; DLB 15
Starbuck, George (Edwin) 1931-1996**CLC 53; DAM POET**
  See also CA 21-24R; 153; CANR 23
Stark, Richard
  See Westlake, Donald E(dwin)
Staunton, Schuyler
  See Baum, L(yman) Frank
Stead, Christina (Ellen) 1902-1983**CLC 2, 5, 8, 32, 80**
  See also CA 13-16R; 109; CANR 33, 40; MTCW
Stead, William Thomas 1849-1912 **TCLC 48**
Steele, Richard 1672-1729 .... **LC 18**
  See also CDBLB 1660-1789; DLB 84, 101
Steele, Timothy (Reid) 1948- .... **CLC 45**
  See also CA 93-96; CANR 16, 50; DLB 120
Steffens, (Joseph) Lincoln 1866-1936 **T C L C 20**
  See also CA 117
Stegner, Wallace (Earle) 1909-1993**CLC 9, 49, 81; DAM NOV; SSC 27**
  See also AITN 1; BEST 90:3; CA 1-4R; 141; CAAS 9; CANR 1, 21, 46; DLB 9; DLBY 93; MTCW
Stein, Gertrude 1874-1946**TCLC 1, 6, 28, 48; DA; DAB; DAC; DAM MST, NOV, POET; PC 18; WLC**
  See also CA 104; 132; CDALB 1917-1929; DLB 4, 54, 86; DLBD 15; MTCW
Steinbeck, John (Ernst) 1902-1968 **CLC 1, 5, 9, 13, 21, 34, 45, 75; DA; DAB; DAC; DAM DRAM, MST, NOV; SSC 11; WLC**
  See also AAYA 12; CA 1-4R; 25-28R; CANR 1, 35; CDALB 1929-1941; DLB 7, 9; DLBD 2; MTCW; SATA 9
Steinem, Gloria 1934- .... **CLC 63**
  See also CA 53-56; CANR 28, 51; MTCW
Steiner, George 1929- ... **CLC 24; DAM NOV**
  See also CA 73-76; CANR 31; DLB 67; MTCW; SATA 62
Steiner, K. Leslie
  See Delany, Samuel R(ay, Jr.)
Steiner, Rudolf 1861-1925 .... **TCLC 13**
  See also CA 107
Stendhal 1783-1842**NCLC 23, 46; DA; DAB; DAC; DAM MST, NOV; SSC 27; WLC**
  See also DLB 119
Stephen, Leslie 1832-1904 .... **TCLC 23**
  See also CA 123; DLB 57, 144
Stephen, Sir Leslie
  See Stephen, Leslie
Stephen, Virginia
  See Woolf, (Adeline) Virginia
Stephens, James 1882(?)-1950 .... **TCLC 4**
  See also CA 104; DLB 19, 153, 162
Stephens, Reed
  See Donaldson, Stephen R.
Steptoe, Lydia
  See Barnes, Djuna
Sterchi, Beat 1949- .... **CLC 65**
Sterling, Brett
  See Bradbury, Ray (Douglas); Hamilton, Edmond
Sterling, Bruce 1954- .... **CLC 72**

See also CA 119; CANR 44
Sterling, George 1869-1926 .... **TCLC 20**
  See also CA 117; DLB 54
Stern, Gerald 1925- .... **CLC 40, 100**
  See also CA 81-84; CANR 28; DLB 105
Stern, Richard (Gustave) 1928- ....**CLC 4, 39**
  See also CA 1-4R; CANR 1, 25, 52; DLBY 87; INT CANR-25
Sternberg, Josef von 1894-1969 .... **CLC 20**
  See also CA 81-84
Sterne, Laurence 1713-1768**LC 2; DA; DAB; DAC; DAM MST, NOV; WLC**
  See also CDBLB 1660-1789; DLB 39
Sternheim, (William Adolf) Carl 1878-1942 **TCLC 8**
  See also CA 105; DLB 56, 118
Stevens, Mark 1951- .... **CLC 34**
  See also CA 122
Stevens, Wallace 1879-1955 **TCLC 3, 12, 45; DA; DAB; DAC; DAM MST, POET; PC 6; WLC**
  See also CA 104; 124; CDALB 1929-1941; DLB 54; MTCW
Stevenson, Anne (Katharine) 1933-**CLC 7, 33**
  See also CA 17-20R; CAAS 9; CANR 9, 33; DLB 40; MTCW
Stevenson, Robert Louis (Balfour) 1850-1894 **NCLC 5, 14, 63; DA; DAB; DAC; DAM MST, NOV; SSC 11; WLC**
  See also CDBLB 1890-1914; CLR 10, 11; DLB 18, 57, 141, 156, 174; DLBD 13; JRDA; MAICYA; YABC 2
Stewart, J(ohn) I(nnes) M(ackintosh) 1906-1994 .... **CLC 7, 14, 32**
  See also CA 85-88; 147; CAAS 3; CANR 47; MTCW
Stewart, Mary (Florence Elinor) 1916-**CLC 7, 35; DAB**
  See also CA 1-4R; CANR 1, 59; SATA 12
Stewart, Mary Rainbow
  See Stewart, Mary (Florence Elinor)
Stifle, June
  See Campbell, Maria
Stifter, Adalbert 1805-1868**NCLC 41; SSC 28**
  See also DLB 133
Still, James 1906- .... **CLC 49**
  See also CA 65-68; CAAS 17; CANR 10, 26; DLB 9; SATA 29
Sting
  See Sumner, Gordon Matthew
Stirling, Arthur
  See Sinclair, Upton (Beall)
Stitt, Milan 1941- .... **CLC 29**
  See also CA 69-72
Stockton, Francis Richard 1834-1902
  See Stockton, Frank R.
  See also CA 108; 137; MAICYA; SATA 44
Stockton, Frank R. .... **TCLC 47**
  See also Stockton, Francis Richard
  See also DLB 42, 74; DLBD 13; SATA-Brief 32
Stoddard, Charles
  See Kuttner, Henry
Stoker, Abraham 1847-1912
  See Stoker, Bram
  See also CA 105; DA; DAC; DAM MST, NOV; SATA 29
Stoker, Bram 1847-1912**TCLC 8; DAB; WLC**
  See also Stoker, Abraham
  See also CA 150; CDBLB 1890-1914; DLB 36, 70, 178
Stolz, Mary (Slattery) 1920- .... **CLC 12**
  See also AAYA 8; AITN 1; CA 5-8R; CANR 13, 41; JRDA; MAICYA; SAAS 3; SATA 10, 71
Stone, Irving 1903-1989 ..**CLC 7; DAM POP**
  See also AITN 1; CA 1-4R; 129; CAAS 3;

CANR 1, 23; INT CANR-23; MTCW; SATA 3; SATA-Obit 64
Stone, Oliver (William) 1946- .... **CLC 73**
  See also AAYA 15; CA 110; CANR 55
Stone, Robert (Anthony) 1937-**CLC 5, 23, 42**
  See also CA 85-88; CANR 23; DLB 152; INT CANR-23; MTCW
Stone, Zachary
  See Follett, Ken(neth Martin)
Stoppard, Tom 1937-**CLC 1, 3, 4, 5, 8, 15, 29, 34, 63, 91; DA; DAB; DAC; DAM DRAM, MST; DC 6; WLC**
  See also CA 81-84; CANR 39; CDBLB 1960 to Present; DLB 13; DLBY 85; MTCW
Storey, David (Malcolm) 1933-**CLC 2, 4, 5, 8; DAM DRAM**
  See also CA 81-84; CANR 36; DLB 13, 14; MTCW
Storm, Hyemeyohsts 1935- ...... **CLC 3; DAM MULT**
  See also CA 81-84; CANR 45; NNAL
Storm, (Hans) Theodor (Woldsen) 1817-1888 **NCLC 1; SSC 27**
Storni, Alfonsina 1892-1938 . **TCLC 5; DAM MULT; HLC**
  See also CA 104; 131; HW
Stoughton, William 1631-1701 .... **LC 38**
  See also DLB 24
Stout, Rex (Todhunter) 1886-1975 ..... **CLC 3**
  See also AITN 2; CA 61-64
Stow, (Julian) Randolph 1935- .. **CLC 23, 48**
  See also CA 13-16R; CANR 33; MTCW
Stowe, Harriet (Elizabeth) Beecher 1811-1896 **NCLC 3, 50; DA; DAB; DAC; DAM MST, NOV; WLC**
  See also CDALB 1865-1917; DLB 1, 12, 42, 74; JRDA; MAICYA; YABC 1
Strachey, (Giles) Lytton 1880-1932 **TCLC 12**
  See also CA 110; DLB 149; DLBD 10
Strand, Mark 1934- **CLC 6, 18, 41, 71; DAM POET**
  See also CA 21-24R; CANR 40; DLB 5; SATA 41
Straub, Peter (Francis) 1943- **CLC 28; DAM POP**
  See also BEST 89:1; CA 85-88; CANR 28; DLBY 84; MTCW
Strauss, Botho 1944- .... **CLC 22**
  See also CA 157; DLB 124
Streatfeild, (Mary) Noel 1895(?)-1986**CLC 21**
  See also CA 81-84; 120; CANR 31; CLR 17; DLB 160; MAICYA; SATA 20; SATA-Obit 48
Stribling, T(homas) S(igismund) 1881-1965 **CLC 23**
  See also CA 107; DLB 9
Strindberg, (Johan) August 1849-1912**T C L C 1, 8, 21, 47; DA; DAB; DAC; DAM DRAM, MST; WLC**
  See also CA 104; 135
Stringer, Arthur 1874-1950 .... **TCLC 37**
  See also DLB 92
Stringer, David
  See Roberts, Keith (John Kingston)
Stroheim, Erich von 1885-1957 ..... **TCLC 71**
Strugatskii, Arkadii (Natanovich) 1925-1991 **CLC 27**
  See also CA 106; 135
Strugatskii, Boris (Natanovich) 1933-**CLC 27**
  See also CA 106
Strummer, Joe 1953(?)- .... **CLC 30**
Stuart, Don A.
  See Campbell, John W(ood, Jr.)
Stuart, Ian
  See MacLean, Alistair (Stuart)
Stuart, Jesse (Hilton) 1906-1984**CLC 1, 8, 11, 14, 34**

See also CA 5-8R; 112; CANR 31; DLB 9, 48, 102; DLBY 84; SATA 2; SATA-Obit 36
Sturgeon, Theodore (Hamilton) 1918-1985 **CLC 22, 39**
See also Queen, Ellery
See also CA 81-84; 116; CANR 32; DLB 8; DLBY 85; MTCW
Sturges, Preston 1898-1959 .... **TCLC 48**
See also CA 114; 149; DLB 26
Styron, William 1925-**CLC 1, 3, 5, 11, 15, 60; DAM NOV, POP; SSC 25**
See also BEST 90:4; CA 5-8R; CANR 6, 33; CDALB 1968-1988; DLB 2, 143; DLBY 80; INT CANR-6; MTCW
Suarez Lynch, B.
See Bioy Casares, Adolfo; Borges, Jorge Luis
Su Chien 1884-1918
See Su Man-shu
See also CA 123
Suckow, Ruth 1892-1960 .... **SSC 18**
See also CA 113; DLB 9, 102
Sudermann, Hermann 1857-1928 '.. **TCLC 15**
See also CA 107; DLB 118
Sue, Eugene 1804-1857 .... **NCLC 1**
See also DLB 119
Sueskind, Patrick 1949- .... **CLC 44**
See also Suskind, Patrick
Sukenick, Ronald 1932- .... **CLC 3, 4, 6, 48**
See also CA 25-28R; CAAS 8; CANR 32; DLB 173; DLBY 81
Suknaski, Andrew 1942- .... **CLC 19**
See also CA 101; DLB 53
Sullivan, Vernon
See Vian, Boris
Sully Prudhomme 1839-1907 .... **TCLC 31**
Su Man-shu .... **TCLC 24**
See also Su Chien
Summerforest, Ivy B.
See Kirkup, James
Summers, Andrew James 1942- .... **CLC 26**
Summers, Andy
See Summers, Andrew James
Summers, Hollis (Spurgeon, Jr.) 1916-**CLC 10**
See also CA 5-8R; CANR 3; DLB 6
Summers, (Alphonsus Joseph-Mary Augustus) Montague 1880-1948 .... **TCLC 16**
See also CA 118
Sumner, Gordon Matthew 1951- ...... **CLC 26**
Surtees, Robert Smith 1803-1864 .. **NCLC 14**
See also DLB 21
Susann, Jacqueline 1921-1974 .... **CLC 3**
See also AITN 1; CA 65-68; 53-56; MTCW
Su Shih 1036-1101 .... **CMLC 15**
Suskind, Patrick
See Sueskind, Patrick
See also CA 145
Sutcliff, Rosemary 1920-1992**CLC 26; DAB; DAC; DAM MST, POP**
See also AAYA 10; CA 5-8R; 139; CANR 37; CLR 1, 37; JRDA; MAICYA; SATA 6, 44, 78; SATA-Obit 73
Sutro, Alfred 1863-1933 .... **TCLC 6**
See also CA 105; DLB 10
Sutton, Henry
See Slavitt, David R(ytman)
Svevo, Italo 1861-1928 . **TCLC 2, 35; SSC 25**
See also Schmitz, Aron Hector
Swados, Elizabeth (A.) 1951- .... **CLC 12**
See also CA 97-100; CANR 49; INT 97-100
Swados, Harvey 1920-1972 .... **CLC 5**
See also CA 5-8R; 37-40R; CANR 6; DLB 2
Swan, Gladys 1934- .... **CLC 69**
See also CA 101; CANR 17, 39
Swarthout, Glendon (Fred) 1918-1992**CLC 35**
See also CA 1-4R; 139; CANR 1, 47; SATA 26
Sweet, Sarah C.
See Jewett, (Theodora) Sarah Orne

Swenson, May 1919-1989**CLC 4, 14, 61; DA; DAB; DAC; DAM MST, POET; PC 14**
See also CA 5-8R; 130; CANR 36, 61; DLB 5; MTCW; SATA 15
Swift, Augustus
See Lovecraft, H(oward) P(hillips)
Swift, Graham (Colin) 1949- ...... **CLC 41, 88**
See also CA 117; 122; CANR 46
Swift, Jonathan 1667-1745 **LC 1; DA; DAB; DAC; DAM MST, NOV, POET; PC 9; WLC**
See also CDBLB 1660-1789; DLB 39, 95, 101; SATA 19
Swinburne, Algernon Charles 1837-1909 **TCLC 8, 36; DA; DAB; DAC; DAM MST, POET; WLC**
See also CA 105; 140; CDBLB 1832-1890; DLB 35, 57
Swinfen, Ann .... **CLC 34**
Swinnerton, Frank Arthur 1884-1982**CLC 31**
See also CA 108; DLB 34
Swithen, John
See King, Stephen (Edwin)
Sylvia
See Ashton-Warner, Sylvia (Constance)
Symmes, Robert Edward
See Duncan, Robert (Edward)
Symonds, John Addington 1840-1893 **N C L C 34**
See also DLB 57, 144
Symons, Arthur 1865-1945 .... **TCLC 11**
See also CA 107; DLB 19, 57, 149
Symons, Julian (Gustave) 1912-1994 **CLC 2, 14, 32**
See also CA 49-52; 147; CAAS 3; CANR 3, 33, 59; DLB 87, 155; DLBY 92; MTCW
Synge, (Edmund) J(ohn) M(illington) 1871-1909 ... **TCLC 6, 37; DAM DRAM; DC 2**
See also CA 104; 141; CDBLB 1890-1914; DLB 10, 19
Syruc, J.
See Milosz, Czeslaw
Szirtes, George 1948- .... **CLC 46**
See also CA 109; CANR 27, 61
Szymborska, Wislawa 1923-.............. **CLC 99**
See also CA 154; DLBY 96
T. O., Nik
See Annensky, Innokenty (Fyodorovich)
Tabori, George 1914- .... **CLC 19**
See also CA 49-52; CANR 4
Tagore, Rabindranath 1861-1941**TCLC 3, 53; DAM DRAM, POET; PC 8**
See also CA 104; 120; MTCW
Taine, Hippolyte Adolphe 1828-1893 . **N C L C 15**
Talese, Gay 1932- .... **CLC 37**
See also AITN 1; CA 1-4R; CANR 9, 58; INT CANR-9; MTCW
Tallent, Elizabeth (Ann) 1954- .... **CLC 45**
See also CA 117; DLB 130
Tally, Ted 1952- .... **CLC 42**
See also CA 120; 124; INT 124
Tamayo y Baus, Manuel 1829-1898 **NCLC 1**
Tammsaare, A(nton) H(ansen) 1878-1940 **TCLC 27**
Tam'si, Tchicaya U
See Tchicaya, Gerald Felix
Tan, Amy (Ruth) 1952-**CLC 59; DAM MULT, NOV, POP**
See also AAYA 9; BEST 89:3; CA 136; CANR 54; DLB 173; SATA 75
Tandem, Felix
See Spitteler, Carl (Friedrich Georg)
Tanizaki, Jun'ichiro 1886-1965**CLC 8, 14, 28; SSC 21**
See also CA 93-96; 25-28R; DLB 180
Tanner, William

See Amis, Kingsley (William)
Tao Lao
See Storni, Alfonsina
Tarassoff, Lev
See Troyat, Henri
Tarbell, Ida M(inerva) 1857-1944 . **TCLC 40**
See also CA 122; DLB 47
Tarkington, (Newton) Booth 1869-1946**TCLC 9**
See also CA 110; 143; DLB 9, 102; SATA 17
Tarkovsky, Andrei (Arsenyevich) 1932-1986 **CLC 75**
See also CA 127
Tartt, Donna 1964(?)- .... **CLC 76**
See also CA 142
Tasso, Torquato 1544-1595 .... **LC 5**
Tate, (John Orley) Allen 1899-1979**CLC 2, 4, 6, 9, 11, 14, 24**
See also CA 5-8R; 85-88; CANR 32; DLB 4, 45, 63; MTCW
Tate, Ellalice
See Hibbert, Eleanor Alice Burford
Tate, James (Vincent) 1943- ..... **CLC 2, 6, 25**
See also CA 21-24R; CANR 29, 57; DLB 5, 169
Tavel, Ronald 1940- .... **CLC 6**
See also CA 21-24R; CANR 33
Taylor, C(ecil) P(hilip) 1929-1981 .... **CLC 27**
See also CA 25-28R; 105; CANR 47
Taylor, Edward 1642(?)-1729 ..... **LC 11; DA; DAB; DAC; DAM MST, POET**
See also DLB 24
Taylor, Eleanor Ross 1920- .... **CLC 5**
See also CA 81-84
Taylor, Elizabeth 1912-1975 ..... **CLC 2, 4, 29**
See also CA 13-16R; CANR 9; DLB 139; MTCW; SATA 13
Taylor, Frederick Winslow 1856-1915 **T C L C 76**
Taylor, Henry (Splawn) 1942- .... **CLC 44**
See also CA 33-36R; CAAS 7; CANR 31; DLB 5
Taylor, Kamala (Purnaiya) 1924-
See Markandaya, Kamala
See also CA 77-80
Taylor, Mildred D. .... **CLC 21**
See also AAYA 10; BW 1; CA 85-88; CANR 25; CLR 9; DLB 52; JRDA; MAICYA; SAAS 5; SATA 15, 70
Taylor, Peter (Hillsman) 1917-1994**CLC 1, 4, 18, 37, 44, 50, 71; SSC 10**
See also CA 13-16R; 147; CANR 9, 50; DLBY 81, 94; INT CANR-9; MTCW
Taylor, Robert Lewis 1912- .... **CLC 14**
See also CA 1-4R; CANR 3; SATA 10
Tchekhov, Anton
See Chekhov, Anton (Pavlovich)
Tchicaya, Gerald Felix 1931-1988 .. **CLC 101**
See also CA 129; 125
Tchicaya U Tam'si
See Tchicaya, Gerald Felix
Teasdale, Sara 1884-1933 .... **TCLC 4**
See also CA 104; DLB 45; SATA 32
Tegner, Esaias 1782-1846 .... **NCLC 2**
Teilhard de Chardin, (Marie Joseph) Pierre 1881-1955 .... **TCLC 9**
See also CA 105
Temple, Ann
See Mortimer, Penelope (Ruth)
Tennant, Emma (Christina) 1937-**CLC 13, 52**
See also CA 65-68; CAAS 9; CANR 10, 38, 59; DLB 14
Tenneshaw, S. M.
See Silverberg, Robert
Tennyson, Alfred 1809-1892 ... **NCLC 30, 65; DA; DAB; DAC; DAM MST, POET; PC 6; WLC**

Townshend, Peter (Dennis Blandford) 1945-
CLC 17, 42
See also CA 107
Tozzi, Federigo 1883-1920............. TCLC 31
See also CA 160
Traill, Catharine Parr 1802-1899 .. NCLC 31
See also DLB 99
Trakl, Georg 1887-1914 .... TCLC 5
See also CA 104
Transtroemer, Tomas (Goesta) 1931-CLC 52,
65; DAM POET
See also CA 117; 129; CAAS 17
Transtromer, Tomas Gosta
See Transtroemer, Tomas (Goesta)
Traven, B. (?)-1969 .... CLC 8, 11
See also CA 19-20; 25-28R; CAP 2; DLB 9,
56; MTCW
Treitel, Jonathan 1959- .... CLC 70
Tremain, Rose 1943- .... CLC 42
See also CA 97-100; CANR 44; DLB 14
Tremblay, Michel 1942- CLC 29, 102; DAC;
DAM MST
See also CA 116; 128; DLB 60; MTCW
Trevanian .... CLC 29
See also Whitaker, Rod(ney)
Trevor, Glen
See Hilton, James
Trevor, William 1928- . CLC 7, 9, 14, 25, 71;
SSC 21
See also Cox, William Trevor
See also DLB 14, 139
Trifonov, Yuri (Valentinovich) 1925-1981
CLC 45
See also CA 126; 103; MTCW
Trilling, Lionel 1905-1975 ...... CLC 9, 11, 24
See also CA 9-12R; 61-64; CANR 10; DLB 28,
63; INT CANR-10; MTCW
Trimball, W. H.
See Mencken, H(enry) L(ouis)
Tristan
See Gomez de la Serna, Ramon
Tristram
See Housman, A(lfred) E(dward)
Trogdon, William (Lewis) 1939-
See Heat-Moon, William Least
See also CA 115; 119; CANR 47; INT 119
Trollope, Anthony 1815-1882NCLC 6, 33; DA;
DAB; DAC; DAM MST, NOV; SSC 28;
WLC
See also CDBLB 1832-1890; DLB 21, 57, 159;
SATA 22
Trollope, Frances 1779-1863 .... NCLC 30
See also DLB 21, 166
Trotsky, Leon 1879-1940................ TCLC 22
See also CA 118
Trotter (Cockburn), Catharine 1679-1749L C
8
See also DLB 84
Trout, Kilgore
See Farmer, Philip Jose
Trow, George W. S. 1943- .... CLC 52
See also CA 126
Troyat, Henri 1911- .... CLC 23
See also CA 45-48; CANR 2, 33; MTCW
Trudeau, G(arretson) B(eekman) 1948-
See Trudeau, Garry B.
See also CA 81-84; CANR 31; SATA 35
Trudeau, Garry B. .... CLC 12
See also Trudeau, G(arretson) B(eekman)
See also AAYA 10; AITN 2
Truffaut, Francois 1932-1984 .. CLC 20, 101
See also CA 81-84; 113; CANR 34
Trumbo, Dalton 1905-1976................ CLC 19
See also CA 21-24R; 69-72; CANR 10; DLB
26
Trumbull, John 1750-1831 .... NCLC 30
See also DLB 31

Trundlett, Helen B.
See Eliot, T(homas) S(tearns)
Tryon, Thomas 1926-1991 . CLC 3, 11; DAM
POP
See also AITN 1; CA 29-32R; 135; CANR 32;
MTCW
Tryon, Tom
See Tryon, Thomas
Ts'ao Hsueh-ch'in 1715(?)-1763 .... LC 1
Tsushima, Shuji 1909-1948
See Dazai, Osamu
See also CA 107
Tsvetaeva (Efron), Marina (Ivanovna) 1892-
1941 .... TCLC 7, 35; PC 14
See also CA 104; 128; MTCW
Tuck, Lily 1938- .... CLC 70
See also CA 139
Tu Fu 712-770.. PC 9
See also DAM MULT
Tunis, John R(oberts) 1889-1975 ...... CLC 12
See also CA 61-64; CANR 62; DLB 22, 171;
JRDA; MAICYA; SATA 37; SATA-Brief 30
Tuohy, Frank .... CLC 37
See also Tuohy, John Francis
See also DLB 14, 139
Tuohy, John Francis 1925-
See Tuohy, Frank
See also CA 5-8R; CANR 3, 47
Turco, Lewis (Putnam) 1934- ...... CLC 11, 63
See also CA 13-16R; CAAS 22; CANR 24, 51;
DLBY 84
Turgenev, Ivan 1818-1883 .... NCLC 21; DA;
DAB; DAC; DAM MST, NOV; DC 7; SSC
7; WLC
Turgot, Anne-Robert-Jacques 1727-1781 L C
26
Turner, Frederick 1943- .... CLC 48
See also CA 73-76; CAAS 10; CANR 12, 30,
56; DLB 40
Tutu, Desmond M(pilo) 1931- CLC 80; BLC;
DAM MULT
See also BW 1; CA 125
Tutuola, Amos 1920-1997CLC 5, 14, 29; BLC;
DAM MULT
See also BW 2; CA 9-12R; 159; CANR 27; DLB
125; MTCW
Twain, Mark TCLC 6, 12, 19, 36, 48, 59; SSC
26; WLC
See also Clemens, Samuel Langhorne
See also AAYA 20; DLB 11, 12, 23, 64, 74
Tyler, Anne 1941- . CLC 7, 11, 18, 28, 44, 59,
103; DAM NOV, POP
See also AAYA 18; BEST 89:1; CA 9-12R;
CANR 11, 33, 53; DLB 6, 143; DLBY 82;
MTCW; SATA 7, 90
Tyler, Royall 1757-1826 .... NCLC 3
See also DLB 37
Tynan, Katharine 1861-1931 .... TCLC 3
See also CA 104; DLB 153
Tyutchev, Fyodor 1803-1873 .... NCLC 34
Tzara, Tristan 1896-1963 ...... CLC 47; DAM
POET
See also Rosenfeld, Samuel; Rosenstock, Sami;
Rosenstock, Samuel
See also CA 153
Uhry, Alfred 1936- ... CLC 55; DAM DRAM,
POP
See also CA 127; 133; INT 133
Ulf, Haerved
See Strindberg, (Johan) August
Ulf, Harved
See Strindberg, (Johan) August
Ulibarri, Sabine R(eyes) 1919-CLC 83; DAM
MULT
See also CA 131; DLB 82; HW
Unamuno (y Jugo), Miguel de 1864-1936
TCLC 2, 9; DAM MULT, NOV; HLC; SSC

11
See also CA 104; 131; DLB 108; HW; MTCW
Undercliffe, Errol
See Campbell, (John) Ramsey
Underwood, Miles
See Glassco, John
Undset, Sigrid 1882-1949TCLC 3; DA; DAB;
DAC; DAM MST, NOV; WLC
See also CA 104; 129; MTCW
Ungaretti, Giuseppe 1888-1970CLC 7, 11, 15
See also CA 19-20; 25-28R; CAP 2; DLB 114
Unger, Douglas 1952- .... CLC 34
See also CA 130
Unsworth, Barry (Forster) 1930- ..... CLC 76
See also CA 25-28R; CANR 30, 54
Updike, John (Hoyer) 1932-CLC 1, 2, 3, 5, 7,
9, 13, 15, 23, 34, 43, 70; DA; DAB; DAC;
DAM MST, NOV, POET, POP; SSC 13, 27;
WLC
See also CA 1-4R; CABS 1; CANR 4, 33, 51;
CDALB 1968-1988; DLB 2, 5, 143; DLBD
3; DLBY 80, 82; MTCW
Upshaw, Margaret Mitchell
See Mitchell, Margaret (Munnerlyn)
Upton, Mark
See Sanders, Lawrence
Urdang, Constance (Henriette) 1922-CLC 47
See also CA 21-24R; CANR 9, 24
Uriel, Henry
See Faust, Frederick (Schiller)
Uris, Leon (Marcus) 1924- CLC 7, 32; DAM
NOV, POP
See also AITN 1, 2; BEST 89:2; CA 1-4R;
CANR 1, 40; MTCW; SATA 49
Urmuz
See Codrescu, Andrei
Urquhart, Jane 1949- .... CLC 90; DAC
See also CA 113; CANR 32
Ustinov, Peter (Alexander) 1921- .... CLC 1
See also AITN 1; CA 13-16R; CANR 25, 51;
DLB 13
U Tam'si, Gerald Felix Tchicaya
See Tchicaya, Gerald Felix
U Tam'si, Tchicaya
See Tchicaya, Gerald Felix
Vaculik, Ludvik 1926- .... CLC 7
See also CA 53-56
Vaihinger, Hans 1852-1933 .... TCLC 71
See also CA 116
Valdez, Luis (Miguel) 1940- .. CLC 84; DAM
MULT; HLC
See also CA 101; CANR 32; DLB 122; HW
Valenzuela, Luisa 1938- CLC 31, 104; DAM
MULT; SSC 14
See also CA 101; CANR 32; DLB 113; HW
Valera y Alcala-Galiano, Juan 1824-1905
TCLC 10
See also CA 106
Valery, (Ambroise) Paul (Toussaint Jules) 1871-
1945 ..... TCLC 4, 15; DAM POET; PC 9
See also CA 104; 122; MTCW
Valle-Inclan, Ramon (Maria) del 1866-1936
TCLC 5; DAM MULT; HLC
See also CA 106; 153; DLB 134
Vallejo, Antonio Buero
See Buero Vallejo, Antonio
Vallejo, Cesar (Abraham) 1892-1938TCLC 3,
56; DAM MULT; HLC
See also CA 105; 153; HW
Vallette, Marguerite Eymery
See Rachilde
Valle Y Pena, Ramon del
See Valle-Inclan, Ramon (Maria) del
Van Ash, Cay 1918- .... CLC 34
Vanbrugh, Sir John 1664-1726 LC 21; DAM
DRAM
See also DLB 80

Van Campen, Karl
See Campbell, John W(ood, Jr.)
Vance, Gerald
See Silverberg, Robert
Vance, Jack .... **CLC 35**
See also Kuttner, Henry; Vance, John Holbrook
See also DLB 8
Vance, John Holbrook 1916-
See Queen, Ellery; Vance, Jack
See also CA 29-32R; CANR 17; MTCW
Van Den Bogarde, Derek Jules Gaspard Ulric
Niven 1921-
See Bogarde, Dirk
See also CA 77-80
Vandenburgh, Jane .... **CLC 59**
Vanderhaeghe, Guy 1951- .... **CLC 41**
See also CA 113
van der Post, Laurens (Jan) 1906-1996 **CLC 5**
See also CA 5-8R; 155; CANR 35
van de Wetering, Janwillem 1931- ... **CLC 47**
See also CA 49-52; CANR 4, 62
Van Dine, S. S. .... **TCLC 23**
See also Wright, Willard Huntington
Van Doren, Carl (Clinton) 1885-1950 **T C L C**
18
See also CA 111
Van Doren, Mark 1894-1972 .... **CLC 6, 10**
See also CA 1-4R; 37-40R; CANR 3; DLB 45;
MTCW
Van Druten, John (William) 1901-1957 **TCLC**
2
See also CA 104; DLB 10
Van Duyn, Mona (Jane) 1921- **CLC 3, 7, 63;**
DAM POET
See also CA 9-12R; CANR 7, 38, 60; DLB 5
Van Dyne, Edith
See Baum, L(yman) Frank
van Itallie, Jean-Claude 1936- .... **CLC 3**
See also CA 45-48; CAAS 2; CANR 1, 48; DLB
7
van Ostaijen, Paul 1896-1928 .... **TCLC 33**
Van Peebles, Melvin 1932- **CLC 2, 20; DAM**
MULT
See also BW 2; CA 85-88; CANR 27
Vansittart, Peter 1920- .... **CLC 42**
See also CA 1-4R; CANR 3, 49
Van Vechten, Carl 1880-1964 .... **CLC 33**
See also CA 89-92; DLB 4, 9, 51
Van Vogt, A(lfred) E(lton) 1912- .... **CLC 1**
See also CA 21-24R; CANR 28; DLB 8; SATA
14
Varda, Agnes 1928- .... **CLC 16**
See also CA 116; 122
Vargas Llosa, (Jorge) Mario (Pedro) 1936-
CLC 3, 6, 9, 10, 15, 31, 42, 85; DA; DAB;
DAC; DAM MST, MULT, NOV; HLC
See also CA 73-76; CANR 18, 32, 42; DLB 145;
HW; MTCW
Vasiliu, Gheorghe 1881-1957
See Bacovia, George
See also CA 123
Vassa, Gustavus
See Equiano, Olaudah
Vassilikos, Vassilis 1933- .... **CLC 4, 8**
See also CA 81-84
Vaughan, Henry 1621-1695 .... **LC 27**
See also DLB 131
Vaughn, Stephanie .... **CLC 62**
Vazov, Ivan (Minchov) 1850-1921 . **TCLC 25**
See also CA 121; DLB 147
Veblen, Thorstein (Bunde) 1857-1929 **T C L C**
31
See also CA 115
Vega, Lope de 1562-1635 .... **LC 23**
Venison, Alfred
See Pound, Ezra (Weston Loomis)
Verdi, Marie de

See Mencken, H(enry) L(ouis)
Verdu, Matilde
See Cela, Camilo Jose
Verga, Giovanni (Carmelo) 1840-1922 **T C L C**
3; SSC 21
See also CA 104; 123
Vergil 70B.C.-19B.C. ... **CMLC 9; DA; DAB;**
DAC; DAM MST, POET; PC 12; WLCS
Verhaeren, Emile (Adolphe Gustave) 1855-1916
TCLC 12
See also CA 109
Verlaine, Paul (Marie) 1844-1896 **NCLC 2, 51;**
DAM POET; PC 2
Verne, Jules (Gabriel) 1828-1905 **TCLC 6, 52**
See also AAYA 16; CA 110; 131; DLB 123;
JRDA; MAICYA; SATA 21
Very, Jones 1813-1880 .... **NCLC 9**
See also DLB 1
Vesaas, Tarjei 1897-1970 .... **CLC 48**
See also CA 29-32R
Vialis, Gaston
See Simenon, Georges (Jacques Christian)
Vian, Boris 1920-1959 .... **TCLC 9**
See also CA 106; DLB 72
Viaud, (Louis Marie) Julien 1850-1923
See Loti, Pierre
See also CA 107
Vicar, Henry
See Felsen, Henry Gregor
Vicker, Angus
See Felsen, Henry Gregor
Vidal, Gore 1925- **CLC 2, 4, 6, 8, 10, 22, 33, 72;**
DAM NOV, POP
See also AITN 1; BEST 90:2; CA 5-8R; CANR
13, 45; DLB 6, 152; INT CANR-13; MTCW
Viereck, Peter (Robert Edwin) 1916- . **CLC 4**
See also CA 1-4R; CANR 1, 47; DLB 5
Vigny, Alfred (Victor) de 1797-1863 **NCLC 7;**
DAM POET
See also DLB 119
Vilakazi, Benedict Wallet 1906-1947 **TCLC 37**
Villiers de l'Isle Adam, Jean Marie Mathias
Philippe Auguste Comte 1838-1889
NCLC 3; SSC 14
See also DLB 123
Villon, Francois 1431-1463(?) .... **PC 13**
Vinci, Leonardo da 1452-1519 .... **LC 12**
Vine, Barbara .... **CLC 50**
See also Rendell, Ruth (Barbara)
See also BEST 90:4
Vinge, Joan D(ennison) 1948- **CLC 30; SSC 24**
See also CA 93-96; SATA 36
Violis, G.
See Simenon, Georges (Jacques Christian)
Visconti, Luchino 1906-1976 .... **CLC 16**
See also CA 81-84; 65-68; CANR 39
Vittorini, Elio 1908-1966 .... **CLC 6, 9, 14**
See also CA 133; 25-28R
Vizenor, Gerald Robert 1934- **CLC 103; DAM**
MULT
See also CA 13-16R; CAAS 22; CANR 5, 21,
44; DLB 175; NNAL
Vizinczey, Stephen 1933- .... **CLC 40**
See also CA 128; INT 128
Vliet, R(ussell) G(ordon) 1929-1984 **CLC 22**
See also CA 37-40R; 112; CANR 18
Vogau, Boris Andreyevich 1894-1937(?)
See Pilnyak, Boris
See also CA 123
Vogel, Paula A(nne) 1951- .... **CLC 76**
See also CA 108
Voight, Ellen Bryant 1943- .... **CLC 54**
See also CA 69-72; CANR 11, 29, 55; DLB 120
Voigt, Cynthia 1942- .... **CLC 30**
See also AAYA 3; CA 106; CANR 18, 37, 40;
CLR 13; INT CANR-18; JRDA; MAICYA;
SATA 48, 79; SATA-Brief 33

Voinovich, Vladimir (Nikolaevich) 1932- **CLC**
10, 49
See also CA 81-84; CAAS 12; CANR 33;
MTCW
Vollmann, William T. 1959- ... **CLC 89; DAM**
NOV, POP
See also CA 134
Voloshinov, V. N.
See Bakhtin, Mikhail Mikhailovich
Voltaire 1694-1778 . **LC 14; DA; DAB; DAC;**
DAM DRAM, MST; SSC 12; WLC
von Daeniken, Erich 1935- .... **CLC 30**
See also AITN 1; CA 37-40R; CANR 17, 44
von Daniken, Erich
See von Daeniken, Erich
von Heidenstam, (Carl Gustaf) Verner
See Heidenstam, (Carl Gustaf) Verner von
von Heyse, Paul (Johann Ludwig)
See Heyse, Paul (Johann Ludwig von)
von Hofmannsthal, Hugo
See Hofmannsthal, Hugo von
von Horvath, Odon
See Horvath, Oedoen von
von Horvath, Oedoen
See Horvath, Oedoen von
von Liliencron, (Friedrich Adolf Axel) Detlev
See Liliencron, (Friedrich Adolf Axel) Detlev
von
Vonnegut, Kurt, Jr. 1922- **CLC 1, 2, 3, 4, 5, 8,**
12, 22, 40, 60; DA; DAB; DAC; DAM MST,
NOV, POP; SSC 8; WLC
See also AAYA 6; AITN 1; BEST 90:4; CA 1-
4R; CANR 1, 25, 49; CDALB 1968-1988;
DLB 2, 8, 152; DLBD 3; DLBY 80; MTCW
Von Rachen, Kurt
See Hubbard, L(afayette) Ron(ald)
von Rezzori (d'Arezzo), Gregor
See Rezzori (d'Arezzo), Gregor von
von Sternberg, Josef
See Sternberg, Josef von
Vorster, Gordon 1924- .... **CLC 34**
See also CA 133
Vosce, Trudie
See Ozick, Cynthia
Voznesensky, Andrei (Andreievich) 1933-
CLC 1, 15, 57; DAM POET
See also CA 89-92; CANR 37; MTCW
Waddington, Miriam 1917- .... **CLC 28**
See also CA 21-24R; CANR 12, 30; DLB 68
Wagman, Fredrica 1937- .... **CLC 7**
See also CA 97-100; INT 97-100
Wagner, Linda W.
See Wagner-Martin, Linda (C.)
Wagner, Linda Welshimer
See Wagner-Martin, Linda (C.)
Wagner, Richard 1813-1883 .... **NCLC 9**
See also DLB 129
Wagner-Martin, Linda (C.) 1936- .... **CLC 50**
See also CA 159
Wagoner, David (Russell) 1926- **CLC 3, 5, 15**
See also CA 1-4R; CAAS 3; CANR 2; DLB 5;
SATA 14
Wah, Fred(erick James) 1939- .... **CLC 44**
See also CA 107; 141; DLB 60
Wahloo, Per 1926-1975 .... **CLC 7**
See also CA 61-64
Wahloo, Peter
See Wahloo, Per
Wain, John (Barrington) 1925-1994 . **CLC 2,**
11, 15, 46
See also CA 5-8R; 145; CAAS 4; CANR 23,
54; CDBLB 1960 to Present; DLB 15, 27,
139, 155; MTCW
Wajda, Andrzej 1926- .... **CLC 16**
See also CA 102
Wakefield, Dan 1932- .... **CLC 7**
See also CA 21-24R; CAAS 7

Literary Criticism Series
Cumulative Topic Index

This index lists all topic entries in Gale's *Classical and Medieval Literature Criticism, Contemporary Literary Criticism, Literature Criticism from 1400 to 1800, Nineteenth-Century Literature Criticism,* and *Twentieth-Century Literary Criticism.*

Topic Index

Topic Index

Topic Index

Twentieth-Century Literary Criticism
Cumulative Nationality Index

Nationality Index

Martinez Sierra, Maria (de la O'LeJarraga) **6**
Miro (Ferrer), Gabriel (Francisco Victor) **5**
Ortega y Gasset, Jose **9**
Pereda (y Sanchez de Porrua), Jose Maria de
   16
Perez Galdos, Benito **27**
Salinas (y Serrano), Pedro **17**
Unamuno (y Jugo), Miguel de **2, 9**
Valera y Alcala-Galiano, Juan **10**
Valle-Inclan, Ramon (Maria) del **5**

SWEDISH
Bengtsson, Frans (Gunnar) **48**
Dagerman, Stig (Halvard) **17**
Ekelund, Vilhelm **75**
Heidenstam, (Carl Gustaf) Verner von **5**
Key, Ellen **65**
Lagerloef, Selma (Ottiliana Lovisa) **4, 36**
Soderberg, Hjalmar **39**
Strindberg, (Johan) August **1, 8, 21, 47**

SWISS
Ramuz, Charles-Ferdinand **33**
Rod, Edouard **52**
Saussure, Ferdinand de **49**
Spitteler, Carl (Friedrich Georg) **12**
Walser, Robert **18**

SYRIAN
Gibran, Kahlil **1, 9**

TURKISH
Sait Faik **23**

UKRAINIAN
Aleichem, Sholom **1, 35**
Bialik, Chaim Nachman **25**

URUGUAYAN
Quiroga, Horacio (Sylvestre) **20**
Sanchez, Florencio **37**

WELSH
Davies, W(illiam) H(enry) **5**
Lewis, Alun **3**
Machen, Arthur **4**
Thomas, Dylan (Marlais) **1, 8, 45**

Nationality Index